Delinquency, Crime, and Social Process

Delinquency, Crime, and Social Process

Donald R. Cressey
University of California, Santa Barbara

David A. Ward
University of Minnesota

HARPER & ROW, PUBLISHERS
New York, Evanston, and London

LIBRARY OF CONGRESS CATALOG CARD NUMBER: 69-14982

Contents

Preface

We have attempted to make this book more than a convenient compendium of well-known criminological research studies and theories. Some college and university instructors might—in light of their own course outlines and theoretical dispositions—ask students to read only some of our selections, and in a different sequence. But we have organized the book to provide a framework from which students—and instructors—can examine not only the major theories of criminologists, but also the statements of judges, legislators, law enforcement officials, and others who express views about "the crime problem," "crime in the streets," and "law and order." The selections are organized around a central theoretical position, which we elaborate progressively in the discussions that introduce each of the ten Parts.

Big-city riots, increasing rates of assaults upon persons, and increasing delinquency rates have made crime a major public concern and a major political issue in this country. Most criminology students will not become criminologists, but sooner or later it will become necessary for them to make decisions about proposed solutions to "the crime problem." As citizens they will be asked to vote for candidates advocating certain courses of action or for tax-dollars to support programs related to crime—ranging from poverty relief to hiring more police officers. They may participate in public discussions about crime, and some may serve as members of citizens' committees established to assist public agencies, suggest new programs, or lobby for new governmental action. Whether students take actions as citizens or in some professional capacity their decisions will be effect-tive only if they are based on factual information about the extent and character of crime and delinquency in our society. We believe that these decisions will be even more effective if they are also based upon knowl-edge of a general perspective which "makes sense" of the statistics on crime and delinquency *and* the nature of criminal and delinquent behavior.

Students, then, as well as scientists and scholars studying crime and delinquency, have to deal with two separate but interrelated phenomena. One is the statistical distribution of criminal and delinquent behavior in time and space. ("Why is the delinquency rate of this group, city, region, or na-tion higher than the delinquency rate of that group, city, region, or nation?") The other is the process by which individuals come to behave criminally or in a delinquent manner. ("How did Johnny happen to go wrong?") Parts I–IV of this book are designed to describe, among other things, the character and location of crime and delinquency in the social structure of America. Parts V–X are designed to articulate and provide support for our con-tention that criminal and delinquent behaviors can most accurately be un-derstood within the framework of symbolic interactionist social psychology.

The need to consider the relationship between these two sets of crimino-logical data cannot be overemphasized. Earlier research and writing on crime and criminality did not make this point clear, principally because criminology was characterized by an informal division of labor: sociologists spent most of their time studying the nature and distribution of crime and de-linquency; psychiatrists and psychologists directed most of their attention to the developmental histories of certain types of individual offenders, most frequently those who committed crimes of violence. The literature of criminology thus contains few studies of delinquent subcultures by psy-chiatrists and psychologists and few studies of murderers and rapists by sociologists. In recent years, however, there has emerged in the field of social psychology a body of theory that emphasizes the impact of culture and patterns of social interaction upon the behavior of individuals. Social psychology may be seen as a bridge over the gap between traditional so-ciological and psychological perspectives. This bridge has not been established by poaching on both preserves, but by setting forth a distinctive theoretical perspective.

The emphasis in this book, however, is not exclusively on the prob-lems of explaining what statistical distributions of crime and delinquency mean and how individuals become criminals and delinquents. We want our readers to be aware that as one examines statistical distributions of delinquency and crime rates and offender characteristics he must pay close attention to variables that relate to the settings and circumstances under which the statistics were collected. Once social scientists simply analyzed the available statistical "facts." Now we know that the datum for study is the process by which the statistical information is assembled, not just the final assembly. For example, arrest statistics are often used as the basis of generalizations about the social-class distribution of delinquency and crime, but they systematically underreport the crimes of the "respectable" segments of the society. Early criminology books acknowledged that criminal and delinquent behavior was to be found in the middle and upper classes, as well as in the lower class, but they also noted that little was known about the extent and variety of these offenses or the persons who committed them. In many of these books the discussion of "white-collar crime" constituted the only analysis of criminal behavior outside the lower socioeconomic class.

In recent years, sociologists have devised methods of data collection which make it unnecessary to rely so heavily upon arrest statistics or other compilations of official statistics. Techniques such as participant-observation, interviews, questionnaires, standardized tests, and surveys of unreported crimes and unreported victimizations have not promoted studies which give a broader and more accurate view of the extent of criminal law violations and of criminal law violators. Thus, among the selections we have been able to reprint in this book are research studies, descriptive accounts, and essays devoted to the illegal activities of businessmen, labor union officials, physicians, politicians, policemen, and middle-class youngsters. The theoretical framework of this book is designed to make these violations just as understandable as the criminal violations of persons in the lower socioeconomic class.

Correcting the deficiencies of crime statistics is not merely a matter of making better counts, however. Our concern for a two-part explanation of crime—its epidemiology and the expression of individual criminal conduct—reflects a concern for the fact that the very conception of some behaviors as "criminal" or "delinquent" depends upon conditions outside the behavior itself. Not only do official crime statistics underestimate middle- and upper-class crime, but a number of studies, including a survey conducted for the President's Commission on Law Enforcement and Administration of Justice, have made it clear that official statistics based on crimes reported to the police underestimate law violations for all segments of the population.

Even known violations of the law are not automatically followed by arrest, trial, conviction, and sentencing. The legal apparatus selects some persons for counting and ignores others. Some laws are strictly enforced, others are ignored; laws vary from time to time and from place to place, and so do law enforcement activities. Furthermore, the kind of crime a person is said to have committed and the decision about whether he is to be designated a "criminal" or not depends, in many cases, upon the outcome of a series of negotiations he or his counsel conduct with representatives of the crimiinal justice system. Experienced offenders, and offenders with experienced attorneys, bargain over pleas, charges, and dispositions. The sum total of the outcome of all such negotiations, conducted by thousands of persons, has obvious implications for the accuracy of our crime statistics. Since the bargaining process and arrangements are not officially recorded, we have included eight selections, which, in one way or another, make the point that both criminological theorists and those who administer criminal justice must recognize that the process of designating a person as a "delinquent" or "criminal" is a selective process. The view of the editors is that *criminality is not "in" people; rather it is a status conferred upon certain persons for certain acts at certain times in certain places.*

Part X poses some interesting problems for sociological theory. Here we present materials on crimes which seem to be "individualistic" and, hence, not readily understandable when examined from the social psychological framework presented in the previous Parts. We believe, however, that key features of the behavior of solitary offenders such as the rapists, physician narcotic addicts, check forgers, embezzlers, and "compulsive criminals" such as pyromaniacs and kleptomaniacs, described in Part X, can be placed within the theory articulated in the preceding Parts.

As editors, we present materials which we hope will help establish, illustrate, support, and elaborate points relevant to the sociology and social psychology of crime and delinquency. The decidedly contemporary character of the selections—about two-thirds were published since 1960—reflects our judgment that the most recent criminological research and writing is also the most important. (This certainly is not true of some other areas of sociology or of certain areas of other academic disciplines such as biology and physics.) It was a fortunate coincidence that as our volume was being prepared, the President's Crime Commission was conducting the most heavily financed and best staffed national survey of crime and delinquency ever made in the United States. In the spring and summer of 1967 the Commission published over fifty volumes of data and discussions pertaining to almost every aspect of criminology. Many of the selections in this book were written by persons who were consultants, advisors, or ghost writers for the Commission, and we have reprinted a number of their reports.

In the process of preparing this volume, we became authors before we became editors. Much of our time and energy went into the preparation of the statements which introduce each of the ten Parts. These introductions are not simply reviews or critiques of the selections that follow. In fact, with the exception of the introduction to Part I, they did not start out as introductions. The basic points of the book were laid out and linked together in ten essays, and *then* readings were selected to illustrate these points, to extend the descriptions or discussions, or provide empirical evidence that supports or raises doubts about their validity. How well we have achieved our general aim or how convincing we have made our specific arguments is, of course, not the responsibility of the authors of the readings which follow.

Our decisions to write ourselves into a book of readings did establish some limits. One of these was that the book could not be a collection of all the best contributions to criminology made by sociologists, let alone those made by psychologists, psychiatrists, anthropologists, and others who have sought to understand the causes and character of crime and delinquency. Another limitation was that some criminological "classics" not directly related to the organizational theme had to be omitted. Most of these classics are, however, discussed in detail in the standard textbooks and have been reprinted many times in other books. Moreover, we believe that these limitations do not outweigh the positive gains which can come from making students aware that the findings of well-conducted criminological studies are relevant not only to propositions about criminal behavior, but also to more general propositions about noncriminal behavior.

DONALD R. CRESSEY
DAVID A. WARD

PART I
Crime in America

Introduction

The Challenge of Crime in a Free Society, which is the general report of The President's Commission on Law Enforcement and Administration of Justice, provides the best summary statement ever made about the state of crime, law enforcement, and justice in the United States. Part of this general report, "Crime in America," was chosen as the first selection because it identifies the principal dimensions of the problem with which this book is concerned. This piece sets the stage for those later selections that deal with the problems of determining "true" crime and delinquency rates. It also suggests answers to basic questions: How much crime is there? Is the crime rate increasing? What is the economic impact of crime? Where do most crimes occur? Is the crime rate among Negroes higher than that among whites? Who are the victims of various types of criminal activity? These questions are concerned with the statistical distribution of crime in time, space, and social location. Understanding the conditions producing such distributions is a necessary prerequisite to understanding how individuals come to be involved in delinquency and crime.

In later Parts some of these questions are examined in more detail. The student should refer to "Crime in America" when he reads the selections which discuss unreported crime and the epidemiological aspects of delinquency and crime. The Commission's discussion of victims should be reviewed when the student reaches Part IX, which is concerned with interactions between criminals and other persons.

1 Crime in America

THE PRESIDENT'S COMMISSION
ON LAW ENFORCEMENT
AND ADMINISTRATION OF JUSTICE

The most natural and frequent question people ask about crime is "Why?" They ask it about individual crimes and about crime as a whole. In either case it is an almost impossible question to answer. Each single crime is a response to a specific situation by a person with an infinitely complicated psychological and emotional makeup who is subject to infinitely complicated external pressures. Crime as a whole is millions of such responses. To seek the "causes" of crime in human motivations alone is to risk losing one's way in the impenetrable thickets of the human psyche. Compulsive gambling was the cause of an embezzlement, one may say, or drug addiction the cause of a burglary or madness the cause of a homicide; but what caused the compulsion, the addiction, the madness? Why did they manifest themselves in those ways at those times?

There are some crimes so irrational, so unpredictable, so explosive, so resistant to analysis or explanation that they can no more be prevented or guarded against than earthquakes or tidal waves.

At the opposite end of the spectrum of crime are the carefully planned acts of professional criminals. The elaborately organized robbery of an armored car, the skillfully executed jewel theft, the murder of an informant by a Cosa Nostra "enforcer" are so deliberate, so calculated, so rational,

Reprinted from "Crime in America," *The Challenge of Crime in a Free Society*, Report by the President's Commission on Law Enforcement and Administration of Justice (Washington: Government Printing Office, 1967), ch. 2, pp. 17–46.

that understanding the motivations of those who commit such crimes does not show us how to prevent them. How to keep competent and intelligent men from taking up crime as a life work is as baffling a problem as how to predict and discourage sudden criminal outbursts.

To say this is not, of course, to belittle the efforts of psychiatrists and other behavioral scientists to identify and to treat the personality traits that are associated with crime. Such efforts are an indispensable part of understanding and controlling crime. Many criminals can be rehabilitated. The point is that looking at the personal characteristics of offenders is only one of many ways, and not always the most helpful way, of looking at crime.

It is possible to say, for example, that many crimes are "caused" by their victims. Often the victim of an assault is the person who started the fight, or the victim of an automobile theft is a person who left his keys in his car, or the victim of a loan shark is a person who lost his rent money at the race track, or the victim of a confidence man is a person who thought he could get rich quick. The relationship of victims to crimes is a subject that so far has received little attention. Many crimes, no matter what kind of people their perpetrators were, would not have been committed if their victims had understood the risks they were running.

From another viewpoint, crime is "caused" by public tolerance of it, or reluctance or inability to take action against it. Corporate and business—"white-collar"—crime is closely associated with a widespread notion that, when making money is involved, anything goes. Shoplifting and employee theft may be made more safe by their victims' reluctance to report to the police—often due to a recognition that the likelihood of detection and successful prosecution are negligible. Very often slum residents feel they live in territory that it is useless for them even to try to defend. Many slum residents feel overwhelmed and helpless in the face of the flourishing vice and crime around them; many have received indifferent treatment from the criminal justice system when they have attempted to do their duty as complainants and witnesses; many fear reprisals, especially victims of rackets. When citizens do not get involved, criminals can act with relative impunity.

In a sense, social and economic conditions "cause" crime. Crime flourishes, and always has flourished, in city slums, those neighborhoods where overcrowding, economic deprivation, social disruption and racial discrimination are endemic. Crime flourishes in conditions of affluence, when there is much desire for material goods and many opportunities to acquire them illegally. Crime flourishes when there are many restless, relatively footloose young people in the population. Crime flourishes when standards of morality are changing rapidly.

Finally, to the extent that the agencies of law enforcement and justice, and such community institutions as schools, churches and social service agencies, do not do their jobs effectively, they fail to prevent crime. If the police are inefficient or starved for manpower, otherwise preventable crimes will occur; if they are overzealous, people better left alone will be drawn into criminal careers. If the courts fail to separate the innocent from the guilty, the guilty may be turned loose to continue their depredations and the innocent may be criminalized. If the system fails to convict the guilty with reasonable certainty and promptness, deterrence of crime may be blunted. If correctional programs do not correct, a core of hardened and habitual criminals will continue to plague the community. If the community institutions that can shape the characters of young people do not take advantage of their opportunities, youth rebelliousness will turn into crime.

The causes of crime, then, are numerous and mysterious and intertwined. Even to begin to understand them, one must gather statistics about the amounts and trends of crime, estimate the costs of crime, study the conditions of life where crime thrives, identify criminals and the victims of crime, survey the public's attitudes toward crime. No one way of describing crime describes it well enough.

THE AMOUNT OF CRIME

There are more than 2800 Federal crimes and a much larger number of State and local ones. Some involve serious bodily harm, some stealing, some public morals or public order, some governmental revenues, some the creation of hazardous conditions, some the regulation of the economy. Some are perpetrated ruthlessly and systematically; others are spontaneous derelictions. Gambling and prostitution are willingly undertaken by both buyer and seller; murder and rape are violently imposed upon their victims. Vandalism is predominantly a crime of the young; driving while intoxicated, a crime of the adult. Many crime rates vary significantly from place to place.

The crimes that concern Americans the most are those that affect their personal safety—at home, at work, or in the streets. The most frequent and serious of these crimes of violence against the person are willful homicide, forcible rape, aggravated assault, and robbery. National statistics regarding the number of these offenses known to the police either from citizen complaints or through independent police discovery are collected from local police officials by the Federal Bureau of Investigation and published annually as a part of its report, "Crime in the United States, Uniform Crime Reports." The FBI also collects "offenses known" statistics for three property crimes: Burglary, larceny of $50 and over and motor vehicle theft. These seven crimes are grouped together in the UCR to form an Index of serious crimes. Figure 1 shows the totals for these offenses for 1965.

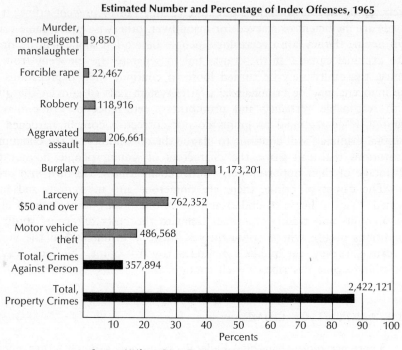

SOURCE: Uniform Crime Reports, *1965*, p. 51.

Figure 1

The Risk of Harm

Including robbery, the crimes of violence make up approximately 13 percent of the Index. The Index reports the number of incidents known to the police, not the number of criminals who committed them or the number of injuries they caused.

The risk of sudden attack by a stranger is perhaps best measured by the frequency of robberies since, according to UCR and other studies, about 70 percent of all willful killings, nearly two-thirds of all aggravated assaults and a high percentage of forcible rapes are committed by family members, friends, or other persons previously known to their victims. Robbery usually does not involve this prior victim-offender relationship.

Robbery, for UCR purposes, is the taking of property from a person by use or threat of force with or without a weapon. Nationally, about one-half of all robberies are street robberies, and slightly more than one-half involve weapons. Attempted robberies are an unknown percentage of the robberies reported to the UCR. The likelihood of injury is also unknown, but a survey by the District of Columbia Crime Commission of 297 rob-

beries in Washington showed that some injury was inflicted in 25 percent
of them. The likelihood of injury was found higher for "yokings" or
"muggings" (unarmed robberies from the rear) than for armed robberies.
Injuries occurred in 10 of 91 armed robberies as compared with 30 of
67 yokings.

Aggravated assault is assault with intent to kill or for the purpose of
inflicting severe bodily injury, whether or not a dangerous weapon is
used. It includes all cases of attempted homicide, but cases in which bodily
injury is inflicted in the course of a robbery or a rape are included with
those crimes rather than with aggravated assault. There are no national
figures showing the percentage of aggravated assaults that involve injury,
but a survey of 131 cases by the District of Columbia Crime Commission
found injury in 84 percent of the cases; 35 percent of the victims required
hospitalization. A 1960 UCR study showed that juvenile gangs committed
less than 4 percent of all aggravated assaults.

Forcible rape includes only those rapes or attempted rapes in which
force or threat of force is used. About one-third of the UCR total is
attempted rape. In a District of Columbia Crime Commission survey of
151 cases, about 25 percent of all rape victims were attacked with dangerous
weapons; the survey did not show what percentage received bodily harm
in addition to the rape.

About 15 percent of all criminal homicides, both nationally and in
the District of Columbia Crime Commission surveys, occurred in the
course of committing other offenses. These offenses appear in the homicide
total rather than in the total for the other offense. In the District of
Columbia Crime Commission surveys, less than one-half of 1 percent of
the robberies and about 1 percent of the forcible rapes ended in homicide.

Some personal danger is also involved in the property crimes. Burglary
is the unlawful entering of a building to commit a felony or a theft, whether
force is used or not. About half of all burglaries involve residences, but the
statistics do not distinguish inhabited parts of houses from garages and
similar outlying parts. About half of all residential burglaries are committed
in daylight and about half at night. A UCR survey indicates that 32 percent
of the entries into residences are made through unlocked doors or windows.
When an unlawful entry results in a violent confrontation with the occupant, the offense is counted as a robbery rather than a burglary. Of
course, even when no confrontation takes place there is often a risk of
confrontation. Nationally such confrontations occur in only one-fortieth
of all residential burglaries. They account for nearly one-tenth of all
robberies.

In summary, these figures suggest that, on the average, the likelihood
of a serious personal attack on any American in a given year is about 1 in

550; together with the studies available they also suggest that the risk of serious attack from spouses, family members, friends, or acquaintances is almost twice as great as it is from strangers on the street. Commission and other studies, moreover, indicate that the risks of personal harm are spread very unevenly. The actual risk for slum dwellers is considerably more; for most Americans it is considerably less.

Except in the case of willful homicide, where the figures describe the extent of injury as well as the number of incidents, there is no national data on the likelihood of injury from attack. More limited studies indicate that while some injury may occur in two-thirds of all attacks, the risk in a given year of injury serious enough to require any degree of hospitalization of any individual is about 1 in 3,000 on the average, and much less for most Americans. These studies also suggest that the injury inflicted by family members or acquaintances is likely to be more severe than that from strangers. As shown by table 1, the risk of death from willful homicide is about 1 in 20,000.

Criminal behavior accounts for a high percentage of motor vehicle deaths and injuries. In 1965 there were an estimated 49,000 motor vehicle deaths. Negligent manslaughter, which is largely a motor vehicle offense, accounted for more than 7,000 of these. Studies in several States indicate that an even higher percentage involve criminal behavior. They show that driving while intoxicated is probably involved in more than one-half of all motor vehicle deaths. These same studies show that driving while intoxicated is involved in more than 13 percent of the 1,800,000 nonfatal motor vehicle injuries each year.

For various statistical and other reasons, a number of serious crimes against or involving risk to the person, such as arson, kidnapping, child molestation, and simple assault, are not included in the UCR Index. In a study of 1,300 cases of delinquency in Philadelphia, offenses other than the

TABLE 1. DEATHS FROM OTHER THAN
NATURAL CAUSES IN 1965
(Per 100,000 inhabitants)

Motor vehicle accidents	25
Other accidents	12
Suicide	12
Falls	10
Willful homicide	5
Drowning	4
Fires	4

SOURCE: National Safety Council, "Accident Facts," 1965; Population Reference Bureau.

seven Index crimes constituted 62 percent of all cases in which there was physical injury. Simple assault accounted for the largest percentage of these injuries. But its victims required medical attention in only one-fifth of the cases as opposed to three-fourths of the aggravated assaults, and hospitalization in 7 percent as opposed to 23 percent. Injury was more prevalent in conflicts between persons of the same age than in those in which the victim was older or younger than the attacker.

Property Crimes

The three property crimes of burglary, automobile theft, and larceny of $50 and over make up 87 percent of Index crimes. The Index is a reasonably reliable indicator of the total number of property crimes reported to the police, but not a particularly good indicator of the seriousness of monetary loss from all property crimes. Commission studies tend to indicate that such non-Index crimes as fraud and embezzlement are more significant in terms of dollar volume. Fraud can be a particularly pernicious offense. It is not only expensive in total but all too often preys on the weak.

Many larcenies included in the Index total are misdemeanors rather than felonies under the laws of their own States. Auto thefts that involve only unauthorized use also are misdemeanors in many States. Many stolen automobiles are abandoned after a few hours, and more than 85 percent are ultimately recovered according to UCR studies. Studies in California indicate that about 20 percent of recovered cars are significantly damaged.

Other Criminal Offenses

The seven crimes for which all offenses known are reported were selected in 1927 and modified in 1958 by a special advisory committee of the International Association of Chiefs of Police on the basis of their serious nature, their frequency, and the reliability of reporting from citizens to police. In 1965 reporting for these offenses included information supplied voluntarily by some 8,000 police agencies covering nearly 92 percent of the total population. The FBI tries vigorously to increase the number of jurisdictions that report each year and to promote uniform reporting and classification of the reported offenses.

The UCR Index does not and is not intended to assist in assessing all serious national crime problems. For example, offense statistics are not sufficient to assess the incidence of crime connected with corporate activity, commonly known as white-collar crime, or the total criminal acts committed by organized crime groups. Likewise, offense and arrest figures alone do not aid very much in analyzing the scope of professional crime—that is, the number and types of offenses committed by those whose principal employment and source of income are based upon the commission of criminal acts.

Except for larceny under $50 and negligent manslaughter, for which there are some national offenses-known-to-the-police data, knowledge of the volume and trends of non-Index crimes depends upon arrest statistics. Since the police are not able to make arrests in many cases, these are necessarily less complete than the "offenses known" statistics. Moreover, the ratio between arrests and the number of offenses differs significantly from offense to offense—as is shown, for example, by the high percentage of reported cases in which arrests are made for murder (91 percent) and the relatively low percentage for larceny (20 percent). Reporting to the FBI for arrests covers less than 70 percent of the population. However, because arrest statistics are collected for a broader range of offenses—28 categories including the Index crimes—they show more of the diversity and magnitude of the many different crime problems. Property crimes do not loom so large in this picture.

Nearly 45 percent of all arrests are for such crimes without victims or against the public order as drunkenness, gambling, liquor law violations, vagrancy, and prostitution. As table 2 shows, drunkenness alone accounts

TABLE 2. NUMBER AND RATE OF ARRESTS
FOR THE 10 MOST FREQUENT OFFENSES, 1965
(4,062 agencies reporting; total population 134,095,000)

Rank	Offense	Number	Rate (per 100,000 population)	Percent of total arrests
1	Drunkenness	1,535,040	1,144.7	31.0
2	Disorderly conduct	570,122	425.2	11.5
3	Larceny (over and under $50)	385,726	286.2	7.7
4	Driving under the influence	241,511	180.1	4.9
5	Simple assault	207,615	154.8	4.2
6	Burglary	197,627	147.4	4.0
7	Liquor laws	179,219	133.7	3.6
8	Vagrancy	120,416	89.8	2.4
9	Gambling	114,294	85.2	2.3
10	Motor vehicle theft	101,763	75.9	2.1
	Total, 10 most frequent offenses	3,651,333	2,722.9	73.7
	Arrests for all offenses[1]	4,955,047	3,695.2	100.0

[1] Does not include arrests for traffic offenses.

SOURCE: "Uniform Crime Reports," 1965, pp. 108–109.

for almost one-third of all arrests. This is not necessarily a good indication of the number of persons arrested for drunkenness, however, as some individuals may be arrested many times during the year. Arrest statistics measure the number of arrests, not the number of criminals.

Federal Crimes

More than 50 percent of all Federal criminal offenses relate to general law enforcement in territorial or maritime jurisdictions directly subject to Federal control, or are also State offenses (bank robberies, for example). Police statistics for these offenses are normally reported in the UCR, particularly when local law enforcement is involved. Such other Federal crimes as antitrust violations, food and drug violations and tax evasion are not included in the UCR. Although Federal crimes constitute only a small percentage of all offenses, crimes such as those shown in table 3 are an important part of the national crime picture.

TABLE 3.   SELECTED FEDERAL CRIMES
(Cases filed in court—1966)

Antitrust	7
Food and drug	350
Income tax evasion	863
Liquor revenue violations	2,729
Narcotics	2,293
Immigration	3,188

SOURCE: Department of Justice.

The Extent of Unreported Crime

Although the police statistics indicate a lot of crime today, they do not begin to indicate the full amount. Crimes reported directly to prosecutors usually do not show up in the police statistics. Citizens often do not report crimes to the police. Some crimes reported to the police never get into the statistical system. Since better crime prevention and control programs depend upon a full and accurate knowledge about the amount and kinds of crime, the Commission initiated the first national survey ever made of crime victimization. The National Opinion Research Center of the University of Chicago surveyed 10,000 households, asking whether the person questioned, or any member of his or her household, had been a victim of crime during the past year, whether the crime had been reported and, if not, the reasons for not reporting.

TABLE 4. COMPARISON OF SURVEY AND UCR RATES
(Per 100,000 population)

Index Crimes	NORC survey 1965–66	UCR rate for individuals 1965 [1]	UCR rate for individuals and organizations 1965 [1]
Willful homicide	3.0	5.1	5.1
Forcible rape	42.5	11.6	11.6
Robbery	94.0	61.4	61.4
Aggravated assault	218.3	106.6	106.6
Burglary	949.1	299.6	605.3
Larceny ($50 and over)	606.5	267.4	393.3
Motor vehicle theft	206.2	226.0	251.0
Total violence	357.8	184.7	184.7
Total property	1,761.8	793.0	1,249.6

[1] "Uniform Crime Reports," 1965, p. 51. The UCR national totals do not distinguish crimes committed against individuals or households from those committed against businesses or other organizations. The UCR rate for individuals is the published national rate adjusted to eliminate burglaries, larcenies, and vehicle thefts not committed against individuals or households. No adjustment was made for robbery.

More detailed surveys were undertaken in a number of high and medium crime rate precincts of Washington, Chicago, and Boston by the Bureau of Social Science Research of Washington, D.C., and the Survey Research Center of the University of Michigan. All of the surveys dealt primarily with households or individuals, although some data were obtained for certain kinds of businesses and other organizations.

These surveys show that the actual amount of crime in the United States today is several times that reported in the UCR. As table 4 shows, the amount of personal injury crime reported to NORC is almost twice the UCR rate and the amount of property crime more than twice as much as the UCR rate for individuals. Forcible rapes were more than 3½ times the reported rate; burglaries three times, aggravated assaults and larcenies of $50 and over more than double, and robbery 50 percent greater than the reported rate. Only vehicle theft was lower and then by a small amount. (The single homicide reported is too small a number to be statistically useful.)

Even these rates probably understate the actual amounts of crime. The national survey was a survey of the victim experience of every member of a household based on interviews of one member. If the results are tabulated only for the family member who was interviewed, the amount of unreported victimization for some offenses is considerably higher. Apparently,

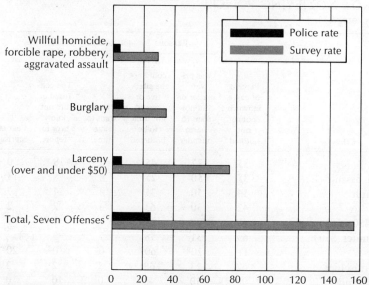

Estimated Rates of Offense[a]
Comparison of Police[b] **and BSSR Survey Data**
3 WASHINGTON, D. C., PRECINCTS   Rates per 1000 Residents 18 Years or Over

Willful homicide, forcible rape, robbery, aggravated assault

Burglary

Larceny (over and under $50)

Total, Seven Offenses[c]

Police rate
Survey rate

0   20   40   60   80   100   120   140   160

[a]Incidents involving more than one victim adjusted to count as only one offense. A victimization rate would count the incidence for each individual.

[b]Police statistics adjusted to eliminate nonresident and commercial victims and victims under 18 years of age.

[c]Willful homicide, forcible rape, robbery, aggravated assault, burglary, larceny (over and under $50), and motor vehicle theft.

Figure 2

the person interviewed remembered more of his own victimization than that of other members of his family.

The Washington, Boston, and Chicago surveys, based solely on victimization of the person interviewed, show even more clearly the disparity between reported and unreported amounts of crime. The clearest case is that of the survey in three Washington precincts, where, for the purpose of comparing survey results with crimes reported to the police, previous special studies made it possible to eliminate from police statistics crimes involving business and transient victims. As figure 2 indicates, for certain specific offenses against individuals the number of offenses reported to the survey per thousand residents 18 years or over ranged, depending on the offense, from 3 to 10 times more than the number contained in police statistics.

The survey in Boston and in one of the Chicago precincts indicated about three times as many Index crimes as the police statistics, in the other Chicago precinct about 1½ times as many. These survey rates are not fully comparable with the Washington results because adequate information did not exist for eliminating business and transient victims from the police

TABLE 5. VICTIM'S MOST IMPORTANT REASON
FOR NOT NOTIFYING POLICE[1]
(In percentages)

Crimes	Percent of cases in which police not notified	Felt it was private matter or did not want to harm offender	Police could not be effective or would not want to be bothered	Did not want to take time	Too confused or did not know how to report	Fear of reprisal
		Reasons for not notifying police				
Robbery	35	27	45	9	18	0
Aggravated assault	35	50	25	4	8	13
Simple assault	54	50	35	4	4	7
Burglary	42	30	63	4	2	2
Larceny ($50 and over)	40	23	62	7	7	0
Larceny (under $50)	63	31	58	7	3	(*)
Auto theft	11	20[2]	60[2]	0[2]	0[2]	20[2]
Malicious mischief	62	23	68	5	2	2
Consumer fraud	90	50	40	0	10	0
Other fraud (bad checks, swindling, etc.)	74	41	35	16	8	0
Sex offenses (other than forcible rape)	49	40	50	0	5	5
Family crimes (desertion, non-support, etc.)	50	65	17	10	0	7

* Less than 0.5%.

[1] Willful homicide, forcible rape, and a few other crimes had too few cases to be statistically useful, and they are therefore excluded.

[2] There were only 5 instances in which auto theft was not reported.

SOURCE: NORC survey.

statistics. If this computation could have been made, the Boston and Chicago figures would undoubtedly have shown a closer similarity to the Washington findings.

In the national survey of households those victims saying that they had not notified the police of their victimization were asked why. The reason most frequently given for all offenses was that the police could not do anything. As table 5 shows, this reason was given by 68 percent of those not reporting malicious michief, and by 60 or more percent of those not reporting burglaries, larcenies of $50 and over, and auto thefts. It is not clear whether these responses are accurate assessments of the victims' inability to help the police or merely rationalizations of their failure to report. The next most frequent reason was that the offense was a private matter or that the victim did not want to harm the offender. It was given by 50 percent or more of those who did not notify the police for aggravated and simple assaults, family crimes, and consumer frauds. Fear of reprisal, though least often cited, was strongest in the case of assaults and family crimes. The extent of failure to report to the police was highest for consumer fraud (90 percent) and lowest for auto theft (11 percent).

The survey technique, as applied to criminal victimization, is still new and beset with a number of methodological problems. However, the Commission has found the information provided by the surveys of considerable value, and believes that the survey technique has a great untapped potential as a method for providing additional information about the nature and extent of our crime problem and the relative effectiveness of different programs to control crime.

TRENDS IN CRIME

There has always been too much crime. Virtually every generation since the founding of the Nation and before has felt itself threatened by the spectre of rising crime and violence.

A hundred years ago contemporary accounts of San Francisco told of extensive areas where "no decent man was in safety to walk the street after dark; while at all hours, both night and day, his property was jeopardized by incendiarism and burglary." Teenage gangs gave rise to the word "hoodlum"; while in one central New York City area, near Broadway, the police entered "only in pairs, and never unarmed." A noted chronicler of the period declared that "municipal law is a failure * * * we must soon fall back on the law of self preservation." "Alarming" increases in robbery and violent crimes were reported throughout the country prior to the Revolution. And in 1910 one author declared that "crime, especially its more violent forms, and among the young is increasing steadily and is threatening to bankrupt the Nation."

Crime and violence in the past took many forms. During the great railway strike of 1877 hundreds were killed across the country and almost 2 miles of railroad cars and buildings were burned in Pittsburgh in clashes between strikers and company police and the militia. It was nearly a half century later, after pitched battles in the steel industry in the late thirties, that the Nation's long history of labor violence subsided. The looting and takeover of New York for 3 days by mobs in the 1863 draft riots rivaled the violence of Watts, while racial disturbances in Atlanta in 1907, in Chicago, Washington, and East St. Louis in 1919, Detroit in 1943 and New York in 1900, 1935, and 1943 marred big city life in the first half of the 20th century. Lynchings took the lives of more than 4,500 persons throughout the country between 1882 and 1930. And the violence of Al Capone and Jesse James was so striking that they have left their marks permanently on our understanding of the eras in which they lived.

However, the fact that there has always been a lot of crime does not mean that the amount of crime never changes. It changes constantly, day and night, month to month, place to place. It is essential that society be able to tell when changes occur and what they are, that it be able to distinguish normal ups and downs from long-term trends. Whether the amount of crime is increasing or decreasing, and by how much, is an important question—for law enforcement, for the individual citizen who must run the risk of crime, and for the official who must plan and establish prevention and control programs. If it is true, as the Commission surveys tend to indicate, that society has not yet found fully reliable methods for measuring the volume of crime, it is even more true that it has failed to find such methods for measuring the trend of crime.

Unlike some European countries, which have maintained national statistics for more than a century and a quarter, the United States has maintained national crime statistics only since 1930. Because the rural areas were slow in coming into the system and reported poorly when they did, it was not until 1958, when other major changes were made in the UCR, that reporting of rural crimes was sufficient to allow a total national estimate without special adjustments. Changes in overall estimating procedures and two offense categories—rape and larceny—were also made in 1958. Because of these problems figures prior to 1958 and particularly those prior to 1940, must be viewed as neither fully comparable with nor nearly so reliable as later figures.

For crimes of violence the 1933–65 period, based on newly adjusted unpublished figures from the UCR, has been, as figure 3 shows, one of sharply divergent trends for the different offenses. Total numbers for all reported offenses have increased markedly; the Nation's population has increased also—by more than 47 percent since 1940. The number of offenses per 100,000 population has tripled for forcible rape and has doubled for aggravated assault during the period, both increasing at a fairly constant pace. The willful homicide rate has decreased somewhat to about 70 percent of its high in 1933, while robbery has fluctuated from a high in 1933 and a low during World War II to a point where it is now about 20 percent above the beginning of the postwar era. The overall rate for violent crimes, primarily due to the increased rate for aggravated assault, now stands at its highest point, well above what it has been throughout most of the period.

Property crime rates, as shown in figure 4, are up much more sharply than the crimes of violence. The rate for larceny of $50 and over has shown the greatest increase of all Index offenses. It is up more than 550 percent over 1933. The burglary rate has nearly doubled. The rate for auto theft

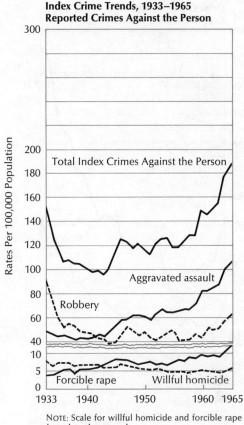

Index Crime Trends, 1933–1965
Reported Crimes Against the Person

Total Index Crimes Against the Person

Aggravated assault

Robbery

Forcible rape Willful homicide

NOTE: Scale for willful homicide and forcible rape enlarged, to show trend.
SOURCE: FBI, Uniform Crime Reports Section; unpublished data.

Figure 3

has followed an uneven course to a point about the same as the rate of the early thirties.

The upward trend for 1960–65 as shown in table 6 has been faster than the long-term trend, up 25 percent for the violent crimes and 36 percent for the property crimes. The greatest increases in the period came in 1964, in forcible rape among crimes of violence and in vehicle theft among property crimes. Preliminary reports indicate that all Index offenses rose in 1966.

Arrest rates are in general much less complete and are available for many fewer years than are rates for offenses known to the police. However, they do provide another measure of the trend of crime. For crimes of violence, arrest rates rose 16 percent during 1960–65, considerably less than

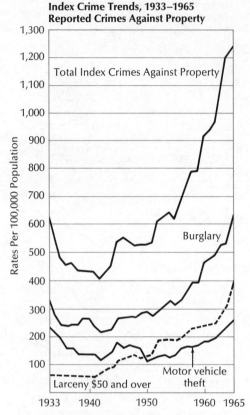

Index Crime Trends, 1933–1965
Reported Crimes Against Property

Total Index Crimes Against Property

Rates Per 100,000 Population

Burglary

Motor vehicle
theft

Larceny $50 and over

1933   1940   1950   1960 1965

NOTE: The scale for this figure is not comparable
with that used in Figure 3.

SOURCE: FBI, Uniform Crime Reports Section; unpublished data.

Figure 4

the 25 percent increase indicated by offenses known to the police. For
property crimes, arrest rates have increased about 25 percent, as opposed
to a 36 percent increase in offenses known to the police during 1960–65.
Figure 5 compares the 1960–65 trend for arrests and offenses known for
both crimes of violence and property crimes.

Prior to the year 1933, shown in figures 3 and 4, there is no estimated
national rate for any offenses. UCR figures for a sizable number of individual cities, however, indicate that the 1930–32 rates, at least for those
cities, were higher than the 1933 rates. Studies of such individual cities as
Boston, Chicago, New York, and others indicate that in the twenties and
the World War I years reported rates for many offenses were even higher.
A recent study of crime in Buffalo, N.Y., from 1854 to 1946 showed arrest
rates in that city for willful homicide, rape, and assault reaching their

TABLE 6. OFFENSES KNOWN TO THE POLICE, 1960–65
(Rates per 100,000 population)

Offense	1960	1961	1962	1963	1964	1965
Willful homicide	5.0	4.7	4.5	4.5	4.8	5.1
Forcible rape	9.2	9.0	9.1	9.0	10.7	11.6
Robbery	51.6	50.0	51.1	53.0	58.4	61.4
Aggravated assault	82.5	82.2	84.9	88.6	101.8	106.6
Burglary	465.5	474.9	489.7	527.4	580.4	605.3
Larceny $50 and over	271.4	277.9	296.6	330.9	368.2	393.3
Motor vehicle theft	179.2	179.9	193.4	212.1	242.0	251.0
Total crimes against person	148.3	145.9	149.6	155.1	175.7	184.7
Total property crimes	916.1	932.7	979.7	1,070.4	1,190.6	1,249.6

SOURCE: FBI, Uniform Crime Reports Section, unpublished data.

highest peak in the early 1870's, declining, rising again until 1918, and declining into the forties.

Trends for crimes against trust, vice crimes, and crimes against public order, based on arrest rates for 1960–65, follow a much more checkered pattern than do trends for Index offenses. For some offenses this is in part due to the fact that arrest patterns change significantly from time to time, as when New York recently decided not to make further arrests for public drunkenness. Based on comparable places covering about half the total population, arrest rates during 1960–65 rose 13 percent for simple assault, 13 percent for embezzlement and fraud, and 36 percent for narcotics violations, while for the same period, the rates declined 24 percent for gambling and 11 percent for drunkenness.

The picture portrayed by the official statistics in recent years, both in the total number of crimes and in the number of crimes per 100,000 Americans, is one of increasing crime. Crime always seems to be increasing, never going down. Up 5 percent this year, 10 the next, and the Commission's surveys have shown there is a great deal more crime than the official statistics show. The public can fairly wonder whether there is ever to be an end.

This official picture is also alarming because it seems so pervasive. Crimes of violence are up in both the biggest and smallest cities, in the suburbs as well as in the rural areas. The same is true for property crimes. Young people are being arrested in ever increasing numbers. Offense rates for most crimes are rising every year and in every section of the country. That there are some bright spots does not change this dismal outlook. Rates for some offenses are still below those of the early thirties and perhaps of

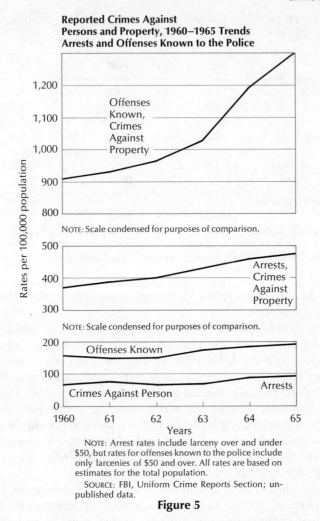

**Reported Crimes Against
Persons and Property, 1960–1965 Trends
Arrests and Offenses Known to the Police**

NOTE: Scale condensed for purposes of comparison.

NOTE: Scale condensed for purposes of comparison.

NOTE: Arrest rates include larceny over and under
$50, but rates for offenses known to the police include
only larcenies of $50 and over. All rates are based on
estimates for the total population.

SOURCE: FBI, Uniform Crime Reports Section; unpublished data.

Figure 5

earlier periods. Willful homicide rates have been below the 1960 level
through most of the last few years. Robbery rates continue to decline in
the rural areas and small towns, and arrest rates for many non-Index
offenses have remained relatively stable.

Because the general picture is so disturbing and the questions it raises
go to the very heart of concern about crime in the United States today,
the Commission has made a special effort to evaluate as fully as possible the
information available. It has tried to determine just how far this picture
is accurate, to see whether our cities and our countryside are more dangerous than they were before, to find out whether our youth and our citizens
are becoming more crime prone than those who were in their same cir-

cumstances in earlier years, to see what lies behind any increases that may have occurred, and to determine what if anything this information tells us can be done to bring the crime rate down.

What is known about the trend of crime—in the total number of offenses; in the ratio of offenses to population, which measures roughly the risk of victimization; and in the relationship of crime trends to changes in the composition of the population, which measures roughly the crime proneness of various kinds of people—is almost wholly a product of statistics. Therefore the Commission has taken a particularly hard look at the current sources of statistical knowledge.

Factors Affecting the Reporting of Crime

From the time that police statistics first began to be maintained in France in the 1820's, it has been recognized that the validity of calculations of changes in crime rates was dependent upon a constant relationship between reported and unreported crime. Until the Commission surveys of unreported crime, however, no systematic effort of wide scale had ever been made to determine what the relationship between reported and unreported crime was. As shown earlier, these surveys have now indicated that the actual amount of crime is several times that reported to the police, even in some of the precincts with the highest reported crime rates. This margin of unreported crime raises the possibility that even small changes in the way that crime is reported by the public to the police, or classified and recorded by the police, could have significant effects on the trend of reported crime. There is strong reason to believe that a number of such changes have taken place within recent years.

CHANGING EXPECTATIONS. One change of importance in the amount of crime that is reported in our society is the change in the expectations of the poor and members of minority groups about civil rights and social protection. Not long ago there was a tendency to dismiss reports of all but the most serious offenses in slum areas and segregated minority group districts. The poor and the segregated minority groups were left to take care of their own problems. Commission studies indicate that whatever the past pattern was, these areas now have a strong feeling of need for adequate police protection. Crimes that were once unknown to the police, or ignored when complaints were received, are now much more likely to be reported and recorded as part of the regular statistical procedure.

The situation seems similar to that found in England. The University of Cambridge's Institute of Criminology, which in 1963 conducted an exhaustive study of the sharp rise in crimes of violence, concluded in its report that:

One of the main causes for an increase in the recording of violent crime appears to be a decrease in the toleration of aggressive and violent behaviour, even in those slum and poor tenement areas where violence has always been regarded as a normal and accepted way of settling quarrels, jealousies or even quite trivial arguments.

POLICE PRACTICE. Perhaps the most important change for reporting purposes that has taken place in the last 25 years is the change in the police. Notable progress has been made during this period in the professionalization of police forces. With this change, Commission studies indicate, there is a strong trend toward more formal actions, more formal records and less informal disposition of individual cases. This trend is particularly apparent in the way the police handle juveniles, where the greatest increases are reported, but seems to apply to other cases as well. It seems likely that professionalization also results in greater police efficiency in looking for crime. Increases in the number of clerks and statistical personnel, better methods for recording information, and the use of more intensive patrolling practices also tend to increase the amount of recorded crime. Because this process of professionalization has taken place over a period of time and because it is most often a gradual rather than an abrupt change, it is difficult to estimate what its cumulative effect has been.

Wholly different kinds of changes have occurred in a number of cities. In 1953 Philadelphia reported 28,560 Index crimes plus negligent manslaughter and larceny under $50, an increase of more than 70 percent over 1951. This sudden jump in crime, however, was not due to an invasion by criminals but to the discovery by a new administration that crime records had for years minimized the amount of crime in the city. One district had actually handled 5,000 complaints more than it had recorded.

The Commission could not attempt an exhaustive study of such changes in reporting procedures. It has noted in table 7 a number of instances in which the UCR indicated changes in reporting procedures for major cities during 1959–65. All of these changes have resulted in an increase in the level of reporting for all subsequent years. It has also noted that changes of this sort are still taking place, being indicated in 1966 for Detroit, Chattanooga, Worcester, Mass., and New York City among others.

Perhaps the clearest illustration of the impact that changes in reporting systems can have is that shown by the history of such changes in New York City and Chicago. These cities are two of the Nation's largest police jurisdictions, accounting in 1965 for 20 percent of all reported robberies and 7 percent of all reported burglaries. Changes in their reporting systems have several times produced large paper increases in crime. Figure 6 illustrates the pattern dramatically.

Although Chicago, with about 3 million people, has remained a little

TABLE 7.   REPORTING SYSTEM CHANGES—UCR INDEX
FIGURES NOT COMPARABLE WITH PRIOR YEARS

Name of city	Years of increase	Amount of increase (Index offenses)		Percent increase
		From	To	
Baltimore	1964–65	18,637	26,193	40.5
Buffalo	1961–63	4,779	9,305	94.7
Chicago	1959–60	56,570	97,253	71.9
Cleveland	1963–64	10,584	17,254	63.0
Indianapolis	1961–62	7,416	10,926	47.3
Kansas City, Mo.	1959–61[1]	4,344	13,121	202.0
Memphis	1963–64	8,781	11,533	31.3
Miami	1963–64	10,750	13,610	26.6
Nashville	1962–63	6,595	9,343	41.7
Shreveport	1962–63	1,898	2,784	46.7
Syracuse	1963–64	3,365	4,527	34.5

[1] No report was published for Kansas City, Mo., for 1960.

SOURCE: "Uniform Crime Reports," 1959–1965.

less than half the size of New York City with 7½ million throughout the
period covered in figure 6, it was reporting in 1935 about 8 times as many
robberies. It continued to report several times as many robberies as New
York City until 1949, when the FBI discontinued publication of New
York reports because it no longer believed them. In 1950 New York discontinued its prior practice of allowing precincts to handle complaints
directly and installed a central reporting system, through which citizens
had to route all calls.

In the first year, robberies rose 400 percent and burglaries 1,300 percent, passing Chicago in volume for both offenses. In 1959 Chicago installed
a central complaint bureau of its own, reporting thereafter several times
more robberies than New York. In 1966 New York, which appeared to
have had a sharp decline in robberies in the late fifties, again tightened its
central controls and found a much higher number of offenses. Based on
preliminary reports for 1966, it is now reporting about 25 percent more
robberies than Chicago.

The existence of the UCR system has been one of the strongest forces
pushing toward the adoption of better and more complete reporting. The
FBI has been alert both to the need to encourage better reporting and to
the problem that sizable changes in reporting present to the national statistical system. Through a careful system of checks the FBI is able to identify

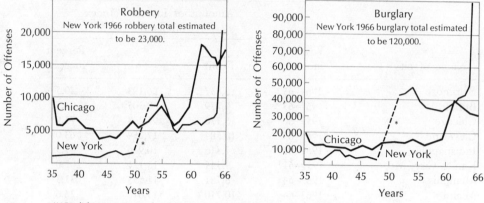

Robbery and Burglary Trends for Chicago and New York, 1935–1966

*UCR did not report any data for New York, 1949–1951.
SOURCE: *Uniform Crime Reports, 1936–1966.* 1966 figures estimated from 11 months' report.

Figure 6

the units that are reporting on a different basis than the previous year. It then restricts its computations of trends from one year to the next to those police agencies that have had comparable records and reporting practices. In 1965, for example, computation of changes from 1964 were limited to agencies representing 82 percent of the U.S. population; 147 reporting agencies representing about 10 percent of the population were eliminated because of changes in reporting practices.

In order to make comparisons for periods greater than 1 year the UCR assumes that the city that underwent the change in reporting practices has had the same experience as other cities of its size and State throughout the period and reestimates the amount of crime for all prior years back to its base period of the 1937–40 average. In the 1960–65 period, use of this system reduces the 36 percent increase in Index crimes against the person based on published rates to a 25 percent increase, and the 39 percent increase in crimes against property to 36 percent. Cities are returned to the trend computation after they have had 2 years of comparable experience under the new system.

This system is perhaps as good as can be devised. It is obviously very hard, however, to estimate how much crime would have been reported in a major city in the year prior to that in which the system of reporting was changed, and even harder to say what the crime rate was 5 years earlier. It seems unlikely that the level of robbery in New York today is 13 times what it was in 1940 or triple what it was in 1960, but how does one decide for the purpose of long-term comparisons? The cities that have significantly changed their reporting systems since 1959 account for nearly 25 percent of all reported Index crimes against the person and about 16 percent of all reported Index property crimes. The real question is not the method of estimation, but whether the yardstick at the present time is too changeable to allow significant trend comparisons to be made at the national level.

A further problem is raised by the fact that a number of other large cities have not yet adopted the central complaint bureaus and strong staff controls necessary for an effective reporting program. In one of these cities Commission staff members were informed of a precinct file 13, where citizen complaints not forwarded to the central statistical office were filed for the purpose of answering insurance inquiries. The President's Commission on Crime in the District of Columbia recently criticized Washington's failure to record all offenses reported to the police. It is not clear how large this group of cities is, but disparities between cities of the same size for each of the Index offenses are so great that they seem most unlikely in the absence of some variation in reporting practice.

The reporting problem arises at least in part from the tendency of some cities, noted in 1931 by the Wickersham Commission, to "use these reports in order to advertise their freedom from crime as compared with other municipalities." This tendency has apparently not yet been fully overcome. It sometimes arises from political pressure outside the police department and sometimes from the desire of the police to appear to be doing a good job of keeping the crime rate down. Defective or inefficient recording practices may also prevent crimes reported by citizens from becoming a part of the record.

The Commission believes that each city administration and each agency of justice has a duty to insure that its citizens are being informed of the full rate of reported crime in the community. Not to do so means that the community is being misled and that it has no benchmark to measure the effectiveness of its prevention and control program. It may also mean that the community is unaware of an increasing problem. In the case of large cities, not to report crime accurately also penalizes those administrations and police departments that are honest with their citizens by causing them to suffer unjust comparisons with other cities. . . .

INSURANCE. Another factor that probably increases the amount of reporting for some crimes is the sizable increase in insurance coverage against theft. It is difficult to evaluate this factor. However, because many persons believe that they must report a criminal event to the police in order to collect insurance, more reporting seems likely. Although not the only factor involved, one indication that this may be the case is the high rate of reporting for auto theft noted by the NORC survey. Insurance is usually involved in auto theft.

Factors Indicating an Increase in Crime

Many factors affect crime trends but they are not always easy to isolate. Murder is a seasonal offense. Rates are generally higher in the summer, except for December, which is often the highest month and almost always 5 to 20 percent above the yearly average. In December 1963, following the assassination of President Kennedy, murders were below the yearly average by 4 percent, one of the few years in the history of the UCR that this occurred. Since 1950 the pace of auto thefts has increased faster than but in the same direction as car registrations. During World War II, however, when there was rationing and a shortage of cars, rates for auto theft rose sharply. And in 1946 when cars came back in production and most other crimes were increasing, auto thefts fell off rapidly.

The introduction to the UCR provides a checklist of some of the many factors that must be taken into account in interpreting changes in crime rates and in the amount and type of crime that occurs from place to place:

Density and size of community population and the metropolitan area of which it is a part.

Composition of the population with reference particularly to age, sex, and race.

Economic status and mores of the population.

Relative stability of population, including commuters, seasonal, and other transient types.

Climate, including seasonal weather conditions.

Educational, recreational, and religious characteristics.

Effective strength of the police force.

Standards governing appointments to the police force.

Policies of the prosecuting officials and the courts.

Attitude of the public toward law enforcement problems.

The administrative and investigative efficiency of the local law enforcement agency.

A number of these factors have been changing in ways that would lead one to expect increases in the amounts of certain kinds of crime.

CHANGING AGE COMPOSITION. One of the most significant factors affecting crime rates is the age composition of the population. In 1965 more than 44 percent of all persons arrested for forcible rape, more than 39 percent for robbery, and more than 26 percent for willful homicide and aggravated assault were in the 18- to 24-year-old age group. For property crimes the highest percentages are found in the under 18 group—nearly 50 percent of all those arrested for burglary and larceny and more than 60 percent for auto theft.

For most of these offenses the rate of offense per individual in these age groups is many times that in older groups. Of course the differences are based on arrest figures, and the national figures on offenses cleared by arrest show that 75 to 80 percent of burglaries, larcenies, and auto thefts are unsolved. It is possible that older persons committing offenses against property are more successful at evading arrest, so that the age figures for arrests give a somewhat biased picture.

Because of the unusual birth rate in the postwar years, the youthful high-risk group—those in their teens and early twenties—has been increasing much faster than other groups in the population. Beginning in 1961 nearly 1 million more youths have reached the ages of maximum risk each year than did so in the prior year. Thus the volume of crime and the overall crime rate could be expected to grow whether the rate for any given age increased or not.

Commission studies based on 1960 arrest rates indicate that between 1960 and 1965 about 40 to 50 percent of the total increase in the arrests reported by UCR could have been expected as the result of increases in population and changes in the age composition of the population.

URBANIZATION. Rates for most crimes are highest in the big cities. Twenty-six core cities of more than 500,000 people, with less than 18 percent of the total population, account for more than half of all reported Index crimes against the person and more than 30 percent of all reported Index property crimes. One of every three robberies and nearly one of every five rapes occurs in cities of more than 1 million. The average rate for every Index crime except burglary, as table 8 shows, is at least twice as great—and often more—in these cities as in the suburbs or rural areas. With a few exceptions, average rates increase progressively as the size of the city becomes larger.

Suburban rates are closest to those of the smaller cities except for forcible rape where suburban rates are higher. Suburban rates appear to be going up as business and industry increase—shopping centers are most frequently blamed by local police officials for rises in suburban crime.

Although rural rates are lower generally than those for cities, the differences have always been much greater for property crimes than for crimes against the person. Until the last few years rural rates for murder were close to those of the big cities, and rural rates for murder and rape still exceed those for small towns.

The country has for many years seen a steady increase in its urban population and a decline in the proportion of the population living in rural areas and smaller towns. Since 1930 the rural population has increased by less than 2 percent while the city population has increased by more than 50 percent. The increase in the cities and their suburbs since 1960 alone has

TABLE 8.   OFFENSES KNOWN BY CITY SIZE, 1965
(Rates per 100,000 population)

Group	Will- ful homi- cide	Forc- ible rape	Rob- bery	Aggra- vated assault	Bur- glary	Larceny $50 and over	Motor vehicle theft
Cities over 1 million	10	26	221	246	930	734	586
500,000 to 1 million	10	20	165	182	1,009	555	640
250,000 to 500,000	7	15	122	142	1,045	550	468
100,000 to 250,000	6	11	73	151	871	556	353
50,000 to 100,000	4	8	49	85	675	492	297
25,000 to 50,000	3	6	33	71	562	443	212
10,000 to 25,000	2	6	19	67	462	309	141
Under 10,000	2	5	12	62	369	236	99
Rural	4	9	10	58	308	176	51
Suburban area	3	10	28	66	545	359	160
All places	5	12	61	107	605	420	251

SOURCE: "Uniform Crime Reports," 1965, table 1, p. 51 and table 6, p. 94.

been about 10 percent. Because of the higher crime rates in and around the larger cities, this trend toward urbanization has a considerable effect on the national rate for most Index crimes. Commission studies show that if metropolitan, small city, and rural crime rates for 1960 had remained constant through 1965, the increase that could have been expected due to urbanization would have been about 7 to 8 percent of the increase reported by the UCR.

It would obviously tell us a great deal about the trend of crime if we could analyze all together the changes that have been taking place in urbanization, age composition of the population, number of slum dwellers, and other factors such as sex, race, and level of income. The Commission has spent a considerable amount of time trying to make this kind of analysis. However, it was unable to analyze satisfactorily more than one or two factors in conjunction with each other on the basis of present information. As more factors were brought into the analysis the results differed in some instances substantially from those obtained when only one factor was analyzed. It also seemed clear that as the number of factors was increased, a more accurate picture of the effect of changing conditions on the rate of crime emerged.

On the basis of its study, the Commission estimates that the total expected increase in crime from 1960 to 1965 from these kinds of changes would be at least half, and possibly a great deal more, of the total increase in crime rates actually observed. The Commission's study clearly indicates the need for fuller reporting of arrest information and for the development of more compatibility between police statistics and information collected by other statistical agencies. The FBI has already made substantial progress in this direction in recent years but further steps are still needed.

SOME UNEXPLAINED VARIATIONS. Some crimes are not so heavily concentrated in the urban areas as the Index offenses. Vandalism, liquor law violations, driving while intoxicated, forgery and counterfeiting, and embezzlement and fraud are much more evenly spread over cities of all sizes and rural areas. Narcotics violations, gambling, drunkenness, vagrancy, and disorderly conduct generally follow the same pattern as Index offenses.

The explanations that have been offered for urban areas having higher rates of crime than rural areas have usually centered around the larger number of criminal opportunities available, a greater likelihood of association with those who are already criminals, a more impersonal life that offers greater freedom and, in many cases, the harsher conditions of slum life—often in sharp and visible contrast to the affluence of nearby areas. That these factors operate differently with regard to crimes of violence and crimes against property, and with regard to more serious offenses, suggests that the relationship between the rate of crime and the degree of urbanization is a very complicated one.

This seems to be borne out by the disparities in rates between cities of the same size. While average rates clearly vary by categories of population, the rates of individual cities seem much more helter-skelter. Of the 56 cities in the country with more than 250,000 in population, only one, Los Angeles, of the 10 cities with the highest rates for all Index offenses is a city of over 1 million. Newark, the city with the highest rate for all Index offenses, is in the 250,000–500,000 category, as are 4 others. Philadelphia ranks 51st and New York, before its change in reporting, ranked 28th.

The patterns vary markedly from offense to offense even within the broad categories of crimes against the person and crimes against property. Los Angeles is 1st for rape and 4th for aggravated assault but 20th for murder, with a murder rate less than half that of St. Louis. Chicago has the highest rate for robbery but a relatively low rate for burglary. New York is 5th in larcenies $50 and over, but 54th for larcenies under $50. The risk of auto theft is about 50 percent greater in Boston than anywhere else in the country, but in Boston the likelihood of other kinds of theft is about the average for cities over 250,000. Table 9 shows the robbery rates for the country's 14 largest cities.

Not very much study has been devoted to this kind of difference and the Commission was able to do little more than survey the literature already in existence. Some of the difference, perhaps a great deal, seems clearly

TABLE 9.   ROBBERY RATES IN 1965—14 LARGEST CITIES
IN ORDER OF SIZE
(Per 100,000 population)

New York	114	Cleveland	213
Chicago	421	Washington	359
Los Angeles	293	St. Louis	327
Philadelphia	140	Milwaukee	28
Detroit	335	San Francisco	278
Baltimore	229	Boston	168
Houston	135	Dallas	79

SOURCE: FBI, Uniform Crime Reports Section, unpublished data.

attributable to differences in reporting. Disparities as great as 17 to 1 between Newark and Jersey City, or 10 to 1 between St. Louis and Milwaukee for certain offenses seem most unlikely in the absence of some reporting variation. There are significant differences, however, among cities in such factors as age, sex, race, and other population characteristics, economic status, character of industry, climate, and the like and it seems clear that there are real and substantial differences in the true amounts of crime.

The few studies that have been done in this area have failed altogether to account for the differences in offense rates in terms of characteristics such as these. These studies suggest that whatever factors are operating affect personal and property crimes differently, and substantially refute the idea that crime rate variations can be accounted for by any single factor such as urbanization, industrialization, or standard of living. These studies take us very little further, however, than the differences in the rates themselves. Even when they offer some explanation of the differences between cities, the explanations they offer are not able to account for the variations within the cities themselves.

Given the large, often gigantic, differences in rates between cities, the Commission has been struck that so little has been done to learn the causes of these variations. If only a little were known as to why the robbery rate was 12 times as high in Chicago as in San Jose, it would be much easier to figure out what to do about robbery in Chicago. While no simple answers can be expected, the Commission strongly believes that further exploration of these differences could make an important contribution to the prevention and control of crime.

INCREASED AFFLUENCE.   Another change that may result in more crime is increasing affluence. There are more goods around to be stolen. National wealth and all categories of merchandise have increased in terms of constant dollars more than fourfold since 1940—significantly more than the population or the rate of reported theft.

Increased affluence may also have meant that property is now protected less well than formerly. More than 40 percent of all auto thefts involve cars with the keys inside or the switch left open. A substantial percentage of residential burglaries occur in unlocked houses. Bicycles, whose theft constitutes 15 percent of all reported larcenies, are frequently left lying around. Larceny of goods and accessories from cars accounts for another 40 percent of all reported larceny.

Some increased business theft seems directly due to less protection. The recent rise in bank robbery seems due in large part to the development of small, poorly protected branch banks in the suburbs.

In retail establishments, managers choose to tolerate a high percentage of shoplifting rather than pay for additional clerks. Discount stores, for example, experience an inventory loss rate almost double that of the conventional department store. Studies indicate that there is in general more public tolerance for theft of property and goods from large organizations than from small ones, from big corporations or utilities than from small neighborhood establishments. Restraints on conduct that were effective in a more personal rural society do not seem as effective in an impersonal society of large organizations.

Inflation has also had an impact on some property crimes. Larcency, for example, is any stealing that does not involve force or fraud. The test of the seriousness of larceny is the value of the property stolen. The dividing line between "grand" and "petty" larceny for national reporting purposes is $50. Larceny of $50 and over is the Index offense that has increased the most over the history of the UCR, more than 550 percent since 1933. Because the purchasing power of the dollar today is only 40 percent of what it was in 1933, many thefts that would have been under $50 then are over $50 now. UCR figures on the value of property stolen, for example, indicate that the average value of a larceny has risen from $26 in 1940 to $84 in 1965.

Other Countries

Crime is a worldwide problem. For most offenses it is difficult to compare directly the rates between countries because of great differences in the definitions of crime and in reporting practices. It is clear, however, that there are great differences in the rates of crime among the various countries, and in the crime problems that they face. These differences are illustrated to some extent by the homicide rates for a number of countries shown in table 10. The comparisons show only the general range of differences, as definitions and reporting even of homicide vary to some extent. In the years covered by the table, Colombia had the highest rate for all countries and Ireland the lowest.

TABLE 10. HOMICIDE RATES FOR SELECTED
COUNTRIES (Per 100,000 population)

Country	Rate	Year reported
Colombia	36.5	1962
Mexico	31.9	1960
South Africa	21.8	1960
United States	4.8	1962
Japan	1.5	1962
France	1.5	1962
Canada	1.4	1962
Federal Republic of Germany	1.2	1961
England/Wales	.7	1962
Ireland	.4	1962

SOURCE: "Demographic Yearbook," 15th issue, United Nations Publications, 1963, pp. 594–611.

A comparison between crime rates in 1964 in West Germany and the north central United States, prepared by the FBI, indicates that the Federal Republic, including West Berlin, had a crime rate of 0.8 murders per 100,000 inhabitants, 10.6 rapes, 12.4 robberies, 1,628.2 larcenies, and 78.2 auto thefts, as opposed to 3.5 murders per 100,000 inhabitants for north central United States, 10.5 rapes, 76.2 robberies, 1,337.3 larcenies, and 234.7 auto thefts.

Commission and other studies of crime trends indicate that in most other countries officially reported rates for property offenses are rising rapidly, as they are in the United States, but that there is no definite pattern in the trend of crimes of violence in other countries. Since 1955 property crime rates have increased more than 200 percent in West Germany, the Netherlands, Sweden, and Finland, and over 100 percent in France, England and Wales, Italy, and Norway. Of the countries studied, property crime rates in Denmark, Belgium, and Switzerland remained relatively stable.

Crimes of violence could be studied in only a few countries. Rates declined in Belgium, Denmark, Norway, and Switzerland, but rose more than 150 percent in England and Wales between 1955 and 1964. Sexual offenses, which are usually kept as a separate statistic in Europe, also showed a mixed trend.

Assessing the Amount and Trend of Crime

Because of the grave public concern about the crime problem in America today, the Commission has made a special effort to understand the amount and trend of crime and has reached the following conclusions:

1. The number of offenses—crimes of violence, crimes against property and most others as well—has been increasing. Naturally, population growth is one of the significant contributing factors in the total amount of crime.

2. Most forms of crime—especially crimes against property—are increasing faster than population growth. This means that the risk of victimization to the individual citizen for these crimes is increasing, although it is not possible to ascertain precisely the extent of the increase. All the economic and social factors discussed above support, and indeed lead to, this conclusion.

The Commission found it very difficult to make accurate measurements of crime trends by relying solely on official figures, since it is likely that each year police agencies are to some degree dipping deeper into the vast reservoir of unreported crime. People are probably reporting more to the police as a reflection of higher expectations and greater confidence, and the police in turn are reflecting this in their statistics. In this sense more efficient policing may be leading to higher rates of reported crime. The diligence of the FBI in promoting more complete and accurate reporting through the development of professional police reporting procedures has clearly had an important effect on the completeness of reporting, but while this task of upgrading local reporting is under way, the FBI is faced with the problem, in computing national trends, of omitting for a time the places undergoing changes in reporting methods and estimating the amount of crime that occurred in those places in prior years.

3. Although the Commission concluded that there has been an increase in the volume and rate of crime in America, it has been unable to decide whether individual Americans today are more criminal than their counterparts 5, 10, or 25 years ago. To answer this question it would be necessary to make comparisons between persons of the same age, sex, race, place of residence, economic status and other factors at the different times: in other words, to decide whether the 15-year-old slum dweller or the 50-year-old businessman is inherently more criminal now that the 15-year-old slum dweller or the 50-year-old businessman in the past. Because of the many rapid and turbulent changes over these years in society as a whole and in the myriad conditions of life which affect crime, it was not possible for the Commission to make such a comparison. Nor do the data exist to make even simple comparisons of the incidence of crime among persons of the same age, sex, race, and place of residence at these different years.

4. There is a great deal of crime in America, some of it very serious, that is not reported to the police, or in some instances by the police. The national survey revealed that people are generally more likely to report serious crimes to the police, but the percent who indicated they did report to the police ranged from 10 percent for consumer fraud to 89 percent for auto theft. Estimates of the rate of victimization for Index offenses ranged from 2 per 100 persons in the national survey to 10 to 20 per 100 persons in the individual districts surveyed in 3 cities. The surveys produced rates of victimization that were from 2 to 10 times greater than the official rates for certain crimes.

5. What is needed to answer questions about the volume and trend of crime satisfactorily are a number of different crime indicators showing trends over a period of time to supplement the improved reporting by police agencies. The Commission experimented with the development of public surveys of victims of crime and feels this can become a useful supplementary yardstick. Further development of the procedure is needed to improve the reliability and accuracy of the findings. However, the Commission found these initial experiments produced useful results that justify more intensive efforts to gather such information on a regular basis. They should also be supplemented by new types of surveys and censuses which would provide better information about crime in areas where good information is lacking such as crimes by or against business and other organizations. The Commission also believes that an improved and greatly expanded procedure for the collection of arrest statistics would be of immense benefit in the assessment of the problem of juvenile delinquency.

6. Throughout its work the Commission has noted repeatedly the sharp differences in the amount and trends of reported crimes against property as compared with crimes against persons. It has noted that while property crimes are far more numerous than crimes against the person, and so dominate any reported trends, there is much public concern about crimes against persons. The more recent reports of the UCR have moved far toward separating the reporting of these two classes of crime altogether.

.   .   .

7. The Commission believes that age, urbanization, and other shifts in the population already under way will likely operate over the next 5 to 10 years to increase the volume of offenses faster than population growth. Further dipping into the reservoirs of unreported crime will likely combine with this real increase in crime to produce even greater increases in reported crime rates. Many of the basic social forces that tend to increase the amount of real crime are already taking effect and are for the most part irreversible. If society is to be successful in its desire to reduce the amount of real crime, it must find new ways to create the kinds of conditions and inducements—social, environmental, and psychological—that will bring about a greater commitment to law-abiding conduct and respect for the law on the part of all Americans and a better understanding of the great stake that all men have in being able to trust in the honesty and integrity of their fellow citizens.

THE ECONOMIC IMPACT OF CRIME

One way in which crime affects the lives of all Americans is that it costs all Americans money. Economic costs alone cannot determine attitudes about crime or policies toward crime, of course. The costs of lost or damaged lives, of fear and of suffering, and of the failure to control critical events cannot be measured solely in dollars and cents. Nor can the requirements of justice and law enforcement be established solely by use of economic measures. A high percentage of a police department's manpower may have to be committed to catch a single murderer or bombthrower. The poor, unemployed defendant in a minor criminal case is entitled to all the protections our constitutional system provides—without regard to monetary costs.

However, economic factors relating to crime are important in the formation of attitudes and policies. Crime in the United States today imposes a very heavy economic burden upon both the community as a whole and individual members of it. Risks and responses cannot be judged with maximum effectiveness until the full extent of economic loss has been ascertained. Researchers, policymakers, and operating agencies should know which crimes cause the greatest economic loss, which the least; on whom the costs of crime fall, and what the costs are to prevent or protect against it; whether a particular or general crime situation warrants further expenditures for control or prevention and, if so, what expenditures are likely to have the greatest impact.

The number of policemen, the size of a plant security staff, or the amount of insurance any individual or business carries are controlled to some degree by economics—the balance of the value to be gained against the burden of additional expenditures. If the protection of property is the objective, the economic loss from crime must be weighed directly against the cost of better prevention or control. In view of the importance and the frequency of such decisions, it is surprising that the cost information on which they are based is as fragmentary as it is. The lack of knowledge about which the Wickersham Commission complained 30 years ago is almost as great today.

Some cost data are now reported through the UCR and additional data are available from individual police forces, insurance companies, industrial security firms, trade associations, and others. However, the total amount of information is not nearly enough in quantity, quality, or detail to give an accurate overall picture.

The information available about the economic cost of crime is most usefully presented not as an overall figure, but as a series of separate private and public costs. Knowing the economic impact of each separate crime aids in identifying important areas for public concern and guides officials in making judgments about priorities for expenditure. Breakdowns of money now being spent on different parts of the criminal justice system, and within each separate part, may afford insights into past errors. For example, even excluding value judgments about rehabilitative methods, the fact that an adult probationer costs 38 cents a day and an adult offender in prison costs $5.24 a day suggests the need for reexamining current budget allocations in correctional practice.

Figure 7 represents six different categories of economic impacts both

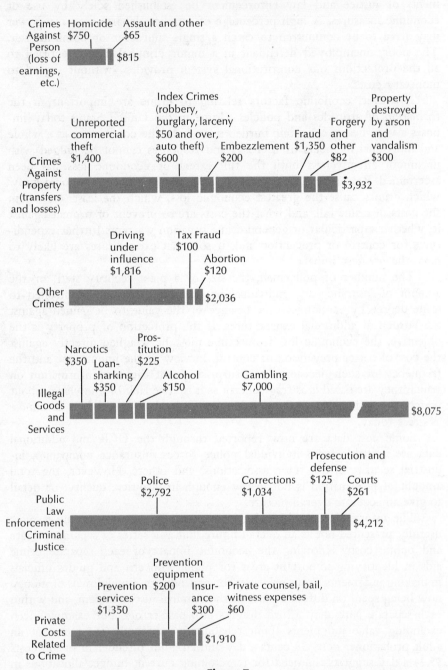

Economic Impact of Crimes and Related Expenditures
(Estimated in millions of dollars)

Crimes Against Person (loss of earnings, etc.)
Homicide $750
Assault and other $65
$815

Crimes Against Property (transfers and losses)
Unreported commercial theft $1,400
Index Crimes (robbery, burglary, larceny $50 and over, auto theft) $600
Embezzlement $200
Fraud $1,350
Forgery and other $82
Property destroyed by arson and vandalism $300
$3,932

Other Crimes
Driving under influence $1,816
Tax Fraud $100
Abortion $120
$2,036

Illegal Goods and Services
Narcotics $350
Loansharking $350
Prostitution $225
Alcohol $150
Gambling $7,000
$8,075

Public Law Enforcement Criminal Justice
Police $2,792
Corrections $1,034
Prosecution and defense $125
Courts $261
$4,212

Private Costs Related to Crime
Prevention services $1,350
Prevention equipment $200
Insurance $300
Private counsel, bail, witness expenses $60
$1,910

Figure 7

private and public. Numerous crimes were omitted because of the lack of figures. Estimates of doubtful reliability were used in other cases so that a fuller picture might be presented. Estimates do not include any amounts for pain and suffering. Except for alcohol, which is based on the amount of tax revenue lost, estimates for illegal goods and services are based on the gross amount of income to the seller. (Gambling includes only the percentage retained by organized crime, not the total amount gambled.) The totals should be taken to indicate rough orders of magnitude rather than precise details.

Economic Impact of Individual Crimes

The picture of crime as seen through cost information is considerably different from that shown by statistics portraying the number of offenses known to the police or the number of arrests:

- ☐ Organized crime takes about twice as much income from gambling and other illegal goods and services as criminals derive from all other kinds of criminal activity combined.
- ☐ Unreported commercial theft losses, including shoplifting and employee theft, are more than double those of all reported private and commercial thefts.
- ☐ Of the reported crimes, willful homicide, though comparatively low in volume, yields the most costly estimates among those listed on the UCR crime index.
- ☐ A list of the seven crimes with the greatest economic impact includes only two, willful homicide and larceny of $50 and over (reported and unreported), of the offenses included in the crime Index.
- ☐ Only a small proportion of the money expended for criminal justice agencies is allocated to rehabilitative programs for criminals or for research.

Employee theft, embezzlement, and other forms of crime involving business, which appear in relatively small numbers in the police statistics, loom very large in dollar volume. Direct stealing of cash and merchandise, manipulation of accounts and stock records, and other forms of these crimes, along with shoplifting, appear to constitute a tax of one to two percent on the total sales of retail enterprises, and significant amounts in other parts of business and industry. In the grocery trade, for example, the theft estimates for shoplifting and employee theft almost equal the total amount of profit. Yet Commission and other studies indicate that these crimes are largely dealt with by business itself. Merchants report to the police fewer than one-quarter of the known offenses. Estimates for these crimes are particularly incomplete for nonretail industries.

Fraud is another offense whose impact is not well conveyed by police statistics. Just one conspiracy involving the collapse of a fraudulent salad oil empire in 1964 created losses of $125–$175 million. Fraud is especially vicious when it attacks, as it so often does, the poor or those who live on the margin of poverty. Expensive nostrums for incurable diseases, home-improvement frauds, frauds involving the sale or repair of cars, and other criminal schemes create losses which are not only sizable in gross but are also significant and possibly devastating for individual victims. Although a very frequent offense, fraud is seldom reported to the police. In consumer and business fraud, as in tax evasion, the line between criminal conduct and civil fraud is often unclear. And just as the amount of civil tax evasion is much greater than the amount of criminal tax fraud, the amount of civil fraud probably far exceeds that of criminal fraud.

Cost analysis also places the crimes that appear so frequently in police statistics—robbery, burglary, larceny, and auto theft—in somewhat different perspective. The number of reported offenses for these crimes accounts for less than one-sixth the estimated total dollar loss for all property crimes and would constitute an even lower percentage if there were any accurate way of estimating the very large sums involved in extortion, blackmail, and other property crimes.

This is not to say, however, that the large amounts of police time and effort spent in dealing with these crimes are not important. Robbery and burglary, particularly residential burglary, have importance beyond the number of dollars involved. The effectiveness of the police in securing the return of better than 85 percent of the $500 million worth of cars stolen annually appears to be high, and without the efforts of the police the costs of these crimes would doubtless be higher. As with all categories of crime, the total cost of property crimes cannot be measured because of the large volume of unreported crimes; however, Commission surveys suggest that the crimes that are unreported involve less money per offense than those that are reported.

The economic impact of crimes causing death is surprisingly high. For 1965 there were an estimated 9,850 homicide victims. Of the estimated 49,000 people who lost their lives in highway accidents, more than half were killed in accidents involving either negligent manslaughter or driving under the influence of alcohol. An estimated 290 women died from complications resulting from illegal abortions (nearly one-fourth of all maternal deaths). Measured by the loss of future earnings at the time of death, these losses totaled more than $1½ billion.

The economic impact of other crimes is particularly difficult to assess. Antitrust violations reduce competition and unduly raise prices; building code violations, pure food and drug law violations, and other crimes affecting the consumer have important economic consequences, but they cannot be easily described without further information. Losses due to fear of crime, such as reduced sales in high crime locations, are real but beyond measure.

Economic impact must also be measured in terms of ultimate costs to society. Criminal acts causing property destruction or injury to persons not only result in serious losses to the victims or their families but also the withdrawal of wealth or productive capacity from the economy as a whole. Theft on the other hand does not destroy wealth but merely transfers it involuntarily from the victim, or perhaps his insurance company, to the thief. The bettor purchasing illegal betting-services from organized crime may easily absorb the loss of a 10-cent, or even 10-dollar, bet. But from the point of view of society, gambling leaves much less wealth available for legitimate business. Perhaps more important, it is the proceeds of this crime tariff that organized crime collects from those who purchase its illegal wares that form the major source of income that organized crime requires to achieve and exercise economic and political power.

Expenditures for Crime Prevention and Control

Public expenditures, shown on figure 8, for the police, courts, and corrections—currently estimated at more than $4 billion a year—are borne primarily by taxpayers at the State and local level.

Both corrections costs and police costs have been growing, with corrections costs expanding at a more rapid rate. About 85–90 percent of all police costs are for salaries and wages, leaving only a small proportion for equipment or research. Ten to 15 percent of local police time and greater amounts for some State police units is spent on traffic control. Because it is difficult to distinguish the civil from the criminal allocations of police time, no adjustment has been made in figure 8. A small percentage of all correctional costs is spent for the treatment—as opposed to custody—of institutionalized offenders.

Many other public expenditures play a direct and important role in the prevention of crime. These include antipoverty, recreational, educational, and vocational programs. They have not been included in this tabulation, however, because most have social purposes that go far beyond preventing crime.

Private costs related to crime are also difficult to determine, particularly those for crime prevention and protection. While the $200 million spent annually for burglar alarms and other protective equipment clearly relates only to crime, the night watchman's additional duties indicate that only an undetermined percentage of his salary should be attributed to crime costs. Insurance awards neither increase nor decrease the total loss from crime, but merely spread it among all premium payers. The substantial overhead cost

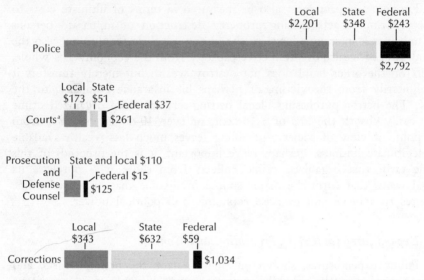

Public Expenditures for Prevention and Control of Crime
(Estimated in millions of dollars)

^aTotal court costs are estimated at $782 million—$109 Federal, $155 State, and $518 local; criminal court costs were estimated at one-third of the total based on studies in several jurisdictions.

SOURCE: Bureau of the Census, Division of Governments (corrections and police); Bureau of the Budget (courts); Commission studies. All figures are for fiscal year ending June 30, 1965.

Figure 8

of insuring—the cost shown in figure 7—is, however, an additional burden that must be borne by those who seek protection from crime.

. . .

CRIME AND THE INNER CITY

One of the most fully documented facts about crime is that the common serious crimes that worry people most—murder, forcible rape, robbery, aggravated assault, and burglary—happen most often in the slums of large cities. Study after study in city after city in all regions of the country have traced the variations in the rates for these crimes. The results, with monotonous regularity, show that the offenses, the victims, and the offenders are found most frequently in the poorest, and most deteriorated and socially disorganized areas of cities.

Studies of the distribution of crime rates in cities and of the conditions of life most commonly associated with high crime rates have been conducted for well over a century in Europe and for many years in the United States. The findings have been remarkably consistent. Burglary, robbery, and serious assaults occur in areas characterized by low income, physical deterioration, dependency, racial and ethnic concentrations, broken homes, working mothers, low levels of education and vocational skill, high unemployment, high proportions of single males, overcrowded and substandard housing, high rates of tuberculosis and infant mortality, low rates of home ownership or single family dwellings, mixed land use, and high population density. Studies that have mapped the relationship of these factors and crime have found them following the same pattern from one area of the city to another.

Crime rates in American cities tend to be highest in the city center and decrease in relationship to distance from the center. This typical distribution of crime rates is found even in medium sized cities. . . . This pattern has been found to hold fairly well for both offenses and offenders, although it is sometimes broken by unusual features of geography, enclaves of socially well integrated ethnic groups, irregularities in the distribution of opportunities to commit crime, and unusual concentrations of commercial and industrial establishments in outlying areas. The major irregularity found is the clustering of offenses and offenders beyond city boundaries in satellite areas that are developing such characteristics of the central city as high population mobility, commercial and industrial concentrations, low economic status, broken families and other social problems. . . .

The big city slum has always exacted its toll on its inhabitants, except where those inhabitants are bound together by an intense social and cultural solidarity that provides a collective defense against the pressures of slum living. Several slum settlements inhabited by people of oriental ancestry have shown a unique capacity to do this. However, the common experience of the great successive waves of immigrants of different racial and ethnic backgrounds that have poured into the poorest areas of our large cities has been quite different.

An historic series of studies by Clifford R. Shaw and Henry D. McKay of the Institute of Juvenile Research in Chicago documented the disorganizing impact of slum life on different groups of immigrants as they moved through the slums and struggled to gain a foothold in the economic and social life of the city. Throughout the period of immigration, areas with high delinquency and crime rates kept these high rates, even though members of new nationality groups successively moved in to displace the older residents. Each nationality group showed high rates of delinquency among its members who were living near the center of the city and lower rates for those living in the better outlying residential areas. Also for each nationality group, those living in the poorer areas had more of all the other social problems commonly associated with life in the slums.

This same pattern of high rates in the slum neighborhoods and low rates in the better districts is true among the Negroes and members of other minority groups who have made up the most recent waves of migration to the big cities. As other groups before them, they have had to crowd into the areas where they can afford to live while they search for ways to live better. The disorganizing personal and social experiences with life in the slums are producing the same problems for the new minority group residents, including high rates of crime and delinquency. As they acquire a stake in urban society and move to better areas of the city, the crime rates and the incidence of other social problems drop to lower levels.

However, there are a number of reasons to expect more crime and related problems among the new migrants to the city than among the older immigrants. There have been major changes in the job market, greatly reducing the demand for unskilled labor, which is all most new migrants have to offer. At the same time the educational requirements for jobs have been rising. Discrimination in employment, education, and housing, based on such a visible criterion as color, is harder to break than discrimination based on language or ethnic background.

What these changes add up to is that slums are becoming ghettos from which escape is increasingly difficult. It could be predicted that this frustration of the aspirations that originally led Negroes and other minority groups to seek out the city would ultimately lead to more crime. Such evidence as exists suggests this is true.

.   .   .

THE VICTIMS OF CRIME

One of the most neglected subjects in the study of crime is its victims: the persons, households, and businesses that bear the brunt of crime in the United States. Both the part the victim can play in the criminal act and the part he could have played in preventing it are often overlooked. If it could be determined with sufficient specificity that people or businesses with certain characteristics are more likely than others to be crime victims, and that crime is more likely to occur in some places than in others, efforts to control and prevent crime would be more productive. Then the public could be told where and when the risks of crime are greatest. Measures such as preventive police patrol and installation of burglar alarms and special locks could then be pursued more efficiently and effectively. Individuals could then substitute objective estimation of risk for the general apprehensiveness that today restricts—perhaps unnecessarily and at best haphazardly—their enjoyment of parks and their freedom of movement on the streets after dark.

Although information about victims and their relationships to offenders is recorded in the case files of the police and other criminal justice agencies,

TABLE 11.   VICTIMIZATION BY INCOME
(Rates per 100,000 population)

Offenses	Income			
	$0 to $2,999	$3,000 to $5,999	$6,000 to $9,999	Above $10,000
Total	2,369	2,331	1,820	2,237
Forcible rape	76	49	10	17
Robbery	172	121	48	34
Aggravated assault	229	316	144	252
Burglary	1,319	1,020	867	790
Larceny ($50 and over)	420	619	549	925
Motor vehicle theft	153	206	202	219
Number of respondents	(5,232)	(8,238)	(10,382)	(5,946)

SOURCE: NORC survey.

it is rarely used for systematic study of those relationships or the risks of victimization. To discover variations in victimization rates among different age, sex, race, and income groupings in the population, the Commission analyzed information on these items obtained in the national survey by NORC.

Rather striking variations in the risk of victimization for different types of crime appear among different income levels in the population. The results shown in table 11 indicate that the highest rates of victimization occur in the lower income groups when all Index offenses except homicide are considered together. The risks of victimization from forcible rape, robbery, and burglary, are clearly concentrated in the lowest income group and decrease steadily at higher income levels. The picture is somewhat more erratic for the offenses of aggravated assault, larceny of $50 and over, and vehicle theft. Victimization for larceny increases sharply in the highest income group.

National figures on rates of victimization also show sharp differences between whites and nonwhites (table 12). Nonwhites are victimized disproportionately by all Index crimes except larceny $50 and over.

The rates of victimization shown for Index offenses against men (table 13) are almost three times as great as those for women, but the higher rates of burglary, larceny and auto theft against men are in large measure an artifact of the survey procedure of assigning offenses against the household to the head of the household.

The victimization rate for women is highest in the 20 to 29 age group. In fact the victimization rates for women for all the Index offenses reported,

TABLE 12. VICTIMIZATION BY RACE
(Rates per 100,000 population)

Offenses	White	Nonwhite
Total	1,860	2,592
Forcible rape	22	82
Robbery	58	204
Aggravated assault	186	347
Burglary	822	1,306
Larceny ($50 and over)	608	367
Motor vehicle theft	164	286
Number of respondents	(27,484)	(4,902)

SOURCE: NORC survey.

TABLE 13. VICTIMIZATION BY AGE AND SEX
(Rates per 100,000 population)

Offense	Male						
	10–19	20–29	30–39	40–49	50–59	60 plus	All ages
Total	951	5,924	6,231	5,150	4,231	3,465	3,091
Robbery	61	257	112	210	181	98	112
Aggravated assault	399	824	337	263	181	146	287
Burglary	123	2,782	3,649	2,365	2,297	2,343	1,583
Larceny ($50 and over)	337	1,546	1,628	1,839	967	683	841
Motor vehicle theft	31	515	505	473	605	195	268
	Female						
Total	334	2,424	1,514	1,908	1,132	1,052	1,059
Forcible rape	91	238	104	48	0	0	83
Robbery	0	238	157	96	60	81	77
Aggravated assault	91	333	52	286	119	40	118
Burglary	30	665	574	524	298	445	314
Larceny ($50 and over)	122	570	470	620	536	405	337
Motor vehicle theft	0	380	157	334	119	81	130

SOURCE: NORC survey.

with the exception of larceny, are greatest in this age group. The concentration of offenses against women in this age group is particularly noticeable for forcible rape and robbery and much less apparent in aggravated assault and the property crimes.

For men the highest Index total rate falls in the 30–39 age category, a result heavily influenced by the burglaries assigned to men as heads of households. Actually, all the Index property offenses against men show peak rates in the older age categories. This is probably due not only to their role as household heads but also to the fact that at older ages they are likely to possess more property to be stolen. Crimes against the person, such as aggravated assault and robbery, are committed relatively more often against men who are from 20 to 29 years of age.

Thus, the findings from the national survey show that the risk of victimization is highest among the lower income groups for all Index offenses except homicide, larceny, and vehicle theft; it weighs most heavily on the nonwhites for all Index offenses except larceny; it is borne by men more often than women, except, of course, for forcible rape; and the risk is greatest for the age category 20 to 29, except for larceny against women, and burglary, larceny, and vehicle theft against men.

Victim-Offender Relationships in Crimes of Violence

The relations and interactions of victims and offenders prior to and during the criminal act are important facts to know for understanding and controlling crime and assessing personal risks more accurately. The relationships most often studied have been those involving crimes of violence against the person, especially homicide and forcible rape. Typical of the findings of these inquiries are the results of an analysis of criminal homicides in Philadelphia between 1948 and 1952. This study clearly demonstrated that it is not the marauding stranger who poses the greatest threat as a murderer. Only 12.2 percent of the murders were committed by strangers. In 28.2 percent of the cases studied, the murderer was a relative or a close friend. In 24.7 percent he was a member of the family. The murderer was an acquaintance of the victim in 13.5 percent of the cases.

These findings are very similar to those reported nationally in the UCR:

In 1965 killings within the family made up 31 percent of all murders. Over one-half of these involved spouse killing spouse and 16 percent parents killing children. Murder outside the family unit, usually the result of altercations among acquaintances, made up 48 percent of the willful killings. In the latter category romantic triangles or lovers' quarrels comprised 21 percent and killings resulting from drinking situations 17 percent. Felony murder, which is defined in this Program as those killings resulting from robberies, sex motives, gangland slayings, and other felonious activities, made up 16 percent of these offenses. In another 5 percent of the total police were unable to identify the reasons for the killings; however, the circumstances were such as to suspect felony murder.

Unfortunately, no national statistics are available on relationships between victims and offenders in crimes other than criminal homicide. However, the District of Columbia Crime Commission surveyed a number of other crimes. Its findings on victim-offender relationships in rape and aggravated assault closely resemble those for murder:

Almost two-thirds of the 151 [rape] victims surveyed were attacked by persons with whom they were at least casually acquainted. Only 36 percent of the 224 assailants about whom some identifying information was obtained were complete strangers to their victims: 16 (7 percent) of the attackers were known to the victim by sight, although there had been no previous contact. Thirty-one (14 percent) of the 224 assailants were relatives, family friends or boy friends of the victims, and 88 (39 percent) were either acquaintances or neighbors.

And among 131 aggravated assault victims, only 25 (19 percent) were not acquainted with their assailants:

Fourteen (11 percent) of the victims were attacked by their spouses, 13 (10 percent) were attacked by other relatives, and 79(60 percent) were assaulted by persons with whom they were at least casually acquainted.

Again, as in murder, a substantial number (20 percent) of the aggravated assaults surveyed by the District of Columbia Crime Commission involved a victim and offender who had had trouble with each other before.

Another source of the concern about crime, in addition to its violence and its frequency, is the extent to which it is assumed to involve interracial attacks. Therefore a key question in any assessment of the crime problem is to what extent men or women of one racial group victimize those of another. For evidence on the way in which the race and sex of victims and offenders might affect the probability of criminal assault, the Commission, with the cooperation of the Chicago Police Department, studied 13,713 cases of assaultive crimes against the person, other than homicide.

As shown in table 14, it is Negro males and females who are most likely to be victimized in crimes against the person. A Negro man in Chicago runs the risk of being a victim nearly six times as often as a white man, a Negro woman nearly eight times as often as a white woman.

The most striking fact in the data is the extent of the correlation in race between victim and offender. Table 14 shows that Negroes are most likely to assault Negroes, whites most likely to assault whites. Thus, while Negro males account for two-thirds of all assaults, the offender who victimizes a white person is most likely also to be white.

The President's Commission on Crime in the District of Columbia discovered similar racial relationships in its 1966 survey of a number of serious crimes. Only 12 of 172 murders were interracial. Eighty-eight per-

TABLE 14. VICTIM-OFFENDER RELATIONSHIPS BY RACE
AND SEX IN ASSAULTIVE CRIMES AGAINST THE PERSON
(EXCEPT HOMICIDE)

	Offenses attributable to—				
	White offenders		Negro offenders		All types of
Victim rate for each 100,000:[1]	Male	Female	Male	Female	offenders
White males	201	9	129	4	342
White females	108	14	46	6	175
Negro males	58	3	1,636	256	1,953
Negro females	21	3	1,202	157	1,382
Total population [1]	130	10	350	45	535

[1] The rates are based only on persons 14 years of age or older in each race-sex category. The "total population" category in addition excludes persons from racial groups other than Negro or white.

Source: Special tabulations from Chicago Police Department, Data Systems Division, for period September 1965 to March 1966.

cent of rapes involved persons of the same race. Among 121 aggravated assaults for which identification of race was available, only 9 percent were interracial. Auto theft offenders in the District are three-fourths Negroes, their victims two-thirds Negroes. Robbery, the only crime of violence in which whites were victimized more often than Negroes, is also the only one that is predominantly interracial: in 56 percent of the robberies committed by Negroes in the District of Columbia, the victims are white.

The high proportions of both acquaintance between victim and offender and the intraracial character of offenses are further borne out by the findings of another study developed for the Commission. Analyzing data obtained from the Seattle Police Department, this study compared the census tract where the crime occurred with the tract (or other place) in which the offender lived. It found that a relatively large percentage of crimes against persons, as contrasted with crimes against property, had been committed in the offender's home tract—an area likely to be racially homogeneous and in which he is most likely to be known at least by sight.

This analysis shows that a failure to collect adequate data on victim-offender relationships may lead to a miscalculation of the source and nature of the risk of victimization. At present the Nation's view of the crime problem is shaped largely by official statistics which in turn are based on offenses known to the police and statistics concerning arrested offenders; they include very little about victims.

Place Where Victimization Occurs

Crime is more likely to occur in some places than in others, just as some persons are more likely than others to be the victims of criminal offenders. The police often distribute their preventive patrols according to spot maps that locate the time and place of occurrence of different types of crimes. Such information, however, has not been developed well enough to inform the public of the places it should avoid.

A well-designed information system should also provide crime rate figures for different types of business premises in different areas of the city. Victimization rates based upon the number of drugstores, cleaning establishments, gas stations, taxicabs, banks, supermarkets, taverns, and other businesses in a neighborhood would furnish better indicators of the likelihood of crime in that neighborhood than exist at present. Determining such rates would require enumerating premises of different types and locating them by area. This information would help to test the effectiveness of control measures and to identify the nature of increases in crime by making it possible to detect changes in the pattern of risk for various businesses. It would also permit more refined calculations of risk for insurance purposes and guide the placement of alarm systems and other crime prevention devices.

TABLE 15. VICTIMIZATION BY SEX AND PLACE OF OCCURRENCE FOR MAJOR CRIMES (EXCEPT HOMICIDE) AGAINST THE PERSON
(In percent)

	Victims of major crimes against person	
Place of occurrence	Male	Female
School property	3.2	2.4
Residence	20.5	46.1
Transport property	1.4	.4
Taxis and delivery trucks	2.6	—
Businesses	3.2	1.1
Taverns and liquor stores	5.7	2.8
Street	46.8	30.7
Parks	.8	.5
All other premises	16.0	16.0
Total percent	100.0	100.0
Total number	(8,047)	(5,666)

SOURCE: Special tabulations from Chicago Police Department, Data Systems Division, for period September 1965 to March 1966.

The study of victimization of individuals carried out in cooperation with the Chicago Police Department recorded the types of premises for all major crimes against the person except homicide. Table 15 classifies victims by sex in relation to the place where the offense occurred. For assaultive crimes against the person, the street and the home are by far the most common places of occurrence. Men are more likely to be victimized on the street, and women are more likely to be victimized in residences.

The findings in general are closely related to the characteristic patterns of interaction among men and women in our society. Men are more likely to meet one another outside the home. A substantial portion of assaults arises from drinking—the tavern is the third most common setting for men to be victims of assault and battery—and some of the conflicts among drunks later erupt into street fights. Men and women more frequently engage in conflicts with each other in domestic settings.

. . .

Commercial Establishments and Organizations as Victims of Crime

It is very difficult to discover the exact extent to which businesses and organizations are the victims of crime. Few attempts are made to keep systematic records or report such crimes to any central place. Police agencies do not ordinarily separate the crimes against individuals from those against organizations. It was not possible in the short time available to the Commission to undertake a systematic census of victimization of different types of industrial, business, professional, religious, or civic organizations throughout the Nation. This task ought to be undertaken, and some assessment procedure developed, using reports, special sample surveys or similar devices.

The Commission was able to make a pilot survey, however, of a sample of neighborhood businesses and organizations in eight police precincts in Chicago, Washington, and Boston. The objective was to discover through interviews what types of victimization businesses and organizations had experienced from crimes such as burglary, robbery, shoplifting, passing of fraudulent checks, and employee theft.

BURGLARY AND ROBBERY. Reports to the UCR indicate that nationally about half of all burglaries in 1965 were nonresidential, and that the average worth of the property stolen in such burglaries was about $225. In the Commission survey almost one of every five businesses and organizations in the eight neighborhood police precincts surveyed was burglarized at least once during the one-year period covered by the survey. Considering only those that were burglarized, 62 percent had from two to seven burglaries.

In both Chicago and Washington, but for some reason not in Boston, the burglary victimization rates were highest in the districts where the overall crime rates were highest. Precinct 13 in the District of Columbia, for example, had a victimization rate of 51.8 per 100 organizations—nearly twice that of the precinct with the fewest burglaries—and a third of all the businesses and organizations sampled in that area had been victimized.

Nationally, reports to the UCR indicate that in 1965 9 percent of all robberies were of service stations or chainstores, almost 1 percent were of banks, and more than 20 percent were of other types of commercial establishments. The average value of the property reported stolen varies from $109 for service station robberies to $3,789 for bank robberies.

In the Commission survey the picture that emerges for victimization by robbery is similar to that for burglary, which occurs more frequently. Among the organizations that were robbed, 80 percent reported only one robbery but 2 percent had as many as five. While any business in a high crime rate area is obviously in danger, it appears that some businesses, like some people, are more likely than others to be victimized by crime. Clearly, the reasons for the differences need investigation as guides in prevention. The findings of the President's Commission on Crime in the District of Columbia with respect to the circumstances of housebreaking are suggestive of the way risks vary:

In 21 (7 percent) of the 313 commercial burglaries surveyed housebreakers entered through unlocked doors and in 70 instances (22 percent) through unlocked windows. In 111 instances the housebreakers broke windows to gain entry, and locks were forced in 95. A total of 105 of the commercial establishments victimized were reported to have had burglar-resistant locks; 65 of these establishments, however, were entered other than by tampering with the lock. Sixty-four percent of the burglarized commercial establishments were located on the first floor.

SHOPLIFTING. Shoplifting usually involves the theft of relatively small and inexpensive articles, although the professional shoplifter may steal expensive furs, clothes, and jewelry. It is heaviest in the chainstores and other larger stores which do the most retail business. However, it is the smaller establishments, particularly those that operate on a low margin of profit, to which shoplifting may make the difference between success and failure.

In the Commission survey, 35 percent of the neighborhood wholesale and retail establishments surprisingly reported no problem with shoplifting, while sizable percentages of other types of businesses, such as construction companies (30 percent), manufacturers of nondurables (33 percent), finance, insurance, and real estate firms (25 percent), which might not be expected to have any problem, reported some shoplifting difficulties. The average amount of shoplifting experienced by the nontrade establishments was considerably less than that for retail establishments.

As one might expect, the highest rates of shoplifting were reported in the high crime rate districts. The most common items carried off by shoplifters were food, liquor or beer, clothing and footwear, and miscellaneous small items worth less than $10. However, it is the total volume, rather than individual acts, that makes shoplifting a serious problem for most commercial enterprises.

Nationally most large retail businesses estimate their overall inventory shrinkage due to shoplifting, employee theft, and accounting errors at between 1 and 2 percent of total inventory. Experts in industrial and commercial security estimate that 75 to 80 percent of the inventory shrinkage is probably attributable to some type of dishonesty. Among the neighborhood businesses found by the Commission survey to have high rates of shoplifting, 60 percent placed their losses at less than 2 percent of total inventory; another 28 percent estimated they had lost between 2 and 6 percent. Surprisingly, 23 percent were unable to give any estimate at all of the amount of their losses due to shoplifting.

EMPLOYEE THEFT.   According to security experts for retail and other commercial establishments, theft by employees accounts for a considerably larger volume of theft than shoplifting. Theft of merchandise or equipment by employees is particularly hard to control because detection is so difficult. Employees have opportunities for theft every working day, whereas the shoplifting customer cannot steal merchandise regularly from the same establishment without arousing suspicion.

Employee theft is also a problem in many industrial concerns. A recent survey by the National Industrial Conference Board of 473 companies indicated that 20 percent of all companies and nearly 30 percent of those with more than 1,000 employees had a serious problem with employee theft of tools, equipment, materials or company products. More than half of the companies with a problem of employee theft indicated trouble with both white and blue collar workers.

In neighborhood establishments surveyed by the Commission only 14 percent reported the discovery of any employee dishonesty. Among those, 40 percent estimated losses at no more than $50 a year. Most managers or owners surveyed attempted to establish the honesty of employees before hiring them. Nearly one-third made an effort to check references or to clear the employee with the local police department but 74 percent did not report to the police the discovery of theft by their own employees, preferring to discharge the employee or handle the matter in some other way by themselves.

Crime Against Public Organizations and Utilities

Public organizations and utilities are repeatedly victimized by crime. While some of the crime committed against these organizations is reported to the police, it is not clear just how much goes unreported and how widespread it is.

To obtain some estimation, the Commission surveyed 48 such organizations in Boston, Chicago, and Washington with special attention to the police districts in which other surveys were being conducted.

The most prevalent and persistent problem reported was vandalism of buildings and equipment. Telephone companies, electric companies, schools, libraries, traffic and highway departments, parks, public transportation, and housing all are victims. Estimates of damage ranging up to $200,000 a year were quoted for such facilities as public housing, transportation, public parks, and recreation facilities in schools. The public school system in Washington, D.C., for example, provided data for 1965 showing a total of 26,500 window panes broken and replaced at a cost of $118,000. A similar report was received in Boston.

Larceny was also a frequently mentioned problem, involving such thefts as stealing loose equipment and personal possessions, theft from coin meters, and breaking and entering. Some organizations make a distinction between amateur and professional theft. For example, the telephone companies distinguish between the organized coinbox larceny using forged keys and the amateur forcible entry involving damage to the equipment. Employee theft was not reported as a serious problem except in hospitals where it represents the most common reason for the apprehension and discharge of employees.

Many public facilities reported problems with various forms of violence within their boundaries. Assaults and child molestation occur in parks, libraries, and schools. Emergency rooms of hospitals cited disturbances by drunken and disorderly persons. The threat of violent behavior or the presence of disorderly persons was reported to affect markedly the patronage of parks, libraries and after-school activities, especially in areas with high crime rates.

CHARACTERISTICS OF OFFENDERS

There is a common belief that the general population consists of a large group of law-abiding people and a small body of criminals. However, studies have shown that most people, when they are asked, remember having committed offenses for which they might have been sentenced if they had been apprehended. These studies of "self-reported" crime have generally been of juveniles or young adults, mostly college and high school students. They uniformly show that delinquent or criminal acts are committed by people at all levels of society. Most people admit to relatively petty delinquent acts, but many report larcenies, auto thefts, burglaries, and assaults of a more serious nature.

One of the few studies of this type dealing with criminal behavior by adults was of a sample of almost 1,700 persons, most of them from the State of New York. In this study, 1,020 males and 670 females were asked which of 49 offenses they had committed. The list included felonies and misdemeanors, other than traffic offenses, for which they might have been sentenced under the adult criminal code.

Ninety-one percent of the respondents admitted they had committed one or more offenses for which they might have received jail or prison sentences. Thirteen percent of the males admitted to grand larceny, 26 percent to auto theft, and 17 percent to burglary. Sixty-four percent of the males and 27 percent of the females committed at least one felony for which they had not been apprehended. Although some of these offenses may have been reported to the police by the victims and would thus appear in official statistics as "crimes known to the police," these offenders would not show up in official arrest statistics.

Such persons are part of the "hidden" offender group. They evidently at one time or another found themselves in situations that led them to violate the criminal law. However, most people do not persist in committing offenses. For many the risk of arrest and prosecution is deterrence enough, while others develop a stake in a law-abiding way of life in which their youthful "indiscretions" no longer have a place.

What is known today about offenders is confined almost wholly to those who have been arrested, tried, and sentenced. The criminal justice process may be viewed as a large-scale screening system. At each stage it tries to sort out the better risks to return to the general population. The further along in the process that a sample of offenders is selected, the more likely they are to show major social and personal problems.

From arrest records, probation reports, and prison statistics a "portrait" of the offender emerges that progressively highlights the disadvantaged character of his life. The offender at the end of the road in prison is likely to be a member of the lowest social and economic groups in the country, poorly educated and perhaps unemployed, unmarried, reared in a broken home, and to have a prior criminal record. This is a formidable list of personal and social problems that must be overcome in order to restore offenders to law-abiding existence. Not all offenders, of course, fit this composite profile, as a more detailed examination of the arrest, probation, and prison data reveals.

Arrest Data on Offenders

National arrest statistics, based on unpublished estimates for the total population, show that when all offenses are considered together the majority of offenders arrested are white, male, and over 24 years of age. Offenders over 24 make up the great majority of persons arrested for fraud, embezzlement, gambling, drunkenness, offenses against the family, and vagrancy. For many other crimes the peak age of criminality occurs below 24.

The 15-to-17-year-old group is the highest for burglaries, larcenies and auto theft. For these three offenses, 15-year-olds are arrested more often than persons of any other age with 16-year-olds a close second. For the three common property offenses the rate of arrest per 100,000 persons 15 to 17 in 1965 was 2,467 as compared to a rate of 55 for every 100,000 persons 50 years old and over. For crimes of violence the peak years are those from 18 to 20, followed closely by the 21 to 24 group. Rates for these groups are 300 and 297 as compared with 24 for the 50-year-old and over group.

One of the sharpest contrasts of all in the arrest statistics on offenders is that between males and females. Males are arrested nearly seven times as frequently as females for Index offenses plus larceny under $50. The rate for males is 1,097 per 100,000 population and the corresponding rate for females is 164. The difference is even greater when all offenses are considered.

The differences in the risks of arrest for males and females seem to be diminishing, however. Since 1960 the rate of arrest for females has been increasing faster than the rate for males. In 1960 the male arrest rate for Index offenses plus larceny under $50 was 926 per 100,000 and in 1965 it was 1,097, an increase in the rate of 18 percent. However, the female rate increased by 62 percent during this same period, from 101 per 100,000 females to 164. Most of the increase was due to the greatly increased rate of arrest of women for larcenies. The larceny arrest rate for women increased 81 percent during this same period in marked contrast to an increase of 4 percent for aggravated assault, the next highest category of arrest for women among these offenses.

The factor of race is almost as important as that of sex in determining whether a person is likely to be arrested and imprisoned for an offense. Many more whites than Negroes are arrested every year but Negroes have a significantly higher rate of arrest in every offense category except certain offenses against public order and morals. For Index offenses plus larceny under $50 the rate per 100,000 Negroes in 1965 was four times as great as that for whites (1,696 to 419).

In general, the disparity of rates for offenses of violence is much greater than comparable differences between the races for offenses against property. For instance, the Negro arrest rate for murder is 24.1 compared to 2.5 for whites, or almost 10 times as high. This is in contrast to the difference between Negroes and whites for crimes against property. For example, the rate of Negro arrest (378) for burglary is only about 3½ times as high as that for whites (107). The statistics also show that the difference between the white and Negro arrest rates is generally greater for those over 18 years of age than for those under 18. Negroes over 18 are arrested about 5 times as often as whites (1,684 to 325). In contrast, the ratio for those under 18 is approximately three to one (1,689 to 591).

The differences between the Negro and white arrest rates for certain crimes of violence have been growing smaller between 1960 and 1965. During that period, considering together the crimes of murder, rape, and aggravated assault, the rate for Negroes increased 5 percent while the rate for whites increased 27 percent. In the case of robbery, however, the white rate increased 3 percent while the Negro rate increased 24 percent. For the crimes of burglary, larceny, and auto theft the Negro rate increased 33 percent while the white rate increased 24 percent.

Many studies have been made seeking to account for these differences in arrest rates for Negroes and whites. They have found that the differences become very small when comparisons are made between the rates for whites and Negroes living under similar conditions. However, it has proved difficult to make such comparisons, since Negroes generally encounter more barriers to economic and social advancement than whites do. Even when Negroes and whites live in the same area the Negroes are likely to have poorer housing, lower incomes, and fewer job prospects. The Commission is of the view that if conditions of equal opportunity prevailed, the large differences now found between the Negro and white arrest rates would disappear.

Probation Data on Offenders

Arrest statistics supply only a limited amount of information about offenders. More detailed descriptions can be obtained from the probation records maintained by the courts. An illustration of what such records reveal is provided in a report by the Stanford Research Institute to the President's Commission on Crime in the District of Columbia. The study examined the background characteristics contained in the probation records of a sample of 932 felons convicted during the years 1964 and 1965 in Washington, D.C.

Among those offenders for whom income information was available, 90 percent had incomes of less than $5,000. At the time of the 1960 census, 56 percent of the adult population in Washington earned less than $5,000. The highest median incomes were found among those who had been convicted of forgery, fraud, and embezzlement. Of the sample, 78 percent were Negro, as contrasted with an estimated 61 percent of Negroes in the population of Washington. The median age of arrest was 29.2 years, and approximately three-fourths of the sample was between 18 and 34 years, a proportion very much higher than that for the same age group in the general population of the District. Adult criminal records were found in 80 percent of the cases. More than half, 52 percent, had six or more prior arrests and 65 percent had previously been confined in some type of juvenile or adult institution.

The picture that emerges from this data is of a group of young adult males who come from disorganized families, who have had limited access to educational and occupational opportunities, and who have been frequently involved in difficulties with the police and the courts, both as juveniles and adults.

Prison Data on Offenders

An even more disadvantaged population can be identified from the characteristics of prisoners tabulated in the 1960 U.S. Census of Population. Every 10 years, the census lists the characteristics of persons in custodial institutions, including Federal and State prisons and local jails and workhouses. These tabulations show the median years of school completed for the State and Federal prison and reformatory population is 8.6 years, in contrast to 10.6 years for the general population in the country. It also shows that 23.9 percent of the offenders were laborers, compared to 5.1 percent in the total population. Only 5.8 percent of the offender population engaged in high status occupations, such as professional, technical work, manager, official, proprietor, and similar groupings, compared to 20.6 percent of the general population. Prisoners are also much more likely to be unmarried than other males 14 or over in the general population. Only 31.1 percent of the prisoners are married compared to 69.1 percent of males generally. The comparable rates for single status are 43.7 percent and 25.1 percent, and for separated, widowed and divorced, 24.6 and 7.2.

Recidivism

The most striking fact about offenders who have been convicted of the common serious crimes of violence and theft is how often how many of them continue committing crimes. Arrest, court, and prison records furnish insistent testimony to the fact that these repeated offenders constitute the hard core of the crime problem. One of the longest and most painstaking followup studies was conducted by Sheldon and Eleanor Glueck on a sample of 510 Massachusetts reformatory inmates released between 1911 and 1922. It showed that 32 percent of the men who could be followed over a 15-year period repeatedly committed serious crimes during this period, and many others did so intermittently.

A recent study of adults granted probation by 56 of the 58 county courts in California from 1956 to 1958 showed that by the end of 1962, 28 percent of the more than 11,000 probationers had been taken off probation because almost half of them had committed new offenses, and others had absconded or would not comply with regulations. Because judges select the better risks for probation, one would expect that men discharged or paroled from prison would be more likely to commit further crimes, and the facts show that they do. A California study of parolees released from 1946 through 1949 found that 43 percent had been reimprisoned by the end of 1952; almost half for committing further felonies and the rest (almost one-third of whom were thought also to have committed further felonies) for other parole violations.

A review of a number of such studies in the various States and in the Federal prison system leads to the conclusion that despite considerable variation among jurisdictions, roughly a third of the offenders released from prison will be reimprisoned, usually for committing new offenses, within a 5-year period. The most frequent recidivists are those who commit such property crimes as burglary, auto theft, forgery, or larceny, but robbers and narcotics offenders also repeat frequently. Those who are least likely to commit new crimes after release are persons convicted of serious crimes of violence—murder, rape, and aggravated assault.

These findings are based on the crimes of released offenders that officials learn about. Undoubtedly many new offenses are not discovered. Furthermore released offenders continue to come to the attention of the police, even though not always charged or convicted for new offenses. A 2-year followup by the UCR of the arrest records of 6,907 offenders released from the Federal system between January and June 1963 shows that 48 percent had been arrested for new offenses by June 1965. Complete figures on the percent convicted are not available.

Studies made of the careers of adult offenders regularly show the importance of juvenile delinquency as a forerunner of adult crime. They support the conclusions that the earlier a juvenile is arrested or brought to court for an offense, the more likely he is to carry on criminal activity into adult life; that the more serious the first offense for which a juvenile is arrested, the more likely he is to continue to commit serious crimes, especially in the case of major crimes against property; and that the more frequently and extensively a juvenile is processed by the police, court, and correctional system the more likely he is to be arrested, charged, convicted, and imprisoned as an adult. These studies also show that the most frequent pattern among adult offenders is one that starts with petty stealing and progresses to much more serious property offenses. . . .

PART II
The Definition of Behavior as "Criminal"

Introduction

One who would understand criminal behavior or crime rates must understand something of the process by which conduct comes to be defined as criminal by the legislative and judicial processes of societies. "Crime" is a legal category, and the criminologist is, strictly speaking, solely concerned with behavior falling within this category. He may, of course, choose to study deviant behavior of all sorts, legal and illegal, but if he restricts himself to studying crime and criminal behavior, he necessarily restricts himself to studying conduct prohibited by the criminal law.

A prohibited act is not a crime unless it is in violation of the criminal law. Each criminal law identifies and defines a prohibited kind of conduct, then specifies that whoever engages in such conduct shall be subject to a prescribed punishment. Criminal behavior is, thus, behavior which is punishable by law. Criminal law prohibits both positive acts such as those described in larceny and burglary statutes, and negative acts such as those described in statutes making it an offense to fail to file an income tax return.[1]

Crime rates tend to increase as societies become more complex and as the number of different values among the members increases. In some nonliterate societies, the bonds between the members are strong and continuous, and conformity to the dominant values held by members is inspired by informal processes such as gossip, ridicule, ostracism, and

[1] See Jerome Hall, *General Principles of Criminal Law*, 2nd ed. (Indianapolis: Bobbs-Merrill, 1960), pp. 14–26.

banishment. In such societies, Emile Durkheim argued, an act is criminal when it offends strongly endorsed beliefs and sentiments which are held in common by the citizens. Criminal behavior is thus behavior which offends the "collective conscience." Accordingly, "we must not say that an action shocks the common conscience because it is criminal, but rather that it is criminal because it shocks the common conscience."[2]

In more complex societies, those characterized as "states," the informal ways of stimulating and maintaining conformity give way to formalized procedures. The dominant values are made official by means of the criminal law, and the responsibility for dealing with those who do not conform to the official values is delegated to representatives of the state—policemen, prosecutors, judges, wardens, executioners, and similar officials. In fact, the designation of acts as crime and the assignment of officials to "enforce the law" are necessary only when there is concern about the extent of the deviation from the dominant values of a society. If all members of our society were in complete agreement about the proper regard for private property, it would not be necessary to designate as crime (e.g., burglary, larceny, and robbery) that conduct which shows disregard for property rights.

Since conduct designated as criminal is in violation of the official values of a society, and since societies vary in what values they hold to be important, definitions of what is crime and what is not crime vary from place to place. Some types of conduct, such as incest, are prohibited in all societies, but many varieties of behavior that are prohibited in one society are not in another. In a large and complex society like the United States there is even variation among the several states—what is crime in Kansas is not necessarily crime in New York. Furthermore, societies change many of their own definitions of crime over time. For example, a study of criminal actions brought before the Essex County Court in Massachusetts from 1636 to 1682 indicates that the Puritans could be convicted of such "crimes" as disturbing the congregation, absence from church, contempt of the clergy, criticism of the government, and "delivering the first child within too short a period after the wedding," in addition to such current crimes as theft and assault.[3] The passing and then repeal of the Prohibition laws represents a more recent example of changing definitions of criminal behavior. At present, designations of other areas of behavior as criminal are being criticized with an eye to changing the laws that so designate them. Already several states have passed statutes permitting, in certain circumstances, abortions that here-

[2] Emile Durkheim, *The Division of Labor in Society* (New York: Free Press, 1947), p. 81. This book was first published, in French, in 1893.

[3] Kai T. Erikson, *Wayward Puritans* (New York: Wiley, 1966), p. 171.

tofore were prohibited. Homosexual behavior between consenting adults in private is no longer a crime in the State of Illinois. Efforts to remove the heavy penalties attached to the possession or smoking of marijuana and the establishment of state-operated or state-controlled lotteries and other gambling activities give further evidence that changes in public morality are reflected in changes in the criminal law.[4]

The selection from Hoebel's *Law of Primitive Man* indicates that the Comanches had many customs similar to the rules of modern criminal law, but they had no "state" in the contemporary sense of the word. Accordingly, one essential element of criminal law systems, *politicality*, was missing. Only violations of rules made by the state are crimes, but the distinction between the state and other groups is difficult to make in societies such as that of the Comanches, where there was patriarchal power, private self-help, and a kind of "popular justice." It is clear that in Comanche society homicide was not an offense against the entire tribe— the "state"—but repeated sorcery was such an offense. *Specificity*, another characteristic of criminal law systems, also was not clearly present in the Comanche law-ways. In modern societies, and especially in democratic societies, the criminal law carefully defines each prohibited act, and if there is any question about whether or not the legal rule in question defines the behavior of the persons accused of crime, the court must find the defendant not guilty.[5] For example, in one famous case a man took an airplane that did not belong to him. He was accused of violating a statute making it a crime to take other people's "self-propelled vehicles," but he was found not guilty on the ground that at the time the law was enacted there were so few airplanes around that the concept "vehicles" could not have included airplanes.[6] In Comanche society, even "excessive sorcery," which came close to being a "crime" in the modern sense, was not precisely defined.

Societies with criminal law systems have developed a set of procedures for protecting the interests of the state by means of rules indicating that whoever violates the law is subject to punishment by the

---

[4] For an excellent discussion of the debates about whether those who violate the laws in regard to abortion, homosexuality, and drug addiction are criminals, sick people, or just "different," see Edwin M. Schur, *Crimes Without Victims* (Englewood Cliffs, N.J.: Prentice-Hall, 1965).

[5] However, some general statutes do not precisely define the specific acts which are prohibited. Whether a specific act is a crime or is not a crime under such statutes depends upon the findings of courts as to whether the act is covered by the statute. Examples are laws dealing with pornography, "outrages of public morality" and "indecent conduct." In recent years, the constitutionality of such statutes has been tested by wearers of topless bathing suits, by topless waitresses, and by the publishers of nudist magazines.

[6] *McBoyle* v. *United States*, 283 U.S. 25 (1931).

society acting as a collectivity. Hoebel's discussion of wife-stealing among the Comanches indicates that the society did not take such collective action against the offender. Accordingly, it may be concluded that another fundamental attribute of criminal law systems, *penal sanction,* was not present in the rule-making and rule-enforcing system of Comanche society. A Comanche husband whose wife was carried off demanded payment from the abductor, but the society did not, collectively, impose a fine or other penalty on him. The Sun and the Earth, not people, had the power to impose penalties on individuals for the collective good. Neither did Comanche society's law-ways provide for *uniformity,* an attribute of criminal law systems which means that justice is supposed to be administered in an even-handed manner without regard for the status of the person who has committed, or is accused of committing, a crime. Theoretically, at least, an act described as a crime is a crime, no matter who perpetrates it.

The process of defining some form of behavior as criminal involves competition between groups of people participating in the legislative process and in the judicial process. Even in reference to the most ancient of criminal laws, the process of declaring an act to be crime involves a number of persons who are behaving in a certain way and a number of persons who disapprove of this conduct, then a struggle for legislative or judicial dominance between these two groups, the victory in the struggle going to the persons opposing the behavior. For example, wilful killing of others became a crime because some persons persisted in such conduct despite *mores* to the contrary. Other members of society, through their political institution, centralized and formalized the mechanisms for social control of the conduct, and the taboo against killing became the "law of the land." Many of our modern criminal laws prohibit conduct that is regarded as taboo—that is, considered morally repulsive—by a vast majority of the members of society. Some contemporary criminal laws, however, have come to institutionalize folkways, values which do not have the broad support such as underlies *mores.* Such legal codification of folkways represents the consensus of only a rather small segment of the society. Fuller's article gives a number of examples of such law.

It is also the case that later revisions of the criminal law may come about because some of the people who engage in certain activities that are prohibited by the law struggle for changes in the definition of that behavior. The current efforts of groups advocating changes in the laws dealing with abortion, drug use, homosexuality and gambling are cases in point. Thus, there are some acts about whose proscription there is general agreement in a society, but there are other forms of behavior about which there is no such consensus. In the latter case there may be competition between groups, each of which claims to represent the larger communities' views and interests. In issues of this sort the main question often is whether the behavior is inappropriate, immoral, or illegal. Perhaps the best illustrations of this kind of behavior are found in controversies about "white-collar crime."

The white-collar crimes of businessmen, especially, are outlawed by means of the criminal law, but prohibited acts such as price fixing, fraudulent advertising, and restraint of trade are not regarded as immoral by general community consensus.[7] Moreover, there is a prevailing belief that business offenses are not "real crime," despite the argument that the invention of special procedures in the administration of criminal laws pertaining to business does not make the offenses any less criminal. In his selection, Aubert argues convincingly that the most significant characteristic of white-collar crime is the fact that persons disagree about whether this kind of conduct is in fact crime. In an earlier study of price control and rationing in Norway, Professor Aubert showed that the interpretation of white-collar offenses as "crime" or "not crime" depends in part upon political, economic, and social conditions.[8] In order to demonstrate its economic power, the politically ascendant group (labor) in Norway outlawed violations of price-control regulations and rationing regulations. If, however, these regulations had been clearly defined and enforced as "criminal laws," a rift between the ascendant group and the descendant group (businessmen) would have occurred.

By keeping open the question of whether violations are or are not crimes (despite the fact that they are designated as crimes on the statute books), and by establishing an inefficient enforcement machinery, "social peace" is maintained between the elected officials and the persons whose behavior is being regulated. The governmental officials in power get credit for attacking a serious social problem by means of criminal law legislation, but they also get credit for creating among the violators a feeling of harmlessness. The earlier selection from the Report of the President's Commission (Part I) made essentially the same point when it said, "Crime is 'caused' by public tolerance of it, or reluctance or inability to take action against it. Corporate and business—'white collar' —crime is closely associated with a widespread notion that, when makeing money is involved, anything goes." Selection 5 in Part III, which deals with the processing of white-collar criminals through our criminal justice machinery, shows the implications of uncertainty in societal definitions of behavior.

[7] See Edwin H. Sutherland, *White Collar Crime* (New York: Dryden, 1949). See also "White-Collar Criminality," in the present book, pp. 349–360.

[8] Vilhelm Aubert, *Priskontroll og Rajonering* ("Price Control and Rationing") (Oslo: Institute for Social Research, 1950).

Aubert's discussion of white-collar crime also demonstrates how changing economic and social conditions create new legal problems for societies in terms of pressures for change. No society can enact a set of criminal law "once and for all" unless it is prepared to overlook the non-criminal practice of exploiting one's fellows by seeking "loopholes" in the law. It is in the period during which such "loopholes" are found that there occur the great debates about whether a specific act is, or is not, a crime. In the selection from *Theft, Law and Society,* Hall shows, for example, that the development of the rules making embezzlement a crime closely paralleled the economic development in England. Before an act can properly be called "larceny," one person must illegally take something from the possession of another. In the sixteenth century, if a servant converted to his own use some money handed to him by a man who instructed him to give it to his master, he had not committed larceny because the money was never in the master's possession. This was no great legal problem because servants were servants and masters were masters—it was almost unthinkable that the servant would be trusted with funds for the master. However, as business expanded and servants became in fact clerks and cashiers, "trusted servants" became a problem. They found a loophole in the law, a loophole arising because of changing economic conditions and, consequently, changed relationships between "masters" and "servants."[9] One "servant" of the Bank of England took bonds worth a fortune, but he did not commit larceny.

Slowly, the legislative and judicial authorities solved the problem. First, it became the rule that if a clerk placed money received from a third person in a cashbox or drawer belonging to the master, the money came into possession of the master, and subsequent conversion by the servant was larceny. But if the clerk put the money directly into his pocket there was no crime. Second, embezzlement statutes specifically prohibiting the behavior in question were passed. The early statutes of this kind pertained only to narrow categories of servants, such as those working for the Bank of England, the South Sea Island Company, or the Post Office. Third, in 1799 the first general embezzlement statute was passed. In the decade 1790–1800 about four hundred banks were organized in England, but the law of larceny did not cover defalcations by their employees. In 1799, but prior to the enactment of the statute, a bank teller who credited a hundred-pound note to a customer's account and then put it directly into his pocket was prosecuted and found not guilty of larceny. Even the general embezzlement statute was narrowly construed—on the principle of "specificity" discussed above. In 1812 a stockbroker (an "agent" not a "servant") converted money given him to invest, but the court held that

[9] Jerome Hall, *Theft, Law and Society*, 2nd ed., (Indianapolis: Bobbs-Merrill, 1952), p. 35.

his act did not come within the statute. New legislation to cover brokers, agents, and similar personnel was passed almost immediately, and in the next fifty years the law of embezzlement was further extended and clarified.

From this brief history it may be observed that as trade and commerce increased and modern business practices arose, it became necessary to modify the former legal relationships between employers and employees in respect to trust. In essence, merchants and bankers found that business could not be conducted unless servants were trusted. At the same time these merchants and bankers had impressed upon them the fact that the common law of fraud and larceny had been designed for a relatively simple economy in which there was no need to trust servants with business transactions. Embezzlement statutes were invented to cover the new offenses that arose with the new economic structure. The selection by Hall is a more detailed example of the criminal law which came with changes in the character of financial organizations.

Changing definitions of what is deviant behavior result in the passing of new laws, failure to apply existing laws, overruling of earlier holdings by the courts, and occasional repeal of existing laws by legislatures. Each of these forms of official conduct has important implications for individual actors because each of them involves a decision as to whether a specific form of deviant conduct will be "criminalized." The selection from Professor Schur's book argues that declaring a person's act to be deviant, and prosecuting it as delinquency or crime, is a crucial step in the individual's progress toward a criminal career. This point is elaborated in Part VI. Moreover, the variations in official conduct make it difficult to compare the crime rates of various geographic areas, and even make comparisons of crime rates for different periods of American history all but impossible. Changes in official definitions, based on changing public reactions about what is "deviant" makes it necessary for administrators of criminal justice to select—intentionally or unwittingly—which few offenders out of hundreds of offenders shall have their conduct "criminalized," by the law-enforcement and judicial processes. This selection process is the subject of Part III.

1 Plains Indian Law in Development: The Comanche

E. ADAMSON HOEBEL

Men have occupied the Great Plains of the West for a good ten thousand years or more. They came in, apparently, when the last ice sheet was in its northward retreat, and their archaeological culture seems to have been fairly stable over long periods of time. But the horse-riding, buffalo-hunting, tipi-dwelling culture of the eighteenth-century Plains Indian was something quite new in its development.

Before the coming of Columbus the Indians of the Plains were largely riverbound and not overly inclined to venture afar into the vast, poorly watered stretches of open grasslands. They had to go afoot.

The coming of the European altered the situation with drastic effect. The Spaniard to the south introduced the horse and thereby provided the means for extensive penetration of the Plains by native populations, for which the thick herds of buffalo and fleet antelope were an enticing lure. On the eastern frontier the French and British were working to cause a far-reaching displacement of the Woodland tribes. White settlements forced some tribes to move westward at an early date. And out beyond the frontier, other displacements were accelerated ahead of the line of settlement by the imperialistic rivalry of the fur trade.

The fur trading tribes sought ever to enlarge their trapping and hunt-

Reprinted by permission of the publishers and the author from E. Adamson Hoebel, *The Law of Primitive Man: A Study in Comparative Legal Dynamics*, Cambridge, Mass.: Harvard University Press, Copyright, 1954, by the President and Fellows of Harvard College, pp. 127–142.

ing domains at the expense of some of their neighbors. The British companies encouraged their tribes to drive off the French-allied tribes, and they gave them guns wherewith to do it. The French responded in kind, and the tribes of either party used their new weapons to drive the unarmed tribes on the western frontier before them. Thus with pressure behind them and an attractive lure before them, a number of the tribes of the Mississippi Valley sought sanctuary and prosperity in the relatively unpopulated lands of the West. The Comanches were among them.

. . .

The Comanches . . . appear in the sixteenth century to have occupied the country that lay around the headwaters of the Yellowstone and Missouri Rivers. They were an eastern branch of the far-flung Shoshonean group of tribes and at that time it is unlikely that they would have been distinguishable from other eastern Shoshoneans. But in the eighteenth century the Comanches moved down into the southern Plains, while the Shoshones were driven back over the Rocky Mountains by invaders from the east. The Comanches became a discrete entity and one of the first, if not the first, of the Plains tribes to acquire horses.[1]

. . .

The Comanche cultural background was that of the so-called "Digger Indians" of the Great Basin. In the tradition of these tribes there was no great social organization. People moved and lived in small isolated family bands. Each was autonomous and economically self-sufficient on a low subsistence level. Religion was vaguely defined and almost wholly devoid of ceremonial structure. Arts were thin, and life offered little of richer satisfactions. War was a thing to be avoided, for the Basin Shoshoneans had no military organization and were wholly lacking in fighting prowess.[2]

In the Plains the Comanches never wholly shed this heritage, but in the new setting they wrought some mighty changes in their way of life. With adequate food resources and the horse they were able to prosper in numbers and so to enlarge the size of their bands. Yet they never forsook band autonomy for tribal government. Religion remained to the very end almost wholly an individual enterprise with few group rituals and no tribal ceremonials.

It was in warring and raiding that the great transformation took place.

[1] Ernest Wallace and E. A. Hoebel, *The Comanches: Lords of the South Plains* (Norman, 1952) pp. 3–16.

[2] J. H. Steward, *Basin–Plateau Aboriginal Socio-political Groups* (Bureau of American Ethnology, Bulletin 120, 1938).

Out of apparent weakness emerged the wildest marauding brigandage. The Comanches whipped and drove the Apaches from the southern Plains. They stalemated the Spanish. They decimated the pueblo of Pecos. They ranged far below the Rio Grande on slave- and booty-taking raids into Old Mexico. They blocked the westward expansion of the Texas frontier for several decades. They became "The Spartans of the Prairies." They were rough, tough, aggressive and militant individualists. They gave trouble to all their enemies and to themselves. And in their way, out of the nothingness of Shoshone legal backgrounds they shaped a crude but effective system of law to cope with the clashes of individual with individual within their ranks.

. . .

The basic postulates of the Comanche way of life are simple and few. They express a strong individualism and man-to-man aggressiveness in the following terms:

Postulate I. The individual is supreme in all things.

Postulate II. The self of the male is realized in striving for accumulated war honors, horses, and women.

Postulate III. Women are sexually and economically desirable but are inferior and subordinate to men.

Corollary 1. The sex rights of a husband to his wife are limited to himself and his brothers.

Postulate IV. The strongest social tie is that of brother to brother.

Postulate V. Sexual relations between kin (incest) constitutes subhuman behavior.

Postulate VI. War is essential to the prosperity of the tribe and the individual self-expression of the male.

Postulate VII. The great spirits (Sun and Earth) have powers of "legal" judgment.

Postulate VIII. Each Comanche ought to cooperate with others and help them in their life's activities.

Corollary 1. Altruism and sharing of goods is socially desirable.

Corollary 2. The killing of a fellow tribesman is not permissible.

Postulate IX. Horses, especially favorite horses, have quasi-human personalities.

The simple needs of Comanche society did not impose any great social pressure for governmental controls, and the high value placed upon individual freedom of action also worked to hold government at a minimum. If a Comanche had been invited to subscribe to a political slogan, he would have given his assent to the proposition that "that government is best which governs least." So fully was this precept expressed in a lack of political action that That's It, one of the most acute of our Comanche informants, in commenting on the band headmen, or peace chiefs, remarked, "I hardly known how to tell about them; they never had much to do except to hold the band together." The headman was a magnet at the core of the band, but his influence was so subtle that it almost defies explicit description. He worked through precept, advice, and good humor, expressing his wisdom through well-chosen words and persuasive common sense. He was not elected to office or even chosen. "He just got that way." His role and status were only slightly more institutionalized than were those of the Eskimo headman. In the making of any important decisions of group policy all men were free to have their say. Yet among them all, the wiser old head, whose time-tested judgment the people respected, was the leader. In matters of daily routine, such as camp moving, he merely made the decisions himself, announcing them through a camp crier. Anyone who did not like his decision simply ignored it. If in time a good many people ignored his announcements and preferred to stay behind with some other man of influence, or perhaps to move in another direction with that man, the chief had then lost his following. He was no longer chief, and another had quietly superseded him.

War chiefs were outstanding fighters whose accumulated records of honored deeds were tangible evidence of their prestige status. Any Comanche was free to initiate a raid or organize a war party—if he could muster a band of followers. The Comanches were chronically at war with the Ute, Pawnee, Apache, Osage, Tonkaway, and sundry other tribes. In later days, the whites of Texas and the Mexicans on both sides of the Rio Grande were fair game. War, for the Comanches, was certainly a national pastime, if not the conscious practice of a national political policy. We suspect it was both. But so far as it was a national policy, it was not explicitly directed by a governing military or political body. It was a matter of individual motivation, prepared by training since infancy and spurred by a social system that gave rich psychological rewards to the men who were bravest in the face of the enemy or most successful in running off the horses of hostile tribes or the horses and cattle of Texas ranchers.

On the raid the leader of the war party—the man who had organized it—had temporary dictatorial powers such as a peace chief never enjoyed. He determined the objectives of the raid; he appointed scouts, cooks and water carriers; he set the camping places and the route of march; he divided the booty, if booty there was. In all his directives he was implicitly obeyed. If anyone seriously objected, he was free to leave the party and go his own way. Success on the raid demanded tough leadership, and the followers of a war chief submitted to it. Yet so strong was the Comanche sense of individual freedom that at any point a man could pick up his arrows and go home.

In view of their basic values of individual supremacy and the related ambiguity of powers of the chieftains, it is not surprising that in this tribe there were no public officials endowed with law-speaking or law-enforcing authority. The law of the Comanche was neither legislative nor judge-made. It was, as we have written elsewhere, "hammered out on the hard anvil of individual cases by claimant and defendant pressing the issues in terms of Comanche notions of individual rights and tribal standards of right conduct."[3] Thus it was almost exclusively a system of private law: a system of individual responsibility and individual action; a law that was case made.

The Comanches surely had no love of legalistic formalism, but they were a most litigious people. Their way of life engendered considerable internal friction. It might almost be said that the Comanches savored trouble-making. Their own accounts of their war parties as often as not begin with a laconic "once there was a bunch of Comanches out looking for trouble."

So, also, a man was often moved to take steps that made trouble. He stole another man's wife, or he secretly consorted with her. When this was done, the husband had no choice but to initiate legal action. Magnanimity on his part would bring no praise, for there was no doctrine of turning the other cheek. A man's status turned on his bravery, and for an offended husband not to act reflected merely on his courage; it was seen not as an act of forgiveness but as an expression of lily-livered cowardice. Wife-stealing and adultery were not the result of any sexual deprivation on the part of the offender; they were in effect deliberate challenges to the prestige of the husband. As such, he was forced in the eyes of the people to respond to them.

The way was open to him in legal action. Custom impelled men to violate the marital rights of other men. The culture also provided a legal remedy for the wronged man. Except in a few rare and extreme cases, the wrongdoer fully expected to pay the legal price—and did so without forcing the injured husband to a violent bodily attack. He knew well that he would have to pay a price, but he also knew that if he was steadfast and could outface the other man, the price would be light. In that case he would come out of the affair with greater public respect than the husband and he might get the woman to boot. So he took the risk.

In the memory of a dozen old Comanche informants still living in 1933 forty-five cases of old-time legal actions involving wife-stealing and adultery were still vivid enough for detailed recording.[4] Twenty-two were wife-absconding cases and twenty-three involved adultery.

As it takes two to make a contract it also takes two to commit adultery or a wife-absconding (Comanche women were not forcibly stolen). The woman's role in these affairs was very frequently an expression of individual revolt against the workings of Postulate III. Theoretically in all instances,

---

[3] Wallace and Hoebel, p. 224.

[4] Cf. Hoebel, *Political Organization and Law-ways*, pp. 49–59.

and actually in many, a girl had no formal voice in the choice of her husband. Her brothers gave her away in exchange for a consideration. The takers were usually older and established warriors and hunters who had the goods. In the Comanche ideal such arrangements made for the best marriages. But they were marriages in which the woman was at the mercy of her husband. Working against the stability of such marriages was a strong current of romantic idealism among the young. The ambition of the adolescent girl was to be a *naiβi*,[5] i.e., a beautiful maiden with lustrous, black hair hanging in long braids, and dressed in a fine fringed buckskin dress. The young bucks for their part strove to attract the attention of the girls by playing the role of *tuiβitsi*: "a handsome young man who looks good on a horse." Wife-absconding was really an escape in which a frustrated wife sought a more romantic match with a daring warrior.

Comanche elopements were invariably linked to a war party. The man in the case would be going on a raid with his friends, and he would make an assignation with the woman to go along. It was a way provided by custom to violate the marriage rights of the rightful husband as defined by custom and sustained by law! A nice example of internal inconsistency in the ways of a culture.

When a woman and her lover took off with a war party, two courses were open to the jilted husband. He could mount in hot pursuit in the hope that he could overtake them before they reached enemy territory. Or he could bide his time until they returned from the raid. In enemy country he could not press his suit; here all Comanches had to stand shoulder to shoulder. Aside from this, he could institute his action wherever he might be able to confront his tortfeasor. He might take along some compatriots—brothers, real or putative—to strengthen his courage and his arm, if need be. A real man, however, went alone. It was not necessary for him to gather witnesses, for a Comanche legal action was in no sense a trial. Questions of evidence rarely, if ever, entered. The wife-stealer, or even the adulterer, had no desire to conceal his deed; his aim was to flaunt his prestige in the face of the challenged husband.

If he followed the dictates of decorum, he politely addressed the defendant as "brother." The defendant replied in kind. Did not Comanche brothers share their wives? Syllogistically the reasoning runs:

> Men who share a wife are brothers.
> This man has assumed a share in my wife.
> Therefore, he is my brother.
> (But he is going to pay for the privilege!)

The immediate goal of the prosecuting husband was to get *nanεwɔkə*, restitutive damages. As an opening gambit he placed his demands high,

---

[5] Phonetic symbols are used as in the International Phonetics System.

customarily asking for four different kinds of articles (four was the mystic number in which most Indians conceived things). Horses were always demanded, numbering from one to ten. The size of the demand varied directly with the wealth of the defendant and the fortitude of the husband and inversely with the war record of the defendant. The husband hoped to squeeze out as much as the traffic would bear and the wrongdoer was willing to yield.

The defendant on his side would pay in the end, but it would be unseemly to yield readily or to first demands. The procedure was one of higgling and haggling—with always the risk of a violent breakdown in the offing. For the husband, if mean-tempered or short of patience, might well cut the palavering short with a quick attack upon the defendant. Theoretically, then, the injured husband had recourse to use of physical force, if the offender failed to recognize his duty to pay up with a settlement that was reasonable in the eyes of the injured party. In fact, however, this was not a genuine legal privilege-right, since in event of homicide retaliation prevailed. The husband who pressed his suit to the killing point was bound to be slain in turn by the defendant's kinsmen. Here was the fatal weakness of the primitive system of the Comanches. Yet in forty-one of the forty-five recorded adultery and absconding cases the offender paid up and the matter became *res judicata* with an award in favor of the plaintiff. It is evident that the Comanches had a strong sense of the fitness of the law and that, willful as they were, wrongdoers submitted to its dictates.

This condition was implemented by two facts: (1) action was not initiated unless the facts were predetermined—guilt, as we have said, was rarely an issue except in sorcery cases; (2) the elopement pattern worked to tone down the first burst of anger; (3) usage saw to it that the husband could in the final resort always muster a greater amount of force than could the defendant.

In the nature of things, the adulterer or wife-absconder was (or thought he was) a more dangerous man than the husband he was wronging. If he had been left wholly to his own resources, the aggrieved husband would more often than not have been in a poor way to exact restitution. In the achievement of justice Comanche practice saw to it that if the husband were man-to-man on the short end of the power stick, he could marshal his brothers or friends to go a-lawing with, or for, him. When confronted with this deputation, the defendant rarely had recourse to marshaling *his* friends or brothers. It was not good form. And more than that—he had made his bid for prestige, and he would surely look bad if he failed to carry it through alone.

The plaintiff who called to his brothers for help naturally lost prestige to some degree, and in addition he had to turn over all that he received in damages. His "lawyers" got the a' of it.

Comanche society in the nineteenth century was constantly recouping its losses by incorporating captives into the tribe. Such captives were taken as children and mildly exploited as houseworkers, if they were girls, or put to work as herders, if boys. The girls were ultimately married by their captors and so acquired full citizenship. The boys were allowed to join war parties and they, too, were incorporated after a time into the kinship system through adoption as "brothers" or "sons" by their captors or some other Comanche friend. Some captives, however, although they achieved free status in manhood, were not absorbed into a family by adoption. Conversely, attrition so decimated a number of Comanche families that only one or two males were left as survivors. These men and unadopted captives had no brothers upon whom to call when hard put to prosecute a wrong. In such a plight there could be no justice for them if left to their own resources. Aggressors would have a free hand.

At this point the Comanches met the social need for a check on aggression and the provision of redress by means of a simple utilization of the materials at hand. They held no constitutional convention to devise new instruments of government. Personal power was the recognized basis of social relations between men. Power out of control was the threat. Controlled power was the countercheck naturally hit upon. The weak-kneed victim of aggression who had no kin to back him turned to some great warriors to press his cause for him "A brave, well-known warrior," runs the stock phrase.

The brave, well-known warrior simply took over the case on behalf of the injured party and prosecuted it as his own. It gave him a neat chance to face down an upstart warrior, to serve his own ends of self-glorification while acting in the interest of the general social welfare—not against it. He could add to the luster of his status while upholding the law of marriage, instead of flouting it. Vanity and social altruism were wedded in one act and both were exploited for the social good. Their gratification was the sole reward, for the warrior champion received no compensation nor any share of the damages collected.

The intervening warrior was acting as a legal champion. He made no pretense of judging the case or of mediating. He entered with the aim of *forcing* the defendant to pay damages exactly as the injured party would have forced him, if he could. And if damages could not be squeezed out, he personally assaulted the defendant with all the violence he could muster. The ultimate sanction was his to use, if need be.

Comanche procedure in the wife absconding cases never involved questions of fact, for fact and evidence were cleared in preliminary investigation by the husband. He had no problem; the presence of the wife with her lover was enough. Adultery, however, was usually surreptitious. And this posed problems. To meet them the suspecting husband had recourse to several violent privilege-rights. A married woman could be wholly at the mercy of her husband's whim. He was free to extort from her a confession, as well as the name of her lover, by use of the cruelest third-degree methods. He either choked her until she gasped out the required information, or he took her out to a spot some distance from the camp where he built a fire over which he slowly lowered his terrorized wife until she gave him the information he wanted.

More refined men put the matter in the hands of the Sun and Earth. They took their wives to a lonely spot for *taß ßekat*, "sun killing." The suspecting husband filled his ceremonial pipe and smoked to the great powers, addressing first the sun. "You, Father, know the truth of this matter. As you look down upon them don't let them live until fall." Then to the Earth he said, "You, Mother Earth, as you know what is true, don't let them live a happy life on you."

Thereupon the wife smoked the pipe and avowed her innocence with an appeal to the Sun and Earth to kill her if she lied. Comanche dogma has it, and supporting cases are offered, that when women made this ritual conditioned curse, the Sun knew if they were guilty, and it killed them. Its penalty for perjury was death.[6]

Women, for their part, had no demand-rights against their husbands that they be faithful in marriage; they could exact no penalties from them. Hence, they had no opportunities to put their husbands to the test. But in recent decades some did turn the tables by demanding of the Sun and Earth, when they took the oath, that the powers kill the husband if the wife were innocent of the act.

Finally, it should be noted that when the issue was put to the Sun and Earth, no legal action against the corespondent followed. The death of the wife ended the matter.

On the other hand, the collecting of damages from the offending male did not necessarily absolve the wife. If her absconder was strong enough, she had a good chance of escaping her husband's ire. But she ran terrible risks. In seven of forty-five Comanche adultery and wife-absconding cases the women were slain by their husbands—one in seven! Three of these were adulteresses; four were absconders. Of the twenty other adulteresses five were mutilated by their husbands; four had their noses cut off, and one had the soles of her feet slashed so she could not walk.

One may wonder that any Comanche woman played the game against such odds. We see it as additional evidence that mere severity of the law is not enough by itself to make people behave.

The Comanche law of murder was most simple. For a Comanche husband to kill his wife—with or without good cause—was not murder.

6 Hoebel, *Political Organization and Law-ways*, pp. 90–91.

It was an absolute privilege-right, which not even her family would move to challenge.

On the other hand, for one Comanche male to kill another was never a privilege-right, even when applying force to an over-stubborn defendant. Any willful killing required a revenge killing of the slayer. Here was the fatal weakness of Comanche law, as indeed of so much primitive law. The culture provided right ways of procedure and defined the substance of tortious acts. But the primacy of the kin group came to the fore whenever a prosecutor felt he had pushed negotiation as far as it would carry and then had taken recourse to arms. The kin of the defendant whom he had killed did not accept the killing, although general public opinion may have held that the victim had it coming to him. The Comanche kinsmen took revenge on the prosecutor regardless of the rightness of his original grievance. In enforcing the law he lost his life, a victim of *lex talionis*.

However much Comanche law fell short in this respect, custom remedied the defect in another. Blood-revenge killing was only of the first killer and retaliation did not lead to feud. The kinship principle, while extant, was nevertheless weak among the Comanches, and general fighting within the tribe was not to be countenanced when there were always outside enemies to be confronted. The killer, and the killer alone, had to die. There it stopped. No religious sanction, no tribal authority, was necessary to suppress the feuding tendency. Custom was sufficient restraint, and in this the Comanches were fortunate, for thereby they escaped the self-renewing curse that plagues so many primitive law systems.

Willful killing of a man's favorite horse was an act akin to murder, especially if the horse had been bequeathed to him by a best friend. Retaliation was taken not in killing the favorite horse of the transgressor but in slaying the transgressor himself. A favorite horse had a legal personality and was equated with a human being. Consequently, no further blood revenge followed, for things were already equal: a man for a horse.

Every Comanche male at one time or another went on a vision quest in search of power. He did not abase himself before the supernatural spirits or masochistically mutilate and torture himself to arouse their compassion. Nor did he weep before them to arouse their pity. Unlike the tribesmen of the Plains to the north, he assumed that the spirits were generally benign toward him; they needed no coaxing to share the benefits of their power with him. If he fasted and waited in a lonely place, they would help him. Nor did they interfere in his daily living except as they put conditions on the use of the power they gave him. A Comanche had to observe no supernatural tabus save those that went with his own personal medicine. Under Postulate VIII most Comanche medicine men used their powers to help the people. They cured and used their medicine to bring success in war and the hunt. They even, for a contractual consideration, helped others to get a share in their power. Although they were paid for their healing efforts, they did not attempt to milk the public or use their supernatural potency for exploitative purposes. Comanche magic was mostly white.

Occasional older medicine men, however, became "mean medicine men." Unable any longer to maintain their prestige by war prowess, they struck out at enterprising youngsters. They shot their medicine into them. The detection of sorcery was the job of a curing medicine man. In the first instance, after diagnosing the nature of the illness and who caused it, he always tried to effect a cure with a counter medicine. If he was successful, nothing more was done. If he failed, legal action was in order. The brothers of the sorcerized victim would call upon the sorcerer to remove the curse. If he refused, which he usually did by denying that he had anything to do with the affair, they could move to an attack with weapons or the threat of such an attack. But whether they did or not depended upon their strength of character. In sorcery cases where the aggrieved party was a weakling (and apparently not backed by brothers) there was no prosecution; and one Comanche, Salt Worn Out, even shifted to another band, to get out of the sorcerer's sphere of influence.[7] In one instance where the aggrieved brothers started an apparently forceful prosecution, they backed down when the sorcerer put up an even more forceful defense—a threat of *more* sorcery.[8] In the event both parties took equally strong positions, one accused sorcerer took a voluntary conditional curse on the sun—and was killed by lightning the following spring. Thus he paid the price of his guilt.[9]

In another instance the alleged sorcerer was forthwith stabbed and killed by his own sister's son, the brother of his victim. The slayer's elder brother was appalled by the act. But Chew Up, the knife wielder, retorted, "Is it as nothing that I should sit and watch my brother being murdered? Should I have done nothing?" And here there was no blood revenge in counteraction, "Because" in the very words of a Comanche, "the quarrel was in the family, no one else could take it up or do anything about it."[10] Homicide was not legally a tribal or public affair.

The cases in general indicate that the Comanches preferred not to tangle with sorcerers. A cure by a good doctor was much to be preferred. This failing, a kinsman did not have to prosecute as did a cuckolded husband, but he legitimately could, if he had the guts. Otherwise the individual act of sorcery went unpunished. Brave warriors as champions at law did not enter these cases. A warrior outfacing another warrior was one thing, but to have to threaten a sorcerer was not an inviting prospect for even the bravest.

[7] Hoebel, *Political Organization and Law-ways*, case 25, p. 92.
[8] *Ibid.*, case 24, p. 91.
[9] *Ibid.*, case 23, pp. 89–90.
[10] *Ibid.*, case 27, pp. 94–95.

Repeated sorcery was another matter. As among the Eskimos it became a threat to all the people—a threat not to be borne. The fact that the sorcerer was believed to have killed a number of people was evidence that he was "getting away with murder," evidence that no one dared to face up to him. In the need to remove the threat to their common security the members of the band drew together in the sole communal action that the Comanches took against any sort of offender. They lynched him. Or together they tricked him into breaking his tabus so that he died of the effects of his own powers. In each of these instances his fate was discussed and ordained in a meeting of all the men of the band. Excessive sorcery thus became the sole crime in the Comanche legal system.

2 Morals and the Criminal Law

RICHARD C. FULLER

What are the possibilities of the criminal law as an agency of social control in contemporary American life? No satisfactory answer to this question can be ventured until we have explored the intricate relationships which exist between current patterns of morality and the prohibitions of criminal statutes. Roscoe Pound has long insisted that the law in action is greatly influenced if not determined by custom and public opinion.[1] Yet we sometimes forget his dictum in our zeal to criticize the shortcomings of such law enforcement agencies as the police and criminal courts.

It is the objective in this paper to examine the role played by the criminal law in a dynamic and highly differentiated society such as ours and to suggest certain problems which arise when we resort to new criminal legislation in order to enforce standards of morality held by certain groups in the general population.

LEGAL CONCEPTION OF CRIME

A crime, considered as a legal category, is an act punishable by the state. For conduct to be considered criminal in this legal sense, it must be

Reprinted by special permission from *The Journal of Criminal Law, Criminology and Police Science*, Copyright © 1942 by the Northwestern University School of Law, Volume 32, Number 6 (March-April, 1942), pp. 624–630.

[1] See Roscoe Pound, *Criminal Justice in America*, New York, 1930.

something more than the violation of group morality or custom. A person's conduct may deviate from some social norm and be regarded as eccentric, bad manners, highly improper, or even downright immoral, but it is not criminal conduct in the legal aspect unless it is also a deviation from the criminal code established and enforceable by the state.

This juridical conception of crime has its logic in expediency, rather than in sociological realism. It conveniently delimits misconduct which is the domain of police, prosecutor and judge from misconduct which must be regulated exclusively by the pressures of public opinion. Sociologically speaking, however, a criminal statute is simply the formal embodiment of someone's moral values (usually the group dominant in political authority) in an official edict, reinforced with an official penal sanction. Moreover, the mere fact that a given act is made punishable by law does not settle the question of the immorality of the prohibited conduct; it does not preclude people from passing moral judgments on the rightfulness or wrongfulness of the behavior. The dominant group whose values are expressed in the law is only one of many groups which are integrated in the moral and political fabric of the community. When the moral values of one or more of these other groups are not in accord with the moral values of the dominant group we are likely to have a persistent problem of law enforcement. Thus viewed, the problem of the criminal law in action reduces to the problem of conflicting moral values held by different groups and classes in the community.

"CRIMINAL" AND "IMMORAL" NOT ALWAYS SYNONYMOUS

If we are to study crime in its widest social setting, we will find a variety of conduct which, although criminal in the legal sense, is not offensive to the moral conscience of a considerable number of persons. Traffic violations do not often brand the offender as guilty of moral turpitude. In fact, the recipient of a traffic ticket is usually simply the butt of some good-natured joking by his friends. Newspapers in reporting chronic traffic violators who come before the courts are prone to play up the humorous rather than the ominous side of such incidents. Although there may be indignation among certain groups of citizens against gambling and liquor law violations, these activities are often tolerated if not openly supported by numerous residents of the community. Indeed, certain church groups and service clubs regularly conduct gambling games and lotteries for the purpose of raising funds. Professional gamblers rationalize that there cannot be anything very unethical about their games when "legitimate" groups are in the same business. With social drinking now morally acceptable in most communities, the operation of drinking emporiums during prohibited hours, the sale of liquor to minors, and many other infractions of local liquor laws are regarded by many with apathy, if not approval. Some communities tolerate such conditions in order to profit from the license fees paid by those who operate such dispensaries.[2] Even brothels, which normally carry a stigma of disrepute, are in some of our municipalities accepted with a shrug by citizens who are inclined to view them as inevitable appurtenances of the community. The thousand and one forms of political graft and corruption which infest our urban centers only sporadically excite public condemnation and official action.

ROLE OF PUBLIC OPINION

There are several reasons why the criminal behavior in the examples cited is not regarded as immoral by general community consensus. Such deviations simply do not carry the same opprobrium of vicious immorality as do other offenses such as murder, kidnapping, rape, arson, and robbery. They do not threaten our physical and pecuniary survival in the same way as do the more heinous offenses against person and property. Even more significant is the fact that such violations are essential to the normal conduct of business of persons engaged in liquor, gambling, and vice enterprises. Moreover, the direct pecuniary interest of these entrepreneurs is shared indirectly by innumerable public officials and plain citizens whose bread and butter are dependent upon the continued operation of such commercial activities. Finally, the survival of these forms of crime is made possible by the patronage of a public whose personal tastes and morals diverge from the values expressed in the criminal law.

So far as the support of public opinion is concerned, the situation is much the same in a relatively new sphere of criminal definitions—that of business and industrial relations. Offenses of this character include violations of laws pertaining to trusts and combines, insurance, marketing of securities, traffic in food and drugs, the employment of children, collective bargaining, and wage and hour standards. The broker who profits from an illegal stock or insurance transaction, the employer of child labor contrary to government codes, the anti-union boss who flaunts the National Labor Relations Act, the manufacturer who defiantly violates wage and hour legislation—all are engaging in criminal behavior in the legal sense. But are these persons regarded as immoral or anti-social in their conduct by the community in general?

With respect to these white-collar crimes of businessmen, there is

[2] The town council in one small Michigan community recently renewed the license of a saloon operator who was flagrantly violating the law because, in the words of one councilman: "We need the fee to pay for our new fire truck."

usually no militant and community-wide public opinion which will reinforce the legal sanction and put down the legally wrongful behavior.[3] The
social philosophy underlying recent governmental regulations of employer-
employee and buyer-seller relations is not yet understood, much less accepted by the general public. Indeed, as regards conduct in business, there is
a "live and let live" attitude abroad in the community. Business relations
have traditionally been left to individual enterprise and there are a great
many who feel that if business is to prosper personal conscience rather than
public conscience should be the arbiter in these matters.

The degree to which the sphere of conduct defined as criminal coincides with the sphere defined as immoral depends upon the relative homogeneity of moral values within the society represented in any political
jurisdiction. Theoretically, in a primitive society where there is almost
complete agreement on moral values the public opinion enforced mores
for all practical purposes comprise the unwritten criminal code of the tribe.
What is immoral is by hypothesis criminal. In societies other than the
primitive where there is little social change, such as the small rural communities of early nineteenth century America, there would likewise be a
very small area of criminal conduct not defined as immoral. In advanced,
industrialized societies, characterized by urbanization, where there is only a
small core of common values, surrounded by numerous conflicting codes of
behavior, the sphere of conduct generally agreed upon as wrongful grows
smaller as the segmentation and differentiation of the society continues.
Yet the number of criminal laws rapidly increases.

NO COHESIVE OPINION—MANY LAWS

As societies become more differentiated and complex, opinion enforced mores no longer suffice to guarantee uniform norms of conduct.
With increasing disparity in values some common denominator for conduct
is needed and hence resort is made to the codes of the criminal law which
apply to everyone within the same political jurisdiction. Not only are the
older and generally accepted mores which punish such offenses as murder,
rape, and robbery perpetuated in the criminal code, but a host of new laws
spring up which seek to define new areas of behavior where conduct is
impinging on the values held by the group in dominant political authority.
Sutherland and Gehlke, examining the essential trends in the criminal laws

[3] In his discussion of white-collar criminality, E. H. Sutherland has shown that the
community is not organized solidly against such behavior. ". . . The law is pressing in
one direction, and other forces are pressing in the opposite direction. In business, the
'rules of the game' conflict with the legal rules . . . The Better Business Bureaus and
Crime Commissions, composed of business and professional men, attack burglary,
robbery, and cheap swindles, but overlook the crimes of their own members." "White-
Collar Criminality," *American Sociological Review*, Vol. 5, No. 1, p. 11 (February, 1940).

of the United States between 1900 and 1930, discovered very little increase in criminal laws dealing with the "bolder offenses"—the felonies such as murder, robbery, rape, assault, and arson upon which there is very general agreement in any community that they are threats to the general welfare. The large increase in criminal laws has come precisely in an area of behavior where there is no cohesive public opinion branding the conduct as immoral. It is an area of disparate and conflicting values such as public morals, business ethics, and standards of health and public safety.[4] Even more recently the great depression facilitated new definitions of offenses in tax and banking laws, social insurance legislation, and collective bargaining regulations.[5] Such social legislation, perhaps acquiesced to in principle by the masses, opposed in principle by powerful business groups, and often militantly supported only by a vigorous minority of socially conscious individuals, gives rise to an entirely new sphere of criminal behavior.

ORIGIN OF PRESSURE GROUPS

This trend toward new criminal definitions presents a neat dilemma so far as law enforcement is concerned. When a modern community is faced with new conditions such as traffic hazards, liquor and gambling institutions open to all ages and classes of the population, consumer exploitation by business interests, cut-throat business competition, oppression of wage labor by employers, those whose values are shocked by such conditions feel that they cannot wait until there is a spontaneous ground-swell of community indignation. Indeed, if all groups in the population frowned on such practices there would be little need of any criminal legislation to suppress them. So the socially minded reformers, or special groups whose interests are being hurt, although often numerically in the minority, put pressure on the legislatures to outlaw the disapproved of behavior. Our parliamentary democracy is so constituted that much of our legislation is, in fact, the legislation of well-organized, articulate, and powerful minorities. Such minorities, in effect, become the dominant groups in casting the new moral molds of the criminal law. The notion that legislatures, in enacting new criminal legislation, are intervening for the "common good" or "general welfare" cannot be reconciled with the harsh realism of our politics. Such intervention is usually simply the result of effective pressure exerted by some group with important political influence.[6] Yet without general com-

---

[4] E. H. Sutherland and C. E. Gehlke, "Crime and Punishment," Chap. 22 in *Recent Social Trends in the United States*, pp. 1116–1120, New York, 1933.

[5] See Thorsten Sellin, *Research Memorandum on Crime in the Depression*, pp. 6–7, Social Science Research Council, New York, 1937.

[6] See Harwood L. Childs, *Pressure Groups and Propaganda*, American Academy of Political and Social Sciences, Philadelphia, 1936.

munity support in these laws, enforcement proves a troublesome problem and the criminal definition may prove to be nothing more than a paper law, not a law in action.

"MORAL" AND "AMELIORATIVE" PROBLEMS

It is probably true that our criminal codes do contain the *moral minimum* of our day and age. That is to say, those values which we hold most sacred and least dispensable are elevated by public opinion to the status of protection by the criminal law. Thus, many of the statutory enactments of our modern criminal codes merely redefine as criminal certain behavior which for many generations has been outlawed by the unwritten mores of our ancestors. These moral minima are found in the many criminal laws which punish offenses against property, such as burglary and robbery; against the person, such as murder, assault, and rape; against the marriage institution, such as incest and bigamy; against public order and decency, such as disturbing the peace and public immorality; against the state, such as insurrection and treason. All these instances represent behavior which the vast majority of the community deems to be injurious to its best interests, welfare, and survival. No matter what an individual's age, sex, race, nationality, religion, or income, he will likely subscribe to the moral values protected by such laws. Offenses of this type are condemned by all "respectable" and "right-thinking" citizens, and even abhorred by criminals themselves when committed against members of their in-group. There are no well-organized pressure groups contending openly in community forum for legal approval of such conduct. Rather, the conduct is not only criminal by legal definition but also by the common moral definition of the community. The "social problem" involved in crimes of this type is *ameliorative* rather than moral in nature. That is to say, the problem is not one of convincing the community that such behavior is wrongful and that it should be put down. Rather, the essential difficulty is one of amelioration, of working out solutions and getting people to agree upon programs of prevention and penology.[7]

On the other hand, contemporary criminal codes go far beyond the

---

[7] Even where there is a basic agreement throughout the community that the conduct is wrongful, there is not likely to be the same unanimity of opinion as to what should be done with the offender. Social attitudes come into conflict over such provocative issues as capital punishment, probation and parole, prison industries, the juvenile court, and prevention programs. Popular sentiments addicted to traditional policies of punishment and retribution obstruct effective programs of control based upon newer conceptions of individualized treatment and rehabilitation. See Logan Wilson, "Public Opinion and the Individualized Treatment of Criminals," *The Journal of Criminal Law and Criminology*, Vol. 28, No. 5, pp. 674–683 (January-February, 1938).

moral minimum in prohibiting various forms of conduct which are not viewed as wrongful by important groups and classes in the community. Violations of such laws constitute a second type of offenses which exploit a high threshold of community tolerance or endorsement. Crimes of this category are exemplified by circumvention of new social legislation, bribery of public officials to secure favorable contracts and legislation, fraud and misrepresentation in the financial statemets of corporations, manipulations on the stock exchange, embezzlement and misapplication of funds, illegal transactions of public utility companies, gambling syndicates, liquor law violations, and commercialized vice. These crimes are committed either by white-collar upper-class businessmen who have the respect of most of the community, or by organized criminal rings which have the support and patronage of a sizeable segment of the citizenry. White-collar crime and organized racketeering are not in the first instance ameliorative problems. Rather they are *moral* problems, because the fundamental issue is the moral unwillingness of the community as a whole to organize to put down wrong. No questions of prevention or punishment can arise until there has been effective action by law enforcement officials backed by an indignant community opinion. Crimes in this moral category persist because the violations themselves are an integral part of the community pattern of living. "Good" citizens may abhor the corruption of their public officials, protest the illegal practices of bankers, doctors, and business executives, and they are even more likely to rise against organized gambling and vice. The fact remains that these practices and practitioners are woven into the economic and moral fabric of the community as an established part of "business as usual," and because of this people cannot agree on the basic moral question of whether or not such conduct should be tolerated.

So it is that in contemporary society behavior often comes to be defined as criminal where the opinion of many individuals and groups is not in support of the definition. This is perhaps inevitable in any culture which is split into so many diversified groups having so very little in common, but it is manifest that legal controls alone will not suffice to guarantee the high standards of moral behavior desired by those who support a given law. If the criminal definitions are to become incorporated into our central core of moral sanctions, many more people, representative of the community as a whole, must be won over to their support.

ADMINISTRATION AN EDUCATIONAL TECHNIQUE

It is not that the law must in all instances wait for widespread moral support. It is possible that the very administration of the law itself, if wisely undertaken, may serve as a technique of popular education through which to mold opinion in its favor. The enforcement of a law inevitably awakens popular discussion as to its merits. This is the case with some of the recent social legislation such as the Securities and Exchange Act regulating transactions on the stock exchange. Moreover, even in the instance of a very unpopular law, people are likely to observe it for some time after its passage simply because it is the law of the land. We have respect for *the law*, as an institution, even though we may have little or no respect for a specific legal measure. There were instances where even the much despised Prohibition act was obeyed in letter and in spirit by socially responsible citizens whose sentiments were not in accord with the law itself. But we cannot depend upon the habit of law obedience exclusively. Ultimately the problem is one of supplementing the political sanctions of the law, which operate through threat of punishment more or less externally on individuals, with spontaneous moral sanctions which operate on the habits, attitudes, and conscience of individuals. Moral sanctions rarely originate in legislatures, but rather in the more primary social groupings of the family, neighborhood discussion groups, school and church. Even where the law is so technical or specialized in subject matter that it must necessarily come in advance of an enlightened public opinion, as in the case of public health measures and conservation of game statutes, it has little chance of permanent success so long as its social objectives remain unintelligible to the general public.

EDUCATION VERSUS THE "BIG STICK"

Should we not rely less on the "big stick" of the law and more on techniques of popular education to the values implicit in the law? There are significant instances where the dominant group has not stopped with control by legal fiat, but has sought by other methods to educate persistent offenders to its way of thinking. Witness traffic schools for adults and programs of safety instruction for child pedestrians; temperance movements supplementing legal restrictions on the liquor business; conservation films and lectures explaining the objectives of new fishing and hunting regulations; and the intensive educational programs of the Federal government relative to new social insurance, wage and hour, and collective bargaining laws. These appeals are directed to the self-interest of individuals as well as to their social conscience, but in any case they seek to lighten the burdensome problem of law enforcement by changing obstructive attitudes and values. Many more experiments in this direction will likely replace the "crack down and educate later" technique which has too often characterized our passion for legislating against things which we do not like.

CONCLUSION

Sociologists interested in the problem of crime in contemporary America should further explore the implications of this relationship between moral and legal patterns. We have been prone to think of crime too much in terms of its legalistic aspects, and too little in terms of its community or cultural sources. The behavior of a criminal is always abnormal or atypical in the restricted sense that it is a deviation from some social norm established in the criminal law, but it is perfectly normal and typical when it subscribes to some cultural conduct norm other than that implicit in the law.[8] If we are to do away with the forms of crime which are supported by the cultural values of the community, we must change these values. The failure of legal controls to eradicate such behavior is merely symptomatic of our failure to alter fundamentally the real source of the conduct which we condemn.

[8] A. R. Lindesmith and H. Warren Dunham have suggested that criminals be classified for sociological investigation according to the degree and manner in which their crimes are related to or spring from cultural definitions. "Some Principles of Criminal Typology," *Social Forces*, Vol. 19, No. 3 (March, 1941).

3 White-Collar Crime and Social Structure[*]

VILHELM AUBERT

One sign of maturity in a research field is the constant and conscious utilization of specific empirical findings to throw light on general theoretical problems. As long as this takes place only as a caprice of occasional deviants, a science has not reached the stage where research becomes genuinely cumulative. The study of crime is in this respect a pertinent example of missed opportunities. The numerous studies in the etiology of criminal and delinquent behavior have by and large constituted an applied field, where research might instead also have been oriented toward basic social theory, or at least toward theories of the middle range.

One main obstacle to the development of a fruitful theoretical orientation is to be found in the tendency to treat criminal behavior, on the one hand, and the system of legal sanctions, on the other, as two separate problems. In our opinion, crime and punishment are most fruitfully handled as two aspects of a group process or two links in a specific type of social interaction.

It is frequently impossible to discover the socio-psychological origins and functions of criminal behavior without insight into the social processes behind the enactment of the corresponding parts of the criminal legislation.

Reprinted from *American Journal of Sociology*, 58 (November, 1952), 263–271, by permission of The University of Chicago Press. Copyright 1952 by The University of Chicago. Also by permission of the author.

[*] I wish to thank Dr. Daniel Katz, Ragnar Rommetveit, and Knut Sveri who gave me many helpful suggestions for this article.

The social norms and mores that gave impetus to the enactment, and the groups that uphold these norms, are important to know for purposes, also, of tracing the criminal recruitment mechanisms. The nature of the norms thus legally sanctioned may, for instance, to some extent determine whether the criminals tend to be rebels, psychopaths, or rational profit-seekers.

The interdependence of the origin and function of social norms and the origin of deviations is seen very clearly in societies which make political activities criminal. Unless we know fairly well the location and scope of the groups supporting the legislation, the function it serves in those groups, and the social norms it is based upon, we shall not succeed in explaining and predicting offenses. As we shall see later, this type of interdependence is apparent in the study of white-collar crimes. In the study of more "orthodox" or "classical" crimes it has, however, been largely ignored, in spite of occasional programmatic pleas for an interaction approach, notably one from Thorsten Sellin.[1]

There are some fairly obvious reasons why the origin and functions of deviant behavior—criminal or not—have been the main focus of scientific attention, to the neglect of the complementary phenomenon of norm-conformity and pressure to conform. It seems somehow to be "natural" to ask why the deviants become deviants, and not why the conforming majority conform and support definitions of specific types of behavior and attitudes as deviations, and prosecute them as such. Robert Merton made the parallel observation concerning the sociology of knowledge that it seems more "natural" to search for a causal explanation of scientific and other intellectual "errors" than to inquire into the whys and wherefores of "truth." But, he proceeds, the "Copernican revolution" in the sociology of knowledge came when scientists began to ask for explanations not only of the mistakes but also of the true, plausible, or valid knowledge.[2] A similar revolution is much needed in the study of criminology and criminal law.

It is, by the way, likely that its close relationship to law explains why criminology in this respect has remained a more obedient servant of society's conventions than many other fields of social science. There is an understandable resistance on the part of lawmakers, judges, and lawyers to become the object of scientific studies, as the criminals are. And this resistance becomes effective by virtue of the close association between them and the criminologists.

There are other factors which may help us to understand the strong scientific attraction inherent in deviant behavior. In contrast to conformity, deviant behavior is dramatic and often highly entertaining. In *Gestalt*

[1] Thorsten Sellin, *Culture Conflict and Crime* (Social Science Research Council Bull. 41 [New York, 1938]), chap. ii.

[2] Robert Merton, "The Sociology of Knowledge," *Social Theory and Social Structure* (Glencoe, Ill.: Free Press, 1950), p. 222.

terminology, deviation is the "figure" against the "ground" of conformity. There can be little doubt that much scientific effort in sociology has been drawn to the outstanding and dramatic, although theoretically isolated, events, at the expense of the dull trivialities which frequently may provide us with better keys to the understanding of general problems.

The recent concern among social scientists with white-collar crime tends to bring long-neglected relationships between criminal behavior, criminal law, penal sanctions, and social structure into focus. The unexpected and somehow deviant nature of many recent laws defining white-collar crimes has made it natural to ask for an explanation of the norms themselves and not only of their infringements. As soon as this happens new theoretical vistas are immediately opened.

Although white-collar crime today in itself is a very important practical problem, its research importance does not lie within the specific field itself. What is theoretically important is that white-collar crime seems to be one of those phenomena which are particularly sensitive to—and therefore highly symptomatic of—more pervasive and generalizable features of the social structure. That is why the field merits even more attention than it is given today.

Although the selection of white-collar crime as a field of research is a real achievement, the discussion has had an unfortunate slant. Not the least responsible for this is the pioneer in the study of white-collar crime, the late E. H. Sutherland. His formulation of the problem, "Is white-collar crime a crime?"[3], has given rise to futile terminological disputes, which are apt to become clouded by class identifications and ideological convictions.

The discussion in the *American Journal of Sociology* some years ago between Hartung and Burgess demonstrates some dangers inherent in this way of phrasing the problem.[4] Professor Hartung seemed to interpret the question of whether white-collar crimes are crimes or not as a research problem, and gave an affirmative answer as if it were a significant result of his studies. Although the material presented by Hartung is of considerable interest, the conclusion seems less significant since the problem mentioned is largely a matter of definition. Burgess on the other hand rejects Hartung's (and Sutherland's) answer on the basis of a theory about differences in causation, the implication being that there exists a specific "criminal-making process" common to all traditional crimes but not white-collar crimes, providing these former crimes with a uniform explanation. In view of the evidence, this seems hardly less dogmatic than the opposite view.

When Burgess suggests that "a criminal is a person who regards himself

[3] *American Sociological Review*, X (April, 1945), 132–39.

[4] Frank E. Hartung, "White-Collar Offenses in the Wholesale Meat Industry in Detroit," *American Journal of Sociology*, LV (July, 1950), 25–31; and Ernest W. Burgess, "Comment," p. 34.

as a criminal and is so regarded by society," he is suggesting a subtle and—in some ways—significant criterion. It has the disadvantage, however, that only very careful attitude studies can reveal if it applies or not in a concrete case. For this end a unifying concept of those who fulfil the criterion is much needed. But if it were to be taken for granted without further research that all traditional crimes fulfil the criterion while none of the white-collar crimes do, it is merely a way to dispose of a complicated empirical problem in the guise of mere conceptual clarification and definition.

Sutherland defined "white-collar crime . . . as a crime committed by a person of respectability and high social status in the course of his occupation."[5] As a prototype of white-collar crimes, he focused special attention on crimes committed by businessmen in the course of their business activities. Hartung uses a somewhat narrower definition: "A white-collar offense is defined as a violation of law regulating business, which is committed for a firm by the firm or its agents in the conduct of its business."[6] Cressey seems implicitly to be using a wider concept—in accordance with Sutherland's explicit definition—a concept broad enough to include also embezzlement.[7] In the following we shall primarily have in mind white-collar crimes in the more narrow sense, those crimes which all the cited writers would accept as such.

The following characteristics of white-collar crimes are claimed to be established by the research done on these problems, primarily Sutherland's.

As far as the "law in books" is concerned, white-collar crimes have much in common with most "traditional" crimes. Statutes define a penal sanction against them. According to Norwegian law these may be quite severe; for price violation they may amount to as much as three years' imprisonment. It is maintained that the situation is similar according to American law, although the evidence is not equally clear.

The "law in action" is, however, in this field characterized by slow, inefficient, and highly differential implementation. And, it is maintained, more so than in other areas of the criminal law. Sometimes the lack of efficient implementation is foreshadowed already in the "law in books" by the setting up of special types of enforcement machinery or the failing to solve obvious enforcement problems. Frequently, however, there is a real gap between the two levels of the law.

White-collar crimes are numerous and, as it follows from the definition, committed by people of high social status, which usually also means high income.

[5] *White Collar Crime* (New York: Dryden Press, 1949), p. 9.
[6] *Op. cit.*, p. 25.
[7] Donald R. Cressey, "The Criminal Violation of Financial Trust," *American Sociological Review*, XV (December, 1950), 741.

A trivial conclusion to be drawn from this is that low socio-economic status and associated factors cannot be considered crucial in the explanation of crime *in general*, that is, if white-collar crimes were to be considered crimes. It is, moreover, possible that the acknowledged existence of white-collar crimes may tend to draw some of the attention away from these factors in other areas of criminal behavior also. The same may happen to theories that explain crimes in terms of personality disorganization, low intelligence, physical type, or the like, although such theories are not meant to cover white-collar crime.

There is usually no clear-cut opposition between the white-collar criminals and the general public, who are themselves often violating the same laws on a modest scale. The public has customarily a condoning, indifferent, or ambivalent attitude. It must be admitted that this conclusion is based to a large extent upon impressionistic observation rather than systematic surveys, although some surveys exist.

It has been established in some studies that the white-collar criminal finds support for his behavior in group-norms, thus tending to break down further the view that violations of laws are rooted in man's raw nature, in his unrestrained biological impulses. We must agree with Merton's statement that "certain phases of social structure generate the circumstances in which infringement of social codes constitutes a "normal response."[8] It is nothing new in criminology that crimes are frequently committed by persons who give each other social (and other) support in groups in pursuance of criminal careers.[9] But what distinguishes the white-collar criminal in this respect is that his group often has an elaborate and widely accepted ideological rationalization for the offenses, and is a group of great social significance outside the sphere of criminal activity—usually a group with considerable economic and political power.

This brief survey does not give a definite answer to the question: "Is white-collar crime a crime?" The definition of an activity as "crime" is always, apart from its scientific merits, a "persuasive definition."[10] It contains an element of propaganda. The terminology one accepts in the present controversy will depend upon how much one wants to get rid of these white-collar activities. Disregarding that for the moment, we have seen that white-collar crimes have at least one characteristic in common with all the conventional crimes: they are forbidden by law, and the law stipulates a penal sanction against infringements. But with respect to the other char-

[8] "Social Structure and Anomie," *American Sociological Review*, III (October, 1938), 672.

[9] Cf. chap. x in Muzafer Sherif and Hadley Cantril, *The Psychology of Ego-Involvements* (New York: John Wiley & Sons, Inc., 1947).

[10] See Charles L. Stevenson, *Ethics and Language* (New Haven: Yale University Press, 1944), pp. 210 ff.

acteristics mentioned (respectively: differential and inefficient implementation, status of violators, tolerance of public, and social support of offenders), they seem to differ somewhat from many other types of law violations. It should be noted, however, that some of these differences are only differences in degree and emphasis. Furthermore, the crimes which fall outside the white-collar category are not as homogeneous as some writers seem to believe, which makes comparisons even more difficult.

For purposes of theoretical analysis it is of prime importance to develop and apply concepts which preserve and emphasize the ambiguous nature of the white-collar crimes and not to "solve" the problem by classifying them as either "crimes" or "not crimes." Their controversial nature is exactly what makes them so interesting from a sociological point of view and what gives us a clue to important norm conflicts, clashing group interests, and maybe incipient social change. One main benefit to be derived from the study of white-collar crimes springs from the opportunity which the ambivalence in the citizen, in the businessman, and among lawyers, judges, and even criminologists offers as a barometer of structural conflicts and change—potential in the larger social system of which they and the white-collar crimes are parts.

The laws against white-collar crime are usually not in obvious and apparent harmony with the mores. They are largely an outcome of the increased complexity of modern industrial society, a complexity which requires legal control of activities with long-range and often very indirectly damaging effects. Price regulation, intending to curb inflation, is a pertinent example. An illegal price will frequently create no immediate reaction and invoke no sanctions from the mores in the community. A tie-in with the mores can only be established through public acceptance of relatively complicated means-end hypotheses from modern economic science. As long as these hypotheses have not become integrated parts of the individual's moral system there will be a gap between the letter of the law and the requirements of the informal norms of the daily interaction between the members of society.

There can be small doubt that this gap exists in many modern societies, for example, in Europe. And in some areas, in relation to some groups, there is not only a gap but a conflict between the laws and the mores or ideologies which are traditionally accepted. In such cases, ambivalence may arise in the attitudes toward white-collar crimes, originating in a loyalty divided between the laws and the traditional beliefs. These ambivalent attitudes, their detailed structures and functions, are the most fruitful starting point for empirical research on white-collar crime in its relation to social structure.

With detailed surveys of these attitudes in hand, research should be further oriented toward the actual external cross pressures that operate in this area of opinion formation. What is, more specifically, the content of the partly conflicting group norms? How can we locate the opinion leaders ("norm speakers") and followers ("norm receivers") within the relevant groups? How can we give an adequate description of an individual's position as a member of more than one group, as illustrated by his conflicting roles as a law-abiding member of the nation and as a loyal member of the business community? How does group-membership affect the perception of specific white-collar crimes and of sanctions against them? Under what conditions of group-membership, previous norms, personal interests, etc., do the threat of penal sanctions exert pressure (and how strong pressure) toward conformity with the legal norms? What are the sanctions that exert pressure toward conformity with conflicting norms?[11]

All these problems, selected at random, have fairly obvious empirical implications. Answers would be highly relevant to current social theory. One basic methodological problem will, of course, be to develop precise and psychologically meaningful criteria of group membership.

Our approach does not lead to any extensive search for the idiosyncratic motivation of individual deviations from legal norms. It is assumed as a working hypothesis that the white-collar criminal is usually no "genuine deviant." He is only apparently so, as long as his group and its norms are unknown. Leon Festinger has recently pointed out the fallacy of attributing deviant behavior or opinions to an individual when his group affiliations are not adequately understood.[12] Here lies a field of the utmost theoretical importance, requiring the most subtle research techniques.

We assume that white-collar crimes are determined by social norms, accepted and enforced by groups and individuals with whom the individual identifies, groups which tend to give social support to the illegal activity. On the other hand, the legal rules and their enforcement are also determined by social norms, accepted and enforced by other kinds of social groups with which the legislators and enforcement agencies identify themselves and with which even the violators often have some measure of identification. The problems of the etiology of crime and of punishment seem then to relate to the same set of basic theoretical concepts. Moreover, it must be assumed that there is a constant process of interaction between the groups involved and some interdependence of the conflicting social norms. The individual's behavior and attitudes, under cross-pressure from both, can no more be understood on the basis of the one alone than on the basis of the other alone.

In the light of the preceding, I shall present a few aspects of two

[11] A theoretical outline of many of the concepts involved in such studies is to be found in Torgny T. Segerstedt, *Social Control as a Sociological Concept* (Uppsala Universitet's Arsskrift, No. 5 [Uppsala, 1948]).

[12] "Informal Communication in Small Groups," in *Groups, Leadership and Men* [Ed. H. Guetzkow] (Pittsburgh: Carnegie Press, 1951), p. 32.

studies that have recently been carried out in Oslo. Both of them are concerned with types of behavior which fulfil, or nearly so, Sutherland's definition of white-collar crimes.

In the first study we made a survey of the attitudes of certain types of businessmen to the rationing of goods and price regulation and to their violation. It was already known that the number of such violations was great, as shown by the criminal statistics for postwar years. The general impression of the survey confirmed the statistics, although we made no systematic attempt to discover violations within our probability sample from a few business branches in Oslo. The survey concentrated on perceptions and attitudes only.[13]

The roles and attitudes of our subjects seem to be analyzable in terms of Stouffer's concepts, "universalistic" and "particularistic obligations."[14] The businessman has conflicting roles as a law-abiding citizen and as a member of the business community. The felt universalistic obligation is to obey the law, an obligation which finds some support in the "general sense of justice," but which is not fortified by very strong or efficient sanctions against breach. The felt particularistic obligation implies avoidance only of certain blatant offenses and, on the other hand, resistance to these laws in general. This is an obligation to business colleagues, supported by their ideology and frequently also by profit motives. In general it seems that the particularistic obligation takes precedence over the universalistic obligation. Subjects do, however, vary considerably in this respect. Our data do not, unfortunately, permit us to explain these variations.

The attitude to the legal regulations was negative in general. But on a more specific level it was frequently admitted that parts of the legal structure were necessary. This ambivalence was even more marked in the attitudes to violations and violators of the laws. On the one hand these were frequently condemned in principle, on a general level. Most often, however, the respondents defended and tried to justify many types of specific violation. It was apparent that they perceived at least two general types of violators, "the good established firms" and "the outsiders" (including new firms, small firms, disreputable firms, etc.). Violations by the former category were considered much more harmless than those committed by the "outsiders." It seems that the businessmen in this case have developed norms of their own, more tolerant and therefore partly contrasting with the legal norms.

Here lies a problem of more general importance. Burgess and others pointed out that legal definitions of crimes are inadequate in the study of

---

[13] Full report in Vilhelm Aubert *Priskontroll og Rasjonering.* ("Price Control and Rationing") (Oslo: Institute for Social Research, 1950).

[14] Samuel A. Stouffer and Jackson Toby, "Role Conflict and Personality," *American Journal of Sociology*, LVI (March, 1951), 395–406.

causation because the types of behavior legally classified together need not show any uniformity in terms of etiology. The perception of an act as criminal on the part of violators and public is presented as a more suitable criterion. We have found that on the basis of such a criterion it will be necessary to classify some violations of a specific law as criminal and others as not. Detailed studies of attitudes to specific laws would therefore be necessary in order to make any kind of statement about criminal behavior, if Burgess' criterion were to be accepted.

There was a tendency on the part of our respondents to structure their attitudes in a way which did not correspond to legal definitions. Irrespective of the terminology one accepts, we shall expect different motivation on the part of those who violate the regulations in an "acceptable" way and those who do it with less decorum, as, for example, a free-lance black marketeer. We notice furthermore that some of those who violate the laws in non-acceptable ways engage in behavior which does not possess all the characteristics ascribed to white-collar crimes by Sutherland, in spite of the fact that they meet his explicit definition of white-collar crime.

The results indicate that the concept "white-collar crime" may not be of such general usefulness in building up hypotheses about crime causation as some have believed. Most likely the main merit of the concept has been to draw attention to new and important data useful in showing the one-sidedness of many previous generalizations about criminal behavior. The concept does, furthermore, take on increased significance if we look at the phenomena discussed from the other side, that is, if we focus on the etiology of criminal law and law enforcement.

Most of the laws and a very significant part of the enforcement machinery that make up the legal background of economic regulation in Norway aim specifically at the business group, which contains at least a large segment of people with high socio-economic status. It seems justified to interpret the growing number of *legally defined* crimes in this area as a symptom of a slow change in Norwegian social structure, where two partly competing social hierarchies, each with its own marks of distinction, are existing peacefully side by side. Of these, the labor movement and the government agencies it controls represent the ascendant hierarchy, while the business group and its fringes represent the descendant hierarchy. It seems that the definition of new legal crimes of the white-collar brand has served an important social function by giving the ascendant group a feeling of possessing the economic power corresponding to its political supremacy. We do, on the other hand, find traces of resistance to implementation in the social structure in general and in the enforcement machinery. The result is slowness and inefficiency which creates a feeling of harmlessness among the violators. This may then serve the function of pacifying the businessmen and in that way insure the social peace which Norway has enjoyed after the war.[15]

If the preceding speculations prove to have some basis in reality, it appears that causes and functions of white-collar crime legislation differ significantly in some respects from other types of criminal legislation.

The second study[16] referred to dealt with a type of behavior which can only be characterized as white-collar crime according to a fairly wide interpretation of Sutherland's definition. We investigated a new piece of social legislation, regulating the working conditions of domestic help. Violations of this law are committed by housewives, frequently citizens of relatively high socio-economic status, in the course of their occupation. Violations are punishable, although a penal sanction presupposes persistence in violation in spite of warnings. It must be admitted that both the position of the violators and the nature of the sanction make this behavior marginal to current discussions about white-collar crimes. Nevertheless, it raises so many of the same problems that it merits some attention in the present context.

Viewed as a study of criminal—or "criminaloid"—behavior and of crime causation, the survey had some peculiar features. It was, in the first place, not based upon any prison population or population identifiable through police or court records. It was entirely a study of "hidden criminality" and it revealed close to 100 per cent "criminality" in the probability sample which was studied. The identification of violations was based upon a fairly intricate interview, eliciting factual information about the respondent's own behavior and (in interviews with housemaids) their employer's behavior. The respondent was usually ignorant of the laws pertaining to her behavior. A procedure like the one we applied seems to be the logical consequence of a strictly legal definition of criminal behavior. It did, however, give a rather frightening demonstration of the technical problems involved in the mapping of criminal behavior in this sense.

As for the correlates, or possible causes, they differed considerably from those which usually predominate in criminological theory. It turned out that the age of the victim was associated with the incidence of violation. The insight into the content of the legal norms on the part of the potential violators was another factor of some importance. The size of the family also seemed to have something to do with violations. The factor, however, which seemed most significantly (negatively) associated with violation, was

---

[15] It will be seen that our interpretation has borrowed something from Thurman Arnold, *The Folklore of Capitalism*, and *Symbols of Government* (New Haven: Yale University Press, 1937 and 1935, respectively).

[16] Full report in Vilhelm Aubert, Torstein Eckhoff, and Knut Sveri, *En lov i søkelyset* ("A Law in the Searchlight") (Oslo: Institute for Social Research, 1952).

the clarity and scope of the contract upon which the work relationship was based.

The aforementioned factors differentiated our respondents. If we want to understand why there are so many "crimes" in the whole group, the newness of the law is significant, and its reformative nature likewise. The relative isolation of the victims and the uncontrollability of the illegal behavior probably also have a great deal to do with the high incidence of violations.

If those variables that are mentioned here are significant causally, it goes once more to show that specific types of law violations need specific types of explanations.[17] Using the legal definition of "crime," there is probably little in common between all the phenomena covered by the concept. And the same seems to be true of white-collar crime. This type can also differ very much in its nature, and may need quite different causal explanations. We disregard then such global and rather empty principles as that "all criminal behavior is learned."

In the present study we made an attempt to examine rather carefully the conditions determining the form and content of the criminal clause in the new law. This revealed a striking ambivalence on the part of the legislators to the behavior in question. Most likely this ambivalence reflects the existence of two groups in the legislature, groups which are frequently divided on issues of social legislation. This division corresponds roughly to the one described previously, i.e., between the left and the right. The legislators expressed a serious wish to put teeth into the new law by supporting it with penal sanctions. On the other hand, however, it was emphasized that the aim of the law was already achieved and sanctions were therefore unnecessary. Furthermore, it would be impossible to enforce the law through inspection in the homes. The resulting criminal clause was a hybrid. It did stipulate a penal sanction, but it was at the same time made practically unenforceable.[18]

The function of this social legislation as it was finally formulated seems again to be the avoidance of a serious split on the issue between contrasting ideological factions in the legislature and corresponding groups in the population. Perhaps the mere existence of a criminal clause goes some way to satisfy those who on ideological grounds demand action against employers who misuse their housemaids. Its lack of enforcement, on the other hand, protects the opposite interest group against any immediate serious

[17] For additional evidence from another "unorthodox" kind of crime see Arnold M. Rose, "The Social Psychology of Desertion from Combat," *American Sociological Review*, XVI (October, 1951), 629.

[18] The social functions of such statutes have previously been analyzed by Thurman Arnold, *op. cit.*, and Jerome Frank, *Courts on Trial* (Princeton: Princeton University Press, 1949).

bother. It looks as if, in the kind of social structure one finds in Norway today, this sort of purely formal criminalization serves primarily to preserve "the groupness of the group," according to K. N. Llewellyn the basic "law-job."[19]

Let us now summarize some of the experiences from the two Norwegian studies, in so far as they pertain to the discussion of white-collar crime.

The public's and the violators' perceptions of crimes in general are frequently not congruent with legal definitions, the implication being that we may find important differences in motivation and other causal mechanisms within even very specific legal categories. Consequently, we find differences to an even higher degree within broader concepts like white-collar crime.

According to the definition that "a criminal is a person who regards himself as a criminal and is so regarded by society" some white-collar offenses are crimes while others are not.

But it looks as if at least the large bulk of laws stipulating penalties for white-collar offenses have something in common sociologically. This needs much further study, however. The major variables which account for the defining of such acts as crimes seem to be connected with the concept of multiple social hierarchies or diverse status systems.

Legal definitions of white-collar crime imply a need for the study of hidden criminality, which constitutes the vast majority of these offenses. Out of this arise methodological problems of vast cope, severely limiting the possibility of answering the problem of causation.

In the area of research discussed in this paper, it seems that the most fruitful orientation in the research is a study of the interaction between the legal stimulus and the response of violators and the public. This requires careful study of the legislative process and the machinery of enforcement, as well as the study of individual motives, attitudes, and social situation of offenders.

Finally, the basic concepts involved in such a study should not be of a specifically criminological or legal nature but belong in a general theory of social psychology.

[19] "Law and the Social Sciences, Especially Sociology," *American Sociological Review*, XIV (August, 1949), 454.

4 Crime and the Commercial Revolution

JEROME HALL

The era of discoveries and the Commercial Revolution whose advent substantially coincided with them poured into Europe specie in quantities sufficient to turn existing values topsy-turvy. This influx of specie, vastly increasing the supply of liquid capital, must be regarded as one potent factor in stimulating economic enterprise.

Moreover, by shifting trade routes from land to sea the discoveries made possible the carriage of merchandise in bulk theretofore unknown. A trade which had been limited largely to spices and other luxuries now became available to sugar, tobacco, tea—and in quantities sufficient to broaden the market enormously and to multiply transactions geometrically. At the same time, England, in particular, moved into the focus of trade, indeed, in time, into a position almost analogous to that the Italian cities had occupied in the days of the caravan.

Late-comer in the exploration, England's road ran over conquest. Her sailors, led by Drake, preyed on the Spanish fleets—while Elizabeth hanged petty thieves at home. Beginning in 1607, advancing rapidly with the emigration consequent on the civil disturbances, the colonial expansion followed, 1640–1664 presenting a peak.

Immediately the colonies served a double purpose. They supplied raw materials. They also furnished a market for the sale of goods manufactured at home; and the home manufacturers were prompt to protect that market.[1] The tremendous change in the organization of industry is the first development of major importance which closely touches the law of the eighteenth century. Trade became increasingly impersonal and free from supervision. In this transformation of the economic organization of England, it will be recalled, four stages are usually distinguished. In the Middle Ages goods were produced by individuals, their families and neighbors, for local consumption. Next came regulation and close supervision by crafts and gilds in villages and small towns. This was still rather largely a primary group organization until the modern period set in. There followed a period of individual and group production, but with an increasing trend toward large-scale marketing. And, finally, with the Industrial Revolution, came large-scale production.

All this was accompanied by changes in the economic organization of society. The growing wool industry aided by the recurrent enclosure movements had swept and continued to sweep away a vast number of tenant farmers. This movement was a symptom of the transition from an agricultural economy toward a dominantly manufacturing system. It permitted the introduction of more modern methods of raising sheep; it supplied labor for expanding industries; it led to the rise of cities.

There was another eighteenth century development of the greatest importance, namely, the rise of credit and banking facilities and the use of modern instruments to facilitate trade. Banking had been of slow growth in England.[2] Up to the end of the sixteenth century, financial affairs had remained largely in the control of foreigners. But the new possibilities of accumulation of large amounts of precious metals had effect. In 1545 it became legal to lend money at interest rates not exceeding ten per cent. Overseas trade and expansion of business made financing essential. The goldsmiths, who had long functioned as depositories for precious metals,

---

[1] In 1651 the Navigation Act was passed compelling her colonies to use English ships manned by English seamen; and ten years later it was required, also, that the ships be built and owned by Englishmen.

[2] The lending of money at interest was condemned by the Church. A detailed statement of the rise of risk enterprise would necessarily include the theories of the effect of the Reformation upon commerce. Max Weber's famous theory relegates such factors as the accumulation of precious metals from America, the reaction of large markets upon industry, improvement in technology, etc., to a secondary place, as occasions, but not causes, of capitalism. The real cause of the construction of the rationalist economic system which characterized capitalism, was, according to Weber, the sixteenth century religious revolution. Calvinism, in particular, taught that the accumulation of wealth was a duty. This theology, it is urged, completely motivated the new bourgeoisie. "Thus the pursuit of riches, which once had been feared as the enemy of religion, was now welcomed as its ally." Tawney, Foreword to Max Weber's The Protestant Ethic and the Spirit of Capitalism (Parsons' transl.) 4. See also, Weber, General Economic History (Knight's transl.) c. 3, 354. . . .

began to make loans. Their rates were very high; the risk of defalcation was great. Thus, when Charles II in 1672 repudiated a debt of almost one and a half million pounds to the goldsmiths, they in turn were unable to meet their obligations to the merchants who had deposited these funds.

In 1691 William Paterson made his famous proposal to establish a Bank of England which would loan money at reasonable rates, do a general banking business, and assure security. For political reasons, in reality, but avowedly because the government objected to the legalizing of paper money,[3] Paterson's scheme was rejected. However, it was taken up later and arrangements for loans to the government being made, the Bank was organized in 1694. The growth of provincial banks, however, was a very slow process. Burke stated in 1750, and his opinion is generally accepted, that there were not more than "twelve banker's shops out of London";[4] and the Clearing House was not established until 1775. From the middle of the century on, however, the careers of many prominent merchants gravitated from business to banking; and by 1793 there were over four hundred county banks in England. In 1759, the Bank of England, which had not issued notes for less than £20, began to issue £10 notes. Paper had, indeed, been used for several centuries by merchants, but ordinary traders were compelled in the eighteenth century to carry considerable amounts of coin with them. Payment by check apparently did not begin until the end of the eighteenth century.

This growth in banking and the use of paper currency and instruments of credit affected the law of theft in several important respects. The effect upon the law of embezzlement was direct and sharply marked. We have met the Act of 1742, the first true embezzlement statute passed by a Whig parliament, anxious to protect the greatest Whig mercantile institution in the country; but this, it will be recalled, applied only to officers and servants of the Bank of England. Just prior to the passage of this Act, one John Waite, a cashier of the Bank, had taken six East India bonds of the value of 13,300 pounds. He could not be convicted under the common law rule incorporated into 2 Geo. II, and was discharged. The second embezzlement statute, enacted in 1751, applied to officers and employees of the South Sea Company; and the third (1763) extended only to employees of the Post Office. This last followed a large number of cases involving the theft of paper money and valuable instruments sent through the mail. These three statutes were enacted between the years 1742 and 1763. . . .

Whig mercantile interests and the importance of the three corporations

---

[3] "The political enemies of the bank were supported by the goldsmiths and other financial men whose monopoly of money lending was assailed by the new institution." C. A. Conant, A History of Modern Banks of Issue (1927) 84. . . .

[4] Quoted by Toynbee, Industrial Revolution of the 18th Century in England (4th ed. 1894) 55.

concerned account for the special acts. In all three statutes the offense was made a felony without benefit of clergy. The appearance of the general act of 1799 followed shortly after the organization of some four hundred banks in the last decade of the century.

The pattern of conditions which gave rise to embezzlement may therefore be delineated as follows: (1) the expansion of mercantile and banking credit and the use of credit mechanisms, paper money, and securities; (2) the employment of clerks in important positions with reference to dealing with and, in particular, receiving valuables from third persons; (3) the interests of the commercial classes and their representation in Parliament; (4) a change in attitude regarding the public importance of what could formerly be dismissed as merely a private breach of trust; and (5) a series of sensational cases of very serious defalcation which set the pattern into motion and produced immediate action.[5]

Fast upon the heels of the sixteenth and seventeenth century colonization and as a phase of the changing financial organization, came the joint-stock companies, promoted for the conduct of the new colonial commerce.[6] These companies required enormous investment of capital and led to the formation of a type of limited partnership and to popular investment which grew very rapidly and soon took on huge proportions.

The first true joint-stock company was the Russia Company, formed in 1553 with 240 shareholders who had paid £25 each. The Hudson Bay Company was chartered in 1670. Between these dates the Levant, the East India, the Virginia, and other stock companies were formed. These companies paid enormous dividends. The stock of the East India Company, to pick an extreme case, paid 245 per cent in profits in 1676. But extreme cases fire popular fancy. The South Sea venture is familiar to all; but there had been previous investment "phrensies" in 1694, 1695 and 1698. "London, at this time [1698] abounded with many new projects and schemes promising mountains of gold, the Royal Exchange was crowded with projects, wagers,

---

[5] "Peculiarly interesting results are obtained by the intensive study of criminal statistics in particular countries. It appears that in nations whose modern economic development is recent or as yet incomplete the more involved forms of dishonesty increase rapidly from year to year. We therefore expect to find, and do find, that in Germany and Austria, frauds, embezzlements and forgeries are for the time being on the increase. On the other hand, a nation that is advancing very slowly in economic standing, such as Italy, or scarcely at all, such as Spain, displays no increase in these more refined offenses of modern life, while retaining a conspicously high average in the unpremeditated and savage crimes, such as homicide, rape, assault and battery." Raymond B. Fosdick, European Police Systems (1915) 12.

[6] Several reasons are assigned for the rise of regular stock exchange dealings. Macaulay states that during 1661–1688 large amounts of capital had accumulated; and that the high price of land and houses led to the formation of joint-stock companies to provide avenues for investment.

airy companies of new manufactures and inventions, and stock-jobbers, and the like."[7]

The South Sea Company itself was formed in 1711 with the encouragement of the government. Its stock rose like a meteor from £100 to over £1000. Brokerage offices were opened everywhere. In coffee houses, bars, at milliners and dressmakers, men and women in all walks of life placed their orders for stock—and not only in the South Sea Company, but in dozens of others promoted upon most fantastic projects.[8]

In 1721 came the crash. The panic which ensued recalls the United States in 1930. Public indignation demanded strong repressive measures against the directors of the South Sea Company. Walpole, although he had himself made a neat fortune in this stock, was recalled into office as the one man who could exercise some control in the crisis. Even he could not prevent the passage of drastic legislation to satisfy the public clamor. The Chancellor of the Exchequer was impeached. A bill was carried to compensate the victims out of the private assets of the promoters. The grandfather of Gibbon, the historian, forfeited almost his entire fortune of £60,000; others suffered like treatment. "There is," writes Thorold Rogers, "I believe, no other instance in our history in which a fraud has been punished by an *ex post facto* law."[9] Prior to this financial panic the Bubble Act of 1719 had been passed, ironically enough at the instigation of directors of the South Sea Company in order to check competition. It prohibited the formation of companies with transferable shares unless chartered by the Crown or Parliament. In 1734 an act was passed "to prevent the infamous Practice of Stock Jobbing." But although speculation stopped for a time, it began again and by 1769 had become common. Still, the more flagrant practices of promoters were checked, and most people turned to safer investments.

So striking and far-reaching was this experience in the promotion of stock that it must necessarily have formed an important factor in the change of social attitudes regarding false representations, which expressed itself later in the criminal law. Yet the connection was not avowed. Repression of fraudulent stock promotion did take specific form, but the thought did not transfer itself to ordinary commercial transactions for some time. Nevertheless, it is impossible to read the vivid accounts of wholesale ruin produced by reliance upon fraudulent representations without placing stock specu-

---

[7] Quoted by H. R. Fox-Bourne, English Merchants (1886) 282.

[8] Companies were organized for the purpose of making salt water fresh, planting mulberry trees and breeding silkworms in Chelsea Park, importing jackasses from Spain, "as if, remarks a later writer with some severity, there were not already jackasses enough in London alone." Gibbons [Industry in England], 303.

[9] The Industrial and Commercial History of England, (1892) 79.

lation high among the factors that changed attitudes regarding misrepresentations in general. . . .

There were a number of other less dramatic developments which influenced the law of criminal fraud. They were the disappearance of gild regulation, the concomitant rise of intercommunity transactions; and the development of vast, new types of business enterprises, particularly at the end of the eighteenth century.

The decline of the gilds was accompanied by an increase in commercial frauds but, as we have been, it was not until the end of the eighteenth century that the law was adjusted to meet the new conditions. The gilds were designed for a local trade economy. "What the public desired, above everything else," writes Ashley, "was that the wares should be of good or standard quality. This was the main purpose of the whole system of regulation by gild wardens and town authorities."[10] From the fourteenth to the sixteenth century the gild system was at its height. Then decay set in and it passed away completely in the eighteenth century.

With the growth of large scale production and the marketing of goods on a wide national basis the personal, immediate relationship that existed between manufacturer, merchant and buyer in the manorial system and under the gilds gave way to an impersonal, distant relationship. As a result, buyers of merchandise were without the first-hand protection they had previously enjoyed.

Instead, the rule *caveat emptor* was invoked, and buyers were required to safeguard their own interests, lest trade be smothered by claims raised after sale. Yet the combination of large-scale marketing and the purchase of goods at a distance in reliance on representations of the seller, produced conditions which in due course could be seen to make safeguards against fraud necessary. Again, the transition from a system of cash on delivery transactions to a credit economy made the sale of goods on time a vital factor. Accordingly it became necessary to safeguard merchants against an extension of credit upon misrepresentations. Finally, the breakdown of primary groups by a succession of enclosure movements concomitant with greatly increased mobility in population and the rise of cities produced new alignments of persons unknown to one another—a condition of affairs which lent itself to fraud quite apart from commercial transactions.

The most significant result of the commercial changes described above was the rise of large-scale dealing in stolen goods. This was dramatically exhibited in the case of Jonathan Wild. In the early part of the eighteenth century Jonathan Wild, the most remarkable receiver of stolen goods on record in the modern world, made his distinctive contribution to a com-

10 The Economic Organization of England 40.

mercial age. A case study of Wild would be most profitable, perhaps especially for those well-intentioned souls who imagine that by any simple device such as passing a new law or restoring capital punishment on a wholesale scale, anti-social behavior can be made to disappear. The study of crimes against property without violence and particularly of this offense of receiving stolen property shows that criminal behavior must be viewed in relation to the culture of which it forms a part.

Wild, notorious organizer of criminal bands on a scale that would make most gangs of today (except those involved in gambling, narcotics, and prostitution) seem ordinary, was an original thinker and a shrewd, capable executive. His career has captured the imagination and engaged the pens of Fielding and Defoe. His exploits have been recorded in numerous monographs.[11]

The following quotation from Gordon presents the salient facts:

"But he dealt extensively in stolen goods, so much so, that he bought a sloop (Captain Roger Johnson), to trade to Holland and Flanders, in which were carried over gold watches, rings, snuff-boxes, and articles of plate, and sometimes bank notes, the proceeds of some mail robbery. His chief-trading port was Ostend, whence Bruges, Ghent, Brussels, and other large towns were easily accessible, and a market existed for his wares. A lading of Hollands and other goods was then shipped, and on the return to England, the custom-house was never troubled.

"An epitome of his villanies is to be found in some sworn informations handed in at his trial.—1. That for many years he had been a confederate with great numbers of highwaymen, pickpockets, housebreakers, shoplifters, and other thieves. 2. That he had formed a kind of corporation of thieves, of which he was the head, or director; and that, notwithstanding his pretended services in detecting and prosecuting offenders, he procured such only to be hanged as concealed their booty, or refused to share it with him. 3. That he divided the town and country into so many districts, and appointed distinct gangs to each, who regularly accounted to him for their robberies. That he had also a particular set to steal at churches in time of divine services; and, likewise, other moving detachments to attend at court, on birthdays, balls, etc.; and at both Houses of Parliament, circuits, and county fairs. 4. That the persons employed by him were, for the most part, felons convict, who had returned from transportation before the time for which they were transported was expired; and that he made choice of them to be his agents, because they could not be legal evidence against

---

[11] See the various Newgate Calendars; Charles Gordon, The Old Bailey and Newgate 134 et seq.; . . . Pike, [A History of Crime in England (1873)] 255 et seq.; A. L. Hayward (Ed.), Lives of the Most Notable Criminals (1927), collected from original papers published in 1735. For an account of his trial, see 2 Select Trials at the Session House at the Old Bailey (1742) 212–18 and 635.

him, and because he had it in his power to take from them what part of the stolen goods he thought fit, and otherwise use them ill, or hang them, as he pleased. 5. That he had from time to time supplied such convicted felons with money and clothes, and lodged them in his own house, the better to conceal them, particularly some, against whom there are now informations for counterfeiting and diminishing broad pieces and guineas. 6. That he had not only been a receiver of stolen goods, as well as of writings of all kinds, for nearly fifteen years past, but had frequently been a confederate, and robbed along with the abovementioned convicted felons. 7. That, in order to carry on these vile practices, to gain some credit with the ignorant multitude, he usually carried a short silver staff, as a badge of authority from the Government, which he used to produce, when he himself was concerned in robbery. 8. That he had under his care and protection several warehouses for receiving and concealing stolen goods; and also a ship for carrying off jewels, watches, and other valuable goods to Holland, where he had a superannuated thief for his factor. 9. That he kept in pay several artists to make alterations, and to transform watches, seals, snuff-boxes, rings, and other valuable things, that they might not be known, several of which he used to present to such persons as he thought might be of service to him. 10. That he seldom, or never, helped the owners to the notes and papers they had lost, unless he found them able exactly to specify and describe them, and then often insisted on more than half their value. 11. And lastly, it appears that he has often sold human blood, by procuring false evidence to swear persons into facts they were not guilty of; sometimes to prevent them from being evidence against himself, and, at other times, for the sake of the great reward given by the Government."[12]

Pike summarizes the situation thus:

"In the republic of the thieves' guild Jonathan Wild became as it were a dictator; but like many of the great men of the middle ages, he owned his greatness to double-dealing. From small beginnings he became in London at least, the receiver-in-chief of all stolen goods. He acquired and maintained this position by the persistent application of two simple principles; he did his best to aid the law in convicting all those misdoers who would not recognise his authority, and he did his best to repair the losses of all who had been plundered and who took him into their confidence. By degrees he set up an office for the recovery of missing property, at which the government must, for a time, have connived. Here the robbed sought an audience of the only man who could promise them restitution; here the robbers congregated like workmen at a workshop, to receive the pay for the work they had done.

"Wild was, in some respects, more autocratic than many kings, for

[12] The Old Bailey and Newgate (1923) 139–40.

he had the power of life and death. If he could reward the thief who submitted to him, he could hang the robber who omitted to seek his protection."[13]

We need to note one other phase of Wild's activities which was a tribute to the man's originality and a contribution to large-scale theft that has persisted to this day. After the enactment of . . . [several new laws], the risk of operating as a buyer of stolen goods was greatly increased. The techniques Wild had applied to protect himself, of concealing the thief or having him executed for another offense, were not helpful in this new situation. Wild, thereupon, refined his *modus operandi*. He became a self-nominated quasi-public police department. He would, for a "reward," and upon receipt of a detailed description of stolen property, undertake to find and restore it to the owner.[14] The new venture flourished, until in 1718 the statute of 4 Geo. I, c. 11, sec. 4 was passed directed at this very activity.[15]

Wild's career ended on the gallows in 1725, but only after three trials. First, he was indicted for a misdemeanor in receiving [stolen] goods, . . . [but was acquitted].

Wild was again indicted, this time for privately stealing in the shop

---

[13] Pike, *op. cit.* 256–8.

[14] "Among the *Egyptians* there was a remarkable Law, or rather custom, which had the sanction of Law, with regard to robbers and sharpers. Whoever entered himself of their gang, gave his name to the Chief, promising to deliver to him all the booty that he should from time to time purloin. On this account, it was customary for such as had anything stolen from them, to apply to the chief of the gang, and give a more particular account and description in writing of what they had lost; as also of the day, hour, and place, when and where they had lost it. This information being given, the stolen goods were easily found, and restored to the right owner, upon his paying a fourth part of the value.

"The institutors of this extraordinary Law, probably thought, that since it was impossible to prevent thieving entirely, it would be more tolerable for the injured party to lose a fourth, by way of redemption than the whole." Henry Dagge, Considerations on Criminal Law (Dublin 1772) 390–1.

[15] This statute is most interesting, and throws light upon a situation which has remained typical until the present day. It provided: "And whereas there are several persons who have secret acquaintance with felons, and who make it their business to help persons to their stolen goods, and by that means gain money from them, which is divided between them and the felons, whereby they greatly encourage such offenders: be it enacted by the authority aforesaid, That wherever any person taketh money or reward, directly or indirectly, under pretence or upon account of helping any person or persons to any stolen goods or chattels, every such person so taking money or reward, as aforesaid, (unless such person doth apprehend, or cause to be apprehended, such felon who stole the same, and cause such felon to be brought to his trial for the same, and give evidence against him) shall be guilty of felony. . . .".

We have here the remarkable instance of the passage of a law aimed directly at the activities of a particular criminal, and of his being indicted, convicted and executed for a violation of this law. . . .

of Catherine Stetham fifty yards of lace, value £40, on January 22, 1725. "But it appearing from the testimony of *Henry Kelly, the principal felon* who had actually stolen the lace, and *who was admitted an evidence for the Crown*, that Wild was not in the shop at the time, but only waited at the corner of the street to receive the goods, he was acquitted on this indictment."[16] The Crown was not, however, deterred. Again Wild was immediately arraigned, tried and, this time, convicted of the offense of receiving a reward of ten guineas from Catherine Stetham for helping her to recover the box of lace stolen by Henry Kelly, who again testified against him.[17]

Wild's elimination in 1725 did not stop the business of dealing in stolen goods. Other receivers continued and appeared; other thief-takers operated upon the same plan. It is a significant commentary that the reward became established as a principal method of recovering stolen property. It became customary to advertise publicly that a reward would be paid for the return of the property, that no inquiries would be made of the person who returned it, and that no attempt would be made to cause his arrest.[18] The inability of the police and other officials to cope adequately with the problem of theft perpetuated the system, and encouraged the intervention of laymen who specialized in the recovery of stolen property.

The legal measures taken to control the criminal receiving of stolen property became prominent at the end of the seventeenth century, and in the first quarter of the eighteenth century they are accentuated in statutes aimed directly at the business of dealing in stolen goods. . . . In general, it was necessary to deal with the problem under handicap of the traditional view of the receiver as an accessory after the fact. Various methods were employed to compensate for this perspective but it was not until 1782 when commerce, including that in stolen goods, had greatly expanded that a

[16] Leach 21, n. a; 168 E. R. 111.

[17] Pike informs us how Wild finally came to his end. "A highwayman was apprehended near Bow: Wild came to the rescue, and aided him to escape from his captor. For this offense Wild was committed to Newgate. When he was thus rendered powerless, the fear with which he had been regarded began to be diminished, and witnesses were less reluctant to give their evidence against him . . . information after information was sworn respecting his past deeds . . . He was hanged on May 24, 1725." Pike, *op. cit.* 259.

And see *N.* [15] *supra.*

[18] "But at present, instead of meeting with any such Discouragement, the Thief disposes of his Goods with almost as much Safety as the honest Tradesman; For first, if he hath made a Booty of any Value, he is almost sure of seeing it advertised within a Day or two, directing him *to bring the Goods to a certain Place where he is to receive a Reward* (sometimes the full value of the Booty) *and no Questions asked.*" Henry Fielding, An Enquiry Into The Causes of the Late Increase of Robbers, etc. 68–9. . . .

major objective was achieved—the use of the thief's testimony in prosecution of the receiver was established by statute.

. . .

We may summarize and conclude this discussion by noting that the last twenty years of the eighteenth century produced the most rapid and extensive growth of the entire law of theft. What conditions influenced this accelerated development? To the continuing and cumulative effects of the social and economic conditions described thus far, it is necessary to add that trade was increasing at enormous strides as the Commercial Revolution advanced to its peak. But most important were the effects of the Industrial Revolution. Both of these factors were aspects of the same movement.

. . .

Whether regarded as the peak of the Commercial Revolution or regarded partly as the era which also ran well into the Industrial Revolution or as a transition, there is unanimity that with reference to the volume of business done, the nature of commerce, and the prevailing types of social and economic organization, the century, as a whole, stands out clearly against all preceding periods in English history. It would be extraordinary if this had left no mark on the growth of the law on crimes against property without violence.

In each development of the law, the particular step taken was a resultant of forces determined largely by social and economic conditions, the existing legal sanctions, the whole body of precedent, and the established judicial techniques. The interplay of law, case, and conditions can be understood only when the meaning of each factor is known.

5 Deviance
and Public Policy

EDWIN M. SCHUR

THE "CREATION" OF DEVIANCE

In the study of deviant behavior and crime, much more attention has been focused on the deviating individuals than on the social "definitions" of the deviance. Yet, as Howard S. Becker has pointed out:

Deviance is *not* a quality of the act the person commits, but rather a consequence of the application by others of rules and sanctions to an "offender." The deviant is one to whom that label has successfully been applied; deviant behavior is behavior that people so label.[1]

When definitions of deviance take the specific form of criminal laws, the sociologist may be particularly likely to neglect their bearing on the behavior in question. Understandably, sociologists are somewhat less interested in law than lawyers are. Furthermore, there has been a general

From Edwin M. Schur, *Crimes Without Victims: Deviant Behavior and Public Policy—Abortion, Homosexuality, Drug Addiction* (pp. 1–8), © 1965. Reprinted by permission of Prentice-Hall, Inc., Englewood Cliffs, New Jersey. Also by permission of the author.

[1] Howard S. Becker, *Outsiders: Studies in the Sociology of Deviance* (New York: The Free Press of Glencoe, Inc., 1963), p. 9. See also Kai Erickson, "Notes on the Sociology of Deviance," *Social Problems*, 9 (Spring 1962), 307–14; and John Kitsuse, "Societal Reaction to Deviant Behavior," *Social Problems*, 9 (Winter 1962), 247–56.

tendency for sociologists to focus greater attention on informal mechanisms of social control. In many instances, however, no real sociological understanding of the deviance problem being considered is possible unless the role of legal norms is examined. This is not to suggest that the sociologist need engage himself in detailed or technical legal analysis; rather, he must consider the important ways in which specific legal definitions and law enforcement policies influence the development of such problems.

Sociology has expanded the analysis of deviance well beyond the narrow individual-centered (even body-centered) schemes that once prevailed. Attempts to relate deviance to the general social structure have helped to balance the treatment (even by some sociologists) of deviant and criminal acts as though they were aberrations rather than integral elements of social life. Yet the particular forms of deviance are frequently ignored. They are considered mere symptoms of underlying social strains and disruptions—in a way that may reveal the impact of psychological theories in this area. And the researcher or analyst is likely to be more concerned with developing a theory of deviance than with understanding any specific form of deviant behavior. This has been evident in the tendency to seek research populations of "criminals" or "delinquents" (as such), with little concern for the varying categories of behavior subsumed under such a rubric. Certainly it is natural for sociologists, in their search for generalizations, to seek out the common elements in diverse behavior patterns and processes. At the same time, however, the search for correlates of deviance should not be allowed to obscure other related sociological concerns. Thus, the *very existence* of a particular deviant behavior pattern in a society is an important datum for research, as is the nature of the social reaction to that behavior and the interplay between the two.

The concept of deviance has itself exerted a helpful influence—especially in underlining the point that deviance can be fully understood only in relation to conformity. On the other hand, it would be most unfortunate if it inadvertently served to perpetuate the preoccupation with deviating individuals.[2] A difficulty has been that in those social problem areas in which deviant or offending individuals are reasonably identifiable, research has concentrated on the question of cause, narrowly construed. It has been the compelling concern, for example, to determine *why* some individuals turn to crime though others do not. When attention is almost exclusively focused on the underlying forces pushing individuals into deviance, there is relatively little consideration of just *what* the deviance itself is. Indeed, various specific forms of deviance are often viewed as being caused by the same underlying forces.

[2] See Edwin M. Schur, "Recent Social Problems Texts: An Essay-Review," *Social Problems*, 10 (Winter 1963), 287–92.

DEVIANCE AS A PROCESS

The notion of deviance as a social process suggests an alternative approach. This concept reflects the basic recognition that deviant behavior, like other forms of social behavior, is learned through social interaction. This is not a new idea, even if it is now being given new emphasis by one group of sociologists. A classic statement of the view, as it has developed in the study of crime, was made by Frank Tannenbaum:

No more self-defeating device could be discovered than the one society has developed in dealing with the criminal. It proclaims his career in such loud and dramatic forms that both he and the community accept the judgment as a fixed description. He becomes conscious of himself as a criminal, and the community expects him to live up to his reputation, and will not credit him if he does not live up to it.[3]

A central thesis in this kind of analysis is that self-fulfilling prophecy mechanisms[4] help to explain deviance.

One of the most systematic efforts to elucidate a theory of deviance in interactional or processual terms has been made by Edwin Lemert. A key feature of his analysis is the recognition that deviance cannot be understood without reference to the societal reactions it invokes. Viewing deviance as but one aspect of social differentiation, Lemert goes on to examine the interplay between the deviant and his judges, highlighting the significant ways in which the deviance comes to be shaped by the attitudes and actions of others. He particularly notes the impact of societal reactions on the organization of deviants, and also draws a highly important distinction between primary and secondary deviation:

When a person begins to employ his deviant behavior or a role based upon it as a means of defense, attack, or adjustment to the overt and covert problems created by the consequent societal reaction to him, his deviation is secondary.[5]

A valuable elaboration of this approach—as seen in recent writings of Erving Goffman and Howard Becker—has involved the application of the "career" concept to deviant behavior. The idea of a criminal career—to describe the actions of professional and habitual offenders—is not new. But there is a broader sense in which every deviant has a "career." This is not simply a sequence of discrete events in the individual's life history; it is

---

[3] Frank Tannenbaum, *Crime and the Community* (New York: Ginn & Company, 1938), p. 477.

[4] Robert K. Merton, *Social Theory and Social Structure*, rev. ed. (New York: The Free Press of Glencoe, Inc., 1957), pp. 421–36.

[5] Edwin Lemert, *Social Pathology* (New York: McGraw-Hill Book Company, Inc., 1951), p. 75.

the subtle and continuous interplay that Goffman describes as a person's "moral career"—"the regular sequence of changes that career entails in the person's self and in his framework of imagery for judging himself and others."[6]

Also highly useful in this regard is the concept of "career contingencies." Just as it can be said that mental patients "distinctively suffer not from mental illness, but from contingencies,"[7] deviants, too, may be generally viewed as displaying contingencies. The actions of others have crucially shaped the deviant outcome. This fact has been recognized by sociologists, who are now increasingly turning their attention to the administration of criminal justice and the intricacies of correctional organizations and techniques.

Important emphasis has been placed on the impact on the individual of being caught, labeled, and publicly "processed" as a deviant. And, as Becker has stated: "Whether a person takes this step [or steps] depends not so much on what he does as on what other people do, on whether or not they enforce the rule he has violated."[8]

The societal reaction to the deviant, then, is vital to an understanding of the deviance itself and a major element in—if not a cause of—the deviant behavior. A related point of some significance, long realized by sociologists, is that the definition of some behavior as "deviant" serves positive functions for the conformists, enhancing group cohesion and strengthening the sense of group membership among such individuals.[9] An appreciation of these functions is also necessary for a complete explanation of deviance.

In his perceptive study, *Stigma*,[10] Erving Goffman discusses some problems of identity and of interpersonal relations which face many stigmatized individuals. For purposes of that analysis, the fact of stigmatization is assumed as a point of departure. Certain personal characteristics are such, of course, that other people can very easily use them as bases for social stigmatization. Highly visible physical handicaps and disfigurements, and membership in a minority racial group, fall into this category. Because of the crucial relevance of sex to questions of personal identity, confirmed homosexuality (if recognized) seems also to carry a built-in stigma. But not all kinds of "differentness" or deviating behavior are equally stigmatizable, nor

[6] Erving Goffman, "The Moral Career of the Mental Patient," in *Asylums* (New York: Doubleday & Company, Inc., 1961), p. 128.

[7] *Ibid.*, p. 135.

[8] Becker, *op. cit.*, p. 31.

[9] Emile Durkheim, *Division of Labor in Society*, translated by G. Simpson (New York: The Free Press of Glencoe, Inc., 1960), pp. 96–110; also see Erickson, *op. cit.*, and Lewis A. Coser, "Some Functions of Deviance and Normative Flexibility," *American Journal of Sociology*, 68 (September 1962), 172–81.

[10] Erving Goffman, *Stigma: Notes on the Management of Spoiled Identity* (Englewood Cliffs, N.J.: Prentice-Hall, Inc., 1963).

is being easily stigmatizable the same as actually being stigmatized. In any case, as Goffman himself rightly notes, "the perceived undesirability of a *particular* personal property, and its capacity to trigger off these stigma-normal processes, has a history of its own, a history that is regularly changed by purposeful social action."[11]

THE CRIMINALIZATION OF DEVIANCE

The definition of behavior as "criminal" is an extreme form of stigmatization. Defining behavior as "deviant" has profound effects on those individuals engaging in it; what might be termed *the criminalization of deviance* pushes the process one step further. As already indicated, public branding as the perpetrator of a specific "criminal" act is a crucial step in the indivdiual's progress toward a criminal "career." Criminal conviction—perhaps even mere prosecution—may automatically and retrospectively effect crucial modifications in a person's identity. Criminal proceedings are, in Harold Garfinkel's phrase, status-degradation ceremonies:

The work of the denunciation effects the recasting of the objective character of the perceived other: The other person becomes in the eyes of his condemners literally a different and new person . . . the former identity stands as accidental; the new identity is the "basic reality." What he is now is what, "after all," he was all along.[12]

But the impact on the deviant of this criminalization of his behavior transcends any actual experience of official reaction. Even when he is not publicly identified and officially dealt with, he is only too aware that his behavior is legally proscribed as well as socially disapproved. Sensing that he is different or is doing an unusual act is one thing; feeling that his act is strongly disapproved is another; and knowledge that he has become a lawbreaker yet another.

Just as the mere knowledge that he has become a "criminal" may alter the individual's self-image, so too may legal proscription drive him into various behavior patterns that reinforce this image and that create new problems for himself and for society at large. As will be seen in the specific examples that follow, the formation of deviant subcultures, as well as the occurrence of certain types of secondary deviation (including secondary crime), may be crucially related to the criminalization of particular forms of socially disapproved behavior. And beyond the significant impact on particular deviating individuals, criminalization may also produce broader

[11] *Ibid.*, p. 138.
[12] Harold Garfinkel, "Conditions of Successful Degradation Ceremonies," *American Journal of Sociology*, 61 (March 1956), 421–22.

alterations of a deviant behavior situation—as when it establishes the economic basis for black-market operations or helps to produce situations in which police efficiency is impaired and police corruption encouraged. With respect to these latter points, the direct influence of the law may be fairly clear. On the other hand, the influence of criminalization on the self-image, the secondary deviance, and the subcultural involvement of the offender are more elusive. It is, after all, extremely difficult to separate (even for purposes of analysis) the influence of the law itself from that of the social disapproval inevitably accompanying it. Only rarely is it possible to make a partially controlled comparative analysis—for example, of the behavior and outlooks of a particular class of deviants in a jurisdiction where social and legal proscription prevail with those of the same class of deviants in a comparable jurisdiction in which there is only social disapproval of the deviance in question. . . .

Sociologists have, perhaps, been too much impressed by the fact that criminal laws do not always effectively curb the behavior they proscribe. One must be on guard against assuming that, because a law does not prevent certain acts from occurring, it is therefore without effect. [Abortion, drug addiction and homosexuality] all involve laws which are highly ineffective from the standpoint of sheer deterrence, yet they may have pronounced impact—through their influence on the social meanings read into various acts or behavior patterns, and through their role in structuring total problem situations. Indeed, it is precisely the criminal laws which fail to deter which may be of greatest interest to the sociologist. In a sense, no existing criminal law ever fully achieves its stated goals. As Sutherland pointed out:

> Laws have accumulated because the mores have been weak and inconsistent; and because the laws have not had the support of the mores they have been relatively ineffective as a means of control. When the mores are adequate laws are unnecessary; when the mores are inadequate, the laws are ineffective.[13]

But some criminal laws are a good deal less enforceable than others. Unenforceable criminal law serves as an indicator of inconsistencies in a society's value system; it may reveal conflicts of interest (both economic and more general) underlying the legal structure and may serve to pinpoint significant loci of social change.

The persistence of manifestly unworkable criminal laws provides an interesting illustration of the key role which latent functions[14] may play in underpinning legally institutionalized norms. Such latent functions of unenforceable laws represent really just another facet of the functions of crime. As already noted, crime or other deviance promotes solidarity in

[13] Edwin Sutherland and Donald Cressey, *Principles of Criminology*, 6th ed. (Philadelphia: J. B. Lippincott Co., 1960), p. 11.

[14] See Merton, *op. cit.*, pp. 19–84.

the group. It may serve psychological functions for conforming individuals and, may also serve quite definite economic functions which may—in turn—give rise to a variety of vested interests in its continuation (on the part of specialized law enforcement agencies, for example, as well as on the part of professionalized offenders). As Willard Waller pointed out some years ago: "Social problems are not solved because people do not want to solve them. . . . Solving social problems would necessitate a change in the organizational mores from which they arise."[15] This realization should strengthen the conviction that problems of deviance are rooted in a great deal more than the characteristics of deviating individuals. Such considerations suggest also the value of attempting to bring the legal reaction into the sociological analysis of deviance. In studies of this sort, the basic unit of analysis should be what may be called a "specific deviance complex." *Specific*, because more attention must be paid to particular types of offending behavior; *complex*, because neither the behavior itself nor the legal norm-and-process is to be considered separately. Rather, the entire sociolegal problem situation must be viewed as a complex of inter-related elements. . . . The relation between deviance and public policy is reciprocal.

· · ·

[15] Willard Waller, "Sociology and the Mores," *American Sociological Review*, 1 (December 1936), 928.

PART III

The Administration of Justice as a Selective Process

Introduction

Besides understanding the process by which societies classify acts as "delinquency" or "crime," one who would understand criminal behavior and crime rates must resign himself to the fact that only an unknown proportion of all crimes are reported to the police, are recorded by the police, and are compiled in the sets of statistics sent to the Federal Bureau of Investigation for publication in *Uniform Crime Reports*. Even though this annual report lists "index crimes," it is not a true index of the crime rate. A statistical index, such as a "cost of living index" is a compilation of the fluctuations in a sample of items taken from the whole. But a set of statistics on crime cannot be such a sample, for the crime rate of the whole population cannot be specified. A set of statistics on delinquency, for example, does not include the vast amount of "undetected" delinquency discussed in the selection by Erickson and Empey. Their study provides evidence that only a small proportion of the actual number of violations of the law by adolescent males are detected and acted upon by the courts. Further, it is clear that there is a substantial drop in the numbers as one moves from the number of crimes known to the police, to those cases where an arrest is made, to those arrests which lead to a court appearance, to those court appearances which result in a conviction, and finally to those convictions which lead to imprisonment.

The sifting process occurring as cases move through the criminal justice system has been the subject of sociological discussion for generations. In 1942, for example, Courtland Van Vechten reported that the men who end up in our prisons represent a very small proportion of those whose crimes are known to the police.[1] In addition, law enforcement agencies have long used the differences between crimes known to them and the number of arrests made in these cases (the "clearance rate") as a measure of organizational efficiency. Somewhat more recently, the selective character of criminal justice system procedures has been the basis for Supreme Court decisions designed to extend full coverage of constitutional rights to all persons. Sociologists, convinced that earlier studies of crime causation conducted in prisons were not studies of representative groups of lawbreakers, have directed attention to populations in other outcome categories of the criminal justice system.

It would be expected, then, that any study of the administration of justice in the United States would report what is so widely known to those working in the field. And this is the case with the 1967 President's Commission. The selective process that characterizes the operation of the criminal justice system is obvious from even a quick look at Figure 9, which is an adaptation of a chart prepared by the Commission.[2] Of the 727,000 cases involving "index crimes" (the most serious violations of our laws) which entered the system by means of an arrest, only a small number—approximately 11 per cent—resulted in imprisonment either by direct commitment or via violation of probation.

Part of the answer to the question of what happens as cases are processed is to be found in the use of fines, suspended sentences, probation, and jail (rather than prison terms) for those convicted. However, even if we exclude cases processed as juveniles, the sum of all the remaining cases in which some punitive sanction was taken still amounts to only about one-third of the cases that entered the process. Clearly, decisions made in early stages of the justice process result in the dropping of cases into categories other than those which follow from guilty pleas and convictions in court. The selections in this Part (III) discuss some of these decisions—decisions not to arrest persons who have violated the law, not to prosecute them, to acquit them, or to permit them to plead guilty to lesser charges.

Police officers, prosecuting attorneys, and courts use discretion in dealing with adults as well as in dealing with juveniles. Offenders and suspected offenders are either released or held for further action at the various stages of the justice process for reasons having to do with their probable guilt or innocence and with seriousness of offense. They also

[1] Courtland C. Van Vechten, "Differential Criminal Case Mortality in Selected Jurisdictions," *American Sociological Review*, 7 (December, 1942), 833–839.

[2] The original diagram appears in *The Challenge of Crime in a Free Society*, A Report by the President's Commission on Law Enforcement and Administration of Justice (Washington: Government Printing Office, 1967), pp. 262–263.

Criminal Justice System Model

(With estimates of flow of offenders for Index Crimes in the United States in 1965)

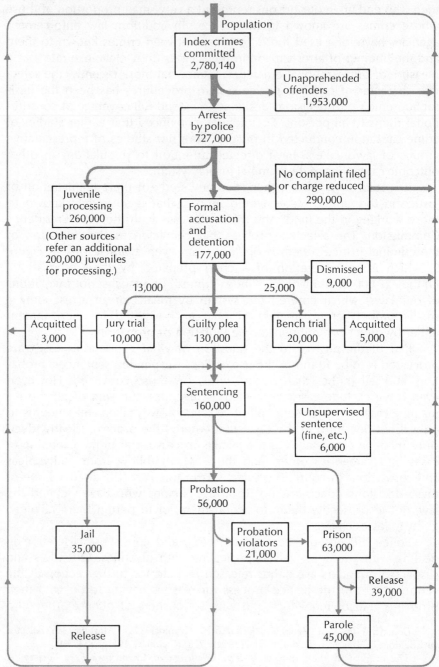

SOURCE: Adapted from the President's Commission on Law Enforcement and Administration of Justice, *The Challenge of Crime in a Free Society* (Washington, D. C.: Government Printing Office, 1967), pp. 262-263.

Figure 9

are either released or held for reasons that run from concern for organizational overcrowding to personal prejudice. Under the notion that ours is a government of laws rather than a government of men, the police and courts are expected simply to enforce the law. Yet police and court officials regularly and frequently make decisions not to invoke the criminal process, and as a result, they sometimes in effect "take the law into their own hands." These decisions, however, do not always or necessarily reflect dishonesty, immorality, personal prejudice, or inefficiency on the part of those who represent the criminal justice system. Policemen, prosecutors, and judges have no easy task in governing men who have some degree of freedom.

One who has a "sense of duty" to his governing body, or a "sense of loyalty" about his society, or a "sense of decency" about his own conduct has given his consent to be governed. Yet governing bodies, whether they be those of a nation, of a community, or of smaller organizations such as prisons or family units, must constantly be trying to establish and maintain, among the members of the unit being governed, this consent to be governed. Further, they must constantly be seeking appropriate measures for the coercive and custodial control of those members of the unit whose "sense of duty," "sense of loyalty," or "sense of decency" does not stop them from violating the rules considered necessary for peace, harmony, or efficiency within the unit. The selection by Piliavin and Briar shows that police tended to hold for further action older juveniles who were Negroes, who had well-oiled hair, who wore black jackets and soiled blue jeans, who had prior offense records and, especially, who did not display appropriate signs of "respect for the police." This selection shows that the "official delinquent," as distinguished from the juvenile who simply commits a juvenile act, is in part a product of a judgment made by the police. Perhaps it shows, also, that the police more readily select for official action those juveniles whose appearance and demeanor makes it easy to conclude that they have withdrawn their consent to be governed.

The rule-making bodies of societies and social groups seldom have a unitary ideology regarding the mechanisms for inspiring and maintaining conformity. A father, for example, may at one time punish his children for violation of family rules, whereas at another time he will overlook known violations, all the while believing that whatever action he takes is for "the good of the child" or "the good of the family." In a nation or community, the comparable inconsistencies in implementing a desire for a maximum amount of conformity are found among law-enforcement and court personnel and, supporting these personnel, in penal legislation and penal theory.

On the one hand, we have developed one penal law theory that maintains that conformity to criminal laws is maximized by swift, certain, and uniform punishment of those who deviate. Consistently, penal laws call for punishment of this kind. The underlying principle of behavioral and social control here seems to be that of deterrence. Swift, certain and uniform punishment of wrongdoers is supposed to help maximize conformity both by frightening others who might contemplate wrongdoing and by reforming the wrongdoer himself. Implementation of this deterrence theory has been found to be very difficult in various periods of history, and there is considerable evidence that when the official punishments are "too severe" they are mitigated in various ways. For example, when English law made most offenses capital crimes, juries used discretion and either refused to convict or mitigated the official penalties by finding defendants guilty of lesser offenses.[3]

On the other hand, another penal theory contends that law violations and law violators must be handled individually, so far as punishment is concerned. "Individualization" of punishment means, of course, that *judicial* discretion but not police discretion, necessarily, is to be exercised. Here, ideologies which lead to mitigation of penalties are incorporated into the official set of rules for judicial handling of offenders. The basic notion is that the entire circumstances of the offense and the entire character of the offender are to be taken into account when a judge decides what the punishment shall be and when, in fact, he decides whether there shall be any punishment at all. Authorization of such judicial discretion is, in the last analysis, an attempt to implement a penal theory that contradicts the notion that conformity will be maximized if all offenders are swiftly and uniformly punished. It is maintained that conformity will in the long run be maximized if some instances of nonconformity are not reacted to with punishment.

The arguments concerning these two penal law theories are ordinarily stated in terms of the contributions the two systems of control make to "justice." For example, it is sometimes considered unjust to assign a severe penalty to one man who has, say, committed murder, while assigning a lesser penalty to another man who also has committed murder. At the same time, it is sometimes considered unjust to impose identical sentences on men who have committed the same offense under quite different circumstances.

Such arguments can, of course, be stated with reference to the society's attempts to maximize the amount of conformity, rather than from the perspective of justice. Viewed in this way, the principal prob-

---

[3] See Leon Radzinowicz, *A History of English Criminal Law and Its Administration from 1750*, vols. 1-3 (New York: Macmillan, 1948, 1957), at vol. 1, pp. 83–164 and 660–698; and Jerome Hall, *Theft, Law and Society*, 2nd ed. (Indianapolis: Bobbs-Merrill, 1952), pp. 110–152.

lem is, again, one of securing and maintaining the consent of the governed. While swift and uniform punishment will tend to increase the amount of conformity, it can be argued that if the legally stipulated punishment is too severe ("unjust"), then imposing it will stimulate rebellion both in the recipients and in their supporters, with the result that some consent of the governed and the degree of conformity will diminish. Further, if the punishment legislated as appropriate for certain types of crimes by the lawmakers is viewed as too severe by the public, then that public will no longer give its consent to be governed by the lawmakers and will tend to shield criminals from the law-enforcement process. Even if the shielders do not themselves commit crimes, it is argued, they learn to overlook crimes, with the result that the law's effectiveness in maximizing conformity diminishes. A balance must be struck between severity and leniency of punishments, and between imposing punishments uniformly and imposing them irregularly. In recent times, a "treatment" response also has become available. To the degree that treatment is an alternative to punishment, not a supplement to it, this process also can be viewed as an attempt to mitigate penalties, officially, in an attempt to maximize the degree of consent of the governed and, thus, the amount of conformity.

Another factor underlying the way that the criminal law is applied has been discussed in Part II. There the point was made that the definition of many forms of behavior as criminal does not reflect either unanimous or unchanging public opinion. Police officers, district attorneys, and judges are public officials who attempt to represent communities that are often divided in opinion about what to do, if anything, about certain types of violations of the law, or that may be disinterested altogether in having the police "crack down" on certain violations of the law. Withholding criminal sanctions by these officials may in many cases be the result of a "reading" of public sentiment, just as campaigns or crusades to "clean up the city" or "do something about delinquency" reflect bursts of public concern.

The President's Commission selection dealing with white-collar crime and the criminal process represents a good example of the ambiguous status of certain forms of criminal behavior. In this report it is argued that some types of white-collar crime might best be countered without criminal sanctions. In view of the alternative theories contained in the penal laws of contemporary societies, we cannot expect police departments, or even individual policemen, to be consistent in their methods of dealing with lawbreakers and potential lawbreakers. At least in regard to the problem of maximizing the amount of conformity, police departments are microcosms of the society that they represent.

One pervasive concern of policemen, however, is a concern for justice. As legislators attempt to maximize conformity by incorporating divergent conceptions of justice in penal laws and in rules of conduct for the sentencing behavior of judges, so policemen attempt to maximize conformity by being "just" in the course of their daily encounters with the public. The policeman does his job in the rather routine way that any workingman does his job. Nevertheless, he tries to operate according to basic assumptions he has learned to make about the proper and efficient ways of maximizing the amount of law-obedience in the society he represents. This is no easy task. As Jerome Skolnick has pointed out, the police respond to pressures that ask them to reconcile two sets of ideals which conflict:

> The police in a democratic society are required to maintain order and to do so under the rule of law. As functionaries charged with maintaining order, they are part of the bureaucracy. The ideology of democratic bureaucracy emphasizes initiative rather than disciplined adherence to rules and regulations. By contrast, the rule of law emphasizes the rights of individual citizens and constraints upon the initiative of legal officials. This tension between the operational consequences of ideas of order, efficiency, and initiative, on the one hand, and legality, on the other, constitutes the principle problem of police as a democratic legal organization.[4]

The police, then, must necessarily implement, on a concrete level, the general but conflicting theories which their society has developed in its attempt to maximize conformity. If a society's mechanisms for maximizing conformity include the use of judicial discretion, the police in that society must be more than "law-enforcement officers." They must "enforce the law," but they also must be "fair" and "just," as the courts are supposed to be. In his selection, Goldstein discusses the argument that is sometimes made that policemen should "enforce the law" by uniformly and dispassionately invoking the penal process (i.e., arrest-trial-punishment) whenever a violation occurs, on the ground that if this procedure is not followed, an undesirable system of "government by men" rather than a desirable system of "government by law" will prevail.[5] But this notion is

---

[4] Jerome Skolnick, *Justice Without Trial* (New York: Wiley, 1966), p. 6. See also, David J. Bordua, ed., *The Police* (New York: Wiley, 1967).

[5] See Christopher Williams, "Turning a Blind Eye," *Criminal Law Review* (1954), 271: "And so to demand that he (the policeman) should exercise some sort of discretion, and refrain from enforcing certain laws is neither fair nor correct. In the first place, it demands of him a judgment and a sense of responsibility which is scarcely reflected in our treatment of him when we fix his salary in relation to that of other public officers. But, more important, such a process must inevitably subject all police activity to the personal likes and dislikes of individual policemen." Quoted by Frank J. Remington, "The Law Relating to 'On the Street' Detention, Questioning and Frisking of Suspected Persons and Police Arrest Privileges in General," in Claude R. Sowle, ed., *Police Power and Individual Freedom: The Quest for Balance* (Chicago: Aldine, 1962), p. 20.

complicated by its implication that the rules to be enforced are clear and of equal importance, as well as by its implication that police action is to be *ex post facto*. If the police were only to "enforce the law," in contrast to *interpreting* or *administering* the law, they could ignore no crimes; they would make arrests or issue summonses in all instances of observed law violation. Further, the police could not forestall the commission of crimes; they could only issue summonses and make arrests of persons observed in the process of breaking the law. The view that the policeman is a "law-enforcement officer" and nothing else is not warranted. It should not be assumed that all laws are perfectly clear, that lawmakers actually want all violators brought into court, or that the police are not necessarily to be alert to potential violations. As Remington has said:

It is obvious that arrests are not made for every offense which comes to the attention of the police. So great has been the proliferation of criminal statutes that arrest of all violators would cause a breakdown of the criminal justice system. There must therefore be a limitation upon the number of persons subjected to the criminal process. As a practical matter, this limitation must take place, in large part, at the arrest stage since this is ordinarily the first official decision relating to the offender's conduct. The power and responsibility which this discretion gives police is immense. Too often the existence of this discretion is denied and its exercise is, therefore, left without guidance and control from the legal system.[6]

When the penal theories of a society are conflicting, as they are in most contemporary societies, the police and courts are assigned at least four interrelated functions, so far as maximizing conformity is concerned, and only one of them is concerned with "law enforcement" in the strict sense of that term.

First, law-enforcement officials symbolize a system of justice of the kind stipulating that the pains of retribution for nonconformity will be distributed "equally" among the persons who deserve them. This is the basis of the expectation, stemming from deterrence theory, that the police will "enforce the law" by making arrests or issuing summonses for any violation of the criminal law. "Justice" and "fairness" require that punishments for similar deviations, and rewards for similar kinds of conformity, be distributed uniformly, without regard for the social status or other characteristics of the offender. The police implement this system of justice by being "honest" and "incorruptible," which means that they do not take into account the social characteristics of the offender or the circumstances of the offense and then, on the basis of them, make adjustments by deciding not to invoke the penal process.

Second, the police, like court officials, symbolize a system of justice of the kind stipulating that officially prescribed punishments must, in specific cases, be mitigated in various ways, depending upon the circum-

[6] *Ibid.,* p. 20.

stances of the offense or the characteristics of the offender. According to the so-called "Classical School" in criminal law theory, equal punishments were to be imposed on men who committed the same offense, as that offense was defined in the penal law. But this conception of justice was soon modified by the so-called "Neo-Classical School," which exempted young children and "lunatics" from punishment, even if their overt deviant acts were identical with those perpetrated by other persons. As the idea promulgated by the Neo-Classical School developed, it became acceptable, in the process of "individualization" of punishments, for courts to dispense justice by stipulating a punishment only after first determining whether the "real" offense committed by the defendant was in fact similar to the "real" offenses committed by defendants who received the same punishment in the past. The circumstances of the offense and the characteristics of the offender, rather than the description of the offense specified in the criminal law, were, then, used to determine whether two defendants deserved the same punishment.

When police systems were later invented, the power of judicial discretion was not officially extended to them. Nevertheless, the police symbolize this system of dispensing justice by making adjustments. According to the law-enforcement ideology, policemen must, as indicated, be "honest" and "incorruptible," thus symbolizing justice of the kind requiring uniform and equal punishments—a government of law, not of men. But according to what we might call the "adjustment ideology" police also must be "kind," "fair," and "understanding," thus symbolizing the system of taking similarities and differences into account. The policeman is being "just" when he behaves in terms of his duty to invoke the penal process whenever he observes a violation, regardless of the consequences to the offender, for punishments are to be distributed equally. But he also is being "just" when he overlooks offenses by using discretion, for in doing so he is symbolizing a system of justice which takes "mitigating circumstances" into account. The selection by Goldstein raises an alarm about the fact that the day-to-day decisions of the police are not visible to the public, not about the fact that the police use discretion. "Total enforcement" or "full enforcement" is not expected of the policemen dealing with adults any more than it is expected of policemen dealing with juveniles, despite the fact that police ordinarily are not officially delegated discretion not to invoke the criminal process.

Third, the police and courts, like parents and theologians, have a function of inspiring conformity to proper standards as defined in the criminal law.[7] In any society the formal legal apparatus consisting of

[7] See Johannes Andenaes, "General Prevention—Illusion or Reality?", *Journal of Criminal Law, Criminology, and Police Science, 43* (July, 1952), 176–198; and Johannes Andenaes, "The General Preventive Effects of Punishment," *University of Pennsylvania Law Review, 114* (May, 1966), 949–983.

police, courts, and prisons is principally an apparatus of the last resort, to be used when more informal processes of inspiring conformity have failed. Thus, if the family were completely successful in socializing children in the values that lawmakers view as right and proper, then the need for a formal apparatus to punish persons who do not adhere to those values would be minimal. But because the family cannot be completely successful in this regard, officials of other institutions, including the government, also are expected to participate in the socialization process. Among these officials are the police and judges.

Fourth, the policeman's presence, like the presence of a court, a judge, or a prison, serves the function of giving "advance notice" that deviants will be made to suffer. As the policeman's presense deters persons from committing crimes, and inspires "morality," it also stimulates conformity by making punishment of wrongdoers seem "just." Especially in Western societies with long traditions of barring ex *post facto* legislation, a system for warning the citizens that nonconformity of certain kinds will have punishment as its consequence stimulates rather docile acceptance of official punishments when they are in fact ordered by the courts and executed by prison officials and others. In other words, Western societies operate on the basic assumption that conformity can be maximized only if the punitive system has a rational base. If punishments were imposed irrationally or capriciously, the citizen would be unable to discern just which rules he is to conform to. Moreover, the infliction of punishments in an apparently arbitrary way would be viewed as "unjust" and would, then, contribute to divisiveness in the society. Perhaps it is for this reason that even the conviction and sentencing processes are seriously affected by considerations other than a finding that the defendant is guilty of the offense for which he was arrested. Newman's first selection shows that a promise of the prosecutor's recommendation for probation is one of the most common values given in exchange for a plea of guilty. It is conceivable that other alternatives are viewed as "unjust" in the circumstances of individual cases.

Just as the prohibitions stipulated in criminal law themselves give advance notice that wrongdoers will be punished, the police and courts are utilized to give advance notice that whoever violates a criminal law risks punishment. But, as we have already noted, it is not correct to assume that all criminal laws are perfectly clear or that all offenders are to be ordered into court by police. Police discretion, specifically in the form of warnings that further violations will have punishment as a consequence is necessary. Newman's second selection indicates that courts sometimes attempt to influence police methods by acquitting the guilty. It is a worthy hypothesis, at least, that such attempts are designed to encourage police to use *more* discretion. Perhaps it is believed that when a policeman "entices" a prostitute or a homosexual, as described by Newman, he is not giving them sufficent "advance notice" that the deviant behavior in question will have punishment as its consequence. Generally speaking, the remedy for such an error on the part of a policeman is one of freeing the offender, rather than one of issuing a reprimand, imposing a fine, instituting a criminal proceeding, or instituting proceedings for the demotion or discharge of the policeman.

1 Court Records, Undetected Delinquency, and Decision-Making*

MAYNARD L. ERICKSON
AND LAMAR T. EMPEY

There is almost universal dissatisfaction with the accuracy of official records on delinquency.[1] Yet, at present, there are few realistic alternatives. Official records must be used, not only to provide statistical information on delinquent trends, but to act as an information base on the qualitative characteristics (i.e., delinquent types) of offenders. It is this base upon which many important practical and theoretical decisions are presently dependent.

Reprinted by special permission from *The Journal of Criminal Law, Criminology and Police Science*, Copyright © 1963 by the Northwestern University School of Law, Volume 54, Number 4 (December, 1963), pp. 456–469. Also by permission of the authors.

* Grateful acknowledgement is expressed by the authors to Monroe J. Paxman for his cooperation and support and to the Ford Foundation for the grant under which this research was conducted. Appreciation is also extended to Stanton Wheeler, Peter Garabedian, and James Short for their helpful criticisms.

[1] Discussions and criticisms are legion. A sample might include: Cressey, *The State of Criminal Statistics*, 3 NAT'L PROBATION & PAROLE ASS'N J. 230 (1957); McQueen, *A Comparative Prospective on Juvenile Delinquency*, in A SYMPOSIUM ON DELINQUENCY: PATTERNS, CAUSES AND CURES 1–21 (1960); Sellin, *The Basis of a Crime Index*, 22 J. CRIM. L. & C. 335 (1931); SUTHERLAND, PRINCIPLES OF CRIMINOLOGY 29–30 (1947); TAFT, CRIMINOLOGY 61–65 (1956); and VanVechten, *Differential Criminal Case Mortality in Selected Jurisdictions*, 7 AM. SOC. REV. 833 (1942).

On the other hand, Perlman and Schwartz, noting a high degree of agreement in trends between police and court records on juveniles, feel the two are subject to common determining factors. See Perlman, *The Meaning of Juvenile Delinquency Statistics*, 13 Fed. Prob. 63 (Sept. 1949). See also Perlman, *Reporting Juvenile Delinquency*, 3 NAT'L PROBATION & PAROLE ASS'N J. 242 (1957); and Schwartz, *Statistics of Juvenile Delinquency in the United States*, 261 ANNALS 9 (1949).

A host of provocative problems relative to each of these uses merits serious attention. Two are discussed below.

The first has to do with the currently increasing emphasis on preventing delinquency.[2] If prevention is to be successful, it must forestall delinquent behavior before it becomes a matter of official record. But how much is known about the whole body of delinquent acts which do not become a matter of official concern? How accurately do official statistics reveal the *actual* extent and types of offenses committed? Answers to these questions are needed before revisions in control strategies can proceed rationally toward desired goals.

At present most control decisions are without the benefit of answers to important questions. Most people are left in a quandary as to whether official records understate or overstate the problem. For example, as a result of finding a vast number of undetected violations in their study, Murphy, Shirley and Witmer concluded that "even a moderate increase in the amount of attention paid to [them] by law-enforcement authorities could create a semblance of a 'delinquency wave' without there being the slightest change in adolescent behavior."[3]

Therefore, perhaps even more basic than deciding what should be done, we need more information in deciding whether, to what extent, or along what dimensions anything needs to be done. A greater knowledge of the nature of *undetected offenses* among the adolescent population might be important in determining prevention (and treatment) strategies.

A second problem has to do with the research on delinquency. Few authorities would dispute the value of using legal norms, in contrast to diffuse moral or extralegal concepts, to define a delinquent act. But the extension of this use to practical purposes often results in the development of extreme, either-or dichotomies: delinquent or nondelinquent, institutionalized or noninstitutionalized.

It is an obvious oversimplification to believe in the validity of such dichotomies. Delinquent behavior is not an attribute—something which one either is or is not, such as male or female, plant or animal. It is "a more or less thing,"[4] possibly distributed along one or more continua.

---

[2] A good example is President Kennedy's creation of the President's Committee on Juvenile Delinquency and Youth Crime; see Executive Order 10940, and THE FEDERAL DELINQUENCY PROGRAM OBJECTIVE AND OPERATION UNDER THE PRESIDENT'S COMMITTEE ON JUVENILE DELINQUENCY AND YOUTH CRIME, AND THE JUVENILE DELINQUENCY AND YOUTH OFFENSES CONTROL ACT OF 1961 (1962).

[3] Murphy, Shirley & Witmer, *The Incidence of Hidden Delinquency*, 16 AM. J. ORTHOPSYCHIATRY 696 (1946). See also, PORTERFIELD, YOUTH IN TROUBLE (1946); and a summary of studies in COHEN, DELINQUENT BOYS: THE CULTURE OF THE GANG 36–44 (1955).

[4] Short, *The Sociocultural Context of Delinquency*, 6 CRIME & DELINQUENCY 365, 366 (1960).

Even so, many sophisticated efforts to develop specific criminal or delinquent typologies based on this premise must still depend on the either-or nature of official records as the major criterion for selecting samples for study.

Once this is done, analyses tend to proceed in one of two directions: (1) either to rely further upon official records for specific information on such things as offense patterns; or (2) to reject as unimportant the official offense pattern in favor of psychological, cultural, or interactional factors.[5] This latter action is usually taken on the premise that the delinquent act is merely a symptom of some more basic cause and that to understand or perhaps remove the cause is what is important. But, in either case, the paradox remains: the court record serves as the basic criterion for sample selection.[6] Any strong bias in it will likely color what is found. Thus, it may be that refined analyses based upon official samples are based also upon a rather questionable foundation.

So long as samples are selected on this basis, there is a possibility that important information is being excluded. What of the possibility, for example, that there are patterns of delinquent activity which are etiologically distinct?[7] What of the possibility that the search for different configurations of variables has been inadequate because of the incompleteness of official records on delinquent activity? Even further, what of the possibility that official records do not even reveal the pattern of offenses which most commonly characterizes an offender?

The fact that many studies have found age and sex to be more highly correlated with delinquency than a host of other supposedly more important etiological variables,[8] suggests the need to explore these questions. The addition of information on the actual, not official, amount and type of delinquency in which an individual has been involved might be an aid in filling many of the gaps which exist. One important gap would have to do with the extent to which, and under what circumstances, the delinquent offense

[5] For excellent summaries and bibliographies on typological developments in criminology, see: Gibbons & Garrity, *Some Suggestions for the Development of Etiological and Treatment Theory in Criminology*, 38 Social Forces 51 (1960); Grant, *Inquiries Concerning Kinds of Treatment for Kinds of Delinquents*, California Board of Corrections Monograph No. 2, at 5 (1961).

[6] For example, such diverse typologies as those produced by Clyde Sullivan, Douglas and Marguerite Grant, in *The Development of Interpersonal Maturity, Applications to Delinquency*, 20 Psychiatry 373 (1957), and Gresham Sykes, in The Society of Captives (1958), must still rely upon official definition for their basic samples of offenders.

[7] This question has been raised in Gibbons & Garrity, *supra* note 5, at 51; Short, *supra* note 4, at 366.

[8] Short, "The Study of Juvenile Delinquency by Reported Behavior—An Experiment in Method and Preliminary Findings" at 12 (unpublished paper read at the annual meeting of the American Sociological Association, 1955).

pattern should be treated as an *independent* rather than as a dependent variable. What might be revealed if it were viewed as a variable which helps to explain rather than one which is always explained by other factors?

THE PRESENT RESEARCH

This research is a modest attempt to provide some information on the questions just raised:

1. What is revealed about the total volume of delinquency when undetected offenses are enumerated? What offenses are most common?
2. To what degree do violations go undetected? To what extent do they go unacted upon in the courts?[9]
3. Do non-official delinquents—young people that have never been convicted—commit delinquencies equal in number and seriousness to those committed by officially designated offenders?[10]
4. How useful are traditional dichotomies—delinquent or nondelinquent, institutionalized or noninstitutionalized—in distinguishing groups of offenders one from another?
5. How valid are court records as an index of the total volume and types of offenses in which individuals are most commonly involved?

In seeking answers to such questions as these, this research sought: (1) to examine reported lawbreaking across an adolescent continuum extending from those who had never been officially declared delinquent, through those who had appeared in court once, to those who were "persistent" offenders; and (2) to question adolescent respondents across the whole spectrum of legal norms for which they might have been taken to court. In all, they were asked about 22 violations.[11]

The Sample

The sample included only males, ages 15–17 years. It was made up of four subsamples:

1. A subsample of 50 randomly selected high school boys who had never been to court.

[9] For studies dealing with the problem of undetected delinquency, see: Murphy, Shirley & Witmer, *supra* note 3; Wallerstein & Wyle, *Our Law-Abiding-Lawbreakers*, 25 Fed. Prob. 110 (April 1947); Wilson, *How To Measure the Extent of Juvenile Delinquency*, 41 J. Crim. L. & C. 435 (1950).

[10] Porterfield's work, *op. cit. supra* note 3, throws some light on this question; however, the evidence is not conclusive.

[11] Unfortunately, no data on sex violations can be presented. Two things stood

2. A subsample of 30 randomly selected boys who had been to court once.[12]
3. A subsample of 50 randomly selected, repeat offenders who were on probation. The respondents in this sample were assigned to a special community treatment program. If the program had not existed, 32 percent of these offenders would have been incarcerated, and 68 percent on regular probation.[13]
4. A subsample of 50 randomly selected, incarcerated offenders. Subsamples 1, 2, and 3 were drawn from the same community population. Subsample 4 was drawn from a statewide population of incarcerated offenders.

It was necessary to keep the number of respondents relatively small because each respondent was questioned at length about the whole spectrum of legal norms for which he might have been taken to court—22 different violations in all. As will be seen, this questioning resulted in the accumulation of a large mass of data which turned out to be expensive and difficult to handle.

Data Collection

All respondents were contacted in person by the authors. The study was explained to them and they were asked to participate. There were no refusals. Data were gathered by means of a detailed interview which was conducted as follows:

First, each of the 22 offenses was described in detail. For example, under the section regarding breaking and entering, it is not enough to ask a boy, "Have you ever broken into a place illegally?" He wants to know what constitutes "a place": a car, a barn in the country, an unlocked garage? All of these had to be defined.

---

in the way. The first was a general policy of high school administrators against questions on sex. The second had to do with possible negative reactions by parents against questions because of the brutal sex slaying of an 11-year-old girl and several attacks on women which occurred at the very time we began our study. For these reasons we did not attempt to gather these data for fear they might endanger the whole study.

[12] Since this study was part of a larger study comparing persistent delinquents—incarcerated and unincarcerated—with nondelinquent high school students, data were not collected initially from one-time offenders. Consequently, they had to be collected especially for this group. However, time and budgetary considerations required that the sample of one-time offenders be limited at 30.

[13] They are assignees to the Provo Experiment in Delinquency Rehabilitation. All assignees are, by design, persistent offenders. Assignment is made on a random basis and includes both offenders who might otherwise be left on regular probation and offenders who might otherwise be incarcerated in the State Industrial School. See Empey & Rabow, *The Provo Experiment in Delinquency Rehabilitation*, 26 Am. Soc. Rev. 693 (1961).

Second, after the act was defined, the respondent was asked if he had ever committed the offense. In judging his response, attention was paid to nonverbal cue—blushes, long pauses, nervousness—as well as to verbal cues. These cues served as guides to further questions, probes and reassurances.

Third, if the respondent admitted having committed the offense, he was asked how many times he had done so. Again, considerable time and effort were spent in obtaining an estimate, the idea being that the greater accuracy could be obtained by this means than by fitting answers to a predetermined code or having him respond to such general categories as "none," "a few times," or "a great many times." In the case of habitual offenders, however, it was necessary on some offenses to have them estimate a range—15–20 times, 200–250 times—rather than a specific number.

Finally, the respondent was asked if he had ever been *caught*, *arrested*, or *to court* for each type of offense. If so, he was asked how many times this had occurred.

Methodological Problems

Besides the methodological problems inherent in any reported data, there are others peculiar to the nature of this type of study.[14] Perhaps the most important has to do with the method of obtaining data. An extended pilot study[15] and pretests, using both interviews and questionnaires, suggested that interviews could provide more complete and reliable data. Two main considerations led to this conclusion.

The first had to do with the lack of literacy skills among persistent delinquents. Two 15-year-olds in this study could neither read nor write; others had great trouble with simple instructions and questions. In our opinion, therefore, an interview was the only alternative for the delinquent subsamples.

Second, in addition to the need for comparable data, our pilot studies indicated that high school samples had trouble understanding specific questions and supplying the data wanted. Therefore, the value of using an interview for this group, as for delinquents, seemed to outweigh the virtues of an anonymous questionnaire.

We did not find the confrontation of an interview to be generally harmful. By using only three skilled interviewers, it became possible to anticipate recurring difficulties and to deal more effectively with them. These

[14] See Short, *supra* note 8; and Short & Nye, *Reported Behavior as a Criterion of Deviant Behavior*, 5 Social Problems 210 (Winter 1957–1958).

[15] Erickson, "An Experiment To Determine the Plausibility of Developing an Empirical Means of Differentiating Between Delinquents and Nondelinquents Without Consideration to Involvement in Legal Process," (unpublished Masters Thesis, Brigham Young University, 1960).

interviewers encountered two types of problems.

The first was the resistance on the part of high school students to revealing offenses. Patience, skepticism regarding replies, probes, and reassurances seemed to encourage candor. The second was a memory problem. Habitual offenders were not so reluctant to admit offenses, but they had often committed them so frequently that they could make an easy estimate neither as to number nor the age at which they began. Probes and extended discussions helped considerably here in settling upon a reasonable estimate.

One possible problem regarding the validity of these data has to do with the perceptions of respondents regarding the "social desirability" of answering questions according to social expectation. What is each respondent's reference group? How does he perceive the interviewer? Are his responses biased by special perceptions of each?

For example, if, among delinquents, it is desirable to exhibit extensive delinquent behavior, then, at least up to a certain point, the less delinquent an individual is, the more likely he may be to inflate his own actual violations. The converse might also be true for the conventional boy. Actually, as will be seen later, our findings tended to question the premise that social expectation influences boys' answers (or at least they failed to establish its validity). Nondelinquents reported so much delinquent behavior that it became difficult to assess the extent to which official delinquents, by contrast, might have inflated their own illegal behavior.

By way of determining validity, the names of all respondents were run through court records. None of those who had been to court failed to say so in the interview, nor did anyone fail to describe the offense(s) for which he was charged.

Few responses were so distorted as to be questionable. For example, no one maintained complete detachment from lawbreaking; no one admitted having committed all offenses. These findings tended to parallel the experience of Short and Nye in this regard.[16]

FINDINGS

1. *What is revealed about the total volume of delinquency when undetected offenses are enumerated? What offenses are most common?*

The number of violations which respondents admitted having committed was tremendous. So great was the volume that it posed some difficulty for display and analysis. A comprehensive table, Table 1, was prepared for use throughout the paper. The reader's patience is requested in referring to it.

[16] Short & Nye, *supra* note 14, at 211.

TABLE 1. EXTENT OF VIOLATIONS AND PER CENT UNDETECTED AND UNACTED UPON

Offense	Rank	Entire Adolescent Sample[1]			Subsamples												
					Non-Delinquents[2]			One-Time Offenders[3]			Delinquents Community[4]			Delinquents Incarcerated[5]		
		Total Offenses	% Undetected	% Unacted Upon	Total Offenses	% Undetected	% Unacted Upon	Total Offenses	% Undetected	% Unacted Upon	Total Offenses	% Undetected	% Unacted Upon	Total Offenses	% Undetected	% Unacted Upon
Traffic Offenses	1															
Driving Without License		11,796	98.9	99.7	1,845	99.6	100.0	512	98.7	98.7	2,386	98.0	99.1	7,053	99.1	99.9
Traffic Viol. (not lic.)		12,150	98.2	99.3	2,040	98.3	99.9	2,142	98.4	98.7	3,068	96.8	98.4	4,900	99.0	98.8
Total		23,946	98.6	99.5	3,885	98.9	100.0	2,654	98.4	98.6	5,454	97.3	98.7	11,953	99.0	99.8
Theft	2															
Articles less than $2		15,175	97.1	99.8	966	91.7	100.0	1,738	96.5	99.6	7,886	98.6	99.8	4,585	95.6	99.8
Articles worth $2 to $50		7,396	97.1	99.1	60	83.3	100.0	80	93.8	95.8	4,671	98.5	99.2	2,585	94.8	99.-
Articles more than $50		294	71.0	92.8	1	100.0	100.0	2	100.0	100.0	90	66.7	91.1	201	72.6	93.5
Auto Theft		822	88.9	95.5	4	100.0	100.0	0	0.0	0.0	169	84.6	93.5	649	90.0	96.0
Forgery		512	93.4	97.5	0	0.0	0.0	0	0.0	0.0	60	70.0	90.0	452	96.5	98.5
Total		24,199	96.3	99.3	1,031	91.3	100.0	1,820	96.3	99.4	12,876	98.0	99.4	8,472	94.5	99.0
Alcohol and Narcotics	3															
Buying Beer or Liquor		8,890	99.6	99.9	18	100.0	100.0	57	94.1	100.0	1,453	99.6	100.0	7,362	99.6	99.9
Drinking Beer or Liquor		12,808	98.8	99.8	219	100.0	100.0	270	100.0	100.0	4,173	99.0	99.7	8,146	98.6	99.8
Selling Narcotics		1	100.0	100.0	0	0.0	0.0	0	0.0	0.0	0	0.0	0.0	1	100.0	100.0
Using Narcotics		74	100.0	100.0	0	0.0	0.0	0	0.0	0.0	3	100.0	100.0	71	100.0	100.0
Total		21,773	99.1	99.9	237	100.0	100.0	327	99.0	100.0	5,629	99.1	99.8	15,580	99.1	99.9
Open Defiance of Authority	4															
Defying Parents		8,142	99.7	99.9	138	100.0*	100.0	128	100.0*	100.0	4,804	99.7*	99.9	3,072	99.8*	99.9
Defying Others		6,497	99.4	99.7	124	100.0*	100.0	170	100.0*	100.0	1,478	99.3*	99.3	4,725	99.5*	99.9
Total		14,639	99.5	99.9	262	100.0*	100.0	298	100.0*	100.0	6,282	99.6*	99.8	7,797	99.6*	99.9

TABLE 1 (*Continued*)

Property Violations 5															
Breaking and Entering	1,622	85.6	94.4	67	94.0	100.0	102	98.4	100.0	527	84.4	93.5	926	84.9	94.2
Destroying Property	10,645	98.5	99.7	477	97.1	100.0	800	98.5	99.7	4,927	98.7	99.6	4,441	98.7	99.4
Setting Fires (Arson)	11	40.0	90.0	2	0.0	0.0	2	0.0	100.0	0	0.0	0.0	7	100.0	100.0
Total	12,278	96.8	99.0	546	96.7	100.0	904	96.5	99.6	5,454	97.3	99.0	5,374	96.4	98.5
Retreatist Activities 6															
Running Away from Home	578	86.8	94.7	19	100.0	100.0	19	100.0	100.0	103	75.0	87.4	437	89.0	96.1
Skipping School	9,375	93.9	99.8	377	94.7	100.0	698	93.1	100.0	3,478	93.2	99.8	4,822	94.4	99.8
Total	9,953	93.5	99.5	396	94.9	100.0	717	93.2	100.0	3,581	92.6	99.5	5,259	94.0	99.5
Offenses Against Person 7															
Armed Robbery	46	80.4	91.3	0	0.0	0.0	0	0.0	0.0	22	68.2	90.9	24	91.7	91.7
Fighting, Assault	8,980	99.7	99.9	354	100.0*	100.0	103	100.0*	100.0	2,207	99.9*	99.8	6,316	99.6*	99.9
Total	9,026	99.6	99.9	354	100.0*	100.0	103	100.0*	100.0	2,229	99.6*	99.7	6,340	99.5*	99.9
Others 8															
Gambling	6,571	99.9	99.8	1,185	100.0	100.0	2,400	100.0	100.0	1,186	99.3	99.5	2,800	99.9	100.0
Smoking (habitually)	86	87.1	91.8	1	...*	100.0	3	50.0	100.0	39	...*	94.9	43	...*	88.4

[1] Number of Respondents = 180, except on Arson (N = 136) and Gambling (N = 171).

[2] N = 50.

[3] Actual N = 30. However, figures in this column have been inflated as though N = 50. This was done to make frequencies comparable with other subsamples.

[4] N = 50, except on Arson (N = 15) and Gambling (N = 41).

[5] N = 50, except on Arson (N = 41).

* Because of their nature, these offenses almost never remain undetected by someone in authority. Thus, these figures refer to per cent *unarrested*, rather than *undetected*.

The first two columns of Table 1 deal with the total volume of reported delinquency. These columns rank types of offenses in terms of the total frequency with which they were reported by all four samples. The frequencies reported for one-time offenders ($N = 30$) has been inflated by two-fifths in order to make them comparable to the other subsamples ($N = 50$). This inflation is also reflected in the *totals column* of Table 1 for the entire sample.[17] (Many other refinements and differences among subsamples in this comprehensive table will be discussed later.)

Three types of offenses were most common: theft (24,199)—especially of articles worth less than $2 (15,175)—, traffic (23,946), and the purchase and drinking of alcohol (21,698).

Grouped somewhat below these three were open defiance of authority—parents and others—(14,639); violations of property, including breaking and entering (12,278); retreatist activities such as running away (9,953); offenses against person (9,026); and finally such offenses as gambling (6,571). In the case of smoking, the total number of respondents who smoke habitually, rather than the estimated number of times all have smoked, was obtained. Of the 200, 86 reported smoking habitually.

2. *To what degree do violations go undetected? To what extent do they go unacted upon in the courts?*

The reader is again referred to Table 1 where, along with the volume of delinquent violations, the percentage of each of those violations which went (1) *undetected* and (2) *unacted upon* in court is presented.

With regard to detection, respondents were asked after each reported violation to tell whether they had been *caught by anyone*: parents, police, or others. With regard to court action, they were asked to report *any* appearance, *formal or informal*, before *any* officer of the court: judge, referee, or probation officer. (It was this question which served as an outside check on reliability. As noted above, respondents were generally very accurate.)

More than nine times out of ten—almost ten times out of ten—most offenses go *undetected* and *unacted upon*. This is especially true with respect to so-called minor violations: traffic offenses, theft of articles worth less than $50, buying and drinking liquor, destroying property, skipping school, and so on.

As might be expected, the picture changes with respect to more serious violations—theft of articles worth more than $50, auto theft, breaking and entering, forgery, and so on. Fewer of these offenses went undetected and

[17] It is impossible to assess any increase in error which might have resulted from this inflation. If there is bias in the sample of 30, it will have been magnified. See HANSEN, HURWITZ & MADOW, SAMPLE SURVEY METHOD AND THEORY (1953). Insofar as sample size, *per se*, is concerned, error would not have been significantly decreased had this sample of 30 been increased to 50. Both ($N = 30$) and ($N = 50$) are very small proportions of the total population of one-time offenders.

unacted upon. Yet, even in these cases, eight out of ten reported that their violations went undetected and nine out of ten did not result in court action.

3. *Do nonofficial delinquents—young people who have never been con-victed—commit delinquencies equal in number and seriousness to those committed by officially designated offenders?*

The answer to this question illustrates the extreme importance of dis-tinguishing between the *frequency* with which a given norm or set of norms is violated by two different samples and the proportion of respondents in each sample who report having violated them. The distinction helps to avoid the pitfall of concluding that, because large *proportions* of two dif-ferent samples—i.e., students and institutionalized delinquents—have com-mitted various offenses, the samples are equally delinquent in terms of total volume. Because of early studies, this impression regarding the total volume of delinquency in different samples has become almost traditional, even though it was not embraced by the authors of these studies.[18] The fact is that the *frequency*, as well as the types of offenses, with which individuals violated certain statutes turns out to be vitally important.

By way of example, consider Table 2. It presents the *proportions* of respondents in the four different samples who reported committing various offenses. On some offenses—theft of articles worth less than $2, traffic vio-lations, and destroying property—there is little to choose among the four samples. Most young people in each sample reported having committed them.

The proportions of all 180 boys who reported committing various offenses were as follows: petty theft (93%), gambling (85%), driving without a license (84%), skipping school (83%), destroying property (80%), other traffic offenses (77%), drinking (74%), fighting (70%), defying others (64%), and thefts of from $2 to $50 (59%).

However, it would be premature and superficial to conclude that, because large *proportions* of the entire sample have committed these of-fenses, the subsamples are equally delinquent. On only two offenses—gambling and traffic—did the proportions of nondelinquents exceed those of the delinquent subsamples. (However, the proportions for the nonde-linquents and one-time offenders were very much the same.)

Furthermore, a re-examination of Table 1 reveals that the *frequency* with which official offenders violate the law is in excess of the *frequency* with which non-official offenders violate it. (Again, however, non-official and one-time offenders differ very little. More will be said on them later.) The chief distinctions were between non- and one-time offenders, on the one hand, and the two subsamples of persistent offenders on the other.

If non- and one-time offenders are combined—because of their similar-ity—the cumulative violations of persistent offenders exceed their violations

18 See PORTERFIELD, *op. cit. supra* note 3.

TABLE 2. PROPORTION OF RESPONDENTS COMMITTING OFFENSES

Offense	Rank	Per Cent of Total[1]	Non-Delinquents[2]	One-Time Offenders[3]	Delinquents Community[4]	Delinquents Incarcerated[5]
				Subsamples		
Theft	1					
Less than $2		93	92	98	96	86
Worth $2 to $50		59	22	36	78	90
More than $50		26	2	2	46	54
Auto Theft		29	2	2	54	60
Forgery		13	0	0	16	34
Others	2					
Gambling		85	90	100	56	72
Smoking (habitually)		42	2	4	76	86
Traffic Offenses	3					
Driving Without License		84	72	78	94	92
Traffic Viol. (not lic.)		77	84	84	72	66
Retreatist Activities	4					
Running Away from Home		38	22	24	46	60
Skipping School		83	66	68	96	100
Property Violations	5					
Breaking and Entering		59	32	46	74	84
Destroying Property		80	66	84	86	84
Setting Fires (Arson)		6	2	2	0	8
Alcohol and Narcotics	6					
Buying Beer or Liquor		29	4	8	46	58
Drinking Beer or Liquor		74	52	66	84	94
Selling Narcotics		0.5	0	0	0	2
Using Narcotics		4	0	0	2	12
Offenses Against Person	7					
Armed Robbery		5	0	0	4	14
Fighting, Assault		70	52	60	82	86
Open Defiance of Authority	8					
Defying Parents		53	40	44	64	64
Defying Others		64	52	54	72	78

[1] Number of Respondents = 200, except on Arson (N = 156) and Gambling (N = 191). [2] N = 50. [3] N = 30. [4] N = 50, except on Arson (N = 15) and Gambling (N = 41). [5] N = 50, except on Arson (N = 41).

by thousands: theft, excluding forgery (20,836 vs. 2,851); violations of property (10,828 vs. 1,450); violations of person (8,569 vs. 457); and violations involving the purchase and drinking of alcohol (21,134 vs. 564).

In addition, as shown in Table 2, far smaller proportions of non- and one-time offenders committed offenses of a "serious" nature than did persistent offenders: theft of articles worth more than $50 (2% vs. 50%), auto theft (2% vs. 52%), forgery (0% vs. 25%), and armed robbery (0% vs. 9%).

The significance of these data, then, seems to be that one should guard against the use of *proportions* of total populations as a measure of delinquent involvement without also taking into account the *frequency* with which these proportions commit violations. Although in two cases proportionately fewer of the delinquent samples had committed certain violations, those who had committed them did so with much greater *frequency* than official nondelinquent samples.

4. *How useful are traditional dichotomies—delinquent or nondelinquent, institutionalized or noninstitutionalized—in distinguishing groups of offenders one from another?*

A series of tests was run, beginning on the nondelinquent end of the continuum, to discover where, if any, there were discriminating dichotomies on the volume of delinquent offenses, either between delinquent and nondelinquent subsamples or between institutionalized and noninstitutionalized offenders.

Chi Square was used as a test of significance. This test examines the possibility that any difference between groups could have occurred by chance. If differences are so great as to suggest that factors other than chance are responsible, it then suggests the confidence one might have in making that assumption.

To lend further refinement, a measure of association (T) was used to indicate the degree of relationship, when any difference was significant,[19] between official status and total volume of delinquency. For example, if Chi Square indicated that a delinquent and nondelinquent sample differed significantly on a given offense, the measure of association (T) suggests the power of that offense to distinguish between these two samples.

An effort was made to increase the validity of all comparisons by diminishing the impact of the large number of offenses committed by a few individuals. Thus, instead of making a gross comparison between two samples on the total number of times an offense was committed, respondents in each sample were ordered according to the number of times they reported committing an offense (i.e., 1–3 times, 4–6 times, etc.). Comparisons were then made between the number of respondents from each sample found in each category.

[19] Hagood & Price, Statistics for Sociologists 370–71 (1952).

The wisdom of doing this can be illustrated by examining Table 1. Persistent delinquents in the community reported having committed more petty theft than institutionalized offenders, while the reverse is true for auto theft. But these differences were largely due to the excessive activities of a few individuals. By taking them into account, the tests could more accurately reflect real, overall differences. If we had not accounted for them, excessively large differences between samples might have been suggested when, in fact, they did not exist.

Official Nondelinquents vs. Official One-time Offenders. The first comparison was between the subsamples of 50 high school boys who had *no* court record and the 30 one-time offenders.[20] In this particular comparison, only one significant difference past the .05 level of confidence was found; the offense was *destruction of property*. Official offenders were more likely to have been involved.

Comparisons on such offenses as stealing articles worth more than $50, auto theft, armed robbery, forgery, etc., were meaningless because they were seldom, if ever, reported by either group. This in itself tells us much about the similarity of these two groups.

This dichotomy, then—official nondelinquent vs. one-time offenders— did not prove to be discriminating.

Official One-time vs. Persistent Offenders. The second comparison was between one-time offenders and the subsample of 50 boys who were non-incarcerated persistent offenders. Differences between these two on most offenses were marked.

Persistent offenders were significantly—that is, 99 times out of 100— more inclined than one-time offenders, as a group, to have stolen expensive and inexpensive items, skipped school, defied parents, bought and drunk liquor, smoked regularly, stolen autos, fought, and driven without a license. There was also a significant difference past the .05 level with regard to forgery.

They did not differ significantly from one-time offenders on such things as running away from home, breaking and entering, destroying property, or committing most types of traffic violations. They could not be compared on such offenses as armed robbery, arson, or selling and using narcotics because of the small number of violations by both groups, but especially by one-time offenders.

[20] This and other comparisons have the serious weakness of dealing with only a limited number of boys. But, at the same time, two things must be recalled: (1) that such comparisons involve an enumeration of violations which, in most cases, was very large; and (2) that it was necessary to limit the number of respondents because of the time and money involved in gathering and analyzing data on such a large number of violations.

This dichotomy, then—*one-time* vs. *persistent* offenders in the community—was generally discriminating.

Institutionalized vs. Noninstitutionalized Offenders. The final comparisons had to do with the institutionalized vs. noninstitutionalized dichotomy. First, the sample of institutionalized offenders (Subsample 4) was compared with those noninstitutionalized offenders who had been to court *once* (Subsample 2). As might be expected, differences were significant on virtually all offenses. The samples seemed to represent two different populations because of the much heavier involvement of the institutionalized offenders (Subsample 4) in delinquency.

Second, institutionalized offenders (Subsample 4) were compared with the subsample of persistent offenders who had not been institutionalized (Subsample 3). The two did not differ significantly.

Persistent institutionalized offenders as a group reported having committed more traffic offenses, forgeries, auto thefts, offenses involving alcohol, and fights than persistent noninstitutionalized offenders. The latter, meanwhile, reported considerably more petty thefts, thefts of items worth up to $50, defying parents, and destruction of property. But these differences were due largely to a few extreme individuals. Consequently, as explained earlier, when tests of significance took this fact into account, the modal behavior of boys in the two samples tended to be very much the same.

Consequently, the only significant difference between these two subsamples was on habitual smoking; more boys in the reformatory smoked regularly. Otherwise, the two samples might be taken as representative of the same population insofar as the modal volume and nature of their offenses were concerned.

The significance of this finding is diluted somewhat by the fact that only two-thirds of the noninstitutionalized group (Subsample 3) would have been on probation (and free in the community) had they not been attending a special rehabilitative program. Nevertheless, the findings strongly support the idea that a dichotomy which distinguishes, without qualification, between *institutionalized* and *noninstitutionalized* offenders may not be valid. *Persistency* rather than institutionalization seems to be the more important variable in distinguishing groups. In this study, for example, the clearest distinction among official offenders was between *one-time* offenders, on one hand, and persistent offenders—whether institutionalized or noninstitutionalized—on the other.

This finding suggests that where persistent offenders are involved, the decision to incarcerate one group and to leave the other in the community may be highly subjective. Factors other than the extent and seriousness of these offenses seem to determine whether they are incarcerated or not.

Because of the significance of this finding, both samples of persistent offenders were combined and compared with the two subsamples on the nondelinquent end of the continuum (Subsamples 1 and 2, the official non-delinquents and one-time offenders) which likewise had been found not to differ. By combining samples in this way, comparisons could be made more reliable because of larger numbers with which to work. The results are displayed in Table 3.

Differences were strong and striking. On virtually all offenses, the chances were less than one in a thousand that they could have occurred by chance (see Table 3). Furthermore, all relationships were positive as indicated by the measures of association (T). This means that persistent offenders report having committed more of virtually every offense. Those offenses which best distinguished them from official non- or one-time offenders were smoking regularly (T = .78) skipping school (T = .50), theft of articles worth $2 to $50 (T = .46), theft of articles worth more than $50 (T = .45), auto theft (T = .45), and drinking alcohol (T = .42).

This finding re-emphasizes the idea that the old dichotomies may be misleading. Persistency is the most distinguishing variable.

To what extent this finding may be generalized is hard to say. Many of the most significant differences—smoking regularly, all kinds of theft, drinking, fighting, and skipping school—are associated with behavior often thought to be more characteristic of the lower than the middle class. Other offense patterns may have been characteristic of their setting in a Mormon subculture. However, such offenses as auto theft, forgery, breaking and entering, or stealing items worth more than $50 were also highly discriminating between these two samples and are likely to draw strong official reaction anywhere.

The implication of these findings for both practice and research seems to be that the unqualified use of traditional dichotomies—i.e., delinquent vs. nondelinquent or institutionalized vs. noninstitutionalized—may be unreliable. A further examination of undetected offenses on other populations, to test the validity of these dichotomies, might be an important prerequisite to their future use as an important source of data.

5. *How valid are court records as an index of the total volume and types of offenses which are committed?*

Court Records as an Index of Volume. Evidence presented earlier indicated that the great majority of all delinquent offenses remain undetected and unacted upon. It might be concluded, therefore, that official records do not accurately reflect the total volume of delinquency. However, this might not be true.

It may be that official records are useful in reflecting volume by (1) distinguishing between those who have been heavily delinquent from those who have not; and/or (2) reflecting a tiny but consistently accurate portion of all offenses.

TABLE 3. COMPARISON OF OFFICIAL NON- AND ONE-TIME
OFFENDERS WITH PERSISTENT OFFENDERS

Offense	Probability that Differences Could be Due to Chance	Degree of Association Between Volume and Official Classification
Theft		
Articles less than $2	.001	.28
Articles worth $2 to $50	.001	.46
Articles more than $50	.001	.45
Auto Theft	.001	.45
Forgery	.001	.31
Property Violations		
Breaking and Entering	.001	.34
Destroying Property	.001	.24
Setting Fires (Arson)	*	
Offenses Against Person		
Armed Robbery	*	
Fighting, Assault	.001	.41
Open Defiance of Authority		
Defying Parents	.001	.27
Defying Others	.001	.34
Retreatist Activities		
Running Away from Home	.001	.32
Skipping School	.001	.50
Traffic Offenses		
Driving Without License	.001	.36
Traffic Viol. (not lic.)	.05	.17
Alcohol and Narcotics		
Buying Beer or Liquor	.001	.40
Drinking Beer or Liquor	.001	.42
Selling Narcotics	*	
Using Narcotics	*	
Others		
Gambling	.001	.29
Smoking (habitually)	.001	.78

* Offense not committed enough times to test differences.

One method of treating these possibilities is to calculate the correlation
between the actual number of court appearances for a given population and
the number of violations it reports having committed. This calculation was
made.

A coefficient of correlation was calculated for all 180 respondents. To do this and still maintain specificity, court appearances were broken into 9 categories—never been to court, been to court one time, two times, three times . . . nine or more times. The total number of reported violations was broken into 11 categories—never, 1–50, 51–100, 101–150 . . . 501 or more. The degree of association between these two variables was then calculated.

A correlation of .51 was obtained. This coefficient is statistically significant, indicating the existence of a relationship between appearing in court and the total number of violations one has committed; that is, the greater the number of reported violations, the greater likelihood that an individual will have appeared in court.

On one hand, this coefficient leaves much to be desired in terms of accurate predictability. A coefficient of .51 means that 26 percent of the variation in the number of court appearances among the 180 respondents could be associated with variations in the number of delinquent offenses they reported having committed.

When only 26 percent of the variation in violation rates, using specific categories, is explained in terms of court appearances, the ability of these appearances to supply a good index of the actual number of violations may be highly questionable.

To further illustrate this point we found a correlation of .56 between dropping out of school and the number of reported violations. This suggested that whether or not individuals had dropped out of school was as accurate or possibly more accurate a predictor of reported violations than court records. (For those respondents incarcerated in the Utah State Industrial School, this meant dropping out of school prior to incarceration, not because of incarceration.)

One would not expect official delinquency rates to be an exact match of the volume of delinquency. Seriousness is also very important. Society demands that stronger measures be taken for serious violations.

In order to examine its significance, correlation coefficients were run between court appearance and a series of single violations, extending all the way from misdemeanors to felonies. The results are displayed in Table 4.

As might be expected, reported felonies correlated more highly with court appearances than did reported misdemeanors. However, taken singly, the correlation between any one of the felonies (theft of articles worth more than $50, auto theft, breaking and entering, and forgery)[21] was not so high as that between the total *volume* of violations and court appearance.

Furthermore, even though the total number of reported violations for

[21] Armed robbery, arson, and the selling and use of narcotics were not included in this analysis because the number reporting such violations was small.

TABLE 4. CORRELATION COEFFICIENT BETWEEN COURT
APPEARANCES AND REPORTED NUMBER OF VIOLATIONS

Offense	Correlation	Percentage of Variation Explained
Misdemeanors		
A. Taken Singly		
Skipping School	.17	.03
Theft (less than $2)	.19	.04
Theft ($2 to $50)	.20	.04
Traffic Violations (all types)	.18	.03
B. Combined	.15	.02
*Felonies**		
A. Taken Singly		
Theft (more than $50)	.25	.06
Auto Theft	.43	.18
Breaking and Entering	.40	.15
Forgery	.05	.003
B. Combined	.29	.08

* Armed robbery, arson and the selling and use of narcotics were not included because the number reporting such violations was small.

the four felonies, when they were combined and then correlated with court appearance, produced a higher coefficient (.29) than did the combined misdemeanors (.15), this correlation (.29) was considerably lower than the correlation (.51) between the total volume of offenses and court appearance.

This finding raises questions regarding the traditional assumption that the court record is a better index of serious violations than it is of the total number of offenses an individual has committed. One might speculate, however, that the finding is due to the inaccuracy of reported data. But if one were to discard these reported data as inaccurate, he would have to ignore the fact that, except for seriousness, these findings met other assumptions rather consistently regarding distinctions between persistent and non-persistent offenders, as to both frequency and seriousness. And they also seemed capable of making more precise distinctions in the direction of theoretical expectations among various dichotomies than court records.

Thus, these findings also raise important questions regarding the accuracy of official records as an index of volume and seriousness. But it is difficult either to assess the amount of combined error inherent in these court and reported data or to generalize from this to other police and court jurisdictions.

Court Records and Types of Offenses. One of the major problems raised in the introduction had reference to the adequacy of official records for the purpose of conducting typological research. There are at least two different levels of complication.

The first has to do with the validity of the official dichotomies—delinquent or nondelinquent, institutionalized or noninstitutionalized—which are used as the major criteria for distinguishing groups and setting up research samples. The foregoing analysis has already suggested some possible difficulties. It suggests that important qualifications may be needed.

The second level of complication comes in specific attempts to establish delinquent typologies based not only upon basic dichotomies but upon the offense patterns which are revealed by court records. To be accurate, these records would have to reflect reliably an individual's major offense pattern, with respect to both number and seriousness. Some test of their ability to do so was made.

The first part of the analysis was concerned with volume. It sought to determine how well the court record reflected, without special regard to seriousness, the offense which each respondent reported having committed *most often*. The court record proved to be a fair index for offenders who had been to court only once. Sixteen of 30, half of them, had appeared in court for the types of offenses they reported having committed most often.

But this was not the case for the more persistent offenders. The more delinquent they tended to be, the less predictive the court record was of their most commonly reported violations. For example, only 26 of the 100 official, persistent delinquents had appeared in court more often for their major areas of offense than for other offenses. Nineteen of the 100 had *never* appeared in court for their reported major areas of offense. Thus, if these reported data are valid, the court record for this latter group would not give any clues as to the types of offenses they reported having committed most frequently.

In between these two extremes were 55 other boys, all of whom had been to court for their major patterns of offense, but they had also been there equally as often for other offenses. Consequently, even for them court records would fail to provide a clear picture of the most commonly reported offense patterns.

With regard to seriousness, the foregoing analysis has already suggested that court records may be a relatively poor index of the total number of *serious* violations. But what of individual offenders rather than their total offenses? How well does the court record eventually select boys who report having committed *serious* violations?

Answers to such questions are important. Although an offender may have a long record of petty violations, his commission of a serious offense, such as breaking and entering, will more likely type him as a burglar than a petty thief.

In order to examine this dimension, a crude "seriousness" classification was established. Five judges and five chief probation officers from Utah's six juvenile judicial districts[22] were asked to rank 25 offenses according to seriousness. The first ten of these offenses were then selected to serve as the *serious* criterion. They were:

1. Rape[23]
2. Selling narcotics
3. Arson
4. Using narcotics
5. Armed robbery
6. Breaking and entering
7. Forgery
8. Auto theft
9. Homosexuality[23]
10. Theft of items worth more than $50

Two specific questions were examined: (1) How accurate is the court record in reflecting the most *serious* offense each respondent has committed (in terms of the hierarchy of eight serious violations)? (2) How accurate is the court record in reflecting each offender's most frequently committed *serious* violation?

For a relatively large group, the court record could supply no information regarding these questions. This group was comprised primarily of the official nondelinquents and one-time offenders. Twenty-three of the 50 nondelinquents (46%) and 14 of the 30 one-time offenders (47%) had committed one or more of the serious violations, but none had ever been to court for any of them. (The close similarity between the nondelinquents and one-time offenders in this study is again illustrated.)

By contrast, a much higher proportion of the two most delinquent samples had not only committed serious offenses—i.e., 88 of 100—but had also been to court for committing them—i.e., 77 of the 88 (or 88%).

Upon reading such information one might conclude that official records are likely biased against persistent offenders. It should be recalled from Table 1, however, that respondents in the two most delinquent samples reported having committed many more serious offenses than the less delinquent subsamples. Court records, therefore, may simply reflect the greater probability of being caught because of excessive violations.

For this group of 77 persistent offenders who had been to court, the

[22] Utah has one of the two State Juvenile Court Systems in the United States. Connecticut has the other. Judges are appointed for six-year terms; they must be members of the bar. Chief probation officers are selected on the basis of a state merit system examination and training and experience in correctional work.

[23] It will be recalled that data on rape and homosexuality are not presented in this paper. Therefore, the seriousness classification includes the eight remaining offenses.

court record was accurate for 65 percent of them in reflecting the most serious offense they had committed. It said nothing of the remaining 35 percent. If, therefore, the premise is accepted that an offender would likely be typed on the basis of his most serious known offense, the court record would be accurate approximately two-thirds of the time for this select group. This is encouraging in some ways because it is persistent offenders with whom officials and researchers have been most concerned.

On the other hand, the large proportion of juveniles whose serious offenses remained undetected might easily have been typed in the same way had they been apprehended. Yet, without official action, many of them apparently make a reasonable, conventional adjustment.

A second qualification has to do with the ability of the court record to reflect not only an individual's most *serious* violation, but the type(s) of *serious* violation(s) he commits most frequently. Another premise might be that an individual should be typed on the basis of frequency of seriousness rather than extremity of seriousness. For example, it may be preferable to type an individual as an auto thief for having been to court three times for auto theft than to type him as an armed robber for having been to court once for armed robbery.

The court records were somewhat less accurate in this regard. About half (39) of the 77 persistent offenders who had appeared in court for serious violations had appeared there more often for the types of *serious* violations they reported committing most often than for any other *serious* violation. However, the picture for this group of 39 was muddied somewhat because 52 percent of them had appeared in court just as often, or more often, for other offenses not considered serious.

For the other half of the 77 offenders who had not been to court more often for their most common serious violation, 20 (26%) had *never* been to court for their most common *serious* offense. And 18 (23%) had been to court just as often for other *serious* offenses. In these cases, the court record would not be an accurate means for typing an individual according to *serious* offense.

CONCLUSION

In conclusion, official records seemed more accurate in reflecting an individual's single most *serious* violation than the pattern of offenses, either *serious* or *nonserious*, which he most commonly commits.

On the surface, these findings may seem more encouraging from the treatment and control, than the research, standpoints. That is, court records, when compared with reported behavior, did distinguish persistent offenders (with whom officials are most concerned) from one-time offenders or nondelinquents, in terms of both number and seriousness of violation. Furthermore, they seemed quite efficient in indicating the most *serious* violations which persistent offenders had committed.

However, a great deal of refined information regarding types of offenders is needed if treatment and control strategies are to be effective. And, even though such information may be most needed for the persistent offender, it cannot be supplied, even for him, until more is known about two things: (1) about any differences or similarities between him and those juveniles who, if they were apprehended, might be typed the same way; and (2) about the offense patterns of him and others who, though they are apprehended, often remain largely unincorporated into the official record. Varying degrees of such information are needed no matter what theoretical orientation one takes towards developing typologies for treatment and control purposes.

Obviously, the findings which led to these conclusions must be qualified because of the data from which they were derived and the methodological problems inherent in obtaining them. Yet, even if they are only partially correct, they indicate one possible reason why we have encountered so much difficulty in pinpointing important etiological and treatment variables.

If different patterns of delinquency have important significance for the administration of justice, for prevention and treatment strategies, and for research purposes, data which could be used to supplement official records seem needed. At least it would seem important to explore the possibility that reported data on undetected offenses might be helpful in understanding delinquency.

The methods for obtaining such data need not be greatly different from those which are used in a variety of other areas, clinical and scientific. Possible legal and constitutional questions would have to be explored. Yet, we are not without precedent in the clinical field where the communication of important information is privileged.

Furthermore, reported data might also open avenues to more detailed examination of the circumstances surrounding the commission of delinquent acts: Who is present? How are the acts carried out? What social and psychological variables seem to be operating? And then attempts might be made to relate such questions to court, control, and research strategies.

2 Police Encounters with Juveniles*

IRVING PILIAVIN AND SCOTT BRIAR

As the first of a series of decisions made in the channeling of youthful offenders through the agencies concerned with juvenile justice and corrections, the disposition decisions made by police officers have potentially profound consequences for apprehended juveniles. Thus arrest, the most severe of the dispositions available to police, may not only lead to confinement of the suspected offender but also bring him loss of social status, restriction of educational and employment opportunities, and future harassment by law-enforcement personnel.[1] According to some criminologists, the stigmatization resulting from police apprehension, arrest, and detention actually reinforces deviant behavior.[2] Other authorities have suggested, in

Reprinted from *American Journal of Sociology,* 70 (September, 1964), 206–214, by permission of The University of Chicago Press. Copyright 1964 by The University of Chicago. Also by permission of the authors.

* This study was supported by Grant MH–06328–02, National Institute of Mental Health, United States Public Health Service.

[1] Richard D. Schwartz and Jerome H. Skolnick, "Two Studies of Legal Stigma," *Social Problems,* X (April, 1962), 133–42; Sol Rubin, *Crime and Juvenile Delinquency* (New York: Oceana Publications, 1958); B. F. McSally, "Finding Jobs for Released Offenders," *Federal Probation,* XXIV (June, 1960), 12–17; Harold D. Lasswell and Richard C. Donnelly, "The Continuing Debate over Responsibility: An Introduction to Isolating the Condemnation Sanction," *Yale Law Journal,* LXVIII (April, 1959), 869–99.

[2] Richard A. Cloward and Lloyd E. Ohlin, *Delinquency and Opportunity* (Glencoe, Ill.: Free Press, 1960), pp. 124–30.

fact, that this stigmatization serves as the catalytic agent initiating delinquent careers.[3] Despite their presumed significance, however, little empirical analysis has been reported regarding the factors influencing, or consequences resulting from, police actions with juvenile offenders. Furthermore, while some studies of police encounters with adult offenders have been reported, the extent to which the findings of these investigations pertain to law-enforcement practices with youthful offenders is not known.[4]

The above considerations have led the writers to undertake a longitudinal study of the conditions influencing, and consequences flowing from, police actions with juveniles. In the present paper findings will be presented indicating the influence of certain factors on police actions. Research data consist primarily of notes and records based on nine months' observation of all juvenile officers in one police department.[5] The officers were observed in the course of their regular tours of duty.[6] While these data do not lend themselves to quantitative assessments of reliability and validity, the candor shown by the officers in their interviews with the investigators and their use of officially frowned-upon practices while under observation provide some assurance that the materials presented below accurately reflect the typical operations and attitudes of the law-enforcement personnel studied.

The setting for the research, a metropolitan police department serving an industrial city with approximately 450,000 inhabitants, was noted within the community it served and among law-enforcement officials elsewhere for the honesty and superior quality of its personnel. Incidents involving criminal activity or brutality by members of the department had been extremely rare during the ten years preceding this study; personnel standards were comparatively high; and an extensive training program was provided to both new and experienced personnel. Juvenile Bureau members, the primary subjects of this investigation, differed somewhat from other

[3] Frank Tannenbaum, *Crime and the Community* (New York: Columbia University Press, 1936), pp. 17–20; Howard S. Becker, *Outsiders: Studies in the Sociology of Deviance* (New York: Free Press of Glencoe, 1963), chaps. i and ii.

[4] For a detailed accounting of police discretionary practices, see Joseph Goldstein, "Police Discretion Not To Invoke the Criminal Process: Low Visibility Decisions in the Administration of Justice," *Yale Law Journal*, LXIX (1960), 543–94; Wayne R. LaFave, "The Police and Non-enforcement of the Law—Part I," *Wisconsin Law Review*, January, 1962, pp. 104–37; S. H. Kadish, "Legal Norms and Discretion in the Police and Sentencing Processes," *Harvard Law Review*, LXXV (March, 1962), 904–31.

[5] Approximately thirty officers were assigned to the Juvenile Bureau in the department studied. While we had an opportunity to observe all officers in the Bureau during the study, our observations were concentrated on those who had been working in the Bureau for one or two years at least. Although two of the officers in the Juvenile Bureau were Negro, we observed these officers on only a few occasions.

[6] Although observations were not confined to specific days or work shifts, more observations were made during evenings and weekends because police activity was greatest during these periods.

members of the department in that they were responsible for delinquency prevention as well as law enforcement, that is, juvenile officers were expected to be knowledgeable about conditions leading to crime and delinquency and to be able to work with community agencies serving known or potential juvenile offenders. Accordingly, in the assignment of personnel to the Juvenile Bureau, consideration was given not only to an officer's devotion to and reliability in law enforcement but also to his commitment to delinquency prevention. Assignment to the Bureau was of advantage to policemen seeking promotions. Consequently, many officers requested transfer to this unit, and its personnel comprised a highly select group of officers.

In the field, juvenile officers operated essentially as patrol officers. They cruised assigned beats and, although concerned primarily with juvenile offenders, frequently had occasion to apprehend and arrest adults. Confrontations between the officers and juveniles occurred in one of the following three ways, in order of increasing frequency: (1) encounters resulting from officers' spotting officially "wanted" youths; (2) encounters taking place at or near the scene of offenses reported to police headquarters; and (3) encounters occurring as the result of officers' directly observing youths either committing offenses or in "suspicious circumstances." However, the probability that a confrontation would take place between officer and juvenile, or that a particular disposition of an identified offender would be made, was only in part determined by the knowledge that an offense had occurred or that a particular juvenile had committed an offense. The bases for and utilization of non-offenses related criteria by police in accosting and disposing of juveniles are the focuses of the following discussion.

SANCTIONS FOR DISCRETION

In each encounter with juveniles, with the minor exception of officially "wanted" youths,[7] a central task confronting the officer was to decide what official action to take against the boys involved. In making these disposition decisions, officers could select any one of five discrete alternatives:

1. outright release
2. release and submission of a "field interrogation report" briefly describing the circumstances initiating the police-juvenile confrontation
3. "official reprimand" and release to parents or guardian
4. citation to juvenile court
5. arrest and confinement in juvenile hall.

[7] "Wanted" juveniles usually were placed under arrest or in protective custody, a practice which in effect relieved officers of the responsibility for deciding what to do with these youths.

Dispositions 3, 4, and 5 differed from the others in two basic respects. First, with rare exceptions, when an officer chose to reprimand, cite, or arrest a boy, he took the youth to the police station. Second, the reprimanded, cited, or arrested boy acquired an official police "record," that is, his name was officially recorded in Bureau files as a juvenile violator.

Analysis of the distribution of police disposition decisions about juveniles revealed that in virtually every category of offense the full range of official disposition alternatives available to officers was employed. This wide range of discretion resulted primarily from two conditions. First, it reflected the reluctance of officers to expose certain youths to the stigmatization presumed to be associated with official police action. Few juvenile officers believed that correctional agencies serving the community could effectively help delinquents. For some officers this attitude reflected a lack of confidence in rehabilitation techniques; for others, a belief that high case loads and lack of professional training among correctional workers vitiated their efforts at treatment. All officers were agreed, however, that juvenile justice and correctional processes were essentially concerned with apprehension and punishment rather than treatment. Furthermore, all officers believed that some aspects of these processes (e.g., judicial definition of youths as delinquents and removal of delinquents from the community), as well as some of the possible consequences of these processes (e.g., intimate institutional contact with "hard-core" delinquents, as well as parental, school, and conventional peer disapproval or rejection), could reinforce what previously might have been only a tentative proclivity toward delinquent values and behavior. Consequently, when officers found reason to doubt that a youth being confronted was highly committed toward deviance, they were inclined to treat him with leniency.

Second, and more important, the practice of discretion was sanctioned by police-department policy. Training manuals and departmental bulletins stressed that the disposition of each juvenile offender was not to be based solely on the type of infraction he committed. Thus, while it was departmental policy to "arrest and confine all juveniles who have committed a felony or misdemeanor involving theft, sex offense, battery, possession of dangerous weapons, prowling, peeping, intoxication, incorrigibility, and disturbance of the peace," it was acknowledged that "such considerations as age, attitude and prior criminal record might indicate that a different disposition would be more appropriate."[8] The official justification for discretion in processing juvenile offenders, based on the preventive aims of the Juvenile Bureau, was that each juvenile violator should be dealt with

[8] Quoted from a training manual issued by the police department studied in this research.

solely on the basis of what was best for him.[9] Unofficially, administrative legitimation of discretion was further justified on the grounds that strict enforcement practices would overcrowd court calendars and detention facilities, as well as dramatically increase juvenile crime rates—consequences to be avoided because they would expose the police department to community criticism.[10]

In practice, the official policy justifying use of discretion served as a demand that discretion be exercised. As such, it posed three problems for juvenile officers. First, it represented a departure from the traditional police practice with which the juvenile officers themselves were identified, in the sense that they were expected to justify their juvenile disposition decisions not simply by evidence proving a youth had committed a crime—grounds on which police were officially expected to base their dispositions of non-juvenile offenders[11]—but in the *character* of the youth. Second, in disposing of juvenile offenders, officers were expected, in effect, to make judicial rather than ministerial decisions.[12] Third, the shift from the offense to the offender as the basis for determining the appropriate disposition substantially increased the uncertainty and ambiguity for officers in the situation of apprehension because no explicit rules existed for determining which disposition different types of youths should receive. Despite these problems, officers were constrained to base disposition decisions on the character of the apprehended youth, not only because they wanted to be fair, but because persistent failure to do so could result in judicial criticism, departmental censure, and, they believed, loss of authority with juveniles.[13]

DISPOSITION CRITERIA

Assessing the character of apprehended offenders posed relatively few difficulties for officers in the case of youths who had committed serious crimes such as robbery, homicide, aggravated assault, grand theft, auto theft, rape, and arson. Officials generally regarded these juveniles as con-

---

[9] Presumably this also implied that police action with juveniles was to be determined partly by the offenders' need for correctional services.

[10] This was reported by beat officers as well as supervisory and administrative personnel of the juvenile bureau.

[11] In actual practice, of course, disposition decisions regarding adult offenders also were influenced by many factors extraneous to the offense per se.

[12] For example, in dealing with adult violators, officers had no disposition alternative comparable to the reprimand-and-release category, a disposition which contained elements of punishment but did not involve mediation by the court.

[13] The concern of officers over possible loss of authority stemmed from their belief that court failure to support arrests by appropriate action would cause policemen to "lose face" in the eyes of juveniles.

firmed delinquents simply by virtue of their involvement in offenses of this magnitude.[14] However, the infraction committed did not always suffice to determine the appropriate disposition for some serious offenders;[15] and, in the case of minor offenders, who comprised over 90 per cent of the youths against whom police took action, the violation per se generally played an insignificant role in the choice of disposition. While a number of minor offenders were seen as serious delinquents deserving arrest, many others were perceived either as "good" boys whose offenses were atypical of their customary behavior, as pawns of undesirable associates or, in any case, as boys for whom arrest was regarded as an unwarranted and possibly harmful punishment. Thus, for nearly all minor violators and for some serious delinquents, the assessment of character—the distinction between serious delinquents, "good" boys, misguided youths, and so on—and the dispositions which followed from these assessments were based on youths' personal characteristics and not their offenses.

Despite this dependence of disposition decisions on the personal characteristics of these youths, however, police officers actually had access only to very limited information about boys at the time they had to decide what to do with them. In the field, officers typically had no data concerning the past offense records, school performance, family situation, or personal adjustment of apprehended youths.[16] Furthermore, files at police headquarters provided data only about each boy's prior offense record. Thus both the decision made in the field—whether or not to bring the boy in—and the decision made at the station—which disposition to invoke—were based largely on cues which emerged from the interaction between the officer and the youth, cues from which the officer inferred the youth's character. These cues included the youth's group affiliations, age, race, grooming, dress, and demeanor. Older juveniles, members of known delinquent gangs, Negroes, youths with well-oiled hair, black jackets, and soiled denims or jeans (the presumed uniform of "tough" boys), and boys who in their interactions with officers did not manifest what were considered to be appropriate signs of respect tended to receive the more severe dispositions.

[14] It is also likely that the possibility of negative publicity resulting from the failure to arrest such violators—particularly if they became involved in further serious crime—brought about strong administrative pressure for their arrest.

[15] For example, in the year preceding this research, over 30 per cent of the juveniles involved in burglaries and 12 per cent of the juveniles committing auto theft received dispositions other than arrest.

[16] On occasion, officers apprehended youths whom they personally knew to be prior offenders. This did not occur frequently, however, for several reasons. First, approximately 75 per cent of apprehended youths had no prior official records; second, officers periodically exchanged patrol areas, thus limiting their exposure to, and knowledge about, these areas; and third, patrolmen seldom spent more than three or four years in the juvenile division.

Other than prior record, the most important of the above clues was a youth's *demeanor*. In the opinion of juvenile patrolmen themselves the demeanor of apprehended juveniles was a major determinant of their decisions for 50–60 per cent of the juvenile cases they processed.[17] A less subjective indication of the association between a youth's demeanor and police disposition is provided by Table 1, which presents the police dispositions for sixty-six youths whose encounters with police were observed in the course of this study.[18] For purposes of this analysis, each youth's demeanor in the encounter was classified as either co-operative or unco-operative.[19] The results clearly reveal a marked association between youth demeanor and the severity of police dispositions.

The cues used by police to assess demeanor were fairly simple. Juveniles who were contrite about their infractions, respectful to officers, and fearful of the sanctions that might be employed against them tended to be viewed by patrolmen as basically law-abiding or at least "salvageable." For these youths it was usually assumed that informal or formal reprimand would suffice to guarantee their future conformity. In contrast, youthful offenders who were fractious, obdurate, or who appeared nonchalant in their encounters with patrolmen were likely to be viewed as "would-be tough guys" or "punks" who fully deserved the most severe sanction: arrest. The following excerpts from observation notes illustrate the importance attached to demeanor by police in making disposition decisions.

1. The interrogation of "A" (an 18-year-old upper-lower-class white male accused of statutory rape) was assigned to a police sergeant with long experience on the force. As I sat in his office while we waited for the youth to arrive for questioning, the sergeant expressed his uncertainty as to what he should do with this young man. On the one hand, he could not ignore the fact that an

[17] While reliable subgroup estimates were impossible to obtain through observation because of the relatively small number of incidents observed, the importance of demeanor in disposition decisions appeared to be much less significant with known prior offenders.

[18] Systematic data were collected on police encounters with seventy-six juveniles. In ten of these encounters the police concluded that their suspicions were groundless, and consequently the juveniles involved were exonerated; these ten cases were eliminated from this analysis of demeanor. (The total number of encounters observed was considerably more than seventy-six, but systematic data-collection procedures were not instituted until several months after observations began.)

[19] The data used for the classification of demeanor were the written records of observations made by the authors. The classifications were made by an independent judge not associated with this study. In classifying a youth's demeanor as co-operative or unco-operative, particular attention was paid to: (1) the youth's responses to police officers' questions and requests; (2) the respect and deference—or lack of these qualities—shown by the youth toward police officers; and (3) police officers' assessments of the youth's demeanor.

TABLE 1. SEVERITY OF POLICE DISPOSITION
BY YOUTH'S DEMEANOR

Severity of Police Disposition	Youth's Demeanor		
	Co-op-erative	Unco-op-erative	Total
Arrest (most severe)	2	14	16
Citation or official reprimand	4	5	9
Informal reprimand	15	1	16
Admonish and release (least severe)	24	1	25
Total	45	21	66

offense had been committed; he had been informed, in fact, that the youth was prepared to confess to the offense. Nor could he overlook the continued pressure from the girl's father (an important political figure) for the police to take severe action against the youth. On the other hand, the sergeant had formed a low opinion of the girl's moral character, and he considered it unfair to charge "A" with statutory rape when the girl was a willing partner to the offense and might even have been the instigator of it. However, his sense of injustice concerning "A" was tempered by his image of the youth as a "punk," based, he explained, on information he had received that the youth belonged to a certain gang, the members of which were well known to, and disliked by, the police. Nevertheless, as we prepared to leave his office to interview "A," the sergeant was still in doubt as to what he should do with him.

As we walked down the corridor to the interrogation room, the sergeant was stopped by a reporter from the local newspaper. In an excited tone of voice, the reporter explained that his editor was pressing him to get further information about this case. The newspaper had printed some of the facts about the girl's disappearance, and as a consequence the girl's father was threatening suit against the paper for defamation of the girl's character. It would strengthen the newspaper's position, the reporter explained, if the police had information indicating that the girl's associates, particularly the youth the sergeant was about to interrogate, were persons of disreputable character. This stimulus seemed to resolve the sergeant's uncertainty. He told the reporter, "unofficially," that the youth was known to be an undesirable person, citing as evidence his membership in the delinquent gang. Furthermore, the sergeant added that he had evidence that this youth had been intimate with the girl over a period of many months. When the reporter asked if the police were planning to do anything to the youth, the sergeant answered that he intended to charge the youth with statutory rape.

In the interrogation, however, three points quickly emerged which profoundly affected the sergeant's judgment of the youth. First, the youth was polite and co-operative; he consistently addressed the officer as "sir," answered all questions quietly, and signed a statement implicating himself in numerous counts of statutory rape. Second, the youth's intentions toward the girl appeared to have been honorable; for example, he said that he wanted to marry her eventually. Third, the youth was not in fact a member of the gang in question. The sergeant's attitude became increasingly sympathetic, and after we left the interrogation room he announced his intention to "get 'A' off the hook," meaning that he wanted to have the charges against "A" reduced, or if possible, dropped.

2. Officers "X" and "Y" brought into the police station a seventeen-year-old white boy who, along with two older companions, had been found in a home having sex relations with a fifteen-year-old girl. The boy responded to police officers' queries slowly and with obvious disregard. It was apparent that his lack of deference toward the officers and his failure to evidence concern about his situation were irritating his questioners. Finally, one of the officers turned to me and, obviously angry, commented that in his view the boy was simply a "stud" interested only in sex, eating, and sleeping. The policemen conjectured that the boy "probably already had knocked up half a dozen girls." The boy ignored these remarks, except for an occasional impassive stare at the patrolmen. Turning to the boy, the officer remarked, "What the hell am I going to do with you?" And again the boy simply returned the officer's gaze. The latter then said, "Well, I guess we'll just have to put you away for a while." An arrest report was then made out and the boy was taken to Juvenile Hall.

Although anger and disgust frequently characterized officers' attitudes toward recalcitrant and impassive juvenile offenders, their manner while processing these youths was typically routine, restrained, and without rancor. While the officers' restraint may have been due in part to their desire to avoid accusation and censure, it also seemed to reflect their inurement to a frequent experience. By and large, only their occasional "needling" or insulting of a boy gave any hint of the underlying resentment and dislike they felt toward many of these youths.[20]

PREJUDICE IN APPREHENSION AND DISPOSITION DECISIONS

Compared to other youths, Negroes and boys whose appearance matched the delinquent stereotype were more frequently stopped and interrogated by patrolmen—often even in the absence of evidence that an

---

[20] Officers' animosity toward recalcitrant or aloof offenders appeared to stem from two sources: moral indignation that these juveniles were self-righteous and indifferent about their transgressions, and resentment that these youths failed to accord police the respect they believed they deserved. Since the patrolmen perceived themselves as honestly and impartially performing a vital community function warranting respect and deference from the community at large, they attributed the lack of respect shown them by these juveniles to the latters' immorality.

offense had been committed[21]—and usually were given more severe dispositions for the same violations. Our data suggest, however, that these selective
apprehension and disposition practices resulted not only from the intrusion
of long-held prejudices of individual police officers but also from certain
job-related experiences of law-enforcement personnel. First, the tendency
for police to give more severe dispositions to Negroes and to youths whose
appearance corresponded to that which police associated with delinquents
partly reflected the fact, observed in this study, that these youths also were
much more likely than were other types of boys to exhibit the sort of
recalcitrant demeanor which police construed as a sign of the confirmed
delinquent. Further, officers assumed, partly on the basis of departmental
statistics, that Negroes and juveniles who "look tough" (e.g., who wear
chinos, leather jackets, boots, etc.) commit crimes more frequently than
do other types of youths.[22] In this sense, the police justified their selective
treatment of these youths along epidemiological lines: that is, they were
concentrating their attention on those youths whom they believed were
most likely to commit delinquent acts. In the words of one highly placed
official in the department:

If you know that the bulk of your delinquent problem comes from kids
who, say, are from 12 to 14 years of age, when you're out on patrol you are
much more likely to be sensitive to the activities of juveniles in this age bracket
than older or younger groups. This would be good law enforcement practice.
The logic in our case is the same except that our delinquency problem is largely
found in the Negro community and it is these youths toward whom we are
sensitized.

As regards prejudice per se, eighteen of twenty-seven officers interviewed openly admitted a dislike for Negroes. However, they attributed
their dislike to experiences they had, as policemen, with youths from this
minority group. The officers reported that Negro boys were much more

[21] The clearest evidence for this assertion is provided by the overrepresentation of
Negroes among "innocent" juveniles accosted by the police. As noted, of the seventy-six
juveniles on whom systematic data were collected, ten were exonerated and released
without suspicion. Seven, or two-thirds of these ten "innocent" juveniles were Negro,
in contrast to the allegedly "guilty" youths, less than one-third of whom were Negro.
The following incident illustrates the operation of this bias: One officer, observing a
youth walking along the street, commented that the youth "looks suspicious" and
promptly stopped and questioned him. Asked later to explain what aroused his suspicion,
the officer explained, "He was a Negro wearing dark glasses at midnight."

[22] While police statistics did not permit an analysis of crime rates by appearance,
they strongly supported officers' contentions concerning the delinquency rate among
Negroes. Of all male juveniles processed by the police department in 1961, for example,
40.2 per cent were Negro and 33.9 per cent were white. These two groups comprised
at that time, respectively, about 22.7 per cent and 73.6 per cent of the population in
the community studied.

likely than non-Negroes to "give us a hard time," be unco-operative, and show no remorse for their transgressions. Recurrent exposure to such attitudes among Negro youth, the officers claimed, generated their antipathy toward Negroes. The following excerpt is typical of the views expressed by these officers:

They (Negroes) have no regard for the law or for the police. They just don't seem to give a damn. Few of them are interested in school or getting ahead. The girls start having illegitimate kids before they are 16 years old and the boys are always "out for kicks." Furthermore, many of these kids try to run you down. They say the damnedest things to you and they seem to have absolutely no respect for you as an adult. I admit I am prejudiced now, but frankly I don't think I was when I began police work.

IMPLICATIONS

It is apparent from the findings presented above that the police officers studied in this research were permitted and even encouraged to exercise immense latitude in disposing of the juveniles they encountered. That is, it was within the officers' discretionary authority, except in extreme limiting cases, to decide which juveniles were to come to the attention of the courts and correctional agencies and thereby be identified officially as delinquents. In exercising this discretion policemen were strongly guided by the demeanor of those who were apprehended, a practice which ultimately led, as seen above, to certain youths, (particularly Negroes[23] and boys dressed in the style of "toughs") being treated more severly than other juveniles for comparable offenses.

But the relevance of demeanor was not limited only to police disposition practices. Thus, for example, in conjunction with police crime statistics the criterion of demeanor led police to concentrate their surveillance activities in areas frequented or inhabited by Negroes. Furthermore, these youths were accosted more often than others by officers on patrol simply because their skin color identified them as potential troublemakers. These discriminatory practices—and it is important to note that they are discriminatory, even if based on accurate statistical information—may well have self-fulfilling consequences. Thus it is not unlikely that frequent encounters with police, particularly those involving youths innocent of wrongdoing, will increase the hostility of these juveniles toward law-enforcement personnel. It is also not unlikely that the frequency of such encounters will in time reduce their significance in the eyes of apprehended juveniles, thereby

[23] An unco-operative demeanor was presented by more than one-third of the Negro youths but by only one-sixth of the white youths encountered by the police in the course of our observations.

leading these youths to regard them as "routine." Such responses to police encounters, however, are those which law-enforcement personnel perceive as indicators of the serious delinquent. They thus serve to vindicate and reinforce officers' prejudices, leading to closer surveillance of Negro districts, more frequent encounters with Negro youths, and so on in a vicious circle. Moreover, the consequences of this chain of events are reflected in police statistics showing a disproportionately high percentage of Negroes among juvenile offenders, thereby providing "objective" justification for concentrating police attention on Negro youths.

To a substantial extent, as we have implied earlier, the discretion practiced by juvenile officers is simply an extension of the juvenile-court philosophy, which holds that in making legal decisions regarding juveniles, more weight should be given to the juvenile's character and life-situation than to his actual offending behavior. The juvenile officer's disposition decisions—and the information he uses as a basis for them—are more akin to the discriminations made by probation officers and other correctional workers than they are to decisions of police officers dealing with non-juvenile offenders. The problem is that such clinical-type decisions are not restrained by mechanisms comparable to the principles of due process and the rules of procedure governing police decisions regarding adult offenders. Consequently, prejudicial practices by police officers can escape notice more easily in their dealings with juveniles than with adults.

The observations made in this study serve to underscore the fact that the official delinquent, as distinguished from the juvenile who simply commits a delinquent act, is the product of a social judgment, in this case a judgment made by the police. He is a delinquent because someone in authority has defined him as one, often on the basis of the public face he has presented to officials rather than of the kind of offense he has committed.

3 Police Discretion Not to Invoke the Criminal Process: Low-Visibility Decisions in the Administration of Justice*

JOSEPH GOLDSTEIN

Police decisions not to invoke the criminal process largely determine the outer limits of law enforcement. By such decisions, the police define the ambit of discretion throughout the process of other decisionmakers—prosecutor, grand and petit jury, judge, probation officer, correction authority, and parole and pardon boards. These police decisions, unlike their decisions to invoke the law, are generally of extremely low visibility and consequently are seldom the subject of review. Yet an opportunity for review and appraisal of non-enforcement decisions is essential to the func-

Reprinted by permission of the Yale Law Journal Company and Fred B. Rothman & Company, from the *Yale Law Journal*, vol. 69 (March, 1960), pp. 543–588. Adapted with the permission of the publishers and the author.

* This Article was suggested by discussions during a seminar on Research in Criminal Law Administration conducted under a grant from the Ford Foundation during the summer of 1958 at the University of Wisconsin Law School. With Herman Goldstein of the Public Administration Service in Chicago, to whom I am especially indebted, I was responsible for leading discussion on police activity. Other participants in the seminar, for whose comments I am grateful, were Professors Francis Allen of the University of Chicago Law School, Richard Cloward of the New York School of Social Work, William Burnett Harvey of the University of Michigan Law School, Lloyd Ohlin of the New York School of Social Work, and Frank Remington of the University of Wisconsin Law School. I am also appreciative of the contributions made by many of my students in my courses in Criminal Law and Criminal Procedure.

tioning of the rule of law in our system of criminal justice.[1] This Article will therefore be an attempt to determine how the visibility of such police decisions may be increased and what procedures should be established to evaluate them on a continuing basis, in the light of the complex of objectives of the criminal law and of the paradoxes toward which the administration of criminal justice inclines.

I

The criminal law is one of many intertwined mechanisms for the social control of human behavior.[2] It defines behavior which is deemed intolerably disturbing to or destructive of community values and prescribes sanctions which the state is authorized to impose upon persons convicted or suspected of engaging in prohibited conduct. Following a plea or verdict of guilty, the state deprives offenders of life, liberty, dignity, or property through convictions, fines, imprisonments, killings, and supervised releases, and thus seeks to punish, restrain, and rehabilitate them, as well as to deter others from engaging in proscribed activity. Before verdict, and despite the presumption of innocence which halos every person, the state deprives the suspect of life, liberty, dignity, or property through the imposition of deadly force, search and seizure of persons and possessions, accusation, imprisonment, and bail, and thus seeks to facilitate the enforcement of the criminal law.

These authorized sanctions reflect the multiple and often conflicting purposes which now surround and confuse criminal law administration at and between key decision points in the process. The stigma which accompanies conviction, for example, while serving a deterrent, and possibly retributive, function, becomes operative upon the offender's release and thus impedes the rehabilitation objective of probation and parole. Similarly, the restraint function of imprisonment involves the application of rules and procedures which, while minimizing escape opportunities, contributes to

---

[1] A judge dismissing criminal charges without trial, upon his own motion, must record his reasons so that all may know why this great power was exercised, and such public declaration is indeed a purposeful restraint, lest magistral discretion sweep away the government of laws.

People v. Winters, 342 P.2d 538, 542 (Cal. Super. Ct. App. Dep't 1959). See also Jaffe, *The Right to Judicial Review*, 71 Harv. L. Rev. 401 (1958).

[2] The criminal law may increase, decrease, or leave unaffected the impact on individual behavior, if any, of family, education, religion, "civil" law, the arts, science, freedom, mass communication, economic conditions, local, state, national, foreign and international governing bodies, and membership or nonmembership in many other formal and informal, large and small, groups including unions, country clubs, and gangs.

the deterioration of offenders confined for reformation.[3] Since police decisions not to invoke the criminal process may likewise further some objectives while hindering others, or, indeed, run counter to all, any meaningful appraisal of these decisions should include an evaluation of their impact throughout the process on the various objectives reflected in authorized sanctions and in the decisions of other administrators of criminal justice.[4]

Under the rule of law, the criminal law has both a fair-warning function for the public and a power-restricting function for officials. Both post- and preverdict sanctions, therefore, may be imposed only in accord with author-

---

[3] See, e.g., SYKES, THE SOCIETY OF CAPTIVES 73, 75–76 (1958):

Regulation by a bureaucratic staff is felt far differently than regulation by custom. . . . Most prisoners express an intense hostility against their far-reaching dependence on the decisions of their captors and the restricted ability to make choices must be included among the pains of imprisonment along with restrictions of physical liberty, the possession of goods and services, and heterosexual relationships.

. . . .

The important point, however, is that the frustration of the prisoner's ability to make choices and the frequent refusals to provide an explanation for the regulations and commands descending from the bureaucratic staff involve a profound threat to the prisoner's self-image because they reduce the prisoner to the weak, helpless, dependent status of childhood . . . the imprisoned criminal finds his picture of himself as a self-determining individual being destroyed by the regime of the custodians.

[4] Conflicts of purpose and function arise not only among the administrators of criminal justice within a single jurisdiction, but also between administrators in different jurisdictions. See United States v. Candelaria, 131 F. Supp. 797 (S.D. Cal. 1955), in which Federal Judge Tolin reduced a five-year sentence for a robbery of a California bank to sixty days, because the District Attorney of Los Angeles County refused to remove a California detainer, based on the same "offense," from the convicted offender. The detainer meant that Candelaria, following his release from the federal prison system, might be prosecuted by California for the same "offense" of which he was convicted and sentenced in federal court. It also meant, under Federal Parole Board policy then, but no longer in effect, that the offender could not be released on parole. Letter From James V. Bennett, Director of Federal Bureau of Prisons, to Joseph Goldstein, March 12, 1958. The court said:

When a Federal Judge, acquainted with the type of corrective treatment which will be administered to an offender, determines that five years of it is sufficient, it changes the character of the penalty when local police or prosecutors can administratively place a detainer which will alter the entire course of treatment of the prisoner and keep him from receiving much of what the sentencing Judge intended when the length of term was prescribed.

United States v. Candelaria, supra at 807. A subsequent conviction of Candelaria for robbery under the California laws was reversed as a violation of the State's double jeopardy statute. People v. Candelaria, 139 Cal. App. 2d 432, 294 P.2d 120 (Dist. Ct. App. 1956). Candelaria was then tried for burglary and convicted a third time on the basis of the same underlying set of facts. The conviction was affirmed. People v. Candelaria, 153 Cal. App. 2d 879, 315 P.2d 386 (Dist. Ct. App. 1957).

ized procedures. No sanctions are to be inflicted other than those which have been prospectively prescribed by the constitution, legislation, or judicial decision for a particular crime or a particular kind of offender. These concepts, of course, do not preclude differential disposition, within the authorized limits, of persons suspected or convicted of the same or similar offenses. In an ideal system differential handling, individualized justice, would result, but only from an equal application of officially approved criteria designed to implement officially approved objectives. And finally a system which presumes innocence requires that preconviction sanctions be kept at a minimum consistent with assuring an opportunity for the process to run its course.[5]

A regularized system of review is a requisite for insuring substantial compliance by the administrators of criminal justice with these rule-of-law principles. Implicit in the word "review" and obviously essential to the operation of any review procedure is the visibility of the decisions and conduct to be scrutinized. Pretrial hearings on motions, the trial, appeal and the writ of habaes corpus constitute a formal system for evaluating the actions of officials invoking the criminal process. The public hearing, the record of proceedings, and the publication of court opinions—all features of the formal system—preserve and increase the visibility of official enforcement activity and facilitate and encourage the development of an informal system of appraisal. These proceedings and documents are widely reported and subjected to analysis and comment by legislative, professional, and other interested groups and individuals.

But police decisions not to invoke the criminal process, except when reflected in gross failure of service, are not visible to the community. Nor are they likely to be visible to official state reviewing agencies, even those within the police department. Failure to tag illegally parked cars is an example of gross failure of service, open to public view and recognized for what it is. An officer's decision, however, not to investigate or report adequately a disturbing event which he has reason to believe constitutes a

---

[5] "Booking," charging and arraigning, with all its concomitant inconveniences and embarrassments, will have to be borne by many citizens who would otherwise have been given an opportunity to make clear their innocence without being subjected to such difficulties or stigma.

United States v. Bonnano (S.D.N.Y. Dec. 2, 1959), in N.Y. Times, Dec. 3, 1959, p. 38, col. 2.

> This practice [the police holding a suspect in detention before they are ready to prefer charge] has one feature which may be of advantage to the detained person; if innocent he has a good prospect of being released without any publicity or stigma. It may be a real hardship to an innocent man to have to appear in open court, even to be discharged as guiltless . . . .

Royal Commission on Police Powers and Procedure, *Report*, CMD. No. 3297, at 58 (1929).

violation of the criminal law does not ordinarily carry with it consequences sufficiently visible to make the community, the legislature, the prosecutor, or the courts aware of a possible failure of service. The police officer, the suspect, the police department, and frequently even the victim, when directly concerned with a decision not to invoke, unlike the same parties when responsible for or subject to a decision to invoke, generally have neither the incentive nor the opportunity to obtain review of that decision or the police conduct associated with it. Furthermore, official police records are usually too incomplete to permit evaluations of nonenforcement decisions in the light of the purposes of the criminal law.[6] Consequently, such decisions, unlike decisions to enforce, are generally not subject to the control which would follow from administrative, judicial, legislative, or community review and appraisal.

Confidential reports detailing the day-to-day decisions and activities of a large municipal police force have been made available to the author by the American Bar Foundation. These reports give limited visibility to a wide variety of police decisions not to invoke the criminal process.[7] Three groups of such decisions will be described and analyzed. Each constitutes a police "program" of nonenforcement either based on affirmative departmental policy or condoned by default. All of the decisions, to the extent that the officers concerned thought about them at all, represent well-intentioned, honest judgments, which seem to reflect the police officer's conception of his job. None of the decisions involve bribery or corruption, nor do they concern "obsolete," though unrepealed, criminal laws. Specifically, these programs involve police decisions (1) not to enforce the narcotics laws against certain violators who inform against other "more serious" violators; (2) not to enforce the felonious assault laws against an assailant whose victim does not sign a complaint; and (3) not to enforce gambling laws against persons engaged in the numbers racket, but instead to harass them. Each of these decisions is made even though the police

[6] Lack of any basic records of the squad's activities thwarts a penetrating view of the services performed; but what is not available to this survey is by the same token also denied to superior officers of the force. The plain fact is that no one, not even the officers of the squad, has any means of reviewing that unit's conduct, work, or abiding value, because the underlying and complex pattern of precinct boundaries is controlling in such matters.
Smith, The New York Police Survey 20 (Institute of Public Administration 1952).

[7] The low visibility of these decisions must in a sense be preserved because of the author's obligation not to identify informants or the police department involved by specific citations to American Bar Foundation, Pilot Project Report—The Survey of the Administration of Criminal Justice (1957), or to supporting field reports. To effectuate the Foundation's policy of maintaining the anonymity of the police department and its officers, no citations to statutes, case law, or legislative hearings of the state or local jurisdiction, as well as congressional hearings, will be given when such citations would compromise confidentiality.

"know" a crime has been committed, and even though they may "know" who the offender is and may, in fact, have apprehended him. But before describing and evaluating these nonenforcement programs, as an agency of review might do, it is necessary to determine what discretion, if any, the police, as invoking agents, have, and conceptually to locate the police in relation to other principal decisionmakers in the criminal law process.

II

The police have a duty not to enforce the substantive law of crimes unless invocation of the process can be achieved within bounds set by constitution, statute, court decision, and possibly official pronouncements of the prosecutor. *Total enforcement*, were it possible, is thus precluded, by generally applicable due-process restrictions on such police procedures as arrest, search, seizure, and interrogation. *Total enforcement* is further precluded by such specific procedural restrictions as prohibitions on invoking an adultery statute unless the spouse of one of the parties complains, or an unlawful-possession-of-firearms statute if the offender surrenders his dangerous weapons during a statutory period of amnesty.[8] Such restrictions of general and specific application mark the bounds, often ambiguously, of an area of *full enforcement* in which the police are not only authorized but expected to enforce fully the law of crimes. An area of *no enforcement* lies, therefore, between the perimeter of *total enforcement* and the outer limits of *full enforcement*. In this *no enforcement* area, the police have no authority to invoke the criminal process.

Within the area of *full enforcement*, the police have not been delegated discretion not to invoke the criminal process. On the contrary, those state statutes providing for municipal police departments which define the responsibility of police provide:

It shall be the duty of the police . . . under the direction of the mayor and chief of police and in conformity with the ordinances of the city, and the laws of the state, . . . to pursue and arrest any persons fleeing from justice . . . to apprehend any and all persons in the act of committing any offense against the laws of the state . . . and to take the offender forthwith before the proper court or magistrate, to be dealt with for the offense; to make complaints to the proper officers and magistrates of any person known or believed by them to be guilty of the violation of the ordinances of the city

[8] N.Y. PENAL LAW § 1899. (4) provides:
Notwithstanding any other provision of law, no person shall be prosecuted for . . . the illegal possession of any pistol, . . . [or any other] dangerous weapon . . . if he surrenders such weapon to . . . [the police] . . . between the first and thirtieth days of June, nineteen hundred and fifty-nine.

or the penal laws of the state; and at all times diligently and faithfully to enforce all such laws. . . .[9]

Even in jurisdictions without such a specific statutory definition, declarations of the *full enforcement* mandate generally appear in municipal charters, ordinances or police manuals. Police manuals, for example, commonly provide, in sections detailing the duties at each level of the police hierarchy, that the captain, superintendent, lieutenant, or patrolman shall be responsible, so far as is in his power, for the prevention and detection of crime and the enforcement of all criminal laws and ordinances. Illustrative of the spirit and policy of *full enforcement* is this protestation from the introduction to the Rules and Regulations of the Atlanta, Georgia, Police Department:

> Enforcement of all Criminal Laws and City Ordinances, is my obligation. There are no specialties under the Law. My eyes must be open to traffic problems and disorders, though I move on other assignments, to slinking vice in back streets and dives though I have been directed elsewhere, to the suspicious appearance of evil wherever it is encountered. . . . I must be impartial because the Law surrounds, protects and applies to all alike, rich and poor, low and high, black and white. . . .

Minimally, then, *full enforcement*, so far as the police are concerned, means (1) the investigation of every disturbing event which is reported to or observed by them and which they have reason to suspect may be a violation of the criminal law; (2) following a determination that some crime has been committed, an effort to discover its perpetrators; and (3) the presentation of all information collected by them to the prosecutor for his determination of the appropriateness of further invoking the criminal process.

Full enforcement, however, is not a realistic expectation. In addition to ambiguities in the definitions of both substantive offenses and due-process boundaries, countless limitations and pressures preclude the possibility of the police seeking or achieving *full enforcement*. Limitations of time, personnel, and investigative devices—all in part but not entirely functions of budget— force the development, by plan or default, of priorities of enforcement. Even if there were "enough police" adequately equipped and trained, pressures from within and without the department,[10] which is after all a human

---

[9] Mich. Stat. Ann. § 5.1752 (1949) . . . [The full enforcement mandate is reinforced in many other similar state statutes.]

[10] . . . For a reflection of external pressures, see PORTLAND, ME., POLICE DEP'T RULES & REGS. § 2040.11, reprinted in WILSON, POLICE PLANNING 405 (2d ed. 1957):

> He [the Intelligence Officer] shall guard himself against being forced into ill-advised action against minor non-commercial violators that may result in arousing public indignation; raids on church buildings, homes, and privately occupied hotel rooms not used for commercial purposes are occasionally examples.

See also GLUECK, FINAL REPORT OF THE N.Y. RESEARCH PROJECT FOR THE STUDY AND

institution, may force the police to invoke the criminal process selectively. By decisions not to invoke within the area of *full enforcement*, the police largely determine the outer limits of *actual enforcement* throughout the criminal process. . . . They may reinforce, or they may undermine, the legislature's objectives in designating certain conduct "criminal" and in authorizing the imposition of certain sanctions following conviction. A police decision to ignore a felonious assault "because the victim will not sign a complaint," usually precludes the prosecutor or grand jury from deciding whether to accuse, judge or jury from determining guilt or innocence, judge from imposing the most "appropriate" sentence, probation or correctional authorities from instituting the most "appropriate" restraint and rehabilitation programs, and finally parole or pardon authorities from determining the offender's readiness for release to the community. This example is drawn from one of the three programs of nonenforcement about to be discussed.

III

Trading enforcement against a narcotics suspect for information about another narcotics offense or offender may involve two types of police decisions not to invoke fully the criminal process. First, there may be a decision to ask for the dismissal or reduction of the charge for which the informant is held; second, there may be a decision to overlook future violations while the suspect serves as an informer. The second type is an example of a relatively pure police decision not to invoke the criminal process while the first requires, at a minimum, tacit approval by prosecutor or judge. But examination of only the pure types of decisions would oversimplify the problem. They fail to illustrate the extent to which police nonenforcement decisions may permeate the process as well as influence, and be influenced by, prosecutor and court action in settings which fail to prompt appraisal of such decisions in light of the purpose of the criminal

TREATMENT OF PERSONS CONVICTED OF CRIMES INVOLVING SEXUAL ABERRATIONS 3–4 (1956):

> One . . . variable [explaining in part differences in percentage of "sex offenders" in state prison populations] is the difference in enforcement of various laws in different jurisdictions. Police activity varies from community to community, and within the same community, depending on the number of men available for patrol duty, the amount of immediate public pressure to do something about sexual offenses, and the individual variable of the enforcement officer's own attitudes toward sexual behavior of all types. The variation in mores within a culture, which may be very rapid in periods of social tension, as have prevailed in this country for the past fifteen years, can produce abrupt shifts in attitude about sexual behavior, so that behavior that may be legally wrong becomes socially acceptable.

law. Both types of decisions, pure and conglomerate, are nonetheless primarily police decisions. They are distinguishable from a prosecutor's or court's decision to trade information for enforcement under an immunity statute, and from such parliamentary decisions as the now-repealed seventeenth century English statutes which gave a convicted offender who secured the conviction of his accomplice an absolute right to pardon. Such prosecutor and parliamentary decisions to trade information for enforcement, unlike the police decisions to be described, have not only been authorized by a legislative body, but have also been made sufficiently visible to permit review.

In the municipality studied, regular uniformed officers, with general law enforcement duties on precinct assignments, and a special narcotics squad of detectives, with citywide jurisdiction, are responsible for enforcement of the state narcotics laws. The existence of the special squad acts as a pressure on the uniformed officer to be the first to discover any sale, possession, or use of narcotics in his precinct. Careful preparation of a case for prosecution may thus become secondary to this objective. Indeed, approximately eighty per cent of those apprehended for narcotics violations during one year were discharged. In the opinion of the special squad, which processes each arrested narcotics suspect, either the search was illegal or the evidence obtained inadequate. The precinct officer's lack of interest in carefully developing a narcotics case for prosecution often amounts in effect to a police decision not to enforce but rather to harass.[11]

But we are concerned here primarily with the decisions of the narcotics squad, which, like the Federal Narcotics Bureau, has established a policy of concentrating enforcement efforts against the "big supplier."[12] The chief of the squad claimed that informers must be utilized to implement that policy, and that in order to get informants it is necessary to trade "little ones for big ones." Informers are used to arrange and make purchases of

[11] Another pure-form decision not to invoke the law against unlawful sales may result from a police decision that it is more important to preserve the anonymity of the informant than to proceed against a known offender. See, e.g., People v. McMurray, 340 P.2d 335, 337, 339 (Cal. Dist. Ct. App. 1959).

[12] See STAFF OF SUBCOMM. ON NARCOTICS, HOUSE COMM. ON WAYS AND MEANS, 84TH CONG., 2D SESS., ILLICIT TRAFFIC IN NARCOTICS, BARBITURATES, AND AMPHETAMINES IN THE UNITED STATES 11 (Comm. Print 1956).

Upon questioning individuals on the street, the police are frequently told "I'm working for the Bureau" or "I'm working for Sergeant --------'s crew." For example, the officers of a cruiser car stopped a car to question the occupants. The driver told the officers that he was working for the Narcotics Squad and was trying to make a purchase from the other person in the car. The other person, who was questioned separately, told the officers that he, too, was an informer—but for the Federal agency, and that he was associating with the driver in hopes that he would obtain some information relating to the sale of narcotics.

narcotics, to elicit information from suspects, including persons in custody, and to recruit additional informants.

Following arrest, a suspect will generally offer to serve as an informer to "do himself some good." If an arrestee fails to initiate such negotiations, the interrogating officer will suggest that something may be gained by disclosing sources of supply and by serving as an informer. A high mandatory minimum sentence for selling, a high maximum sentence for possession, and, where users are involved, a strong desire on their part to avoid the agonies of withdrawal, combine to place the police in an excellent bargaining position to recruit informers. To assure performance, each informer is charged with a narcotics violation, and final disposition is postponed until the defendant has fulfilled his part of the bargain. To protect the informer, the special squad seeks to camouflage him in the large body of releasees by not disclosing his identity even to the arresting precinct officer, who is given no explanation for release.[13] Thus persons encountered on the street by a uniformed patrolman the day after their arrest may have been discharged, or they may have been officially charged and then released on bail or personal recognizance to await trial or to serve as informers.

While serving as informers, suspects are allowed to engage in illegal activity. Continued use of narcotics is condoned; the narcotics detective

[13] The informer is contacted by the police away from public view. Members of the Squad refrain from apprehending a suspect making a sale to an informer during a supervised purchase. See KENNEY, A GUIDE FOR POLICE PLANNING NARCOTICS OPERATIONS 10 (1954), pp. 10–11.

A. How to cultivate narcotic informants.
    . . . .
    2. Above all, do not make arrest with the informant present when said informant has introduced the officer to the peddler. This is called a "burn." Once an officer or unit secures the reputation of "burning" informants it will be hard pressed in securing information from informants.

B. How to use narcotic informants for information on other crimes.
    . . . .
    2. The officer should keep in mind that the disclosure of an informant's identity will in all probability result in serious injury or possible death to the informant.

    . . . .
D. How to properly use informants.
    1. Informants must be protected at all times by not revealing identiy [sic] or disclosing the fact that they are giving information or assistance.
    2. Avoid making arrests when informants are present, or so close after informant-officer-contact that informants are suspected by the violator of "burning him." This is called a "buy and a bust" with a "burn" of the informant.
    3. Always build up in the informant's mind that the officer will never "burn" him.

                        . . .

generally is not concerned with the problem of informants who make buys and use some of the evidence themselves.[14] Though informers are usually warned that their status does not give them a "license to peddle," possession of a substantial amount of narcotics may be excused. In one case, a defendant found guilty of possession of *marijuana* argued that she was entitled to be placed on probation since she had cooperated with the police by testifying against three persons charged with the sale of narcotics. The sentencing judge denied her request because he discovered that her cooperation was related to the possession of a substantial amount of *heroin*, an offense for which she was arrested (but never charged) while on bail for the marijuana violation. A narcotics squad inspector, in response to an inquiry from the judge, revealed that the defendant had not been charged with possession of *heroin* because she had been cooperative with the police on that offense.[15]

[14] In one case an informer, who had just made a buy handed the officer ten red capsules of heroin wrapped in tinfoil and stated that he was keeping two for his trouble. In no cases observed did the police directly furnish informers with narcotics.

In other jurisdictions, the supplying of addict informers with narcotics by the police apparently is not uncommon. DEUTSCH, THE TROUBLE WITH COPS 98 (2d ed. 1955), reports:

> The chief of one of our best-policed cities gave me an elaborate rationalization for the practice:
>
> "We don't hand out dope to an addict who supplies us with information. But if one comes in, desperate for want of the addicting drug that he can't obtain for one reason or another, and if he gives us information that we deem valuable, we send him to the public hospital where a doctor can administer an injection of the drug for medical reasons, to relieve his suffering."
>
> This chief, along with others who defend the practice, claimed it is almost impossible to apprehend dope peddlers without the cooperation of their addict customers.

On quite the other hand, Deutsch reports:

> Police Chief John Holstrom of Berkeley, California, makes this observation:
> . . .
> "In Berkeley, we don't trade immunity for information, in so far as toleration of continued violations is concerned. But we trade in another way. For instance, if a man is arrested for a petty theft and he tells us he will give us convicting information on a big narcotics operator if I recommend dismissal of the charge against him, I wouldn't hesitate to do it—if he comes through with the goods."

Id. at 97.

. . . For some evidence on the extent to which the courts may be involved with the police in the trading of enforcement for information, see Griffin v. Renkert, 121 N.E.2d 171 (Ohio C.P. 1954) (ordering reinstatement of police detective dismissed for obtaining modification of sentence and release of a person convicted on charge of possession of lottery slips in order to aid him in "his subversive" work in checking communism "in certain colored circles").

[15] On imposing a sentence of two to ten years, the judge said that her cooperation in the heroin offense did not place any moral obligation on him or the police department as to her sentence for the marijuana charge. Had she been charged and convicted on both counts, the maximum could have been twenty years. A third conviction for

In addition to granting such outright immunity for some violations, the police will recommend to the prosecutor either that an informer's case be *nolle prossed* or, more frequently, that the charge be reduced to a lesser offense. And, if the latter course is followed, the police usually recommend to the judge, either in response to his request for information or in the presentence report, that informers be placed on probation or given relatively light sentences. Both the prosecutor and judge willingly respond to police requests for reducing a charge of sale to a lesser offense because they consider the mandatory minimum too severe.[16] As a result, during a four year period in this jurisdiction, less than two and one-half per cent of all persons charged with the sale of narcotics were convicted of that offense.

The narcotics squad's policy of trading *full enforcement* for information is justified on the grounds that apprehension and prosecution of the "big supplier" is facilitated. The absence of any in the city is attributed to this policy. As one member of the squad said, "[The city] is too hot. There are too many informants." A basic, though untested, assumption of the policy is that ridding the city of the "big supplier" is the key to solving its narcotics problem. Even if this assumption were empirically validated, the desirability of continuing such a policy cannot be established without taking into account its total impact on the administration of criminal justice in the city, the state, and the nation. Yet no procedure has been designed to enable the police and other key administrators of criminal justice to obtain such an appraisal. . . .

. . .

IV

Another low visibility situation . . . stems from police decisions not to invoke the felonious assault laws unless the victim signs a complaint. Like

---

possession would carry a mandatory twenty years minimum with a possible maximum of forty years.

In another case an informer for the Federal Bureau of Narcotics sold heroin capsules to an informer of the city narcotics squad. The Federal informer was arrested by the city police and charged. Following consultation with Federal agents the case was *nolle prossed*.

On the widespread use of informers and police protection of them, see Kooken, *Ethics in Police Service*, 38 J. Crim. L. & Criminology 172, 174–75 (1947).

[16] The police work under specific instructions from the judges to notify them of those cases in which they wish to have imposed the heavy mandatory sentences prescribed by statute. For an example of a trial court penalizing a defendant because of her failure to cooperate as an informant, see State v. Carter, Conn. L.J., Nov. 4, 1958, pp. 14, 15 (Sentence Rev. Div.) (sentence review decision reducing sentence).

the addict-informer, the potential complainant in an assault case is both the victim of an offense and a key source of information. But unlike him, the complainant, who is not a suspect, and whose initial contact with the police is generally self-imposed, is not placed under pressure to bargain. And in contrast with the informer program, the police assault program was clearly not designed, if designed at all, to effectuate an identifiable policy.

During one month under the nonenforcement program of a single precinct, thirty-eight out of forty-three felonious assault cases, the great majority involving stabbings and cuttings, were cleared "because the victim refused to prosecute."[17] This program, which is coupled with a practice of not encouraging victims to sign complaints, reduces the pressure of work by eliminating such tasks as apprehending and detaining suspects, writing detailed reports, applying for warrants to prefer charges and appearing in court at inconvenient times for long periods without adequate compensation.[18] As one officer explained, "run-of-the-mill" felonious assaults are so common in this precinct that prosecution of each case would force patrolmen to spend too much time in court and leave too little time for investigating other offenses. This rationalization exposes the private value system of individual officers as another policy-shaping factor. Some policemen feel,

[17] The police are frequently made aware of the offense by victims apparently more anxious to obtain ambulance service to the hospital than to initiate apprehension and prosecution of an assailant. If hospitalization is required, the police arrest the offender even though the complainant may not wish to prosecute. When such arrests are made, the police conduct a "minimum type" investigation to assure that the basic facts will be available should the victim die and murder or manslaughter become the more appropriate charge for the state, as complainant, to lodge against the offender. The police decision to arrest, however, does not reflect any intention to further invoke the process because of the seriousness of the injury inflicted. For soon after the disturbing event, in an effort to close the case, the police will ask the hospitalized victim to decide whether prosecution should be initiated. Though his condition may cast doubt about his competence to understand and respond to such an inquiry, in at least one case the victim demonstrated complete awareness. Shortly before his death for which the assailant was subsequently charged with murder, he replied from his hospital bed, "I want to see whether or not I live first."

The police will also make arrests, even if the complainant does not wish to prosecute, if the suspect has offered to pay off the complainant or if the suspect is a "known criminal" whom the police wish to get off the street. The decision to invoke the process in these cases is equally a reflection of the private value system of the police. In these cases the state acts as complainant and the victim is subpoenaed to appear at trial. See Miller, *The Compromise of Criminal Cases*, 1 So. CAL. L. REV. 1, & nn.3–5 (1927) (on compounding crime as a separate offense).

[18] A decision to arrest may be influenced by the time an offense occurs and the time the police officer is scheduled to go off and return to duty. An officer assigned to the vice squad explained, for example, that officers will not make an arrest on Saturday night if they can avoid it since court appearance is likely to be scheduled for their day off. And no matter what the duration of his court appearance, the officer receives credit for only two hours work.

for example, that assault is an acceptable means of settling disputes among Negroes, and that when both assailant and victim are Negro, there is no immediately discernible harm to the public which justifies a decision to invoke the criminal process.[19] Anticipation of dismissal by judge and district attorney of cases in which the victim is an uncooperative witness, the police claim, has been another operative factor in the development of the assault policy. . . .

. . .

V

Police decisions to harass, though generally perceived as overzealous enforcement, constitute another body of nonenforcement activities. . . . Harassment is the imposition by the police, acting under color of law, of sanctions prior to conviction as a means of ultimate punishment, rather than as a device for the invocation of criminal proceedings. Characteristic of harassment are efforts to annoy certain "offenders" both by temporarily detaining or arresting them without intention to seek prosecution and by destroying or illegally seizing their property without any intention to use it as evidence.[20] Like other police decisions not to invoke the criminal process, harassment is generally of extremely low visibility, probably because the police ordinarily restrict such activity to persons who are unable to afford the costs of litigation, who would, or think they would, command little respect even if they were to complain, or wish to keep themselves out of public view in order to continue their illicit activities. Like the informer program, harassment is conducted by the police in an atmosphere of cooperation with other administrators of criminal justice. . . .

[In some jurisdictions one] would discover, for example, a mixture of

[19] In such cases the police do not attribute their unwillingness to act on any legal restriction placed upon them or any particular difficulty which they may encounter in taking the case to court. Other expressions of private and possibly community value systems are found in police decisions, for example, not to proceed against an elderly gentleman for larceny of a ham ("You are 74 years old—for crying out loud we don't want to lock you up for something like that . . ." the lieutenant said), or to take home an upper class drunk while locking up a "drunken bum."

[20] This definition of harassment excludes, therefore, the lawful arrests of "golden rule" drunks whom the police intend to release the next morning, the apprehension and detention of material witnesses, arrests or searches of doubtful legality engaged in to determine the limits of due process, and finally "letter of the law" enforcement which is frequently mislabled harassment. For an account of the development of the Golden Rule Police Policy in late nineteenth century, see Bremmer, *Police, Penal and Parole Policies in Cleveland and Toledo: The Civic Revival in Ohio*, 14 Am. J. Economics & Sociology 387 (1955).

enforcement and harassment in a police program designed to regulate the gambling operations of mutual-numbers syndicates.[21] The enforcement phase is conducted by a highly trained unit of less than a dozen men who diligently gather evidence in order to prosecute and convict syndicate operators of conspiracy to violate the gambling laws. This specialized unit, which operates independently of and without the knowledge of other officers, conducts all its work within the due-process boundaries of *full enforcement*. Consequently, the conviction rate is high for charges based upon its investigations. The harassment phase is conducted by approximately sixty officers who tour the city and search on sight, because of prior information, or such telltale actions as carrying a paper bag, a symbol of the trade, persons who they suspect are collecting bets. They question the "suspect" and proceed to search him, his car, or home without first making a valid arrest to legalize the search. If gambling paraphernalia are found, the police, fully aware that the exclusionary rule prohibits its use as evidence in this jurisdiction, confiscate the "contraband" and arrest the individual without any intention of seeking application of the criminal law.[22]

Gambling operators treat the harassment program as a cost of doing business, "a risk of the trade." Each syndicate retains a bonding firm and an

[21] Betting on the numbers is a poor man's hobby. Wagers are for small amounts—may be for as low as a nickel or a dime, although occasionally an affluent player may invest $100 on a number. . . . [T]he player places his bet on any combination of three numbers. He wins if the three numbers he has chosen correspond to three numbers appearing in the same order in a previously designated portion of the day's parimutuel betting total at a selected race track.

. . . .

The usual payoff is at 600 to 1. However, the player usually gets only 500 to 1, the remaining 100 being kept as commission by the man who took his bet. In addition, the policy operators lower the odds further on the most popular numbers and those that have won most frequently. Actually, the player should receive 999 to 1 odds, because that represents the number of possible winning combinations.

There is a business hierarchy in the conduct of numbers gambling. Low man in the operation is the "runner," often an elevator operator, a doorman, an orderly in a large hospital, a worker in a factory or office, a housewife or just a plain out-of-work guy who picks up bets from customers on his beat. Players also can make their wagers in candy stores, bars, restaurants and other retail establishments, known as "drops."

Bets made with runners and at drops are picked up by an employe called a collector. He brings the slips with their bets to a controller, who can be likened to the branch manager of a bank. The controller in turn delivers the slips to the "bank," which is headquarters of the betting ring.

N.Y. Times, Jan. 10, 1960, § 4, p. 6, cols. 5–6 (description of current practices in New York).

For a description of the numbers racket during another era and its relation to bribery and corruption of the police, see Whyte, *The Social Structure of Racketeering*, in PRINCIPLES OF SOCIOLOGY 494 (Freedman, Hawley, Landecker, Lenski & Miner rev. ed. 1956).

[22] If the searchers uncover only one or two number slips, no one is taken into custody. If an individual attempts to dispose of gambling paraphernalia which he has

attorney to service members who are arrested. When a "runner" or "bag-man" is absent from his scheduled rounds, routine release procedures are initiated. The bondsman, sometimes premateurely, checks with the police to determine if a syndicate man has been detained. If the missing man is in custody, the syndicate's attorney files an application for a writ of habeas corpus and appears before a magistrate who usually sets bail at a nominal amount and adjourns hearing the writ, at the request of the police, until the following day. Prior to the scheduled hearing, the police usually advise the court that they have no intention of proceeding, and the case is closed. Despite the harassee's release, the police retain the money and gambling paraphernalia. If the items seized are found in a car, the car is confiscated, with the cooperation of the prosecutor, under a nuisance abatement statute. Cars are returned, however, after the harassee signs a "consent decree" and pursuant to it, pays "court costs"—a fee which is based on the car's value and which the prosecutor calls "the real meat of the harassment program."[23] The "decree," entered under a procedure devised by the court and prosecutor's office, enjoins the defendant from engaging in illegal activity and, on paper, frees the police from any tort liability by an acknowledgment that seizure of the vehicle was lawful and justified—even though one prosecutor has estimated that approximately eighty per cent of the searches and seizures were illegal. A prosecuting attorney responsible for car confiscation initially felt that such procedures "in the ordinary practice of law would be un-ethical, revolting, and shameful," but explained that he now understands why he acted as he did:

> To begin with . . . the laws in . . . [this state] with respect to gambling are most inadequate. This is equally true of the punishment feature of the law. To illustrate . . . a well-organized and productive gambling house or numbers racket would take in one quarter of a million dollars each week. If, after a long and vigorous period of investigation and observation, the defendant was charged with violating the gambling laws and convicted therefore, the resulting punishment is so obviously weak and unprohibitive that the defendants are willing to shell out a relatively small fine or serve a relatively short time in prison. The . . . [city's] gamblers and numbers men confidently feel that the odds are in their favor. If they operate for six months or a year, and accumulate

---

on his person within the presence of the officers, the police may then proceed to effect a legal arrest and the evidence may be introduced at trial.

Though the bulk of arrests are labeled "investigative arrests" by the police, there is no indication that harassment is a device for recruiting informants. Though a "runner" or "bagman," as the collector of bets is called, may not know that his rights have been violated or that he is entitled to immediate release, he does know that his syndicate will arrange an early release and that he will gain nothing by incriminating his "benevolent" and powerful associates.

[23] For example, "court costs" may be $120 for a 1957 car or $70 for a 1953 model. Assessments are made even though actual court costs have been estimated at approximately $20, although the legality of such retribution is in doubt in some jurisdictions.

untold thousands of dollars from the illegal activity, then the meager punishment imposed upon them if they are caught is well worth it. Then, too, because of the search and seizure laws in . . . [this state], especially in regard to gambling and the number rackets, the hands of the police are tied. Unless a search can be made prior to an arrest so that the defendant can be caught in the act of violating the gambling laws, or a search warrant issued, there is no other earthly way of apprehending such people along with evidence sufficient to convict them that is admissible in court.

Because of these two inadequacies of the law (slight punishment and conservative search and seizure laws with regard to gambling) the prosecutor's office and the police department are forced to find other means of punishing, harassing and generally making life uneasy for gamblers.

This position, fantastic as it is to be that of law-trained official, a guardian of the rule of law, illustrates how extensively only one of many police harassment programs in this jurisdiction can permeate the process and be tolerated by other decisionmakers in a system of criminal administration where decisions not to enforce are of extremely low visibility.[24]

. . .

VI

The mandate of *full enforcement*, under circumstances which compel selective enforcement, has placed the municipal police in an intolerable

---

[24] Some indication of the extensiveness of police harassment in this jurisdiction can be gleaned from a single precinct's arrest and release statistics on "prostitutes" and "gamblers." During a six-month period criminal prosecutions were initiated against only 75 out of 3000 women arrested for prostitution and against only 25 out of 600 persons arrested for gambling. During that same period eighty raids on alleged gambling operations were staged accounting for more than 580 of the 600 gambling arrests and the confiscation of approximately $9,000 in "gambling money." . . .

In raids, called "tipovers," the police enter premises, search, seize, and arrest illegally, fully aware that by resorting to such techniques they are forfeiting a court case. This harassment policy may partially explain why fewer than thirty search warrants have been issued annually by the courts in recent years to the police of the more than dozen precincts in the city, not just to the police of the precinct described. A member of the prosecutor's office explained the small number of warrants issued by noting that (1) in cases involving deadly weapons and narcotics found outside a dwelling place the exclusionary rule does not apply—though criteria of lawful searches and seizures continue to have in theory general application; (2) officers wait until they have sufficient evidence to substantiate an arrest and to conduct a lawful search pursuant to an arrest without a warrant; (3) by avoiding a search warrant, officers minimize the chances of leaking information about a raid; (4) "probable cause" is difficult to prove; and (5) it is useless to go to the trouble, time, and expense of obtaining a warrant since it is so easy to conduct a search without a warrant. . . .

position. As a result, nonenforcement programs have developed undercover, in a hit-or-miss fashion, and without regard to impact on the overall administration of justice or the basic objectives of the criminal law. Legislatures, therefore, ought to reconsider what discretion, if any, the police must or should have in invoking the criminal process, and what devices, if any, should be designed to increase visibility and hence reviewability of these police decisions.

The ultimate answer is that the police should not be delegated discretion not to invoke the criminal law. It is recognized, of course, that the exercise of discretion cannot be completely eliminated where human beings are involved. The frailties of human language and human perception will always admit of borderline cases (although none of the situations analyzed in this Article are "borderline"). But nonetheless, outside this margin of ambiguity, the police should operate in an atmosphere which exhorts and commands them to invoke impartially all criminal laws within the bounds of *full enforcement*.[25] If a criminal law is ill-advised, poorly defined, or too costly to enforce, efforts by the police to achieve *full enforcement* should generate pressures for legislative action.[26] Responsibility for the enactment,

---

[25] This, of course, does not mean that the police must *arrest* every violator.

For an example of a statute under which *full enforcement* might mean no more than the issuance of a warning to the offender, see Street Offenses Act, 7 & 8 Eliz. 2, c. 57, § 2. In accord with this section the Home Office issued a circular stating the procedure to be adopted by the Metropolitan Police, which provides, *inter alia*:

> On the first occasion when a woman who has not previously been convicted of loitering or soliciting for the purpose of prostitution is seen loitering or soliciting in a street or public place for that purpose, the officer seeing her will obtain the assistance of a second officer as a witness, and when both officers, after having kept the woman under observation, are satisfied by her demeanor and conduct that she is in fact loitering or soliciting for the purpose of prostitution, they will tell her what they have seen and caution her. Details of the caution will subsequently be recorded at the police station and in a central register for the Metropolitan Police District. The two officers, after administering the caution, will ask the woman if she is willing to be put in touch with a moral welfare organization or a probation officer, and invite her to call at the police station at a convenient time to see a woman police officer for these arrangements to be made, unless she prefers her name and address to be given to a welfare organization or a probation officer without going to the station. If the woman continues to loiter or solicit for the purpose of prostitution, a second formal caution will be given in the street and recorded and a second offer will be made to put her in touch with a welfare officer or probation officer. She will not be arrested until she is seen loitering or soliciting on the third occasion.

G.B. Home Office Circular No. 109/1959, Aug. 13, 1959, reprinted in 23 J. Crim. Law (Eng.) 299 (1959).

[26] Essentially this position was taken and the result achieved by New York City's police commissioner when in 1955 he declared that bingo would be treated as a violation of the state's gambling laws, that "anyone who goes ahead with bingo in this city does so at his peril . . . . If people do not like it they should take the necessary steps to

amendment, and repeal of the criminal laws will not, then, be abandoned to the whim of each police officer or department, but retained where it belongs in a democracy—with elected representatives.

Equating *actual enforcement* with *full enforcement*, however, would be neither workable nor humane nor humanly possible under present conditions in most, if not all, jurisdictions. Even if there were "enough police" (and there are not) to enforce all of the criminal laws, too many people have come to rely on the nonenforcement of too many "obsolete" laws to justify the embarrassment, discomfort, and misery which would follow implementation of *full enforcement* programs for every crime. *Full enforcement* is a program for the future, a program which could be initiated with the least hardship when the states, perhaps stimulated by the work of the American Law Institute, enact new criminal codes clearing the books of obsolete offenses.

. . .

---

repeal it. But while it is on the books, we [policemen] must enforce it." N.Y. Times, Sept. 26, 1955, p. 25, col. 8. The New York legislature responded by legalizing bingo conducted by religious, charitable, veterans, volunteer firemen, and similar nonprofit organizations. N.Y. Munic. Law §§ 477–99. On the stringent set of rules promulgated for the conduct of legalized bingo by the State Lottery Control Commission to keep the game out of the hands of racketeers, see N.Y. Times, Sept. 23, 1958, p. 35, cols. 1–2.

4 Noninvocation of the Criminal Law by Police

WAYNE R. LAFAVE

There are not sufficient resources available to the police for them to proceed against all the conduct which the legislature may actually desire subjected to enforcement. As a consequence, discretion must be exercised in deciding how to allocate the resources that do exist. As Thurman Arnold has said, to deny discretion at this point would be "like directing a general to attack the enemy on all fronts at once."[1] The police and other enforcement agencies are given the general responsibility for maintaining law and order under a body of criminal law defining the various kinds of conduct against which they may properly proceed. They are then furnished with enforcement resources less than adequate to accomplish the entire task. Consequently, discretionary enforcement occurs in an attempt to obtain the best results from these limited means. In this sense, the budgetary appropriation is an establishment of policy (the general level of enforcement for which the public is willing to pay) and an indirect delegation of power by the legislative to the administrative branch.[2]

Much of the criminal conduct coming to the attention of the police does not lead to arrest. Often a warning is given; this is the form of action

Reprinted from Wayne R. LaFave, *Arrest: The Decision to Take a Suspect into Custody* (Boston: Little, Brown and Company, 1965), pp. 102–124, by permission of the publisher and the author.

[1] Arnold, The Symbols of Government 1953 (1935).
[2] See Wilson. Police Planning 20 (2d ed. 1957).

least demanding on available enforcement resources.[3] Though warnings are generally issued on a haphazard basis, they are regularly used in some situations where the conduct is thought not serious enough to justify an arrest.

Even more serious offenses do not necessarily lead to arrest, however. This may occur, for example, when the police view the conduct as conforming to the normal standards of the group involved; when the victim is not seriously interested in prosecution; or when the victim's plight, considering his own misconduct, is not thought worthy of official attention. Factors such as these influence the police in their adjustment of enforcement priorities.[4]

Before discussing the particular criteria employed, one general observation can be made. Although police decisions not to arrest do lessen the burden upon the prosecutor's office, the courts, the prisons, and the correctional agencies, there is no evidence to indicate that they are especially prompted by this consideration.[5] Rather, the practice of not arresting is generally adopted to conserve *police* resources, either those which would be used to arrest, book, and detain the suspect or those necessarily involved later in the process, such as for police testimony at the trial.

This is not to say that the predictable action at later stages of the process has no bearing on police allocation of enforcement resources. Police may not arrest if they believe that there is no likelihood of prosecution or conviction. Also, if the predictable punishment is thought to be either too strict or too lenient, arrest is less likely unless the police have means of influencing the nature of the penalty.[6] Finally, if the conduct is

[3] In this analysis, warning is not considered a form of invocation of the process. Warning might be viewed as one kind of invocation, inasmuch as the offender learns that his violation has come to official attention and the warning, hopefully, serves to prevent future offenses. However, no established policy exists with regard to the issuance of a warning, except that some police manuals state that a warning may be given for "minor offenses." See note 8 *infra*. It is generally quite an arbitrary matter whether a decision not to invoke, as the phrase is used here, is accompanied by a warning. Thus any attempt to select for separate discussion decisions to invoke by warning would tend to give a distorted picture of current practice.

[4] Of course, not all police attempts to allocate law enforcement resources take the form of decisions on whether or not to arrest a particular offender. Priorities of enforcement are largely set by the manner in which a particular police agency is organized. An examination of the distribution of manpower among specialized subagencies may be particularly revealing in this respect.

[5] Criticism of police lack of consideration for these other agencies was noted only once. A judge of Recorder's Court, Detroit, was critical of the police going into a bar to arrest a drunk, and said: "If the police did this in every bar in Detroit they would have time for nothing else, and if they did the jails would not hold all the drunks."

[6] Thus if the officer views the punishment as too severe, he may attempt to have a lesser offense charged. In Wisconsin, the officer can often significantly alter the possible punishment by channeling the case through the ordinance violation process

such that it is thought that the criminal process cannot provide the appropriate punishment, deterrence, or rehabilitation, the police may again devote their resources to other cases.[7] Combinations of these factors will appear in the situations which follow.

A. TRIVIAL OFFENSES

Police manuals often advise the officer that warning rather than arrest is appropriate when only minor violations are concerned.[8] This has the effect of conserving enforcement resources for more serious conduct.

---

rather than the state statute process. Since city ordinance violations in Wisconsin are not criminal, they involve no jail sentence, and the fines are correspondingly lower than those for violations of state statutes. Conversely, in more serious cases, particularly in those involving second offenders, the person may be charged under the state statutes because the officer thinks that time in jail will be beneficial.

The Michigan State Police indicated that they were able to influence the penalty by their choice of the justice of the peace to whom they sent the violator. Thus, if they felt the violation was not serious enough to warrant the usual penalty, they would send the violator to a lenient justice. Conversely, if they desired a more severe penalty, the offender would be sent to a justice who usually imposed such penalties.

[7] The police may consider the alternative methods available. The conduct may be best dealt with by a private agency of a civic, recreational, religious, educational, or welfare nature, or by a governmental agency not under the criminal justice system.

Where the conduct calls for penal treatment, it would appear that it could be effectively dealt with by the criminal administration process. However, the distinction between penal treatment and the administration of welfare services is often not clear, even in theory. See Allen, The Borderland of the Criminal Law: Problems of "Socializing" Criminal Justice, 32 Social Serv. Rev. 107 (1958). Even when welfare services are called for, law enforcement agencies may have to handle the situation because of a lack of appropriate public or private welfare facilities. Thus Allen notes that unmarried pregnant women were convicted when they were unable to pay for the necessary hospital expenses and the subsequent care of the child, so that the burden was shifted to the state. Id. at 109.

[8] Detroit and Milwaukee police are cautioned that "a polite warning" will suffice for "minor offenses" and that arrests should not be made in such cases unless the violations are "willful or repeated." Detroit Police Dept., Revised Police Manual, chap. 16, §34 (1955); Milwaukee Police Dept., Rules & Regulations, Rule 30, §31 (1950). Wichita police, in their "square deal code," are cautioned to "save unfortunate offenders from unnecessary humiliation, inconvenience and distress" and "never to arrest if a summons will suffice; never to summons if a warning would be better." Wichita Police Dept., Duty Manual i (undated). Similarly, Kansas City police are instructed, "Don't make trivial arrests when a warning will suffice." Kansas City Police Dept., Rules & Regulations, Reg. 121(2) (1956). Pontiac (Michigan) police are told to use warnings, but are then "enjoined against the indiscriminate use of this rule to the detriment of the peace and order of the city, and will be held accountable for undue leniency toward offenders." Pontiac Police Dept., Rules & Regulations §237 (undated).

1. *Traffic violations.*

Illustration No. 1: A police officer saw a motorist make an illegal left turn. The officer stopped the driver, brought the violation to his attention, but did not make an arrest and did not write a ticket.

The use of a warning rather than making an arrest or issuing a ticket is common in cases involving minor traffic offenses. Indeed, the discretion which the officer has the power to exercise in such cases is so well known to the motoring public that an indivdual motorist is likely to protest if arrested or given a ticket.[9] The practical necessity for the warning alternative in traffic cases is widely acknowledged even by those who deny the propriety of police discretion for more serious offenses.[10] The volume of minor traffic cases is so great that it would be very costly to subject them all to the formal criminal process.[11]

Officers engaged in traffic enforcement in each of the three states studied indicated that the decision to issue a warning rather than a regular citation in a given case is left to the discretion of the individual patrolman. Specific guidance as to what kind of case deserves only a warning is rarely given, except for some written policy on the toleration levels on speeding.[12]

[9] Because it is generally recognized that the police engage in the practice of warning offending drivers, pressures are increased to expand the area of nonenforcement. In Wichita the point has been reached where the police often avoid arresting for traffic offenses because of the loss of respect engendered by such action. Assigning men to traffic work has become a personnel problem because the officers are subjected to considerable abuse and vituperation by the citizenry. When a traffic offense is written up, the officer really has to "sell" the ticket, sometimes having to talk to the offender for as much as fifteen minutes. In Milwaukee traffic violators sometimes complain to police supervisors about the fact that they were given a ticket instead of a mere warning. Another study has also concluded that "for the policeman the traffic violator represents an unpleasant experience." Westley, The Police: A Sociological Study of Law, Custom and Morality 109 (unpublished Ph.D. thesis No. 1197, Dept. of Sociology, Univ. of Chicago, 1951).

[10] For example, one writer, after asserting that the police should enforce *all* the law, adds: "Nor is it really relevant to point out that the police in this country do already exercise some degree of discrimination in the enforcement of the law. Many traffic offenders, for example, receive a word of advice on the spot instead of a summons. That speaks merely for the good sense of the police, and for our good fortune in being served by sensible officers. The point is that these are exceptions to the general rule, and are made under strictly controlled conditions, for a particular purpose; . . ." Williams, Turning a Blind Eye, 1954 Crim. L. Rev. (Eng.) 272. His justification for the exception seems questionable, as it is not readily apparent that there is any greater control over noninvocation here than in other areas.

[11] In one study it was concluded that in Berkeley, California, three million traffic violations were occurring daily, and that full enforcement would require 14,000 traffic officers. Cal. State Dept. of Education, Cal. Peace Officers Training Publication No. 71, Police Supervisory Control 26 (1957).

[12] Thus the radar unit in one Wisconsin community was instructed that when operating in a 25 m.p.h. zone, speeds up to 32 m.p.h. were to be ignored, speeds

The result is that warnings are sometimes given for illegal turns, rolling stops, and the like, but the process is invoked for the same conduct on other occasions, and it is not possible to observe any uniform enforcement pattern in this area. Invocation is the rule, however, if the violation results in a person actually being injured or put in a dangerous situation.[13] Of course, when a warning proves ineffective, then invocation of the process against the violator can be expected. But, unless warnings are made a matter of record, these repeated violations usually are not known.[14]

2. Juvenile offenses.

Illustration No. 2: Residents near a drive-in restaurant complained to the police that a disturbance of the peace was occurring in their neighborhood. A patrol car was dispatched to the scene, and the officers found a group of teenagers singing, shouting, and racing the engines of their cars, which created a considerable disturbance. The officers administered severe warnings to the youths and then left.

Minor offenses by juveniles are not usually considered important enough to warrant expenditure of any substantial amount of police enforcement resources. The usual opinion is that such conduct, while proscribed by the penal statutes, is merely a consequence of the minor's immature judgment or youthful exuberance and poses no major threat to society if not proceeded against fully. Thus youthful offenders are often given a warning and sent on their way when the violation is not serious. This frequently occurs in small cities,[15] but in the larger metropolitan areas, such as Detroit and Milwaukee, the warning is more likely to come after arrest.[16] Even in large urban areas, however, it is still common for individual

---

from 32 to 38 m.p.h. were to be considered cases for warning cards, and drivers going above 38 m.p.h. were to receive regular traffic citations.

[13] Therefore, whereas a speeder on a lonely road might not be arrested, another person driving at the same place, and at the same speed, would be if the traffic were heavy.

[14] Probably the best system observed was in Eau Claire, Wisconsin. There, when a warning is issued, the driver signs a warning card, a copy of which is placed on file. Should a particular driver receive three warnings within a year, the process is invoked with respect to the third violation.

[15] Thus the chief of police in a small Michigan community indicated that petty juvenile offenses there are dealt with on a informal basis and without an arrest routinely being made. He said that this method of settling these kinds of cases "behind the kitchen stove" is particularly suited to a small town, but would probably not be possible in a larger city.

[16] In a smaller town the officer may know whether the youth is a first offender or a habitual troublemaker, or, in any event, whether he can be easily located later. But arrest is more usual in the larger city. The Detroit Police Manual instructs: "All violators under the age of twenty-one (21) years [who are guilty of purchasing, possessing, or transporting intoxicating beverages] shall be brought into the Precinct Station, and if it is determined that this is their first offense and there are

patrolmen to dispose of cases by some means other than arrest.[17]

The level of toleration of juvenile offenses cannot be stated with any great degree of certainty.[18] However, the chance of arrest is great when force or violence has been used against an innocent victim outside the juvenile's social group. Nonviolent property crimes are not thought to warrant arrest unless the amount of damage involved is great or the technique employed is professional in nature.[19] The juvenile's past record is considered

---

no aggravated conditions involved, all such minors or juveniles may be released with a warning except juvenile girls [who will be transported home by the Women's Division]. . . . The provisions of this procedure may be applied to other types of cases involving juveniles and minors found in disorderly parties or other difficulties where liquor violations are not involved." Detroit Police Dept., Revised Police Manual, chap. 12, §74(a)(1), (b)(4) (1955). The Milwaukee regulations put the invocation question in the hands of supervisory officers, which suggests that arrest will be the first step. "Whenever a juvenile case is brought before any commanding officer, and in his judgment the offense involved is of a minor nature and the case can consistently be kept out of the Juvenile Court, such commanding officer may release the offender with a reprimand." Milwaukee Police Dept., Rules & Regulations, Rule 32, §9 (1950). In Wichita, juvenile officers are told to "dispose of all juvenile offenders in the way that will be to the best interest of the offender and to society in general." Wichita Police Dept., Duty Manual 61 (undated). Sometimes these juvenile officers do not enter the case until after the arrest, but it is not uncommon for a patrolman in Wichita to radio for a juvenile officer and to have him make the determination on the spot.

[17] See Carr, Delinquency Control 150 (1940), where it is said that in a city such as Detroit the police annually make from 10,000 to 14,000 nonofficial contacts in which youngsters may be reproved or admonished because of undesirable conduct. Of these, only one in three will be apprehended and placed in the detention home, and less than one in seven will be brought before juvenile court.

[18] Field research for this study did not focus upon crimes by juveniles as a special problem. Consequently, the factual data reported here are rather limited, having been obtained merely incidentally to other inquiries. For a recent study on the appropriate degree of toleration of juvenile offenses, see Myren and Swanson, Police Work With Children (1962).

[19] The limited observations are entirely consistent with the conclusion reached in another study, which focused on juvenile offenders. It was there noted that auto theft was considered a serious offense by the police and that burglary and robbery generally resulted in arrest unless they were very minor and restitution was made. Sexual relations between juveniles without coercion do not often result in arrest unless they are abnormal. Purse snatching is usually looked upon as a grave offense —an attack on the weaker sex—and restitution will rarely prevent arrest. Shoplifting and other larceny is not generally considered worthy of arrest if the victim will accept restitution (but see note 23 infra). The mode of commission of the offense may be significant. Carefully planned offenses, professional in nature, such as burglary with burglary tools, are viewed as much more serious than offenses committed on impulse. Use of force is an important factor, as is the fact that the offense was committed at night. Goldman, The Differential Selection of Juvenile Offenders for Court Appearance 148–156 (unpublished Ph.D. thesis, Dept. of Sociology, Univ. of Chicago, 1950).

very important; it is for this reason that the decision whether to proceed against the juvenile must sometimes wait until after arrest, when it can be determined whether the youth has a record.[20]

The most obvious reason why the police do not feel that petty juvenile offenders need to be arrested is that the offenses are not serious enough to justify official concern. In many cases a warning appears to accomplish all that is necessary. In other cases, although the police consider the juvenile's conduct serious enough to merit punishment, no arrest is made because the officer feels that the juvenile court is too lenient.[21]

The fact that special treatment is given to the juvenile offender following arrest, during trial, and in sentencing and correction might be thought to bring nonenforcement in this area into question. Since these procedures are designed to rehabilitate, it might be argued that it is desirable to subject all youths who commit crimes to arrest and thus to rehabilitative treatment.[22] This consideration does sometimes prompt a police officer to make an arrest in circumstances which would not be thought to merit the expenditure of police resources were an adult involved.[23] However, in many other cases, the police conclude either that the need for rehabilitative treatment is not great enough to justify the expenditure of their resources or that an arrest would have harmful consequences for the juvenile regardless of what the objectives of the juvenile process are in theory.

3. *Drunkenness.*

Illustration No. 3: A patrolman came upon a man staggering down the street. The man was clearly intoxicated but, while his gait was unsteady, he was able to walk without any great risk of falling. Upon questioning the man, the patrolman learned that he was on his way home and that he lived about a block away. No arrest was made.

Another offense which occurs frequently but is not subject to full enforcement is drunkenness. Even though the statutes in Kansas and

---

[20] While taking a juvenile offender to headquarters for a check on his record is considered an arrest, it may not be recorded as such if it is later decided that the youth will be released with a warning.

[21] Such opinions were not infrequently voiced by the police, and were particularly vehement when the police had expended a considerable amount of their resources. For example, one Detroit officer said, "We may go around here for months trying to figure out who in hell is committing a bunch of petty crimes. We finally apprehend the guy and bring him before a judge. But, since he is a juvenile, he gets off easy."

[22] For a discussion of police responsibilities in handling juvenile offenders see, Myren and Swanson, *Police Work With Children, op. cit.*

[23] Thus, although police do not usually arrest a shoplifter unless there is a prior assurance from the merchant that he desires prosecution [see page 198], some juvenile offenders are arrested for shoplifting without such assurance. This is because the officers know that the juvenile will be given special consideration later in the process, and they feel that this presents an opportunity for his guidance.

Michigan[24] prohibit being intoxicated in public, a substantial number of persons observed in such condition are not arrested.[25] If the person is not a habitual drunk, it is unusual for him to be taken into custody unless he cannot care for his own safety[26] or is likely to cause harm to another. If the drunk is creating a nuisance, this will increase the probability of arrest, but if the disturbance can be stopped and there does not appear to be a significant likelihood of further trouble, an arrest still might not be made.[27] Drunks are often told at the time of arrest that they are being arrested for their own protection, and this fact may be incorporated into the arrest report. An arrest is not usually made when the person evinces a willingness and ability to go home, and in this respect the proximity of the offender's home is a relevant factor.[28] In practice there is a lower level of tolerance for the "skid row" drunk, but this is because arrest is the only way in which to insure his safety.[29]

The intoxicated person who is most likely to cause harm to others is the one who is driving or who is likely to drive if not arrested. While arrest under these circumstances is more likely, the police sometimes utilize an alternative if one is available. Persons under the influence of alcohol who are seen entering cars may be allowed to take a cab home, and even those who have been stopped for erratic driving are sometimes permitted to

[24] Kan. Gen. Stat. §41–802 (1949). In Michigan a disorderly person is "any person who shall be drunk or intoxicated . . . in any public place." Mich. Stat. Ann. §28.364 (1938).

[25] Statutory language tending to reflect legislative recognition of such discretionary action is to be found only in Michigan. There the provision setting forth the duties of the chief of police of a city says: "He shall arrest upon view, and with or without process, any person found in the act of committing any offense against the laws of the state or the ordinances of the city amounting to a breach of the peace, and forthwith take such person before the proper magistrate or court for examination or trial, and *may* also without process *arrest and imprison persons found drunk in the streets.*" Mich. Stat. Ann. §5.1674 (1949) (emphasis supplied).

[26] The statutory definition of a drunken person in Wisconsin is "A person who is so intoxicated that he is unable to care for his own safety and is found in a public place in such condition." Wis. Stat. §947.03 (1955). This is not significantly different from the prior provision in Wis. Stat. §351.59 (1953).

[27] Thus, in Detroit, a drunk who had been arguing with patrons in a restaurant calmed down upon the arrival of the police and so was allowed to leave, whereas another highly intoxicated man who was found urinating on the sidewalk was arrested.

[28] Milwaukee officers entered a tavern in which the bartender pointed to a man slumped over a drink and said that he had refused to pay for his drink. When the officers ordered the man to pay, he did so and then stumbled off the stool and weaved toward the door. The officers learned that he lived only four doors away at a hotel, so they told him to get to the hotel as fast as he could or he would be arrested.

[29] This type of drunk creates the greatest problem in Detroit. A specialized "bum squad" patrols the skid row there, picking up the habituals and those who are "down and out."

park their car and resume their journey home by taxi.[30] One tactic which an officer may use when he finds a drunk sleeping in a car is to remove the keys from the ignition and either take them with him or hide them in the back seat of the car, or under the floor rug, thus insuring that the person will not drive until he is sufficiently sober to recover the keys.[31]

One situation which appears to provoke some disagreement between different agencies in the process, particularly in Michigan, is that concerning drunks found in taverns. The police apply the same test to these persons as that applied to those found drunk on the street. If the person appears to be unable to care for himself, and no responsible person is available to help him reach home safely,[32] an arrest is made. This practice is not approved by some judges,[33] who apparently feel that no arrest should be made unless a risk of harm on the street or highway is directly shown by actions of the drunk.

The police practice in all three states is substantially the same, though only Wisconsin has a statute which defines intoxication as a crime only when the person thereby puts himself in a helpless condition. The case of the occasional drunk is not considered serious, and even arresting the habitual drunk does not accomplish much, since there is little the system can do for him. The officer's knowledge of postarrest alternatives may influence his decision. Thus in Kansas, where the only procedure following arrest is prosecution, fewer arrests are made than in Detroit, where many arrests are followed by release without prosecution.[34]

Although the practice of not arresting for minor offenses is not limited to the three kinds of cases described above, the policy factors usually involved are indicated by these examples.

[30] Other drunks who are driving recklessly may not be so leniently treated, even though they are but a few blocks from home, if it is known by the officers that they have been apprehended for such conduct in the past.

[31] A Dane County, Wisconsin, deputy upheld this practice by stating that in his opinion a person who is intoxicated but who does get off the road should be commended and not punished by being brought in as a drunk. He indicated that the "hidden key" trick was commonly used in the county.

[32] While the police feel justified in telling bartenders or owners to see that the drunk gets home safely, they may doubt whether these persons are sufficiently reliable to be entrusted with the drunk's safety.

[33] An officer in one Michigan community ignored persons whom he found to be "stone drunk" while checking a local bar. He said: "Why bother to arrest them? There is just no use to this type of enforcement. The case will get thrown out of court in the municipal court."

[34] In a case observed in Recorder's Court, Detroit, the judge severely criticized the arresting officers for their actions in such a case. He said that although the defendant might have been drunk, he could not understand why the police were checking bars for drunks in the first place or why they had attempted to arrest the defendant when he was not "doing anything." [See note 5 supra.]

B. CONDUCT THOUGHT TO REFLECT THE STANDARDS OF A COMMUNITY SUBGROUP

Illustration No. 4: A report that a stabbing had taken place came in to the station of a precinct predominantly Negro in population. An officer reported to the address and learned that a Negro woman had seriously stabbed her husband with a pair of scissors. The husband commented that there had been a little argument and requested transportation to the hospital. The officer, who had served in the precinct for some time, had reported to such calls in the past and had received similar responses. Although the conduct constituted a felonious assault, no official action was taken.

Differential treatment of racial groups may take many forms in law enforcement. One possibility is that members of minority groups may be arrested or may have even more serious action taken against them when they have not in fact engaged in criminal conduct.[35] This quite obviously is improper. A second possibility is that laws which generally are not enforced may be enforced only when violated by members of certain minority groups. Such a practice is not so easy to evaluate, and it is harder for the individual defendant to establish, because it is almost impossible to present adequate proof of the discrimination.[36] A third possibility, and the one of concern here, is the failure to enforce certain laws which are enforced when members of certain minority groups are not involved. This obviously is not thought disadvantageous by the offender himself, but it may be of concern to the victim or to other members of the minority group.[37]

This kind of unequal enforcement of the law frequently occurs when

[35] E.g., Thompson v. City of Louisville, 362 U.S. 199, 80 Sup. Ct. 624, 4 L. Ed. 2d 654 (1960).

[36] In People v. Winters, 171 Cal. App. 2d Supp. 876, 342 P.2d 538 (Super. Ct. 1959), when a Negro trial judge dismissed a case on the basis of discriminatory enforcement of the gambling laws against Negroes, the court reversed his decision but without prejudice to the defendant's right to prove intentional or deliberate discriminatory enforcement. This would appear a formidable task, however.

While no instances of this kind of discriminatory law enforcement were observed, allegations to this effect were made. A Negro attorney objected to a police lieutenant in one Michigan community that while Negro gambling was proceeded against, a horse racing book for whites only two blocks from the police station was not. The lieutenant offered to make an arrest if the attorney would make a formal complaint, but the attorney declined the offer. These same charges were repeated in the Negro press shortly thereafter.

[37] "Equality of treatment implies also that there will be one standard of law enforcement in all areas within the community. Respectable members of a minority group do not appreciate the fact that minor criminals in their areas are sometimes treated like children, or are laughed at, when their violations are the type that run down the minority community, but do not seriously annoy the police or vocal complainants. It becomes particularly galling to them when, on the other hand, they

Negroes are involved, particularly in large metropolitan areas such as Detroit. Such offenses as bigamy and open and notorious cohabitation are overlooked by law enforcement officials,[38] and arrests often are not made for carrying knives[39] or for robbery of other Negroes.[40] However, the practice is most strikingly illustrated by the repeated failure of the police to arrest Negroes for a felonious assault upon a spouse or acquaintance unless the victim actually insists upon prosecution.

This practice is most apparent in one predominantly Negro precinct in Detroit. The average officer, after spending several months in that precinct, becomes accustomed to the offenses which he is regularly called upon to handle; he accepts the double standard and applies it without question.[41] He does not look upon a stabbing, for example, with the same degree of seriousness as would an officer in one of the other precincts. While settling differences with a knife cannot properly be called the established standard of behavior for Negroes, the officer repeatedly called to cases of this kind is apt to conclude that it is, particularly since his contacts with Negroes are usually confined to the law-breaking, and not the law-abiding, Negro. Thus what might appear to be an aggravated assault to an officer assigned elsewhere would, to the officer in this precinct, be looked upon merely as a family disturbance.

Usually the victim of such an assault does not wish to have the offender prosecuted. Even arrest is not usually desired; the police are called because they are able to provide the victim with ambulance service to the hospital. While the attitude of the victim is an important factor in the exercise of police discretion generally, the assault cases between Negroes are the only apparent situations in which the victim controls the arrest decision when the offense is a serious one. Although the reluctance of the victim to

feel that excessive police attention is given to other violations by their members. They sometimes allege the police make or fail to make arrests of their members to suit police convenience rather than the ends of justice." Brown, The Police and Community Conflict 19–20 (1962). This is a pamphlet distributed by the National Conference of Christians and Jews. It is prepared by a retired inspector of the New York City Police Department who had twenty-two years of service.

[38] These offenses came to official attention principally when aid to dependent children was sought or when a domestic dispute was being dealt with.

[39] A car occupied by ten Negro youths was stopped and switch-blade knives were found on each of them. The knives were taken, but no arrests were made.

[40] Only one such case was observed, and the facts are unusual because the offender recouped his losses at gunpoint from his co-gamblers but then returned the money before the police located him.

[41] One exception was the officer who reflected that perhaps the department should begin signing complaints in these cases despite the protest of the victim. This officer appeared principally concerned with decreasing the number of calls to the police. This proposal would seem to approve the present lower standard of enforcement in Negro communities, since, if successful, it would result not in less crimes being committed, but in less crimes coming to police attention.

cooperate makes successful prosecution difficult and in many cases impossible, the willingness of the police to accept the decision of the victim indicates that they are not greatly concerned about the problem.

The Negro press sometimes accuses the police of discrimination solely on the grounds that more Negroes are being arrested than whites.[42] Nonenforcement in Negro assault cases has the effect of keeping down Negro arrest statistics and thus is sometimes thought to have the added benefit of deterring criticism. While there is no reason to believe that this is the only cause of the practice, the attitude of the Negro press is hardly conducive to the adoption of a nondiscriminatory policy.[43]

The fact that the practice of not arresting in Negro assault cases is more prevalent in Detroit than elsewhere[44] undoubtedly reflects the higher

[42] Frequent criticism of the Negro press was heard. Similarly, one Philadelphia policeman is quoted in another study as saying: "I don't know what the answer is. I think the Negro press plays up the wrong angle. Sometimes they hurt things instead of helping. It's got so now that some white cops hate to arrest a Negro. They know if there's any trouble the press will play it up to look bad for the cop." Kephart, Racial Factors and Urban Law Enforcement 66 (1957). Similarly, a Negro patrolman, when asked if he was discouraged by the high Negro crime rate, replied: "No, I don't get discouraged. It's just being handled all wrong. The cops, the magistrates, the judges—everybody's afraid to crack down, especially with the Negro press yelling discrimination all the time." Id. at 119. Kephart reports that police of all ranks and both races were interviewed and all condemned local Negro newspapers. Id. at 147.

[43] Chief Parker of Los Angeles, in one of a series of interviews on the American character published by the Center for the Study of Democratic Institutions, said: "One of the real problems has been the resentment of some minority groups because of the publication of the high amount of crime attributed to these groups. From the police standpoint, however, that incidence of crime is a fact. The social and economic conditions that contribute to this high rate of criminal activity is another matter. . . . In the last meeting with the commission on human rights I made it clear that I was disturbed about the consistently inflammatory criticism of the police in the press published by one of these minority groups. I challenged this group. . . . They accepted the challenge. A little later there was a most amazing editorial in the leading newspaper of this group. It stated, calmly and objectively, that their people must stop blaming the police for their own criminal activity. It admitted that there was a great deal of crime and it went on to say that a man who holds up another person with a gun must expect vigorous and prompt action by the police, regardless of whether he is a member of a minority group or not. It was a magnificent, thorough treatise on the subject and represents a real breakthrough in this matter. We had never seen such an editorial." Center for the Study of Democratic Institutions, The Police 15–16 (1962).

[44] In Milwaukee a definite attempt has been made to eliminate any prejudice against, and unfair treatment of, the Negro section of the community. Great care is taken in the selection of officers for duty in Negro areas. Police commanders said that, if a policeman was believed to be prejudiced against Negroes, he was assigned to an area where he was not likely to be called upon to deal with them; and cases of overt prejudice would be grounds for disciplinary action. The Negro in Milwaukee VII, The Milwaukee Journal, May 30, 1960, p. 22, col. 1–5. On more than

concentration of Negro population there.[45] In such areas, there is apt to be more of a disparity between Negro crime and the resources which the police administrator has to deal with the problem.

The basic question is: To what extent, if at all, is it ever justifiable to take into account the customs, practices, and prevailing standard of conduct of an identifiable subcultural group in determining whether the process should be invoked against a member of that group?[46] The problem was defined by a Negro assistant prosecutor in these terms:

Negroes have been struggling for many years to secure their civil and legal rights through such organizations as the NAACP, but there has been too little emphasis placed upon the Negro's duty to assume responsibility for acts of violence and not to expect differential treatment. But it will take cooperation by the white people as well. There is too much of a tendency on the part of police officers, juries, and even judges to dismiss Negro crimes of violence with the saying, "It's only Negroes, and they've always been like that." Too many Negroes expect to escape lightly in crimes of this nature, and with some justification, as those in authority have actually condoned such offenses by taking them so lightly.

The obvious dilemma is that the Negro continues to be judged by a different standard because it is assumed that he has a greater tolerance for certain kinds of antisocial conduct, and existing differences in attitude are probably reinforced by the fact that different standards are applied by enforcement agencies.

C. VICTIM DOES NOT OR WILL NOT REQUEST PROSECUTION

Police nonenforcement is also the rule when the victim of a minor offense does not wish to expend his own time in the interests of successful

---

one occasion observation was made of the courteous manner in which these officers treated Negroes.

It might be argued that the double standard can still prevail despite these highly successful attempts to combat the other manifestations of discrimination. The data from Milwaukee do not allow a conclusive judgment, as noninvocation against Negroes was observed only with regard to lesser assaults. But in some of the instances it appeared likely that an arrest would have resulted had the parties been white.

[45] Detroit had a population 16.2 per cent Negro in the 1950 census, while Milwaukee had only 3.4 per cent. See Kephart, Racial Factors and Urban Law Enforcement 135 (1957).

[46] The criminal law has rarely considered cultural differences, although the problem has arisen when a given set of laws has been imposed upon territories with a population unlike that of the lawmakers. See Howard, What Colour Is the "Reasonable Man"? 1961 Crim. L. Rev. (Eng.) 41; Marsack, Provocation in Trials for Murder, 1959 Crim. L. Rev. (Eng.) 697.

prosecution. This occurs not only with minor property crimes, when the victim is concerned primarily with restitution, but also with many offenses arising out of family relationships or other associations, such as that between landlord and tenant or employer and employee.

The reluctance of the victim to prosecute makes conviction difficult or impossible and is at least some indication that the offense is not serious enough to justify the expenditure of time and effort of the police and prosecutor.[47] In those cases arising out of a private relationship, resolution of the difficulty without prosecution may appear to be a more desirable alternative. For these reasons, the police frequently decide to apply their resources to other offenses.

1. *Victim interested only in restitution.*

Illustration No. 5: A merchant called the police after having apprehended a shoplifter in his store. When the merchant was asked by the officer whether he was willing to appear in court to testify, he replied that he could not take time out from his work for this. The officer declined to arrest the shoplifter.

When small amounts of property have been taken without force or violence, the criminal process is not usually invoked unless the victim indicates that he is willing to cooperate in the prosecution of the case. In cases in which the police recover all or a substantial portion of the stolen property, it is likely that the victim will ask that the matter be dropped so that he need not take the time to appear in court. The police usually do not take further action in such cases.[48] Cases of larceny are frequently

---

[47] The fact that the victim does not desire prosecution will be disregarded in some offenses where the damage is minor if the police consider the conduct serious. The following excerpt, from a newspaper report on enforcement against the hit-and-run offender, is particularly revealing. "Often his offense is minor, but affects the owner of the other car disproportionately. In a routine case handled in the traffic court last week, for example, the owner of a damaged parked car spent an entire morning 'doing nothing,' he said, 'but following the policeman around.'

"In this case, the other driver pleaded not guilty, said he did not think he had damaged the other car much, accepted a fine of $10 (with costs, it came to $24.50) and went home. The owner of the damaged car received assurances that his car would be fixed, collected a witness fee of $5.50 but lost $25 in wages because he had to appear in court instead of at his job.

"Some car owners, not wanting to be bothered with the lengthy processes of justice, refuse to sign complaints against hit-run drivers if they know their own damages will be taken care of.

"This attitude, needless to say, does not serve the cause of justice. Investigating officers, questioning a witness reluctant to give information about a hit-runner, ask: 'How would you feel if it had been your car—or your child—that was hit?' The witnesses usually come through." Milwaukee Journal, Dec. 10, 1959, pt. 1m, p. 4, col. 3.

[48] For example, in Wichita, a man found that his wallet, containing $750, was missing the morning after he had been on a drinking spree with two other men. He could not recall the events of the prior evening. The police suggested that his

concluded in this way, as is an occasional burglary. If force or violence has been used in obtaining the property, however, the victim's desire is seldom determinative, although action might not be taken if the act was impulsive and the victim is an acquaintance of the offender.[49] In any of these cases, if the police have already expended considerable resources in investigating the offense, they are less likely to abide by the victim's wishes. In fact, in such a case steps will probably be taken to persuade the victim to commit himself to cooperate in the prosecution.[50]

Probably the most significant category of conduct in which recovery of the stolen property concludes the victim's interest in prosecution is shoplifting. When shoplifters are caught, they are usually apprehended in the act, which results in immediate recovery of the stolen goods. Merchants generally are unwilling to prosecute, asserting that they cannot afford the time away from the store to testify in court or that they do not want to risk a loss of good will.[51] The police reaction is typified by the following statement by an experienced officer to a "rookie":

---

two companions of that evening take a lie detector test. One did so, but the other refused. The police continued to pressure the latter, who eventually reported that he had "found" $680 in his clothes. He agreed to turn this over to the victim. The police learned that the victim did not wish to prosecute, so no arrest was made.

[49] For example, when a man who had been participating in a gambling game retrieved his losses by taking $64 from the other players at gunpoint, the victims complained to the police and a warrant was obtained, apparently because the offender's whereabouts was then unknown. An attempt to serve the warrant was made a few days later, and the offender told the officers that when he had sobered up after this incident he had had feelings of remorse and had since returned the money and given the gun to a friend. The officers told him the incident could be closed if he would turn the gun in to the police, which he promised to do. No arrest was made.

[50] A Wichita barber reported a burglary from his shop. After considerable investigation, the missing items were found in local pawnshops by the police. The pawn tickets bore the name of a recent employee of the barber. The barber indicated that he did not want to prosecute. This was probably because he had recovered the property and he would have had to spend time away from his shop as a witness. Nonetheless, the detectives pressured him into signing a complaint, and a search for the offender was begun. Very likely the victim's attitude was not honored here because the police had already expended considerable time in investigation of the crime. The fact that the former employee had a long criminal record, including two prior felony convictions, may also be significant.

[51] In a recent commentary on the increase of shoplifting and the means being employed to combat it, the following appears with regard to shoplifting by youths. "Reactions of parents are equally distressing: a few bring the child back to the store to apologize, but most parents in this well-to-do community either (a) stop trading at that particular store or (b) become highly indignant and overprotective, claiming the manager doesn't know what he's talking about: 'Why, Junior goes around all the time with $5 in his pocket!'" Wharton, Shoplifting—Newest Crime Wave, Family Weekly, March 17, 1963, p. 8.

Now if that situation ever comes up with you, don't take the person to the station unless you can get somebody to agree to sign a complaint. When I first got on, I went to this store just like we did tonight. I took the shoplifter to the station, booked him through, and then one of the policewomen came up and asked me who the complainant was. Being green, I just looked at her and said, "I don't know." The policewoman informed me that the best thing to do was to turn the individual loose, and that it was a good thing we had not booked him in county jail.

For a while this store manager would not sign complaints; all he wanted the police to do was to throw a little scare into the suspect and get him out of his hair. Now, however, since we have adopted the policy of not taking them unless he will sign a complaint, things have improved, and he only calls when he intends to sign a complaint.

Thus nonenforcement in this type of situation conserves police resources in two ways: no further action need be taken in the particular case, and calls for police service from merchants are substantially diminished.[52]

Illustration No. 6: A merchant turned over a "no account" check to the police, requesting apprehension of the writer. The merchant was asked whether he was willing to appear in court when the offender was prosecuted, and he replied that he only wanted to collect the amount of the check. The police refused to take any action.

Usually, when a minor property crime is reported, the police ask whether the victim is willing to prosecute before deciding whether to arrest. While this issue may arise in a variety of situations,[53] it occurs most often in reports of bad checks by merchants.

It is important at the outset to distinguish between three kinds of bad checks. One is the check with a forged signature; the second is the no-account check, to which the writer has signed his own name but which is written on a bank where he has no account; and the third is the "NSF" check, to which the writer has signed his own name but for which his account has insufficient funds. Police view the forgery as the most serious and the no-account check as more serious than the check written without sufficient funds. The victim's reluctance to prosecute, therefore, is likely to be given the greatest weight in the insufficient funds situation.

[52] For similar conclusions, see Goldman, The Differential Selection of Juvenile Offenders for Court Appearance 161–166 (unpublished Ph.D. thesis No. T 914, Dept. of Sociology, Univ. of Chicago, 1950).

[53] Thus when a woman called a Detroit precinct and reported that in the course of paying for her meal in a restaurant she had been cheated of some money, the lieutenant answering the call suggested she report to the station so that a complaint could be made out against the person who had cheated her. When the woman replied that she only wanted her money back, the lieutenant said: "Then, madam, you have the wrong department. Please call the Lonely Hearts Club of the Detroit Free Press."

In Michigan, the practice is to proceed against forgers regardless of the attitude of the victim, although forgery ordinarily requires the expenditure of police time and resources to identify the offender.[54] In some parts of Kansas, on the other hand, the police are hesitant to proceed with investigations unless the victim promises to cooperate in prosecution of the offender after he is found. The Milwaukee policy is to refer these check complaints to the documents examiner. After identification is made, the complainant is contacted, and, if he is willing to appear in court, a warrant is obtained and the case is assigned to detectives, who then arrest the suspect. The fact that in Milwaukee the investigation is made first suggests that the police will make an effort to prosecute regardless of the victim's desires if the case involves a serious forgery or a repeating offender.

The victim's attitude is most often decisive in the case of insufficient funds checks and is only slightly less so in the case of no-account checks. Many of these cases are not brought to the attention of the police. Instead, complainants go directly to the prosecutor's office, probably because it is widely known that the prosecutor sometimes aids in the collection of bad checks.[55] In cases which do come directly to the police, the victim is first asked whether he is willing to take the time to appear in court to testify, and if the answer is negative the police indicate that they will take no action in the case. Thus in Detroit a set of instructions for the use of precinct detectives in such cases asks: "Is the complainant willing to prosecute? (If the check is being reported merely as an aid to collection, the police department is not interested, and the check cannot be accepted as a complaint.)" Insuring that the complainant will prosecute may be more essential when considerable expense will be involved in preparing the case for prosecution. These instructions continue:

It is well to caution the complainant that in the event that the check is drawn on an out-of-state bank account, unless the writer of the check admits that he has no account (or insufficient funds in that bank) it will be necessary for the county to bring in an officer from that bank to testify as to the status of the defendant's account (or lack of it). For that reason, the complainant may be required to post a cash bond guaranteeing prosecution in the case.

Customarily in Wisconsin, and to a somewhat lesser extent in the other two states, bad check complainants are referred by the police to the prose-

---

[54] In Detroit, forged checks are handled by a specialized unit, the check detail of the general services bureau of the detective division. The Michigan State Police have a fraudulent check section of the special investigation squad, which maintains a statewide central record file on bogus checks passed in Michigan. A highly developed system is employed for determining, from examination of the check, whether it was written by a known forger.

[55] On complainants going directly to the prosecutor, see page 36 [LaFave, *Arrest: The Decision to Take a Suspect into Custody*].

cutor's office, thus leaving the decision whether to invoke the process to the prosecutor.[56] There appear to be several reasons for this. First, there is usually no need for immediate police action, so that the decision whether to arrest can be made after such investigations as the prosecutor wishes to make. Second, except in forgery cases there is no particular need for police investigative skills, as the identity of the offender is known. Also, the typical bad check case is not of particular concern to the police because there is no connection with organized crime. Another important factor is that resort to the complaint-warrant process, which involves the prosecutor, tends to commit the complainant to further cooperation. Finally, the police view restitution as insufficient cause for expenditure of their resources,[57] and they are also concerned with the possibility of tort liability resulting from an arrest to effect restitution.[58]

A decision not to invoke is clearly involved here, in the sense that the police are aware of an offense but take no affirmative action. This becomes more apparent when one considers the general facts already noted concerning the practice in the three states: (a) the initial inquiry of the police is always as to whether the complainant is willing to prosecute; (b) arrests, if any, are made only when the police are certain that the victim agrees to prosecution;[59] (c) referral to the prosecutor is not always made, since reluctant victims are sometimes told that nothing can be done for them; and (d) even when there is referral, the police do not try to determine whether the victim will cooperate, leaving the burden solely on the prosecutor.

[56] On police referral to the prosecutor generally, see page 47 [LaFave, *ibid*.].

[57] The police policy of not aiding merchants seeking only restitution results in fewer complaints being made to the police. One inspector in the Detroit department, after reading some statistical sheets, said: "There was an 11% drop in complaints, department wide, from 1955 to 1956. This was due to greater selectivity in taking a case from a merchant who would indicate immediately his unwillingness to prosecute on an NSF check."

[58] Bergeron v. Peyton, 106 Wis. 377, 82 N.W. 291 (1900). An officer took Bergeron to the bank where he had been overpaid on a check, and, when Bergeron refused to return the excess, the officer took him to the magistrate. Since the jury found the arrest was "for the sole purpose of compelling and inducing him to repay . . . the $43 thus overpaid . . . ," the court held the arrest illegal and the officer liable for damages, even though the officer had taken the offender directly to the magistrate when he refused the opportunity to make restitution. But in a Kansas case, apparently in answer to an assertion that an arrest had been made to influence payment of a debt, the court said that "if the arrest was lawful the motive for it was immaterial" but that the arrest must have been made "in good faith." Atchison, T. & S.F. Ry. v. Hinsdell, 76 Kan. 74, 90 Pac. 800 (1907).

[59] In Detroit, the police also usually give the offender an opportunity to make restitution and thus avoid being arrested. There is some evidence that this is less usual in other parts of Michigan, where the offender may be arrested and brought before a justice of the peace, and only then given the opportunity to make restitution.

2. *Victim in continuing relationship with offender.*

Illustration No. 7: An officer responding to a call learned that the complainant wanted his neighbor arrested for tearing down a part of his fence. The officer's investigation disclosed that this was merely the latest chapter in a continued neighborhood dispute between the complainant and offender. Although the property destruction was a criminal violation, the officer declined to take any official action.

A combination of factors may result in nonenforcement when the criminal conduct involves two persons who are in a continuing legitimate relationship with each other, such as neighbors, landlord and tenant, or parties to a contract. Generally, the police feel that such disputes are principally private in nature and that so long as the conduct is not serious, enforcement resources need not be diverted to it.

Obviously an arrest should not be made when the conduct is not criminal and would warrant only a civil action. The police are warned against acting in such cases[60] and in fact do refuse assistance.[61] However, they may not arrest even when the conduct is criminal if a civil remedy is available to the injured party. The availability of a civil remedy is thought adequate by the police, and their hesitation to act may be increased by a fear of giving an undue advantage to one of the parties. Also, the fact that the victim can resolve his difficulty by terminating his relationship with the offender is important. Thus a landlord was advised to evict his tenant when he wanted criminal action brought against a member of the tenant's household who caused malicious damage to the premises.[62] Similarly, an employer

[60] Detroit police are told: "Members of the Department shall render no assistance whatever in civil cases, or advise parties involved, except to prevent a breach of the peace or to quell a disturbance actually commenced." Detroit Police Dept., Revised Police Manual, chap. 10, §25 (1955). Similarly, in Wichita the police are instructed: "Officers shall not render assistance in civil cases, except to prevent an immediate breach of the peace or to quell a disturbance actually commenced." Wichita Police Dept., Duty Manual 11 (undated).

[61] For example, a Detroit station lieutenant received a call from a man who said that his wife had left him and was now in a bar. The lieutenant told the complainant that no police action was warranted in this case and that the man should go to the bar himself and tell his wife to come home. "You want an officer to be a witness in a civil matter and we are not going to do it. I will give you help if it is a criminal matter and a criminal matter only. If she is leaving you that is a civil matter."

[62] The Michigan state policeman responding to the call learned that the landlord's primary interest was in having his door replaced. The trooper advised: "That won't do very much good. He probably is smart enough to know that there is not much that can be done unless you swear out a complaint form. And then if you do that there is no telling what will happen after that. If the man does go to jail for thirty days, you still haven't got your door repaired, and in a sense you are still paying for it because you are supporting him while he is in jail. It may be that you will have to handle this case civilly. Frankly, I think the best thing for you to do would be to order these people to move and get rid of the problem that way."

was told that he could handle the situation himself when a minor burglary was found to be an "inside job" perpetrated by an employee.

In such cases, the police are not likely to take any action unless the victim asserts a strong desire for prosecution. They may even discourage the complainant if they feel that he is motivated by spite and that prosecution would only strain a necessarily continuing relationship, such as that between neighbors. The continuing relationship also makes it more likely that the victim will change his mind about prosecution.

Often the police refer these matters to another agency. Putting the burden on the victim to see the prosecutor or magistrate conserves police resources in two ways: first, no action is necessary unless the victim fails to "cool off" and continues his demand for prosecution;[63] and, second, future complaints of this kind to the police are likely to diminish. The police feel that other agencies should take care of restitution cases. The exception is Detroit, where a specialized agency within the police department itself will aid insistent complainants in obtaining restitution.[64]

3. *Victim a member of offender's family.*

Illustration No. 8: A call was received at the precinct reporting a disturbance of the peace. The officer responding to the call found that the disturbance was due to a family squabble. Although the man was still hitting his wife when the officer arrived, the officer did not make an arrest but merely restored order and left.

The police are sometimes advised to avoid arrest in domestic disputes where possible. For example, the Detroit Police Manual provides:

When a police officer is called to a disturbance in a private home having family difficulties, he should recognize the sanctity of the home and endeavor diplomatically to quell the disturbance and create peace without making an arrest.[65]

[63] The clerk of police court in Wauwatosa, Wisconsin, said that the police often refer complainants in neighborhood quarrels to the justice of the peace for the determination of whether a warrant should be issued. It does not appear that the police believe that this justice is any more qualified to make the determination. Rather, this referral, which usually entails a "cooling-off" period since the justice is available only on Mondays and Tuesdays, again tests the complainant's willingness to see the case through prosecution.

[64] This specialized agency is the prosecutor's bureau of the detective division. Within this bureau is the Misdemeanor Complaint Bureau, which handles neighborhood disputes and other quasi-civil cases. In 1956 this bureau investigated 5791 cases, of which 123 were found to be civil in nature, which may mean either purely civil or primarily civil. Also within the prosecutor's bureau is the felony detail, which handles embezzlement, larceny by conversion, false pretenses and other frauds, blue sky violations, and similar offenses. Unlike the average patrolman, felony detail personnel are not concerned with the motive of the complainant; if restitution appears to be the motive they work toward this result.

[65] Of course, if the offense is only a misdemeanor, arrest without warrant is not

In any case where an officer suspects that a disturbance may result in the injury of any person, it is advisable for the officer to take the person causing such disturbance into custody, at least temporarily, even though it may be against the wishes of the family involved.[66]

This is the policy generally followed in all three states.[67] The police dislike becoming involved in family disputes,[68] and calls for service may be refused when it does not appear that arrest is essential to maintain order,[69] or when demands upon police services are particularly heavy.[70]

In any event, an officer is unlikely to make an arrest in cases of intra-family disturbances involving minor offenses such as unaggravated assaults[71] if the offended spouse does not insist upon prosecution.[72] Even if the victim-spouse asserts a desire to prosecute, the officers may still refrain from arresting if it appears likely that the victim will later change his or

---

possible, except in Wisconsin, if it occurred prior to the officer's arrival. But the officers could obtain a warrant, and if immediate arrest were actually desired they might resort to a variety of devices to accomplish this. . . .

[66] Detroit Police Dept., Revised Police Manual, chap. 16, §22 (1955).

[67] For example, when a Detroit officer reported to a family dispute in which a man had struck his wife, the officer told the man that he was acquainted with the man's employer and cautioned him that any further trouble might result in his losing his job. When the husband promised not to resort to physical violence again the officer departed.

[68] Confirming this is the statement of a police official quoted in another study: "You know, if there is one thing these men hate more than anything else it is to go out on a call for a family quarrel. You ought to see their faces when they hear that call come over the radio." Westley, The Police: A Sociological Study of Law, Custom and Morality 115 (unpublished Ph.D. thesis No. 1197, Dept. of Sociology, Univ. of Chicago, 1951).

[69] For example, a woman called a Michigan State Police post to complain about domestic trouble. The corporal on duty suggested that the woman spend the night elsewhere and then reprimanded the husband over the phone, but declined to send an officer out to make an arrest. Both parties were informed that the state police have no right to take action in a problem such as this except to preserve the peace.

[70] Especially during the hours when police patrol cars are most busy, Detroit precinct dispatchers screen out those family disturbances in which there does not appear to be any threat of excessive violence.

[71] Occasionally officers also decide not to arrest in cases of intrafamily felonious assault, but this was rarely observed except where the parties were Negroes [see page 194] or persons the police referred to as "hillbillies."

[72] Undoubtedly the law could be drafted so as to require such demand by the spouse in this case, just as with adultery and intrafamily thefts. See Model Penal Code §§206.13(4), 207.1, Comment (10) (Tent. Draft No. 4, 1955). The adultery provision was subsequently deleted from the Code, and the theft provision was changed so that misappropriation of household and personal effects, or other property normally accessible to both spouses, is characterized as theft only if the parties have ceased living together. Model Penal Code §223.1(4) (Proposed Official Draft, 1962).

her mind.[73] Because the police do not wish to expend resources on cases in which the victim will later refuse to cooperate in prosecution, steps are sometimes taken to make it difficult for the insistent victim to change his mind later. In Wichita, the victim-spouse may be taken to the station immediately to sign a complaint before arrest,[74] or the victim may also be arrested in an attempt to insure appearance in court the following day. In Milwaukee the police determine the victim's true desires by giving him a referral memorandum which may later be used to obtain a warrant. The clerk of municipal court, who issues warrants in both ordinance and statute violation cases, will issue warrants under a charge of common drunk or assault upon complaint of the spouse only after a three-day "cooling-off" period.[75] In Detroit the police try to discourage prosecution by the victim-spouse, but they may refer the spouse to the Misdemeanor Complaint Bureau, which does undertake to mediate more serious family disputes. The full burden is on the victim, who must go to the Misdemeanor Complaint Bureau, and no arrest is made in cases where mediation is the goal.[76]

There are exceptions to this policy. Sometimes the circumstances are such that arrest becomes necessary regardless of the offended spouse's attitude. For example, if the police have had to respond to the same address on a number of occasions, an arrest will be made. Also, if the officer feels that the incident cannot be closed by a brief lecture, the offender will be taken into custody.[77] Finally, a threat of subsequent serious harm will

[73] A Detroit scout car was dispatched to a family dispute. Questioning disclosed that each party was guilty of having assaulted the other. Both asserted that they desired to have the other party prosecuted. However, one officer recalled having been called to this household on a previous occasion and having made an arrest because the victim expressed a desire to prosecute. But he also recalled that the victim had undergone a change of heart the following day, which resulted in the offender's release. Therefore no arrest was made on this occasion. Rather the husband was told to leave the house for the remainder of the night.

[74] Use of this method may also be prompted by an attempt to circumvent the in-presence arrest requirement.

[75] Occasionally, in an aggravated case such as one in which it appears that the husband is likely to resume the conduct, an attempt may be made by the prosecutor to have the warrant issued immediately.

[76] The Misdemeanor Complaint Bureau which handles neighborhood and family disputes seeks to avoid criminal prosecution. Because the offenses within its jurisdiction usually arise out of private transactions and are of such a nature that they would also be a basis for civil action, it is thought best to settle the matter by resort to mediation where possible. Only when a private settlement cannot be reached is a criminal prosecution undertaken.

[77] Of course, the police are not always able to predict whether any further trouble is likely. In the situation described in note 73 *supra*, the husband later returned to the house and the dispute was resumed. This time the officers arrested without any inquiry concerning the victim's desire to prosecute.

prompt a decision to arrest even when the victim does not desire prosecution.[78]

D. VICTIM INVOLVED IN MISCONDUCT

Illustration No. 9: A man entered a precinct station and complained that
he had just been cheated of $20. Asked to explain, he said that he had given
the money to a prostitute who had agreed to meet him at a certain time and
place, but that she had failed to appear. The police, although familiar with
this kind of racket, subjected the complainant to some ridicule, suggested that
he had learned his lesson, and sent him on his way.

In some situations a crime is committed upon a person who is himself
engaged in criminal conduct at the time. Indeed, the person's misconduct
often increases the likelihood that he will become a victim of criminal
action. Such is the case, for example, when a prostitute is mistreated as a
direct result of her illegal activity,[79] or when both parties to a fight are at
fault. Despite the fact that the criminal activity of the victim would not be
a defense in a criminal prosecution of the other party, the police are reluctant to arrest in such cases.[80]

The most frequently observed situation of this kind is that in which
a man has been tricked out of funds given to a prostitute or pimp. If the
victim is insistent the police may attempt to shame him out of desiring
police action, but if this is unsuccessful they may proceed to arrest the
offender. Often the police will question the victim in an attempt to determine the extent of his own culpability. He will be asked how long he has
lived in the vicinity, and an attempt will be made to learn whether he was
sufficiently familiar with the area to know that he was exposing himself
to this kind of offense by going there.

There is no established department policy to refuse to arrest under
these circumstances, and informal policy has not developed to the point
where all such cases are treated in the same way. An officer may detain
the prostitute long enough to obtain a return of the victim's money; he

[78] When Kansas City Police, in response to a call, found a woman cowering in
a corner and were told by her that her mentally unbalanced son had threatened
her with violence, they attempted to find the son so that he could be arrested, despite
the fact that the mother did not want him jailed.

[79] One case of this kind in which the police will take action is that in which
a prostitute is beaten or otherwise mistreated by her pimp. The police strongly
desire to prosecute panderers, and such a situation is about the only one in which
they can hope to have the prostitute testify against her pimp.

[80] No similar police reaction is to be found regarding the multitude of offenses
which involve what might be termed a "willing victim," such as prostitution, gambling,
and the illegal sale of liquor or narcotics.

may arrest and jail the prostitute; he may detain for a while both the prostitute and the man; or he may release the prostitute but detain the victim for a short time. Those officers who refuse to take action in these cases probably do so in part because they know that such a case cannot be successfully prosecuted. It is not likely that a warrant will be issued if the complainant does not have "clean hands," and judges are reluctant to convict in cases of this kind.[81]

[81] For example, in one case the judge asked the complainant to explain what had happened. The complainant stated that he had given the defendant $15 upon the defendant's promise to obtain some girls, and that the defendant had disappeared with the money. The judge asked again, "And you gave him the money?" The complainant answered, "Yes." The judge said, "And you did this on Hastings Street?" Again the complainant nodded in the affirmative. The judge dismissed the case.

5 White-Collar Crime and the Criminal Process

THE PRESIDENT'S COMMISSION
ON LAW ENFORCEMENT
AND ADMINISTRATION OF JUSTICE

EFFECTIVENESS OF CRIMINAL SANCTIONS

. . . Most persons convicted of common law crimes are likely to be young and to have serious educational and vocational lacks which rehabilitation programs can help meet. Presumably such programs are far less significant and will often be irrelevant for the white-collar offender.

Furthermore, with respect to many kinds of white-collar offenders long periods of incarceration or supervision are not needed to protect society from further criminality. For example, there appears to be only a negligible amount of recidivism among those convicted of certain white-collar crimes. Thus of the 1,186 persons convicted of criminal tax fraud in 1963 and 1964, only 2 persons were repeat offenders.[1] On the other hand, among some classes of white-collar offenders, such as those guilty of cheating consumers, recidivism may be a serious problem.

There is, unfortunately, no hard evidence available regarding the deterrent effect of criminal sanctions. This was vividly illustrated when in a 1964 tax case the Justice Department was asked to submit a memorandum

Reprinted from "White Collar Crime," *Task Force Report: Crime and Its Impact—An Assessment*, Task Force on Assessment—The President's Commission on Law Enforcement and Administration of Justice (Washington: Government Printing Office, 1967), ch. 8, pp. 104–108.

[1] See Robert E. Lane, "Why Businessmen Violate the Law," 44 *J. Crim. L., C. & P.S.* 151 (1953).

to the court justifying imposition of a 4-month jail term and a $10,000 fine as a deterrent. The only significant data produced were figures indicating that recidivism among tax violators was minimal, and a case study from Israel which indicated that since 1956, when the government had adopted a program of criminal prosecutions for tax evasion, there had been a graphic increase in the amount of income declared for taxation.[2] There is a clear need for further research into the effectiveness of criminal sanctions in this area. We need to know, for example, more about the comparative deterrent effects of prosecution, publicity, a jail sentence, a criminal fine, and civil damages. To this end, the IRS and the Justice Department recently engaged the National Opinion Research Center of the University of Chicago to conduct a survey of public attitudes toward the administration, enforcement and infringement of the tax laws.

Despite the lack of hard evidence, common sense notions about how people behave support the thesis that the condemnatory and deterrent aspects of criminal sanctions are likely to be peculiarly effective in the white-collar area. Persons who have standing and roots in a community, and are prepared for and engaged in legitimate occupations, can be expected to be particularly susceptible to the threat of criminal prosecution. Criminal proceedings and the imposition of sanctions have a much sharper impact upon those who have not been hardened by previous contact with the criminal justice system. Moreover, white-collar crimes as a class are more likely than common law crimes to be preceded by some deliberation; there is therefore more often an opportunity to calculate the risk objectively.

It appears further that jail sentences, however short, would constitute particularly significant deterrents for white-collar crime. The imposition of jail sentences may be the only way adequately to symbolize society's condemnation of the behavior in question, particularly where it is not on its face brutal or repulsive. And jail may be the only sanction available which will serve as an adequate deterrent.

These impressions are supported by the opinions of those who have had experience with the enforcement of the tax and antitrust laws.

No one in direct contact with the living reality of business conduct in the United States is unaware of the effect the imprisonment of seven high officials in the Electrical Machinery Industry in 1960 had on the conspiratorial price fixing in many areas of our economy; similar sentences in a few cases each decade would almost completely cleanse our economy of the cancer of collusive price fixing and the mere prospect of such sentences is itself the strongest available deterrent to such activities.[3]

---

[2] Government brief, *United States v. Dugan* (Dist. Ct. Mass., 1964), U.S. Department of Justice files 5–36–2843.

[3] Spivack (Director of Operations, Antitrust Division, U.S. Department of Justice), "Antitrust Enforcement, A Primer," 37 Conn. B. J. 375, 382 (1963).

The Department of Justice believes that imprisonment may often be the appropriate penalty for a clear-cut antitrust violation, such as price fixing. The attached paper [refers to Attachment A, pp. 109–112, not included in this selection] points out that criminal fines or civil damages may be inadequate for a number of reasons: present statutory maximums often make criminal fines trivial for corporations[4] in proportion both to their ability to pay and to the profits resulting from the criminal violations; in a number of States corporate executives may be lawfully reimbursed by the corporation for fines imposed on them; and since discovery of criminal violations of the antitrust laws is very difficult, even substantial civil penalties may not constitute adequate deterrents.[5]

Significantly, the Antitrust Division does not feel that lengthy prison sentences are ordinarily called for. It "rarely recommends jail sentences greater than 6 months—recommendations of 30-day imprisonment are most frequent."

In tax cases, the Justice Department also considers criminal sanctions, and jail sentences in particular, of significant value as deterrents. It is the Tax Division's policy to recommend jail sentences for all defendants convicted of tax fraud whenever the court requests a recommendation. James V. Bennett, former Director of the Federal Bureau of Prisons, has taken the position that the effort to deter misconduct by imposing relatively harsh penalties, while often a feeble thing in regard to traditional crime, "has had a most benign effect on those who do not like to pay taxes."[6]

But it is clear that the criminal law is not an appropriate means of dealing with all kinds of white-collar misconduct. Since white-collar misconduct usually does not involve an act which, like robbery, burglary or rape, is of a simple and dramatic predatory nature, it is inevitable that one of the critical and difficult issues is determining when the violation is clear-cut enough to warrant use of society's ultimate method of control. A great deal of business is now subject to regulations whose interpretation is not at all clear. The language of the Sherman Act, for example, is extremely broad and abstract, and has been subject to varying administrative and judicial interpretations. As pointed out in the attached paper, the Antitrust Division's solution has been to seek criminal sanctions only where there has been an intentional violation of clear and established rules of law. Where misconduct does not constitute such a violation, the Antitrust Division pursues civil remedies in place of criminal sanctions.

But the law is often adequately unambiguous. The offenders in the

[4] Between 1890 and 1955 the Sherman Act provided for a fine not to exceed $5,000. This amount was raised to $50,000 in 1955.

[5] See Alan M. Dershowitz, "Increasing Community Control Over Corporate Crime: A Problem in the Law of Sanctions," 71 *Yale L. J.* 280 (1961).

[6] James V. Bennett, "After Sentence—What?" 45 *J. Crim., L., C. & P.S.* 537 (1955).

Electrical Equipment cases were, for example, quite aware that their activities were in violation of the law. As one of the violators testified:

> [I]t was considered discreet to not be too obvious and to minimize telephone calls, to use plain envelopes if mailing material to each other, not to be seen together traveling, and so forth * * * not leave wastepaper, of which there was a lot, strewn around a room when leaving.[7]

The list of executives in attendance at meetings was referred to as the "Christmas card list," and the meetings as "choir practice."[8] The executives filed false travel vouchers in order to conceal their visits to the cities in which meetings were held.[9]

Aside from the question of ambiguity of the violation, it is important to recognize that a decision to use criminal sanctions involves costs and disadvantages which must be analyzed against the gains to be achieved and the alternative methods available to seek compliance. As discussed above, against many types of white-collar offenders application of criminal sanctions is likely to be highly effective in terms of deterrence. But this "economy" of sanction does not argue for an indiscriminate increase in the use of criminal sanctions. Among the economic and social costs involved in using criminal sanctions are the loss of services or serious curtailment of the usefulness of highly productive members of society, and the danger that greatly increased use of the criminal law would dilute its condemnatory effect. And there are many situations in which use of criminal sanctions may not be the most effective means of obtaining compliance with the law. Thus it is apparent that use of the withholding tax scheme has proved an extraordinarily efficient and effective method of preventing tax fraud. This is of course true in other areas of the law as well. Increased use of locks may be far more effective in reducing burglary and auto theft than an increase in police patrol. But the threat of criminal sanctions will often be an economical way to obtain compliance. In the tax area, for example, 80 million income tax returns are filed annually. It would be impractical to audit all of these and investigate all cases in which there was some reason for suspicion. The Tax Division audits only 4 percent of all returns filed. And the withholding tax scheme, while highly effective, can only ensure that income earned in the course of some regular employment is reported. The Government must therefore depend to a great extent on the deterrent effect of the threat of criminal sanctions.

Careful thought must be given to determining those areas in which use

[7] U.S. Senate, Subcommittee on Antitrust and Monopoly, Committee on the Judiciary, 87th Cong., 1st Sess., 1961, "Administered Price Hearings," pt. 28, p. 17395 [hereinafter cited as *Hearings*].

[8] Id., pt. 27, p. 17100.

[9] Id., pt. 27, p. 16760.

of criminal sanctions is appropriate and in which other means of enforcement will suffice. And sound prosecutorial discretion must be exercised in deciding which cases, among those that might technically involve criminal violations, should be selected for prosecution.

PRACTICAL PROBLEMS WITH THE USE OF CRIMINAL SANCTIONS

There are practical obstacles to enforcement of the laws relating to white-collar crime because of factors peculiar to this kind of criminality.

As noted previously, it is often extremely difficult even to discover the existence of white-collar crimes; it is similarly difficult to secure evidence of criminal guilt. White-collar crime may not stand out as unusual conduct when committed as would, for example, theft, burglary or assault. It may involve acts of omission rather than commission, which are less likely to be observed or noticed. It is often committed in the privacy of a business office or home. In addition, there may be no single victim or group of victims to complain to law enforcement authorities. Or victims may be unaware at the time of the offense that they have been victimized. Victims of consumer fraud are but one example. Moreover, the crime itself may be difficult to identify. It is often committed in the course of ordinary business activity and may not be significantly distinguishable from noncriminal business conduct. Especially where financial offenses are involved, the crime may be so technical that discovery is possible only after detailed and lengthy audit or economic analysis by specially trained law enforcement personnel with expertise in fields such as accounting and economics. Careful scrutiny of a huge mass of data for weeks or months may be necessary to produce the required evidence of criminality. A complicated security fraud investigation, for example, may involve several years of investigation by a team of law enforcement personnel.

A pervasive problem affecting enforcement is the fact that white-collar crime is often business crime and business crime is often corporate crime. Where corporate defendants are involved, the only criminal sanction available is the fine. As noted previously, fines may be inadequate as deterrents for a variety of reasons. There are also serious practical problems in imposing sanctions upon corporate employees. It is very difficult to obtain the conviction of the true policy formulators in large, complex corporations. The top executives do not ordinarily carry out the overt criminal acts—it is the lower or middle management officials who, for example, attend price-fixing meetings. Under traditional doctrines of complicity, to hold a superior responsible he must be shown actually to have participated in his subordinate's criminal activities, as by ordering the conduct or encouraging or aiding in its performance. It is very difficult to obtain evidence of such participation. Difficulties of proof have prevented the prosecution of top management in many Sherman Act cases.[10]

RESISTANCE TO THE USE OF CRIMINAL SANCTIONS

As important as the practical obstacles to effective law enforcement is society's reluctance to impose criminal sanctions upon the white-collar offender. Thus despite the apparent effect of the *Electrical Equipment* cases, in which seven individual executives received and served jail sentences, since that case no antitrust defendant has been imprisoned. In seven cases since then, involving 45 individual defendants, prison sentences were imposed, but in each case the sentence was suspended. During this time the Government has recommended that, out of 58 cases in which individual defendants were charged with criminal violations, prison sentences be imposed but suspended in seven cases, and imposed and served in 27 cases. The recommendations covered 105 individual defendants. Similarly, Marshall Clinard's study of a variety of rationing and other controls during the second World War revealed that the sentences imposed on OPA violators after conviction were relatively mild.[11]

While little is known of the public attitude toward white-collar crime, it is apparent that the present concern with crime is not directed at white-collar crime but at "crime on the streets." As one executive convicted and sentenced to jail in the *Electrical Equipment* conspiracy said:

[O]n the bright side for me personally have been the letters and calls from people all over the country, the community, the shops and offices here, expressing confidence in me and support. This demonstration has been a warm and humbling experience for me.[12]

But one attempt to measure public reactions to a form of white-collar crime—violations of the Federal Food, Drug and Cosmetic Act—indicated that the public would treat offenders more severely than the courts, although not as severely as persons guilty of such crimes as larceny and burglary. Consumers were asked to judge cases of food law violation in terms of how they would punish the offender. Six actual cases were selected, representing three types of violation—misbranding, distasteful but not physically harm-

---

[10] Dershowitz has recommended imposing upon corporate executives a duty, enforceable by criminal sanctions, to exercise reasonable care in preventing acquisitive crime within the area of corporate business under their control. Alan M. Dershowitz, supra n. 5.

[11] Marshall Clinard, "Criminological Theories of Violations of Wartime Regulations," 11 *Amer. Soc. Rev.* 258, 261 (1946).

[12] Schenectady & Union-Star, Feb. 10, 1961.

ful adulteration, and physically harmful adulteration. Fifty-eight percent of the consumers felt that penalties should have been more severe than the actual court decisions, and yet within the maximum penalty provided by the Federal law, a one-year prison sentence on first conviction. Twenty-two percent of the sample chose penalties equal to or less harsh than the one actually imposed, while almost 20 percent felt that the violators should receive a prison term longer than a year.[13]

The very characteristics which make white-collar criminals particularly deterrable may make it difficult to obtain the sanctions necessary to deter. They generally have families, an established place in the community, and a spotless record. They often occupy managerial or executive roles in their business and a leadership position in their community.

In the *Electrical Equipment* cases the defendants included several vice presidents of the General Electric Corporation and the Westinghouse Electric Corporation. They were described by a newspaper reporter as "typical business men in appearance, men who would never be taken for lawbreakers."[14] Several were deacons or vestrymen of their churches. One was president of his local Chamber of Commerce, another a hospital board member, another chief fund raiser for the Community Chest, another a bank director, another director of the taxpayer's association, another organizer of the local little league.

The highest paid executive to be given a jail sentence was a General Electric vice president, earning $135,000 a year. He was married, and the father of three children. He had served in the Navy during the second World War, rising to the rank of lieutenant commander, was director of the Schenectady Boy's Club, on the board of trustees of a girl's finishing school, and was a member of the Governor's Temporary State Committee on Economic Expansion in New York.

Obviously there is resistance to subjecting defendants who are performing useful functions in society to criminal sanctions and especially to prison sentences. Clinard's study of OPA violators found that one reason for the light sentences imposed was "the fact that the offenders seldom had a criminal past or other circumstances which would warrant a severe sentence. As the judges on occasion stated from the bench, they 'would not make criminals of reputable businessmen.' "[15] On the other hand Judge Skelly Wright, in considering the question of whether an income tax violator ought to be sentenced to jail, took the position that "the only real purpose of an income tax sentence is its deterrent value. Unless we use the income

---

[13] Donald J. Newman, "Public Attitudes Toward a Form of White Collar Crime," 4 *Social Problems* 228, 230, 231 (Jan. 1957).

[14] New York Times, Feb. 7, 1961, p. 1, p. 26, col. 3.

[15] Marshall Clinard, "Criminological Theories of Violations of Wartime Regulations," 11 *Amer. Soc. Rev.* 258, 263 (1946).

tax sentence as a deterrent, we are overlooking one of our responsibilities as judges."[16]

In addition to the standing of the offenders, there are a number of aspects of white-collar offenses that may encourage public and official reluctance to use criminal sanctions, as well as provide rationalizations for the violators themselves. Thus Cressey's study of embezzlement found rationalization to be an important factor in offenders' patterns of misconduct. They distinguished embezzlement sharply from robbery or theft. He found, for example, that independent buisnessmen who converted "deposits" which had been entrusted to them because of their business positions, convinced themselves "either (a) that they were merely borrowing the money which they converted, or (b) that the funds entrusted to them were really theirs."[17] It has been argued that use of criminal sanctions to enforce much of the law in this area is inappropriate because the conduct proscribed is "morally neutral."[18] The soundness of some of the regulatory laws that have grown up in recent decades is a subject of continuing debate. And the very fact that they are so recent in comparison with the laws prohibiting such conduct as larceny and assault makes it unlikely that they will enjoy similar acceptance for some time. Many of the defendants in the *Electrical Equipment* cases argued that their behavior, while technically criminal, had really served a worthwhile purpose by "stabilizing prices." They frequently combined this altruistic interpretation with an attempted distinction among illegal, criminal, and immoral acts, expressing the view that what they had done might have been designated by the statutes as criminal, but either they were unaware of such a designation or they thought it unreasonable that acts with admirable consequences should be considered criminal. The fact that the line between legitimate and illegitimate behavior is sometimes fuzzy and seems occasionally arbitrary does not help in obtaining popular support for the law. Thus the fine line between legal tax avoidance and illegal evasion may make it hard for the violator himself or others to accept the appropriateness of criminal sanctions even where the violation is not close to the line.

But most white-collar crime is not at all morally neutral. Most fraud involves preying upon the weak and ignorant; violation of food and drug laws may cause death or serious injury; embezzlement is, very simply, a form of theft; tax fraud involves cheating the Government and, indirectly, other taxpayers.

[16] Wright, "Sentencing the Income Tax Violator, Statement of the Basic Problem," delivered before the Sentencing Institute for the Fifth Circuit, 30 F.R.D. 185, 302, 304–305 (1962).

[17] Cressey, *Other People's Money* 102 (The Free Press: Glencoe, Ill., 1953).

[18] Sanford H. Kadish, "Some Observations on the Use of Criminal Sanctions in Enforcing Economic Regulations," 30 *U. Chi. L. Rev.* 423, 435 (1963).

Reluctance to see criminal sanctions used in the white-collar area derives also from the fact that there is often no particular victim, or group of victims. The harm is not as apparent, and certainly not as dramatic. Where loss is spread throughout society, the harm to any particular individual is minimal. As Sanford H. Kadish has pointed out,

it is possible to reason convincingly that the harm done to the economic order by violations of many of these regulatory laws are of a magnitude that dwarf in significance the lower class property offenses. But the point is that these perceptions require distinguishing and reasoning processes that are not the normal governors of the passion of moral disapproval, and are not dramatically obvious to a public long conditioned to responding approvingly to the production of profit through business shrewdness, especially in the absence of live and visible victims.[19]

Moreover, where corporate misconduct is involved, the offenders—and particularly the offenders against whom evidence of guilt can be obtained—act as part of a corporate hierarchy and, ordinarily, follow a pattern of corporate behavior. Individual responsibility is therefore reduced—the offenders are often following orders from above, either explicit or implicit. Moreover, the fact that acts are performed to further the interests of the corporation, and not merely the offenders' personal interests, helps to rationalize misconduct. Thus in the *Electrical Equipment* cases, personal explanations for the acts were, for the most part, sought in the structure of corporate pressures. The defendants almost invariably testified that they came new to a job, found price-fixing an established way of life, and simply entered into it as they did into other aspects of their job. This is illustrative of a pattern that Senator Everett Dirksen of Illinois, during the subcommittee hearings, labeled "imbued fraud."[20] There was testimony that, if one employee refused to engage in price-fixing, the responsibility would simply be delegated to another. Prior to imposing sentence in the *Electrical Equipment* cases, Judge T. Cullen Ganey criticized the corporations as the major culprits, but he did not excuse the offenders:

they were torn between conscience and an approved corporate policy, with the rewarding objectives of promotion, comfortable security, and large salaries. They were the organization or company men, the conformist who goes along with his superiors and finds balm for his conscience in additional comforts and security of his place in the corporate setup.[21]

And in his study of embezzlement Cressey found that offenders rationalized on the basis "that 'everyone' in business in some way or other converts or

19 Id. at 436.
20 *Hearings*, pt. 27, p. 16773.
21 New York Times, Feb. 7, 1961, p. 26.

misapplies deposits so that it is not entirely wrong."[22] Criminal conduct that accords with such an accepted "system" and is in response to such pressures is not unique to white-collar offenders, as the Commission's work on juvenile delinquency, organized crime and professional crime indicates.

There is strong evidence that many white-collar offenders do not think of themselves as criminals. Cameron's study of middle-class shoplifters who had stolen from a large department store in Chicago gave some indication of the potential educative effect of the use of criminal sanctions. Shoplifters generally do not think of themselves as thieves, Cameron points out, and "even when arrested, they resist strongly being pushed to admit their behavior is theft. Again and again store people explain to pilferers, that they are under arrest as thieves, that they will, in the normal course of events, be taken in a police van to jail, held in jail until bond is raised, and tried in a court before a judge and sentenced." Interrogation procedures at the store are directed specifically and consciously toward breaking down any illusion that the shoplifter may possess that his behavior is merely regarded as "naughty" or "bad."

In the course of this investigation, it becomes increasingly clear to the pilferer that he is considered a thief and is in imminent danger of being hauled into court and publicly exhibited as such. This realization is often accompanied by a dramatic change in attitude and by severe emotional disturbance.[23]

*   *   *   *   *

Because the adult pilferer does not think of himself, prior to his arrest, as a thief and can conceive of no in-group support for himself in that role, his arrest forces him to reject the role * * * [and] is in itself sufficient to cause him to redefine his situation.[24]

And Cressey found that "among the violators interviewed, the accountants, bankers, business executives and independent businessmen all reported that the possibility of stealing or robbing to obtain the needed funds never occurred to them, although many objective opportunities for such crimes were present."[25]

Application of criminal sanctions in this area raises some of the most delicate and perplexing problems confronting the criminal justice system. The sensitivity of successful members of society to the threat of criminal prosecution is indicative not only of the potential success of criminal sanctions in deterring misconduct, but of their potentially destructive effect upon the offenders. Criminal sanctions may help to educate the public to realize the seriousness of misconduct which is not on its face abhorrent, yet

[22] Cressey, *supra* n. 17 at 102.
[23] Mary Cameron, *The Booster and The Snitch* 162 (New York: Free Press, 1965).
[24] Id. at 165.
[25] Cressey, *supra* n. 17 at 140.

their indiscriminate use in areas where public opinion has not crystallized may seriously weaken the condemnatory effect of the criminal law. Imprisonment may be unnecessary for purposes of rehabilitation and incapacitation, although very effective as a deterrent.

. . .

6 Pleading Guilty
for Considerations:
A Study of Bargain Justice

DONALD J. NEWMAN

One of the major problems faced by social scientists interested in studying criminal behavior involves obtaining samples of offenders to be used as units of research. Ordinarily such samples are drawn from prisons or probation files because the study of unapprehended criminals is extremely difficult. Conviction by a court or authorized agency is, therefore, the usual basis of sample selection.[1] Virtually all sociologists admit the inadequacy of such a technique and qualify their samples as non-representative of any kind of a criminal universe. At the same time, the conviction record of the offenders who are selected for study from prisons and courts is used as the basis for typing the offenders and for various statistical computations. In general, the man's conviction record is assumed to be a quasi-automatic legal stamp which defines those activities which make him a criminal.

Of course very few researchers would treat a person such as Al Capone as merely an income tax violator, but this is because they would

Reprinted by special permission from *The Journal of Criminal Law, Criminology and Police Science*, Copyright © 1956 by the Northwestern University School of Law, Volume 46, Number 6 (March-April, 1956), pp. 780–790. Also by permission of the author.

[1] See PAUL TAPPAN, *Who is the Criminal?* in: AMER. SOCIOL. REV., Vol. 12, no. 1, pp. 96–102 and DONALD R. CRESSEY, *Criminological Research and the Definitions of Crimes*, AMER. JOUR. OF SOCIOL., Vol. 57 (May 1951) pp. 546–551.

know, or think that they know that such an individual had committed other offenses or had different patterns of criminal behavior than those for which he was sentenced. In less notorious cases, however, the type of offense and the severity of the sentence, remain the pivotal points around which research is pursued and prison classification systems are built.

This does not mean that sociologists naively accept conviction on a specific charge as definitive nor that they have little interest in the mechanics of justice. The reverse, of course, is more accurate. But the emphasis of both sociological exposition and research has been on the *gross* misuse of justice, on methods used by criminals, political officials and the business elite to avoid conviction. It is also true that some sociological interest has been shown in procedural variation, particularly brutal, and in many cases, illegal, arrest and interrogation methods. The police particularly have come under sociological scrutiny.[2] Nevertheless, apart from the "fix" and the "third degree", the conviction process has generally been neglected in research as of minor importance in the complicated process of defining "criminal" as the basic unit of research.

METHODS OF STUDYING THE CONVICTION PROCESS

In order to bring to light some of the less apparent factors influencing the procedural steps by which society labels the criminal, a sample of men, all convicted of "conventional" felonies in one court district was interviewed in regard to the processes involved in their own convictions. Men from a single county were selected in order to keep formal legal procedures and court and prosecuting officials constant for each case. The lawyers and judges of this district had been interviewed previously by the author,[3] so that information was available about conviction processes from the legal participants viewpoints. The county was located in the mid-west (Wisconsin) and was of "medium" size, neither rural nor metropolitan. The county seat had a population of approximately 100,000 persons. Furthermore, the district was politically clean, having no widespread organized crime or vice nor a tradition of "fixing" criminal cases by bribery or intimidation. Supposedly in such a setting, felony convictions would follow a quasi-automatic, "combat" theory of criminal justice, involving a jury trial or at least an unconditional plea of guilty.

---

[2] William Westley, *Violence and the Police* (in: Amer. Jour. of Sociol., July, 1953) pp. 34–41 and Ernest J. Hopkins, Our Lawless Police (New York: Viking Press, 1931).

[3] This study took place in 1951 and 1952 as part of the American Bar Association's study entitled *Criminal Law and Litigation*.

MOST CONVICTIONS THE RESULT OF GUILTY PLEAS

The felons who were interviewed, a group of ninety-seven representing all men from the district under active sentence, had all been convicted of felonies ranging from non-support to murder. There were no white-collar criminals in the group, except for three clerks serving sentence for embezzlements, nor were there any racketeers or professional criminals such as confidence men, and no individuals sentenced from Juvenile Court were included. The men were serving sentences under the following conditions:

State prison	34
State reformatory	6
Parole	9
Probation	48
Total	97

Most of the convictions (93.8 percent) were not convictions in a combative, trial-by-jury sense, but merely involved sentencing after a plea of guilty had been entered. On the surface this might lend support to the contention that most convictions are mere rubber stamps of the court applied to the particular illegal behavior involved in each case.

On closer analysis, however, it was seen that over a third (38.1 percent) of the men had originally entered a not guilty plea, changing to guilty only at a later procedural stage short of an actual trial. The question immediately arose; why did these men change their minds? Was it because of a promise of leniency or some such bargain as suggested by the Wickersham report, Moley and other writers of a decade ago?[4] A second question followed. Did the men who pleaded guilty immediately do so unconditionally to the charge as contained in the complaint or was there any evidence of informal "arranging" of the sentence so widely alleged in criminology texts?

Pursuing these lines of inquiry, an interesting difference between the two groups of men was seen. Men entering an initial plea of not guilty were significantly more often represented by defense attorneys than the men pleading guilty immediately. On all other demographic characteristics, age, gross type of offense for which sentenced (personal, property, sex,

---

[4] NATIONAL COMMISSION ON LAW OBSERVANCE AND ENFORCEMENT, *Report on Prosecution*, Bulletin 4 (Washington, D.C.: Government Printing Office, 1931); and RAYMOND MOLEY, OUR CRIMINAL COURTS (New York: Minton, Balch Co., 1930) and POLITICS AND CRIMINAL PROSECUTION (New York: Minton, Balch Co., 1929). See also NEWMAN F. BAKER and EARL H. DELONG, *The Prosecuting Attorney: Powers and Duties in Criminal Prosecution* (in: JOUR. OF CRIM. L. AND CRIMINOL., Vol. 24, No. 6, March–April 1934) and NEWMAN F. BAKER, *The Prosecutor—Initiation of Prosecution* (in JOUR. OF CRIM. L. AND CRIMINOL., Vol. 23, No. 5, September, 1933).

TABLE 1. TYPE OF PLEA BY RETENTION OF COUNSEL

Retention of Counsel	Type of Plea		
	Guilty	Changed not guilty to guilty	Total
Offenders with lawyers	21	24	45
	(23.2)	(26.3)	(49.5)
Offenders without lawyers	39	7	46
	(42.7)	(7.8)	(50.5)
Total	60	31	91*
percent	(65.9)	(34.1)	(100.0)

* Offenders pleading not guilty and retaining this plea through a jury trial were eliminated. All, however, had counsel.

$\chi^2 = 14.713$, d.f. $= 1$, significant at the 5 percent level. Yules Q $= -.728$ indicating a negative correlation between initial admission of guilt and the retention of counsel.

and miscellaneous violations such as carrying a concealed weapon), education, occupation, residence and so on, the groups showed no significant differences. Furthermore, on the eventual disposition of the cases, e.g., whether sent to prison or placed on probation, the groups did not differ. In fact, only one other difference besides the retention of counsel was noted. It was found that the men who initially pleaded guilty and who more often than not did not hire or request counsel were recidivists, whereas the men with lawyers, who at first pleaded innocent, were more often experiencing their first conviction.

This phenomenon is rather curious when it is recalled that the groups showed no differences in the frequency of being placed on probation. It might logically be expected, in the light of current sentencing practices, that first offenders would more likely receive probation than men with previous convictions, particularly if, as was the case, there was no significant variation in the types of crimes for which they were sentenced. The implications of this lack of difference in sentences for the role of the lawyer in the conviction process was so great that the men were further analyzed by dividing them into two groups, one characterized by the retention of counsel, the other comprising men who pleaded without an attorney.

The outcome of the conviction process from the point of view of the offender is satisfactory or unsatisfactory depending upon the actual sentence he receives compared to his expectations of punishment at the time he is arrested. It might be supposed that a violator who expected a severe sentence would seek legal advice. However, an analysis of the responses of the men showed that their expectations was not the determining factor in their decisions to retain counsel or to plead without counsel.

TABLE 2. EXPECTED PUNISHMENT BY
RETENTION OF COUNSEL

Punishment Expected at time of Arrest	Retention of Counsel		
	Offenders with lawyers	Offenders without lawyers	Total
Expected same as actual or didn't know what to expect	3 (3.2)	10 (10.3)	13 (13.5)
Expected less severe than actual	11 (11.3)	11 (11.3)	22 (22.6)
Expected more severe than actual	37 (38.1)	25 (25.8)	62 (63.9)
Total	51	46	97
percent	(52.6)	(47.4)	(100.0)

$\chi^2 = 5.827$, d.f. $= 2$, not significant at five percent level.

TABLE 3. NON-REPRESENTED OFFENDERS REASONS
FOR NOT RETAINING COUNSEL

	Percent
Obviously guilty, hoped for mercy from the court	19.5
Made deal for concurrent sentence or had charges dropped	30.4
Made deal for lesser charge or a light sentence	23.9
Don't trust lawyers	4.4
Had no money, didn't know about court-assigned lawyers	13.0
Other*	4.4
Not ascertained	4.4
Total	100.0

* These cases claimed that they were subjected to long and arduous questioning and "confessed" to "get it over with" and thus had neither the time nor the inclination to get a lawyer.

REASONS FOR PLEADING GUILTY WITHOUT A LAWYER

The reasons given for claiming or for disdaining counsel varied from confessions of "obvious" guilt and a hope for mercy from the court to poverty coupled with ignorance of provisions for state-paid defense attorneys. The chief reason, however, appeared to be an expedient one, related to the factor of past experience in going through the conviction process. The recidivists were both conviction wise and conviction susceptible in the dual sense that they knew of the possibility of bargaining a guilty plea for a light sentence and at the same time were vulnerable, because of their records, to threats of the prosecutor to "throw the book" at them unless they confessed. Over half (54.3 percent) of the men claimed that they had bargained for their sentences, and 84 percent of these men had been convicted previously. A number of factors, all interrelated, seem to account for this. First, a general fear expressed by multiple offenders of facing a jury or of antagonizing sentencing officials was revealed in most cases. Some felt that their records would be held against them by a jury (actually the admission in court of the offender's previous criminal record is closely regulated by law to assure a fair trial on the current charge). They felt conviction would be more certain because in the public mind they were "ex-cons". A more general fear, however, was that the judge would be especially severe in sentencing if they did decide to fight and then lost. They felt that pleading not guilty and hiring a lawyer would only irritate the various officials, particularly the prosecutor, whose recommendation at the time of sentencing is an important consideration of the court. One of the men said:

When the day comes to go and the D.A. stands up and says you're a dirty rat and a menace to society and should be locked up and have the key thrown away—then look out! You're going away for a few years.

These fears, whether justified or not, undoubtedly made these men more amenable to an informal "settling" of their cases.

A second factor making for bargaining and the rejection of counsel was the experience of these men gained in previous convictions. Many of the recidivists, particularly those with two or more convictions, knew the sentencing judges and some of the prosecutors quite well and all of the offenders knew most of the police. They were on a first name basis with many of these men and could bargain in a friendly or even a jocular manner. One man (on probation) said:

Old —— told me he was going to throw the book at me. I told him he didn't have a damn thing on me. He said I'd get five to ten. I told him he couldn't even book me, that's how little he had. I knew he was riding me; he didn't mean a thing by it. I've known him for years. He just likes to act tough.

Men who had been convicted in other states or in other counties but never before in this district were quite conscious of this "friendship" factor in the bargaining processes. Each of them expressed the belief that had he been a "local" he would have fared better.

Previous sentences served in institutions also seemed to be relevant to bargaining without a lawyer. Former inmates were more legal-wise; their conceptions of their offenses were not primarily in terms of guilt or innocence but contained more references to evidence and its relation to the outcome of the conviction process. They referred to how much the prosecutor "had on me" and the ability of the prosecution to make a charge stick. One of the men expressed it this way:

The D.A. needed my help. His evidence was all circumstances (*sic*). He knew I done it but he couldn't ever prove it. But I couldn't go to court and take a chance with my record. When I saw he was going to stick me with something, I was willing to make the best deal.

Not only does a quasi-legal knowledge evidently develop in incarceration (most of these men knew the statute numbers of their offenses and all knew such terms as "preliminary hearing", "arraignment" and "pre-sentence investigation") but those men seemed better able to recognize a good bargain when they saw one. Although all offenders recognized probation as the best break, of course, and many knew the possible length of sentence for their particular crime, recidivists knew customary sentences (and court district variations) for their offenses. In short, they recognized a "good-as-compared-to-other-guys-I-know" sentence when they faced it.

OFFENDERS WHO RETAIN COUNSEL

Over half (52.6%) of the men in the total sample retained lawyers and proceeded through more of the formal stages of the conviction process (preliminary hearing, arraignment) than those men who pleaded without attorneys. As anticipated from the analysis of the group of non-represented offenders, the factor of recidivism with its accompanying implication of bargaining skills learned from past experience was almost completely absent from this group. As one of these men expressed it:

I'd never been in trouble before. I didn't know which end was up. I thought sure I was going to prison. It seemed as if they had a million laws I'd broken. The only thing I could think of was calling my wife to get me a lawyer.

These men with their lawyers, either privately hired or court assigned, significantly more often pleaded not guilty when first apprehended, changing their pleas only later in the process. On the surface, this observation might lead to one of two conflicting conclusions. The fact that the retention of counsel correlated with a change of plea to guilty might mean that the lawyers, having a better grasp of the legal worth of the evidence against their clients, advised them to plead guilty and that the clients followed their advice. Or, it could with equal validity indicate that perhaps the lawyers, through informal bargaining skills similar to the non-represented recidivists, had arranged satisfactory charges or more lenient sentences than originally expected by their clients. The latter would seem to be the most convincing in view of the offenders' responses. When asked their lawyer's advice in regard to pleading, 75 percent of those first pleading not guilty and then guilty, responded that their counsel's advice was to maintain a not guilty plea "until something can be arranged." This they did. The remainder were advised to plead guilty without promise of any arrangement, although bargaining is not thus ruled out.

Only fifteen of the represented offenders said that their convictions were the result of unconditional pleas of guilty. The remainder, including not only the offenders whose lawyers' advice was to hold off pleading guilty until settlement was made, but twelve of the men who entered initial guilty pleas as well, claimed to have received some consideration in the nature of the charge or type and length of sentence in exchange for their admissions of guilt.

TYPES OF BARGAINING WHERE ATTORNEY HAS BEEN RETAINED

While the frequency of claimed bargaining does not differ significantly between the groups of offenders without lawyers and with lawyers, there is some difference in the frequencies of the various types reported. Men without attorneys significantly more often mentioned as the consideration they received in exchange for a guilty plea either the reduction of the charge or the promise of a suitable, fixed sentence.

TABLE 4. OFFENDERS PLEADING GUILTY AFTER
BARGAINING OVER CHARGE OR SENTENCE

Retention of Counsel	Offenders Pleading Guilty		
	Pleaded guilty for consideration	Pleaded guilty without bargaining	Total
Offenders with lawyers	30	15	45
	(33.0)	(16.5)	(49.5)
Offenders without lawyers	25	21	46
	(27.4)	(23.1)	(50.5)
Total	55	36	91
percent	(60.4)	(39.6)	(100.0)

$\chi^2 = 1.443$, d.f. $= 1$, not significant at 5 percent level.

It would seem from this that lawyers are more likely to be retained by offenders who fear a severe punishment or in cases involving a disputable charge whereas violators with many charges against them "cop a plea" directly from the prosecution or the court without a lawyer as intermediary. This would also seem to substantiate the evidence from the unrepresented defendants that the function of the lawyer in bargaining is not essential for all offenders, and that men experienced in the conviction process can informally and successfully arrange their own legal fate.

TYPES OF INFORMAL CONVICTION AGREEMENTS

The considerations received by the offenders in exchange for their guilty pleas were of four general types:

1. *Bargain concerning the charge.* A plea of guilty was entered by the offenders in exchange for a reduction of the charge from the one alleged in the complaint. This ordinarily occurred in cases where the offense in question carried statutory degrees of severity such as homicide assault, and

TABLE 5. FREQUENCY OF TYPES OF BARGAINING
BY RETENTION OF COUNSEL*

	With Offenders Lawyers	Offenders Without Lawyers	Total
1. Pleading to a lesser charge	8	3	11
	(14.5)	(5.5)	(20.0)
2. Pleading for a light sentence	17	8	25
	(30.9)	(14.6)	(45.5)
3. Pleading for concurrent sentences	3	9	12
	(5.5)	(16.3)	(21.8)
4. Pleading for the dismissal of charges	2	5	7
	(3.6)	(9.1)	(12.7)
Total	30	25	55
percent	(54.5)	(45.5)	(100.0)

* Combining the first two types (lesser charge, light sentence) and comparing them with the last two (concurrent sentence, charge dismissed) a significant difference between types of bargaining and retention of counsel is seen. $\chi^2 = 23.72$, d.f. $= 1$, significant at 5 percent level. Yules $Q = -.732$ indicating a negative correlation between retention of lawyer and pleading guilty for considerations of concurrent sentences or dismissed charges.

sex offenses. This type was mentioned as a major issue in twenty percent of the cases in which bargaining occurred. The majority of offenders in these instances were represented by lawyers.

2. *Bargain concerning the sentence.* A plea of guilty was entered by the offenders in exchange for a promise of leniency in sentencing. The most commonly accepted consideration was a promise that the offender would be placed on probation, although a less-than-maximum prison term was the basis in certain instances. All offenses except murder, serious assault, and robbery were represented in this type of bargaining process. This was by far the most frequent consideration given in exchange for guilty pleas, occurring in almost half (45.5 percent) of the cases in which any bargaining occurred. Again, most of these offenders were represented by attorneys.

3. *Bargain for concurrent charges.* This type of informal process occurred chiefly among offenders pleading without counsel. These men exchanged guilty pleas for the concurrent pressing of multiple charges, generally numerous counts of the same offense or related violations such as breaking and entering and larceny. This method, of course, has much the same effect as pleading for consideration in the sentence. The offender with concurrent convictions, however, may not be serving a reduced sentence; he is merely serving one sentence for many crimes. Altogether, concurrent convictions were reported by 21.8 percent of the men who were convicted by informal methods.

4. *Bargain for dropped charges.* This variation occurred in about an eighth of the cases who reported bargaining. It involved an agreement on the part of the prosecution not to press formally one or more charges against the offender if he in turn pleaded guilty to (usually) the major offense. The offenses dropped were extraneous law violations contained in, or accompanying, the offense alleged in the complaint such as auto theft accompanying armed robbery and violation of probation where a new crime had been committed. This informal method, like bargaining for concurrent charges, was reported chiefly by offenders without lawyers. It occurred in 12.6 percent of cases in which bargaining was claimed.

The various types of informal conviction agreements were described in the majority of the cases and, as mentioned, only six members of the sample went to jury trial. The remainder of the sample (37.1 percent) pleaded guilty, they said, without any considerations. It is possible, however, that in those 15 instances where the men had counsel, the attorney had bargained, or had attempted to bargain, without the knowledge of the offender.

In instances where informal methods were used, the roles of the various participants were cooperative rather than combative. Central to the entire process were the roles of offender and prosecutor; the defense attorney played a significant part chiefly in cases of first offenders and in instances where the nature of the charge was in dispute. The judge sometimes played an informal role in cases involving a fixed sentence, but even here the prosecutor's role dominated because of the common practice in the court whereby the judge asks for, and generally follows, the prosecutor's recommendation as to sentence in cases pleading guilty.

THE BARGAIN THEORY OF CRIMINAL JUSTICE

The most significant general finding of the study was that the majority of the felony convictions in the district studied were not the result of the formal, combative theory of criminal law involving in effect a legal battle between prosecution and defense, but were compromise convictions, the result of bargaining between defense and prosecution. Such informal conviction processes were observed in over half of the cases studied.

In the informal process the accused, directly or through his attorney, offered to plead guilty to the offense for which he was arrested, providing it was reduced in kind or degree, or in exchange for a given type or length of sentence. The prosecutor benefitted from such a bargain in that he was assured of a conviction, yet did not have to spend the time and effort to prepare a trial case. He also avoided the ever-present risk of losing even a clear-cut case should the accused have gone before a jury. The court, too, benefitted. Court calendars were, and are, crowded and the entire court system would be admittedly inadequate to cope with criminal trials should all, or even a fraction of the felony arrests decide to go to trial. This, coupled with a generally favorable attitude toward bargaining processes on the part of the lawyers, civil and criminal, in the local bar, made informal methods of conviction almost inevitable.

Instead of proceeding through all the formal stages of conviction such as hearing before a magistrate, preliminary hearing, arraignment, etc., the majority of the offenders waived most of these procedures and because of informal promises of leniency or threats of long sentences, entered guilty pleas and were sentenced. About half (50.5 percent) of the sample went to preliminary hearings of their cases but only 6.2 percent proceeded through a jury trial.

CONCLUSIONS: SIGNIFICANCE OF INFORMAL
CONVICTION PROCESSES TO CRIMINOLOGY

Criminological research has generally ignored methods of conviction in conventional felony cases except the illegal "fix" and brutal "third-degree" as primarily legal steps automatically defining the unit to be studied. The automatism of conviction has here been challenged, and within the limits of the present research, interaction processes of sociological interest in themselves, have been outlined.

It was felt in conducting this research that, if informal methods of convictions were discovered, they would be of a nature to negate the use of conviction records in many types of research and correctional administration. In the typology of criminals, in prison classification, and in other applied fields such as parole prediction, bargaining techniques would rule out the accuracy of the "paper" convictions as an index of the offender's actual patterns of criminality. In spite of the high incidence (56.7 percent) of admitted bargaining in the sample, however, only a very small proportion of cases admitted guilt to offenses grossly different from those alleged in the complaint, and only a small proportion had offenses dismissed so that they did not appear at all on the offenders' records. In other words, the informal conviction processes tended to result in guilty pleas to the same or very similar offenses, so that the offenses for which convicted did not usually deviate greatly from the crime actually committed. The greater proportion of the bargaining was concerned with directly gaining a lighter sentence regardless of the offense, rather than indirectly by pleading to a lesser charge.

One of the most important implications of the informal methods is the effect of these processes on selection for probation. A promise of the prosecutor's recommendation for probation was one of the most common values given in exchange for a guilty plea. This occurred in 34.5 percent of the cases reporting bargaining. With such informal tactics, selection for placement on probation is determined by the skill of the offender or his lawyer in bargaining, rather than on factors of the case which would have more relevance to successful rehabilitation by field rather than institutional placement.

The existence of informal methods also has broader significance to law and law enforcement as well as to criminology and related areas. The use of such methods involves a differential implementation of the law comparable to the discrepancies noted by Reckless in his "categoric risk" of conviction and Sutherland in his conceptions of white collar crime.[5] An analysis of the sample of offenders showed no clear cut categories separating bargained from non-bargained convictions, yet the fact that some offenders, without going to trial, pleaded guilty without any considerations in the charge or in sentencing while others "settled" their cases informally, raises again the sociological, and presumably the moral, problems of criminal justice.

[5] See WALTER RECKLESS, THE CRIME PROBLEM, 2nd edition, (New York: Appleton-Century-Crofts, Inc., 1955) pp. 26–42; and EDWIN H. SUTHERLAND, WHITE COLLAR CRIME (New York: Dryden Press, 1949) pp. 3–14.

Evidently the criminal law is not only differentially enforced in general, but as far as this study shows, this also occurs within groups of offenders convicted of the ordinary (or conventional) felonies of robbery, homicide, burglary, larceny and sex offenses. Certain proportions of these violators (56.7 percent in this sample), without resorting to bribery or other methods of the professional "fix", can modify the nature of the charge against them or the length or type of their sentences in much the same manner as the white collar offender.

Whether bargaining is legal, that is, whether men convicted as the result of bargaining are convicted by due process of law, is a difficult question to answer without referring the decision to a specific case. Likewise, whether bargaining is ethical cannot be summarily answered. Certainly in cases where bargaining is misused, where the accused is exploited or the community subjected to danger, the issue is clear. Under these conditions bargaining is not only unethical but would probably be held unconstitutional, as a violation of the "due process" clauses of the Constitution.

When compromise is used, however, to gain a certain conviction of a surely guilty offender, the question is not so clear. Defense lawyers, prosecutors, and criminal court judges interviewed in an earlier study overwhelmingly favored bargain-justice where judiciously used. They felt it to be the most expedient way of gaining justice. Likewise the offenders who bargained successfully were well satisfied with this process. It was the men who went to trial or who failed to bargain successfully who more often claimed injustice in their cases.

As the lawyers said, bargaining appears to be an expedient method of answering numerous problems of the administration of justice. Our criminal procedure is cumbersome. Legal defense is expensive both for the state and the accused. Court calendars are crowded and would not be able to cope with the number of trials which would ensue if all arrestees pleaded not guilty. Furthermore, no conviction is ever a sure thing, no matter how overwhelming the evidence, if the case goes before a jury. Prosecutors, who need convictions to be successful, know this. For these reasons, "bargain-justice" appears the natural answer to lawyers and court officials and, of course, to offenders who are guilty. For these reasons, too, the problem of bargaining cannot easily be corrected, if it should be corrected at all. Bargain-justice appears as a natural, expedient outgrowth of deficiencies in the administration of our "trial-by-combat" theory of justice. It is supported by both the attitudes of offenders who see justice as a purely personal thing, how well they fare in sentencing, and by the attitudes of lawyers and court officials who can only "get things done" in this way.

While bargain-justice may thus be an expedient and at present even a necessary and legitimate legal phenomenon in certain cases, some broader implications of bargaining should be mentioned. Cases of conventional felonies that are "settled" may well result in strengthening attitudes which favor a general disregard for law and for justice, in much the same way as does the differential legal treatment of business and political violators. If conviction on a charge is to be determined in great part by skill of the offender in bargaining with the court or in hiring a lawyer to bargain for him, then our concept of impartial justice based upon facts and rules of evidence becomes meaningless. Furthermore, the fact that opportunities and techniques for bargaining exist in our system can have an adverse effect upon attempts to rehabilitate offenders and generally to decrease crime rates. What happens, for example, when one man, merely because he is unsophisticated, does not know of bargaining techniques nor of the right lawyer to contact, is sentenced to prison while another more sophisticated offender, a recidivist who commits the same offense, arranges a sentence to be served on probation? Certainly the rationalizations of the man sentenced to prison to the effect that he is a "fall guy", and his conception of himself gained from serving prison time, make rehabilitation far more complex if not impossible. The way bargaining now works, the more experienced criminals can manipulate legal processes to obtain light sentences and better official records while the less experienced, occasional offenders receive more harsh treatment. Under these conditions the effectiveness of law as a means of social control is seriously jeopardized and any long range attempts to build respect for the law and law abiding attitudes will prove extremely difficult.

7 Acquittal of the Guilty to Control Police Enforcement Methods

DONALD J. NEWMAN

There appears to be a trend in recent years to give the trial judge greater responsibility for controlling police policy and practice. In *Mapp v. Ohio*[1] the Supreme Court of the United States held that state trial judges must exclude evidence obtained by police in violation of the constitutional rights of the defendant. In announcing its decision, the court said that it was convinced that this is the only effective way of controlling police practice.[2] Furthermore, a minority but increasingly common view of the defense of entrapment reiterates the court's responsibility for supervising police practices. Mr. Justice Frankfurter has said with respect to entrapment: "The crucial question . . . is whether the police conduct revealed in the particular case falls below standards, to which common feelings respond, for the proper use of governmental power."[3] This is a position now adopted in the American Law Institute Model Penal Code.[4]

Both the so-called exclusionary rule and the defense of entrapment

Reprinted from Donald J. Newman, *Conviction: The Determination of Guilt or Innocence Without Trial* (Boston: Little, Brown and Company, 1966), pp. 188–196,

[1] Mapp v. Ohio, 367 U.S. 643, 81 Sup. Ct. 1684, 6 L. Ed. 2d 1081 (1961).
by permission of the publisher and the author.
[2] 367 U.S. at 660, 81 Sup. Ct. at 1694, 6 L. Ed. 2d at 1093.
[3] Sherman v. United States, 356 U.S. 369, 382, 78 Sup. Ct. 819, 825, 2 L. Ed. 2d 848, 856 (1958).
[4] Model Penal Code §2.13 (Proposed Official Draft, 1962).

as well as their respective effects upon police practices are discussed in detail in other volumes in this series.[5] Both are subject to an increasing effort by appellate courts to articulate their purposes and scope.[6]

The types of acquittals discussed here are based on less formal criteria than those which underlie entrapment proposals as in the Model Penal Code and the exclusionary rule. The court's basic purpose of disciplining the police and of controlling police practices is, however, the same. In effect these informal methods of control represent an extension of the scope of the trial court's customary supervisory responsibility over the police; an extension that depends heavily on the proclivities of particular judges, is often based on unclear criteria, and is not always uniformly applied even in a single court.

In the federal system of criminal justice, the superintending responsibility of the court over police is acknowledged in situations where there are no constitutional issues involved. For example, federal courts will exclude a confession obtained in violation of Rule 5 of the Federal Rules of Criminal Procedure even though Rule 5 has not been declared a mandate of the Constitution.[7] At the state court level, however, there is less recognition of a general responsibility of the trial judge to superintend police practices. Commonly state appellate courts limit the trial court's responsibility to concern with constitutional violations by police. In practice, however, some trial judges do acquit defendants because they have been dealt with by police in ways thought improper by the trial judge even though the impropriety is not of constitutional dimensions. Along with extension of entrapment and the exclusionary rule, it is this informal, seldom-acknowledged, function of the trial judge that underlies the acquittals analyzed here.

[5] See LaFave, Arrest: The Decision to Take a Suspect into Custody (1965); the forthcoming volume on Detection of Crime.

[6] An interesting example of an attempt by a trial judge to influence appellate court consideration of police practices occurred in a recent case arising in a federal district court. In a trial of a defendant for manslaughter, after both sides had rested, the trial judge denied a motion by the defendant's counsel for acquittal. The judge then learned that the government had a written confession from the defendant which was not introduced in evidence because the prosecutor recognized its dubious status since the conditions under which the statement was obtained would probably not be acceptable under the Mallory Rule. The trial judge stated that the government should use the "signed statement in order to bring a test case . . . because the circuits are at loggerheads as to what constitutes undue delay under the Mallory Rule." Cunningham v. United States, 340 F.2d 787, 788 (D.C. Cir. 1964). The trial judge then announced that unless the statement were offered in evidence, the case would be dismissed despite his earlier ruling to the contrary. The case was reopened and the confession was admitted and read to the jury. The defendant was convicted and appealed. The case was reversed by the circuit court.

[7] Mallory v. United States, 354 U.S. 449, 77 Sup. Ct. 1356, 1 L. Ed. 2d 1479 (1957).

A. ACQUITTAL BECAUSE THE TRIAL JUDGE DISAGREES WITH THE INTENSITY OF THE LAW ENFORCEMENT EFFORT

Some trial judges are in obvious disagreement with police as to how active enforcement should be with regard to certain kinds of criminal conduct. This is reflected in some judicial antagonism over current police activity in respect to consensual vice crimes like prostitution and public solicitation by homosexuals. Since trial judges seldom articulate the exact nature of their concern it is not easy to be certain whether it relates primarily to the propriety of the methods being used, the wisdom of devoting a considerable amount of police time and resources to those activities, a disagreement over the meaning of the substantive criminal statute, or a general sense of frustration with the lack of effectiveness of the criminal justice process in dealing with sexual misconduct.

1. The enticement of prostitutes

Illustration No. 1: The court in acquitting a female defendant of charges of accosting and soliciting for immoral purposes commented: "The vice officer purchased dance hall tickets with state funds and deliberately set out to arrest one of the girls. This is going too far; this is deliberate enticement and it will not be tolerated."

An area of conflict between the courts and the police, particularly in Detroit, has to do with the arrest of prostitutes for accosting and soliciting for immoral purposes. Part of this conflict results from differing views of judges and police as to the meaning of the law which makes accosting and soliciting a crime in Michigan. Another part, however, relates to what the courts consider unfair detection techniques, which at least one judge refers to as "enticement," a word chosen to distinguish this from the formal, recognized defense of entrapment. Enticement involves arrests by plain-clothes officers of prostitutes who typically are fully aware of the illegality of their conduct and who certainly are not first introduced to such behavior by the police. The objection of the courts to enticement is based squarely on the belief that police methods in these cases are unfair and improper, and acquittals are used in a frank attempt to change these practices. The vice squad, in order to fulfill what they consider their mandate of arresting prostitutes, use plainclothes detectives placed strategically where they may be solicited by both streetwalkers and pick-up prostitutes. Some judges feel that the zealousness of these officers extends beyond merely being in a position to be solicited and includes a number of techniques whereby the original accosting is by the officer, not the defendant.

It is evident that trial judges differ in their reactions to the propriety of these police practices and that there is no systematic communication of the criteria for enticement to persons involved in police administration. Reports of judge's attitudes are sporadic, generally coming from individual officers who were involved in cases which resulted in acquittal, particularly when the officer has been chastised by the judge in open court. As a consequence, extreme cases are told and retold and come to be looked upon by police as typical illustrations of the difficulty they have with the judiciary.

For example, police officers report acquittals in these illustrative cases: An officer spent about twenty minutes in a bar buying drinks for a girl before she made a proposition. The court felt that "too long a time" had elapsed for a true accosting case. In another instance, defendants charged with accosting and soliciting were acquitted when it was revealed that the plainclothes vice officers were in an unmarked Cadillac automobile when the typical vice squad car was an unmarked Ford. In still another case, a waitress was acquitted when she accompanied the officer to a hotel. The court said that "too much time and too much traveling was involved" and that "this is not the type of case the accosting and soliciting law was intended to cover." Analysis of the situation is difficult because it is not clear whether the trial judge is most concerned over the intensity of the police detection efforts on grounds of general policy or whether he reads the "accosting and soliciting" statute as requiring an aggressiveness on the part of the female which is lacking when the officer plays an active role. In all likelihood both are involved. If the substantive ambiguity in the meaning of the crime were resolved legislatively, it would make it possible to deal more accurately with such difference of opinion as exists between judges and the police over enforcement policy in respect to prostitution.

2. *Enticement of homosexuals*

Illustration No. 2: A psychiatrist who, on court order, has seen many homosexual defendants for diagnosis, notified the court of what he feels is the "typical" operation of the vice squad in such cases: "The arresting officer goes to a public rest room or to some other location which is frequented by homosexuals. Upon seeing a potential defendant, the officer will stare or smile or will even affect feminine mannerisms. While urinating the officer will handle his genitalia in such a manner as to excite or arouse the interested defendant. The defendant then will make an oral proposition which results in his arrest. In my opinion this form of practice is not only entrapment but is harmful to the defendant in that the individual may have succumbed to the officer's enticement while under ordinary circumstances he would not have been aroused enough to make such a solicitation."

When apprised of such techniques by this psychiatrist and being familiar with the use of the peephole in public rest rooms, one judge was moved to remark that such practices are "atrocious," "appalling," "horrible," and "miserable." This judge is convinced that plainclothes officers make a practice of visiting places where homosexuals congregate, such as the rest rooms of large department stores and bus stations, in order to be accosted. When confronted with a homosexual accosting and soliciting case, the judge puts the police officer on the stand and asks him three "key questions." The first is, "Did you go to the bus station rest room due to nature's call or did you go there for the specific purpose of being accosted and solicited by a homosexual?" The second is, "When did you make the arrest—in the rest room or after you got out?" The third is, "How much time elapsed between the initial contact with the defendant and the arrest?" On the basis of answers to these questions, the judge establishes the facts of entice-ment. He concludes that officers who testify that they went to the rest room to answer nature's call are "obviously lying" because "a police officer driv-ing around town would certainly not go to a department store rest room or to a bus depot rest room. There are many other places available." The questions of when the officer made the arrest and the length of time in-volved are usually even more narrowly defined in cases of homosexuals than of prostitutes. The judge explained, "If an officer spends over three or four minutes, then there is definitely enticement and I will dismiss the case." About 40 per cent of all accosting and soliciting cases in the Detroit area involve homosexual defendants, and the enticement concept is used by the courts to acquit these persons with perhaps even more regularity than with prostitutes.

3. Overzealous enforcement

Illustration No. 3: A judge in dismissing drunk and disorderly charges against some defendants arrested in a tavern commented that it is "not a proper police function to go into bars to see who is drunk or not. I don't believe this is your duty. The police have plenty of other things to do rather than making the rounds and bothering tavern patrons."

Judges occasionally acquit defendants when it appears to them that the police have been overzealous in enforcement. Such acquittals apparently reflect the judge's opinion that the violation is of a de minimis nature and should be so considered at the enforcement level. In general, courts do not wish to be bothered with cases of minor law infraction and it is easier all around if criminal procedures are not started. In dismissing some minor disorderly conduct charges, for example, one judge commented, "This should have been handled at the precinct level." Another judge called police arrests in minor gambling cases a "fantastic waste" of police manpower. Another judge commented, "It is ridiculous that the vice squad will assign 28 men to investigate a misdemeanor while we have only 22 men on the homicide squad." The prevailing opinion is that intensive, unrelenting en-forcement of minor vice, vagrancy, disorderly conduct, and similar laws is an unwise allocation of police resources and perhaps improper where, for example, a disproportionate number of Negro defendants are involved. The assumption is that systematic acquittal of such defendants will be translated into police nonenforcement in de minimis cases or into the informal settling of problems, such as domestic disputes, by methods short of court appearance.

A major difficulty arises in situations where the judge's conception of de minimis differs substantially from the police view. What may appear to the judge as an isolated case of prostitution, for example, may appear to the police as an integral part of organized vice in the community or what to the judge may seem to be an isolated case of solicitation by a homosexual may, to the police, be one instance of a general pattern of homosexual activity which has caused a department store or a hotel to exert pressure on the police to clean up an intolerable pattern of solicitation in men's washrooms. Seldom will the judge see the individual case in the context of the larger law enforcement problem which confronts the police, and it is rare for the police to systematically communicate this over-all enforcement picture to the trial judiciary. Undoubtedly communication of such information to the judge would be improper if it were done for the purpose of influencing his evaluation of whether there is sufficient evidence of guilt to convict the defendant, but it would seem most relevant and proper if addressed to the judge's concern with whether the police were "overzealous" given the circumstances of the case and its relationship to the over-all enforcement problem.

B.   ACQUITTAL BECAUSE OF DISAGREEMENT OVER THE MEANING AND PURPOSE OF THE LAW

Illustration No. 4: A Detroit judge, in acquitting two female defendants of charges of accosting and soliciting for immoral purposes, commented: "It is clear that this entire affair was initiated and staged by the police officers who made the arrest and not by the defendants. The officers made the first contacts, they bought the defendants a number of drinks, and they suggested illicit relations. Under such conditions, the charge cannot stand. The crime charged is not prostitution; it is soliciting and accosting."

An acknowledged function of the trial judge is the interpretation of the substantive law relevant to the particular case. In accosting and soliciting cases in Michigan, some trial judges construe the statute[8] to require the female to have engaged in an "accosting," that is, to have been fairly aggressive in solicitation of a male. Where the plainclothes police officer actively encourages solicitation, this may remove the essential "accosting" element of the offense. The difficulty is that trial court opinions seldom attempt to differentiate clearly between an interpretation of the statute

[8] Mich. Comp. Laws §750.448 (1948).

defining the crime, an evaluation of the adequacy of the evidence of guilt, or a ruling on the propriety of the police detection methods which were involved. As a consequence, it is seldom apparent to the police or to the prosecutor whether the trial judge is performing his traditional function of law interpretation or his less traditional function of using his acquittal power to control arrest and charging practices.

Since minor offenses, such as prostitution or homosexual offenses, are seldom appealed, there is little opportunity for an appellate court to construe the statute defining the crime; nor, amid this uncertainty, is there any substantial pressure on the legislature to clarify the meaning of the accosting and soliciting statute. In prostitution cases particularly, the courts typically give literal meaning to the "accosting and soliciting" elements of the offense, while the police, on the other hand, broadly interpret the law to be a prohibition against prostitution and prostitutes per se and translate this into a mandate to "clean the streets" of all prostitutes. Since both the courts and the vice squad hold rather tenaciously to each of these different perspectives, the conflict comes to focus on the intensity of the in-court examination in accosting cases to discover who accosted whom and under what circumstances.

C. ACQUITTAL OF THE GUILTY
TO SUPPORT POLICE CRIME DETECTION METHODS

While there is little doubt that acquittal is sometimes used by trial judges as a device to control unfair police practices, it is also used to lend support to certain crime detection methods. This most often involves the freeing of police informants or of co-defendants whose testimony or other assistance has led to the conviction of their co-conspirators or to the solution of other crimes. All metropolitan police departments use informants, with particular frequency in the enforcement of laws relating to narcotics, gambling, and prostitution. It is general practice not to arrest or charge informants, but there are occasional exceptions, particularly when the arrest is made by police for whom the informant does not work. Federal informants, for example, are occasionally arrested by municipal police. Once their identity is proved, however, it is the practice to dismiss the charges against them.

In general, the courts support the giving of immunity to informants so long as they do not use their status as a "license to expand their own operations." An informant who is arrested for a crime unrelated to his undercover services will ordinarily be charged and convicted, unless he is of exceptional value to future enforcement plans. Furthermore, informants who have lost their usefulness (through being forced to testify or otherwise exposing their identity) will not ordinarily be fully acquitted; instead charges against them are commonly reduced to lesser offenses. Acquittal to support the activities of the police or prosecutor commonly involves the freeing of defendants who turn state's witness. This often means the acquittal of one member of some sort of criminal gang in exchange for his testimony against his co-defendants. Acquittal is also used as an attempt to control organized crime by offering immunity to gambling runners to get information about higher-up criminals or to prostitutes to obtain evidence against their procurers. In fact, Michigan has a statutory provision granting such immunity in prostitution investigations.[9]

D. THE EFFECT OF USE OF ACQUITTAL TO CONTROL POLICE CONDUCT

The effect of informal methods of trial court control over police practice is much like the effect of efforts at control by means of the formally recognized exclusionary rule and defense of entrapment. Efforts at informal control by trial judges do, however, create some additional problems. The informality itself results in greater differences in attitude between judges than is true in their interpretation of formally recognized and articulated rules. As a consequence of this trial court disparity in attitude the police vary their enforcement objectives, depending upon who the trial court judge is at a particular time. This is especially noticeable in multi-judge courts where there is rotation of assignment. There is often a noticeable decrease in emphasis on enforcement of certain crimes like prostitution or homosexual solicitation when the cases have to be brought before a judge who opposes an intensive enforcement program. On the other hand, when the assignment is given to a judge more sympathetic to the enforcement program, the intensity of police effort is increased.

Whether the judicial use of acquittal power as an informal means of controlling police practice has a constructive or destructive effect upon law enforcement would seem to depend upon several factors: (a) whether the trial judge's decision is based upon adequate understanding, not only of the facts of the particular case but of the law enforcement context out of which the case arises; (b) whether the judge or judges are consistent in their reactions to law enforcement practices; (c) whether the judge's reasons are made clear and effectively communicated to those in the police department who have the authority to change police practice; and (d) whether informal judicial control causes police to re-evaluate their practices rather than to resort to alternatives like harassment, which continues old practices but avoids bringing these matters to the attention of the trial judge.

[9] Mich. Comp. Laws §§750.453 and 750.461 (1948).

To the extent that generalization is possible, it is apparent in current administration that there is wide disparity in attitudes of trial judges toward police practices; there is no effective communication between police and judges; and the judges' efforts at control are resisted by police, who do not rethink the propriety of the enforcement program but rather adopt alternative methods of achieving their objectives. The common result is that police harass prostitutes and homosexuals by arresting them for other offenses such as disorderly conduct or vagrancy, taking only selected cases of accosting and soliciting to court. When acquittal results in even these "strong" cases, the only diminution is in the frequency of court appearances; arrests on other grounds continue as long as the police feel a mandate to proceed against vice crimes. This serves once again to illustrate the difficulty of effective control of one part of the criminal justice process by authority elsewhere. Just as trial judges avoid legislative sentencing mandates by systematically downgrading charges, so the police avoid trial court controls by arresting vice offenders for lesser crimes. This not only demonstrates the operational complexity of the process but questions the assumption commonly made that conformity of practice with court decisions is the inevitable result of trial or appellate holdings which are intended to discipline and control other agencies.

PART IV

The Epidemiology of Delinquency and Crime

Introduction

A theory of social behavior in general, or of criminality in particular, should include two distinct but interrelated aspects. For one thing, there should be an explanation of statistical distributions of behavior in terms of time, space, and social location. Secondly, there should be an explanation of the social-psychological process by which individuals come to exhibit the behavior in question. This aspect of the theory must be logically consistent with the first because a high crime rate, if it is accurate, is simply a summary figure indicating that some criminality-producing process is taking place among persons belonging to one social group or category more frequently than it is taking place among persons in some other social group or category. For example, the fact that the rate of narcotic law violations is higher among Negroes than among whites means that more Negroes than whites, proportionately, are undergoing some social-psychological process that makes them into narcotics violators. And the fact that the arrest rate for fraud is higher for whites than it is for Negroes means that, proportionately, more whites than Negroes are undergoing some social-psychological process leading them to commit this type of crime.

Behavioral explanations based on this kind of "dual" theoretical statement about rates and individual conduct cannot always be formulated, because data on both aspects are sometimes not available. For example, statistics on white-collar crime are not routinely collected by law-enforcement agencies, so theoretical concern for this crime focuses primarily on the conduct of individual white-collar criminals. In other cases, the researcher's personal interests may dispose him to concentrate on only the statistical distribution of the behavior or on only the process by which individuals take on the behavior.

The shorthand term for the distribution of crime and delinquency in time, space, and social location is "epidemiology." This concept has been borrowed from medicine, and, like other analogies with the biological or physical sciences, it can be misleading when applied to social phenomena. Nevertheless, the concept directs attention to concern for variations in rates of crime and delinquency among various social groups and categories. There is no comparable shorthand term describing criminological concern for the behavior of individual offenders. The processes by which individuals become criminals will be discussed in Parts V and VI.

The statistics pertaining to the epidemiological distribution of delinquency and crime are "location data." Such data signal criminologists to prepare theoretical statements which, hopefully, will account for the character of the statistical findings. For example, the general crime and delinquency rates are higher for young adults than for persons in later life, higher for persons reared in broken homes than for persons reared in unbroken homes, higher for blacks than for whites, higher for males than for females, higher for native-born than for foreign-born persons, higher for urban residents than for rural residents, and higher for working-class persons than for middle- and upper-class persons.[1] The difference between the crime rates of each of these pairs is not constant, however. For example, males in the United States have much higher general crime and delinquency rates than do females, but the extent of the difference varies by race, by age, by offense, and by other social conditions. What accounts for these variations?

The papers in this Part do not provide complete answers to these questions, but they steer us in the right direction. We have not presented papers on many of the epidemiological aspects of delinquency and crime traditionally discussed and analyzed by sociologists and criminologists. We concentrate on the distribution of crime and delinquency in the various social classes because in recent years epidemiological analyses have shown that most other distributions are associated with some aspect of social class position. Moreover, the theoretical questions regarding epidemiology have been most adequately raised with reference to relationships between poverty and lower-class status on the one hand, and delinquency and crime on the other. Until recently, it was widely asserted that "poverty" somehow "caused" delinquency and crime, but careful and precise statements about how poverty might work to produce either high delinquency rates or individual delinquencies were few and far be-

[1] See Part I above.

tween. Moreover, theoretical arguments about the relationship between delinquency (or crime) and poverty are countered with the argument that delinquent acts really are not more frequent in areas of poverty than in other areas; they just appear to be. Part IV addresses both the question of the adequacy of statistical information about the class distribution of delinquency and crime—a question raised in Part III—and some of the theoretical questions regarding the relationship between that distribution and other epidemiological distributions.

The selection by Robert K. Merton is a revision and extension of a classic sociological statement first published in 1938. It illustrates the need for integrated, "dual" theories of epidemiology and individual conduct. The essay purports, among other things, to account for an excess of property crimes in the working-class population. Briefly stated, Merton's theory asserts that the value structure of a society identifies both the "good things of life" in that society and the culturally approved means of achieving those goals. Further, in some societies, such as ours, the value structure includes the claim that these good things of life ("success goals") are equally available to *all* segments of the population, while in fact the social structure effectively blocks access to the goals for certain groups. A number of different systems for coping with this disparity between culturally approved goals and socially structured avenues for achieving them are evoked. One adaptation, "innovation," involves the use of illegitimate means to achieve legitimate goals. This adaptation is of particular relevance to students of criminology. To the extent that the illegitimate means include the use of illegal means, innovation is criminal behavior.

If Merton's analysis of innovation is viewed as a theory about delinquent and criminal behavior, rather than as a theory about how delinquent and criminal values came to be invented,[2] then the following hypothesis can be derived from it: Those sections of the population most frustrated in their efforts to achieve success will have the highest rate of delinquency and crime. Since it is easy to argue that the lower class has the highest rate of crime and delinquency, it is easy to conclude that the excess of delinquency in the lower class is due to restricted opportunities to acquire some of the good things of life. However, this analysis leaves unanswered, and to some extent unasked, both the question of why only a small proportion of the "structurally frustrated" working-class persons become property offenders, and the question of why "successful" middle- and upper-class persons engage in white-collar crime.

Although a few sociologists in the 1940s and early 1950s paid attention to Merton's theory in their studies of the epidemiology of delinquency and crime, psychiatric theory continued to dominate explanations

2 See Part VII below.

of the involvement of working-class (and other) individuals.[3] Only since about 1955 have there been attempts to identify the processes by which the blocking of legitimate means for achieving success, posed by Merton, might work to produce the criminality of individual working-class persons. Most of these efforts have continued to concentrate on variations in socially structured opportunities for success and for deviation, rather than on the social-psychological mechanisms through which individuals become involved in illegal activity. One of the most important extensions of Merton's theory was made by Richard Cloward, whose essay makes the point that for some persons the opportunities to achieve success goals by *illegitimate* means may also be blocked. Such persons are "double failures," in the sense that neither legitimate nor illegitimate means for achieving success are available to them. Like legitimate means to success goals, illegitimate avenues to such goals are differentially available to various segments of the population. Cloward and Ohlin have carried this theory further by considering opportunities to learn the skills necessary for participating in either the legitimate or illegitimate paths to success. This important theoretical development will be discussed later.[4]

A differing view of the relationship between social class and delinquency and crime is taken by Walter Miller, who hints at what many sociologists and social psychologists have suspected for some time, namely that the significant determinant of high delinquency rates in the lower class is a set of values which are conducive to individual delinquencies. He contends, in other words, that lower-class delinquency can best be understood as a consequence of involvement with a particular set of values ("subculture") rather than as a reaction to blocked legitimate means for achieving success. Bordua has noted that the lower-class subculture described by Miller has emerged from the shaking-down process of immigration, internal migration, and vertical mobility in the United States.[5] Miller sees street groups as training grounds for lower-class boys.

[3] For a critical analysis of this area of criminological research, see Frank E. Hartung, "A Critique of the Sociological Approach to Crime and Correction," *Law and Contemporary Problems, 23* (Autumn, 1958), 703–734; and Michael Hakeem, "A Critique of the Psychiatric Approach to Crime and Correction," *ibid.*, 650–682.

[4] See "The Evolution of Delinquent Subcultures" and "The Differentiation of Delinquent Subcultures" in Parts VII and VIII below.

[5] David J. Bordua, "Delinquent Subcultures: Sociological Interpretations of Gang Delinquency," *Annals of the American Academy of Political and Social Science, 338* (November, 1961), 120–136. This is an excellent critique of Miller's work as well as of the sociological work stemming from Merton's theory. The classic study of informal groups of boys in a slum area is William F. Whyte's *Street Corner Society*, Chicago: The University of Chicago Press, 1943. Daniel Bell's article, "Crime as an American Way of Life," *The Antioch Review, 13* (June, 1953), 131–154, is a well-known statement that organized crime and racketeering have provided an alternative opportunity structure for young Italian men disadvantaged in competing for legitimate opportunities.

Boys who grow up in the lower-class areas of large cities rather automatically violate the law because the values of the lower class are in conflict with those of the larger society. It is not necessary that their opportunities for achieving success goals be blocked; it is necessary only that they participate in the values of the lower-class subculture.

In our introduction to Part II we stated that crime rates tend to increase as societies become more complex and as the number of different values among the members increases. But it is also true that as societies have become complex and as conflicting values have appeared, feelings of *unjust* deprivation also have increased. Merton does not argue that poverty, or even low status, evokes the innovation response. His basic notion is that the unavailability of the good things of life is relevant to delinquency and crime when there is a blocking of *aspirations*. Mere differences in degrees of affluence among segments of the population are not relevant. What is relevant is structural frustration. The value system of the society must include the implication that the poor are *deprived*. Moreover, the frustration need not be a frustration of desires for basic needs; it can be a frustration of culturally induced desires for equality of affluence. Toby has gone a long way toward confirming this notion by showing that crime rates are rising most rapidly in those countries of the world characterized not by the greatest poverty but by the greatest affluence. This fact cannot be readily explained by those who claim that criminal and delinquent behavior are rooted in the conditions caused by poverty. The sociological concept "relative deprivation" may be useful here to distinguish the reactions of the disadvantaged in an affluent society from the reactions of the disadvantaged in a poor society. A feeling of unjust deprivation depends upon knowledge of what goals one should expect to achieve, but cannot, and upon opportunities to see that others with no more ability have achieved them.

The theory developed by Merton and extended by Cloward has particular relevance to an understanding of why there is more crime among the poor in an affluent society like the United States than there is among the destitute and starving people of India. The same conceptual framework is also useful in explaining why the most serious racial disturbances in American cities have occurred in areas of Los Angeles and Detroit, where employment opportunities and living conditions for Negroes were considered to be superior to conditions in cities where trouble either did not occur or was less serious. The mere existence of success goals which some cannot achieve is not sufficient to explain either delinquency or riots. Until recently, most black Americans had little hope of ever achieving the success goals which were available to many white persons. Southern Negroes, for example, traditionally resolved the problem of deprivation in the present by seeking their rewards in the "hereafter." However, as American society has begun, officially at least, to move toward equalizing opportunities for its black citizens—through court decisions, civil rights legislation, and other governmental actions— participation in the "American Dream" has begun to be expected. Negroes living in northern ghettoes and in the South have been continually reminded by civil rights workers, militant black organizations, and the mass media that in the United States *all* citizens have a right to be full and equal partners in this country's affluence. Hope has been raised. But the rate of progress has been slow, political promises have been unfilled, and there have been numerous reminders that the legitimate means of achievement, particularly employment opportunities, have been unduly and unfairly restricted. The differential between achievement and aroused hope has produced a potential for direct action involving crime. In other words, it is after expectations have been revised upward and attempts to achieve new success goals have been frustrated that criminal means may be used.

It should be noted, however, that most of the Negroes living in ghettoes do not participate in riots and that most Negroes are not criminals. One could argue that this low rate of involvement in illegality arises because only a few Negroes have had their hopes raised, or because many whose hopes have been raised have been able to achieve success legally. One also could argue that the crime rate of most Negroes remains low because structural frustration does not cast them into contact with sets of delinquent and criminal values. Perhaps the most important theoretical problem now confronting criminologists who would "make sense" of the epidemiology of delinquency and crime is the one of resolving these two alternative arguments. Such a resolution probably will combine the structural frustration idea discussed by Merton and Cloward with the "automatic participation" idea advanced by Miller. Some persons might automatically participate extensively in a delinquent or criminal subculture while others need to be motivated, by structural frustration, for such participation. In either case, participation in a delinquent or criminal value system is essential. To a large degree the location of persons in the social structure determines both whether they will become structurally frustrated and whether they will participate in a delinquent or criminal value system. This is best illustrated in observations of the delinquency rates and crime rates of social categories whose members only infrequently appear in police stations and courts.

The American middle-class youth culture, for example, is not such that a participant automatically violates the law. Moreover, middle-class youth are not clearly frustrated in their desires to acquire the good things of life. But, as Vaz shows, a competitive system for gaining status among middle-class youth is somewhat the equivalent of structural frustration.

As middle-class boys explore the boundaries of legitimacy, principally as a competitive status-gaining device, they develop "game rules" which make delinquency seem rather routine. Similarly, it might be argued that the competitive system for gaining status among businessmen is the equivalent of structural frustration, or that there is a literal blocking of businessmen's aspirations for success as *they* see it, not as poor persons see it. Sutherland makes neither of these arguments in his classic article on white-collar crime. Rather, he implies that businessmen rather routinely commit crimes in the course of "doing business," just as Miller's lower-class boys rather routinely commit delinquencies in the course of "growing up." Businessmen have developed "game rules" which make business crimes seem rather routine while at the same time making the street crimes of working-class persons appear to be a difficult and serious social problem.

The effects of a combination of structural frustration and subcultural participation become even clearer when two or more epidemiological variables are considered at the same time. As indicated earlier, it can readily be concluded that the relatively high delinquency rate of lower-class persons stems from structural frustration in the form of restricted opportunities. But when the delinquency rates of additional categories are considered along with social class, it becomes obvious that only some sets of lower-class persons have high delinquency rates. For example, lower-class females and lower-class rural persons have low delinquency rates. The difference between the delinquency rates of lower-class females and of lower-class males, and the difference between the delinquency rates of lower-class rural dwellers and lower-class urban dwellers might be due to differences in status frustration. Alternatively, the differences might be due to differences in opportunities to participate in value systems favorable to delinquency. By considering the social-class distribution of delinquency and the rural-urban distribution of delinquency at the same time, Polk discovered that in nonmetropolitan areas, at least, the important delinquency-producing process involves *both* structural frustration and participation in a delinquent subculture. In the excerpt from the report he wrote for the President's Crime Commission he notes that earlier studies concluded that distinct delinquent and criminal subcultures are rarely found in rural areas and that, generally speaking, the relatively low delinquency rates of nonmetropolitan areas were attributed to this condition. He notes, further, that such delinquency as is found in nonmetropolitan areas tends to be located in the lower class. From these observations it could be concluded that some social class variable other than participation in a delinquent subculture was producing the excess of delinquency in the lower class of nonmetropolitan areas. In an earlier study, Polk found that variable to be structural frustration—blue-collar students who were at the same level of achievement as were white-collar students did not have an excess of delinquency. Conversely, about one-fifth to one-fourth of the students doing poor or failing work in school (a measure of structural frustration) became delinquent regardless of their social class.[6] But in the selection reprinted below Polk argues that small towns contain a "trouble making subculture." School failures are "locked out" of the system supporting accomplishments by legitimate means, and they drift into the "trouble making subculture." Even when they migrate to urban areas they are not able to participate fully in the legitimate opportunity structures because they are economically, educationally, socially, and culturally disadvantaged. A combination of structural frustration and participation in a deviant subculture, then, is seen as the important delinquency-producing condition.

It should not be concluded from Polk's analysis that structural frustration, in school or elsewhere, drives students into participation in a delinquent subculture. After all, 75 to 80 percent of the school failures studied by Polk did not become delinquent. Structural frustration seems to be relevant to delinquent and criminal conduct because persons are motivated to seek relief from it, but only some of them find relief by participating in delinquent subcultures. Others find different solutions, while still others might merely drift into participation.[7] Clark and Wenninger discuss some of these variations. Their selection summarizes a study which found, basically, that "location" is more important to delinquency than is "social class" in its pure form. The authors found no differences in the self-reported delinquency rates among the social classes of rural areas and small urban areas, a finding consistent with that of other persons studying self-reported delinquency rather than official statistics. However, they did find significant differences when communities were compared on a "status area" basis. The analysis of the self-reported delinquency rates of these areas indicates that the lower-class areas have the highest rates, particularly for the more serious types of offenses. Differences among the socio-economic classes *within* these areas were generally insignificant. Without saying so, Clark and Wenninger conclude that the "working class" discussed by Merton and by Cloward consists of the lower-class persons living in the lower-class areas of large urban communities. They make clear, further, that Miller is discussing the lower-class persons living in particular ("lower class") areas of large cities, not all lower-class persons. Furthermore, the middle-class children living in the same areas report delinquencies in about the same measures as do the lower-class children. Clark and Wenninger's findings also suggest that

[6] Kenneth Polk and David S. Halferty, "Adolescence, Commitment, and Delinquency," *Journal of Research in Crime and Delinquency, 3* (July, 1966), 82–96.

[7] See David Matza, *Delinquency and Drift* (New York: Wiley, 1964).

the earlier studies reporting no significant interclass differences in delinquency rates were studies of areas similar to the areas they call "rural farm," "upper urban," and "lower urban." Conceivably, processes similar to those giving "industrial city" boys high delinquency rates also occur in some middle-class and upper-class areas, giving members of these classes high white-collar crime rates.

Generally speaking, Clark and Wenninger have confirmed earlier conclusions regarding the relevance of "poverty" to delinquency. It is quite clear that something more than "poverty" is involved. Poverty in the modern city customarily means segregation in low-rent areas, isolation from anticriminal values and behavior patterns, and contact with delinquent and criminal subcultural values. It also means low status (and status frustration), with little to respect and little to lose, and little to encourage or sustain efforts at self-advancement. Further, it frequently means, in the midst of affluence, bad housing conditions, poor health, unemployment, and contact with drunks, prostitutes, pimps, beggars, vagrants, delinquents, and criminals. These are the conditions characterizing the living conditions of Negroes in many American metropolitan areas, and these probably are the conditions characterizing the "lower class" described by Miller and the "status areas" whose delinquency rates Clark and Wenninger found to be high.

The results of Erickson's and Empey's study are consistent with those found by Clark and Wenninger, but these authors go into more detail regarding the mechanisms of participation in the deviant subcultures of "status areas." They treat Merton's paradigm as a theory of delinquency rather than as a theory about the origin of delinquent subcultures, and they provide a rough test of that theory. In effect, they ask whether lower-class children, assumed to be experiencing the frustrations leading to Merton's "innovation" reaction, are in fact more frequently delinquent than are middle- or upper-class children. Using the self-reporting technique, the investigators determined that about nine out of ten violations of law reported by the two hundred boys in their sample went undetected. When the undetected violations were correlated with social class affiliation, statistically significant differences between the classes appeared. This was due to the strong negative relationship between upper-class status and delinquent activities. The samples of middle-class and lower-class boys did not differ significantly from each other. Further analysis indicated that the upper-class boys associated less frequently with delinquents, and identified less often with delinquent peers, than did middle- and lower-class boys. Generally, peer variables (associates and commitment to peer expectations) were found to be more efficient predictors of delinquency than was social class.

In Part V we shall introduce the "differential association" theory of delinquency and crime, a theory which places great emphasis on the importance to delinquency of learning to be guided by deviant values. This theory has to some extent been neglected in epidemiological research because it has been viewed mainly as an alternative to psychiatric theories about the process by which individuals become delinquents and criminals. But the implications of differential association as a theory for explaining differences in the delinquency and crime rates of various categories of lower-class and upper-class persons have been explored to some extent in the research on which the article by Erickson and Empey is based. We will show later that the theory of differential association does not precisely portray the process by which individuals become delinquents and criminals but that its capacity to explain the distribution of delinquency and crime rates is quite high.[8] Here it need only be noted that Erickson and Empey found that the respondents who had been most delinquent were also those who were most likely to have delinquent associates.

---

[8] See "Epidemiology and Individual Conduct" in Part V below.

1 Social Structure and Anomie

ROBERT K. MERTON

Until recently, and all the more so before then, one could speak of a marked tendency in psychological and sociological theory to attribute the faulty operation of social structures to failures of social control over man's imperious biological drives. The imagery of the relations between man and society implied by this doctrine is as clear as it is questionable. In the beginning, there are man's biological impulses which seek full expression. And then, there is the social order, essentially an apparatus for the management of impulses, for the social processing of tensions, for the "renunciation of instinctual gratifications," in the words of Freud. Nonconformity with the demands of a social structure is thus assumed to be anchored in original nature.[1] It is the biologically rooted impulses which from time to time break through social control. And by implication, conformity is the result of an utilitarian calculus or of unreasoned conditioning.

With the more recent advancement of social science, this set of conceptions has undergone basic modification. For one thing, it no longer appears so obvious that man is set against society in an unceasing war

Reprinted with permission of The Macmillan Company from *Social Theory and Social Structure* by Robert K. Merton. Copyright 1957 by The Free Press, a Corporation, pp. 131–160.

[1] See, for example, S. Freud, *Civilization and Its Discontents* (*passim*, and esp. at 63); Ernest Jones, *Social Aspects of Psychoanalysis* (London 1924) 28. If the Freudian notion is a variety of the "original sin" doctrine, then the interpretation advanced in this paper is a doctrine of "socially derived sin."

between biological impulse and social restraint. The image of man as an untamed bundle of impulses begins to look more like a caricature than a portrait. For another, sociological perspectives have increasingly entered into the analysis of behavior deviating from prescribed patterns of conduct. For whatever the role of biological impulses, there still remains the further question of why it is that the frequency of deviant behavior varies within different social structures and how it happens that the deviations have different shapes and patterns in different social structures. Today, as then, we have still much to learn about the processes through which social structures generate the circumstances in which infringement of social codes constitutes a "normal" (that is to say, an expectable) response.[2] This . . . is an essay seeking clarification of the problem.

The framework set out in this essay is designed to provide one systematic approach to the analysis of social and cultural sources of deviant behavior. Our primary aim is to discover how some *social structures exert a definite pressure upon certain persons in the society to engage in nonconforming rather than conforming conduct.* If we can locate groups peculiarly subject to such pressures, we should expect to find fairly high rates of deviant behavior in these groups, not because the human beings comprising them are compounded of distinctive biological tendencies but because they are responding normally to the social situation in which they find themselves. Our perspective is sociological. We look at variations in the *rates* of deviant behavior, not at its incidence.[3] Should our quest be at all successful, some forms of deviant behavior will be found to be as

---

[2] "Normal" in the sense of the psychologically expectable, if not culturally approved, response to determinate social conditions. This statement does not, of course, deny the role of biological and personality differences in fixing the *incidence* of deviant behavior. It is simply that *this* is not the problem considered here. It is in this same sense, I take it, that James S. Plant speaks of the "normal reaction of normal people to abnormal conditions." See his *Personality and the Cultural Pattern* (New York, 1937), 248.

[3] The position taken here has been perceptively described by Edward Sapir. ". . . problems of social science differ from problems of individual behavior in degree of specificity, not in kind. Every statement about behavior which throws the emphasis, explicitly or implicitly, on the actual, integral experiences of defined personalities or types of personalities is a datum of psychology or psychiatry rather than of social science. Every statement about behavior which aims, not to be accurate about the behavior of an actual individual or individuals or about the expected behavior of a physically and psychologically defined type of individual, but which abstracts from such behavior in order to bring out in clear relief certain expectancies with regard to those aspects of individual behavior which various people share, as an interpersonal or 'social' pattern, is a datum, however crudely expressed, of social science." I have here chosen the second perspective; although I shall have occasion to speak of attitudes, values and function, it will be from the standpoint of how the social structure promotes or inhibits their appearance in specified types of situations. See Sapir, "Why cultural anthropology needs the psychiatrist," *Psychiatry*, 1938, 1, 7–12.

psychologically normal as conformist behavior, and the equation of deviation and psychological abnormality will be put in question.

PATTERNS OF CULTURAL GOALS AND INSTITUTIONAL NORMS

Among the several elements of social and cultural structures, two are of immediate importance. These are analytically separable although they merge in concrete situations. The first consists of culturally defined goals, purposes and interests, held out as legitimate objectives for all or for diversely located members of the society. The goals are more or less integrated—the degree is a question of empirical fact—and roughly ordered in some hierarchy of value. Involving various degrees of sentiment and significance, the prevailing goals comprise a frame of aspirational reference. They are the things "worth striving for." They are a basic, though not the exclusive, component of what Linton has called "designs for group living." And though some, not all, of these cultural goals are directly related to the biological drives of man, they are not determined by them.

A second element of the cultural structure defines, regulates and controls the acceptable modes of reaching out for these goals. Every social group invariably couples its cultural objectives with regulations, rooted in the mores or institutions, of allowable procedures for moving toward these objectives. These regulatory norms are not necessarily identical with technical or efficiency norms. Many procedures which from the standpoint of particular individuals would be most efficient in securing desired values—the exercise of force, fraud, power—are ruled out of the institutional area of permitted conduct. At times, the disallowed procedures include some which would be efficient for the group itself—*e.g.*, historic taboos on vivisection, on medical experimentation, on the sociological analysis of "sacred" norms—since the criterion of acceptability is not technical efficiency but value-laden sentiments (supported by most members of the group or by those able to promote these sentiments through the composite use of power and propaganda). In all instances, the choice of expedients for striving toward cultural goals is limited by institutionalized norms.

Sociologists often speak of these controls as being "in the mores" or as operating through social institutions. Such elliptical statements are true enough, but they obscure the fact that culturally standardized practices are not all of a piece. They are subject to a wide gamut of control. They may represent definitely prescribed or preferential or permissive or proscribed patterns of behavior. In assessing the operation of social controls, these variations—roughly indicated by the terms *prescription, preference, permission* and *proscription*—must of course be taken into account.

To say, moreover, that cultural goals and institutionalized norms operate jointly to shape prevailing practices is not to say that they bear a constant relation to one another. The cultural emphasis placed upon certain
goals varies independently of the degree of emphasis upon institutionalized
means. There may develop a very heavy, at times a virtually exclusive,
stress upon the value of particular goals, involving comparatively little
concern with the institutionally prescribed means of striving toward these
goals. The limiting case of this type is reached when the range of alternative
procedures is governed only by technical rather than by institutional norms.
Any and all procedures which promise attainment of the all-important goal
would be permitted in this hypothetical polar case. This constitutes one type
of malintegrated culture. A second polar type is found in groups where
activities originally conceived as instrumental are transmuted into self-
contained practices, lacking further objectives. The original purposes are
forgotten and close adherence to institutionally prescribed conduct becomes
a matter of ritual.[4] Sheer conformity becomes a central value. For a time,
social stability is ensured—at the expense of flexibility. Since the range of
alternative behaviors permitted by the culture is severely limited, there is
little basis for adapting to new conditions. There develops a tradition-bound,
'sacred' society marked by neophobia. Between these extreme types are
societies which maintain a rough balance between emphases upon cultural
goals and institutionalized practices, and these constitute the integrated and
relatively stable, though changing, societies.

An effective equilibrium between these two phases of the social structure is maintained so long as satisfactions accrue to individuals conforming
to both cultural constraints, *viz.*, satisfactions from the achievement of
goals and satisfactions emerging directly from the institutionally canalized
modes of striving to attain them. It is reckoned in terms of the product and
in terms of the process, in terms of the outcome and in terms of the
activities. Thus continuing satisfactions must derive from sheer participation
in a competitive order as well as from eclipsing one's competitors if the
order itself is to be sustained. If concern shifts exclusively to the outcome
of competition, then those who perenially suffer defeat may, understandably enough, work for a change in the rules of the game. The sacrifices
occasionally—not, as Freud assumed, invariably—entailed by conformity
to institutional norms must be compensated by socialized rewards. The
distribution of statuses through competition must be so organized that
positive incentives for adherence to status obligations are provided *for
every position* within the distributive order. Otherwise, as will soon become

---

[4] This ritualism may be associated with a mythology which rationalizes these
practices so that they appear to retain their status as means, but the dominant pressure
is toward strict ritualistic conformity, irrespective of the mythology. Ritualism is thus
most complete when such rationalizations are not even called forth.

plain, aberrant behavior ensues. It is, indeed, my central hypothesis that aberrant behavior may be regarded sociologically as a symptom of dissociation between culturally prescribed aspirations and socially structured avenues for realizing these aspirations.

Of the types of societies which result from independent variation of cultural goals and institutionalized means, we shall be primarily concerned with the first—a society in which there is an exceptionally strong emphasis upon specific goals without a corresponding emphasis upon institutional procedures. If it is not to be misunderstood, this statement must be elaborated. No society lacks norms governing conduct. But societies do differ in the degree to which the folkways, mores and institutional controls are effectively integrated with the goals which stand high in the hierarchy of cultural values. The culture may be such as to lead individuals to center their emotional convictions upon the complex of culturally acclaimed ends, with far less emotional support for prescribed methods of reaching out for these ends. With such differential emphases upon goals and institutional procedures, the latter may be so vitiated by the stress on goals as to have the behavior of many individuals limited only by considerations of technical expediency. In this context, the sole significant question becomes: Which of the available procedures is most efficient in netting the culturally approved value?[5] The technically most effective procedure, whether culturally legitimate or not, becomes typically preferred to institutionally prescribed conduct. As this process of attenuation continues, the society becomes unstable and there develops what Durkheim called "anomie" (or normlessness).[6]

The working of this process eventuating in anomie can be easily

---

[5] In this connection, one sees the relevance of Elton Mayo's paraphrase of the title of Tawney's well-known book. "Actually the problem is *not that of the sickness of an acquisitive society; it is that of the acquisitiveness of a sick society*." *Human Problems of an Industrial Civilization*, 153. Mayo deals with the process through which wealth comes to be the basic symbol of social achievement and sees this as arising from a state of anomie. My major concern here is with the social consequences of a heavy emphasis upon monetary success as a goal in a society which has not adapted its structure to the implications of this emphasis. A complete analysis would require the simultaneous examination of both processes.

[6] Durkheim's resurrection of the term "anomie" which, so far as I know, first appears in approximately the same sense in the late sixteenth century, might well become the object of an investigation by a student interested in the historical filiation of ideas. Like the term "climate of opinion" brought into academic and political popularity by A. N. Whitehead three centuries after it was coined by Joseph Glanvill, the word "anomie" (or anomy or anomia) has lately come into frequent use, once it was reintroduced by Durkheim. Why the resonance in contemporary society? For a magnificent model of the type of research required by questions of this order, see Leo Spitzer, "*Milieu* and *Ambiance*: an essay in historical semantics," *Philosophy and Phenomenological Research*, 1942, 3, 1–42, 169–218.

glimpsed in a series of familiar and instructive, though perhaps trivial, episodes. Thus, in competitive athletics, when the aim of victory is shorn of its institutional trappings and success becomes construed as "winning the game" rather than "winning under the rules of the game," a premium is implicitly set upon the use of illegitimate but technically efficient means. The star of the opposing football team is surreptitiously slugged; the wrestler incapacitates his opponent through ingenious but illicit techniques; university alumni covertly subsidize "students" whose talents are confined to the athletic field. The emphasis on the goal has so attenuated the satisfactions deriving from sheer participation in the competitive activity that only a successful outcome provides gratification. Through the same process, tension generated by the desire to win in a poker game is relieved by successfully dealing one's self four aces or, when the cult of success has truly flowered, by sagaciously shuffling the cards in a game of solitaire. The faint twinge of uneasiness in the last instance and the surreptitious nature of public delicts indicate clearly that the institutional rules of the game are *known* to those who evade them. But cultural (or idiosyncratic) exaggeration of the success-goal leads men to withdraw emotional support from the rules.[7]

This process is of course not restricted to the realm of competitive sport, which has simply provided us with microcosmic images of the social macrocosm. The process whereby exaltation of the end generates a literal *demoralization*, i.e., a de-institutionalization, of the means occurs in many[8] groups where the two components of the social structure are not highly integrated.

Contemporary American culture appears to approximate the polar type in which great emphasis upon certain success-goals occurs without equivalent emphasis upon institutional means. It would of course be fanciful to assert that accumulated wealth stands alone as a symbol of success just as it would be fanciful to deny that Americans assign it a place high in their scale of values. In some large measure, money has been consecrated as a value in itself, over and above its expenditure for articles of consumption or its use for the enhancement of power. "Money" is peculiarly well adapted

[7] It appears unlikely that cultural norms, once interiorized, are wholly eliminated. Whatever residuum persists will induce personality tensions and conflict, with some measure of ambivalence. A manifest rejection of the once-incorporated institutional norms will be coupled with some latent retention of their emotional correlates. Guilt feelings, a sense of sin, pangs of conscience are diverse terms referring to this unrelieved tension. Symbolic adherence to the nominally repudiated values or rationalizations for the rejection of these values constitute a more subtle expression of these tensions.

[8] "Many," not all, unintegrated groups, for the reason mentioned earlier. In groups where the primary emphasis shifts to institutional means, the outcome is normally a type of ritualism rather than anomie.

to become a symbol of prestige. As Simmel emphasized, money is highly abstract and impersonal. However acquired, fraudulently or institutionally, it can be used to purchase the same goods and services. The anonymity of an urban society, in conjunction with these peculiarities of money, permits wealth, the sources of which may be unknown to the community in which the plutocrat lives or, if known, to become purified in the course of time, to serve as a symbol of high status. Moreover, in the American Dream there is no final stopping point. The measure of "monetary success" is conveniently indefinite and relative. At each income level, as H. F. Clark found, Americans want just about twenty-five per cent more (but of course this "just a bit more" continues to operate once it is obtained). In this flux of shifting standards, there is no stable resting point, or rather, it is the point which manages always to be "just ahead." An observer of a community in which annual salaries in six figures are not uncommon, reports the anguished words of one victim of the American Dream: "In this town, I'm snubbed socially because I only get a thousand a week. That hurts."[9]

To say that the goal of monetary success is entrenched in American culture is only to say that Americans are bombarded on every side by precepts which affirm the right or, often, the duty of retaining the goal even in the face of repeated frustration. Prestigeful representatives of the society reinforce the cultural emphasis. The family, the school and the workplace—the major agencies shaping the personality structure and goal formation of Americans—join to provide the intensive disciplining required if an individual is to retain intact a goal that remains elusively beyond reach, if he is to be motivated by the promise of a gratification which is not redeemed. As we shall presently see, parents serve as a transmission belt for the values and goals of the groups of which they are a part—above all, of their social class or of the class with which they identify themselves. And the schools are of course the official agency for the passing on of the prevailing values, with a large proportion of the textbooks used in city schools implying or stating explicitly "that education leads to intelligence and consequently to job and money success."[10] Central to this process of disciplining people to maintain their unfulfilled aspirations are the cultural prototypes of success, the living documents testifying that the American Dream can be realized if one but has the requisite abilities. Consider in this connection the following excerpts from the business journal, *Nation's Buisness*, drawn from a large amount of comparable materials found in mass communications setting forth the values of business class culture.

[9] Leo. C. Rosten, *Hollywood* (New York, 1940), 40.

[10] Malcolm S. MacLean, *Scholars, Workers and Gentlemen* (Harvard University Press, 1938), 29.

The Document
(*Nation's Business, Vol. 27, No. 8, p. 7*)

Its Sociological Implications

'You have to be born to those jobs, buddy, or else have a good pull.'

Here is a heretical opinion, possibly born of continued frustration, which rejects the worth of retaining an apparently unrealizable goal and, moreover, questions the legitimacy of a social structure which provides differential access to this goal.

That's an old sedative to ambition.

The counter-attack, explicitly asserting the cultural value of retaining one's aspirations intact, of not losing "ambition."

Before listening to its seduction, ask these men:

A clear statement of the function to be served by the ensuing list of "successes." These men are living testimony that the social structure is such as to permit these aspirations to be achieved, *if one is worthy*. And correlatively, failure to reach these goals testifies only to one's own personal shortcomings. Aggression provoked by failure should therefore be directed inward and not outward, against oneself and not against a social structure which provides free and equal access to opportunity.

Elmer R. Jones, president of Wells-Fargo and Co., who began life as a poor boy and left school at the fifth grade to take his first job.

Success prototype I: *All* may properly have the *same* lofty ambitions, for however lowly the starting-point, true talent can reach the very heights. Aspirations must be retained intact.

Frank C. Ball, the Mason fruit jar king of America, who rode from Buffalo to Muncie, Indiana, in a boxcar along with his brother George's horse, to start a little business in Muncie that became the biggest of its kind.

Success prototype II: Whatever the present results of one's strivings, the future is large with promise; for the common man may yet become a king. Gratifications may seem forever deferred, but they will finally be realized as one's enterprise becomes "the biggest of its kind."

J. L. Bevan, president of the Illinois Central Railroad, who at twelve was a messenger boy in the freight office at New Orleans.

Success prototype III: If the secular trends of our economy seem to give little scope to small business, then one may rise within the giant bureaucracies of private enterprise. If one can no longer be a king in a realm of his own creation, he may at least become a president in one of the economic democracies. No matter what one's present station, messenger boy or clerk, one's gaze should be fixed at the top.

From diverse sources there flows a continuing pressure to retain high ambition. The exhortational literature is immense, and one can choose only at the risk of seeming invidious. Consider only these: The Reverend Russell H. Conwell, with his *Acres of Diamonds* address heard and read by hundreds of thousands and his subsequent book, *The New Day*, or *Fresh Opportunities: A Book for Young Men*; Elbert Hubbard, who delivered the famous *Message to Garcia* at Chautauqua forums throughout the land; Orison Swett Marden, who, in a stream of books, first set forth *The Secret of Achievement*, praised by college presidents, then explained the process of *Pushing to the Front*, eulogized by President McKinley and finally, these democratic testimonials notwithstanding, mapped the road to make *Every Man a King*. The symbolism of a commoner rising to the estate of economic royalty is woven deep in the texture of the American culture pattern, finding what is perhaps its ultimate expression in the words of one who knew whereof he spoke, Andrew Carnegie: "Be a king in your dreams. Say to yourself, 'My place is at the top.' "[11]

Coupled with this positive emphasis upon the obligation to maintain lofty goals is a correlative emphasis upon the penalizing of those who draw in their ambitions. Americans are admonished "not to be a quitter" for in the dictionary of American culture, as in the lexicon of youth, "there is no such word as 'fail.' " The cultural manifesto is clear: one must not quit, must not cease striving, must not lessen his goals, for "not failure, but low aim, is crime."

Thus the culture enjoins the acceptance of three cultural axioms: First, all should strive for the same lofty goals since these are open to all; second, present seeming failure is but a way-station to ultimate success; and third, genuine failure consists only in the lessening or withdrawal of ambition.

In rough psychological paraphrase, these axioms represent, first, a symbolic secondary reinforcement of incentive; second, curbing the threatened extinction of a response through an associated stimulus; third, increasing the motive-strength to evoke continued responses despite the continued absence of reward.

In sociological paraphrase, these axioms represent, first, the deflection

---

[11] *Cf.* A. W. Griswold, *The American Cult of Success* (Yale University doctoral dissertation, 1933); R. O. Carlson, "*Personality Schools*": A Sociological Analysis, (Columbia University Master's Essay, 1948).

of criticism of the social structure onto one's self among those so situated in the society that they do not have full and equal access to opportunity; second, the preservation of a structure of social power by having individuals in the lower social strata identify themselves, not with their compeers, but with those at the top (whom they will ultimately join); and third, providing pressures for conformity with the cultural dictates of unslackened ambition by the threat of less than full membership in the society for those who fail to conform.

It is in these terms and through these processes that contemporary American culture continues to be characterized by a heavy emphasis on wealth as a basic symbol of success, without a corresponding emphasis upon the legitimate avenues on which to march toward this goal. How do individuals living in this cultural context respond? And how do our observations bear upon the doctrine that deviant behavior typically derives from biological impulses breaking through the restraints imposed by culture? What, in short, are the consequences for the behavior of people variously situated in a social structure of a culture in which the emphasis on dominant success-goals has become increasingly separated from an equivalent emphasis on institutionalized procedures for seeking these goals?

TYPES OF INDIVIDUAL ADAPTATION

Turning from these culture patterns, we now examine types of adaptation by individuals within the culture-bearing society. Though our focus is still the cultural and social genesis of varying rates and types of deviant behavior, our perspective shifts from the plane of patterns of cultural values to the plane of types of adaptation to these values among those occupying different positions in the social structure.

We here consider five types of adaptation, as these are schematically set out in the following table, where (+) signifies "acceptance," (−) signifies "rejection," and (±) signifies "rejection of prevailing values and substitution of new values."

A Typology of Modes of Individual Adaptation[12]

Modes of Adaptation	Culture Goals	Institutionalized Means
I. Conformity	+	+
II. Innovation	+	−
III. Ritualism	−	+
IV. Retreatism	−	−
V. Rebellion[13]	±	±

[12] There is no lack of typologies of alternative modes of response to frustrating conditions. Freud, in his *Civilization and Its Discontents* (p. 30 ff.) supplies one;

Examination of how the social structure operates to exert pressure upon individuals for one or another of these alternative modes of behavior must be prefaced by the observation that people may shift from one alternative to another as they engage in different spheres of social activities. These categories refer to role behavior in specific types of situations, not to personality. They are types of more or less enduring response, not types of personality organization. To consider these types of adaptation in several spheres of conduct would introduce a complexity unmanageable within the confines of this paper. For this reason, we shall be primarily concerned with economic activity in the broad sense of "the production, exchange, distribution and consumption of goods and services" in our competitive society, where wealth has taken on a highly symbolic cast.

I. Conformity

To the extent that a society is stable, adaptation type I—conformity to both cultural goals and institutionalized means—is the most common and widely diffused. Were this not so, the stability and continuity of the society could not be maintained. The mesh of expectancies constituting every social order is sustained by the modal behavior of its members representing conformity to the established, though perhaps secularly chang-

---

derivative typologies, often differing in basic details, will be found in Karen Horney, *Neurotic Personality of Our Time* (New York, 1937); S. Rosenzweig, "The experimental measurement of types of reaction to frustration," in H. A. Murray *et al.*, *Explorations in Personality* (New York, 1938), 585–99; and in the work of John Dollard, Harold Lasswell, Abram Kardiner, Erich Fromm. But particularly in the strictly Freudian typology the perspective is that of types of individual responses, quite apart from the place of the individual within the social structure. Despite her consistent concern with "culture," for example, Horney does not explore differences in the impact of this culture upon farmer, worker and businessman, upon lower-, middle-, and upper-class individuals, upon members of various ethnic and racial groups, *etc.* As a result, the role of "inconsistencies in culture" is *not* located in its differential impact upon diversely situated groups. Culture becomes a kind of blanket covering all members of the society equally, apart from their idiosyncratic differences of life-history. It is a primary assumption of our typology that these responses occur with different frequency within various sub-groups in our society precisely because members of these groups or strata are differentially subject to cultural stimulation and social restraints. This sociological orientation will be found in the writings of Dollard and, less systematically, in the work of Fromm, Kardiner and Lasswell. On the general point, see note 3.

[13] This fifth alternative is on a plane clearly different from that of the others. It represents a transitional response seeking to *institutionalize* new goals and new procedures to be shared by other members of the society. It thus refers to efforts to *change* the existing cultural and social structure rather than to accommodate efforts *within* this structure.

ing, culture patterns. It is, in fact, only because behavior is typically oriented toward the basic values of the society that we may speak of a human aggregate as comprising a society. Unless there is a deposit of values shared by interacting individuals, there exist social relations, if the disorderly interactions may be so called, but no society. It is thus that, at mid-century, one may refer to a Society of Nations primarily as a figure of speech or as an imagined objective, but not as a sociological reality.

Since our primary interest centers on the sources of *deviant* behavior, and since we have briefly examined the mechanisms making for conformity as the modal response in American society, little more need be said regarding this type of adaptation, at this point.

II. Innovation

Great cultural emphasis upon the success-goal invites this mode of adaptation through the use of institutionally proscribed but often effective means of attaining at least the simulacrum of success—wealth and power. This response occurs when the individual has assimilated the cultural emphasis upon the goal without equally internalizing the institutional norms governing ways and means for its attainment.

From the standpoint of psychology, great emotional investment in an objective may be expected to produce a readiness to take risks, and this attitude may be adopted by people in all social strata. From the standpoint of sociology, the question arises, which features of our social structure predispose toward this type of adaptation, thus producing greater frequencies of deviant behavior in one social stratum than in another?

On the top economic levels, the pressure toward innovation not infrequently erases the distinction between business-like strivings this side of the mores and sharp practices beyond the mores. As Veblen observed, "It is not easy in any given case—indeed it is at times impossible until the courts have spoken—to say whether it is an instance of praiseworthy salesmanship or a penitentiary offense." The history of the great American fortunes is threaded with strains toward institutionally dubious innovation as is attested by many tributes to the Robber Barons. The reluctant admiration often expressed privately, and not seldom publicly, of these "shrewd, smart and successful" men is a product of a cultural structure in which the sacrosanct goal virtually consecrates the means. This is no new phenomenon. Without assuming that Charles Dickens was a wholly accurate observer of the American scene and with full knowledge that he was anything but impartial, we cite his perceptive remarks on the American

love of "smart" dealing: which gilds over many a swindle and gross breach of trust; many a defalcation, public and private; and enables many a knave to hold up his head with the best, who well deserves a halter. . . . The merits of a broken speculation, or a bankruptcy, or of a successful scoundrel, are not gauged by its or his observance of the golden rule, "Do as you would be done by," but are considered with reference to their smartness. . . . The following dialogue I have held a hundred times: "Is it not a very disgraceful circumstance that such a man as So-and-so should be acquiring a large property by the most infamous and odious means, and notwithstanding all the crimes of which he has been guilty, should be tolerated and abetted by your Citizens? He is a public nuisance, is he not?" "Yes, sir." "A convicted liar?" "Yes, sir." "He has been kicked and cuffed, and caned?" "Yes, sir." "And he is utterly dishonorable, debased, and profligate?" "Yes, sir." "In the name of wonder, then, what is his merit?" "Well, sir, he is a smart man."

In this caricature of conflicting cultural values, Dickens was of course only one of many wits who mercilessly probed the consequences of the heavy emphasis on financial success. Native wits continued where alien wits left off. Artemus Ward satirized the commonplaces of American life until they seemed strangely incongruous. The "crackerbox philosophers," Bill Arp and Petroleum Volcano [later Vesuvius] Nasby, put wit in the service of iconoclasm, breaking the images of public figures with unconcealed pleasure. Josh Billings and his alter ego, Uncle Esek, made plain what many could not freely acknowledge, when he observed that satisfaction is relative since "most of the happiness in this world konsists in possessing what others kant git." All were engaged in exhibiting the social functions of tendentious wit, as this was later to be analyzed by Freud, in his monograph on *Wit and Its Relation to the Unconscious*, using it as "a weapon of attack upon what is great, dignified and mighty, [upon] that which is shielded by internal hindrances or external circumstance against direct disparagement. . . ." But perhaps most in point here was the deployment of wit by Ambrose Bierce in a form which made it evident that *wit* had not cut away from its etymological origins and still meant the power by which one knows, learns, or thinks. In his characteristically ironical and deep-seeing essay on "crime and its correctives," Bierce begins with the observation that "Sociologists have long been debating the theory that the impulse to commit crime is a disease, and the ayes appear to have it—the disease." After this prelude, he describes the ways in which the successful rogue achieves social legitimacy, and proceeds to anatomize the discrepancies between cultural values and social relations.

The good American is, as a rule, pretty hard on roguery, but he atones for his austerity by an amiable toleration of rogues. His only requirement is that he must personally know the rogues. We all "denounce" thieves loudly enough if we have not the honor of their acquaintance. If we have, why, that is different—unless they have the actual odor of the slum or the prison about them. We may know them guilty, but we meet them, shake hands with them, drink with them and, if they happen to be wealthy, or otherwise great, invite them to our houses, and deem it an honor to frequent theirs. We do not "approve their methods"—let that be understood; and thereby they are sufficiently punished. The notion that a knave cares a pin what is thought of his ways by one who is civil and friendly to himself appears to have been invented by a humorist. On the vaudeville stage of Mars it would probably have made his fortune.

[And again:] If social recognition were denied to rogues they would be fewer by many. Some would only the more diligently cover their tracks along the devious paths of unrighteousness, but others would do so much violence to their consciences as to renounce the disadvantages of rascality for those of an honest life. An unworthy person dreads nothing so much as the withholding of an honest hand, the slow, inevitable stroke of an ignoring eye.

We have rich rogues because we have "respectable" persons who are not ashamed to take them by the hand, to be seen with them, to say that they know them. In such it is treachery to censure them; to cry out when robbed by them is to turn state's evidence.

One may smile upon a rascal (most of us do many times a day) if one does not know him to be a rascal, and has not said he is; but knowing him to be, or having said he is, to smile upon him is to be a hypocrite—just a plain hypocrite or a sycophantic hypocrite, according to the station in life of the rascal smiled upon. There are more plain hypocrites than sycophantic ones, for there are more rascals of no consequence than rich and distinguished ones, though they get fewer smiles each. The American people will be plundered as long as the American character is what it is; as long as it is tolerant of successful knaves; as long as American ingenuity draws an imaginary distinction between a man's public character and his private—his commercial and his personal. In brief, the American people will be plundered as long as they deserve to be plundered. No human law can stop, none ought to stop it, for that would abrogate a higher and more salutary law: "As ye sow, ye shall reap."[14]

[14] The observations by Dickens are from his *American Notes* (in the edition, for example, published in Boston: Books, Inc., 1940), 218. A sociological analysis which would be the formal, albeit inevitably lesser, counterpart of Freud's psychological analysis of the functions of tendentious wit and of tendentious wits is long overdue. The doctoral dissertation by Jeannette Tandy, though not sociological in character, affords one point of departure: *Crackerbox Philosophers: American Humor and Satire* (New York: Columbia University Press, 1925). In Chapter V of *Intellectual America* (New York: Macmillan, 1941), appropriately entitled "The Intelligentsia," Oscar Cargill has some compact observations on the role of the nineteenth century masters of American wit, but this naturally has only a small place in this large book on the "march of American ideas." The essay by Bierce from which I have quoted at such length will be found in *The Collected Works of Ambrose Bierce* (New York and Washington: The Neale Publishing Company, 1912), volume XI, 187–198. For what it is worth, I must differ with the harsh and far from justified judgment of Cargill on Bierce. It seems to be less a judgment than the expression of a prejudice which, in Bierce's own understanding of "prejudice," is only "a vagrant opinion without visible means of support."

Living in the age in which the American robber barons flourished, Bierce could not easily fail to observe what became later known as "white-collar crime." Nevertheless, he was aware that not all of these large and dramatic departures from institutional norms in the top economic strata are known, and possibly fewer deviations among the lesser middle classes come to light. Sutherland has repeatedly documented the prevalence of "white-collar criminality" among business men. He notes, further, that many of these crimes were not prosecuted because they were not detected or, if detected, because of "the status of the business man, the trend away from punishment, and the relatively unorganized resentment of the public against white-collar criminals."[15] A study of some 1,700 prevalently middle-class individuals found that "off the record crimes" were common among wholly "respectable" members of society. Ninety-nine per cent of those questioned confessed to having committed one or more of 49 offenses under the penal law of the State of New York, each of these offenses being sufficiently serious to draw a maximum sentence of not less than one year. The mean number of offenses in adult years—this excludes all offenses committed before the age of sixteen—was 18 for men and 11 for women. Fully 64% of the men and 29% of the women acknowledged their guilt on one or more counts of felony which, under the laws of New York is ground for depriving them of all rights of citizenship. One keynote of these findings is expressed by a minister, referring to false statements he made about a commodity he sold, "I tried truth first, but it's not always successful." On the basis of these results, the authors modestly conclude that "the number of acts legally constituting crimes are far in excess of those officially reported. Unlawful behavior, far from being an abnormal social or psychological manifestation, is in truth a very common phenomenon."[16]

But whatever the differential rates of deviant behavior in the several social strata, and we know from many sources that the official crime statistics uniformly showing higher rates in the lower strata are far from complete or reliable, it appears from our analysis that the greatest pressures toward deviation are exerted upon the lower strata. Cases in point permit us to detect the sociological mechanisms involved in producing these pressures. Several researches have shown that specialized areas of vice and crime constitute a "normal" response to a situation where the cultural em-

[15] E. H. Sutherland, "White collar criminality," *op. cit.*; "Crime and business," *Annals, American Academy of Political and Social Science*, 1941, 217, 112–118; "Is 'white collar crime' crime?", *American Sociological Review*, 1945, 10, 132–139; Marshall B. Clinard, *The Black Market: A Study of White Collar Crime* (New York: Rinehart & Co., 1952); Donald R. Cressey, *Other People's Money: A Study in the Social Psychology of Embezzlement* (Glencoe: The Free Press, 1953).

[16] James S. Wallerstein and Clement J. Wyle, "Our law-abiding law-breakers," *Probation*, April, 1947.

phasis upon pecuniary success has been absorbed, but where there is little access to conventional and legitimate means for becoming successful. The occupational opportunities of people in these areas are largely confined to manual labor and the lesser white-collar jobs. Given the American stigmatization of manual labor *which has been found to hold rather uniformly in all social classes,*[17] and the absence of realistic opportunities for advancement beyond this level, the result is a marked tendency toward deviant behavior. The status of unskilled labor and the consequent low income cannot readily compete *in terms of established standards of worth* with the promises of power and high income from organized vice, rackets and crime.[18]

For our purposes, these situations exhibit two salient features. First, incentives for success are provided by the established values of the culture *and* second, the avenues available for moving toward this goal are largely limited by the class structure to those of deviant behavior. It is the *combination* of the cultural emphasis and the social structure which produces intense pressure for deviation. Recourse to legitimate channels for "getting in the money" is limited by a class structure which is not fully open at each level to men of good capacity.[19] Despite our persisting open-class-ideology,[20] advance toward the success-goal is relatively rare and notably difficult for those armed with little formal education and few economic

[17] National Opinion Research Center, *National Opinion on Occupations*, April, 1947. This research on the ranking and evaluation of ninety occupations by a nation-wide sample presents a series of important empirical data. Of great significance is their finding that, despite a slight tendency for people to rank their own and related occupations higher than do other groups, there is a substantial agreement in ranking of occupations among all occupational strata. More researches of this kind are needed to map the cultural topography of contemporary societies. (See the comparative study of prestige accorded major occupations in six industrialized countries: Alex Inkeles and Peter H. Rossi, "National comparisons of occupational prestige," *American Journal of Sociology*, 1956, 61, 329–339.)

[18] See Joseph D. Lohman, "The participant observer in community studies," *American Sociological Review*, 1937, 2, 890–98 and William F. Whyte, *Street Corner Society* (Chicago, 1943). Note Whyte's conclusions: "It is difficult for the Cornerville man to get onto the ladder [of success], even on the bottom rung. . . . He is an Italian, and the Italians are looked upon by upper-class people as among the least desirable of the immigrant peoples . . . the society holds out attractive rewards in terms of money and material possessions to the 'successful' man. For most Cornerville people these rewards are available only through advancement in the world of rackets and politics." (273–74.)

[19] Numerous studies have found that the educational pyramid operates to keep a large proportion of unquestionably able but economically disadvantaged youth from obtaining higher formal education. This fact about our class structure has been noted with dismay, for example, by Vannevar Bush in his governmental report, *Science: The Endless Frontier*. Also, see W. L. Warner, R. J. Havighurst and M. B. Loeb, *Who Shall Be Educated?* (New York, 1944).

[20] The shifting historical role of this ideology is a profitable subject for exploration.

resources. The dominant pressure leads toward the gradual attenuation of legitimate, but by and large ineffectual, strivings and the increasing use of illegitimate, but more or less effective, expedients.

Of those located in the lower reaches of the social structure, the culture makes incompatible demands. On the one hand, they are asked to orient their conduct toward the prospect of large wealth—"Every man a king," said Marden and Carnegie and Long—and on the other, they are largely denied effective opportunities to do so institutionally. The consequence of this structural inconsistency is a high rate of deviant behavior. The equilibrium between culturally designated ends and means becomes highly unstable with progressive emphasis on attaining the prestige-laden ends by any means whatsoever. Within this context, Al Capone represents the triumph of amoral intelligence over morally prescribed "failure," when the channels of vertical mobility are closed or narrowed *in a society which places a high premium on economic affluence and social ascent for* all *its members*.[21]

This last qualification is of central importance. It implies that other aspects of the social structure, besides the extreme emphasis on pecuniary success, must be considered if we are to understand the social sources of deviant behavior. A high frequency of deviant behavior is not generated merely by lack of opportunity or by this exaggerated pecuniary emphasis. A comparatively rigidified class structure, a caste order, may limit opportunities far beyond the point which obtains in American society today. It is only when a system of cultural values extols, virtually above all else, certain *common* success-goals *for the population at large* while the social structure rigorously restricts or completely closes access to approved modes of reaching these goals *for a considerable part of the same population*, that deviant behavior ensues on a large scale. Otherwise said, our egalitarian ideology denies by implication the existence of non-competing individuals and groups in the pursuit of pecuniary success. Instead, the same body of success-symbols is held to apply for all. Goals are held to transcend class lines, not to be bounded by them, yet the actual social organization is such that there exist class differentials in accessibility of the goals. In this setting, a cardinal American virtue, "ambition," promotes a cardinal American vice, "deviant behavior."

This theoretical analysis may help explain the varying correlations

[21] The role of the Negro in this connection raises almost as many theoretical as practical questions. It has been reported that large segments of the Negro population have assimilated the dominant caste's values of pecuniary success and social advancement, but have "realistically adjusted" themselves to the "fact" that social ascent is presently confined almost entirely to movement within the caste. See Dollard, *Caste and Class in a Southern Town*, 66 ff.; Donald Young, *American Minority Peoples*, 581; Robert A. Warner, *New Haven Negroes* . (New Haven, 1940), 234. See also the subsequent discussion.

between crime and poverty.[22] "Poverty" is not an isolated variable which operates in precisely the same fashion wherever found; it is only one in a complex of identifiably interdependent social and cultural variables. Poverty as such and consequent limitation of opportunity are not enough to produce a conspicuously high rate of criminal behavior. Even the notorious "poverty in the midst of plenty" will not necessarily lead to this result. But when poverty and associated disadvantages in competing for the culture values approved for *all* members of the society are linked with a cultural emphasis on pecuniary success as a dominant goal, high rates of criminal behavior are the normal outcome. Thus, crude (and not necessarily reliable) crime statistics suggest that poverty is less highly correlated with crime in southeastern Europe than in the United States. The economic life-chances of the poor in these European areas would seem to be even less promising than in this country, so that neither poverty nor its association with limited opportunity is sufficient to account for the varying correlations. However, when we consider the full configuration—poverty, limited opportunity and the assignment of cultural goals—there appears some basis for explaining the higher correlation between poverty and crime in our society than in others where ridigified class structure is coupled with *differential class symbols of success.*

The victims of this contradiction between the cultural emphasis on pecuniary ambition and the social bars to full opportunity are not always aware of the structural sources of their thwarted aspirations. To be sure, they are often aware of a discrepancy between individual worth and social rewards. But they do not necessarily see how this comes about. Those who do find its source in the social structure may become alienated from that structure and become ready candidates for Adaptation V (rebellion). But others, and this appears to include the great majority, may attribute their difficulties to more mystical and less sociological sources. For as the distinguished classicist and sociologist-in-spite-of-himself, Gilbert Murray, has remarked in this general connection, "The best seed-ground for superstition is a society in which the fortunes of men seem to bear practically no relation to their merits and efforts. A stable and well-governed society does tend, speaking roughly, to ensure that the Virtuous and In-

---

[22] This analytical scheme may serve to resolve some of the apparent inconsistencies in the relation between crime and economic status mentioned by P. A. Sorokin. For example, he notes that "not everywhere nor always do the poor show a greater proportion of crime . . . many poorer countries have had less crime than the richer countries. . . . The economic improvement in the second half of the nineteenth century, and the beginning of the twentieth, has not been followed by a decrease of crime." See his *Contemporary Sociological Theories,* (New York, 1928), 560–61. The crucial point is, however, that low economic status plays a different dynamic role in different social and cultural structures, as is set out in the text. One should not, therefore, expect a linear correlation between crime and poverty.

dustrious Apprentice shall succeed in life, while the Wicked and Idle Apprentice fails. And in such a society people tend to lay stress on the reasonable or visible chains of causation. But in [a society suffering from anomie] . . ., the ordinary virtues of diligence, honesty, and kindliness seem to be of little avail."[23] And in such a society people tend to put stress on mysticism: the workings of Fortune, Chance, Luck.

In point of fact, both the eminently "successful" and the eminently "unsuccessful" in our society not infrequently attribute the outcome to "luck." Thus, the prosperous man of business, Julius Rosenwald, declared that 95% of the great fortunes were "due to luck."[24] And a leading business journal, in an editorial explaining the social benefits of great individual wealth, finds it necessary to supplement wisdom with luck as the factors accounting for great fortunes: "When one man through wise investments—aided, we'll grant, by good luck in many cases—accumulates a few millions, he doesn't thereby take something from the rest of us."[25] In much the same fashion, the worker often explains economic status in terms of chance. "The worker sees all about him experienced and skilled men with no work to do. If he is in work, he feels lucky. If he is out of work, he is the victim of hard luck. *He can see little relation between worth and consequences.*"[26]

But these references to the workings of chance and luck serve distinctive functions according to whether they are made by those who have reached or those who have not reached the culturally emphasized goals. For the successful, it is in psychological terms, a disarming expression of modesty. It is far removed from any semblance of conceit to say, in effect, that one was lucky rather than altogether deserving of one's good fortune. In sociological terms, the doctrine of luck as expounded by the successful serves the dual function of explaining the frequent discrepancy between merit and reward while keeping immune from criticism a social structure which allows this discrepancy to become frequent. For if success is primarily a matter of luck, if it is just in the blind nature of things, if

[23] Gilbert Murray, *Five Stages of Greek Religion* (New York, 1925), 164–5. Professor Murray's chapter on "The Failure of Nerve," from which I have taken this excerpt, must surely be ranked among the most civilized and perceptive sociological analyses in our time.

[24] See the quotation from an interview cited in Gustavus Meyers, *History of the Great American Fortunes* (New York, 1937), 706.

[25] *Nation's Business*, Vol. 27, No. 9, pp. 8–9.

[26] E. W. Bakke, *The Unemployed Man* (New York, 1934), p. 14 (I have supplied the emphasis.) Bakke hints at the structural sources making for a belief in luck among workers. "There is a measure of hopelessness in the situation when a man knows that *most of his good or ill fortune is out of his own control and depends on luck.*" (Emphasis supplied) In so far as he is forced to accommodate himself to occasionally unpredictable decisions of management, the worker is subject to job insecurities and anxieties: another "seed-ground" for belief in destiny, fate, chance. It would be instructive to learn if such beliefs become lessened where workers' organizations reduce the probability that their occupational fate will be out of their own hands.

it bloweth where it listeth and thou canst not tell whence it cometh or whither it goeth, then surely it is beyond control and will occur in the same measure *whatever the social structure.*

For the unsuccessful and particularly for those among the unsuccessful who find little reward for their merit and their effort, the doctrine of luck serves the psychological function of enabling them to preserve their self-esteem in the face of failure. It may also entail the dysfunction of curbing motivation for sustained endeavor.[27] Sociologically, as implied by Bakke,[28] the doctrine may reflect a failure to comprehend the workings of the social and economic system, and may be dysfunctional inasmuch as it eliminates the rationale of working for structural changes making for greater equities in opportunity and reward.

This orientation toward chance and risk-taking, accentuated by the strain of frustrated aspirations, may help explain the marked interest in gambling—an institutionally proscribed or at best permitted rather than preferred or prescribed mode of activity—within certain social strata.[29]

Among those who do not apply the doctrine of luck to the gulf between merit, effort and reward there may develop an individuated and cynical attitude toward the social structure, best exemplified in the cultural cliché that "it's not what you know, but who you know, that counts."

In societies such as our own, then, the great cultural emphasis on pecuniary success for all and a social structure which unduly limits practical recourse to approved means for many set up a tension toward innovative practices which depart from institutional norms. But this form of adaptation presupposes that individuals have been imperfectly socialized so that they abandon institutional means while retaining the success-aspiration. Among those who have fully internalized the institutional values, however, a comparable situation is more likely to lead to an alternative response in which the goal is abandoned but conformity to the mores persists. This type of response calls for further examination.

III. Ritualism

The ritualistic type of adaptation can be readily identified. It involves the abandoning or scaling down of the lofty cultural goals of great pecuniary success and rapid social mobility to the point where one's aspirations can

[27] At its extreme, it may invite resignation and routinized activity (Adaptation III) or a fatalistic passivism (Adaptation IV), of which more presently.

[28] Bakke, *op. cit.*, 14, where he suggests that "the worker knows less about the processes which cause him to succeed or have no chance to succeed than business or professional people. There are more points, therefore, at which events appear to have their incidence in good or ill luck."

[29] *Cf.* R. A. Warner, *New Haven Negroes* and Harold F. Gosnell, *Negro Politicians* (Chicago, 1935), 123–5, both of whom comment in this general connection on the great interest in "playing the numbers" among less-advantaged Negroes.

be satisfied. But though one rejects the cultural obligation to attempt "to get ahead in the world," though one draws in one's horizons, one continues to abide almost compulsively by institutional norms.

It is something of a terminological quibble to ask whether this represents genuinely deviant behavior. Since the adaptation is, in effect, an internal decision and since the overt behavior is institutionally permitted, though not culturally preferred, it is not generally considered to represent a social problem. Intimates of individuals making this adaptation may pass judgment in terms of prevailing cultural emphases and may "feel sorry for them," they may, in the individual case, feel that "old Jonesy is certainly in a rut." Whether this is described as deviant behavior or no, it clearly represents a departure from the cultural model in which men are obliged to strive actively, preferably through institutionalized procedures, to move onward and upward in the social hierarchy.

We should expect this type of adaptation to be fairly frequent in a society which makes one's social status largely dependent upon one's achievements. For, as has so often been observed,[30] this ceaseless competitive struggle produces acute status anxiety. One device for allaying these anxieties is to lower one's level of aspiration—permanently. Fear produces inaction, or more accurately, routinized action.[31]

The syndrome of the social ritualist is both familiar and instructive. His implicit life-philosophy finds expression in a series of cultural clichés: "I'm not sticking *my* neck out," "I'm playing safe," "I'm satisfied with what I've got," "Don't aim high and you won't be disappointed." The theme threaded through these attitudes is that high ambitions invite frustration and danger whereas lower aspirations produce satisfaction and security. It is a response to a situation which appears threatening and excites distrust. It is the attitude implicit among workers who carefully regulate their output to a constant quota in an industrial organization where they have occasion to fear that they will "be noticed" by managerial personnel and "something will happen" if their output rises and falls.[32] It is the perspective of the frightened employee, the zealously conformist bureaucrat in the teller's cage of the private banking enterprise or in the front office of the public works enterprise. It is, in short, the mode of adaptation of individually seeking a *private* escape from the dangers and frustrations which seem to

[30] See, for example, H. S. Sullivan, "Modern conceptions of psychiatry," *Psychiatry*, 1940, 3, 111–12; Margaret Mead, *And Keep Your Powder Dry* (New York, 1942), Chapter VII; Merton, Fiske and Curtis, *Mass Persuasion*, 59–60.

[31] P. Janet, "The fear of action," *Journal of Abnormal Psychology*, 1921, 16, 150–60, and the extraordinary discussion by F. L. Wells, "Social maladjustments: adaptive regression," *op. cit.*, which bears closely on the type of adaptation examined here.

[32] F. J. Roethlisberger and W. J. Dickson, *Management and the Worker*, Chapter 18 and 531 ff.; and on the more general theme, the typically perspicacious remarks of Gilbert Murray, *op. cit.*, 138–39.

them inherent in the competition for major cultural goals by abandoning these goals and clinging all the more closely to the safe routines and the institutional norms.

If we should expect *lower-class* Americans to exhibit Adaptation II— "innovation"—to the frustrations enjoined by the prevailing emphasis on large cultural goals and the fact of small social opportunities, we should expect *lower-middle class* Americans to be heavily represented among those making Adaptation III, "ritualism." For it is in the lower middle class that parents typically exert continuous pressure upon children to abide by the moral mandates of the society, and where the social climb upward is less likely to meet with success than among the upper middle class. The strong disciplining for conformity with mores reduces the likelihood of Adaptation II and promotes the likelihood of Adaptation III. The severe training leads many to carry a heavy burden of anxiety. The socialization patterns of the lower middle class thus promote the very character structure most predisposed toward ritualism,[33] and it is in this stratum, accordingly, that the adaptive pattern III should most often occur.[34]

But we should note again, as at the outset of this paper, that we are here examining *modes of adaptation* to contradictions in the cultural and

[33] See, for example, Allison Davis and John Dollard, *Children of Bondage* (Washington, 1940), Chapter 12 ("Child Training and Class"), which, though it deals with the lower- and lower-middle class patterns of socialization among Negroes in the Far South, appears applicable, with slight modification, to the white population as well. On this, see further M. C. Erickson, "Child-rearing and social status," *American Journal of Sociology*, 1946, 53, 190–92; Allison Davis and R. J. Havighurst, "Social class and color differences in child-rearing," *American Sociological Review*, 1946, 11, 698–710: ". . . *the pivotal meaning of social class* to students of human development is that it defines and systematizes different learning environments for children of different classes." "Generalizing from the evidence presented in the tables, we would say that middle-class children [the authors do not distinguish between lower-middle and upper-middle strata] are subjected earlier and more consistently to the influences which make a child an orderly, conscientious, responsible, and tame person. In the course of this training middle-class children probably suffer more frustration of their impulses."

[34] This hypothesis still awaits empirical test. Beginnings in this direction have been made with the "level of aspiration" experiments which explore the determinants of goal-formation and modification in specific, experimentally devised activities. There is, however, a major obstacle, not yet surmounted, in drawing inferences from the laboratory situation, with its relatively slight ego-involvement with the casual task— pencil-and-paper mazes, ring-throwing, arithmetical problems, *etc.*—which will be applicable to the strong emotional investment with success-goals in the routines of everyday life. Nor have these experiments, with their *ad hoc* group formations, been able to reproduce the acute social pressures obtaining in daily life. (What laboratory experiment reproduces, for example, the querulous nagging of a modern Xantippe: "The trouble with you is, you've got no ambition; a real man would go out and do things"?) Among studies with a definite though limited relevance, see especially R. Gould, "Some sociological determinants of goal strivings," *Journal of Social Psychology*, 1941, 13, 461–73; L. Festinger, "Wish, expectation and group standards as factors

social structure: we are not focusing on character or personality types. Individuals caught up in these contradictions can and do move from one type of adaptation to another. Thus it may be conjectured that some ritualists, conforming meticulously to the institutional rules, are so steeped in the regulations that they become bureaucratic virtuosos, that they over-conform precisely because they are subject to guilt engendered by previous nonconformity with the rules (*i.e.*, Adaptation II). And the occasional passage from ritualistic adaptation to dramatic kinds of illicit adaptation is well-documented in clinical case-histories and often set forth in insightful fiction. Defiant outbreaks not infrequently follow upon prolonged periods of over-compliance.[35] But though the psychodynamic mechanisms of this

influencing level of aspiration," *Journal of Abnormal and Social Psychology*, 1942, 37, 184–200. For a resume of researches, see Kurt Lewin *et al.*, "Level of Aspiration," in J. McV. Hunt, ed., *Personality and the Behavior Disorders* (New York, 1944), I, Chap. 10.

The conception of "success" as a ratio between aspiration and achievement pursued systematically in the level-of-aspiration experiments has, of course, a long history. Gilbert Murray (*op. cit.*, 138–9) notes the prevalence of this conception among the thinkers of fourth century Greece. And in *Sartor Resartus*, Carlyle observes that "happiness" (gratification) can be represented by a fraction in which the numerator represents achievement and the denominator, aspiration. Much of the same notion is examined by William James (*The Principles of Psychology* [New York, 1902], I, 310). See also F. L. Wells, *op. cit.*, 879, and P. A. Sorokin, *Social and Cultural Dynamics* (New York, 1937), III, 161–164. The critical question is whether this familiar insight can be subjected to rigorous experimentation in which the contrived laboratory situation adequately reproduces the salient aspects of the real-life situation or whether disciplined observation of routines of behavior in everyday life will prove the more productive method of inquiry.

[35] In her novel, *The Bitter Box* (New York, 1946), Eleanor Clark has portrayed this process with great sensitivity. The discussion by Erich Fromm, *Escape from Freedom* (New York, 1941), 185–206, may be cited, without implying acceptance of his concept of "spontaneity" and "man's inherent tendency toward self-development." For an example of a sound sociological formulation: "As long as we assume . . . that the anal character, as it is typical of the European lower middle class, is caused by certain early experiences in connection with defecation, we have hardly any data that lead us to understand why a specific class should have an anal social character. However, if we understand it as one form of relatedness to others, rooted in the character structure and resulting from the experiences with the outside world, we have a key for understanding why the whole mode of life of the lower middle class, its narrowness, isolation, and hostility, made for the development of this kind of character structure." (293–4) For an example of a formulation stemming from a kind of latter-day benevolent anarchism here judged as dubious: ". . . there are also certain psychological qualities inherent in man that need to be satisfied. . . . The most important seems to be the tendency to grow, to develop and realize potentialities which man has developed in the course of history—as, for instance, the faculty of creative and critical thinking. . . . It also seems that this general tendency to grow—which is the psychological equivalent of the identical biological tendency—results in such specific tendencies as the desire for freedom and the hatred against oppression, since freedom is the fundamental condition for any growth." (287–88)

type of adaptation have been fairly well identified and linked with patterns of discipline and socialization in the family, much sociological research is still required to explain why these patterns are presumably more frequent in certain social strata and groups than in others. Our own discussion has merely set out one analytical framework for sociological research focused on this problem.

IV. Retreatism

Just as Adaptation I (conformity) remains the most frequent, Adaptation IV (the rejection of cultural goals and institutional means) is probably the least common. People who adapt (or maladapt) in this fashion are, strictly speaking, *in* the society but not *of* it. Sociologically, these constitute the true aliens. Not sharing the common frame of values, they can be included as members of the *society* (in distinction from the *population*) only in a fictional sense.

In this category fall some of the adaptive activities of psychotics, autists, pariahs, outcasts, vagrants, vagabonds, tramps, chronic drunkards and drug addicts.[36] They have relinquished culturally prescribed goals and their behavior does not accord with institutional norms. This is not to say that in some cases the source of their mode of adaptation is not the very social structure which they have in effect repudiated nor that their very existence within an area does not constitute a problem for members of the society.

From the standpoint of its sources in the social structure, this mode of adaptation is most likely to occur when *both* the culture goals and the institutional practices have been thoroughly assimilated by the individual and imbued with affect and high value, but accessible institutional avenues are not productive of success. There results a twofold conflict: the interiorized moral obligation for adopting institutional means conflicts with pressures to resort to illicit means (which may attain the goal) and the individual is shut off from means which are both legitimate and effective. The competitive order is maintained but the frustrated and handicapped individual who cannot cope with this order drops out. Defeatism, quietism and resignation are manifested in escape mechanisms which ultimately lead him to "escape" from the requirements of the society. It is thus an expedient which arises from continued failure to near the goal by legitimate measures

[36] Obviously, this is an elliptical statement. These individuals may retain some orientation to the values of their own groupings within the larger society or, occasionally, to the values of the conventional society itself. They may, in other words, shift to other modes of adaptation. But Adaptation IV can be easily detected. Nels Anderson's account of the behavior and attitudes of the bum, for example, can readily be recast in terms of our analytical scheme. See *The Hobo* (Chicago, 1923), 93–98, *et passim*.

and from an inability to use the illegitimate route because of internalized prohibitions, *this process occurring while the supreme value of the success-goal has not yet been renounced.* The conflict is resolved by abandoning *both* precipitating elements, the goals and the means. The escape is complete, the conflict is eliminated and the individual is asocialized.

In public and ceremonial life, this type of deviant behavior is most heartily condemned by conventional representatives of the society. In contrast to the conformist, who keeps the wheels of society running, this deviant is a non-productive liability; in contrast to the innovator who is at least "smart" and actively striving, he sees no value in the success-goal which the culture prizes so highly; in contrast to the ritualist who conforms at least to the mores, he pays scant attention to the institutional practices.

Nor does the society lightly accept these repudiations of its values. To do so would be to put these values into question. Those who have abandoned the quest for success are relentlessly pursued to their haunts by a society insistent upon having all its members orient themselves to success-striving. Thus, in the heart of Chicago's Hobohemia are the book stalls filled with wares designed to revitalize dead aspirations.

The Gold Coast Book Store is in the basement of an old residence, built back from the street, and now sandwiched between two business blocks. The space in front is filled with stalls, and striking placards and posters.

These posters advertise such books as will arrest the attention of the down-and-out. One reads: ". . . Men in thousands pass this spot daily, but the majority of them are not financially successful. They are never more than two jumps ahead of the rent men. Instead of that, they should be more bold and daring," "Getting Ahead of the Game," before old age withers them and casts them on the junk heap of human wrecks. If you want to escape this evil fate—the fate of the vast majority of men—come in and get a copy of *The Law of Financial Success*. It will put some new ideas in your head, and put you on the highroad to success. 35 cents.

There are always men loitering before its stalls. But they seldom buy. Success comes high, even at thirty-five cents, to the hobo.[37]

But if this deviant is condemned in real life, he may become a source of gratification in fantasy-life. Thus Kardiner has advanced the speculation that such figures in contemporary folklore and popular culture bolster "morale and self-esteem by the spectacle of man rejecting current ideals and expressing contempt for them." The prototype in the films is of course Charlie Chaplin's bum.

He is Mr. Nobody and is very much aware of his own insignificance. He is always the butt of a crazy and bewildering world in which he has no place and from which he constantly runs away into a contented do-nothingness. *He*

[37] H. W. Zorbaugh, *The Gold Coast and the Slum* (Chicago, 1929), 108.

is free from conflict because he has abandoned the quest for security and prestige, and is resigned to the lack of any claim to virtue or distinction. [A precise characterological portrait of Adaptation IV.] He always becomes involved in the world by accident. There he encounters evil and aggression against the weak and helpless which he has no power to combat. Yet always, in spite of himself, he becomes the champion of the wronged and oppressed, not by virtue of his great organizing ability but by virtue of homely and insolent trickiness by which he seeks out the weakness of the wrongdoer. He always remains humble, poor, and lonely, but is contemptuous of the incomprehensible world and its values. He therefore represents the character of our time who is *perplexed by the dilemma either of being crushed in the struggle to achieve the socially approved goals of success and power* (he achieves it only once—in *The Gold Rush*) *or of succumbing to a hopeless resignation and flight from them.* Charlie's bum is a great comfort in that he gloats in his ability to outwit the pernicious forces aligned against him if he chooses to do so and affords every man the satisfaction of feeling that the ultimate flight from social goals to loneliness is an act of *choice* and not a symptom of his defeat. Mickey Mouse is a continuation of the Chaplin saga.[38]

This fourth mode of adaptation, then, is that of the socially disinherited who if they have none of the rewards held out by society also have few of the frustrations attendant upon continuing to seek these rewards. It is, moreover, a privatized rather than a collective mode of adaptation. Although people exhibiting this deviant behavior may gravitate toward centers where they come into contact with other deviants and although they may come to share in the subculture of these deviant groups, their adaptations are largely private and isolated rather than unified under the aegis of a new cultural code. The type of collective adaptation remains to be considered.

V. Rebellion

This adaptation leads men outside the environing social structure to envisage and seek to bring into being a new, that is to say, a greatly modified social structure. It presupposes alienation from reigning goals and standards. These come to be regarded as purely arbitrary. And the arbitrary is precisely that which can neither exact allegiance nor possess legitimacy, for it might as well be otherwise. In our society, organized movements for rebellion apparently aim to introduce a social structure in which the cultural standards of success would be sharply modified and provision would be made for a closer correspondence between merit, effort and reward.

But before examining "rebellion" as a mode of adaptation, we must

[38] Abram Kardiner, *The Psychological Frontiers of Society* (New York, 1945), 369–70. (Emphases supplied.)

distinguish it from a superficially similar but essentially different type, *ressentiment*. Introduced in a special technical sense, by Nietzsche, the concept of *ressentiment* was taken up and developed sociologically by Max Scheler.[39] This complex sentiment has three interlocking elements. First, diffuse feelings of hate, envy and hostility; second, a sense of being powerless to express these feelings actively against the person or social stratum evoking them; and third, a continual re-experiencing of this impotent hostility.[40] The essential point distinguishing *ressentiment* from rebellion is that the former does not involve a genuine change in values. *Ressentiment* involves a sour-grapes pattern which asserts merely that desired but unattainable objectives do not actually embody the prized values—after all, the fox in the fable does not say that he abandons all taste for sweet grapes; he says only that these particular grapes are not sweet. Rebellion, on the other hand, involves a genuine transvaluation, where the direct or vicarious experience of frustration leads to full denunciation of previously prized values—the rebellious fox simply renounces the prevailing taste for sweet grapes. In *ressentiment*, one condemns what one secretly craves; in rebellion, one condemns the craving itself. But though the two are distinct, organized rebellion may draw upon a vast reservoir of the resentful and discontented as institutional dislocations become acute.

When the institutional system is regarded as the barrier to the satisfaction of legitimized goals, the stage is set for rebellion as an adaptive response. To pass into organized political action, allegiance must not only be withdrawn from the prevailing social structure but must be transferred to new groups possessed of a new myth.[41] The dual function of the myth is to locate the source of large-scale frustrations in the social structure and to portray an alternative structure which would not, presumably, give rise to frustration of the deserving. It is a charter for action. In this context,

---

[39] Max Scheler, *L'homme du ressentiment* (Paris, n. d.). This essay first appeared in 1912; revised and completed, it was included in Scheler's *Abhandlungen und Aufsätze,* appearing thereafter in his *Vom Umsturz der Werte* (1919). The last text was used for the French translation. It has had considerable influence in varied intellectual circles. For an excellent and well-balanced discussion of Scheler's essay, indicating some of its limitations and biases, the respects in which it prefigured Nazi conceptions, its anti-democratic orientation and, withal, its occasionally brilliant insights, see V. J. McGill, "Scheler's theory of sympathy and love," *Philosophy and Phenomenological Research,* 1942, 2, 273–91. For another critical account which properly criticizes Scheler's view that social structure plays only a secondary role in *ressentiment*, see Svend Ranulf, *Moral Indignation and Middle-Class Psychology: A Sociological Study* (Copenhagen, 1938), 199–204.

[40] Scheler, *op. cit.,* 55–56. No English word fully reproduces the complex of elements implied by the word *ressentiment*; its nearest approximation in German would appear to be *Groll.*

[41] George S. Pettee, *The Process of Revolution* (New York, 1938), 8–24; see particularly his account of "monopoly of the imagination."

the functions of the counter-myth of the conservatives—briefly sketched in an earlier section of this chapter—become further clarified: whatever the source of mass frustration, it is not to be found in the basic structure of the society. The conservative myth may thus assert that these frustrations are in the nature of things and would occur in *any* social system: "Periodic mass unemployment and business depressions can't be legislated out of existence; it's just like a person who feels good one day and bad the next."[42] Or, if not the doctrine of inevitability, then the doctrine of gradual and slight adjustment: "A few changes here and there, and we'll have things running as ship-shape as they can possibly be." Or, the doctrine which deflects hostility from the social structure onto the individual who is a "failure" since "every man really gets what's coming to him in this country."

The myths of rebellion and of conservatism both work toward a "monopoly of the imagination" seeking to define the situation in such terms as to move the frustrate toward or away from Adaptation V. It is above all the renegade who, though himself successful, renounces the prevailing values that becomes the target of greatest hostility among those in rebellion. For he not only puts the values in question, as does the out-group, but he signifies that the unity of the group is broken.[43] Yet, as has so often been noted, it is typically members of a rising class rather than the most depressed strata who organize the resentful and the rebellious into a revolutionary group.

THE STRAIN TOWARD ANOMIE

The social structure we have examined produces a strain toward anomie and deviant behavior. The pressure of such a social order is upon outdoing one's competitors. So long as the sentiments supporting this competitive system are distributed throughout the entire range of activities and are not confined to the final result of "success," the choice of means will remain largely within the ambit of institutional control. When, however, the cultural emphasis shifts from the satisfactions deriving from competition itself to almost exclusive concern with the outcome, the resultant stress makes for the breakdown of the regulatory structure. With this attenuation of institutional controls, there occurs an approximation to the situation erroneously held by the utilitarian philosophers to be typical of society, a situation in which calculations of personal advantage and fear of punishment are the only regulating agencies.

This strain toward anomie does not operate evenly throughout the

[42] R. S. and H. M. Lynd, *Middletown in Transition* (New York, 1937), 408, for a series of cultural clichés exemplifying the conservative myth.

[43] See the acute observations by Georg Simmel, *Soziologie* (Leipzig, 1908), 276-77.

society. Some effort has been made in the present analysis to suggest the strata most vulnerable to the pressures for deviant behavior and to set forth some of the mechanisms operating to produce those pressures. For purposes of simplifying the problem, monetary success was taken as the major cultural goal, although there are, of course, alternative goals in the repository of common values. The realms of intellectual and artistic achievement, for example, provide alternative career patterns which may not entail large pecuniary rewards. To the extent that the cultural structure attaches prestige to these alternatives and the social structure permits access to them, the system is somewhat stabilized. Potential deviants may still conform in terms of these auxiliary sets of values.

But the central tendencies toward anomie remain, and it is to these that the analytical scheme here set forth calls particular attention.

THE ROLE OF THE FAMILY

A final word should be said drawing together the implications scattered throughout the foregoing discussion concerning the role played by the family in these patterns of deviant behavior.

It is the family, of course, which is a major transmission belt for the diffusion of cultural standards to the oncoming generation. But what has until lately been overlooked is that the family largely transmits that portion of the culture accessible to the social stratum and groups in which the parents find themselves. It is, therefore, a mechanism for disciplining the child in terms of the cultural goals and mores characteristic of this narrow range of groups. Nor is the socialization confined to direct training and disciplining. The process is, at least in part, inadvertent. Quite apart from direct admonitions, rewards and punishments, the child is exposed to social prototypes in the witnessed daily behavior and casual conversations of parents. Not infrequently, *children detect and incorporate cultural uniformities even when these remain implicit and have not been reduced to rules.*

Language patterns provide the most impressive evidence, readily observable in clinical fashion, that children, in the process of socialization, detect uniformities which have not been explicitly formulated for them by elders or contemporaries and which are not formulated by the children themselves. Persistent errors of language among children are most instructive. Thus, the child will spontaneously use such words as "mouses" or "moneys," *even though he has never heard such terms or been taught "the rule for forming plurals."* Or he will create such words as "falled," "runned," "singed," "hitted," though he has not been taught, at the age of three, "rules" of conjugation. Or, he will refer to a choice morsel as "gooder" than another less favored, or perhaps through a logical extension, he may describe it as "goodest" of all. Obviously, he has detected the implicit paradigms for the expression of plurality, for the conjugation of verbs, and the inflection of adjectives. The very nature of his error and misapplication of the paradigm testifies to this.[44]

It may be tentatively inferred, therefore, that he is also busily engaged in *detecting and acting upon the implicit paradigms of cultural evaluation, and categorization of people and things, and the formation of estimable goals* as well as assimilating the explicit cultural orientation set forth in an endless stream of commands, explanations and exhortations by parents. It would appear that in addition to the important researches of the depth psychologies on the socialization process, there is need for supplementary types of direct observation of culture diffusion within the family. It may well be that the child retains the implicit paradigm of cultural values detected in the day-by-day behavior of his parents even when this conflicts with their explicit advice and exhortations.

The projection of parental ambitions onto the child is also centrally relevant to the subject in hand. As is well known, many parents confronted with personal "failure" or limited "success" may mute their original goal-emphasis and may defer further efforts to reach the goal, attempting to reach it vicariously through their children. "The influence may come through the mother or the father. Often it is the case of a parent who hopes that the child will attain heights that he or she failed to attain."[45] In a recent research on the social organization of public housing developments, we have found among both Negroes and Whites on lower occupational levels, a substantial proportion having aspirations for a professional career for their children.[46] Should this finding be confirmed by further research it will have large bearing upon the problem in hand. For if compensatory projection of parental ambition onto children is widespread, then it is precisely those parents least able to provide free access to opportunity for their children—the "failures" and "frustrates"—who exert great pressure upon their children for high achievement. And this syndrome of lofty aspirations and limited realistic opportunities, as we have seen, is precisely the pattern which invites deviant behavior. This clearly points to the need for investigation focused upon occupational goal-formation in the several social strata if the inadvertent role of family disciplining in deviant behavior is to be understood from the perspectives of our analytical scheme.

[44] W. Stern, *Psychology of Early Childhood* (New York, 1924), 166, notes the *fact* of such errors (*e.g.,* "drinked" for "drank"), but does not draw the inferences regarding the detection of implicit paradigms.

[45] H. A. Murray *et al., Explorations in Personality,* 307.

[46] From a study of the social organization of planned communities by R. K. Merton, Patricia S. West and M. Jahoda, *Patterns of Social Life.*

CONCLUDING REMARKS

It should be apparent that the foregoing discussion is not pitched on a moralistic plane. Whatever the sentiments of the reader concerning the moral desirability of coordinating the goals-and-means phases of the social structure, it is clear that imperfect coordination of the two leads to anomie. In so far as one of the most general functions of social structure is to provide a basis for predictability and regularity of social behavior, it becomes increasingly limited in effectiveness as these elements of the social structure become dissociated. At the extreme, predictability is minimized and what may be properly called anomie or cultural chaos supervenes.

This essay on the structural sources of deviant behavior remains but a prelude. It has not included a detailed treatment of the structural elements which predispose toward one rather than another of the alternative responses open to individuals living in an ill-balanced social structure; it has largely neglected but not denied the relevance of the social-psychological processes determining the specific incidence of these responses; it has only briefly considered the social functions fulfilled by deviant behavior; it has not put the explanatory power of the analytical scheme to full empirical test by determining group variations in deviant and conformist behavior; it has only touched upon rebellious behavior which seeks to refashion the social framework.

It is suggested that these and related problems may be advantageously analyzed by use of this scheme.

2 Affluence and Adolescent Crime

JACKSON TOBY

In 1960 a United Nations Congress on "The Prevention of Crime and the Treatment of Offenders" met in London. Delegates from countries on every continent compared notes. The verdict was pessimistic: Crime rates were increasing in nearly all countries, especially among adolescents, and rich countries were having as serious problems as poor countries.[1] In 1964 another United Nations Congress met in Stockholm and came to similar conclusions about adolescent crime. Economic growth, though it raised living standards, did not seem to reduce crime rates. Some criminological experts went further: Affluence was itself a causal factor in the worsening crime problems of contemporary society.

What did these crime problems consist of? Rape? Murder? Assault? From crime reports in the daily newspapers of the large cities of the world— New York, London, Tokyo—one might think that crimes of violence were rising rapidly and constituted a major component of "the crime problem." In some places this was happening, but it was not a consistent trend. For example, in Scotland and in England and Wales, there was a steep rise in the crime rate between 1927 and 1962, . . . but in neither country were crimes

Reprinted from *Task Force Report: Juvenile Delinquency and Youth Crime*, Report on Juvenile Justice and Consultants' Papers, Task Force on Juvenile Delinquency— The President's Commission on Law Enforcement and Administration of Justice (Washington: Government Printing Office, 1967), Appendix H, pp. 132–144.

[1] Second United Nations Congress on the Prevention of Crime and the Treatment of Offenders, "Report Prepared by the Secretariat," New York: Department of Economic and Social Affairs, 1960, pp. 8–18.

against the person an important factor. In Great Britain, crimes against the person consisted of less than 5 percent of crime in general. Furthermore, crimes against the person were not increasing faster than all crimes together; in Scotland, crimes against the person rose more slowly. Criminologists who disregarded the selective horror stories of daily newspapers and looked at crime statistics coldly have observed that the crime problem revolved mainly around theft. Insofar as crimes of violence increased, they were mainly crimes like armed robbery rather than rape and murder. This thought may not console the gas station attendant shot during a holdup attempt, but it helps to explain the motivations of people who behave in ways summarized in the unrevealing category, "crime."

CRIME AND THE REVOLUTION OF RISING EXPECTATIONS

The preponderance of crimes against property sheds light on the tendency of crime rates to rise in the most affluent countries. People steal, not because they are starving, but because they are envious, and they are more likely to be envious of the possessions of others in countries with rising standards of living. Why should this be so? Because the rise in living standards is associated not only with an improvement of the style of life of elite groups; it is associated also with the trickling down of television sets, refrigerators, transistor radios, and automobiles to segments of the population who had not anticipated such good fortune. Industrial societies, which produce the new luxuries, distribute them more democratically than the less affluent agrarian societies did. Paradoxically though, the trend toward increasing equality in the distribution of consumer goods generates expectations of further equality. When expectations are rising faster than the standard of living, the greater availability of consumer goods makes for greater rather than less dissatisfaction. This revolution of rising expectations is both cause and effect of the soaring ownership of automobiles, television sets, and radios not just in the United States or even in Europe but in Africa, Asia, and South America (see table 1A). Traffic jams are now fully as serious in Tokyo as they have long been in New York and London; rivers of cars flow toward Tokyo every morning from as far away as Mount Fuji.[2] Suburbanization is no longer an American phenomenon; the automobile has transformed the world.

[2] In 1964, the number of registered automobiles in Japan was 6,775,971, about 47 times as many as were registered in 1945. The number of traffic deaths in Tokyo was 1,050, about 9.8 per 100,000 population and about 9.9 per 10,000 registered automobilies. The latter rate is much higher than for large cities in the United States. "Summary of the White Paper on Crime, 1965," Tokyo: Training and Research Institute, Ministry of Justice, March 1966, p. 6.

TABLE 1A. INDICES OF AFFLUENCE FOR SELECTED COUNTRIES, 1963

Country	Number of radios per 100 population	Rank	Number of TV's per 100 population	Rank	Number of cars per 100 population	Rank
U.S.A.	97	1	33	1	36	1
Canada	48	2	25	2	25	2
Sweden	39	3	24	3	20	5
Denmark	35	4	20	5	13	11
Belgium	33	5	12	10	11	13
Luxembourg	33	6	5	21	15	7
West Germany	31	7	15	8	13	9
Finland	31	8	10	11	7	19
France	30	9	9	12	17	6
United Kingdom	29	10	24	4	14	8
Norway	29	11	8	14	10	14
Austria	29	12	6	17	9	15
Switzerland	28	13	6	18	13	10
Iceland	28	14	(1)	(1)	12	12
Netherlands	26	15	13	9	7	18
Argentina	25	16	6	20	3	22
Chile	24	17	0.4	31	1	30
New Zealand	24	18	6	19	24	3
Israel	24	19	(1)	(1)	2	25
Panama	22	20	4	22	2	26
Australia	20	21	16	7	23	4
Japan	20	22	16	6	1	29
Venezuela	20	23	7	16	4	21
Ireland	19	24	7	15	8	16
Italy	19	25	8	13	8	17
Peru	18	26	1	26	1	31
Mexico	17	27	3	24	2	28
Jamaica	13	28	1	30	3	23
Spain	13	29	3	23	2	27
Portugal	12	30	1	27	2	24
Greece	9	31	(1)	(1)	1	32
Paraguay	9	32	(1)	(1)	0.4	36
South Africa	7	33	(1)	(1)	6	20
U.A.R.	7	34	1	29	0.3	39
Ghana	7	35	(1)	(1)	0.4	37
Brazil	6	36	2	25	0.1	40
South Korea	6	37	(2)	34	(2)	—
Turkey	5	38	(2)	35	(2)	—
Philippines	4	39	0.2	32	0.3	38

TABLE 1A (*Continued*)

Country	Number of radios per 100 population	Rank	Number of TV's per 100 population	Rank	Number of cars per 100 population	Rank
Ceylon	4	40	([1])	([1])	1	33
Iraq	2	41	0.7	28	1	34
Burma	1	42	([1])	([1])	0.1	35
India	1	43	([2])	36	0.1	42
Nigeria	1	44	([2])	33	0.1	45
Pakistan	0.5	45	([1])	([1])	0.1	41

[1] Statistics not available.

[2] Less than 0.05 per 100 population.

SOURCE: "United Nations Statistical Yearbook, 1964," New York Statistical Office of the United Nations, 1965, pp. 23–42, 391–398, 714–716.

Table 1A reflects the level of affluence in selected countries—at least insofar as radios, television sets, and automobiles can be regarded as indices of affluence. Thus, table 1A shows the United States, Canada, and Sweden to be among the countries of the world rich in durable consumer goods whereas India, Nigeria, and Pakistan are among the poor countries. But for persons interested in the effect of affluence on crime, it is not only the level of affluence that is important, but the rate at which affluence is increasing. Table 1B shows that the rate at which affluence is increasing is comparatively slow for the richest countries. Thus, the rate of increase of ownership of radios in the United States and Canada is of the order of 12 percent per year. India's annual rate of increase of radio ownership was 36 percent in the decade 1954–64, and Nigeria's was 89 percent. True, these countries started from very low levels of ownership. Still, if we are interested in the impact of affluence on the revolution of rising expectations, the increases are dramatic. The situation with respect to automobile ownership is somewhat different. The richest countries have a comparatively slow rate of increase in automobile ownership. But it is not the poorest countries that have the fastest rate of increase but countries of the second rank: Italy, Greece, Spain. (Germany and Japan also have high rates of increase, but this can be interpreted as due to "catching up" after the Second World War.) The poorest countries have annual rates of increase only slightly higher than the richest countries, doubtless because an automobile is such a large investment in poor countries. If the increases in ownership of durable consumer goods contribute as much or more to envy as the level of ownership, this would help to explain why crime is increasing in most countries of the world.

TABLE 1B.   CHANGES IN AFFLUENCE, 1954–64*

Country	Percent increase in radio ownership per 1,000 population	Percent increase in automobile ownership per 1,000 population
U.S.A.	134	125
Canada	111	147
Sweden	116	292
West Germany	127	469
Argentina	132	136
Japan	155	977
Switzerland	114	296
Italy	175	581
Spain	227	499
Greece	152	457
Philippines	388	165
Ceylon	339	53
Burma	797	184
India	362	172
Nigeria	891	176

* For Argentina, Japan, and the United States, the 10-year interval was 1953–63. For Burma and India, the 10-year interval was 1952–62.

SOURCE: Calculated from data in various volumes of "United Nations Statistical Yearbook."

Industrialization and suburbanization may be thought of in relation to the world of adults. But the revolution of rising expectations has consequences for the young too. As car registrations grow, so do the desires of adolescents to drive (as well as to own cameras, transitor radios, and new clothes). Few adolescents can get legitimate access to a car, partly because of the age of licensing drivers, partly because of the cost of vehicles. In Japan, for example, the custom is to pay workers in accordance with age as well as skill; so adolescent workers (as well as schoolboys) have almost no chance to buy a car unless they come from rich families. Relative to adults, they are impoverished despite the growing affluence of Japanese society. Interestingly enough, the crime rate in Japan has risen most rapidly for the 14 to 17 age group (see table 2), and has not increased at all for adults.[3] In 1941, the Japanese police apprehended 334,417 suspects of whom 7 percent were 14 to 17 years of age; in 1964, 726,910 suspects were apprehended of whom 19 percent were 14 to 17. Although table 2 shows the

[3] "Crime rate" refers to the number of persons investigated by the Japanese police for a penal code violation per thousand persons of the base population.

TABLE 2. INCREASE IN JUVENILE CRIME IN JAPAN

	Suspects apprehended by the Japanese police											
	In 1941		In 1946		In 1951		In 1956		In 1961		In 1964	
Age of suspects	Number	Percent	Number	Percent	Number	Percent	Number	Percent	Number	Percent	Number	Percent
Over 20	281,708	84	333,694	75	452,602	73	427,192	77	422,430	66	488,080	67
18 and 19	19,780	6	51,910	11	58,030	10	48,301	9	62,758	10	55,208	8
14–17	22,731	7	47,479	11	75,626	12	52,457	9	96,126	15	135,334	18
Under 14	10,198	3	12,401	3	32,777	5	26,663	5	57,572	9	48,388	7
Total	334,417	100	445,484	100	619,035	100	554,613	100	638,886	100	726,910	100

SOURCE: "Juvenile Problems in Japan," Tokyo: Central Council on Juvenile Problems, Prime Minister's Office, 1962, p. 38; "Summary of the White Paper on Crime, 1965," Tokyo: Training and Research Institute of the Ministry of Justice, March 1966, pp. 17–18.

crime trend for the entire 14 to 17 age group, in 1954 the 14- and 15-year-olds and the 16- and 17-year-olds were separated in Japanese crime statistics, making it possible to study arrest data since then in greater detail.[4] For ages 20 to 24, the crime rate was 17.1 per thousand persons of those ages in 1955, and it was still 17.1 in 1964. For ages 18 and 19, the crime rate increased from 13.1 per thousand persons of those ages in 1955 to 17.8 in 1964. For ages 16 to 17, the crime rate increased from 8.8 per thousand in 1955 to 14.5 per thousand in 1964. For ages 14 and 15, the increase was the greatest of all: From 5.8 [per] thousand persons of those ages in 1955 to 14.1 in 1964.

Can the increase in the crime rate of Japanese 14- and 15-year-olds be fully explained by a desire to share in the new affluence? Probably not. There are other factors, including the decreased authority of adults over children since the defeat of the Japanese in the Second World War. A case history of a Japanese delinquent shows some of these interrelated motivations in vivid form. The following are excerpts from 3 days of conversation with a 19-year-old boy interviewed recently in a training school for delinquents near Tokyo.[5]

At 15, Toshiko graduated from junior high school and enrolled in a vocational school to learn how to drive and repair cars. He stayed 6 months although the course was supposed to last 1 year. He said that his friends urged him to quit in order to "live an adult life." He wanted to smoke, to stay out late at night in the entertainment districts of Tokyo, to play *pachinko* [a popular Japanese slot machine game], and to wear fashionable clothing. Before he was imprisoned Toshiko wore bell-bottomed trousers and short jackets, the costume of a *chimpira* gang. He and his friends wished to feel superior to other Japanese and therefore wore what they thought to be American-style clothing. Toshiko's mother disapproved, but his father, a hard-working clerk, did not say anything. Like his friends, Toshiko wore thin underwear instead of the heavy underwear worn by the older generation. [There is very little central heating in Japan, and heavy underwear is protection against a cold, damp climate.]

After leaving the vocational school, Toshiko and his friends maintained their interest in cars. They broke into at least 11 cars over a period of several weeks, using a master key to get inside and shorting the ignition wires to start them. They picked up bread in the early morning from in front of grocery stores and ate it while driving around. When the gasoline was used up, they would abandon the cars—first taking care to remove the radios, which they sold for as much as 2,000 yen [$5.50] each.

[4] "Summary of the White Paper on Crime, 1965," p. 18, op. cit. n. 2.

[5] The interviews were conducted in Japanese with the help of a skilled interpreter, Masahiko Kikuchi, during March and April of 1964. The opportunity to visit the training school and interview inmates was graciously provided by the Correction Bureau of the Ministry of Justice and in particular by Director Osawa, Mr. Kakuichiro Ogino, and Mr. Akira Tanigawa.

Toshiko and his friends also broke into shops at night. They would select a little shop without a watchman. It would have to be located where a car, previously stolen for the purpose, could be parked nearby while the break-in was in progress. There were usually three to five in the group, one or two looking out for the police. They would either jimmy the door or apply a chemical paste to a window and set it aflame, enabling it to break easily and quietly.

Sometimes they picked a quarrel with a drunk, beat him up, and went through his pockets. Aside from drunks, however, they did not usually bother conventional people. More usually, they would extort money from members of rival *chimpira* groups. Toshiko would walk down the street until he saw a likely victim. Two confederates would be nearby but not visible. "Hello, fine fellow. Lend me your face." This was a challenge for the victim to go to a less busy place for a fight. Not seeing Toshiko's friends, the victim would agree; he was angry. After the fight started, the confederates would join in, using wooden bats as well as fists. Soon the victim had enough and was willing to agree to give the victors what they wanted. They preferred money. But the victim might not have any. If not, they would take his fountain pen, watch, railroad ticket, and even his clothing. If he had on expensive shoes or a new suit, they might accompany him to a pawn shop where he would exchange these things for old clothes and cash, the latter for Toshiko and his friends. (They would give a small amount to the victim, 10 percent or less.)

Since Toshiko was stealing and extorting yen with his friends, he had enough money to spend long evenings in the entertainment districts of Tokyo. Subways and buses stopped running at midnight, whereas he did not usually leave his favorite bars until 2 a.m., so he was forced to pay expensive night rates to taxis in order to get home. This dissatisfied him; he preferred to pay for beer and whiskey or, if he was looking for cut-rate intoxication, for sleeping pills rather than for transportation. He asked his father to buy him a car so that he might drive himself home in the small hours of the morning. His father was outraged. Toshiko did not work; he slept until noon or later every day; he spent his nights in the bars of Shibuya [an entertainment district]; and he had the effrontery to ask his father, a poorly paid clerk, to buy him a car. [His father did not himself have a car.] A violent argument ensued in the course of which his father hit him; he hit his father back.

This blow must have been even more surprising to Toshiko's father than the original request for a car. While paternal authority is not now what it was once in Japan, it is still considerable. In traditional homes, the wife and children do not eat with the father, who is served literally on bended knee. That a son would dare to argue openly with his father is a sign of the increased equality between the generations in urban Japan. That he would hit his father, no matter what the provocation, is, to a Japanese, almost unbelievable.

Toshiko's father ordered him out of the house. He left home and moved in with a friend where he stayed for a week. Then he came home and apologized.

His father would not forgive him. For a few weeks he stayed first with one *chimpira* and then with another. As soon as he found a girl who worked in a bar as a hostess and could help support him, he rented an apartment. [Such a girl is called *dambe* in Japanese slang, meaning "one who pulls money in on a string."] It was important to him that she not become pregnant because she could not continue to work, so Toshiko was careful to use contraceptives during sexual intercourse. This was not his usual practice with casual pickups.

The significance of Toshiko is not that he is Japanese or even that he is delinquent but that he represents one aspect of the revolution of rising expectations: the dissatisfaction of adolescents with their share in the new affluence. From this point of view, Toshiko is an international phenomenon that can be observed in Stockholm and Tel-Aviv as well as in Tokyo and Newark. Sweden offers an unusual opportunity to observe the effect of affluence on delinquency because circumstances that tend to raise the delinquency rates of other countries are, for the most part, absent from the richest country in Europe. Sweden was not a belligerent during the Second World War and did not suffer the disruptive effects of bombing and population loss, as did Japan. Sweden has no ethnic minorities, except for Lapp reindeer herders in the northern section, and therefore need not be concerned about prejudice and discrimination as a cause of crime. Sweden is culturally homogeneous; except for temporary workers from Latin countries, there has been no large-scale immigration for centuries. In the United States and Great Britain, on the other hand, an appreciable part of the crime problem results from the limited economic and social opportunities of colored persons. In Israel, much crime results from "melting-pot" problems. Since immigrants from the Middle East and Africa are more difficult to educate and to train for industrial occupations than those from Europe and America, young Israeli from "Oriental" backgrounds are more likely to feel materially deprived. Statistics show that Oriental youngsters become delinquent more frequently than European youngsters.[6] The following are excerpts from an interview with a 20-year-old Yemenite prisoner in an Israeli reformatory; they illustrate one byproduct of the revolution of rising expectations in a culturally heterogeneous society:[7]

Happy's parents came to Israel in 1939 from a town in Yemen when they were young adults. Born in 1944, Happy does not seem to have many pleasant

[6] Children born in Israel had a delinquency rate in 1960 of 5.6 per thousand of juvenile court age. Children born in Europe or America had exactly the same rate. But children born in Asia had a delinquency rate of 11.4 per thousand in the base population, and children born in Africa a rate of 17.6 per thousand. "Statistical Abstract of Israel, 1963," Jerusalem: Central Bureau of Statistics, 1963, p. 688.

[7] The interview was conducted in Hebrew with the help of an Israeli colleague, Aryeh Leissner. The opportunity to visit a reformatory and interview prisoners was graciously provided by Dr. Zvi Hermon, Scientific Director, Prison Service of Israel.

childhood memories. He mentioned two birthday parties when he was very young. I think he mentioned them to suggest how little his parents did for him as he grew older. He stopped going to synagogue at the age of 10. By the age of 15, he began smoking and gambling on the Sabbath. This was shocking behavior to his Orthodox parents, and they objected. "But I did not hear." Happy finished elementary school at 15 and went for a year to a vocational school.

When he was free, he lived in Tel-Aviv. He would wake up about 10:30 a.m. Although his mother was in the house, he would take something to eat for himself. Then he would go to a street with trees and benches where he would meet his friends. If any of the boys had money, they would go to play snooker [a form of pool] or to a day performance in the movies, taking a girl if possible. If there were unaccompanied girls near the meeting place who didn't work and had nothing to do, they might be picked up. If the boys had no money, they sat, talked, got bored, and annoyed people. If there was a plan to steal a car in the evening and break in, they talked about the job. If no job was planned, they talked about girls, about jobs they did pull or would pull.

Happy wanted to be considered *bomba* [tough] rather than *fryer* [a sucker]. A *fryer* wants to be accepted by the gang, but he never succeeds. "This kind of boy hasn't had the kind of childhood we had, and he doesn't know how to take care of himself." He is permitted to associate with the *chevra* [gang] because he gets money [presumably from his parents] for gasoline, for a party, or to pay the bill in a restaurant. A *bomba*, on the other hand, is daring and aggressive. He steals the latest model cars, and he is successful with *fryereet* [girls who are easy to seduce].

The *chevra* gambled three or four evenings a week for about 5 hours at a time, playing poker, rummy, 21, coin tossing, dice, or a game with a numbered board called "7 times 3." Happy was not usually very lucky. He lost as much as $50 in an evening. Gambling usually started on Friday evening, stopped at 2 or 3 a.m. and began again at about 10:30 a.m. on Saturday morning. The gambling stopped by Saturday evening when the *chevra* went to the movies or to a dance club. Sometimes a boy won too much, and the others suspected him of cheating. They might beat him up and take his money.

Happy and his friends drank liquor at every opportunity, sometimes during a card game, sometimes at a coffee shop, sometimes at a party. They drank Stock 84, for which they paid $1.20 to $1.40 for a half pint. When they had little money, they bought a big bottle of medicinal brandy for 70 cents.

Alcohol increased the probability of fights. "When you are a little drunk, sometimes you start pushing someone around." Once Happy kicked a dog when he was "high." The lady who owned the dog shouted at him; he shouted back. The owner's husband joined the argument. Soon the *doda* [literally "aunts" in Hebrew but meaning "police"] were called. But fights occurred for other reasons. Happy recalled one time when he was playing cards out-of-doors on a Saturday afternoon. A member of an extremely Orthodox sect came over to the *chevra* and told them to stop gambling on the Sabbath. In the course of the furious argument that ensued, the Orthodox man threw a nearby bicycle in the middle of the game. They stopped the game and beat him up badly. If members of the *chevra* made remarks about a girl in the movies, and her boyfriend resented them, this could start a fight. Or sometimes a member of the group took a couple of friends and *laredet alay* [literally "went down on" but meaning "beat up"] a boy who was saying insulting things about him or about the group.

On Happy's right hand is a tatoo consisting of a half moon and three stars, which [he said] means, "We are against the law." Although he made this tatoo in the reformatory, this could well have been the motto of his *chevra* in the community. Car thefts were a favorite activity. At first cars were stolen only for joyrides. The competition consisted of stealing newer model cars and large cars. "The car is always full—as many as the car will hold." Girls were sometimes reluctant to come for fear of getting involved. Once Happy left his straw hat with a feather in a car he had tried to start unsuccessfully. The gang went back to get the hat after having stolen another car. The *doda* gave chase; but Uri, the driver, outdistanced them. After a while, they decided to use the cars they stole to help in burglaries. For example, they broke into a supermarket through airvents in the back—forcing the grill—and took cigarettes and cognac and chocolate away in the car. Then they went back to the room of one of the boys and had a party.

Once, when they passed a Willys station wagon filled with appliances, they stole them and sold them to a *client* [fence] recommended by a friend. The loot consisted of: Clothes, irons, fans, transistor radios, and electric shavers. Four boys each got $200. Happy hid his share under a tile in the courtyard of his house and continued to ask his mother for a pound or two [33 or 66 cents] for spending money. Happy spent all of his share in a month. (He kept the clothes he bought in a pal's house—so as not to arouse his mother's suspicions.) This success aroused the interest of the *chevra* in transistor radios, and they broke into appliance stores, preferably from the back but sometimes from the front when the street was clear. Sometimes they broke into two stores in a week, sometimes none at all. They also broke into dry goods stores—but this was not so profitable. From every car they stole, they took the radio. Sometimes they stripped cars without moving them.

In some ways, the crimes of Happy and his gang are not startling. They remind criminologists of the Irish, Polish, and Italian juvenile gangs in Chicago a half century ago—or of Negro gangs today in Philadelphia, New York, or Cleveland. Gangs consisting of the sons of poverty-stricken migrants to the city are commonplace. But the juvenile gangs of Sweden are less easy to understand because poverty, in the old sense of hunger, ragged clothes, and disease, does not exist in Sweden. As in many countries, there has been a housing shortage in Sweden, especially in the cities; this shortage dates from the postwar rise in the birth rate. But existing housing is modern and pleasant. Slums cannot be the breeding place of crime in Stockholm, Malmö, or Gothenburg, the three largest cities of Sweden, because there are no slums. Nevertheless, delinquency has been a troublesome problem for the Swedes. Table 3 shows the rise in adolescent offenders

TABLE 3. NUMBER OF OFFENDERS RECORDED
IN THE PENAL REGISTER OF SWEDEN PER 100,000
OF THE BASE POPULATION, 1946–55

	Age of offenders and their crime rates		
Year	15–17 years	18–20 years	21 years and older
1946	485	473	155
1947	469	506	148
1948	482	460	128
1949	485	535	144
1950	522	569	157
1951	637	697	188
1952	651	697	204
1953	634	718	202
1954	677	708	210
1955	671	743	235

SOURCE: "Post-War Juvenile Delinquency in Sweden," Stockholm: Department of Justice and the Swedish Institute, July 1960,
p. 6 (mimeographed).

from 1946 to 1955. During those years, the conviction rate rose 38 percent
in the age group, 15 to 17; the corresponding rise for the 18 to 20 age group
was 57 percent. Note that the increase in Swedish delinquency rates, unlike
the increase in Japanese delinquency, was more pronounced among older
adolescents. There may be a good explanation for this. Sweden is a radically
equalitarian country, where as Japanese tradition stresses the submission of
the young to the old. Swedish youngsters, 15 to 17, are the beneficiaries of
many governmental services including excellent youth clubs, and they can
earn almost as much as adults if they choose to leave school and go to work.
So even though they may feel deprived, they are not likely to feel as
deprived as Japanese youngsters of the same age.

In spite of these favorable circumstances, Swedish adolescents commit
crimes. And in addition to committing crimes, they behave in ways that
are, if not illegal, disturbing to adults. For example, in the 1950's gangs of
raggare [cruisers] drove around the downtown districts of the large cities
in American-made cars looking for girls. At one time *raggare* automobiles
interfered sufficiently with traffic flow in Stockholm that city officials
invited leaders of the main groups, the Car Angels, the Car Comets, the
Teddy Boys, and the Car Devils, to City Hall to discuss the problem. On
New Year's Eve of 1957, a crowd of 3,000 persons, about two-thirds of
them under 21, gathered in the center of Stockholm and bombarded police

with empty tin cans and other objects. They forced several cars to stop and wrenched off their doors. One car was overturned and wrecked.[8] Gate-crashing has also been a problem in Sweden, as it has in the United States.[9] As a Swedish governmental report put it, "Groups of young people force their way uninvited into a party, or break into a private house or apartment, in the absence of the owners, and proceed to break china, mutilate furniture and deface walls."[10]

That the rise in Swedish delinquency is indirectly related to Swedish prosperity is not self-evident. But there does not seem to be any major social trend—except the increase in affluence—to blame for the delinquency problem. There are also some direct connections between delinquency and affluence. In Sweden, as in the United States, auto theft is predominantly a crime of adolescents.[11] Furthermore, while the rate of auto theft in Sweden rose from 29 per 100,000 population in 1950 to 126 per 100,000 population in 1957, the rate computed per 10,000 automobiles registered rose only from 90 per 10,000 registrations in 1950 to 116 per 10,000 registrations in 1957.[12] What does this mean? That the temptation to steal cars was proportional to the number of cars in use and the number of adolescents who felt dissatisfied with their share of them. Of course, older Swedish adolescents did not have to steal cars in order to drive them. Unlike the situation in Japan, teenage boys in Sweden who work in unskilled jobs may nevertheless earn enough to afford a secondhand car. The *raggare* gangs do not consist entirely of delinquents any more than the American hotrod clubs consist of delinquents. But some *raggare* boys and girls are not satisfied with their share in Sweden's high living standards. And they can be very delinquent indeed, as the following excerpts from an interview with a former member of the Road Devils show:[13]

[8] "Post-War Juvenile Delinquency in Sweden," Stockholm: Department of Justice and the Swedish Institute, July 1960, p. 19 (mimeographed).

[9] Robert Wallace, "Where's the Party—Let's Crash It!" "Life," vol. 55 (July 5, 1963), pp. 62–67.

[10] "Post-War Juvenile Delinquency in Sweden," op. cit., p. 20.

[11] In 1965 there were 486,600 auto thefts reported in the United States, 51 percent more than in 1960 and more than double the percentage increase in automobile registrations. Sixty-two percent of the persons arrested for auto theft were under 18; 88 percent of the persons arrested for auto theft were under 25. Federal Bureau of Investigation, "Uniform Crime Reports of the United States, 1965," Washington: Government Printing Office, 1966, pp. 17–18.

[12] "Post-War Juvenile Delinquency in Sweden," op. cit. n. 8, p. 14.

[13] This interview was conducted in English in a reception center for young offenders near Uppsala, Sweden, in 1960. In addition to studying English in school, as all Swedes do, the prisoner had been a merchant seaman and had visited English-speaking countries. The opportunity to visit a reception center and interview inmates was graciously provided by Torsten Erikson, Director-General, Swedish National Prisons Board.

Lappen was an unwanted child. He arrived just as the marriage of his parents was breaking up. Shortly after Lappen's birth, his father left his mother for another woman. Lappen's brother Bengt, 2 years older than he, was kept at home, and Lappen was temporarily sent to live with his maternal grandparents in Lapland; his mother could not take care of both children.[14] Lappen's mother earned 600 crowns a month [about $120] in a butcher shop. By Swedish standards this was a low income, and Lappen reported that he envied the clothes and spending money of some of his friends whose family earned 1,600 crowns a month [the man of the family earned a thousand and the woman 600]. When Lappen was 9 or 10 years old, he and three friends from relatively poor families began stealing candy and fruit from local stores so that they could have the same things as the other boys in the neighborhood. (Stig was 1 year older than Lappen, Borje 1 year older, and Jan 1 year younger.) The other neighborhood boys admired the courage of the thieves. "We took greater and greater chances because we had to show that we were just as good as those whose parents had a lot of money." The boys who did not need to steal stole anyway out of a sense of adventure. Lappen and his three friends became the leaders of a gang. Lappen's gang controlled 10 or 15 square blocks. Between the ages of 10 and 15, Lappen participated in many fights. As many as 200 boys were involved in some of the biggest fights. The fights were with gangs from outside the neighborhood and were usually over "honor and girls, if I may say so." Lappen differentiated between two types of boys from outside the neighborhood: Boys who came from essentially the same class and boys who were *sossar* [important]. Fights with boys from the same social level were relatively friendly. "We only fought to show who was best. After the fight, we were all friends." In addition to fighting, Lappen and his friends increased the scope of their stealing activities. They "borrowed" rowboats and bicycles. They also "borrowed" automobiles for joyrides.

When Lappen attended school he played hookey at least 1 day a week. He said it was because he "had it so easy. The next day I came back and knew what they had talked about." The teachers did not find out about his truancy because he would write notes to them and forge his mother's signature. His mother urged him to go to school. However, she didn't tell the teacher he played hookey when she had an interview with the teacher because "* * * she wanted it to be good for me in school. Mother wanted me to be something, to go to the university, but I wouldn't. My interest was motors. I wouldn't sit on a book." Lappen's relationship with his mother has never been very good. "She lives her life and I live mine. I like her but I do not love her."

At the age of 15, just about the time he quit school, Lappen had his first sex experience. His gang [the South End Club] had obtained a meeting room in a local youth club. Lappen had carefully observed the caretaker's keys, and he had made a duplicate from memory. Consequently, he, Stig, and Borje had a

[14] "Lappen" is a nickname meaning Laplander. At the age of 6, he spent 6 months in Lapland with his maternal grandparents when his mother was too sick to take care of him. When he returned to Stockholm, his friends noticed a trace of a Lapland accent and dubbed him "Lappen." "I liked that name because not everyone knew my real name. If someone told it to the police, they might not catch me."

key to the meeting room. One evening he took a girl friend into the room and locked the door. Stig and Borje were outside to see that members of the youth club did not try to come in. Other members of the gang were in the game rooms of the club to keep the caretaker busy enough so that he would not disturb Lappen. Since there was no bed or sofa in the room, his first experience with *knulla* [intercourse] occurred on a table. Subsequently, he engaged in *knulla* frequently, usually in the home of girls whose parents were working. Although he and his friends were *raggarbrud* [promiscuous], they resented it when girls were unfaithful. He told me of one member of the gang who was in love with a girl. When he discovered that he had been sharing her with numerous others, he was enraged. He told his friends. On some pretext the jealous lover and seven of his friends, including Lappen, rowed to a deserted island near Stockholm with the girl. They confronted her with her infidelity and, as punishment, forced her to remove her clothes, and then all except the injured boy friend had sexual relations with her in turn. They rowed back to the mainland leaving her to swim back as best she could.

When he left school, Lappen got a job as a car mechanic. On and off for the next 3 or 4 years, he worked in this occupation, earning 200–250 crowns a week [$40–$50]. Like many other Swedish boys of similar social background, he is fascinated by cars, especially big American cars. He eventually became a member of one of the four most important *raggare* clubs of Stockholm, the Road Devils. Lappen and his friends drank heavily, drove recklessly, and cruised around the city of Stockholm picking up girls who were "looking for a good time." They held noisy parties and dances. Some members stole accessories for their cars. Those who did not own a car "borrowed" cars for joyrides. Lappen was probably more delinquent than most of the *raggare*. He rolled homosexuals and drunks. He burglarized stores with one or two confederates— usually using *schmacha* [the smash and grab technique]. His last *schmacha* was a jewelry store window. He got enough jewelry and watches to sell to a fence for 2,000 crowns. With this money he bought his own car and gave up stealing.

As Lappen described his life as a *raggare* boy, it was a life of fun, of laughs. "I lived an expensive life and I done exactly what I want. If I wanted to go to Copenhagen, I gotta go to Copenhagen. When we would drive to a little town, the girls knew we came from Stockholm and looked up to us." There was dancing and singing in the streets. "When I want to dance, I dance." Every weekend there would be parties in the homes of various girls or boys that he knew. He would start out on a Saturday evening at one party and would move on to others as the inclination moved him. He would usually bring vodka or Scotch or Spanish brandy as his contribution to the merriment. Ten to twenty young people would be present at a given party at one time, but there would be constant comings and goings. For example, Lappen would usually get to three or four parties by Sunday morning. "If I didn't have fun, I'd get home by 3 or 4 a.m. If I had fun, I'd get home by 6 or 7." Sometimes, however, the parties lasted all through Sunday.

In 1957 Lappen was convicted for breaking and entering and sent to Fagared, a youth prison near Gothenburg. When he was released, he did not return to Stockholm. Instead he took a room in Gothenburg and got a job as an auto mechanic. Somehow, while he was in the institution, he had fallen in love with a local girl. He distinguished his love for this 17-year-old girl from the many intimate relationships that he has had with girls in his neighborhood and in the *raggare*. (Girls are also members of the *raggare* clubs, but they rarely own cars.) "That year 1958 I shall never forget. It was the happiest year of my life. For the first time, I had a family. I played cards with her father and listened to the radio." The girl's father, an office worker, took a liking to Lappen. He discovered that the boy was living in a lonely furnished room and offered to rent a room to him in their house. Lappen eagerly accepted. During the period when he lived in his girl friend's house, he was, according to his account, a model young man. He didn't drink; he went to bed early; he worked steadily; and he spent his spare time with his girl friend. Unfortunately, she became pregnant. When they told her parents, he at first thought that they would allow him to marry her, which is what both of them wanted. But a few days later the father told him that he "was no longer welcome in the house." Without further discussion, Lappen left. The girl, being only 17, could not marry without her parent's consent. They insisted that she go to a hospital and have an abortion. Lappen returned to Stockholm. His letters to her were returned unopened. Soon he went back to his old life with the *raggare*. Twice he and another Road Devil broke into safes although Lappen was very nervous, and he let his partner handle the explosives.

"The boys in this place are like gamblers. If we win, we get money. If we lose, we are locked up. Because we are good losers, we can smile." He recognized that, when he got out of prison, he faced a choice between two very different ways of life. "I know that the right kind of life is to work and have a family, something to hope at. Maybe I had it too easy the last year now and it is difficult to get back to normal life. On the one side, I found a lot of fun and on the other side, the right side, there was only a hard life." I asked Lappen what the chances were of his not getting into trouble any more. "If I learn to trust people, I won't have any more trouble." I think what he meant was that he would not commit further crimes if he developed another relationship like the one he had with the girl from Gothenburg and her family.

Case studies like those of Lappen, Happy, and Toshiko illustrate the mechanisms whereby affluence leads to crime: through arousing feelings of material deprivation that cannot be satisfied legitimately. It is unlikely that adolescents from such different cultures would react to affluence so similarly unless there were a common causal process at work. Bear in mind though that the Lappens, Happys, and Toshikos are in the minority in their countries. Feelings of deprivation do not inevitably lead to crime. On the contrary, they are rarely acted upon. Under what conditions does the impulse to steal lead to theft? If affluence not only arouses predatory motives but gives the potential predator some prospect for "getting away with it," it greatly increases the probability that the motives will find expression in action. As the next section of this report will show, urban industrial societies do precisely that for adolescents: They loosen social controls and thus provide the opportunity for delinquency.

AFFLUENCE AND PARENTAL CONTROL
OVER CHILDREN

One of the effects of affluence is to increase the life expectancy of everybody in the society, including, of course, parents. This means that a child in a rich industrial society has a far better chance of having both his parents alive and well during his adolescence. Another effect of affluence is to increase the divorce and separation rate. Why? Because industrialization enables women to support themselves—and their children, if need be.[15] Hence marital unhappiness is more likely to result in divorce or separation in rich industrial societies than in poor underdeveloped societies. But the most important effect of affluence on the family is to strip it down to jetage size (mother, father, and their dependent children) and to isolate it physically and emotionally from other relatives. This is not true of all families even in the United States. And some industrial societies—Japan is a good example—have gone less far in deemphasizing generational ties than has Sweden, Israel, and the United States. Still, families in industrial societies are characteristically small; they move from community to community as employment opportunities arise; they lack the bulwark of kinship and communal support that poorer societies had.

These effects of affluence on the family help to explain why delinquents come from broken or inadequate families in industrial societies. Broken and inadequate families cause delinquency in rich societies because these societies assign major responsibility to parents for the control of their children. In poorer rural societies, where in addition to their biological parents, neighbors, grandparents, uncles, aunts and other assorted relatives supervise children the death or divorce of parents does not lead to juvenile delinquency. In short, a truism of criminologists, that delinquents come from less stable families than nondelinquents, is a truism only for affluent industrial societies. And even for us it is not clear *why* it is true. Two quite different mechanisms have been suggested by experts to explain this relationship between parental inadequacy and juvenile delinquency:

Mechanism 1. Parental rejection and neglect damage the personality of

[15] In 1890, women constituted 15.8 percent of the white civilian labor force; in 1957, they constituted 34.1 percent. In 1890, divorced, separated, and widowed women constituted 28.6 percent of working women; in 1957, these categories constituted 40.4 percent of working women. U.S. Bureau of the Census, "Historical Statistics of the United States, Colonial Times to 1957," Washington: Government Printing Office, 1960, p. 72.

the developing child. Lack of impulse control results from pathological socialization. The psychopathic or neurotic boy reacts with violence to trivial provocations, sets fires, and steals purposelessly.

Mechanism 2. Parental inadequacy and neglect, by reducing family control, thereby orient the boy toward his agemates in the neighborhood. The family and the peer group are in a sense competing for the allegiance of boys in high-delinquency neighborhoods. If the peer group is delinquent, a boy's desire for acceptance by his peers tempts him to participate in delinquent activities.

Some evidence supports both mechanisms; research is needed to distinguish the more important one. Such clarification would be useful because if mechanism 1 predominates, juvenile delinquency will probably continue to rise in all urban industrial countries. It is unlikely that most family catastrophes can be prevented. Assuming that the emotional scars resulting from death, divorce, or the mental illness of a parent cause delinquency, then delinquency may be part of the price of living in a rich society. On the other hand, if mechanism 2 predominates, more effective programs of delinquency control can be designed than are available at present. Assuming that the main problem is a breakdown of family control over the child, thereby exposing him to the corrupting influences of the street corner gang, then supportive institutions can be developed to backstop parents.[16]

Supportive institutions may be needed anyway. After all, although "problem" families have less effective control over adolescents than "normal" families in affluent societies, under contemporary conditions all families have weak control over adolescents, especially over boys. This weakness of adult control is most obvious under pathological circumstances such as slum neighborhoods or broken homes. Its ultimate source, however, is not pathology but the increasing social fluidity resulting from the allocation of education, recreation, work, and family life to separate institutional contexts. These changes in social organization affect everyone in contemporary societies, but their impact is especially great on adolescents because adolescence is a period of transition. Youngsters must disengage themselves from the family into which they were born and raised and establish themselves in a new family unit. They must eventually withdraw from the system of formal education and assume an occupational role. While preparing to make these transitions and learning preparatory skills, many adolescents are socially adrift—except for such solidarities as they form with youngsters in

---

[16] In Sweden, unmarried mothers not only receive allowances for their children. They are visited regularly by social workers who attempt to give some of the guidance that a husband-father might provide. Nevertheless, children from broken families have a higher delinquency rate than children from intact families. The supportive institution is not fully successful.

the same situation as they. This is one reason for the development of "teenage culture." It is not the whole explanation. The affluence of industrial societies creates the material basis for an adolescent market. That is to say, adults in the United States, Sweden, Great Britain, the Soviet Union, Israel, and other industrial societies give adolescents substantial discretionary purchasing power, which enables adolescents to demand (and obtain) distinctive clothing, motion pictures, phonograph records, recreational facilities, and eating and drinking places.[17]

Teenage culture helps to ease the transition between the family into which the child was born and the family the young adult will create by marriage. Peers give the adolescent an emotional anchorage, but they constitute an unpredictable influence. Unless adolescents are organized under adult sponsorship, as boy's clubs, Scouts, and church youth groups are, they may mutually encourage one another to engage in a wide variety of unconventional or rebellious behavior. Delinquent gangs represent an antisocial development of adolescent autonomy; they are of course less pleasing to adults than scouting or 4–H clubs. Gang formation is possible in contemporary societies because the institutional structure, in adjusting to the requirements of urban industrial life, has (unintentionally) undermined effective adult supervision of adolescents. Of course, some families maintain better control over adolescents than others; and adolescent girls are generally better supervised than adolescent boys. The very technology of industrial societies emphasizes the independence of the adolescent from parental observation. In the age of the automobile, an adolescent's home may be the place where he sleeps and little else. The car is not the only means of avoiding adult surveillance, but the car symbolizes the looseness of the ties between adults and adolescents because it is such an effective instrument for escaping the eyes of adults.

The increased freedom of adolescents from adult control cannot be revoked. Not only technology but ideology is on the side of youthful independence. Contemporary societies are organized with the unit of participation the individual rather than the family. The child is not a representative of his family in the classroom or in the play group; as an adult he will participate in the economic and political systems as an individual also. This principle of individualism, implicitly embodied in social organization, is explicitly defined (outside of Iron Curtain countries) in the concept of "freedom." Adolescents are jealous of this prerogative. The freedom offered to adolescents is not always used wisely; the freedom to choose is the freedom to make mistakes. Delinquency is one mistake. On the other hand, many adolescents use their period of unsupervised freedom creatively: to establish commitments to educational and occupational goals, to learn how to relate to the opposite sex and, ultimately, to marry and have children.

[17] Mark Abrams, "The Teenage Consumer," London: London Press Exchange, 1960.

It would be throwing out the baby with the bath water to attempt to establish preindustrial control over adolescents to prevent some of them from using their freedom destructively.

AFFLUENCE AND EDUCATION:
COUNTERVAILING FORCES ON DELINQUENCY

The new affluence has an important impact on the material aspirations of young people: on the desire for cars, transitor radios, cameras, and clothes. But affluence has also an impact on education. As table 4 shows, substantial proportions of adolescents in industrial countries now remain

TABLE 4. SCHOOL ATTENDANCE IN CONTEMPORARY NATIONS IN VARIOUS RECENT YEARS

Country	Base year	Percent of age group enrolled in school			
		5–14 years	15–19 years	20–24 years	5–24 years
United States	1958	89.9	66.2	12.0	69.9
Iceland	1957	73.2	57.9	6.8	56.7
Soviet Union	1958	71.5	48.6	8.2	49.1
Canada	1958	87.3	45.9	9.3	63.0
Norway	1957	77.3	35.7	9.5	55.2
Netherlands	1958	85.5	32.8	4.7	57.4
Sweden	1960	82.6	32.3	11.0	54.0
Belgium	1957	95.4	31.5	5.5	60.2
France	1958	90.1	30.8	3.8	58.6
Luxembourg	1957	76.3	25.2	5.4	44.0
Switzerland	1956	78.6	22.9	3.4	48.7
Ireland	1957	92.6	19.6	4.2	59.3
Denmark	1957	76.4	18.5	5.6	48.9
Germany, F.R.	1958	80.2	17.6	4.6	42.3
United Kingdom	1957	98.8	17.6	3.9	59.6
Yugoslavia	1956	66.3	16.9	4.1	37.8
Greece	1956–57	74.5	16.9	3.3	40.8
Italy	1957	78.8	15.7	3.9	42.5
Spain	1958–59	74.9	13.3	3.3	39.6
Austria	1957	84.8	13.1	3.7	46.5
Portugal	1957–58	56.2	8.8	3.1	32.6
Turkey	1959–60	44.7	3.3	1.1	25.1

After Ingvar Svennilson (in association with Friedrich Edding and Lional Elvin), "Targets for Education in Europe in 1970," Paris: Organization for Economic Cooperation and Development, January 1962, pp. 107–108.

TABLE 5. THE INCREASING NUMBER OF
HIGH SCHOOL GRADUATES IN THE
UNITED STATES, 1870–1956

	High school graduates	
School year ending	Number	Percent of population 17 years old
1870	16,000	2.0
1880	23,634	2.5
1890	43,731	3.5
1900	94,883	6.4
1910	156,429	8.8
1920	311,266	16.8
1930	666,904	29.0
1940	1,221,475	50.8
1950	1,199,700	59.0
1956	1,414,800	62.3

SOURCE: U.S. Bureau of the Cencus, "Historical
Statistics of the United States, Colonial Times to 1957,"
Washington: Government Printing Office, 1960, p. 207.

in school instead of going to work, which was the usual pattern up to a
generation ago. Even for the United States, the first country to embark
on mass secondary education, the change is recent, as table 5 shows.

Why does affluence have this effect on educational aspirations? One
reason is the increased public support of education made possible by large
national incomes. Another is the greater resources of individual families,
making it possible for them to forego the financial contributions of working adolescents. Both of these factors make for an increased supply of educational opportunities. Education is a substantial investment, both for society
and for the individual family; rich countries can make this investment more
easily. The demand for education—as opposed to the supply—depends on
the motivation of young people themselves. This has been negatively
demonstrated in recent crash programs in slum schools (e.g., the Higher
Horizon program in New York) where substantial new resources did not
make dramatic improvements in student accomplishments. Research is
needed to clarify the conditions under which students are motivated to
seek as much education as they can master. It is known that parental encouragement is important. And what if parents are not encouraging? Can
teachers and other school personnel make up for this deficit? To some as
yet unknown extent, they can.

The potentialities of fostering educational aspirations can perhaps be gauged by an unplanned experiment in the consequences of high aspirations. American children of Japanese, Chinese, and Jewish backgrounds do extraordinarily well in school and go to colleges and universities in disproportionate numbers. They also have extremely low delinquency rates.[18] What is the connection? These same ethnic groups are often considered drivingly ambitious. Do not their educational aspirations reflect this ambition? Japanese, Chinese, and Jewish parents want to insure their children a share in business and professional occupations; education is the means to this end. Being members of minority groups, they are perhaps more keenly aware of the necessity of education for socioeconomic success, but they are motivated in essentially the same way as white Anglo-Saxon Protestants. The connection between higher education and high-income employment is well understood and provides a principal motivation for college attendance.[19]

What about Negroes? Unlike the Japanese, Chinese, and Jews, American Negroes show massive educational disadvantage. But recent studies prove that Negro educational retardation does not reflect lack of interest in education. Negro school children, even though they may be performing poorly in the classroom, are as likely as white children to say that they want to to to college.[20] They are less likely to perceive education as feasible for them; hence they are less likely to plan on going and to put in the consistent studying that can make college attendance a reality. In the light of their underutilization of the educational escalator, it is no coincidence that Negro adolescents have a high delinquency rate. Whereas education is a legitimate opportunity for Japanese adolescents, delinquency constitutes for Negro adolescents a tempting alternative to poverty—what one sociologist has called an "illegitimate opportunity."[21] It would be oversimplifying to maintain (1) that all delinquents are envious and (2) that they would not be delinquent had they realized that education could get them a high standard of living. Some delinquents are not envious. Some envious adolescents are not delinquent. Some adolescents are not willing or able to wait

[18] Jackson Toby, "Educational Maladjustment as a Predisposing Factor in Criminal Careers: A Comparative Study of Ethnic Groups," Ph. D. Dissertation, Department of Social Relations, Harvard University, 1950.

[19] Jackson Toby, "The American College Student: A Candidate for Socialization," "American Association of University Professors Bulletin," vol. 43 (June 1957), pp. 319–322.

[20] U.S. Office of Education, "Equality of Educational Opportunity," Washington: Government Printing Office, 1966.

[21] Richard A. Cloward, "Illegitimate Means, Anomie and Deviant Behavior," "American Sociological Review," vol. 24 (April 1959), pp. 164–176.

for the economic payoff of education; they share the sentiments of a famous economist who said, "In the long run we are all dead."

Nevertheless, there is fragmentary but consistent evidence from various industrialized countries that the longer a youngster stays in school the smaller are the chances that he will commit crimes. For example, table 6 presents some Swedish data showing that the criminal conviction rate for boys born in Stockholm in 1940 was 10 times as great if they completed primary school than if they completed *gymnasium*. The data in table 6 are unusually clean cut; few countries have as good criminal records as Sweden where it was possible to trace 94 percent of the cohort of Stockholm boys from birth until the age of 21.

Table 6 shows clearly that educational accomplishment prevents criminality, but it does not tell why. Therefore it does not immediately suggest policy recommendations. Would raising the age for compulsory school attendance reduce adolescent delinquency? Not unless mere custody of children in school is the reason for the correlation between educational attainment and nondelinquency. This is rather unlikely to be the case. The correlation almost certainly reflects the motivations of young people themselves. That is to say, the significance of graduation from *gymnasium* is that graduation from *gymnasium* fulfills the aspirations of Swedish young people. Most of them were interested in obtaining business and professional occupations. Some may have been interested in education for its own sake. But committing crimes would be incompatible with the fulfillment of either of these goals. Arrests label a boy to himself as well as to his classmates and teachers as belonging to a different world, a world the values of which are opposed to those of the school and incompatible with it.

TABLE 6. BOYS BORN IN STOCKHOLM IN 1940 WHO, BY THE AGE OF 21, ACQUIRED A RECORD IN THE CRIMINAL REGISTER, BY EDUCATIONAL ATTAINMENT

Highest educational attainment	Boys with criminal records		All boys
	Number	Percent	
Gymnasium	10	2.0	488
Realskola	34	9.9	445
Primary school	185	20.2	918
Unknown	7	14.3	49
Total	236	12.4	1900

SOURCE: Unpublished study of comparative adolescent delinquency being conducted by Jackson Toby, Carl-Gunnar Janson, and Shuichi Miyake.

TABLE 7. THE CRIME RATES OF BOYS BORN IN STOCKHOLM
IN 1940, BY EDUCATIONAL ATTAINMENT AND THE
SOCIOECONOMIC STATUS OF THEIR FAMILIES

Highest educational attainment	Boys with criminal records					
	In the upper class		In the middle class		In the working class	
	Number	Percent	Number	Percent	Number	Percent
Gymnasium	4	1.7	3	1.6	3	4.2
Realskola	4	5.3	15	8.6	15	8.0
Primary school	0	—	57	20.0	128	20.7
Unknown (49 cases)	—	—	—	—	—	—
Total	8	2.4	75	11.8	146	16.6

SOURCE: Unpublished study of comparative adolescent delinquency being conducted
by Jackson Toby, Carl-Gunnar Janson, and Shuichi Miyake.

Table 7 is a refinement of the data of table 6 taking into account the
fact that the 1900 boys came from different socioeconomic circumstances.
It is known that boys from working class families are less likely to seek
higher education than boys from business, professional, and white-collar
families. It is also known that boys from working class families are more
likely to be arrested for delinquent behavior than boys from more elite
occupational backgrounds. Table 7 examines the joint effect of socioeconomic background and educational attainment on criminality, thus providing an answer to the question: Which takes precedence? The answer is
fairly clear. Those Stockholm boys who graduated from gymnasium had a
low offense rate, and it did not make much difference whether their fathers
were high status or low status. Three of the 71 working class boys who
completed gymnasium had a criminal record as compared with 2 of the
235 boys from upper class families. At the minimal education level, on the
other hand, parental status had an appreciable effect on criminality. Whereas
21 percent of the 618 working class boys with minimal education had a
criminal record, none of the 25 upper class boys with minimal education
had one. What are the implications of this finding? That a youngster who
commits himself to education is unlikely to become delinquent regardless
of his family background.

But why does educational commitment have this effect? Criminologists
do not know for sure. One likely possibility is that youngsters who pursue
successful careers at school are consciously doing so in order to enjoy the
"good life" as adults. They desire to share in the material rewards of an afflu-

ent society, just as delinquents do, but they utilize a legitimate path to socio-economic advancement. This is probably not the whole explanation. Whatever the initial motivation for desiring success at school—to please concerned parents, to obtain a well-paying job as an adult, to learn—involvement in the school program has consequences for the student's conception of the world. A relatively uneducated delinquent does not know as much about the pleasures an affluent society can offer as a university student. The university student may obtain pleasure out of reading a book, attending a concert or ballet, visiting a museum, appreciating natural beauty, fighting for social justice—as well as out of driving a powerful car, getting "high," and wearing fashionable clothes. Delinquents in affluent societies characteristically desire material pleasures intensely—so much so that they are willing to risk freedom for them—but they are aware only of a small part of the opportunities for gratification that their societies offer. Furthermore, opportunities they are unaware of are those that are awakened or cultivated by the educational system. These considerations suggest that another reason that education prevents crime is that education broadens the range of desires of young people and stimulates some desires that bear little relation to money income. This is, of course, speculation. Research is needed to establish the precise mechanism whereby educational achievement prevents crime.

CONCLUSION

Poverty is nothing new. It is affluence that is new. But the relationship between subjective dissatisfaction and objective deprivation is more complicated than was at first thought. Poverty cannot cause crime but resentment of poverty can, and, curiously enough, resentment of poverty is more likely to develop among the relatively deprived of a rich society than among the objectively deprived in a poor society. This is partly because affluent industrial societies are also secular societies; the distribution of goods and services here and now is a more important preoccupation than concern with eternal salvation. It is also because the mass media—to which television has been a recent but important addition—stimulate the desire for a luxurious style of life among all segments of the population. These considerations explain why the sting of socioeconomic deprivation can be greater for the poor in rich societies than for the poor in poor societies. They also throw light on the high crime rates of affluent societies and on the increase of adolescent delinquency rates with the increase in general prosperity. Relative to adults, adolescents feel like a poverty stricken and powerless minority, and how they feel has consequences for how they behave.

The fact that adolescents mostly go to school and adults mostly go to work helps to explain the phenomenon of "teenage culture." It is not the whole explanation. The affluence of industrial societies creates the material basis for cultural differentiation. That is to say, industrial societies allocate to adolescents substantial discretionary purchasing power, and this enables adolescents to demand (and obtain) distinctive clothing, motion pictures, phonograph records, recreational facilities, and eating and drinking establishments. From the viewpoint of understanding delinquency, however, the extension of formal education is probably more important than the development of the adolescent market. The reason for this is that mass formal education has created serious problems of life goals for adolescents with educational disabilities. For academically successful adolescents, school is a bridge between the world of childhood and the world of adulthood. For children unwilling or unable to learn, school is a place where the battle against society is likely to begin.

Orientation to consumption seems to be an increasing characteristic of industrial societies. It permeates most strata, not merely adolescents, and it contributes to other phenomena besides delinquency, e.g., ostentatious expenditures for food, clothing, travel, housing. However, the impact of commercialism is greatest on working class adolescents because the impact on them of the educational system is less positive than for middle class youth. If they leave school as soon as they legally may, they have less opportunity to experience art, literature, serious music, science, religion, and meaningful work, than they have of being attracted to the gadgets and entertainments available in the marketplace. This isolation of school-leaving youths from what are generally conceded to be the accomplishments of industrial civilization may partially account for violent crimes. As Nelson Algren put it in his paraphrase of a literary idea of Richard Wright, "* * * when a crime is committed by a man who has been excluded from civilization, civilization is an accomplice of the crime."[22] Selective exposure to industrial society is not merely an internal problem. Anthropologists have called attention to the selective "diffusion" of culture traits to underdeveloped societies. Trinkets, tools, hard liquor, and Coca Cola are easier to export than arts and sciences or even religion.

H. G. Wells once remarked, "Human history becomes more and more a race between education and catastrophe." Is delinquency a catastrophe? Some might argue that delinquency is a small price to pay for life in a rich society where most people, including adolescents, have the freedom to choose the direction of their destiny. It is true that delinquency is rare in subsistence economies (where there is less to envy) and in totalitarian states (where social controls coerce would-be rebels). On the other hand, crime does cost a society something, not only the losses to victims but also

[22] Nelson Algren, "Remembering Richard Wright," "The Nation," vol. 192 (Jan. 28, 1961), p. 85.

the wasted years of delinquent youths. Most ex-delinquents regard the years spent in raising hell on the streets as well as those in prison as irretrievable mistakes. Mass education can prevent some of this waste. The appeal of education, like adolescent delinquency itself, is stimulated by affluence. But affluence needs reinforcement if youngsters from homes where parents do not value education are to believe that education is for them too. The primary benefit of education is of course intrinsic: the greater realization of the potentialities of young people. But a secondary consequence is to deflect adolescents from the destructive possibilities open to them in a free society. If the experience of American society with its Japanese, Chinese, and Jewish minorities is any precedent, the indirect consequence of educational upgrading will be the reduction of adolescent delinquency. True, these ethnic groups possessed special cultural values favorable to education, which were transmitted to children without planning. However, it seems likely that planned programs of educational upgrading, adequately financed and enthusiastically publicized, could duplicate the Japanese, Chinese, and Jewish unintended experiments in delinquency prevention. Is it worth a try?

3 Illegitimate Means, Anomie, and Deviant Behavior

RICHARD A. CLOWARD

This paper[1] represents an attempt to consolidate two major sociological traditions of thought about the problem of deviant behavior. The first, exemplified by the work of Emile Durkheim and Robert K. Merton, may be called the anomie tradition.[2] The second, illustrated principally by the studies of Clifford R. Shaw, Henry D. McKay, and Edwin H. Sutherland, may be called the "cultural transmission" and "differential association" tradition.[3] Despite some reciprocal borrowing of ideas, these intellectual tradi-

Reprinted from *American Sociological Review, 24* (April, 1959), 164–176, by permission of The American Sociological Association and the author.

[1] This paper is based on research conducted in a penal setting. For a more detailed statement see Richard A. Cloward, *Social Control and Anomie: A Study of a Prison Community* (to be published by The Free Press).

[2] See especially Emile Durkheim, *Suicide,* translated by J. A. Spaulding and George Simpson, Glencoe, Ill.: Free Press, 1951; and Robert K. Merton, *Social Theory and Social Structure,* Glencoe, Ill.: Free Press, 1957, Chapters 4 and 5.

[3] See especially the following: Clifford R. Shaw, *The Jack-Roller,* Chicago: The University of Chicago Press, 1930; Clifford R. Shaw, *The Natural History of a Delinquent Career,* Chicago: The University of Chicago Press, 1931; Clifford R. Shaw *et al., Delinquency Areas,* Chicago: The University of Chicago Press, 1940; Clifford R. Shaw and Henry D. McKay, *Juvenile Delinquency and Urban Areas,* Chicago: The University of Chicago Press, 1942; Edwin H. Sutherland, editor, *The Professional Thief,* Chicago: The University of Chicago Press, 1937; Edwin H. Sutherland, *Principles of Criminology,* 4th edition, Philadelphia: Lippincott, 1947; Edwin H. Sutherland, *White Collar Crime,* New York: Dryden, 1949.

tions developed more or less independently. By seeking to consolidate them, a more adequate theory of deviant behavior may be constructed.

DIFFERENTIALS IN AVAILABILITY OF LEGITIMATE MEANS: THE THEORY OF ANOMIE

The theory of anomie has undergone two major phases of development. Durkheim first used the concept to explain deviant behavior. He focussed on the way in which various social conditions lead to "overweening ambition," and how, in turn, unlimited aspirations ultimately produce a breakdown in regulatory norms. Robert K. Merton has systematized and extended the theory, directing attention to patterns of disjunction between culturally prescribed goals and socially organized access to them by *legitimate* means. In this paper, a third phase is outlined. An additional variable is incorporated in the developing scheme of anomie, namely, the concept of *differentials in access to success-goals by illegitimate means.*[4]

Phase I: Unlimited Aspirations and the Breakdown of Regulatory Norms. In Durkheim's work, a basic distinction is made between "physical needs" and "moral needs." The importance of this distinction was heightened for Durkheim because he viewed physical needs as being regulated automatically by features of man's organic structure. Nothing in the organic structure, however, is capable of regulating social desires; as Durkheim put it, man's "capacity for feeling is in itself an insatiable and bottomless abyss."[5] If man is to function without "friction," "the passions must first be limited. . . . But since the individual has no way of limiting them, this must be done by some force exterior to him." Durkheim viewed the collective order as the external regulating force which defined and ordered the goals to which men should orient their behavior. If the collective order is disrupted or disturbed, however, men's aspirations may then rise, exceeding all possibilities of fulfillment. Under these conditions, "de-regulation or anomy" ensues: "At the very moment when traditional rules have lost their authority, the richer prize offered these appetites stimulates them and makes them more exigent and impatient of control. The state of de-regulation or anomy is thus further heightened by passions being less disciplined precisely when

---

[4] "Illegitimate means" are those proscribed by the mores. The concept therefore includes "illegal means" as a special case but is not coterminous with illegal behavior, which refers only to the violation of legal norms. In several parts of this paper, I refer to particular forms of deviant behavior which entail violation of the law and there use the more restricted term, "illegal means." But the more general concept of illegitimate means is needed to cover the wider gamut of deviant behavior and to relate the theories under review here to the evolving theory of "legitimacy" in sociology.

[5] All of the excerpts in this section are from Durkheim, *op. cit.,* pp. 247–257.

they need more disciplining." Finally, pressure toward deviant behavior were said to develop when man's aspirations no longer matched the possibilities of fulfillment.

Durkheim therefore turned to the question of *when* the regulatory functions of the collective order break down. Several such states were identified, including sudden depression, sudden prosperity, and rapid technological change. His object was to show how, under these conditions, men are led to aspire to goals extremely difficult if not impossible to attain. As Durkheim saw it, sudden depression results in deviant behavior because "something like a declassification occurs which suddenly casts certain individuals into a lower state than their previous one. Then they must reduce their requirements, restrain their needs, learn greater self-control. . . . But society cannot adjust them instantaneously to this new life and teach them to practice the increased self-repression to which they are unaccustomed. So they are not adjusted to the condition forced on them, and its very prospect is intolerable; hence the suffering which detaches them from a reduced existence even before they have made trial of it." Prosperity, according to Durkheim, could have much the same effect as depression, particularly if upward changes in economic conditions are abrupt. The very abruptness of these changes presumably heightens aspirations beyond possibility of fulfillment, and this too puts a strain on the regulatory apparatus of the society.

According to Durkheim, "the sphere of trade and industry . . . is actually in a chronic state [of anomie]." Rapid technological developments and the existence of vast, unexploited markets excite the imagination with the seemingly limitless possibilities for the accumulation of wealth. As Durkheim said of the producer of goods, "now that he may assume to have almost the entire world as his customer, how could passions accept their former confinement in the face of such limitless prospects"? Continuing, Durkheim states that "such is the source of excitement predominating in this part of society. . . . Here the state of crisis and anomie [are] constant and, so to speak, normal. From top to bottom of the ladder, greed is aroused without knowing where to find ultimate foothold. Nothing can calm it, since its goal is far beyond all it can attain."

In developing the theory, Durkheim characterized goals in the industrial society, and specified the way in which unlimited aspirations are induced. He spoke of "dispositions . . . so inbred that society has grown to accept them and is accustomed to think them normal," and he portrayed these "inbred dispositions": "It is everlastingly repeated that it is man's nature to be eternally dissatisfied, constantly to advance, without relief or rest, toward an indefinite goal. The longing for infinity is daily represented as a mark of moral distinction. . . ." And it was precisely these pressures to strive for "infinite" or "receding" goals, in Durkheim's view, that generate a breakdown in regulatory norms, for "when there is no other aim but to outstrip constantly the point arrived at, how painful to be thrown back!"

Phase II: Disjunction Between Cultural Goals and Socially Structured Opportunity. Durkheim's description of the emergence of "overweening ambition" and the subsequent breakdown of regulatory norms constitutes one of the links between his work and the later development of the theory by Robert K. Merton. In his classic essay, "Social Structure and Anomie," Merton suggests that goals and norms may vary independently of each other, and that this sometimes leads to malintegrated states. In his view, two polar types of disjunction may occur: "There may develop a very heavy, at times a virtually exclusive, stress upon the value of particular goals, involving comparatively little concern with the institutionally prescribed means of striving toward these goals. . . . This constitutes one type of malintegrated culture."[6] On the other hand, "A second polar type is found where activities originally conceived as instrumental are transmuted into self-contained practices, lacking further objectives. . . . Sheer conformity becomes a central value." Merton notes that "between these extreme types are societies which maintain a rough balance between emphases upon cultural goals and institutionalized practices, and these constitute the integrated and relatively stable, though changing societies."

Having identified patterns of disjunction between goals and norms, Merton is enabled to define anomie more precisely: "Anomie [may be] conceived as a breakdown in the cultural structure, occurring particularly when there is an acute disjunction between cultural norms and goals and the socially structured capacities of members of the group to act in accord with them."

Of the two kinds of malintegrated societies, Merton is primarily interested in the one in which "there is an exceptionally strong emphasis upon specific goals without a corresponding emphasis upon institutional procedures." He states that attenuation between goals and norms, leading to anomie or "normlessness," comes about because men in such societies internalize an emphasis on common success-goals under conditions of varying access to them. The essence of this hypothesis is captured in the following excerpt: "It is only when a system of cultural values extols, virtually above all else, certain *common* success-goals for the population at large while the social structure rigorously restricts or completely closes access to approved modes of reaching these goals *for a considerable part of the same population*, that deviant behavior ensues on a large scale." The focus, in short, is on the way in which the social structure puts a strain upon the cultural structure. Here one may point to diverse structural differentials in access to

---

[6] For this excerpt and those which follow immediately, see Merton, *op. cit.*, pp. 131–194.

culturally approved goals by legitimate means, for example, differentials of age, sex, ethnic status, and social class. Pressures for anomie or normlessness vary from one social position to another, depending on the nature of these differentials.

In summary, Merton extends the theory of anomie in two principal ways. He explicitly identifies types of anomic or malintegrated societies by focussing upon the relationship between cultural goals and norms. And, by directing attention to patterned differentials in the access to success-goals by legitimate means, he shows how the social structure exerts a strain upon the cultural structure, leading in turn to anomie or normlessness.

Phase III: The Concept of Illegitimate Means. Once processes generating differentials in pressures are identified, there is then the question of how these pressures are resolved, or how men respond to them. In this connection, Merton enumerates five basic categories of behavior or role adaptations which are likely to emerge: conformity, innovation, ritualism, retreatism, and rebellion. These adaptations differ depending on the individual's acceptance or rejection of cultural goals, and depending on his adherence to or violation of institutional norms. Furthermore, Merton sees the distribution of these adaptations principally as the consequence of two variables: the relative extent of pressure, and values, particularly "internalized prohibitions," governing the use of various illegitimate means.

It is a familiar sociological idea that values serve to order the choices of deviant (as well as conforming) adaptations which develop under conditions of stress. Comparative studies of ethnic groups, for example, have shown that some tend to engage in distinctive forms of deviance; thus Jews exhibit low rates of alcoholism and alcoholic psychoses.[7] Various investigators have suggested that the emphasis on rationality, fear of expressing aggression, and other alleged components of the "Jewish" value system constrain modes of deviance which involve "loss of control" over behavior.[8] In contrast, the Irish show a much higher rate of alcoholic deviance because, it has been argued, their cultural emphasis on masculinity encourages the excessive use of alcohol under conditions of strain.[9]

[7] See, e.g., Seldon D. Bacon, "Social Settings Conducive to Alcoholism—A Sociological Approach to a Medical Problem," *Journal of the American Medical Association*, 16 (May, 1957), pp. 177–181; Robert F. Bales, "Cultural Differences in Rates of Alcoholism," *Quarterly Journal of Studies on Alcohol*, 16 (March, 1946), pp. 480–499; Jerome H. Skolnick, "A Study of the Relation of Ethnic Background to Arrests for Inebriety," *Quarterly Journal of Studies on Alcohol*, 15 (December, 1954), pp. 451–474.

[8] See Isidor T. Thorner, "Ascetic Protestantism and Alcoholism," *Psychiatry*, 16 (May, 1953), pp. 167–176; and Nathan Glazer, "Why Jews Stay Sober," *Commentary*, 13 (February, 1952), pp. 181–186.

[9] See Bales, *op. cit.*

Merton suggests that differing rates of ritualistic and innovating behavior in the middle and lower classes result from differential emphases in socialization. The "rule-oriented" accent in middle-class socialization presumably disposes persons to handle stress by engaging in ritualistic rather than innovating behavior. The lower-class person, contrastingly, having internalized less stringent norms, can violate conventions with less guilt and anxiety.[10] Values, in other words, exercise a canalizing influence, limiting the choice of deviant adaptations for persons variously distributed throughout the social system.

Apart from both socially patterned pressures, which give rise to deviance, and from values, which determine choices of adaptations, a further variable should be taken into account: namely, *differentials in availability of illegitimate means*. For example, the notion that innovating behavior may result from unfulfilled aspirations and imperfect socialization with respect to conventional norms implies that illegitimate means are freely available— as if the individual, having decided that "you can't make it legitimately," then simply turns to illegitimate means which are readily at hand whatever his position in the social structure. However, these means may not be available. As noted above, the anomie theory assumes that conventional means are differentially distributed, that some individuals, because of their social position, enjoy certain advantages which are denied to others. Note, for example, variations in the degree to which members of various classes are fully exposed to and thus acquire the values, education, and skills which facilitate upward mobility. It should not be startling, therefore, to find similar variations in the availability of illegitimate means.

Several sociologists have alluded to such variations without explicitly incorporating this variable in a theory of deviant behavior. Sutherland, for example, writes that "an inclination to steal is not a sufficient explanation of the genesis of the professional thief."[11] Moreover, "the person must be appreciated by the professional thieves. He must be appraised as having an adequate equipment of wits, front, talking-ability, honesty, reliability nerve and determination." In short, "a person can be a professional thief only if he is recognized and received as such by other professional thieves." But recognition is not freely accorded: "Selection and tutelage are the two necessary elements in the process of acquiring recognition as a professional thief. . . . A person cannot acquire recognition as a professional thief until he has had tutelage in professional theft, *and tutelage is given only to a few persons selected from the total population*." Furthermore, the aspirant is judged by high standards of performance, for only "a very small percentage

---

[10] Merton, *op. cit.*, p. 151.

[11] For this excerpt and those which follow immediately, see Sutherland, *The Professional Thief*, pp. 211–213.

of those who start on this process ever reach the stage of professional theft." The burden of these remarks—dealing with the processes of selection, induction, and assumption of full status in the criminal group—is that motivations or pressures toward deviance do not fully account for deviant behavior. The "self-made" thief—lacking knowledge of the ways of securing immunity from prosecution and similar techniques of defense—"would quickly land in prison." Sutherland is in effect pointing to differentials in access to the role of professional thief. Although the criteria of selection are not altogether clear from his analysis, definite evaluative standards do appear to exist; depending on their content, certain categories of individuals would be placed at a disadvantage and others would be favored.

The availability of illegitimate means, then, is controlled by various criteria in the same manner that has long been ascribed to conventional means. Both systems of opportunity are (1) limited, rather than infinitely available, and (2) differentially available depending on the location of persons in the social structure.

When we employ the term "means," whether legitimate or illegitimate, at least two things are implied: first, that there are appropriate learning environments for the acquisition of the values and skills associated with the performance of a particular role; and second, that the individual has opportunities to discharge the role once he has been prepared. The term subsumes, therefore, both *learning structures* and *opportunity structures*.

A case in point is recruitment and preparation for careers in the rackets. There are fertile criminal learning environments for the young in neighborhoods where the rackets flourish as stable, indigenous institutions. Because these environments afford integration of offenders of different ages, the young are exposed to "differential associations" which facilitate the acquisition of criminal values and skills. Yet preparation for the role may not insure that the individual will ever discharge it. For one thing, more youngsters may be recruited into these patterns of differential association than can possibly be absorbed, following their "training," by the adult criminal structure. There may be a surplus of contenders for these elite positions, leading in turn to the necessity for criteria and mechanisms of selection. Hence a certain proportion of those who aspire may not be permitted to engage in the behavior for which they have been prepared.

This illustration is similar in every respect, save for the route followed, to the case of those who seek careers in the sphere of legitimate business. Here, again, is the initial problem of securing access to appropriate learning environments, such as colleges and post-graduate school of business. Having acquired the values and skills needed for a business career, graduates then face the problem of whether or not they can successfully discharge the roles for which they have been prepared. Formal training itself is not sufficient for occupational success, for many forces intervene to determine who shall succeed and fail in the competitive world of business and industry—as throughout the entire conventional occupational structure.

This distinction between learning structures and opportunity structures was suggested some years ago by Sutherland. In 1944, he circulated an unpublished paper which briefly discusses the proposition that "criminal behavior is partially a function of opportunities to commit specific classes of crimes, such as embezzlement, bank burglary, or illicit heterosexual intercourse."[12] He did not, however, take up the problem of differentials in opportunity as a concept to be systematically incorporated in a theory of deviant behavior. Instead, he held that "opportunity" is a necessary but not sufficient explanation of the commission of criminal acts, "since some persons who have opportunities to embezzle, become intoxicated, engage in illicit heterosexual intercourse or to commit other crimes do not do so." He also noted that the differential association theory did not constitute a full explanation of criminal activity, for, notwithstanding differential association, "it is axiomatic that persons who commit a specific crime must have the opportunity to commit that crime." He therefore concluded that "while opportunity may be partially a function of association with criminal patterns and of the specialized techniques thus acquired, *it is not determined entirely in that manner*, and consequently differential association is not the sufficient cause of criminal behavior." (emphasis not in original)

In Sutherland's statements, two meanings are attributed to the term "opportunity." As suggested above, it may be useful to separate these for analytical purposes. In the first sense, Sutherland appears to be saying that opportunity consists in part of learning structures. The principal components of his theory of differential association are that "criminal behavior is learned," and, furthermore, that "criminal behavior is learned in interaction with other persons in a process of communication." But he also uses the term to describe situations conducive to carrying out criminal roles. Thus, for Sutherland, the commission of a criminal act would seem to depend upon the existence of two conditions: differential associations favoring the acquisition of criminal values and skills, and conditions encouraging participation in criminal activity.

This distinction heightens the importance of identifying and questioning the common assumption that illegitimate means are freely available. We can now ask (1) whether there are socially structured differentials in access to illegitimate learning environments, and (2) whether there are differentials limiting the fulfillment of illegitimate roles. If differentials exist and can be identified, we may then inquire about their consequences for the behavior of persons in different parts of the social structure. Before pursuing this

[12] For this excerpt and those which follow immediately, see Albert Cohen, Alfred Lindesmith and Karl Schuessler, editors, *The Sutherland Papers,* Bloomington: Indiana University Press, 1956, pp. 31–35.

question, however, we turn to a fuller discussion of the theoretical tradition established by Shaw, McKay, and Sutherland.

DIFFERENTIALS IN AVAILABILITY OF ILLEGITIMATE MEANS: THE SUBCULTURE TRADITION

The concept of differentials in availability of illegitimate means is implicit in one of the major streams of American criminological theory. In this tradition, attention is focussed on the processes by which persons are recruited into criminal learning environments and ultimately inducted into criminal roles. The problems here are to account for the acquisition of criminal roles and to describe the social organization of criminal activities. When the theoretical propositions contained in this tradition are reanalyzed, it becomes clear that one underlying conception is that of variations in access to success-goals by illegitimate means. Furthermore, this implicit concept may be shown to be one of the bases upon which the tradition was constructed.

In their studies of the ecology of deviant behavior in the urban environment, Shaw and McKay found that delinquency and crime tended to be confined to delimited areas and, furthermore, that such behavior persisted despite demographic changes in these areas. Hence they came to speak of "criminal tradition," of the "cultural transmission" of criminal values.[13] As a result of their observations of slum life, they concluded that *particular importance must be assigned to the integration of different age-levels of offenders.* Thus:

Stealing in the neighborhood was a common practice among the children and approved by the parents. Whenever the boys got together they talked about robbing and made more plans for stealing. I hardly knew any boys who did not go robbing. The little fellows went in for petty stealing, breaking into freight cars, and stealing junk. The older guys did big jobs like stick-up, burglary, and stealing autos. The little fellows admired the "big shots" and longed for the day when they could get into the big racket. Fellows who had "done time" were the big shots and looked up to and gave the little fellow tips on how to get by and pull off big jobs.[14]

In other words, access to criminal roles depends upon stable associations with others from whom the necessary values and skills may be learned. Shaw and McKay were describing deviant learning structures—that is, alternative routes by which people seek access to the goals which society holds to be worthwhile. They might also have pointed out that, in areas where such learning structures are unavailable, it is probably difficult

[13] See especially *Delinquency Areas,* Chapter 16.
[14] Shaw, *The Jack-Roller,* p. 54.

for many individuals to secure access to stable criminal careers, even though motivated to do so.[15]

The concept of illegitimate means and the socially structured conditions of access to them were not explicitly recognized in the work of Shaw and McKay because, probably, they were disposed to view slum areas as "disorganized." Although they consistently referred to illegitimate activities as being organized, they nevertheless often depicted high-rate delinquency areas as disorganized because the values transmitted were criminal rather than conventional. Hence their work includes statements which we now perceive to be internally inconsistent, such as the following:

> This community situation [in which Sidney was reared] was not only disorganized and thus ineffective as a unit of control, but it was characterized by a high rate of juvenile delinquency and adult crime, not to mention the widespread political corruption which had long existed in the area. Various forms of stealing and many organized delinquent and criminal gangs were prevalent in the area. These groups exercised a powerful influence and tended to create a community spirit which not only tolerated but actually fostered delinquent and criminal practices.[16]

Sutherland was among the first to perceive that the concept of social disorganization tended to obscure the stable patterns of interaction among carriers of criminal values. Like Shaw and McKay, he had been influenced by the observation that lower-class areas were organized in terms of both conventional and criminal values, but he was also impressed that these alternative value systems were supported by patterned systems of social relations. He expressly recognized that crime, far from being a random, unorganized activity, was typically an intricate and stable system of human arrangements. He therefore rejected the concept of "social disorganization" and substituted the concept of "differential group organization."

> The third concept, social disorganization, was borrowed from Shaw and McKay. I had used it but had not been satisfied with it because the organization of the delinquent group, which is often very complex, is social disorganization only from an ethical or some other particularistic point of view. At the suggestion of Albert K. Cohen, this concept has been changed to differential group

---

[15] We are referring here, and throughout the paper, to stable criminal roles to which persons may orient themselves on a career basis, as in the case of racketeers, professional thieves, and the like. The point is that access to stable roles depends in the first instance upon the availability of learning structures. As Frank Tannenbaum says, "it must be insisted on that unless there were older criminals in the neighborhood who provided a moral judgement in favor of the delinquent and to whom the delinquents could look for commendation, the careers of the younger ones could not develop at all." *Crime and the Community*, New York: Ginn, 1938, p. 60.

[16] Shaw, *The Natural History of a Delinquent Career*, p. 229.

organization, with organization for criminal activities on one side and organization against criminal activities on the other.[17]

Having freed observation of the urban slum from conventional evaluations, Sutherland was able to focus more clearly on the way in which its social structure constitutes a "learning environment" for the acquisition of deviant values and skills. In the development of the theory of "differential association" and "differential group organization," he came close to stating explicitly the concept of differentials in access to illegitimate means. But Sutherland was essentially interested in learning processes, and thus he did not ask how such access varies in different parts of the social structure, nor did he inquire about the consequences for behavior of variations in the accessibility of these means.[18]

William F. Whyte, in his classic study of an urban slum, advanced the empirical description of the structure and organization of illegitimate means a step beyond that of Sutherland. Like Sutherland, Whyte rejected the earlier view of the slum as disorganized:

It is customary for the sociologist to study the slum district in terms of "social disorganization" and to neglect to see that an area such as Cornerville has a complex and well-established organization of its own. . . . I found that in every group there was a hierarchical structure of social relations binding the individuals to one another and that the groups were also related hierarchically to one another. Where the group was formally organized into a

---

[17] Cohen, Lindesmith and Schuessler, *op. cit.,* p. 21.

[18] It is interesting to note that the concept of differentials in access to *legitimate* means did not attain explicit recognition in Sutherland's work, nor in the work of many others in the "subculture" tradition. This attests to the independent development of the two traditions being discussed. Thus the ninth proposition in the differential association theory is stated as follows:

> (9) *Though criminal behavior is an expression of general needs and values, it is not explained by those general needs and values since noncriminal behavior is an expression of the same needs and values.* Thieves generally steal in order to secure money, but likewise honest laborers work in order to secure money. The attempts by many scholars to explain criminal behavior by general drives and values, such as the happiness principle, striving for social status, the money motive, or frustration, have been and must continue to be futile since they explain lawful behavior as completely as they explain criminal behavior.

Of course, it is perfectly true that "striving for status," the "money motive" and similar modes of socially approved goal-oriented behavior do not as such account for both deviant and conformist behavior. But if goal-oriented behavior occurs under conditions of socially structured obstacles to fulfillment by legitimate means, the resulting pressures might then lead to deviance. In other words, Sutherland appears to assume that the distribution of access to success-goals by legitimate means is uniform rather than variable, irrespective of location in the social structure. See his *Principles of Criminology,* 4th edition, pp. 7–8.

political club, this was immediately apparent, but for informal groups it was no less true.[19]

Whyte's contribution to our understanding of the organization of illegitimate means in the slum consists primarily in showing that individuals who participate in stable illicit enterprise do not constitute a separate or isolated segment of the community. Rather, these persons are closely integrated with the occupants of conventional roles. In describing the relationship between racketeers and politicians, for example, he notes that "the rackets and political organizations extend from the bottom to the top of Cornerville society, mesh with one another, and integrate a large part of the life of the district. They provide a general framework for the understanding of the actions of both 'little guys' and 'big shots.' "[20] Whyte's view of the slum differs somewhat from that conveyed by the term "differential group organization." He does not emphasize the idea that the slum is composed of two different systems, conventional and deviant, but rather the way in which the occupants of these various roles are integrated in a single, stable structure which organizes and patterns the life of the community.

The description of the organization of illegitimate means in slums is further developed by Solomon Kobrin in his article, "The Conflict of Values in Delinquency Areas."[21] Kobrin suggests that urban slum areas vary in the degree to which the carriers of deviant and conventional values are integrated with one another. Hence he points the way to the development of a "typology of delinquency areas based on variations in the relationship between these two systems," depicting the "polar types" on such a continuum. The first type resembles the integrated areas described in preceding paragraphs. Here, claims Kobrin, there is not merely structural integration between carriers of the two value systems, but reciprocal participation by each in the value system of the other. Thus:

> Leaders of [illegal] enterprises frequently maintain membership in such conventional institutions of their local communities as churches, fraternal and mutual benefit societies and political parties. . . . Within this framework the influence of each of the two value systems is reciprocal, the leaders of illegal enterprise participating in the primary orientation of the conventional elements in the population, and the latter, through their participation in a local power structure sustained in large part by illicit activity, participating perforce in the alternate, criminal value system.

[19] William F. Whyte, *Street Corner Society*, (original edition, 1943). Chicago: The University of Chicago Press, 1955, p. viii.

[20] *Ibid.*, p. xviii.

[21] *American Sociological Review*, 16 (October, 1951), pp. 657–658, which includes the excerpts which follow immediately.

Kobrin also notes that in some urban slums there is a tendency for the relationships between carriers of deviant and conventional values to break down. Such areas constitute the second polar type. Because of disorganizing forces such as "drastic change in the class, ethnic, or racial characteristics of its population," Kobrin suggests that "the bearers of the conventional culture and its value system are without the customary institutional machinery and therefore in effect partially demobilized with reference to the diffusion of their value system." At the same time, the criminal "value system remains implicit" since this type of area is "characterized principally by the absence of systematic and organized adult activity in violation of the law, despite the fact that many adults in these areas commit violations." Since both value systems remain implicit, the possibilities for effective integration are precluded.

The importance of these observations may be seen if we ask how accessibility of illegal means varies with the relative integration of conventional and criminal values from one type of area to another. In this connection, Kobrin points out that the "integrated" area apparently constitutes a "training ground" for the acquisition of criminal values and skills.

The stable position of illicit enterprise in the adult society of the community is reflected in the character of delinquent conduct on the part of children. While delinquency in all high rate areas is intrinsically disorderly in that it is unrelated to official programs for the education of the young, in the [integrated community] boys may more or less realistically recognize the potentialities for personal progress in local society through access to delinquency. In a general way, therefore, delinquent activity in these areas constitutes a training ground for the acquisition of skill in the use of violence, concealment of offense, evasion of detection and arrest, and the purchase of immunity from punishment. Those who come to excel in these respects are frequently noted and valued by adult leaders in the rackets who are confronted, as are the leaders of all income-producing enterprises, with problems of the recruitment of competent personnel.

With respect to the contrasting or "unintegrated area," Kobrin makes no mention of the extent to which learning structures and opportunities for criminal careers are available. Yet his portrayal of such areas as lacking in the articulation of either conventional or criminal values suggests that the appropriate learning structures—principally the integration of offenders of different age levels—are not available. Furthermore, his depiction of adult violative activity as "unorganized" suggests that the illegal opportunity structure is severely limited. Even if youngsters were able to secure adequate preparation for criminal roles, the problem would appear to be that the social structure of such neighborhoods provides few opportunities for stable, criminal careers. For Kobrin's analysis—as well as those of Whyte and others before him—leads to the conclusion that illegal opportunity structures tend to emerge in lower-class areas only when stable patterns of accommodation and integration arise between the carriers of conventional and deviant values. Where these values remain unorganized and implicit, or where their carriers are in open conflict, opportunities for stable criminal role performance are more or less limited.[22]

Other factors may be cited which affect access to criminal roles. For example, there is a good deal of anecdotal evidence which reveals that access to the upper echelons of organized racketeering is controlled, at least in part, by ethnicity. Some ethnic groups are found disproportionately in the upper ranks and others disproportionately in the lower. From an historical perspective, as Bell has shown, this realm has been successively dominated by Irish, East-European Jews, and more recently, by Italians.[23] Various other ethnic groups have been virtually excluded or at least relegated to lower-echelon positions. Despite the fact that many rackets (especially "policy") have flourished in predominantly Negro neighborhoods, there have been but one or two Negroes who have been known to rise to the top in syndicated crime. As in the conventional world, Negroes are relegated to the more menial tasks. Moreover, access to elite positions in the rackets may be governed in part by kinship criteria, for various accounts of the blood relations among top racketeers indicate that nepotism is the general rule.[24] It has also been noted that kinship criteria sometimes govern access to stable criminal roles, as in the case of the pickpocket.[25] And there are, of course, deep-rooted sex differentials in access to illegal means. Although women are often employed in criminal vocations—for example, thievery, confidence games, and extortion—and must be employed in

[22] The excellent work by Albert K. Cohen has been omitted from this discussion because it is dealt with in a second article, "Types of Delinquent Subcultures," prepared jointly with Lloyd E. Ohlin (mimeographed, December, 1958, New York School of Social Work, Columbia University). It may be noted that although Cohen does not explicitly affirm continuity with either the Durkheim-Merton or the Shaw-McKay-Sutherland traditions, we believe that he clearly belongs in the former. He does not deal with what appears to be the essence of the Shaw-McKay-Sutherland tradition, namely, the crucial social functions performed by the integration of offenders of differing age-levels and the integration of adult carriers of criminal and conventional values. Rather he is concerned primarily with the way in which discrepancies between status aspirations and possibilities for achievement generate pressures for delinquent behavior. The latter notion is a central feature in the anomie tradition.

[23] Daniel Bell, "Crime as an American Way of Life," The Antioch Review (Summer, 1953), pp. 131–154.

[24] For a discussion of kinship relationships among top racketeers, see Stanley Frank, "The Rap Gangsters Fear Most," The Saturday Evening Post (August 9, 1958), pp. 26ff. This article is based on a review of the files of the United States Immigration and Naturalization Service.

[25] See David W. Maurer, Whiz Mob: A Correlation of the Technical Argot of Pickpockets with Their Behavior Pattern, Publication of the American Dialect Society, No. 24, 1955.

others—such as prostitution—nevertheless females are excluded from many criminal activities.[26]

Of the various criteria governing access to illegitimate means, class differentials may be among the most important. The differentials noted in the preceding paragraph—age, sex, ethnicity, kinship, and the like—all pertain to criminal activity historically associated with the lower class. Most middle- or upper-class persons—even when interested in following "lower-class" criminal careers—would no doubt have difficulty in fulfilling this ambition because of inappropriate preparation. The prerequisite attitudes and skills are more easily acquired if the individual is a member of the lower class; most middle- and upper-class persons could not easily unlearn their own class culture in order to learn a new one. By the same token, access to many "white collar" criminal roles is closed to lower-class persons. Some occupations afford abundant opportunities to engage in illegitimate activity; others offer virtually none. The businessman, for example, not only has at his disposal the means to do so, but, as some studies have shown, he is under persistent pressure to employ illegitimate means, if only to maintain a competitive advantage in the market place. But for those in many other occupations, white collar modes of criminal activity are simply not an alternative.[27]

SOME IMPLICATIONS OF A CONSOLIDATED APPROACH TO DEVIANT BEHAVIOR

It is now possible to consolidate the two sociological traditions described above. Our analysis makes it clear that these traditions are oriented to different aspects of the same problem: differentials in access to opportunity. One tradition focusses on legitimate opportunity, the other on illegitimate. By incorporating the concept of differentials in access to *illegitimate* means, the theory of anomie may be extended to include seemingly unrelated studies and theories of deviant behavior which form a part of the literature of American criminology. In this final section, we try to show

[26] For a discussion of racial, nationality, and sex differentials governing access to a stable criminal role, see *ibid.*, Chapter 6.

[27] Training in conventional, specialized occupational skills is often a prerequisite for the commission of white collar crimes, since the individual must have these skills in hand before he can secure a position entailing "trust." As Cressey says, "it may be observed that persons trained to carry on the routine duties of a position of trust have at the same time been trained in whatever skills are necessary for the violation of that position, and the technical skill necessary to trust violation is simply the technical skill necessary to holding the position in the first place." (Donald R. Cressey, *Other People's Money*, Glencoe, Ill.: Free Press, 1953, pp. 81–82.) Thus skills required in certain crimes need not be learned in association with criminals; they can be acquired through conventional learning.

how a consolidated approach might advance the understanding of both rates and types of deviant conduct. The discussion centers on the conditions of access to *both* systems of means, legitimate and illegitimate.

The Distribution of Criminal Behavior. One problem which has plagued the criminologist is the absence of adequate data on social differentials in criminal activity. Many have held that the highest crime rates are to be found in the lower social strata. Others have suggested that rates in the middle and upper classes may be much higher than is ordinarily thought. The question of the social distribution of crime remains problematic.

In the absence of adequate data, the theorist has sometimes attacked this problem by assessing the extent of pressures toward normative departures in various parts of the social structure. For example, Merton remarks that his "primary aim is to discover how some social structures exert a definite pressure upon certain persons in the society to engage in non-conforming rather than conforming conduct."[28] Having identified structural features which might be expected to generate deviance, Merton suggests the presence of a correlation between "pressures toward deviation" and "rate of deviance."

But whatever the differential rates of deviant behavior in the several social strata, and we know from many sources that the official crime statistics uniformly showing higher rates in the lower strata are far from complete or reliable, *it appears from our analysis that the greater pressures toward deviation are exerted upon the lower strata.* . . . Of those located in the lower reaches of the social structure, the culture makes incompatible demands. On the one hand they are asked to orient their behavior toward the prospect of large wealth . . . and on the other, they are largely denied effective opportunities to do so institutionally. *The consequence of this structural inconsistency is a high rate of deviant behavior.*[29]

Because of the paucity and unreliability of existing criminal statistics, there is as yet no way of knowing whether or not Merton's hypothesis is correct. Until comparative studies of crime rates are available the hypothesized correlation cannot be tested.

From a theoretical perspective, however, questions may be raised about this correlation. Would we expect, to raise the principal query, the correlation to be fixed or to vary depending on the distribution of access to illegitimate means? The three possibilities are (1) that access is distributed uniformly throughout the class structure, (2) that access varies inversely with class position, and (3) that access varies directly with class position. Specification of these possibilities permits a more precise statement of the conditions under which crime rates would be expected to vary.

[28] Merton, *op. cit.*, p. 132.
[29] *Ibid.*, pp. 144–145.

If access to illegitimate means is *uniformly distributed* throughout the class structure, then the proposed correlation would probably hold—higher rates of innovating behavior would be expected in the lower class than elsewhere. Lower-class persons apparently experience greater pressures toward deviance and are less restrained by internalized prohibitions from employing illegitimate means. Assuming uniform access to such means, it would therefore be reasonable to predict higher rates of innovating behavior in the lower social strata.

If access to illegitimate means varies *inversely* with class position, then the correlation would not only hold, but might even be strengthened. For pressures toward deviance, including socialization that does not altogether discourage the use of illegitimate means, would coincide with the availability of such means.

Finally, if access varies *directly* with class position, comparative rates of illegitimate activity become difficult to forecast. The higher the class position, the less the pressure to employ illegitimate means; furthermore, internalized prohibitions are apparently more effective in higher positions. If, at the same time, opportunities to use illegitimate methods are more abundant, then these factors would be in opposition. Until the precise effects of these several variables can be more adequately measured, rates cannot be safely forecast.

The concept of differentials in availability of illegitimate means may also help to clarify questions about varying crime rates among ethnic, age, religious, and sex groups, and other social divisions. This concept, then, can by systematically employed in the effort to further our understanding of the distribution of illegitimate behavior in the social structure.

Modes of Adaptation: The Case of Retreatism. By taking into account the conditions of access to legitimate *and* illegitimate means, we can further specify the circumstances under which various modes of deviant behavior arise. This may be illustrated by the case of retreatism.[30]

As defined by Merton, retreatist adaptations include such categories of behavior as alcoholism, drug addiction, and psychotic withdrawal. These adaptations entail "escape" from the frustrations of unfulfilled aspirations by withdrawal from conventional social relationships. The processes leading to retreatism are described by Merton as follows: "[Retreatism] arises from continued failure to near the goal by legitimate measures and from an inability to use the illegitimate route because of internalized prohibitions, *this process occurring while the supreme value of the success-goal has not yet*

[30] Retreatist behavior is but one of many types of deviant adaptations which might be re-analyzed in terms of this consolidated theoretical approach. In subsequent papers, being prepared jointly with Lloyd E. Ohlin, other cases of deviant behavior—e.g., collective disturbances in prisons and subcultural adaptations among juvenile delinquents—will be examined. In this connection, see footnote 22.

been renounced. The conflict is resolved by abandoning *both* precipitating elements, the goals and means. The escape is complete, the conflict is eliminated and the individual is asocialized."[31]

In this view, a crucial element encouraging retreatism is internalized constraint concerning the use of illegitimate means. But this element need not be present. Merton apparently assumed that such prohibitions are essential because, in their absence, the logic of his scheme would compel him to predict that innovating behavior would result. But the assumption that the individual uninhibited in the use of illegitimate means becomes an innovator presupposes that successful innovation is only a matter of motivation. Once the concept of differentials in access to illegitimate means is introduced, however, it becomes clear that retreatism is possible even in the absence of internalized prohibitions. For we may now ask how individuals respond when they fail in the use of *both* legitimate and illegitimate means. If illegitimate means are unavailable, if efforts at innovation fail, then retreatist adaptations may still be the consequence, and the "escape" mechanisms chosen by the defeated individual may perhaps be all the more deviant because of his "double failure."

This does not mean that retreatist adaptations cannot arise precisely as Merton suggests: namely, that the conversion from conformity to retreatism takes place in one step, without intervening adaptations. But this is only one route to retreatism. The conversion may at times entail intervening stages and intervening adaptations, particularly of an innovating type. This possibility helps to account for the fact that certain categories of individuals cited as retreatists—for example, hobos—often show extensive histories of arrests and convictions for various illegal acts. It also helps to explain retreatist adaptations among individuals who have not necessarily internalized strong restraints on the use of illegitimate means. In short, retreatist adaptations may arise with considerable frequency among those who are failures in both worlds, conventional and illegitimate alike.[32]

Future research on retreatist behavior might well examine the interval between conformity and retreatism. To what extent does the individual entertain the possibility of resorting to illegitimate means, and to what extent does he actually seek to mobilize such means? If the individual turns to innovating devices, the question of whether or not he becomes a retreatist

---

[31] Merton, *op. cit.*, pp. 153–154.

[32] The processes of "double failure" being specified here may be of value in re-analyzing the correlation between alcoholism and petty crime. Investigation of the *careers* of petty criminals who are alcoholic may reveal that after being actively oriented toward stable criminal careers they then lost out in the competitive struggle. See, e.g., Irwin Deutscher, "The Petty Offender: A Sociological Alien," *The Journal of Criminal Law, Criminology and Police Science*, 44 (January-February, 1954), pp. 592–595; Albert D. Ullman *et al.*, "Some Social Characteristics of Misdemeanants," *The Journal of Criminal Law, Criminology and Police Science*, 48 (May-June, 1957), pp. 44–53.

may then depend upon the relative accessibility of illegitimate means. For although the frustrated conformist seeks a solution to status discontent by adopting such methods, there is the further problem of whether or not he possesses appropriate skills and has opportunities for their use. We suggest therefore that data be gathered on preliminary responses to status discontent—and on the individual's perceptions of the efficacy of employing illegitimate means, the content of his skills, and the objective situation of illegitimate opportunity available to him.

Respecification of the processes leading to retreatism may also help to resolve difficulties entailed in ascertaining rates of retreatism in different parts of the social structure. Although Merton does not indicate explicitly where this adaptation might be expected to arise, he specifies some of the social conditions which encourage high rates of retreatism. Thus the latter is apt to mark the behavior of downwardly mobile persons, who experience a sudden breakdown in established social relations, and such individuals as the retired, who have lost major social roles.[33]

The long-standing difficulties in forecasting differential rates of retreatism may perhaps be attributed to the assumption that retreatists have fully internalized values prohibiting the use of illegitimate means. That this prohibition especially characterizes socialization in the middle and upper classes probably calls for the prediction that retreatism occurs primarily in those classes—and that the hobohemias, "drug cultures," and the ranks of the alcoholics are populated primarily by individuals from the upper reaches of society. It would appear from various accounts of hobohemia and skid row, however, that many of these persons are the products of slum life, and, furthermore, that their behavior is not necessarily controlled by values which preclude resort to illegitimate means. But once it is recognized that retreatism may arise in response to limitations on both systems of means, the difficulty of locating this adaptation is lessened, if not resolved. Thus retreatist behavior may vary with the particular process by which it is generated. The process described by Merton may be somewhat more characteristic of higher positions in the social structure where rule-oriented socialization is typical, while in the lower strata retreatism may tend more often to be the consequence of unsuccessful attempts at innovation.

SUMMARY

This paper attempts to identify and to define the concept of differential opportunity structures. It has been suggested that this concept helps to extend the developing theory of social structure and anomie. Furthermore, by linking propositions regarding the accessibility of *both* legitimate and

[33] Merton, *op. cit.*, pp. 188–189.

illegitimate opportunity structures, a basis is provided for consolidating various major traditions of sociological thought on nonconformity. The concept of differential systems of opportunity and of variations in access to them, it is hoped, will suggest new possibilities for research on the relationship between social structure and deviant behavior.

4 Lower Class Culture as a Generating Milieu of Gang Delinquency

WALTER B. MILLER

The etiology of delinquency has long been a controversial issue, and is particularly so at present. As new frames of reference for explaining human behavior have been added to traditional theories, some authors have adopted the practice of citing the major postulates of each school of thought as they pertain to delinquency, and going on to state that causality must be conceived in terms of the dynamic interaction of a complex combination of variables on many levels. The major sets of etiological factors currently adduced to explain delinquency are, in simplified terms, the physiological (delinquency results from organic pathology), the psychodynamic (delinquency is a "behavioral disorder" resulting primarily from emotional disturbance generated by a defective mother-child relationship), and the environmental (delinquency is the product of disruptive forces, "disorganization," in the actor's physical or social environment).

This paper selects one particular kind of "delinquency"[1]—law-violating acts committed by members of adolescent street corner groups in lower

Reprinted from *Journal of Social Issues, 14*, No. 3 (1958), 5–19, by permission of the Society for the Study of Social Issues and the author.

[1] The complex issues involved in deriving a definition of "delinquency" cannot be discussed here. The term "delinquent" is used in this paper to characterize behavior or acts committed by individuals within specified age limits which if known to official authorities could result in legal action. The concept of a "delinquent" individual has little or no utility in the approach used here; rather, specified types of *acts* which may be committed rarely or frequently by few or many individuals are characterized as "delinquent."

class communities—and attempts to show that the dominant component of motivation underlying these acts consists in a directed attempt by the actor to adhere to forms of behavior, and to achieve standards of value as they are defined within that community. It takes as a premise that the motivation of behavior in this situation can be approached most productively by attempting to understand the nature of cultural forces impinging on the acting individual as they are perceived *by the actor himself*—although by no means only that segment of these forces of which the actor is consciously aware—rather than as they are perceived and evaluated from the reference position of another cultural system. In the case of "gang" delinquency, the cultural system which exerts the most direct influence on behavior is that of the lower class community itself—a long-established, distinctively patterned tradition with an integrity of its own—rather than a so-called "delinquent subculture" which has arisen through conflict with middle class culture and is oriented to the deliberate violation of middle class norms.

The bulk of the substantive data on which the following material is based was collected in connection with a service-research project in the control of gang delinquency. During the service aspect of the project, which lasted for three years, seven trained social workers maintained contact with twenty-one corner group units in a "slum" district of a large eastern city for periods of time ranging from ten to thirty months. Groups were Negro and white, male and female, and in early, middle, and late adolescence. Over eight thousand pages of direct observational data on behavior patterns of group members and other community residents were collected; almost daily contact was maintained for a total time period of about thirteen worker years. Data include workers' contact reports, participant observation reports by the writer—a cultural anthropologist—and direct tape recordings of group activities and discussions.[2]

FOCAL CONCERNS OF LOWER CLASS CULTURE

There is a substantial segment of present-day American society whose way of life, values, and characteristic patterns of behavior are the product of a distinctive cultural system which may be termed "lower class." Evidence indicates that this cultural system is becoming increasingly dis-

[2] A three year research project is being financed under National Institutes of Health Grant M—1414, and administered through the Boston University School of Social Work. The primary research effort has subjected all collected material to a uniform data-coding process. All information bearing on some seventy areas of behavior (behavior in reference to school, police, theft, assault, sex, collective athletics, etc.) is extracted from the records, recorded on coded data cards, and filed under relevant categories. Analysis of these data aims to ascertain the actual nature of customary behavior in these areas, an the extent to which the social work effort was able to effect behavioral changes.

tinctive, and that the size of the group which shares this tradition is increasing.[3] The lower class way of life, in common with that of all distinctive cultural groups, is characterized by a set of focal concerns—areas or issues which command widespread and persistent attention and a high degree of emotional involvement. The specific concerns cited here, while by no means confined to the American lower classes, constitute a distinctive *patterning* of concerns which differs significantly, both in rank order and weighting from that of American middle class culture. [Chart 1]

CHART 1. FOCAL CONCERNS OF LOWER CLASS CULTURE

Area	Perceived Alternatives (state, quality, condition)	
1. *Trouble:*	law-abiding behavior	law-violating behavior
2. *Toughness:*	physical prowess, skill; "masculinity"; fearlessness, bravery, daring	weakness, ineptitude; effeminacy; timidity, cowardice, caution
3. *Smartness:*	ability to outsmart, dupe, "con"; gaining money by "wits"; shrewdness, adroitness in repartee	gullibility, "con-ability"; gaining money by hard work; slowness, dull-wittedness, verbal maladroitness
4. *Excitement:*	thrill; risk, danger; change, activity	boredom; "deadness," safeness; sameness, passivity
5. *Fate:*	favored by fortune, being "lucky"	ill-omened, being "unlucky"
6. *Autonomy:*	freedom from external constraint; freedom from super-ordinate authority; independence	presence of external constraint; presence of strong authority; dependency, being "cared for"

[3] Between 40 and 60 per cent of all Americans are directly influenced by lower class culture, with about 15 per cent, or twenty-five million, comprising the "hard-core" lower class group—defined primarily by its use of the "female-based" household as the basic form of child-rearing unit and of the "serial monogamy" mating pattern as the primary form of marriage. The term "lower class culture" as used here refers most specifically to the way of life of the "hard core" group; systematic research in this area would probably reveal at least four to six major subtypes of lower class culture, for some of which the "concerns" presented here would be differently weighted, especially for those subtypes in which "law-abiding" behavior has a high overt valuation. It is impossible within the compass of this short paper to make the finer intra-cultural distinctions which a more accurate presentation would require.

presents a highly schematic and simplified listing of six of the major concerns of lower class culture. Each is conceived as a "dimension" within which a fairly wide and varied range of alternative behavior patterns may be followed by different individuals under different situations. They are listed roughly in order of the degree of *explicit* attention accorded each, and, in this sense represent a weighted ranking of concerns. The "perceived alternatives" represent polar positions which define certain parameters within each dimension. As will be explained in more detail, it is necessary in relating the influence of these "concerns" to the motivation of delinquent behavior to specify *which* of its aspects is oriented to, whether orientation is *overt* or *covert, positive* (conforming to or seeking the aspect), or *negative* (rejecting or seeking to avoid the aspect).

The concept "focal concern" is used here in preference to the concept "value" for several interrelated reasons: (1) It is more readily derivable from direct field observation. (2) It is descriptively neutral—permitting independent consideration of positive and negative valences as varying under different conditions, whereas "value" carries a built-in positive valence. (3) It makes possible more refined analysis of subcultural differences, since it reflects actual behavior, whereas "value" tends to wash out intracultural differences since it is colored by notions of the "official" ideal.

Trouble

Concern over "trouble" is a dominant feature of lower class culture. The concept has various shades of meaning; "trouble" in one of its aspects represents a situation or a kind of behavior which results in unwelcome or complicating involvement with official authorities or agencies of middle class society. "Getting into trouble" and "staying out of trouble" represent major issues for male and female, adults and children. For men, "trouble" frequently involves fighting or sexual adventures while drinking; for women, sexual involvement with disadvantageous consequences. Expressed desire to avoid behavior which violates moral or legal norms is often based less on an explicit commitment to "official" moral or legal standards than on a desire to avoid "getting into trouble," e.g., the complicating consequences of the action.

The dominant concern over "trouble" involves a distinction of critical importance for the lower class community—that between "law-abiding" and "non-law-abiding" behavior. There is a high degree of sensitivity as to where each person stands in relation to these two classes of activity. Whereas in the middle class community a major dimension for evaluating a person's status is "achievement" and its external symbols, in the lower class, personal status is very frequently gauged along the law-abiding-non-law-abiding dimension. A mother will evaluate the suitability of her daughter's boyfriend less on the basis of his achievement potential than on the basis of his innate "trouble" potential. This sensitive awareness of the opposition of "trouble-producing" and "non-trouble-producing" behavior represents both a major basis for deriving status distinctions, and an internalized conflict potential for the individual.

As in the case of other focal concerns, which of two perceived alternatives—"law-abiding" or "non-law-abiding"—is valued varies according to the individual and the circumstances; in many instances there is an overt commitment of the "law-abiding" alternative, but a covert commitment to the "non-law-abiding." In certain situations, "getting into trouble" is overtly recognized as prestige-conferring; for example, membership in certain adult and adolescent primary groupings ("gangs") is contingent on having demonstrated an explicit commitment to the law-violating alternative. It is most important to note that the choice between "law-abiding" and "non-law-abiding" behavior is still a choice *within* lower class culture; the distinction between the policeman and the criminal, the outlaw and the sheriff, involves primarily this one dimension; in other respects they have a high community of interests. Not infrequently brothers raised in an identical cultural milieu will become police and criminals respectively.

For a substantial segment of the lower class population "getting into trouble" is not in itself overtly defined as prestige-conferring, but is implicitly recognized as a means to other valued ends, e.g., the covertly valued desire to be "cared for" and subject to external constraint, or the overtly valued state of excitement or risk. Very frequently "getting into trouble" is multi-functional, and achieves several sets of valued ends.

Toughness

The concept of "toughness" in lower class culture represents a compound combination of qualities or states. Among its most important components are physical prowess, evidenced both by demonstrated possession of strength and endurance and athletic skill; "masculinity," symbolized by a distinctive complex of acts and avoidances (bodily tatooing; absence of sentimentality; non-concern with "art," "literature," conceptualization of women as conquest objects, etc.); and bravery in the face of physical threat. The model for the "tough guy"—hard, fearless, undemonstrative, skilled in physical combat—is represented by the movie gangster of the thirties, the "private eye," and the movie cowboy.

The genesis of the intense concern over "toughness" in lower class culture is probably related to the fact that a significant proportion of lower class males are reared in a predominantly female household, and lack a consistently present male figure with whom to identify and from whom to learn essential components of a "male" role. Since women serve as a primary object of identification during pre-adolescent years, the almost obsessive lower class concern with "masculinity" probably resembles a type of compulsive reaction-formation. A concern over homosexuality runs like a persistent thread through lower class culture. This is manifested by the institutionalized practice of baiting "queers," often accompanied by violent physical attacks, an expressed contempt for "softness" or frills, and the use of the local term for "homosexual" as a generalized pejorative epithet (e.g., higher class individuals or upwardly mobile peers are frequently characterized as "fags" or "queers"). The distinction between "overt" and "covert" orientation to aspects of an area of concern is especially important in regard to "toughness." A positive overt evaluation of behavior defined as "effeminate" would be out of the question for a lower class male; however, built into lower class culture is a range of devices which permit men to adopt behaviors and concerns which in other cultural milieux fall within the province of women, and at the same time to be defined as "tough" and manly. For example, lower class men can be professional short-order cooks in a diner and still be regarded as "tough." The highly intimate circumstances of the street corner gang involve the recurrent expression of strongly affectionate feelings towards other men. Such expressions, however, are disguised as their opposite, taking the form of ostensibly aggressive verbal and physical interaction (kidding, "ranking," roughhousing, etc.).

Smartness

"Smartness," as conceptualized in lower class culture, involves the capacity to outsmart, outfox, outwit, dupe, "take," "con" another or others, and the concomitant capacity to avoid being outwitted, "taken," or duped oneself. In its essence, smartness involves the capacity to achieve a valued entity—material goods, personal status—through a maximum use of mental agility and a minimum use of physical effort. This capacity has an extremely long tradition in lower class culture, and is highly valued. Lower class culture can be characterized as "non-intellectual" only if intellectualism is defined specifically in terms of control over a particular body of formally learned knowledge involving "culture" (art, literature, "good" music, etc.), a generalized perspective on the past and present conditions of our own and other societies, and other areas of knowledge imparted by formal educational institutions. This particular type of mental attainment is, in general, overtly disvalued and frequently associated with effeminacy; "smartness" in the lower class sense, however, is highly valued.

The lower class child learns and practices the use of this skill in the street corner situation. Individuals continually practice duping and outwitting one another through recurrent card games and other forms of gambling, mutual exchanges of insults, and "testing" for mutual "con-ability." Those who demonstrate competence in this skill are accorded considerable prestige. Leadership roles in the corner group are frequently allocated according to demonstrated capacity in the two areas of "smartness" and "toughness"; the ideal leader combines both, but the "smart" leader is often accorded more prestige than the "tough" one—reflecting a general lower class respect for "brains" in the "smartness" sense.[4]

The model of the "smart" person is represented in popular media by the card shark, the professional gambler, the "con" artist, the promoter. A conceptual distinction is made between two kinds of people: "suckers," easy marks, "lushes," dupes, who work for their money and are legitimate targets of exploitation; and sharp operators, the "brainy" ones, who live by their wits and "getting" from the suckers by mental adroitness.

Involved in the syndrome of capacities related to "smartness" is a dominant emphasis in lower class culture on ingenious aggressive repartee. This skill, learned and practiced in the context of the corner group, ranges in form from the widely prevalent semi-ritualized teasing, kidding, razzing, "ranking," so characteristic of male peer group interaction, to the highly ritualized type of mutual insult interchange known as "the dirty dozens," "the dozens," "playing house," and other terms. This highly patterned cultural form is practiced on its most advanced level in adult male Negro society, but less polished variants are found throughout lower class culture—practiced, for example, by white children, male and female, as young as four or five. In essence, "doin' the dozens" involves two antagonists who vie with each other in the exchange of increasingly inflammatory insults, with incestuous and perverted sexual relations with the mother a dominant theme. In this form of insult interchange, as well as on other less ritualized occasions for joking, semi-serious, and serious mutual invective, a very high premium is placed on ingenuity, hair-trigger responsiveness, inventiveness, and the acute exercise of mental faculties.

Excitement

For many lower class individuals the rhythm of life fluctuates between periods of relatively routine or repetitive activity and sought situations of great emotional stimulation. Many of the most characteristic features of lower class life are related to the search for excitement or "thrill." Involved here are the highly prevalent use of alcohol by both sexes and the widespread use of gambling of all kinds—playing the numbers, betting on horse

[4] The "brains-brawn" set of capacities are often paired in lower class folk lore or accounts of lower class life, e.g., "Brer Fox" and "Brer Bear" in the Uncle Remus stories, or George and Lennie in "Of Mice and Men."

races, dice, cards. The quest for excitement finds what is perhaps its most vivid expression in the highly patterned practice of the recurrent "night on the town." This practice, designated by various terms in different areas ("honky-tonkin' "; "goin' out on the town"; "bar hoppin' "), involves a patterned set of activities in which alcohol, music, and sexual adventuring are major components. A group or individual sets out to "make the rounds" of various bars or night clubs. Drinking continues progressively throughout the evening. Men seek to "pick up" women, and women play the risky game of entertaining sexual advances. Fights between men involving women, gambling, and claims of physical prowess, in various combinations, are frequent consequences of a night of making the rounds. The explosive potential of this type of adventuring with sex and aggression, frequently leading to "trouble," is semi-explicitly sought by the individual. Since there is always a good likelihood that being out on the town will eventuate in fights, etc., the practice involves elements of sought risk and desired danger.

Counterbalancing the "flirting with danger" aspect of the "excitement" concern is the prevalence in lower class culture of other well established patterns of activity which involve long periods of relative inaction, or passivity. The term "hanging out" in lower class culture refers to extended periods of standing around, often with peer mates, doing what is defined as "nothing," "shooting the breeze," etc. A definite periodicity exists in the pattern of activity relating to the two aspects of the "excitement" dimension. For many lower class individuals the venture into the high risk world of alcohol, sex, and fighting occurs regularly once a week, with interim periods devoted to accommodating to possible consequences of these periods, along with recurrent resolves not to become so involved again.

Fate

Related to the quest for excitement is the concern with fate, fortune, or luck. Here also a distinction is made between two states—being "lucky" or "in luck," and being unlucky or jinxed. Many lower class individuals feel that their lives are subject to a set of forces over which they have relatively little control. These are not directly equated with the supernatural forces of formally organized religion, but relate more to a concept of "destiny," or man as a pawn of magical powers. Not infrequently this often implicit world view is associated with a conception of the ultimate futility of directed effort towards a goal: if the cards are right, or the dice good to you, or if your lucky number comes up, things will go your way; if luck is against you, it's not worth trying. The concept of performing semi-magical rituals so that one's "luck will change" is prevalent; one hopes that as a result he will move from the state of being "unlucky" to that of being "lucky." The element of fantasy plays an important part in this area. Related to and complementing the notion that "only suckers work" (Smartness) is the idea that once things start going your way, relatively independent of your own effort, all good things will come to you. Achieving great material rewards (big cars, big houses, a roll of cash to flash in a fancy night club), valued in lower class as well as in other parts of American culture, is a recurrent theme in lower class fantasy and folk lore; the cocaine dreams of Willie the Weeper or Minnie the Moocher present the components of this fantasy in vivid detail.

The prevalence in the lower class community of many forms of gambling, mentioned in connection with the "excitement" dimension, is also relevant here. Through cards and pool which involve skill, and thus both "toughness" and "smartness"; or through race horse betting, involving "smartness"; or through playing the numbers, involving predominantly "luck," one may make a big killing with a minimum of directed and persistent effort within conventional occupational channels. Gambling in its many forms illustrates the fact that many of the persistent features of lower class culture are multi-functional—serving a range of desired ends at the same time. Describing some of the incentives behind gambling has involved mention of all of the focal concerns cited so far—Toughness, Smartness, and Excitement, in addition to Fate.

Autonomy

The extent and nature of control over the behavior of the individual—an important concern in most cultures—has a special significance and is distinctively patterned in lower class culture. The discrepancy between what is overtly valued and what is covertly sought is particularly striking in this area. On the overt level there is a strong and frequently expressed resentment of the idea of external controls, restrictions on behavior, and unjust or coercive authority. "No one's gonna push *me* around," or "I'm gonna tell him he can take the job and shove it. . . ." are commonly expressed sentiments. Similar explicit attitudes are maintained to systems of behavior-restricting rules, insofar as these are perceived as representing the injunctions, and bearing the sanctions of superordinate authority. In addition, in lower class culture a close conceptual connection is made between "authority" and "nurturance." To be restrictively or firmly controlled is to be cared for. Thus the overtly negative evaluation of superordinate authority frequently extends as well to nurturance, care, or protection. The desire for personal independence is often expressed in such terms as "I don't need *nobody* to take care of me. I can take care of myself!" Actual patterns of behavior, however, reveal a marked discrepancy between expressed sentiment and what is covertly valued. Many lower class people appear to seek out highly restrictive social environments wherein stringent external controls are maintained over their behavior. Such institutions as the armed forces, the mental hospital, the disciplinary school, the prison or correctional institution, provide environments which incorporate a strict and detailed set of rules defining and limiting behavior, and enforced by an authority system which controls and applies coercive sanctions for deviance from these rules. While under the jurisdiction of such systems, the lower class person generally expresses to his peers continual resentment of the coercive, unjust, and arbitrary exercise of authority. Having been released, or having escaped from these milieux, however, he will often act in such a way as to insure recommitment, or choose recommitment voluntarily after a temporary period of "freedom."

Lower class patients in mental hospitals will exercise considerable ingenuity to insure continued commitment while voicing the desire to get out; delinquent boys will frequently "run" from a correctional institution to activate efforts to return them; to be caught and returned means that one is cared for. Since "being controlled" is equated with "being cared for," attempts are frequently made to "test" the severity or strictness of superordinate authority to see if it remains firm. If intended or executed rebellion produces swift and firm punitive sanctions, the individual is reassured, at the same time that he is complaining bitterly at the injustice of being caught and punished. Some environmental milieux, having been tested in this fashion for the "firmness" of their coercive sanctions, are rejected, ostensibly for being too strict, actually for not being strict enough. This is frequently so in the case of "problematic" behavior by lower class youngsters in the public schools, which generally cannot command the coercive controls implicitly sought by the individual.

A similar discrepancy between what is overtly and covertly desired is found in the area of dependence-independence. The pose of tough rebellious independence often assumed by the lower class person frequently conceals powerful dependency cravings. These are manifested primarily by obliquely expressed resentment when "care" is not forthcoming rather than by expressed satisfaction when it is. The concern over autonomy-dependency is related both to "trouble" and "fate." Insofar as the lower class individual feels that his behavior is controlled by forces which often propel him into "trouble" in the face of an explicit determination to avoid it, there is an implied appeal to "save me from myself." A solution appears to lie in arranging things so that his behavior will be coercively restricted by an externally imposed set of controls strong enough to forcibly restrain his inexplicable inclination to get in trouble. The periodicity observed in connection with the "excitement" dimension is also revelant here; after involvement in trouble-producing behavior (assault, sexual adventure, a "drunk"), the individual will actively seek a locus of imposed control (his wife, prison, a restrictive job); after a given period of subjection to this control, resentment against it mounts, leading to a "break away" and a search for involvement in further "trouble."

FOCAL CONCERNS OF THE LOWER CLASS ADOLESCENT STREET CORNER GROUP

The one-sex peer group is a highly prevalent and significant structural form in the lower class community. There is a strong probability that the prevalence and stability of this type of unit is directly related to the prevalence of a stabilized type of lower class child-rearing unit—the "female-based" household. This is a nuclear kin unit in which a male parent is either absent from the household, present only sporadically, or, when present, only minimally or inconsistently involved in the support and rearing of children. This unit usually consists of one or more females of child-bearing age and their offspring. The females are frequently related to one another by blood or marriage ties, and the unit often includes two or more generations of women, e.g., the mother and/or aunt of the principal child-bearing female.

The nature of social groupings in the lower class community may be clarified if we make the assumption that it is the *one-sex peer unit* rather than the two-parent family unit which represents the most significant relational unit for both sexes in lower class communities. Lower class society may be pictured as comprising a set of age-graded one-sex groups which constitute the major psychic focus and reference group for those over twelve or thirteen. Men and women of mating age leave these groups periodically to form temporary marital alliances, but these lack stability, and after varying periods of "trying out" the two-sex family arrangement, gravitate back to the more "comfortable" one-sex grouping, whose members exert strong pressure on the individual *not* to disrupt the group by adopting a two-sex household pattern of life.[5] Membership in a stable and solidary peer unit is vital to the lower class individual precisely to the extent to which a range of essential functions—psychological, educational, and others, are not provided by the "family" unit.

The adolescent street corner group represents the adolescent variant of this lower class structural form. What has been called the "delinquent gang" is one subtype of this form, defined on the basis of frequency of participation in law-violating activity; this subtype should not be consid-

---

[5] Further data on the female-based household unit (estimated as comprising about 15 per cent of all American "families") and the role of one-sex groupings in lower class culture are contained in Walter B. Miller, Implications of Urban Lower Class Culture for Social Work. *Social Service Review*, 1959, *33*, No. 3.

ered a legitimate unit of study per se, but rather as one particular variant of the adolescent street corner group. The "hanging" peer group is a unit of particular importance for the adolescent male. In many cases it is the most stable and solidary primary group he has ever belonged to; for boys reared in female-based households the corner group provides the first real opportunity to learn essential aspects of the male role in the context of peers facing similar problems of sex-role identification.

The form and functions of the adolescent corner group operate as a selective mechanism in recruiting members. The activity patterns of the group require a high level of intra-group solidarity; individual members must possess a good capacity for subordinating individual desires to general group interests as well as the capacity for intimate and persisting interaction. Thus highly "disturbed" individuals, or those who cannot tolerate consistently imposed sanctions on "deviant" behavior cannot remain accepted members; the group itself will extrude those whose behavior exceeds limits defined as "normal." This selective process produces a type of group whose members possess to an unusually high degree both the *capacity* and *motivation* to conform to perceived cultural norms, so that the nature of the system of norms and values oriented to is a particularly influential component of motivation.

Focal concerns of the male adolescent corner group are those of the general cultural milieu in which it functions. As would be expected, the relative weighting and importance of these concerns pattern somewhat differently for adolescents than for adults. The nature of this patterning centers around two additional "concerns" of particular importance to this group—concern with "belonging," and with "status." These may be conceptualized as being on a higher level of abstraction than concerns previously cited, since "status" and "belonging" are achieved *via* cited concern areas of Toughness, etc.

Belonging

Since the corner group fulfills essential functions for the individual, being a member in good standing of the group is of vital importance for its members. A continuing concern over who is "in" and who is not involves the citation and detailed discussion of highly refined criteria for "in-group" membership. The phrase "he hangs with us" means "he is accepted as a member in good standing by current consensus"; conversely, "he don't hang with us" means he is not so accepted. One achieves "belonging" primarily by demonstrating knowledge of and a determination to adhere to the system of standards and valued qualities defined by the group. One maintains membership by acting in conformity with valued aspects of Toughness, Smartness, Autonomy, etc. In those instances where conforming to norms of this reference group at the same time violates norms of other reference groups (e.g., middle class adults, institutional "officials"), immediate reference group norms are much more compelling since violation risks invoking the group's most powerful sanction: exclusion.

Status

In common with most adolescents in American society, the lower class corner group manifests a dominant concern with "status." What differentiates this type of group from others, however, is the particular set of criteria and weighting thereof by which "status" is defined. In general, status is achieved and maintained by demonstrated possession of the valued qualities of lower class culture—Toughness, Smartness, expressed resistance to authority, daring, etc. It is important to stress once more that the individual orients to these concerns *as they are defined within lower class society;* e.g., the status-conferring potential of "smartness" in the sense of scholastic achievement generally ranges from negligible to negative.

The concern with "status" is manifested in a variety of ways. Intra-group status is a continued concern, and is derived and tested constantly by means of a set of status-ranking activities; the intra-group "pecking order" is constantly at issue. One gains status within the group by demonstrated superiority in Toughness (physical prowess, bravery, skill in athletics and games such as pool and cards), Smartness (skill in repartee, capacity to "dupe" fellow group members), and the like. The term "ranking," used to refer to the pattern of intra-group aggressive repartee, indicates awareness of the fact that this is one device for establishing the intra-group status hierarchy.

The concern over status in the adolescent corner group involves in particular the component of "adultness," the intense desire to be seen as "grown up," and a corresponding aversion to "kid stuff." "Adult" status is defined less in terms of the assumption of "adult" responsibility than in terms of certain external symbols of adult status—a car, ready cash, and, in particular, a preceived "freedom" to drink, smoke, and gamble as one wishes and to come and go without external restrictions. The desire to be seen as "adult" is often a more significant component of much involvement in illegal drinking, gambling, and automobile driving than the explicit enjoyment of these acts as such.

The intensity of the corner group member's desire to be seen as "adult" is sufficiently great that he feels called upon to demonstrate qualities associated with adultness (Toughness, Smartness, Autonomy) to a much greater degree than a lower class adult. This means that he will seek out and utilize those avenues to these qualities which he perceives as available with greater intensity than an adult and less regard for their "legitimacy." In this sense the adolescent variant of lower class culture represents a maximization or an intensified manifestation of many of its most characteristic features.

Concern over status is also manifested in reference to other street corner groups. The term "rep" used in this regard is especially significant, and has broad connotations. In its most frequent and explicit connotation, "rep" refers to the "toughness" of the corner group as a whole relative to that of other groups; a "pecking order" also exists among the several corner groups in a given interactional area, and there is a common perception that the safety or security of the group and all its members depends on maintaining a solid "rep" for toughness vis-a-vis other groups. This motive is most frequently advanced as a reason for involvement in gang fights: "We *can't* chicken out on this fight; our rep would be shot!"; this implies that the group would be relegated to the bottom of the status ladder and become a helpless and recurrent target of external attack.

On the other hand, there is implicit in the concept of "rep" the recognition that "rep" has or may have a dual basis—corresponding to the two aspects of the "trouble" dimension. It is recognized that group as well as individual status can be based on both "law-abiding" and "law-violating" behavior. The situational resolution of the persisting conflict between the "law-abiding" and "law-violating" bases of status comprises a vital set of dynamics in determining whether a "delinquent" mode of behavior will be adopted by a group, under what circumstances, and how persistently. The determinants of this choice are evidently highly complex and fluid, and rest on a range of factors including the presence and perceptual immediacy of different community reference-group loci (e.g., professional criminals, police, clergy, teachers, settlement house workers), the personality structures and "needs" of group members, the presence in the community of social work, recreation, or educational programs which can facilitate utilization of the "law-abiding" basis of status, and so on.

What remains constant is the critical importance of "status" both for the members of the group as individuals and for the group as a whole insofar as members perceive their individual destinies as linked to the destiny of the group, and the fact that action geared to attain status is much more acutely oriented to the fact of status itself than to the legality or illegality, morality or immorality of the means used to achieve it.

LOWER CLASS CULTURE AND THE MOTIVATION OF DELINQUENT BEHAVIOR

The customary set of activities of the adolescent street corner group includes activities which are in violation of laws and ordinances of the legal code. Most of these center around assault and theft of various types (the gang fight; auto theft; assault on an individual; petty pilfering and shoplifting; "mugging"; pocketbook theft). Members of street corner gangs are well aware of the law-violating nature of these acts; they are not psychopaths, nor physically or mentally "defective"; in fact, since the corner group supports and enforces a rigorous set of standards which demand a high degree of fitness and personal competence, it tends to recruit from the most "able" members of the community.

Why, then, is the commission of crimes a customary feature of gang activity? The most general answer is that the commission of crimes by members of adolescent street corner groups is motivated primarily by the attempt to achieve ends, states, or conditions which are valued, and to avoid those that are disvalued within their most meaningful cultural milieu, through those culturally available avenues which appear as the most feasible means of attaining those ends.

The operation of these influences is well illustrated by the gang fight—a prevalent and characteristic type of corner group delinquency. This type of activity comprises a highly stylized and culturally patterned set of sequences. Although details vary under different circumstances, the following events are generally included. A member or several members of group A "trespass" on the claimed territory of group B. While there they commit an act or acts which group B defines as a violation of its rightful privileges, an affront to their honor, or a challenge to their "rep." Frequently this act involves advances to a girl associated with group B; it may occur at a dance or party; sometimes the mere act of "trespass" is seen as deliberate provocation. Members of group B then assault members of group A, if they are caught while still in B's territory. Assaulted members of group A return to their "home" territory and recount to members of their group details of the incident, stressing the insufficient nature of the provocation ("I just *looked* at her! Hardly even said anything!"), and the unfair circumstances of the assault ("About *twenty* guys jumped just the *two* of us!"). The highly colored account is acutely inflammatory; group A, perceiving its honor violated and its "rep" threatened, feels obligated to retaliate in force. Sessions of detailed planning now occur; allies are recruited if the size of group A and its potential allies appears to necessitate larger numbers; strategy is plotted, and messengers dispatched. Since the prospect of a gang fight is frightening to even the "toughest" group members, a constant rehearsal of the provocative incident or incidents and the essentially evil nature of the opponents accompanies the planning process to bolster possibly weakening motivation to fight. The excursion into "enemy" territory sometimes results in a full scale fight; more often group B cannot be found, or the police appear and stop the fight, "tipped off" by an anonymous informant. When this occurs, group members express disgust and disappointment; secretly there is much relief; their honor has been avenged without incurring injury; often the anonymous tipster is a member of one of the involved groups.

The basic elements of this type of delinquency are sufficiently stabilized and recurrent as to constitute an essentially ritualized pattern, resembling both in structure and expressed motives for action classic forms such as the European "duel," the American Indian tribal war, and the Celtic clan feud. Although the arousing and "acting out" of individual aggressive emotions are inevitably involved in the gang fight, neither its form nor motivational dynamics can be adequately handled within a predominantly personality-focused frame of reference.

It would be possible to develop in considerable detail the processes by which the commission of a range of illegal acts is either explicitly supported by, implicitly demanded by, or not materially inhibited by factors relating to the focal concerns of lower class culture. In place of such a development, the following three statements condense in general terms the operation of these processes:

1. Following cultural practices which comprise essential elements of the total life pattern of lower class culture automatically violates certain legal norms.

2. In instances where alternate avenues to similar objectives are available, the non-law-abiding avenue frequently provides a relatively greater and more immediate return for a relatively smaller investment of energy.

3. The "demanded" response to certain situations recurrently engendered within lower class culture involves the commission of illegal acts.

The primary thesis of this paper is that the dominant component of the motivation of "delinquent" behavior engaged in by members of lower class corner groups involves a positive effort to achieve states, conditions, or qualities valued within the actor's most significant cultural milieu. If "conformity to immediate reference group values" is the major component of motivation of "delinquent" behavior by gang members, why is such behavior frequently referred to as negativistic, malicious, or rebellious? Albert Cohen, for example, in *Delinquent Boys* (Glencoe: Free Press, 1955) describes behavior which violates school rules as comprising elements of "active spite and malice, contempt and ridicule, challenge and defiance." He ascribes to the gang "keen delight in terrorizing 'good' children, and in general making themselves obnoxious to the virtuous." A recent national conference on social work with "hard-to-reach" groups characterized lower class corner groups as "youth groups in conflict with the culture of their *(sic)* communities." Such characterizations are obviously the result of taking the middle class community and its institutions as an implicit point of reference.

A large body of systematically interrelated attitudes, practices, behaviors, and values characteristic of lower class culture are designed to support and maintain the basic features of the lower class way of life. In areas where these differ from features of middle class culture, action oriented to the achievement and maintenance of the lower class system may violate norms of middle class culture and be preceived as deliberately non-conforming or malicious by an observer strongly cathected to middle class norms. This does not mean, however, that violation of the middle class norm is the dominant component of motivation; it is a by-product of action primarily oriented to the lower class system. The standards of lower class culture cannot be seen merely as a reverse function of middle class culture—as middle class standards "turned upside down"; lower class culture is a distinctive tradition many centuries old with an integrity of its own.

From the viewpoint of the acting individual, functioning within a field of well-structured cultural forces, the relative impact of "conforming" and "rejective" elements in the motivation of gang delinquency is weighted preponderantly on the conforming side. Rejective or rebellious elements are inevitably involved, but their influence during the actual commission of delinquent acts is relatively small compared to the influence of pressures to achieve what is valued by the actor's most immediate reference groups. Expressed awareness by the actor of the element of rebellion often represents only that aspect of motivation of which he is explicitly conscious; the deepest and most compelling components of motivation—adherence to highly meaningful group standards of Toughness, Smartness, Excitement, etc.—are often unconsciously patterned. No cultural pattern as well-established as the practice of illegal acts by members of lower class corner groups could persist if buttressed primarily by negative, hostile, or rejective motives; its principal motivational support, as in the case of any persisting cultural tradition, derives from a positive effort to achieve what is valued within that tradition, and to conform to its explicit and implicit norms.

5 White-Collar Criminality

EDWIN H. SUTHERLAND

This paper[1] is concerned with crime in relation to business. The economists are well acquainted with business methods but not accustomed to consider them from the point of view of crime; many sociologists are well acquainted with crime but not accustomed to consider it as expressed in business. This paper is an attempt to integrate these two bodies of knowledge. More accurately stated, it is a comparison of crime in the upper or white-collar class, composed of respectable or at least respected business and professional men, and crime in the lower class, composed of persons of low socioeconomic status. This comparison is made for the purpose of developing the theories of criminal behavior, not for the purpose of muck-raking or of reforming anything except criminology.

The criminal statistics show unequivocally that crime, *as popularly conceived and officially measured*, has a high incidence in the lower class and a low incidence in the upper class; less than two percent of the persons committed to prisons in a year belong to the upper class. These statistics refer to criminals handled by the police, the criminal and juvenile courts, and the prisons, and to such crimes as murder, assault, burglary, robbery, larceny,

Reprinted from *American Sociological Review, 5* (February, 1940), 1–12, by permission of The American Sociological Association and the author.

[1] Thirty-fourth Annual Presidential Address delivered at Philadelphia, Pa., Dec. 27, 1939 in joint meeting with the American Economic Society (its Fifty-second) at which President Jacob Viner spoke on the relations of economic theory to the formulation of public policy.

sex offenses, and drunkenness, but exclude traffic violations.

The criminologists have used the case histories and criminal statistics derived from these agencies of criminal justice as their principal data. From them, they have derived general theories of criminal behavior. These theories are that, since crime is concentrated in the lower class, it is caused by poverty or by personal and social characteristics believed to be associated statistically with poverty, including feeblemindedness, psychopathic deviations, slum neighborhoods, and "deteriorated" families. This statement, of course, does not do justice to the qualifications and variations in the conventional theories of criminal behavior, but it presents correctly their central tendency.

The thesis of this paper is that the conception and explanations of crime which have just been described are misleading and incorrect, that crime is in fact not closely correlated with poverty or with the psychopathic and sociopathic conditions associated with poverty, and that an adequate explanation of criminal behavior must proceed along quite different lines. The conventional explanations are invalid principally because they are derived from biased samples. The samples are biased in that they have not included vast areas of criminal behavior of persons not in the lower class. One of these neglected areas is the criminal behavior of business and professional men, which will be analyzed in this paper.

The "robber barons" of the last half of the nineteenth century were white-collar criminals, as practically everyone now agrees. Their attitudes are illustrated by these statements: Colonel Vanderbilt asked, "You don't suppose you can run a railroad in accordance with the statutes, do you?" A. B. Stickney, a railroad president, said to sixteen other railroad presidents in the home of J. P. Morgan in 1890, "I have the utmost respect for you gentlemen, individually, but as railroad presidents I wouldn't trust you with my watch out of my sight." Charles Francis Adams said, "The difficulty in railroad management . . . lies in the covetousness, want of good faith, and low moral tone of railway managers, in the complete absence of any high standard of commercial honesty."

The present-day white-collar criminals, who are more suave and deceptive than the "robber barons," are represented by Krueger, Stavisky, Whitney, Mitchell, Foshay, Insull, the Van Sweringens, Musica-Coster, Fall, Sinclair, and many other merchant princes and captains of finance and industry, and by a host of lesser followers. Their criminality has been demonstrated again and again in the investigations of land offices, railways, insurance, munitions, banking, public utilities, stock exchanges, the oil industry, real estate, reorganization committees, receiverships, bankruptcies, and politics. Individual cases of such criminality are reported frequently, and in many periods more important crime news may be found on the financial pages of newspapers than on the front pages. White-collar criminality is found in every occupation, as can be discovered readily in casual conversation with a representative of an occupation by asking him, "What crooked practices are found in your occupation?"

White-collar criminality in business is expressed most frequently in the form of misrepresentation in financial statements of corporations, manipulation in the stock exchange, commercial bribery, bribery of public officials directly or indirectly in order to secure favorable contracts and legislation, misrepresentation in advertising and salesmanship, embezzlement and misapplication of funds, short weights and measures and misgrading of commodities tax frauds, misapplication of funds in receiverships and bankruptcies. These are what Al Capone called "the legitimate rackets." These and many others are found in abundance in the business world.

In the medical profession, which is here used as an example because it is probably less criminalistic than some other professions, are found illegal sale of alcohol and narcotics, abortion, illegal services to underworld criminals, fraudulent reports and testimony in accident cases, extreme cases of unnecessary treatment, fake specialists, restriction of competition, and fee-splitting. Fee-splitting is a violation of a specific law in many states and a violation of the conditions of admission to the practice of medicine in all. The physician who participates in fee-splitting tends to send his patients to the surgeon who will give him the largest fee rather than to the surgeon who will do the best work. It has been reported that two thirds of the surgeons in New York City split fees, and that more than one half of the physicians in a central western city who answered a questionnaire on this point favored fee-splitting.

These varied types of white-collar crimes in business and the professions consist principally of violation of delegated or implied trust, and many of them can be reduced to two categories: misrepresentation of asset values and duplicity in the manipulation of power. The first is approximately the same as fraud or swindling; the second is similar to the double-cross. The latter is illustrated by the corporation director who, acting on inside information, purchases land which the corporation will need and sells it at a fantastic profit to his corporation. The principle of this duplicity is that the offender holds two antagonistic positions, one of which is a position of trust, which is violated, generally by misapplication of funds, in the interest of the other position. A football coach, permitted to referee a game in which his own team was playing, would illustrate this antagonism of positions. Such situations cannot be completely avoided in a complicated business structure, but many concerns make a practice of assuming such antagonistic functions and regularly violating the trust thus delegated to them. When compelled by law to make a separation of their functions, they make a nominal separation and continue by subterfuge to maintain the two positions.

An accurate statistical comparison of the crimes of the two classes is not available. The most extensive evidence regarding the nature and prevalence of white-collar criminality is found in the reports of the larger investigations to which reference was made. Because of its scattered character, that evidence is assumed rather than summarized here. A few statements will be presented, as illustrations rather than as proof of the prevalence of this criminality.

The Federal Trade Commission in 1920 reported that commercial bribery was a prevalent and common practice in many industries. In certain chain stores, the net shortage in weights was sufficient to pay 3.4 percent on the investment in those commodities. Of the cans of ether sold to the Army in 1923–1925, 70 percent were rejected because of impurities. In Indiana, during the summer of 1934, 40 percent of the ice cream samples tested in a routine manner by the Division of Public Health were in violation of law. The Comptroller of the Currency in 1908 reported that violations of law were found in 75 percent of the banks examined in a three months' period. Lie detector tests of all employees in several Chicago banks, supported in almost all cases by confessions, showed that 20 percent of them had stolen bank property. A public accountant estimated, in the period prior to the Securities and Exchange Commission, that 80 percent of the financial statements of corporations were misleading. James M. Beck said, "Diogenes would have been hard put to it to find an honest man in the Wall Street which I knew as a corporation lawyer" (in 1916).

White-collar criminality in politics, which is generally recognized as fairly prevalent, has been used by some as a rough gauge by which to measure white-collar criminality in business. James A. Farley said, "The standards of conduct are as high among officeholders and politicians as they are in commercial life," and Cermak, while mayor of Chicago, said, "There is less graft in politics than in business." John Flynn wrote, "The average politician is the merest amateur in the gentle art of graft, compared with his brother in the field of business." And Walter Lippmann wrote, "Poor as they are, the standards of public life are so much more social than those of business that financiers who enter politics regard themselves as philanthropists."

These statements obviously do not give a precise measurement of the relative criminality of the white-collar class, but they are adequate evidence that crime is not so highly concentrated in the lower class as the usual statistics indicate. Also, these statements obviously do not mean that every business and professional man is a criminal, just as the usual theories do not mean that every man in the lower class is a criminal. On the other hand, the preceding statements refer in many cases to the leading corporations in America and are not restricted to the disreputable business and professional men who are called quacks, ambulance chasers, bucket-shop operators, dead-beats, and fly-by-night swindlers.[2]

---

[2] Perhaps it should be repeated that "white-collar" (upper) and "lower" classes merely designate persons of high and low socioeconomic status. Income and amount

The financial cost of white-collar crime is probably several times as great as the financial cost of all the crimes which are customarily regarded as the "crime problem." An officer of a chain grocery store in one year embezzled $600,000, which was six times as much as the annual losses from five hundred burglaries and robberies of the stores in that chain. Public enemies numbered one to six secured $130,000 by burglary and robbery in 1938, while the sum stolen by Krueger is estimated at $250,000,000, or nearly two thousand times as much. *The New York Times* in 1931 reported four cases of embezzlement in the United States with a loss of more than a million dollars each and a combined loss of nine million dollars. Although a million-dollar burglar or robber is practically unheard of, these million-dollar embezzlers are small-fry among white-collar criminals. The estimated loss to investors in one investment trust from 1929 to 1935 was $580,000,000 due primarily to the fact that 75 percent of the values in the portfolio were in securities of affiliated companies, although it advertised the importance of diversification in investments and its expert services in selecting safe securities. In Chicago, the claim was made six years ago that householders had lost $54,000,000 in two years during the administration of a city sealer who granted immunity from inspection to stores which provided Christmas baskets for his constituents.

The financial loss from white-collar crime, great as it is, is less important than the damage to social relations. White-collar crimes violate trust and therefore create distrust, which lowers social morale and produces social disorganization on a large scale. Other crimes produce relatively little effect on social institutions or social organization.

White-collar crime is real crime. It is not ordinarily called crime, and calling it by this name does not make it worse, just as refraining from calling it crime does not make it better than it otherwise would be. It is called crime here in order to bring it within the scope of criminology, which is justified because it is in violation of the criminal law. The crucial question in this analysis is the criterion of violation of the criminal law. Conviction in the criminal court, which is sometimes suggested as the criterion, is not adequate because a large proportion of those who commit crimes are not convicted in criminal courts. This criterion, therefore, needs to be supplemented. When it is supplemented, the criterion of the crimes of one class must be kept consistent in general terms with the criterion of the crimes of the other class. The definition should not be the spirit of the law for white-collar crimes and the letter of the law for other crimes, or in other

of money involved in the crime are not the sole criteria. Many persons of "low" socioeconomic status are "white-collar" criminals in the sense that they are well-dressed, well-educated, and have high incomes, but "white-collar" as used in this paper means "respected," "socially accepted and approved," 'looked up to." Some people in this class may not be well-dressed or well-educated, nor have high incomes, although the "upper" usually exceed the "lower" classes in these respects as well as in social status.

respects be more liberal for one class than for the other. Since this discussion is concerned with the conventional theories of the criminologists, the criterion of white-collar crime must be justified in terms of the procedures of those criminologists in dealing with other crimes. The criterion of white-collar crimes, as here proposed, supplements convictions in the criminal courts in four respects, in each of which the extension is justified because the criminologists who present the conventional theories of criminal behavior make the same extension in principle.

First, other agencies than the criminal court must be included, for the criminal court is not the only agency which makes official decisions regarding violations of the criminal law. The juvenile court, dealing largely with offenses of the children of the poor, in many states is not under the criminal jurisdiction. The criminologists have made much use of case histories and statistics of juvenile delinquents in constructing their theories of criminal behavior. This justifies the inclusion of agencies other than the criminal court which deal with white-collar offenses. The most important of these agencies are the administrative boards, bureaus, or commissions, and much of their work, although certainly not all, consists of cases which are in violation of the criminal law. The Federal Trade Commission recently ordered several automobile companies to stop advertising their interest rate on installment purchases as 6 percent, since it was actually 11½ percent. Also it filed complaint against *Good Housekeeping*, one of the Hearst publications, charging that its seals led the public to believe that all products bearing those seals had been tested in their laboratories, which was contrary to fact. Each of these involves a charge of dishonesty, which might have been tried in a criminal court as fraud. A large proportion of the cases before these boards should be included in the data of the criminologists. Failure to do so is a principal reason for the bias in their samples and the errors in their generalizations.

Second, for both classes, behavior which would have a reasonable expectancy of conviction if tried in a criminal court or substitute agency should be defined as criminal. In this respect, convictability rather than actual conviction should be the criterion of criminality. The criminologists would not hesitate to accept as data a verified case history of a person who was a criminal but had never been convicted. Similarly, it is justifiable to include white-collar criminals who have not been convicted, provided reliable evidence is available. Evidence regarding such cases appears in many civil suits, such as stockholders' suits and patent-infringement suits. These cases might have been referred to the criminal court but they were referred to the civil court because the injured party was more interested in securing damages than in seeing punishment inflicted. This also happens in embezzlement cases, regarding which surety companies have much evidence.

In a short consecutive series of embezzlements known to a surety company, 90 percent were not prosecuted because prosecution would interfere with restitution or salvage. The evidence in cases of embezzlement is generally conclusive, and would probably have been sufficient to justify conviction in all of the cases in this series.

Third, behavior should be defined as criminal if conviction is avoided merely because of pressure which is brought to bear on the court or substitute agency. Gangsters and racketeers have been relatively immune in many cities because of their pressure on prospective witnesses and public officials, and professional thieves, such as pickpockets and confidence men who do not use strong-arm methods, are even more frequently immune. The conventional criminologists do not hesitate to include the life histories of such criminals as data, because they understand the generic relation of the pressures to the failure to convict. Similarly, white-collar criminals are relatively immune because of the class bias of the courts and the power of their class to influence the implementation and administration of the law. This class bias affects not merely present-day courts but to a much greater degree affected the earlier courts which established the precedents and rules of procedure of the present-day courts. Consequently, it is justifiable to interpret the actual or potential failures of conviction in the light of known facts regarding the pressures brought to bear on the agencies which deal with offenders.

Fourth, persons who are accessory to a crime should be included among white-collar criminals as they are among other criminals. When the Federal Bureau of Investigation deals with a case of kidnapping, it is not content with catching the offenders who carried away the victim; they may catch and the court may convict twenty-five other persons who assisted by secreting the victim, negotiating the ransom, or putting the ransom money into circulation. On the other hand, the prosecution of white-collar criminals frequently stops with one offender. Political graft almost always involves collusion between politicians and business men but prosecutions are generally limited to the politicians. Judge Manton was found guilty of accepting $664,000 in bribes, but the six or eight important commercial concerns that paid the bribes have not been prosecuted. Pendergast, the late boss of Kansas City, was convicted for failure to report as a part of his income $315,000 received in bribes from insurance companies but the insurance companies which paid the bribes have not been prosecuted. In an investigation of an embezzlement by the president of a bank, at least a dozen other violations of law which were related to this embezzlement and involved most of the other officers of the bank and the officers of the clearing house, were discovered but none of the others was prosecuted.

This analysis of the criterion of white-collar criminality results in the conclusion that a description of white-collar criminality in general terms will be also a description of the criminality of the lower class. The respects in which the crimes of the two classes differ are the incidentals rather than the essentials of criminality. They differ principally in the implementation of the criminal laws which apply to them. The crimes of the lower class are handled by policemen, prosecutors, and judges, with penal sanctions in the form of fines, imprisonment, and death. The crimes of the upper class either result in no official action at all, or result in suits for damages in civil courts, or are handled by inspectors, and by administrative boards or commissions, with penal sanctions in the form of warnings, orders to cease and desist, occasionally the loss of a license, and only in extreme cases by fines or prison sentences. Thus, the white-collar criminals are segregated administratively from other criminals, and largely as a consequence of this are not regarded as real criminals by themselves, the general public, or the criminologists.

This difference in the implementation of the criminal law is due principally to the difference in the social position of the two types of offenders. Judge Woodward, when imposing sentence upon the officials of the H. O. Stone and Company, bankrupt real estate firm in Chicago, who had been convicted in 1933 of the use of the mails to defraud, said to them, "You are men of affairs, of experience, of refinement and culture, of excellent reputation and standing in the business and social world." That statement might be used as a general characterization of white-collar criminals for they are oriented basically to legitimate and respectable careers. Because of their social status they have a loud voice in determining what goes into the statutes and how the criminal law as it affects themselves is implemented and administered. This may be illustrated from the Pure Food and Drug Law. Between 1879 and 1906, 140 pure food and drug bills were presented in Congress and all failed because of the importance of the persons who would be affected. It took a highly dramatic performance by Dr. Wiley in 1906 to induce Congress to enact the law. That law, however, did not create a new crime, just as the federal Lindbergh kidnapping law did not create a new crime; it merely provided a more efficient implementation of a principle which had been formulated previously in state laws. When an amendment to this law, which would bring within the scope of its agents fraudulent statements made over the radio or in the press, was presented to Congress, the publishers and advertisers organized support and sent a lobby to Washington which successfully fought the amendment principally under the slogans of "freedom of the press" and "dangers of bureaucracy." This proposed amendment, also, would not have created a new crime, for the state laws already prohibited fraudulent statements over the radio or in the press; it would have implemented the law so it could have been enforced. Finally, the Administration has not been able to enforce the law as it has desired because of the pressures by the offenders against the law, sometimes brought to bear through the head of the Department of Agriculture, sometimes through congressmen who threaten cuts in the appropriation, and sometimes by others. The statement of Daniel Drew, a pious old fraud, describes the criminal law with some accuracy, "Law is like a cobweb; it's made for flies and the smaller kinds of insects, so to speak, but lets the big bumblebees break through. When technicalities of the law stood in my way, I have always been able to brush them aside easy as anything."

The preceding analysis should be regarded neither as an assertion that all efforts to influence legislation and its administration are reprehensible nor as a particularistic interpretation of the criminal law. It means only that the upper class has greater influence in moulding the criminal law and its administration to its own interests than does the lower class. The privileged position of white-collar criminals before the law results to a slight extent from bribery and political pressures, principally from the respect in which they are held and without special effort on their part. The most powerful group in medieval society secured relative immunity by "benefit of clergy," and now our most powerful groups secure relative immunity by "benefit of business or profession."

In contrast with the power of the white-collar criminals is the weakness of their victims. Consumers, investors, and stockholders are unorganized, lack technical knowledge, and cannot protect themselves. Daniel Drew, after taking a large sum of money by sharp practice from Vanderbilt in the Erie deal, concluded that it was a mistake to take money from a powerful man on the same level as himself and declared that in the future he would confine his efforts to outsiders, scattered all over the country, who wouldn't be able to organize and fight back. White-collar criminality flourishes at points where powerful business and professional men come in contact with persons who are weak. In this respect, it is similar to stealing candy from a baby. Many of the crimes of the lower class, on the other hand, are committed against persons of wealth and power in the form of burglary and robbery. Because of this difference in the comparative power of the victims, the white-collar criminals enjoy relative immunity.

Embezzlement is an interesting exception to white-collar criminality in this respect. Embezzlement is usually theft from an employer by an employee, and the employee is less capable of manipulating social and legal forces in his own interest than is the employer. As might have been expected, the laws regarding embezzlement were formulated long before laws for the protection of investors and consumers.

The theory that criminal behavior in general is due either to poverty or to the psychopathic and sociopathic conditions associated with poverty can now be shown to be invalid for three reasons. First, the generalization is based on a biased sample which omits almost entirely the behavior of white-collar criminals. The criminologists have restricted their data, for reasons of convenience and ignorance rather than of principle, largely to cases dealt with in criminal courts and juvenile courts, and these agencies are used principally for criminals from the lower economic strata. Consequently, their data are grossly biased from the point of view of the economic status of criminals and their generalization that criminality is closely associated with poverty is not justified.

Second, the generalization that criminality is closely associated with poverty obviously does not apply to white-collar criminals. With a small number of exceptions, they are not in poverty, were not reared in slums or badly deteriorated families, and are not feebleminded or psychopathic. They were seldom problem children in their earlier years and did not appear in juvenile courts or child guidance clinics. The proposition, derived from the data used by the conventional criminologists that "the criminal of today was the problem child of yesterday" is seldom true of white-collar criminals. The idea that the causes of criminality are to be found almost exclusively in childhood similarly is fallacious. Even if poverty is extended to include the economic stresses which afflict business in a period of depression, it is not closely correlated with white-collar criminality. Probably at no time within fifty years have white-collar crimes in the field of investments and of corporate management been so extensive as during the boom period of the twenties.

Third, the conventional theories do not even explain lower class criminality. The sociopathic and psychopathic factors which have been emphasized doubtless have something to do with crime causation, but these factors have not been related to a general process which is found both in white-collar criminality and lower class criminality and therefore they do not explain the criminality of either class. They may explain the manner or method of crime—why lower class criminals commit burglary or robbery rather than false pretenses.

In view of these defects in the conventional theories, an hypothesis that will explain both white-collar criminality and lower class criminality is needed. For reasons of economy, simplicity, and logic, the hypothesis should apply to both classes, for this will make possible the analysis of causal factors freed from the encumbrances of the administrative devices which have led criminologists astray. Shaw and McKay and others, working exclusively in the field of lower class crime, have found the conventional theories inadequate to account for variations within the data of lower class crime and from that point of view have been working toward an explanation of crime in terms of a more general social process. Such efforts will be greatly aided by the procedure which has been described.

The hypothesis which is here suggested as a substitute for the conventional theories is that white-collar criminality, just as other systematic criminality, is learned; that it is learned in direct or indirect association with those who already practice the behavior; and that those who learn this criminal behavior are segregated from frequent and intimate contacts with law-abiding behavior. Whether a person becomes a criminal or not is determined largely by the comparative frequency and intimacy of his contacts with the two types of behavior. This may be called the process of differential association. It is a genetic explanation both of white-collar criminality and lower class criminality. Those who become white-collar criminals generally start their careers in good neighborhoods and good homes, graduate from colleges with some idealism, and with little selection on their part, get into particular business situations in which criminality is practically a folkway and are inducted into that system of behavior just as into any other folkway. The lower class criminals generally start their careers in deteriorated neighborhoods and families, find delinquents at hand from whom they acquire the attitudes toward, and techniques of, crime through association with delinquents and in partial segregation from law-abiding people. The essentials of the process are the same for the two classes of criminals. This is not entirely a process of assimilation, for inventions are frequently made, perhaps more frequently in white-collar crime than in lower class crime. The inventive geniuses for the lower class criminals are generally professional criminals, while the inventive geniuses for many kinds of white-collar crime are generally lawyers.

A second general process is social disorganization in the community. Differential association culminates in crime because the community is not organized solidly against that behavior. The law is pressing in one direction, and other forces are pressing in the opposite direction. In business, the "rules of the game" conflict with the legal rules. A business man who wants to obey the law is driven by his competitors to adopt their methods. This is well illustrated by the persistence of commercial bribery in spite of the strenuous efforts of business organizations to eliminate it. Groups and individuals are individuated; they are more concerned with their specialized group or individual interests than with the larger welfare. Consequently, it is not possible for the community to present a solid front in opposition to crime. The Better Business Bureaus and Crime Commissions, composed of business and professional men, attack burglary, robbery, and cheap swindles, but overlook the crimes of their own members. The forces which impinge on the lower class are similarly in conflict. Social disorganization affects the two classes in similar ways.

I have presented a brief and general description of white-collar criminality on a framework of argument regarding theories of criminal behavior. That argument, stripped of the description, may be stated in the following propositions:

1. White-collar criminality is real criminality, being in all cases in violation of the criminal law.

2. White-collar criminality differs from lower class criminality princi-

pally in an implementation of the criminal law which segregates white-collar criminals administratively from other criminals.

3. The theories of the criminologists that crime is due to poverty or to psychopathic and sociopathic conditions statistically associated with poverty are invalid because, first, they are derived from samples which are grossly biased with respect to socioeconomic status; second, they do not apply to the white-collar criminals; and third, they do not even explain the criminality of the lower class, since the factors are not related to a general process characteristic of all criminality.

4. A theory of criminal behavior which will explain both white-collar criminality and lower class criminality is needed.

5. An hypothesis of this nature is suggested in terms of differential association and social disorganization.

6 Juvenile Delinquency in the Middle-Class Youth Culture*

EDMUND W. VAZ

A youth culture of middle-class adolescents is not endemic to a society. Adolescents have not always been as freely available to one another as they are today. Their community of interests, consensus of opinion, and the uniformities of action that spotlight the contemporary scene constitute a relatively new phenomenon in society, one not easily envisaged in the past. Seventy-five years ago the social structure of society, the organization of family life, educational standards, rights and obligations of the student role, and the routine activities among middle-class youth tended to handicap the emergence of a middle-class youth culture.

Few are the middle-class children today who are reared in an atmosphere of Puritan severity. No longer must children be seen and not heard, kept indoors, and off the streets. Patterns of hard work and hard saving are apt to be a thing of the past. No longer is it enough for a boy to enjoy the right to the opportunity of an education; there exists the felt right to a high school diploma, and a college degree is becoming more a matter of

* Part of this article is taken from "Middle-Class Adolescents: Self-Reported Delinquency and Youth Culture Activities," *The Canadian Review of Sociology and Anthropology*, Vol. 2, No. 1 (February, 1965), 52–70. Reprinted by permission of the editor.

perseverance than of burning the midnight oil. Relaxed parental control in today's middle-class family, and the general freedom enjoyed by adolescents have been used traditionally to explain lower-class adolescent behavior. Use of the now popular term "street-corner society" is no longer warranted to describe the joint activities of lower-class boys only. The corner drug store, the drive-in, and the coffee bar are as much a precinct of the middle-class teen-ager as of his lower-class brother.

The world of middle-class boys is largely peer oriented, conspicuously non-intellectual, and is outstanding for its concern with status and the pursuit of "fun and games." Notwithstanding the diversity and size of groups among these boys, they possess a relatively common system of values, norms, and practices, and their collective behavior patterns are distinguishable. Their tacit ratification of norms, and conformity to existing practices, foster the flow of teen-age behavior and reflect its legitimacy within the culture. This has helped strengthen the role of adolescent in the middle-class, given it newly won status, and has contributed to the stability of the youth culture.

The content of the middle-class youth culture is neither delinquent nor rebellious, and seldom does it antagonize middle-class sentiments. Usually it reflects adult expectations, values, and institutions, and adult groups have encouraged development of the youth culture, advertised its prominence, and utilized its resources which has strengthened its position within the larger system. The proliferation of "extracurricular" activities has received widespread parental approval and mirrors the proclaimed educational value of the "life adjustment" and "social maturity" of the child. This congruence of attitudes between parents and educators lends structural support to the youth culture. Not only do parents encourage youth participation in social events, they also organize opportunities for regular teen-age activities. The respectability and popularity of these activities help convince parents (and adolescents) of their value, and the variety of programs testifies to widespread adult concern for adolescent participation. This tends to strengthen adolescent relationships and helps build mutual respect between adolescents and adults in the community.

Similarly, communal support of high school athletics has kept pace with the rapid growth of college and professional sports. High schools serve as preparatory training grounds for professional talent, and organized sports (e.g., Little League Baseball) has contributed widely to the general popularity of sports in the high school and community. Successful high school teams enhance community status and the reputation of families of participating athletes. Communal moral support and financial subsidization contribute to the development of athletic talent for schools, and spotlight its value for the community. The convergence of common purpose and action between community and schools reaffirms common values. Continued interest and participation by students comply with adult expectations, and promote the general reputation of schools, coaches, and of athletes in the youth culture, which helps consolidate the youth culture within the larger institutional network.

Full "membership" in the adolescent system is contingent largely upon the exercise of one's role, which requires active participation in youth culture activities and relationships. Learning the skills and nuances of a role often occurs through trial and error, but it also requires instruction from others. Middle-class youngsters are tutored early in the conduct required for future social success. Participation in age-restricted, sometimes adult-supervised social events, introduces youngsters to incipient forms of hetero-sexual relations and teen-age games. Older boys and the mass media are also valuable sources of instruction in the details and marginal maneuvers used in "handling" the opposite sex.

The significance of "socializing" for the middle-class adolescent cannot be overemphasized. Both teachers and parents expect the child to be a "joiner," and, to perform his role adequately, active participation in teen-age events is mandatory. Boys who pursue academic interests only are noticeably disapproved. Yet the student who excels both academically and socially is fully acceptable and mirrors the success of the educational system.

The pursuit of status is intense among middle-class adolescents, and often it is to his peers that the adolescent looks for respect. Peer-group membership and conformity to role expectations confer social approbation and tend to publicize (through frequency of interaction) collective teen-age solidarity. In a newly developing culture where norms are not fully institutionalized, where structural stability and internal coherence are only partially realized, and where traditional role expectations are obscure, conformity as a moral imperative is especially helpful and desirable.

COMPETITION

Competition pervades all parts of a boy's life in the middle-class youth culture. It influences his choice of clothes, his preference in music and girls, his necking techniques, and the manipulation of his car. Peer-group standards are often the critical criteria by which a boy forms his opinions and gauges his behavior. Throughout his daily activities competition prevails, and peers stand alert to criticize, to pass judgment, and to offer approval. Ultimately, competition with "everyman" becomes "internalized" and the "generalized other" becomes an ubiquitous audience always keeping score. The absence of others, or the fact that only strangers are present, fails to deter a boy's struggle for attention. Continuously on parade even when he is alone, the adolescent "guns" his engine, "drags" the streets, squeals the tires of his automobile ("lays a patch"), coercing attention, seeking approval.

Were competition uncontrolled in the youth culture, it might corrode friendships and damage group relationships. The conditions under which current teen-age activities occur tend to preserve social ties and strengthen group cohesion. Typically, adolescent activity occurs under a veneer of non-competitive good-fellowship and fun. This unserious quality to their joint activity fosters their belief in the impression that they create. And the rhetoric in terms of which they describe their behavior, "It's all in fun," "It's just for kicks," or "We were just having a few laughs," enables them to escape opprobrium should they be accused of more deliberate competitive-ness. Increasing use of this vocabulary of motives obscures underlying com-petition, and tends to prevent them from making clear-cut distinctions among their everyday practices and games. Thus, "heavy" necking, "hooliganism," "playing chicken" at 100 m.p.h., drinking bouts, and sexual escapades are often described as merely "having fun."

MARGINAL DIFFERENTIATION

Throughout the daily legitimate activities (dating, dances, riding about with friends, "hanging" about the drug store, playing sports, etc.) of middle-class boys, veiled competition for status stimulates their experimentation in behavior. These "operating inventions"[1] attract others, win approval and nourish competition, and take the form of behavioral nuances, sufficiently novel to distinguish them from existing patterns and competing efforts of peers. Although all behavior is, perhaps, partly exploratory, stabs at marginal differentiation are likely to be guarded, tentative, ambiguous, and to transpire in a situation characterized by "joint exploration and elabora-tion" of behavior.[2] Yet extreme conduct of any kind is apt to be strongly disapproved among "sophisticated" youths, and there exist strong motivations to conform to prevailing norms and patterns. But the boundaries of legit-imacy are not impregnable, and it is during these legitimate fun-ridden activities, where boys are encouraged to join in, that unobtrusive acts lead gradually to unanticipated elaboration beyond the precincts of legitimacy. Since adolescent activities occur in a spirit of good will, creative efforts are applauded, encouraged, and behavioral novelty is seldom considered delinquent. However, innovation is tolerated only within the limits of

[1] Robert Dubin, "Deviant Behavior and Social Structure: Continuities in Social Theory," *American Sociological Review*, 24 (April, 1959), 152.

[2] The basic idea is taken from Albert K. Cohen, *Delinquent Boys*, Glencoe, Ill.: Free Press, 1955, p. 60.

acceptable adolescent interests. In this way behavioral differentiation does little injury to existing norms and values, and group status is not undermined. As newly developing practices gain approval, they acquire their own morality, and each move becomes circumscribed by game rules. In this setting delinquency needs not emerge from anti-social motives. Delinquent acts, rooted in anti-social impulses, are apt to transgress acceptable conduct, violate middle-class norms, and be disapproved altogether. The motives for much middle-class delinquency are learned through sustained participation in everyday respectable, adolescent activities. In this manner delinquency becomes gradually routine in the middle-class youth culture.

To help substantiate some of the ideas in this paper, evidence is presented from a larger study of middle-class delinquency. Data on the self-reported delinquency of 850 middle-class boys are offered and interpreted according to their social roles in the youth culture. Evidence is presented on the relationship between differential delinquency involvement and (a) the active participation of boys in legitimate teen-age activities, and (b) their peer orientation. Data are included on the relationship between the seriousness with which boys perceive engaging in delinquent acts and their differential participation in legitimate teen-age activities. To emphasize the delinquent content of the middle-class youth culture, the relationship between differential delinquency involvement and the seriousness with which boys define engaging in delinquent acts is investigated.

RESEARCH

During the spring of 1963 questionnaires were administered to 1,639 white high school boys in grades 9 through 13 in five coeducational high schools located in four Canadian communities. Appropriate techniques were used to minimize collusion and maximize anonymity of subjects. The communities differ in size and are urban or semi-urban in character, and the high schools are located in middle-class socioeconomic areas.

Delinquency was measured by a check list of 21 items of behavior. The items are violations of the law or are offenses on the basis of which juveniles can be adjudicated as delinquent. Both serious and minor offenses are included, such as driving a car beyond the speed limit, breaking and entering, intoxication, and the use of drugs for kicks. Offenses such as gang fights, armed robbery, and rape were not included. The boys were asked how often they had committed each offense; response categories included very often, quite often, several times, once or twice, never.

To establish the socioeconomic position of subjects, three indicators were used in the following order: (a) father's occupation, (b) father's level of education, and (c) size of organization in which father works. Using father's occupation, subjects were first classified according to the Blishen Occupational Class Scale.[3] Questionnaires initially difficult to classify, or that included only father's level of education, were reviewed and grouped according to the second indicator. Subjects whose fathers had "completed high school" or completed "some college" were classified into Group III, and those who had "finished college" or higher were sorted into Group II. A small number of remaining questionnaires, with ambiguously reported job titles only, were categorized with the help of the third indicator according to the writer's judgment. All subjects classified into Groups II ($n =$ 337) and III ($n = 513$) were combined and hereafter are termed "middle-class."

Table 1 reveals sharp differences in the responses of younger and older boys. Important considerations in interpreting the data are the social roles of middle-class boys and the rights and obligations—varying sets of role criteria—by which boys may claim status to their roles. To the extent that a boy conforms to these criteria his peers will judge and reward him accordingly.

Some of the delinquent practices are more realistically possible and readily available for older boys as relevant criteria of status. For younger boys these practices are less meaningful to their social role. To learn the rules and tricks of smoking marijuana or of purchasing liquor takes time and effort and requires the opportunity. Youngsters are apt not to claim status in terms of these practices. Nevertheless, younger and older boys share in part, a relatively common frame of experience. In and out of school, on and off the playing field, youngsters show deference to their teen-age elders, strengthen growing identifications, and they are eager to learn and anxious to participate. Thus, drinking games, sexual intimacy with girls, and truancy are not uncommon among these boys.

As youngsters assume gradually the role of older teen-ager new attitudes and practices are required of them. New criteria become applicable in terms of which peers judge them and, depending upon their ego-involvement in their role, they evaluate themselves. Older boys care less about the practices and criteria of status that matter to younger lads. What a youngster considers serious an older boy will define as "kid stuff." Delinquent activities that are relatively popular among boys occupying different roles will depend on the alternative criteria available for status gain.

Table 1 shows that petty theft is the only offense committed by the majority of younger boys. Other popular delinquencies, among younger boys, include fist fighting, vandalism, gambling, stealing money, and drink-

---

[3] See Bernard Blishen, "The Construction and Use of an Occupational Class Scale," *Canadian Journal of Economics and Political Science*, 24 (November, 1958), 519–531.

TABLE 1. SELF-REPORTED DELINQUENT BEHAVIOR OF MIDDLE-CLASS BOYS BY AGE GROUP

Type of Offense[a]	Percent Admitting Commission of Offense Age		Percent Admitting Commission of Offense More than Once or Twice Age	
	13–14	15–19	13–14	15–19
Driven a car without a driver's license	28.6	62.3	9.1	27.9
Taken little things that did not belong to you	61.0	67.2	10.4	16.7
Skipped school without a legitimate excuse	23.6	40.8	3.9	13.6
Driven beyond the speed limit	5.8	51.2	1.3	39.7
Participated in drag-races along the highway with your friends	6.5	31.1	2.0	16.3
Engaged in a fist fight with another boy	45.8	56.0	7.1	8.7
Been feeling "high" from drinking beer, wine or liquor	11.7	39.0	2.6	17.9
Gambled for money at cards, dice, or some other game	42.2	66.0	16.9	37.4
Remained out all night without parents' permission	19.5	25.8	5.2	9.5
Taken a car without owner's knowledge	5.2	12.5	0.7	3.1
Placed on school probation or expelled from school	0.7	5.6	0.0	1.2
Destroyed or damaged public or private property of any kind	44.8	52.0	11.7	14.8
Taken little things of value (between $2 and $50) which did not belong to you	9.7	16.0	0.7	3.5
Tried to be intimate with a member of the opposite sex	18.2	37.8	7.8	17.6
Broken into or tried to break and enter a building with the intention of stealing	5.2	7.5	0.7	1.0
Sold, used or tried to use drugs of some kind	1.3	1.0	0.0	0.3
Bought or tried to buy beer, wine, or liquor from a store or adult	3.3	24.8	0.7	11.7
Taken money of any amount from someone or place which				

TABLE 1 (*Continued*)

Type of Offense[a]	Percent Admitting Commission of Offense Age		Percent Admitting Commission of Offense More than Once or Twice Age	
	13–14	15–19	13–14	15–19
did not belong to you	30.5	32.7	7.1	6.9
Taken a glass of beer, wine, or liquor at a party or elsewhere with your friends	32.5	64.8	8.4	35.2
	n = 154	682[b]		

[a] Two items are omitted because they were used solely as reliability check measures.
[b] Fourteen cases of boys over 19 years are omitted.

ing liquor. These offenses are popular also among older teen-agers, but in some cases the difference in responses is small. There is a difference of only 11 percentage points between younger and older boys who fist fight. Less than 7 percentage points separate younger and older boys who admit petty theft. About 45 percent of younger boys and 52 percent of older teen-agers report vandalic behavior.

Ironically, the world of younger boys is a masculine world, girls occupy little of their time. Their role in the middle class (perhaps among all social classes) is characterized by a particular image of masculinity. The values of adventure, bravado, manliness, and muscular prowess circumscribe their role, and usually they make every effort to prove that they are "all boy." Most younger lads approve of practices that enable them to display their courage, exhibit their physical strength, and thereby "improve" their self-image. To "take a dare," to engage in varying kinds of vandalism, fighting, and petty theft are practiced frequently among younger boys. Failure to participate in at least one of these types of games may deny a boy's claim to being "all boy" among his peers. The data indicate that typical of these boys are the more masculine offenses.

The older adolescent role requires increased participation in dominant youth culture activities. Parties, dances, sport events, cars, and girls occupy a larger part of a boy's time. "Sophistication" replaces masculinity, and a premium is put on the cultivation of social skills and a "social personality." The rougher habits of younger lads are taboo. Yet a change in roles and the gradual transformation of a boy's self-image take time and involve uncertainty and strain. Under such conditions boys are apt to revert, occasionally, to an earlier set of responses and standards to which they are still partly committed. Thus, older boys continue temporarily their earlier delinquencies. But once they learn their new role, feel committed to its standards, and begin to judge themselves by it, earlier practices, no longer serviceable, are seldom recruited. Petty theft, vandalism, stealing money, and aggressive behavior concomitant with the role of the youngster, become relics of an earlier role.

If the role of older teen-ager calls for sophisticated behavior, it tends also to generate a more sophisticated brand of delinquency. Yet, theirs is no criminal world, there is no community of delinquent gangs, no body of criminal values, malicious attitudes, and predatory skills. The young hoodlum, the adolescent thug, and the gang leader are types of a nether world. It is the crew-cut and the clean look, the "nice guy," and the high school star who claim status among these boys. Drinking, drag-racing, speeding, sex practices, truancy, and gambling assume a larger part of later adolescent behavior. At age 16 a boy immediately acquires greater access to an automobile. Besides being a symbol of status the car allows the teen-ager to expand his circle of friends, makes available girls otherwise inaccessible to him, and also offers him increased opportunity to break the law. Sixty-two percent of older boys admit having driven without a permit. Over 50 percent have driven beyond the speed limit, and 31 percent admit dragging along the highway. Admittedly, the values of courage and daring underlie the practice of dragging, but its value for these boys is less to demonstrate their masculinity than it is to exhibit their driving skills and to highlight the efficiency of their cars. Since the automobile is an extension of self, these practices enable a boy to increase his popularity among peers.

Drinking practices (at parties, sport events, in cars during intermission at high school dances), sex games with girls, and gambling are symbolic of adolescent sophistication, serviceable for youth culture participation, and very likely a means for acquiring popularity. Sixty-five percent of older boys admit drinking liquor at a party; 39 percent admit having felt "high," and over 37 percent have tried to "go the limit" with a girl. And once boys begin to drink they are expected to buy their liquor.

New interests and non-academic, time-consuming activities are necessary in maintaining a boy's popularity and very likely subvert his interest in school work. Thus, truancy tends to gain popularity among older youths. Similarly, gambling very likely increases among boys who gradually obtain larger sums of money. Most of these activities are predominantly sociable forms of delinquency and, apart from the intimate stages of sexual congress, are seldom practiced in private. They strengthen peer-group relationships, consolidate normative patterns among teen-agers, and contribute to the cohesion of the middle-class youth culture.

Table 1 shows also that sociable delinquencies such as automobile offenses, drinking, gambling, and sex violations rank highest among older boys who admit committing offenses more than once or twice.

DELINQUENCY INVOLVEMENT AMONG MIDDLE-CLASS BOYS

In order to establish the differential delinquency involvement of boys, two Guttman scales were obtained.[4] Eleven items were selected on the basis that they might measure a common dimension of middle-class delinquency and using 850 boys, aged 13–19, eight of the items scale satisfactorily. Dichotomizing each item, a reproducibility coefficient of .920 was obtained with random distribution of error. Scale items include: taken little things that did not belong to you; gambled for money at cards, dice, or other games; driven a car beyond the speed limit; skipped school without a legitimate excuse; been feeling "high" from drinking beer, wine, or liquor; bought or tried to buy beer, wine, or liquor from a store or adult; taken a glass of beer, wine, or liquor at a party or elsewhere with your friends; and tried to be intimate (go the limit) with a member of the opposite sex.

A second scale was obtained for 682 boys aged 15 to 19. Dichotomizing each item, eight items scale satisfactorily giving a reproducibility coefficient of .914. Scale items include: taken little things that did not belong to you; taken a glass of beer, wine, or liquor at a party or elsewhere with your friends; driven a car beyond the speed limit; been feeling "high" from drinking beer, wine, or liquor; driven a car without a driver's license or permit; tried to be intimate (go the limit) with a member of the opposite sex; bought or tried to buy beer, wine, or liquor; and skipped school. Each delinquency scale was trichotomized into low, medium, and high categories.

Not all boys engage actively in the social events of the middle-class youth culture, and not all delinquency is found among those who do. However, it is noteworthy that our scales highlight a non-violent component of delinquency. Items such as drinking liquor, skipping school, speeding, purchasing liquor, and sexual intimacy are noticeably sociable practices, and are conspicuously in accord with the typical, legitimate affairs of the youth culture. This kind of conduct seems to "fit" the sophisticated self-image of the older middle-class adolescent.

Two situation-type items (each with two response categories) were used to establish the peer orientation of boys. Three items were used to measure the active participation of boys in typical teen-age activities. One item deals

---

[4] See also the work of F. Ivan Nye and James Short, Jr., "Scaling Delinquent Behavior," *American Sociological Review*, 22 (June, 1957), 326–331. Also, John F. Scott, "Two Dimensions of Delinquent Behavior," *American Sociological Review*, 24 (April, 1959), 240–243.

with the time a boy spends riding about with his friends in the evenings. The second concerns the frequency of dating girls. The third item enquires about the time a boy spends around the local "hangout" in the evenings. Each item has five weighted response categories, and cases were distributed into high, medium, and low categories.

DIFFERENTIAL DELINQUENCY INVOLVEMENT AND PEER-GROUP ORIENTATION

Ordinarily adolescents are preoccupied with those of their own kind, friends and acquaintances who hold their values, share their opinions, and talk their language. Recurrent participation in peer activities tends to increase one's status in the eyes of peers, and opportunities (dates, parties, dances, etc.) for further social activity are the cherished rewards for conformity to prevailing norms. Under these conditions, to be a "loner" is a passport to pariahdom, but from our perspective the "loner," the boy who is not peer-oriented, is less apt to engage in delinquency.

When each peer orientation item is tested against delinquent participation, results are significant ($p < .001$). In each case the majority of peer-oriented boys rates high in delinquency. Boys who favor parents rank lower in delinquency. To substantiate further these results, composite results of the peer orientation items were cross tabulated with delinquency involvement.

Table 2 indicates that over 80 percent of high peer-orientated boys aged 15 to 19 rank high or medium in delinquency. Being parent-oriented is no guarantee against delinquency, but considerably fewer parent-oriented boys are highly delinquent. If we are correct, peer-oriented boys are more in

TABLE 2. COMBINED ITEMS ON PEER ORIENTATION BY DIFFERENTIAL DELINQUENCY INVOLVEMENT: MIDDLE-CLASS ADOLESCENTS BY AGE GROUPS

| | Delinquency Involvement | | | | | |
| | 15–19 Years | | | All Ages | | |
Peer Orientation	High	Med.	Low	High	Med.	Low
High	13.2	14.1	6.2	14.0	11.8	6.0
Medium	7.9	18.5	18.0	10.0	18.2	17.4
Low	2.9	7.8	9.4	3.7	6.5	10.7
Non-responses	0.0	0.0	0.0	0.0	0.0	0.0
		$n = 682$			850	
	$x^2 = 58.03$, 4df, $p < .001$			$x^2 = 75.36$, 4df, $p < .001$		
	$C = .283$ $\overline{C} = .346$			$C = .287$ $\overline{C} = .352$		

demand in the typical carrousel of teen-age activities of which delinquency is an unanticipated result. The more a boy engages in such events the greater the likelihood of his becoming delinquent.

DIFFERENTIAL DELINQUENCY INVOLVEMENT AND YOUTH CULTURE PARTICIPATION

We have described the middle-class youth culture as predominantly social in character. We have implied that the boy who has ready access to an automobile, who dates girls, attends dances, who goes to parties, and who is regularly engaged in sports is more likely to begin drinking, drag-racing, gambling, and to become partner to sexual practices and other sophisticated forms of delinquency. The more restricted, unsociable adolescent is less apt to become so involved.

When responses to the question, "How often do you drive about with friends in the evening" were cross tabulated with delinquency involvement, results revealed that approximately 90 percent of boys, aged 15 to 19, who drive about with friends three or more times per week, rank high or medium in delinquency. Boys who drive about once a week or less, are much less likely to rank high in delinquency. The same pattern holds for boys of all ages ($p < .001$).

The majority of boys who date girls three or more times a week are highly involved in delinquency. Most boys who seldom or never date rank low in delinquency. Again the pattern holds for both age groups ($p < .001$).

The third item asked was, "How often do you spend some time about the local 'hangout' in the evenings throughout the whole week?" When

TABLE 3. COMBINED SCORES ON ACTIVE PARTICIPATION IN YOUTH CULTURE BY DIFFERENTIAL DELINQUENCY INVOLVEMENT: MIDDLE-CLASS ADOLESCENTS BY AGE GROUPS

Youth Culture Activities	Delinquency Involvement					
	15–19 Years			All Ages		
	High	Med.	Low	High	Med.	Low
High	15.1	16.0	3.5	16.9	10.1	3.1
Medium	7.0	18.0	15.3	9.2	18.9	12.4
Low	2.0	6.9	15.7	1.9	7.9	19.4
Non-responses	0.2	0.0	0.2	0.1	0.1	0.0
	$n = 682$			850		
	$\chi^2 = 151.26$, 4df, $p < .001$			$\chi^2 = 251.67$, 4df, $p < .001$		
	$C = .426$ $\overline{C} = .522$			$C = .478$ $\overline{C} = .586$		

responses are matched against delinquency involvement, the results are significant ($p < .001$). With an increase in the social pursuits of boys, there is an increase in their delinquent behavior. Table 3 is important because it indicates the overall youth culture participation scores of boys and their delinquency involvement. Among boys highly active in legitimate activities about 90 percent fall into the two highest delinquent categories. Among low participants about 35 percent rank high in delinquency.

ACTIVE PARTICIPATION IN YOUTH CULTURE AND BOYS' PERCEPTION OF DELINQUENT ACTS AS SERIOUS CONDUCT

The adolescent who is actively engrossed in social affairs is especially susceptible to current teen-age perspectives, attitudes, and opinions. Absorbed with his peers, listening to what they say, watching their actions, engaging in their games, prevailing teen-age attitudes gradually become part of his own behavioral and motivational baggage. Delinquency in the middle-class youth culture is an unanticipated consequence of conformity to the expected patterns of respectable teen-age behavior. Seldom is it defined illegal, and these boys rarely develop an image of themselves as delinquent. Under these circumstances certain types of delinquent practices are apt not to be taken seriously by middle-class boys. Paradoxically this relatively unserious attitude towards delinquency is learned while engaging in typically non-delinquent activities.

Twelve items were used to measure the seriousness felt by boys toward selected delinquent acts, and the distribution of scores was trichotomized into low, medium, and high categories. When responses to youth culture items are matched separately against scores on the perceived seriousness of delinquent acts, Chi-square values are significant in each instance ($p < .001$). Boys who are highly active in teen-age affairs (dating, driving about with friends, etc.) define delinquent acts less seriously than do boys who participate infrequently in such pursuits. More important is the association between overall scores on both variables (see Table 4). Again Chi-square values are significant ($p < .05$) for both age groups.

Teen-agers who are caught in the vortex of typical social activities are especially popular and enhance their social standing among peers. This is difficult to relinquish and they are apt to persist in their quest for social rewards. Through prolonged youth culture involvement they learn the prevailing attitudes and definitions and ultimately become involved in delinquency. But since this is seldom discovered and accords with routine events, neither the behavior nor the boys are apt to be considered delinquent. The seductive appeal of the middle-class youth culture and the rewards that reside therein very likely contain the seeds of delinquency.

TABLE 4. SEPARATE AND COMBINED SCORES ON THE
RELATIONSHIP BETWEEN YOUTH CULTURE ACTIVITIES
AND THE PERCEPTION OF DELINQUENT ACTS AS SERIOUS:
MIDDLE-CLASS ADOLESCENTS BY AGE GROUP

Youth Culture Activities by Perceived Seriousness of Delinquent Acts	15–19 Years			All Ages		
	x^2	C	$\overline{C}$	x^2	C	$\overline{C}$
Driving about with friends in evening	77.94 S^a	.319	.368	106.71 S	.333	.384
Takes out a girl in evening	36.72 S	.225	.275	41.11 S	.214	.262
Spends time about local "hangout"	82.80 S	.340	.380	104.13 S	.330	.369
Youth Culture Activities: Combined Scores	83.08 S	.109	.133	113.91 S	.343	.420

$^a S$ = Significant at .05 level.

A difficulty in appreciating delinquency among middle-class adolescents is that the majority of their everyday activities receive the blessing of parents, which tends to inhibit the development of a socially recognized image of the middle-class delinquent. This seeming immunity from the delinquent role perhaps confirms the teen-ager in his delinquent ways. Since delinquent practices emerge so unobtrusively from non-delinquent activities, middle-class teen-agers are apt less to define them as serious practices. Yet middle-class delinquency is not a happenstance affair. It is one thing for boys to break the rules, define their acts as serious and, perhaps, feel guilty. But boys who break rules and are indifferent about their violations are certainly to be viewed in a different light. The association between delinquency involvement and the seriousness with which they define delinquent acts suggests strongly a delinquent content to the middle-class youth culture. Moreover, it lends stability to the delinquent norms developing in the culture.

Table 5 reveals that the definition of engaging in delinquency as serious behavior tends to correspond with the differential involvement in delinquency. These results subvert the idea that delinquency among middle-class boys is an occasional phenomenon.

Because behavior is illegal does not exempt it from having objective consequences for the adjustment of boys and for the middle-class youth culture. In the first place, as long as delinquency remains relatively faithful to middle-class values, it tends to reaffirm the social standing of the adolescent. Drinking games, dragging a car, "scoring" with a girl, or getting mildly drunk at a party are apt to be normative practices among these boys and are congruent with the dominant social orientation of the middle-class youth culture. Since these kinds of conduct emerge from societally endorsed

TABLE 5. THE PERCEPTION OF DELINQUENT ACTS AS SERIOUS BEHAVIOR BY DIFFERENTIAL DELINQUENCY INVOLVEMENT: MIDDLE-CLASS ADOLESCENTS BY AGE GROUPS

Perceived Seriousness of Delinquency	Delinquency Involvement					
	15–19 Years			All Ages		
	High	Med.	Low	High	Med.	Low
Not very serious	15.4	11.7	6.3	15.8	9.9	5.4
Moderately serious	7.2	18.0	12.2	9.5	16.9	10.4
Serious	1.8	11.0	16.1	2.8	10.1	19.1
Non-responses	0.0	0.2	0.0	0.0	0.1	0.0
	$n = 682$			850		
	$\chi^2 = 102.04$, 4df, $p < .001$			$\chi^2 = 187.58$, 4df, $p < .001$		
	$C = .360$ $\bar{C} = .441$			$C = .425$ $\bar{C} = .521$		

activities, and once they do not get "out of hand," they are likely perceived by parents as signs of maturity. This will prevent a boy from developing a delinquent self-conception, confirm his image of himself as an "average boy," and legitimize his claim to the adolescent role.

In addition, conformity to legitimate teen-age norms serves to sustain existing delinquent patterns. Until middle-class delinquency openly violates middle-class values and sentiments it is not likely to arouse collective parental concern over the teen-age culture. The fact that periodic outbursts among these boys are blamed on a few "troublemakers"—whose behavior is attributed typically to personality pathology—prevents delinquency from being considered normative within the culture. Since the recreational programs of middle-class youngsters coincide with current educational programs and reflect strongly felt values of adults, this helps deflect attention from the youth culture, and its relationship to the larger social structure, as a major source of juvenile delinquency among middle-class youth.

7 Delinquency and Community Action in Nonmetropolitan Areas

KENNETH POLK

The swell of concern in the United States over problems found in metropolitan slums gives rise to the possible danger of viewing phenomena such as poverty or delinquency as the exclusive province of megalopolis. This thinking would be in error. Over two-thirds of the poor persons in the United States, for example, reside outside major metropolitan centers. Furthermore, while the crime rates are higher in metropolitan areas, still well over 1 million offenses were reported by the police of rural areas and small cities in 1965. However legitimate, vital, and immediate our concerns may be with social action in our slums, we should not be blinded to the problems that occur elsewhere as well.

This paper will deal with delinquency and community action in the rural areas and smaller cities of the United States. In so doing, it covers a wide range of people and communities. In 1960, over 65 million persons resided in areas outside the standard metropolitan statistical areas as defined by the U.S. census. These individuals are spread over a number of different kinds of communities and regions. There are diverse kinds of nonmetropolitan communities, including the rural-farm community, which typically has a mix of residents in a small urban center surrounded by a more sparsely settled farming area; the small but concentrated rural-nonfarm community devoted to such activities as mining, fishing, or lumbering; and the small

Reprinted from *Task Force Report: Juvenile Delinquency and Youth Crime,* Report on Juvenile Justice and Consultants' Papers, Task Force on Juvenile Delinquency—The President's Commission on Law Enforcement and Administration of Justice (Washington: Government Printing Office, 1967), Appendix R, pp. 343–347.

city that can serve varied economic, educational, technical, and service functions.

As we look at the problems found in these nonmetropolitan communities, we do so knowing that we are becoming an increasingly urban nation. Since 1890, when roughly one-third of our population lived in cities, there has been a steady urbanizing trend, so that by 1960 slightly over two-thirds (69.9 percent) of the population of the United States resided in urban areas. Without questioning the clear implication of this trend, some cautions can be offered in the interpretation of these data. The U.S. census defines an area as urban if it contains more than 2,500 persons, so that a large number of persons classified as urban residents reside in small cities whose size ranges from 2,500 to 50,000. When the proportion of residents in these small cities, 33.7 percent of the Nation's total population, is added to the 30.1 percent residing in rural areas, it can be seen that while we are an urban nation, this does not mean that our population is concentrated in the major cities of the United States.

In addition, the growth of the urban population is not a result of an increase in population in the largest cities. The proportion of the population residing in cities over 1 million has actually declined since 1930 (from 12.3 percent then to 9.8 in 1960). Further, the proportion of individuals living in cities of 50,000 or over has remained relatively stable since 1930. In that year, the proportion of individuals living in medium to large cities, i.e., in cities over 50,000, was 34.9; in 1940 it was 34.4; in 1950, 35.7; and in 1960 it rose slightly to 36.2.[1] The great increase in the urban population that has occurred in recent years, in other words, is to be accounted for in the growth of small rather than large cities.

While it is true that many of these growing cities are satellites to larger metropolitan centers, they nonetheless will exhibit patterns of youthful deviance which in all probability are different from those found in the slums of the urban centers. The organization of deviance, and the organization of the community itself, are different enough so that community action taken to prevent or control such behavior in these nonmetropolitan areas, as well as in more rural settings, will require a different focus and strategy than that enunciated for the larger metropolitan communities.

DELINQUENCY AND CRIME IN
NONMETROPOLITAN AREAS: A DESCRIPTION

Delinquency and crime are not evenly distributed throughout the United States. Rural areas typically report a lower incidence of both

[1] *Census of the Population: 1960*, Vol. 1, Characteristics of the Population; Part A: Number of Inhabitants. Washington, D.C.: U.S. Department of Commerce, Bureau of the Census, pp. 1–14.

juvenile and adult deviance. Recent figures on delinquency released by the U.S. Children's Bureau, for example, show that in 1963 the rate of delinquency (per 1,000 child population) was 10.3 in rural areas, compared with 22.6 in semiurban and 31.8 in urban areas.[2] Analysis of rates for adult criminality yields comparable results. Highest rates are observed in cities over 50,000 population, with lower rates in cities under 50,000, and the lowest rates in rural areas.[3]

But even though the rates of deviance are lower in nonmetropolitan areas they still reflect the presence of a problem of public concern. In 1964, over 1 million offenses were known to the police agencies in rural and small city communities. Recent evidence suggests that even in nonmetropolitan communities as many as one in five youngsters is delinquent some time before he reaches adulthood.[4] The lower rates, in other words, should not blind us to the fact that large numbers of individuals do engage in delinquent activities outside megalopolis.

There is also some evidence that the increase in population in smaller communities is being accompanied by an increase in criminality. The average yearly increase in crime reports for cities under 100,000 between 1960 and 1964 was roughly twice that in cities of over 1 million. The actual yearly mean increase in small cities varied somewhat by city size, but fell within 8.9 and 9.4, compared with 4.6 for the largest cities; i.e., those over 1 million. The mean yearly increase in rural areas (4.7), however, was roughly comparable to that in the largest cities. (See Table 1.)

Considerable evidence has been amassed showing that nonmetropolitan delinquency differs in character as well as incidence. Earlier studies of delinquency have suggested that rural youth in general commit offenses of a less serious nature than their urban counterparts. In his study of youth in a State institution in Wisconsin, Lentz reports that rural boys more often than urban boys were institutionalized for offenses such as nominal burglary and general misconduct, but less often for the more serious offenses such as auto theft and serious burglary. There were no substantial differences between the groups in their commission of sex offenses, theft, and truancy.[5]

[2] *Juvenile Court Statistics*—1963, Washington, D.C.: U.S. Children's Bureau, 1964, p. 11.

[3] *Uniform Crime Reports*—1964, Washington, D.C.: Department of Justice, 1965, p. 106.

[4] Current studies in Lane County, Oreg., indicate that among male graduates of 13 small city and rural high schools in Lane County, approximately 19.5 percent have had at least one delinquency referral to the juvenile court. This is comparable to estimates of John C. Ball, et al., "Incidence and Estimated Prevalence of Recorded Delinquency in a Metropolitan Area," *American Sociological Review*, 29 (February 1964), pp. 90–93.

[5] William P. Lentz, "Rural-Urban Differentials and Juvenile Delinquency," *Journal of Criminal Law, Criminology, and Police Science*, 47 (October 1956), pp. 331–339.

TABLE 1. MEAN YEARLY INCREASE IN OFFENSES
REPORTED TO POLICE, 1960–64, BY COMMUNITY SIZE

Size of community	Mean yearly increase	Size of community	Mean yearly increase
1. Over 1,000,000	4.6	6. 25,000 to 50,000	9.1
2. 500,000 to 1,000,000	7.8	7. 10,000 to 25,000	9.4
3. 250,000 to 500,000	7.5	8. Under 10,000	8.9
4. 100,000 to 250,000	8.2	9. Rural areas	4.7
5. 50,000 to 100,000	9.0		

SOURCE: Uniform Crime Reports from 1961, 1962, 1963, and 1964.

Similar findings emerge from the self-report study of public school youth in Illinois conducted by Clark and Wenninger. In comparing youth from different kinds of community environments, they found that rural youth differ very little from urban youth in the extent to which they confess to minor theft, the telling of lies, loitering, beating up other youngsters without specific reason, the use of narcotics (rare in all groups), and arson (also rare). In contrast, rural-farm youth engage less, according to Clark and Wenninger, in such activities as major theft, consumption of alcohol, taking money on the pretence that it would be repaid, and skipping school.[6]

Not only are the acts less serious, but, as we might expect, one uniform finding is that delinquent youth from nonmetropolitan areas are much less sophisticated in their delinquencies than are the urban boys. Clinard has found that rural offenders do not exhibit the characteristics of a definite criminal social type as defined by (a) an early start in criminal behavior, (b) progressive knowledge of criminal techniques and crime in general, (c) resort to crime as the sole means of livelihood, and (d) a self-concept of being a criminal.[7] Partial support for these findings is contained in the work of Lentz who reports that rural offenders were less likely to be repeat offenders and that they displayed much less knowledge of criminal practices in the commission of their offenses.[8]

Among rural youth, the existence of a distinct criminal or delinquent subculture is reported only rarely. In his early study of rural criminal offenders, Clinard finds a comparative absence of gangs in the life histories of his subjects; even where companions are noted, usually only two or three

[6] John P. Clark and Eugene P. Wenninger, "Socio-Economic Class and Area as Correlates of Illegal Behavior Among Juveniles," American Sociological Review, 27 (December 1962), pp. 826–834.

[7] Marshall B. Clinard, "Rural Criminal Offenders," American Journal of Sociology, 50 (July 1944), pp. 38–50.

[8] Lentz, op. cit.

persons rather than a gang are involved.[9] Lentz reports that 52 percent of the rural boys compared with only 16 percent of urban boys in Wisconsin were lone offenders. Further, 22 percent of rural boys compared with 87 percent of urban boys were members of gangs known to be composed of delinquent boys.[10] Clinard emphasizes the role of the criminal culture in the explanation of rural crime and delinquency:

To develop a criminal social type there must be in existence some organized criminal culture which is at least tolerated in the area and through which deviant norms are transmitted. Criminal techniques, argot, and progressive association with others having criminal associations are necessary for a criminal career; and without their presence an offender may commit a crime in the legal sense without being a criminal in a sociological sense. The division of labor and heterogeneity of standards of an urban world make possible the existence of a criminal culture independent of the traditional culture. Where there exists the opposite characteristics of urbanization, such as general homogenetity of culture and more general personal behavior, it is difficult to identify one's self with a criminal world. Rural offenders are not criminal social types, owing to the fact that in areas of limited urbanization there have been few opportunities to become identified with a separate criminal culture.[11]

Present-day support for Clinard's early observation can be found in the distribution of adult offenses in nonmetropolitan and metropolitan communities. Looking at the crime rate figures for 1964, it can be observed that the offenses which derive from professional criminal activity occur much more commonly in the largest cities. Such offenses as robbery, auto theft, prostitution, narcotics violations, and gambling occur three or more times as often in the largest cities (over 250,000 population) than in rural areas, and are without exception more common in cities over 50,000 population than in the smaller jurisdiction. In contrast, little if any consistent variation by community size is associated with violations of financial trust (forgery, fraud, and embezzlement), offenses against family and children, and manslaughter by negligence. (See table 2.)

NONMETROPOLITAN DELINQUENCY: THE LOCKING-OUT PROCESS

While this descriptive information is useful in providing some understanding of the general nature of the delinquency problem in nonmetropolitan

[9] Marshall B. Clinard, "The Process of Urbanization and Criminal Behavior," *American Journal of Sociology*, 48 (September 1942), pp. 202–213.

[10] Lentz, *op. cit.*

[11] Clinard, "Process of Urbanization," *op. cit.*, p. 211.

TABLE 2. ARRESTS AND RATE, 1964, BY POPULATION GROUPS
(RATE PER 100,000; 1964 ESTIMATED POPULATION)

	Criminal murder, non-negligent man-slaughter	Homicide, man-slaughter by negligence	Forcible rape	Robbery	Aggravated assault	Burglary; breaking or entering	Larceny theft	Auto theft	Arson
Group I (52 cities, over 250,000)	8.3	1.9	11.2	62.5	96.9	183.8	314.9	102.6	4.8
Rural area (830 agencies)	3.5	2.3	5.6	23.6	47.4	138.2	320.7	78.6	3.6
Group II (76 cities, 100,000 to 250,000)	2.8	2.3	4.2	16.6	42.5	130.4	343.9	71.9	3.5
Group III (187 cities, 50,000 to 100,000)	2.1	1.4	3.4	9.8	39.0	108.1	286.3	61.6	3.8
Group IV (351 cities, 25,000 to 50,000)	2.0	1.3	3.7	8.5	43.2	113.1	249.4	53.4	4.1
Group V (867 cities, 10,000 to 25,000)	3.3	2.5	5.4	7.6	27.2	104.4	108.9	36.9	3.4
Group VI (1,476 cities, under 10,000)	5.6	2.2	7.8	28.6	87.3	165.0	385.5	93.6	3.8
Total all offenses	4.8	2.0	7.1	29.5	60.3	141.2	270.7	73.5	3.9

	Forgery and counter-feiting	Fraud	Embezzle-ment	Weapons; carrying, possessing, etc.	Prostitution and com-mercialized vice	Narcotic drug laws	gam-bling	Offenses against family and children	Total, all offenses
Group I (52 cities, over 250,000)	21.3	30.6	5.2	52.9	57.3	71.0	199.1	37.6	4,641.0
Group II (76 cities, 100,000 to 250,000)	33.9	51.2	9.3	53.5	17.5	18.0	60.8	70.9	4,977.0
Group III (187 cities, 50,000 to 100,000)	26.8	35.7	6.5	36.1	6.5	17.4	26.7	38.9	3,594.8
Group IV (351 cities, 25,000 to 50,000)	25.6	38.4	10.4	33.2	2.7	10.8	24.1	38.9	3,537.5
Group V (867 cities, 10,000 to 25,000)	19.9	30.8	5.6	25.9	2.1	5.6	16.1	32.4	3,148.4
Group VI (1,476 cities, under 10,000)	18.0	23.9	4.5	28.1	2.7	3.6	11.5	26.8	3,356.2
Rural area (830 agencies)	23.0	35.4	5.9	13.4	2.4	4.0	19.0	42.4	1,462.5
Total all offenses	23.1	34.7	6.5	35.7	21.3	28.5	78.4	43.4	3,460.4

SOURCE: Uniform Crime Reports—1965.

communities, development of a community action program depends much more on an understanding of the forces within the community that generate this behavior. Of many possible relevant factors, sociologists have long been concerned with the importance of social class position in the development of delinquency. Cohen and Cloward and Ohlin have argued persuasively that the delinquency observed in urban areas arises out of the peculiar problems of adjustment faced by working class youth.[12] Empirical studies of delinquency suggest the relevance of this variable in rural and small city areas as well. In the River City study, for example it is reported that a great majority of delinquencies among males, and all the delinquency observed among females, occurs in the lower social class groupings.[13]

In addition to the economic theme which runs through accounts of nonmetropolitan delinquency, there is also a theme having to do with school adjustment. Again in the River City study, Havighurst and his associates report that all of the youth in their population who had committed serious delinquencies, and well over three-fourths of those committing moderately serious offenses, were individuals who had withdrawn from school before graduation.[14] In his analysis of delinquency in a small city, Polk reports not only a close link between school achievement and delinquency, but also that when the comparison is between students at the same level of academic achievement, virtually no relationship is found between social class and delinquency.[15] This suggests that there may be occurring over time a shift in the role that social class plays in the life of an individual, with the predominant relevance of economic status noted in the small town studies by Hollingshead in the early 1940's being eroded to some degree by an emerging search for talent and a consequent increase in emphasis on achievement. Cicourel and Kitsuse have suggested the importance of one specific aspect of the changing function of the school; namely, the preparation of youth for college:

The differentiation of college-going and non-college-going students defines the standards of performance by which they are evaluated by the school personnel and by which students are urged to evaluate themselves. It is the college-going student more than his non-college-going peer who is continually reminded by his teachers, counselor, parents, and peers of the decisive importance of academic achievement to the realization of his ambitions and who becomes

[12] Albert K. Cohen, *Delinquent Boys,* Glencoe: The Free Press, 1955; and Richard A. Cloward and Lloyd E. Ohlin, *Delinquency and Opportunity,* Glencoe: The Free Press, 1961.

[13] Robert J. Havighurst, et al., *Growing up in River City,* New York: John Wiley, 1962.

[14] *Ibid.*

[15] Kenneth Polk and David Halferty, "Adolescence, Commitment, and Delinquency," *Journal of Research in Criminology,* 3 (July 1966), in press.

progressively committed to this singular standard of self-evaluation. He becomes the future-oriented student interested in a delimited occupational specialty, with little time to give thought to the present or to question the implications of his choice and the meaning of his strivings.[16]

It is within this framework that the functional relationship between class background and school behavior may be changing:

> . . . we suggest that the influence of social class upon the way students are processed in the high school today is reflected in new and more subtle family-school relations than the direct and often blatant manipulation of family class pressure documented by Hollingshead. . . . Insofar as the high school is committed to the task of identifying talent and increasing the proportion of college-going students, counselors will tend to devote more of their time and activities to those students who plan and are most likely to go to college and whose parents actively support their plans and make frequent inquiries at the school about their progress—namely, the students from the middle and upper social classes.[17]

Such a view emphasizes the role of the school in the life of the individual and focuses on the question of the consequences that accrue to those who are unable to achieve within the school system. Vinter and Sarri have pointed out that the school has a multitude of punishments which it can mete out to the malperforming youngster.[18] In "Valley City," Call reports that not only were delinquent youth likely to do poor academic work, they were also less likely to participate in school activities and more likely to see themselves as outsiders in the school setting.[19]

For such youth the future begins to take on a different meaning. If they lack an orientation to the future, and appear unwilling to defer immediate gratifications in order to achieve long-range future goals, it may be that they see fairly clearly that for them there is little future. Pearl suggests that such youth—

> . . . develop a basic pessimism because they have a fair fix on reality. They rely on fate because no rational transition by system is open to them. They react against schools because schools are characteristically hostile to them.[20]

---

[16] Aaron V. Cicourel and John I. Kitsuse, *The Educational Decision-Makers*, New York: Bobbs-Merrill, 1963, p. 146.

[17] *Ibid.*, pp. 144–145.

[18] Robert D. Vinter and Rosemary C. Sarri, "Malperformance in the Public School: A Group Work Approach," *Social Work*, 10 (January 1965), pp. 3–13, see especially p. 9.

[19] Donald J. Call, "Delinquency, Frustration, and Non-Commitment," Unpublished Ph.D. dissertation, University of Oregon, Eugene, Oreg., 1965.

[20] Arthur Pearl, "Youth in Lower Class Settings," in M. Sherif and C. Sherif, *Problems of Youth*, Chicago: Aldine Press, pp. 89–109.

The hostility engendered is not simple individual hostility. While a professional criminal culture may not exist in nonmetropolitan areas, there seems to occur a troublemaking subculture which may have its roots in the locking-out process of the school. Such an interpretation is not inconsistent with the observations of Empey and Rabow in a small city in Utah:

Despite the fact that Utah County is not a highly urbanized area when compared to large metropolitan centers, the concept of a "parent" delinquent subculture has real meaning for it. While there are no clear-cut gangs, per se, it is surprising to observe the extent to which delinquent boys from the entire county, who have never met, know each other by reputation, go with the same girls, use the same language, or can seek each other out when they change high schools. About half of them are permanently out of school, do not participate in any regular institutional activities, are reliant almost entirely upon the delinquent system for social acceptance and participation.[21]

Call presents evidence from a small city in Oregon which suggests that delinquent youth are more likely to spend their spare time with friends and that their friends are much more likely to be outside the school system.[22] Polk's factor analytic study suggests that delinquency fits into a pattern of rejection of commitment to school success accompanied by a concomitant involvement in a pattern of peer rebellion against adults.[23] Pearl expresses the role such processes play in enabling youngsters to cope with the locking-out process:

A limited gratification exists in striving for the impossible and as a consequence poor youth create styles, coping mechanisms, and groups in relation to the systems which they can and cannot negotiate. Group values and identifications emerge in relation to the forces opposing them.[24]

The point of this discussion is that these youth are not passive receptors of the stigma that develops within the school setting. When locked out they respond by seeking an interactional setting where they can function comfortably. The fact that the resulting subculture has built-in oppositional forces becomes an important aspect of the delinquency problem encountered in a community. We deal not with isolated alienated youth, but with a loosely organized subculture which provides important group supports for the deviancy observed. Individualized treatment aimed at such youth which does not take into account the importance and functioning of the group supports within this culture can have limited, if any, impact. What

[21] Lamar T. Empey and Jerome Rabow, "The Provo Experiment in Delinquency Rehabilitation," *American Sociological Review*, 26 (October 1961), pp. 674–695.

[22] Call, *op. cit.*

[23] Polk and Halferty, *op. cit.*

[24] Pearl, *op. cit.*

is needed is an approach that will counteract the system processes which generate this subcultural response.

THE SITUATIONAL MATRIX
OF NONMETROPOLITAN YOUTH

Change in the World of Work

The full plight of the delinquent and malperforming student in the nonmetropolitan community can be understood only when the problem is cast against its economic backdrop. The urbanizing trend in the United States is accompanied by processes related to industrialization which have a profound and dramatic impact on rural youth in general and the delinquent in particular. None is more basic than the changing work world. On the one hand, there has been a drastic reduction in the demand for agricultural labor. Since the turn of the century, the proportion of the labor force engaged in agricultural work has declined from 37.3 to 6.0 percent in 1960. Especially dramatic is the fact that the actual size of the labor force engaged in agriculture was more than cut in half between 1940 (when 8.9 million persons were employed in agriculture) and 1960 (4.1 million so employed.)[25]

Cross-cutting this trend is the decline in the demand for unskilled labor. Automation is taking an ever-increasing toll of unskilled occupations. Not only is the nonmetropolitan worker squeezed out of agricultural jobs, in other words, but alternatives at the same skill level are increasingly unavailable.

Rural to Urban Migration

Another factor affecting the situation of the nonmetropolitan youth is geographic mobility. High rates of geographic mobility are a fact of life in modern American society. One person in every four now lives in a State other than the one in which he was born[26] and nearly one American in five changes his residential address every year.[27] Such internal movement in the American population over the past 75 years has not been a random phe-

[25] *Census of the Population:* 1960, Vol. 1, Characteristics of the Population; Part A: Number of Inhabitants. Washington, D.C.: U.S. Department of Commerce, Bureau of the Census, pp. 1–14.

[26] *A Place To Live: The Yearbook of Agriculture, 1963.* U.S. Department of Agriculture, Washington, D.C., 1963, p. 10.

[27] Bureau of Census, *Mobility of the Population of the United States,* March 1960 to March 1961, U.S. Department of Commerce, Washington, D.C., 1962.

nomenon and appears to press particularly hard on the rural-farm population. The fact of steady migration from rural areas to large urban centers has been well documented. It has been estimated that a net migration of 2 million farm males who were 5 years of age or older in 1960 will occur during the 1960–70 decade. This means that only three out of five farm males in 1960 who survive to 1970 will be on the farm by the end of that decade.[28]

The impact of rural migration is now reaching its apex. In the 1950–60 decade, 8.6 million persons migrated from farm areas. This rural-to-urban migration involves more people than those of the peak years of the great migrations to this country.[29] Two-thirds (5.8 million) of the farm migrants in the 1950–60 decade were under 20 years of age.[30] In western United States, two out of every three males in the 15–24 age category in 1960 might be expected to leave the farm over the next 10 years.[31] The majority of these youth will migrate to large metropolitan centers.

It is also well documented that the typical rural migrant is not able to compete successfully with urban residents for employment in metropolitan centers since, in general, he is disadvantaged economically, educationally, socially, and culturally. Considerable evidence points to continuing differences between rural educational systems and those serving urban children and youth. Nonmetropolitan high schools have given little attention to the task of preparing youth for entrance into a metropolitan world, especially with regard to employment.[32] Particularly acute inadequacies in rural education are found in such areas as occupational exploration and guidance and educational background for later specialized occupational training in post-high-school centers or actual job placements.[33]

In addition to differences in quality of education, urban dwellers derive many benefits from simply having grown up in the centers where they will compete for jobs. Nonmetropolitan youth, by virtue of having lived in less complex social systems, are not familiar with the routine

[28] "Unemployment prospects for rural communities," G. S. Tolley, Report No. 36, National Conference on Problems of Rural Youth in a Changing Environment, Stillwater, Okla., September 1963, p. 9.

[29] *A Place To Live: The Yearbook of Agriculture, 1963, op. cit.,* p. 15.

[30] *Ibid.,* p. 31.

[31] C. E. Bishop and G. S. Tolley, *Manpower in Farming and Related Occupations,* prepared for the President's Panel of Consultants on Vocational Education, July 1962, pp. 15–16.

[32] See Lee G. Burchinal and James D. Cowhig, "Rural Youth in an Urban Society," *Children,* Vol. 10, 1963, pp. 167–172, and *Education for a Changing World of Work,* Report of the Panel of Consultants on Vocational Education, U.S. Department of Health, Education, and Welfare, Washington, D.C., 1963, pp. 116–118.

[33] Gerald B. James, "Vocational and Technical Education at the Post High School Level for Rural Youth," paper read at the National Conference on Problems of Rural Youth in a Changing Environment, Stillwater, Okla., September 1963, p. 1.

problems of working and living in cities.[34] This is the first component of a split-level infirmity which exists for nonmetropolitan entrants into an adult world of work. They are literally being pushed out of farm labor and off the farm, but, upon migration, they find themselves ill equipped to compete successfully with urban dwellers for industrial jobs in an alien urban environment. A recent Government report noted:

Every year, mechanization is driving tens of thousands of farm-workers and their families from their homes. Fields hands flock to town looking for jobs. Whole families unrooted from small farms which have been their homes for generations abandon their birthplaces and go into the cities to start entirely new ways of life. Because of technological advances, a strong back counts for far less than it did on the farm.[35]

Changes in the world of work and these migration trends pose a challenge for nonmetropolitan communities that is especially relevant for the malperforming youth. Innovative educational programs are needed which direct themselves to the two-pronged problem of improving the ability of youth to contend with the urbanizing world and reversing the locking-out process that characterizes the community's response to youthful deviance.

. . .

[34] See Lee G. Burchinal and Ward W. Bauder, "Adjustments to the New Institutional Environment," 1964 (mimeo), and Lyle W. Shannon, "Occupational and Residential Adjustments of Rural Migrants," *Labor Mobility, and Population in Agriculture*, Iowa State University Press, 1961, pp. 122–123.

[35] *Education for a Changing World of Work*, Washington, D.C.: U.S. Department of Health, Education, and Welfare, Office of Education, 1963, p. 13.

8 Socio-Economic Class and Area as Correlates of Illegal Behavior Among Juveniles[*]

JOHN P. CLARK AND
EUGENE P. WENNINGER

Until recently almost all efforts to discover characteristics that differentiate juveniles who violate legal norms from those who do not have compared institutional and non-institutional populations. Though many researchers still employ a "delinquent" or "criminal" sample from institutions,[1] there is a growing awareness that the process through which boys and girls are selected to populate our "correctional" institutions may cause such comparison studies to distort seriously the true picture of illegal behavior in our society. Therefore, conclusions based upon such studies are subject to considerable criticism[2] if generalized beyond the type of population of that particular institution at the time of the study. Although the study of adjudicated offenders is important, less encumbered studies of the violation of legal norms hold more promise for those interested in the more general concept of deviant behavior.

Reprinted from *American Sociological Review,* 27 (December, 1962), 826–834, by permission of The American Sociological Association and the authors.

[*] The total project of which this paper is a part was sponsored by the Ford Foundation and the University of Illinois Graduate Research Board. Professor Daniel Glaser was very helpful throughout the project and in the preparation of this paper.

[1] An outstanding example of this type of research design is Sheldon and Eleanor Glueck, *Unraveling Juvenile Delinquency*, New York: The Commonwealth Fund, 1950.

[2] See Marshall B. Clinard, *Sociology of Deviant Behavior*, New York: Rinehart, 1958, p. 124, for his assessment of the validity of the study by Sheldon and Eleanor Glueck, *Unraveling Juvenile Delinquency*.

Though it, too, has methodological limitations, the anonymous-questionnaire procedure has been utilized to obtain results reflecting the rates and patterns of illegal behavior among juveniles from different social classes, ages, sexes, and ethnic groups in the general population.[3] The results of these studies have offered sufficient evidence to indicate that the patterns of illegal behavior among juveniles may be dramatically different than was heretofore thought to be the case.

Some of the most provocative findings have been those that challenge the almost universally-accepted conclusion that the lower socio-economic classes have higher rates of illegal behavior than do the middle or upper classes. For example, neither the Nye-Short study[4] nor that of Dentler and Monroe[5] revealed any significant difference in the incidence of certain illegal or "deviant" behaviors among occupational-status levels—a finding quite at odds with most current explanations of delinquent behavior.

Although most of the more comprehensive studies in the social class tradition have been specifically concerned with a more-or-less well-defined portion of the lower class (i.e., "delinquent gangs,"[6] or "culture of the gang," or "delinquent subculture"[7]), some authors have tended to generalize their findings and theoretical formulations rather specifically to the total lower class population of juveniles.[8] These latter authors certainly do not profess that *all* lower class children are equally involved in illegal behavior, but by implication they suggest that the incidence of illegal conduct (whether brought to the attention of law enforcement agencies or not) is more pervasive in this class than others because of some unique but fundamental characteristics of the lower social strata. For example, Miller has

---

[3] Most outstanding are those by Austin L. Porterfield, *Youth in Trouble*, Fort Worth, Texas: Leo Potishman Foundation, 1946: F. Ivan Nye and James F. Short, "Scaling Delinquent Behavior," *American Sociological Review*, 22 (June, 1957), pp. 326–331; and Robert A. Dentler and Lawrence J. Monroe, "Early Adolescent Theft," *American Sociological Review*, 26 (October, 1961), 733–743; Fred J. Murphy, Mary M. Shirley, and Helen L. Witmer, "The Incidence of Hidden Delinquency," *American Journal of Orthopsychiatry*, 16 (October, 1946), pp. 686–696.

[4] James F. Short, "Differential Association and Delinquency," *Social Problems*, 4 (January, 1957), pp. 233–239; F. Ivan Nye, *Family Relationships and Delinquent Behavior*, New York: John Wiley, 1958; James F. Short and F. Ivan Nye, "Reported Behavior as a Criterion of Deviant Behavior," *Social Problems*, 5 (Winter, 1957–1958), pp. 207–213; F. Ivan Iye, James F. Short, and Virgil J. Olson, "Socio-Economic Status and Delinquent Behavior," *American Journal of Sociology*, 63 (January, 1958), pp. 381–389.

[5] Dentler and Monroe, *op. cit.*

[6] Richard A. Cloward and Lloyd E. Ohlin, *Delinquency and Opportunity: A Theory of Delinquent Gangs,* New York: The Free Press of Glencoe, 1961.

[7] Albert K. Cohen, *Delinquent Boys: The Culture of the Gang*, Glencoe, Ill.: Free Press, 1955.

[8] Walter B. Miller, "Lower Class Culture as a Generating Milieu of Gang Delinquency," *Journal of Social Issues*, 14 (No. 3, 1958), pp. 5–19.

compiled a list of "focal concerns" toward which the lower class supposedly is oriented and because of which those in this class violate more legal norms with greater frequency than other classes.[9] Other authors point out that the lower classes are disadvantaged in their striving for legitimate goals and that they resort to deviant means to attain them.[10] Again, the result of this behavior is higher rate of illegal behavior among the lower socio-economic classes.

Therefore, there *appears* to be a direct conflict between the theoretical formulations of Miller, Cohen, Merton, Cloward and Ohlin, and those findings reported by Nye and Short and Dentler and Monroe. This apparent discrepancy in the literature can be resolved, however, if one hypothesizes that the rates of illegal conduct among the social classes vary with the type of community[11] in which they are found. Were this so, it would be possible for studies which have included certain types of communities to reveal differential illegal behavior rates among social classes while studies which have involved other types of communities might fail to detect social class differences.

Whereas the findings and formulations of Merton, Cohen, Cloward and Ohlin, and Miller are oriented, in a sense, toward the "full-range" of social situations, those of Nye-Short and Dentler-Monroe are very specifically limited to the types of populations used in their respective studies. It is important to note that the communities in which these latter studies were conducted ranged only from rural to small city in size. As Nye points out, "They are thus urban but not metropolitan."[12] Yet, most studies of "delinquent gangs" and "delinquent subcultures" have been conducted in metropolitan centers where these phenomena are most apparent. Perhaps, it is only here that there is a sufficient concentration of those in the extreme socio-economic classes to afford an adequate test of the "social class hypothesis."

In addition to the matter of social class concentration and size, there is obviously more than one "kind" of lower class and each does not have rates or types of illegal behavior identical to that of the others. For example, most rural farm areas, in which occupations, incomes, and educational levels are indicative of lower class status, as measured by most social class indexes,

[9] *Ibid.* The matter of class differences in "focal concerns" or values will be explored in subsequent articles.

[10] Cohen, *op. cit.*, Cloward and Ohlin, *op. cit.*, and Robert K. Merton, *Social Theory and Social Structure*, Glencoe, Ill.: Free Press, 1957, pp. 146–149.

[11] In this report "type of community" is used to refer in a general way to a geographic and social unit having certain distinctive demographic qualities, such as occupational structure, race, social class, and size. Designations such as "rural farm," or "Negro lower class urban," or "middle class suburbia," have long been utilized to describe such persistent physical-social characteristics.

[12] Nye, Short, and Olson, *op. cit.*, p. 383.

consistently have been found to have low rates of misconduct—in fact lower than most urban middle class communities.

Therefore, to suggest the elimination of social class as a significant correlate to the quantity and quality of illegal behavior before it has been thoroughly examined in a variety of community situations, seems somewhat premature. Reiss and Rhodes concluded as a result of study of class and juvenile court rates by school district that "it is clear, that there is no simple relationship between ascribed social status and delinquency."[13] In order to isolate the factor of social class, to eliminate possible effects of class bias in the rate of which juvenile misbehavior is referred to court, as well as to vary the social and physical environs in which it is located, we chose in this study to compare rates of admitted illegal behavior among diverse communities within the northern half of Illinois. Our hypotheses were:

1. Significant differences in the incidence of illegal behavior exist among communities differing in predominant social class composition, within a given metropolitan area.

2. Significant differences in the incidence of illegal behavior exist among similar social class strata located in different types of community.

3. Differences in the incidence of illegal behavior among different social class populations within a given community are not significant.

THE STUDY

The data to test the above hypotheses were gathered in 1961 as part of a larger exploratory study of illegal behavior (particularly theft) among juveniles, and its relationship to socio-economic class, type of community, age, race, and various attitudinal variables, such as attitude toward law, feelings of alienation, concept of self, and feelings of being able to achieve desired goals. Subsequent reports will deal with other aspects of the study.

A total of 1154 public school students from the sixth through the twelfth grades in the school systems of four different types of communities were respondents to a self-administered, anonymous questionnaire given in groups of from 20 to 40 persons by the senior author. Considerable precaution was taken to insure reliability and validity of the responses. For example, assurances were given that the study was not being monitored by the school administration; questions were pretested to eliminate ambiguity; and the administration of the questionnaire was made as threat-free as possible.

The four communities represented in the study were chosen for the

[13] Albert J. Reiss and Albert L. Rhodes, "The Distribution of Juvenile Delinquency in the Social Class Structure," *American Sociological Review*, 26, (October, 1961), pp. 720–732.

unique social class structure represented by each. The Duncan "Socio-Economic Index for All Occupations,"[14] was used to determine the occupational profile of each community by assigning index scores to the occupation of the respondents' fathers. The results are summarized in Table 1.

The overwhelming majority of the respondents comprising the *rural farm* population live on farms, farming being by far the most common occupation of their fathers. Many of the fathers who were not listed as farmers were, in fact, "part-time" farmers. Therefore, though the Duncan Index would classify most of the residents in the lower class, most of these public school children live on farms in a prosperous section of the Midwest. The sixth, seventh, and eighth graders were drawn from schools located in very small villages. Grades 9–12 were drawn from the high school which was located in open-farm land.

The *lower urban* sample is primarily composed of children of those with occupations of near-equal ranking but certainly far different in nature from those of the rural farm community. The lower urban sample was drawn from a school system located in a very crowded and largely-Negro area of Chicago. The fathers (or male head of the family) of these youngsters are laborers in construction, waiters, janitors, clean-up men, etc. Even among those who place relatively high on the Duncan Scale are many who, in spite of their occupational title, reside, work, and socialize almost exclusively in the lower class community.

As Table 1 demonstrates, the occupational structure of the *industrial city* is somewhat more diffuse than the other communities, though consisting primarily of lower class occupations. This city of about 35,000 is largely autonomous, although a small portion of the population commutes daily to Chicago. However, about two-thirds of these students have fathers who work as blue-collar laborers in local industries and services. The median years of formal education of all males age 25 or over is 10.3.[15] The median annual family income is $7,255.[16] The population of this small city contains substantial numbers of Polish and Italian Americans and about fifteen per cent Negroes.

Those in the *upper urban* sample live in a very wealthy suburb of Chicago. Nearly three-fourths of the fathers in these families are high-level executives or professionals. The median level of education for all males age 25 or over is 16 plus.[17] The median annual family income is slightly over $20,000—80 per cent of the families make $10,000 or more annually.[18]

[14] Albert J. Reiss, Jr., Otis Dudley Duncan, Paul K. Hatt, and Cecil C. North, *Occupations and Social Status*, New York: The Free Press of Glencoe, 1961, especially pp. 109–161 prepared by Otis D. Duncan.

[15] *U.S. Census of Population: 1960.* Final Report PC (1)–15C, p. 15–296.

[16] *Ibid.*, p. 15–335.

[17] *Ibid.*, p. 15–305.

[18] *Ibid.*, p. 15–344.

TABLE 1. DUNCAN SOCIO-ECONOMIC-INDEX SCORES BASED ON OCCUPATION OF FATHER

| | Type of Community | | | |
| | Rural Farm | Lower Urban | Industrial City | Upper Urban |
Score	%	%	%	%
(1) 0–23	75.9	40.4	36.4	5.7
(2) 24–47	9.9	15.5	19.3	4.8
(3) 48–71	4.7	12.5	22.9	41.9
(4) 72–96	1.5	4.2	10.0	34.6
(5) Unclassifiable*	8.0	27.4	11.4	11.0
Total	100 (N—274)	100 (N—265)	100 (N—280)	100 (N—335)

* This category included those respondents from homes with no father and those respondents who did not furnish adequate information for reliable classification. The 27.4 per cent figure in the lower urban community reflects a higher proportion of "father-less" homes rather than greater numbers of responses which were incomplete or vague in other ways.

With two exceptions, representative sampling of the public school children was followed within each of these communities: (1) those who could not read at a fourth grade level were removed in all cases, which resulted in the loss of less than one-half per cent of the total sample, and (2) the sixth-grade sample in the industrial city community was drawn from a predominantly Negro, working class area and was, therefore, non-representative of the total community for that grade-level only. All the students from grade six through twelve were used in the rural farm community "sample."

MEASURE OF ILLEGAL BEHAVIOR

An inventory of 36 offenses was initially assembled from delinquency scales, legal statutes, and the FBI Uniform Crime Reports. In addition to this, a detailed list of theft items, ranging from candy to automobiles, was constructed. The latter list was later combined into two composite items (minor theft, and major theft) and added to the first list, enlarging the number of items in this inventory to 38 items as shown in Table 2. No questions on sex offenses were included in this study, a restriction found necessary in order to gain entrance into one of the school systems.

All respondents were asked to indicate if they had committed each of these offenses (including the detailed list of theft items) *within the past*

TABLE 2. PERCENTAGE OF RESPONDENTS ADMITTING INDIVIDUAL OFFENSES AND SIGNIFICANCE OF DIFFERENCES BETWEEN SELECTED COMMUNITY COMPARISONS

	Community				Significance of Differences*		
Offense	(1) Indus- trial City N=280	(2) Lower Urban N=265	(3) Upper Urban N=335	(4) Rural Farm N=274	(1-2)	(2-3)	(3-4)
1. Did things my parents told me not to do.	90	87	85	82	X	X	X
2. Minor theft (compilation of such items as the stealing of fruit, pencils, lipstick, candy, cigarettes, comic books, money less than $1, etc.)	79	78	80	73	X	X	X
3. Told a lie to my family, principal, or friends.	80	74	77	74	X	X	X
4. Used swearwords or dirty words out loud in school, church, or on the street so other people could hear me.	63	58	54	51	X	X	X
5. Showed or gave someone a dirty picture, a dirty story, or something like that.	53	39	58	54	1	3	X
6. Been out at night just fooling around after I was supposed to be home.	49	50	51	35	X	X	3
7. Hung around other people who I knew had broken the law lots of times or who were known as "bad" people.	49	47	27	40	X	2	4
8. Threw rocks, cans, sticks, or other things at passing car, bicycle, or person.	41	37	33	36	X	X	X
9. Slipped into a theater or other place without paying.	35	40	39	22	X	X	3
10. Major theft (compilation of such items as the stealing of auto parts, autos, money over $1, bicycles, radios and parts, clothing, wallets, liquor, guns, etc.)	37	40	29	20	X	2	3
11. Gone into another person's house, a shed, or other building without their permission.	31	16	31	42	1	3	4

TABLE 2 (*Continued*)

	Community				Significance of Differences*		
Offense	(1) Indus- trial City N=280	(2) Lower Urban N=265	(3) Upper Urban N=335	(4) Rural Farm N=274	(1-2)	(2-3)	(3-4)
12. Gambled for money or something else with people other than my family.	30	22	35	26	X	3	3
13. Got some money or something from others by saying that I would pay them back even though I was pretty sure I wouldn't.	35	48	26	14	2	2	3
14. Told someone I was going to beat-up on them unless they did what I wanted them to do.	33	28	24	32	X	X	4
15. Drank beer, wine, or liquor without my parents permission.	38	37	26	12	X	2	3
16. Have been kicked out of class or school for acting up.	27	28	31	22	X	X	3
17. Thrown nails, or glass, or cans in the street.	31	29	21	17	X	X	X
18. Used a slug or other things like this in candy, coke, or coin machines.	24	35	18	12	2	2	3
19. Skipped school without permission.	24	36	18	11	2	2	3
20. Helped make a lot of noise outside a church, or school, or any other place in order to bother the people inside.	17	37	18	15	X	2	X
21. Threw rocks, or sticks or any other thing in order to break a window, or street light, or thing like that.	24	26	22	16	X	X	3
22. Said I was going to tell something on someone unless they gave me money, candy, or something else I wanted.	23	28	17	19	X	2	X
23. Kept or used something that I knew had been stolen by someone else.	29	36	15	16	X	2	X
24. Tampered or fooled with another person's car, tractor,							

TABLE 2 (*Continued*)

Offense	Community				Significance of Differences*		
	(1) Indus-trial City N=280	(2) Lower Urban N=265	(3) Upper Urban N=335	(4) Rural Farm N=274	(1-2)	(2-3)	(3-4)
or bicycle while they weren't around.	26	13	19	24	1	3	X
25. Started a fist fight.	26	22	15	18	X	2	X
26. Messed up a restroom by writing on the wall, or leaving the water running to run onto the floor, or upsetting the waste can.	18	33	14	17	X	2	X
27. Hung around a pool hall, bar, or tavern.	21	18	10	23	X	2	4
28. Hung around the railroad tracks and trains.	16	13	23	16	X	3	3
29. Broken down or helped break down a fence, gate, or door on another person's place.	15	14	8	8	X	2	X
30. Taken part in a "gang fight."	12	18	7	7	X	2	X
31. Ran away from home.	12	12	8	7	X	X	X
32. Asked for money, candy, a cigarette or other things from strangers.	12	12	6	7	X	2	X
33. Carried a razor, switchblade, or gun to be used against other people.	8	16	3	4	2	2	X
34. "Beat up" on kids who hadn't done anything to me.	8	5	5	6	X	X	X
35. Broke or helped break up the furniture in a school, church, or other public building.	8	4	2	8	X	X	4
36. Attacked someone with the idea of killing them.	3	6	1	3	2	n	n
37. Smoked a reefer or used some sort of dope (narcotics).	3	4	1	3	X	n	n
38. Started a fire or helped set a fire in a building without the permission of the owner.	3	2	1	3	X	n	n

* Code: X = No significant difference.
[Note continues on page 397.]

year, thus furnishing data amenable to age-level analysis.[19] If the respondents admitted commission of an offense, they so indicated by disclosing the number of times (either 1, 2, 3, or 4 or more) they had done so. The first four columns of Table 2 reveal the percentage of students who admitted having indulged in each specific behavior one or more times *during the past year*.

Specific offense items were arranged in an array from those admitted by the highest percentage of respondents to those admitted by the lowest percentage of respondents. Obviously the "nuisance" offenses appear near the top while the most serious and the more situationally specific fall nearer the end of the listing.[20] Several offenses are apparently committed very infrequently by school children from the sixth to twelfth grades regardless of their social environs.

FINDINGS

In order to determine whether significant differences exist in the incidence of illegal behavior among the various types of communities, a two-step procedure was followed. First, each of the four communities was assigned a rank for each offense on the basis of the percentage of respondents admitting commission of that offense. These ranks were totaled across all offenses for each community. The resultant numerical total provided a very crude over-all measure of the relative degree to which the sample population from each community had been involved in illegal behavior during the past year. The results were (from most to least illegal behavior): industrial city, lower urban, upper urban, and rural farm. However, there was little over-all difference in the sum of ranks between upper urban and rural farm and even less difference between the industrial city and lower urban areas.

[19] Rates of illegal behavior were found to increase until age 14–15 and then to decrease.

[20] Ordinarily, not receiving 100 per cent admission to the first few offenses listed would have raised doubt as to the validity of those questionnaires on which these extremely common offenses were not admitted. In the Nye-Short study such questionnaires were discarded. However, since the respondents were asked in this study to admit their offenses during the past year only, it was thought that less than 100 per cent admission would be highly possible when one considers the entire age range. Undoubtedly some of the respondents who did not admit these minor offenses were falsifying their questionnaires.

1, 2, 3, or 4 = significant differences at .05 level or higher. The numbers indicate which of the communities in the comparison is higher in incidence of the offense.

n = too few offender cases to determine significant level.

In the second step the communities were arranged in the order given above and then the significance of the difference between adjacent pairs was determined by applying the Wilcoxon matched-pairs signed-ranks test. Only those comparisons which involve either industrial city or lower urban versus upper urban or rural farm result in any significant differences.[21] This

1–2—P .35	1–3—P .00006
2–3—P .0034	1–4—P .0006
3–4—P .90	2–4—P .016

finding is compatible with the above crude ranking procedure.

On the basis of these findings the first hypothesis is supported, while the second hypothesis received only partial support. Lower urban juveniles reported significantly more illegal behavior than did the juveniles of the upper urban community, and the two lower class communities of industrial city and lower urban appear to be quite similar in their high rates, but another lower class area composed largely of farmers has a much lower rate, similar to that of the upper urban area.

Much more contrast among the rates of juvenile misconduct in the four different communities, than is indicated by the above results, becomes apparent when one focuses on individual offenses. As the last column in Table 2 reveals, and as could be predicted from the above, there are few significant differences in the rates on each offense between the industrial city and lower urban communities. The few differences that do occur hardly fall into a pattern except that the lower urban youth seem to be oriented more toward violence (carrying weapons and attacking persons) than those in the industrial city.

However, 16 of a possible 35 relationships are significantly different in the upper urban-rural farm comparison, a fact that could not have been predicted from the above results. Apparently, variation in one direction on certain offenses tends to be neutralized by variation in the opposite direction on other offenses when the Wilcoxon test is used. There are greater actual differences in the nature of illegal behavior between these two communities than is noticeable when considered in more summary terms. (It might be pointed out here, parenthetically, that this type of finding lends support to the suggestion by Dentler and Monroe that the comparison of criterion groups on the basis of "omnibus scales" may have serious shortcomings.)[22]

Rural farm youngsters are more prone than those in the upper urban area to commit such offenses as trespassing, threatening to "beat up" on persons, hanging around taverns and being with "bad" associates—all relatively unsophisticated acts. Although some of the offenses committed more

[21] Significance of differences were calculated between pairs of communities across *all* 38 offenses by using the Wilcoxon Matched-Pairs Signed-Ranks test (described in Sidney Siegel, *Non-Parametric Statistics*, New York: McGraw-Hill Book Company, Inc., 1956, pp. 75–83). The results of this procedure were:

[22] Dentler and Monroe, *op. cit.*, p. 734.

often by those who live in the upper urban community are also unsophisticated (throwing rocks at street lights, getting kicked out of school classes,
and hanging around trains), others probably require some skill to perform
successfully and probably depend on supportive peer-group relationships.
For example, these data reveal that upper urban juveniles are more likely
than their rural farm counterparts to be out at night after they are supposed
to be at home, drink beer and liquors without parents permission, engage
in major theft, gamble, skip school, and slip into theaters without paying.
In addition to their likely dependence upon peer-groups, perhaps these
offenses are more easily kept from the attention of parents in the urban
setting than in open-farm areas.

The greatest differences between rates of illegal conduct occur between
the lower urban and upper urban communities, where 21 of a possible 35
comparisons reach statistical significance, the lower urban rates being higher
in all except five of these. Although the upper urban youngsters are more
likely to pass "dirty pictures," gamble, trespass, hang around trains, and
tamper with other people's cars, their cousins in the lower class area are
more likely to steal major items, drink, skip school, destroy property, fight,
and carry weapons. The latter offenses are those normally thought to be
"real delinquent acts" while the upper urban offenses (with the exception
of vehicle tampering) are not generally considered to be such.

To summarize briefly, when the rates of juvenile misconduct are compared on individual offenses among communities, it appears that as one
moves from rural farm to upper urban to industrial city and lower urban,
the incidence of most offenses becomes greater, especially in the more
serious offenses and in those offenses usually associated with social structures
with considerable tolerance for illegal behavior.

While most emphasis is placed here on the differences, one obvious
finding, evident in Table 2, is that in most of the nuisance offenses (minor
theft, lying to parents, disobeying parents, swearing in public, throwing
objects to break things or into the streets) there are no differences among
the various communities. Differences appear to lie in the more serious offenses and those requiring a higher degree of sophistication and social
organization.

The Reiss-Rhodes findings tend to refute theories of delinquent behavior which imply a high delinquency proneness of the lower class
regardless of the "status area" in which it is found.[23] In view of this report,
and since Nye-Short and Dentler-Monroe were unable to detect inter-class
differences, inter-class comparisons were made within the four community
types of this study. Following the technique employed by Nye and Short,
only those students age 15 and younger were used in these comparisons in

[23] Reiss and Rhodes, op. cit., p. 729. The concept of "status areas" is used here as
it was used by Reiss and Rhodes to designate residential areas of a definite social class
composition.

order to neutralize the possible effects of differential school drop-out rates by social classes in the older categories.

With the exception of the industrial city, no significant inter-class differences in illegal behavior rates were found within community types when either the Wilcoxon test was used for all offenses or when individual offense comparisons were made.[24] This finding supports hypothesis #3. It could account for the inability of Nye-Short and Dentler-Monroe to find differences among the socio-economic classes from several relatively similar communities in which their studies were conducted. It is also somewhat compatible with the Reiss and Rhodes findings. However, we did not find indications of higher rates of illegal conduct in the predominant socio-economic class within most areas, as the Reiss and Rhodes data suggested.[25] This may have been a function of the unique manner in which the socio-economic categories had to be combined for comparison purposes in this study. These findings, however, are logical in that boys and girls of the minority social classes within a "status area" would likely strive to adhere to the norms of the predominant social class as closely as possible whether these norms were legal or illegal.

Within the industrial city the second socio-economic category (index scores 24–47) was slightly significantly lower than either extreme category when the Wilcoxon test was used. Since the largest percentage of the sample of the industrial city falls in the lowest socio-economic category (0–23) and since this category evidences one of the highest rates of misconduct, the finding for this community is somewhat similar to the Reiss-Rhodes findings.

CONCLUSIONS

The findings of this study tend to resolve some of the apparent conflicts in the literature that have arisen from previous research concerning the

[24] Because of small numbers in social classes within certain communities, categories were collapsed or ignored for comparison purposes as shown below. Refer to Table 1 for designation of categories. The Wilcoxon matched-pairs signed-ranks test was used.

Rural farm	category 1 versus 2, 3, 4	insignificant
Lower urban	category 1 versus 2, 3, 4	insignificant
	category 1 versus 5	insignificant
	categories 2, 3, 4 versus 5	insignificant
Industrial		
city	category 1 versus 2	significant
	category 2 versus 3, 4	significant
	category 1 versus 3, 4	insignificant
Upper urban	category 3 versus 4	insignificant

[25] Reiss and Rhodes, *op. cit.*, p. 729.

relationship between the nature of illegal behavior and socio-economic class. However, some of the results contradict earlier reports.

Our findings are similar to those of Nye-Short and Dentler-Monroe in that we failed to detect any significant differences in illegal behavior rates among the social classes of rural and small urban areas. However, in keeping with the class-oriented theories, we did find significant differences, both in quantity and quality of illegal acts, among communities or "status areas," each consisting of one predominant socio-economic class. The lower class areas have higher illegal behavior rates, particularly in the more serious types of offenses. Differences among the socio-economic classes within these "status areas" were generally insignificant (which does not agree with the findings of Reiss and Rhodes), although when social class categories were compared across communities, significant differences were found. All this suggests some extremely interesting relationships.

1. The pattern of illegal behavior within small communities or within "status areas" of a large metropolitan center is determined by the predominant class of that area. Social class differentiation within these areas is apparently not related to the incidence of illegal behavior. This suggests that there are community-wide norms which are related to illegal behavior and to which juveniles adhere regardless of their social class origins. The answer to the obvious question of how large an urban area must be before socio-economic class becomes a significant variable in the incidence of illegal behavior is not provided by this study. It is quite likely that in addition to size, other considerations such as the ratio of social class representation, ethnic composition, and the prestige of the predominant social class relative to other "status areas" would influence the misconduct rates. The population of 20,000 of the particular upper urban community used in this study is apparently not of sufficient size or composition to provide for behavior autonomy among the social classes in the illegal behavior sense. There is some evidence, however, that an industrial city of roughly 40,000 such as the one included here is on the brink of social class differentiation in misconduct rates.

2. Though the juveniles in all communities admitted indulgence in several nuisance offenses at almost equal rates, serious offenses are much more likely to have been committed by lower class urban youngsters. Perhaps the failure of some researchers to find differences among the social classes in their misconduct rates can be attributed to the relatively less-serious offenses included in their questionnaires or scales. It would seem to follow that any "subculture" characterized by the more serious delinquencies, would be found only in large, urban, lower-class areas. However, the data of this study, at best, can only suggest this relationship.

3. Lastly, these data suggest that the present explanations that rely heavily on socio-economic class as an all-determining factor in the etiology

of illegal behavior should be further specified to include data such as this study provides. For example, Cohen's thesis that a delinquent subculture emerges when lower class boys discover that they must satisfy their need for status by means other than those advocated in the middle class public schools should be amended to indicate that this phenomenon apparently occurs only in large metropolitan centers where the socio-economic classes are found in large relatively-homogeneous areas. In the same manner, Miller's theory of the relationship between the focal concerns of the lower class culture and delinquency may require closer scrutiny. If the relationship between focal concerns to illegal behavior that Miller has suggested exists, then those in the lower social class (as determined by father's occupation) who live in communities or "status areas" that are predominantly of some other social class, are apparently not participants in the "lower class culture;" or, because of their small numbers, they are being successfully culturally intimidated by the predominant class. Likewise, those who are thought to occupy middle class positions apparently take on lower class illegal behavior patterns when residing in areas that are predominantly lower class. This suggests either the great power of prevailing norms within a "status area" or a limitation of social class, as it is presently measured, as a significant variable in the determination of illegal behavior.

RESEARCH QUESTIONS

At least three general questions that demand further research emerge from this study:

1. What dimension (in size and other demographic characteristics) must an urban area attain before socio-economic class becomes a significant variable in the determination of illegal behavior patterns?

2. What are the specific differences between lower class populations and social structures located in rural or relatively small urban areas and those located in large, concentrated areas in metropolitan centers that would account for their differential illegal behavior rates, especially in the more serious offenses?

3. The findings of this study suggest that the criteria presently used to determine social class levels may not be the most conducive to the understanding of variation in the behavior of those who fall within these classes, at least for those within the juvenile ages. A substitute concept is that of "status area" as operationalized by Reiss and Rhodes. For example, the differentiating characteristics of a large, Negro, lower-class, urban "status area" could be established and would seem to have greater predictive and descriptive power than would the social class category as determined by present methods. Admittedly, this suggestion raises again the whole messy

affair of "cultural area typologies" but area patterns of behaviors obviously exist and must be handled in some manner. Research effort toward systematically combining the traditional socio-economic class concept with that of cultural area might prove extremely fruitful by providing us with important language and concepts not presently available.

9 Class Position, Peers and Delinquency[*]

MAYNARD L. ERICKSON
AND LAMAR T. EMPEY

A major theoretical theme in explaining delinquency has been concerned primarily with forces *external to*, rather than *within*, the family. Its main focus has been upon the location of the family unit in the larger social class structure.[1]

Class position is thought to be vitally important because it implies the presence or lack of educational and other opportunities for the child and determines the kinds of persons and activities, values and standards, barriers and gratifications which will influence him in virtually all areas of his life. Insofar as eventual lawbreaking is concerned, these influences are be-

Reprinted from *Sociology and Social Research, 49* (April, 1965), 268–282, by permission of the publisher and the authors.

[*] This work was financed in part by grants from the Ford Foundation and the Office of Juvenile Delinquency and Youth Development, United States Department of Health, Education and Welfare. Grateful acknowledgement is expressed to both.

[1] The volume of literature is large. For examples see Richard A. Cloward and Lloyd E. Ohlin, *Delinquency and Opportunity: A Theory of Delinquent Gangs* (New York: The Free Press of Glencoe, 1960); Albert K. Cohen, *Delinquent Boys: The Culture of the Gang* (New York: The Free Press of Glencoe, 1955); Robert K. Merton, *Social Theory and Social Structure* (New York: The Free Press of Glencoe, 1957), Chapters IV–V; Walter B. Miller, "Lower Class Culture as a Generating Milieu of Gang Delinquency." *The Journal of Social Issues*, Vol. 14, No. 3 (1958), 5–19; and Clifford R. Shaw, Henry D. McKay, *et al., Juvenile Delinquency and Urban Areas* (Chicago: University of Chicago Press, 1931):

lieved to leave a more lasting imprint than those limited primarily to the internal, emotional climate of the home.[2]

One variation of this theoretical theme suggests that low-class children are in a difficult social-psychological position. On one hand, it suggests that they are very much aware of middle-class values and standards, successes and satisfactions, having been socialized in a middle-class dominated society. But, on the other, because of inadequate access to these successes and satisfactions, they are more inclined than children from other class levels to become delinquent. A delinquent response is, for many of them, a natural reaction to problems they have in common. However, rather than isolated and pathological, this response is collective and shared. A low-class child joins with delinquent peers and participates in delinquent activities because these things represent an alternative means for acquiring many of the social and emotional satisfactions which other children obtain from conventional sources.[3]

This study is concerned with this latter explanation. If it is accurate certain things should be empirically demonstrable:

1. Low social class position should be more predictive of delinquency than middle- or upper-class position.

2. Juveniles from low-class homes should be more inclined to associate with delinquent peers and to exhibit more commitment to peer standards and expectations than juveniles from other class levels.

3. Associations with other delinquents and commitment to peer expectations should be more predictive of delinquent behavior than low-class family position; that is, if delinquency is a collective response to class position, then peer relationships should be demonstrable as a vitally important and intervening variable between low-class family position and habitual delinquent behavior.

ACTUAL VS. OFFICIAL DELINQUENCY

Prior to examining these issues, there is another matter of extreme importance. It concerns the accuracy of official statistics as a source of data on delinquency. Much of the theory building just described is based upon them. Yet, official statistics really measure several things: (1) the delinquent acts which juveniles commit; (2) the responses of society to these acts; and (3) the whole context of familial and social forces which, according

---

[2] See especially Cohen, *Delinquent Boys, op. cit.*; Cloward and Ohlin, *Delinquency and Opportunity, op. cit.*; and Shaw and McKay, *Juvenile Delinquency and Urban Areas, op. cit.*

[3] Cloward and Ohlin, *Delinquency and Opportunity, op. cit.*; Cohen, *Delinquent Boys, op. cit.*; and Merton, *Social Theory and Social Structure, op. cit.*

to the juvenile court law, are taken into consideration in dealing with juveniles. But official statistics do not make clear the contribution of each of these factors to the total. Theory and research, therefore, cannot be sure which of the many they are describing.[4]

The problem is that, until more evidence is available on the *actual* rather than the official amount and nature of delinquency, investigators will be hampered in their efforts to explain delinquent acts, *per se*, and to isolate the specific influences and processes which lead to them. It will be impossible to tell whether official records represent the total iceberg or only the tip that is observable above the surface of the water.

This study attempts to remedy this situation by basing its analysis upon self-reported rather than official data. All of the respondents were contacted in person by the authors. Data were gathered by means of a detailed interview which was conducted as follows: (1) each of 22 different delinquent acts, ranging from traffic to very serious offenses, was defined in detail; (2) each respondent was asked if he had ever committed the offense; (3) if so, how many times he had committed it; and, (4) if he had ever been caught, arrested, or brought to court for the offense. Reliability and validity checks were made.[5] Results were encouraging, supporting similar findings in other studies.[6]

It is complex and difficult to relate each of the 22 offenses to a number of family, class, and peer variables. Therefore, attempts were made to construct scales which represent the kinds of offenses which form unidimensional patterns. The attempts were successful. Three Guttman scales were developed:

1. A *general theft* scale made up of dichotomous items and including theft of articles or money valued at less than $2, theft of articles or money valued from $2–$50 and theft of articles worth more than $50. The coefficient of reproducibility for the scale is .91.

2. A *serious theft scale* made up of dichotomous items and including theft of articles or money worth more than $50, auto theft, and theft involv-

---

[4] Official records have been suspect for a long time. Our own work, for example, suggests that more than 9 out of 10 violations may go undetected and unacted upon. See Maynard L. Erickson and LaMar T. Empey, "Court Records, Undetected Delinquency and Decision Making," *The Journal of Criminal Law, Criminology and Police Science*, 54 (December, 1963), 456–69; and for a critical review of statistics, Donald R. Cressey, "A State of Criminal Statistics," *National Probation and Parole Association Journal*, 3 (July, 1957), 230–34.

[5] Maynard L. Erickson and LaMar T. Empey, "Court Records, Undetected Delinquency and Decision Making," *op. cit.*

[6] F. Ivan Nye, James F. Short, Jr., and V. J. Olsen, "Socio-Economic Status and Delinquent Behavior," *American Journal of Sociology*, 63 (January, 1958), 381–89; and Martin Gold, "Socio-Economic Distributions of Juvenile Delinquency," University of Michigan, Institute for Social Research, paper presented at the Annual Meetings of the American Psychological Association, Los Angeles, September 5, 1964.

ing breaking and entering. The coefficient of reproducibility for this scale was .93.

3. A *common delinquency* scale made up of dichotomous items and including illegal drinking, petty theft, open defiance of people in authority, skipping school and fighting. The coefficient of reproducibility was .91.

The use of these scales has the deficiency of eliminating some of the more serious offenses—narcotics sale and use, forgery, arson—because relatively few people had committed them and it eliminates other items such as running away and destroying property because they did not scale.

THE SAMPLE

The sample was drawn in Utah and included only white males, ages 15–17 years. Negro and Mexican boys were excluded because: (1) they constitute a very small minority in Utah; and (2) their exclusion permitted ethnic status to be controlled as a contributing influence.

The over-all sample was made up of four subsamples: (1) 50 randomly selected high school boys who had never been to court; (2) 30 randomly selected boys who had been to court once; (3) 80 randomly selected offenders who were on probation; and (4) 40 randomly selected offenders who were incarcerated.

The first three subsamples were drawn from a county population of 110,000 people. The fourth subsample was drawn from a state-wide population of incarcerated offenders.

MEASUREMENT OF SOCIAL CLASS

The occupational status of the father or guardian was used as the criterion for defining class level for each family. Occupation was used because it has proven to be the most important single measure of class.[7]

Occupational status was determined by means of an occupational prestige scale which was formed by combining the Hatt-North[8] and Smith[9] scales, whose common occupations correlated .97 with each other.[10] The

---

[7] W. Lloyd Warner, M. Meeker and K. Eels, *Social Class in America* (Chicago: Social Science Research Associates, Inc., 1949), 167–68; Nye, Short and Olsen, *op. cit.*; and Leona Tyler, *The Psychology of Human Differences* (New York: Appleton-Century-Crofts, 1947), 145–46.

[8] Paul K. Hatt and C. C. North, "Jobs and Occupations: A Popular Evaluation," in *Class, Status and Power*, ed. by R. Bendix and S. M. Lipset (New York: The Free Press of Glencoe, 1953), 411–26.

[9] Mapheus Smith, "An Empirical Scale of Prestige of Occupations," *American Sociological Review*, 8 (April, 1943), 185–92.

[10] LaMar T. Empey, "Social Class and Occupational Aspiration: A Comparison of Absolute and Relative Measurement," *American Sociological Review*, 21 (December, 1956), 705–6.

rankings of 250 test occupations using this combined scale also correlated .75 with a socioeconomic index by the National Opinion Research Center.[11]

The combined scale ranks occupations from 0 to 100. It was collapsed for purposes of this analysis into three major categories: (1) *low*, including unskilled or semi-skilled occupations; (2) *middle*, including skilled occupations, owners of small businesses and a variety of white collar jobs; and (3) *upper*, including most of the professions, corporate positions, scientists, and artists.

CLASS MEMBERSHIP AND DELINQUENCY

There was a statistically significant correlation between low-class position and a greater amount of delinquency as indicated by all three of the delinquency scales. However, the degree of association was low making the predictive efficiency of class position extremely poor: for *general* theft the correlation was only .20, explaining only 4 per cent of the variance; for serious theft .17, explaining only 3 per cent of the variance; and for *common* delinquency .17, explaining only 3 per cent of the variance.[12]

Because of this apparent low degree of association, it was decided to examine the matter further using analysis of variance. This statistical tool seemed well suited for the purpose because it is a means of tracing down sources of variation. In this case it was important to learn two things: (1) whether there might be greater variation within the classes than between them, and (2) whether the correlation coefficient was simply indicating a general tendency for delinquency to be located toward the bottom end of the class ladder rather sharply distinguishing between the two classes there. For example, the correlation coefficient could be measuring a very low tendency for upper-class respondents to be delinquent rather than a very high tendency for low-class children to exceed the other two.

The analysis provided answers for the two questions. The major source of variation was between rather than within classes. The F-ratio was significant at the .001 level. However, the variance did not conform precisely to theoretical expectation; that is, it was not located most strongly beween low-class respondents and both other groups but between upper-class respondents and both other groups.

The correlation coefficient presented earlier had correctly indicated a

[11] Albert Reiss, Jr., *Occupations and Social Status* (New York: The Free Press of Glencoe, 1961), 259–95.

[12] Nye, Short and Olsen, "Socio-Economic Status and Delinquent Behavior," *op. cit.*, were not able to find consistent differences among classes. Gold, "Socio-Economic Distributions of Juvenile Delinquency," *op. cit.*, reported a statistically reliable relationship between white low-status boys and delinquency.

relationship between class and delinquency but, in this case, it was due more to a low amount of delinquency on the extreme upper end of the class ladder rather than a high amount on the extreme lower end. On all three delinquency scales, low and middle-class respondents did not differ significantly from each other. Yet, at the same time, the difference between both of them and the upper-class group was significant beyond the .001 level.

Thus, the correlation coefficients were measuring a general tendency for delinquency to be concentrated toward, but not primarily at, the bottom end of the class ladder. With respect to the theoretical position that delinquency is primarily a low-class phenomenon, therefore, there are two striking things about these findings: (1) that low- and middle-class respondents did not differ significantly and (2) that class was really a poor predictor of delinquency, explaining only a small proportion of the variance. For this sample, at least, they heighten the importance of considering other variables.

DELINQUENT ASSOCIATES

As mentioned earlier, the body of theory under consideration suggests that the low-class child may be more inclined than other children to associate with delinquent peers. Hypothetically, they represent a source of support and a means for establishing identity and status not otherwise available. In order to determine whether, in fact, low-class respondents were any more inclined to associate with delinquent peers, the following steps were taken.

A special instrument was created, the rationale for which was provided by Sutherland's Theory of Differential Association and its emphasis upon three things: the duration, priority and intensity of delinquent associations.[13] In order to provide some assessment of these variables, each boy was asked to list his 5 best friends, how long he had known each of them and the number of times each week he associated with them. The names of these friends were then checked through court records to determine their official delinquent-nondelinquent standing.

Once this information was known, an index of delinquent-nondelinquent associations was constructed. A high score on the index indicates extensive and regular association with delinquents while a low score indicates the opposite. One primary weakness with the instrument is its reliance upon official data. This makes it subject to many of the limitations mentioned earlier. It is difficult, therefore, to determine whether delinquent, but not officially designated, peers are any more important to one than another.

Findings. The findings were a repeat of those already presented with

[13] Edwin H. Sutherland and Donald R. Cressey, *Principles of Criminology* (New York: J. B. Lippincott Co., 5th ed., 1955), Chapter IV.

respect to class and delinquency. The significant variance was between rather than within classes and it was the *upper* rather than the lower-class group that differed from the others. The low and middle-class groups were similar in their tendencies to associate with known delinquents but both differed significantly from the upper-class group. In fact, the extent of difference was greater between the middle- and upper-class groups ($P<.001$) than it was between the low- and upper-class groups ($P<.01$).

Coupled with the previous findings, a pattern begins to emerge. So far it indicates that those respondents who had been most delinquent were also those who were most inclined to have delinquent associates. But it does not indicate that such a pattern is primarily a low-class phenomenon. Rather it includes middle- as well as low-class respondents and excludes only the upper class.

PEER COMMITMENT

This is a significant finding but association alone is not the only dimension of peer relationships. An important distinction has been made in the literature between one's "membership" group and his "reference" group. Membership in a particular group need not connote a strong identification with that group. One's point of reference may be elsewhere.

Therefore, because mere association with delinquents or nondelinquents alone may not connote identification with them, it was thought important to determine the extent to which each respondent identifies with, or was committed in an ideological way to, the expectations of his peers. Would he be inclined to do what the group asked of him? Would he go along with them? Would he protect them?

Three Guttman scales were developed as a method of studying this dimension. The first scale includes 4 items and measures commitment to peer-defined, but nondelinquent expectations. Typical of the items included in this and the other two scales is the following:

Suppose you were planning to go to church one Sunday morning and your friends called and wanted you to do something else with them, would you go with them?

Other items involved making a choice between watching TV or going to a bowling alley with the boys, doing homework or riding around with friends, allowing or refusing a friend to copy school work. The coefficient of reproducibility for this scale is .93.

The second scale contains 7 items which were constructed in the same way as those in the first. It measures commitment to delinquent peer expectations: refusing to or going along with friends who want to steal gas, helping a friend to hide if he is wanted by the police, joining others who want to skip school, joining in a gang fight or hiding a friend who has run away from home. The coefficient of reproducibility is .90.

The third scale was designed to determine if a boy would "rat" or "fink" on his friends. It asked if he would tell parents, teachers or police about friends in trouble. This "fink" scale has 3 items and a coefficient of reproducibility of .99.

Findings. These findings contributed to the emerging pattern. On the nondelinquent peer scale, low and middle-class respondents did not differ significantly from each other but both differed, and to the same extent (P<.01), from upper-class respondents. Both were significantly more committed to the expectations of peers, even though in this case the expectations were nondelinquent.

On the delinquent peer scale the pattern was generally the same except that it was the middle rather than the low-class group which displayed the greatest commitment to delinquent expectations. Whereas the level of significance between the low and upper-class groups on this scale was only .05, it was at the .001 level for the middle- and upper-class groups.

On the "fink" scale, there were no significant differences, either within or between classes. The implication was clear that, whether delinquent or nondelinquent, lower or upper class, these adolescents were ideologically opposed to informing on a peer. This finding was at variance with the emerging pattern in the sense this scale made no distinctions and would not be useful in predicting delinquency.

The pattern thus far has not conformed closely to theoretical expectation. It has suggested that delinquency is concentrated toward, but not primarily at, the bottom of the class ladder. Middle-class respondents report having been about as delinquent as low-class respondents. Only the upper-class group differs.

Similarly, the tendency has been greater among low and middle-class boys to associate with, and be committed to, delinquent peers than upper class boys. The question that is significant, therefore, is whether peer relationships are themselves a more, or less, efficient predictor of delinquency than social class. Hypothetically, they might be a key, intervening variable. The last part of the analysis is concerned with this issue.

PEER RELATIONS AND DELINQUENCY

The importance of peer relations will be examined through the use of simple and multiple correlation. A series of tables are presented which compare the single and combined relationships of class and peer variables with the three delinquency scales. These tables are complex and it is difficult to repeat in the text all they reveal. The reader is urged, therefore to devote considerable attention to them.

General Theft. The first table presents the data for the general theft scale. It is divided into three sections: the first shows the relationship between such single variables as class and general theft, delinquent associates and theft, commitment to nondelinquent peers and theft and so on; the second takes two of these variables at a time and relates them through multiple correlation to general theft; and the third relates three variables at a time to general theft. This does not exhaust all the possible combinations but demonstrates some important trends.

It will be observed in Table 1 that peer variables are considerably more efficient as single predictors than social class. A general commitment to peers as revealed by the nondelinquent peer index is the most highly correlated with general theft ($r = .41$) followed by commitment to delinquent peer standards ($r = .35$), associations with known delinquents ($r = .31$) and an unwillingness to "fink" ($r = .30$). These relationships and their explained variance are in sharp contrast to the much lower predictability of social class, ($r = .20$).

The same kind of picture is presented in the correlation of variables, taken two at a time, with general theft. The most efficient combinations in terms of rank are the delinquent associates and nondelinquent peer scales ($r = .46$), the nondelinquent and "fink" scale ($r = .44$) and the nondelinquent scales combined with social class ($r = .44$). The striking thing is the apparently much greater influence of a general commitment to peers in explaining general theft than delinquent associates or, especially, social class.

Predictive efficiency increases again when three variables are correlated. Three combinations were approximately equal having a correlation of .48 and accounting for 23 per cent of the variance. Apparently delinquent associates and commitment to nondelinquent expectations are the most important variables, appearing in all three combinations. The three less significant variables were social class commitment to delinquent expectations and the "fink" scale.

The least predictive combination of all ($r = .41$) included class, delinquent associates and the "fink" scales. This triple combination was less efficient than several combinations of just two variables. Again, social class seemed relatively less important than other variables and in future analyses might better be removed.

Serious Theft. The same process of analysis was followed in examining serious theft. The results are displayed in Table 2. One important difference that is immediately observable is that none of the variables is as predictive of serious theft as it was of general theft. The most efficient combination of

TABLE 1. CORRELATES WITH *GENERAL* THEFT

Variables Correlated	Correlation Coefficient	Explained Variance
Simple Correlation		
General Theft with:		
(1) Social Class	.20	.04
(2) Delinquent Associates	.31	.10
(3) Nondelinquent Comm.	.41	.17
(4) Delinquent Comm.	.35	.12
(5) "Fink" Scale	.30	.09
Multiple Correlation		
General Theft with:		
(1) (2)	.35	.12
(1) (3)	.44	.19
(1) (4)	.38	.14
(1) (5)	.33	.11
(2) (3)	.46	.22
(2) (4)	.43	.18
(2) (5)	.40	.16
(3) (4)	.43	.19
(3) (5)	.44	.19
(4) (5)	.39	.16
General Theft with:		
(1) (2) (3)	.48	.23
(1) (2) (4)	.44	.19
(1) (2) (5)	.41	.17
(1) (3) (4)	.45	.20
(1) (3) (5)	.45	.20
(1) (4) (5)	.41	.17
(2) (3) (4)	.48	.23
(2) (3) (5)	.48	.23
(2) (4) (5)	.45	.20
(3) (4) (5)	.45	.20

three variables, for example, is capable of explaining only 14 per cent of the variance contrasted to 23 per cent for general theft.

The second thing is striking is that, again, the most predictive variable is the nondelinquent peer scale, one which measures a general, but not necessarily delinquent, commitment to peers. But, along with it, delinquent associa-

TABLE 2. CORRELATES WITH *SERIOUS* THEFT

Variables Correlated	Correlation Coefficient	Explained Variance
	Simple Correlation	
Serious Theft with:		
(1) Social Class	.17	.03
(2) Delinquent Associates	.27	.07
(3) Nondelinquent Comm.	.32	.10
(4) Delinquent Comm.	.21	.04
(5) "Fink" Scale	.20	.04
	Multiple Correlation	
Serious Theft with:		
(1) (2)	.30	.09
(1) (3)	.34	.11
(1) (4)	.25	.06
(1) (5)	.24	.06
(2) (3)	.37	.14
(2) (4)	.31	.10
(2) (5)	.31	.10
(3) (4)	.32	.10
(3) (5)	.33	.11
(4) (5)	.25	.06
Serious Theft with:		
(1) (2) (3)	.39	.15
(1) (2) (4)	.33	.11
(1) (2) (5)	.33	.11
(1) (3) (4)	.34	.12
(1) (3) (5)	.35	.12
(1) (4) (5)	.28	.08
(2) (3) (4)	.37	.14
(2) (3) (5)	.38	.14
(2) (4) (5)	.33	.11
(3) (4) (5)	.33	.11

tions were almost as important. Taken together they accounted for as much variation (14 per cent) as did any combination of three variables, including themselves.

The third thing that is striking is the relative inefficiency of social class in explaining serious theft, especially when combined with two other indexes, the one measuring commitment to delinquent peer expectations and the one

TABLE 3. CORRELATES WITH *COMMON* DELINQUENCY

Variables Correlated	Correlation Coefficient	Explained Variance
Simple Correlation		
Common Delinquency with:		
(1) Social Class	.17	.03
(2) Delinquent Associates	.27	.07
(3) Nondelinquent Comm.	.20	.04
(4) Delinquent Comm.	.42	.18
(5) "Fink" Scale	.41	.17
Multiple Correlation		
Common Delinquency with:		
(1) (2)	.37	.14
(1) (3)	.47	.22
(1) (4)	.45	.20
(1) (5)	.38	.15
(2) (3)	.47	.22
(2) (4)	.47	.22
(2) (5)	.41	.17
(3) (4)	.46	.21
(3) (5)	.46	.21
(4) (5)	.45	.20
Common Delinquency with:		
(1) (2) (3)	.50	.25
(1) (2) (4)	.49	.24
(1) (2) (5)	.44	.20
(1) (3) (4)	.49	.24
(1) (3) (5)	.49	.24
(1) (4) (5)	.48	.23
(2) (3) (4)	.50	.25
(2) (3) (5)	.49	.24
(2) (4) (5)	.50	.25
(3) (4) (5)	.49	.24

measuring willingness to fink. Social class is the most inefficient but the other two are almost as bad. In various combinations of two, they are capable of explaining only about half the variance (6 vs. 11 to 14 per cent) of which some other combinations are capable.

Finally, the data on common delinquency are presented in Table 3. They are intriguing because they seem to attest to the validity of these instruments in measuring different kinds of delinquency. The scale which measures common delinquency seems to be getting at different phenomena than the theft scales. The reason is that the general predictive efficiency of the independent variables changed markedly. In general, they went up. But some of those which had been the most predictive previously declined in this case.

The most glaring example is the nondelinquent peer index which on the theft scales had been most efficient. In this case, it is second only to social class in its lack of ability to predict. Social class accounts for only 3 per cent of the variance while the nondelinquent peer index accounts for only 4 per cent.

Meanwhile, the predictive efficiency of the delinquent peer and "fink" scales went up while the importance of delinquent associates remained about the same. The delinquent peer scale—i.e., a willingness to go along with others in getting into trouble—accounts for 18 per cent of the variance, the highest of any variable on any kind of offense pattern. The "fink" scale was not far behind with 17 per cent. Apparently, common delinquency—drinking, fighting, petty theft, skipping school—is more closely associated for the sample with what is traditionally thought to be delinquent standards and expectations than is either of the unidimensional patterns of general or serious theft.

Some further evidence for this conclusion appeared when these two variables were combined for purposes of calculating multiple correlation. They seemed to be measuring somewhat the same thing because together they did not account for as much variance as did each of them when combined with other variables.

The highest multiple correlations always involved some combination of delinquent associate and peer commitment variables. The largest amount of variance, 25 per cent, was accounted for by a combination of indexes of delinquent associates, nondelinquent and delinquent peer commitments. Other combinations which added the "fink" scale were not far behind (24 per cent).

These findings are important but at the same time must not be overrated. They are important because, for this sample, they find delinquent associates and an identification with peers to be far more predictive of delinquency than social class position. In the cast of single variables, they were as much as 6 times more efficient; in the case of multiple variables as much as 16 times more efficient.

On the other hand, the highest per cent of variance explained by any combination of variables was only 25 per cent for common delinquency (in the case of serious theft only 14 per cent). This leaves 75 per cent unexplained. Thus, these findings are important, not so much because they explain delinquency, but suggest the need for qualitatively different emphases in both theory and research.

SUMMARY AND CONCLUSIONS

This paper was based upon self-reported rather than official delinquency. It attempted to examine certain assumptions regarding the relation of class and peer variables to delinquency. The findings were these:

1. There was a slight but statistically reliable relationship between social class and delinquency. However, when variance was traced it was discovered that the correlation was significant more because upper-class respondents differed from the other two than that low-class respondents differed from the other two. Middle and low-class did not differ significantly from each other.

2. The same pattern characterized the relationship of social class to delinquent associates. The upper-class group was significantly less inclined than the other two to have delinquent associates. Middle and low-class respondents did not differ.

3. The pattern was confirmed even more in the analysis of respondent commitment to peer expectations. Upper-class respondents were significantly less committed than others to the expectations of their peers, delinquent or nondelinquent. But, in addition, there was some suggestion that it was the middle rather than the low-class group which had the greatest commitment of all.

The data would definitely not support the notion that peer standards have more importance for the low than the middle-class juvenile. In fact, these findings might lead one to hypothesize that, because they are departing perhaps even further from the expectations of their parents than low-class children, middle class offenders have greater need for peer support than low-class offenders.

4. Delinquent associates and peer commitment variables proved to be far more predictive of delinquent behavior than did social class. As a part of an overall pattern, it strongly implied the need to examine more carefully the role of peers, as contrasted to class, in attempting to understand delinquency.

The need for qualification is always present. There are two ways in which this need is apparent here. In the first place, the sample was drawn in a Western State and from relatively small communities. Therefore, the fact that delinquency and commitment to peers showed up so strongly among the middle-class group might come as some surprise. One might expect family and community influences to exert greater control.

Yet, on the other hand, the sample did not include Negro and other minorities. What this inclusion might have meant cannot be determined and might paint a different picture elsewhere. It would also add other complexities which were controlled here.

The second need for qualification is related. The amount of variance explained by these variables was not great. In most cases, over three-quarters of it remained unexplained. This kind of a problem occurs almost every time the investigator turns from the warming logic of theory to the icy experience of empirical investigation. It points to the tremendous lack of certainty as to what the issues really are, as to whether the problem is theoretical, methodological or both. Perhaps it changes so fast with respect to time, location and system that different models than ones now used are needed for postulating and explaining, ones which do not seek generalizations but are related almost entirely to contemporary issues and decision-making.

PART V

Crime and Delinquency as Products of Interaction

Introduction

In his classic statement of the theory of "differential association," the late Edwin H. Sutherland described the variables which he considered to be fundamental components of any adequate explanation of delinquent and criminal behavior. His statement is a "dual theory" of the kind described in the introduction to Part IV. One can best understand the "individual conduct" part of this theory, in contrast to the "epidemiological" part, if it is viewed as a set of directives about the kinds of things that ought to be included in a theory of criminality, rather than as an actual statement of theory. The variables Sutherland pointed to are the same variables included in the social psychological theory of "symbolic interaction." According to this theory, and according to Sutherland, behavior is learned through a process of communication—interaction—with others. Communications take many forms, from physical appearance to gestures, but the principal form is verbal expression. All communications consist of symbols or stimuli which have learned meanings and values for the actors.[1]

Sutherland shared with the "symbolic interactionists" the assertion that the basic elements of any kind of social behavior are verbalizations which represent norms, values, definitions, attitudes, rationalizations,

[1] For general statements of symbolic interaction theory see Tamotsu Shibutani, *Society and Personality* (Englewood Cliffs: Prentice-Hall, 1961); and Arnold M. Rose, ed., *Human Behavior and Social Processes: An Interactionist Approach* (Boston: Houghton Mifflin, 1962).

rules, etc. He also agreed that the process of taking on (learning) behavior patterns is importantly influenced by the persons and groups with whom one interacts. Specifically in regard to criminology, Sutherland argued that we should stop looking for emotional disturbances and personality traits as the bases of delinquency, and that we should start looking at the verbalizations of groups in which individuals participate. For it is in the context of interactions composed of verbalizations that the individual learns criminalistic attitudes, precepts, and behavior. Feldman's article criticizes the psychoanalytic perspective in criminology precisely because it has not taken sufficient cognizance of the fact that a learning process must occur before the personality of the criminal can be established and before his actions come to include violations of the law.

The shift in perspective called for by Feldman involves empirical investigation of variables other than "emotional traits," "personality" or "early childhood experiences." William Sewell (a general symbolic inter-action theorist, not a criminologist) contends that research into those particular aspects of personality most likely to be directly influenced by others, such as attitudes, values, and aspirations, would be more promising than studies concerned with "deeper personality characteristics."[2] The increasing influence of symbolic interactionist theory reflected in Sewell's recommendations for general social psychological research has also been reflected in criminological research and theory. Daniel Glaser, for one, has noted such a trend:

The process of rationalization reconciles crime or delinquency with conventionality; it permits a person to maintain a favorable conception of himself, while acting in ways which others see as inconsistent with a favorable self-conception. In this analysis of motivation by the verbal representation of the world with which a person justifies his behavior, sociologists are converging with many psychologists. This seems to be an individualistic analysis of behavior, but the so-called "symbolic interactionists" viewpoint is gaining acceptance, and it sees individual human thought as essentially a social interaction process: the individual "talks to himself" in thinking and reacts to his own words and gestures in "working himself" into an emotional state in much the same manner as he does in discussion or in emotional interaction with others.[3]

When Sutherland told us to look at symbolic behavior (e.g., words) in order to explain why most people are law abiding and only a small proportion are criminal, he was aligning himself with a group of social scientists whose assumptions about human behavior were quite different from those whose theoretical base was Freudian psychology. The latter

[2] William H. Sewell, "Social Class and Childhood Personality," *Sociometry,* 24 (1961), 340–356.

[3] Daniel Glaser, "The Sociological Approach to Crime and Correction," *Law and Contemporary Problems,* 23 (Autumn, 1958), 683–702.

view asserts that personality is an outgrowth of an inevitable conflict between individual needs and the requirements of the social order.[4] Sutherland and many contemporary social psychologists conceive of "personality" as an inseparable part of the social organization, not as an "adjustment" to it. Man is born into a social setting, and his personality is shaped not by conflict with a restricting social order but by participation in social relationships. Through these relationships he learns the values, norms, rules, rituals, customs, and regulations that comprise the culture around him.

Man behaves according to the rules of social groups, and since he participates in many groups, he must sometimes reconcile conflicting normative directives. Criminality, like other aspects of behavior—attitudes, beliefs, and values—is the property of groups, not of individuals, much as the French language or the English language is the property of a collectivity rather than of an individual.

Two questions are frequently directed toward those who study criminal behavior from the interactionist perspective. One asks how the influence of the dominant culture is diminished so that definitions favorable to violation of the law assume first priority. The selections which follow Sutherland's theory and Feldman's supporting view deal with this question. The other question asks how this theory explains the "loner" in crime. Responses to this question will be considered in Part X.

Maurer makes a distinction between the dominant culture where anti-criminal behavior patterns predominate and the subculture of pickpockets which consists principally of pro-criminal behavior patterns. According to Sutherland, one becomes a criminal if he has an excess of associations with criminal values (such as those making up the subculture of pickpockets), as compared with the law-abiding values of the dominant culture. Maurer shows that children of pickpockets live in a cultural environment such that exposure to an excess of associations with values favorable to theft is inevitable. In addition, they have very little association with values that hold stealing to be undesirable or unacceptable. It is not necessary to block their legitimate paths to success in order to motivate them to pick pockets. Once having absorbed the values of the subculture through participation in everyday social interaction, these children have no real opportunity to choose a noncriminal occupation. Maurer provides a description of a colorful criminal subculture whose own special language, symbolizing special skills and special norms, is so pervasive that the rather remote conventional community with its rules and opportunities cannot effectively compete with it.

In most delinquent and criminal learning, the variables are not nearly

[4] See Sigmund Freud, *Civilization and Its Discontents* (New York: Jonathan Cape and Harrison Smith, 1930).

as clear as they are in the case of professional pickpockets. The process of internalizing norms and learning patterns of behavior involves multiple social interactions—interactions that are so entangled, so complicated, and so subtle that even the participants are unable to describe clearly how they came to hold certain attitudes or act in certain ways. It is not yet possible to reduce the effects of these interactions to a simple equation by adding the factors for and against law violation, and determining the valence, plus or minus, that prevails.

According to Sutherland's theory, and that of general symbolic interaction, the impact upon individual conduct of all the relationships in which a person participates is determined by the symbols (language, action, appearance) he learns from other people. In simplified form, this view regards cultures and subcultures as comprised of collections of symbols, the meaning of which is shared by participants. In order to study and explain subcultural behavior (whether criminal, adolescent, or middle-class) it is essential to know its symbols and understand their significance for its members. Symbols make certain behavior appropriate when directed toward "outsiders" but inappropriate toward in-group members. What is right, and when, and to whom is represented symbolically in the group norms in the same way that what is wrong or illegitimate is defined. The legality of an act is in the statutes or the criminal code, but the legitimacy of that act can vary situationally. What is "all right," in some instances at least, may also be illegal. In our culture there are a number of ideologies that sanction criminal behavior. To give some easy examples: "Honesty is the best policy but business is business." "It is all right to steal a loaf of bread when you are starving." "All people steal when they get into a tight spot." "Some of our most respectable citizens got their start in life by using other people's money temporarily." "He is a dishonest merchant who cheats his customers and he therefore deserves to be robbed." The selection by Hartung gives examples of how certain vocabularies of motives legitimize forms of behavior that are violations of the law.[5]

Research conducted by the Schwendingers demonstrates that a specific vocabulary of motives emerges from interacting with others who have already adopted it. Their study compared the role-playing responses of noninstitutionalized delinquents and nondelinquents to hypothetical situations involving probable victims. They found that members of delinquent groups expressed a different rhetoric than that did nondelinquent groups. Delinquent dialogues focused on instrumental or tactical aspects of the crime; they were indifferent to the moral considerations that

[5] Hartung's selection is a restatement in the language of symbolic interaction of Gresham Sykes and David Matza's thesis in "Techniques of Neutralization: A Theory of Delinquency," *American Sociological Review, 22* (August, 1957), 664–670.

characterized nondelinquent dialogues. As youngsters engage in initial forms of delinquency, they learn to stereotype victims in ways that make them appear to be rather proper subjects of victimization. The delinquents studied had learned, more effectively than had the nondelinquents, that victims were "worthless," "cowardly," "untrustworthy." A similar point was made some years ago by Howard Becker in his study of the process of becoming a marihuana user. In his article, he shows that definitions learned from experienced users determine whether or not an inexperienced marihuana smoker becomes "high" and whether he enjoys the sensation. The selection by Bryan presents another example of the important role that social relationships and special vocabularies of motives play in the process of becoming involved in illegal careers—in this case, prostitution. Before becoming call girls, all the women studied had prior contact with someone in the profession. These contacts provided opportunities for the novice to learn the profession's ideology and to receive specific instructions on how to deal appropriately with customers and colleagues.[6]

A number of modifications of the differential association principle have been proposed. Hartung's article reformulates the principle in the language of contemporary symbolic interactionist theory. The final selections also represent important efforts to improve the theory.

Glaser makes the important point that Sutherland's concept of an "excess of definitions" (favorable or unfavorable to law violation) does not clearly indicate what specific mechanisms are involved in the learning process. Further, "association" seems to be equated with "contact" in face-to-face relationships. Like other symbolic interactionists, Glaser is concerned with the fact that individuals "identify" with imaginary persons and reference groups. He argues that the concept "differential identification" describes the criminal learning process more precisely than does "differential association." Like Glaser, Burgess and Akers note that "excess of definitions" does not adequately describe the subtle process of behavioral exchange. They base their revision of the differential association principal on a theory of human learning which is somewhat of an alternative to symbolic interactionist theory. In terms of "reinforcement theory," or "operant behavior theory," or "operant conditioning theory," they specify conditions and mechanisms through which criminal behavior is learned.[7] The express purpose of this reformulation of the components of differential association theory is to seek propositions that can be empirically tested.

    [6] The classic statement of the genesis of criminal behavior based upon selection and tutelage is contained in Edwin H. Sutherland, *The Professional Thief* (Chicago: University of Chicago Press, 1937).

    [7] See B. F. Skinner, *Science and Human Behavior* (New York: Macmillan, 1953).

The final selection reviews most of the research and writing involving differential association up to 1960. The criticisms of the principle are discussed, and Cressey concludes that it can organize and make sense of statistical information on crime and delinquency and specify the process by which individuals become criminals. The arguments contained in this selection comprise the major elements of the theoretical foundation upon which this book is based.

1 A Sociological Theory of Criminal Behavior

EDWIN H. SUTHERLAND
AND DONALD R. CRESSEY

THE PROBLEM FOR CRIMINOLOGICAL THEORY

If criminology is to be scientific, the heterogeneous collection of "multiple factors" known to be associated with crime and criminality should be organized and integrated by means of an explanatory theory which has the same characteristics as the scientific explanations in other fields of study. That is, the conditions which are said to cause crime should always be present when crime is present, and they should always be absent when crime is absent. Such a theory would stimulate, simplify, and give direction to criminological research, and it would provide a framework for understanding the significance of much of the knowledge acquired about crime and criminality in the past. Furthermore, it would be useful in control of crime, providing it could be "applied" in much the same way that the engineer "applies" the scientific theories of the physicist.

There are two complementary procedures which may be used to put order into criminological knowledge, to develop a causal theory of criminal behavior. The first is logical abstraction. Negroes, urban-dwellers, and young adults all have comparatively high crime rates. What do they have in common that results in these high crime rates? Research studies have shown that criminal behavior is associated in greater or less degree with

Reprinted from Edwin H. Sutherland and Donald R. Cressey, *Principles of Criminology* (7th ed.; Philadelphia: J. B. Lippincott Co., 1966), pp. 77–83, with the permission of the publisher.

the social and personal pathologies, such as poverty, bad housing, slum-residence, lack of recreational facilities, inadequate and demoralized families, feeble-mindedness, emotional instability, and other traits and conditions. What do these conditions have in common which apparently produces excessive criminality? Research studies have also demonstrated that many persons with those pathological traits and conditions do not commit crimes and that persons in the upper socio-economic class frequently violate the law, although they are not in poverty, do not lack recreational facilities, and are not feeble-minded or emotionally unstable. Obviously, it is not the conditions or traits themselves which cause crime, for the conditions are sometimes present when criminality does not occur, and they also are sometimes absent when criminality does occur. A causal explanation of criminal behavior can be reached by abstracting, logically, the mechanisms and processes which are common to the rich and the poor, Negroes and whites, urban- and the rural-dwellers, young adults and old adults, and the emotionally stable and the emotionally unstable who commit crimes.

In arriving at these abstract mechanisms and processes, criminal behavior must be precisely defined and carefully distinguished from non-criminal behavior. The problem in criminology is to explain the criminality of behavior, not behavior, as such. The abstract mechanisms and processes common to the classes of criminals indicated above should not also be common to non-criminals. Criminal behavior is human behavior, has much in common with non-criminal behavior, and must be explained within the same general framework used to explain other human behavior. However, an explanation of criminal behavior should be a specific part of a general theory of behavior. Its specific task should be to differentiate criminal from non-criminal behavior. Many things which are necessary for behavior are not for that reason important to the criminality of behavior. Respiration, for instance, is necessary for any behavior, but the respiratory process cannot be used in an explanation of criminal behavior, for it does not differentiate criminal behavior from non-criminal behavior.

The second procedure for putting order into criminological knowledge is differentiation of levels of analysis. This means that the problem is limited to a particular part of the whole situation, largely in terms of chronology. The causal analysis must be held at a particular level. For example, when physicists stated the law of falling bodies they were not concerned with the reasons why a body began to fall except as this might affect the initial momentum. It made no difference to the physicist whether a body began to fall because it was dropped from the hand of an experimental physicist or rolled off the edge of a bridge because of vibration caused by a passing vehicle. Also, a round object would have rolled off the bridge more readily than a square object, but this fact was not significant for the law of falling bodies. Such facts were considered as existing on a different level of explanation and were irrelevant to the problem with which the physicists were concerned. Much of the confusion regarding criminal behavior is due to a failure to define and hold constant the level of explanation. By analogy, many criminologists would attribute some degree of causal power to the "roundness" of the object in the illustration above. However, consideration of time sequences among the factors associated with crime and criminality may lead to simplicity of statement. In the heterogeneous collection of factors associated with criminal behavior, one factor often occurs prior to another factor (in much the way that "roundness" occurs prior to "vibra-tion," and "vibration" occurs prior to "rolling off a bridge"), but a theoretical statement about criminal behavior can be made without referring to those early factors. By holding the analysis at one level, the early factors are combined with or differentiated from later factors or conditions, thus reducing the number of variables which must be considered in a theory.

A motion picture several years ago showed two boys engaged in a minor theft; they ran when they were discovered; one boy had longer legs, escaped, and became a priest; the other had shorter legs, was caught, committed to a reformatory, and became a gangster. In this comparison, the boy who became a criminal was differentiated from the one who did not become a criminal by the length of his legs. But "length of legs" need not be considered in a criminological theory for, in general, no significant relationship has been found between criminality and length of legs and certainly many persons with short legs are law-abiding and many persons with long legs are criminals. The length of the legs does not determine criminality and has no necessary relation to criminality. In the illustration, the differential in the length of the boys' legs may be observed to be significant to subsequent criminality or non-criminality only to the degree that it determined the subsequent experiences and associations of the two boys. It is in these experiences and associations, then, that the mechanisms and processes which are important to criminality or non-criminality are to be found. A "one-level" theoretical explanation of crime would be concerned solely with these mechanisms and processes, not with the earlier factor "length of legs."

TWO TYPES OF EXPLANATIONS OF CRIMINAL BEHAVIOR

Scientific explanations of criminal behavior may be stated either in terms of the processes which are operating at the moment of the occurrence of crime or in terms of the processes operating in the earlier history of the criminal. In the first case, the explanation may be called "mechanistic," "situational," or "dynamic"; in the second, "historical" or "genetic." Both types of explanation are desirable. The mechanistic type of explanation has been favored by physical and biological scientists, and it probably could be the more efficient type of explanation of criminal behavior. However, criminological explanations of the mechanistic type have thus far been notably unsuccessful, perhaps largely because they have been formulated in connection with the attempt to isolate personal and social pathologies among criminals. Work from this point of view has, at least, resulted in the conclusion that the immediate determinants of criminal behavior lie in the person-situation complex.

The objective situation is important to criminality largely to the extent that it provides an opportunity for a criminal act. A thief may steal from a fruit stand when the owner is not in sight but refrain when the owner is in sight; a bank burglar may attack a bank which is poorly protected but refrain from attacking a bank protected by watchmen and burglar alarms. A corporation which manufactures automobiles seldom or never violates the Pure Food and Drug Law, but a meat-packing corporation might violate this law with great frequency. But in another sense, a psychological or sociological sense, the situation is not exclusive of the person, for the situation which is important is the situation as defined by the person who is involved. That is, some persons define a situation in which a fruit-stand owner is out of sight as a "crime-committing" situation, while others do not so define it. Furthermore, the events in the person-situation complex at the time a crime occurs cannot be separated from the prior life experiences of the criminal. This means that the situation is defined by the person in terms of the inclinations and abilities which the person has acquired up to date. For example, while a person could define a situation in such a manner that criminal behavior would be the inevitable result, his past experiences would for the most part determine the way in which he defined the situation. An explanation of criminal behavior made in terms of these past experiences is an historical or genetic explanation.

The following paragraphs state such a genetic theory of criminal behavior on the assumption that a criminal act occurs when a situation appropriate for it, as defined by the person, is present. The theory should be regarded as tentative, and it should be tested. . . .

GENETIC EXPLANATION OF CRIMINAL BEHAVIOR

The following statement refers to the process by which a particular person comes to engage in criminal behavior.

1. *Criminal behavior is learned.* Negatively, this means that criminal behavior is not inherited, as such; also, the person who is not already trained in crime does not invent criminal behavior, just as a person does

not make mechanical inventions unless he has had training in mechanics.

2. *Criminal behavior is learned in interaction with other persons in a process of communication.* This communication is verbal in many respects but includes also "the communication of gestures."

3. *The principal part of the learning of criminal behavior occurs within intimate personal groups.* Negatively, this means that the impersonal agencies of communication, such as movies and newspapers, play a relatively unimportant part in the genesis of criminal behavior.

4. *When criminal behavior is learned, the learning includes (a) techniques of committing the crime, which are sometimes very complicated, sometimes very simple; (b) the specific direction of motives, drives, rationalizations, and attitudes.*

5. *The specific direction of motives and drives is learned from definitions of the legal codes as favorable or unfavorable.* In some societies an individual is surrounded by persons who invariably define the legal codes as rules to be observed, while in others he is surrounded by persons whose definitions are favorable to the violation of the legal codes. In our American society these definitions are almost always mixed, with the consequence that we have culture conflict in relation to the legal codes.

6. *A person becomes delinquent because of an excess of definitions favorable to violation of law over definitions unfavorable to violation of law.* This is the principle of differential association. It refers to both criminal and anti-criminal associations and has to do with counteracting forces. When persons become criminal, they do so because of contacts with criminal patterns and also because of isolation from anti-criminal patterns. Any person inevitably assimilates the surrounding culture unless other patterns are in conflict; a Southerner does not pronounce "r" because other Southerners do not pronounce "r." Negatively, this proposition of differential association means that associations which are neutral so far as crime is concerned have little or no effect on the genesis of criminal behavior. Much of the experience of a person is neutral in this sense, e.g., learning to brush one's teeth. This behavior has no negative or positive effect on criminal behavior except as it may be related to associations which are concerned with the legal codes. This neutral behavior is important especially as an occupier of the time of a child so that he is not in contact with criminal behavior during the time he is so engaged in the neutral behavior.

7. *Differential associations may vary in frequency, duration, priority, and intensity.* This means that associations with criminal behavior and also associations with anti-criminal behavior vary in those respects. "Frequency" and "duration" as modalities of associations are obvious and need no explanation. "Priority" is assumed to be important in the sense that lawful behavior developed in early childhood may persist throughout life, and also that delinquent behavior developed in early childhood may persist

throughout life. This tendency, however, has not been adequately demonstrated, and priority seems to be important principally through its selective influence. "Intensity" is not precisely defined but it has to do with such things as the prestige of the source of a criminal or anti-criminal pattern and with emotional reactions related to the associations. In a precise description of the criminal behavior of a person these modalities would be stated in quantitative form and a mathematical ratio be reached. A formula in this sense has not been developed, and the development of such a formula would be extremely difficult.

8. *The process of learning criminal behavior by association with criminal and anti-criminal patterns involves all of the mechanisms that are involved in any other learning.* Negatively, this means that the learning of criminal behavior is not restricted to the process of imitation. A person who is seduced, for instance, learns criminal behavior by association, but this process would not ordinarily be described as imitation.

9. *While criminal behavior is an expression of general needs and values, it is not explained by those general needs and values since non-criminal behavior is an expression of the same needs and values.* Thieves generally steal in order to secure money, but likewise honest laborers work in order to secure money. The attempts by many scholars to explain criminal behavior by general drives and values, such as the happiness principle, striving for social status, the money motive, or frustration, have been and must continue to be futile since they explain lawful behavior as completely as they explain criminal behavior. They are similar to respiration, which is necessary for any behavior but which does not differentiate criminal from non-criminal behavior.

It is not necessary, at this level of explanation, to explain why a person has the associations which he has; this certainly involves a complex of many things. In an area where the delinquency rate is high, a boy who is sociable, gregarious, active, and athletic is very likely to come in contact with the other boys in the neighborhood, learn delinquent behavior from them, and become a gangster; in the same neighborhood the psychopathic boy who is isolated, introverted, and inert may remain at home, not become acquainted with the other boys in the neighborhood, and not become delinquent. In another situation, the sociable, athletic, aggressive boy may become a member of a scout troop and not become involved in delinquent behavior. The person's associations are determined in a general context of social organization. A child is ordinarily reared in a family; the place of residence of the family is determined largely by family income; and the delinquency rate is in many respects related to the rental values of the houses. Many other aspects of social organization affect the kinds of associations a person has.

The preceding explanation of criminal behavior purports to explain the criminal and non-criminal behavior of individual persons. As indicated earlier, it is possible to state sociological theories of criminal behavior which explain the criminality of a community, nation, or other group. The problem, when thus stated, is to account for variations in crime rates and involves a comparison of the crime rates of various groups or the crime rates of a particular group at different times. The explanation of a crime rate must be consistent with the explanation of the criminal behavior of the person, since the crime rate is a summary statement of the number of persons in the group who commit crimes and the frequency with which they commit crimes. One of the best explanations of crime rates from this point of view is that a high crime rate is due to social disorganization. The term "social disorganization" is not entirely satisfactory and it seems preferable to substitute for it the term "differential social organization." The postulate on which this theory is based, regardless of the name, is that crime is rooted in the social organization and is an expression of that social organization. A group may be organized for criminal behavior or organized against criminal behavior. Most communities are organized both for criminal and anti-criminal behavior and in that sense the crime rate is an expression of the differential group organization. Differential group organization as an explanation of variations in crime rates is consistent with the differential association theory of the processes by which persons become criminals.

2 Psychoanalysis and Crime

DAVID FELDMAN

Psychoanalysis is, of course, best known for its contibutions to the understanding and treatment of mental disorders. Yet, almost from its inception, psychoanalytic theory was conceived by Sigmund Freud as having equal explanatory value in areas quite beyond what is usually considered the realm of the psychopathological. And in accordance with this conception, psychoanalysts have, over the years, expanded their theoretical interests to include very nearly every facet of the subject-matters treated in the social sciences and arts.[1] But perhaps the most assiduously cultivated extracurricular interest for psychoanalysis has been the problem of criminal behavior. Indeed, what may be called psychoanalytic criminology is already close to half a century in age and remains still among the foremost influences in shaping current programs of dealing with criminal and delinquent offenders. However, as has been the case in all of the behavioral disciplines, the fundamental theoretical framework of psychoanalysis has received differential interpretations, resulting in the development of diverse psychoanalytic accounts of criminality. In this survey of psychoanalytic criminology

Reprinted with permission of The Macmillan Company from *Mass Society in Crisis*, edited by Bernard Rosenberg, Israel Gerver, and F. William Howton. Copyright by The Macmillan Company, 1964, pp. 50–58.

[1] See, e.g., the range of subject-matters covered in S. Lorand (ed.), *Psychoanalysis Today* (New York, 1944) and in G. Roheim (ed.), *Psychoanalysis and the Social Sciences*, (New York, 1947).

what follows, then, is, first, a brief sketch of its underlying theoretical orientation and, second, a consideration of some of the important recent trends in the various applications of that orientation.

Logically, psychoanalytic theory starts out with the commonplace, but crucial, assumption that all human behavior is motivated and, hence, goal-oriented or teleological in character. To begin with, this means that human behavior is functional, that it is undertaken to fulfill a given need or desire, and that it has consequences for other patterns of behavior. But since the same action can have many different purposes, it follows that neither the motives nor the functions of any given act can be ascertained by observing the overt action itself. This implies that, as a matter of general principle, a proper grasp of human behavior requires that this behavior be understood in terms of the subjective meanings and significances which the actor himself attaches to his action. This principle of subjective understanding now occupies a well-established, though not undisputed, position in contemporary sociological theory. But for psychoanalysis the situation is further complicated by its concept that the subjective meaning which an actor attaches to his action may be quite unconscious, so that the actor himself is consciously unaware of the functions he imputes to his own action. Thus, in addition to any manifest functions which an overt act may have for the actor, the same act can also have latent functions which, while of equal or more importance, remain unconscious.[2]

With respect to the problem of criminal behavior, this principle of motivational functionalism implies that a concentration of analysis on the manifest criminal act itself cannot hope to provide a proper etiological understanding of the crime. For like any other behavior, criminal behavior is a form of self-expression and what is intended to be expressed in the act of crime is not only unobservable in the act itself, but also may even be beyond the awareness of the criminal actor himself. So, for example, an overt criminal act of stealing may be undertaken for the attainment of purposes which are far removed from, and even contrary to, that of simple illegal aggrandizement; indeed, it may even be, as shall be seen in the sequel, that the criminal, in stealing, seeks not material gain by self-punishment. The etiological basis of a criminal act can, therefore, be understood only in terms of the functions, latent as well as manifest, which the act was intended to accomplish.[3]

[2] It is worth emphasizing that the distinction between manifest and latent functions, currently something of an issue in sociological discussion, was not imported for use in the present context. The distinction is actually very much a part of the psychoanalytic conception of motivation and was originated by Freud in his theory of dreams. In fact, it was Merton who popularized the notion in sociology and borrowed the terms from Freud. See R. K. Merton, *Social Theory and Social Structure* (Glencoe, Ill., rev. ed., 1957), p. 60 ff.

[3] The concept of motivational functionalism is most explicitly formulated in psychoanalytic criminology in W. Healy and A. Bronner, *New Light on Delinquency and*

But, of course, to know that a criminal act is functional and may have both manifest and latent functions is not yet to know anything about the specific causal determinants of that act. Accordingly, the methodological principle of motivational functionalism has to be supplemented with substantive concepts of the actual functions involved. Now crime, however it is defined, represents a behavioral violation of one or more social norms. Since the cognition of, and conformity to, social norms are resultants of the socialization process, it follows that the individual who engages in a pattern of criminal behavior has, in some sense, been defectively socialized or that the norms demanding his conformity are themselves, in some sense, defective. In either case, it also follows that prerequisite to a resolution of the problem of crime causation is a theoretical explication of the processes comprising the socialization of the individual. And such an analysis is precisely what constitutes the heart of the psychoanalytic conception of ego psychology.

In a gross way, it may be said that, as an analytic schema of the socialization process, psychoanalytic ego psychology revolves around, and reflects, the fact that the human individual, born into a family, group, and class, has in some way to come to terms with the operative norms which are arbitrarily imposed upon him as regulators of his behavior. Thus there is a certain tension built up within the individual as a result of the competing requirements of the social group and his own private and original impulses. In the Freudian view, these original impulses are part of the biological equipment of the individual and are essentially antisocial in nature, consisting of the sexual, aggressive, and destructive "instinct."[4] Left to his own devices, therefore, the individual would necessarily undertake actions which, in substance and aim, run counter to the normative demands of his social group. But since he is not allowed such license and is, moreover, for a long time after his birth, in a physical condition of total helplessness of dependency, thereby making him highly susceptible to both the danger of his environment and the threat of punishment, the individual has little choice in the matter and must find means of adapting himself to the "reality" of his situation. And he must do so because his needs for the support, protection, and acceptance of his family and group are far more urgent than are his needs to satisfy his antisocial drives.

Its Treatment (New Haven, Conn., 1936). Today, of course, functionalism is highly fashionable, and it is no longer required to be a Freudian to think of crime in terms of its latent functions. See, e.g., A. K. Cohen, *Delinquent Boys* (Glencoe, Ill., 1955), which sets down a theory of the latent functions of gang delinquency.

[4] It should be noted that Freud's German term for "instinct" is "trieb," which, as Freudians are forever pointing out, does not have the connotations of rigidity and immutability associated with the English usage of "instinct." See, e.g., the discussion in O. Fenichel, *The Psychoanalytic Theory of Neurosis* (New York, 1945), pp. 12 f. 54 ff.

However, one fundamental aspect of being born dependent and power-less is that the individual is, willy-nilly, subjected to an inexorable process of indoctrination in the group norms under a pedagogical technique consisting largely of a differential application of reward and punishment (love and rejection) and relying heavily on the individual's role-taking capacity. The individual manages his adaptation in primarily two ways: on the one hand, he resorts to reasoned calculations and compromises of what can and cannot be done, which of his original impulses he may seek to satisfy with impunity and which he must not act upon lest he suffer penalty. And, on the other hand, he incorporates and accepts for himself the group norms and evaluates his own impulses in their terms. This he does by means of identification, involving what Mead called "taking the role of the other," first with the immediate authority figures in his life, then with an expanding number of "significant others," and lastly with the social group as a whole representing the "generalized other."[5]

In short, there are three basic psychological processes operating within the individual comprising the original impulses, the mechanisms of adjust-ment, and the internalized group norms. Each of these processes tends to be in potential or active conflict with the others, and the individual is able to maintain a stable existence only to the extent that a viable "balance of power" obtains among them and functions to temper the conflicts and pre-vent an explosive eruption. And this balance, in turn, depends upon a minimally favorable equilibrium between the kinds and amounts of com-pensatory gratifications and enforced renunciations the individual experi-ences.[6]

Combining now the principle of motivational functionalism and the socialization schema of ego psychology, the basic etiological formula of psychoanalytic criminology becomes apparent; it simply states that crimi-nality is undertaken as a means of maintaining psychic balance or as an effort to rectify a psychic balance which has been disrupted. On this general formula, a substantial consensus of opinion has been attained among psycho-analytic criminologists. At the same time, however, a considerable diversity

[5] G. H. Mead, *Mind, Self, and Society* (Chicago, 1934), Chs. III and IV.

[6] In Freudian theory the three psychic processes are referred to as id, ego, and superego respectively. But, of course, these analytic categories entail a good deal more than has here been set down. The primary sources of ego psychology are S. Freud, *The Ego and The Id* (London, 1947) and S. Freud, *The Problem of Anxiety* (New York, 1936); less technical discussions are contained in S. Freud, *New Introductory Lectures on Psychoanalysis* (New York, 1933) and S. Freud, *An Outline of Psychoanalysis* (New York, 1936). The Freudian schema of socialization has been taken over prac-tically intact by contemporary structural-functionalism in sociology and has already found expression in the textbook literature. See the interesting discussion in H. M. Johnson, *Sociology: A Systematic Introduction* (New York, 1960), Ch. 5.

of views has developed as to exactly what it is in the socialization of the individual which compels him to resort to crime and as to precisely how criminal behavior fulfills the function of helping retain psychic balance. In fact, there are at present at least five more or less contrasting psychoanalytic views available for consideration.

Among the first and still persistently maintained interpretations of the etiological formula is the view that criminality is a form of neurosis. The criminal is a person suffering from a neurotic illness which, in no fundamental way, differs from any of the other forms of neurotic phenomena. Psychodynamically, so it is held, the only difference between the common symptomatic neurosis and criminal neurosis is merely that the latter is alloplastically manifested in overt acts, while the former finds expression in the autoplastic symbolism of symptom formation. But exactly like the symptoms of the symptomatic neurosis, the criminal acts of the criminal neurosis have the function of providing neurotic gratifications and resolutions of unconscious conflicts over which the individual has partially lost control. Generally, it is believed that the criminal neurotic suffers from a compulsive need for punishment to alleviate intolerable guilt feelings stemming from unconscious, and poorly sublimated, incestuous strivings. Thus the criminal engages in illegal activity so that he may be apprehended and penalized for his crimes. From the subjective standpoint of the criminal, the real crime demanding punishment in his incestuous wish; but by a form of neurotic compromise, the punishment he receives for his overt crimes functions to expiate his guilt and ameliorate the debilitating effects of his emotional conflicts.[7]

A more recent, and contrasting, conception of the etiological formula holds that, far from suffering guilt and needing punishment, the criminal feels no guilt and strenuously avoids being subjected to penalty. On this view, the criminal is an "antisocial character" who has been defectively socialized so that he is unable to cope properly with the normative requirements of his external situation. Realistically, every individual is frequently compelled to postpone gratification of his needs or to modify them in a manner more acceptable to his group and to himself. But the antisocial character, due to certain deformities in his rearing, is chronically unable to orient his conduct in accordance with the dictates of this "reality principle." He simply cannot endure temporary frustrations and he cannot postpone the quest for satisfaction, and so he impulsively engages in antisocial, criminal behavior as a means of seeking immediate gratification. Because the internalization of social norms is, for the antisocial character, in a weakened state,

[7] An early and still influential statement of this view is F. Alexander and H. Staub, *The Criminal, The Judge, and the Public* (Glencoe, Ill., rev. ed., 1956). The original edition was published in translation in 1931.

he has no strong internal guides to evaluate his actions; and because his mechanisms of adjustment are poorly developed, he permits himself kinds of activities which a properly socialized individual would not undertake. Basically, he regards his behavior and his relationships to others sheerly in terms of pleasure and penalty. If actions can provide pleasure without penalty he will perform them, and if, upon misjudgment, he is penalized for these actions, he does not react with remorse but with hatred and frustration at having to put up with displeasure.[8]

A third, and extremely influential, interpretation of the etiological formula is that criminal activity is undertaken as a means of obtaining substitutive and compensatory gratifications of needs and desires which would ordinarily be met and fulfilled within the network of familial relationships. These are the needs and desires which are fundamental in determining the nature of the individual's maturation and involve such matters as the inherent needs for security, recognition, acceptance, adequacy, status, and self-assertion. When the individual finds that these basic needs are frustrated in the interpersonal channels of his family environment, he inevitably experiences painful feelings of being thwarted and deprived. In these circumstances, it is a natural response for the individual to divert his activities into the illegal channels of delinquency and crime as a means of securing some substitute satisfactions and to pacify his frustrations. Where his family fails, the delinquent gang can succeed in giving the individual the necessary sense of acceptance, recognition, and adequacy; and if the family cannot, or will not, allow outlets for the individual's expression of independence, self-assertion, and self-direction, he may wreak his vengeance and demonstrate his inner capacities to his own satisfaction in the act of crime. Criminality, therefore, is a consequence of a disturbance in the psychic balance and the criminal or delinquent is an emotionally frustrated and perturbed individual who unconsciously seeks in his offensive actions a resolution to his emotional problems in the form of compensatory satisfactions which have been denied him in his familial relationships.[9]

A quite recently developed fourth conception of the etiological formula is somewhat akin to the idea of the criminal as an antisocial character. However, according to this newer view the deficiency within the criminal stems not from impoverished mechanisms of adjustment and internalized norms, but from the unconscious permissiveness of parental figures who are themselves ambivalent towards the acceptance of the norms prohibiting criminal-

---

[8] The concept of the antisocial character is most closely associated with K. Friedlander, *The Psychoanalytical Approach to Juvenile Delinquency* (New York, 1945); a briefer statement is K. Friedlander, "Latent Delinquency and Ego Development," in K. R. Eissler (ed.), *Searchlights on Delinquency* (New York, 1949).

[9] The most prominent statement of this position is W. Healy and A. Bronner, *op. cit.*, which has practically become a classic of psychoanalytic criminology.

ity. The delinquent or criminal, it is held, suffers from "superego lacunae," or unformed segments in his normative orientation; he may be fully oriented toward acceptance of most social norms, while toward some other norms he has not evolved an orientation of acceptance and conformity. These lacunae derive from similar defective normative orientations in his parents who unconsciously encourage criminal activities in their child as a means of obtaining vicarious gratifications for their own unconscious strivings. Thus the child, seeking the approbation of his parents, engages in delinquent acts because he believes that his delinquencies would be gratifying to them or because he rightly senses that such actions can be used as a weapon in his relations with his family.[10]

The concept of superego lacunae seems to hint slightly at a notion that the norms prohibiting criminal behavior are not strongly or consistently maintained as regulators of conduct; there is at least something of an implication that, aside from any psychological deficiencies within the criminal, criminality may also ensue from the internalization of defective norms. This implication has recently received some further development in yet a fifth interpretation of the etiological formula which, in many respects, bears a close resemblance to the theory of anomie currently so popular in sociological circles.[11] According to this psychoanalytic conception of anomie, criminal behavior occurs in the context of a social situation in which an extremely high value is placed on the individual achievement of economic success, but which, at the same time, stringently limits the legitimate means of obtaining this goal. The value of individual initiative and success, it is maintained, is an historical hangover from the period of the open frontier, when the emphasis on personal effort and achievement was feasible economically and, therefore, a natural ideological outgrowth of the prevailing conditions. Since that period, however, the available opportunities for achieving success have been progressively exhausted, and a heavy expenditure of individual initiative can no longer be expected to be rewarded by economic success. But while the underlying socioeconomic conditions for achieving success have changed, the ideological superstructure has been retained. In these circumstances, there must develop definite tensions for the individual who has been socialized to incorporate the norms of personal initiative and achievement and who finds himself placed socially in a situation of deprivation or poverty where the legitimate exercise of these values can only lead to frustration and failure. Yet this discrepancy between social structure and

[10] For an exposition of this view, see A. M. Johnson, "Sanctions for Superego Lacunae of Adolescents," in K. R. Eissler, *op. cit.*, and A. M. Johnson, "Juvenile Delinquency," in S. Arieti (ed.), *American Handbook of Psychiatry* (New York, 1959), Vol. I.

[11] The sociological theory of anomie was originally developed by Durkheim and further extended by Merton. See R. K. Merton, *op. cit.*, Chs. IV and V.

cultural norms does not uniformly affect all individuals in like degree; it will, instead, have its greatest psychological impact upon those individuals who are least equipped psychically to undertake the unrewarding pursuit of success. Such individuals who are, by nature, more passive, compliant and dependent than the average are trapped in an intolerable conflict with their internalization of the norms of personal achievement. Compelled to define their passivity and dependency as personal weakness and incompetence, they will tend to repress these qualities and, by the process of reaction-formation, overcomform to the social norms by adopting an excessively individualistic aggressiveness. But barred from success by their social position and the social structure, this exaggerated individualism will naturally find outlet in criminal behavior, which serves the dual purpose of denying their unconscious dependency while accruing material benefits. And so it is the social structure which generates tendencies towards criminality among select individuals who, as a result of a combination of social position and psychic nature, are unable to make the necessary adjustments.[12]

Now looking over these variant interpretations of the same basic etiological formula, it is readily noted that they form something of a sequence ranging in scope from an exclusive emphasis on internal factors operating within the psychological constitution of the criminal to a fairly liberal concentration on external situational conditions confronting him. Partially, at least, this shift in perspective probably derives from the obvious vulnerability of the idea that all of the etiological sources of criminality are to be located in the personality of the criminal. Thus the notion of the neurotic criminal compulsively intent on self-punishment is plainly vitiated by the fact that most criminals seem to expend a great deal of energy and effort on escaping the clutches of the law and, on the whole, as is commonly acknowledged, are inordinately successful at it. Moreover, available evidence of the mental states of convicted criminals unmistakably points to the conclusion that the vastly major portion of them are simply not neurotic.[13] Again, the concept of the criminal as an antisocial character bent on obtaining immediate gratifications patently ignores the commonplace fact that criminality frequently demands much laborious training and planning of techniques and strategies, all of which belie the naive idea that the criminal is psychologically unable to endure temporary frustrations. And, indeed, if professional, organized,

[12] A clear statement of the psychoanalytic conception of anomie can be found in F. Alexander, *Our Age of Unreason*, p. 301 ff. An earlier adumbration of this view is F. Alexander and W. Healy, *The Roots of Crime* (New York, 1935).

[13] See, e.g., the important study by W. Bromberg and C. B. Thompson, "The Relation of Psychosis, Mental Defect, and Personality Types to Crime," in *J. Crimin. Law & Criminology*, Vol. 28. Studying a random sample of close to ten thousand convicted criminals, Bromberg and Thompson found that 82.0 per cent were "average or normal."

and white-collar crime are to be given their due, it must be acknowledged that much, if not most, criminality rather strongly adheres to the "reality principle" of Freudian theory.

Empirical considerations of this and other cognate sorts have, no doubt, persuaded many psychoanalytic criminologists to attempt an integration of sociological materials. Yet even the psychoanalytic concept of anomie, which probably comes as close to a distinctively sociological perspective as psychoanalysis has yet achieved, remains rooted in the idea that there must be something special and different about the personality of the criminal which induces him to behave in a criminal fashion. And while it cannot be said that criminological research has definitively disposed of this idea, evidence accumulated to date strongly suggests that the distribution of normality, pathology, and general personality traits among criminals is in approximately the same proportion as that found for the rest of the noncriminal population.[14] Thus it would seem that there is nothing in the criminal personality, apart from his criminality, to differentiate him from the noncriminal. And if this is so, it must follow that criminality is not to be considered a function of the psychic state of the individual.

Nor has psychoanalytic criminology taken sufficient cognizance of the fact that the criminal does not spontaneously invent patterns of criminality. Criminal behavior, it hardly needs saying, is a social phenomenon, and a learning process has, therefore, to intervene between the personality of the criminal and his criminal actions. Typically, this learning process entails a wide assortment of techniques, ideas, and skills, all of which take time and practice to master and assimilate. Moreover, this learning process requires the individual's participation in the formation and maintenance of relationships with others who dispose of the necessary knowledge and put it to use. It is in the context of these relationships that the individual learns his criminality and adopts for himself distinctive criminalistic attitudes and precepts. Presumably, the experiences of such a learning process must have an effect on the personality of the individual undergoing them. Yet this reciprocating influence of criminal experience on the personality of the criminal appears to have received no consideration in psychoanalytic criminology. Indeed, all the interpretations of the basic etiological formula share this common implicit assumption that the personality differentials to which causal status is attributed are temporally antecedent to the individual's par-

[14] See the excellent review of research in this area by L. G. Lowrey, "Delinquent and Criminal Personalities," in J. M. Hunt (ed.), *Personality and the Behavior Disorders* (New York, 1944), Vol. II; see also K. F. Schuessler and D. R. Cressey, "Personality Characteristics of Criminals," in *Am. J. Socio.*, Vol. 55, and M. B. Clinard, "Criminological Research," in R. K. Merton, *et al.*, (eds.), *Sociology Today* (New York, 1959), p. 515 ff.

ticipation in criminal activity. Nevertheless, it is, at least, a plausible alternative possibility that such personality differentials are consequential precipitants of the individual's induction into criminality. And in failing to take this possibilty into account, the entire structure of psychoanalytic criminology becomes vulnerable to the charge that it merely begs the question from the outset.

3 The Skills and Training of the Pickpocket

DAVID W. MAURER

. . . This [discussion is] concerned almost exclusively with the technology of pickpockets, or, in a broader sense, the ways they make a living, together with those peripheral activities which are functionally related to making a living. Sometimes it has been difficult to draw the line between what is functional and what is not, in which cases the policy has been, usually, to omit this peripheral material. It would be manifestly impossible to cover all phases of the life pattern of a specialized group of thieves in a study so limited in both size and scope. In this [paper] then, several of these peripheral areas will be considered, but only insofar as they contribute to the general picture of making a living. . . .

This area of the subculture is comparable to *Education* in the dominant culture; most pickpockets have certain cross-cultural traits, since they are all, to some extent even if that extent is minimal, exposed to the education system of the dominant culture. The slight degree to which most of them respond is evident from the high incidence of illiteracy among them. This lack of response to the education system of the dominant culture is a result of several forces. First, the traditions of the subculture are all against it; there is, from birth on, a suspicion and distrust of the dominant culture which is intense; thieves tend to resent any attempt (however well meant) by the dominant culture to educate the children of the subculture in the

Reprinted from David W. Maurer, *Whiz Mob: A Correlation of the Technical Argot of Pickpockets with Their Behavior Pattern*, American Dialect Society, 24 (1955), 153–165, by permission of College and University Press Services, Inc., and the author.

ways of the *square John*; this suspicion is intense in direct proportion to the lack of formal education experienced by the parents.

The following comment by a professional shows the dichotomy between the institutions and values of the subculture and those of the dominant culture. It also shows the conflict in the mind of the father over denying his boy the advantages of the dominant culture, at least while he is a child.

I had that problem occur just a short while ago. You remember I told you we've got a little boy. And here some time ago, just a few months ago, he wanted to join the Cub Scouts. And I always had an idea when them things come up, I'd call a spade, a spade. I mean it's all right to think that, but when the time comes, it's a little different. So he wants to join the Cub Scouts. And he's with my mother, his grandmother, and we're not rich or anything like that, but I'd say he's got a very good home. And he wants to join the Cub Scouts, the junior Boy Scouts. So I know that the Cub Scouts make stool pigeons out of all those kids. All them organizations do. They make the cop on the corner look like something, but they don't tell them that when they grow up, he'll put them in the penitentiary, if he gets a chance to do it. And I know that they're going to train him to be a perfect little stool pigeon. So I turned that over in my mind for two or three days. After all, it's going to affect his whole life. So I finally come to the conclusion, well, let him be a stool pigeon, if he wants to be, but at least let him be normal. Let him get what the other kids get and when he is just a little older I can tell him straight, "Now that cop out there, he's a dirty son-of-a-bitch. He'll put you away. That's a kind of an oath he took to get that kind of a job, and he wouldn't only arrest you, he'd frame you and put you in prison."

Second, the educational system of the dominant culture teaches little for which the subculture has any direct use. Perhaps a bare minimum of reading is harmless, since it permits reading of form-sheets and train schedules and, on occasion, newspapers; enough writing to correspond is also accepted, though not considered essential, for communication is mainly verbal in this subculture; and the *grapevine* (a loosely organized but very effective arrangement for transmitting messages for great distances by word of mouth) has worked effectively for centuries, so why discard it?

True, some thieves later in life realize some of the advantages of literacy, and learn to read and write fluently—sometimes in prison schools.

Well I'll tell you there's a lot of guys, ashamed as I am to say it, well I ain't ashamed to say it though because why should I be? It's their own damn fault if they ain't got any education; they've been in enough joints. Half of them have spent half their lives in the penitentiary. And can't spell "cat." And they got a library there and schools and everything. I don't know; it's just that "dese," "dose," and "dem" kind of guys are ignoramuses.

They know all the answers, as far as their racket is concerned. They don't know anything else. You know there's pickpockets that will freeze themselves to death and not steal an overcoat? In the winter time. If they can't get the money out of the leather to go buy an overcoat, they wouldn't step inside a joint and beat it for an overcoat. They think that's beneath them.

But pickpockets with the attitude of this informant are rare. Most of the skills they need are manual, psychological, almost intuitive. They have to learn to *work on the sneak*, and the public school system seems to neglect or omit entirely this phase of the thief-child's development.

Last, almost everything taught in the public schools is directly opposed to the values and techniques of living in the subculture. Everyone is taught to conform, to coöperate, to take orders. "I learned to stall and I learned to hook, too, and I broke in many a stall. A lot of stalls won't break in, you see, because they're thieves and they won't be told. That's the reason they are thieves. They don't want people to tell them what to do. So if you can't tell a man what to do, then he can't stall." Public education teaches property rights which are quite the reverse of most of those recognized by the pickpocket. It attempts to instill respect for law and order. It tries to develop in children the desires and abilities to function in the dominant culture. It develops attitudes and motives which, viewed by the pickpocket, are not only useless but definitely subversive—if one is going out on the *whiz*.

And so there is a general disregard for public education, and all the institutions associated therewith. As a result, pickpockets have little incentive to keep their children in school even for the minimum number of years required by law, and they are inclined to wink at truancy, general incorrigibility, and delinquency. These children are often problems in the schools, for the parents regard the teacher as a kind of female *hack*, *screw*, or *shack* (prison guard) and are likely to encourage or approve anything Junior does to make trouble for her. If he gives her a hard enough way to go, they feel that this indicates promise for the future; if he is by chance expelled, that is fine with them. He can learn rapidly then to work with his elders. On the other hand, there are a few enlightened pickpockets who send their children to school and even to college, for they want them to have a better life than their parents had.

Of course, not all pickpockets come from pickpocket families, or even from families of the subculture; some come from the dominant culture, are rejected by it or reject it, and by chance or by choice find a way to associate with members of the subculture; these associations are usually with children of the subculture, often enough older than the child of the dominant culture to be looked up to, identified with, and finally associated with professionally. While juvenile cross-cultural ventures from legitimate society into the pickpocket subculture are not common, they do happen.

Most often, however, the pickpocket is born into a family living within some criminal subculture; from earliest consciousness he learns the attitudes of this group, cultivates hostility for the dominant culture, and shows vocational aptitude in various techniques calculated to separate members of the dominant culture from their money. Once an individual has grown to adulthood in this subculture and acquired professional status, only the most unrealistic type of thinking on the part of members of the dominant culture would expect him to change his ways. One hears of religious conversions which have suddenly changed the lives of pickpockets and made them pillars of the dominant culture; I do not know of any such cases personally, nor have I reason to believe that they exist on a bona fide basis. Likewise, I have never known psychiatry to create a similar conversion and adjustment, once the pickpocket has become established.

In fact, I have never known any professional thief to reform—which is another way of saying that he changes culture completely and permanently. He may *pack the racket in* because things get too *hot*, or because with advancing age he fears imprisonment more than he once did and at the same time has to depend on diminishing reactions in the practice of a highly skilled manual craft. "Then we could work until it got too hot and by 'too hot' I mean there'd be too many beefs coming in. So then you'd have to pack it in." "Joe Goss knows about my last fall, but no previous episodes. I handle over ten grand a season but do not carry a key to the money boxes. Don't believe I'd be tempted anyway, for at 59 there is a real fear of consequences" (letter from a professional who has *packed it in*). He may *square up* permanently or temporarily because there is a life sentence hanging over him as an habitual criminal. "But I said, 'I'm gonna square up. I'm gonna do the right thing.'" "Society don't give a guy a decent chance to square up. In a hell of a lot of cases they make it so goddamned hard." But he only conforms to the dominant culture superficially. Basically his motives, his attitudes, and his values remain unchanged. He has simply been forced to stop doing what he had been doing to make a living. Often he substitutes something less likely to *put him away*, such as dealing in a gambling joint, or touting at a racetrack, or working at some very minor *racket* like *pimping*.

But we have gone far ahead of the child in the subculture. There are no organized schools or systems of education within the subculture; it has been said that there are "schools" for pickpockets in large cities, run by professional *fagins* who turn youngsters into expert pickpockets; it has been said that they go so far as to set up dummies, fully dressed, which have bells attached to their pockets; the children are then taught to pick the dummy's pockets without ringing any of the bells. This suggests a touching scene, with all the little scholars chanting *left britch, right britch, prat kick, raust,* under the baton of a slyly beaming old Fagin. It smacks more of Dickens and sentimental journalism than anything taking place in the modern pickpocket's subculture. While it may have been a fact somewhere and at some time in the past, I can find no evidence that it has been practiced recently in the United States. Says an experienced *road man* with a wide knowledge of the criminal subculture: "I never had no such training. I never heard tell of a school for the whiz, and I never in all my life heard any cannon mention such a thing. One thief turns out another. That is, he teaches him. I was taught to reef a britch from the bottom so a tweezer poke would wind up in the palm of my hand. Back in them days there was nothing but tweezer pokes out in the corn belt."

What is the child-thief to be taught? Most of his early education is very informal. He absorbs a knowledge of the *racket* from those about him even before he is old enough to think of himself as a participant. Perhaps the most important factor is his early realization that it is possible to commit theft from the person; this has the same sort of impact that learning that it is possible to drive an automobile has on a young child. Very shortly he likes to be up behind the wheel, driving like a fireball, though actually the car is not in motion. When it is in motion, he identifies with the driver, and long before he is old enough to drive, he knows exactly how it is done; had he never seen anyone drive a car, he would never think of it in motion, and would have to make an entirely new set of adjustments to accept it as a vehicle. And so with the child in the house. Once he realizes that theft from the person is possible without *rumbling* the victim, whole new horizons have opened.

Anyone who has raised children knows that stealing comes to them as naturally as breathing. The attitudes of the parents and especially the other siblings toward this tendency are all-important in determining the attitudes of the child. After much careful and patient teaching, he may eventually learn that stealing is not acceptable behavior in the dominant culture; he learns something of property rights, and develops feelings of guilt when he violates them. But the thief-child has exactly the opposite experience. He knows not only about stealing, but about theft. He learns, no one knows how early, that his parents or his older brothers and sisters not only approve it, but are adept at it. The other children he is likely to play with have similar knowledge, or participate in a culture where this behavior is accepted, at least by the males. The aura of secrecy surrounding it, the taboo nature of the craft, the knowing looks, the brief, cryptic discussions of it in undertones, serve to emphasize its importance. Very early he is pretty thoroughly indoctrinated with the idea not only that it is all right to steal, but that it is a fine and admirable thing, and carries status.

About this time, he learns one very important thing. He is taught that it is laudable indeed to steal from a *sucker*, but that stealing from his own family or, later, his own friends, is a low and reprehensible thing; sometimes the emphasis falls so heavily upon the former principle, and so lightly upon the latter one, that he never fully grasps the idea that one must not steal from his own kind. This boy will never make a *class cannon*, though he may become a thief.

Thus he learns to recognize and identify the subculture as contrasted to the dominant culture, and soon collects a set of appropriate symbols for each. Not only does he learn to respect the craft of thievery, but he learns all the other standards and values of the subculture, and embraces them. Throughout boyhood and adolescence he has these reënforced by experience and precept, and by the time he is fourteen or fifteen years old, he is ready to support himself by thievery, though by this age he is seldom anything like an accomplished pickpocket. He probably simply steals anything he can and sells it wherever he can, his pickings being limited by the range of technology which his older friends and associates have at their disposal. He knows the general argot of the subculture, but as yet not the specialized aspects of it. He is just a growing hoodlum, and may never get any specialized training whatever.

The first word of the whiz lingo I can remember hearing was "poke," but I can't be sure that was actually the first one. This is just the first one I remember. All the lingo of the whiz was foreign to me then. That was when I was turning out. Then I learned some more. After I got around with other cannons, I heard some more and picked it up. By the time I was twenty, I could spin the lingo like an old-timer, or at least I thought I could.

His development has not, however, gone unnoticed by his elders and others who could use him in the subculture. He must be known to have *grift sense, grift know*, or *larceny sense* before anyone will further his education in any way.

Yeah, that takes a lot of grift sense. There's a thousand different ways you have to maneuver, in other words the whiz is a lot of psychology. You've got to maneuver a man, particularly if you are by yourself. You got to think twice as fast as him and faster than all the coppers that are looking for you, so you got to do some thinking. So wherever the spot might be, you got to take the whole thing into consideration. Suppose you had been going up in an elevator, it would have been an entirely different thing. Well what would I have done then? Going up in an elevator, I might have burned him in the neck with a cigarette or pulled his hat down over his ears or something. I had to make him take his hand off, I had to make him let go of that money. I couldn't take it out of his hand. I had to make him take his hand off it. You have to make the situation. . . . You got to make the break yourself. You understand what I mean? The play is there, the dough is there, the man's got money in his pocket. You've got to have grift sense to take it away from him.

Also, he must know someone who can use a boy with light fingers, a good personality, and strong affiliations with the subculture. This last is very important, for it determines whether he will be loyal to his associates and his work, or whether he will yield to the first police pressures, or sell out at the first opportunity. In other words, he must also have *grift guts*. Without a doubt, he already has some sort of police record, even though it may be happily concealed behind the well-meaning anonymity of juvenile court.

Let us say that there is a professional *whiz* who has noted him around the hangouts and has taken a liking to him. The boy responds. The first stages of this relationship remind one of a dog finding a new master. The boy runs errands for the thief. He does his bidding in every way. He curries favor by catering to every whim of the professional. He takes messages to his lady-loves, "That's one of the first jobs I ever had—reading his mail. I used to have to read it for him. A lot of notes from broads that was carrying the torch for him. He'd say, 'You are just a punk kid, but you are OK. You come up to the hotel with me, because I want you to read my mail.' That made me feel like somebody. And why not? He was the best guy in the world, a prince among men."

He finds *connections* where he can buy narcotics for his hero; he probably begins to *chippy around* himself, despite the warnings which the professional is likely to give him. This friendly relationship goes on for some time, off and on, as the thief is in town or in the neighborhood. By the time he is eighteen or so, he is ready to be *brought out* or *turned out*. He is also probably a full-fledged heroin addict, having learned how to use the needle and to take *main line shots* from other youngsters, if indeed not from the hero himself.

Already the professional has come to like the boy, and has made up his mind that perhaps he could be taught. The thief likes to have the boy build up his ego with loyalty, with praises behind his back, and by defending him against all critics. The boy may already know a good deal about the thief; he may even have asked him to teach him to be a pickpocket too. Also, the boy is already *grifting* in a crude way, cheating at cards or dice, and selling *hot* merchandise, and always has some cash in reserve. The pickpocket cannot be free on the streets, and successful, without a certain streak of cynicism; he reasons that if the boy is going to be a thief, he might as well be a good one; he remembers his own youth, when someone *turned him out*. "Old John Snarley turned me out." "I was turned out by Windy Dick Preston." "Well, I turned out in the Village before the hangout was Hinky Dink's scatter." And so, when there is a convention in town, he may take the boy along as a stall.

After some rather solemn instructions and admonitions, they go to work in the crowd. The boy must know who is boss. He instructs the boy to watch him for an *office* indicating which victim to take, then *put his hump up* as he has been shown. The tool picks *easy scores* and *kick outs*, letting the tough ones go. The boy isn't much help, but he is in there trying. They take two or three *pokes* during the evening. He gives the new man his share, and says maybe he'll use him again sometime. There is also a conference afterward in which the tool criticizes every move the boy made, and analyzes every mistake he made. If the boy can take this kind of "chewing out," it is one sign that he may make a good stall. If he blows up, or loses his head, or becomes defensive, he will never make a pickpocket. At least, he can hardly work with a good mob.

This venture may be repeated from time to time; the thief is in town without his stall; the boy knows the city and likes the work. They make several such tentative forays, with no *falls*. Then the tool takes his new stall to a state fair in another city for a day or two; the boy is learning fast and responds to teaching. Some day he may make a *bang up stall*. But he is still working on a very tentative basis with the tool, who has his own stall who travels on the road with him, or works regularly in some other big city. Suppose this steady stall "goes sour," or has some woman trouble, or *takes a fall* which looks as if it is easy to *fix*, but is not a *turn out* after all, and he has to go away for two years. The tool, who can *muzzle around* a bit *single o*, but who isn't by any means a *single handed gun*, comes back for the boy and makes a proposition to *fill him in*. The boy has saved up some money, and has $300 which he will put up for *fall dough*, which is welcome, for the tool has just *dropped a man* and that is always expensive. "We dropped a man before we hardly made a score."

The boy has *busted out*. He has been *joined out*. He is part of a mob. He has *mobbed it up*, though he might be stretching this phrase a bit to apply it to a boy making his debut in a two-handed *outfit*. He is a *cannon* now, and *on the whiz*. He is subject to all the trials, troubles, and pleasures which have long been the lot of the second oldest profession. And lest his *joining out* go to his head and he become a *sensational punk*, his mentor continues his instruction indefinitely. In fact, he rides the boy unmercifully.

Many a night in a hotel room they *punch gun* or *punch whiz* and the whole lore of the subculture is gradually made familiar to him. "Guns like to punch whiz when they get together and they tell funny things about eggs they have pushed around. Peter men don't punch much guff as a rule, but sometimes the scat will loosen them up for some good yarns. But guns learn that way, from the mistakes other fellows made." Every mistake he makes is called to his attention, and ways are suggested to overcome that one next time. He learns to take more and more of the responsibility of a stall, and may become quite proficient. This is mechanical proficiency. However, most of what he has to learn goes beyond the rather elementary physical act of theft; he goes out "big-timing it" and meets other *guns*; he has to learn about people, about the psychology of the mark, about ways and means to handle a *fall*, about the police and their ways, about travel and hangouts and *fixers* and bondsmen and various jails and prisons and a thousand other things which an effective *gun* needs to know.

He discovers how important a *good front* is; consequently he buys expensive clothes and keeps them *sharp*; sooner or later he sees sad examples of how disastrous it can be to *look bad*. He hears about the *seams* and learns to use them. He learns about *plants* of all kinds, ranging from a secret hiding place for drugs in the flush-box of a toilet in his hotel room to a *heel plant* for money or drugs in the hollowed heels of his shoes. "A fellow also plants for a heel touch, but this isn't a heel plant, unless the guy is a heel" (humor). In various *cans* and *joints* he learns about the more intimate *kiester plant*, and volumes more to make him prison-wise.

More than that, he begins to meet other *cannons* of all levels and kinds. They begin to know him, and he may get a *monicker* or underworld name, which means that he is known and accepted. He learns more and more about protecting himself and the tool too. He learns how to *bring a mark out* or *take a mark out* of a bank or station or other place where he has acquired or *flashed* a fat wallet. He learns how to *case* a mark after the *touch* has come off, following him to his train or bus and being sure that he didn't *blow* before he was safely away. He learns how to *shade the duke* and how to *cop the score* from the tool. He learns all the tool can teach him, and from then on he will be self-taught, because no pickpocket knows all the answers, and every *touch* presents variables which may be disastrous if not understood or controlled. Eventually he will learn from other *cannons* he meets or works with, including those he meets in jails and prisons.

He meets some *cannon broads*, who can be shapely girls indeed, and who may interest him if heroin is not already his only mistress; he has the experience of getting *nailed*, *snatched in the neck*, *clawed down* and *guzzled*, not once, but many times. He learns how to differentiate between a *shake-down* and a *bad fall*, and how to deal with each. He may get *lagged* and do some time in prison; in fact, it will be surprising if he does not. He will learn when to *lay dead* and when to *go out*, and if he gets *raw* or out of practice, he will find how to *sharp up*, and after a year or so in *stir*, he may find that he has lost some of his confidence. "When I got off the road, I would lay dead for a few weeks." Little by little he accumulates the spoken wisdom of the *grift*, which is passed from mouth to mouth when the boys are *punching the guff* or *chopping up old touches* or *cutting them up* or *punching gun*. He learns the code of the subculture as he has never known it before, and understands how important it is that he observe it. He now knows the specialized argot, or at least much of it. If he is going to stay *with it*—and he is now *hooked* beyond redemption—he will need every bit of wisdom and philosophy he can get, and if one cannot be a philosopher of sorts, he can never be happy on the *whiz*.

If he is unusually ambitious, he may try his hand at becoming a tool also, and he may prosper; he may fall back on card-sharping, and become a dealer or stick-man in some gambling joint in order to earn *side money*. He learns how to always keep *fresh money* coming in so that he does not have to bite into his savings except in great emergencies. "One of the best angles is that it's fresh money every day." His income may be good, as incomes for pickpockets go, and he may cultivate cultural pursuits like improving the breed in bookie-joints, or playing at craps for large stakes, or fancying women. However, the chances are that he will stay with his first love, the needle, and that the habit will lose the glorious drive and tingle that it had at first, and become the *chinaman on his back* who drives him like a slave to get more money to buy more *junk*. "And when I did take junk, I'll say this, when I did take junk, although it drove me like a mule, the only satisfaction I ever found in life I found in junk. They could take me out there and behead me in the morning. . . . That wouldn't mean anything, but I'd use junk tonight if I could get it."

His attitudes become case-hardened. He finds that, as a young man with plenty of money, he is very popular amongst his kind; he can *fix a beef*, and have some illusions of his own importance; however, he has to learn that when he is broke, his friends will *chill* on him quickly, that people are not so anxious to lend him money as they were to borrow it, and that the *fix* is a relentless animal which eats lettuce steadily, and in large quantities; otherwise he goes to *stir*. He finds his only security, however, in the subculture; the dominant culture has turned against him completely, and he has rejected most of its values. He knows that all *suckers* are against him, and he is against them. He is a professional thief. And once he has become a specialized thief like a pickpocket, he will probably continue in that activity all his life. The chances are that he will never go back into the dominant culture, and they are equally good that he will not climb out of his pedestrian craft in this subculture to bigger *rackets*. It has been tried—and in some cases it has been accomplished—but the average pickpocket does not change.

But usually if a guy's a pickpocket, he knows what the score is as far as he's concerned. He knows that he's got a living there. So he goes out and if he only gets ten pokes a day, he's got grocery money, anyway. But if he goes out on one of them other capers, he don't know what he's got, because you have to specialize. If you're going to specialize in a certain subject, you have to concentrate on that. A man's capabilities is only going to carry him so far, and he can't do it. I have never knew—I have never known—I have never known a pickpocket to be successful at another racket.

In fact, the mere framework of specialization seems to keep a pickpocket where he is, to "freeze" him in his occupation. He has no need to learn anything else to practice his *racket*. The very practice of it precludes his learning anything else; while he may be highly skilled at removing a wallet, there his abilities, legitimate and illegitimate, usually end.

No, that wouldn't change your way of thinking. The moral of what he just said a minute ago is this: ninety-nine and ninety-nine one-hundredths percent of organized society as we know it today are not going to give a thief with a record . . . they're not going to give him a chance. Our chances of squaring up . . . well, we've got two. A bum chance and no chance at all. If you've gone this far down the river, there's no way back. Just like he said. . . .

Well, he might have a chance. But he's a heavy. In between his criminal activities and a prison sentence here and there, he's become an expert welder. And an iron-worker. He can do a lot of different jobs. And this boy [a short-change artist] has a lot of qualifications. He has a good education, he can read and write very well, and there is a lot of things he can do that he has picked up in the world.

Now you take a guy like me. . . . I don't know anything. I've centered everything I know on how to make an illegitimate dollar. I don't think about trying to make money any other way. Every time I've had a legitimate job, always one of those tornados strikes, or a windstorm comes up, and first thing you know I find myself out in the cold again. So I center all my alleged brain, my thinking power, whatever it may be, on trying to make an illegitimate dollar . . . which of course big business is trying to do the same. They're trying to phenagle [finagle] us all out of a dollar.

And so the pickpocket, however expert he may be in his *racket*, is limited to that craft. Nothing he learns in the subculture can be applied in the dominant culture; his very professional skill inhibits him psychologically from learning anything he can use while he is in prison, where educational facilities are available. And he sees no way of learning anything in the dominant culture which might be applied in the subculture. Consequently he remains a pickpocket, usually on whatever level he was *turned out* originally.

4 A Vocabulary of Motives for Law Violations

FRANK E. HARTUNG

Sykes and Matza use the concept "techniques of neutralization" to indicate the process of reasoning in which the boy engages before he commits his delinquency or after it, or both.[1] It emphasizes that delinquency, being purposive in one way or another, results, in part, from the way in which the individual conceives of himself in relation to others. I must add that it also implies that lawful behavior results from the same process of rationalization, but with a different vocabulary of reasons being employed. This conclusion is in keeping with the social-psychological analysis of motivation. The following discussion will show, I hope, that the juvenile delinquent and the adult offender are engaging in deliberate action accompanied by reasoning, and that they are therefore rational. This analysis presents a very different conception, therefore, of the juvenile delinquent and the criminal from that presented by psychiatry, which tends to view them as being emotionally disturbed or mentally ill—to use terms often regarded as synonyms.

An individual is not culpable and therefore not legally punishable if

Reprinted from *Crime, Law and Society*, pp. 62–83, by Frank E. Hartung, by permission of The Wayne State University Press. Copyright © 1965 by The Wayne State University Press, Detroit 2, Michigan. Also by permission of the author.

[1] The following discussion draws on Gresham M. Sykes and David Matza, "Techniques of Neutralization: A Theory of Delinquency," *American Sociological Review*, 22, August 1957, pp. 664–70.

he can prove the absence of criminal intent in the act he committed.[2] Much delinquency is based on what is essentially an unrecognized extension to crimes, in the form of justifications for deviance that are held valid by the delinquent but denied validity by the criminal law and by society at large.[3] These justifications comprise a vocabulary of motives. The delinquent learns them from a number of sources, for they are abundantly supplied by the community, as we shall see. They are thus sociocultural products and not individually invented. In social-psychological analysis the term "motivation" refers to the process through which an individual, as a participant in a group (or perhaps by himself through sociocultural action such as reading or thinking) symbolically (by means of language) defines a situation as calling for the performance of a particular act with, symbolically, more or less expected consummation and consequences.[4] Motives, then, are linguistic constructs organizing actions in particular situations.[5] They are rationalizations of acts, or symbolic constructs, which not only organize the acts in particular situations, but make them recognizably recurrent in the life-history of any group or individual. The pattern of recurrence is part of what is referred to as the group's culture and part of the individual's self. The use of these motives can be examined empirically, as we shall presently indicate.

The reader may have noticed that the psychiatric meaning of "to rationalize" is radically different from the historically long established social-psychological mean. The former means that one advances plausible or socially conforming reasons for his conduct, as a substitute for the supposedly true and socially unacceptable reasons. The "true" reasons, psychiatry also claims, are "in" the actor's unconscious (wherever may that organ be?) and therefore unknowable to him but discoverable by a psychiatrist. The psychiatric meaning thus enables one to disregard and to discredit the conclusions and motives of other people. Kenneth Burke has said of the psychiatric meaning of rationalization that "as people tend to round out their orientations verbally, we sometimes show our approval of the verbalizations by the term 'reasoning' and our disapproval by the term 'rationalizing.' "[6] But in social psychology the symbolic constructs applied by an individual to his own

---

[2] This does not apply to "strict liability": "In problems relevant to criminal law, strict liability means liability to punitive sanctions despite the lack of *mens rea*," Jerome Hall, *General Principles of Criminal Law*, rev. ed., Indianapolis: Bobbs-Merrill Co., Inc., 1960, p. 325.

[3] Sykes and Matza, *op. cit.*, p. 666, paraphrased. Following references to Sykes and Matza are to this study, pp. 667–70.

[4] Nelson N. Foote, "Identification as a Basis for a Theory of Motivation," *American Sociological Review*, 16, February 1951, pp. 14–21, at p. 15.

[5] C. Wright Mills, "Situated Actions and Vocabularies of Motives," *American Sociological Review*, 5, December 1940, pp. 904–13.

[6] Kenneth Burke, *Permanence and Change*, rev. ed., Los Altos, Calif.: Hermes Publications, 1954, p. 11.

behavior in a given situation are motives. The complete process in which these verbalizations are used is motivation.

It will be seen later that the social-psychological conceptions of motivation and rationalization are important in the understanding of the allegedly "senseless" actions that are supposed to comprise "compulsive" crimes. It is therefore appropriate to emphasize in the present discussion of juvenile delinquency that a person acts because he has already rationalized, and that the rationalization is his motive. The psychiatric notion that rationalization is "merely" an *ex post facto* justification of action resulting from "deep-seated and unconscious motives" is erroneous. It not only disregards the reasoning that precedes the act, but denies that it occurred.

Some vocabularies of motives are more systematized and widely held than others. When an individual—say, a juvenile delinquent—draws upon the rationalizations of his group, he will observe himself as conforming because the rationalizations that he shares with the others support and sanction him in his actions. This comforting experience of conforming applies of course, to other people, including the lawful. One may also suppose it to be the experience of all or practically all of the forty-five executives from the twenty-nine corporations who were defendants in the Incredible Electrical Conspiracy, for violation of the Sherman Anti-Trust Act, including, according to Fortune's account, "men in the highest echelons of the corporations."[7] Judge J. Cullen Ganey, chief judge of the United States District Court of Philadelphia, referred to "the company man, the conformist, who goes along with his superiors and finds balm for his conscience in additional comforts and the security of his place in the corporate setup." If the corporate executives had acted on the basis of the rationalization "All businessmen are crooks," a rationalization that seems not to be widely held by businessmen, they would perhaps not have experienced the support and sanction that they evidently did.

One can also speculate that the conspirators apprehended late in 1961 in the province of Ontario for the sale of uninspected and contaminated meat drew personal comfort from the fact that they were acting in concert. They could not have acted on the basis of the maxim that a number of legitimate small meat-packers have expressed to me, "Anybody who sells uninspected meat should be forced to feed his own family with it."

We can therefore say, in the case of juveniles who are learning delinquency, that the disapproval they would otherwise apply to their own conduct, and the disapproval that they believe others would express, can be neutralized in advance by the use of one or more of the rationalizations provided by the delinquent vocabulary of motives. Through this means a delinquent can (a) remain committed to the conventional code but so qualify

[7] Richard Austin Smith, "The Incredible Electrical Conspiracy," *Fortune*, April 1961, pp. 132 ff., and May 1961, pp. 161 ff.

its moral imperatives that violations of them are not only "acceptable" but "right," and (b) not seriously endanger his own self-conception. It is well known that many, if not most, delinquent children do not progress from delinquency as a game to being career delinquent. It may very well be that a major reason for this is that the boys are possessed by conventional norms. Perhaps research can provide a valid answer. These rationalizations, as Sykes and Matza state, comprise a significant component of Sutherland's "definitions favorable to the violation of law." We shall discuss five of them.

First, *the denial of responsibility*. This rationalization seems to be the most frequently resorted to by delinquents, one reason being, perhaps, that it is so firmly a part of the professional ideology of many people in authoritative positions who handle delinquents: social workers, juvenile-court judges, psychiatrists and other employees of the court, probation officers, and the like. The denial of responsibility asserts that delinquent acts are due to agencies beyond the control of the individual. The delinquency, it may be asserted, is the result of such things as being a member of a minority group, living in a slum with inadequate housing, having a broken home or drunken parents, bad companions, and lack of recreation. Judge Leibowitz' "two strikes" theory, previously cited, is an illustration of the kind of statement through which a delinquent can deny his responsibility for his actions: ". . . we are supporting them [children and families] in the most wretched and degrading environment which prevents the moral development of the child . . . A child brought here [New York City] to live in crowded slums begins life with two strikes against him."

The delinquents do not, of course, express themselves in such correct English. Their speech is typically ungrammatical and vulgar, but in their slogan—with the obscenities removed—"I couldn't help it," and similar expressions, one can discern the self-conception advanced to the person in authority. It is a conception of themselves as billiard balls. Helpless subjects of agents that knock them around the billiard table, they are acted upon rather than acting. It will have been recognized that this rationalization repeats some of the psychiatric, psychological, and sociological theories advanced to explain delinquency. If the boy does not know the juvenile version of the mechanistic explanation of his misdeeds the first time he is in juvenile court—"I couldn't help it"—he will have learned it by the second time. He plays back to the social worker the explanation that the social worker originally advanced, the explanation that relieves the delinquent of his responsibility. Virginia P. Held provides an excellent illustration in the rationalization, "It's not my fault":

"A 15-year-old boy came here the other day," Dr. [Melitta] Schmideberg told me, "with a handful of clippings that said that delinquency is the fault of the parents, and that parents should talk with and try to understand their

children. He said his parents didn't understand him, so it wasn't his fault that
he held up a store." Another delinquent blamed his mother, saying she was
impossibly neurotic: she made him straighten up his room. "One would like
simply to laugh at these cases," Dr. Schmideberg said, "but one can't, because
they have unfortunately become quite typical."[8]

As the psychiatrist Plant says, "Juvenile delinquency is a thing that
happens to an individual, not a thing that he does." This conception is
reinforced when the boy is repeatedly told by those in legal authority,
"We are here to help you." The juvenile court was invented, in part, just
for that purpose: to help the juvenile, and not to blame, punish, or hold
him responsible. When the delinquent can present a conception of himself
as an innocent victim of evil forces, he can steal without danger to his
self-conception, while at the same time not having to reject the conventional
moral code. Respectable society has told him, "It isn't your fault because
you couldn't help yourself."

An illustration of this type of thinking may be drawn from a juvenile-
court hearing that I attended in one of the more populous counties of Iowa,
in July 1963. The complaint alleged that a twelve-year-old boy had stolen
several purses, removed the money, and then thrown them away. A fourteen-
year-old girl was also involved, but she had only acted as an overseer and
had taken none of the money. Both children were in the courtroom, as
were the boy's divorced parents, the county probation officer, and the woman
who was to receive the boy when he was placed in her foster home. The
judge began by praising the boy's appearance and smile, saying that he could
go far in life if he continued to have such a winning smile. "You are a good
boy," he said, and proceeded to question him about the theft. The boy,
to judge from his frequent smiling, was pleased indeed to hear himself praised
so fulsomely.

After a few moments of silence and in the presence of the two children,
the judge verbally excoriated the boy's parents. When they were divorced,
he said, they were thoroughly selfish and thought only of their own bodies
(he had himself granted the divorce in August 1962). They ought to be
ashamed of themselves and be horsewhipped, and if the state law allowed
it he would have a whipping post erected in the courtyard and do the
whipping himself. He forced the mother to admit that she had had sexual
relations in her home since the divorce and that she was now pregnant out
of wedlock. He said, further, that he was going to declare the boy a ward
of the court, not because he was delinquent but because he was a dependent
and neglected child from an unfit home, repeating the charge of "unfit
home" loudly and emotionally three times. In reply to his questions, the

[8] Virginia P. Held, "The Formless Years—What Can We do about 'J.D.,'"
Hearings before the Subcommittee to Investigate Juvenile Delinquency of the Committee on the Judiciary, United States, 86th Congress, 1st Session, 1959, p. 474.

mother said that she was twenty-seven years of age and had six children, the oldest of whom was the twelve-year-old boy presently in court. He then said she was a good-looking woman, but that while she was good-looking now she would be old tomorrow; if she did not mend her ways, she would lose everything and wind up in the gutter before she was thirty. He then repeated his comments about horsewhipping and the parents' shameful behavior. He then told both parents twice that they were responsible for their son's thefts, that the boy was not, and that therefore they should be ashamed.

The judge then told the boy that he was a good boy, that he had friends—namely, himself (the judge), the probation officer, and the woman who was to be his foster mother. He then threatened the parents with jail if they bothered the foster parents, told the boy once more that he was a good boy, announced that the session was over, and walked around the table with his right hand extended to shake hands with the parents, which neither parent wanted to do. At the end of the hearing the boy was still smiling.

During a conversation with the probation officer the next day I commented on the judge's remarks and asked, "Does he usually talk that way to the parents when their children are present?" She replied, "No, he has several speeches, and he talks that way only to those parents who deserve it." She added that the mother had "come by her immorality honestly, so to speak," because *her* mother had been pregnant out of wedlock when she was fifteen years old.

Perhaps in ten years that twelve-year-old will say and believe, as the young man in the Iowa State Reformatory said in effect, "The reason why I commit evil is because my father was evil":

Well starting at an early age I was living in B——, Iowa with my mother, father & 15 Brothers and Sisters which was 9 Boys and 7 Girls and we were in hard times and my dad and two Brothers worked on W.P.A. Making about $110.00 a month and my Brothers were married with small familys and all we got to eat was what the W.P.A. workers and familys were issued which wasn't very much and my older Brothers and myself had to steal food in Order for the family to live and we even stoled milk so we could fed the smaller Babys. we didn't have enough clothing for all of us to go to school each day so we would change off wearing clothes so we could all get at least 1½ to 2 days a week in school. And soon after some of the girls got married and left home and the Boys as well and so that left me and My younger brothers to help out at home so I had to quit school to Help my dad make a living for the rest of us kids and if we did do everything we were Beat and I mean Beat not whipped And we were brought up to fight with every one who said a word wrong to us I am pretty sure that if I or any of my brothers would of come from a family of 5 or 6 we would of had had a better chance of Being like we wanted to Be able to complete school had plenty of clothes and shoes on are feet and Not Been treated so mean and made to do wrong things I am now seving a five year sentence which I Believe and always will Believe I got it from Being treated like i was treated at home my dad is responsible for my wrong and all my Brothers wrongs . . . I am suffering from the wrong rearing I had at home. . . .[9]

The young man's disclaimer of responsibility for his crimes is matched by the one reported by Dr. William Glasser. While eating lunch with five newly admitted inmates at the Ventura School for Girls, one girl said, "Doc, you know why I'm here—it's because I'm emotionally disturbed." The other four also claimed that they needed help because they were emotionally disturbed, and that was why they were committed. In relating how the girls then admitted that they were incarcerated because they had violated a criminal law, Glasser described what he and Dr. G. L. Harrison call "reality therapy," which they contrast with "conventional therapy." In discussing the girls' claim of "emotional disturbance," Glasser writes:

What this example illustrates is how the application of modern psychiatry, psychology, sociology, and criminology is understood by these delinquent girls and most children in trouble. It is a function of the effect of our whole psychotherapeutic profession that these girls feel they are basically emotionally disturbed and what they did is much less important, because it is only a part of a deep emotional disturbance over which they have little control. They feel that they are psychologically upset and therefore not particularly responsible for their behavior.

This is not something they would be aware of on their own. They have learned that to get along well in a modern, treatment-conscious institution, this is the most comfortable attitude to take.[10]

Both Glasser and Harrison "disagree completely" with both the conception of the child as emotionally disturbed and the assumption that the child's understanding of his unconscious conflicts will lead him to rational behavior:

. . . this is most obvious with delinquent children, that just the opposite will occur. The more they are convinced by traditional therapy that they are

[9] The author of the quotation was reared in a village in Iowa. Harold Dwight Eastman, "The Process of Urbanization and Criminal Behavior: A Restudy of Culture Conflict," unpublished Ph.D. dissertation, State University of Iowa, 1954, p. 190.

[10] William Glasser, "Reality Psychiatry: An Effective Treatment for Delinquents," Reference Bulletin No. 24, San Diego County Probation Department (mimeographed). Reproduced from a speech delivered before the National Institute on Crime and Delinquency, Seattle, during July 1962, p. 2.

Dr. Glasser is Consulting Psychiatrist at the Ventura School for Girls. Dr. Harrison is a psychiatrist at the Los Angeles Veterans Administration Neuropsychiatric Hospital. Both employ reality therapy exclusively in their respective institutions as well as in their private practice.

disturbed and have good reason to be so, the worse they will act in or out of custody. There is nothing in the traditional therapy which leads to responsible behavior, only the vague hope that understanding one's actions will motivate one in the right direction.[11]

Traditional therapy, Glasser concludes, is ineffective because it never puts the responsibility for disturbed behavior or thought processes on the patient; and indeed, it does just the opposite:

Its stated purpose is to remove the responsibility for the behavior from the patient and place it on his unconscious conflicts, conflicts caused by parents, environment, society, or usually a combination of all three. The argument is that a child never takes narcotics because he consciously wants to, it is because his unconscious conflicts left him desperately in need of the feeling of security that narcotics provide.

Thus, in the words again of my lunch companions, "it is because we are emotionally disturbed that we're in trouble." Carried a step further, the up-to-date delinquent child expects therapist to ask "why?" It's part of the therapy game and when the traditional therapist complies it is as if the child never really broke the law. What happened didn't really happen, it is only a surface manifestation of an unconscious conflict.

There is nothing in the traditional therapy which presents the patient with the responsibility for his actions, there is no personal responsibility even implied. The present reality is less important than the reasons why he got into trouble. In working with delinquent children this is a serious handicap. Relieved by the well-meaning therapist of the responsibility for their actions, they often react with violent behavior, partly in an effort to be helped now, rather than to be dragged through disturbing memories which both incite and justify their activities.

In his eagerness to be accepted and to help, the traditional therapist emphasizes that the patient has little responsibility for what he did as long as he understands why he did it, but the patient, unfortunately, interprets this as meaning "I have no responsibility for anything I do that is wrong because I have problems."

There is nothing in the concept of traditional therapy which will help him to stop except the hope that reason and understanding will prevail. . . . the inclusion of traditional therapy in an institution which previously had no psychiatric treatment program often leads to acting out, discipline breakdown, increased emotional upset and conflict between the old personnel and the new traditional therapists.[12]

Reality therapy, as presented by Glasser, is the opposite of conventional therapy. It never excuses any conduct, past or present, directly or indirectly, by asking "Why?" or by seeking the reason in the unconscious.

[11] *Ibid.*, p. 3.
[12] *Ibid.*, pp. 4–5.

It ignores the unconscious completely, and works only with the conscious and present situation.

> We always ask *what*, we never ask *why*. We will say to a girl who breaks an institutional rule, "What did you do?" We ask this even if what she did was obvious, because, accustomed to the traditional way and expecting us to ask *why*, she has already dismissed what she really did and formed an excuse, an excuse which relieves her of the responsibility for what she did.[13]

Reality therapy thus never asks, "Why did you do it?" because to do so is to admit that there may be an excuse. The child is held primarily responsible regardless of what causes his bad behavior. There is never any intimation that psychiatric treatment relieves him of the responsibility for what he has done. He is held accountable to his own principles for what he does. It is assumed—which is rarely if ever the case in conventional therapy—that he has a workable set of principles, standards, or values. The delinquent, Glasser believes, knows right from wrong, and good from bad in some absolute way for himself. Glasser is at one with sociology when he maintains that, no matter how severe the personality disorder is, when removed from a situation in which excuses are accepted, the boy has adequate standards: "We have never met anyone who lacks adequate standards."[14]

---

[13] *Ibid.*, p. 5.

[14] *Ibid.*, p. 6. Somewhat parallel developments seem to have occurred independently of each other in psychiatry and sociology. Much of what Glasser and Harrison refer to as "reality therapy" has, as far as one can judge, been known for some years to sociology under the heading of "guided group interaction," and other names. Two examples of this concept and technique, and their application and development are the experimental project for the treatment of youthful offenders at Highfields, New Jersey, and "The Provo Experiment" with adjudicated delinquents in Provo, Utah. Both are explicitly based on the sociological theory of delinquency and crime, toward which "reality therapy" seems to have converged remarkably.

See Donald R. Cressey, "Changing Criminals: The Application of the Theory of Differential Association," *American Journal of Sociology*, 61, July 1955, pp. 116–20; Lloyd W. McCorkle and Richard Korn, "Resocialization within Walls," *Annals of the American Academy of Political and Social Science*, 293, May 1954, pp. 88–98; Joseph Abrahams and Lloyd W. McCorkle, "Group Psychotherapy of Military Offenders," *American Journal of Sociology*, 51, March 1946, pp. 455–64; Joseph Abrahams and Lloyd W. McCorkle, "Group Psychotherapy at an Army Rehabilitation Center," *Diseases of the Nervous System*, February 1947; Lloyd W. McCorkle, "Group Therapy in Correctional Institutions," *Federal Probation*, 13, June 1949, pp. 34–37; F. Lovell Bixby and Lloyd W. McCorkle, "Guided Group Interaction and Correctional Work," *American Sociological Review*, 16, August 1951, pp. 455–59; Lloyd W. McCorkle, "Group Therapy," in Paul W. Tappan, ed., *Contemporary Correction*, New York: McGraw-Hill Book Co., Inc., 1951, pp. 211–23; Lloyd W. McCorkle, Albert Elias, and F. Lovell Bixby, *The Highfields Story*, New York: Henry Holt & Co., 1958; H. Ashley Weeks, *Youthful Offenders at Highfields*, Ann Arbor: University of Michigan Press, 1958; Albert Elias and Jerome Rabow, "Post-Release Adjustment of Highfields Boys,

This is in accord with the experience of Redl and Wineman, who report that "the strength of the conscience may vary from child to child but *we have never seen a child in whom it is totally absent.*"[15]

The assertion that reality therapy is an effective treatment for delinquents has yet to be tested. There are at present no departments of psychiatry in medical schools or schools of social work that train graduate students in its practice and theory, and it may be years before any do. Even so, it surely bolsters the sociological analysis of the denial of responsibility. It presents clinical, empirical evidence that the delinquent transforms the scientifically based and authoritatively presented reasons explaining his delinquency into excuses and justifications for it. One can generalize and state that there seems to be a continual tendency for reasons to be used as excuses and justifications.

Second, *the denial of injury.* The delinquent may rest the matter of whether his actions were wrong on the point of whether or not anyone was unquestionably hurt by them. This, of course, is a matter of judgment, and of interpretation. He may say that he "borrowed" an automobile and had no intention of stealing or stripping it; he just wanted a joyride. "After all," he may say, "I didn't wreck it," and it isn't damaged and I didn't even empty the gas tank. So, who's hurt?" The police very often recognize the distinction made by the delinquent, and the complaint will be "Unlawfully Driving Away an Automobile," rather than a complaint of automobile theft. Vandalism, especially when committed against the property of an impersonal agent—say, a corporation or an absentee owner—may be defined as "fun," or as "having a good joke."

If the delinquent can break the relation between what he did and its consequences, he does not have to judge himself adversely and can reject the otherwise expected adverse judgments of respectable, lawful people. It must be said that society at large presents the delinquent with many reasons for using this rationalization, just as it does for the first: "Providing there is not serious injury to property, the American public tends to view

---

1955–57," *Welfare Reporter*, January 1960, pp. 7–11; LaMar T. Empey and Jerome Rabow, "The Provo Experiment in Delinquency Rehabilitation," *American Sociological Review*, 26, October 1961, pp. 679–96; LaMar T. Empey, "The Application of Sociological Theory to Sociological Problems," and the "Discussion" of Empey's paper by Edward J. Abramson, Gilbert L. Geis, and Harold Finestone, Annual Meeting of the Society for the Study of Social Problems, Statler-Hilton Hotel, Los Angeles, August 23–25, 1963; and Rita Volkman and Donald R. Cressey, "Differential Association and the Rehabilitation of Drug Addicts," *American Journal of Sociology*, 69, September 1963, pp. 129–42.

[15] Fritz Redl and David Wineman, *The Aggressive Child*, Glencoe: Free Press, 1957, p. 261. My italics.

pranks with a kind of careless tolerance, probably because most American males were once participants in this kind of activity."[16]

Whether a given action is vandalism, good clean fun, or just a lark, seems to depend, in large part, on time, place and social context. In the past that is beyond the memory of perhaps, most of my readers, it was permissible "skylarking" to overturn farm wagons or outhouses on Halloween, or to dismantle a farmer's wagon and reassemble it on the roof of his barn. But today the overturning of a truck is "malicious destruction of property." There was often widespread vandalism in college towns on the evening of a "homecoming" football game, or after the victory of the home team over a hated rival—or after its defeat. Liberty Street in Ann Arbor, Michigan, and State Street in Madison, Wisconsin, have in the past been the victims of such good, clean, and expensive destruction by the students at the two universities. Occasionally, a few students were placed on probation. Had that destruction of property, and the rioting, been the work of the "town" youth, rather than the "grown" youth it would without question have resulted in a demand for stricter enforcement of the law, a call to stop the mollycoddling of delinquents, and an effort to re-establish the woodshed as a place for punishing the deserving delinquent or youthful criminal. This distinction between the good, clean fun of college boys and the vandalism of delinquents is also made in England:

[T]he party of public schoolboys who damage property during a "rag" are behaving very differently from the street corner gang who smash street lamps or shop windows "just for the fun of it." . . . The mores of the Public School community allow and even encourage such explosively expressive behavior and the scholar's participation in its restricted setting, whereas the casual destructiveness of promiscuous gangs has no such social approval to sustain it.[17]

There is probably no college fraternity that does not have its traffic signs, stolen from the municipality and the state, and its laboratory equipment—stolen from the college's laboratories in a completely selfish disregard of the other students. But this is defined as "good, clean fun," and not as larceny. The newspapers and magazines make much of the physical and sometimes savage attacks in which juvenile gangs sometimes engage. Perhaps a stir should be created over that violence. Those same newspapers and magazines will not, however, devote the same amount of time to the brutal, corporal attacks of upper-class college students on freshmen. Hazing is not as brutal as it used to be; one still learns, however, of an occasional homicide. A recent case that comes to mind is that of a young man killed while

[16] Marshall B. Clinard and Andrew L. Wade, "Toward the Delineation of Vandalism as a Sub-Type in Juvenile Delinquency," *Journal of Criminal Law, Criminology, and Police Science,* 48, January-February, 1958, p. 497.

[17] John Barron Mays, *Growing Up in the City,* Liverpool: University of Liverpool Press, 1954, pp. 18–19.

being initiated into the fraternity of a university in southern California, in 1959. He had been forced by his brothers [sic] to swallow a piece of oil-soaked liver that lodged in his throat; he choked to death. His life might have been saved had his "brothers" not lied to the internes on the ambulance that was called, as to what his trouble was. No sanctions were imposed on the other students involved; yet, had this happened in a gang of boys from the other side of the tracks they would very likely have been charged with either negligent or nonnegligent manslaughter. (If they were of juvenile-court age, and the judge refused to waive jurisdiction to the criminal court, the complaint would be the same, but they could be found to have "committed a delinquent act," and then be subject to the juvenile court's sanctions.)

About two weeks after the above event, two freshmen at Michigan State University, in East Lansing, were involved in a hazing "incident." They had been kidnapped near the campus on Saturday night, November 7, 1959, by six or seven fraternity members who forced the two into an automobile and drove them about fifty miles northeast. There, on an unlighted side road, they were undressed, bound, and spattered with red, black, yellow, and brown paint and shellac; tape was placed over their eyes and mouths and they were then abandoned. One victim was able to chew through the tape covering his mouth, and then managed to chew through his companion's bonds. They were taken to a hospital by a motorist who passed their way. No charges were brought against the young men who perpetrated the kidnapping and the assault. In some states it is a capital offense to commit bodily harm on the person who has been kidnapped.

Sororities and fraternities have been prohibited by law in the public high schools of Michigan since 1911. Some high schools have allowed the formation of what are called "social clubs," as a substitute. The social clubs are in addition to the usual high school activity clubs. In January of 1962 the principal of Redford High School in Detroit announced that social clubs were thenceforward to be banned at that school.

The principal blamed cruel and brutal hazing and the practice of beating unwanted members, for the ban. He had received repeated complaints of hazing from parents, students, and ministers. "It was so bad," the principal was quoted as saying, "that I dreaded coming to school on Thursday mornings because I knew there would be a flood of calls about the meetings held the night before. Parents were supposed to supervise the meetings but I discovered that many of them were not supervised." He further said that it was difficult to identify the boys who were the subjects of brutal hazing. It was not only that they were frightened of a subsequent beating. They were more "scared" of being known as "crybaby" or "chicken" to their fellow students. A number of boys who were beaten went to their ministers for help rather than to their parents or to the school's administration.

Since the social clubs at Redford High School were not permitted to blackball any students assigned to them as members, the older members resorted to beating unwelcome new members with a paddle until they quit. This practice was ungrammatically but picturesquely referred to as a "swat-out." The "swat-out" could not be ignored when public attention was called to it. Late in January 1962, a swimming instructor asked the principal to come to the swimming pool. Two of the boys "were black and blue from their waists to the backs of their knees." The banning of the "social" clubs followed.

No attempt to identify the assailants of the boys was reported.

The admission of injury and the denial of injury thus depend partly on the respective social class of the victim and his assailant; and also partly on the context in which the crimes or delinquencies are perpetrated. To repeat, the rationalization, *the denial of injury*, shows that the community supplies its members with a host of motivations, and free of charge.[18]

Third, *the denial of the victim*. The moral disapproval of self and of respectable people that can be expected for delinquencies may be neutralized in advance by insisting that the misdeed was not wrong in the given circumstances. In this rationalization the delinquent reverse the positions of himself and his victim. The victim, it may be insisted, "had it coming to him"; so the injury is rationalized as being nothing more nor less than a just punishment, and, if anything, less than the victim really deserved. Sykes and Matza list some types of victims who may be "justly" punished on the basis of this motivation. Assaults on homosexuals are not only justified by delinquents on this basis, but the police seem often to condone such attacks, if not actively to approve them. A fifteen-year-old boy in Chicago described briefly how the four members of his gang "pulled off our trick in a slick way":

West Madison Street and vicinity was a rather dark section of the city, so it was easy to strongarm. . . . There were a lot of homosexuals and we played our game on them. We would let them approach one of us, usually me, because I was so little and they like little fellows, and then I'd follow

[18] Many sociologists would deny delinquents the comfort and support of this rationalization. An example is provided by J. P. Shalloo, who says, "The plain fact is that such vandals are fully aware of the nature of their actions and are as completely normal mentally as juveniles who do not engage in such conduct." He then refers to "incontrovertible evidence that such juveniles (delinquents) are not subnormal or abnormal." The overwhelming proportion of vandals, he asserts, "are as normal and as intelligent and resourceful as juveniles who find socially acceptable means of solving the problems that are an inherent part of the very trying process of growing up." J. P. Shalloo, "Vandalism: Whose Responsibility?" *Federal Probation,* 18, March 1954, pp. 6–8.

The same issue of *Federal Probation* contains a valuable symposium on vandalism, placing it with stealing in the cultural matrix of the versatility and meanness that characterize much of the delinquent subculture.

him to his room or to a vacant house to do the act. My pals would follow us to our destination and then we'd rob him.[19]

Other types of victims who are "justly punished" because "they had it coming" are members of minority groups who have "gotten out of their place," and "crooked" store owner, the unfair teacher, and the harsh principal. Lawful society provides the delinquents with a store of respectable examples of lawbreakers who are held in high esteem. Robin Hood and Zorro are two. It will be recalled that the psychiatrist, Lauretta Bender, described *Superman Comics* as being "good," because Superman righted wrongs and imposed "just punishment" outside the law, according to his conception of justice. The National Association for Better Radio and Television, in its Tenth Annual Survey of Children's Programs, classified "Superman" as the "Most objectionable":

The essence of Superman is violence to those whom he thinks deserve it. He is permitted to commit crimes under the pretense of imposing punishment. He is immortal and has powers beyond any physical, natural, or religious law. Clark Kent as Superman shows up at just the right place to fight for "truth, justice and the American way." There is no division between reality and fantasy. Crimes are solved because, and only because, a reporter can turn into an extra-terrestrial investigator. Murder, kidnapping, and other crimes make this an outstanding example of exploitation of children, serving them poisoned mental food, to make sales and money. A most distasteful program.[20]

Examples are by no means confined to fiction and folklore. Many members of the lawful community will on occasion "justly punish" members of minority groups who are "trying to get out of their place." During 1963 thousands of Negroes were arrested in the United States while attempting to exercise their constitutional rights. Many were beaten, some seriously, and others assaulted. Some were murdered. Arson, dynamiting, and other forms of vandalism were committed on homes, churches, and places of business. It was necessary in several situations to mobilize United States marshals and part of the military. Most of the instances in which lawful citizens resorted to the rationalization, the denial of the victim, occurred in the former Confederate states of the southeast. An example from a northern state is provided by Dearborn, Michigan, a satellite of Detroit. In the fall of 1963 a home was ruined by a crowd of white vandals who thought that it had been sold to a Negro family. The Dearborn police did not interfere, and its

[19] Clifford R. Shaw and Henry D. McKay, *Social Factors in Juvenile Delinquency: A Study of the Community, the Family, and the Gang in Relation to Delinquent Behavior*, for the National Commission on Law Observance and Enforcement, *Report on the Causes of Crime*, No. 13, Vol. II, Washington: Government Printing Office, 1931, p. 228.

[20] *Hearings* before the Subcommittee to Investigate Juvenile Delinquency of the Committee on the Judiciary, United States, 87th Congress, 1963, p. 1937.

mayor praised them for their "fine work" in maintaining order. The home had been purchased by a white family; the company moving their furniture in had Negro employees.

The existence of these victims and the use of this motivation show once again that delinquency, like lawfulness, is selective, ordered, and sociocultural, rather than unselective, random and individualistic. This is so, regardless of the race, nationality, religion, or personality of the delinquent, —all of which further shows that delinquency involving vandalism, theft, and physical assault is deliberate and willful. It is therefore erroneous to describe the vandalism and bodily assaults committed by teen-age hoodlums as "senseless," and as having "no purpose, no rhyme, no reason," as many psychiatrists, social workers, psychologists, policemen, sociologists and other people do. It is correct to describe them as being often malicious, savage, and vicious.

Our repugnance for some of the delinquents' actions and our inability to conceive of ourselves as committing them should not lead us to accept the erroneous and misleading hypothesis of the irresistible impulse or compulsive crime.

Fourth, *the condemnation of the condemners.* This is the phrase used by Sykes and Matza, whereas McCorkle and Korn refer to *the rejection of the rejectors.* Both phrases refer to the same rationalization, which focuses attention on the motives and behavior of those who would morally disapprove of the delinquent's action.[21] Those who would condemn, disapprove, or reject him, the delinquent may argue, are hypocrites, motivated by spite, or are themselves undetected criminals or delinquents. The forms of this rationalization reported by Dr. Melitta Schmideberg from her questioning of delinquent children are commonly heard: "When I ask them why they were sent [to training schools or to jail], they tell me the judge didn't like them, or their lawyer was no good, or the jury was rigged. Almost never do they say, 'I stole' or 'I shot a man. . . .' "[22]

The present rationalization, in common with the first three, is supplied in one or more forms by, and confirmed by, the larger society. Thus, the delinquent may say that the police are corrupt and brutal. Despite the remarkable professionalization of police departments since about 1930, including many state systems, there is enough corruption to give a degree of validity to the assertion. It is no secret that in the United States this

---

[21] "In many ways the inmate social system [of the prison] may be viewed as providing a way of life which enables the inmate to avoid the devastating psychological effects of internalizing and converting social rejection into self-rejection. In effect, it permits the inmate to reject his rejectors rather than himself." Lloyd W. McCorkle and Richard Korn, "Resocialization within Walls," *Annals of the American Academy of Political and Social Science*, 293, May 1954, p. 88.

[22] Virginia P. Held, *op. cit.*, p. 475.

conception of the police is widely held in all segments of the population. The municipal police in the United States have, in fact, come to the point at which their effective functioning is dependent upon their developing a positive conception of themselves among the general population. They are confronted by no problem more pressing and serious. It is admittedly very difficult to solve when members of police departments, widely separated geographically, are themselves revealed as being burglars.

The delinquent's use of this rationalization is facilitated by newspaper reports of widespread crookedness on the part of retail grocery store operators, service establishments such as watch and jewelry repair, radio and television service and repair, automobile garages, and the like. These assist the adolescent in adopting the rationalization "Everyone has his own racket." This reaches its finest flower among (1) the young narcotics addict who claims that everyone is an "operator" who is always "shooting the angles" (except the Square John, who is so stupid that he works at a regular job); (2) the convict's ideal of the "real man," who knows that there are only two kinds of people: the "suckers" who work, and the "smart guys" who "skim it off the top"; and (3) the honest policeman who believes that "everyone has larceny in his heart."

The world of the delinquent and of the juvenile-becoming-delinquent is also populated—according to the boys—with teachers who always have their pets; with hypocritical male probation officers who are lushes (excessive drinkers), or who are having extramarital sexual affairs with female probation officers or policewomen; with the homosexual Boy Scout master and the like. The juvenile is assisted in coming to believe and to use this rationalization, "Everybody's got it in for me," or, "He's worse than I am," by respectable organizations and lawful individuals in positions of authority. Thus—with no attempt on my part to evaluate or deny the validity of their assertions—organizations ranging from the United States Department of Justice to the National Association for the Advancement of Colored People often assert and confirm, or attempt to confirm, the existence of various kinds and degrees of discrimination. The newspapers, including the Negro press, also report this as a matter of course.

Some professional people also confirm the delinquent's rationalization "They're just picking on me, "Everybody's against me." Anyone with the experience in dealing with delinquents and near-delinquents soon learns that he must guard against the boy's attempt to manipulate him through the use of the verbalization "They're picking on me." But there are some professional people who never learn this lesson. Bruno Bettelheim is one who seems, on the basis of his own words, firmly to believe that every delinquent does in fact and in actuality believe his jaundiced rationalization, "Everybody's against me; I didn't have a chance." In giving evidence before the Committee on the Judiciary, United States Senate, he said, ". . . we believe that basically every delinquent is an individual who is convinced that society has not given him a fair break, that society is against him, that he hasn't gotten [sic] a chance to succeed, he feels very much degraded."[23]

The boys regard as fair game for "conning," or manipulating, any adult representing the lawful world who takes them at their own word, as Bettelheim seems to. But the boys, as I have tried to show, begin early to learn the "scientific" explanations for their behavior that they acquire from their peers, from the mass media of communication, and from the professional and semi-professional persons with whom they come to have dealings. The song, "Gee! Officer Kruppke," in *West Side Story*, is an excellent example of delinquents' mastery of the psychiatric, psychological, and sociological theories of juvenile delinquency.

Bettelheim had much more to say in justifying the delinquent's use of the rationalization "They're picking on me." He said, concerning a boy with a stick in his hand:

Let there be a plate glass window unexpectedly, it is too bad for the window, but there we already come to very fancy business because if he is a poor kid and he gets picked up, he probably won't be punished, but he might be booked. But if it is a rich man's son, you know, he doesn't get booked, and that isn't only true for plate glass windows. . . . That is true for stealing cars, that is true for major acts of crime, and the delinquents of our big city know there is a great difference when they are picked up on the West Side of Chicago and one of our fancy suburbs.[24]

He further developed the psychoanalytic statement of the delinquents' condemnation of the condemners:

. . . the court process against juvenile delinquency is [not] the best way to rehabilitate them, but it is a miserable way when all delinquents know whether they are subject to the punishment by the court or not depends on the parental pocketbook; or influence, because you see, youngsters have a much finer sense of justice. . . . we definitely have two classes of justice, and if you are a rich man's son and have all the other breaks in your favor, good food, and good housing and, hopefully, a good home, and what have you, and you commit a delinquent act, you get a psychiatrist as a reward, and very often, "Well, we are going to provide psychiatry for the boy," so he gets psychiatry [sic] services as a reward, and the poor boy who has none of these advantages is sent to St. Charles, and the youngsters know that. . . .[25]

No one would want to be so unrealistic as to claim that a completely even-handed justice is dispensed in the legal system of any country. But the refutation of Bettelheim's conception of the police and the courts,

[23] Statement of Bruno Bettelheim, *Hearings, op. cit.*, 86th Congress, 1959, p. 187.
[24] *Ibid.*, p. 187–88.
[25] *Ibid.*, p. 188.

accepting as it does without question the criminal's and the delinquent's claim of absolute and unremitting injustice perpetrated against the poor, down-trodden and exploited masses, would be merely tedious rather than difficult. It is sufficient to note that Bettelheim's statement is one kind of respectable and lawful source from which the delinquent derives the rationalization for his offense, "The cops are picking on me."

It is thus necessary to indicate that some professionally trained people justify the delinquent's use of the motive "It isn't fair and they're only hypocrites anyway." One more example will be sufficient. Gibney's *The Operators* depicts the American nation as being a population most of which falls into one or the other of two classes. One class is composed of individuals who are Operators. They thrive on immoral, unethical, and illegal prac-tices. The second class is composed of individuals who are Corruptibles. They are either already receiving unethical or illegal gains from the Opera-tors or are eager to do so. Gibney contends that Americans today live in a climate of fraud, a "Genial Society" that practices the corruption it hypo-critically condemns and secretly applauds the shunting of the ethical precepts that it professes to believe and practice. Gibney writes that "our national future is being misshaped, far more than we realize, by the witless optimist gulled into phony stock purchases, by the two-bit chiseler padding his out-size expense account, by the corporate dodger who writes off his Florida yacht as a business expense [and by] the influence peddler who tampers with legislation."[26] He discusses "retailers who shortchange their customers, advertising men who misrepresent their products, income-tax cheats, expense-account wizards and stockmarket sharpers." By the time one finishes reading the book, he may be convinced that the "real man" convict is correct in saying that there are only two classes: the smart guys who skim it off the top and the suckers who work. One may also conclude that the delinquent is justified in using the motive, "Everybody's got his own racket, and those squares [lawful people] are only hypocrites, anyway."

Fifth, *the appeal to higher loyalty*. The delinquent may violate the moral demands of the larger society, and neutralize the expected moral con-demnation by appealing to a smaller group in the community. He may claim loyalty to his brothers, or to a friend, or to the corner gang. The occasional necessity of having to choose between the demands of the law, on the one hand, and the claims of fraternity or friendship, on the other, is by no means confined to the delinquent. As Sykes and Matza observe, this theme has long been recognized both in literature and social science as a fairly common problem. Both the criminal and the lawful adolescent and adult know that one must "never squeal on a pal." Nobody, it seems—not even the police who use them—loves an informer; or depending on one's particular view, a squealer, a rat, a stool-pigeon, or a courageous, patriotic citizen.

26 Frank Gibney, *The Operators*, New York: Harper & Bros., 1960, p. 252.

The delinquent confronted with choosing between the law and a friend is in a situation familiar to many. To decide in favor of his friends enables him to violate the conventional code without rejecting it. This acceptance and negation is a property common to the other rationalizations. The delinquent is unusual only in that he is perhaps able to appreciate the fact that his action in behalf of his small group is a justification for the violation of the larger society's norms. This, however, is only a distinction of degree between the delinquent and the lawful person.

The vocabulary of motives discussed above is a presentation in academic language of what delinquent boys say, and of what boys who are becoming delinquent are learning to say. It is a translation of the ungrammatical, vulgar, and often colorful speech that can be heard in their conversation in the streets and alleys, and in formal and informal interviews and discussions. They may say, "I couldn't help it," "I didn't really hurt anybody, " "He had it coming," "Everybody's picking on me," or "I did it for my friend." These expressions are, in social-psychological terminology, definitions of the situation. They are learned from family, friends, social workers, juvenile-court employees, psychiatrists, and others; and from newspapers, the cinema, radio, and television. They are criminal conceptions of thought and action. Their mastery requires time and practice. This is why we have said that it is a positive achievement to become a delinquent. The boy learns reasons for committing delinquencies and also a conception of himself in relation to others that enables him to admit his offenses to himself without damaging his own self-conception.

The above discussion has not evaluated the truth or validity of the delinquent's motives nor has it evaluated the twofold classification of the American population into Operators and Corruptibles. The distinction between criminal and lawful people is not as sharp as the latter seem to want to believe. Even so, it is unlikely that there will ever be an empirical verification of the criminal's "everybody has his own racket," and the honest policeman's "everybody has larceny in his heart." The discussion has indicated that (1) delinquents learn a number of motives for the committing of delinquency and (2) the stock of motives exists as habits of thought held by professional people and the general public, as well as by delinquents.

Habits and patterns of thought and the learning of those patterns by delinquents have been emphasized. Association with given individuals has not been emphasized. As we have shown, lawful people as well as criminals and delinquents can be and sometimes are involved in a young person's learning to be delinquent. Patterns of action have also been emphasized, rather than patterns of personal association. This is an important point in understanding both the types of offenders already considered and those to be discussed subsequently.

There is good evidence that the delinquent's use of the vocabulary of motives is inclusive in the sense that the motives may be innervated in situations not defined as delinquent by the juvenile but in which he may nevertheless believe that others may impute guilt to him. We may quote from Redl and Wineman in this connection, although their thesis cannot be presented in detail here:

We want the basic mechanisms described here to be considered applicable to a much wider range of situations, even to such where the word "delinquent" in its original meaning loses its sense. That means that what we described here under the title of defense techniques of the "delinquent ego" are actually techniques of defense anywhere, *whenever an ego makes up its mind to stick to impulsive demands or to its pathology against changes which the educator or clinician is trying to bring about.*[27]

We have tried to show that the vocabulary of motives consist of rationalizations in the public domain, that delinquents make use of them, and that therefore their motivations are sociocultural rather than individual in origin. . . .

[27] Redl and Wineman, *op. cit.*, p. 195.

5 Delinquent Stereotypes of Probable Victims

HERMAN SCHWENDINGER
AND JULIA SCHWENDINGER

What values are held by delinquents? Are they similar or different from those of other youth? Is there a unique delinquent view of life? To date, these questions have been answered in divergent ways. Albert Cohen has suggested that delinquent values are the inverse of those held by middle class persons.[1] Solomon Kobrin speaks of two antithetical value systems in high delinquency areas; one held by delinquents, the other reflected in the activity of conforming youth.[2] Walter Miller presents a description of lower class youth concerned about being in trouble with the police and maintaining a tough, masculine image of themselves.[3] In Walter Miller's view, these values are continuous with traditional lower class culture. In contrast, Sykes and Matza stress the continuity between delinquent values and an ethos of prior leisure or upper class relationships.[4]

Most of these beliefs about the nature of delinquent values and views

Reprinted from *Juvenile Gangs in Context*, ed. Malcolm W. Klein (Englewood Cliffs, N.J.: Prentice-Hall, Inc., 1967), pp. 92–105, by permission of the authors and the publisher.

[1] Albert K. Cohen, *Delinquent Boys* (New York: Free Press of Glencoe, Inc., 1955).

[2] Solomon Kobrin, "The Conflict of Values in Delinquency Areas," *American Sociological Review*, XVI (October 1951), 653–61.

[3] Walter B. Miller, "Lower Class Culture as a Generating Milieu of Gang Delinquency," *Journal of Social Issues*, XVI (1958), 5–19.

[4] David Matza and Gresham M. Sykes, "Juvenile Delinquency and Subterranean Values," *American Sociological Review*, XXVI 5 (October 1961), 712–19.

of life are predicated on the researcher's personal impressions, on a review of the literature, or on observations made by social workers. Thus, theoretical accounts of delinquent perspectives are generally marked by analysis of data from secondary sources, the presence of highly impressionistic categories, and the absence of controlled measurement. This state of affairs is primarily dictated by enormous difficulties in obtaining responses from delinquents under controlled experimental conditions.

In a previous paper we presented a study of experimentally controlled delinquent and non-delinquent verbal responses to the same set of conditions; namely, instructions to imagine themselves in a debate about victimizing a person.[5] The participants were instructed first to argue about, and then to decide to victimize particular kinds of people. The analysis focused on statements that might be made if an act of victimization were to be discussed and questioned among small groups of closely associated adolescents.

Thirty-nine role plays were conducted among fifty-four delinquent and non-delinquent youths.[6] Each role play enactment contained no less than three subjects. Almost all the fifty-four adolescents acted in three role plays each and performed a total of 162 roles. The delinquents were non-institutionalized youth and among them were boys who were currently active but non-apprehended thieves, drug users, and participants in acts of violence—to mention only a few of the types of illegalities involved.

Although the deviant status of these groups was known as a result of extensive participant observation of delinquent cliques, crowds, and clubs from different communities over several years, a questionnaire was ad-

TABLE 1. AVERAGE OF GROUP MEMBERS RESPONSES
TO FIGHTING AND THIEVING QUESTIONS

Group	Fight-ing Alone	Rank	Fight-ing Gang	Rank	Theft $2.00	Rank	Theft $2.00 to $5.00	Rank	Theft Over $50	Rank	Sum of Ranks
A	2.1	1	1.1	1	2.1	1	1.5	1	1.0	1	5
B	2.4	2	1.4	2	2.3	2	1.9	2	1.2	2	10
C	3.3	4	1.9	3	2.5	3	2.1	3	1.5	3	16
D	3.0	3	2.0	4	3.1	4	3.0	4	1.7	4	19
E	3.8	5	4.2	5	3.3	5	3.1	5	2.8	5	25

Rank Correlation: .97 (Kendall coefficient of concordance)

[5] Herman and Julia Schwendinger, "Delinquent Stereotypes of Probable Victims, Part I," read at Pacific Sociological Association Conference, Sacramento, April 1962.

[6] The delinquents were selected from lowest strata youth in a community. For definition of the term "lowest strata," see Herman Schwendinger. *The Instrumental Theory of Delinquency*, unpublished doctoral dissertation, University of California at Los Angeles, 1963.

ministered which was composed of items developed by Nye and Short.[7]
These items provided the degree to which the respondent admitted engaging
in different types of thieving and fighting, up to the time the questionnaire
was administered. The analysis of responses, as summarized in Table 1,
indicates the increasing involvement in fighting and thievery as one moves
from Group A to Group E.

At the beginning of each role play some of the male subjects were
instructed to argue for and against proposals to commit specified deviant
acts. Those who were assigned roles against the deviant act will be referred
to in this paper as *Objectors*. The role players justifying the act will be
called *Proponents*. The participants were given the following instructions:

> I want you to act out this story; some teenagers are arguing over whether
> they should beat up an Outsider who insulted their club. An Outsider is some-
> one outside their circle of friends. Those who are in favor of beating him up
> argue with the others about it. The others are finally *convinced* that the
> Outsider should be beaten up by the *entire* group.

The same general format was followed in additional enactments involving victimization of a Rich Teenager and a Businessman, with the following
modifications in instructions:

> Some teenagers are arguing over whether to take advantage of a teenager
> in order to get money to go to Disneyland, or Pacific Ocean Park, or get club
> jackets. Those who are in favor . . .
> Some teenagers are arguing over whether to rob a local businessman's
> store. Those who are in favor . . .

The role play dialogues were taped and transcribed and the dialogues
of each group were analyzed.

In the earlier paper, referred to above, we presented findings which
were felt to be contradictory to Sykes and Matza's interpretation of the
function of delinquent rationalizations. It was pointed out that if these
authors were correct, we would find some moral ambivalence, or a sensitivity to a "societal generalized other."[8] It was reasoned that if this sensitivity
among delinquents exists, at least the delinquent Objectors would seize upon
moral issues in challenging the legitimacy of the delinquent act. They would
take the standpoint of the conventional moral perspective and utter such
statements as "its not fair," "put yourself in the other guy's shoes," "he
worked for his money and has a right to keep it," or "where would we all
be if everyone stole from each other?" These utterances mirror the moral

[7] F. Ivan Nye and James F. Short, Jr., "Scaling Delinquent Behavior," *American
Sociological Review*, XXII (June 1957), 326–31.

[8] Gresham M. Sykes and David Matza, "Techniques of Neutralization: A Theory
of Delinquency," *American Sociological Review*, XXII (December 1957), 664–70.

implications of the act which Sykes and Matza believe are situationally neutralized by delinquent rationalizations.

However, the *delinquent* Objectors were almost entirely concerned with tactical rather than moral issues. They countered the Proponent's arguments with such tactical problems as possible defeat at the hands of the Outsider's friends, apprehension by the police, or stakes too small for the risk involved in robbing the businessman. In contrast, it was in the dialogues of the *non*-delinquent Objectors that concern for moral issues was revealed.

Since the non-delinquent dialogues manifested the dynamics that Sykes and Matza believed would take place among delinquents, it was concluded from these findings that these authors, like our non-delinquent actors, might have unwittingly placed themselves in the roles of the delinquents. They may have fashioned their theoretical dynamics of delinquent behavior out of the moral concerns aroused while imagining themselves in these roles.

In the prior paper we also attempted to show that the moral utterances of delinquent and non-delinquent role players could only be explained by assuming the existence of two different working ethics, and two different modes by which moral utterances were structured. A mode of moral utterances consists of basic assumptions about the nature of human relationships which are deeply rooted in our culture and which usually unwittingly influence the form in which good reasons for conduct are shaped. For example, in earlier religious rhetorics deviant persons were often defined as instruments of the devil or persons fallen from the grace of God.

Today, most conforming persons construct their good reasons for moral activity out of what might be called a "rhetoric of egoism." A model of this rhetoric has been described more fully elsewhere.[9] There are other rhetorics organized around kinship, religious, political, or humanistic principles. However, the rhetoric of egoism is the most commonly shared mode of discourse, even though tacit shifts are often made between it and other modes. We will also refer to the rhetoric of egoism as the "conventional mode of moral discourse."

The underlying assumptions contained in the conventional moral rhetoric are that all men possess inherently egoistic interests; human relationships consist of atomistic individuals who are competitively arraigned against each other; and each man confronts the other as an equal and engages in myriad interactions in which goods and services are exchanged. The general form of these exchanges is an acquisitive, laissez-faire society. In this framework, the moral weight of any man's decision is seen to rest on free choice; therefore, he is responsible for his own actions. In this rhetoric, the weight of moral decision is placed on responsibility to fulfill obligations inherent in the definition of the rules governing conduct. Moral conduct is lawfully

[9] Herman Schwendinger, *op. cit.* See Chapter 3, Section V, "Models of Rhetoric and Linguistic Structures of Moral Conversations," pp. 164–93.

regulated conduct, and society would disintegrate without moral contracts. There are other principles which underlie this rhetoric, but these are sufficient to understand the relationship between the rhetoric of egoism and the mode by which the rationalizations of our non-delinquents were constructed.

The rhetoric of egoism can be used to justify legal activity. This is primarily achieved by placing emphasis on the legitimacy of the conventional *rules* of the game. In objecting to the illegal means *and* ends—for no means is completely divorced from ends—the users of this rhetoric invoke the legitimacy of "playing fair," of "going by the rules," "keeping up one's obligations," or "acting right because if we acted wrong then where would we be?"

Another way in which this rhetoric structures the utterances of those who support conventionally governed activity is by maintaining the moral worthiness of possible victims. (The "self" cannot easily justify abrogation of typical rules, especially when "others" have maintained their obligations.)

Finally, this rhetoric can be used to justify conventionally governed activity by reweighing the comparative value of the ends that may serve to legitimate an illegal means. One can then claim that the ends are not worth the price that may have to be paid for the use of an illegal means. In order to do this in the company of like-minded peers, one has to question the value of the ends served by the means. In the role plays, for example, the values of club honor and money must be brought into question.

The user of this rhetoric can also justify a questionable, deviant act in terms of this mode. This is done by construing a deviant act as an act of moral sanction, or as an act not governed by those rules stipulating "typical" responses, or as an act which is justified in terms of the value of the ends involved.

One can see examples of this use of the rhetoric in Cressey's study of men who have committed the act of embezzlement for the *first* time.[10] The paradigm which is used by some of them to structure the relation between themselves and their victims is that of two persons competing for a value. In their justifications, the victim is defined as a deviant in order to maintain a typically moral self-definition. In this sense, the criminal defines his criminal act as an act of a morally indignant man.

In the course of the role plays, the non-delinquent Proponents fashioned the image of the Businessman to be that of a "monopolistic miser" or a "dishonest merchant" who cheats his customers and therefore *deserves* to be victimized. The illegal act was defined as an act of moral indignation. In response to this, the non-delinquent Objectors countered with positive images of the victim; images of worthy, compassionate, and moral human beings.

[10] Donald R. Cressey, *Other People's Money* (New York: Free Press of Glencoe, Inc., 1953).

Through a content analysis of the dialogues we found that it was the *non*-delinquent Objectors who structured their discourse in terms of the rhetoric of egoism. They were more likely to invoke the conventional rules governing conduct, to question the value of the ends to be served by the deviant act, to refer to the image of the victim in positive terms. On the other hand, the delinquent Objectors were more likely to raise the tactical issues, to *affirm* and not question the value of club honor or money even while objecting to the act, and to ascribe negative attributes to the victim.

In the main, the delinquents *were indifferent to* the concerns that seemed to have shaped the non-delinquent dialogues. We tried to show with these findings that a different kind of moral rhetoric structured the delinquent dialogues. We termed this the *instrumental rhetoric*.

In another mode of discourse, the humanistic rhetoric, persons are defined in terms of an ever widening potentiality. In the conventional, egoistic rhetoric, individuals are ideally seen in a contractually governed exchange relation bounded and judged in terms of their obligations. In the instrumental rhetoric, the images of human beings are stripped of all humanistic or conventional sentiment and their definitions are carved solely out of their utility for the private ends of those powerful enough to command their use. In its most systematic form, the instrumental rhetoric depicts a world of Givers and Takers, and the Takers are accorded superior status. The habituated delinquent fashions his interpretation of the moral character of his act out of the assumption that successful persons achieve their positions in life primarily through the manipulation of less powerful human beings. This view of life emerges when habituated delinquents conceptually abstract the internecine character of their interpersonal milieu and generalize it to all social relationships. Older career delinquents often share this view of life.

Of course, not every delinquent subscribes to a systematic and general instrumental view, but such variation is unimportant on the level of analysis dealt with here. Even though there may be many delinquents who do not stereotype a large range of persons, it is suggested that these youth are publicly constrained to frame their reasons for acting in terms of an instrumental ideology. Otherwise these reasons would be evaluated either as false or incomprehensible by delinquent audiences. Further, even though they may not privately subscribe to their public utterances, it is suggested that they *act* on the basis of their public rather than their private vocabularies of motive.

We analyzed the statements of those who were given the role of Objectors to show that they were constrained to express those rationalizations which were believable from the standpoint of the working ethic of these groups. In this sense, for example, even though both delinquent and non-delinquent Objectors might have challenged the legitimacy of the act by referring to the victim as a person who did not deserve to be victimized—that is, by maintaining a positive image of the victim—the delinquents were more likely to say, "I *know* he is a *punk*, but we shouldn't swing him because we'll get caught." There seemed to be a tacit agreement among the delinquents from the very beginning of the plays that the victim was a worthless human being.

This paper presents additional data that reinforce the assumption that delinquents tacitly hold a common attitude toward the victim. These data are based upon the use of semantic differentials to measure the existence of stereotypic definitions of victims.[11]

The theoretical reasoning that gave rise to the construction of the differentials is that delinquents tend to develop stereotypic definitions of social types early in their careers. However, *along with their deviant motives*, these definitions do *not* emerge *prior* to experiencing deviant behavior. Instead, they develop out of this experience.

As they engage in initial forms of deviant activity, youngsters legitimate their behavior by developing consensually validated images of victims. At this stage, some youth focus on the moral issues involved and fashion the images of the victim out of the conventional moral rhetoric. After this stage, however, the stereotypic images become standardized in the form of metaphors which catalogue persons by typical kinds of victim terms; words like Punk, Chump, Box, Pigeon, and Fag emerge and represent the standardization of the typical moral relations with the victim as perceived from the standpoint of the victimizer's ideology. These terms do not emerge in isolation from others, but rather through social processes in which peers are persuaded by prestigeful members to engage in deviant activity.

As such, these terms are created in the first place because they function as linguistic coordinates for collective activity. It is suggested that for most youth these terms function as symbolic coordinates for the individual, as part of his personal belief system, after the terms have been standardized in collective usage.

[11] A stereotypic relation, as defined here, is a special case of an institutionalized role-axis. In this case, the definition of the other is fashioned so as to legitimate specific manipulations, often but not always illegal. Two major types of definitions exist. The first is fashioned out of the attributions of inferior virtues; the second is constructed solely along the dimension of the relative power that distinguishes the victimizer from the victim. This latter type is functionally more rational to the institutional structures that develop among older delinquents. We use the term "role-axis" as it is conceived by Ralph H. Turner, "Role-Taking: Process Versus Conformity" in *Human Relations and Social Processes: An Interactionist Approach*, ed. Arnold M. Rose (Boston: Houghton Mifflin Company, 1962), pp. 20–40. For application of this concept to criminal-victim role-axis, see W. Phillips, "Criminal Self-Conceptions and the Respectable Others," an unpublished manuscript. For the investigation of stereotypic conceptions of outgroup members under conditions of adolescent intergroup rivalry, see Muzafer Sherif and Carolyn W. Sherif, *Groups in Harmony and Tension* (New York: Harper & Row, Publishers, 1953).

Most delinquents stereotype persons in the context of delimited situations. Certain honorific codes specify the conditions under which persons are legitimate objects of victimization. However, particularly under those conditions wherein illegal marketplace activities exist,[12] the career delinquent tends to define everyone as a probable victim; society itself is seen as one vast assemblage of instrumentally defined persons. The instrumental rhetoric obtains its most systematic form under these marketplace conditions, and even in-group members are stereotyped in the proverbs and maxims that abound among these youth. Examples of pithy commentaries on the nature of reality are:

It's fuck your buddy week, fifty-two weeks of the year.
Do unto others as they would do unto you . . . only do it first.
If I don't cop (steal) it . . . somebody else will.
You know man, everybody's got their little game.

To obtain evidence of the existence of stereotyping processes among the delinquents, three semantic differentials were presented to the subjects prior to any hint as to the nature of the role plays. These differentials contained possible meanings of the types of persons who served as the victims. We shall refer to these differentials as the Outsider, Rich Teenager, and Businessman differentials.

The subjects were asked to define an "average" Outsider, Rich Teenager, or Businessman on the differential. Thus, the first differentials defined these persons as general types. A differential was then presented to them after the decision to victimize was reached and the subjects were asked to respond to it from the viewpoint of the actor whose role they played. These differentials corresponded to the specific plays; the Outsider differential was given to the role players after the enactment about the Outsider, the Rich Teenager differential after the enactment about the Rich Teenager, and so on. Finally, after the actors had filled out the differential the second time, they were asked to respond to a third differential of the same type. At this third time, they responded to the differential from their own personal perspective—that is, as they "really" saw the social type. Usually, the subjects would complain that they did this the first time. However, we insisted that they do it again.

In brief, the subjects filled out three differentials. Each social type was defined as an "average" type prior to the instruction for the first play; that is, players were not to think of a particular individual. Then after each play, a differential based on the victim represented in the play was defined from the standpoint of the actor. When this was done, we asked the subjects to define the type of victim from their personal point of view.

[12] Julia and Herman Schwendinger, "The Illegal Marketplace Among Adolescents," read at Pacific Sociological Association Conference, Portland, Oregon, May 1963.

The differentials were constructed in the following way: we obtained adjectives from a selected group of delinquent "jive studs" who described the following types in the delinquent lexicon—the Punk, the Chump, and a powerless Dealer. Once this was done, we attached an antonym secured from our informants to each adjectival term. These polar adjectival dimensions were used as the semantic dimensions of the differentials. The dimensions which the informants used to describe the Punk were used for the Outsider differential, the terms based on the word Chump were used for the Rich Teenager differential, and those related to the Dealer were used for the Businessman differential. The words Punk, Chump, and Dealer did not appear at all on the differentials. Rather, the semantic dimensions which could be used to define these terms appeared under the words: Outsider, Rich Teenager, and Businessman.

For example, the Outsider could be defined as a "worthless," "untrustworthy," "cowardly" person who "should be taken advantage of" and who "deserves no sympathy." These were the most negative meanings possible in defining this type. On the other hand, the Outsider could be defined in opposite terms: as a "valuable," "trustworthy," "courageous" person who "should not be taken advantage of" and who "deserves sympathy."

By standardizing the response scores that most closely approximated the negative meanings at zero, we obtained a differential profile score that represented the same meanings that had been used to define a Punk, or Chump, or Dealer. All other profile scores were also standardized so that they would range between the most negative and positive meanings; any actual score represented a quantitative distance from the standard stereotypic score—i.e., zero.

The first hypothesis tested with the use of this instrument was that before the role play instructions were first given to the actors, delinquent groups would tend to stereotype the Outsider, Rich Teenager, and Businessman (when defined as general social types) more negatively than would the non-delinquents. This hypothesis is confirmed in Table 2.

The range of scores possible for any differential is dependent upon the number of semantic dimensions it contains. The Outsider differential contained five dimensions and the range of scores could vary from zero to 13.42. The Rich Teenager differential contained four dimensions and the range was from zero to 12.0. The Businessman differential contained three dimensions and the range was from zero to 5.19.[13]

The mid-points of the differentials (6.7, 6.0, and 5.1) represent the undecided boundary which separates the positive from the negative profiles.

[13] The dimensions of the Rich Teenager differential were: Hep (wise)-Gullible, Can be Used-Can't be Used, Flunkey-Independent, Sympathetic-Unsympathetic. The dimensions of the Businessman were: Unselfish-Out for Himself, Dishonest-Honest, Sympathetic-Unsympathetic.

TABLE 2. GROUP MEANS OF STANDARD STEREOTYPE FIRST DIFFERENTIAL SCORES

Differential	Group A	Rank	Group B	Rank	Group C	Rank	Group D	Rank	Group E	Rank
Outsider	8.95	1	8.51	2	7.96	3	6.93	4	6.35	5
Rich teen	6.15	2	7.14	1	5.78	3	3.19	5	3.70	4
Businessman	5.52	1	5.05	2	4.81	3	3.35	4	3.30	5
Sum of ranks		4		5		9		13		14

Rank correlation: .91 (Kendall coefficient of concordance).

It can be seen that the delinquent responses, although more negative than the non-delinquent ones, are either clustered around the "undecided" mid-point and therefore represent problematic concepts to the delinquents, or they are on the negative side of the mid-point.

We have indicated that the role plays performed by the delinquents began with a tacit assumption regarding the stereotypic nature of the victim. In light of this, whether or not the social types were problematic—that is, as they appeared prior to the plays where they were defined in terms of "undecided" responses—we would expect the delinquents to sharply define the types negatively as actors when the role plays were terminated.

We also have indicated in our analysis that the non-delinquents, confronted by the problem of legitimating their deviant decision, constructed images that legitimated such a decision out of the rhetoric of egoism.

It is assumed that the symbolic content that has been long standardized in the development of many delinquents is now created by the non-delinquents in their role plays. It was expressed, argued about, and standardized in their dialogues. For a short moment they were like new delinquents who developed categories of the victim in some ideal isolation from older deviant youth.

In line with these interpretations, the second hypothesis is that all groups, delinquent and non-delinquent, will define the victim more stereotypically at the end of the role play, when they respond to the second differential as actors. Table 3 indicates that all groups do shift negatively without exception.[14]

The third hypothesis, which involves the selective reinforcement effects of the role play experiences and the theory underlying it, cannot be discussed within the limits of this paper.

Certain theoretical observations and conclusions can be drawn from this study.

[14] The lower magnitude of the negative shifts among delinquents is an artifact. Since the delinquent differentials were less positive to begin with, the degree to which the shifts were possible is smaller than the non-delinquent shifts.

TABLE 3. DIFFERENCE BETWEEN GROUP MEANS OF
SEMANTIC DIFFERENTIALS ADMINISTERED BEFORE (FIRST
DIFFERENTIAL) AND AT THE END (FROM THE VIEWPOINT
OF THE ACTOR) OF THE ROLE PLAY

Group	Differential	First	Second (Actor)	Difference
A	Outsider	8.948	4.609	−4.339
	Rich teen	6.151	4.588	−1.563
	Businessman	5.519	3.503	−2.016
B	Outsider	8.510	5.340	−3.170
	Rich teen	7.130	4.780	−2.350
	Businessman	5.050	2.510	−2.499
C	Outsider	7.955	4.895	−3.060
	Rich teen	5.782	4.193	−1.589
	Businessman	4.808	4.531	−0.277
D	Outsider	6.930	0.110	−6.820
	Rich teen	3.192	0.560	−2.632
	Businessman	3.345	3.170	−0.175
E	Outsider	6.350	4.930	−1.420
	Rich teen	3.700	2.190	−1.510
	Businessman	3.300	2.848	−0.452

Summary: All groups shifted negatively toward greater stereotypy.

The psychoanalytic tradition has long pointed to the discrepancy between the justifications that persons express for their action and the "real"
underlying motives. However, while the psychoanalysts utilize the frustrated
motive as the independent variable for deviant behavior, Sykes and Matza
point instead to the rationalization. On one level, both these authors and the
psychoanalysts fragment the motive and the rationale as a "mechanism"
or "technique" which expiates individual guilt, or, in Sykes and Matza's
terms, "neutralizes the moral implications of the act." But on another level,
while utilizing similar components in their scheme, one theoretical approach
uses the rationale as the causal locus, while the other uses the frustrated
motive.[15]

[15] The major theories of delinquency today contain references to the *necessary*
function of repression or "neutralization" of guilt in the development of delinquent
careers. However, we feel that such processes, while important in some cases, are
still not necessary for understanding factors effecting other delinquent career-lines.
Some youth are ideologically marginal and subscribe to both conventional and instrumental perspectives simultaneously. Their guilt is never fully "neutralized" throughout
their entire career. Because important interests are at stake, they act in consort with
delinquent others irrespective of the guilt they feel. Other youth (very early in their
play group experiences) come into contact with stereotypic definitions that have been
highly stablized in the community for many years. They quickly learn these definitions

In order to ascribe a causal role to the rationalization, Sykes and Matza indicate that other symbolic relationships—such as values, moral imperatives, or attitudes of delinquents—are similar to those of "dominant society." In their words:

It is by learning these techniques [of neutralization] that the juvenile becomes delinquent *rather* than by learning moral imperatives, values or attitudes standing in direct contradiction to those of the dominant society.[16]

We have tried to show that if dominant society is mirrored in the moral standpoint of our non-delinquents, then differences in values, moral imperatives, definitions of persons, and mode by which rationalizations are structured exist between our non-delinquent and delinquent subjects. This has been shown in the analysis of the collective rhetorics of these youths.

A relationship between the institutional arrangements within which delinquent biographies are enacted and the institutions of society at large can be shown once one has stipulated the institutional sources of humanistic, religious, egoistic, and instrumental rhetorics. To do this, one must analyze the very different kinds of moral relationships that exist within our society. These moral relationships do not have their locus within small groups of frustrated individuals or imitative patterns of past leisure class relationships. They emerge in concrete religious, economic, political, and other institutions, and they cut across class lines.

In light of Davis and Moore's suggestion that social class relations of any society be analyzed in terms of dominant institutional frameworks,[17] one might say that the structuring of social class relations primarily around values of competition and invidious ownership of commodities, combined with the use of these values as guides to the estimation of human worth, represents the pervasive influence of economic institutions on the formation of status groups in our society. Among Elmtown adults, for example, Hollingshead has pointed out that occupational achievement, stocks, bonds, property, and money are the prevailing criteria by which honor is estimated.[18]

---

from older youth. In fact, delinquent relationships around them may be so stabilized and pervasive, that the age-graded transition in perspectives occurs with very little concern as to contradictory moralities. Finally, there exist youth who have never subscribed to a conventional moral perspective to begin with. Instead, they have learned to define conventional moral relations in stereotypic terms (and all "respectable" persons as hypocrites) from earliest family experience. These youth do not repress guilt that is allegedly aroused by the thoughts of their immoral conduct. They have never felt guilty in the first place.

[16] Sykes and Matza, *op. cit.*, p. 666; our emphasis.

[17] Kingsley Davis and Wilbert E. Moore, "Some Principles of Stratification," *American Sociological Review*, X (April 1945), 242–49.

[18] August B. Hollingshead, *Elmtown's Youth* (New York: John Wiley & Sons, Inc., Science Editions, 1961), pp. 449–50.

Youth, however, are not directly involved in economic institutions. The institutional effects of the market which they experience are mediated through the occupational ideologies subscribed to by their parents, or by mass communications media. They perceive and interpret life from the standpoint of their own childish consciousness, and instead of conventional property, it is styles of dress, transistor radios, customized cars, and owning relationships with the opposite sex that are among the many commodities serving as guides to human worth.

From seven to fourteen years of age, status groups begin to emerge among youth who give preeminent subscription to values of this sort. By junior high, the system composed of these status arrangements begins to differentiate into various strata. It becomes most differentiated within communities with families of heterogeneous social class composition. In these communities, two major adolescent strata, and often an intermediary one, emerge.

The proportional sizes of these strata vary considerably from community to community. In some communities this system is populated by almost three quarters of the youth inhabiting the area; in other communities only one third may be so involved. While there is an overlap between this system of strata and those youths outside of it, the majority of conforming youth are not within the system.

Besides the overlapping between those inside the system and those outside of it, there are youth who take on different strata roles at different times and shift between the strata. In order to analytically grasp the constancies of this highly fluctuating and ephemeral system, one has to perceive it independently of these fluctuations—as a set of institutional arrangements independent of the fluctuations of the individuals who move about within it and separate from the private attitudes of those who assume its roles.

For example, Short, Strodtbeck, and Cartwright[19] have pointed to the discrepancy that exists in regard to public and private attitudes expressed by delinquent boys. They found that the attitudes expressed in private to adult interviewers (regarding marriage and relations with girls) were much different from the attitudes expressed in public among peers. The privately expressed views were highly conventional, while the publicly expressed attitudes supported deviant sexual relationships. It was the *public rhetoric* that closely approximated the kinds of attitudes facilitating their delinquent activity.

We had become aware of this profound schism between public and private attitudes of delinquents early in our investigation of delinquent behavior. It not only exists in regard to their attitudes toward sexual rela-

19 James F. Short, Jr., Fred L. Strodtbeck, Desmond S. Cartwright, "A Strategy for Utilizing Research Dilemmas: A Case Study from the Study of Parenthood in a Street Corner Gang," *Sociological Inquiry*, XXXII 2 (Spring 1962), 189.

tionships, but is also characteristic of their attitudes toward a large number of persons and relationships. The schism arises, in part, out of the conflict between their public views and more conventional perspectives. Since their relationships are never wholly independent of conventional ones, we can expect to find that, among some youth, extreme shifts between conventional and deviant modes of discourse are, under certain conditions, characteristic not only of their public but also of their private rhetorics.

It is believed that one cannot begin to understand the complexities involved until delinquent behavior is lifted out of reductionist frameworks and first understood as institutionalized forms of behavior. In doing this, the personalistic categories that involve only the relationships between the individual and his motives, rationales, and acts should be replaced with such sociological categories as ideology, vocabularies of motive, and institutional arrangements.

In the context of prevailing modes by which deviant behavior is interpreted, delinquent biographies are made comprehensible primarily by constructing theoretical models of atomistic, troubled youth and setting these models into motion with categories of frustrated motives or learned mechanisms, by which guilt is expiated. However, once the broader institutional class patterns are made clear, it can be seen that deviant motives and rationales for action only emerge when youth have already experienced deviant relationships and have conceptually grasped them through acts of conversation among peers.

6 Becoming a Marihuana User*

HOWARD S. BECKER

The use of marihuana is and has been the focus of a good deal of attention on the part of both scientists and laymen. One of the major problems students of the practice have addressed themselves to has been the identification of those individual psychological traits which differentiate marihuana users from nonusers and which are assumed to account for the use of the drug. That approach, common in the study of behavior categorized as deviant, is based on the premise that the presence of a given kind of behavior in an individual can best be explained as the result of some trait which predisposes or motivates him to engage in the behavior.[1]

Reprinted from *American Journal of Sociology, 59* (November, 1953), 235–242, by permission of The University of Chicago Press. Copyright 1953 by The University of Chicago. Also by permission of the author.

* Paper read at the meetings of the Midwest Sociological Society in Omaha, Nebraska, April 25, 1953. The research on which this paper is based was done while I was a member of the staff of the Chicago Narcotics Survey, a study done by the Chicago Area Project, Inc., under a grant from the National Mental Health Institute. My thanks to Solomon Kobrin, Harold Finestone, Henry McKay, and Anselm Strauss, who read and discussed with me earlier versions of this paper.

[1]See, as examples of this approach, the following: Eli Marcovitz and Henry J. Meyers, "The Marihuana Addict in the Army," *War Medicine,* VI (December, 1944), 382–91; Herbert S. Gaskill, "Marihuana, an Intoxicant," *American Journal of Psychiatry,* CII (September, 1945), 202–4; Sol Charen and Luis Perelman, "Personality Studies of Marihuana Addicts," *American Journal of Psychiatry,* CII (March, 1946), 674–82.

This study is likewise concerned with accounting for the presence or absence of marihuana use in an individual's behavior. It starts, however, from a different premise: that the presence of a given kind of behavior is the result of a sequence of social experiences during which the person acquires a conception of the meaning of the behavior, and perceptions and judgments of objects and situations, all of which make the activity possible and desirable. Thus, the motivation or disposition to engage in the activity is built up in the course of learning to engage in it and does not antedate this learning process. For such a view it is not necessary to identify those "traits" which "cause" the behavior. Instead, the problem becomes one of describing the set of changes in the person's conception of the activity and of the experience it provides for him.[2]

This paper seeks to describe the sequence of changes in attitude and experience which lead to *the use of marihuana for pleasure.* Marihuana does not produce addiction, as do alcohol and the opiate drugs; there is no withdrawal sickness and no ineradicable craving for the drug.[3] The most frequent pattern of use might be termed "recreational." The drug is used occasionally for the pleasure the user finds in it, a relatively casual kind of behavior in comparison with that connected with the use of addicting drugs. The term "use for pleasure" is meant to emphasize the noncompulsive and casual character of the behavior. It is also meant to eliminate from consideration here those few cases in which marihuana is used for its prestige value only, as a symbol that one is a certain kind of person, with no pleasure at all being derived from its use.

The analysis presented here is conceived of as demonstrating the greater explanatory usefulness of the kind of theory outlined above as opposed to the predispositional theories now current. This may be seen in two ways: (1) predispositional theories cannot account for that group of users (whose existence is admitted)[4] who do not exhibit the trait or traits considered to cause the behavior and (2) such theories cannot account for the great variability over time of a given individual's behavior with reference to the drug. The same person will at one stage be unable to use the drug for pleasure, at a later stage be able and willing to do so, and, still later, again be unable to use it in this way. These changes, difficult to explain from a predispositional or motivational theory, are readily understandable in terms of changes in the individual's conception of the drug as is the existence of "normal" users.

[2] This approach stems from George Herbert Mead's discussion of objects in *Mind, Self, and Society* (Chicago: University of Chicago Press, 1934), pp. 277–80.

[3] Cf. Roger Adams, "Marihuana," *Bulletin of the New York Academy of Medicine,* XVIII (November, 1942), 705–30.

[4] Cf. Lawrence Kolb, "Marihuana," *Federal Probation,* II (July, 1938), 22–25; and Walter Bromberg, "Marihuana: A Psychiatric Study," *Journal of the American Medical Association,* CXIII (July 1, 1939), 11.

The study attempted to arrive at a general statement of the sequence of changes in individual attitude and experience which have always occurred when the individual has become willing and able to use marihuana for pleasure and which have not occurred or not been permanently maintained when this is not the case. This generalization is stated in universal terms in order that negative cases may be discovered and used to revise the explanatory hypothesis.[5]

Fifty interviews with marihuana users from a variety of social backgrounds and present positions in society constitute the data from which the generalization was constructed and against which it was tested.[6] The interviews focused on the history of the person's experience with the drug, seeking major changes in his attitude toward it and in his actual use of it and the reasons for these changes. The final generalization is a statement of that sequence of changes in attitude which occurred in every case known to me in which the person came to use marihuana for pleasure. Until a negative case is found, it may be considered as an explanation of all cases of marihuana use for pleasure. In addition, changes from use to nonuse are shown to be related to similar changes in conception, and in each case it is possible to explain variations in the individual's behavior in these terms.

This paper covers only a portion of the natural history of an individual's use of marihuana,[7] starting with the person having arrived at the point of willingness to try marihuana. He knows that others use it to "get high," but he does not know what this means in concrete terms. He is curious about the experience, ignorant of what it may turn out to be, and afraid that it may be more than he has bargained for. The steps outlined below, if he undergoes them all and maintains the attitudes developed in them, leave him willing and able to use the drug for pleasure when the opportunity presents itself.

I

The novice does not ordinarily get high the first time he smokes marihuana, and several attempts are usually necessary to induce this state. One explanation of this may be that the drug is not smoked "properly," that is, in a way that insures sufficient dosage to produce real symptoms of intoxica-

[5] The method used is that described by Alfred R. Lindesmith in his *Opiate Addiction* (Bloomington: Principia Press, 1947), chap. i. I would like also to acknowledge the important role Lindesmith's work played in shaping my thinking about the genesis of marihuana use.

[6] Most of the interviews were done by the author. I am grateful to Solomon Kobrin and Harold Finestone for allowing me to make use of interviews done by them.

[7] I hope to discuss elsewhere other stages in this natural history.

tion. Most users agree that it cannot be smoked like tobacco if one is to get high:

Take in a lot of air, you know, and . . . I don't know how to describe it, you don't smoke it like a cigarette, you draw in a lot of air and get it deep down in your system and then keep it there. Keep it there as long as you can.

Without the use of some such technique[8] the drug will produce no effects, and the user will be unable to get high:

The trouble with people like that [who are not able to get high] is that they're just not smoking it right, that's all there is to it. Either they're not holding it down long enough, or they're getting too much air and not enough smoke, or the other way around or something like that. A lot of people just don't smoke it right, so naturally nothing's gonna happen.

If nothing happens, it is manifestly impossible for the user to develop a conception of the drug as an object which can be used for pleasure, and use will therefore not continue. The first step in the sequence of events that must occur if the person is to become a user is that he must learn to use the proper smoking technique in order that his use of the drug will produce some effects in terms of which his conception of it can change.

Such a change is, as might be expected, a result of the individual's participation in groups in which marihuana is used. In them the individual learns the proper way to smoke the drug. This may occur through direct teaching:

I was smoking like I did an ordinary cigarette. He said, "No, don't do it like that." He said, "Suck it, you know, draw in and hold it in your lungs till you . . . for a period of time."
I said, "Is there any limit of time to hold it?"
He said, "No, just till you feel that you want to let it out, let it out." So I did that three or four times.

Many new users are ashamed to admit ignorance and, pretending to know already, must learn through the more indirect means of observation and imitation:

I came on like I had turned on [smoked marihuana] many times before, you know. I didn't want to seem like a punk to this cat. See, like I didn't know the first thing about it—how to smoke it, or what was going to happen, or what. I just watched him like a hawk—I didn't take my eyes off him for a second, because I wanted to do everything just as he did it. I watched how he held it, how he smoked it, and everything. Then when he gave it to me I just came

[8] A pharmacologist notes that this ritual is in fact an extremely efficient way of getting the drug into the blood stream (R. P. Walton, *Marihuana: America's New Drug Problem* [Philadelphia: J. B. Lippincott, 1938], p. 48).

on cool, as though I knew exactly what the score was. I held it like he did and took a poke just the way he did.

No person continued marihuana use for pleasure without learning a technique that supplied sufficient dosage for the effects of the drug to appear. Only when this was learned was it possible for a conception of the drug as an object which could be used for pleasure to emerge. Without such a conception marihuana use was considered meaningless and did not continue.

II

Even after he learns the proper smoking technique, the new user may not get high and thus not form a conception of the drug as something which can be used for pleasure. A remark made by a user suggested the reason for this difficulty in getting high and pointed to the next necessary step on the road to being a user:

I was told during an interview, "As a matter of fact, I've seen a guy who was high out of his mind and didn't know it."

I expressed disbelief: "How can that be, man?"

The interviewee said, "Well, it's pretty strange, I'll grant you that, but I've seen it. This guy got on with me, claiming that he'd never got high, one of those guys, and he got completely stoned. And he kept insisting that he wasn't high. So I had to prove to him that he was."

What does this mean? It suggests that being high consists of two elements: the presence of symptoms caused by marihuana use and the recognition of these symptoms and their connection by the user with his use of the drug. It is not enough, that is, that the effects be present; they alone do not automatically provide the experience of being high. The user must be able to point them out to himself and consciously connect them with his having smoked marihuana before he can have this experience. Otherwise, regardless of the actual effects produced, he considers that the drug has had no effect on him: "I figured it either had no effect on me or other people were exaggerating its effect on them, you know. I thought it was probably psychological, see." Such persons believe that the whole thing is an illusion and that the wish to be high leads the user to deceive himself into believing that something is happening when, in fact, nothing is. They do not continue marihuana use, feeling that "it does nothing" for them.

Typically, however, the novice has faith (developed from his observation of users who do get high) that the drug actually will produce some new experience and continues to experiment with it until it does. His failure to get high worries him, and he is likely to ask more experienced users or provoke comments from them about it. In such conversations he is made aware of specific details of his experience which he may not have noticed or may have noticed but failed to identify as symptoms of being high:

I didn't get high the first time. . . . I don't think I held it in long enough. I probably let it out, you know, you're a little afraid. The second time I wasn't sure, and he [smoking companion] told me, like I asked him for some of the symptoms or something, how would I know, you know. . . . So he told me to sit on a stool. I sat on—I think I sat on a bar stool—and he said, "Let your feet hang," and then when I got down my feet were real cold, you know.

And I started feeling it, you know. That was the first time. And then about a week after that, sometime pretty close to it, I really got on. That was the first time I got on a big laughing kick, you know. Then I really knew I was on.

One symptom of being high is an intense hunger. In the next case the novice becomes aware of this and gets high for the first time:

They were just laughing the hell out of me because like I was eating so much. I just scoffed [ate] so much food, and they were just laughing at me, you know. Sometimes I'd be looking at them, you know, wondering why they're laughing, you know, not knowing what I was doing. [Well, did they tell you why they were laughing eventually?] Yeah, yeah, I come back, "Hey, man, what's happening?" Like, you know, like I'd ask, "What's happening?" and all of a sudden I feel weird, you know. "Man, you're on you know. You're on pot [high on marihuana]." I said, "No, am I?" Like I don't know what's happening.

The learning may occur in more indirect ways:

I heard little remarks that were made by other people. Somebody said, "My legs are rubbery," and I can't remember all the remarks that were made because I was very attentively listening for all these cues for what I was supposed to feel like.

The novice, then, eager to have this feeling, picks up from other users some concrete referents of the term "high" and applies these notions to his own experience. The new concepts make it possible for him to locate these symptoms among his own sensations and to point out to himself a "something different" in his experience that he connects with drug use. It is only when he can do this that he is high. In the next case, the contrast between two successive experiences of a user makes clear the crucial importance of the awareness of the symptoms in being high and re-emphasizes the important role of interaction with other users in acquiring the concepts that make this awareness possible:

[Did you get high the first time you turned on?] Yeah, sure. Although, come to think of it, I guess I really didn't. I mean, like that first time it was more or less of a mild drunk. I was happy, I guess, you know what I mean. But I didn't really know I was high, you know what I mean. It was only after the second time I got high that I realized I was high the first time. Then I knew that something different was happening.

[How did you know that?] How did I know? If what happened to me that night would of happened to you, you would've known, believe me. We played the first tune for almost two hours—one tune! Imagine, man! We got on the stand and played this one tune, we started at nine o'clock. When we got finished I looked at my watch, it's quarter to eleven. Almost two hours on one tune. And it didn't seem like anything.

I mean, you know, it does that to you. It's like you have much more time or something. Anyway, when I saw that, man, it was too much. I knew I must really be high or something if anything like that could happen. See, and then they explained to me that that's what it did to you, you had a different sense of time and everything. So I realized that that's what it was. I knew then. Like the first time, I probably felt that way, you know, but I didn't know what's happening.

It is only when the novice becomes able to get high in this sense that he will continue to use marihuana for pleasure. In every case in which use continued, the user had acquired the necessary concepts with which to express to himself the fact that he was experiencing new sensations caused by the drug. That is, for use to continue, it is necessary not only to use the drug so as to produce effects but also to learn to perceive these effects when they occur. In this way marihuana acquires meaning for the user as an object which can be used for pleasure.

With increasing experience the user develops a greater appreciation of the drug's effects; he continues to learn to get high. He examines succeeding experiences closely, looking for new effects, making sure the old ones are still there. Out of this there grows a stable set of categories for experiencing the drug's effects whose presence enables the user to get high with ease.

The ability to perceive the drug's effects must be maintained if use is to continue; if it is lost, marihuana use ceases. Two kinds of evidence support his statement. First, people who become heavy users of alcohol, barbiturates, or opiates do not continue to smoke marihuana, largely because they lose the ability to distinguish between its effects and those of the other drugs.[9] They no longer know whether the marihuana gets them high. Second, in those few cases in which an individual uses marihuana in such quantities that he is always high, he is apt to get this same feeling that the drug has no effect on him, since the essential element of a noticeable difference between feeling high and feeling normal is missing. In such a situation, use is likely to be given up completely, but temporarily, in order that the user may once again be able to perceive the difference.

9 "Smokers have repeatedly stated that the consumption of whiskey while smoking negates protency of the drug. They find it very difficult to get 'high' while drinking whiskey and because of that smokers will not drink while using the "weed" (cf. New York City's Mayor's Committee on Marihuana, The Marihuana Problem in the City of New York [Lancaster, Pa.: Jacques Cattell Press, 1944], p. 13).

III

One more step is necessary if the user who has now learned to get high is to continue use. He must learn to enjoy the effects he has just learned to experience. Marihuana-produced sensations are not automatically or necessarily pleasurable. The taste for such experience is a socially acquired one, not different in kind from acquired tastes for oysters or dry martinis. The user feels dizzy, thirsty; his scalp tingles; he misjudges time and distances; and so on. Are these things pleasurable? He isn't sure. If he is to continue marihuana use, he must decide that they are. Otherwise, getting high, while a real enough experience, will be an unpleasant one he would rather avoid.

The effects of the drug, when first perceived, may be physically unpleasant or at least ambiguous:

It started taking effect, and I didn't know what was happening, you know, what it was, and I was very sick. I walked around the room, walking around the room trying to get off, you know; it just scared me at first, you know. I wasn't used to that kind of feeling.

In addition, the novice's naïve interpretation of what is happening to him may further confuse and frighten him, particularly if he decides, as many do, that he is going insane:

I felt I was insane, you know. Everything people done to me just wigged me. I couldn't hold a conversation, and my mind would be wandering, and I was always thinking, oh, I don't know, weird things, like hearing music different. . . . I get the feeling that I can't talk to anyone. I'll goof completely.

Given these typically frightening and unpleasant first experiences, the beginner will not continue use unless he learns to redefine the sensations as pleasurable:

It was offered to me, and I tried it. I'll tell you one thing. I never did enjoy it at all. I mean it was just nothing that I could enjoy. [Well, did you get high when you turned on?] Oh, yeah, I got definite feelings from it. But I didn't enjoy them. I mean I got plenty of reactions, but they were mostly reactions of fear. [You were frightened?] Yes. I didn't enjoy it. I couldn't seem to relax with it, you know. If you can't relax with a thing, you can't enjoy it, I don't think.

In other cases the first experiences were also definitely unpleasant, but the person did become a marihuana user. This occurred, however, only after a later experience enabled him to redefine the sensations as pleasurable:

[This man's first experience was extremely unpleasant, involving distortion of spatial relationships and sounds, violent thirst, and panic produced by these systems.] After the first time I didn't turn on for about, I'd say, ten months to a year. . . . It wasn't a moral thing; it was because I'd gotten so frightened, bein' so high. An' I didn't want to go through that again, I mean, my reaction was, "Well, if this is what they call bein' high, I don't dig [like] it." . . . So I didn't turn on for a year almost, accounta that. . . .

Well, my friends started, an' consequently I started again. But I didn't have any more, I didn't have that same initial reaction, after I started turning on again.

[In interaction with his friends he became able to find pleasure in the effects of the drug and eventually became a regular user.]

In no case will use continue without such a redefinition of the effects as enjoyable.

This redefinition occurs, typically, in interaction with more experienced users who, in a number of ways, teach the novice to find pleasure in this experience which is at first so frightening.[10] They may reassure him as to the temporary character of the unpleasant sensations and minimize their seriousness, at the same time calling attention to the more enjoyable aspects. An experienced user describes how he handles newcomers to marihuana use:

Well, they get pretty high sometimes. The average person isn't ready for that, and it is a little frightening to them sometimes. I mean, they've been high on lush [alcohol], and they get higher that way than they've ever been before, and they don't know what's happening to them. Because they think they're going to keep going up, up, up till they lose their minds or begin doing weird things or something. You have to like reassure them, explain to them that they're not really flipping or anything, that they're gonna be all right. You have to just talk them out of being afraid. Keep talking to them, reassuring, telling them it's all right. And come on with your own story, you know: "The same thing happened to me. You'll get to like that after awhile." Keep coming on like that; pretty soon you talk them out of being scared. And besides they see you doing it and nothing horrible is happening to you, so that gives them more confidence.

The more experienced user may also teach the novice to regulate the amount he smokes more carefully, so as to avoid any severely uncomfortable symptoms while retaining the pleasant ones. Finally, he teaches the new user that he can "get to like it after awhile." He teaches him to regard those ambiguous experiences formerly defined an unpleasant as enjoyable. The older user in the following incident is a person whose tastes have shifted in this way, and his remarks have the effect of helping others to make a similar redefinition:

A new user had her first experience of the effects of marihuana and became frightened and hysterical. She "felt like she was half in and half out of the room" and experienced a number of alarming physical symptoms. One of the more experienced users present said, "She's dragged because she's high like that. I'd give anything to get that high myself. I haven't been that high in years."

[10] Charen and Perelman, *op. cit.*, p. 679.

In short, what was once frightening and distasteful becomes, after a taste for it is built up, pleasant, desired, and sought after. Enjoyment is introduced by the favorable definition of the experience that one acquires from others. Without this, use will not continue, for marihuana will not be for the user an object he can use for pleasure.

In addition to being a necessary step in becoming a user, this represents an important condition for continued use. It is quite common for experienced users suddenly to have an unpleasant or frightening experience, which they cannot define as pleasurable, either because they have used a larger amount of marihuana than usual or because it turns out to be a higher-quality marihuana than they expected. The user has sensations which go beyond any conception he has of what being high is and is in much the same situation as the novice, uncomfortable and frightened. He may blame it on an overdose and simply be more careful in the future. But he may make this the occasion for a rethinking of his attitude toward the drug and decide that it no longer can give him pleasure. When this occurs and is not followed by a redefinition of the drug as capable of producing pleasure, use will cease.

The likelihood of such a redefinition occurring depends on the degree of the individual's participation with other users. Where this participation is intensive, the individual is quickly talked out of his feeling against marihuana use. In the next case, on the other hand, the experience was very disturbing, and the aftermath of the incident cut the person's participation with other users to almost zero. Use stopped for three years and began again only when a combination of circumstances, important among which was a resumption of ties with users, made possible a redefinition of the nature of the drug:

It was too much, like I only made about four pokes, and I couldn't even get it out of my mouth, I was so high, and I got real flipped. In the basement, you know, I just couldn't stay in there anymore. My heart was pounding real hard, you know, and I was going out of my mind; I thought I was losing my mind completely. So I cut out of this basement, and this other guy, he's out of his mind, told me, "Don't, don't leave me, man. Stay here." And I couldn't.

I walked outside, and it was five below zero, and I thought I was dying, and I had my coat open; I was sweating, I was perspiring. My whole insides were all . . ., and I walked about two blocks away, and I fainted behind a bush. I don't know how long I laid there. I woke up, and I was feeling the worst, I can't describe it at all, so I made it to a bowling alley, man, and I was trying to act normal, I was trying to shoot pool, you know, trying to act real normal, and I couldn't lay and I couldn't stand up and I couldn't sit down, and I went up and laid down where some guys that spot pins lay down, and that didn't help me, and I went down to a doctor's office. I was going to go in there and tell the doctor to put me out of my misery . . . because my heart was pounding so hard, you know. . . . So then all week end I started flipping, seeing things there and going through hell, you know, all kinds of abnormal things. . . . I just quit for a long time then.

[He went to a doctor who defined the symptoms for him as those of a nervous breakdown caused by "nerves" and "worries." Although he was no longer using marihuana, he had some recurrences of the symptoms which led him to suspect that "it was all his nerves."] So I just stopped worrying, you know; so it was about thirty-six months later I started making it again. I'd just take a few pokes, you know. [He first resumed use in the company of the same user-friend with whom he had been involved in the original incident.]

A person, then, cannot begin to use marihuana for pleasure, or continue its use for pleasure, unless he learns to define its effects as enjoyable, unless it becomes and remains an object which he concieves of as capable of producing pleasure.

IV

In summary, an individual will be able to use marihuana for pleasure only when he goes through a process of learning to conceive of it as an object which can be used in this way. No one becomes a user without (1) learning to smoke the drug in a way which will produce real effects; (2) learning to recognize the effects and connect them with drug use (learning, in other words, to get high); and (3) learning to enjoy the sensations he perceives. In the course of this process he develops a disposition or motivation to use marihuana which was not and could not have been present when he began use, for it involves and depends on conceptions of the drug which could only grow out of the kind of actual experience detailed above. On completion of this process he is willing and able to use marihuana for pleasure.

He has learned, in short, to answer "Yes" to the question: "Is it fun?" The direction his further use of the drug takes depends on his being able to continue to answer "Yes" to this question and, in addition, on his being able to answer "Yes" to other questions which arise as he becomes aware of the implications of the fact that the society as a whole disapproves of the practice: "Is it expedient?" "Is it moral?"[11] Once he has acquired the ability to get enjoyment out of the drug, use will continue to be possible for him. Considerations of morality and expediency, occasioned by the reactions of society, may interfere and inhibit use, but use continues to be a possibility in terms of his conception of the drug. The act becomes impossible only when the ability to enjoy the experience of being high is lost, through a change in the user's conception of the drug occasioned by certain kinds of experience with it.

[11] Another paper will discuss the series of developments in attitude that occurs as the individual begins to take account of these matters and adjust his use to them.

In comparing this theory with those which ascribe marihuana use to motives or predispositions rooted deep in individual behavior, the evidence makes it clear that marihuana use for pleasure can occur only when the process described above is undergone and cannot occur without it. This is apparently so without reference to the nature of the individual's personal makeup or psychic problems. Such theories assume that people have stable modes of response which predetermine the way they will act in relation to any particular situation or object and that, when they come in contact with the given object or situation, they act in the way in which their makeup predisposes them.

This analysis of the genesis of marihuana use shows that the individuals who come in contact with a given object may respond to it at first in a great variety of ways. If a stable form of new behavior toward the object is to emerge, a transformation of meanings must occur, in which the person develops a new conception of the nature of the object.[12] This happens in a series of communicative acts in which others point out new aspects of his experience to him, present him with new interpretations of events, and help him achieve a new conceptual organization of his world, without which the new behavior is not possible. Persons who do not achieve the proper kind of conceptualization are unable to engage in the given behavior and turn off in the direction of some other relationship to the object or activity.

This suggests that behavior of any kind might fruitfully be studied developmentally, in terms of changes in meanings and concepts, their organization and reorganization, and the way they channel behavior, making some acts possible while excluding others.

[12] Cf. Anselm Strauss, "The Development and Transformation of Monetary Meanings in the Child," *American Sociological Review,* XVII (June, 1952), 275–86.

7 Apprenticeships in Prostitution*

JAMES H. BRYAN

    While theoretical conceptions of deviant behavior range from role strain to psychoanalytic theory, orientations to the study of the prostitute have shown considerable homogeneity. Twentieth century theorizing concerning this occupational group has employed, almost exclusively a Freudian psychiatric model. The prostitute has thus been variously described as masochistic, of infantile mentality, unable to form mature interpersonal relationships, regressed, emotionally dangerous to males and as normal as the average woman.[1] The call girl, the specific focus of this paper, has been

Reprinted from *Social Problems*, Volume 12, Number 3 (Winter, 1965), 287–297, by permission of The Society for the Study of Social Problems and the author.

* This data was collected when the author was at the Neuropsychiatric Institute, UCLA Center for the Health Sciences. I wish to acknowledge the considerable aid of Mrs. Elizabeth Gordon, Miss Carol Kupers, and Mr. Saul Sherter in the preparation and the analysis of his data. I am greatly indebted to Dr. Evelyn Hooker for both her intellectual and moral support, and to Vivian London for her excellent editorial advice. I particularly wish to express my great gratitude to my wife, Virginia, for her tolerance, encouragement, and understanding.

[1] H. Benjamin "Prostitution Reassessed," *International Journal of Sexology,* 26 (1951), pp. 154–160; H. Benjamin & A. Ellis, "An Objective Examination of Prostitution," *International Journal of Sexology,* 29 (1955), pp. 100–105; E. Glover, "The Abnormality of Prostitution," In A. M. Krich, editor, *Women,* New York: Dell Publishing Company, Inc., 1953; M. H. Hollander, "Prostitution, The Body, and Human Relatedness," *International Journal of Psychoanalysis,* XLII (1961), pp. 404–413; M. Karpf, "Effects of Prostitution on Marital Sex Adjustment," *International Journal of Sexology,* 29 (1953),

accused of being anxious, possessing a confused self-image, excessively dependent, demonstrating gender-role confusion, aggressive, lacking internal controls and masochistic.[2]

The exclusive use of psychoanalytic models in attempting to predict behavior, and the consequent neglect of situational and cognitive processes, has been steadily lessening in the field of psychology. Their inadequacy as models for understanding deviancy has been specifically explicated by Becker, and implied by London.[3] The new look in the conceptualization and study of deviant behavior has focused on the interpersonal processes which help define the deviant role, the surroundings in which the role is learned, and limits upon the enactment of the role. As Hooker has indicated regarding the study of homosexuals, one must not only consider the personality structure of the participants, but also the structure of their community and the pathways and routes into the learning and enactment of the behavior.[4] Such "training periods" have been alluded to by Maurer in his study of the con man, and by Sutherland in his report on professional thieves. More recently, Lindesmith and Becker have conceptualized the development of drug use as a series of learning sequences necessary for the development of steady use.[5]

This paper provides some detailed, albeit preliminary, information concerning induction and training in a particular type of deviant career: prostitution, at the call girl level. It describes the order of events, and their surrounding structure, which future call girls experience in entering their occupation.

The respondents in this study were 33 prostitutes, all currently or previously working in the Los Angeles area. They ranged in age from 18 to 32, most being in their mid-twenties. None of the interviewees were

pp. 149–154; J. F. Oliven, *Sexual Hygiene and Pathology,* Philadelphia: J. B. Lippincott Co., 1955; W. J. Robinson, *The Oldest Profession in The World,* New York: Eugenics Publishing Co., 1929.

[2] H. Greenwald, *The Call Girl,* New York: Ballantine Books, 1960.

[3] H. S. Becker, *Outsiders: Studies in the Sociology of Deviance,* New York: Free Press of Glencoe, 1963. Also see *The Other Side,* H. S. Becker, editor, New York: Free Press of Glencoe, 1964. P. London, *The Modes and Morals of Psychotherapy,* New York: Holt, Rinehart and Winston, Inc. 1964. For recent trends in personality theory, see N. Sanford, "Personality: Its Place in Psychology" and D. R. Miller, "The Study of Social Relationships: Situation, Identity, and Social Interaction." Both papers are presented in S. Koch, editor *Psychology: A Study of a Science,* Vol. 5, New York: McGraw-Hill Book Co., Inc. 1963.

[4] Evelyn Hooker, "The Homosexual Community." *Proceedings of the XIV International Congress of Applied Psychology,* 1961, pp. 40–59. See also A. Reiss, "The Social Integration of Queers and Peers." *Social Problems,* 9 (1961), pp. 102–120.

[5] D. W. Maurer, *The Big Con,* New York: Signet Books, 1940. H. S. Becker, *Outsiders, op. cit.* E. H. Sutherland, *The Professional Thief,* Chicago: University of Chicago Press, 1937. A. R. Lindesmith, *Opiate Addiction,* Evanston: Principia Press, 1955.

obtained through official law enforcement agencies, but seven were found within the context of a neuropsychiatric hospital. The remaining respondents were gathered primarily through individual referrals from previous participants in the study. There were no obvious differences between the "psychiatric sample" and the other interviewees on the data to be reported.

All subjects in the sample were call girls. That is, they typically obtained their clients by individual referrals, primarily by telephone, and enacted the sexual contract in their own or their clients' place of residence or employment. They did not initiate contact with their customers in bars, streets, or houses of prostitution, although they might meet their customers at any number of locations by pre-arrangement. The minimum fee charged per sexual encounter was $20.00. As an adjunct to the call girl interviews, three pimps and two "call boys" were interviewed as well.[6]

Approximately two thirds of the sample were what are sometimes known as "outlaw broads"; that is, they were not under the supervision of a pimp when interviewed. There is evidence that the majority of pimps who were aware of the study prohibited the girls under their direction from participating in it. It should be noted that many members of the sample belonged to one or another clique; their individually expressed opinions may not be independent.

The interviews strongly suggest that there are marked idiosyncrasies from one geographical area to another in such practices as fee-splitting, involvement with peripheral occupations (e.g., cabbies), and so forth. For example, there appears to be little direct involvement of peripheral occupations with call girl activities in the Los Angeles area, while it has been estimated that up to 10% of the population of Las Vegas is directly involved in activities of prostitutes.[7] What may be typical for a call girl in the Los Angeles area is not necessarily typical for a girl in New York, Chicago, Las Vegas, or Miami.

Since the professional literature (e.g., Greenwald; Pomeroy) concerning this occupation and its participants is so limited in quantity, and is not concerned with training per se, the present data may have some utility for the social sciences.[8]

[6] This definition departs somewhat from that offered by Clinard. He defines the call girl as one dependent upon an organization for recruiting patrons and one who typically works in lower-class hotels. The present sample is best described by Clinard's category high-class independent professional prostitute. M. D. Clinard, *Sociology of Deviant Behavior,* New York: Rinehart & Co., Inc., 1957.

[7] E. Reid and O. Demaris, *The Green Felt Jungle,* New York: Pocket Books, Inc., 1963.

[8] H. Greenwald, *op. cit.* W. Pomeroy, *Some Aspects of Prostitution,* unpublished paper.

All but two interviews were tape recorded. All respondents had prior knowledge that the interview would be tape recorded. The interviewing was, for the most part, done at the girls' place of work and/or residence. Occasional interviews were conducted in the investigator's office, and one in a public park. Interviews were semistructured and employed open-ended questions. One part of the interview concerned the apprenticeship period or "turning out" process.

THE ENTRANCE

I had been thinking about it [becoming a call girl] before a lot. . . . Thinking about wanting to do it, but I had no connections. Had I not had a connection, I probably wouldn't have started working. . . . I thought about starting out. . . . Once I tried it [without a contact]. . . . I met this guy at a bar and I tried to make him pay me, but the thing is, you can't do it that way because they are romantically interested in you, and they don't think that it is on that kind of basis. You can't all of a sudden come up and want money for it, you have to be known beforehand. . . . I think that is what holds a lot of girls back who might work. I think I might have started a year sooner had I had a connection. You seem to make one contact or another . . . if it's another girl or a pimp or just someone who will set you up and get you a client. . . . You can't just, say, get an apartment and get a phone in and everything and say, "Well, I'm gonna start business," because you gotta get clients from somewhere. There has to be a contact.

Immediately prior to entrance into the occupation, all but one girl had personal contact with someone professionally involved in call girl activities (pimps or other call girls). The one exception had contact with a customer of call girls. While various occupational groups (e.g., photographers) seem to be peripherally involved, often unwittingly, with the call girl, there was no report of individuals involved in such occupations being contacts for new recruits. The novice's initial contact is someone at the level at which she will eventually enter the occupation: not a street-walker, but a call girl; not a pimp who manages girls out of a house of prostitution, but a pimp who manages call girls.

Approximately half of the girls reported that their initial contact for entrance into the profession was another "working girl." The nature of these relationships is quite variable. In some cases, the girls have been long standing friends. Other initial contacts involved sexual relationships between a Lesbian and the novice. Most, however, had known each other less than a year, and did not appear to have a very close relationship, either in the sense of time spent together or of biographical information exchanged. The relationship may begin with the aspiring call girl soliciting the contact. That is, if a professional is known to others as a call girl, she will be sought out and approached by females who are strangers:[9]

I haven't ever gone out and looked for one. All of these have fell right into my hands. . . . They turned themselfs out. . . . They come to me for help.

Whatever their relationship, whenever the professional agrees to aid the beginner, she also, it appears, implicitly assumes responsibility for training her. This is evidenced by the fact that only one such female contact referred the aspirant to another girl for any type of help. Data are not available as to the reason for this unusual referral.

If the original contact was not another call girl but a pimp, a much different relationship is developed and the career follows a somewhat different course. The relationship between pimp and girl is typically one of lovers, not friends:

. . . because I love him very much. Obviously, I'm doing this mostly for him. . . . I'd do anything for him. I'm not just saying I will, I am. . . . [After discussing his affair with another woman] I just decided that I knew what he was when I decided to do this for him and I decided I had two choices—either accept it or not, and I accepted it, and I have no excuse.

Occasionally, however, a strictly business relationship will be formed:

Right now I am buying properties, and as soon as I can afford it, I am buying stocks. . . . It is strictly a business deal. This man and I are friends, our relationship ends there. He handles all the money, he is making all the investments and I trust him. We have a legal document drawn up which states that half the investments are mine, half of them his, so I am protected.

Whether the relationship is love or business, the pimp solicits the new girl.[10] It is usually agreed that the male will have an important managerial role in the course of the girl's career, and that both will enjoy the gains from the girl's activities for an indefinite period:

Actually a pimp has to have complete control or else its like trouble with him. Because if a pimp doesn't, if she is not madly in love with him or something in some way, a pimp won't keep a girl.

Once the girl agrees to function as a call girl, the male, like his female counterpart, undertakes the training of the girl, or refers the girl to another

[9] A point also made in the autobiographical account of a retired call girl. Virginia McManus, *Not For Love,* New York: Dell Publishing Co., Inc., 1960, p. 160.

[10] Two of the pimps denied that this was very often so and maintained that the girls will solicit them. The degree to which they are solicited seems to depend upon the nature and extent of their reputations. It is difficult to judge the accuracy of these reports as there appears to be a strong taboo against admitting to such solicitation.

call girl for training. Either course seems equally probable. Referrals, when employed, are typically to friends and, in some cases, wives or ex-wives.

Although the data are limited, it appears that the pimp retains his dominance over the trainee even when the latter is being trained by a call girl. The girl trainer remains deferential to the pimp's wishes regarding the novice.

APPRENTICESHIP

Once a contact is acquired and the decision to become a call girl made, the recruit moves to the next stage in the career sequence: the apprentice-ship period. The structure of the apprenticeship will be described, followed by a description of the content most frequently communicated during this period.

The apprenticeship is typically served under the direction of another call girl, but may occasionally be supervised by a pimp. Twenty-four girls in the sample initially worked under the supervision of other girls. The classroom is, like the future place of work, an apartment. The apprentice typically serves in the trainer's apartment, either temporarily residing with the trainer or commuting there almost daily. The novice rarely serves her apprenticeship in such places as a house of prostitution, motel, or on the street. It is also infrequent that the girl is transported out of her own city to serve an apprenticeship. Although the data are not extensive, the number of girls being trained simultaneously by a particular trainer has rarely been reported to be greater than three. Girls sometimes report spending up to eight months in training, but the average stay seems to be two or three months. The trainer controls all referrals and appointments, novices seem-ingly not having much control over the type of sexual contract made or the circumstances surrounding the enactment of the contract.

The structure of training under the direction of a pimp seems similar, though information is more limited. The girls are trained in an apartment in the city they intend to work and for a short period of time. There is some evidence that the pimp and the novice often do not share the same apartment as might the novice and the girl trainer. There appear to be two reasons for the separation of pimp and girl. First, it is not uncommonly thought that cues which suggest the presence of other men displease the girl's customers:

Well, I would never let them know that I had a lover, which is something that you never ever let a john know, because this makes them very reticent to give you money, because they think you are going to go and spend it with your lover, which is what usually happens.

(Interestingly, the work of Winick suggests that such prejudices may not actually be held by many customers.)[11] Secondly, the legal repercussions are much greater, of course, for the pimp who lives with his girl than for two girls rooming together. As one pimp of 19 years experience puts its:

> It is because of the law. There is a law that is called the illegal cohabitation that they rarely use unless the man becomes big in stature. If he is a big man in the hustling world, the law then employs any means at their command. . . .

Because of the convenience in separation of housing, it is quite likely that the pimp is less directly involved with the day-to-day training of the girls than the call girl trainer.

The content of the training period seems to consist of two broad, inter-related dimensions one philosophical, the other interpersonal. The former refers to the imparting of a value structure, the latter to "do's" and "don'ts" of relating to customers and, secondarily, to other "working girls" and pimps. The latter teaching is perhaps best described by the concept of a short range perspective. That is, most of the "do's" and "don'ts" pertain to ideas and actions that the call girl uses in problematic situations.[12] Not all girls absorb these teachings, and those who do incorparate them in varying degrees.

Insofar as a value structure is transmitted it is that of maximizing gains while minimizing effort, even if this requires transgressions of either a legal or moral nature. Frequently, it is postulated that people, particularly men, are corrupt or easily corruptible, that all social relationships are but a reflection of a "con," and that prostitution is simply a more honest or at least no more dishonest act than the everyday behavior of "squares." Furthermore, not only are "johns" basically exploitative, but they are easily exploited; hence they are, in some respects, stupid. As explained by a pimp:

> . . . [in the hustling world] the trick or the john is known as a fool . . . this is not the truth. . . . He [the younger pimp] would teach his woman that a trick was a fool.

Since the male is corrupt, or honest only because he lacks the opportunity to be corrupt, then it is only appropriate that he be exploited as he exploits.

[11] C. Winick, "Prostitutes' Clients' Perception of the Prostitute and Themselves," *International Journal of Social Psychiatry,* 8 (1961-62), pp. 289–297.

[12] H. S. Becker, Blanche Geer, and E. C. Hughes, A. L. Strauss, *Boys In White,* Chicago: University of Chicago Press, 1961.

Girls first start making their "scores"—say one guy keeps them for a while or maybe she gets, you know, three or four grand out of him, say a car or a coat. These are your scores. . . .

The general assumption that man is corrupt is empirically confirmed when the married male betrays his wife, when the moralist, secular or religious, betrays his publicly stated values, or when the "john" "stiffs" (cheats) the girl. An example of the latter is described by a girl as she reflects upon her disillusionment during her training period.

It is pretty rough when you are starting out. You get stiffed a lot of times. . . . Oh sure. They'll take advantage of you anytime they can. And I'm a trusting soul, I really am. I'll believe anybody till they prove different. I've made a lot of mistakes that way. You get to the point, well, Christ, what the heck can I believe in people, they tell me one thing and here's what they do to me.

Values such as fairness with other working girls, or fidelity to a pimp, may occasionally be taught. To quote a pimp:

So when you ask me if I teach a kind of basic philosophy, I would say that you could say that. Because you try to teach them in an amoral way that there is a right and wrong way as pertains to this game . . . and then you teach them that when working with other girls to try to treat the other girl fairly because a woman's worst enemy in the street [used in both a literal and figurative sense] is the other woman and only by treating the other women decently can she expect to get along. . . . Therefore the basic philosophy I guess would consist of a form of honesty, a form of sincerity and complete fidelity to her man [pimp].

It should be noted, however, that behavior based on enlightened self-interest with concomitant exploitation is not limited to customer relationships. Interviewees frequently mentioned a pervasive feeling of distrust between trainer and trainee, and such incidents as thefts or betrayal of confidences are occasionally reported and chronically guarded against.

Even though there may be considerable pressure upon the girl to accept this value structure, many of them (perhaps the majority of the sample) reject it.

People have told me that I wasn't turned out, but turned loose instead. . . . Someone who is turned out is turned out to believe in a certain code of behavior, and this involves having a pimp, for one thing. It also involves never experiencing anything but hatred or revulsion for "tricks" for another thing. It involves always getting the money in front [before the sexual act] and a million little things that are very strictly adhered to by those in the "in group," which I am not. . . . Never being nice or pleasant to a trick unless you are doing it for the money, getting more money. [How did you learn that?] It was explained to me over a period of about six months. I learned that you were doing it to make money for yourself so that you could have nice things and security. . . . [Who would teach you this?] [The trainer] would teach me this.[13]

It seems reasonable to assume that the value structure serves, in general, to create in-group solidarity and to alienate the girl from "square" society, and that this structure serves the political advantage of the trainer and the economic gains of the trainee more than it allays the personal anxieties of either. In fact, failure to adopt these values at the outset does not appear to be correlated with much personal distress.[14] As one girl describes her education experiences:

Some moral code. We're taught, as a culture . . . it's there and after awhile you live, breathe, and eat it. Now, what makes you go completely against everything that's inside you, everything that you have been taught, and the whole society, to do things like this?

Good empirical evidence, however, concerning the functions and effectiveness of this value structure with regard to subjective comfort is lacking.

A series of deductions derived from the premises indicated above serve to provide, in part, the "rules" of interpersonal contact with the customer. Each customer is to be seen as a "mark," and "pitches" are to be made.

[Did you have a standard pitch?] It's sort of amusing. I used to listen to my girl friend [trainer]. She was the greatest at this telephone type of situation. She would call up and cry and say that people had come to her door. . . . She'd cry and she'd complain and she'd say "I have a bad check at the liquor store, and they sent the police over," and really . . . a girl has a story she tells the man. . . . Anything, you know, so he'll help her out. Either it's the rent or she needs a car, or doctor's bills, or any number of things.

Any unnecessary interaction with the customer is typically frowned upon, and the trainee will receive exhortations to be quick about her business. One girl in her fourth week of work explains:

[What are some of the other don't's that you have learned about?] Don't take so much time. . . . The idea is to get rid of them as quickly as possible.

Other content taught concerns specific information about specific customers.

---

[13] The statements made by prostitutes to previous investigators and mental helpers may have been parroting this particular value structure and perhaps have misled previous investigators into making the assumption that "all whores hate men." While space prohibits a complete presentation of the data, neither our questionnaire nor interview data suggest that this is a predominant attitude among call girls.

[14] There is, from the present study, little support for the hypothesis of Reckless concerning the association of experience trauma and guilt with abruptness of entry into the occupation. W. C. Reckless, *The Crime Problem*, New York: Appleton-Century-Crofts, Inc., 1950.

. . . she would go around the bar and say, now look at that man over there, he's this way and that way, and this is what he would like and these are what his problems are. . . .

. . . she would teach me what the men wanted and how much to get, what to say when I got there . . . just a line to hand them.

Training may also include proprieties concerning consuming alcohol and drugs, when and how to obtain the fee, how to converse with the customers and, occasionally, physical and sexual hygiene. As a girl trainer explains:

First of all, impress cleanliness. Because, on the whole, the majority of girls, I would say, I don't believe there are any cleaner women walking the streets, because they've got to be aware of any type of body odor. . . . You teach them to French [fellatio] and how to talk to men.

[Do they [pimps] teach you during the turning out period how to make a telephone call?] Oh, usually, yes. They don't teach you, they just tell you how to do it and you do it with your good common sense, but if you have trouble, they tell you more about it.

Interestingly, the specific act of telephoning a client is often distressing to the novice and is of importance in her training. Unfortunately for the girl, it is an act she must perform with regularity as she does considerable soliciting.[15] One suspects that such behavior is embarrassing for her because it is an unaccustomed role for her to play—she has so recently come from a culture where young women do *not* telephone men for dates. Inappropriate sex-role behavior seems to produce greater personal distress than does appropriate sex-role behavior even when it is morally reprehensible.

Well, it is rather difficult to get on the telephone, when you've never worked before, and talk to a man about a subject like that, and it is very new to you.

What is omitted from the training should be noted as well. There seems to be little instruction concerning sexual techniques as such, even though the previous sexual experience of the trainee may have been quite limited. What instruction there is typically revolves around the practice of fellatio. There seems to be some encouragement not to experience sexual orgasms with the client, though this may be quite variable with the trainer.

. . . and sometimes, I don't know if it's a set rule or maybe it's an unspoken rule, you don't enjoy your dates.

Yes, he did [teach attitudes]. He taught me to be cold. . . .

It should be stressed that, if the girls originally accepted such instructions and values, many of them, at least at the time of interviewing, ver-

---

[15] The topic of solicitation will be dealt with in a forthcoming paper.

balized a rejection of these values and reported behavior which departed considerably from the interpersonal rules stipulated as "correct" by their trainers. Some experience orgasms with the customer, some show considerable affect toward "johns," others remain drunk or "high" throughout the contact.[16] While there seems to be general agreement as to what the rules of interpersonal conduct are, there appears to be considerable variation in the adoption of such rules.

A variety of methods are employed to communicate the content described above. The trainer may arrange to eavesdrop on the interactions of girl and client and then discuss the interaction with her. One trainer, for example, listened through a closed door to the interaction of a new girl with a customer, then immediately after he left, discussed, in a rather heated way, methods by which his exit may have been facilitated. A pimp relates:

> The best way to do this [teaching conversation] is, in the beginning, when the phone rings, for instance . . . is to listen to what she says and then check and see how big a trick he is and then correct her from there.
> . . . with everyone of them [trainees] I would make it a point to see two guys to see how they [the girls] operate.

In one case a girl reported that her pimp left a written list of rules pertaining to relating to "johns." Direct teaching, however, seems to be uncommon. The bulk of whatever learning takes place seems to take place through observation.

> It's hard to tell you, because we learn through observations.
> But I watched her and listened to what her bit was on the telephone.

To summarize, the structure of the apprenticeship period seems quite standard. The novice receives her training either from a pimp or from another more experienced call girl, more often the latter. She serves her initial two to eight months of work under the trainer's supervision and often serves this period in the trainer's apartment. The trainer assumes responsibility for arranging contacts and negotiating the type and place of the sexual encounter.

The content of the training pertains both to a general philosophical stance and to some specifics (usually not sexual) of interpersonal behavior with customers and colleagues. The philosophy is one of exploiting the exploiters (customers) by whatever means necessary and defining the colleagues of the call girl as being intelligent, self-interested and, in certain important respects, basically honest individuals. The interpersonal techniques addressed during the learning period consist primarily of "pitches," telephone conversations, personal and occasionally sexual hygiene, prohibi-

---

[16] In the unpublished paper referred to above, Pomeroy has indicated that, of 31 call girls interviewed, only 23% reported never experiencing orgasms with customers.

tions against alcohol and dope while with a "john," how and when to obtain the fee, and specifics concerning the sexual habits of particular customers. Specific sexual techniques are very rarely taught. The current sample included a considerable number of girls who, although capable of articulating this value structure, were not particularly inclined to adopt it.

CONTACTS AND CONTRACTS

While the imparting of ideologies and proprieties to the prospective call girl is emphasized during the apprenticeship period, it appears that the primary function of the apprenticeship, at least for the trainee, is building a clientele. Since this latter function limits the degree of occupational socialization, the process of developing the clientele and the arrangements made between trainer and trainee will be discussed.

Lists ("books") with the names and telephone numbers of customers are available for purchase from other call girls or pimps, but such books are often considered unreliable. While it is also true that an occasional pimp will refer customers to girls, this does not appear to be a frequent practice. The most frequent method of obtaining such names seems to be through contacts developed during the apprenticeship. The trainer refers customers to the apprentice and oversees the latter in terms of her responsibility and adequacy in dealing with the customer. For referring the customer, the trainer receives forty to fifty per cent of the total price agreed upon in the contract negotiated by the trainer and customer.[17] The trainer and trainees further agree, most often explicitly, on the apprentice's "right" to obtain and to use, on further occasions, information necessary for arranging another sexual contract with the "john" without the obligation of further "kick-back" to the trainer. That is, if she can obtain the name and telephone number of the customer, she can negotiate another contract without fee-splitting. During this period, then, the girl is not only introduced to other working colleagues (pimps and girls alike) but also develops a clientele.

There are two obvious advantages for a call girl in assuming the trainer role. First, since there seems to be an abundant demand for new girls, and since certain service requirements demand more than one girl, even the well established call girl chronically confronts the necessity for making referrals. It is then reasonable to assume that the extra profit derived from

[17] The fee-splitting arrangement is quite common at all levels of career activity. For example, cooperative activity between two girls is often required for a particular type of sexual contract. In these cases, the girl who has contracted with the customer will contact a colleague, usually a friend, and will obtain 40%–50% of the latter's earnings. There is suggestive evidence that fee-splitting activities vary according to geographical areas and that Los Angeles is unique for both its fee-splitting patterns and the rigidity of its fee-splitting structure.

the fee-splitting activities, together with the added conveniences of having a girl "on call," allows the trainer to profit considerably from this arrangement. Secondly, contacts with customers are reputedly extremely difficult to maintain if services are not rendered on demand. Thus, the adoption of the trainer role enables the girl to maintain contacts with "fickle" customers under circumstances where she may wish a respite from the sexual encounter without terminating the contacts necessary for re-entry into the call girl role. It is also possible that the financial gains may conceivably be much greater for most trainers than for most calls girls, but this is a moot point.

A final aspect of the apprenticeship period that should be noted is the novice's income. It is possible for the novice, under the supervision of a competent and efficient trainer, to earn a great deal of money, or at least to get a favorable glimpse of the great financial possibilities of the occupation and, in effect, be heavily rewarded for her decision to enter it. Even though the novice may be inexperienced in both the sexual and interpersonal techniques of prostitution, her novelty on the market gives her an immediate advantage over her more experienced competitors. It seems quite likely that the new girl, irrespective of her particular physical or mental qualities, has considerable drawing power because she provides new sexual experience to the customer. Early success and financial reward may well provide considerable incentive to continue in the occupation.

A final word is needed regarding the position of the pimp vis-à-vis the call girl during the apprenticeship period. While some pimps assume the responsibility for training the girl personally, as indicated above, as many send the novice to another girl. The most apparent reason for such referral is that it facilitates the development of the "book." Purposes of training appear to be secondary for two reasons: (1) The pimp often lacks direct contact with the customers, so he personally cannot aid directly in the development of the girl's clientele; (2) When the pimp withdraws his girl from the training context, it is rarely because she has obtained adequate knowledge of the profession. This is not to say that all pimps are totally unconcerned with the type of knowledge being imparted to the girl. Rather, the primary concern of the pimp is the girl's developing a clientele, not learning the techniques of sex or conversation.

The apprenticeship period usually ends abruptly, not smoothly. Its termination may be but a reflection of interpersonal difficulties between trainer and trainee, novice and pimp, or between two novices. Occasionally termination of training is brought about through the novice's discovery and subsequent theft of the trainer's "book." Quite frequently, the termination is due to the novice's developing a sufficient trade or other business opportunities. The point is, however, that no respondent has reported that the final disruption of the apprenticeship was the result of the completion of adequate training. While disruptions of this relationship may be due to personal or impersonal events, termination is not directly due to the development of sufficient skills.

DISCUSSION AND SUMMARY

On the basis of interviews with 33 call girls in the Los Angeles area, information was obtained about entrance into the call girl occupation and the initial training period or apprenticeship therein.

The novice call girl is acclimated to her new job primarily by being thoroughly immersed in the call girl subculture, where she learns the trade through imitation as much as through explicit tutoring. The outstanding concern at this stage is the development of a sizable and lucrative clientele. The specific skills and values which are acquired during this period are rather simple and quickly learned.

In spite of the girls' protests and their extensive folklore, the art of prostitution, at least at this level, seems to be technically a low-level skill. That is, it seems to be an occupation which requires little formal knowledge or practice for its successful pursuit and appears best categorized as an unskilled job. Evidence for this point comes from two separate sources. First, there seems to be little technical training during this period, and the training seems of little importance to the career progress. Length or type of training does not appear correlated with success (i.e., money earned, lack of subjective distress, minimum fee per "trick," etc.). Secondly, the termination of the apprenticeship period is often brought about for reasons unrelated to training. It seems that the need for an apprenticeship period is created more by the secrecy surrounding the rendering or the utilization of the call girl service than by the complexity of the role. In fact, it is reasonable to assume that the complexity of the job confronting a street-walker may be considerably greater than that confronting a call girl. The tasks of avoiding the police, sampling among strangers for potential customers, and arrangements for the completion of the sexual contract not only require different skills on the part of the street-walker, but are performances requiring a higher degree of professional "know-how" than is generally required of the call girl.[18]

As a pimp who manages both call girls and "high-class" street-walkers explains:

[18] Needless to say, however, all of the sample of call girls who were asked for status hierarchies of prostitution felt that the street-walker had both less status and a less complex job. It *may* well be that the verbal exchange required of the call girl requires greater knowledge than that required of a street-walker, but the nonverbal skills required of the street-walker may be considerably greater than those of the call girl.

The girl that goes out into the street is the sharper of the two, because she is capable of handling herself in the street, getting around the law, picking out the trick that is not absolutely psycho . . . and capable of getting along in the street. . . . The street-walker, as you term her, is really a prima donna of the prostitutes . . . her field is unlimited, she goes to all of the top places so she meets the top people. . . .

The fact that the enactment of the call girl role requires little training, and the introduction of the girl to clients and colleagues alike is rather rapid, gives little time or incentive for adequate occupational socialization. It is perhaps for this reason rather than, for example, reasons related to personality factors, that occupational instability is great and cultural homogeneity small.

In closing, while it appears that there is a rather well defined apprenticeship period in the career of the call girl, it seems that it is the secrecy rather than the complexity of the occupation which generates such a period. While there is good evidence that initial contacts, primarily with other "working girls," are necessary for entrance into this career, there seems no reason, at this point, to assume that the primary intent of the participants in training is anything but the development of an adequate clientele.

8 Criminality Theories and Behavioral Images[*]

DANIEL GLASER

This article attempts to appraise the scientific utility of alternative theories proposed for the explanation of that individual behavior which is most uniformly designated "crime" in our society. All such theories are derived, explicitly or implicity, from more general psychological or social-psychological theories applicable to the larger class of behavior of which crime is considered an instance.

THEORIES AND IMAGERY

The language which explains a human act evokes imagery by which certain aspects of the act are abstractly conceived and are related to other phenomena. For example, an act may be explained as the rational pursuit of a purpose, as the expression of inner drives, as a conditioned neural response, or as a mechanical resultant of external pressures. Each type of

Reprinted from *American Journal of Sociology, 61* (March, 1956), 433–444, by permission of The University of Chicago Press. Copyright 1956 by The University of Chicago. Also by permission of the author.

* Acknowledgment is made of useful comments, leading to revisions of this article, which were received from Drs. J. E. Hulett, Jr., Alvin W. Gouldner, Bernard Farber, and others, all of the University of Illinois, and from Martin U. Martel, now of the University of Washington.

explanatory language evokes a somewhat different image of how human beings behave—as rational, as driven from within, as internally mechanical, or as atoms in fields of external forces. Each set of terms for explaining behavior and the associated imagery constitutes a psychological frame of reference. When made explicit, they are called "models" or "paradigms."

"Language is, by its very nature and essence, metaphorical," Cassirer observed.[1] For example, such psychological concepts as "force," "stimulus," and "response" were imported from physics and physiology, where they were first developed to deal with phenomena other than those to which they are applied by psychologists. These concepts evoke images which give meaning to our observations by interrelating them. But since considerable compression, deletion, or extension of available observations of behavior are usually necessary to fit our observations into our frame of reference, these conceptual frameworks determine both what we look for and what we overlook.[2]

As a theory is more rigorously tested, it becomes increasingly formalized. Ultimately, it may be expressed as mathematical relations between quantitative variables which are operationally defined by objectively specified rules of observational procedure. It then evokes little in the way of concrete images. While any theory may be formalized, more or less adequately, the imagery evoked when the theory is first formulated limits what later testing seeks. As testing proceeds, the theory may be delimited on the basis of negative findings. But additions to scientific theory have always depended upon the introduction of new imagery, from the theory of evolution to time-space relativity to any hypothesis which is clearly new to a particular research situation (though probably metaphorically drawn from another situation). If we focus on explaining an empirical phenomenon, a theory may be sufficiently tested to provoke extensive revision before it is highly formalized. That is a justification for this article. If we focus on developing and applying techniques for formalizing theory, we are likely to select theories on the basis of their amenability to the techniques of formalization rather than by their relevance to the phenomenon which we initially sought to explain.[3]

Crime, like most topics in social psycholgy, refers to a class of behavior the separate instances of which have many and diverse subjective and ob-

[1] Ernst Cassirer, *An Essay on Man* (Garden City, N.Y.: Doubleday, 1953), p. 142.

[2] Cf. Herbert Blumer, "Science without Concepts," *American Journal of Sociology,* XXXVI (January, 1931), 515–33; Kenneth Burke, *Permanence and Change* (New York: New Republic, 1936); Susanne K. Langer, *Philosophy in a New Key* (Cambridge: Harvard University Press, 1942), esp. chap. iv.

[3] Cf. A. H. Maslow, "Problem Centering versus Means Centering in Science," *Philosophy of Science,* XIII (October, 1946), 326–31; Gordon W. Allport, "The Psychologist's Frame of Reference," *Psychological Bulletin,* XXXVII (January, 1940), 1–28; Paul H. Furfey, "The Formalization of Sociology," *American Sociological Review,* XIX (October, 1954), 525–28.

jective aspects.[4] Our theoretical conceptions of criminal or other behavior necessarily simplify this complexity, and in our effort to comprehend such behavior we may distort it. Nevertheless, we strive for the most valid theoretical image of actual behavior, assuming thereby that this effort will ultimately produce the most fruitful basis for prediction or control of behavior.

In distinguishing the images which various criminality theories evoke, a somewhat imperfect distinction will be made between (1) "monistic" theories, which are based upon a single type of simple behavioral image; (2) "pluralistic" theories, which involve two or more distinct behavioral images; and (3) "integrative" theories, which attempt to subsume the aspects of behavior dealt with in pluralistic theories under a single relatively complex behavioral image. These theories will be appraised with respect to the interconnectedness of their explanatory imagery,[5] their comprehensiveness (the types or aspects of crime to which they apply), and their implications for the continuity and validity of empirical research.

MONISTIC THEORIES

Underlying prevailing monistic criminality theories, the following types of imagery may be distinguished: spontaneity, possession, rationality, external

---

[4] The term "crime" is here confined primarily to felonies, as felonies are defined by criminal courts in their prosecution and adjudication of cases, to which we add misdemeanors, such as petty larceny and assault, which are identified by lesser forms of the same attributes which identify felonies. This usage, which we believe corresponds to the usual connotation of "crime," excludes those misdemeanors which do not become felonies when "exaggerated," such as most disorderly conduct, vagrancy, and indecent exposure. It also excludes those "white-collar crimes" not commonly prosecuted as felonies. We also include as crime any act legally called "delinquency" if the only attribute which is the basis for its being considered delinquency rather than crime is the fact the doer is below a particular age.

We believe that there is a predominantly stable and uniform content to this reference of "crime" in Western society, despite some variation in its limits under different legal jurisdictions. Indicative of the complexity of crime as a topic for social-psychological study are the facts that crimes (a) occur in diverse situations; (b) must be identified by the symbolic interpretation given the behavior by the actors in the situation (e.g., identifying the victim's property as "owned" or his compliance as "involuntary"); (c) can be experienced or imputed subjectively as symbolic processes (ideation) and feelings (reflected in such legal language as "wilfully," "maliciously," etc.).

[5] The significance of interconnectedness in theory was indicated when, in a lecture at the University of Chicago in 1939, Bertrand Russell distinguished mysticism from science by saying that mysticism accepts the possibility of distance between cause and effect, while "science cannot accept action at a distance." As Hume suggested, this distinction is relative rather than absolute, since the connection is conceived rather than directly observed. In terms of that philosophy of science which eschews the language of "causality," disconnectedness refers to the failure to specify intervening variables between a dependent and an independent variable.

forces, internal mechanism, and role.

An image of behavior as spontaneous underlies that "pure" free-will criminality theory which is still voiced in lay discussions of crimes and is implicit in the judicial notion of "choosing" between right and wrong. Such an explanation is the epitome of disconnectedness, since it indicates inability or unwillingness to relate the behavior to anything else. Actually, "pure" free-will theory is seldom maintained continuously, for, when practical problems are considered, it must be modified to reflect other types of imagery.[6]

Possession imagery, which involves an image of a prepotent force resident in the person and determining his behavior, has been evoked by biological determinism theories of criminality, from Lombroso to Sheldon. While criminal behavior is asserted to be caused by malformed biological structures, no direct connection between the specific actions involved in crime and the defective structure is indicated, at least not in terms of specific known functions of organic structures. Much use of the term "psychopath," especially when explicitly or implicitly modified by the adjective "constitutional," still conveys this image of determination by an ill-defined condition. Another such disconnected explanation is that implied in the assertions that criminality is correlated with hypoglycemia or with organic brain damage. These hypotheses have never been tested on representative samples of persons with these ailments. However, if such correlation were established, there would be pressure to focus theory and research on establishing a conceptual connection between the correlated data. As an explanation for crime, it would still be "disconnected," as we use this adjective, because of the large conceptual gaps between organic phenomena and complex behavior.[7]

[6] We are implying that the free-will position in most debate on free-will versus determinism in criminology involves simultaneous employment of several definitions of "free will." No one endeavors to educate or to persuade without assuming that an individual's behavior is influenced by the experience to which he is exposed and that when this experience brings alternative choices to an individual's attention, he has the experience of choosing between alternative courses of action. Neither of these assumptions contradicts the notion of universal determinism in nature on which all science rests, nor has either the remotest relationship to the question of the indeterminancy of quantum particles, to which the free-will issue is often referred (cf. C. H. Cooley, *Social Organization* [New York: Charles Scribner's Sons, 1929], pp. 20–21; and *Human Nature and the Social Order* [rev. ed.; New York: Charles Scribner's Sons, 1922], pp. 38–43 and 55, n.).

[7] When comparing delinquents and non-delinquents from high-delinquency areas, the Gluecks found the delinquents to be stronger and more athletic (mesomorphic) anatomically than the non-delinquents, as well as more aggressive and extroverted in what they call "temperament." An example of conceptual connection between such "biological" data and criminality is the following earlier statement by Sutherland (which is amenable to empirical validation): "In an area where the delinquency rate is high a boy who is sociable, gregarious, active and athletic is very likely to come in contact with the other boys in the neighborhood, learn delinquent behavior from them, and become a gangster. . . . In another situation the sociable, athletic, aggressive boy may

Freudian criminologists have ascribed criminality to instinct.[8] This conception also involves possession imagery. However, in psychoanalysis, controls by the rational mind (ego) and society (superego) are seen as repressing or redirecting the instinctive criminal force (id), latent and manifest criminality being ascribed to the failure of the controls. Like other possession images, this conception fails to explain any aspect of criminality in which learning can be observed (such as complex criminal techniques, pride in conception of self as criminal, and pious loyalty to a criminal group). In the purely Freudian conception, we are possessed of criminal impulses, and we learn or fail to learn to control them; there is no learning of distinctively new criminality.

The frustration-equals-aggression formula, and amalgamation of behavioristic and psychoanalytic theory, provides another variation of possession imagery. A sum of vaguely defined emotional energy is seen as fixed in an individual. If the steady and relatively moderate expression of this energy is blocked, one of two alternative results is predicted: either there is an immediate outburst of unusually violent and reckless behavior, or there is a slow accumulation of "blocked energy" which must ultimately be expressed. The immediate outburst may explain some "crimes of passion" which seem unplanned, but it is inapplicable where blockage does not lead to immediate aggression. The "blockage-leads-to-ultimate-expression-in-some-other-manner" formulation provides a disconnected explanation for any emotional behavior; early frustration, perhaps in infancy or even prenatal, can always be demonstrated or assumed and can then be cited as the cause of later behavior without a clearly connecting causal mechanism.

Observations of aggression following frustration are explained in less disconnected imagery by certain older theories of emotional behavior which also account more adequately for observations contradicting the frustration-equals-aggression formula. We may develop the habit of reacting to frustration by violence, growing more set in the habit with each occasion of it. The current reaction against extreme permissiveness in child-rearing, which had been advocated as preventing children from accumulating aggression, is based on the newer tenet that tolerance of their aggression develops aggressive children. The James-Lange theory of emotions, that "we are afraid be-

become a member of a scout troop and not become involved in delinquent behavior" (E. H. Sutherland, *Principles of Criminology* [4th ed.; Chicago: J. B. Lippincott Co., 1947], p. 8; cf. also S. and E. Glueck, *Unravelling Juvenile Delinquency* [New York: Commonwealth Fund, 1950]).

[8] E.g., "The ideal criminal has not structured his personality in accordance with any value system. . . . Instinctual forces drive him on without any opposition from a restraining conscience" (K. R. Eissler, "General Problems of Delinquency," in K. R. Eissler [ed.], *Searchlights on Delinquency* [New York: International Universities Press, 1949], p. 7). Similar quotations from several other psychoanalytic writers are presented in Albert K. Cohen, *Delinquent Boys* (Glencoe, Ill.: Free Press, 1955), pp. 181–82.

cause we run," can be restated as: When habitual behavior is frustrated, we mobilize attention and energy for initiating a new course of behavior. Emotions are sense-experiences of bodily changes concomitant with such mobilization. We experience anger when we react by mobilizing to strike, and fear when we mobilize to flee. Mobilization may be inhibited before completion; we may only raise our voice rather than strike. Different experience leads to different habits of mobilization for given types of frustrating situation: one person mobilizes to fight, another flees, another deliberates. Different emotional experience accompanies each of these behavioral patterns.

The "classical" theory of criminality, identified with utilitarian philosophy and expressed in most criminal law, implies free will but immediately modifies it with the notion that man's behavior is determined by the nearness and efficacy of the choosable means for obtaining happiness. (Crime is to be prevented by making it produce unhappiness.) This is really a pluralistic theory, since the image of man shifts from a purely spontaneous actor to a rational calculator and, finally, to an atom moved by its external field of pleasant and painful forces.

Economic determinism in criminology is simply classical theory which assumes that economic ends are the primary means to the ultimate end of happiness. Crime is viewed as an alternative means to such ends when other means fail. The behavioral image of rational man in classical theory provides an insufficiently comprehensive explanation of irrational habits, predilections, and prejudices in specific cases of criminality; it also does not explain the absence of criminality in people whose economic need is equal to, or greater than, that of criminals. The imagery of external forces does not connect economic, geographic, and other abstract forces to specific criminal techniques and loyalties. Extreme cultural determinism theories may also arouse an imagery of external forces. They have been criticized for implying greater homogeneity of criminal subcultures than can be established empirically.

An image of internal mechanism (personality) developing through conditioning underlies many psychological explanations of crime which dispense with the concept of instinct. Its adequacy depends in part on the answer to the question of whether conditioning explains the acquisition of new responses rather than the association of new stimuli with old responses. Indicative of the issue of disconnectedness is the current debate on reductionism in the behavioral sciences: whether "voluntary" human behavior, in which images and symbolic evaluations of completed acts continuously enter into the initiation of new acts, can usefully be reduced to the conditioned-reflex model which physiologists verify from the study of isolated muscles or glands.[9] The discovery of the extreme diversity of personality in

[9] Still highly relevant are the questions raised in John Dewey, "The Reflex-Arc Concept in Psychology," *Psychological Review,* III (July, 1896), 357–70. New response learning seems accounted for by the concept of operants as response components which

criminals and of the frequency of allegedly criminal categories of personality among non-criminals supports the view that ascribing criminality to the habitual modes of behavior which psychologists usually connote by the term "personality" is based on an invalid image of criminal behavior.[10]

The image of behavior as role-playing, borrowed from the theater, presents people as directing their actions on the basis of their conceptions of how others see them. The choice of another, from whose perspective we view our own behavior, is the process of identification. It may be with the immediate others or with distant and perhaps abstractly generalized others of our reference groups. (The "amateur" criminal may identify himself with the highly professional "master"-criminal whom he has never met.) Rationalization is seen as a necessary concomitant of voluntary behavior, particularly when role conflicts exist. Acceptance by the group with which one identifies one's self and conceptions of persecution by other groups are among the most common and least intellectual bases for rationalization by criminals. Role imagery provides the most comprehensive and interconnected theoretical framework for explaining the phenomena of criminality.[11] We shall take up the problem of articulating the specific relationship of role theory with criminality in discussing "integrative" criminality theories.

---

are "emitted rather than elicited" and which are continuously shaped into even the most complex behavior through reinforcement of those components yielding favorable consequences and extinction of the remainder (cf. B. F. Skinner, *Science and Human Behavior* [New York: Macmillan Co., 1953]). While mechanistic data on animal learning may support this theory, such data are related only by gross analogy to human learning of complex "voluntary" behavior like crime, since we have negligible evidence of animal ability to learn complex behavior through symbolic communication (hence accumulation of learning from one generation to the next) or of animals reinforcing their acts by verbal rationalization. Apart from the need to learn those gross principles applicable to both human and animal learning, further "control" of such human learning as that involved in crime requires more discriminating analysis and more reliable data on human verbal processes, feelings, and relationships.

[10] Where the measure of personality is a measure of the extent of criminal behavior (psychopathy scales), the empirical correlation discovered is that between criminality and itself. This has no explanatory value and does not compare with the fruitful logical reduction of complex theories to quasi-tautological relations between distinct conceptual frameworks (cf. Karl F. Schuessler, review of Hathaway and Monachesi, "Analyzing and Predicting Juvenile Delinquency with the MMPI," *American Journal of Sociology,* LX [November, 1954], 321–22; Donald R. Cressey and Karl F. Schuessler, "Personality Characteristics of Criminals," *American Journal of Sociology,* LV [March, 1950], 476–84).

[11] Cf. Nelson N. Foote, "Identification as the Basis for a Theory of Motivation," *American Sociological Review,* XVI (February, 1951), 14–22; C. Wright Mills, "Situated Actions and Vocabularies of Motive," *American Sociological Review,* V (December, 1940), 904–13; Tamotsu Shibutani, "Reference Groups as Perspectives," *American Journal of Sociology,* LX (May, 1955), 562–69.

PLURALISTIC AND INTEGRATIVE THEORIES

Serendipity—the influence of "unanticipated, anomalous and strategic"[12] observations—in causing us to revise theory, has usually resulted in patch-work eclecticism rather than the systematic revision of criminality theory. Where one behavioral image does not fit, we skip to another. Most textbooks in criminology present a cluster of disparate monistic theories as "the theory of multiple causation." These should be regarded as temporary expedients in the course of revising theory. Instead, since the nineteenth-century writ-ings of Enrico Ferri, they have been repeatedly extolled as the ultimate, most satisfactory formulations.

Pluralistic theories evoke a mixed metaphorical image—the criminal is possessed, pushed, rationally chooses, or interpretively interacts. The major practical objection is that no rules are provided for interrelating component theories and for shifting from one to another. Starting an analysis from the standpoint of one theory, one is likely to persevere in that theory in analyzing behavior and thus may be blinded to observations which might be revealed, were one to start with another theory. For example, even sociologists repeatedly find themselves neglecting social relationships through the natural tendency to look only at individual traits when trying to explain an indi-vidual's criminality. Both the defects and the merits of the component theories thereby remain in the multiple-causation mixtures.

There are precedents in the physical sciences for the simultaneous ac-ceptance of alternative theoretical images of phenomena, such as the wave and the corpuscular conceptions of light, each being employed to explain different types of observation. This is considered a temporary and unsatis-factory state of affairs pending the appearance of a more general integrative theory which will account for all the observations. The old theories often become special cases of the more general theory (e.g., as Newtonian physics is a special case of Einsteinian physics).

The outstanding attempt to formulate an integrative theory of crimi-nality is the "differential association" theory, proposed by the late Edwin H. Sutherland, who summarized his theory in the statement: "A person becomes delinquent because of an excess of definitions favorable to violation of law."[13] Personality, economic conditions, and other elements of monistic criminality theories are related to crime by this theory only to the extent that they lead to the procurement of an excess of definitions favorable to violation of law. Unlike the pluralistic approaches, such theory interrelates

[12] Robert K. Merton, *Social Theory and Social Structure* (Glencoe, Ill.: Free Press, 1949), p. 98.

[13] E. H. Sutherland, *Principles of Criminology*, prepared by Donald R. Cressey (5th ed.; Chicago: J. B. Lippincott Co., 1955), p. 78 (p. 6 in 4th ed.).

the separate monistic factors in each case. Differential association theory channels research by knitting diverse data together, whereas multiple-factor conceptions lead to the collection of disparate observations.

Sutherland's formal statement of this theory actually conveys a rather mechanistic image of criminality, which differs from the multiple-factor conception in one major respect. While the multiple-factor imagery presents the criminal as an atom in a multi-dimensional field, the differential association conception involves imagery of the criminal on a unidimensional continuum. Criminality is at one extreme of this continuum and non-criminality at the other, with the individual's associations pushing him toward one extreme or the other. This imagery is not altered essentially when Sutherland observes that criminal and non-criminal associations may vary in "frequency, duration, priority and intensity." The phrase "excess of definitions" itself lacks clear denotation in human experience.

Probably, the failure of Sutherland's language to evoke a clearly recognizable behavioral image is responsible for the limited acceptance of his theory. The criticisms have been of two principal types. First, there have been assertions that the differential learning of crime is more complex than the critics assume Sutherland's conception of differential association to be. Some critics have interpreted "association" in Sutherland's writings as synonymous with "contact."[14] Sutherland seems to have been dismayed by an assumption that "association" is distinct from "identification."[15] Donald R. Cressey has suggested modification of differential association theory by:

> the substitution of a different conception of the process by which criminality is learned for the conception of a differential in the quantity and quality of con-

[14] E.g.: "While this theory of crime explains the delinquent behavior of many juveniles, it does not adequately explain why some individuals who have extensive contacts with criminal norms and with persons who engage in criminal behavior do not themselves commit delinquencies" (Martin H. Neumeyer, *Juvenile Delinquency in Modern Society* [New York: D. Van Nostrand Co., 1949], p. 226); "[Sutherland's theory] . . . does not adequately explain why two or more children in the same home often respond differently to the situation of delinquent and criminal members of the family" (Milton L. Barron, *The Juvenile in Delinquent Society* [New York: A. A. Knopf, 1954], p. 147). We might also note the recurrent question by students: Why doesn't the prison guard become a criminal, since his association is primarily with criminals?

[15] Cf. "The opposition to 'differential association' as an explanation seems to be based on a misconception of a meaning of that process, as indicated by the sentence, 'Identification with a group of boys who stole was as important as contact with the differential association'" (Sutherland, *op. cit.*, n. 25, pp. 157–58; p. 138 in 4th ed.). In his posthumous revision of Sutherland, Cressey added to the above: "Differential identification is a clearly implied and congruous aspect of the differential association theory." The reformulation of "differential identification" set forth below supports everything in this added sentence except the world "clearly." Sutherland's theory has been very diversely interpreted.

tacts with the two varieties of behavior patterns. For example . . . a search for the differences in the typical vocabularies used by criminals and non-criminals in specific situations might reveal that it is the presence or absence of a specific, learned verbal label in a specific situation which determines the criminality or non-criminality of a particular person.[16]

These diverse comments suggest the need for a restatement of Sutherland's theory so as to make its behavioral referent less ambiguous.

A second criticism of Sutherland's theory consists of arguments for certain pluralistic criminality theories on the grounds that Sutherland's theory accounts for only one of several distinct types of criminality. The most common of these views evokes a dualistic image of criminality as manifesting either differential association or personality, or both.[17] It frequently ignores Sutherland's reference to personality as one of several factors determining patterns of differential association and therefore related to crime indirectly (cf. our n. 6). Usually it also involves the assumption that the major aspects of personality determining crime are relatively fixed from childhood on. A conception of personality reconcilable with Sutherland's theory would be as the sum total of a person's regular role patterns in a given period. This includes, as personality, aspects of roles which develop only in adulthood, such as class and occupational roles. Criminality itself would then be considered a component of personality, and the theory for explaining criminality presumably would be analogous with the theory for explaining other components of personality; it would go beyond descriptive designation of criminality as a component of the referent for the term "personality."

Some critics of Sutherland augment the dualism of personality and association by also calling for recognition of accidental and transitory situational causes of crime.[18] Such criticism, prompted by the premises of pluralistic theory, implies that Sutherland's theory either should be radically revised or should be applied to a much more limited range of criminality than he and his students believed. But neither of these changes is necessary if we reconceptualize Sutherland's theory in terms which we call "differential identification."

[16] Donald R. Cressey, "Application and Verification of the Differential Association Theory," *Journal of Criminal Law, Criminology, and Police Science*, XLIII (May–June, 1952), 43–52.

[17] Cf. Paul W. Tappan, *Juvenile Delinquency* (New York: McGraw-Hill Book Co., Inc., 1949), pp. 82 ff.; S. Kirson Weinberg, "Theories of Criminality and Problems of Prediction," *Journal of Criminal Law, Criminology, and Police Science*, XIV (November–December, 1954), 412–24.

[18] Cf. "The theory of differential association does not explain the incidental, the highly emotional, or the accidental crimes, but applies only to the confirmed types of criminality in which the offender accepts anti-social behavior as a suitable way of life" (Mabel A. Elliott, *Crime in Modern Society* [New York: Harper & Bros., 1952], p. 402).

DIFFERENTIAL IDENTIFICATION
AS AN INTEGRATIVE CRIMINALITY THEORY

We describe identification somewhat unconventionally as "the choice of another, from whose perspective we view our own behavior." What we have called "differential identification" reconceptualizes Sutherland's theory in role-taking imagery, drawing heavily on Mead as well as on later refinements of role theory.[19] Most persons in our society are believed to identify themselves with both criminal and non-criminal persons in the course of their lives. Criminal identification may occur, for example, during direct experience in delinquent membership groups, through positive reference to criminal roles portrayed in mass media, or as a negative reaction to forces opposed to crime. The family probably is the principal non-criminal reference group, even for criminals. It is supplemented by many other groups of anti-criminal "generalized others."

The theory of differential identification, in essence, is that *a person pursues criminal behavior to the extent that he identifies himself with real or imaginary persons from whose perspective his criminal behavior seems acceptable.* Such a theory focuses attention on the interaction in which choice of models occurs, including the individual's interaction with himself in rationalizing his conduct. This focus makes differential identification theory integrative, in that it provides a criterion of the relevance, for each individual case of criminality, of economic conditions, prior frustrations, learned moral creeds, group participation, or other features of an individual's life. These features are relevant to the extent that they can be shown to affect the choice of the other from whose perspective the individual views his own behavior. The explanation of criminal behavior on the basis of its imperfect correlation with any single variable of life-situations, if presented without specifying the intervening identification, evokes only a disconnected image of the relationship between the life-situation and the criminal behavior.

Sutherland supported the differential association theory by evidence that a major portion of criminality is learned through participation in criminal groups. Differential identification is a less disconnected explanation for such learning, and it also does not seem vulnerable to most of the objections to differential association. Because opposing and divisive roles frequently develop within groups, because our identification may be with remote reference groups or with imaginary or highly generalized others, and because identifications may shift rapidly with dialectical processes of role change

---

[19] Cf. D. Glaser, "A Reconsideration of Some Parole Prediction Factors," *American Sociological Review,* XIX (June, 1954), 335–41; G. H. Mead, *Mind, Self, and Society* (Chicago: University of Chicago Press, 1934); Foote, *op. cit.*; Mills, *op. cit.*; Shibutani, *op. cit.*

and rationalization during social interaction, differential association, as ordinarily conceived, is insufficient to account for all differential identification.

In practice, the use of differential identification to explain lone crimes the source of learning which is not readily apparent (such as extremes of brutality or other abnormality in sex crimes) gives rise to speculation as to the "others" involved in the identification. The use of this theory to explain a gang member's participation in a professional crime against property presents fewer difficulties. In so far as the former types of offense are explained by psychiatrists without invoking instincts or other mystical forces, they usually are interpreted, on a necessarily speculative basis, in terms of the self-conception which the offender develops in supporting his behavior and the sources of that self-conception. Such differential identification, in the case of most unusual and compulsive crimes, offers a less disconnected explanation than explanations derived from the alternative theories.[20]

The one objection to the theory of differential association which cannot be met by differential identification is that it does not account for "accidental" crimes. Differential identification treats crime as a form of voluntary (i.e., anticipatory) behavior, rather than as an accident. Indeed, both legal and popular conceptions of "crime" exclude acts which are purely accidental, except for some legislation on felonious negligence, to which our discussion of criminality must be considered inapplicable. Even for the latter offenses, however, it is noteworthy that the consequences of accidentally committing a crime may be such as to foster identification with criminal-role models (whether one is apprehended for the accidental crime or not).

During any period, *prior identifications* and *present circumstances* dictate the selection of the persons with whom we identify ourselves. Prior identifications which have been pleasing tend to persist, but at any time the immediate circumstances affect the relative ease (or salience) of alernative identifications. That is why membership groups so frequently are the reference groups, although they need not be. That, too, is why those inclined to crime usually refrain from it in situations where they play satisfying conventional roles in which crime would threaten their acceptance. From the latter situations their identification with non-criminal others may eventually make them anticriminal. This is the essence of rehabilitation.[21]

There is evidence that, with the spread of urban secularism, social situations are becoming more and more deliberately rather than traditionally

[20] For an outstanding illustration of what becomes differential identification rather than the usual conception of differential association, applied to compulsive crimes, see Donald R. Cressey, "Differential Association and Compulsive Crimes," *Journal of Criminal Law, Criminology, and Police Science,* XLV (May–June, 1954), 29–40.

[21] Cf. Donald R. Cressey, "Contradictory Theories in Correctional Group Therapy Programs," *Federal Probation,* XVIII (June, 1954), 20–26.

organized. Concurrently, roles are increasingly adjusted on the basis of the apparent authority or social pressure in each situation.[22] Our culture is said to give a common level of aspiration but different capacities of attainment according to socioeconomic class. At the same time, it is suggested, economic sources of status are becoming stronger while non-economic sources are becoming weaker. Therefore, when conventional occupational avenues of upward mobility are denied, people are more and more willing to seek the economic gains anticipated in crime, even at the risk of losing such non-economic sources of status as acceptance by non-criminal groups.[23] All these alleged features of urbanism suggest a considerable applicability of differential identification to "situational" and "incidental" crimes; focus on differential identification with alternative reference groups may reveal "situational imperatives" in individual life-histories.

Differential identification may be considered tautological, in that it may seem merely to make "crime" synonymous with "criminal identification." It is more than a tautology, however, if it directs one to observations beyond those necessary merely for the classification of behavior as criminal or noncriminal. It is a fruitful empirical theory leading one to proceed from the legalistic classification to the analysis of behavior as identification and role-playing.[24]

IMPLICATIONS

Three general hypotheses are derived from the assumption that the image of criminal behavior evoked by the theory of differential identification is more valid than evoked by alternative formulations.

[22] This evidence has come most dramatically from recent studies of race relations. Cf. Joseph D. Lohman and Dietrich C. Reitzes, "Note on Race Relations in Mass Society," *American Journal of Sociology,* LVIII (November, 1952), 240–46; Dietrich C. Reitzes, "The Role of Organizational Structures," *Journal of Social Issues,* IX, No. 1 (1953), 37–44; William C. Bradbury, "Evaluation of Research in Race Relations," *Inventory of Research in Racial and Cultural Relations,* V (winter–spring, 1953), 99–133.

[23] Cf. Merton, *op. cit.,* chap. iv. It may be noteworthy here that classification of Illinois parolees by status ratings of the jobs to which they were going was more predictive than classification by the status of their father's occupation or by whether their job was of higher, lower, or equal status than their father's occupation. Regardless of their class background, the parolee's infractions seemed primarily to be a function of their failure to approach middle-class status (cf. Daniel Glaser, "A Reformulation and Testing of Parole Prediction Factors" [unpublished Ph.D. dissertation, University of Chicago, 1954], pp. 253–59).

[24] A number of examples of useful tautologies in social science are presented in Arnold Rose, *Theory and Method in the Social Sceinces* (Minneapolis: University of Minnesota Press, 1954), pp. 328–38. In so far as a proposition is of heuristic use, however, one may question whether it is appropriately designated a "tautology."

The first hypothesis is that the imagery invoked by the theory of differential identification is the most adequate and parsimonious theoretical framework with which to account for the findings of criminology. We have shown the more disconnected imagery and the failure to comprehend major aspects of criminality inherent in theories which do not evoke an image of criminality as role-expressive activity. Parsimony of preconception is indicated by (1) its "integrative" function in interrelating the diverse phenomena which may be associated with crime through specifying intervening behavior; (2) its relating of criminal behavior to other behavior rather than to conceptually more distant phenomena; (3) its capacity to comprehend a tremendous diversity of criminal behavior. The theory of differential identification, by indicating the relevance of phenomena grossly correlated with crime, promotes continuity in research and theoretically should direct attention to phenomena having higher correlations with crime. Even more than differential association, as that theory is ordinarily conceived, differential identification should facilitate the recognition of "behavior systems" in crime.[25]

The second hypothesis is that differential identification orients one to evaluate soundly the rehabilitative effects of correctional techniques. Tests of this hypothesis will require more extensive and sophisticated research than that now applied to the appraisal of rehabilitative efforts.[26] However, some suggestive clues are available, for example, from studies of inmate social systems. These systems are seen as coercing each prison inmate into identification with fellow-inmates and hampering, if not preventing, his identification with non-criminal persons. Many prison policies sometimes considered "progressive," such as housing men in large dormitories, facilitating freedom of contact between inmates, assigning prison social workers to cope with prisoners' grievance claims, and keeping relations between inmates and the rest of the institution staff highly formal, may be criticized from the standpoint of their effects upon identifications.[27]

The third hypothesis is that research workers of diverse background are converging on a differential identification type of theory. While the proposition can be tested only by time, illustrations of the trend can be provided from several areas.

1. Psychoanalysts are supplied by adult neurotic patients with a wealth of volunteered verbal data on which to speculate freely. When juvenile

[25] Cf. Sutherland, op. cit., chap. xiii.

[26] Cf. Daniel Glaser, "Testing Correctional Decisions," Journal of Criminal Law, Criminology, and Police Science, XLV (March–April, 1955), 679–84.

[27] A sophisticated analysis of the impact of inmate social systems on correctional programs is presented in Lloyd W. McCorkle and Richard Korn, "Resocialization within Walls," Annals, CXCIII (May, 1954), 88–98; see also Donald Clemmer, The Prison Community (Boston: Christopher Publishing House, 1940); Richard McCleery, "The Strange Journey," University of North Carolina Extension Bulletin, Vol. XXXII (March, 1953).

delinquents are referred to analysts, however, such co-operation is not always forthcoming. Milieu therapy, which developed in part to meet this contingency, requires that the analyst (*a*) live intimately with small groups of delinquents, (*b*) capture his data when manifested in their interaction, and (*c*) exert a therapeutic influence by counseling and manipulating the environment when strategic moments arise. It is interesting that milieu therapists increasingly seem to be forced by their data to interpret their observations and justify their treatment techniques by analysis of simple role expression. Their efforts to fit their data into traditional psychoanalytic frameworks then seem superfluous and the strain obvious. Aichhorn's pioneer discussion of the ego ideal in milieu therapy provides considerable analysis of differential identification in both group and individual delinquency. Redl and Wineman, who drop Aichhorn's postulation of instincts, are even more dependent on role analysis to interpret behavior and to justify therapeutic techniques. When superimposing Freudian conceptions on role analysis, they are forced to contradictory portrayals of the delinquent's reified ego as both weak and strong, depending on which chapter one reads. It is quite easy to reconceptualize their data as illustrating ambivalent and undefined roles in the case of the weak ego, highly organized learned delinquent roles in the case of delinquent egos and superegos, and therapy as a shift of identification from delinquent to non-delinquent persons.[28]

2. The Gluecks once wrote: "It is the presence or absence of certain traits and characteristics in the constitution and early environment of the different offenders which determines . . . what such offenders will ultimately become and what will become of them."[29] This preconception is reflected in their choice of alternative possible explanations of their findings. For example, they have been criticized for dismissing their datum that gang membership was the feature most differentiating delinquents from non-delinquents.[30] It is interesting that, of three of the Glueck's delinquency prediction scales, two based on personality traits and one on early parent-child relationships ("Social Background Scale"), only the latter has been

[28] As another psychoanalytic milieu therapist has put it: "The basic requirement in all education [of delinquents] is that the adult place himself in relation to the child whereby the child accepts him and therefore accepts his social concepts and community values" (S. R. Slavson, *Re-educating the Delinquent through Group and Community Participation* [New York: Harper & Bros., 1954], p. 242. Cf. August Aichhorn, *Wayward Youth* [New York: Viking Press, 1935]; F. Redl and D. Wineman, *Children Who Hate* [Glencoe, Ill.: Free Press, 1951]; and Redl and Wineman, *Controls from Within* [Glencoe, Ill.: Free Press, 1952]).

[29] S. and E. Glueck, *Criminal Careers in Retrospect* (New York: Commonwealth Fund, 1943, p. 285 (original italicized).

[30] Cf. E. W. Burgess, review of Gluecks' *Unravelling Juvenile Delinquency,* in *Federal Probation,* XV (March, 1951), 53–54; A. J. Reiss, Jr., "*Unravelling Juvenile Delinquency*. II. An Appraisal of the Research Methods," *American Journal of Sociology,* LVII (September, 1951), 115–20.

validated.[31] Warm and consistent relationships with parents are the basis for predicting non-delinquency by this scale, for, say the Gluecks, such relationships create personalities free of criminal tendencies. Yet there is no evidence that early personality classifications are as predictive of delinquency as classifications of the social relationships themselves. A more adequate explanation for the predictive value of the data on social relationship may be that warm relationships inside the family strengthen the identifications with it. These latter, which are predominantly non-criminal, compete with the identifications developing from delinquent and criminal contacts.

3. Psychologists studying delinquency have increasingly been forced by their data to focus on peer-group relations rather than on personality traits. Harris, in summarizing research findings, stated:

It is interesting to note that Hart's factor analysis of 25 traits in 300 delinquent boys yielded six factors, at least four of which have a distinct group reference. . . .

There is ample evidence that the delinquent is quite conversant with the wide social code, yet there are suggestions that on an absolute basis as well as on a relative basis his values are scaled somewhat differently than are similar values in the experience of non-delinquents. Much more research is needed, not only on the values that are accepted, but also on the process by which they become "interiorized."[32]

The differential identification theory, we suggest, offers a fruitful theoretical orientation for the fulfilment of the above-mentioned need.

Editors from diverse backgrounds in behavioral science have asserted: "The role concept provides the principal theoretical point of articulation between analyses of the behavior of groups by anthropologists and sociologists and analyses of individual motivation by psychologists and psychiatrists."[33] We have submitted differential identification as a frame of reference for fruitfully integrating criminality theory by giving that theory an image of behavior as role-playing.

[31] Cf. Richard E. Thompson, "A Validation of the Glueck Social Prediction Scale for Proneness to Delinquency," *Journal of Criminal Law, Criminology, and Police Science,* XLIII (November–December, 1952), 451–70; S. Axelrad and S. J. Glick, "Application of the Glueck Social Prediction Table to 100 Jewish Delinquent Boys," *Jewish Social Service Quarterly,* XXX (winter, 1953), 127–36.

[32] Dale B. Harris, "The Socialization of the Delinquent," *Child Development,* XIX (September, 1948), 1943–53.

[33] H. A. Murray, Clyde Kluckhohn, and D. M. Schneider, *Personality in Nature, Society, and Culture* (New York: A. A. Knopf, 1953), p. 361.

9 A Differential Association-Reinforcement Theory of Criminal Behavior

ROBERT L. BURGESS
AND RONALD L. AKERS

INTRODUCTION

In spite of the body of literature that has accumulated around the differential association theory of criminal behavior,[1] it has yet to receive crucial

Reprinted from *Social Problems,* Volume 14, Number 2 (Fall, 1966), 128–147, by permission of The Society for the Study of Social Problems and the authors.

[1] By 1960, Cressey had collected a 70-item bibliography on the theory; see Edwin H. Sutherland and Donald R. Cressey, *Principles of Criminology,* 6th ed., Chicago: J. B. Lippincott Co., 1960, p. vi. He has presented an exhaustive review of the mistaken notions, criticisms, attempted reformulations, and empirical tests of the theory contained in a sizable body of literature. Donald R. Cressey, "Epidemiology and Individual Conduct: A Case from Criminology," *Pacific Sociological Review,* 3 (Fall, 1960), pp. 47–58. For more recent literature see Donald R. Cressey, "The Theory of Differential Association: An Introduction," *Social Problems,* 8 (Summer, 1960), pp. 2–5. James F. Short, Jr., "Differential Association as a Hypothesis: Problems of Empirical Testing," *Social Problems,* 8 (Summer, 1960), pp. 14–25. Henry D. McKay, "Differential Association and Crime Prevention: Problems of Utilization," *Social Problems,* 8 (Summer, 1960), pp. 25–37. Albert J. Reiss, Jr., and A. Lewis Rhodes, "An Empirical Test of Differential Association Theory," *The Journal of Research in Crime and Delinquency,* 1 (January, 1964), pp. 5–18. Harwin L. Voss, "Differential Association and Reported Delinquent Behavior: A Replication," *Social Problems,* 12 (Summer, 1964), pp. 78–85. Siri Naess, "Comparing Theories of Criminogenesis," *The Journal of Research in Crime and Delinquency,* 1 (July, 1964), pp. 171–180. C. R. Jeffery, "Criminal Behavior and Learning Theory," *The Journal of Criminal Law, Criminology and Police Science,* 56 (September, 1965), pp. 294–300.

empirical test or thorough restatement beyond Sutherland's own revision in 1947. Recognizing that the theory is essentially a learning theory, Sutherland rephrased it to state explicitly that criminal behavior is learned as any behavior is learned. In Cressey's two revisions of the textbook, the theory has been deliberately left unchanged from Sutherland's revision. Thus, the theory as it stands now is postulated upon the knowledge of the learning process extant 20–25 years ago.[2]

Sutherland, himself, never was able to test directly or find specific empirical support for his theory, but he was convinced that the two-edged theory—(1) genetic, differential association and (2) structural, differential social organization—accounted for the known data on the full range of crimes, including conventional violations and white-collar crimes.[3] The theory has received some other empirical support,[4] but negative cases have also been found.[5] The attempts to subject the theory to empirical test are marked by inconsistent findings both within the same study and between studies, as well as by highly circumscribed and qualified findings and conclusions. Whether the particular researcher concludes that his findings do or do not seem to support the theory, nearly all have indicated difficulty in operationalizing the concepts and recommend that the theory be modified in such

[2] The original formal statement appeared in Edwin H. Sutherland, *Principles of Criminology,* 3rd ed., Philadelphia: J. B. Lippincott Co., 1939, pp. 4–8. The terms, "systematic" and "consistency" along with some statements referring to social disorganization and culture conflict were deleted in the revised theory. Two sentences stating that criminal behavior is learned were added and the terms "learned" and "learning" were included in other sentences. The modalities of duration, priority, and intensity were added. The revised theory is in Sutherland and Cressey, *op. cit.,* pp. 77–79. For Cressey's discussion of why he left the theory in its 1947 form see *ibid.,* p. vi.

[3] *Ibid.,* pp. 77–80. Edwin H. Sutherland, *White Collar Crime,* New York: Holt, Rinehart and Winston, 1961, pp. 234–256 (originally published 1949). See also Cressey's "Foreword," *ibid.,* p. x.

[4] John C. Ball, "Delinquent and Non-Delinquent Attitudes Toward the Prevalence of Stealing," *The Journal of Criminal Law, Criminology and Police Science,* 48 (September-October, 1957), pp. 259–274. James F. Short, "Differential Association and Delinquency," *Social Problems,* 4, (January, 1957), pp. 233–239. Short, "Differential Association with Delinquent Friends and Delinquent Behavior," *Pacific Sociological Review,* 1 (Spring, 1958, pp. 20–25. Short, "Differential Association as a Hypothesis," *op. cit.* Voss, *op. cit.* Donald R. Cressey, "Application and Verification of the Differential Association Theory," *The Journal of Criminal Law, Criminology and Police Science,* 43 (May-June, 1952), pp. 47–50. Cressey, *Other People's Money,* Glencoe, Ill.: The Free Press, 1953, pp. 147–149. Glaser, *op. cit.,* pp. 7–10.

[5] Marshall Clinard, *The Black Market,* New York: Rinehart Co., 1952, pp. 285–329. Marshall Clinard, "Rural Criminal Offenders," *American Journal of Sociology,* 50 (July, 1944), pp. 38–45. Edwin M. Lemert, "An Isolation and Closure Theory of Naive Check Forgery," *The Journal of Criminal Law, Criminology and Police Science,* 44, (September–October, 1953), pp. 293–307. Reiss and Rhodes, *op. cit.* Cressey, "Application and Verification of the Differential Association Theory," *op. cit.,* pp. 51–52. Cressey, *Other People's Money, op. cit.,* pp. 149–151. Glaser, *op. cit.,* pp. 12–13.

a way that it becomes more amenable to empirical testing.

Suggested theoretical modifications have not been lacking, but the difficulty with these restatements is that they are no more readily operationalized than Sutherland's.[6] One recent paper, however, by DeFleur and Quinney,[7] offers new promise that the theory can be adequately operationalized. They have presented a detailed strategy for making specific deductions for empirical testing. But while they have clarified the problems in the derivation and generation of testable hypotheses from differential association, they still see its empirical validation as a very difficult, though not impossible task.

Regardless of the particular criticisms, the exceptions taken, and the difficulties involved in testing and reformulating the theory that have been offered, few take exception to the central learning assumptions in differential association. If we accept the basic assumption that criminal behavior is learned by the same processes and involves the same mechanisms as conforming behavior, then we need to recognize and make use of the current knowledge about these processes and mechanisms. Neither the extant statement of the theory nor the reformulations of it make explicit the nature of the underlying learning process involved in differential association. In short, no major revisions have been made utilizing established learning principles.

That this type of revision of the theory is needed has been recognized and some criticism of differential association has revolved around the fact that it does not adequately portray the process by which criminal behavior is learned. But as Cressey explains:

> It is one thing to criticise the theory for failure to specify the learning process accurately and another to specify which aspects of the learning process should be included and in what way.[8]

Sutherland, of course, was as interested in explaining the "epidemiology" of crime as in explaining how the individual comes to engage in behavior in violation of the law and insisted that the two explanations must be consistent.[9] Differential social organization (normative conflict) has been successful in "making sense" of variations in crime rates. But differential

---

[6] See Daniel Glaser, "Criminality Theories and Behavioral Images," *American Journal of Sociology,* 61 (March, 1956), pp. 433–444. Glaser, "Differential Association and Criminological Prediction," *op. cit.,* pp. 10–13. Naess, *op. cit.,* pp. 174–179.

[7] Melvin DeFleur and Richard Quinney, "A Reformulation of Sutherland's Differential Association Theory and a Strategy for Empirical Verification," *Journal of Research in Crime and Delinquency,* 3 (January, 1966), p. 13.

[8] Cressey, "Epidemiology and Individual Conduct," *op. cit.,* p. 54.

[9] Sutherland and Cressey, *op. cit.,* p. 80. Albert K. Cohen, Alfred R. Lindesmith, and Karl F. Schuessler (eds.), *The Sutherland Papers,* Bloomington: Indiana University Publications, Social Science Series, No. 15, 1956, pp. 5–42. That Sutherland intended an explanation of the two-fold problem of rates of crime and individual criminal behavior is, of course, the basic point of Cressey's paper, "Epidemiology and Individual Conduct," *op. cit.*

association has been less successful in explicating the process by which this differential organization produces individual criminality. This seems to be due not to the lack of importance of associations for criminal behavior but:

> . . . rather to the fact that the theory outran the capacity of either psychology or social psychology to give adequate, scientific answers to the question of why there are such qualitative (selective) differences in human association.[10]

It now appears, however, that there is a body of verified theory which is adequate to the task of accurately specifying this process. Modern learning theory seems capable of providing insights into the problem of uniting structural and genetic formulations. While sociologists know a great deal about the structure of the environment from which deviants come, we know very little about the determining variables operating within this environment. The burden of criminological theory today is to combine knowledge of structural pressures with explanations of "why only *some* of the persons on whom this pressure is exerted become non-conformists."[11]

It is for this reason that the recent effort by C. R. Jeffery to re-examine differential association in light of modern learning theory marks a new departure in the abundance of thinking and writing that has characterized the intellectual history of this theory.[12] In spite of their intricate axiomatization of the theory, DeFleur and Quinney, for example, recognize that even they have left the learning process in differential association unspecified. But, they note, "modern reinforcement learning theory would handle this problem. . . ."[13] This is precisely what Jeffery proposed to do and to the extent that this objective is served by discussing learning theory and criminal behavior together, he is at least partially successful. However, Jeffery does not in fact make it clear just how Sutherland's differential association theory may be revised. His explanation incorporates differential reinforcement:

> . . . [A] criminal act occurs in an environment in which in the past the actor has been reinforced for behaving in this manner, and the aversive consequences attached to the behavior have been of such a nature that they do not control or prevent the response.[14]

This statement, as it stands, bears no obvious or direct relation to Sutherland's differential association, and nowhere else does Jeffery make it clear how differential reinforcement is a reformulation of differential association. Jeffery does discuss modern learning principles but he does not show how

---

[10] George B. Vold, *Theoretical Criminology*, New York: Oxford University Press, 1958, p. 198.

[11] Cressey, "The Theory of Differential Association," *op. cit.*, p. 5.

[12] Jeffery, *op. cit.*

[13] DeFleur and Quinney, *op. cit.*, p. 3.

[14] *Ibid*, p. 295.

these principles may be incorporated within the framework of Sutherland's theory, nor how these principles may lead to explanations of past empirical findings.

Jeffery's theory and his discussion of criminal behavior and learning theory remains not so much incorrect as unconvincing. His presentation of learning principles is supported wholly by reference to experiments with lower organisms and his extension to criminal behavior is mainly through anecdotal and illustrative material. The potential value and impact of Jeffery's article is diminished by not calling attention to the already large and growing body of literature in experimental behavioral science, especially evidence using human subjects, that has direct implications for differential association theory. We are basically in agreement with Jeffery that learning theory has progressed to the point where it seems likely that differential association can be restated in a more sophisticated and testable form in the language of modern learning theory. But that restatement must be attempted in a thorough fashion before we can expect others to accept it. Jeffery begins to do this and his thoughts are significant, but they do not take into account the theory as a whole.

The amount of empirical research in the social psychology of learning clearly has shown that the concepts in learning theory are susceptible to operationalization. Therefore, applying an integrated set of learning principles to differential association theory should adequately provide the revision needed for empirical testing. These learning principles are based on literally thousands of experimental hours covering a wide range of the phylogenetic scale and more nearly constitute empirically derived *laws* of behavior than any other set of principles. They enable the handling of a great variety of observational as well as experimental evidence about human behavior.

It is the purpose of this paper to take the first step in the direction to which Jeffery points. A restatement of the theory, not an alternative theory, will be presented, although, of necessity, certain ideas not intrinsic to differential association will have to be introduced and additions will be made to the original propositions. It should be pointed out that DeFleur and Quinney have been able to demonstrate that Sutherland's propositions when stated in the form of set theory, appear to be internally consistent. By arranging the propositions in axiomatic form, stating them in logical rather than verbal symbols, they have brought the theoretical grammar up to date.[15] Such is not our intention in this paper, at all. We recognize and appreciate the importance of stating the propositions in a formal, deductive fashion. We do feel, however, that this task is, at the present time, subsidiary to the more urgent task of: (1) making explicit the learning process, as it is now understood by modern behavioral science, from which the propositions of differential association can be derived; (2) fully reformulating the theory,

---

[15] DeFleur and Quinney, *op. cit.*

statement by statement, in light of the current knowledge of this learning process; and (3) helping criminologists become aware of the advances in learning theory and research that are directly relevant to an explanation of criminal behavior.[16] No claim is made that this constitutes a final statement. If it has any seminal value at all, that is, if it provokes a serious new look at the theory and encourages further effort in this direction, our objective will have been served.

DIFFERENTIAL ASSOCIATION AND MODERN BEHAVIOR THEORY

In this section the nine formal propositions in which Sutherland expressed his theory will be analyzed in terms of behavior theory and research and will be reformulated as seven new propositions. (See Table 1.)

I. "Criminal behavior is learned." VIII. "The process of learning criminal behavior by association with criminal and anti-criminal patterns involves all of the mechanisms that are involved in any other learning."

Since both the first and eighth sentences in the theory obviously form a unitary idea, it seems best to state them together. Sutherland was aware that these statements did not sufficiently describe the learning process,[17] but these two items leave no doubt that differential association theory was meant to fit into a general explanation of human behvior and, as much is unambiguously stated in the prefatory remarks of the theory: an "explanation of criminal behavior should be a specific part of a general theory of behavior."[18] Modern behavior theory as a general theory provides us with a good idea of what the mechanisms are that are involved in the process of acquiring behavior.[19]

---

[16] Our main concern here, of course, is with the nine statements of the theory as a genetic explanation of the process by which the individual comes to engage in illegal behavior. We do not lose sight of the fact, however, that this must be integrated with explanations of the variation and location of crime.

[17] Cressey, 1960, *op. cit.,* p. 54.

[18] Sutherland and Cressey, *op. cit.,* p. 75.

[19] It should be mentioned at the outset that there is more than one learning theory. The one we will employ is called Behavior Theory. More specifically, it is that variety of behavior theory largely associated with the name of B. F. Skinner. (*Science and Human Behavior,* New York: Macmillan, 1953.) It differs from other learning theories in that it restricts itself to the relations between observable, measurable behavior and observable, measurable conditions. There is nothing in this theory that denies the existence, or importance, or even the inherent interest of the nervous system or brain. However, most behavioral scientists in this area are extremely careful in hypothesizing intervening variables or constructs, whether they are egos, personalities, response sets, or some sort of internal computers. Generally they adopt the position that the only real value of a construct is its ability to improve one's predictions. If it does not, then it must be excluded in accordance with the rule of parsimony.

According to this theory, there are two major categories of behavior. On the one hand, there is reflexive or *respondent* behavior which is behavior that is governed by the stimuli that elicit it. Such behaviors are largely associated with the autonomic system. The work of Pavlov is of special significance here. On the other hand, there is *operant* behavior: behavior which involves the central nervous system. Examples of operant behavior include verbal behavior, playing ball, driving a car, and buying a new suit. It has been found that this class of behavior is a function of its past and present environmental consequences. Thus, when a particular operant is followed by certain kinds of stimuli, that behavior's frenquency of occurrence will increase in the future. These stimuli are called reinforcing stimuli or re-inforcers[20] and include food, money, clothes, objects of various sorts, social attention, approval, affection and social status. This entire process is called positive reinforcement. One distinguishing characteristic of operant behavior as opposed to respondent behavior, then, is that the latter is a function of its antecedent stimuli, whereas the former is a function of its antecedent environmental consequences.

Typically, operant and respondent behaviors occur together in an individual's everyday behavior, and they interact in extremely intricate ways. Consequently, to fully understand any set of patterned responses, the investigator should observe the effects of the operants on the respondents as well as the effects of the respondents on the operants. The connections between operant and respondent behaviors are especially crucial to an analysis of attitudes, emotional and conflict behaviors.

In everyday life, different consequences are usually contingent upon different classes of behavior. This relationship between behavior and its consequences functions to alter the rate and form of behavior as well as its relationship to many features of the environment. The process of operant reinforcement is the most important process by which behavior is generated and maintained. There are, in fact, six possible environmental consequences

[20] It has been said by some that a tautology is involved here. But there is nothing tautological about classifying events in terms of their effects. As Skinner, *op. cit.,* pp. 72–73, has noted, this criterion is both empirical and objective. There is only one sure way of telling whether or not a given stimulus event is reinforcing to a given individual under given conditions and that is to make a direct test: observe the frequency of a selected behavior, then make a stimulus event contingent upon it and observe any change in frequency. If there is a change in frequency then we may classify the stimulus as reinforcing to the individual under the stated conditions. Our reasoning would become circular, however, if we went on to assert that a given stimulus strengthens the behavior *because* it is reinforcing. Furthermore, not all stimuli, when presented, will increase the frequency of the behavior which *produced* them. Some stimuli will increase the frequency of the behavior which *removes* them, still others will neither strengthen nor weaken the behavior which produced them. See Robert L. Burgess, Ronald L. Akers, "Are Operant Principles Tautological?" *The Psychological Record,* 16 (July, 1966), pp. 305–312.

relative to the Law of Operant Behavior. (1) A behavior may produce certain stimulus events and thereby increase in frequency. As we have indicated above, such stimuli are called positive reinforcers and the process is called positive reinforcement. (2) A behavior may remove, avoid, or terminate certain stimulus events and thereby increase in frequency. Such stimuli are termed negative reinforcers and the process, negative reinforcement. (3) A behavior may produce certain stimulus events and thereby decrease in frequency. Such stimuli are called aversive stimuli or, more recently, punishers.[21] The entire behavior process is called positive punishment. (4) A behavior may remove or terminate certain stimulus events and thereby decrease in frequency. Such stimuli are positive reinforcers and the process is termed negative punishment. (5) A behavior may produce or remove certain stimulus events which do not change the behavior's frequency at all. Such stimuli are called neutral stimuli. (6) A behavior may no longer produce customary stimulus events and thereby decrease in frequency. The stimuli which are produced are neutral stimuli, and the process, extinction. When a reinforcing stimulus no longer functions to increase the future probability of the behavior which produced it, we say the individual is satiated. To restore the reinforcing property of the stimulus we need only deprive the individual of it for a time.[22]

The increase in the frequency of occurrence of a behavior that is reinforced is the very property of reinforcement that permits the fascinating variety and subtlety that occur in operant as opposed to respondent behavior. Another process producing the variety we see in behavior is that of *conditioning*. When a primary or unconditioned reinforcing stimulus such as food is repeatedly paired with a neutral stimulus, the latter will eventually function as a reinforcing stimulus as well. An illustration of this would be as follows. The milk a mother feeds to her infant is an unconditioned reinforcer. If the food is repeatedly paired with social attention, affection, and approval, these latter will eventually become reinforcing as will the mother herself as a stimulus object. Later these *conditioned reinforcers* can be used to strengthen other behaviors by making these reinforcers contingent upon those new behaviors.

Differential reinforcement may also alter the form of a response. This process is called *shaping* or *response differentiation*. It can be exemplified by a child learning to speak. At first, the parent will reinforce any vocalization, but as time wears on, and as the child grows older, the parent will differen-

[21] N. H. Azrin and D. F. Hake, "Conditioned Punishment," *Journal of the Experimental Analysis of Behavior,* 8 (September, 1965), pp. 279–293.

[22] See Jacob L. Gewirtz and Donald M. Baer, "Deprivation and Satiation of Social Reinforcers as Drive Conditions," *Journal of Abnormal and Social Psychology,* 57, 1958, pp. 165–172.

tially reinforce only those responses which successfully approximate certain criteria. The child will be seen to proceed from mere grunts to "baby-talk" to articulate speech.[23]

Of course, organisms, whether pigeons, monkeys or people, do not usually go around behaving in all possible ways at all possible times. In short, behavior does not occur in a vacuum; a given behavior is appropriate to a given situation. By appropriate we mean that reinforcement has been forthcoming only under certain conditions and it is under these conditions that the behavior will occur. In other words, differential reinforcement not only increases the probability of a response, it also makes that response more probable upon the recurrence of conditions the same as or similar to those that were present during previous reinforcements. Such a process is called *stimulus control* or *stimulus discrimination*. For example, a child when he is first taught to say "daddy" may repeat it when any male is present, or even, in the very beginning, when any adult is present. But through differential reinforcement, the child will eventually only speak the word "daddy" when his father is present or in other "appropriate" conditions. We may say that the father, as a stimulus object, functions as a discriminative stimulus (S^D) setting the occasion for the operant verbal response "daddy" because in the past such behavior has been reinforced under such conditions.

It has also been discovered that the pattern or schedule of reinforcement is as important as the amount of reinforcement. For example, a *fixed-interval* schedule of reinforcement, where a response is reinforced only after a certain amount of time has passed, produces a lower rate of response than that obtained with reinforcement based on a fixed-ratio schedule where a response is reinforced only after a certain number of responses have already been emitted. Similarly a response rate obtained with a fixed-ratio schedule is lower than that obtained with a *variable-ratio* schedule, where reinforcement occurs for a certain proportion of responses randomly varied about some central value. A schedule of reinforcement, then, refers to the response *contingencies* upon which reinforcement depends. All of the various schedules of reinforcement, besides producing lawful response characteristics, produce lawful extinction rates, once reinforcement is discontinued. Briefly, behavior reinforced on an intermittent schedule takes longer to extinguish than behavior reinforced on a continuous schedule.

This concept, schedules of reinforcement, is one the implications of which are little understood by many behavioral scientists, so a few additional words are in order. First of all, social reinforcements are for the most part

[23] This seems to be the process involved in learning to become a marihuana user. By successive approximations, the user learns (from others) to close on the appropriate techniques and effects of using marihuana. See Howard S. Becker, *Outsiders*, Glencoe, Ill.: The Free Press, 1963, pp. 41–58.

intermittent. One obvious result of this fact is the resistance to extinction and satiation of much social behavior, desirable as well as undesirable. This is not peculiar to human social behavior, for even lower organisms seldom are faced with a continuous reinforcement schedule. Nevertheless, reinforcements mediated by another organism are probably much less reliable than those produced by the physical environment. This is the case because social reinforcement depends upon behavioral processes in the reinforcer which are not under good control by the reinforcee. A more subtle, though essentially methodological, implication of this is that because most social behaviors are maintained by complex intermittent schedules which have been shaped over a long period of time, a social observer, newly entering a situation may have extreme difficulty in immediately determining exactly what is maintaining a particular behavior or set of behaviors. Nor can the individual himself be expected to be able to identify his own contingencies of reinforcement.[24]

An important aspect of this theory is the presentation of the general ways that stimuli and responses can be formed into complex constellations of stimulus-response events. Although the basic principles are simple and must be separated to distinguish and study them, in actual life the principles function in concert, and consist of complex arrays and constellations.[25] Such complexity can be seen in the fact that single S-R events may be combined into sequences on the basis of conditioning principles. That is, responses can be thought to have stimulus properties. In addition, more than one response may come under the control of a particular stimulus. Thus, when the stimulus occurs, it will tend to set the occasion for the various responses that have been conditioned to it. These responses may be competitive, that is, only one or the other can occur. When this is so, the particular response which does occur may also depend upon other discriminative stimuli present in the situation that control only one or the other response. Finally, while some of the stimuli to which an individual responds emanate from the external environment, social and otherwise, some come from his own behavior. An individual is, then, not only a source of responses, he is also a source of some stimuli—stimuli that can affect his own behavior.

The most general behavioral principle is the Law of Operant Behavior which says that behavior is a function of its past and current environmental consequences. There have been numerous studies with children[26] as well as

---

[24] Cressey encountered this problem in trying to get trust violators to reconstruct past associations. Cressey, *Other People's Money, op. cit.,* p. 149.

[25] Arthur Staats, "An Integrated-Functional Learning Approach to Complex Human Behavior," *Technical Report 28,* Contract ONR and Arizona State University, 1965.

[26] See, for example, S. W. Bijou and P. T. Sturges, "Positive Reinforcers for Experimental Studies with Children—Consumables and Manipulatables," *Child Development,* 30, 1959, pp. 151–170.

adults[27] which indicate that individual behavior conforms to this law. Of much more interest to sociologists is an experiment designed by Azrin and Lindsley in 1956[28] to investigate cooperative social behavior. Their study demonstrated that cooperative behavior could be developed, maintained, eliminated and reinstated solely through the manipulation of the contingency between reinforcing stimuli and the cooperative response. This basic finding has received much subsequent support. It has also been demonstrated that not only cooperative behavior, but also competitive behavior and leading and following behavior are a function of their past and present consequences.

Another of the behavioral principles we mentioned was that of stimulus discrimination. A discriminative stimulus is a stimulus in the presence of which a particular operant response is reinforced. Much of our behavior has come under the control of certain environmental, including social, stimuli because in the past it has been reinforced in the presence of those stimuli. In an experiment by Donald Cohen,[29] a normal 13-year-old boy named Justin, when placed under identical experimental conditions emitted different behaviors depending upon whether his partner was his mother, brother, sister, friend, or a stranger. The results of this investigation demonstrated that Justin's social behavior was differentially controlled by reinforcement; but it also demonstrated that his behavior was different depending upon the social stimuli present, thus reaffirming the principle of stimulus discrimination. In other words, the dynamic properties of his social behavior, whether cooperative, competitive, leading or following, were controlled by his previous extra-experimental history with his teammates, although the experimenter could change those behaviors by experimentally altering the contingencies of reinforcement. It is, of course, almost a truism to say that an individual behaves differently in the presence of different people. The significance of this experiment, however, is that the investigator was able to isolate the determining variables and the principles by which they operated to produce this common phenomenon.

While this is by no means a complete survey of the relevant experimental tests of the behavioral principles outlined above, it may serve to point out that many forms of "normal" social behavior function according to the Law of Operant Behavior. But what about "deviant" behavior? Can we be sure these same principles are operating here? Unfortunately there have been no studies which attempt to test directly the relevance of these behavioral

[27] J. G. Holland, "Human Vigilance," *Science,* 128, 1959, pp. 61–67; Harold Weiner, "Conditioning History and Human Fixed-Interval Performance," *Journal of the Experimental Analysis of Behavior,* 7 (September, 1964), pp. 383–385.

[28] N. H. Azrin and O. R. Lindsley, "The Reinforcement of Cooperation Between Children," *The Journal of Abnormal and Social Psychology,* 52 (January, 1956).

[29] Donald J. Cohen, "Justin and His Peers: An Experimental Analysis of a Child's Social World," *Child Development,* 33, 1962.

principles to criminal behavior. But there have been several experimental investigations of deviant behaviors emitted by mental patients. For example, in a study by Ayllon and Michael,[30] it was shown that the bizarre behaviors of psychotics functioned according to these learning principles. In this particular study various behavioral problems of psychotic patients were "cured" through the manipulation of reinforcement contingencies. Such principles as extinction, negative and positive reinforcement, and satiation were effectively utilized to eliminate the unwanted behaviors.[31] This study was one of the first experimental tests of the contention that not only conforming but also many unusual, inappropriate, or undesirable behaviors are shaped and maintained through social reinforcement. In another experiment Isaacs, Thomas, and Goldiamond[32] demonstrate that complex adjustive behaviors can be operantly conditioned in long-term psychotics by manipulating available reinforcers.

In yet another investigation,[33] the personnel of a mental hospital ward for schizophrenics recorded the behavior of the patients and provided consequences to it according to certain pre-established procedures. Without going into the many important details of this long investigation, we may note that in each of the six experiments that were carried out, the results demonstrate that reinforcement was effective in maintaining desired performances, even though these were "back-ward" psychotics who had resisted all previous therapy, including psychoanalysis, electroshock therapy, lobotomies and so forth.

In each experiment, the performance fell to a near zero level when the established response-reinforcement relation was discontinued. . . . The standard procedure for reinforcement had been to provide tokens . . . [exchanged] for a variety of reinforcers. Performance deceased when this response-reinforcement relation was disrupted (1) by delivering tokens independntly of the response while still allowing exchange of tokens for the reinforcers (Exp II and III), (2) by discontinuing the token system entirely but providing continuing access to the reinforcers (Exp IV), or (3) by discontinuing the delivery of tokens for a previously reinforced response while simultaneously providing tokens for a different, alternative response (Exp I and VI). Further, the effectiveness of the reinforcement

[30] T. Ayllon and J. Michael, "The Psychiatric Nurse, as a Behavioral Engineer," *Journal of the Experimental Analysis of Behavior,* 2, 1959, pp. 323–334.

[31] There is, of course, no intention on our part to equate "mental" illness or similarly severe behavior problems with criminal behavior. The only connection that we are making is that both may be seen to function according to the same basic behavioral principles and both may be in opposition to established norms.

[32] W. Isaacs, J. Thomas, and I. Goldiamond, "Application of Operant Conditioning to Reinstate Verbal Behavior in Psychotics," *Journal of Speech and Disorders,* 25, 1960, pp. 8–12.

[33] T. Ayllon and N. Azrin, "The Measurement and Reinforcement of Behavior of Psychotics," *Journal of the Experimental Analysis of Behavior,* 8 (November, 1965), pp. 357–383.

procedure did not appear to be limited to an all-or-none basis. Patients selected and performed the assignment that provided the larger number of tokens when reinforcement was available for more than one assignment (Exp V).[34]

Again, we cannot review all of the relevant literature, yet perhaps the three investigations cited will serve to emphasize that many forms of deviant behavior are shaped and maintained by various contingencies of reinforcement.[35] Given this experimental evidence we would amend Sutherland's first and eighth propositions to read: I. *Criminal behavior is learned according to the principles of operant conditioning.*

II. "Criminal behavior is learned in interaction with other persons in the process of communication."

As DeFleur and Quinney have noted, the major implication of this proposition is that symbolic interaction is a necessary condition for the learning of criminal behavior.[36] Of direct relevance to this is an experiment designed to test the relative significance of verbal instructions and reinforcement contingencies in generating and maintaining a certain class of behaviors.[37] In brief, the results indicated that behavior could not be maintained solely through verbal instructions. However, it was also discovered that it was an extremely arduous task to shape a set of complex behaviors without using verbal instructions as discriminative stimuli. Behavior was quickly and effectively developed and maintained by a combination of verbal instructions *and* reinforcement consequences. Symbolic interaction is, then, not enough, contingencies of reinforcement must also be present.

From the perspective of modern behavior theory, two aspects of socialization are usually considered to distinguish it from other processes of behavioral change: (1) Only those behavioral changes occurring through learning are considered relevant; (2) only the changes in behavior having their origins in interaction with other persons are considered products of socialization.[38] Sutherland's theory may, then, be seen to be a theory of differential socialization since he, too, restricted himself to learning having its origin in interaction with other persons. While social learning is, indeed, important and even predominant, it certainly does not exhaust the learning process. In

[34] *Ibid,* p. 381.

[35] See also H. J. Eysenck (ed.), *Experiments in Behavior Therapy,* New York: Pergamon Press, The Macmillan Company, 1964. L. Krasner and L. Ullman, *Research in Behavior Modification,* New York: Holt, Rinehart and Winston, 1965. L. Ullman and L. Krasner, *Case Studies in Behavior Modification,* New York: Holt, Rinehart and Winston, 1964.

[36] DeFleur and Quinney, *op. cit.,* p. 3.

[37] T. Ayllon and N. Azrin, "Reinforcement and Instructions with Mental Patients," *Journal of the Experimental Analysis of Behavior,* 7, 1964, pp. 327–331.

[38] Paul E. Secord and Carl W. Backman, *Social Psychology,* New York: McGraw-Hill, 1964.

short, we may learn (and, thus, our behavior would be modified) without any direct contact with another person. As such, Sutherland's theory may be seen to suffer from a significant lacuna in that it neglected the possibility of deviant behavior being learned in nonsocial situations. Consequently, to be an adequate theory of deviant behavior, the theory must be amended further to include those forms of deviant behavior that are learned in the absence of social reinforcement. Other people are not the only source of reinforcement although they are the most important. As Jeffery[39] has aptly noted, stealing is reinforcing in and by itself whether other people know about it and reinforce it socially or not. The same may be said to apply to many forms of aggressive behaviors.[40]

There are many studies which are relevant to social interaction and socialization on the one hand, and Sutherland's second proposition on the other. For example, in a study by Lott and Lott[41] it was found that when child A was reinforced in the presence of child B, child A would later select child B as a companion. The behavior selecting child B was not the behavior that was reinforced. The experimental conditions simply paired child B with positive reinforcement. In accordance with the principle of conditioning, child B had become a conditioned positive reinforcer. As such any behavior which produced the presence of child B would be strengthened, such behaviors, for example, as verbal responses requesting child B's company. Thus, as Staats[42] has noted, the results of this study indicate that the concepts of reinforcing stimuli and group cohesion are related when analyzed in terms of an integrated set of learning principles.

Glaser[43] has attempted to reformulate Sutherland's differential association theory in terms of social identification. It should be recognized, however, that identification as well as modeling and imitative behavior (which are usually associated with identification) comprise just one feature of the socialization process. Furthermore, such behavior may be analyzed quite parsimoniously with the principles of modern behavior theory. For example, in a study by Bandura and Ross,[44] a child experienced the pairing of one

---

[39] Jeffery, op. cit.

[40] For some evidence that aggressive behavior may be of a respondent as well as an operant nature, see N. Azrin, R. Hutchinson, and R. McLaughlin, "The Opportunity for Aggression as an Operant Reinforcer during Aversive Stimulation," *Journal of the Experimental Analysis of Behavior,* 8 (May, 1965), pp. 171–180.

[41] B. E. Lott and A. J. Lott, "The Formation of Positive Attitudes Toward Group Members," *The Journal of Abnormal and Social Psychology,* 61, 1960, pp. 297–300.

[42] Arthur Staats, *Human Learning,* New York: Holt, Rinehart and Winston, 1964, p. 333.

[43] Glaser, "Criminality Theories and Behavioral Images," *op. cit.*

[44] A. Bandura, D. Ross, and S. Ross, "A Comparative Test of the Status Envy, Social Power and the Secondary Reinforcement Theories of Identification Learning," *Journal of Abnormal and Social Psychology,* 67, 1963, pp. 527–534.

adult with positive reinforcers. Presumably this adult would become a conditioned reinforcer. And indeed, later it was found that the child imitated this adult more than he did an adult who was not paired with positive reinforcers. That is, the one adult, as he became a stronger reinforcer, had also become a stronger S^D for imitating or following behavior. Thus, Bandura and Ross's results demonstrate that imitating or following behavior is at least in part a function of the reinforcing value of people as social stimuli.

On the basis of these results it is suggested that a change in the reinforcing value of an individual will change his power as a stimulus controlling other people's behavior in various ways. An increase in the reinforcing value of an individual will increase verbal and motor approach, or companionable responses, respectful responses, affectionate behavior, following behavior, smiling, pleasant conversation, sympathetic responses and the like.[45]

The relevance of these studies is that they have isolated some of the determining variables whereby the behavior of one person is influenced or changed by the behavior of another as well as the principles by which these variables operate. We have, of course, only scratched the surface. Many other variables are involved. For instance, not all people are equally effective in controlling or influencing the behavior of others. The person who can mediate the most reinforcers will exercise the most power. Thus, the parent, who controls more of his child's reinforcers, will exercise more power than an older sibling or the temporary "baby sitter." As the child becomes older and less dependent upon the parent for many of his reinforcers, other individuals or groups such as his peers may exercise more power. Carrying the analysis one step further, the person who has access to a large range of aversive stimuli will exert more power than one who has not. Thus a peer group may come to exercise more power over a child's behavior than the parent even though the parent may still control a large share of the child's positive reinforcers.

In addition to the reinforcing function of an individual or group, there is, as seen in the Cohen and the Bandura and Ross studies, the discriminative stimulus function of a group. For example, specific individuals as physical stimuli may acquire discriminative control over an individual's behavior. The child in our example above is reinforced for certain kinds of behaviors in the presence of his parent, thus the parent's presence may come to control this type of behavior. He is reinforced for different behaviors in the presence of his peers, who then come to set the occasion for this type of behavior. Consequently this proposition must be amended to read: II. *Criminal behavior is learned both in nonsocial situations that are reinforcing or discrimina-*

[45] Staats, 1964, *op. cit.,* p. 333.

tive, and through that social interaction in which the behavior of other persons is reinforcing or discriminative for criminal behavior.

III. "The principal part of the learning of criminal behavior occurs within intimate personal groups."

In terms of our analysis, the primary group would be seen to be the major source of an individual's social reinforcements. The bulk of behavioral training which the child receives occurs at a time when the trainers, usually the parents, possess a very powerful system of reinforcers. In fact, we might characterize a primary group as a generalized reinforcer (one associated with many reinforcers, conditioned as well as unconditioned). And, as we suggested above, as the child grows older, groups other than the family may come to control a majority of an individual's reinforcers, e.g., the adolescent peer group.

To say that the primary group is the principal molder of an individual's behavioral repertoire is not to ignore social learning which may occur in other contexts. As we noted above, learning from social models can be adequately explained in terms of these behavioral principles. The analysis we employed there can also be extended to learning from the mass media and from "reference" groups. In any case, we may alter this proposition to read: III. *The principal part of the learning of criminal behavior occurs in those groups which comprise the individual's major source of reinforcements.*

IV. "When criminal behavior is learned, the learning includes (a) techniques of committing the crime, which are sometimes very complicated, sometimes very simple; (b) the specific direction of motives, drives, rationalizations, and attitudes."

A study by Klaus and Glaser[46] as well as many other studies[47] indicate that reinforcement contingencies are of prime importance in learning various behavioral techniques. And, of course, many techniques, both simple and complicated, are specific to a particular deviant act such as jimmying, picking locks of buildings and cars, picking pockets, short- and big-con techniques, counterfeiting and safe-cracking. Other techniques in criminal behavior may be learned in conforming or neutral contexts, e.g., driving a car, signing checks, shooting a gun, etc. In any event, we need not alter the first part of this proposition.

The second part of this proposition does, however, deserve some additional comments. Sutherland's major focus here seems to be motivation.

[46] D. J. Klaus and R. Glaser, "Increasing Team Proficiency Through Training," Pittsburgh: American Institute of Research, 1960.

[47] See Robert L. Burgess, "Communication Networks and Behavioral Consequences," forthcoming.

Much of what we have already discussed in this paper often goes under the general heading of motivation. The topic of motivation is as important as it is complex. This complexity is related to the fact that the same stimulus may have two functions: it may be both a reinforcing stimulus and a discriminative stimulus controlling the behavior which is followed by reinforcement.[48] Thus, motivation may be seen to be a function of the processes by which stimuli acquire conditioned reinforcing value and become discriminative stimuli. Reinforcers and discriminative stimuli here would become the dependent variables; the independent variables would be the conditioning procedures previously mentioned and the level of deprivation. For example, when a prisoner is deprived of contact with members of the opposite sex, such sex reinforcers will become much more powerful. Thus, those sexual reinforcers that are available, such as homosexual contact, would come to exert a great deal of influence and would shape behaviors that would be unlikely to occur without such deprivation. And, without going any further into this topic, some stimuli may be more reinforcing, under similar conditions of deprivation, for certain individuals or groups than for others. Furthermore, the satiation of one or more of these reinforcers would allow for an increase in the relative strength of others.

Much, therefore, can be learned about the distinctive characteristics of a group by knowing what the available and effective reinforcers are and the behaviors upon which they are contingent. Basically, we are contending that the nature of the reinforcer system and the reinforcement contingencies are crucial determinants of individual and group behavior. Consequently, a description of an individual's or group's reinforcers, and an understanding of the principles by which reinforcers affect behavior, would be expected to yield a great deal of knowledge about individual and group deviant behavior.

Finally, the rationalizations which Cressey identifies with regard to trust violators and the peculiar extensions of "defenses to crimes" or "tech-

---

[48] A central principle underlying this analysis is that reinforcing stimuli, both positive and negative, elicit certain respondents. Unconditioned reinforcers elicit these responses without training, conditioned reinforcers elicit such responses through respondent conditioning. Staats and Staats (*Complex Human Behavior,* New York: Holt, Rinehart and Winston, 1964) have characterized such respondents as "attitude" responses. Thus, a positive reinforcer elicits a positive attitude. Furthermore, these respondents have stimulus characteristics which may become discriminative stimuli setting the occasion for a certain class of operants called "striving" responses for positive reinforcers and escape and/or avoidance behaviors for negative reinforcers. These respondents and their attendant stimuli may be generalized to other reinforcing stimuli. Thus, striving responses can be seen to generalize to new positive reinforcers since these also will elicit the respondent responses and their characteristic stimuli which have become S^D's for such behavior.

niques of neutralization" by which deviant behavior is justified, as identified by Sykes and Matza,[49] may be analyzed as operant behaviors of the escape or avoidance type which are maintained because they have the effect of avoiding or reducing the punishment that comes from social disapproval by oneself as well as by others. We may, therefore, rewrite this proposition to read: IV. *The learning of criminal behavior, including specific techniques, attitudes, and avoidance procedures, is a function of the effective and available reinforcers, and the existing reinforcement contingencies.*

V. "The specific direction of motives and drives is learned from definitions of the legal codes as favorable or unfavorable."

In this proposition, Sutherland appears to be referring, at least in part, to the concept "norm" which may be defined as a statement made by a number of the members of a group, not necessarily all of them, prescribing or proscribing certain behaviors at certain times.[50] We often infer what the norms of a group are by observing reaction to behavior, i.e., the sanctions applied to, or reinforcement and punishment consequences of, such behavior. We may also learn what a group's norms are through verbal or written statements. The individual group member also learns what is and is not acceptable behavior on the basis of verbal statements made by others, as well as through the sanctions (i.e., the reinforcing or aversive stimuli) applied to his behavior (and other norm violators) by others.

Behavior theory specifies the place of normative statements and sanctions in the dynamics of acquiring "conforming" or "normative" behavior. Just as the behavior and even the physical characteristics of the individual may serve discriminative functions, verbal behavior, and this includes normative statements, can be analyzed as S^D's. A normative statement can be analyzed as an S^D indicating that the members of a group ought to behave in a certain way in certain circumstances. Such "normative" behavior would be developed and maintained by social reinforcement. As we observed in the Ayllon-Azrin study[51] of instructions and reinforcement contingencies, such verbal behavior would not maintain any particular class of behaviors if it were not at least occasionally backed by reinforcement consequences. Extending their analysis, an individual would not "conform" to a norm if he did not have a past history of reinforcement for such conforming behavior. This is important, for earlier we stated that we can learn a great deal about a group by knowing what the effective reinforcers are and the behaviors

[49] Cressey, *Other People's Money, op. cit.,* pp. 93–138. G. M. Sykes and David Matza, "Techniques of Neutralization: A Theory of Delinquency," *American Sociological Review,* 22 (December, 1957), pp. 664–670.

[50] George C. Homans, *Social Behavior: Its Elemetary Forms,* New York: Harcourt, Brace and World, 1961.

[51] Ayllon-Azrin, 1964, *op. cit.*

upon which they are contingent. We may now say that we can learn a great deal about an individual's or a group's behavior when we are able to specify, not only what the effective reinforcers are, but also what the rules or norms are by which these reinforcers are applied.[52] For these two types of knowledge will tell us much about the types of behavior that the individual will develop or the types of behaviors that are dominant in a group.

For example, it has often been noted that most official criminal acts are committed by members of minority groups who live in slums. One distinguishing characteristic of a slum is the high level of deprivation of many important social reinforcers. Exacerbating this situation is the fact that these people, in contrast to other groups, lack the behavioral repertoires necessary to produce reinforcement in the prescribed ways. They have not been and are not now adequately reinforced for lawful or normative behavior. And as we know from the Law of Operant Reinforcement, a reinforcer will increase the rate of occurrence of any operant which produces it. Furthermore, we would predict that given a large number of individuals under similar conditions, they are likely to behave in similar ways. Within such groups, many forms of social reinforcement may become contingent upon classes of behaviors which are outside the larger society's normative requirements. Norms and legal codes, as discriminative stimuli, will only control the behavior of those who have experienced the appropriate learning history. If an individual has been, and is, reinforced for such "normative" behavior, that behavior will be maintained in strength. If he has not been, and is not now reinforced for such behaviors they would be weak, if they existed in his repertoire at all. And, importantly, the reinforcement system may shape and maintain another class of behaviors which do result in reinforcement and such behaviors may be considered deviant or criminal by other members of the group. Thus we may formulate this proposition to read: V. *The specific class of behaviors which are learned and their frequency of occurrence are a function of the reinforcers which are effective and available, and the rules or norms by which these reinforcers are applied.*

VI. "A person becomes delinquent because of an excess of definitions favorable to violation of law over definitions unfavorable to violation of law."

This proposition is generally considered the heart of Sutherland's theory; it is the principle of differential association. It follows directly from proposition V, and we must now refer back to that proposition. In proposition V, the use of the preposition "from" in the phrase, "learned from definitions of the legal codes as favorable or unfavorable," is somewhat misleading. The meaning here is not so much that learning results *from* these definitions as it is that they form part of the *content* of one's learning, deter-

[52] Staats and Staats, *op. cit.*

mining which direction one's behavior will go in relation to the law, i.e., law-abiding or lawbreaking.

These definitions of the law make lawbreaking seem either appropriate or inappropriate. Those definitions which place lawbreaking in a favorable light in a sense can be seen as essentially norms of evasion and/or norms directly conflicting with conventional norms. They are, as Sykes and Matza and Cressey note, "techniques of neutralization," "rationalizations," or "verbalizations" which make criminal behavior seem "all right" or justified, or which provide defenses against self-reproach and disapproval from others.[53] The principle of negative reinforcement would be of major significance in the acquisition and maintenance of such behaviors.

This analysis suggests that it may not be an "excess" of one kind of definition over another in the sense of a cumulative ratio, but rather in the sense of the relative amount of discriminative stimulus value of one set of verbalizations or normative statements over another. As we suggested in the last section, normative statements are, themselves, behaviors that are a function of reinforcement consequences. They, in turn, may serve as discriminative stimuli for other operant behaviors (verbal and nonverbal). But recall that reinforcement must be forthcoming, at least occasionally, before a verbal statement can continue as a discriminative stimulus. Bear in mind, also, that behavior may produce reinforcing consequences even in the absence of any accompanying verbal statements.

In other terms, a person will become delinquent if the official norms or laws do not perform a discriminative function and thereby control "normative" or conforming behavior. We know from the Law of Differential Reinforcement that that operant which produces the most reinforcement will become dominant if it results in reinforcement. Thus, if lawful behavior did not result in reinforcement, the strength of the behavior would be weakened, and a state of deprivation would result, which would, in turn, increase the probability that other behaviors would be emitted which are reinforced, and such behaviors would be strengthened. And, of course, these behaviors, though common to one or more groups, may be labeled deviant by the larger society. And such behavior patterns, themselves, may acquire conditioned reinforcing value and, subsequently, be enforced by the members of a group by making various forms of social reinforcement, such as social approval, esteem, and status contingent upon that behavior.

The concept "excess" in the statement, "excess of definitions favorable

[53] Sykes and Matza, op. cit., Cressey, Other People's Money, op. cit., pp. 93–138; Donald R. Cressey, "The Differential Association Theory and Compulsive Crimes," Journal of Criminal Law, Criminology and Police Science, 45 (May–June, 1954), pp. 29–40; Donald R. Cressey, "Social Psychological Foundations for Using Criminals in the Rehabilitation of Criminals," Journal of Research in Crime and Delinquency, 2 (July, 1965), pp. 45–59. See revised proposition IV.

to violation of law," has been particularly resistant to operationalization. A translation of this concept in terms of modern behavior theory would involve the "balance" of reinforcement consequences, positive and negative. The Law of Differential Reinforcement is crucial here. That is, a person would engage in those behaviors for which he had been reinforced most highly in the past. (The reader may recall that in the Ayllon-Azrin study with schizophrenics, it was found that the patients selected and performed those behaviors which provided the most reinforcers when reinforcement was available for more than one response.) Criminal behavior would, then, occur under those conditions where an individual has been most highly reinforced for such behavior, and the aversive consequences contingent upon the behavior have been of such a nature that they do not perform a "punishment function."[54] This leads us to a discussion of proposition VII. But, first, let us reformulate the sixth proposition to read: VI. *Criminal behavior is a function of norms which are discriminative for criminal behavior, the learning of which takes place when such behavior is more highly reinforced than non-criminal behavior.*

VII. "Differential associations may vary in frequency, duration, priority, and intensity."

In terms of our analysis, the concepts frequency, duration, and priority are straightforward enough. The concept *intensity* could be operationalized to designate the number of the individual's positive and negative reinforcers another individual or group controls, as well as the reinforcement value of that individual or group. As previously suggested the group which can mediate the most positive reinforcers and which has the most reinforcement value, as well as access to a larger range of aversive stimuli, will exert the most control over an individual's behavior.

There is a good reason to suspect, however, that Sutherland was not so much referring to differential associations with other persons, as differential associations with criminal *patterns*. If this supposition is correct, then this proposition can be clarified by relating it to differential contingencies of reinforcement rather than differential social associations. From this perspective, the experimental evidence with regard to the various schedules of reinforcement is of major importance. There are three aspects of the sched-

[54] This, then, is essentially differential reinforcement as Jeffery presents it. We have attempted to show how this is congruent with differential association. Further, while Jeffery ignores the key concepts of "definitions" and "excess" we have incorporated them into the reformulation. These definitions, viewed as verbalizations, become discriminative stimuli; and "excess" operates to produce criminal behavior in two related ways: (1) verbalizations conducive to law violation have greater discriminative stimulus value than other verbalizations, and (2) criminal behavior has been more highly reinforced and has produced fewer aversive outcomes than has law-abiding behavior in the conditioning history of the individual.

ules of reinforcement which are of particular importance here: (1) the *amount* of reinforcement: the greater the amount of reinforcement, the higher the response rate; (2) the *frequency* of reinforcement which refers to the number of reinforcements per given time period: the shorter the time period between reinforcements, the higher the response rate; and (3) the *probability* of reinforcement which is the reciprocal of responses per reinforcement: the lower the ratio of responses per reinforcement, the higher the rate of response.[55]

Priority, frequency, duration, and intensity of association with criminal persons and groups are important to the extent that they insure that deviant behavior will receive greater amounts of reinforcement at more frequent intervals or with a higher probability than conforming behavior. But the frequency, probability, and amount of reinforcement are the crucial elements. This means that it is the coming under the control of contingencies of reinforcement that selectively produces the criminal definitions and behavior. Consequently, let us rewrite this proposition to read: VII. *The strength of criminal behavior is a direct function of the amount, frequency, and probability of its reinforcement.*

IX. "While criminal behavior is an expression of general needs and values, it is not explained by those general needs and values since noncriminal behavior is an expression of the same needs and values."

In this proposition, Sutherland may have been reacting, at least in part, to the controversy regarding the concept "need." This controversy is now essentially resolved. For, we have finally come to the realization that "needs" are unobservable, hypothetical, fictional inner-causal agents which were usually invented on the spot to provide spurious explanations of some observable behavior. Furthermore, they were inferred from precisely the same behavior they were supposed to explain.

While we can ignore the reference to needs, we must discuss values. Values may be seen as reinforcers which have salience for a number of the members of a group or society. We agree with Sutherland to the extent that he means that the nature of these general reinforcers do not necessarily determine which behavior they will strengthen. Money, or something else of general value in society, will reinforce any behavior that produces it. This reinforcement may depend upon noncriminal behavior, but it also may become contingent upon a set of behaviors that are labelled as criminal. Thus, if Sutherland can be interpreted as meaning that criminal and noncriminal behavior cannot be maintained by the same set of reinforcers, we must dis-

[55] R. T. Kelleher and L. R. Gollub, "A Review of Positive Conditioned Reinforcement," *Journal of the Experimental Analysis of Behavior* (October, 1962), pp. 543–597. Because the emission of a fixed ratio or variable ratio of responses requires a period of time, the rate of responding will indirectly determine the frequency of reinforcement.

agree. However, it may be that there are certain reinforcing consequences which only criminal behavior will produce, for the behavior finally shaped will depend upon the reinforcer that is effective for the individual. Nevertheless, it is the reinforcement, not the specific nature of the reinforcer, which explains the rate and form of behavior. But since this issue revolves around contingencies of reinforcement which are handled elsewhere, we will eliminate this last proposition.

TABLE 1. A DIFFERENTIAL ASSOCIATION-REINFORCEMENT THEORY OF CRIMINAL BEHAVIOR

Sutherland's Statements	*Reformulated Statements*
1. "Criminal behavior is learned." 8. "The process of learning criminal behavior by association with criminal and anti-criminal patterns involves all of the mechanisms that are involved in any other learning."	1. Criminal behavior is learned according to the principles of operant conditioning.
2. "Criminal behavior is learned in interaction with other persons in a process of communication."	2. Criminal behavior is learned both in nonsocial situations that are reinforcing or discriminative and through that social interaction in which the behavior of other persons is reinforcing or discriminative for criminal behavior.
3. "The principal part of the learning of criminal behavior occurs within intimate personal groups."	3. The principal part of the learning of criminal behavior occurs in those groups which comprise the individual's major source of reinforcements.
4. "When criminal behavior is learned, the learning includes (a) techniques of committing the crime, which are sometimes very complicated, sometimes very simple; (b) the specific direction of motives, drives, rationalizations, and attitudes."	4. The learning of criminal behavior, including specific techniques, attitudes, and avoidance procedures, is a function of the effective and available reinforcers, and the existing reinforcement contingencies.
5. "The specific direction of motives and drives is learned from definitions of the legal codes as favorable or unfavorable."	5. The specific class of behaviors which are learned and their frequency of occurrence are a function of the reinforcers which are effective and available, and the rules or norms by which these reinforcers are applied.

TABLE 1 (*Continued*)

Sutherland's Statements	Reformulated Statements
6. "A person becomes delinquent because of an excess of definitions favorable to violation of law over definitions unfavorable to violation of law."	6. Criminal behavior is a function of norms which are discriminative for criminal behavior, the learning of which takes place when such behavior is more highly reinforced than noncriminal behavior.
7. "Differential associations may vary in frequency, duration, priority, and intensity."	7. The strength of criminal behavior is a direct function of the amount, frequency, and probability of its reinforcement.
9. "While criminal behavior is an expression of general needs and values, it is not explained by those general needs and values since noncriminal behavior is an expression of the same needs and values."	9. (Omit from theory.)

CONCLUDING REMARKS

The purpose of this paper has been the application of the principles of modern behavior theory to Sutherland's differential association theory. While Sutherland's theory has had an enduring effect upon the thinking of students of criminal behavior, it has, till now, undergone no major theoretical revision despite the fact that there has been a steady and cumulative growth in the experimental findings of the processes of learning.

There are three aspects of deviant behavior which we have attempted to deal with simultaneously, but which should be separated. First, how does an individual *become* delinquent, or how does he learn delinquent behavior? Second, what *sustains* this delinquent behavior? We have attempted to describe the ways in which the principles of modern behavior theory are relevant to the development and maintenance of criminal behavior. In the process, we have seen that the principle of differential reinforcement is of crucial importance. But we must also attend to a third question, namely, what sustains the pattern or *contingency* of reinforcement? We only have hinted at some of the possibly important variables. We have mentioned briefly, for example, structural factors such as the level of deprivation of a particular group with regard to important social reinforcers, and the lack of effective reinforcement of "lawful" behavior[56] and the concomitant fail-

[56] Robert K. Merton, *Sociol Theory and Social Structure*, Glencoe, Ill.: The Free

ure to develop the appropriate behavioral repertoires to produce reinforcement legally.[57] We have also suggested that those behaviors which do result in reinforcement may, themselves, gain reinforcement value and be enforced by the members of the group through the manipulation of various forms of social reinforcement such as social approval and status, contingent upon such behaviors.[58] In short, new norms may develop and these may be termed delinquent by the larger society.

There are many other topics that are of direct relevance to the problem of deviant behavior which we have not been able to discuss given the requirements of space. For instance, no mention has been made of some outstanding research in the area of punishment. This topic is, of course, of prime importance in the area of crime prevention. To illustrate some of this research and its relevance, it has been found experimentally that the amount of behavior suppression produced by response-contingent aversive stimuli is a direct function of the intensity of the aversive stimulus, but that a mild aversive stimulus may produce a dramatic behavior-suppression if it is paired with reinforcement for an alternative and incompatible behavior. Furthermore, it has been discovered that if an aversive stimulus is repeatedly paired with positive reinforcement, and reinforcement is not available otherwise, the aversive stimulus may become a discriminative stimulus (S^D) for reinforcement and, consequently, not decrease the behavior's frequency of occurrence.

There are, in conclusion, numerous criteria that have been used to evaluate theories. One such set is as follows:

(1) The amount of empirical support for the theory's basic propositions.

(2) The "power" of the theory, i.e., the amount of data that can be derived from the theory's higher-order propositions.

(3) The controlling possibilities of the theory, including (a) whether the theory's propositions are, in fact, *causal* principles, and (b) whether the theory's propositions are stated in such a way that they suggest possible *practical* applications.

What dissatisfaction there has been with differential association can be attributed to its scoring low on these criteria, especially (1) and (3). We submit that the reformulated theory presented here answers some of these problems and better meets each of these criteria. It is our contention, more-

---

Press, pp. 161–195. For a more complete discussion of social structure in terms relevant to this paper. See Robert L. Burgess and Don Bushell, Jr., *Behavioral Sociology*, Parts IV and V, forthcoming, 1967.

[57] *Ibid.*, and Richard A. Cloward, "Illegitimate Means, Anomie, and Deviant Behavior," *American Sociological Review*, 24 (April, 1959), pp. 164–177.

[58] Albert K. Cohen, *Delinquent Boys: The Culture of the Gang*, Glencoe, Ill.: The Free Press, 1955.

over, that the reformulated theory not only specifies the conditions under which criminal behavior is learned, but also some of the conditions under which deviant behavior in general is acquired. Finally, while we have not stated our propositions in strictly axiomatic form, a close examination will reveal that each of the later propositions follow from, modify, or clarify earlier propositions.

10 Epidemiology and Individual Conduct

DONALD R. CRESSEY

Sutherland's theory of differential association can best be understood if only that part of it which has become the center of attention and which purports to explain individual criminality is considered first. The essential ideas here are that "criminal behavior is learned in interaction with persons in a pattern of communication," and that the specific direction of motives, drives, rationalizations, and attitudes—whether in the direction of criminality or anti-criminality—is learned from persons who define the legal codes as rules to be observed and from persons whose attitudes are favorable to violation of legal codes. "A person becomes delinquent because of an excess of definitions favorable to violation of law over definitions unfavorable to violation of law."[1] In modern society, the two kinds of definitions of what is expected and desired in reference to legal codes exist side by side, and a person might present contradictory definitions to another person at different times and in different situations. Sutherland called the process of receiving these two kinds of definitions "differential association," because what is learned in association with criminal behavior patterns is in competition with what is learned in association with anti-criminal behavior patterns. "When

Reprinted from Donald R. Cressey, "Epidemiology and Individual Conduct: A Case from Criminology," *Pacific Sociological Review*, 3 (Fall, 1960), 47–58, with the permission of the publisher.

[1] For a complete statement of Sutherland's theory, see Edwin H. Sutherland and Donald R. Cressey, *Principles of Criminology*, 5th edition, New York: Lippincott, 1955, pp. 74–81. Unless otherwise identified, all quotations of Sutherland are from these pages.

persons become criminals, they do so because of contacts with criminal behavior patterns and also because of isolation from anti-criminal patterns." The kind of social psychological process Sutherland seemed to have in mind will became clearer if we consider some of the details of his statement by reviewing both the principal interpretive errors apparently made by his readers and the principal criticisms advanced by his criminological colleagues.

SOME LITERARY ERRORS

The statement of the theory of differential association is not clear. In two pages, Sutherland presented nine propositions, with little elaboration, that purport to explain both the epidemiology of crime and delinquency and the presence of criminality and delinquency in individual cases. It therefore is not surprising that his words do not always convey the meaning he seemed to intend. Most significantly, as we shall see later, the statement gives the impression that there is little concern for explaining variations in crime and delinquency rates. This is a serious error in communication on Sutherland's part. In reference to the delinquent and criminal behavior of individuals, however, the difficulty in communication seems to arise as much from readers' failure to study the words presented as from the words themselves. Five principal errors, and a number of minor ones, have arisen because readers do not always understand what Sutherland seemed to be trying to say.

First, it is common to believe, or (perhaps necessarily) to assume momentarily, if only for purposes of research and discussion, that the theory is concerned only with contacts or associations with criminal and delinquent behavior patterns.[2] Vold, for example, says, "One of the per-

---

[2] Robert G. Caldwell, *Criminology*, New York: Ronald Press, 1956, p. 182; Ruth S. Cavan, *Criminology*, 2nd edition, New York: Crowell, 1955, p. 701; Marshall B. Clinard, "The Process of Urbanization and Criminal Behavior," *American Journal of Sociology*, 48 (September, 1942), pp. 202–213; Rural Criminal Offenders," *American Journal of Sociology*, 50 (July, 1944), pp. 38–45; "Criminological Theories of Violations of Wartime Regulations," *American Sociological Review*, 11 (June, 1946), pp. 258–270; "The Sociology of Delinquency and Crime," in Joseph Gittler, editor, *Review of Sociology*, New York: Wiley, 1957, p. 477; and *Sociology of Deviant Behavior*, New York: Rinehart, 1957, p. 240; H. Warren Dunham and Mary Knauer, "The Juvenile Court in Its Relationship to Adult Criminality," *Social Forces*, 32 (March, 1954), pp. 290–296; Mabel A. Elliott, *Crime in Modern Society*, New York: Harper & Bros., 1952, pp. 347–348; Sheldon Glueck, "Theory and Fact in Criminology," *British Journal of Delinquency*, 7 (October, 1956), pp. 92–109; Robert E. Lane, "Why Businessmen Violate the Law," *Journal of Criminal Law and Criminology*, 44 (July–August, 1953), pp. 151–165; Walter C. Reckless, *The Etiology of Delinquent and Criminal Behavior*, New York: Social Science Council, 1943, p. 60; James F. Short, Jr., "Differential Association and Delinquency," *Social Problems*, 4 (January, 1957), pp. 223–239; and "Differential Asso-

sistent problems that always has bedeviled the theory of differential association is the obvious fact that not everyone in contact with criminality adopts
or follows the criminal pattern."[3] At first glance, at least, such statements
seem to overlook or ignore the words "differential" and "excess" in Sutherland's presentation. After stating that a person becomes delinquent because
of an *excess* of definitions favorable to violation of law over definitions
unfavorable to violation of law, Sutherland continues by saying, "This is
the principle of differential association. It refers to both criminal and anti-
criminal associations and has to do with counter-acting forces." Thus, he
does not say that persons become criminals because of associations with
criminal behavior patterns; he says that they become criminals because of
an *overabundance* of such associations, in comparison with associations with
anti-criminal behavior patterns. Accordingly, it is erroneous to state or
imply that the theory is invalid because a category of persons—such as
policemen, prison workers, or criminologists—have had extensive association with criminal behavior patterns but yet are not criminals.

Second, it is commonly believed that Sutherland says persons become
criminals because of an excess of associations with *criminals*.[4] Because of
the manner in which the theory is stated, and because of the popularity of
the "bad companions" theory of criminality in our society, this error is
easy to make. Sutherland's proposal is concerned with ratios of associations
with *patterns of behavior*, no matter what the character of the person presenting them. Throughout his formal statement, Sutherland uses terms
such as "definitions of legal codes as favorable or unfavorable," "definitions
favorable to violation of law over definitions unfavorable to violation of
law," and "association with criminal and anti-criminal patterns." Thus, if
a mother teaches her son that "Honesty is the best policy" but also teaches

---

ciation with Delinquent Friends and Delinquent Behavior," *Pacific Sociological Review,*
1 (Spring, 1958), pp. 20–25; Harrison M. Trice, 'Sociological Factors in Association with
A.A.," *Journal of Criminal Law and Criminology,* 48 (November–December, 1957), pp.
374–386; George B. Vold, *Theoretical Criminology,* New York: Oxford University
Press, 1958, pp. 194–195.

[3] *Op. cit.,* p. 194.

[4] Harry Elmer Barnes and Negley K. Teeters, *New Horizons in Criminology,* 3rd
edition, Englewood Cliffs, New Jersey: Prentice-Hall, 1959, p. 159; Caldwell, *op. cit.,*
pp. 182–183; Cavan, *op. cit.,* p. 701; Clinard, "The Process of Urbanization and Criminal
Behavior," *op. cit.;* "Rural Criminal Offenders," *op. cit.,* and "Criminological Theories
of Violations of Wartime Regulations," *op. cit.;* Elliott, *op. cit.,* p. 274; Daniel Glaser,
"The Sociological Approach to Crime and Correction," *Law and Contemporary Problems,* 23 (Autumn, 1958), pp. 683–702; and "Differential Association and Criminological
Prediction: "Problems of Measurement," paper read at the annual meetings of the Ameri-
can Sociological Association, Chicago, September, 1959; Glueck, *op. cit.;* Lane, *op. cit.;*
Reckless, *op. cit.,* p. 60; Harry M. Shulman, "The Family and Juvenile Delinquency,"
Annals of the American Academy of Political and Social Science, 261 (January, 1949),
pp. 21–31; Donald R. Taft, *Criminology,* New York: Macmillan, 1956, p. 338.

him, perhaps inadvertently, that "It is all right to steal a loaf of bread when you are starving," she is presenting him with an anti-criminal behavior pattern and a criminal behavior pattern, even if she herself is honest, non-criminal, and even anti-criminal. One can learn criminal behavior patterns from persons who are not criminals, and one can learn anti-criminal behavior patterns from hoods, professional crooks, habitual offenders, and gangsters.

Third, in periods of time ranging from five to twelve years after publication of the formal statement with the word "systematic" omitted, at least five authors have erroneously believed that the theory pertains to "systematic" criminal behavior only.[5] This error is not important to the substance of Sutherland's current statement of the theory, but discussing it does tell something about the nature of the theory. The first formal statement was qualified so that it pertained only to "systematic" criminal behavior, rather than to the more general category "criminal behavior."[6] Sutherland deleted the word "systematic" from the second version of his theory, which first appeared in the Fourth Edition of his Principles of Criminology, in 1947. He explained that it was his belief that all but "the very trivial criminal acts" were "systematic," but he deleted the word because some research workers were unable to identify "systematic criminals," and other workers considered only an insignificant proportion of prisoners to be "systematic criminals."[7] The theory now refers to all criminal behavior. Limitation to "systematic" criminality was made for what seemed to be practical rather than logical reasons, and it was abandoned when it did not seem to have practical utility. Yet, one author (Caldwell) has recently been as critical of the word "systematic" as was an early article that attacked the original statement containing the word "systematic."[8]

Fourth, it is commonplace to say that the theory is defective because

[5] Caldwell, op. cit., pp. 182–184; Cavan, op. cit., p. 701; Elliott, op. cit., p. 274; Richard R. Korn and Lloyd W. McCorkle, Criminology and Penology, New York: Holt, 1959, pp. 297–297; Vold, op. cit., pp. 197–198.

[6] See Edwin H. Sutherland, Principles of Criminology, 3rd edition, New York: Lippincott, 1939, pp. 5–9. This statement proposed generally that systematic criminality is learned in a process of differential association but then went on to use "consistency" as one of the modes of affecting the impact of the various patterns presented in the process of association. Thus, "consistency" of the behavior patterns presented was used as a general explanation of criminality, but "consistency" also we used to describe the process by which differential association takes place. Like the word "systematic," "consistency" was deleted from the next version of the theory.

[7] Edwin H. Sutherland, "Development of the Theory," in Albert K. Cohen, Alfred R. Lindesmith, and Karl F. Schuessler, editors, The Sutherland Papers, Bloomington: Indiana University Press, 1956, p. 21.

[8] Arthur L. Leader, "A Differential Theory of Criminality," Sociology and Social Research, 26 (September, 1941), pp. 45–53.

it does not explain why persons have the associations they have.[9] Although such expressions are valuable statements of what is needed in criminological research, they are erroneous when applied to differential association. Sutherland recognized that determining why persons have the associations they have is a desirable problem for research, and we shall later see that when his theory is viewed as a principle that attempts to account for variations in crime rates it does deal in a general way with differential opportunities for association with an excess of criminal behavior patterns. Nevertheless, the fact that the "individual conduct" part of the theory does not pretend to account for a person's associations cannot be considered a defect in it:

It is not necessary, at this level of explanation, to explain why a person has the associations he has; this certainly involves a complex of things. In an area where the delinquency rate is high a boy who is sociable, gregarious, active, and athletic is very likely to come in contact with other boys in the neighborhood, learn delinquent behavior from them, and become a gangster; in the same neighborhood the psychopathic boy who is isolated, introvert, and inert may remain at home, not become acquainted with other boys in the neighborhood, and not become delinquent. In another situation, the sociable, athletic, aggressive boy may become a member of a scout troop and not become involved in delinquent behavior. The person's associations are determined in the general context of social organization.[10]

Fifth, other authors have erroneously taken "theory" to be synonymous with "bias" or "prejudice," and have condemned Sutherland's statement on this ground. For example, in connection with criticizing Sutherland for deleting "systematic" from the 1947 version of his theory, Caldwell has written that by 1947 "we had not acquired enough additional facts to enable [Sutherland] to explain all criminal behavior."[11] This statement does not clearly recognize that facts themselves do not explain anything, and that theory tries to account for the relationships between known facts, among other things. Confusion about the role of theory also is apparent in Clinard's statement that Sutherland's theory is "arbitrary," Glueck's statement that "social processes are dogmatically shaped to fit into the prejudices

---

[9] Glueck, op. cit.; Clarence R. Jeffery, "An Integrated Theory of Crime and Criminal Behavior," Journal of Criminal Law and Criminology, 49 (March–April, 1959), pp. 533–552; Leader, op. cit.; Martin H. Neumeyer, Juvenile Delinquency in Modern Society, 2nd edition, New York: Van Nostrand, 1955, p. 152; James F. Short, Jr., "Differential Association as a Hypothesis: Problems of Empirical Testing," paper read at the annual meetings of the American Sociological Association, September, 1959; Trice, op. cit.; S. Kirson Weinberg, "Theories of Criminality and Problems of Prediction," Journal of Criminal Law and Criminology, 45 (November–December, 1954), pp. 412–429.

[10] Sutherland and Cressey, op. cit., p. 79.

[11] Op. cit., p. 182.

of the pre-existing theory of 'differential association'," and Jeffery's statement that "the theory does not differentiate between criminal and non-
criminal behavior, since both types of behavior can be learned."[12] Such
statements are not so much errors in interpretation of the differential association statements as they are errors regarding the role of theory, hypotheses,
and facts in scientific research. Later, we will show that Sutherland's whole
theory does organize and integrate known facts about crime. Here, we need
only indicate that Merton, and many others, have dispelled the notion that
sociological theory is arbitrarily imposed on the facts it seeks to explain.[13]

Additional errors stemming from the form of Sutherland's formal statement, from lack of careful reading of the statement, or from assumptions necessary to conducting research, have been made, but not with the frequency
of the five listed above. Among these are confusion of the concept "definition of the situation" with the word "situation,"[14] confusion of the notion
that persons associate with criminal and anti-criminal behavior patterns with
the notion that it is groups that associate on a differential basis,[15] belief that
the theory is concerned principally with learning the *techniques* for committing crimes,[16] belief that the theory refers to learning of behavior patterns that are neither criminal nor anti-criminal in nature,[17] belief that
"differential association," when used in reference to professional thieves,
means maintaining "a certain necessary aloofness from ordinary people,"[18]
failure to recognize that the shorthand phrase "differential association" is
equivalent to "differential association with criminal and anti-criminal behavior patterns," with the consequent assumption that the theory attempts
to explain all behavior, not just criminal behavior,[19] and belief that the

---

[12] Clinard, *Sociology of Deviant Behavior, op. cit.,* p. 204; Glueck, *op. cit.,* p. 99;
Jeffery, *op. cit.,* p. 537.

[13] Robert K. Merton, *Social Theory and Social Structure,* rev. edition, Glencoe: The
Free Press, 1957, pp. 85–117.

[14] Milton L. Barron, *The Juvenile in Delinquent Society,* New York: Knopf, 1954,
p. 101.

[15] Elliott, *op. cit.,* p. 274.

[16] Clinard, "Criminological Theories of Violations of Wartime Regulations," *op. cit.*

[17] Taft writes of differential association "with others who have become relative
failures or criminals," but Sutherland's theory has nothing to say about association with
"failures," unless "failures" and "persons presenting criminal behavior patterns" are used
synonymously. *Op. cit.;* p. 338.

[18] Walter C. Reckless, *The Crime Problem,* 2nd edition, New York: Appleton-
Century-Crofts, 1955, p. 169. This kind of error may stem from Sutherland himself,
for in his work on the professional thief he used the term "differential association" to
characterize the members of the behavior system, rather than to describe the process
presented in the first statement of this theory, two years later. See Edwin H. Sutherland,
The Professional Thief, Chicago: University of Chicago Press, 1937, pp. 206–207.

[19] Howard B. Gill, "An Operational View of Criminology," *Archives of Criminal
Psychodynamics,* October, 1957, p. 284; Jeffery, *op cit.*

theory is concerned only with a raw ratio of associations between the two kinds of behavior patterns and does not contain the statement, explicitly made, that "differential association may vary in frequency, duration, priority, and intensity."[20]

SOME POPULAR CRITICISMS
OF DIFFERENTIAL ASSOCIATION

Identification of some of the defects that various critics have found in Sutherland's statement also should make his theory clearer. Five principal types of criticism have been advanced in the literature. It would be incorrect to assume that a criticism advanced by many readers is more valid or important than one advanced by a single reader, but commenting on every criticism would take us too far afield. We can only mention, without elaboration, some of the criticisms advanced by only one or two authors. It has been stated or implied that the theory of differential association is defective because it omits consideration of free will,[21] is based on a psychology assuming rational deliberation,[22] ignores the role of the victim,[23] does not explain the origin of crime,[24] does not define terms such as "systematic" and "excess,"[25] does not take "biological factors" into account,[26] is of little or no value to "practical men,"[27] is not comprehensive enough because it is not interdisciplinary,[28] is not allied closely enough with more general

[20] Clinard, "Criminological Theories of Violations of Wartime Regulations," *op. cit.* If these "modalities," as Sutherland called them, are ignored, then the theory would equate the impact of a behavior pattern presented once in a radio show with the impact of a pattern presented numerous times to a child who deeply loved and respected the donor. It does not so equate the patterns.

[21] Caldwell, *op. cit.,* p. 182.

[22] Weinberg, *op. cit.*

[23] Clinard, "The Sociology of Delinquency and Crime, *op. cit.,* p. 479.

[24] Jeffery, *op. cit.,* p. 537.

[25] Leader, *op. cit.;* Caldwell, *op. cit.;* Marshall B. Clinard, "Criminological Research," in Robert K. Merton, Leonard Broom, and Leonard Cottrell, editors, *Sociology Today,* New York: Basic Books, 1959, pp. 510–513; Short, "Differential Association and Delinquency," *op. cit.*

[26] Barnes and Teeters, *op. cit.,* p. 159; Caldwell, *op. cit.,* p. 182; Gill, *op. cit.,* pp. 289–291; Glueck, *op. cit.,* pp. 98–99. Olof Kinberg, "Kritiska reflexioner över den differentiella associationhypotesen," Chapter 24, in Ivar Agge, Gunnar Boalt, Bo Gerle, Maths Heuman, Carl-Gunnar Janson, Olof Kinberg, Sven Rengby, Torgny Segerstedt, and Thorsten Sellin, *Kriminologi,* Stockholm: Wahlström and Widstrand, 1955, pp. 415–429.

[27] Barnes and Teeters, *op. cit.,* p. 210.

[28] *Ibid.,* p. 162; Caldwell, *op. cit.,* p. 182; Gill, *op. cit.,* p. 284; Glueck, *op. cit.,* pp. 105, 108; Howard Jones, *Crime and the Penal System,* London: University Tutorial Press, 1956, p. 95.

sociological theory and research,[29] is too comprehensive because it applies to non-criminals,[30] and assumes that all persons have equal access to criminal and anti-criminal behavior patterns.[31] Some of these comments represent pairs of opposites, one criticism contradicting another, and others seem to be based on one or more of the errors described above. Still others are closely allied with the five principal types of criticism, and we shall return to them.

One popular form of "criticism" of differential association is not, strictly speaking, criticism at all. At least ten scholars have speculated that some kinds of criminal behavior are exceptional to the theory. Thus, it has been said that the theory does not apply to rural offenders,[32] to landlords who violated OPA regulations,[33] to criminal violators of financial trust,[34] to "naive check forgers,"[35] to white-collar criminals,[36] to perpetrators of "individual" and "personal" crimes,[37] to irrational and impulsive criminals,[38] to "adventitious" and/or "accidental" criminals,[39] to "occasional," "incidental," and "situational" offenders,[40] to murderers, non-professional shoplifters and non-career type of criminals,[41] to persons who commit crimes of passion,[42] and to men whose crimes were perpetrated under emotional stress.[43] It is significant that only the first five comments—those referring

[29] Clarence Schrag, "Review of Principles of Criminology," *American Sociological Review,* 20 (August, 1955), pp. 500–501.

[30] Gill, *op. cit.,* p. 284; Jeffery, *op. cit.,* p. 537.

[31] Richard A. Cloward, "Illegitimate Means, Anomie and Deviant Behavior," *American Sociological Review,* 24 (April, 1959), pp. 164–176; Short, "Differential Association as a Hypothesis," *op. cit.,* p. 3.

[32] Clinard, "The Process of Urbanization and Criminal Behavior," and "Rural Criminal Offenders," *op. cit.*

[33] Clinard, "Criminological Theories of Violations of Wartime Regulations," *op. cit.*

[34] Donald R. Cressey, "Application and Verification of the Differential Association Theory," *Journal of Criminal Law and Criminology,* 43 (May–June, 1952), pp. 43–52.

[35] Edwin M. Lemert, "Isolation and Closure Theory of Naive Check Forgery," *Journal of Criminal Law and Criminology,* 44 (September–October, 1953), pp. 293–307.

[36] Clinard, *Sociology of Deviant Behavior, op. cit.,* p. 240; Korn and McCorkle, *op. cit.,* pp. 299–300.

[37] Marshall B. Clinard, "Criminal Behavior Is Human Behavior," *Federal Probation,* 13 (March, 1949), pp. 21–27; "Research Frontiers in Criminology," *British Journal of Delinquency,* 7 (October, 1956), pp. 110–122; *Sociology of Deviant Behavior, op. cit.,* p. 229; and "Criminological Research," *op. cit.,* p. 512.

[38] Elliott, *op. cit.,* p. 402; Vold, *op. cit.,* pp. 197–198.

[39] Clinard, "Criminological Research," *op. cit.,* p. 511; Elliott, *op. cit.,* p. 402; Jeffery, *op. cit.;* Daniel Glaser, "Criminality Theories and Behavioral Images," *American Journal of Sociology,* 61 (March, 1956), p. 441.

[40] Elliott, *op. cit.,* p. 402; Clinard, "Criminological Research," *op. cit.,* p. 512.

[41] *Ibid.*

[42] Jeffery, *op. cit.*

[43] Elliott, *op. cit.,* pp. 347–348.

to rural offenders, landlords, trust violators, check forgers, and some white-collar criminals—are based on research. It also is significant that at least two authors have simply stated that the theory is subject to criticism because there are exceptions to it; the kind of behavior thought to be exceptional is not specified.[44]

The fact that most of the comments are not based on research means that the "criticisms" actually are proposals for research. Should a person conduct research on a particular type of offender and find that the theory does not hold, a revision is called for, providing the research actually tested the theory, or part of it. As indicated, this procedure has been used in five instances, and these instances need to be given careful attention. But in most cases, there is no evidence that the kind of behavior said to be exceptional is exceptional. For example, we do not know that "accidental" or "incidental" or "occasional" criminals have not gone through the process specified by Sutherland. Perhaps it is assumed that some types of criminal behavior are "obviously exceptional." However, a theoretical analysis indicated that one type of behavior that appears to be obviously exceptional—"compulsive criminality"—is not necessarily exceptional at all.[45]

A second principal kind of criticism attacks the theory because it does not adequately take into account the "personality traits," "personality factors," or "psychological variables" in criminal behavior. This is real criticism, for it suggests that Sutherland's statement neglects an important determinant of criminality. Occasionally, the criticism is linked with the apparent assumption that some kinds of criminality are "obviously" exceptional. However, at least a dozen authors have proposed that Sutherland's statement is defective because it omits or overlooks the general role of personality traits in determining criminality.[46]

Sutherland took this kind of criticism seriously, and in an early period he stated that his theory probably would have to be revised to take account of personality traits.[47] Later he pointed out what he believed to be the

---

[44] Barnes and Teeters, *op. cit.*, p. 159; Taft, *op. cit.*, p. 340.

[45] Donald R. Cressey, "The Differential Association Theory and Compulsive Crimes," *Journal of Criminal Law and Criminology*, 45 (May–June, 1954), pp. 49–64.

[46] Barnes and Teeters, *op. cit.*, p. 159; Barron, *op. cit.*, p. 147; Caldwell, *op. cit.*, pp. 179, 182, 184; Clinard, "Criminological Theories of Violations of Wartime Regulations, *op. cit.*; "Sociologists and America Criminology," *Journal of Criminal Law and Criminology*, 41 (January–February, 1951), pp. 549–577; "The Sociology of Delinquency and Crime," *op. cit.*; *Sociology of Deviant Behavior, op. cit.*, pp. 204–205, 229, 240–241; Gill, *op. cit.*, p. 286; Glueck, *op. cit.*, p. 97; Kinberg, *op. cit.*; Lane, *op. cit.*; Leader, *op. cit.*; S. F. Lottier, "Tension Theory of Criminal Behavior," *American Sociological Review*, 7 (December, 1942), pp. 840–848; Neumeyer, *op. cit.*, pp. 152–153; Short, "Differential Association as a Hypothesis," *op. cit.*, p. 4; Vold, *op. cit.*, p. 197.

[47] Sutherland, "Development of the Theory," (1942) *op. cit.*, pp. 25–27.

fundamental weakness in his critics' argument: "Personality traits," and "personality" are words that merely specify a condition, like feeblemindedness, without showing the relationship between that condition and criminality. He posed three questions for advocates of "personality traits" as supplements to differential association: (1) What are the personality traits that should be regarded as significant? (2) Are there personal traits, to be used as supplements to differential association, which are not already included in the concept of differential association? (3) Can differential association, which is essentially a *process* of learning, be combined with personal traits, which are essentially the *product* of learning?[48]

Sutherland did not attempt to answer these questions, but the context of his discussion indicates his belief that differential association does explain why some persons with a trait like "aggressiveness" commit crimes, while other persons possessing the same trait do not. It also reveals his conviction that terms like "personality traits," "personality," and "psychogenic trait components" are (when used, with no further elaboration, to explain why a person becomes a criminal) synonyms for "unknown conditions."

Closely allied with the "personality trait" criticism is the assertion that Sutherland's statement does not adequately take into account the "response" patterns, "acceptance" patterns, and "receptivity" patterns of various individuals.[49] The essential notion here is that differential association emphasizes the social process of transmission but minimizes the individual process of reception. Stated in another way, the idea is that the theory of differential association deals only with external variables and does not take into account the meaning to the recipient of the various patterns of behavior presented to him in situations which are objectively quite similar but nevertheless variable, according to the recipient's perception of them. One variety of this type of criticism takes the form of asserting that criminals and noncriminals are sometimes reared in the "same environment"—criminal behavior patterns are presented to two persons, but only one of them becomes a criminal.

Sutherland was acutely aware of the social psychological problem posed by such concepts as "differential response patterns." Significantly, his proposed solution to the problem was his statement of the theory of differ-

[48] Edwin H. Sutherland, *White Collar*, New York: Dryden, 1949, p. 272.

[49] John C. Ball, "Delinquent and Non-Delinquent Attitudes Toward the Prevalence of Stealing," *Journal of Criminal Law and Criminology*, 48 (September–October, 1957), pp. 259–274; Caldwell, *op. cit.*, p. 182; Clinard, "The Process of Urbanization and Criminal Behavior," *op. cit.*; "Sociologists and American Criminology," *op. cit.*; *Sociology of Deviant Behavior, op. cit.*, pp. 240–241; and "Criminological Research," *op. cit.*; Glueck, *op. cit.*; Jeffery, *op. cit.*; Korn and McCorkle, *op. cit.*, p. 298; Leader, *op. cit.*; Neumeyer, *op. cit.*, p. 142; Reckless, *The Crime Problem, op. cit.*, p. 109; and *The Etiology of Delinquent and Criminal Behavior, op. cit.*, p. 62; Trice, *op. cit.*; Vold, *op. cit.*, p. 196; Weinberg, *op. cit.*

ential association.[50] One of the principal objectives of the theory is to account for differences in individual responses to opportunities for crime and in individual responses to criminal behavior patterns presented. To illustrate, one person who walks by an unguarded and open cash register, or who is informed of the presence of such a condition in a nearby store, may perceive the situation as a "crime committing" one, while another person in the identical circumstances may perceive the situation as one in which the owner should be warned against carelessness. The difference in these two perceptions, Sutherland held, is due to differences in the prior associations with the two types of definition of situation, so that the alternatives in behavior are accounted for in terms of differential association. The differential in "response pattern," or the difference in "receptivity" to the criminal behavior pattern presented, then, is accounted for by differential association itself.[51] Elsewhere, we have insisted that one of the greatest defects in Sutherland's theory is its implication that receptivity to any behavior pattern presented is determined by the patterns presented earlier, that receptivity to those early presentations was determined by even earlier presentations, and so on back to birth.[52] But this is an assertion that the theory cannot be tested, not an assertion that it does not take into account the "differential response patterns" of individuals.

If "receptivity" is viewed in a different way, however, the critics appear to be on firm ground.[53] Sutherland did not identify what constitutes a definition "favorable to" or "unfavorable to" the violation of law, but he recognized that the same objective definition might be "favorable" or "unfavorable," depending on the relationship between the donor and the recipient. Consequently, he said that differential associations may vary in "intensity," which was not precisely defined but "has to do with such things as the prestige of the source of a criminal or anti-criminal pattern and with emotional reactions to the associations." This attempt at what is now called "reference group theory" merely begs the question; it tells us that some

[50] See Edwin H. Sutherland, "Susceptibility and Differential Association," in Cohen Lindesmith, and Schuessler, *op. cit.,* pp. 42–43. See also Solomon Kobrin, "The Conflict of Values in Delinquency Areas," *American Sociological Review,* 16 (October, 1951), pp. 653–661.

[51] *Cf.* Ralph L. Beals, "Acculturation," in A. L. Kroeber, editor, *Anthropology Today,* Chicago: University of Chicago Press, 1953, pp. 621–641; and Richard Thurnwald, "The Psychology of Acculturation," *American Anthropologist,* 34 (October–December, 1932), pp. 557–569.

[52] Cressey, "Application and Verification of the Differential Association Theory," *op. cit.*

[53] I am indebted to Albert K. Cohen for assistance with this paragraph and with other points. Also, I am grateful to the following persons for suggested modifications of the original draft: Daniel Glaser, Sheldon Glueck, Michael Hakeem, Frank Hartung, C. Ray Jeffery, Richard T. Morris, Melvin Seeman, James F. Short, Jr., and George B. Vold.

associations are to be given added *weight*, but it does not tell us how, or whether, early associations affect the *meaning* of later associations. If earlier associations determine whether a person will later identify specific behavior patterns as "favorable" or "unfavorable" to law violation, then these earlier associations determine the very meaning of the later ones, and do not merely give added weight to them. In other words, whether a person is prestigeful or not prestigeful to another may be determined by experiences that have nothing to do with criminality and anti-criminality. Nevertheless, these experiences affect the meaning (whether "favorable" or "unfavorable") of patterns later presented to the person and, thus, they affect his "receptivity" to the behavior patterns.[54]

A fourth kind of criticism is more damaging than the first three, for it insists that the ratio of learned behavior patterns used by Sutherland to explain criminality cannot be determined with accuracy in specific cases. A minimum of eight authors have stated this criticism in seven different articles.[55] Short, for example, has pointed out the extreme difficulty of operationalizing terms such as "favorable to" and "unfavorable to"; nevertheless, he has devised various measures of differential association and has used them in a series of significant studies. Glaser has argued that "the phrase 'excess of definitions' itself lacks clear denotation in human experience," and Glueck has asked, "Has anybody actually counted the number of definitions favorable to violation of law and definitions unfavorable to violation of law, and demonstrated that in the pre-delinquency experience of the vast majority of delinquents and criminals, the former exceeds the latter?" In my work on trust violation, I was unable with the methods at my disposal to get embezzlers to identify specific persons or agencies from whom they learned behavior patterns favorable to trust violation. My general conclusion was, "It is doubtful that it can be shown empirically that the differential association theory applies or does not apply to crimes of financial trust violation or even to other kinds of criminal behavior."[56] I have been severely taken to task for not revising Sutherland's statement in light of this conclusion.[57] My reasons for not doing so have to do with the difference in the theory of differential association considered as a gen-

[54] This actually is the important point Vold was making in the quotation cited at footnote 3 above.

[55] Ball, *op. cit.*; Clinard, "Criminological Research," *op. cit.*; Cressey, "Application and Verification of the Differential Association Theory," *op. cit.*; Glaser, "Criminality Theories and Behavioral Images, *op. cit.*; Glueck, *op. cit.*, p. 96; Lane, *op. cit.*; Reckless, *The Etiology of Delinquent and Criminal Behavior, op. cit.*, p. 63; Schrag, *op. cit.*; Short, "Differential Association and Delinquency" *op. cit.*; "Differential Association as a Hypothesis," *op. cit.*

[56] Cressey, "Application and Verification of the Differential Association Theory," *op. cit.*, p. 52.

[57] Caldwell, *op. cit.*, p. 185.

eral principle which organizes and makes good sense of the data on crime rates, as compared to the theory considered only as a statement of the precise mechanism by which a person becomes a criminal. As we shall see below, a principle accounting for the distribution of deviancy, or any other phenomenon, can be valid even if a presumably coordinate theory specifying the process by which deviancy occurs in individual cases is *incorrect*, let alone untestable.

The fifth kind of criticism states in more general terms than the first four that the theory of differential association over-simplifies the process by which criminal behavior is learned. Such criticism ranges from simple assertions that the learning process is more complex than the theory states or implies,[58] to the idea that the theory does not adequately take into account some specific type of learning process, such as differential identification.[59] Between these two extremes are assertions that the theory is inadequate because it does not allow for a process in which criminality seems to be "independently invented" by the actor. I am one of the dozen authors who have advanced this kind of criticism,[60] and in this day of role theory, reference group theory, and complex learning theory, it would be foolhardy to assert that this type of general criticism is incorrect. But it is one thing to criticize the theory for failure to specify the learning process accurately and another to specify which aspects of the learning process should be included and in what way.[61] Clinard's and Glaser's attempts to utilize the process of identification, and Weinberg's, Sykes and Matza's, and my own efforts to utilize more general symbolic interactionist theory, seem to be the only published attempts that specifically substitute alternative learning processes for the mechanistic process specified by Sutherland. Even these attempts are, like Sutherland's statement, more in the nature of general indications of the kind of framework or orientation one should use in formulating a theory of criminality than they are statements of theory.

[58] See, for example, Ball, *op. cit.*

[59] See, for example, Clinard, "The Process of Urbanization and Criminal Behavior," *op. cit.*; and Glaser, "Criminality Theories and Behavior Images, *op. cit.*

[60] Caldwell, *op. cit.*, p. 183; Clinard, "The Sociology of Delinquency and Crime," *op. cit.*; and "Criminological Research," *op. cit.*; Cressey, "Application and Verification of the Differential Association Theory, *op. cit.*; and "The Differential Association Theory and Compulsive Crime," *op. cit.*; Daniel Glaser, "Review of *Principles of Criminology,*" *Federal Probation,* 20 (December, 1956), pp. 66–67; "The Sociological Approach to Crime and Correction," *op. cit.*; and "Differential Association and Criminological Prediction," *op. cit.*; Glueck, *op. cit.*, pp. 93, 97; Korn and McCorkle, *op. cit.*, p. 299; Leader *op. cit.*; Short, "Differential Association as a Hypothesis," *op. cit.*; Gresham Sykes and David Matza, "Techniques of Neutralization: A Theory of Delinquency," *American Sociological Review,* 22 (December, 1957), pp. 664–670; Weinberg, *op. cit.*

[61] Despite the fact that Sutherland described a learning process, it should be noted that he protected himself by saying, "The process of learning criminal and anti-criminal patterns involves all the mechanisms that are involved in any other learning."

DIFFERENTIAL ASSOCIATION
AND THE EPIDEMIOLOGY OF CRIME

Sutherland's short, formal statement emphasizes the problem of explaining variations in the criminality of individuals. Only a careful reader of the statement can discern that it is concerned with making sense of the gross facts about crime, rather than concentrating exclusively on individual criminality.[62] However, examination of Sutherland's writings clearly indicates that he was greatly, if not primarily, concerned with organizing and integrating the factual information about crime rates. In his account of how the theory of differential association developed, he made the following three points, which are sufficient to establish his concern for the epidemiology of crime.

More significant for the development of the theory were certain questions which I raised in class discussions. One of these questions was, Negroes, young-adult males, and city dwellers all have relatively high crime rates: What do these three groups have in common that places them in this position? Another question was, Even if feeble-minded persons have a high crime rate, why do they commit crimes? It is not feeble-mindedness as such, for some feeble-minded persons do not commit crimes. Later I raised another question which became even more important in my search for generalizations. Crime rates have a high correlation with poverty if considered by areas of a city but a low correlation if considered chronologically in relation to the business cycle; this obviously means that poverty as such is not an important cause of crime. How are the varying associations between crime and poverty explained?[63]

It was my conception that a general theory should take account of all the factual information regarding crime causation. It does this either by organizing the multiple factors in relation to each other or by abstracting them from certain common elements. It does not, or should not, neglect or eliminate any factors that are included in the multiple factor theory.[64]

The hypothesis of differential association seemed to me to be consistent with

---

[62] One of Sutherland's own students, colleagues, and editors has said, "Much that travels under the name of sociology of deviant behavior or of social disorganization is psychology—some of it very good psychology, but psychology. For example, Sutherland's theory of differential association, which is widely regarded as pre-eminently sociological, is not the less psychological because it makes much of the cultural milieu. It is psychological because it addresses itself to the question: How do people become the kind of individuals who commit criminal acts? A sociological question would be: What is it about the structure of social systems that determines the kinds of criminal acts that occur in these systems and the way in which such acts are distributed within these systems?" Albert K. Cohen, "The Study of Social Disorganization and Deviant Behavior," Chapter 21 in Robert K. Merton, Leonard Broom and Leonard S. Cottrell, Jr., editors, *Sociology Today,* New York: Basic Books, 1959, p. 462.

[63] Sutherland, "Development of the Theory," *op. cit.,* p. 15.

[64] *Ibid.,* p. 18.

the principal gross findings in criminology. It explained why the Mollaccan children became progressively delinquent with length of residence in the deteriorated area of Los Angeles, why the city crime rate is higher than the rural crime rate, why males are more delinquent than females, why the crime rate remains consistently higher in deteriorated areas of cities, why the juvenile delinquency rate in a foreign nativity is high while the group lives in a deteriorated area and drops when the group moves out of the area, why second-generation Italians do not have the high murder rate their fathers had, why Japanese children in a deteriorated area of Seattle had a low delinquency rate even though in poverty, why crimes do not increase greatly in a period of depression. All of the general statistical facts seem to fit this hypothesis.[65]

It appears, then, that in writing about differential association Sutherland was trying to say, for example, that a high crime rate in urban areas can be considered the end product of social conditions that lead to a situation in which relatively large proportions of persons are presented with an excess of criminal behavior patterns. Similarly, the fact that the rate for all crimes is not higher in some urban areas than it is in some rural areas can be attributed to differences in conditions which affect the probabilities of exposure to criminal behavior patterns.[66] The important general point is that in a multi-group type of social organization, alternative and inconsistent standards of conduct are possessed by various groups, so that an individual who is a member of one group has a high probability of learning to use legal means for achieving success, or learning to deny the importance of success, while an individual in another group learns to accept the importance of success and to achieve it by illegal means. Stated in another way, there are alternative educational processes in operation, varying with groups, so that a person may be educated in either conventional or criminal means of achieving success. Sutherland sometimes called this situation "differential social organization" or "differential group organization," and he proposed that "Differential group organization should explain the crime rate, while differential association should explain the criminal behavior of a person. The two explanations must be consistent with each other."[67]

It should be noted that, in the quotations above, Sutherland referred to his statement as both a "theory" and a "hypothesis," and did not indicate any special concern for distinguishing between differential association as it applies to the epidemiology of crime and differential association as it applies to individual conduct. In order to avoid controversy about the essential characteristics of theories and hypotheses, we prefer to call differential association, as it is used in reference to crime rates, a "principle."

[65] *Ibid.*, pp. 19–20.

[66] *Cf.* Henry D. McKay, "Differential Association and Crime Prevention: Problems of Utilization," unpublished paper read at the annual meetings of the American Sociological Association, Chicago, September, 1959.

[67] Sutherland, "Development of the Theory," *op. cit.*, p. 21.

Because sociology seems to be dominated by a logic and methodology derived from physics, through psychology, sociologists are reluctant to label a statement "theory" unless it is a generalization sufficiently detailed to permit derivation of predictive hypotheses that can be put to test by gathering *new* facts. Nevertheless, it might be argued that many "theories" in sociology are in fact principles that order *known* facts about rates—now called epidemiology—in some way, and that they only in very general ways specify directions for accumulation of new facts that might prove them wrong. Durkheim, for example, invented what may be termed a "principle of group integration" to account for, organize logically, and integrate systematically the data on variations in suicide rates. He did not invent a theory of suicide, derive hypotheses from it, and then collect data to determine whether the hypotheses were correct or incorrect. He tried to "make sense" of known facts about rates, and the principle he suggested remains the most valuable idea available to persons who would understand the differences in the rates of suicide between Protestants and Jews, urban dwellers and rural dwellers, etc.

We suggest, similarly, that Sutherland's statement is a "principle of normative conflict" which proposes that high crime rates occur in societies and groups characterized by conditions that lead to the development of extensive criminalistic subcultures. Sutherland made some attempt to account for the origins of these subcultures,[68] but he did not concentrate on this problem any more than Durkheim concentrated on attempting to account for the fact that Jewish families seemed more closely integrated than non-Jewish families. He "made sense" of variations in crime rates by observing that modern societies are organized for crime as well as against it, and then observing further that crime rates are unequally distributed because of differences in the degree to which various categories of persons participate in this normative conflict.

Darwinism and Sutherlandism

The value of general principles like "normative conflict" can be further established by comparing the work of Darwin and Sutherland. Although such a comparison might seem pretentious when the range of phenomena included in the scope of Darwin's theory is compared with the range included in Sutherland's, each man did try to state a principle accounting for the presence or absence of "deviant" phenomena, and then also tried to specify the process by which "deviancy" comes to be present in individual cases. Although Darwin's contribution is called the "theory of evolution" and Sutherland's is called the "theory of differential association," both had two distinct parts. There is a remarkable similarity in the goals of

[68] See Sutherland and Cressey, *op. cit.*, pp. 82–92.

the two "theories," the logic on which they are based, and the defects in them. Darwin invented the principle of natural selection, with its implication of evolution, to account for the strange distribution of "deviant" biological specimens and the forms of plant and animal life. Next, he tried to specify the process by which this principle of natural selection "works" in individual cases. Sutherland invented the principle of normative conflict to account for the strange distribution of high and low crime rates; he then tried to specify the mechanism by which this principle works to produce individual cases of criminality. The mechanism proposed is differential association:

> The second concept, differential association, is a statement of [normative] conflict from the point of view of the person who commits the crime. The two kinds of culture impinge on him or he has association with the two kinds of cultures and this is differential association.[69]

Darwin had three principle advantages over Sutherland. First, his emphasis was on the "epidemiological" part of his theory, rather than on the "individual conduct" part. His principle of natural selection ordered a wide range of facts that had been minutely detailed by thousands of careful observers. He knew quite precisely what facts his principle had to fit. For at least a century prior to *Origin of Species*, observation of the wonders of nature had been almost a national pastime in England. Great numbers of persons who, like Darwin, had little formal training in science were recording observations of biological and physical phenomena.[70] In the fifty years before *Origin*, at least a half dozen persons, including Darwin's grandfather, tried to put order into all these data by formulating something like a principle of natural selection. After publication of *Origin of Species*, the principle became a "hit" because it stirred up religious controversy, but also because thousands of amateur scientists could, like the professionals, check it against their own small world of observations and agree or disagree.

In contrast, Sutherland presented his theory to a world that knew little about crime and cared little about understanding it. Twenty-five years ago, the study of crime probably was more popular than it is at present, but detailed, precise, observations were being made by only a handful of persons. As today, careful observations were being made largely by academic sociologists, and the amateurs in the field were more concerned with doing something about crime than they were in knowing about it. Moreover, much work in criminology was, and still is, sporadic and slipshod, so that we

---

[69] Sutherland, "Development of the Theory," *op. cit.*, pp. 20–21.

[70] The popularity of scientific concern was a social movement growing out of Calvinism, which admonished its followers to observe God's laws by observing His works, the wonders of nature. Fashionable English ladies carried pocket miscroscopes, which they would train on flowers and insects while strolling through the garden. See Gerald Dennis Meyer, *The Scientific Lady in England, 1650–1750*, Los Angeles: The University of California Press, 1955.

cannot be sure that the "facts" about crime are facts at all. Sutherland tried to induce order in what facts we have, sparse as they may be. His principle organized only a narrow range of observations which were not always valid, and which were known to only a handful of dedicated souls.

Moreover, Sutherland handicapped himself by presenting the principle as an appendage to a well-established textbook, and by not explicitly trying to show in a formal statement how the principle helped to integrate and organize the existing data on crime. He needed to confront the reader with an overwhelming number of valid observations that somehow seemed less likely to be mere happenstance occurrences after his principle was stated than they had seemed before it was stated. It seems likely that Sutherland did not try to promote his principle because of a characteristic he had in common with Darwin—extreme modesty. It is conceivable that he did not completely commit himself to his principle, in the form of a major publication like *Origin*, for the same reason that Darwin published four monographs on barnacles, none of them containing any reference to his principle, between the time he formulated the principle and the time he published it.[71] Sutherland was well aware of the failure of previous theories about crime, and he did not want to get too committed to his own formulation.[72]

Second, it was to Darwin's advantage that *Origin of Species* eventually attracted the attention of his professional colleagues; Sutherland's theoretical work is still so unknown even among sociologists that in at least two instances the words "differential association" have been invented as concepts describing phenomena quite unrelated to crime.[73] Publication in a textbook, as compared to a monograph, probably had some effect on this difference. Also, there is a tendency among sociologists to think of criminology as a distinct discipline, rather than observing that criminologists like Sutherland are interested in data on crime for the same theoretical reasons that other sociologists are interested in data on industry, family life, and politics. Sutherland's principle remains unknown to almost all psychiatrists, psychologists, and social workers.

The third, and by far the most important, advantage Darwin had over Sutherland was a set of research workers who appeared on the scene to correct him as well as criticize him. In simple fact, Sutherland's Mendel, Fisher, and Wright have not appeared. It turned out that Darwin was quite wrong after all. His principle of natural selection became one of the most

---

[71] It is quite possible that Darwin never would have published his principle had it not been independently formulated by Alfred R. Wallace, who threatened to scoop him. See Garrett Hardin, *Nature and Man's Fate,* New York: Rinehart, 1959, pp. 42–45.

[72] Sutherland, "Development of the Theory," *op. cit.,* p. 17.

[73] Ronald Freedman, Amos H. Hawley, Werner S. Landecker, and Horace M. Miner, *Princples of Sociology,* 1st edition, New York: Holt, pp. 235–238; David Gold, "On Description of Differential Association," *American Sociological Review,* 22 (August, 1957), pp. 448–450.

important ideas in the history of man, but it was founded on an erroneous conception of the mechanisms by which heredity takes place in individual cases. Darwin adhered to the incorrect but popular "paint pot" theory that viewed heredity as a blending process, and because of this adherence he eventually had to join the Lamarckian geneticists, holding that mysterious particles called "pangenes" are modified by environmental conditions and are then gathered together to form the hereditary elements of the sperm or egg.[74] Although Mendel "corrected" Darwin when he published his discovery in 1866, his work did not become known and understood until the turn of the century. Since then, research in genetics has given Darwin's principle what it most needed—mathematically precise statements of the process by which natural selection "works." What has remained of Darwin himself is his important first principle, the principle of natural selection, and not his ideas about genetics.

There are no known published accounts of research that would carefully quantify or in some other way induce exact precision in Sutherland's statement of the process by which normative conflict "works" to produce criminality in individual cases. The most significant work has been done by Daniel Glaser and James F. Short, Jr. Although critics agree, as we have indicated, that the differential association statement oversimplifies the process by which normative conflict "gets into" persons and produces criminality, an acceptable substitute that is consistent with the principle of normative conflict has not appeared.

THE VALUE OF DIFFERENTIAL ASSOCIATION

We have suggested that Sutherland, like Darwin, tried to formulate a principle that would organize available factual information on a type of deviation and then tried to specify the process by which that principle operates in individual cases of deviation. Sutherland's critics have argued that his specification of the latter process is incorrect, just as Darwin's specification of the hereditary process was incorrect. But inaccuracy in specifying the mechanism for becoming a criminal does not necessarily negate the value of the general principle, as the history of Darwinism has shown.

As an organizing principle, normative conflict makes understandable most of the variations in crime rates discovered by various researchers and observers, and it also focusses attention on crucial research areas.[75] In a

[74] Hardin, op. cit., p. 118.

[75] Cf. Llewellyn Gross, "Theory Construction in Sociology: A Methodological Inquiry," Chapter 17 in Llewellyn Gross, editor, Symposium on Sociological Theory, Evanston: Row, Peterson, 1959, pp. 548–555.

publication appearing in 1961, I listed over thirty facts about the statistical distribution of crime by age, sex, race, nativity, size of community, and social class; and then examined the capacity of various criminological theories to integrate them logically.[76] The principle of normative conflict does not make good sense out of all the facts, but it seems to make better sense out of more of the facts than do any of the alternative theories. Probably we should not expect the principle to fit all the observations to which it might be applied. As the physicist-philosopher Phillipp Frank has said, "There is certainly no theory which is in complete agreement with all our observations. If we require complete agreement, we can certainly achieve it by merely recording the observations."[77]

On the other hand, it also seems safe to conclude that differential association is not a precise statement of the process by which one becomes a criminal. The idea that criminality is a consequence of an excess of intimate associations with criminal behavior patterns is valuable because, for example, it negates assertions that deviation from norms is simply a product of being emotionally insecure or living in a broken home, and then indicates in a general way why only some emotionally insecure persons and only some persons from broken homes commit crimes. Also, it directs attention to the idea that an efficient explanation of individual conduct is consistent with explanations of epidemiology. Yet the statement of the differential association process is not precise enough to stimulate rigorous empirical test, and it therefore has not been proved or disproved. This defect is shared with broader social psychological theory. As Schrag has pointed out, "The individual internalizes the norms of his group," and "Stimulus patterns that are active at the time of a response eventually acquire the capacity to elicit the response," are illustrations of assertions which cannot be confirmed or denied but which stand, at present, as substitutes for descriptions of the process by which persons learn social behavior.[78] Criminological theory can be no more precise than the general sociological theory and general social psychological theory of which it is a part.

It is important to observe, however, that the "individual conduct" part of Sutherland's statement does order data on individual criminality in a general way and, consequently, might be considered a principle itself. Thus, "differential association" may be viewed as a restatement of the

[76] Donald R. Cressey, "Crime," Chapter 1 in Robert K. Merton and Robert A. Nisbet, eds., *Contemporary Social Problems,* (New York: Harcourt, Brace & World, 1961). See also Donald R. Cressey, "The State of Criminal Statistics," *National Probation and Parole Association Journal,* 3 (July, 1957), pp. 230–241.

[77] *Philosophy of Science,* Englewood Cliffs, New Jersey: Prentice-Hall, 1957, p. 353; quoted by Glaser, "Differential Association and Criminological Prediction," *op. cit.*

[78] Clarence Schrag, "Some Foundations for a Theory of Correction," Chapter 8 in Donald R. Cressey, editor, *The Prison: Studies in Institutional Organization and Change,* New York: Holt, Rinehart and Winston, 1961.

principle of normative conflict, so that this one principle is used to account for the distribution of criminal and non-criminal behavior in both the life of the individual *and* in the statistics on collectivities. In this case, both individual behavior data and epidemiological rate data may be employed as indices of the variables in the principle, thus providing two types of hypotheses for testing it.[79] Glaser has recently shown that differential association makes sense of both the predictive efficiency of some parole prediction items and the lack of predictive efficiency of other items.[80] In effect, he tested the principle by determining whether parole prediction procedures which could have proven it false actually failed to prove it false. First, he shows that a majority of the most accurate predictors in criminological prediction research are deducible from differential association theory while the least accurate predictors are not deducible at all. Second, he shows that this degree of accuracy does not characterize alternative theories. Finally, he notes that two successful predictors of parole violation—type of offense and non-criminal employment opportunities—are not necessarily deducible from the theory, and he suggests a modification that would take this fact into account.

Future research on differential association might specify in more detail the mechanisms by which one becomes a criminal, but it probably will do so only if sociologists recognize the epidemiological principle with which the process is consistent. While it might be argued that Darwin's "theory of evolution" can only be illustrated, not tested, it is clear that genetics has been profoundly affected by Darwin's scientific desire to generalize broadly on his, and others' observations of the distribution of species.[81] Similarly, Sutherland's "theory of normative conflict" tends to be tautological and might not be testable. Nevertheless, it is a starting point for theory of criminal epidemiology, and its counterpart, differential association, indicates in a general way the process which should be closely studied as a first step to development of efficient theory of individual criminal conduct.

[79] I am indebted to Daniel Glaser for calling this point to my attention.

[80] "Differential Association and Criminological Prediction, *op. cit.* See also Daniel Glaser, "A Reconsideration of Some Parole Prediction Factors," *American Sociological Review,* 19 (June, 1954), pp. 335–341; and "The Efficiency of Alternative Approaches to Parole Prediction," *American Sociological Review,* 20 (June, 1955), pp. 283–287; and Daniel Glaser and Richard F. Hangren, "Predicting the Adjustment of Federal Probationers," *National Probation and Parole Association Journal,* 4 (July, 1958), pp. 258–267.

[81] *Cf.* Garrett Hardin, "The Competitive Exclusion Principle," *Science,* 131 (April, 1960), pp. 1292–1298.

PART VI

Societal Reactions to Deviant Behavior

Introduction

Howard S. Becker has in recent years popularized the notion that deviance (which includes more than delinquency and crime) is created in part by the social groups making and applying the rules whose infraction constitutes deviance. Whether a heavy drinker, for example, is considered a deviant or not depends upon the rules his society has formulated about drinking behavior, and also upon the specific reactions to the behavior of the heavy drinker once conduct such as his has been officially condemned in the rules. We have seen, in Part II, that the criminal law officially proclaims as "improper" certain behaviors which, henceforth, are known as "crimes" or "delinquencies." In Part III we saw, further, that administrators of criminal justice apply the rules of criminal law differentially to the crimes and delinquencies committed by various individuals, depending on the circumstances of the offense and the characteristics of the offender. We also have seen that a large proportion of all delinquencies and crimes go undetected and that, hence, no official reaction to the action is officially communicated to the offender. Here, we are concerned with the effects on law violators of the fact that their behavior is "criminalized."[1] As Wheeler and Cottrell say in their selection, "It is not at all clear that doing something is better than doing nothing, or that doing one thing is better than doing another."

There is no question about the fact that, legally speaking, one who violates the criminal law is a criminal. However, it is not at all clear how

[1] See "Deviance and Public Policy" in Part II above.

long he remains a criminal after he has committed a crime. Is one who commits a crime a criminal for the rest of his life, only until he has "paid the penalty" for his offense, or only while he is engaged in the illegal conduct? The question is unanswerable, principally because we use the words "delinquent" and "criminal" to stigmatize law violators, as well as merely to indicate that they have violated the law.

In everyday conversation, we try to differentiate between the law violator or offender (not stigmatized) and the criminal or delinquent (stigmatized) by using phrases such as "hardened criminal," "confirmed criminal," and "incorrigible delinquent" to refer to the latter. Almost all members of modern societies commit delinquencies and crimes. Most of these offenses go undetected. Further, most of those who violate the law do not consider themselves delinquents or criminals. Even a man in prison might admit that he committed the crime for which he was convicted, yet feel inside that he is not really a criminal. Moreover, not all persons who commit delinquencies and crimes are considered delinquents or criminals by their associates, or by law-enforcement agents. The adjectives "hardened," "confirmed," and so on are used as defaming, stigmatizing terms referring to persons who conceive of themselves as criminals, are persistent in their criminality, and are regarded as criminals by others.

The reactions to an individual's initial lawbreaking behavior—on the part of family members, friends, neighbors, teachers, social workers, police officers, judges, and others—play a crucial part in determining whether the individual becomes a "hardened criminal" or "incorrigible delinquent." The undesirable consequences of what Lemert calls "secondary deviation" and of what Wheeler and Cottrell call the "labeling process" are unintentional, of course. For example, in an effort to forestall delinquency or to help a young offender, family members, friends, and community agencies may take actions which unintentionally drive the youngster into groups in which the chances to acquire a conception of self as a delinquent or criminal are greatly increased. This sequence of alienation may be outlined as follows:

1. In the eyes of a child, behavior which is proper as play may include breaking windows, climbing over roofs or, generally, "raising hell." Such definitions of "play" are akin to "fun" on Halloween. But many adults, including parents, policemen, and the victims of the play, may see the behavior as bad, deviant, and delinquent, and they insist that it be curtailed or suppressed. Moreover, it seems to be the case that destructive or bothersome behavior defined as "play" or "fun" by middle-class children is less frequently defined as "bad" by the community than is the same kind of "play" by lower-class children.

2. Demands for suppression of the "bad" behavior are made on the child by community members, sometimes including his parents. The demands may lead to a shift away from definition of the specific *acts* as evil to a definition of the *actor* as evil. Once this shift occurs, Kitsuse shows, a great variety of behavioral forms may be used as evidence of "deviation" or "delinquency" where earlier, or in another situation, the same behavioral forms were used as indications of normality.

3. In the face of this reaction by adults, the child may feel that an injustice is being done to him and, more importantly, that his community and perhaps his parents consider him different from "good children." Parsons has suggested that at this point a youngster may reduce his contacts with, or become isolated from, persons oriented to "good behavior" and become "predisposed toward individualized crime." On the other hand, he might become more closely integrated with the group that shares his "fun" because other members are encountering similar experiences.[2] As Cohen says, "Culture is continually being created, re-created and modified wherever individuals sense in one another like needs, generated by like circumstances, not shared generally in the larger social system."[3]

4. Parents, police, and others may then scrutinize and look with suspicion upon all of a youngster's activities, his companions, his hangouts, his speech, and his personality, thus reinforcing the definition of him as "bad."

5. Once the child discovers that he has been defined as bad and that even his efforts to be good are interpreted as evidence of his badness, he may become even more "predisposed toward individualized crime" or even more closely integrated with his play group, which has been redefined as a "delinquent gang." As Wheeler and Cottrell indicate, the youngster then begins to look upon himself and his companions as bad and organizes his behavior accordingly. He becomes bad because he has been defined as bad.

6. Once the community has defined a youngster as bad, it knows how to cope with him; it does not, in fact, know how to deal with him until it defines him as bad. He may be threatened, avoided, punished, counseled, analyzed, supervised, and committed to institutions. He gets a "record" with police and other agencies. As both Becker and Kitsuse suggest in their selections, the assumption is that he is like other rule breakers—that the boys labeled "delinquent" have had a great deal in common from the beginning. For example, it might be assumed that a

[2] Talcott Parsons, *The Social System*, (New York: Free Press, 1951), p. 284.
[3] See "A General Theory of Subcultures," Part VII, below.

given boy has personality traits similar to the personality traits which are assumed to motivate the deviant behavior of all delinquents. Neither assumption is warranted. Kitsuse shows that once the label "homosexual" has been assigned to an individual, behavior that has previously been regarded as innocuous is reinterpreted as evidence of incipient or characteristic homosexual behavior.

7. As the community copes with the delinquent, its conception of him crystallizes, as does his conception of himself. He now defines himself as he is defined, as an "incorrigible," a "delinquent," or a "criminal." In Lemert's terms, he begins to employ his delinquent behavior "as a means of defense, attack or adjustment to the overt and covert problems created by the consequent societal reaction to him." He might become, as Parsons maintains, "compulsively conformative *within* the deviant subgroup at the same time that he is compulsively alienated from the main institutional structure."[4] He has adopted the community's classification system, which separates the good and the bad, the right and the wrong. He becomes loyal to groups in which the membership consists of bad persons like himself, becomes educated in crime, and learns that the community which has been defining him as bad contains many elements which support his badness.

These steps in a sequence of alienation play an important part in determining whether an actor will continue to deviate and perhaps become a "hardened criminal" with a "criminal personality." Tannenbaum referred to this process, twenty years ago, as a "dramatization of evil."

The first dramatization of "evil" which separates the child out of his group for specialized treatment plays a greater role in making the criminal than perhaps any other experience. It cannot be too often emphasized that for the child the whole situation has become different. He now lives in a different world. He has been tagged. A new and hitherto nonexistent environment has been precipitated out for him.

The process of making the criminal, therefore, is a process of tagging, defining, identifying, segregating, describing, emphasizing, making conscious and self-conscious; it becomes a way of stimulating, suggesting, emphasizing, and evolving the very traits that are complained of.[5]

[4] Parsons, *op. cit.*, p. 286.

[5] Frank Tannenbaum, *Crime and the Community* (Boston: Ginn, 1938), pp. 19–20. For an elaboration of Tannenbaum's observations, see "The Evolution of Delinquent Subcultures" in Part VII, below. Recent studies have indicated that even in physical illness the physician's attention plays a considerable part in bringing on the very symptoms it is designed to diagnose. Scheff points out that false diagnoses of illness, made because the physician is obligated to suspect illness even when the evidence is not clear, often incapacitate the persons being diagnosed. Thomas J. Scheff, "Decision Rules, Types of Error, and Their Consequences in Medical Diagnosis," *Behavioral Science*, 8 (1963), pp. 97–107.

In more recent years, this notion has been discussed by Merton as "the self-fulfilling prophecy."[6] In 1951 Lemert gave the name "secondary deviation" to the outcome of the process. The important point in the selection from Lemert's book is that in attempting to correct "primary deviation" we sometimes present verbalizations that inadvertently make the subjects more deviant. The selection by Werthman carries this kind of analysis one step further by dealing with children who are, at first, members of family groups which do not necessarily own values favorable to delinquency. Werthman dramatically demonstrates how lower-class juvenile gang boys become "autonomous," in the sense that they lose membership in groups owning verbalizations conducive to non-delinquency, and at the same time become members of groups owning verbalizations which sanction stealing and fighting. He suggests that by the time the "delinquent" is ready to assume adult responsibility his choices may have been so severely limited that he is incapable of making the transition to a non-delinquent role.

It is, of course, possible to carry this notion of "dramatization of evil" and "secondary deviation" so far that it can erroneously be deduced that the police and other official agents of the state are more important in producing criminality and other forms of deviant behavior than is informal interaction among peers. For example, at present there seems to be a tendency among some social scientists to view police officers, prison workers, and parole officers as the "bad guys" that are producing criminality, while the crooks and other carriers of crooked values are the "good guys." This is absurd.[7] Despite the absurdity, the emphasis on secondary deviation as well as on primary deviation focuses our attention exactly where it needs to be focused—on the subcultures made up of verbalizations which inadvertently, but nevertheless inexorably, are presented to persons who adopt them and who, in adopting them, become delinquents and criminals.

[6] Robert K. Merton, *Social Theory and Social Structure,* revised ed. (New York: Free Press, 1957), pp. 421–436.

[7] See Edwin M. Lemert, *Human Deviance, Social Problems and Social Control* (Englewood Cliffs, N.J.: Prentice-Hall, 1967), pp. 50–51.

1 Deviance and the Responses of Others

HOWARD S. BECKER

[One sociological view] defines deviance as the infraction of some agreed-upon rule. It then goes on to ask who breaks rules, and to search for the factors in their personalities and life situations that might account for the infractions. This assumes that those who have broken a rule constitute a homogeneous category, because they have committed the same deviant act.

Such an assumption seems to me to ignore the central fact about deviance: it is created by society. I do not mean this in the way it is ordinarily understood, in which the causes of deviance are located in the social situation of the deviant or in "social factors" which prompt his action. I mean, rather, that *social groups create deviance by making the rules whose infraction constitutes deviance*, and by applying those rules to particular people and labeling them as outsiders. From this point of view, deviance is *not* a quality of the act the person commits, but rather a consequence of the application by others of rules and sanctions to an "offender." The deviant is one to whom that label has successfully been applied; deviant behavior is behavior that people so label.[1]

Reprinted with permission of The Macmillan Company from *Outsiders* by Howard S. Becker. Copyright by The Free Press, a Corporation, 1963, pp. 8–14.

[1] The most important earlier statements of this view can be found in Frank Tannenbaum, *Crime and the Community* (Boston: Ginn and Company, 1938), and E. M. Lemert, *Social Pathology* (New York: McGraw-Hill Book Co., Inc., 1951). A recent

Since deviance is, among other things, a consequence of the responses of others to a person's act, students of deviance cannot assume that they are dealing with a homogeneous category when they study people who have been labeled deviant. That is, they cannot assume that these people have actually committed a deviant act or broken some rule, because the process of labeling may not be infallible; some people may be labeled deviant who in fact have not broken a rule. Furthermore, they cannot assume that the category of those labeled deviant will contain all those who actually have broken a rule, for many offenders may escape apprehension and thus fail to be included in the population of "deviants" they study. Insofar as the category lacks homogeneity and fails to include all the cases that belong in it, one cannot reasonably expect to find common factors of personality or life situation that will account for the supposed deviance.

What, then, do people who have been labeled deviant have in common? At the least, they share the label and the experience of being labeled as outsiders. I will begin my analysis with this basic similarity and view deviance as the product of a transaction that takes place between some social group and one who is viewed by that group as a rule-breaker. I will be less concerned with the personal and social characteristics of deviants than with the process by which they come to be thought of as outsiders and their reactions to that judgment.

Malinowski discovered the usefulness of this view for understanding the nature of deviance many years ago, in his study of the Trobriand Islands:

One day an outbreak of wailing and a great commotion told me that a death had occurred somewhere in the neighborhood. I was informed that Kima'i, a young lad of my acquaintance, of sixteen or so, had fallen from a coco-nut palm and killed himself. . . . I found that another youth had been severely wounded by some mysterious coincidence. And at the funeral there was obviously a general feeling of hostility between the village where the boy died and that into which his body was carried for burial.

Only much later was I able to discover the real meaning of these events. The boy had committed suicide. The truth was that he had broken the rules of exogamy, the partner in his crime being his maternal cousin, the daughter of his mother's sister. This had been known and generally disapproved of but nothing was done until the girl's discarded lover, who had wanted to marry her and who felt personally injured, took the initiative. This rival threatened first to use black magic against the guilty youth, but this had not much effect. Then one evening he insulted the culprit in public—accusing him in the hearing of the whole community of incest and hurling at him certain expressions intolerable to a native.

article stating a position very similar to mine is John Kitsuse, "Societal Reaction to Deviance: Problems of Theory and Method," *Social Problems*, 9 (Winter, 1962), 247–256.

For this there was only one remedy; only one means of escape remained to the unfortunate youth. Next morning he put on festive attire and ornamentation, climbed a coco-nut palm and addressed the community, speaking from among the palm leaves and bidding them farewell. He explained the reasons for his desperate deed and also launched forth a veiled accusation against the man who had driven him to his death, upon which it became the duty of his clansmen to avenge him. Then he wailed aloud, as is the custom, jumped from a palm some sixty feet high and was killed on the spot. There followed a fight within the village in which the rival was wounded; and the quarrel was repeated during the funeral. . . .

If you were to inquire into the matter among the Trobrianders, you would find . . . that the natives show horror at the idea of violating the rules of exogamy and that they believe that sores, disease and even death might follow clan incest. This is the ideal of native law, and in moral matters it is easy and pleasant strictly to adhere to the ideal—when judging the conduct of others or expressing an opinion about conduct in general.

When it comes to the application of morality and ideals to real life, however, things take on a different complexion. In the case described it was obvious that the facts would not tally with the ideal of conduct. Public opinion was neither outraged by the knowledge of the crime to any extent, nor did it react directly—it had to be mobilized by a public statement of the crime and by insults being hurled at the culprit by an interested party. Even then he had to carry out the punishment himself. . . . Probing further into the matter and collecting concrete information, I found that the breach of exogamy—as regards intercourse and not marriage—is by no means a rare occurrence, and public opinion is lenient, though decidedly hypocritical. If the affair is carried on *sub rosa* with a certain amount of decorum, and if no one in particular stirs up trouble—"public opinion" will gossip, but not demand any harsh punishment. If, on the contrary, scandal breaks out—everyone turns against the guilty pair and by ostracism and insults one or the other may be driven to suicide.[2]

Whether an act is deviant, then, depends on how other people react to it. You can commit clan incest and suffer from no more than gossip as long as no one makes a public accusation; but you will be driven to your death if the accusation is made. The point is that the response of other people has to be regarded as problematic. Just because one has committed an infraction of a rule does not mean that others will respond as though this had happened. (Conversely, just because one has not violated a rule does not mean that he may not be treated, in some circumstances, as though he had.)

The degree to which other people will respond to a given act as deviant varies greatly. Several kinds of variation seem worth noting. First of all, there is variation over time. A person believed to have committed a

[2] Bronislaw Malinowski, *Crime and Custom in Savage Society* (New York: Humanities Press, 1926), pp. 77–80. Reprinted by permission of Humanities Press and Routledge & Kegan Paul, Ltd.

given "deviant" act may at one time be responded to much more leniently than he would be at some other time. The occurrence of "drives" against various kinds of deviance illustrates this clearly. At various times, enforcement officials may decide to make an all-out attack on some particular kind of deviance, such as gambling, drug addiction, or homosexuality. It is obviously much more dangerous to engage in one of these activities when a drive is on than at any other time. (In a very interesting study of crime news in Colorado newspapers, Davis found that the amount of crime reported in Colorado newspapers showed very little association with actual changes in the amount of crime taking place in Colorado. And, further, that peoples' estimate of how much increase there had been in crime in Colorado was associated with the increase in the amount of crime news but not with any increase in the amount of crime.)[3]

The degree to which an act will be treated as deviant depends also on who commits the act and who feels he has been harmed by it. Rules tend to be applied more to some persons than others. Studies of juvenile delinquency make the point clearly. Boys from middle-class areas do not get as far in the legal process when they are apprehended as do boys from slum areas. The middle-class boy is less likely, when picked up by the police, to be taken to the station; less likely when taken to the station to be booked; and it is extremely unlikely that he will be convicted and sentenced.[4] This variation occurs even though the original infraction of the rule is the same in the two cases. Similarly, the law is differentially applied to Negroes and whites. It is well known that a Negro believed to have attacked a white woman is much more likely to be punished than a white man who commits the same offense; it is only slightly less well known that a Negro who murders another Negro is much less likely to be punished than a white man who commits murder.[5] This, of course, is one of the main points of Sutherland's analysis of white-collar crime: crimes committed by corporations are almost always prosecuted as civil cases, but the same crime committed by an individual is ordinarily treated as a criminal offense.[6]

Some rules are enforced only when they result in certain consequences. The unmarried mother furnishes a clear example. Vincent[7] points

[3] F. James Davis, "Crime News in Colorado Newspapers," *American Journal of Sociology,* LVII (January, 1952), 325–330.

[4] See Albert K. Cohen and James F. Short, Jr., "Juvenile Delinquency," in Robert K. Merton and Robert A. Nisbet, editors, *Contemporary Social Problems* (New York: Harcourt, Brace and World, Inc., 1961), p. 87.

[5] See Harold Garfinkel, "Research Notes on Inter- and Intra-Racial Homicides," *Social Forces,* 27 (May, 1949), 369–381.

[6] Edwin H. Sutherland, "White Collar Criminality," *American Sociological Review,* V (February, 1940), 1–12.

[7] Clark Vincent, *Unmarried Mothers* (New York: The Free Press of Glencoe, 1961), pp. 3–5.

out that illicit sexual relations seldom result in severe punishment or social censure for the offenders. If, however, a girl becomes pregnant as a result of such activities the reaction of others is likely to be severe. (The illicit pregnancy is also an interesting example of the differential enforcement of rules on different categories of people. Vincent notes that unmarried fathers escape the severe censure visited on the mother.)

Why repeat these commonplace observations? Because, taken together, they support the proposition that deviance is not a simple quality, present in some kinds of behavior and absent in others. Rather, it is the product of a process which involves responses of other people to the behavior. The same behavior may be an infraction of the rules at one time and not at another; may be an infraction when committed by one person, but not when committed by another; some rules are broken with impunity, others are not. In short, whether a given act is deviant or not depends in part on the nature of the act (that is, whether or not it violates some rule) and in part on what other people do about it.

Some people may object that this is merely a terminological quibble, that one can, after all, define terms any way he wants to and that if some people want to speak of rule-breaking behavior as deviant without reference to the reactions of others they are free to do so. This, of course, is true. Yet it might be worthwhile to refer to such behavior as *rule-breaking behavior* and reserve the term *deviant* for those labeled as deviant by some segment of society. I do not insist that this usage be followed. But it should be clear that insofar as a scientist uses "deviant" to refer to any rule-breaking behavior and takes as his subject of study only those who have been *labeled* deviant, he will be hampered by the disparities between the two categories.

If we take as the object of our attention behavior which comes to be labeled as deviant, we must recognize that we cannot know whether a given act will be categorized as deviant until the response of others has occurred. Deviance is not a quality that lies in behavior itself, but in the interaction between the person who commits an act and those who respond to it.

2 Societal Reactions to Deviant Behavior: Problems of Theory and Method*

JOHN I. KITSUSE

Sociological theory and research in the area traditionally known as "social pathology" have been concerned primarily with the classification and analysis of *deviant forms of behavior* and relatively little attention has been given to societal reactions to deviance.[1] In a recent paper, Merton has noted this lack of a "systematic *classification* of the responses of the conventional or conforming members of a group to deviant behavior."[2] Similarly, Cohen has observed that "a sociology of deviant behavior-conformity will have to devise ways of conceptualizing responses to deviant behavior from the standpoint of their relevance to the production or extinction of deviant behavior."[3] In this paper, I shall discuss some of the theoretical and methodo-

Reprinted from *Social Problems,* Volume 9, Number 3 (Winter, 1963), 247–256, by permission of The Society for the Study of Socal Problems and the author.

* An earlier form of this paper was read at the meetings of the American Sociological Association, 1960. I have profited from the critical comments and suggestions of Herbert R. Barringer, Aaron V. Cicourel, Sheldon L. Messinger, and H. Jay Shaffer. Troy S. Duster's valuable assistance in the analysis of the data is gratefully acknowledged.

[1] A notable exception is the work of Edwin M. Lemert, who systematically incorporates the concept of societal reaction in his theory of sociopathic behavior. See *Social Pathology,* McGraw-Hill, New York: 1951.

[2] Robert K. Merton, Social Conformity, Deviation, and Opportunity-Structures: A Comment on the Contributions of Dubin and Cloward," *American Sociological Review,* 24 (1959), pp. 177–189.

[3] Albert K. Cohen, "The Study of Social Disorganization and Deviant Behavior," in *Sociology Today,* R. Merton, L. Broom, and L. Cottrell, eds. Basic Books: New York, 1959, pp. 465–466.

logical issues posed by the problem of societal reactions to deviant behavior and report on a preliminary attempt to formulate a research design which specifically takes them into account.

I propose to shift the focus of theory and research from the forms of deviant behavior to the *processes by which persons come to be defined as deviant by others*. Such a shift requires that the sociologist view as problematic what he generally assumes as given—namely, that certain forms of behavior are *per se* deviant and are so defined by the "conventional or conforming members of a group." This assumption is frequently called into question on empirical grounds when the societal reaction to behaviors defined as deviant by the sociologist is non-existent, indifferent, or at most mildly disapproving. For example, in his discussion of "ritualism" as a form of deviant behavior, Merton states that it is not that such behavior is treated by others as deviant which identifies it as deviant "since the overt behavior is institutionally permitted, though not culturally prescribed."[4] Rather, the behavior is deviant because it "clearly represents a departure from the cultural model in which men are obliged to move onward and upward in the social hierarchy."[5] The discrepancy between the theoretically hypothesized and empirically observable societal reaction is also noted by Lemert: "It is fairly easy to think of situations in which serious offenses against laws commanding public respect have only mild penalty or have gone entirely unpunished. Conversely, cases are easily discovered in which a somewhat minor violation of legal rules has provoked surprisingly stringent penalties."[6]

Clearly, the forms of behavior *per se* do not activate the processes of societal reaction which sociologically differentiate deviants from non-deviants. Thus, a central problem for theory and research in the sociology of deviance may be stated as follows: What are the behaviors which are defined by members of the group, community, or society as deviant, and how do those definitions organize and activate the societal reactions by which persons come to be differentiated and treated as deviants? In formulating the problem in this way, the point of view of those who interpret and define behavior as deviant must explicitly be incorporated into a sociological definition of deviance. Accordingly, deviance may be conceived as a process by which the members of a group, community, or society (1) interpret behavior as deviant, (2) define persons who so behave as a certain kind of deviant, and (3) accord them the treatment considered appropriate to such deviants. In the following pages, this conception of deviance and societal reaction will be applied to the processes by which persons come to be defined and treated as homosexuals.

[4] Robert K. Merton, *Social Theory and Social Structure*, revised, Free Press: Glencoe, 1957, p. 150.

[5] *Ibid,* p. 150.

[6] *Op. cit.,* p. 55.

SOCIETAL REACTIONS
TO "HOMOSEXUAL BEHAVIOR"

As a form of deviant behavior, homosexuality presents a strategically important theoretical and empirical problem for the study of deviance. In the sociological and anthropological literature[7] homosexual behavior and the societal reactions to it are conceptualized within the framework of ascribed sex statuses and the socialization of individuals to those statuses. The ascription of sex statuses is presumed to provide a complex of culturally prescribed roles and behaviors which individuals are expected to learn and perform. Homosexual roles and behaviors are conceived to be "inappropriate" to the individual's ascribed sex status, and thus theoretically they are defined as deviant.

With reference to American society, Allison Davis states: "Sex-typing of behavior and privileges is even more rigid and lasting in our society than is age-typing. Indeed, sexual status and color-caste status are the only life-long forms of rank. In our society, one can escape them in approved fashion only by death. Whereas sexual mobility is somewhat less rare today than formerly, sex-inappropriate behavior, social or physical, is still one of the most severely punished infractions of our social code."[8] In Lemert's terminology, norms concerning sex-appropriate behavior have a high degree of "compulsiveness" and social disapproval of violations is stringent and effective.[9] Homosexuals themselves appear to share this conception of the societal reaction to their behavior, activities, and subculture.[10]

Such a view of homosexuality would lead one to hypothesize that "sex-appropriate" (and conversely "sex-inappropriate") behaviors are unambiguously prescribed, deviations from those prescriptions are invariably interpreted as immoral, and the reactions of the conventional and conforming members of the society to such deviations are uniformly severe and effective. The evidence which apparently supports this hypothesis is not difficult to

---

[7] For examples, see Talcott Parsons and Robert F. Bales, *Family Socialization and Interaction Process,* Free Press: Glencoe, 1955, pp. 103–105; Ruth Benedict, "Continuities and Discontinuities in Cultural Conditioning," *Psychiatry,* 1 (1938), pp. 161–167; Abram Kardiner and Associates, *Psychological Frontiers of Society,* Columbia University Press: New York, 1945, pp. 57, 88, etc.; Clifford Kirkpatrick, *The Family,* Ronald Press: New York, 1955, pp. 57–58; Margaret Mead, *Sex and Temperament,* William Morrow: New York, 1955.

[8] Allison Davis, "American Status Systems and the Socialization of the Child," *American Sociological Review,* 6 (1941), p. 350.

[9] *Op. cit.,* Chapter 4.

[10] Evelyn Hooker, "Sequences in Homosexual Identification," read at the meetings of the American Sociological Association, 1960; Donald Webster Cory, *The Homosexual in America,* Greenburg: New York, 1951, esp. Part I.

find, particularly with reference to the definition and treatment of male homosexuals. Individuals who are publicly identified as homosexuals are frequently denied the social, economic, and legal rights of "normal" males. Socially they may be treated as objects of amusement, ridicule, scorn, and often fear; economically they may be summarily dismissed from employment; legally they are frequently subject to interrogation and harassment by police.

In citing such evidence, however, it is important to note that the societal reaction to and the differentiation of homosexuals from the "normal" population is a consequence of the fact that the former are "known" to be homosexuals by some individuals, groups or agencies. Thus, within the framework of the present formulation of homosexuality as a form of deviant behavior, the processes by which individuals come to be "known" and treated as sexually deviant will be viewed as problematic and a problem for empirical investigation. I shall not be concerned here with the so-called "latent homosexual" unless he is so defined by others and differentially treated as a consequence of that definition. Nor will I be concerned with the variety of "internal" conflicts which may form the "clinical" picture of the homosexual except insofar as such conflicts are manifested in behavior leading others to conceive of him as a homosexual. In short, I shall proceed on the principle that it is only when individuals are defined and identified by others as homosexuals and accorded the treatment considered "appropriate" for individuals so defined that a homosexual "population" is produced for sociological investigation.[11] With reference to homosexuality, then, the empirical questions are: What forms of behavior do persons in the social system consider to be "sex-inappropriate," how do they interpret such behaviors, and what are the consequences of those interpretations for their reactions to individuals who are perceived to manifest such behaviors?

In a preliminary attempt to investigate these questions, an interview schedule was constructed[12] and administered to approximately seven hundred individuals, most of whom were college undergraduates. The sample was neither random nor representative of any specified population, and the generalizability of the interview materials is limited except insofar as they are relevant to the previously noted hypothesis that homosexual behavior is uniformly defined, interpreted, and negatively sanctioned. The interview materials will therefore be used for the purpose of illustrating the theory and method of the present conception of deviance and societal reaction.

The objectives of the interview were threefold: It attempted to docu-

[11] This principle has been suggested by Harold Garfinkel. See "Some Sociological Concepts and Methods for Psychiatrists," *Psychiatric Research Reports,* 6 (1956), pp. 181–195.

[12] The interview schedule and methods were conceived and constructed in consultation with Aaron V. Cicourel.

ment (1) the behavior forms which are interpreted as deviant, (2) the processes by which persons who manifest such behaviors are defined and (3) treated as deviant. Thus, in the construction of the interview schedule, what the interviewees considered to be "deviant" behavior, the interpretations of such behavior, and the actions of subjects toward those perceived as deviant were addressed as empirical questions. Labels such as alcoholic, illiterate, illegitimate child, and ex-convict were assumed to be categories employed by persons in everyday life to classify deviants, but the behavioral forms by which they identify individuals as deviants were treated as problematic. "Sexual deviant" was one of ten categories of deviants about which subjects were questioned in the interview. Among the more than seven hundred subjects interviewed, seventy-five stated they had "known" a homosexual and responded to questions concerning their experiences with such individuals. The data presented below are drawn from the protocols of interviews with this group of subjects.

The interview proceeded as follows:

The subject was asked "Have you ever known anyone who was a sexual deviant?" If he questioned the meaning of "deviant," the subject was asked to consider the question using his own meaning of "sexual deviant."

When the subject stated he had known a sexual deviant—a homosexual in this case—as he defined the term, he was asked to think about the most recent incident involving him in an encounter with such a person. He was then asked "When was the first time you noticed (found out) that this person was a homosexual?" followed by "What was the situation? What did you notice about him? How did he behave?" This line of questioning was focused on the interaction between the subject and the alleged deviant to obtain a detailed description of the situation which led the subject to define the person as homosexual. The subject's description of the person's behavior was systematically probed to clarify the terms of his description, particularly those which were interpretive rather than descriptive.

EVIDENCE OF HOMOSEXUALITY

Responses to the question "When was the first time you noticed (found out) that this person was homosexual?" and the related probes suggest that an individual's sexual "normality" may be called into question with reference to two broad categories of evidence (a) *Indirect evidence* in the form of a rumor, an acquaintance's experience with the individual in question subsequently communicated to the subject, or general reputational information concerning the individual's behavior, associates and sexual predilections may be the occasion for suspecting him to be "different." Many subjects reported that they first "found out" or "knew" that the individuals in question concerning the individual's behavior, associates and sexual predilections Such information was generally accepted by the subjects without independent verification. Indeed, the information provided a new perspective for their retrospective as well as prospective observations and interpretations of the individuals' behaviors. An example of how hearsay organizes observation and interpretation is the following statement by a 35-year-old male (a draftsman):

I: Then this lieutenant was a homosexual?

S: Yes.

I: How did you find out about it?

S: The guy he approached told me. After that, I watched him. Our company was small and we had a bar for both enlisted men and officers. He would come in and try to be friendly with one or two of the guys.

I: Weren't the other officers friendly?

S: Sure, they would come in for an occasional drink; some of them had been with the company for three years and they would sometimes slap you on the back, but he tried to get over friendly.

I: What do you mean "over friendly"?

S: He had only been there a week. He would try to push himself on a couple of guys—he spent more time with the enlisted personnel than is expected from an officer.

(b) *Direct observation* by the subject of the individual's behavior may be the basis for calling the latter's sexual "normality" into question. The descriptions of behavior which subjects took to be indicative of homosexuality varied widely and were often vague. Most frequently the behaviors cited were those *"which everyone knows"* are indications of homosexuality. For example, a 20-year-old male subject reports an encounter with a stranger at a bar:

I: What happened during your conversation?

S: He asked me if I went to college and I said I did. Then he asked me what I was studying. When I told him psychology he appeared very interested.

I: What do you mean "interested"?

S: Well, you know queers really go for this psychology stuff.

I: Then what happened?

S: Ah, let's see. I'm not exactly sure, but somehow we got into an argument about psychology and to prove my point I told him to pick an area of study. Well, he appeared to be very pensive and after a great thought he said, "Okay, let's take homosexuality."

I: What did you make of that?

S: Well, by now I figured the guy was queer so I got the hell outta there.

The responses of other subjects suggest that an individual is particularly suspect when he is observed to behave in a manner which deviates from the *behaviors-held-in-common* among members of the group to which he belongs. For example, a behavior which is presumed to be held-in-common among sailors in the U.S. Navy is intense and active sexual activity. When a sailor does not affirm, at least verbally, his interest in such activity, his competence as a "male" may be called into question. A 22-year-old engineer, recently discharged from the Navy, responds to the "how did you first know" question as follows:

All of a sudden you just get suspicious of something. I began to wonder about him. He didn't go in for leave activities that most sailors go for. You know, girls and high times. He just never was interested and when you have been out at sea for a month or two, you're interested. That just wasn't Navy, and he was a career man.

Although the responses of our subjects indicate there are many behavioral gestures which "everyone knows" are indicators of homosexuality in males, there are relatively few such gestures that lead persons to suspect females of homosexuality. Following is an excerpt from a 21-year-old college co-ed whose remarks illustrate this lack of definite indicators *prior* to her labeling of an acquaintance as a homosexual:

I: When was the first time you noticed she was a deviant?
S: I didn't notice it. I thought she had a masculine appearance when I first saw her anyway.
I: What do you mean?
S: Oh, her haircut, her heavy eyebrows. She had a rather husky build.
I: Exactly when did you think she had a masculine appearance?
S: It was long after [the first meeting] that I found out that she was "one."
I: How do you define it?
S: Well, a lesbian. I don't know too much about them. It was —— who told me about her.
I: Did you notice anything else about her [at the first meeting]?
S: No, because you really don't know unless you're looking for those things.

Unlike "effeminate" appearance and gestures in males, "masculine" appearance in females is apparently less likely to be immediately linked to the suspicion or imputation of homosexuality. The statements of the subject quoted above indicate that although "masculine appearance" is an important element in her conception of a lesbian, its significance did not become apparent to her until a third person told her the girl was homosexual. The remarks of other subjects in our sample who state they have "known" female homosexuals reveal a similar ambiguity in their interpretations of what they describe as indicators of sexual deviance.

A third form of evidence by direct observation is behaviors which the subjects interpreted to be *overt sexual propositions*. Descriptions of such propositions ranged from what the subjects considered to be unmistakable evidence of the person's sexual deviance to ambiguous gestures which they did not attempt to question in the situation. The following is an excerpt from an interview with a 24-year-old male school teacher who recounts an experience in a Korean Army barrack:

I: What questions did he [the alleged homosexual] ask?
S: "How long have you been in Korea?" I told him. "What do you think of these Korean girls?" which I answered, "Not too much because they are dirty." I thought he was probably homesick and wanted someone to talk to. I do not remember what he said then until he said, "How much do you have?" I answered him by saying, "I don't know, about average I guess." Then he said, "Can I feel it just once?" To this I responded with, "Get the hell out of here," and I gave him a shove when he reached for me as he asked the question.

In a number of interviews, the subjects' statements indicate that they interpreted the sequence of the alleged deviants' behavior as progressively inappropriate or peculiar in the course of their interaction with them. The link between such behavior and their judgment that a sexual proposition was being made was frequently established by the subjects' growing realization of its deviant character. A 21-year-old male subject recalls the following experience involving his high school tennis coach who had invited him to dinner:

S: Anyway, when I get there he served dinner, and as I think back on it—I didn't notice it at the time—but I remember that he did act sort of effeminate. Finally he got up to change a record and picked up some of my English themes. Then he brought them over and sat down beside me. He began to explain some of my mistakes in my themes, and in the meantime he slipped his arms around me.
I: Would you say that this was done in a friendly manner or with an intent of hugging you or something?
S: Well, no, it was just a friendly gesture of putting his arm around my shoulder. At that time, I didn't think anything of it, but as he continued to explain my mistakes, he started to rub my back. Then he asked me if I want a back rub. So I said, "No! I don't need one." At this time, I began thinking something was funny anyway. So I said that I had to go. . . .

THE IMPUTATION OF HOMOSEXUALITY

When a detailed description of the subject's evidence concerning the alleged homosexual was obtained, he was asked, "What did you make of that?" to elicit information about how he interpreted the person's observed or reported behavior. This line of questioning yielded data on the inferential process by which the subject linked his information about the individual to the deviant category "homosexual."

A general pattern revealed by the subjects' responses to this section of the interview schedule is that when an individual's sexual "normality" is called into question, by whatever form of evidence, the imputation of homosexuality is documented by *retrospective interpretations* of the deviant's behavior, a process by which the subject re-interprets the individual's past behavior in the light of the new information concerning his sexual deviance. This process is particularly evident in cases where the prior relationship between the subject and the alleged homosexual was more than a chance encounter or casual acquaintanceship. The subjects indicate that they reviewed their past interactions with the individuals in question, searching for subtle cues and nuances of behavior which might give further evidence of the alleged deviance. This retrospective reading generally provided the subjects with just such evidence to support the conclusion that "this is what was going on all the time."

Some of the subjects who were interviewed were themselves aware of their retrospective interpretations in defining individuals as sexually deviant. For example, a 23-year-old female graduate student states:

I: Will you tell me more about the situation?

S: Well, their relationship was a continuous one, although I think that it is a friendship now as I don't see them together as I used to; I don't think it is still homosexual. When I see them together, they don't seem to be displaying the affection openly as they did when I first realized the situation.

I: How do you mean "openly"?

S: Well, they would hold each other's hand in public places.

I: And what did you make of this?

S: Well, I really don't know, because I like to hold people's hands, too! I guess I actually didn't see this as directly connected with the situation. What I mean is that, if I hadn't seen that other incident [she had observed the two girls in bed together] I probably wouldn't have thought of it [i.e., hand-holding] very much. . . . Well, actually, there were a few things that I questioned later on that I hadn't thought really very much about. . . . I can remember her being quite affectionate towards me several times when we were in our room together, like putting her arm around my shoulder. Or I remember one time specifically when she asked me for a kiss. I was shocked at the time, but I laughed it off jokingly.

THE INTERACTIONAL CONTEXTS OF
SOCIETAL REACTIONS

When the description of the alleged deviant's behavior and the subject's interpretations of that behavior were recorded, the subject was asked "What did you do then?" This question was directed toward documenting societal reactions to deviant behavior. Forms of behavior *per se* do not differentiate deviants from non-deviants; it is the responses of the conventional and conforming members of the society who identify and interpret behavior as deviant which sociologically transform persons into deviants. Thus, in the formulation of deviance proposed here, if the subject observes an individual's behavior and defines it as deviant but does not accord him differential treatment as a consequence of that definition, the individual is not sociologically deviant.

The reactions of the subjects to individuals they defined as homosexuals ranged from immediate withdrawal from the scene of interaction and avoidance of further encounters with the alleged deviants to the maintenance of the prior relationship virtually unaltered by the imputation of deviance. The following responses to the question "What did you do then?" illustrate the variation in sanctions directed toward persons defined as homosexuals.

Explicit disapproval and immediate withdrawal: The most negatively toned and clearly articulated reaction reported by our subjects is that of the previously quoted Korean War veteran. It is interesting to note that extreme physical punishment as a reaction to persons defined as homosexuals, a reaction which is commonly verbalized by "normal" males as proper treatment of "queers," is not reported by any of the subjects. When physical force is used, it is invariably in response to the deviant's direct physical overtures, and even then it is relatively mild, e.g., "I gave him a shove when he reached for me."

Explicit disapproval and subsequent withdrawal: In the following excerpt, a 20-year-old male college student describes an encounter with a man whom he met in a coffee shop. In the course of their conversation, the man admitted his homosexuality to the subject. The two left the coffee shop and walked together to the subway station.

I: What happened then?
S: We got to the subway whereupon he suggested that he hail a cab and take me up to Times Square—a distance of almost 40 blocks.
I: Did you agree, and what did you think?
S: Yes, I thought he was just being very nice and I had no qualms about getting in a cab with a homosexual since I was quite sure I could protect myself against any advances in a cab.
I: What happened then?
S: When we had ridden a little distance, he put his hand on my knee, and I promptly removed it saying that it just wasn't right and that I wanted nothing of it. However, after a while he put his hand back. This time I didn't take it away for a while because I was interested in what he would do. It was the funniest thing—he rubbed and caressed my knee the same way in which I would have done this to a girl. This time I took his

hand and hit him across the chest with it, telling him to "cut it out." Finally, we got to Times Square, and I got out.

This example and that provided by the Korean War veteran's reaction to behavior interpreted as overt sexual propositions suggest the possibility that responses to persons suspected of homosexuality or defined as homosexuals on the basis of more indirect evidence of appearance, "confessions," hearsay, reputation, or association will vary within an even wider range of applied sanctions. Indeed, the statements of subjects concerning their responses to persons alleged to be deviant on such evidence indicate that the modal reaction is disapproval, implicitly rather than explicitly communicated, and a restriction of interaction through partial withdrawal and avoidance. It should be noted further that although the subject's silent withdrawal from an established relationship with an alleged deviant may represent a stronger disapproval than an explicitly communicated, physically enforced sanction against a stranger, moral indignation or revulsion is not necessarily communicated to the deviant. The subject's prior relationship with the alleged deviant and the demands of propriety in subsequent interactions with him qualify the form and intensity of the sanctions which are applied. Thus, when the organization of the subject's day-to-day activities "forces" him into interaction with the deviant, expressions of disapproval are frequently constrained and diffused by the rules of deference and demeanor.[13] The following excerpts provide illustrations:

Implicit disapproval and partial withdrawal: A 20-year-old co-ed's reaction to a girl she concluded was a homosexual was expressed as follows:

"Well, I don't want to be alone with X [the homosexual] because the four of us had two connecting rooms and I was in the room with X. As much as I liked the girl and felt sorry for her, I knew she could really wring me through the wringer. So the rest decided that I should tell her that if she and Y wanted to be homos, to do it somewhere else and not in the room."

No disapproval and relationship sustained: The "live and let live" response to homosexuals, which is implied in the preceding reaction, was not uncommon among the subjects. Some subjects not only affirmed the right of the homosexual to "live his own life" but also reported that their knowledge of the deviance has had little or no effect upon their subsequent relationships with the deviants. In this regard, the mildest reaction, so mild that it might be considered no reaction at all, was that of a 19-year-old male college student:

I: What was your reaction to him?
S: My reactions to him have always been friendly because he seems like a
     very friendly person. Uh, and he has a very nice sense of humor and

[13] Erving Goffman, "The Nature of Deference and Demeanor," *American Anthropologist,* 58 (1956), pp. 473–502.

I've never been repelled by anything he's said. For one thing, I think he's tremendously interesting because he seems to have such a wide range for background. . . .

I: When was the last time you saw this person?

S: Last night. . . . I was sitting in a restaurant and he walked in with some friends . . . he just stopped in and said hello, and was his usual friendly self.

I: What in particular happened after that?

S: Actually, nothing. He sat down with his friends and we exchanged a few words about the records that were playing on the juke box. But nothing, actually. . . .

The thoretical significance of these data for the conception of deviance and societal reaction presented here is not that the subjects' information is of dubious accuracy or questionable relevance as evidence of homosexuality. Nor is it that the subjects' interpretations of them are unreasonable, unjustifiable, or spurious. They suggest rather that the conceptions of persons in everyday life concerning "sex-appropriate" or "sex-inappropriate" behavior may lead them to interpret a variety of behavioral forms as indications of the same deviation, and the "same" behavioral forms as indications of a variety of deviant as well as "normal" behavior. An individual's sexual "normality" may be made problematic by the interpretations and re-interpretations of his behavior by others, and the interpretive process may be activated by a wide range of situational behaviors which lend new significance to the individual's past and present behavior. His behavior with respect to speech, interests, dress, dating, or relations with other males are not *per se* significant in the deviant-defining process. The data suggest that the critical feature of the deviant-defining process is not the behavior of individuals who are defined as deviant, but rather the interpretations others make of their behaviors, whatever those behaviors may be.

With specific reference to homosexuality as a form of deviant behavior, the interview materials suggest that while reactions toward persons defined as homosexuals tend to be negatively toned, they are far from homogeneous as to the forms or intensity of the sanctions invoked and applied. Indeed, reactions which may appear to the sociological observer or to the deviant himself as negative sanctions, such as withdrawal or avoidance, may be expressions of embarrassment, a reluctance to share the burden of the deviant's problems, fear of the deviant, etc., as well as moral indignation or revulsion. In none of the interviews does the subject react with extreme violence, explicitly define or directly accuse the deviant of being a "queer," "fairy," or other terms of opprobrium, nor did any of them initiate legal actions against the deviant. In view of the extreme negative sanctions against homosexuality which are posited on theoretical grounds, the generally mild reactions of our subjects are striking.

The relative absence of extreme and overtly expressed negative sanctions against homosexuals among our subjects may, of course, reflect the higher than average educational level of the sample. A sample of subjects less biased toward the highly educated, middle-class segment of the population than was interviewed in this preliminary study may be expected to reflect a more definite pattern with reference to such negative reactions. We must, therefore, be cautious in generalizing the range of reactions among our subjects to the general population. It is equally important to note, however, that these data do indicate that reactions to homosexuals in American society are not *societal* in the sense of being uniform within a narrow range; rather, they are significantly conditioned by sub-cultural as well as situational factors. Thus, not only are the processes by which persons come to be defined as homosexuals contingent upon the interpretations of their behavior by others, but also the sanctions imposed and the treatment they are accorded as a consequence of that definition vary widely among conventional members of various sub-cultural groups.

The larger implications of these data are that a sociological theory of deviance must explicitly take into account the variety and range of conceptions held by persons, groups, and agencies within the society concerning any form of behavior. The increasing differentiation of groups, institutions, and sub-cultures in modern society generates a continually changing range of alternatives and tolerance for the expression of sexual as well as other forms of behavior. Consequently, it is difficult if not impossible to theoretically derive a set of *specific behavioral prescriptions* which will in fact be normatively supported, uniformly practiced, and socially enforced by more than a segment of the total population. Under such conditions, it is not the fact that individuals engage in behaviors which diverge from some theoretically posited "institutionalized expectations" or even that such behaviors are defined as deviant by the conventional and conforming members of the society which is of primary significance for the study of deviance. A sociological theory of deviance must focus specifically upon the interactions which not only define behaviors as deviant but also organize and activate the application of sanctions by individuals, groups, or agencies. For in modern society, the socially significant differentiation of deviants from the non-deviant population is increasingly contingent upon circumstances of situation, place, social and personal biography, and the bureaucratically organized activities of agencies of control.[14]

---

[14] For a discussion of such contingencies, see Edwin M. Lemert, *op. cit.*, Chapter 4, and Erving Goffman, "The Moral Career of the Mental Patient," *Psychiatry*, 22 (1959), pp. 123–142.

3 Primary and Secondary Deviation

EDWIN M. LEMERT

There has been an embarrassingly large number of theories, often without any relationship to a general theory, advanced to account for various specific pathologies in human behavior. For certain types of pathology, such as alcoholism, crime, or stuttering, there are almost as many theories as there are writers on these subjects. This has been occasioned in no small way by the preoccupation with the origins of pathological behavior and by the fallacy of confusing *original* causes with *effective* causes. All such theories have elements of truth, and the divergent viewpoints they contain can be reconciled with the general theory here if it is granted that original causes or antecedents of deviant behaviors are many and diversified. This holds especially for the psychological processes leading to similar pathological behavior, but it also holds for the situational concomitants of the initial aberrant conduct. A person may come to use excessive alcohol not only for a wide variety of subjective reasons but also because of diversified situational influences, such as the death of a loved one, business failure, or participating in some sort of organized group activity calling for heavy drinking of liquor. Whatever the original reasons for violating the norms of the community, they are important only for certain research purposes, such as assessing the extent of the "social problem" at a given time or determining the requirements for a rational program of social control. From a narrower sociological viewpoint the deviations are not significant until they are organized subjectively and transformed into active roles and become the social criteria for assigning status. The deviant individuals must react symbolically to their own behavior aberrations and fix them in their socio-psychological patterns. The deviations remain primary deviations or symptomatic and situational as long as they are rationalized or otherwise dealt with as functions of a socially acceptable role. Under such conditions normal and pathological behaviors remain strange and somewhat tensional bedfellows in the same person. Undeniably a vast amount of such segmental and partially integrated pathological behavior exists in our society and has impressed many writers in the field of social pathology.

Just how far and for how long a person may go in dissociating his sociopathic tendencies so that they are merely troublesome adjuncts of normally conceived roles is not known. Perhaps it depends upon the number of alternative definitions of the same overt behavior that he can develop; perhaps certain physiological factors (limits) are also involved. However, if the deviant acts are repetitive and have a high visibility, and if there is a severe societal reaction, which, through a process of identification is incorporated as part of the "me" of the individual, the probability is greatly increased that the integration of existing roles will be disrupted and that reorganization based upon a new role or roles will occur. (The "me" in this context is simply the subjective aspect of the societal reaction.) Reorganization may be the adoption of another normal role in which the tendencies previously defined as "pathological" are given a more acceptable social expression. The other general possibility is the assumption of a deviant role, if such exists; or, more rarely, the person may organize an aberrant sect or group in which he creates a special role of his own. *When a person begins to employ his deviant behavior or a role based upon it as a means of defense, attack, or adjustment to the overt and covert problems created by the consequent societal reaction to him, his deviation is secondary.* Objective evidences of this change will be found in the symbolic appurtenances of the new role, in clothes, speech, posture, and mannerisms, which in some cases heighten social visibility, and which in some cases serve as symbolic cues to professionalization.

ROLE CONCEPTIONS OF THE INDIVIDUAL MUST BE REINFORCED BY REACTIONS OF OTHERS

It is seldom that one deviant act will provoke a sufficiently strong societal reaction to bring about secondary deviation, unless in the process of introjection the individual imputes or projects meanings into the social situation which are not present. In this case anticipatory fears are involved. For example, in a culture where a child is taught sharp distinctions between "good" women and "bad" women, a single act of questionable morality might conceivably have profound meaning for the girl so indulging. However, in the absence of reactions by the person's family, neighbors, or the larger community, reinforcing the tentative "bad-girl" self-definition, it is questionable whether a transition to secondary deviation would take place. It is also doubtful whether a temporary exposure to a severe punitive reaction by the community will lead a person to identify himself with a pathological role, unless, as we have said, the experience is highly traumatic. Most frequently there is a progressive reciprocal relationship between the deviation of the individual and the societal reaction, with a compounding of the societal reaction out of the minute accretions in the deviant behavior, until a point is reached where ingrouping and outgrouping between society and the deviant is manifest.[1] At this point a stigmatizing of the deviant occurs in the form of name calling, labeling, or stereotyping.

The sequence of interaction leading to secondary deviation is roughly as follows: (1) primary deviation; (2) social penalties; (3) further primary deviation; (4) stronger penalties and rejections; (5) further deviation, perhaps with hostilities and resentment beginning to focus upon those doing the penalizing; (6) crisis reached in the tolerance quotient, expressed in formal action by the community stigmatizing of the deviant; (7) strengthening of the deviant conduct as a reaction to the stigmatizing and penalties; (8) ultimate acceptance of deviant social status and efforts at adjustment on the basis of the associated role.

As an illustration of this sequence the behavior of an errant schoolboy can be cited. For one reason or another, let us say excessive energy, the schoolboy engages in a classroom prank. He is penalized for it by the teacher. Later, due to clumsiness, he creates another disturbance and again he is reprimanded. Then, as sometimes happens, the boy is blamed for something he did not do. When the teacher uses the tag "bad boy" or "mischief maker" or other invidious terms, hostility and resentment are excited in the boy, and he may feel that he is blocked in playing the role expected of him. Thereafter, there may be a strong temptation to assume his role in the class as defined by the teacher, particularly when he discovers that there are rewards as well as penalties deriving from such a role. There is, of course, no implication here that such boys go on to become delinquents or criminals, for the mischief-maker role may later become integrated with or retrospectively rationalized as part of a role more acceptable to

[1] Mead, G., "The Psychology of Punitive Justice," *American Journal of Sociology,* 23 (March, 1918), pp. 577–602.

school authorities.[2] If such a boy continues this unaccepable role and becomes delinquent, the process must be accounted for in the light of the general theory of this [paper]. There must be a spreading corroboration of a sociopathic self-conception and societal reinforcement at each step in the process.

The most significant personality changes are manifest when societal definitions and their subjective counterpart become generalized. When this happens, the range of major role choices becomes narrowed to one general class.[3] This was very obvious in the case of a young girl who was the daughter of a paroled convict and who was attending a small Middle Western college. She continually argued with herself and with the author, in whom she had confided, that in reality she belonged on the "other side of the railroad tracks" and that her life could be enormously simplified by acquiescing in this verdict and living accordingly. While in her case there was a tendency to dramatize her conflicts, nevertheless there was enough societal reinforcement of her self-conception by the treatment she received in her relationship with her father and on dates with college boys to lend it a painful reality. Once these boys took her home to the shoddy dwelling in a slum area where she lived with her father, who was often in a drunken condition, they abruptly stopped seeing her again or else became sexually presumptive.

· · ·

THE SYMBOLIC CONSEQUENCES OF CONTROL

Among the unanticipated consequences of therapy, treatment, or administrative manipulations, none are more important than those which are symbolic in nature. More and more we are coming to realize that the actual symbolic impact of a control or therapeutic experience often is a far cry from what has been intended. The way in which a social worker, a psychiatrist, or a judge conceives of his own role and the meaning of the administrative or clinical situation for the deviant may or may not coincide with the average or modal perception of the latter. If we are to understand in a worth-while way the reactions of deviants brought under societal control we must get at the effective rather than the formal or intended symbols in control situations. They are not the whole of the symbolic environment in which deviation develops, but they make up a very significant part of it. Frequently they are instrumental in giving unintended but critical meanings

[2] Evidence for fixed or inevitable sequences from predelinquency to crime is absent. Sutherland, E. H., *Principles of Criminology*, 1939, 4th ed., p. 202.

[3] Sutherland seems to say something of this sort in connection with the development of criminal behavior. *Ibid.*, p. 86.

to deviant conduct. Court hearings, home investigations by social workers, arrests, clinical visits, segregation within the school system and other formal dispositions of deviants under the aegis of public welfare or public protection in many instances are cause for dramatic redefinitions of the self and role of deviants which may or may not be desired.

4 The Labeling Process

STANTON WHEELER AND
LEONARD S. COTTRELL, JR.
With the assistance of ANNE ROMASCO

Delinquency-prevention activities include all efforts expended before the juvenile's behavior has brought him to the attention of such official agencies as the police and the courts, while adjudicative and correctional activities are those that ensue after the youth's contact with these agencies. Important problems emerge at the meeting of the preventive and adjudicative agencies.

A traditional view of the relationship between delinquents and official agencies is that the latter are primarily passive responders to the active behavior or misbehavior of juveniles. The police exist, among other reasons, to detect delinquency, and the courts to adjudicate the cases of those who are detected. Both are reactions to deviant behavior.

A variety of social science theory and evidence leads to the conclusion that such agencies may play a far more important role than is ordinarily ascribed to them. The evidence suggests that official response to the behavior in question may initiate processes that push the misbehaving juveniles toward further delinquent conduct, and, at least, make it more difficult for them to re-enter the conventional world. This hypothesis is based upon the concept of labeling and a theory of its consequences.[1]

Reprinted from Stanton Wheeler and Leonard S. Cottrell, Jr., with the assistance of Anne Romasco, *Juvenile Delinquency: Its Prevention and Control* (New York: Russell Sage Foundation, 1966), pp. 22–27, by permission of the publisher and the authors.

[1] Recent relevant works include: Freidson, Eliot, "Disability as Social Deviance,"

The assumption is that the public responds to a person informally and in an unorganized way unless that person has been defined as falling into a clear category. The official labeling of a misbehaving youth as delinquent has the effect of placing him in such a category. This official stamp may help to organize responses different from those that would have arisen without the official action. The result is that the label has an important effect upon how the individual is regarded by others. If official processing results in an individual's being segregated with others so labeled, an additional push toward deviant behavior may result. Their association with others who are similarly defined may make the category "delinquent" or "criminal" much more salient for them as well as for others' views of them. In other words, the individual begins to think of himself as delinquent, and he organizes his behavior accordingly.

This argument is particularly relevant to the field of delinquency, even though it has been extended to a variety of other forms of deviant behavior. Its special relevance for delinquency is twofold. First, since delinquency is so broadly defined, discretion is necessary in deciding which cases should be officially handled and which dismissed. Most youths may be involved in minor forms of misbehavior during their teens. This means that the official decision to categorize certain youths as delinquent may provide the important cue for public reactions. The second aspect is the nature of the delinquent act itself. There is a very important distinction between engaging in a delinquent *act* and following a delinquent *career* organized around the repetitive commission of such acts. Given the relatively minor, episodic, and perhaps situationally induced character of much delinquency, many who have engaged in minor forms of delinquency once or twice may grow out of this pattern of behavior as they move toward adulthood. For these, the labeling theorists argue, a concerted policy of doing nothing may be more helpful than active intervention, if the long-range goal is to reduce the probability of repetition of the acts. If the labeling hypothesis is correct, official intervention may further define the youth as delinquent in the eyes of neighbors, family members, and peers, thus making it more difficult for him to resume conventional activities.

The counterargument to this view takes two forms. First, if the offender

in Sussman, Marvin B., editor, *Sociology and Rehabilitation,* American Sociological Association and Vocational Rehabilitation Administration, 1965; Becker, Howard S., *Outsiders: Studies in the Sociology of Deviance,* The Free Press of Glencoe, New York, 1963; Lemert, Edwin M., *Social Pathology,* McGraw-Hill, Inc., 1951; and Kitsuse, John I., "Societal Reaction to Deviant Behavior Problems of Theory and Method," in Becker, Howard S., editor, *The Other Side: Perspectives on Deviance,* The Free Press of Glencoe, New York, 1964, pp. 87–102. But the idea is not new in its application to delinquency. Frank Tannenbaum treated it under the concept of "the dramatization of evil" in *Crime and the Community,* Columbia University Press, New York, 1938.

is ignored, he may continue to offend for the same reason he began. The assumption here is that delinquency brings the youth some return and that it will continue to do so unless he is apprehended. It is precisely this argument that provides support for those persons interested in early identification and treatment of problem children.[2] If we assume that their deviant behavior is not a relatively superficial form of expression of adolescence, but symptomatic of something deep within them, some form of official reaction is essential. It is beneficial for the welfare of the delinquent, as well as for the community, that the deviant behavior be dealt with immediately, before it grows worse.

The second strand of the counterargument is that the process of official police handling in court adjudication may have a deterrent effect on the youths so processed. The youths do not want to be treated like delinquents and hence will refrain from further delinquent acts. This argument justifies intervention on much different grounds from the former one, and entails very different assumptions about the nature of delinquent motivations. Indeed, it is the standard argument for the deterrent impact of punishment. As such, it more often appears in arguments about adult crime and penal sanctions. But, although it is a distinctly secondary theme as applied to delinquency, it is still frequently voiced and forms a part of the public concern for dealing too leniently with delinquents.

These competing rationales for official actions are difficult to test empirically. Indeed, as yet there is very little systematic knowledge regarding reactions of offenders to varying types of sanctions. Conceivably, some delinquents refrain from committing further delinquent acts without official sanctions or labeling processes, while others may refrain only after such inhibition. But what are the conditions under which these various alternatives will occur? No other single question in the field of delinquency prevention and control seems so important and so deserving of careful investigation.

Social policy formation, however, may not be able to wait for the results of such research, and it is necessary to formulate a position on these issues without the carefully gathered and assessed data that would support a more clear-cut choice for one or another alternative. The choice seems clear: in the absence of evidence on the beneficial effects of official contacts, every effort should be made to avoid the use of a formal sanctioning system and

[2] The early identification theme appears most clearly in conjunction with the prediction efforts associated with the work of the Gluecks and the tests carried out by the New York City Youth Board. See Glueck, Eleanor T., "Efforts to Identify Delinquents," *Federal Probation*, vol. 24, June, 1960, pp. 49–56. The identification efforts have been subject to detailed criticisms. See, for example, Kahn, Alfred J., "Public Policy and Delinquency Prediction: The Case of the Premature Claims" *Crime and Delinquency*, vol. 11, July, 1965, pp. 217–228; Toby, Jackson, "An Evaluation of Early Identification and Intensive Treatment Programs for Predelinquents," *Social Problems*, vol. 13, no. 2, 1965, pp. 160–175.

particularly the official pronouncement of delinquency. Such a position is justified on grounds of the potentially damaging effects of the labeling process. The primary reason for use of the official sanctions should be the seriousness of the conduct and its potential damage to the community.

A concomitant effort must be devoted to developing new forms of controlling youthful misbehavior without relying on the traditional agencies that usually process deviants. If the school system, for example, can develop programs for truants and potential dropouts, it might be possible to avoid the potentially negative effects of processing offenders by the police and courts. Further, if cases normally coming before the courts can be handled by police referral to family and neighborhood institutions and child welfare agencies, a similar benefit may result. Currently, about one-fourth of all cases handled by the juvenile courts are youth offenses that have no parallel in adult crime: curfew violation, running away from home, ungovernability, and related types of activity. Many of these activities, and perhaps many of the more minor forms of delinquency, could be handled without official court contact.

The aim in all such cases would be to avoid a possibly premature labeling of a young person as delinquent or deviant, except in cases where the action is so repetitive or so clearly dangerous to the community that really major efforts are required. Adherence to such a policy would considerably reduce the number of cases that now come before the juvenile courts. It would clearly be necessary, for at least many of such cases, to provide supportive services at the family and neighborhood level. The goal of all such services would be to keep the juvenile functioning in the family and community as long as possible without recourse to the official sanctioning systems.[3]

The same logic should apply at each point in the process of delinquency control. If it is necessary to take official actions, efforts should first be made to leave the offenders in the community. The burden of proof, any time official intervention occurs, must be on the side of those who feel that the intervention is clearly necessary for the safety of the community and the welfare of the juvenile.

This position is fortified by two features of delinquency control as currently practiced. First, it is not at all clear that doing something is better than doing nothing, or that doing one thing is better than doing another. This is a hard fact that simply must be faced. Indeed, we are finally begin-

---

[3] A different and in some ways more radical suggestion has been offered in the British White Paper on "The Child, The Family, and the Young Offender," published by Great Britain Home Office, London, Her Majesty's Stationery Office, 1965. It recommends that all persons under sixteen years of age be removed from the jurisdiction of the court and placed under local welfare authorities. Family councils, operating on a county level and composed of social workers and others with experience in handling children, would work with parents in devising courses of treatment for the juveniles coming before them.

ning to understand that any intervention has the possibility of harm as well as help, and it is conceivable that the actions of even the well-meaning helpers do as much harm as good. At least in the absence of strong evidence that they are effective, there is reason to guard against intervening in the life of the child or family. In the past such interventions have often been justified less on grounds of the severity of misconduct of a child than on grounds of the seeming problems and pathologies within his family. While it is important not to underestimate the problems of parental and family pathology, it seems similarly important not to overestimate the power of current therapeutic techniques.

Second, the current trends toward professionalization in the field of delinquency prevention and control services may lead toward a broader category of persons being defined as "in need of service" than in the past. For there is at least a modicum of evidence that the more sophisticated personnel become, the greater is their tendency to see symptoms of problem behavior, and therefore the greater the tendency to engage in some form of intervention. It is the very feeling of confidence in the sophisticated techniques of modern intervention methods that may serve as justification for placing children in special therapeutic settings, in residential treatment centers, and in institutions thought to be beneficial for them. Thus a study of police relations with juveniles suggests that the more professionalized police system formally charges a larger percentage of the juvenile population with delinquency. A study of judges suggests that those with more therapeutically oriented attitudes were somewhat more willing to commit children to institutions, and an authority on youth correctional systems who has surveyed them around the country is left with the strong feeling that it is the states with the most professional services that implicate the largest number of children in the official agencies and institutions.[4]

In the absence of greater evidence as to their effectiveness, the wisest policy is to refrain from implicating children in the delinquency control apparatus insofar as possible, and to invoke that apparatus only when it is clear that the conduct of the juvenile in question requires it for the protection of the community. There seems to be support for this position from many of those involved in judicial and correctional work. This is not to argue that professionalism is harmful. Rather, it is to argue simply that intervention techniques, if justified on grounds of therapeutic effectiveness, should be demonstrated to be successful before they are widely employed.

[4] Wilson, James Q., "The Police and the Delinquent in Two Cities," in Wheeler, Stanton, editor, *Controlling Delinquents,* to be published by John Wiley & Sons, Inc., New York, 1966; Wheeler, Stanton, "Legal Justice and Mental Health in the Care and Treatment of Deviants," paper presented at meetings of the American Orthopsychiatric Association, San Francisco, April, 1966.

5 Delinquency and Moral Character*

CARL WERTHMAN

The moral career of the lower-class juvenile gang boy often begins at age 6, 7, or 8 when he is defined by his teachers as "pre-delinquent" for demonstrating to his friends that he is not a "sissy," and it ends between the ages of sixteen and twenty-five when he either takes a job, goes to college, joins the army, or become a criminal.[1] Although much of his behavior during this period can be seen and is seen by him as a voluntary set of claims on one of the temporary social identities available to him as a lower

Editorial adaptation by Carl Werthman of his "The Function of Social Definitions in the Development of Delinquent Careers," *Task Force Report: Juvenile Delinquency and Youth Crime*, Report on Juvenile Justice and Consultants' Papers, Task Force on Juvenile Delinquency—The President's Commission on Law Enforcement and Administration of Justice (Washington: Government Printing Office, 1967), Appendix J, pp. 155–170.

* The research on which this paper is based was initiated by the Survey Research Center at the University of California in Berkeley on a grant from the Ford Foundation and was later moved to the Center for the Study of Law and Society on the Berkeley campus, where funds were made available under a generous grant from the Office of Juvenile Delinquency and Youth Development, Welfare Administration, U.S. Department of Health, Education, and Welfare in cooperation with the President's Committee on Juvenile Delinquency and Youth Crime.

[1] The concept of a moral career has been defined by Erving Goffman as "the regular sequence of changes that career entails in the person's self and in his framework of imagery for judging himself and others." See Erving Goffman, "The Moral Career of the Mental Patient," in *Asylums* (New York: Doubleday & Company, Inc., 1961), p. 128.

class "youth," his final choice of an adult identity will depend in large measure on the way his moral character has been assessed, categorized, and acted upon by his parents, teachers, and officials of the law as well as on the attitudes and actions he has chosen in response. How the boys construct their identities, how adults tend to define and treat them for doing so, and how the boys respond to these definitions and treatments is thus the subject of this paper.[2]

THE DYNAMICS OF CHARACTER CONSTRUCTION

As Erving Goffman has elegantly made clear, there are certain attributes of moral character, particularly those most prized by gang boys, that can only be claimed by aspirants to them in social situations where something of consequence is risked.[3] It is impossible to prove that one is cool, courageous, or "smart," for example, without a situation in which there is something to be cool, courageous, or "smart" about, just as it is difficult to gain a reputation for being "tough" unless the skills involved are occasionally put to a test.

Claiming title to these character traits can sometimes be difficult, however, since risky situations do not arise very often in the course of an average day. In fact, as Goffman points out, most people manage to arrange their lives so that matters of consequence such as one's body and money supply are safely protected, although as a result most people also encounter few situations in which the most heroic of social virtues can actually be claimed.

Yet if someone with an adult status actually decides he desires "action," there is always Las Vegas or a risky job, while a lower-class gang boy is more or less forced to create his own.[4] If he wishes to prove that he is autonomous, courageous, loyal, or has "heart," not only must he

[2] The data on which this study is based consists of taped interviews with fifty-six "core" members of eleven "delinquent" gangs or "jacket clubs," plus observations and more informal conservations involving over one hundred members of these eleven gangs. The boys were drawn from the clientele of a delinquency-prevention program in San Francisco called Youth for Service, and the research was conducted largely out of their offices for a two-year period. Of the fifty-six boys interviewed on tape, thirty-seven were Negro, eleven were Mexican, and eight were Caucasian. This report is thus based primarily on a sample of Negro gang boys.

[3] I am indebted to a recent paper by Goffman for much of the analysis of gang activity that follows. See Erving Goffman, "Where the Action Is: or, Hemingway Revisited," Center for the Study of Law and Society, University of California, Berkeley, 1965.

[4] According to Goffman, "action" is located "wherever the individual knowingly takes chances that are defined as voluntary, and whose conduct is perceived as a reflection on character," Goffman, op. cit., p. 48.

take a chance, he must also construct the situations in which to take it; and for most gang boys this means that risky situations must be created from whatever materials happen to be at hand.[5]

Although the various activities defined as "thefts" provide perhaps the best examples of the way gang boys use laws to generate character while they are on the streets, the situations in which laws against theft are broken must be carefully selected to insure that sufficient risk is present. Unlike the professional thief who takes pride in knowing how to minimize the occupational risks of his trade, most younger gang boys create risks where none need be involved.[6] Joyriding, for example, is ideally suited for this purpose. Not only does it require "cool" to get a stolen car started quickly, once the car is started there is also the courage generated by the generous though not overwhelming chance of getting caught. Moreover, given the wide range of risky activities that can be engaged in once the cars are stolen, joyriding is viewed as an abundant source of the anxiety, excitement, and tension that is often referred to as "kicks."

(Did you guys do much joyriding?) Yeah. When I was about thirteen, I didn't do nothing but steal cars. The guy that I always stole with, both of us liked to drive so we'd steal a car. And then he'd go steal another car and we'd chase each other. Like there would be two in our car, two in the other car, and we'd drive by and stick out our hands, and if you touch them then they have to chase you. Or we'd steal an old car, you know, that have the running boards on it. We'd stand on that and kick the car going past. Kind of fun, but, uh, it's real dangerous. We used to have a ball when we'd do that other game with the hands though.

Although joyriding was almost always done at night, the younger gang boys I studied also located two risky daytime situations in which to engage in theft. On Saturday afternoons they would delight in trying to steal hubcaps from a packed parking lot next to a local supermarket, and on special occasions, they enjoyed breaking into gum and candy machines located in a crowded amusement park. In the parking lot, the challenge consisted of making away with the hubcaps without being seen, while in the equally crowded amusement park, the object was to escape from the police after making sure that the theft itself had been observed.

(What else did you guys used to do when you were in Junior High School?) Well, we would sometimes, three or four of us, maybe go to Playland and rob the machines. That would be a ball cause, see, what we'd do is maybe have two

[5] It was largely on the basis of an argument such as this that Norman Mailer suggested "medieval jousting tournaments in Central Park" and "horse races through the streets of Little Italy" as delinquency prevention programs for the City of New York. See Norman Mailer, *The Presidential Papers* (New York: Bantam Books, 1964), p. 22.

[6] See Edwin H. Sutherland, *The Professional Thief* (Chicago: The University of Chicago Press, 1937).

guys start fighting or maybe jump on a sailor or something like that. In the meantime, the other two guys would go back in there while the police was, you know, chasing the others, while we was back there breaking the machines open, you know. There was about five or six of them machines. So then the cops would always see us cause somebody would yell for them. So they would stop chasing the other guys and start chasing us. We had a lot of fun up there.

In addition to using the laws against theft, gang boys also use each other to demonstrate moral character—a type of risk-taking activity that Goffman calls a "character game."

I assume that when two persons are in one another's presence it will be inevitable that many of the obligations of one will be the expectations of the other (and vice versa), in matters both substantive and ceremonial. Each participant will have a personal vested interest in seeing to it that in this particular case the rules the other ought to obey are in fact obeyed by him. Mutual dependence on the other's proper conduct occurs. Each individual necessarily thus becomes a field in which the other necessarily practices good or bad conduct. In the ordinary course of affairs, compliance, forebearance and the mechanisms of apology and excuse insure that showdowns don't occur. None the less, contests over whose treatment of the other is to prevail are always a possibility, and can almost always be made to occur. The participants will then find themselves committed to producing evidence that will cause a re-assessment of self at the expense of the assessment that will come to be made of the other. A *character game results*.[7]

Goffman suggests that the stake in most character games is a claim to possess *honor*, honor defined as "the property of character which causes the individual to engage in a character contest when his rights have been violated and when the likely cost of the contest is high."[8] Like other forms of "action," then, character games are played at some risk but also presumably for some reward.

As Short and Strodtbeck have pointed out, fighting is perhaps the classic example of a gang activity that is best understood with this model.[9] After observing gang boys in Chicago for a number of years, these authors concluded that most fights take place either when a *"rep"* for toughness is suddenly challenged or when a challenge to within-group rank appears, either from inside or outside the gang.

Although it is quite true that most older gang boys will only fight when their reputations or ranks are threatened, the younger boys can

[7] Goffman, *op. cit.*, p. 60.

[8] *Ibid.*, p. 63.

[9] James F. Short, Jr., and Fred L. Strodtbeck, *Group Process and Gang Delinquency* (Chicago: The University of Chicago Press, 1965), pp. 248–264; also J. Short and F. Strodtbeck, "Why Gangs Fight," *Trans-Action*, 1 (1964).

sometimes be found initiating fights even though they have not been provoked. These fights are consciously sought out or searched for in an attempt to build a reputation where none existed before, and the boys are referred to as "looking for trouble" because they are "coming up." In these situations, also, an attempt is usually made to select the target carefully. Not any rival gang will serve as a suitable object on which to build a rep, and thus, as in the following case, a gang invading "rival territory" may decide to go home if the members cannot find boys who are big or important enough to prove a case.

Remember when them guys from Hunters Point came over looking for us? Man, it got real bad there. Cause when we made the papers, you know, everybody thought we was something. So then they all come lookin' for you. Gonna knock off the big boys. So a whole bunch of these little kids from Hunters Point came lookin' for us one night. They was coming up, and they figured they could beat us or something. (Did you fight?) No. We wasn't in the neighborhood that night. They found a bunch of guys their age but they wasn't interested in that. They just went home.

Regardless of whether fights are entered into voluntarily or involuntarily, however, the basic principal involved in this mode of character construction is clear: the fight is defined as a situation in which reputation or rank can be won or lost, and whether a particular fight will be entered into depends on the expected values of the various outcomes, values that can vary considerably from boy to boy. It is no accident, for example, that situations involving violence are often perceived as "turning points" by ex-gang members when contemplating their past careers. Particularly among older boys, it is easy to see how reputations can get so great as to be too risky to defend.[10] Similarly, in areas where it is tacitly understood that certain affronts can only be revenged by attempting to kill the offender, the person offended may simply decide to leave town or the neighborhood rather than risk being sent to jail or killed defending his honor.[11]

The behavior described by Miller as "verbal aggression," also known variously as "ranking," "capping," or "sounding," seems to involve some of the same principles found in fights.[12] As Matza has pointed out, this

[10] I encountered two boys who dropped out of gang activity for this reason. In one case, the boy decided it was time to leave after he was shot at twice in one week from passing automobiles driven by members of different rival gangs.

[11] Claude Brown cites an incident such as this as his reason for leaving Harlem. See Claude Brown, *Manchild in the Promised Land* (New York: The Macmillan Co., 1965), p. 171.

[12] W. B. Miller, H. Geertz, and S. G. Cutter, "Aggression in a Boy's Street-Corner Group," *Psychiatry* (November, 1961), pp. 283–298.

activity amounts essentially to a process of testing status by insult, and thus honor is the quality of moral character at stake.[13] Goffman has called these encounters "contest contests," situations in which someone forces someone else "into a contest over whether or not there will be a contest."[14] Like fighting, this activity involves risk and thus can have a bearing on status. Unlike fighting, however, it is not engaged in to demonstrate toughness or courage but rather to display a type of verbal agility that gang boys call "smarts."

Short and Strodtbeck have also suggested that the "utility-risk paradigm" might shed some light on the high percentage of illegitimate pregnancies that gang boys produce while engaged in another type of "inter-personal action" discussed by Goffman, i.e., "making out."[15] Sexual activity sometimes begins very early among gang boys, and there is typically a great deal of it throughout a career. Most of the Negro boys claim to have lost their virginity around the age of 8 or 9, and some have intercourse regularly in junior high school. During most of the years spent in a gang, girls are seen primarily as objects for sexual play, and it is not until the age of sixteen or older that they are sometimes treated with anything resembling respect. Ultimately, however, it is marriage that takes most boys out of the gang, thus providing one of the few available legitimate excuses for leaving the streets.[16]

Short and Strodtbeck suggest that two separate risks are involved in illegitimacy, the first being the probability of engaging in sexual intercourse with a given frequency and the second being the probability that these actions will eventuate in parenthood. Success or failure at "making it" with a girl is socially risky, since the outcome affects status in the gang, while the risk involved in gambling without contraception is sometimes used to demonstrate "cool."

The gang boy thus aspires to an identity that puts him in a special relationship to risk. When he is around his friends, he often creates the situations in which he chooses to exist, an act of creation that involves selecting out certain features of the social environment and then transforming them into the conditions that allow him to define a self. Taken together, these risky activities can be interpreted as claims to be treated prematurely as "men," a status that gang boys are culturally and structurally forbidden to occupy until the "delinquent career" comes to an end. Why gang boys rather than others decide to take these risks is a

13 David Matza, *Delinquency and Drift* (New York: John Wiley & Sons, 1964), pp. 42–44.

14 Goffman, *op. cit.,* p. 68.

15 Short and Strodtbeck, *Group Process, op. cit.,* pp. 44–45, 249–250.

16 Walter B. Miller, "The Corner Gang Boys Get Married," *Trans-Action,* Vol. 1 (November, 1963), pp. 10–12.

difficult if not impossible question to answer. Yet it is possible to look at how the gang boy deals with the mechanisms that ordinarily prevent these risks from being taken.

THE GENESIS OF AUTONOMY

Although the absence of adult economic responsibilities can be seen as conducive to the development of unconventional identity formations among youth, young people are also legally dependent on adults. A person under age eighteen is always in the custody of someone; and, if he proves to be beyond control by parents, he can always be adopted by the state.

Yet, in most instances, parental power develops into authority.[17] And it is precisely this authority relationship that allows at least the pre-adolescent to define himself as "a child." He implicitly surrenders his autonomy in return for the feeling of being protected and thus he does not exercise the capacity he might otherwise have to make his own decisions.

In addition to securing their own authority, however, parents also have a vested interest in endowing a variety of adult officials with a temporary "title to rule." For example, to ensure that the authority of school personnel is perceived as legitimate, children are made aware that their parents can be informed of all misadventures. Parents thus become the center of a communications network for other adult authorities; and whether the child is at school or on the streets, he is made to feel none of his behavior can be hidden from his parents.[18]

Yet the youngsters who define themselves as dependent do not mind being the subjects of this friendly conspiracy and most, in fact, would feel very insecure without it. Moreover, as long as parents can manage to have their ideals about the behavior of their offspring either aspired to or even achieved, however vague the achievement, there is precious little chance that policemen and probation officers will end up defining them as "delinquents," provided, of course, that the number of crimes committed is kept to some reasonable limit. Although I encountered a great many parents who had come to look upon the trip to jail as "routine" by the time their sons were sixteen, I found none who said that at an earlier point in life they had not hoped for something better. In practically every case it was possible to locate a set of expectations that was perceived by parents either to have broken down or never to have developed, despite the

[17] Max Weber, *The Theory of Social and Economic Organization,* translated by A. M. Henderson and Talcott Parsons (New York: The Free Press of Glencoe, 1947).

[18] It is largely for this reason that vehicles for public transportation such as buses become scenes of mass confusion when children ride them unsupervised to and from school. The bus drivers do not have access to parents and the children know it.

fact that many had also come to view the news of "trouble" as a more or less "normal" event.

The situation that these parents find themselves in can perhaps best be described with a vocabulary developed by Harold Garfinkel for the analysis of how stable social activity systems are "constituted," can become "disorganized," and can also be "reconstituted."[19] Garfinkel suggests that routine social activities are defined in the most fundamental sense of that word by a set of "constitutive" or "basic" rules, i.e., rules that are used to make behavior recognizable as an act or event in some known order of events. Unlike institutionalized norms (or "preferred rules" as Garfinkel calls them), the "basic" rules do not specify *how* a person is to act in an activity but only the range of possible acts he could perform as well as the social category of person he is if he takes part in them.

Garfinkel further suggests that in order for an activity system to be *stable*, the people involved in the activity must "trust" each other, "trust" defined as a condition in which the participants expect one another to act in compliance with the basic or constitutive rules. If these rules are violated, the activity is in danger of becoming "confused" or "disorganized," since people will find themselves without a context in which to interpret the meaning of the act committed by the violator and thus will not know how to respond to him.

Following this conceptual scheme, we can see that where the participants in an activity include an "authority" as well as others who are seen as "subordinates," the set of basic rules establishing the activity will always include a rule which constitutes this relationship. In addition, we can predict that where an authority has a part in some activity, it will be important to him that his subordinates act in compliance with the basic rule establishing the source of preferred rules, or, put another way, that his subordinates "trust" him. From the point of view of the authority, moreover, the important issue about any act becomes not whether it is performed in accordance with a particular rule but whether it is performed in accordance with the rule establishing authority itself.

This problem is frequently and simply illustrated among the parents of pre-adolescent and "pre-delinquent" boys, many of whom are described simply as "out of control." In these cases, what parents seem to be describing are situations in which no stable pattern of mutual expectations develops at all. Whatever preferred rules they attempt to establish as ways of ordering the activities of the family are more or less randomly ignored, and thus these parents can rarely count on their sons either to be at school, at home for meals, or sometimes even in bed. For example:

[19] Harold Garfinkel, "Some Conceptions of and Experiments with 'Trust' as a Condition of Stable Concerted Actions," MS.

(How do you handle Melvin when he gets into trouble?) Well, we figure that weekends are the main times he looks forward to—parties and going out. So we'd say, "You can't go out tonight." You know, we'd try to keep him from something he really wanted to do. But he usually goes out anyway. Like one night we was watching TV, and Melvin said he was tired and went to bed. So then I get a phone call from a lady who wants to know if Melvin is here because her son is with him. I said, "No, he has gone to bed already." She says, "Are you sure?" I said, "I'm pretty sure." So I went downstairs and I peeked in and saw a lump in the bed but I didn't see his head. So I took a look and he was gone. He came home about 12:30, and we talked for a while. (What did you do?) Well, I told him he was wrong going against his parents like that, but he keeps sneaking out anyway. (What does your husband do about it?) Well, he don't do much. I'm the one who gets upset. My husband, he'll say something to Mel and then he'll just relax and forget about it. (Husband and wife laugh together.) There's little we can do, you know. It's hard to talk to him 'cause he just go ahead and do what he wants anyway.

These children, most between the ages of 6 and 10, were some of the most puzzling people I met on this study. Their behavior always seemed to make perfect sense to them, but it also seemed to make so much sense that they could not produce accounts for it. Although they sometimes exhibited a touch of bravado, they were only rarely defensive, and most managed to carry themselves with what can only be described as miniature adult poise. When they were not in motion or suddenly running away, they assumed the posture of "little old men," often shouldering their autonomy with dignity but rarely with perfect ease.

These children are a testimony to the fact that basic rules about authority are not accepted automatically, even among the young. The assumption of dependence must be cultivated before it can be used as a basis for control; in fact, that becomes quite clear when for some reason the assumption of dependence is never made. In these cases, the children often demonstrate a remarkable capacity to take care of themselves. In fact, one could argue that the pre-adolescent who does not conceive of himself as dependent on his parents also does not really conceive of himself as "a child," particularly when he loses his virginity at eight and supports himself on lunch money taken from classmates. Once the authority rule is rejected, the family as an activity system becomes an entirely new game. Legally the child is not an adult, but sociologically it is hard to argue that he is still a child.[20]

[20] Gans notes the tendency among working-class Italians in Boston to treat their children as "little adults." It could well be that the posture of the boys described in this paper is simply an exaggerated version of lower-class socialization generally. See Herbert J. Gans, *The Urban Villagers* (New York: The Free Press of Glencoe, 1962), p. 59.

Not only is the assumption of autonomy the important issue at home, it also has important implications for the way gang boys are treated by school officials and officers of the law. Most young people adopt a posture of deference in the presence of adult authorities because this posture is a "taken-for-granted" assumption about the self. Yet to gang boys this posture is a matter of choice. They can defer or not defer, depending on their feelings about a teacher or a "cop"; and for most adult authorities, the very existence of the assumption that submissiveness is a matter of choice is either sufficient grounds for the withdrawal of "trust" or is considered a personal affront.

THE MEANING OF "DELINQUENCY" IN THE SCHOOLS

The posture of premature autonomy is carried directly into the schools and the result is the "pre-delinquent." As early as the first and second grade, his teachers find him wild, distracted, and utterly oblivious to their presumed authority. He gets out of chairs when he feels like it; begins fighting when he feels like it; and all of this is done as if the teacher were not present.

Further, once the boys begin to prove that they are "tough," there seems to be little that the schools can do to stop them. If they are suspended, they come to school anyway; and if they are transferred from one class to another, they return to the first class or to whatever teacher they happen to like. Moreover, since the boys seem immune to sanctions, their bullying, thefts, and truancies are often blatantly displayed.

It is not until the fifth or sixth grades that organized gangs begin to form, and, in a certain sense, it is not until this age that the boys can be brought under systematic group control. Since most of my work was done with older boys, however, this discussion must be confined to them.

Although there are many differences between contemporary sociological portraits of the lower-class juvenile delinquent, the same model of his educational problem is used by most authors. Regardless of whether the delinquent is viewed as ambitious and capable,[21] ambitious and incapable,[22] or unambitious and incapable,[23] the school is sketched as a monolith of middle-class personnel against which he fares badly.

[21] Richard A. Cloward and Lloyd E. Ohlin, *Delinquency and Opportunity* (New York: The Free Press of Glencoe, 1960), p. 102.

[22] Albert K. Cohen, *Delinquent Boys* (New York: The Free Press of Glencoe, 1965), p. 116.

[23] Walter B. Miller and William C. Kvaraceus, *Delinquent Behavior: Culture and the Individual*, National Education Association of the United States, 1959, p. 44. See also Walter Miller, "Lower Class Culture as a Generating Milieu of Gang Delinquency," *Journal of Social Issues*, Vol. XIV (1958).

Yet the school difficulties of these boys occur only in some classes and not others, and this fact suggests that pitting middle-class schools against variations in the motivation and capacity of some lower-class boys is at best too simple and at worst incorrect as a model of the problem. Good and bad students alike are consistently able to get through half or more of their classes without friction, and it is only in particular classes with particular teachers that incidents leading to suspension flare up.

We thus need to see how the same gang boy may become a "trouble-maker" in one classroom and an "ordinary student" in another; and to do this, it is again worth using Garfinkel's scheme to look at the classroom as a place where a range of possible activities or "constitutive orders of events" can take place. The most common set is known as "teaching and learning," but these are not the only activities that can take place. Many young people, including gang boys, tend also to see the classroom as a place to see friends, converse by written notes, read comic books, eat, sleep, or stare out the window. For example:

If I'm bored then I have to do something to make it exciting. First, second, and third ain't too bad because I get me two comic books and they last me three periods.

Further, most gang boys will "test" the limits of the classroom situation before making up their minds whether a teacher can be trusted. This is done by purposely violating a rule preferred by the teacher in such a way as to suggest that their participation in the classroom is a voluntary act and should be acknowledged as such with the proper amount of respect.

When confronted with activities other than "learning" or behavior that is clearly designed to "test," most teachers respond by insisting that their rights to teach be respected and their authority be properly maintained. They thus resort to the imperative and begin to issue commands. But this response, in turn, is almost always defined by gang boys as "getting smart." The boys view the teacher's insistence on his rights to authority as a violation of their rights to autonomy, and thus the prospect of a "character contest" arises over whose honor is to remain intact. Moreover, if the boys do not concede the contest for fear of being expelled, they often challenge the authority of the teacher again.

This challenge tends to take one of three forms: it is either done subtly with demeanor, directly with words, or forcefully with violence. All three methods are used in the encounter described below.

The first day I came to school I was late to class so this teacher got smart with me. He didn't know me by name. See a lot of people have to go by the office and see what class they in or something. Like there was lot of new people there. So you know I was fooling around 'cause I know nothing gonna happen to you if you late. 'Cause all you tell them, you got the program mixed or something.

When I came into the class you know I heard a lot of hollering and stuff. Mr. H. was in the class too. He's a teacher, see. I guess he had a student teacher or something, you know, because he was getting his papers and stuff. So Mr. H. went out. Well this new teacher probably wonder if he gonna be able to get along with me or something. 'Cause the class was kinda loud. When I walked in the class got quiet all of a sudden. Like they thought the Principal was coming in or something.

So I walk into class and everybody look up. That's natural, you know, when somebody walk into class. People gonna look up at you. They gonna see who it is coming in or something. So I stopped. You know, like this. Looked around. See if there was any new faces. Then a girl named Diane, she say, "Hey Ray!" You know, when I walk into class they start calling me and stuff. They start hollering at me.

I just smile and walk on. You know. I had my hands in my pocket or something 'cause I didn't have no books and I just walk into class with my hands in my pockets a lot of times. I mean I have to walk where I can relax. I'm not going to walk with my back straight. I mean you know I relax. (What were you wearing?) About what I got on now. I had a pair of black slacks and a shirt on. My hair was long and I had taps on my shoes. I had kinda boots on but they weren't real high boots. They came up to about here.

Then I looked over at the teacher. I see we had a new teacher. He was standing in front of the desks working on some papers and doing something. He looked at me. I mean you enter by the front of the classroom so when you walk into the classroom he's standing right there. You gotta walk in front of him to get to the seats. So then I went to sit down. Soon as I passed his desk he say, "Just go sit down." Just like that.

So I stop. I turn around and look at him, then I went and sat down. (What kind of look did you give him?) You might say I gave him a hard look. I thought you know he might say something else. 'Cause tht same day he came he got to hollering at people and stuff. I don't like people to holler at me. He was short, you know, about medium build. He might be able to do a little bit. So I say to myself, "I better sit down and meditate a little bit."

So I went and sat down. I sat in the last row in the last seat. Then he say, "Come sit up closer." So I scoot up another chair or two. Then he tell me to come sit up in the front. So I sat up there.

Then you know a lot of people was talking. A lot of people begin telling me that he be getting smart all day. You know Stubby? He is a big square but he pretty nice. He told me how the teacher was. And Angela start telling me about how he try to get smart with her. He say, "This is where you don't pick out no boy friend. You come and get your education." I mean just cause you talk to a boy, that don't mean you be scheming on them or nothing. It just that you want to be friends with people.

Then he say something like, "You two shut up or I'll throw you out on your ear!" So he told me he'd throw me out.

So I say, "The best thing you can do is ask me to leave and don't tell me. You'll get your damn ass kicked off if you keep messing!"

Then he told me to move over on the other side. See, I was talking to every-body so he told me to move away from everybody. And so I moved to the other side. He told me to move three times! I had to move three times!

And then he got to arguing at somebody else. I think at somebody else that came in the class. You know, a new person. So while he was talking to them, I left out. I snuck out of class.

So I walked out the class. Went out in the yard and started playing basketball. We were supposed to turn in the basketball out there so I took the ball through the hall on the way back in. I was gonna go back out there and play some more. See I had the ball and I passed by his class and I looked in. I seen him with his back turned and I didn't like him. That's when I hit him. I hit him with the ball. Got him! I didn't miss. Threw it hard too. Real hard!

The issue of who decides what takes place in classrooms is not the only matter of dispute that sometimes arises. For example, although the students may be willing to comply with the rule establishing the teacher as the source of preferred rules, they may also feel that there are limits to the kinds of things a teacher can legitimately make rules about. These issues are most likely to arise when teachers feel it is within their jurisdiction to pass judgment on the dress and physical appearance of their students; and if a gang boy feels that his moral character has been reconstituted by a teacher on the basis of the clothes he wears, he is likely to register his sense of injustice.[24]

A gang boy's career as a "delinquent" in the schools is thus a highly problematic affair, since the genesis and outcome of character contests are in part affected by the conduct of teachers themselves. In many instances, of course, the boys will "test" a teacher to see if a claim to autonomy will be honored. Yet if the teacher is willing to concede the fact that school is meaningless to some boys and that other activities besides "teaching and learning" will necessarily go on in class, and if he is willing to limit the scope of his jurisdiction to the activity of "teaching and learning" itself, then his authority is likely to remain intact. Whether or not he can persuade the boys to join the learning process is another matter again; but it is precisely at this point that we see the merits of defining authority after Bertrand de Juvenel as "the faculty of gaining another man's assent."[25]

THE MEANING OF "DELINQUENCY" TO THE POLICE

As Aaron Cicourel has recently suggested, the transformation of gang boys into official "delinquents" by policemen, probation officers, and

[24] For the general discussion of the problems created by contingent or purposive infraction of irrelevance rules, see Erving Goffman, *Encounters* (Indianapolis: The Bobbs-Merrill Co., 1961), pp. 17–85.

[25] Bertrand de Juvenel, *Sovereignty: An Inquiry Into the Political Good,* translated by J. F. Huntington (Chicago: The University of Chicago Press, 1957), p. 29.

judges of the juvenile court can also be looked upon as an organizational rather than a legal process, since the criteria used to contact, categorize, and dispose of boys often has little to do with breaking the law itself.[26]

In studies of how boys are contacted by the police, the distinction between policemen and juvenile officers is often made, largely because these two groups often tend to organize their work in different ways. Harvey Sacks has suggested that the task of the patrolman can best be defined as "inferring the probability of criminality from the appearances persons present in public places";[27] and, as David Matza has pointed out, this task "is similar in almost every respect to that faced by the sociologist." Both must "classify individuals" into a set of social or legal categories since "true indicators rarely exist";[28] and the indicators of suspicion mentioned most frequently by policemen and gang boys are a combination of race and neighborhood, plus an odd assortment of clothing, hair, and walking styles.[29]

Although it is difficult to imagine how patrolmen could organize their work in any other way, the indicators of suspicion they use provoke considerable outrage among the boys. As soon as a patrolman makes contact with a boy, the structure of the situation itself reveals his mistrust. The boy instantly knows that if he were not a Negro and was not sporting boots and long hair, his moral character would not have been called into question and he could walk the streets without insult, risk, or fear.

Most gang boys respond to these situational insults the way they respond to teachers who challenge their autonomy in the schools. By acquitting themselves with a straightforward nonchalance or indifference and refusing to proffer the expected gestures of respect, the boys insult the authority of the patrolman who then must either arrest, use his billy club, or withdraw from the situation as honorably as he can.

Members of Juvenile Bureaus tend to make contact with gang boys on other grounds. Unlike patrolmen, they attempt to trace particular crimes to their source in a universe of suspects rather than trying to link "suspicious people" to the universe of possible crimes.

Once suspects are contacted, however, both patrolmen and juvenile officers proceed the same way. A variety of interrogation techniques are used, including lies about the amount of information possessed. And the

[26] See Aaron V. Cicourel, *The Social Organization of Juvenile Justice* (New York: Wiley, 1968). See also John I. Kitsuse and Aaron V. Cicourel, "A Note on the Uses of Official Statistics," *Social Problems*, Vol. II (Fall, 1963), pp. 139–152.

[27] Harvey Sacks, "Methods in Use for the Production of a Social Order: A Method for Warrantably Inferring Moral Character," MS., p. 4.

[28] David Matza, "The Selection of Deviants," MS., p. 2.

[29] These indicators are discussed at length in Carl Werthman and Irving Piliavin, "Gang Members and the Police," in David J. Bordua, ed., *The Police* (New York: John Wiley & Sons, Inc., 1966).

success of these techniques is reflected in the fact that over 90 per cent of juvenile convictions in the United States are gotten because boys "confess."

Yet even these confessions do not mean much, since most policemen, like probation officers and judges, define the "delinquent" as a boy with questionable moral character rather than as a boy who has merely committed a crime. Thus, the age of an offender, his family situation, his prior arrest record, and the nature of his offense all enter into dispositions as do the style and speed with which he manages to confess.[30] If he confesses immediately, this act is taken as a sign that the boy "trusts" adults, in which case it is further assumed that his attachment to the basic authority rule is both sound and intact. If he proves to be a "tough nut to crack," however, he is viewed with suspicion. It is said that he is "hardened," does not "trust" authority, and is therefore probably "out of control."

Piliavin and Briar also report that boys who appear frightened, humble, penitent, and ashamed are also more likely to go free.[31] And, conversely, in a study of the differential selection of juvenile offenders for court appearances, Nathan Goldman reports that "defiance on the part of a boy will lead to juvenile court quicker than anything else."[32]

Given the variety of criteria that seem to enter into dispositions, the moral career of a gang boy in the eyes of the courts and the police becomes almost as problematic as his "delinquent" career in the schools, particularly when the techniques used by the police themselves provoke the very defiance that ultimately sends him to jail.

OPPORTUNITIES, CONTINGENCIES, AND RISKS

There is some evidence to suggest that most gang boys have a conception of how and when their careers as "delinquents" will end. As Short and Strodtbeck have recently reported, most look forward to becoming stable and dependable husbands in well-run households, despite their reluctance to voice these expectations around one another and despite the fact that some become fathers out of wedlock along the way.[33] Similarly, although about half the boys interviewed by Short and Strodtbeck anticipate problems in securing "good paying honest jobs," their images of family life make it clear that the great majority expect to be holding down some

---

[30] Cicourel, *The Social Organization of Juvenile Justice, op. cit.*

[31] Irving Piliavin and Scott Briar, "Police Encounters with Juveniles," *American Journal of Sociology,* LXXX (1964).

[32] Nathan Goldman, *The Differential Selection of Juvenile Offenders for Court Appearances,* National Council on Crime and Delinquency, 1963, p. 106.

[33] Short and Strodtbeck, *Group Process, op. cit.,* pp. 25–46.

kind of conventional occupation when they finally do become "adults."[34]

During most of the years the boys spend in gangs, however, these aspirations are neither salient nor relevant, and thus they do not think much about the future at all. They understand that as long as they are defined and define themselves as "youth," they are not the people they will someday become. And since they do not have the responsibility of maintaining a home and a job, they have little to lose by devoting their time to more expressive and entertaining pursuits.

Yet what happens to a boy at the end of a "delinquent" career is very much affected by how he deals with the various contingencies that arise during the course of career itself, particularly those associated with the way he is acted upon by policemen, probation officers, and judges of the juvenile court. For example, although the consequences of taking risks become more serious as arrest records gets longer, a boy who knows that the California Youth Authority awaits him if he is caught for theft or joyriding one more time can demonstrate possession of more courage than the boys who have never been caught. Similarly, the judge who orders a boy to discontinue his association with particular friends also makes it possible for him to demonstate even greater loyalty than before.

Thus, to the extent that boys do not drop out of gangs as the sanctions they face become more severe, they tend to constitute an increasingly select elite. In the identity system of the gang world, reputation increases with the fatefulness of the situation in which a boy is willing to take a risk, and thus the boys who have been sent to the more important prisons can flaunt this fact as evidence that they have paid and were willing to pay a more significant price for maintaining their identity on the streets.

They think they is bad because they have gone to jail. Most of them, that is. They come out with a big build or something like that and they think they is bigger than somebody else, you know, they done learn some slang in jail, and may have won a few fights up there or something and think they can whup everybody when they come out. They think they is halfway bad. They done beat up somebody that was supposed to be the baddest up there in jail where they was. Being in jail doesn't make them badder, but it makes them think different than before they left. The stud who's been in jail expects you to respect him when he comes back. You know, before he goes in you respect him and he respects you, but when he comes back he expects you to respect him more. Like the kid in the Marathons who went in weighing 75 pounds and came out weighing 100, looking for me [laughter].

The identity system of the gang world actually tends to be somewhat more sophisticated than this. In practice, every gang tends to view its own

[34] See James F. Short, Jr., Ramon Rivera, and Ray A. Tennyson, "Opportunities, Gang Membership, and Delinquency," *American Sociological Review,* (February, 1965), p. 60; see also Delbert S. Elliott, "Delinquency and Perceived Opportunity," *Sociological Inquiry* (Spring, 1962), pp. 216–228.

particular situation as the best. When comparing themselves to the gang described above, for example, a somewhat younger group of boys tended to pride themselves on having more boys in school and having been sent to jail less often, all of which seemed to prove to them that they were "smarter."

> The Marathons, they much bigger than us, but half of them crazy. They equip their heads with something else. Like they don't have no imagination, you know, no fear. When they go do something they do it. They act like if they ever got started you have to kill them to stop them. But we got the smartest guys. Half of them (the Marathons) ain't going to school. They all go to jail. If we had to plan something we'd get them. They don't have any sense. Only one they got in there that's smart is Johnny, and he's crazy himself. We just think quicker than they do. You know, when it comes down to going to jail or getting into trouble, we just think quicker. And we been through more than they been through. You know, like where to hit 'em to hurt 'em most. They ain't learned that yet. There's only one club in this district and that's the Conquerors [laughter].

On the other hand, when these same boys compare themselves to nondelinquent neighborhood cliques, they denigrate school and pride themselves on taking more risks.

> No. School ain't going to make you whup them, and it ain't necessarily going to make you smarter neither. It don't teach you nothing about how to get along with the bitches [girls] or all them other dudes [boys]. What are these cafeteria-eaters going to do when they get married or when they go to a dance? Some stud hits on [makes a play for] the bitch they is with, and what they going to do? They gonna talk some more shit in the cafeteria. And those guys never been to jail. They just don't know what's happening. Them books don't teach you nothing about the streets, and that's where them cats is going to spend the rest of their lives.

In addition to the contingencies associated with a boy's situation in the eyes of the law, the progress of his moral career is made even more indeterminate by the fact that it is often difficult for him to assess the consequences of his acts until *after* they have been committed. As we have seen, this is particularly true in cases involving the courts and the police where many more rules are invoked to pass judgment on the offender than were actually involved in the offense.

Also, there is the fact that courts sometimes create their own special rules to judge the "improvement" of a boy, but when these rules are violated, there is a sense in which they have created the very criteria by which the boy is then condemned. Consider, for example, the following conversation between this researcher and a twelve-year-old boy who had just run away from his foster home. He had been living with "Uncle

Eddie," his mother's brother, essentially because his older brothers were in jail, his father deserted the family some years ago, and, as a result of these actions by other members of the family, his mother was declared "unfit" and Danny was forced to go.

(Why did you stay away from school yesterday?) I felt like comin' to San Francisco to see my mother. (Didn't you go back last night?) Yeh, but my cousin Darlene said they was lookin' for me, you know, my probation officer. He came to visit me in school and couldn't find me. I got scared so I came back up here. (Where did you stay last night?) I slept in a friend of mine's car. I figured I better not go home. I don't want to get my mother in dutch. They'll call her and if she says I'm home that'll get her in trouble. (What do you think your probation officer will do when he finds you?) He told me he was going to send me to C.Y.A. like Billy if I got into any trouble down there, you know, at my Uncle Eddie's. I don't want to go to C.Y.A.

(Well, what do you plan to do now?) I don't know. I figure I could keep running. I could stay with my brother up in Tahoe, but it's tough bein' on the run. What do you think I should do? (I don't know either. Let's discuss it. You're the one that has to make the decision. How do you like living down at your Uncle Eddie's?) I don't like it. They talk about me behind my back, and they say bad things about my mother. And Eddie's no good. He won't even buy me gym clothes. They told me at school I can't go to gym class unless I got the clothes, and he won't get them. He said he already bought me some and I lost 'em but he's lyin'. He never bought me no gym clothes. (Would you rather live somewhere else?) Yeh, but they won't let me come home. They say I got too many friends up there and the school won't let me back. But all my friends have left, and I could go to a different school. I know I could make it. But they won't let me. I know they're going to send me to C.Y.A.

(Well, it looks to me like you have two choices. You could either keep running and take your chances on getting caught, or go back and take your chances on getting sent to C.Y.A.) [After a long silence.] Well maybe C.Y.A. wouldn't be so bad after all. [He tries hard to fight back tears and succeeds.]

This is a good example of what can happen with probation restrictions. A boy is sent to a foster home because he comes from a broken one and then plays hookey in order to come back. The truancy is produced by the desire to see his mother, and the terms of his probation make this act an offense unless it is properly approved. The boy is thus in danger of being sent to the California Youth Authority for committing an offense that was actually created by the courts themselves.

Yet the fact remains that boys who remain on the streets take more serious risks than boys who leave them; and thus, in terms of the logic underlying the identity system itself, they justifiably see themselves as more committed than others to this round of life. The most serious change in their situation occurs, however, when the police finally decide to "crack down." The boys are warned to "stay off the streets or else," and after this injunction has been issued, the character of the streets is fundamentally transformed. The neighborhood, the territory, and the hangout cease being places where it is merely dangerous to be found since the probability is nearly perfect that if they remain on the streets they will go to jail.

In summary, then, by viewing the "delinquent career" as a more or less stable sequence of acts taken in risky social situations in order to claim an identity or define a self, often followed by changes in the rules that make up these situations, and followed again by new choices of the self in the new situations, it is possible to see how a gang boy could arrive at the age of 18 or 21 to find that his situation makes it costly, painful, or difficult for him to take the conventional job that he always expected to take, particularly if he has come to view the conventional world as a place full of the kinds of people who have labeled him a "delinquent."[35]

Once a gang boy gets beyond the age of 18, moreover, he has a choice to make about what identity system to enter. He could get married, get a job, and assume the status of a full-fledged "adult"; he could decide to postpone this decision in legitimate ways such as joining the Army or going to school at night; or he could spend a few more years as an elder statesman on the streets.

The decision he makes at this point in his career will depend in part on his situation. If he managed to graduate from high school, he may well decide to go on to college; but if he was expelled from high school, he may feel either bitter or reluctant about getting the high school degree. He knows that he has been administratively reborn in the eyes of the law, and thus the risks he takes by staying on the streets increase considerably, since he now may be processed by the courts as an adult. On the other hand, if his status in the gang world is still high, he may not want to trade it for a low-paying blue-collar job; and he knows he will be rejected by the Army if he has a jail record of any kind.

In short, it is at this point in his career that the "opportunities" available to him will affect his behavior, his attitudes, and the decisions he makes about his life.[36] If there are no legitimate options open to him that would not mean a sudden decrease in status, he may well decide to stay on the streets, despite the greater consequences involved in taking risks.

If he remains on the streets, however, his perception and use of theft becomes increasingly instrumental until it finally turns into a particular version of the "hustle." These hustles still involve risks, but the risks are

[35] This process has been described in somewhat different terms by Lemert as a transformation from "primary" to "secondary" deviance. See Edwin M. Lemert, *Social Pathology* (New York: McGraw-Hill Book Co., 1951), p. 75.

[36] This view suggests that the various processes discussed by Cloward and Ohlin tend to effect outcomes of the transition between youth and adult status at the end of the delinquent career. See Cloward and Ohlin, *Delinquency and Opportunity, op. cit.*

no longer incurred exclusively for the sake of demonstrating something about the self. The boys now need the money, and their relationship to the risky situation changes as both positive and negative outcomes become more consequential. The actual thefts themselves are also talked about less and less: as attempts are made to avoid detection, a boy's source of money becomes more and more his own business.

Along with the hustle comes a full-blown ideology: when a boy views the conventional world as a place he is expected to enter, he tends to develop a "position" on it. Jobs become "slaves"; going to school becomes "serving time"; and the assumptions about marriage and getting a conventional job are replaced by exploitative relations with women and fantasies about a big "score." These are no longer the "delinquent boys described by Cohen.[37] They are the defensive aristocrats described by Finestone, and by Sykes and Matza.[38] They have an answer to everything, and they always "know the score."

By this time the boys are really at the end of their "delinquent" careers. If they do not get jobs, go to jail, or get killed, they simply fade into an underground of pool rooms, pimps, and petty thefts. Most cannot avoid ending up with conventional jobs, however, largely because the "illegitimate opportunities" available simply are not that good.

[37] Cohen, *Delinquent Boys, op. cit.*
[38] Harold Finestone, "Cats, Kicks, and Colors," *Social Problems,* Vol. 5, (July, 1957), pp. 3–13; G. M. Sykes and David Matza, "Techniques of Neutralization: A Theory of Delinquency," *American Sociological Review,* Vol. 22 (December, 1957), pp. 664–670.

PART VII

The Development and Maintenance of Delinquent Subcultures

Introduction

A subculture is a set of conduct norms which cluster together in such a way that they can be differentiated from the broader culture of which they are a part. Thus, if some of the rules for the conduct of working-class persons are different from the rules for the behavior of middle-class persons, it is proper to speak, as Miller does, of a "working-class subculture" and a "middle-class subculture."[1] While a collection of different conduct norms and beliefs may make one segment of the larger society a "subculture," there remain so many beliefs and rules of conduct that are identical for members of all subcultures that they may be considered as belonging to the same culture. In some subcultures, however, some of the conduct norms oppose or inspire violation of the legal standards of the larger society. Such subcultural rules may, for example, indicate that stealing is legitimate under certain conditions, or they may underwrite the notion that stealing is an acceptable method of achieving the legitimate goals of the larger society. Such a set of conduct norms may be referred to as a "stealing subculture" or more generally, as a "delinquent subculture" or a "criminal subculture."[2]

Note that no *people* are involved in subcultures. The components of

[1] See "Lower Class Culture as a Generating Milieu of Gang Delinquency" in Part IV, above.

[2] This is the usage in "The Skills and Training of the Pickpocket," in Part V, above, were Maurer compares the subculture of pickpockets with the "dominant culture."

a subculture are rules of conduct expressed for the most part in verbalizations that define what is proper or improper for whom and under what conditions. It is important to understand that "rules for delinquency" or "delinquent subcultures" existed long before most of today's delinquents and criminals were born. Each generation does not invent its own new and distinctive techniques and vocabularies of motives for violating the law. The verbalizations described by Sykes and Matza and elaborated by Hartung in "A Vocabulary of Motives for Law Violations" (Part V, above) have been used by many generations of offenders. As a boy follows such rules of conduct, he participates in a "delinquent subculture" and commits "subcultural delinquency," whether he acts alone or with others in a gang.

Our understanding of social behavior in general and criminal behavior in particular will be greatly enhanced if we can determine the conditions under which delinquent subcultures originate. This seems to be an obvious research problem, but even a brief look at the history of criminological research indicates that it has been sorely neglected. Criminologists were once concerned primarily with trying to identify anatomic and physiological characteristics which would distinguish criminals from non-criminals. Then, with the emergence of psychology, criminological research became oriented toward studies of the intellectual, emotional, and temperamental characteristics of criminals. Although some of the psychological studies were designed to determine whether criminals differ from non-criminals, other studies sought characteristics that differentiated offenders from some *model* of what was thought to be the distribution of these characteristics in the "normal population." As sociology and social psychology developed, research focused first on the epidemiology of crime and delinquency and then on the processes by which delinquent and criminal values are transmitted from one person to another. The latter development was greatly influenced by Sutherland's theory of differential association. It was not until the mid-1950s that Cohen, and then Cloward and Ohlin, pointed out that in this last endeavor we were looking at only half the problem.[3] They argued that the interest Sutherland and others had shown in the diffusion of the values that make delinquency and crime possible had directed attention away from the equally important question of why these delinquent norms or rules of conduct ("delinquent subcultures") develop in the first place.

The study of how criminal norms originate is not easy because, as already noted, few of the rules of conduct followed by today's delinquents and criminals are new. As Bordua has said, "Each generation does not

[3] Albert K. Cohen, *Delinquent Boys: The Culture of the Gang* (New York: Free Press, 1955); Richard A. Cloward and Lloyd E. Ohlin, *Delinquency and Opportunity: A Theory of Delinquent Gangs* (New York: Free Press, 1960).

meet and solve anew the problems of class structure barriers to opportunity but begins with the solution of its forbears."[4] Since many of these "solutions" (conduct norms and vocabularies of motive) are old, in some cases ancient, studies of the processes by which they were initially established require the skills of anthropologists and historians as well as those of sociologists. However, a number of sociologists have applied sociological analyses to historical and anthropological data and have given us good theoretical leads for studying the process of inventing new social rules. Among these are Emile Durkheim, Max Weber, and Robert Merton, all of whom observed that changes in social structure, i.e., the sets of relationships among people, stimulate the invention of new rules of conduct.[5] Weber, for example, showed that as the economic structure of societies changed, new rules for religious conduct came into being.

Along the same line, but more specifically related to criminology, studies by Jerome Hall and Svend Ranulf make the point that changes in the social structure have implications for the rules governing behavior. The excerpt from Hall's work reprinted in Part II presents evidence that changes in the rules of law follow changes in economic and business structures, and Ranulf's study indicates that as the class structures of societies change, new rules for reacting toward wrongdoers are invented.[6] Inquiries such as these are studies of the "origin of subcultures." There is a great need for similar inquiries into how subcultures with conduct norms favorable to stealing, to violence, to drug use, to embezzlement, to sexual assault, to forgery, and to a host of other behavior patterns, originated.

The selections, reprinted in this Part are not devoted exclusively to concern for the *origin* of "delinquent norms" or, in other words, rules for delinquent conduct. Very little research has been conducted in this area, and we know of no research report or essay devoted exclusively to this subject. Moreover, it is equally important to understand how subcultures are *maintained,* and most authors address both issues simultaneously. Cohen, for example, describes how subcultures arise, but then goes on to say, "Once established, such a subcultural system may persist, but not by sheer inertia. It may achieve a life which outlasts that of the

[4] David Bordua, "Delinquent Subcultures: Sociological Interpretations of Gang Delinquency," *Annals of the American Academy of Political and Social Science, 338* (November, 1961), pp. 134–135.

[5] Emile Durkheim, *Suicide: A Study in Sociology,* trans. John A. Spaulding and George Simpson (New York: The Free Press, 1951), pp. 250–257 (first published in Paris in 1897); Max Weber, *The Protestant Ethic and the Spirit of Capitalism,* trans. Talcott Parsons (London: Allen & Unwin, 1930); Robert K. Merton, "Social Structure and Anomie," *America Sociological Review,* 3 (October, 1938), 672–682.

[6] Svend Ranulf, *Moral Indignation and Middle Class Psychology: A Sociological Study* (Copenhagen: Levin and Munksgaard, 1938).

individuals who participated in its creation, but only so long as it continues to serve the needs of those who succeed its creators." In their selection, Cloward and Ohlin conclude that the "conversation of gestures," a process which Cohen describes as important to the development of subcultures, is also important to the maintenance of delinquent subcultures, since new participants must be recruited if any subculture is to survive. Their discussion is thus more concerned with the emergence of delinquent norms among gangs of boys than with analysis of how changing structural conditions in societies stimulate the invention of new rules of conduct. Like Cohen, Cloward and Ohlin specify the conditions under which delinquent and potential delinquents join with others like themselves to form delinquent gangs. But, unlike Cohen, they are primarily concerned with the structural conditions motivating persons to adopt norms that compete with official rules.

Cloward and Ohlin's explanation of the emergence and continuance of gang delinquency makes use of Merton's structural analysis.[7] However, they argue that more than just limited opportunities for success are involved in the motivation process. The restriction of legitimate opportunities must be perceived as unjust before it becomes effective. Thus, the individual likely to get into "trouble" is one who, finding his aspirations for success frustrated, attributes his frustration or failure to unjust barriers erected by society rather than to personal inadequacy, and then is led to attribute legitimacy to officially *dis*approved modes of conduct.

Although principally concerned with the degree to which subcultural characteristics appear among members of delinquent gangs and not with the question of how these characteristics originated, the study by Short, Rivera, and Tennyson provides some empirical support for the "limited opportunity" or "structural frustration" thesis of Cohen, and Cloward and Ohlin. Their comparison of Chicago gang boys, non-gang boys, and middle-class boys revealed that gang boys perceived their occupational and educational opportunities to be restricted to a greater degree than did members of the other two categories. Gang boys were also more likely to perceive illegitimate opportunities as open to them than were the other boys, and perception of the availability of legitimate opportunities was more strongly associated with delinquency rates than was perception of illegitimate opportunities.

There is some confusion in the sociological writing about the development of delinquent subcultures on the one hand, and the developmental processes involved in the formation of gangs on the other. This confusion is reflected in the frequent use of the terms "gang" and "delinquent subculture" as synonyms. Cloward and Ohlin use the two terms interchangeably. In his first selection in this Part, Cohen argues that status

[7] See "Social Structure and Anomie" in Part IV, above.

deprivation is the fundamental problem for which delinquency is the solution. However, it is unclear whether status deprivation motivates the invention of delinquent rules, the formation of delinquent gangs, or both. Cloward and Ohlin apply their general theory of subcultures to delinquent subcultures, but it is not clear whether this application, elaborated in Part VIII,[8] is concerned with the invention of three different sets of rules for delinquency or with the opportunities and motivations of boys forming delinquent gangs. Most of the research studies and action programs stimulated by these theories seem to have proceeded on the assumption that they are causal explanations of delinquency, rather than theories about the origin of delinquent rules of conduct.

The findings of Miller's research on gang violence challenge Cohen's thesis that the delinquent subculture is "non-utilitarian," by which he seems to mean that activities are oriented to malicious mischief and "hell raising" rather than to acquisition. In a situation of economic and social frustration whereby working-class boys are judged and found wanting in terms of the "middle-class measuring rod," Cohen says, working-class boys have invented a subculture comprised of values that are in direct opposition to middle-class values. Once this subculture has been established, working-class boys can achieve status in their own groups by engaging in activities that symbolize their rejection of the middle-class value and in terms of which they can "measure up." Thus, lower-class delinquent boys are motivated to destroy property instead of acquiring it, to vandalize the school instead of reading books, to waste money instead of saving it, and so forth. But Miller's study indicates that vandalism is relatively uncommon among street gangs. Further, even "non-utilitarian" violence is much rarer than the public is inclined to believe. The bulk of assault incidents among the members of the street gangs observed by Miller involved contests between boys in which the preservation and defense of gang honor was a central issue and where, "little of the deliberately-inflicted property damage represented a diffuse outpouring of accumulated hostility against arbitrary objects." One finding, however, did tend to support Cohen's thesis: the lower status lower-class gang members engaged in violence four times as often as did other boys also of the lower class but of slightly higher status. Miller concludes that a subculture of violence has not developed in American cities, popular opinion to the contrary.

Miller's finding that preservation and defense of honor is a rallying point for delinquent gang activity raises another important question about delinquent gangs: Does their persistence reflect internal or external pressures? After reviewing the theory and research on "delinquent subcultures" (gangs), Empey concludes that the cohesiveness of gangs is

[8] "The Differentiation of Delinquent Subcultures."

decreased if external pressures are decreased. Influences outside the gang, such as each member's position in the class structure, are more significant than is the gratification derived from group activities and relationships themselves. It should be noted that Empey does not address the question of how subcultures begin, perhaps because his overall conclusions question the validity of the "delinquent subcultures" concept itself. He observes that both conventional and delinquent values are parts of the *same* culture, but that the degree to which they are accepted varies. He suggests that we need studies of "the extent to which deviant values are diffused either throughout the entire class structure or through subgroups on all class levels."

The concluding selection, by Cohen, builds upon the discussion of "social structure and anomie" begun in Part IV and resumed in this Part. It takes a further look at the ideas and arguments stemming in part from Cohen's own book, published in 1955. In this article, which first appeared in 1965, Cohen attempts to integrate "anomie theory" and the symbolic interactionist perspective. His is not the first effort at such integration. Cloward and Ohlin made such an effort in developing their theory of delinquent gangs. Cohen takes the basic position that much deviant behavior is the direct outcome of roles being played, or of coveted roles. He notes that disparity between aspirations and opportunities is but one source of deviance, and that another source is the effort of the individual to establish his identity by learning behavior that symbolizes memberships of various kinds. This view shifts the focus from a disjunction between aspiration and achievement (from structural frustration) to the processes involved as a person in a halting, tentative, groping way assumes delinquent roles and becomes progressively involved in delinquent behavior. Some "delinquent subcultures" may in fact be collections of rules about how one is to behave if he is to maintain the image he would like to have of himself, rather than direct "rules for delinquency." The motivation for participating in these rules need not necessarily involve structural frustration.

1 A General Theory of Subcultures

ALBERT K. COHEN

This is [a discussion] about subcultures in general, how they get started and what keeps them going. . . . Any explanation of a particular event or phenomenon presupposes an underlying theory, a set of general rules or a model to which all events or phenomena of the same class are supposed to conform. Indeed, do we not mean by "explanation" a demonstration that the thing to be explained can be understood as a special case of the working out of such a set of general rules? For example, when we explain to a child why the rubber safety valve on a pressure cooker pops off when the interior of the cooker reaches a certain critical temperature, we first tell him that there are certain well-established relationships between pressure and temperature (which have been technically formulated in physics as Boyle's Law) and then we show him that the behavior of the valve is exactly what we should expect if the rules which describe those relationships are true. We do no more nor less when we explain the velocity of a falling body, the acquisition of a habit, an increase in the price of some commodity or the growth of a subculture. In every case, if the general theory which we invoke does not "fit" other phenomena of the same class, the explanation is not considered satisfactory. Thus, if *some* changes in the price level seem to be consistent with the "laws of supply and demand" but *other* changes in the price level are not, then the "laws" are considered unsatisfactory and *none* of the changes are explained by reference to these laws.

Reprinted with permission of The Macmillan Company from *Delinquent Boys: The Culture of the Gang.* Copyright by The Free Press, a Corporation, 1955, pp. 49–72.

Therefore, it is appropriate that we set forth explicitly, if somewhat sketchily, the theory about subcultures in general that underlies our attempt to explain the delinquent subculture. If the explanation is sound, then the general theory should provide a key to the understanding of other subcultures as well. If the general theory does not fit other subcultures as well, then the explanation of this particular subculture is thrown into question.

ACTION IS PROBLEM-SOLVING

Our point of departure is the "psychogenic" assumption that all human action—not delinquency alone—is an ongoing series of efforts to solve problems. By "problems" we do not only mean the worries and dilemmas that bring people to the psychiatrist and the psychological clinic. Whether or not to accept a proffered drink, which of two ties to buy, what to do about the unexpected guest or the "F" in algebra are problems too. They all involve, until they are resolved, a certain tension, a disequilibrium and a challenge. We hover between doing and not doing, doing this or doing that, doing it one way or doing it another. Each choice is an act, each act is a choice. Not every act is a *successful* solution, for our choice may leave us with unresolved tensions or generate new and unanticipated consequences which pose new problems, but it is at least an attempt at a solution. On the other hand, not every problem need imply distress, anxiety, bedevilment. Most problems are familiar and recurrent and we have at hand for them ready solutions, habitual modes of action which we have found efficacious and acceptable both to ourselves and to our neighbors. Other problems, however, are not so readily resolved. They persist, they nag, and they press for novel solutions.

What people do depends upon the problems they contend with. If we want to explain what people do, then we want to be clear about the nature of human problems and what produces them. As a first step, it is important to recognize that all the multifarious factors and circumstances that conspire to produce a problem come from one or the other of two sources, the actor's "frame of reference" and the "situation" he confronts. All problems arise and all problems are solved through changes in one or both of these classes of determinants.

First, the situation. This is the world we live in and where we are located in that world. It includes the physical setting within which we must operate, a finite supply of time and energy with which to accomplish our ends, and above all the habits, the expectations, the demands and the social organization of the people around us. Always our problems are what they are because the situation limits the things we can do and have and the conditions under which they are possible. It will not permit us to satisfy equally potent aspirations, *e.g.*, to enjoy the blessings of marriage and bachelorhood at the same time. The resources it offers may not be enough to "go around," *e.g.*, to send the children to college, to pay off the mortgage and to satisfy a thousand other longings. To some of us it may categorically deny the possibility of success, as we define success. To others, it may extend the possibility of success, but the only means which it provides may be morally repugnant; *e.g.*, cheating, chicanery and bootlicking may be the only road open to the coveted promotion.

But the niggardliness, the crabbiness, the inflexibility of the situation and the problems they imply are always relative to the actor. What the actor sees and how he feels about what he sees depend as much on his "point of view" as on the situation which he encounters. Americans do not see grasshoppers as belonging to the same category as pork chops, orange juice and cereal; other peoples do. Different Americans, confronting a "communist" or a "Negro," have very different ideas of what kind of person they are dealing with. The political office which one man sees as a job, another sees as an opportunity for public service and still another as something onerous and profitless to be avoided at all costs. Our beliefs about what is, what is possible and what consequences flow from what actions do not necessarily correspond to what is "objectively" true. "The facts" never simply stare us in the face. We see them always through a glass, and the glass consists of the interests, preconceptions, stereotypes and values we bring to the situation. This glass is our frame of reference. What is a "barrier" and what an "opportunity," what is a "reward" and what a "punishment," what is a "loss" and what a "gain" depends upon our goals and aspirations; they are not "given" by the bare facts of the situation taken by itself. Things are scarce or plentiful, hard or easy, precious or cheap depending upon our scale of values. Most important of all, perhaps, the moral insufficiency of this or that aspect of the situation, the moral obligation to "do something about it" and the moral impediments to quick and easy solutions derive not from the objective properties of the situation but from the moral standards within our frame of reference. Seen through one frame of reference the world is fraught with dark and frightening dilemmas; seen through another frame of reference, the "same" world is full of promise and cheer.

Our really hard problems are those for which we have no ready-at-hand solutions which will not leave us without feelings of tension, frustration, resentment, guilt, bitterness, anxiety or hopelessness. These feelings and therefore the inadequacy of the solutions are largely the result of the frame of reference through which we contemplate these solutions. It follows that an effective, really satisfying solution *must entail some change in that frame of reference itself*. The actor may give up pursuit of some goal which seems unattainable, but it is not a "solution" unless he can first persuade himself that the goal is, after all, not worth pursuing; in short, his values must change. He may resolve a problem of conflicting loyalties by persuading himself that the greater obligation attaches to one rather than to the other, but this too involves a change in his frame of reference: a commitment to some standard for adjudicating the claims of different loyalties. "Failure" can be transformed into something less humiliating by imputing to others fraud, malevolence or corruption, but this means adopting new perspectives for looking at others and oneself. He may continue to strive for goals hitherto unattainable by adopting more efficacious but "illicit" means; but, again, the solution is satisfying only to the degree that guilt is obviated by a change in moral standards. All these and other devices are familiar to us as the psychologist's and the psychoanalyst's "mechanisms of adjustment"— projection, rationalization, substitution, etc.—and they are all ways of coping with problems by a change within the actor's frame of reference.

A second factor we must recognize in building up a theory of subcultures is that human problems are not distributed in a random way among the roles that make up a social system. Each age, sex, racial and ethnic category, each occupation, economic stratum and social class consists of people who have been equipped by their society with frames of reference and confronted by their society with situations which are not equally characteristic of other roles. If the ingredients of which problems are compounded are likened to a deck of cards, your chances and mine of getting a certain hand are not the same but are strongly affected by where we happen to sit. The problems and preoccupations of men and women are different because they judge themselves and others judge them by different standards and because the means available to them for realizing their aspirations are different. It is obvious that opportunities for the achievement of power and prestige are not the same for people who start out at different positions in the class system; it is perhaps a bit less obvious that their levels of aspiration in these respects and therefore what it will take to satisfy them are likely also to differ. All of us must come to terms with the problems of growing old, but these problems are not the same for all of us. To consider but one facet, the decline of physical vigor may have very different meaning for a steel worker and a physician. There is a large and increasing scholarly literature, psychiatric and sociological, on the ways in which the structure of society generates, at each position within the system, characteristic combinations of personality and situation and therefore characteristic problems of adjustment.

Neither sociologists nor psychiatrists, however, have been sufficiently diligent in exploring the role of the social structure and the immediate social milieu in determining *the creation and selection of solutions*. A way of acting is never completely explained by describing, however convincingly, the problems of adjustment to which it is a response, *as long as there are conceivable alternative responses*. Different individuals *do* deal differently with

the same or similar problems and these differences must likewise be accounted for. One man responds to a barrier on the route to his goal by
redoubling his efforts. Another seeks for a more devious route to the same
objective. Another succeeds in convincing himself that the game is not
worth the candle. Still another accepts, but with ill grace and an abiding
feeling of bitterness and frustration, the inevitability of failure. Here we
shall explore some of the ways in which the fact that we are participants
in a system of social interaction affects the ways in which we deal with our
problems.

PRESSURES TOWARD CONFORMITY

In a general way it is obvious that any solution that runs counter to
the strong interests or moral sentiments of those around us invites punishment or the forfeiture of satisfactions which may be more distressing than
the problem with which it was designed to cope. We seek, if possible, solutions which will settle old problems and not create new ones. A first requirement, then, of a wholly acceptable solution is that it be acceptable to those
on whose cooperation and good will we are dependent. This immediately
imposes sharp limits on the range of creativity and innovation. Our dependence upon our social milieu provides us with a strong incentive to select our
solutions from among those already established and known to be congenial
to our fellows.

More specifically, the consistency of our own conduct and of the frame
of reference on which it is based with those of our fellows is a criterion
of status and a badge of membership. Every one of us wants to be a member
in good standing of some groups and roles. We all want to be recognized
and respected as a full-fledged member of some age and sex category, as an
American, perhaps also as a Catholic, a Democrat, a Southerner, a Yale man,
a doctor, a man-of-the-world, a good citizen of West Burlap. For every
such role there are certain kinds of action and belief which function, as
truly and effectively as do uniforms, insignia and membership cards, as signs
of membership. To the degree that we covet such membership, we are motivated to assume those signs, to incorporate them into our behavior and
frame of reference. Many of our religious beliefs, esthetic standards, norms
of speech, political doctrines, and canons of taste and etiquette are so
motivated.

Not only recognition as members of some social category but also the
respect in which others hold us are contingent upon the agreement of the
beliefs we profess and the norms we observe with their norms and beliefs.
However much we may speak of tolerance of diversity and respect for
differences we cannot help but evaluate others in terms of the measure of

their agreement with ourselves. With people who think and feel as we do we are relaxed. We do not have to defend ourselves to them. We welcome them to our company and like to have them around. But in dissent there is necessarily implied criticism, and he who dissents, in matters the group considers important, inevitably alienates himself to some extent from the group and from satisfying social relationships.

Not only is consensus rewarded by acceptance, recognition and respect; it is probably the most important criterion of the *validity* of the frame of reference which motivates and justifies our conduct. The man who stands alone in holding something dear or in despising some good that others cherish, whether it be a style of art, a political belief, a vocational aspiration, or a way of making money not only suffers a loss of status; he is not likely to hold to his beliefs with much conviction. His beliefs will be uncertain, vacillating, unstable. If others do not question us, on the other hand, we are not likely to question ourselves. For any given individual, of course, some groups are more effective than others as authorities for defining the validity or plausibility of his beliefs. These are his "reference groups." For all of us, however, faith and reason alike are curiously prone to lead to conclusions already current in our reference groups. It is hard to convince ourselves that in cheating, joining the Christian Science Church, voting Republican or falsifying our age to buy beer we are doing the right thing if our reference groups are agreed that these things are wrong, stupid or ridiculous.

We see then why, both on the levels of overt action and of the supporting frame of reference, there are powerful incentives not to deviate from the ways established in our groups. Should our problems be not capable of solution in ways acceptable to our groups and should they be sufficiently pressing, we are not so likely to strike out on our own as we are to shop around for a group with a different subculture, with a frame of reference we find more congenial. One fascinating aspect of the social process is the continual realignment of groups, the migration of individuals from one group to another in the unconscious quest for a social milieu favorable to the resolution of their problems of adjustment.

HOW SUBCULTURAL SOLUTIONS ARISE

Now we confront a dilemma and a paradox. We have seen how difficult it is for the individual to cut loose from the culture models in his milieu, how his dependence upon his fellows compels him to seek conformity and to avoid innovation. But these models and precedents which we call the surrounding culture are ways in which other people think and other people act, and these other people are likewise constrained by models in *their* milieux. *These models themselves, however, continually change.* How is it possible for cultural innovations to emerge while each of the participants in the culture is so powerfully motivated to conform to what is already established? This is the central theoretical problem of this book.

The crucial condition for the emergence of new cultural forms is the existence, *in effective interaction with one another, of a number of actors with similar problems of adjustment.* These may be the entire membership of a group or only certain members, similarly circumstanced, within the group. Among the conceivable solutions to their problems may be one which is not yet embodied in action and which does not therefore exist as a cultural model. This solution, except for the fact that is does not already carry the social criteria of validity and promise the social rewards of consensus, might well answer more neatly to the problems of this group and appeal to its members more effectively than any of the solutions already institutionalized. For each participant, this solution would be adjustive and adequately motivated provided that he could anticipate a simultaneous and corresponding transformation in the frames of reference of his fellows. Each would welcome a sign from the others that a new departure in this direction would receive approval and support. But how does one *know* whether a gesture toward innovation will strike a responsive and sympathetic chord in others or whether it will elicit hostility, ridicule and punishment? *Potential* concurrence is always problematic and innovation or the impulse to innovate a stimulus for anxiety.

The paradox is resolved when the innovation is broached in such a manner as to elicit from others reactions suggesting their receptivity; and when, at the same time, the innovation occurs by increments so small, tentative and ambiguous as to permit the actor to retreat, if the signs be unfavorable, without having become identified with an unpopular position. Perhaps all social actions have, in addition to their instrumental, communicative and expressive functions, this quality of being *exploratory gestures.* For the actor with problems of adjustment which cannot be resolved within the frame of reference of the established culture, each response of the other to what the actor says and does is a clue to the directions in which change may proceed further in a way congenial to the other and to the direction in which change will lack social support. And if the probing gesture is motivated by tensions common to other participants it is likely to initiate a process of *mutual* exploration and *joint* elaboration of a new solution. My exploratory gesture functions as a cue to you; your exploratory gesture as a cue to me. By a casual, semi-serious, non-commital or tangential remark I may stick my neck out just a little way, but I will quickly withdraw it unless you, by some sign of affirmation, stick *yours* out. I will permit myself to become progressively committed but only as others, by some visible sign, become likewise committed. The final product, to which we are jointly committed, is likely to be a compromise formation of all the participants to what we may call a cultural process, a formation perhaps unanticipated by any of them. Each actor may contribute something directly to the growing product, but he may also contribute indirectly by encouraging others to advance, inducing them to retreat, and suggesting new avenues to be explored. The product cannot be ascribed to any one of the participants; it is a real "emergent" on a group level.

We may think of this process as one of mutual conversion. The important thing to remember is that we do not first convert ourselves and then others. The acceptability of an idea to oneself depends upon its acceptability to others. Converting the other is part of the process of converting oneself.

A simple but dramatic illustration may help. We all know that soldiers sometimes develop physical complaints with no underlying organic pathology. We know that these complaints, which the soldier himself is convinced are real, are solutions to problems. They enable the soldier to escape from a hazardous situation without feeling guilty or to displace his anxiety, whose true cause he is reluctant to acknowledge even to himself, upon something which is generally acknowledged to be a legitimate occasion for anxiety. Edward A. Strecker describes an episode of "mass psychoneurosis" in World War I. In a period of eight days, on a certain sector of the front, about 500 "gas casualties" reported for medical aid. There had been some desultory gas shelling but never of serious proportions.

Either following the explosion of a gas shell, or even without this preliminary, a soldier would give the alarm of "gas" to those in his vicinity. They would put on their masks, but in the course of a few hours a large percentage of this group would begin to drift into the dressing stations, complaining of indefinite symptoms. It was obvious upon examination that they were not really gassed.[1]

Strecker tells us that these symptoms were utilized as "a route to escape from an undesirable situation." What he does not tell us, but what seems extremely probable, is that for many and probably most of the soldiers, this route to escape was available only because hundreds of other soldiers were "in the same boat" and in continual communicative interaction before, during and after the shelling. One soldier might be ripe for this delusion but if his buddies are not similarly ripe he will have a hard time persuading them that he has been gassed, and if they persist in not being gassed he will have a hard time persuading himself. If all are ripe, they may, in a relatively short time, collectively fabricate a false but unshakeable belief that all have been gassed. It is most unlikely that these 500 soldiers would have been able to "describe all the details with convincing earnestness and generally some dramatic quality of expression" if they had not been able to communicate with one

[1] Edward A. Strecker, *Beyond the Clinical Frontier* (New York: W. W. Norton and Company, 1940), pp. 77–78.

another and develop a common vocabulary for interpreting whatever subjective states they did experience.

The literature on crowd behavior is another source of evidence of the ability of a propitious interaction situation to generate, in a short time, collective although necessarily ephemeral and unstable solutions to like problems. Students are agreed that the groundwork for violent and destructive mob behavior includes the prior existence of unresolved tensions and a period of "milling" during which a set of common sentiments is elaborated and reinforced. It is incorrect to assume, however, that a certain magic in numbers simply serves to lift the moral inhibitions to the expression of already established destructive urges. Kimball Young observes:

> Almost all commentators have noted that individuals engaged in mass action, be it attack or panic flight, show an amazing lack of what are, under calmer conditions, considered proper morals. There is a release of moral inhibitions, social taboos are off, and the crowd enjoys a sense of freedom and unrestraint.[2]

He goes on to add, however:

> Certainly those engaged in a pogrom, a lynching or a race riot have a great upsurge of moral feelings, the sense of righting some wrong . . . Though the acts performed may be viewed in retrospect as immoral, and may later induce a sense of shame, remorse and guilt, at the time they seem completely justified.[3]

It is true that ordinary moral restraints often cease to operate under mob conditions. These conditions do not, however, produce a suspension of all morality, a blind and amoral outburst of primitive passions. The action of each member of the mob is in accordance with a collective solution which has been worked out during the brief history of the mob itself. This solution includes not only something to do but a positive morality to justify conduct at such gross variance with the mob members' ordinary conceptions of decency and humanity. In short, what occurs under conditions of mob interaction is not the annihilation of morality but a rapid transformation of the moral frame of reference.

Here we have talked about bizarre and short-lived examples of group problem-solving. But the line between this sort of thing and large-scale social movements, with their elaborate and often respectable ideologies and programs, is tenuous. No fundamentally new principles have to be invoked to explain them.

We quote from one more writer on the efficacy of the interaction situation in facilitating transformations of the frame of reference. The late Kurt

[2] Kimball Young, *Social Psychology* (2nd ed.; New York: F. S. Crofts and Company, 1946), p. 398.

[3] *Ibid.,* p. 399.

Lewin, on the basis of his experience in attempts at guided social change, remarks:

. . . Experience in leadership training, in changing of food habits, work production, criminality, alcoholism, prejudices, all seem to indicate that it is usually easier to change individuals formed into a group than to change any one of them separately. As long as group values are unchanged the individual will resist changes more strongly the farther he is to depart from group standards. If the group standard itself is changed, the resistance which is due to the relationship between individual and group standard is eliminated.[4]

The emergence of these "group standards" of this shared frame of reference, is the emergence of a new subculture. It is cultural because each actor's participation in this system of norms is influenced by his perception of the same norms in other actors. It is *sub*cultural because the norms are shared only among those actors who stand somehow to profit from them and who find in one another a sympathetic moral climate within which these norms may come to fruition and persist. In this fashion culture is continually being created, re-created and modified wherever individuals sense in one another like needs, generated by like circumstances, not shared generally in the larger social system. Once established, such a subcultural system may persist, but not by sheer inertia. It may achieve a life which outlasts that of the individuals who participated in its creation, but only so long as it continues to serve the needs of those who succeed its creators.

SUBCULTURAL SOLUTIONS TO STATUS PROBLEMS

One variant of this cultural process interests us especially because it provides the model for our explanation of the delinquent subculture. Status problems are problems of achieving respect in the eyes of one's fellows. Our ability to achieve status depends upon the criteria of status applied by our fellows, that is, the standards or norms they go by in evaluating people. These criteria are an aspect of their cultural frames of reference. If we lack the characteristics or capacities which give status in terms of these criteria, we are beset by one of the most typical and yet distressing of human problems of adjustment. One solution is for individuals who share such problems to gravitate toward one another and jointly to establish new norms, new criteria of status which define as meritorious the characteristics they *do* possess, the kinds of conduct of which they *are* capable. It is clearly necessary for each participant, if the innovation is to solve his status problem, that these new criteria be shared with others, that the solution be a group and

[4] Kurt Lewin, "Frontiers of Group Dynamics," *Human Relations,* I (June, 1947), 35.

not a private solution. If he "goes it alone" he succeeds only in further estranging himself from his fellows. Such new status criteria would represent new subcultural values different from or even antithetical to those of the larger social system.

In general conformity with this pattern, social scientists have accounted for religious cults and sects such as the Oxford Group and Father Divine's Kingdom as attempts on the part of people who feel their status and self-respect threatened to create little societies whose criteria of personal goodness are such that those who participate can find surcease from certain kinds of status anxiety. They have explained such social movements as the Nazi Party as coalitions of groups whose status is unsatisfactory or precarious within the framework of the existing order and who find, in the ideology of the movement, reassurance of their importance and worth or the promise of a new society in which their importance and worth will be recognized. They have explained messianic and revivalistic religious movements among some American Indian and other non-literate groups as collective reactions to status problems which arise during the process of assimilation into a culture and social system dominated by white people. In this new social system the natives find themselves relegated to the lowest social strata. They respond by drawing closer together to one another and elaborating ideologies which emphasize the glories of the tribal past, the merit of membership in the tribe and an early millennium in which the ancient glory and dignity of the tribe will be reestablished. All these movements may seem to have little in common with a gang of kids bent on theft and vandalism. It is true that they have little in common on the level of the concrete content of ideologies and value systems. In later chapters, however, we will try to show that the general principles of explanation which we have outlined here are applicable also to the culture of the delinquent gang.

SOME ACCOMPANIMENTS OF THE CULTURAL PROCESS

The continued serviceability and therefore the viability of a subcultural solution entails the emergence of a certain amount of group solidarity and heightened interaction among the participants in the subculture. It is only in interaction with those who share his values that the actor finds social validation for his beliefs and social rewards for his way of life, and the continued existence of the group and friendly intercourse with its members become values for the actor. Furthermore, to the extent that the new subculture invites the hostility of outsiders—one of the costs of subcultural solutions— the members of the subcultural group are motivated to look to one another for those goods and services, those relationships of cooperation and exchange which they once enjoyed with the world outside the group and which have now been withdrawn. This accentuates still further the separateness of the group, the dependence of the members on the group and the richness and individuality of its subculture. No group, of course, can live entirely unto itself. To some extent the group may be compelled to improvise new arrangements for obtaining services from the outside world. "The fix," for example, arises to provide for the underworld that protection which is afforded to legitimate business by the formal legal system and insurance companies.

Insofar as the new subculture represents a new status system sanctioning behavior tabooed or frowned upon by the larger society, the acquisition of status within the new group is accompanied by a loss of status outside the group. To the extent that the esteem of outsiders is a value to the members of the group, a new problem is engendered. To this problem the typical solution is to devalue the good will and respect of those whose good will and respect are forfeit anyway. The new subculture of the community of innovators comes to include hostile and contemptuous images of those groups whose enmity they have earned. Indeed, this repudiation of outsiders, necessary in order to protect oneself from feeling concerned about what they may think, may go so far as to make nonconformity with the expectations of the outsiders a positive criterion of status within the group. Certain kinds of conduct, that is, become reputable precisely because they are disreputable in the eyes of the "out-group."

One curious but not uncommon accompaniment of this process is what Fritz Redl has called "protective provocation." Certain kinds of behavior to which we are strongly inclined may encounter strong resistances because this behavior would do injury to the interests or feelings of people we care about. These same kinds of behavior would, however, be unequivocally motivated without complicating guilt feelings if those people stood to us in the relation of enemies rather than friends. In such a situation we may be unconsciously motivated to act precisely in those ways calculated to stimulate others to expressions of anger and hostility, which we may then seize upon as evidences of their essential enmity and ill will. We are then absolved of our moral obligations toward those persons and freer to act without ambivalence. The hostility of the "out-group," thus engendered or aggravated, may serve to protect the "in-group" from mixed feelings about its way of life.

CONCLUSION

Our point of departure, we have said, is the psychogenic assumption that innovations, whether on the level of action or of the underlying frame of reference, arise out of problems of adjustment. In the psychogenic model, however, the innovation is independently contrived by the actor. The role of the social milieu in the genesis of the problem is recognized, but its role in the determination of the solution minimized. In the psychogenic model, the fact that others have problems similar to my own may lead them to contrive like solutions, but my problem-solving process runs to its conclusion unaffected by the parallel problem-solving processes of the others.

In the pure or extreme cultural-transmission model, on the other hand, the role of important differences in problems of adjustment and the motivation of newly acquired behavior by those problems tend to drop out of sight. Above all, the pure cultural-transmission view fails completely to explain the origin of new cultural patterns. Indeed, if the view we have proposed is correct, the cultural-transmission model fails to explain even the perpetuation of a cultural pattern through social transmission, for the recruitment of new culture-bearers presupposes life-problems which render them susceptible to the established pattern. The theory we have outlined, couched in terms of group problem-solving, attempts to integrate two views which, in the literature, frequently stand in presumed contrast to one another.

It is to be emphasized that the existence of problems of adjustment, even of like problems of adjustment among a plurality of actors, is not sufficient to insure the emergence of a subcultural solution. The existence of the necessary conditions for effective social interaction prerequisite to such a solution cannot be taken for granted. Who associates with whom is partly a matter of "shopping around" and finding kindred souls. But circumstances may limit this process of mutual gravitation of people with like problems and free and spontaneous communication among them. People with like problems may be so separated by barriers of physical space or social convention that the probability of mutual exploration and discovery is small. Free choice of associates may be regulated by persons in power, as parents may regulate the associates of their children. Where status differences among people with like problems are great, the probability of spontaneous communication relating to private, intimate, emotionally involved matters is small. Where the problems themselves are of a peculiarly delicate, guilt-laden nature, like many problems arising in the area of sex, inhibitions on communication may be so powerful that persons with like problems may never reveal themselves to one another, although circumstances are otherwise favorable for mutual exploration. Or the problems themselves may be so infrequent and atypical that the probability of running into someone else whose interests would be served by a common solution is negligible.

Because of all these restraints and barriers to communication, as well as the costs of participation in subcultural groups, which may sometimes be counted excessive, subcultural solutions may not emerge, or particular individuals may not participate in them. Nonetheless, the problems of adjustment may be sufficiently intense and persistent that they still press for some kind of change that will mitigate or resolve the problem. Since group solutions are precluded, the problem-solving may well take a "private," "personal-social" or "neurotic" direction and be capable of satisfactory description in primarily psychogenic terms.

A complete theory of subcultural differentiation would state more precisely the conditions under which subcultures emerge and fail to emerge, and would state operations for predicting the content of subcultural solutions. . . .

2 The Evolution of Delinquent Subcultures

RICHARD A. CLOWARD
AND LLOYD E. OHLIN

The development and maintenance of a delinquent subculture is obviously a collective enterprise. Delinquent norms are a group product and command the allegiance of individuals as members of a group. Yet many youngsters "resolve" their problems of adjustment by developing essentially solitary or individualistic deviant forms of behavior, especially various types of mental illness. Consequently, in attempting to account for the emergence of delinquent norms, we must also consider what conditions tend to encourage the development of collective rather than individual adaptations.

. . . [T]he tendency to withdraw attributions of legitimacy from established social norms depends in part upon whether the individual attributes failure to the social order or himself. It is our hypothesis that collective adaptations are likely to emerge when failure is attributed to the inadequacy of existing institutional arrangements; conversely, when failure is attributed to personal deficiencies, solitary adaptations are more likely.

In our society success and failure are ideologically explained in essentially individualistic terms. Success is formally attributed to ambition, perseverance, talent, and the like; failure, on the other hand, is regarded as a result of a lack of these traits. In explaining occupational achievements or failures, we do not ordinarily refer to the "life chances" or "objective opportunities" of the individual; we tend, rather, to ask whether he has made

Reprinted with permission of The Macmillan Company from *Delinquency and Opportunity: A Theory of Delinquent Gangs* by Richard A. Cloward and Lloyd E. Ohlin. Copyright by The Free Press, a Corporation 1960, pp. 124–143.

the most of the chances that he has, whether he has been diligent, industrious, and imaginative in the pursuit of success-goals. This tendency to equate success with ability and failure with personal inferiority helps to ensure the stability and continuity of existing arrangements by deflecting criticism from the institutional order and turning it back upon the self.

Those who attribute failure to their own shortcomings in effect accept the prevailing ideology of the society. They use socially accepted evaluative criteria in explaining their adjustment problems. Such persons are not at odds with society; on the contrary, self-blame is an important index of attitudinal conformity, for it is essentially an affirmation of the fairness and moral validity of the prevailing ideology. Individuals who explain failure in this way then have the problem of coping with the psychic consequences of internalized definitions of themselves as unworthy or inferior. It is unlikely that they will join with others to develop a solution, for they see their adjustment problem as essentially personal. They tend to experience feelings of guilt, shame, and loss of self-esteem which lead them to withdraw from others in seeking to solve their difficulties. Such persons may violate established rules of conduct in reaching their personal solutions, but these "solutions," however deviant, do not necessarily involve repudiation of the legitimacy of the prevailing system. The legtimacy of official norms is in fact asserted by the act of blaming oneself. The individual who violates official norms in these circumstances usually experiences strong feelings of guilt.

The individual who attributes his achievement dilemmas to deficiencies in the prevailing institutional arrangements, on the other hand, is at odds with the social order. This alienation generates a great deal of tension in relation to the carriers of the dominant cultural ideology. To some extent, the tension can be relieved if the alienated person can gain the support of others who are in the same position and who share the view that their misfortunes are due to an unjust system of social arrangements. Collective support can provide reassurance, security, and needed validation of a frame of reference toward which the world at large is hostile and disapproving.

The youngster who is motivated by a sense of injustice generally commits his first acts of deviance in a climate of uncertainty and fear of disapproval. The withdrawal of attributions of legitimacy from the dominant social norms is initially tentative and unstable. These first acts are usually minor and often impulsive expressions of resentment against the apparent injustice of the established social order. However, they bring the individual into conflict with the official system and expose him to its arsenal of invidious definitions and punitive sanctions. Members of the conventional community are likely to respond to them with strong efforts at repression, precisely because they recognize the underlying attitude of alienation from the established norms. These early acts of deviance are in effect tentative steps toward the adoption of norms in competition with the official rules. At this stage the deviant needs all the encouragement and reassurance he can muster to defend his position. He finds these by searching out others who have faced similar experiences and who will support one another in common attitudes of alienation from the official system. The deviant who is unable to mobilize such social support will have great difficulty in establishing firm grounds for his defiance of the official system, for he requires not only justifying beliefs but also social validation of the appropriateness of his deviant acts.

The initial contest between the individual and the authorities over the legitimacy of certain social norms and the appropriateness of certain acts of deviance sets in motion a process of definition that marks the offender as different from law-abiding folk. His acts and his person are defined as "evil," and he is caught up in a vicious cycle of norm-violation, repression, resentment, and new and more serious acts of violation. The process of alienation is accelerated, and the chasm between the offender and those who would control and reform him grows wider and deeper. In such circumstances he becomes increasingly dependent on the support of others in his position. The gang of peers forms a new social world in which the legitimacy of his delinquent conduct is strongly reinforced.

Tannenbaum locates the beginning of this alienation process in the innocent, random play activities of youngsters which result in acts that conflict with adult interests and values. The adult response of disapproval defines the acts and subsequently the child himself as "bad." This initiates a process that emphasizes and crystallizes the very behavior that is being proscribed.

In the conflict between the young delinquent and the community there develop two opposing definitions of the situation. In the beginning the definition of the situation by the young delinquent may be in the form of play, adventure, excitement, interest, mischief, fun. Breaking windows, annoying people, running around porches, climbing over roofs, stealing from pushcarts, playing truant—all are items of play, adventure, excitement. To the community, however, these activities may and often do take on the form of nuisance, evil, delinquency, with the demand for control, admonition, chastisement, punishment, police court, truant school. This conflict arises out of a divergence of values. As the problem develops, the attitude of the community hardens definitely into a demand for suppression. There is a gradual shift from the definition of the specific acts as evil to a definition of the individual as evil, so that all his acts come to be looked upon with suspicion. In the process of identification his companions, hangouts, play, speech, income, all his conduct, the personality itself, become subject to scrutiny and question. . . .

Early in his career, then, the incipient professional criminal develops an attitude of antagonism to the regulated orderly life that he is required to lead.

This attitude is hardened and crystallized by opposition. The conflict becomes a clash of wills. . . .

The firm dramatization of the "evil" which separates the child out of his group for specialized treatment plays a greater role in making the criminal than perhaps any other experience. It cannot be too often emphasized that for the child the whole situation has become different. He now lives in a different world. He has been tagged. A new and hitherto nonexistent environment has been precipitated out for him.

The process of making the criminal, therefore, is a process of tagging, defining, identifying, segregating, describing, emphasizing, making conscious and self-conscious; it becomes a way of stimulating, suggesting, emphasizing, and evolving the very traits that are complained of. If the theory of relation of response to stimulus has any meaning, the entire process of dealing with the young delinquent is mischievous in so far as it identifies him to himself or to the environment as a delinquent person.[1]

This process tends to isolate the child from constructive adult influences and make him dependent for security on the support and encouragement of others like himself. As Tannenbaum puts it: "The child's isolation forces him into companionship with other children similarly defined, and the gang becomes his means of escape, his security."

We agree with Tannenbaum and others in assigning central importance to the definitional process and peer-group support in the development of delinquent careers. However, our theoretical position differs from Tannenbaum's in two major respects. First, we assign much less importance to rule violations that grow out of the random play activities of children as the starting point of the alienation process. What Tannenbaum calls the "innocent divergence of the child from the straight road" during "play, adventure, excitement," along with unfavorable adult reactions to such "divergence," is experienced by *all* children in the normal course of socialization; yet relatively few children move toward delinquent *careers* after such experiences. In our view, the factor that distinguishes the children who do become delinquent is their withdrawal of attributions of legitimacy from established social norms. Children who continue to accept the conventional rules of conduct as binding are likely to accept adult disapproval as a justifiable response to their rule violations. They frequently feel guilty about their deviance and become motivated to act in more conforming fashion. However, those who question the legitimacy of the dominant norms are likely to resist being defined as morally inferior, which adult disapproval implies. Indeed, this invidious definition only feeds their resentment and encourages further misconduct. For such children, the definitional process that Tannen-

[1] Frank Tannenbaum, *Crime and the Community* (New York: Columbia University Press, 1938), pp. 17–20.

baum describes increases alienation from conventional norms and fosters the development of a delinquent career. But this occurs because the young offender has already developed an atttiude of alienation from at least some of the required forms of behavior. He is already capable in some measure of viewing his misconduct as justified.

Our second point of difference with Tannenbaum is that we assign an active role in the alienation process to the predispositions of the deviant youngster, whereas Tannenbaum focuses exclusively on the definitions and other responses given by adults to the innocent misconduct of children. The child, to Tannenbaum, is analogous to a pool ball propelled into the pocket of a delinquent career by the definitional thrusts of adults, whatever their intentions.

The person becomes the thing he is described as being. Nor does it seem to matter whether the valuation is made by those who would punish or those who would reform. In either case the emphasis is upon the conduct that is disapproved of. The parents or the policemen, the older brother or the court, the probation officer or the juvenile institution, in so far as they rest upon the thing complained of, rest upon a false ground. Their very enthusiasm defeats their aim. The harder they work to reform the evil, the greater the evil grows under their hands. The persistent suggestion, with whatever good intentions, works mischief, because it leads to bringing out the bad behavior that it would suppress.[2]

Since, according to Tannenbaum, it is the definitional structure of the adult community that creates delinquency, the solution lies in modifying that structure: "The way out is through a refusal to dramatize the evil. The less said about it the better. The more said about something else, still better."[3]

Tannenbaum's tendency to overstress the adult response to youthful misconduct is in part a conscious reaction against the tendency of other writers to ascribe "the cause of the unsocial behavior" to "a personal shortcoming of the offender." He states his opposition to this position in strong terms:

The assumption that crime is caused by any sort of inferiority, physiological or psychological, is here completely and unequivocally repudiated.

This does not mean that morphological or psychological techniques do not have value for the individual. It merely means that they have no greater value in the study of criminology than they would have in the study of any profession.[4]

Once the pressure to adopt a polemical position is removed, it is possible to recognize delinquency as a product of the interaction between certain internalized orientations of the delinquent and the structure of definitions and evaluations with which he is confronted. The adult response to miscon-

[2] *Ibid.*
[3] *Ibid.*
[4] *Ibid.*, p. 22.

duct has different consequences for the youngster who is disposed to question the legitimacy of established norms than for one who is not. Further, we contend, the consequences differ depending upon whether the invidious definitions based on minor acts of misconduct are imposed on those who already view the established order as unjust and deprivational.

TECHNIQUES OF DEFENSE AGAINST GUILT

People who violate rules which they accept as valid are likely to experience strong feelings of guilt, anxiety, or fear, whether or not the rule violations have collective support. With repeated violations, the accumulated anxiety tends to become so intense that the offender gives up his deviant conduct unless he can develop some defense against feelings of guilt. He must find a way of managing the guilt generated by the conflict between what he does and what he feels he should do before he can accept delinquent conduct as a stable solution to his adjustment problem.

The psychological literature dealing with delinquency has concentrated on identifying the devices by which this guilt is handled.[5] We take a somewhat different approach, by drawing a distinction between the legitimacy of social norms and their moral validity. If an individual withdraws sentiments supporting specific official norms and attributes legitimacy instead to officially prohibited modes of conduct, the guilt problem in regard to the violated norms has been solved in advance of the act. He may then engage in delinquent acts without experiencing acute guilt feelings about them because he has come to believe in the legitimacy of these acts, given the social circumstances in which he is placed. Distinguishing between the question of the legitimacy of norms and the question of their moral validity permits the performance of acts that the actor himself may view as morally inferior to some alternative way of behaving but as nevertheless justified. The problem of guilt does not arise for him so long as the specific attribution of legitimacy can be defended. One does not feel very guilty about violating a rule which one does not view as binding on one's conduct.

. . . We have traced the process of alienation by which the potential offender is led to attribute legitimacy to officially disapproved modes of conduct. A person who places blame for failure on the unjust organization of the established social order and who finds support from others for his withdrawal of legitimacy from official norms may be induced to resort to illegitimate means of achieving success-goals as a stable form of adaptation.

[5] See, e.g., August Aichhorn, *Wayward Youth* (New York: Viking Press, 1935); Kate Friedlander, *The Psychoanalytic Approach to Juvenile Delinquency* (New York: International Universities Press, 1944); and K. R. Eisler, ed., *Searchlights on Delinquency* (New York: International Universities Press, 1949).

Having withdrawn his acceptance of officially approved norms, he is psychologically protected against the guilt feelings that would otherwise result from violation of those norms. Successful communication and sharing of discontent with others who are similarly situated furnishes social support for and lends stability to whatever pattern of deviant conduct develops.

These steps are accompanied by the growth of a supporting structure of beliefs and values that provide advance justification for deviant conduct. Those who regard the social order as unjust and evaluate themselves as the equal of persons who have been granted access to legitimate opportunities in effect rationalize their deviance before it occurs. Thus they take steps to preserve their sense of personal integrity as they change their allegiance from conforming to prohibited modes of conduct. The emerging deviant subculture acquires a set of beliefs and values which rationalize the shift in norms as a natural response to a trying situation. These beliefs are in the form of descriptions and evaluations of the social world of the delinquent which contradict those held by conforming persons. Armed with these new conceptions of his social situation, the delinquent is able to adhere to the norms of the delinquent subculture with less vulnerability to the invidious definitions of his actions by law-abiding persons.

Recognizing this sequence in the development of delinquent norms and justifying beliefs and values makes it easier to understand the intractable and apparently conscienceless behavior of the fully indoctrinated members of delinquent subcultures. The absence of guilt feelings and a stubborn resistance to correction have earned such offenders the label of "psychopathic personalities." Most attempts to reform them through clinical therapy have been unsuccessful, largely because it is necessary for the "patient" to have guilt feelings before customary treatment procedures leading to psychological reorganization can be brought into play. This difficulty has been extensively documented in the work of Fritz Redl and his associates.[6] In order to create the requisite conditions for effective clinical treatment, they found it necessary to engage in prolonged and continuous assaults on the delinquents' underlying structure of justificatory beliefs and values. The offenders displayed remarkable ingenuity, skill, and determination in defending these cornerstones of their delinquent style of life. The literature contains descriptions of many individual delinquents who experience strong guilt feelings because they continue in some ambivalent fashion to acknowledge the legitimacy of the rules that they have violated. One even finds accounts of fully indoctrinated members of delinquent subcultures who occasionally give evidence of uncertainty about the validity of their justifying beliefs and values. Generally, however, members of delinquent subcultures effectively fight off these challenges and maintain their commitments

[6] Fritz Redl and David Wineman, *Children Who Hate* (Glencoe, Ill.: Free Press, 1956).

to delinquent norms in appropriate behavior areas. Of course, even members of the delinquent core group conform to conventional codes of conduct in many of their daily activities. In those behavioral areas which make up the delinquent role, however, they have attributed legitimacy to codes of conduct that compete directly with official norms and they staunchly defend the beliefs and values which support these codes.

Recent interpretations offered by Cohen and by Sykes and Matza differ from the foregoing analysis. Both contend that the delinquent retains a belief in the legitimacy of the official norms, although they differ in estimating the delinquent's awareness of this imputation. "The hallmark of the delinquent subculture," according to Cohen, "is the explicit and wholesale repudiation of middle-class standards and the adoption of their very antithesis."[7] However, he suggests that this repudiation is more apparent than real, for the delinquent maintains a secret and repressed desire for what he openly rejects:

> May we assume that when the delinquent seeks to obtain unequivocal status by repudiating, once and for all, the norms of the college-boy culture, these norms really undergo total extinction? Or do they, perhaps, linger on, underground, as it were, repressed, unacknowledged, but an ever-present threat to the adjustment which has been achieved at no small cost? There is much evidence from clinical psychology that moral norms, once effectively internalized, are not lightly thrust aside or extinguished.[8]

This assumption of a basic ambivalence which threatens the stability of the delinquent adaptation makes it possible for Cohen to introduce the psychological concept of reaction-formation to explain the "maliciousness" and "negativism" of some delinquent behavior. Apparently the constant internal and external threats to his adjustment lead the delinquent to exaggerate the extent of his alienation from middle-class norms of conduct.

> If a new moral order is evolved which offers a more satisfactory solution to one's life problems, the old order usually continues to press for recognition, but if this recognition is granted, the applecart is upset. The symptom of this obscurely felt, ever-present threat is clinically known as "anxiety," and the literature of psychiatry is rich with devices for combatting . . . this threat to a hard-won victory. One such device is reaction-formation. Its hallmark is an "exaggerated," "disproportionate," "abnormal" intensity of response, "inappropriate" to the stimulus which seems to elicit it. . . . The "overreaction" . . . has the function of reassuring the actor against an *inner* threat to his defenses as well as the function of meeting an external situation on its own terms. . . . We would expect the delinquent boy, who, after all, has been socialized in a society dominated by a middle-class morality and who can never quite escape the blandishments of middle-class society, to seek to maintain his safeguards against seduction. Reac-

[7] A. K. Cohen, *Delinquent Boys: The Culture of the Gang* (Glencoe, Ill.: Free Press, 1955), p. 129.

[8] *Ibid.*, p. 132.

tion-formation, in his case, should take the form of an "irrational," "malicious," "unaccountable" hostility to the enemy within the gates as well as without: the norms of the respectable middle-class society.[9]

In Cohen's view, then, the delinquent never quite gives up his allegiance to middle-class norms but continues to acknowledge their legitimacy secretly while openly challenging them by his behavior. In fact, the form and content of his behavior are apparently accounted for by this very ambivalence.

Sykes and Matza also see the delinquent as a person who continues to impute legitimacy to the official norms of the society, although they differ from Cohen in believing that this imputation is often quite conscious. As they put it, "The juvenile delinquent frequently recognizes *both* the legitimacy of the dominant social order and its moral rightness."[10] Cohen solves the problem of the discrepancy between the delinquent's conduct and his attribution of legitimacy to middle-class norms by viewing his attachment to these rules as repressed and unconscious. Sykes and Matza solve the problem by citing various techniques which enable the delinquent to escape guilt feelings for his behavior by redefining the applicability of the official norms. The delinquent, they contend, does not repudiate conventional norms; he "neutralizes" them. What makes it possible for him to do this is that accepted rules of conduct "appear as *qualified* guides for action, limited in their applicability in terms of time, place, persons, and social circumstances"[11]—limited, for example, by the forms of justification allowed by the criminal law as defenses against crime. The delinquent subculture simply extends these limitations so as to justify the conduct of its members.

The individual can avoid moral culpability for his criminal action—and thus avoid the negative sanctions of society—if he can prove that criminal intent was lacking. *It is our argument that much delinquency is based on what is essentially an unrecognized extension of defenses to crimes, in the form of justifications for deviance that are seen as valid by the delinquent but not by the legal system or society at large.*[12]

Thus the delinquent seems to concede the legitimacy of the existing structure of social rules, but he redefines the limitations on their applicability in such a way that his misconduct can be justified, at least to himself and his associates. For example, a street gang whose "turf" is invaded by a rival gang might redefine the situation as analogous to that of nations at war and might behave accordingly toward the invaders. Official representatives of the dominant value system and other conventional adults claim that this

---

[9] *Ibid.,* p. 133.

[10] G. M. Sykes and David Matza, "Techniques of Neutralization: A Theory of Delinquency," *American Sociological Review,* Vol. 22 (December, 1957), p. 665.

[11] *Ibid.,* p. 666.

[12] *Ibid.*

is an unwarranted extension of the code of conduct permissible in time of war. Youngsters claim, however, that this redefinition realistically fits the situation that confronts them.

It must be recognized in evaluating the position of Sykes and Matza that the delinquent's qualifications of official norms generally call for markedly different behavior than is conventionally expected in the situations to which they apply. Some established limitations upon the conditions under which otherwise proscribed conduct is justifiable are indispensable to the stability of the official normative system. By challenging the official definitions of these conditions, delinquent norms do compete with official norms.

In our view, the analyses by Cohen and by Sykes and Matza both fail to make four relevant distinctions: (1) between delinquent norms or rules of conduct (prescriptions), on the one hand, and the structure of beliefs (descriptions) and values (evaluations) on the other; (2) between the attribution of legitimacy to norms and the attribution of moral validity; (3) between the normative and moral problems of delinquents who are members of delinquent subcultures and the comparable problems of those who are not; and (4) between the presence of guilt and its absence in relation to the sequential development of justifying beliefs and delinquent norms.

In both these accounts there is a tendency to use the terms "norm," "belief," and "value" interchangeably, which leads to much confusion.[13] It is quite possible that the norms, beliefs, and values of a subculture develop by quite different processes. Unless these three features of a cultural system are kept analytically distinct, it is impossible to identify such developmental differences, to compare the time sequences in their growth, and to analyze how they become integrated into the system.

Secondly, both the Cohen and the Sykes and Matza positions tend to treat the problem of the legitimacy of a set of action prescriptions as equivalent to the problem of their moral validity.[14] They fail to perceive that the individual may regard a given norm as a legitimate guide to behavior under a particular set of circumstances even though at the same time he considers that pattern of action morally inferior to some alternative pattern. He may believe that law-abiding conduct is morally right but inappropriate or impossible in a particular situation. As a consequence of their failure to develop this distinction, Cohen and Sykes and Matza seem to be concerned almost exclusively with the moral judgments of delinquents and the way in which offenders handle problems of guilt. Both accounts assume that delin-

[13] Examples of this practice can be found in the quotations from Cohen's work cited previously and in the following characteristic passage from Sykes and Matza (*op. cit.,* p. 666): "A basic clue is offered by the fact that social rules or norms calling for valued behavior seldom if ever take the form of categorical imperatives. Rather, values or norms appear as *qualified* guides for action. . . ."

[14] Although Sykes and Matza recognize the distinction in a footnote commenting on its use by Weber (*ibid.,* p. 665, n. 4), it plays no part in their analytical scheme.

664   The Development and Maintenance of Delinquent Subcultures

quents consciously or unconsciously impute legitimacy to the norms of the larger society. It is for this reason that Cohen and Short are able to view the work of Sykes and Matza as "an important elaboration of the argument of *Delinquent Boys*."[15] Similarly, both analyses assume that delinquents accept the moral superiority of conventional norms. Cohen and Short, in fact, point to reaction-formation as a mechanism for handling the resulting moral ambivalence and stress the importance of this mechanism in the position of Sykes and Matza as well.

Thirdly, these accounts do not differentiate sufficiently between the problems of members of delinquent subcultures and those of solitary delinquents. Yet this distinction may have strategic theoretical value. For example, it is our impression that the lone delinquent is much more likely to experience feelings of ambivalence toward conventional norms of conduct and moral evaluations. He is therefore more likely to experience severe guilt reactions and to use various psychological mechanisms for controlling them, such as the ones Cohen and Sykes and Matza describe. Further, the withdrawal of sentiments in support of law-abiding norms of conduct and the imputation of legitimacy to a new set of norms seems much more likely to occur among delinquents who have collective support. It is difficult to see how an individual delinquent could maintain such a shift as a stable form of accommodation to his adjustment problems unless he also managed to acquire a rigid structure of supporting conceptions comparable to the delusional system of a paranoic. Generally speaking, the imputation of legitimacy to a model of conduct that is widely disapproved requires continual reassurance from others in order to persist.

Finally, the question of whether or not guilt feelings become a significant problem depends in large measure on when delinquent norms and justifying beliefs are developed. As we have indicated, the problem of guilt is resolved in advance of the delinquent act when the process of alienation has previously brought about a withdrawal of sentiments from official norms and the collective development of a supporting belief structure that justifies adherence to delinquent norms.[16] Sykes and Matza explicitly recognize this fact:

[15] A. K. Cohen and J. F. Short, Jr., "Research in Delinquent Subcultures," *Journal of Social Issues,* Vol 14, No. 3 (1958), p. 21.

[16] This insistence on the sequential priority of the justificatory beliefs to the development of delinquent norms is similar to Cressey's analysis of the relationship of "rationalizations" and acts of embezzlement. (See D. R. Cressey, *Other People's Money* Glencoe, Ill.: Free Press, [1953], esp. pp. 93–138.) Cressey assigns a crucial role to the learning of rationalizations which would permit the offender to embezzle without damaging his self-image as a law-abiding person. He insists that these rationalizing beliefs, such as the assertion that one is "only borrowing," are not *post facto* defenses against accusations of dishonesty but mechanisms that facilitate the act in advance of its performance.

Cressey emphasizes the priority of the rationalization to the act more consistently

These justifications are commonly described as rationalizations. They are viewed as following deviant behavior and as protecting the individual from self-blame and the blame of others after the act. But there is also reason to believe that they precede deviant behavior and make deviant behavior possible. . . . Disapproval flowing from internalized norms and conforming others in the social environment is neutralized, turned back, or deflected in advance. Social controls that serve to check or inhibit deviant motivational patterns are rendered inoperative, and the individual is freed to engage in delinquency without serious damage to his self-image. In this sense the delinquent both has his cake and eats it too, for he remains committed to the dominant normative system and yet so qualifies its imperatives that violations are "acceptable" if not "right." Thus the delinquent represents not a radical opposition to law-abiding society but sometimes more like an apologetic failure, often more sinned against than sinning in his own seyes. We call these justifications of deviant behavior "techniques of neutralization," and we believe these techniques make up a crucial component of Sutherland's "definitions favorable to the violation of law." It is by learning these techniques that the juvenile becomes delinquent, rather than by learning moral imperatives, values or attitudes standing in direct contradiction to those of the dominant society.[17]

They do not develop the implications of the priority of justifying beliefs to delinquent norms for the presence or absence of guilt. Instead they stress the delinquent's continued attribution of legitimacy to the dominant normative system and his consequent need to manage or neutralize the guilt that results.

THE COLLECTIVE PROBLEM-SOLVING PROCESS

In addition to the motivation to seek support from others who feel alienated from the prevailing social norms, collective solutions require a set of conditions in which communication among alienated persons can take place. If there are serious barriers to communication among the disaffected, the chances for the development of a collective solution will be relatively slight. As Cohen points out, "The crucial condition for the emergence of new cultural norms is the existence, *in effective interaction with one another,* of a number of actors with similar problems of adjustment."[18] However,

---

than Sykes and Matza do. However, his usage differs sharply from ours in regard to the attribution of legitimacy. In Cressey's cases, the embezzlers continued to attribute legitimacy to law-abiding norms of conduct and employed rationalizing arguments of their continued adherence to those norms. In contrast, the innovators of delinquent subcultural norms develop beliefs which justify their withdrawal of legitimacy from established norms and their attribution of legitimacy to officially proscribed models of behavior.

[17] Sykes and Matza, *op. cit.,* p. 666.
[18] Cohen, *op. cit.,* p. 59.

as Cohen makes clear, "The existence of problems of adjustment, even of like problems of adjustment, among a plurality of actors is not sufficient to insure the emergence of a subcultural solution."[19] He calls attention to a variety of social conditions that may impede communication and hence the formation of a subculture:

People with like problems may be so separated by barriers of physical space or social convention that the probability of mutual exploration and discovery is small. Free choice of associates may be regulated by persons in power, as parents may regulate the associates of their children. Where status differences among people with like problems are great, the probability of spontaneous communication relating to private, intimate, emotionally involved matters is small. Where the problems themselves are of a particularly delicate, guilt-laden nature, like many problems arising in the area of sex, inhibitions on communication may be so powerful that persons with like problems may never reveal themselves to one another, although circumstances are otherwise favorable for mutual exploration. Or the problems themselves may be so infrequent and atypical that the probability of running into someone else whose interest would be served by a common solution is negligible.[20]

Cohen has described the collective problem-solving process as a "conversation of gestures" in which each participant gradually stimulates the others to reveal themselves. Through "mutual conversion" a "compromise formation" results to which each participant has contributed.

. . . [H]ow does one *know* whether a gesture toward innovation will strike a responsive and sympathetic chord in others or whether it will elicit hostility, ridicule and punishment? *Potential* concurrence is always problematical and innovation or the impulse to innovate a stimulus for anxiety.

The paradox is resolved when the innovation is broached in such a manner as to elicit from others reactions suggesting their receptivity; and when, at the same time, the innovation occurs by increments so small, tentative and ambiguous as to permit the actor to retreat, if the signs be unfavorable, without having become identified with an unpopular position. Perhaps all social actions have, in addition to their instrumental, communicative and expressed functions, this quality of being *exploratory* gestures. For the actor with problems of adjustment which cannot be resolved within the frame of reference of the established culture, each response of the other to what the actor says and does is a clue to the directions in which change may proceed further in a way congenial to the other and to the direction in which change will lack social support. And if the probing gesture is motivated by tensions common to other participants it is likely to initiate a process of *mutual* exploration and *joint* elaboration of a new solution. My exploratory gesture functions as a cue to you; your exploratory gesture as a cue to me. By a casual, semi-serious, noncommittal or tangential remark I may stick my neck out just a little way, but I will quickly withdraw

19 *Ibid.,* p. 70.
20 *Ibid.,* pp. 70–71.

it unless you, by some sign of affirmation, stick *yours* out. I will permit myself to become progressively committed but only as others, by some visible sign, become likewise committed. The final product, to which we are jointly committed, is likely to be a compromise formation of all the participants to what we may call a cultural process, a formation perhaps unanticipated by any of them. Each actor may contribute something directly to the growing product, but he may also contribute indirectly by encouraging others to advance, inducing them to retreat, and suggesting new avenues to be explored. The product cannot be ascribed to any one of the participants; it is a real "emergent" on a group level.

We may think of this process as one of mutual conversion. The important thing to remember is that we do not first convert ourselves and then others. The acceptability of an idea to oneself depends upon its acceptability to others. Converting the other is part of the process of converting oneself.[21]

This conversation of gestures serves at least four important functions. First, it permits the participants to explore the extent and intensity of one another's alienation from the prevailing cultural norms and to determine how far each is willing to go in developing alternative prescriptions for action. Secondly, it permits them to explore their mutual interest in developing a collective as opposed to an individual solution—to estimate the extent to which they will be able to rely upon one another for support if their solution should take a daring, rebellious, or delinquent path. Thirdly, it gives them an opportunity to elaborate and test various justificatory beliefs and values by means of which problems of moral validity and guilt can be neutralized in anticipation of commitment to a deviant course of action. Finally, it permits them to explore a variety of deviant solutions to the common adjustment problem, to assess the merits of each and its chances of success, and to weigh the commitment that the other is willing to undertake to each type of solution. Once they have located the blame for their troubles in the social system and have successfully communicated to one another the extent of their alienation from established norms and their interest in finding an alternative collective solution, the development of delinquent norms and of some type of delinquent subculture becomes possible.

The exploration and adoption of a collective alternative solution are facilitated by the invidious definitions and punitive responses with which the law-abiding adult community reacts to collective acts of deviance. Thus the emerging collectivity is made more acutely aware of its isolation from the conventional community.

It does not become a gang, however, until it begins to excite disapproval and opposition, and thus acquires a more definite group-consciousness. It discovers a rival or an enemy in the gang in the next block; its baseball or football team is pitted against some other team; parents or neighbors look upon it with suspicion and hostility; "the old man around the corner," the storekeepers, or the "cops"

[21] *Ibid.*, pp. 60–61.

begin to give it "shags" (chase it); or some representative of the community steps in and tries to break it up. This is the real beginning of the gang, for now it starts to draw itself more closely together. It becomes a conflict group.[22]

The group members begin to exhibit a greater cohesiveness and sense of mutual dependence. They learn to define more closely those who are friendly or hostile to their activities. The experience of arrest, court adjudication, and correctional treatment of some members of the group casts a new light on the meaning and consequences of their activities.

There is a great deal more delinquency practiced and committed by the young groups than comes to the attention of the police. The boy arrested, therefore, is singled out in specialized treatment. This boy, no more guilty than the other members of his group, discovers a world of which he knew little. His arrest suddenly precipitates a series of institutions, attitudes, and experiences which the other children do not share. For this boy there suddenly appear the police, the patrol wagon, the police station, the other delinquents and criminals found in the police lock-ups, the court with all its agencies such as bailiffs, clerks, bondsmen, lawyers, probation officers. There are bars, cells, handcuffs, criminals. He is questioned, examined, tested, investigated. His history is gone into, his family is brought into court. Witnesses make their appearance. The boy, no different from the rest of his gang, suddenly becomes the center of a major drama in which all sorts of unexpected characters play important roles. And what is it all about? About the accustomed things his gang has done and has been doing for a long time. In this entirely new world he is made conscious of himself as a different human being than he was before his arrest. He becomes classified as a thief, perhaps, and the entire world about him has suddenly become a different place for him and will remain different for the rest of his life.[23]

The development of a delinquent solution thus depends not only on the exploratory gestures that boys direct toward one another but also on their interaction with others in the community. Through its representatives, official and unofficial, its institutions, and its other adolescent collectivities, the community enters into the life of the emerging delinquent gang at every stage. By the definitions it imposes and the opportunities it provides or denies, it helps to shape the final product.

[22] F. M. Thrasher, *The Gang* (Chicago: University of Chicago Press, 1927), p. 30.
[23] Tannenbaum, *op. cit.*, p. 19.

3 Perceived Opportunities, Gang Membership, and Delinquency*

JAMES F. SHORT, JR.,
RAMON RIVERA,
AND RAY A. TENNYSON

Not since the advent of psychoanalysis has a theory had such impact on institutionalized delinquency control as the theory, explicit or implied, in *Delinquency and Opportunity*.[1] Given the impetus of major foundation and federal support, the theory has been extensively adopted as a rationale for action programs in many areas of the country. There is some danger that, like psychoanalysis, "opportunity structure theory" may be rationalized and elaborated so rapidly and extensively as to discourage, if not render impossible, empirical testing, pragmatic validation, or demonstration of worth by any other criterion of "good theory." *Delinquency and Op-*

Reprinted from *American Sociological Review, 30* (February, 1956), 56–67, by permission of The American Sociological Association and the authors.

* This research is supported by grants from the Behavior Science Study Section of the National Institute of Mental Health (M–3301 and MH–07158); the Office of Juvenile Delinquency and Youth Development, Welfare Administration, U.S. Department of Health, Education, and Welfare in cooperation with the President's Committee on Juvenile Delinquency and Youth Crime (#62220); the Ford Foundation; and the Research Committee of Washington State University. We are grateful for this support and for the support and encouragement of staff members at the University of Chicago, Washington State University, and the Program for Detached Workers of the YMCA of Metropolitan Chicago, whose wholehearted cooperation makes the entire enterprise such an exciting "opportunity." An earlier version of this paper was read at the annual meetings of the Pacific Sociological Association, 1963.

[1] Richard A. Cloward and Lloyd E. Ohlin, *Delinquency and Opportunity: A Theory of Delinquent Gangs,* New York: Free Press of Glencoe, 1960.

portunity has been widely praised for its theoretical integration, e.g., as "a logically sound deductive system that is rich in its implications for delinquency causation and control," but the same critic also notes that "examined in terms of its logical, operational, and empirical adequacy, the theory poses a number of questions concerning the accuracy of some of its postulates and theorems."[2] Our papers will bring data to bear on certain aspects of the opportunity structure paradigm as we operationalized it in a study of delinquent gangs in Chicago.

Figure 1 reproduces in paradigm form the principal elements of "opportunity structure theory" concerning *criminal* and *conflict* subcultures. It subdivides the "Innovation" category of Merton's deviance paradigm, referring to acceptance (internalization) of culturally prescribed success goals and rejection (incomplete internalization) of institutional norms or culturally prescribed means, by those for whom legitimate means to success goals are restricted.[3] To this the paradigm adds Cloward's four sets of

FIGURE 1.   SOCIAL CONTEXT AND MODES OF DELINQUENT BEHAVIOR: A PARADIGM

STRUCTURAL FEATURES	TYPE OF SUBCULTURE	
	CRIMINAL	CONFLICT
I. *Independent Variable*	(Integrated Areas)	(Unintegrated Areas)
A. Culturally prescribed success goals	Internalized	Internalized
B. Availability of legitimate means to success goals	Limited; hence intense pressures toward deviant behavior	Limited; hence intense pressures toward deviant behavior
II. *Intervening Variables*		
A. Institutional norms	Incomplete internalization	Incomplete internalization
B. Availability of legiti- means to success goals	Available	Unavailable
1. Relations between adult carriers of conventional and criminal values	Accommodative; each participates in value system of other	Conflicted; neither group well organized; value systems implicit, and opposed to one another

[2] Clarence Schrag, "Delinquency and Opportunity: Analysis of a Theory," *Sociology and Social Research*, 46 (January, 1962), pp. 167–75.

[3] Robert K. Merton, *Social Theory and Social Structure*, New York: Free Press of Glencoe, 1958, Ch. 4.

FIGURE 1 (*Continued*)

2. Criminal learning structure	Available; offenders at different age levels integrated	Unavailable; attenuated relations between offenders at different age levels
3. Criminal opportunity structure	Stable sets of criminal roles graded for different ages and levels of competence; continuous income; protection from detection and prosecution	Unarticulated opportunity structure; individual rather than organized crime; sporadic income; little protection from detection and prosecution
4. Social control	Strong controls originate in *both* legitimate and illegal structures	Diminished social control; "weak" relations between adults and adolescents

III. *Dependent Variable*

A. Expected type of collective response among delinquents	Pressures toward deviance originate in limited accessibility to success goals by legitimate means, but are ameliorated by opportunities for access by illegal means. Hence, delinquent behavior is rational, disciplined, and crime-oriented	Pressures toward deviance originate in blocked opportunity by *any* institutionalized system of means. Hence delinquent behavior displays expressive conflict patterns

defining conditions for the relative availability of illegitimate means to success goals,[4] and the two hypothesized types of "collective response among delinquents" produced by the preceding conditions.[5]

In our research in Chicago we have attempted to measure variables specified in this paradigm and to investigate their inter-relations. For this purpose we have studied lower-class "delinquent gangs" involved in a "detached worker" program of the YMCA of Metropolitan Chicago, control groups of lower-class nongang boys from the same neighborhoods as

[4] Richard A. Cloward, "Illegitimate Means, Anomie, and Deviant Behavior," *American Sociological Review*, 24 (April, 1959), pp. 164–76.

[5] Cloward and Ohlin use a different theoretical rationale to explain "retreatist" subcultures, but our data are not relevant specifically on this aspect of the theory. See Cloward and Ohlin, *op. cit.*, pp. 25–27, 178ff.

the gang boys, and middle-class nongang boys.[6] Elements of the paradigm were operationalized in terms of the *perceptions* reported by the boys studied.[7] In this paper we direct attention to perceptions of legitimate and illegitimate opportunities by Negro and white lower-class gang and nongang boys and middle-class boys of both races, and to the relations among these perceptions. Detailed discussion of the relation of perceived opportunities and patterns of behavior derived from self-reports and, for gang boys only, from detached-worker ratings, is deferred for later presentation.[8]

Data reported elsewhere establish different levels of aspiration among the boys studied, but they show that regardless of race, class, or gang membership, mean levels of both occupational and educational aspirations considerably exceed fathers' achieved levels of occupation and education.[9] In this sense the independent variable—internalization of culturally prescribed success goals—may be said to have a positive value among all the boys

[6] Selection and description of study populations and other characteristics of the research program are described in previous publications and in greatest detail in a forthcoming book. See, for example, James F. Short, Jr., Fred L. Strodtbeck, and Desmond Cartwright, "A Strategy for Utilizing Research Dilemmas: A Case from the Study of Parenthood in a Street Corner Gang," *Sociological Inquiry*, 32 (Spring, 1962), pp. 185–202; James F. Short, Jr., "Street Corner Groups and Patterns of Delinquency: A Progress Report," *American Catholic Sociological Review*, 24 (Spring, 1963), pp. 13–32; and James F. Short, Jr., and Fred L. Strodtbeck, *Group Process and Gang Delinquency* (The University of Chicago Press, forthcoming), esp. Ch. 1.

[7] Cloward and Ohlin refer to "common perceptions" of opportunities, and Schrag explains that one of the basic postulates of the theory is that "perceived disadvantage, regardless of the accuracy of the perception, is for lower-class youth the functional equivalent of objectively verified disadvantage in that it has the same effect on overt behavior." (Schrag, *op. cit.*, p. 168.) This is not to deny the importance of *objective* opportunities, legitimate and illegitimate. The former can be demonstrated to be greater for whites than Negroes, and for middle- than for lower-class persons. It is more difficult to demonstrate gang-nongang differences except in terms of the cumulative *effects*—school performance, relations with the police, etc.—which favor nongang boys. Differences in objective illegitimate opportunities are similarly difficult to demonstrate, though the illegal enterprises are more likely to be present in a lower-class than in a middle-class environment.

[8] Behavior factors based on detached-worker ratings of gang boys are reported in James F. Short, Jr., Ray A. Tennyson, and Kenneth I. Howard, "Behavior Dimensions of Gang Delinquency," *American Sociological Review*, 28 (June, 1963), pp. 411–428. Self-reported behavior factors are presented in Short and Strodtbeck, *op. cit.*, Ch. 7.

[9] See James F. Short, Jr., "Gang Delinquency and Anomie," in Marshall B. Clinard (ed.), *Deviant Behavior and Anomie*, New York: Free Press of Glencoe, 1964; see also Jonathan Freedman and Ramon Rivera, "Education, Social Class, and Patterns of Delinquency," paper read at the annual meetings of the American Sociological Association, 1962. Elliott's study of "200 delinquent and nondelinquent boys attending two adjoining high schools in a large West Coast city" supports these findings. See Delbert S. Elliott, "Delinquency and Perceived Opportunity," *Sociological Inquiry*, 32 (Spring, 1962), pp. 216–27.

studied. For the first intervening variable in the paradigm, however—internalization of institutional norms—our gang members are less positive than the other boys studied. With "values" data from semantic differential scales, we established the fact that all groups assign equally high value and degree of legitimacy to such "middle-class" images as "Someone who works for good grades at school" and "Someone who likes to read good books"— again indicating that certain values are common to all groups—but gang boys of both races hold more positive attitudes toward *deviant* images than do the other boys.[10] These deviant images represented hypothesized "delinquent subcultures"; e.g., conflict ("Someone who is a good fighter with a tough reputation"), criminal ("Someone who knows where to sell what he steals" and "Someone who has good connections to avoid trouble with the law"), and retreatist ("Someone who makes easy money by pimping and other illegal hustles" and "Someone who gets his kicks by using drugs"). Middle-class boys generally attribute to these deviant images a lower value and less legitimacy, as we expected.

This paper is concerned with other elements in the paradigm, based on data from one part of an extensive interview schedule administered by specially trained interviewers to more than 500 boys in the six categories (race by class status and gang membership) under study. Respondents were instructed to indicate whether each of a series of statements was true of the "area where your group hangs out." In this way we hoped to measure perceptions of relatively specific legitimate and illegal opportunities. Perceptions of legitimate means to success goals, for example, were sampled by a series of statements concerning the *educational* and *occupational* orientations, abilities, and prospects for "guys in our area." We hoped by the impersonal referent to avoid the personalized ambitions and expectations which were the subject of inquiry in another part of the interview and thus to obtain measures referring to the boys' perceptions of general opportunities for legitimate and illegal achievement in their respective areas.

Aspects of the availability of illegal means to success goals to which attention was directed concerned the relative integration of the carriers of criminal and noncriminal values (in terms of the respectability of persons making money illegally and the orientation of local police toward law violation); adult "connections" and opportunities for learning and abetting criminal activities; the availability of criminal role models; and the probability of successful criminal enterprise in the area. Finally, because Cloward and Ohlin stress the importance of these matters for social control, perceptions of appropriate adult role models and their interest and sincerity

[10] The data are reported in Robert A. Gordon, James F. Short, Jr., Desmond S. Cartwright, and Fred L. Strodtbeck, "Values and Gang Delinquency: A Study of Street Corner Groups," *American Journal of Sociology,* 69 (September, 1963), pp. 109–128.

concerning the problems of adolescents were also covered. The list of statements is in Table 1, together with the percentage of boys in each group answering "true."[11]

In most cases responses to the statements concerning open legitimate opportunities and adult helpfulness form a gradient: gang boys are least likely to answer "true," followed by nongang and then by middle-class boys of each race. For negatively stated legitimate opportunity questions, and for the two negative adult power ("clout") statements, this gradient is reversed.[12] White gang boys generally are more sanguine than Negro gang boys about occupational opportunities and adult "clout," while Negroes tend to be slightly more optimistic concerning education and adult helpfulness. For all these areas, white middle-class boys have the most *open* view of "opportunities."

Conversely, gang boys are more likely to perceive illegitimate opportunities as open than are other boys, and these perceptions are held by more Negro than white boys in each stratum. The latter finding is somewhat surprising, in view of the acknowledged white domination of organized crime in Chicago. Informal observation suggests that vice organized on a large scale does flourish in Negro communities, and that "independent entrepreneurship" in such forms as small (and large) policy wheels, marijuana peddling, street-walking prostitutes, pool sharks, professional burglars and robbers, and the like, is more common in lower-class Negro than in lower-class white communities.[13] In any case, illegitimate opportunities appeared to be open to more Negro than white boys.

To reduce these data further, we assigned an opportunity structure score to each item. Except for items 17(A) and 18(A) answers were scored 2, 1, or 0, with 2 assigned to *open* opportunity perceptions, whether legitimate or illegitimate. Thus, for questions in Table 1 followed by (—), a "true" answer received a 0, "Don't know," a 1, and "False," a 2. The reverse procedure was applied to questions followed by (+).

Statements 17(A) and 18(A) are difficult to score. At first we assumed that a positive response to these questions indicated that illegitimate opportunities were perceived as closed. Boys were asked these questions only if they had already responded positively to questions 17 and 18. Thus, a "true" response to the statement that "A lot of these guys who make money illegally do not operate alone. They have to answer to people above them

---

[11] In the interview schedule the statements were not labeled according to which "opportunity structures" were being studied, and they were arranged in different order.

[12] Elliott, *op. cit.,* finds that delinquents consistently perceive lower opportunities for educational and occupational "success" than do nondelinquents. For evidence of other gradients among boys in the present study, see Gordon, *et al., op. cit.,* and Short and Strodtbeck, *op. cit.*

[13] See Short and Strodtbeck, *op. cit.,* esp. Ch. 5, "Racial Differentials in Gang Behavior."

TABLE 1. PERCENTAGE OF BOYS ANSWERING "TRUE" TO OPPORTUNITY STRUCTURE QUESTIONS, BY RACE, CLASS, AND GANG STATUS

Interviewer: "Once again I want you to think about the area where your group hangs out. I'm going to read a few statements to you, and all you have to do is say 'True' or 'False' after each statement. If you think the statement is true about the area, say 'True'; if you don't think it's true, say 'False.'"	Per Cent Answering "True"					
	Negro			White		
	Lower Class Gang N = 206	Lower Class Non-gang N = 89	Middle Class N = 26	Lower Class Gang N = 90	Lower Class Non-gang N = 79	Middle Class N = 53
Legitimate Educational Opportunities						
1. In our area it's hard for a young guy to stay in school. (−)*	48.5	28.1	7.7	52.2	21.5	0.0
2. Most kids in our area like school. (+)	43.2	49.4	80.8	32.2	60.8	94.3
3. Most of the guys in our area will graduate from high school. (+)	30.6	44.9	96.2	32.2	65.8	100.0
4. In our area, there are a lot of guys who want to go to college. (+)	37.4	47.2	84.6	16.7	44.3	98.1
5. College is too expensive for most of the guys in the area. (−)	75.7	76.4	53.8	80.0	65.8	7.5
6. As far as grades are concerned, most of the guys in our area could get through college without too much trouble. (+)	46.6	43.8	50.0	43.3	40.5	73.6

* Signs in parentheses indicate the "valence" of a "True" answer relative to the opportunity structure area indicated.

TABLE 1 (*Continued*)

Interviewer: "Once again I want you to think about the area where your group hangs out. I'm going to read a few statements to you, and all you have to do is say 'True' or 'False' after each statement. If you think the statement is true about the area, say 'True'; if you don't think it's true, say 'False.'"	Per Cent Answering "True"					
	Negro			White		
	Lower Class Gang N = 206	Lower Class Non-gang N = 89	Middle Class N = 26	Lower Class Gang N = 90	Lower Class Non-gang N = 79	Middle Class N = 53
Legitimate Occupational Opportunities						
7. It's hard for a young guy in our area to get a good paying honest job. (−)	77.2	62.9	46.2	56.7	31.6	9.4
8. Most of the guys in the area will probably get good paying honest jobs when they grow up. (+)	51.9	59.6	61.5	65.6	79.7	92.5
9. For guys in this area honest jobs don't pay very well. (−)	56.3	47.2	26.9	40.0	22.8	3.8
10. Guys in this area have to have connections to get good paying jobs. (−).	53.9	51.7	30.8	56.7	44.3	22.6
11. In this area it's hard to make much money without doing something illegal. (−)	54.9	38.2	23.1	37.8	13.9	0.0
Integration of the Carriers of Criminal and Non-Criminal Values						
12. Some of the most respectable people in our area make their money illegally. (+)	44.2	19.1	15.4	24.4	10.1	3.8

TABLE 1 (*Continued*)

13. The police in this area get paid off for letting things happen that are against the law. (+)	51.5	37.1	30.8	42.2	36.7	20.8

Criminal Learning Structures

14. There are connections in this area for a guy who wants to make good money illegally. (+)	57.8	49.4	38.5	47.8	35.4	5.7
15. Young guys can learn a lot about crime from older people in the area. (+)	75.2	66.3	34.6	52.2	35.4	11.3
16. There are adults in this area who help young guys make money illegally. (+)	59.2	49.4	30.8	42.2	26.6	15.1

Visibility of Criminal Careers

17. In this area there are some people who make their living by doing things that are against the law. (+)	83.0	73.0	69.2	70.0	60.8	30.2
18. Some of the young guys in our area will be making a living someday by doing things that are against the law. (+)	83.0	79.8	73.1	75.6	59.5	39.6

Elite Criminal Opportunities

17. (A) A lot of these guys who make money illegally do not operate alone. They have to answer to people above them who are calling the shots. (−)	62.6	62.9	65.4	45.6	40.5	18.9

TABLE 1 *(Continued)*

Visibility of Criminal Careers						
18. (A) A lot of these guys won't be operating alone either. They'll have to answer to people above them who'll be calling the shots. (—)	70.4	70.8	65.4	62.2	53.2	30.2
19. A guy from this area has a chance of really making it big in the rackets. (+)	45.1	30.3	34.6	35.6	24.1	3.8
20. None of the people who make big money in the rackets live in this area. (—)	54.4	66.3	38.5	56.7	75.9	60.4
Adult "Clout"						
21. Not many really successful people live in this area. (—)	63.6	59.6	19.2	42.2	26.6	0.0
22. Adults in this area haven't much clout (pull). (—)	55.3	42.7	23.1	48.9	48.1	13.2
Adult Helpfulness						
23. There are adults in this area who help young guys get jobs. (+)	82.5	93.3	92.3	78.9	89.9	94.3
24. Adults in the area do a lot to help young guys keep out of trouble. (+)	67.0	91.0	61.5	50.0	73.4	88.7

who are calling the shots," was taken to mean that the "really big" hoodlums were not available as role models; hence, to this extent illegitimate opportunities for "making it big" were perceived as closed. On the other hand, a boy might answer *"false"* to this statement on the grounds that those who were making money illegally were involved in such petty pursuits as not to warrant concern or control by the syndicate, or, particularly in the case of middle-class white boys, illegal pursuits might be in the nature of white-collar crime and so not subject to syndicate control. In the latter case, a "false" answer still would be consistent with an *open* perception of opportunity, while in the former it would not. Answers to "elite criminal opportunities" questions are the only exceptions to the observed gradient for perceptions of illegitimate opportunities, suggesting that boys within each class of respondents may have interpreted these questions less uniformly than they did the others.

Before answers to these questions are dismissed as invalid, however, they should be examined more carefully. Note that responses to questions 17(A) and 18(A) follow a pattern: more Negro than white boys say that people in their areas who make money illegally have to "answer to people above them." Unfortunately the question did not specify where these "higher ups" lived or whether they were visible to the boys. We may infer, however, that a higher proportion of persons making money illegitimately in the white areas were among the "higher ups" in organized crime than was the case in Negro neighborhoods.

The middle-class boys' answers to the entire set of four "elite" questions are especially interesting. Negro middle-class boys are far more likely to indicate that local area people have "a chance of really making it big in the rackets" and far less likely to say that locals do not "make big money in the rackets." Drake and Cayton[14] and Frazier[15] have described important criminal and otherwise "shady" elements in the Negro middle class. Frazier, in particular, indicates that influential segments of the "black bourgeoisie" are "recruited from the successful underworld Negroes, who have gained their money from gambling, prostitution, bootlegging, and the 'numbers.' "[16] Frazier attributes the flashy consumption patterns of the new Negro middle class to the influence of these elements and contrasts this way of life with that of the old upper and middle classes who "erected an impenetrable barrier between themselves and Negroes who represented the 'sporting' and criminal world."[17] The white middle-class boys, who were chosen precisely because they were the "cream" of YMCA Hi-Y clubs, are very unlikely to be exposed to this sort of community influence. Such differences as these, if they are real, should find expression in other data from these subjects.[18]

[14] St. Clair Drake and Horace R. Cayton, *Black Metropolis: A Study of Negro Life in a Northern City,* New York: Harper and Row, 1962, Vol. II.

[15] E. Franklin Frazier, *Black Bourgeoisie,* New York: Collier Books, 1962.

[16] *Ibid.,* p. 109.

[17] *Ibid.,* pp. 109–110.

[18] We were first alerted to differences between our Negro and white middle-class boys when they came to our offices for testing, and later by analysis of semantic differential data. See Gordon, *et al., op. cit.* It should be emphasized that primary data for this paper represent perceptions rather than objective measures of opportunities or of the communities in which these boys live. Other investigators have emphasized the extent to which middle-class Negroes are like their white counterparts in terms of the char-

TABLE 2. MEAN OPPORTUNITY STRUCTURE SCORES, BY RACE, CLASS, AND GANG STATUS

Aspect of Opportunity Structure*	White			Negro		
	Lower Class Gang N=206**	Lower Class Non-gang N=89	Middle Class N=26	Lower Class Gang N=89	Lower Class Non-gang N=75	Middle Class N=53
Legitimate Educational (0–12)	4.8	5.7	9.0	3.8	6.4	11.2
Legitimate Occupational (0–10)	4.2	5.2	6.6	5.4	7.3	9.1
Integration of Carriers of Criminal and Noncriminal Values (0–4)	2.1	1.4	1.2	1.5	1.0	0.5
Criminal Learning Structures (0–6)	4.0	3.6	2.3	3.0	2.2	0.7
Visibility of Criminal Careers (0–4)	3.4	3.2	3.0	3.0	2.5	1.4
Criminal Opportunities (0–10)	4.7	4.0	4.6	4.7	4.3	4.6
Adult Clout (0–4)	1.5	1.9	3.0	2.0	2.4	3.7
Adult Helpfulness (0–4)	3.0	3.7	3.2	2.6	3.2	3.7
Criminal Opportunities (0–4)	1.8	1.2	1.8	1.5	1.0	0.9
Summary Scores						
Legitimate Educational and Occupational Opportunities (0–22)	9.0	11.0	15.6	9.3	13.7	20.2
Illegitimate Opportunities (0–24)	14.3	12.3	11.0	12.1	10.0	7.2
Illegitimate Opportunities Less Inclusive (0–18)	11.4	9.5	8.2	9.0	6.7	3.5
Adult Power and Helpfulness (0–8)	4.5	5.6	6.2	4.7	5.6	7.4

* Figures in parentheses indicate the possible range for each score.

** Ns vary slightly for some scores, due to nonresponse. Scores are based in each case on the number of boys who actually gave meaningful responses.

acter and stability of their institutions and their community leadership, and in interracial situations. Life styles, interaction patterns with whites, and leadership among middle-class Negroes vary greatly, however. See, for example, the discussion in Robin M. Williams, Jr., et al., Strangers Next Door: Ethnic Relations in American Communities, New York: Prentice-Hall, 1964, esp. Chs. 7–10; also James Q. Wilson, Negro Politics: The Search for Leadership, New York: The Free Press of Glencoe, 1960.

These ambiguities in interpretation led us to score "elite" criminal opportunities in two ways—with and without questions 17(A) and 18(A). When they were included, we followed our original assumptions, adjusting the scoring so that if either question was not asked, implying closed opportunities, the boy was scored zero for the question; if the question was asked and a "true" answer recorded, a score of 1 was given; "undecided" was scored 2, and "false," 3.

Table 2 presents mean opportunity structure scores, by race, class, and gang status of respondents. The trends apparent in Table 1 appear here, also.

In addition, it is clear that for *legitimate* opportunities, gang-nongang and middle-class differences *within* racial categories are greater than the Negro-white differences for each of the three gang and class strata. For *illegitimate* opportunities, differences between races are greater than within-race differences.

PERCEIVED OPPORTUNITIES AND AN OFFICIAL DELINQUENCY RATE

In Table 3, ranking on each of the summary opportunity scores is compared with the official delinquency rates of the six race-by-class-by-gang-status groups.[19] As far as the *ordering* of the six groups is concerned, perception of *legitimate* opportunities is more strongly associated with delinquency rates than is perception of illegitimate opportunities. This is consistent with the assumption that perceived legitimate opportunities are independent variables, while perceived illegitimate opportunities intervene, after legitimate opportunities have been appraised and found wanting. Legitimate achievement tends to be the universal standard in our culture, highly valued even by very deviant individuals.[20] Note, however, that *within* racial categories, perception of illegitimate opportunities does order the groups according to official delinquency rates.

Official delinquency rates measure the hypothesized dependent variables only in a very gross sense. The gang-nongang distinction probably measures participation in delinquent subcultural activity, and adding the middle-class—lower-class division permits a test of the theory in terms somewhat broader than it was originally set forth. Here the theory holds up well: gang boys of both races perceive greater restrictions on legitimate opportunities than do nongang boys in the same neighborhoods or middle-class boys. Thus, the *negative* pressure toward deviance is greater for gang boys. Within each racial group, gang boys perceive better illegitimate opportunities; hence the greater "pull" toward deviance. While perceived

---

[19] These rates refer to the mean number of offenses known to the police, per boy, in each group. Data are based on John M. Wise, "A Comparison of Sources of Data as Indexes of Delinquent Behavior," M.A. thesis, University of Chicago, 1962.

[20] See Gordon, *et al., op. cit.*

TABLE 3. MEAN OPPORTUNITY STRUCTURE SCORES
KNOWN TO THE POLICE, BY RACE, CLASS, AND
GANG STATUS*

Legitimate Educational and Occupational Opportunities (0 to 22)	Perception of Illegitimate Opportunities (Less Inclusive) (0 to 18)	Perception of Adult Power and Helpfulness (0 to 8)	Total Opportunities Score** (−18 to 30)	Mean Number of Offenses Known to Police, Per Boy
NG (9.0)	NG (11.4)	NG (4.5)	NG (2.1)	NG (3.14)
WG (9.3)	NLC (9.5)	WG (4.7)	WG (5.0)	WG (2.73)
NLC (11.0)	WG (9.0)	NLC (5.6)	NLC (7.1)	NLC (0.47)
WLC (13.7)	NMC (8.2)	WLC (5.6)	WLC (12.6)	WLC (0.31)
NMC (15.6)	WLC (6.7)	NMC (6.2)	NMC (13.6)	NMC (0.06)
WMC (20.2)	WMC (3.5)	WMC (7.4)	WMC (24.1)	WMC (0.02)

* NG stands for Negro gang members, NLC for Negro lower-class boys, and so on.
** Total Opportunities Score is designed to reflect both legitimate and illegitimate pressures toward delinquency. It is obtained by adding together legitimate educational and occupational opportunities and adult power and helpfulness scores, and from this sum subtracting illegitimate opportunity scores. Hence it should be negatively correlated with delinquency.

adult power and helpfulness, combined, rank the groups very much as do official delinquency rates, adult power alone turns out, as predicted, to be negatively related to delinquency, while helpfulness, which may be exercised by carriers of criminal as well as noncriminal values, is related inconsistently to delinquency among Negro boys.

Adult power and helpfulness are both hypothesized by Cloward and Ohlin to be negatively related to the emergence and maintenance of conflict subcultures. "The term that the bopper uses most frequently to characterize his relationships with adults is 'weak.' . . . He views himself as isolated and the adult world as indifferent. The commitments of adults are to their own interests and not to his. Their explanations of why he should behave differently are 'weak,' as are their efforts to help him."[21] This description holds up well with respect to "clout." Gang boys score lower than the others and Negro gang boys—by far our most conflict oriented[22]—score lowest of all. But helpfulness scores are comparatively

[21] Cloward and Ohlin, *op. cit.,* pp. 24–25.

[22] For documentation, see Short, Tennyson, and Howard, *op. cit.,* and Short and Strodtbeck, *op. cit.,* esp. Chs. 1, 5, and 9. It was in large part because they were involved in gang fighting that most of the Negro gangs received the attention of newspapers, police, and the Program for Detached Workers with which this research program was associated. Close observation of the gangs over periods ranging from several months to

high for all groups, and they are lowest for the less conflict-oriented white gang boys.[23]

Differences between nongang and gang boys on both scores are sufficient to suggest that these factors are important in selection for gang membership, though their relation to a particular type of delinquent subculture—conflict—is inconsistent with the theory. The previously noted higher illegitimate opportunity scores registered by the Negro boys are also inconsistent, but the greater visibility and availability of petty criminal activities in lower-class Negro communities may account for this. Similarly, the comparatively low Negro middle-class scores on clout and helpfulness are consistent with Frazier's descriptions of the superficial show put on by Negro middle-class "society," which he regards as a somewhat futile attempt to compensate for status insecurities relative to whites.[24]

The hypothesis that perceived adult power is inversely related to gang conflict is essentially a social control argument. But helpfulness, when exercised by illegitimate adults, may be conducive to involvement in a criminal subculture. To investigate this possibility, we examined the relation *between* perceptions of various types of opportunities.

THE RELATION BETWEEN LEGITIMATE AND ILLEGITIMATE OPPORTUNITIES

The product-moment correlations between opportunity scores, for all boys and for gang boys only, by race, are in Table 4. Legitimate opportunity scores tend to be positively correlated with one another, as are illegitimate opportunity scores, and between legitimate and illegitimate scores correlations are negative. There are exceptions to this general pattern, however; for example, perceptions of legitimate educational and occupational opportunities are significantly correlated for all groups except white gang boys. The low correlation in the latter group suggests that perceptions of legitimate educational and occupational opportunities often are not mutually reinforcing.

The relation betwen adult power and perceived illegitimate opportunities suggests greater "integration" of the carriers of criminal and

---

more than three years suggests that nearly all the Negro gangs had at one time been more involved in "conflict subcultures" than had any of the white gangs. Finally, detailed analysis of behavior ratings by detached workers indicates greater conflict involvement by Negro than white gangs.

[23] These findings are consistent with boys' ratings of a series of adult roles in the same interview. See James F. Short, Jr., Ramon Rivera, and Harvey Marshall, "Adult-Adolescent Relations and Gang Delinquency: An Empirical Report," *Pacific Sociological Review* (Fall, 1964).

[24] Frazier, *op. cit.*

TABLE 4. CORRELATIONS AMONG OPPORTUNITY STRUCTURE SCORES, BY RACE***

	Legitimate Educational		Legitimate Occupational		Adult Clout		Adult Helpfulness		Criminal, Noncriminal Integration		Criminal Learning Opportunities		Visibility of Criminal Careers		Criminal Opportunities Elite (Less Inclusive)		Criminal Opportunities Elite (Inclusive)	
	W*	N**	W	N	W	N	W	N	W	N	W	N	W	N	W	N	W	N
Legitimate Educational	1.00		.13	.34	.10	.22	.23	.32	−.26	−.19	−.26	−.20	−.28	−.27	−.21	−.18	−.03	−.05
Legitimate Occupational	.48	.38	1.00		.28	.37	.23	.35	−.18	−.33	−.15	−.31	−.17	−.39	−.24	−.25	−.15	−.07
Adult Clout	.45	.34	.42	.35	1.00		.19	.32	.05	−.23	.16	−.22	.10	−.22	.24	−.04	.19	.01
Adult Helpfulness	.35	.27	.28	.28	.29	.29	1.00		−.27	−.29	−.20	−.19	−.34	−.16	−.32	−.24	−.23	−.15
Criminal, Noncriminal Integration	−.36	−.17	−.26	−.32	−.14	−.25	−.23	−.26	1.00		.59	.52	.37	.34	.60	.31	.32	.08
Criminal Learning Opportunities	−.49	−.22	−.31	−.37	−.13	−.23	−.19	−.15	.49	.51	1.00		.46	.37	.64	.29	.41	−.03
Visibility of Criminal Careers	−.42	−.23	−.26	−.30	−.19	−.23	−.26	−.14	.37	.32	.54	.43	1.00		.38	.21	.16	−.10
Criminal Opportunities Elite (Less Inclusive)	−.27	−.13	−.25	−.23	.04	−.01	−.27	−.21	.46	.32	.52	.27	.38	.21	1.00		.74	.66
Criminal Opportunities Elite (Inclusive)	−.06	−.03	−.10	−.08	.10	.05	−.19	−.13	.20	.14	.19	−.02	.00	−.14	.73	.70	1.00	

*White: p<.05=.13 (all boys); p<.01=.18 (all boys) and .27 (gang boys)
**Negro: p<.05=.11 (all boys); p<.01=.14 (all boys) and .18 (gang boys)
*** Italicized coefficients below the diagonal represent gang boys only; coefficients above the diagonal represent all boys, including gang members.

conventional values in white neighborhoods: the correlations are low but *positive* among white boys, and *negative* among Negroes. For both races, adult helpfulness is negatively correlated with illegitimate opportunities.

Correlations between perceived illegitimate opportunities are higher for white boys, particularly those involving the criminal *elite* measures. Thus, while white boys perceive illegitimate opportunities as less available than do Negro boys, "integration" as we have operationalized it is actually more characteristic of white than Negro gang areas. Negro gang boys perceive illegitimate opportunities as relatively open, but they tend to perceive illegitimate adults as neither powerful nor helpful. White gang boys, however, tend to perceive illegitimate adults as powerful but not very helpful. A similar pattern occurs in data from another section of the interview, in which boys were asked to indicate four characteristics of several adult roles in their local areas. Among Negro gang boys, 38 per cent, compared with 53 per cent of white gang boys, felt that adults making money illegally have "a lot of clout," while only about one boy in five in both racial groups felt that such adults are "interested in the problems of teen-agers." Lower-class nongang boys consistently rated legitimate adult roles higher than gang boys did on scales reflecting their interest in and degree of contact with teen-agers, their "clout," and the extent to which they are considered "right guys."[25]

In the present analysis, the relations between various opportunity scores reveal no significant or consistent differences that explain behavioral differences between gang and nongang lower-class boys. The most striking differences are between middle-class Negro boys and all other groups in the correlation between adult helpfulness and perceived elite criminal opportunities. This correlation is positive for both elite scores (.34 for the more inclusive measure, .20 for the less inclusive measure) among Negro middle-class boys, but both correlations are negative in all other groups. Adult clout was also correlated positively with the two elite criminal opportunity scores among Negro middle-class boys (.22 and .30), and among white gang members, but negatively in the other groups. Again, reference to Frazier's perceptive analysis is pertinent.[26]

SUMMARY

Legitimate occupational opportunities are perceived as available less often by gang than by nongang boys, and most often by middle-class boys. White boys are more likely than Negro boys to perceive such opportunities as available, in each of the strata examined. With respect to legitimate

[25] A more detailed report of these data is in Short, Rivera, and Marshall, *op. cit.*
[26] Frazier, *op. cit.*

educational opportunities, the same pattern occurs, except that the racial difference does not occur among gang boys. Race and class-by-gang-status gradients are both present concerning adult clout, but not perceived adult helpfulness, among lower-class boys. These data are consistent with the apparently greater *protest* orientation of white as compared with Negro gang boys.[27] Gradients within racial groups are consistent with inferences from the Cloward and Ohlin theory.

Differences in perceptions of illegitimate opportunities reverse most of those found for legitimate opportunities, as expected. These differences are inconsistent with the greater conflict orientation of Negro gang boys, but when adult clout is correlated with criminal opportunity scores, and other data are introduced, "integration" of criminal opportunities and between criminal and legitimate opportunities is greater for white than for Negro boys. Even for white gang boys, however, the negative correlations between adult helpfulness and criminal opportunity scores, and their small positive correlations with adult clout suggest a low degree of "integration" between the carriers of criminal and conventional values.[28]

The logic of the theory clearly presumes that perceptions of opportunities *precede* involvement in delinquency, while our data reflect perceptions "after the fact." We cannot fully resolve this problem. Evidence concerning the relations of *individual* gang boys' perceptions of opportunities to their behavior as individuals, is relevant, however, and its mention permits brief discussion of the somewhat different causal model that has emerged from the larger study of which this paper is a partial report. Correlations between opportunity scores and theoretically relevant behavior scores for individual gang boys are low. For example, *conflict factor scores*, consisting of a combination of individual and gang fighting (with and without weapons), assault, and carrying concealed weapons, are not systematically related to perceptions of either legitimate or illegitimate opportunity scores. That is, boys with high scores do not have lower opportunity scores.[29] It seems unlikely, therefore, that data reported in this paper reflect the boys' efforts to rationalize delinquent behavior by "blaming" the lack of opportunity. Although this does not solve the problem of temporal order, it is presumptive evidence against an alternative interpretation based on the assumption of "after-the-fact" (of delinquency or gang membership) influences on perception.

Our argument is not that the latter are unimportant. Other data from

[27] See Short, Tennyson, and Howard, *op. cit.,* and Short and Strodtbeck, *op. cit.,* Ch. 5.

[28] This, perhaps, explains why we had such difficulty locating criminal gangs. See Short and Strodtbeck, *op. cit.,* Chs. 1 and 9.

[29] Derivation of the scores is detailed in Short, Tennyson and Howard, *op. cit.* Full presentation of the data concerning individual opportunity perception and behavior is beyond the scope of this paper.

our study suggest that social structure influences the development of ethnic, class, life-cycle, and perhaps "delinquent" subcultures with relatively distinctive content. Social structural theories are therefore appropriately applied to the social distribution of many phenomena—to delinquency "rates" rather than to individual episodes or degrees of involvement in delinquency. It is to the question of "rates" or the social distribution of delinquent subcultures, that the Cloward and Ohlin theory is addressed—appropriately. To account for selection into subcultures—into gang membership, for example—from the youngsters available, and for individual behavior within the context of a subculture, requires reference to "levels" of explanation other than social structure.[30] We have found it necessary to invoke personality level variables, as Inkeles suggested,[31] and *group process* considerations, to explain delinquent behavior *within* our gangs.[32] The give and take of interaction among gang boys, and between gang boys and others; a variety of role relations within the gang and status considerations related to these roles and to opportunities present in situations of the moment—these are prime determinants of what happens in the gang, of who becomes involved in what type of behavior, and with whom.[33] This *level* of explanation "washes out" variations in perceptions of opportunities related to social structure as a major determinant of individuals' behavior in the gang context.

[30] See David Bordua's critique of social structural theories in this regard. David Bordua, "Delinquent Subcultures: Sociological Interpretations of Gang Delinquency," *Annals of the American Academy of Political and Social Science,* 338 (November, 1961), and his "Sociological Theories and Their Implications for Juvenile Delinquency," Children's Bureau, *Juvenile Delinquency: Facts and Facets,* No. 2, Washington, D. C.: Government Printing Office, 1960. See, also, Short and Strodtbeck, *op. cit.,* and James F. Short, Jr., "Social Structure and Group Process in Explanations of Gang Delinquency," paper read at the Fifth Social Psychology Symposium, University of Oklahoma, 1964, to be published in the Symposium volume.

[31] Alex Inkeles, "Personality and Social Structure," Ch. 11 in *Sociology Today,* Robert K. Merton, Leonard Broom, and Leonard S. Cottrell, Jr., (eds.), New York: Basic Books, 1959. From the present study, see Robert A. Gordon and James F. Short, Jr., "Social Level, Social Disability, and Gang Interaction," Ch. 10 in Short and Strodtbeck, *op. cit.*

[32] See, esp., Short, "Gang Delinquency and Anomie," *op. cit.;* Short and Strodtbeck, *op. cit.,* and by the same authors, "The Response of Gang Leaders to Status Threats: An Observation on Group Process and Delinquent Behavior," *American Journal of Sociology,* 68 (March, 1963), pp. 571–579, and "Why Gangs Fight," *Trans-Action,* 1 (September–October, 1964), pp. 25–29; and Strodtbeck and Short, "Aleatory Risks v. Short-Run Hedonism in Explanation of Gang Action," *Social Problems* (Fall, 1964).

[33] The point is made in more general theoretical terms in Albert K. Cohen, "The Sociology of the Deviant Act: Anomie Theory and Beyond," *American Sociological Review,* 30 (February, 1965), pp. 5–14.

4 Violent Crime in City Gangs

WALTER B. MILLER

The 1960's have witnessed a remarkable upsurge of public concern over violence in the United States. The mass media flash before the public a vivid and multivaried kaleidescope of images of violence. Little attention is paid to those who question the assumption that the United States is experiencing an unparalleled epidemic of violence, who point out that other periods in the past may have been equally violent or more so; that troops were required to subdue rioting farmers in 1790, rioting tax-protesters in 1794, rioting laborers in the 1870's and 1880's, and rioting railroad workers in 1877; that race riots killed fifty people in St. Louis in 1917 and erupted in twenty-six other cities soon after; that fifty-seven whites were killed in a slave uprising in 1831; that the Plug Uglies, Dead Rabbits, and other street gangs virtually ruled parts of New York for close to forty years; that rival bootleg mobs engaged in armed warfare in Chicago and elsewhere during the Capone era; and that the number killed in the 1863 draft riots in New York was estimated at up to 1,000 men. Nevertheless, however much one may question the conviction that the United States today is engulfed in unprecedented violence, one can scarcely question the ascendancy of the *belief* that it is. It is this belief that moves men to action—action whose consequences are just as real as if the validity of the belief were incontrovertible.

Reprinted from *Annals of the American Academy of Political and Social Science,* 343 (March, 1966), 97–112, by permission of the publisher and the author.

Close to the core of the public imagery of violence is the urban street gang. The imagery evokes tableaux of sinister adolescent wolf packs prowling the darkened streets of the city intent on evil-doing, of grinning gangs of teen-agers tormenting old ladies in wheelchairs and ganging up on hated and envied honor students, and of brutal bands of black-jacketed motorcyclists sweeping through quiet towns in orgies of terror and destruction. The substance of this image and its basic components of human cruelty, brutal sadism, and a delight in violence for its own sake have become conventionalized within the subculture of professional writers. The tradition received strong impetus in the public entertainment of the early 1950's with Marlon Brando and his black-jacketed motorcycle thugs, gathered momentum with the insolent and sadistic high-schoolers of *The Blackboard Jungle*, and achieved the status of an established ingredient of American folklore with the Sharks and Jets of the *West Side Story*.

What is the reality behind these images? Is the street gang fierce and romantic like the Sharks and Jets? Is it a tough but good-hearted bunch of rough and ready guys like the "Gang that Sang Heart of My Heart"? Or is it brutal and ruthless like the motorcyclists in *The Wild Ones*? In many instances where an area of interest engages both scholars and the public, most of the public embrace one set of conceptions and most scholars, another. This is not so in the case of the street gang; there is almost as much divergence within the ranks of scholars as there is between the scholars and the public.

One recent book on gangs contains these statements:

Violence [is] the core spirit of the modern gang. . . . The gang boy . . . makes unprovoked violence . . . [senseless rather than premeditated] . . . the major activity or dream of his life. . . . The gang trades in violence. Brutality is basic to its system.[1]

Another recent work presents a different picture:

The very few [gang] boys who persist in extreme aggression or other dangerous exploits are regarded generally as "crazy" by the other boys. . . . Our conservative estimate is that not more than one in five instances of potential violence actually result in serious consequences. . . . For average Negro gang boys the probability of an arrest for involvement in instances of potential violence is probably no greater than .04.[2]

A third important work states:

In [a] second type [of delinquent gang or subculture] violence is the keynote. . . . The immediate aim in the world of fighting gangs is to acquire a

---

[1] L. Yablonsky, *The Violent Gang* (New York: The Macmillan Company, 1963), pp. 4, 6.

[2] J. F. Short and F. L. Strodtbeck, *Group Process and Gang Delinquency* (Chicago: University of Chicago Press, 1965), pp. 224, 258.

reputation for toughness and destructive violence. . . . In the world of violence such attributes as race, socioeconomic position, age, and the like, are irrevelant.[3]

What is the reality behind these differences? The question is readily raised, but is not, unfortunately, readily answered. There exists in this area of high general interest a surprising dearth of reliable information. It is quite possible that discrepancies between the statements of scholars arise from the fact that each is referring to different kinds of gangs in different kinds of neighborhoods in different kinds of cities. We simply do not know. Lacking the information necessary to make general statements as to the nature of violence in the American city gang, it becomes obvious that one major need is a series of careful empirical studies of particular gangs in a range of cities and a variety of neighborhoods. The present paper is an attempt to present such information for one inner-city neighborhood, "Midcity," in a major eastern city, "Port City."

WHAT ARE "VIOLENT" CRIMES?

The term "violence" is highly charged. Like many terms which carry strong opprobrium, it is applied with little discrimination to a wide range of things which meet with general disapproval. Included in this broad net are phenomena such as toy advertising on television, boxing, rock-and-roll music and the mannerisms of its performers, fictional private detectives, and modern art. Used in this fashion the scope of the term becomes so broad as to vitiate its utility severely. Adding the term "crimes" to the designation substantially narrows its focus. It is at once apparent that not all "violence" is criminal (warfare, football, surgery, wrecking cars for scrap), but it is less apparent to some that not all crime is violent. In fact, the great bulk of adolescent crime consists of nonviolent forms of theft and statute violations such as truancy and running away. In the present report "violent crimes" are defined as *legally proscribed acts whose primary object is the deliberate use of force to inflict injury on persons or objects, and, under some circumstances, the stated intention to engage in such acts.* While the scope of this paper prevents discussion of numerous complex issues involved in this definition, for example, the role of "threat of force" as criminally culpable, an idea of the kinds of acts included under the definition may be obtained directly by referring to Tables 3 and 4, pages 701 and 702. Table 3 delineates sixteen forms of "violent" offenses directed at persons and objects, and Table 4 delineates fourteen legal categories. It is to these forms that the term "violent crimes" will apply.

[3] R. A. Cloward and L. E. Ohlin, *Delinquency and Opportunity: A Theory of Delinquent Gangs* (Glencoe, Ill.: Free Press, 1960), pp. 20, 24.

CIRCUMSTANCES AND METHODS OF STUDY

Conclusions presented in subsequent sections are based on the research findings of an extensive study of youth gangs in "Midcity," a central-city slum district of 100,000 persons. Information was obtained on some 150 corner gangs, numbering about 4,500 males and females, aged twelve to twenty, in the middle and late 1950's. Selected for more detailed study were twenty-one of these gangs numbering about 700 members; selection was based primarily on their reputation as the "toughest" in the city. Study data of many kinds were obtained from numerous sources, but the great bulk of data was derived from the detailed field records of workers who were in direct daily contact with gang members for periods averaging two years per gang. Seven of these gangs, numbering 205 members (four white male gangs, one Negro male, one white female, one Negro female) were subject to the most intensive field observation, and are designated "intensive-observation" gangs. Findings presented here are based primarily on the experience of these seven, along with that of fourteen male gangs numbering 293 members (including the five intensive-observation male gangs) whose criminal records were obtained from the state central criminal records division.

Detailed qualitative information on the daily behavior of gang members in sixty "behavioral areas" (for example, sexual behavior, family behavior, and theft) was collected and analyzed; however, the bulk of the findings presented here will be quantitative in nature, due to requirements of brevity.[4] Present findings are based primarily on three kinds of data: (1) *Field-recorded behavior*—all actions and sentiments recorded for the seven intensive-observation gangs which relate to assault ($N = 1,600$); (2) *Field-recorded crimes*—all recorded instances of illegal acts of assault and property damage engaged in by members of the same gangs ($N = 228$); and (3) *Court-recorded crimes*—all charges of assaultive or property damage offenses recorded by court officials for members of the fourteen male gangs between the ages of seven and twenty-seven ($N = 138$).

The analysis distinguishes four major characteristics of gangs: age, sex, race, and social status. Of the seven intensive-observation gangs, five were male ($N = 155$) and two, female ($N = 50$); none of the fourteen court-record gangs was female. Five of the intensive-observation gangs were white ($N = 127$) and two, Negro ($N = 78$); eight of the court-record gangs were white ($N = 169$) and six, Negro ($N = 124$). The ethnic-religious status of the white gangs was multinational Catholic (Irish-

---

[4] Qualitative data on the nature of "violent" and other forms of gang behavior which convey a notion of its "flavor" and life-context will be presented in W. B. Miller, *City Gangs* (New York: John Wiley & Sons, forthcoming).

Italian, with Irish dominant, some French, and Slavic). Social status was determined by a relatively complex method based on a combination of educational, occupational, and other criteria (for example, parents' occupation, gang members' occupation, gang members' education, and families' welfare experience).[5] On the basis of these criteria all gangs were designated "lower class." Three levels *within* the lower class were delineated and were designated, from highest to lowest, Lower Class I, II, and III. Gangs analyzed in the present paper belonged to levels II and III; the former level is designated "higher" status, and the latter, "lower." It should be kept in mind that the terms "higher" and "lower" in this context refer to the lowest and next-lowest of three intra-lower-class social-status levels.[6]

THE PATTERNING OF VIOLENT CRIMES IN CITY GANGS

Study data make it possible to address a set of questions central to any consideration of the reality of violent crime in city gangs. How prevalent are violent crimes, both in absolute terms and relative to other forms of crime? What proportion of gang members engage in violent crimes? Is individual or collective participation more common? Are those most active in such crimes more likely to be younger or older? white or Negro? male or female? higher or lower in social status? What forms do violent crimes take, and which forms are most prevalent? Who and what are the targets of violent crimes? How serious are they? How does violence figure in the daily lives of gang members?

The following sections present data bearing on each of these questions, based on the experience of Midcity gangs in the 1950's. The first section bears on the last of the questions just cited: What was the role of assaultive behavior in the daily lives of gang members?

Assault-Oriented Behavior

Approximately 1,600 actions and sentiments relating to assaultive behavior were recorded by field workers during the course of their work

---

[5] Details of this method are presented in *City Gangs, op. cit.*

[6] IBM processing of court-recorded offenses and preliminary analyses of field-recorded assault behavior and illegal incidents was done by Dr. Robert Stanfield, University of Massachusetts; additional data analysis by Donald Zall, Midcity Delinquency Research Project. Some of the specific figures in the tables may be slightly altered in the larger report; such alterations will not, however, affect the substance of the findings. The research was supported under the National Institute of Health's Grant M–1414, and administered by the Boston University School of Social Work.

with the seven "intensive observation" gangs—a period averaging two years per gang.[7]

This number comprised about 3 per cent of a total of about 54,000 actions and sentiments oriented to some sixty behavioral areas (for example, sexual behavior, drinking behavior, theft, and police-oriented behavior). Assault-oriented behavior was relatively common, ranking ninth among sixty behavioral areas. A substantial portion of this behavior, however, took the form of words rather than deeds; for example, while the total number of assault-oriented actions and sentiments was over two and a half times as great as those relating to theft, the actual number of "arrestable" incidents of assault was less than half the number of theft incidents. This finding is concordant with others which depict the area of assaultive behavior as one characterized by considerably more smoke than fire.

About one half (821) of the 1,600 actions and sentiments were categorized as "approved" or "disapproved" with reference to a specified set of evaluative standards of middle-class adults;[8] the remainder were categorized as "evaluatively neutral." There were approximately thirty "disapproved" assault-oriented actions for every instance of "arrestable" assault, and five instances of arrestable assault for every court appearance on assault charges. Males engaged in assault-oriented behavior far more frequently than females (males 6.3 events per month, females 1.4), and younger males more frequently than older.

Information concerning both actions and sentiments relating to assault —data not generally available—revealed both similarities and differences in the patterning of these two levels of behavior. Expressed sentiments concerning assaultive behavior were about one and a half times as common as actual actions; in this respect, assault was unique among analyzed forms of behavior, since, in every other case, recorded actions were more common

[7] The definition of "violent crimes" used here would call for an analysis at this point of behavior oriented to both assault and property destruction. However, the type of data-processing necessary to an integrated analysis of these two behavioral forms has not been done for "property damage," so that the present section is based almost entirely on behavior involving persons rather than persons and property. Behavior involving property damage was relatively infrequent; 265 actions and sentiments were recorded, ranking this form of behavior forty-fifth of sixty forms; vandalistic behavior was about one-sixth as common as assaultive behavior, a ratio paralleled in officially recorded data (cf. Table 4). Most subsequent sections will utilize findings based on both assault and property damage.

[8] Examples of *approved actions:* "acting to forestall threatened fighting" and "agreeing to settle disputes by means other than physical violence"; *disapproved actions:* "participating in gang-fighting" and "carrying weapons"; *approved sentiments:* "arguing against involvement in gang fighting" and "opposing the use of weapons"; *disapproved sentiments:* "defining fighting prowess as an essential virtue" and "perceiving fighting as inevitable."

than sentiments, for example, theft behavior (actions 1.5 times sentiments) and family-oriented behavior (actions 2.2 times sentiments). The majority of actions and sentiments (70 per cent) were "disapproved" with reference to adult middle-class standards; actions and sentiments were "concordant" in this respect, in that both ran counter to middle-class standards by similar proportions (actions, 74 per cent disapproved and sentiments, 68 per cent). This concordance contrasted with other forms of behavior: in sexual behavior, the level of disapproved action was substantially higher than that of disapproved sentiment; in family-oriented behavior, the level of disapproved sentiment, substantially higher than that of action.

Separate analyses were made of behavior oriented to "individual" assault (mostly fights between two persons) and "collective" assault (mostly gang fighting). With regard to individual assault, the number of actions and the number of sentiments were approximately equal (181 actions, 187 sentiments); in the case of collective assault, in contrast, there was almost twice as much talk as action (239 sentiments, 124 actions). Sentiments with respect both to individual and collective assault were supportive of disapproved behavior, but collective assault received less support than individual. Behavior *opposing* disapproved assault showed an interesting pattern; specific actions aimed to inhibit or forestall collective assault were over twice as common as actions opposing individual assault. Gang members thus appeared to be considerably more reluctant to engage in collective than in individual fighting; the former was dangerous and frightening, with uncontrolled escalation a predictable risk, while much of the latter involved relatively mild set-to's between peers within the "controlled" context of gang interaction.

Assault-oriented behavior, in summary, was relatively common, but a substantial part of this behavior entailed words rather than deeds. Both actions and sentiments ran counter to conventional middle-class adult standards, with these two levels of behavior concordant in this respect. Insofar as there did exist an element of assault-inhibiting behavior, it was manifested in connection with collective rather than individual assault. This provides evidence for the existence within the gang of a set of "natural" forces operating to control collective assault, a phenomenon to be discussed further.

Frequency of Violent Crime

The wide currency of an image of violence as a dominant occupation and preoccupation of street gangs grants special importance to the question of the actual prevalence of violent crimes. How frequently did gang members engage in illegal acts of assault and property damage? Table 1

TABLE 1. FREQUENCY OF VIOLENT CRIMES BY MALE GANG MEMBERS
(by Race and Social Status)

Race and Social Status	Five Intensive-Observation Gangs			Fourteen Court-Record Gangs		
	Number of Individuals	Number of Involve-ments[a]	Rate[b]	Number of Individuals	Number of Charges[c]	Rate[d]
White L.C. III	66	154	8.4	97	81	8.3
Negro L.C. III	—[e]	—	—	58	39	6.7
White L.C. II	50	40	1.5	72	10	1.4
Negro L.C. II	39	34	2.5	66	8	1.2
	155	228	4.7	293	138	4.7

$$\text{L.C.III } (8.4) = \text{L.C.II } (2.0) \times 4.2 \qquad \text{L.C.III } (7.7) = \text{L.C.II } (1.3) \times 5.9$$

$$\text{White } (5.4) = \text{Negro } (2.5) \times 2.1 \qquad \text{White } (5.4) = \text{Negro } (3.8) \times 1.4$$

[a] No incidents assault and property damage $\times$ number of participants.

[b] Involvements per 10 individuals per ten-month period.

[c] Charges on fourteen categories of assault and property-damage offenses (see Table 4, page 702, below).

[d] Charges per ten individuals ages seven through eighteen.

[e] Not included in study population.

shows that members of the five intensive-observation male gangs, on the basis of field records of known offenses, were involved in violent crimes at a rate of somewhat under one offense for each two boys per ten-month period, and that the fourteen male gangs, on the basis of court-recorded offenses, were charged with "violent" crimes at a rate of somewhat under one charge for each two boys during the twelve-year period from ages seven through eighteen.[9] The 228 "violent offense" involvements comprised

[9] Four types of "unit" figure in this and following tables. These are: (1) *Incidents*: An illegal incident is a behavioral event or sequence of events adjudged by a coder to provide a sound basis for arrest if known to authorities. Information as to most incidents was obtained from field records. In the case of assault incidents, this definition ruled out a fair number of moderately to fairly serious instances of actual or intended assault which involved members of the same gang or occurred under circumstances deemed unlikely to produce arrest even if known. (2) *Involvements*: Incidents multiplied by number of participants, for example: two gang members fight two others—one incident, four involvements. (3) *Court Appearances*: The appearance in court of a gang member on a "new" charge or charges (excluded are rehearings, appeals, and the like). (4) *Court Charges*: Appearances multiplied by number of separate charges, for example, an individual's being charged at one appearance with breaking and entering, possession of burglars' tools, and conspiracy to commit larceny counts as three "charges." The "violent crime" charges of Table 1 represent fourteen categories of offense involving

24 percent of all categories of illegal involvements (assault 17 per cent, property damage 7 per cent), with assault about one-half as common as theft, the most common offense, and property damage about one-quarter as common. The 138 court charges comprised 17 per cent of all categories of charge (assault charges 11 per cent, property damage 6 per cent) with assault charges about one-third as common as theft, the most common charge, and property damage about one-fifth as common. The total number of "violence-oriented" actions and sentiments examined in the previous section comprised something under 4 per cent of actions and sentiments oriented to sixty behavioral areas (assault-oriented behavior, 3.2 per cent; property-damage-oriented, 0.5 per cent).

These figures would indicate that violence and violent crimes did not play a dominant role in the lives of Midcity gangs. The cumulative figures taken alone—228 known offenses by 155 boys during a period of approximately two years, and 138 court charges for 293 boys during a twelve-year age span—would appear to indicate a fairly high "absolute" volume of violent crime. If, however, the volume of such crime is compared with that of other forms—with "violent" behavior, both actional and verbal, comprising less than 4 per cent of all recorded behavior, field-recorded "violent" offenses comprising less than one-quarter of all known offenses, and court charges of violent crimes less than one-fifth of all charges—violence appears neither as a dominant preoccupation of city gangs nor as a dominant form of criminal activity. Moreover, one should bear in mind that these rates apply to young people of the most "violent" sex, during the most "violent" years of their lives, during a time when they were members of the toughest gangs in the toughest section of the city.

Race and Social Status

The relative importance of race and social status is indicated in Table 1, with field-recorded and court-recorded data showing close correspondence. Of the two characteristics, social status is clearly more important. Lower-status gang members (Lower Class III) engaged in field-recorded acts of illegal violence four times as often as those of higher status (Lower Class II) and were charged in court six times as often. White and Negro rates, in contrast, differ by a factor of two or less. The finding that boys of lower educational and occupational status both engaged in and were arrested for violent crimes to a substantially greater degree than those of higher status is not particularly surprising, and conforms to much research which shows that those of lower social status are likely to be more active

---

actual or threatened injury to persons or obects. The fourteen offense designations appear in Table 4, and were condensed from forty categories of police-blotter designations.

in criminal behavior. What is noteworthy is the fact that differences of this magnitude appear in a situation where status differences are as small, relatively, as those between Lower Class II and III. One might expect, for example, substantial differences between college boys and high school drop-outs, but the existence of differences on the order of four to six times between groups *within* the lower class suggests that even relatively small social-status differences among laboring-class populations can be associated with relatively large differences in criminal behavior.

Table 1 findings relating to race run counter to those of many studies which show Negroes to be more "violent" than whites and to engage more actively in violent crimes. Comparing similar-status white and Negro gangs in Midcity shows that racial differences were relatively unimportant, and that, insofar as there were differences, it was the whites rather than the Negroes who were more likely both to engage in and to be arrested for violent crimes. White gang members engaged in field-recorded acts of illegal violence twice as often as Negro gang members and were charged in court one and a half times as often. These data, moreover, do not support a contention that Negroes who engage in crime to a degree similar to that of whites tend to be arrested to a greater degree. The one instance where Negro rates exceed those of whites is in the case of field-recorded crimes for higher status gangs (white rate 1.5, Negro 2.5).[10] Court data, however, show that the Negro boys, with a *higher* rate of field-recorded crime, have a slightly *lower* rate of court-recorded crime. An explanation of these findings cannot be undertaken here; for present purposes it is sufficient to note that carefully collected data from one major American city do not support the notion that Negroes are more violent than whites at *similar social status levels*, nor the notion that high Negro arrest rates are invariably a consequence of the discriminatory application of justice by prejudiced white policemen and judges.

Age and Violent Crime

Was there any relationship between the age of gang members and their propensity to engage in violent crimes? Table 2 shows a clear and regular relationship between age and offense-frequency. The yearly rate of changes rises quite steadily between the ages of 12 and 18, reaches a peak of about 9 charges per 100 boys at age 18, then drops off quite rapidly to

[10] This ratio obtains for males only; calculations which include the girls' gangs show higher rates for whites in this category as well as the others. Data on field-recorded crimes on the female gangs are not included in Table 1 for purposes of comparability with court data; there were too few court-recorded offenses for females to make analysis practicable. At the time the field data were collected (1954–1957) Negroes comprised about 35 per cent of the population of Midcity; court data cover the years up to 1964, at which time Negroes comprised about 55 per cent of the population.

TABLE 2. FREQUENCY OF VIOLENT CRIMES BY AGE:
14 MALE GANGS (N = 293): COURT CHARGES (N = 229)

Age	Number of Individuals	Number of Charges[a]	Rate[b]	Assault Charges[c]	Rate	Property Damage Charges[d]	Rate
8	293	—	—	—	—	—	—
9	293	—	—	—	—	—	—
10	293	1	0.3	1	0.3	—	—
11	293	7	2.4	2	0.7	5	1.7
12	293	—	—	—	—	—	—
13	293	6	2.0	1	0.3	5	1.7
14	293	16	5.5	12	4.1	4	1.4
15	293	19	6.5	14	4.8	5	1.7
16	293	26	8.9	21	7.2	5	1.7
17	293	25	8.5	21	7.2	5	1.7
18	293	27	9.2	23	7.8	3	1.0
19	293	21	7.2	18	6.1	3	1.0
20	293	22	7.5	21	7.2	1	0.3
21	293	20	6.8	19	6.5	1	0.3
22	292	9	3.1	8	2.7	1	0.3
23	281	10	3.5	8	2.8	2	0.7
24	247	5	2.0	4	1.6	1	0.4
25	191	7	3.7	6	3.1	1	0.5
26	155	5	3.2	5	3.2	—	—
27	95	3	3.1	3	3.2	—	—

[a] Charges on fourteen categories of offense (see Table 4).
[b] Charges per 100 individuals per year of age.
[c] Categories 1, 3, 4, 5, 5, 7, 8, 9, 13, and 14, Table 4.
[d] Categories 2, 10, 13, 12, Table 4.

age 22, leveling off thereafter to a relatively low rate of about 3 charges per 100 boys per year. The bulk of court action (82 per cent of 229 charges) involved assaultive rather than property-damage offenses. The latter were proportionately more prevalent during the 11–13 age period, after which the former constitute a clear majority.

The age-patterning of theft-connected versus nontheft-connected violence and of intended versus actual violence was also determined. Violence in connection with theft—almost invariably the threat rather than the use thereof—constituted a relatively small proportion of all charges (14 per cent), occurring primarily during the 15–21 age period. Court action based on the threat or intention to use violence rather than on its actual use comprised about one-quarter of all charges, becoming steadily more common between the ages of thirteen and twenty, and less common thereafter. At age twenty the number of charges based on the threat of violence was exactly equal to the number based on actual violence.

These data indicate quite clearly that involvement in violent crimes was a relatively transient phenomenon of adolescence, and did not presage a continuing pattern of similar involvement in adulthood. It should also be noted that these findings do not support an image of violent crimes as erratically impulsive, uncontrolled, and unpredictable. The fact that the practice of violent crime by gang members showed so regular and so predictable a relationship to age would indicate that violence was a "controlled" form of behavior—subject to a set of shared conceptions as to which forms were appropriate, and how often they were appropriate, at different age levels.

Participation in Assaultive Crime

What proportion of gang members engaged in assaultive crimes?[11] During the two-year period of field observation, 53 of the 205 intensive-contact gang members (26 per cent) were known to have engaged in illegal acts of assault—50 out of 155 males (32 per cent), and 3 out of 50 females (6 per cent). Male-participation figures ranged from 22 per cent for the higher status gangs to 42 per cent for the lower. "Heavy" participants (four or more crimes) comprised only 4 per cent (six males, no females) of all gang members. During the same period nineteen gang members (all males) appeared in court on assault charges—about 12 per cent of the male gang members. While there is little doubt that some gang members also engaged in assaultive crimes that were known neither to field workers nor officials, the fact that three-quarters of the gang members and two-thirds of the males were *not* known to have engaged in assaultive crimes during the observation period and that 88 per cent of the males and 100 per cent of the females did not appear in court on charges of assaultive crimes strengthens the previous conclusion that assault was not a dominant form of gang activity.

A related question concerns the relative prevalence of individual and collective assault. One image of gang violence depicts gang members as cowardly when alone, daring to attack others only when bolstered by a clear numerical superiority. Study data give little support to this image. Fifty-one per cent of recorded assault incidents involved either one-to-one engagements or engagements in which a single gang member confronted more than one antagonist. As will be shown in the discussion of "targets," a good proportion of the targets of collective assault were also groups rather than individuals. Some instances of the "ganging-up" phenomenon did occur, but they were relatively infrequent.

[11] Findings do not include data on property damage. See footnote 7.

The Character of Violent Crime

What was the character of violent crime in Midcity gangs? Violent crimes, like other forms of gang behavior, consist of a multiplicity of particular events, varying considerably in form and circumstance. Any classification based on a single system does not account for the diversity of violence. The following sections use five ways of categorizing violent crimes: (1) *forms of crime directed at persons* (distinctions based on age, gang membership, and collectivity of actors and targets); (2) *forms of crime directed at objects* (distinctions based on mode of inflicting damage); (3) *forms of crime directed at persons and objects* (based on official classifications); (4) *targets of crime directed at persons* (distinctions based on age, sex, race, gang membership, collectivity); and (5) *targets of crime directed at objects* (distinctions based on identity of object).

Table 3 (column 1) shows the distribution of eleven specific forms of field-recorded assault directed at persons. In three-quarters of all incidents participants on both sides were peers of the same sex. In 60 per cent of the incidents, gang members acted in groups; in 40 per cent as individuals. Fifty-one per cent of the incidents involved collective engagements between same-sex peers. The most common form was the collective engagement between members of different gangs; it constituted one-third of all forms and was three times as common as the next most common form. Few of these engagements were full-scale massed-encounter gang fights; most were brief strike-and-fall-back forays by small guerrilla bands. Assault on male adults, the second most common form (11 per cent), involved, for the most part, the threat or use of force in connection with theft (for example, "mugging," or threatening a cab-driver with a knife) or attacks on policemen trying to make an arrest. It should be noted that those forms of gang assault which most alarm the public were rare. No case of assault on an adult woman, either by individuals or groups, was recorded. In three of the four instances of sexual assault on a female peer, the victim was either a past or present girl friend of the attacker. Only three incidents involving general rioting were recorded; two were prison riots and the third, a riot on a Sunday excursion boat.

The character of violent crimes acted on by the courts parallels that of field-recorded crimes. Table 4 shows the distribution of fourteen categories of offense for 293 gang members during the age period from late childhood to early adulthood. Charges based on assault (187) were five and a half times as common as charges on property damage (42). About one-third of all assault charges involved the threat rather than the direct use of force. The most common charge was "assault and battery," including, primarily, various kinds of unarmed engagements such as street fighting and barroom brawls. The more "serious" forms of assaultive crime were among the less

TABLE 3. FORMS OF VIOLENT CRIME: FIELD-RECORDED OFFENSES: SEVEN INTENSIVE-OBSERVATION GANGS (N = 205): INCIDENTS (N = 125)

Person-Directed			Object-Directed		
	Number of Incidents	% Known Forms		Number of Incidents	% All Forms
1. Collective engagement: different gangs	27	32.9	1. Damaging via body blow, other body action	10	27.0
2. Assault by individual on individual adult, same sex	9	11.0	2. Throwing of missile (stone, brick, etc.)	10	27.0
3. Two-person engagement: different gangs	6	7.3	3. Scratching, marking, defacing, object or edifice	8	21.6
4. Two-person engagement: gang member, nongang peer	6	7.3	4. Setting fire to object or edifice	4	10.8
5. Two-person engagement: intragang	5	6.1	5. Damaging via explosive	1	2.7
6. Collective assault on same sex peer, non-gang-member	5	6.1	6. Other	4	10.8
7. Threatened collective assault on adult	5	6.1		37	100.0
8. Assault by individual on group	4	4.9			
9. Assault by individual on female peer	4	4.9			
10. Participation in general disturbance, riot	3	3.6			
11. Collective assault on same-sex peer, member of other gang	2	2.4			
12. Other	6	7.3			
13. Form Unknown	6	—			
	88	99.9			

prevalent: armed assault, 8 per cent; armed robbery, 5 per cent; sexual assault, 4 per cent. Not one of the 293 gang members appeared in court on charges of either murder or manslaughter between the ages of seven and twenty-seven.

The use of weapons and the inflicting of injury are two indications that violent crimes are of the more serious kind. Weapons were employed in a minority of cases of assault, actual or threatened, figuring in 16 of the 88 field-recorded offenses, and about 55 of the 187 court offenses.[12] In the 16 field-recorded incidents in which weapons were used to threaten or injure, 9 involved knives, 4 an object used as a club (baseball bat, pool cue), and 3 missiles (rocks, balls). In none of the 88 incidents was a firearm of any description used. The bulk of assaultive incidents, then, involved the direct

[12] On the basis of field-recorded data it was estimated that about one-quarter of "Affray" charges involved sticks or other weapons.

TABLE 4. FORMS OF VIOLENT CRIME: COURT-RECORDED OFFENSES: 14 MALE GANGS (N = 293): COURT CHARGES THROUGH AGE 27 (N = 229)

Offense	Number	Percentage
1. Assault and battery: no weapon	75	32.7
2. Property damage	36	15.7
3. Affray	27	11.8
4. Theft-connected threat of force: no weapon	22	9.6
5. Possession of weapon	18	7.9
6. Assault, with weapon	18	7.9
7. Theft-connected threat of force: with weapon	11	4.8
8. Assault, threat of	8	3.5
9. Sexual assault	8	3.5
10. Arson	6	2.5
11. Property damage, threat of	—	—
12. Arson, threat of	—	—
13. Manslaughter	—	—
14. Murder	—	—
	229	100.0

use of the unarmed body; this finding accords with others in failing to support the notion that gang members engage in assault only when fortified by superior resources.

Serious injuries consequent on assault were also relatively uncommon. There were twenty-seven known injuries to all participants in the eighty-eight incidents of assault; most of these were minor cuts, scratches, and bruises. The most serious injury was a fractured skull inflicted by a crutch wielded during a small-scale set-to between two gangs. There were also two other skull injuries, three cases of broken bones, three broken noses, and one shoulder dislocation (incurred during a fight between girls). While these injuries were serious enough for those who sustained them, it could not be said that the totality of person-directed violence by Midcity gang members incurred any serious cost in maimed bodies. The average week-end of highway driving in and around Port City produces more serious body injuries than two years of violent crimes by Midcity gangs.

Data on modes of property damage similarly reflect a pattern of involvement in the less serious forms. As shown in Table 3, in ten of the thirty-seven field-recorded incidents the body was used directly to inflict damage (punching out a window, breaking fences for slats); another ten involved common kinds of missile-throwing (brick through store window). Most of the "defacing" acts were not particularly destructive, for example, scratching the name of the gang on a store wall. Fire-setting was confined to relatively small objects, for example, trash barrels. No instance was recorded of viciously destructive forms of vandalism such as desecration of churches or cemeteries or bombing of residences. The one case where explosives were used involved the igniting of rifle cartridge powder in a variety store. Of the forty-two cases of court-charged property-destruction, only six involved arson; the actual nature of vandalistic acts was not specified in the legal designations.

Targets of Violent Crime

While much gang violence took the form of "engagements with" rather than "attacks on" other persons, additional insight may be gained by viewing the gang members as "actors," and asking: "What categories of person were targets of gang assault, and what kinds of physical objects targets of damage?" One image of gang violence already mentioned sees the act of "ganging up" on solitary and defenseless victims as a dominant gang practice; another sees racial antagonism as a major element in gang violence. What do these data show?

Table 5 shows the distribution of 88 field-recorded incidents of assault for 13 categories of target, and 43 incidents of damage for 6 categories.[13]

Of 77 targets of assault whose identity was known, a substantial majority (73 per cent) were persons of the same age and sex category as the gang members, and a substantial majority (71 per cent), of the same race. One-half of all targets were peers of the same age, sex, and race category. On initial inspection the data seem to grant substance to the "ganging up" notion; 44 of 77 targets (57 per cent) were individuals. Reference to Table 3, however, shows that 34 of these incidents were assaults on individuals *by* individuals; of the remaining 10, 4 were adult males (police, mugging victims) and one, the female member of a couple robbed at knife point. The remaining 5 were same-sex peers, some of whom were members of rival gangs. There was no recorded instance of collective assault on a child, on old men or women, or on females by males. There was no instance of an attack on a white female by a Negro male. Partly balancing the five cases of collective assault on lone peers were three instances in which a lone gang member took on a group.

These data thus grant virtually no support to the notion that favored targets of gang attacks are the weak, the solitary, the defenseless, and the innocent; in most cases assaulters and assaultees were evenly matched; the bulk of assaultive incidents involved contests between peers in which the preservation and defense of gang honor was a central issue. Some support is

[13] Findings are based on field-recorded data only; official offenses designations seldom specify targets.

TABLE 5. TARGETS OF VIOLENT CRIME: FIELD-RECORDED OFFENSES: SEVEN INTENSIVE-OBSERVATION GANGS (N = 205): INCIDENTS (N = 125)

Persons	Number of Incidents	% Known Targets	Objects	Number of Incidents	% All Targets
1. Groups of adolescents, other gangs, same sex, race	18	23.4	1. Stores, commercial facilities: premises, equipment	11	29.7
2. Groups of adolescents, other gangs, same sex, different race	12	15.5	2. Semipublic facilities: social agencies, gyms, etc.	10	27.0
3. Individual adults, same sex, same race	12	15.5	3. Automobiles	8	21.6
4. Individual adolescents, other gangs, same sex, same race	8	10.4	4. Public facilities: schools, public transportation, etc.	5	13.5
5. Individual adolescents, nongang, same sex, race	6	7.8	5. Private houses: premises, furnishings	3	8.1
6. Individual adolescents, nongang, different sex, same race	4	5.2		37	99.9
7. Individual adolescents, nongang, same sex, different race	4	5.2			
8. Individual adults, same sex, different race	4	5.2			
9. Individual adolescents, own gang	3	3.9			
10. Groups of adolescents, own gang	3	3.9			
11. Individual adolescents, nongang, same sex, different race	2	2.6			
12. Individual adults, different sex, same race	1	1.3			
13. Target unknown	11	—			
	88	99.9			

given to the notion of racial friction; 30 per cent of all targets were of a different race, and racial antagonism played some part in these encounters. On the other hand, of thirty-three instances of collective assault, a majority (55 per cent) involved antagonists of the same race.

Physical objects and facilities suffering damage by gang members were largely those which they used and frequented in the course of daily life. Most damage was inflicted on public and semipublic facilities, little on private residences or other property. There was no evidence of "ideological" vandalism (stoning embassies, painting swastikas on synagogues). Most damage was deliberate, but some additional amount was a semiaccidental consequence of the profligate effusion of body energy so characteristic of male adolescents (breaking a store window in course of a scuffle). Little of the deliberately inflicted property damage represented a diffuse outpouring of accumulated hostility against arbitrary objects; in most cases the gang members injured the possession or properties of particular persons who had angered them, as a concrete expression of that anger (defacing automobile of mother responsible for having gang member committed to correctional institution; breaking windows of settlement house after ejection therefrom). There was thus little evidence of "senseless" destruction; most property damage was directed and responsive.

Gang Fighting

An important form of gang violence is the gang fight; fiction and drama often depict gang fighting or gang wars as a central feature of gang life (for example, *West Side Story*). The Midcity study conceptualized a fully developed gang fight as involving four stages: initial provocation, initial attack, strategy-planning and mobilization, and counterattack.[14] During the study period, members of the intensive-observation gangs participated in situations involving some combination of these stages fifteen times. Despite intensive efforts by prowar agitators and elaborate preparations for war, only one of these situations eventuated in full-scale conflict; in the other fourteen, one or both sides found a way to avoid open battle. A major objective of gang members was to put themselves in the posture of fighting without actually having to fight. The gangs utilized a variety of techniques to maintain their reputation as proud men, unable to tolerate an affront to honor, without having to confront the dangerous and frightening reality of massed antagonists. Among these were the "fair fight" (two champions represent their gangs *à la* David and Goliath); clandestine informing of police by prospective combatants; *reluctantly* accepting mediation by social workers.

Despite the very low ratio of actual to threatened fighting, a short-term observer swept up in the bustle and flurry of fight-oriented activity, and ignorant of the essentially ritualistic nature of much of this activity, might gain a strong impression of a great deal of actual violence. In this area, as in others, detailed observation of gangs over extended periods revealed that gang fighting resembled other forms of gang violence in showing much more smoke than fire.

THE PROBLEM OF GANG VIOLENCE

The picture of gang violence which emerges from the study of Midcity gangs differs markedly from the conventional imagery as well as from that

[14] A description of the gang fight as a form of gang behavior is included in W. B. Miller, "Lower-Class Culture as a Generating Milieu of Gang Delinquency," *Journal of Social Issues,* Vol. XXXI, No. 4 (December, 1957), pp. 17, 18.

presented by some scholars. How is this difference to be explained? The most obvious possibility is that Midcity gangs were somehow atypical of gangs in Port City, and of the "true" American street gang. In important respects the gangs were *not* representative of those in Port City, having been selected on the basis of their reputation as the "toughest" in the city, and were thus *more* violent than the average Port City gang. The possibility remains, in the absence of information equivalent in scope and detail to that presented here, that Port City gangs were atypical of, and less violent than, gangs in other cities. I would like in this connection to offer my personal opinion, based on ten years of contact with gang workers and researchers from all parts of the country, that Midcity gangs were in fact *quite* typical of "tough" gangs in Chicago, Brooklyn, Philadelphia, Detroit, and similar cities, and represent the "reality" of gang violence much more accurately than "the Wild Ones" or the Egyptian Kings represented as the prototypical "violent gang" in a well-known television program.

Even if one grants that actual city gangs are far less violent than those manufactured by the mass media and that the public fear of gangs has been unduly aroused by exaggerated images, the problem of gang violence is still a real one. However one may argue that all social groups need outlets for violence and that gang violence may serve to siphon off accumulated aggression in a "functional" or necessary way, the fact remains that members of Midcity gangs repeatedly violated the law in using force to effect theft, in fighting, and in inflicting damage on property as regular and routine pursuits of adolescence. *Customary* engagement in illegal violence by a substantial sector of the population, however much milder than generally pictured, constitutes an important threat to the internal order of any large urbanized society, a threat which must be coped with. What clues are offered by the research findings of the Midcity study as to the problem of gang violence and its control?

First, a brief summary of what it *was*. Violence as a concern occupied a fairly important place in the daily lives of gang members, but was distinguished among all forms of behavior in the degree to which concern took the form of talk rather than action. Violent crime as such was fairly common during middle and late adolescence, but, relative to other forms of crime, was not dominant. Most violent crimes were directed at persons, few at property. Only a small minority of gang members was active in violent crimes. Race had little to do with the frequency of involvement in violent crimes, but social status figured prominently. The practice of violent crimes was an essentially transient phenomenon of male adolescence, reaching a peak at the age when concern with attaining adult manhood was at a peak. While the nature of minor forms showed considerable variation, the large bulk of violent crime in Midcity gangs consisted in unarmed physical encounters between male antagonists—either in the classic form of combat skirmishes between small bands of warriors or the equally classic form of direct combative engagement between two males.

Next, a brief summary of what it was *not*. Violence was not a dominant activity of the gangs, nor a central reason for their existence. Violent crime was not a racial phenomenon—either in the sense that racial antagonisms played a major role in gang conflict, or that Negroes were more violent, or that resentment of racial injustice was a major incentive for violence. It was not "ganging up" by malicious sadists on the weak, the innocent, the solitary. It did not victimize adult females. With few exceptions, violent crimes fell into the "less serious" category, with the extreme or shocking crimes rare.

One way of summarizing the character of violent crime in Midcity gangs is to make a distinction between two kinds of violence—"means" violence and "end" violence. The concept of violence as a "means" involves the notion of a resort to violence when other means of attaining a desired objective have failed. Those who undertake violence in this context represent their involvement as distasteful but necessary—an attitude epitomized in the parental slogan, "It hurts me more than it does you." The concept of violence as an "end" involves the notion of eager recourse to violence for its own sake—epitomized in the mythical Irishman who says, "What a grand party! Let's start a fight!" The distinction is illustrated by concepts of two kinds of policeman—the one who with great reluctance resorts to force in order to make an arrest and the "brutal" policeman who inflicts violence unnecessarily and repeatedly for pure pleasure. It is obvious that "pure" cases of either means- or end-violence are rare or nonexistent; the "purest" means-violence may involve some personal gratification, and the "purest" end-violence can be seen as instrumental to other ends.

In the public mind, means-violence is unfortunate but sometimes necessary; it is the spectacle of end-violence which stirs deep indignation. Much of the public outrage over gang violence arises from the fact that it has been falsely represented, with great success, as pure end-violence ("senseless," "violence for its own sake") when it is largely, in fact, means-violence.

What are the "ends" toward which gang violence is a means, and how is one to evaluate the legitimacy of these ends? Most scholars of gangs agree that these ends are predominantly ideological rather than material, and revolve on the concepts of prestige and honor. Gang members fight to secure and defend their honor as males; to secure and defend the reputation of their local area and the honor of their women; to show that an affront to their pride and dignity demands retaliation.[15] Combat between males is a major means for attaining these ends.

[15] The centrality of "honor" as a motive is evidenced by the fact that the "detached worker" method of working with gangs has achieved its clearest successes in preventing gang fights by the technique of furnishing would-be combatants with various means of avoiding direct conflict without sacrificing honor.

It happens that great nations engage in national wars for almost identical reasons. It also happens, ironically, that during this period of national concern over gang violence our nation is pursuing, in the international arena, very similar ends by very similar means. At root, the solution to the problem of gang violence lies in the discovery of a way of providing for men the means of attaining cherished objectives—personal honor, prestige, defense against perceived threats to one's homeland—without resort to violence. When men have found a solution to this problem, they will at the same time have solved the problem of violent crimes in city gangs.

5   Delinquent Subcultures: Theory and Recent Research[*]

LAMAR T. EMPEY

DIMENSIONS OF GROUP DELINQUENCY

There are few findings which question seriously the basic proposition that delinquency is typically a group phenomenon. Most studies, including some which use self-reported data, place the incidence of group delinquency somewhere between 60 and 90 percent of the total.[1] It may be that with

Reprinted from LaMar T. Empey, "Delinquency Theory and Recent Research," *Journal of Research in Crime and Delinquency*, Volume 4, Number 1 (January, 1967), 32–42, by permission of the National Council on Crime and Delinquency and the author.

[*] Appreciation is expressed to William Fawcett Hill, Malcolm W. Klein, Solomon Kobrin, Sanford Labovitz, Steven G. Lubeck, George Newland, and James F. Short, Jr. for their review of and comments on this article.

[1] For examples see William Healy and Augusta F. Bronner, *New Light on Delinquency and Its Treatment* (New Haven: Yale University Press, 1936), p. 52; Sheldon and Eleanor Glueck, *Delinquents in the Making* (New York: Harper, 1952), p. 89; Clifford R. Shaw and Henry D. McKay, "Social Factors in Juvenile Delinquency," *Report on the Causes of Crime* (Washington: National Commission on Law Observance and Enforcement, 1931), pp. 195–96; Joseph D. Lohman, *Juvenile Delinquency* (Cook County: Office of the Sheriff, 1957), p. 8; Norman Fenton, *The Delinquent Boy and the Correctional School* (Claremont: Claremont Colleges Guidance Center, 1935), as quoted by Karl G. Garrison, *Psychology of Adolescence* (New York: Prentice-Hall, 1956), p. 350; and Peter Scott, "Gangs and Delinquent Groups in London," *British Journal of Delinquency*, July 1956, pp. 4–26.

. . . Unpublished data in our possession on self-reported delinquency, both from Utah and California, confirm this figure.

more systematic data this range will be extended, since some offenses—defying parents or running away—are by nature less likely to be group-related than others. However, the group aspects of delinquency seem to be well established with a modal figure of about 75 per cent.

What is not well established is a consensus regarding the nature of delinquent groups—their cohesiveness, their structural qualities, their subcultural characteristics. The most commonly used term to refer to delinquent groups has been the word "gang." The term has been so overworked and is so imprecise that its use in scientific discourse may well be questioned. An examination of evidence relative to the cohesiveness and structural qualities of delinquent groups illustrates the elusiveness of the "gang" and other group concepts.

Group Cohesiveness

Conflicting themes run through the literature regarding cohesiveness. The first theme, exemplified most clearly by Thrasher and the Chicago school, emphasizes the idea that delinquent groups are characterized by *internal* cohesion—*esprit de corps*, solidarity, cooperative action, shared tradition, and a strong group awareness.[2] Despite the qualifications which Thrasher placed on this theme—and he did qualify it—there is no denying that a traditional perspective has developed emphasizing the romantic quality of delinquent gangs, the free and easy life, the joint commitments of members to one another. The key to this theme is its emphasis upon the culture-generating qualities and attractiveness of the peer group.

The second theme, as Bordua notes, is irrationalistic and deterministic in its emphasis. "Gang boys are driven," he notes, "not attracted. Their lives are characterized by desperation rather than fun."[3] Such theories as those of Cohen,[4] Cloward and Ohlin,[5] and Miller[6] emphasize the idea that lower-class children are downgraded in both the child and the adult status

[2] Frederic M. Thrasher, *The Gang: A Study of 1,313 Gangs in Chicago*, abridged and with a new introduction by James F. Short, Jr. (Chicago: University of Chicago Press, 1963), pp. 40–46. See also Short's discussion of this theme in his introduction to the abridged edition, *passim*.

[3] David J. Bordua, "Some Comments on Theories of Group Delinquency," *Sociological Inquiry*, Spring, 1962, pp. 245–46; see also David J. Bordua, "A Critique of Sociological Interpretations of Gang Delinquency," *Annals of the American Academy of Political and Social Science*, November 1961, pp. 120–36.

[4] Albert K. Cohen, *Delinquent Boys: The Culture of the Gang* (Glencoe: The Free Press, 1955).

[5] Richard A. Cloward and Lloyd E. Ohlin, *Delinquency and Opportunity: A Theory of Delinquent Gangs* (Glencoe: Free Press, 1960).

[6] Walter B. Miller, "Lower-Class Culture as a Generating Milieu of Gang Delinquency," *Journal of Social Issues*, Summer, 1958, pp. 5–19.

hierarchies of our middle-class institutions. They are ill-prepared by family background and cultural heritage to achieve successfully and, as a consequence, their lives are characterized by frustration, negativistic retaliation, alienation, and radical separation from conventional successes and satisfactions. This theme is much less romantic in its emphasis than the first and implies, not internal attraction, but external pressure as the source of gang cohesion.

It is the role of the individual youngster in the social structure, not his role in the street group, that is of primary significance. He is alienated before he enters the group, not because of it. The group is simply the instrument that translates his individual discontent into a collective solution.[7] By implication, the group can do little to remedy his sensitivity to the middle-class measuring rod, to provide him with the material and social satisfactions to which he aspires.

The fundamental question, then, asks what the forces are that hold delinquent groups together. Are they the group rules and loyalties which emerge from gratifying relationships within the group, as the first theme suggests, or are they due to the position of gang boys in the class structure as suggested by the second theme?

First of all, we are confronted with the apparent fact that, if the delinquent group were not rewarding to the individual, it would cease to exist. In this vein, Short and Strodtbeck have observed that when it comes to assuming adult roles—occupation and marriage—". . . the lure of the gang may spell disaster."[8] Even when challenging jobs are obtained for them, when the pay is good or when gang members are married and have children, the lure of the street is not easily forgotten and any inclination to return to it is supported by the gang. The implication, of course, is one of *internal* cohesiveness and attraction: gang membership has much to offer. However, as might be expected, there are other interpretations.

. . . Klein and Crawford argue that *internal* sources of lower-class gang cohesion are weak.[9] Group goals which might be unifying are minimal, membership stability is low, loyalty is questionable, and even the names of gangs—Gladiators, Vice Lords, Egyptian Kings—are unifying only when external threat is present. When the threat is diminished, cohesion is diminished. It is their feeling that were it not for the external pressures of police and other officials, the threats of rival groups, or the lack of acceptance by parents and employers, many delinquent gangs would have nothing

---

[7] Bordua, *op. cit. supra* note 3, pp. 252–57.

[8] James F. Short, Jr., and Fred L. Strodtbeck, *Group Process and Gang Delinquency* (Chicago: University of Chicago Press, 1965), pp. 221–34.

[9] Malcolm W. Klein and Lois Y. Crawford, "Groups, Gangs and Cohesiveness," *Journal of Research in Crime and Delinquency*, January 1967, p. 63.

to unify them. By themselves, such gangs do not develop the kinds of group goals and instrumentally oriented activities which are indicative of much organization.

Group Cohesion and Delinquent Acts

The commission of delinquent acts seems to illustrate this lack of organization. One of the most striking things about them is not their planned and patterned characteristics but their episodic and highly situational character.[10] One would think that if delinquent groups were highly cohesive or highly structured this would not be the case. Yet, most delinquent acts are more spontaneous than planned and, even though they involve groups, they rarely involve all members of a gang acting together.

Even complex crimes reveal considerable spontaneity and what Matza calls "shared misunderstanding."[11] Thrasher describes three college students who began to phantasize about robbing a post-office.[12] Subsequent interviews with them revealed that none of them wanted to be involved in the actual robbery but the more they talked the deeper they became involved, each hoping, actually believing, that the others would call a halt to this crazy phantasy but each reluctant, on his own, to "chicken out." The result was that, in a state of almost total individual disbelief, they robbed the post-office and found themselves in legal custody.

Careful observation of delinquents reveals countless repetitions of this phenomenon—the wandering kinds of interaction that lead to delinquent acts and the mixed rather than solidary motivations that accompany them. Even in regard to fighting, as Miller points out, "A major objective of gang members is to put themselves in the posture of fighting without actually having to fight."[13]

Group Cohesion and Member Interaction

Observations of delinquent gangs led Short and Strodtbeck, like Klein and Crawford, to depreciate nostalgic references to "that old gang of mine" and to deny the image of the delinquent gang as a carefree and solidary group. They report that such an interpretation may derive more from the projections of middle-class observers than from the realities that domi-

---

[10] Many works allude to this phenomenon. For example see Thrasher, *op. cit. supra* note 2; Short and Strodtbeck, *op. cit. supra* note 8; and Lewis Yablonsky, *The Violent Gang* (New York: Macmillan, 1962).

[11] David Matza, *Delinquency and Drift* (New York: Wiley, 1964), pp. 35–59.

[12] Thrasher, *op. cit. supra* note 2, pp. 300–03.

[13] Walter B. Miller, "Violent Crimes in City Gangs," *Annals of the American Academy of Political and Social Science*, March 1965, p. 110.

nate street life.[14] They document this interpretation with a considerable amount of data.

They found that, compared with others, gang boys were characterized by a long list of "social disabilities": unsuccessful school adjustment, limited social and technical skills, a low capacity for self-assertion, lower intelligence scores, and also a tendency to hold other gang members in low esteem.[15] Interaction within the gang seemed to be characterized by an omnipresent tone of aggression as a result of these disabilities and the insecurities they engendered.

This account is complemented by Matza's use of the term "sounding," which refers to the incessant plumbing and testing through insult by delinquent boys of one another's status and commitment to delinquency.[16] Miller speaks of the "focal concerns" of lower-class gang culture as toughness, smartness, and excitement.[17] Whatever the terms, it appears that delinquent boys are under constant pressure to protect status and assert masculinity.

While this pressure to project a particular image may not be qualitatively different from many of the highly stylized kinds of interaction found in a host of other status-conscious groups, the point is that such interaction is not characteristic, at least hypothetically, of *primary* groups. Primary groups, ideally, are supposed to provide warmth and support. With the constant "sounding" that goes on in delinquent groups it is questionable whether lower-class gangs are conducive to close friendships.[18]

The picture that is painted suggests that gang members, like inmates in a prison, are held together, not by feelings of loyalty and solidarity, but by forces much less attractive. It is not that structure is lacking but that it is defensive and highly stylized, not supportive. Group members stay together simply because they feel they have more to lose than to gain by any breach in their solidarity. While they may appear to the outsider to be dogmatic, rigid, and unyielding in their loyalty to each other, the sources of this loyalty are not internal but external. Remove the pressure and you remove the cohesion.

Seeming to comment on this very point, Short and Strodtbeck report that they "find the capacity of lower-class gangs to elaborate and enforce norms of reciprocity is very much below what might be required to sustain the group if alternative forms of gratification were available."[19] Similarly,

---

[14] Short and Strodtbeck, *op. cit. supra* note 8, p. 231.

[15] *Ibid.*, ch. 10 and 12.

[16] Matza, *op. cit. supra* note 11, pp. 53–55.

[17] Miller, *op. cit. supra* note 6, p. 519.

[18] Short and Strodtbeck, *op. cit. supra* note 8, p. 233. See also Lewis Yablonsky, "The Delinquent Gang as a Near Group," *Social Problems*, Fall, 1959, pp. 108–17.

[19] Short and Strodtbeck, *op. cit. supra* note 8, p. 280.

Matza argues that the majority of delinquents are not strongly committed either to delinquent groups or to a criminal career but are "drifters" who are held together by a kind of pluralistic ignorance.[20] When in the company of others, the boy is inclined to attribute to them a greater commitment to delinquent relationships and values than he has himself.

These points of view indicate the need for more direct investigation of delinquent group cohesiveness *per se* and for the study of middle-class as well as lower-class groups. Our lack of information is so great that we do not have even an adequate baseline from which to begin; that is, we know very little about the cohesiveness and inherent gratifications of adolescent groups in general. Therefore, until we can establish a baseline, it will be difficult either to generalize about delinquent groups or to compare them with other groups. Furthermore, the possible lack of cohesiveness in delinquent groups raises questions regarding the nature of delinquent subculture. If delinquent groups are not cohesive and internally gratifying, can it be expected that delinquents, especially those in the lower class, have either the personal motivation or the organizational skills to promote and maintain a deviant subculture which is in total opposition to prevailing values?

DELINQUENT SUBCULTURE

Such theorists as Cloward and Ohlin have defined the subcultural concept in narrow terms.[21] They see a delinquent subculture as unique and as autonomous. Organization around a specific delinquent activity, they say, distinguishes a delinquent subculture from other subcultures. Such behaviors as truancy, drunkenness, property destruction, or theft are legally delinquent activities but these they would not include as characteristic of a delinquent subculture unless they were the focal activities around which the dominant beliefs and roles of a group were organized.

The narrowness and rigor of their postulates regarding criminal, retreatist, and conflict-oriented subcultures characterize the logical structure of their theory but do these postulates accurately characterize delinquent groups and subculture? Are they this focused? Are they this unique and autonomous?

When Short and his associates set about trying to study these kinds of subcultures, they had extreme difficulty in locating them.[22] They found a number of gangs in which marijuana smoking was rather common and in

---

[20] Matza, *op. cit. supra* note 6, pp. 27–30, 56.
[21] Cloward and Ohlin, *op. cit. supra* note 5, p. 7.
[22] Short and Strodtbeck, *op. cit. supra* note 8, pp. 10–13.

which there was experimentation with heroin and pills, but it took more than a year of extensive inquiries among police and local adults to locate a clearly drug-oriented group. They never did find a full-blown criminal group. Consequently, they concluded that their failure casts doubt on the generality of the Cloward-Ohlin postulates.[23]

Short, et al., had no difficulty in locating a number of gangs who were well-known for their conflict, toughness, and fighting but one still must question what it means to say that the "focal" concern of gangs is conflict. The bulk of even the most delinquent boys' time is spent in nondelinquent activity and their delinquent acts make up a long list of different offenses.[24] How precise can we be, then, in referring to the characteristics of a "conflict" subculture or gang?

In observing "typical," "tough" city gangs over a two-year period, Miller found that assault was *not* the most dominant form of activity.[25] In fact, two-thirds of the male gang members who were observed were not known to have engaged in *any* assaultive crimes over the two-year period and 88 per cent did not appear in court on such a charge. Similarly, Klein and his colleagues in Los Angeles have found that less than 10 per cent of the recorded offenses for gang members are assaultive.[26] Instead, the *frequency* with which adolescents commit a long list of different offenses seems to better characterize their commitments to delinquency than their persistent adherence to a particular offense pattern.[27] There seems to be limited empirical support for the idea of autonomous and highly focused delinquent subcultures and somewhat more support for the notion of a ubiquitous, "parent" subculture of delinquency in which there is a "garden-variety" of delinquent acts.[28]

A ubiquitous, but amorphous, subculture would be more consistent with the notion of weak internal bonds in delinquent groups and highly situational delinquent acts than with the idea of internally cohesive groups who participate in planned and highly patterned delinquent activities. Furthermore, if delinquent subculture is not highly focused and autonomous, question is raised regarding its relation to the larger culture.

[23] *Ibid.*, p. 13.

[24] Short, Introduction in Thrasher, *op cit. supra* note 2, pp. xlvii–xlviii.

[25] Miller, *op. cit. supra* note 13, pp. 105, 111.

[26] Malcolm W. Klein, Youth Studies Center, University of Southern California, Personal Communication, September 1966.

[27] Maynard L. Erickson and LaMar T. Empey, "Court Records, Undetected Delinquency and Decision-Making," *Journal of Criminal Law, Criminology and Police Science*, December 1963, pp. 465–469; and Martin Gold, "Undetected Delinquent Behavior," *Journal of Research in Crime and Delinquency*, January, 1966, pp. 27–46.

[28] Albert K. Cohen and James F. Short, Jr., "Research in Delinquent Subcultures," *Journal of Social Issues*, Summer 1958, pp. 20–36.

Subculture: Contraculture or Infraculture?

Most contemporary theory has suggested that lower-class delinquent subculture is *contra*culture[29] in which status is gained by demonstrated opposition to prevailing middle-class standards.[30] Theories of middle-class delinquency suggests that the delinquent group is a collective response to adolescent efforts to establish sexual identity and to deal with frustrations attendant on the transition from childhood to adulthood.[31] But does this mean that a middle-class delinquent group is, like a lower-class gang, the instrument that translates individual discontent into a delinquent *contra*culture?

Matza takes issue with the notion of *contra*culture on any class level and emphasizes a subtle but important distinction. He argues that "there is a subculture of delinquency but it is not a delinquent subculture."[32] American culture, he believes, is not a simple puritanism exemplified by the middle-class. Instead, it is a complex and pluralistic culture in which, among other cultural traditions, there is a "subterranean" tradition—an *infra*culture of delinquency.[33]

This *infra*culture does not represent ignorance of the law nor even general negation of it; instead, it is a complex relationship to law in a *symbiotic* rather than an oppositional way. It is not a separate set of beliefs which distinguish delinquents from other youth, or youth from adults; it is that part of the overall culture which consists of the personal, more deviant, and less-publicized version of officially endorsed values. The two sets of traditions—conventional and deviant—are held simultaneously by almost everyone in the social system and, while certain groups may be influenced more by one than the other, both determine behavior to a considerable degree.

Daniel Bell's analysis of crime as an American way of life is probably a good illustration of Matza's point.[34] Bell notes that Americans are char-

[29] J. Milton Yinger, "Contraculture and Subculture," *American Sociological Review*, October 1960, pp. 625–35.

[30] Cohen, *op. cit. supra* note 4; Cloward and Ohlin, *op. cit. supra* note 5; and Miller, *op. cit. supra* note 6.

[31] Ralph W. England, Jr., "A Theory of Middle-Class Delinquency," *Journal of Criminal Law, Criminology and Police Science*, April 1960, pp. 535–40; Herbert A. Bloch and Arthur Niederhoffer, *The Gang: A Study of Adolescent Behavior* (New York: Philosophical Library, 1958).

[32] Matza, *op. cit. supra* note 11, p. 33; and David Matza and Gresham M. Sykes, "Juvenile Delinquency and Subterranean Values," *American Sociological Review*, October 1961, pp. 712–19.

[33] The idea of *infra*culture was suggested by J. A. Pitt-Rivers, *The People of the Sierra* (Chicago: University of Chicago Press, 1961), who referred to "infrastructure" rather than "infraculture."

[34] Daniel Bell, *The End of Ideology* (Glencoe: Free Press, 1959), pp. 115–36.

acterized by an "extremism" in morality, yet they also have an "extraordinary" talent for compromise in politics and a "brawling" economic and social history. These contradictory features form the basis for an intimate and symbiotic relationship between crime and politics, crime and economic growth, and crime and social change, not an oppositional relationship. The tradition of wanting to "get ahead" is no less an ethic than wanting to observe the law.

Crime has been a major means by which a variety of people have achieved the American success ideal and obtained respectability, if not for themselves, for their children. The basic question, therefore, is whether this deviant tradition contributes more than we realize to the behavior of younger as well as older people. Rather than delinquent subculture being uniquely the property of young people, it may have roots in the broader culture.

Empirical investigation of the matter would seem to involve two questions: (1) the extent to which adolescents legitimate official, conventional patterns and (2) the extent to which they simultaneously participate in, or espouse in some way, deviant patterns. With reference to the first question both Kobrin[35] and Gordon et al.[36] suggest that adolescents from all strata are inclined to legitimate official patterns. The gang members they studied did not seem to be alienated from the goals of the larger society and ". . . even the gang ethic, is not one of 'reaction formation' *against* widely shared conceptions of the 'good' life." Gang, low-class and middle-class boys, Negro and white, ". . . *evaluated images representing salient features of the middle-class styles of life equally high.*"[37] This finding confirmed that of Gold in Michigan with a much different population[38] and led to the conclusion that ". . . if the finding is valid, three separate theoretical formulations [Cohen, Miller, and Cloward-Ohlin] fail to make sufficient allowance for the meaningfulness of middle-class values to members of gangs."[39] In fact, given the strength of the findings, one wonders whether we are correct in referring to official values as "middle-class" values or whether we should be using some more inclusive term.

The second question, regarding the simultaneous possession of deviant patterns, presents a more confused picture. A curious omission in our conjectures and research has been our failure to examine the extent to which

[35] Solomon Kobrin, "The Conflict of Values in Delinquency Areas," *American Sociological Review*, October 1951, pp. 653–61.

[36] Robert A. Gordon, James F. Short, Jr., Desmond F. Cartwright, and Fred L. Strodtbeck, "Values and Gang Delinquency," *American Journal of Sociology*, September 1963, pp. 109–28, as reproduced in Short and Strodtbeck, *op. cit. supra* note 8, ch. 3.

[37] Short and Strodtbeck, *op cit. supra* note 8, pp. 271,59. Italics theirs.

[38] Martin Gold, *Status Forces in Delinquent Boys* (Ann Arbor: University of Michigan, Institute for Social Research, 1963).

[39] Short and Strodtbeck, *op. cit. supra* note 8, p. 74.

deviant values are widely transmitted to young people. Several elaborate theories hypothesize that all children, including those in the lower class, are conditioned by official, "middle-class" stimuli. They watch television, listen to the radio, go to the movies, read the ads, and attend middle-class dominated schools; as a consequence, they acquire common desires for status, recognition, and achievement. Despite these conjectures, we have not had similar conjectures regarding the possible transmission of deviant patterns.

Kvaraceus and Miller have suggested that middle-class delinquency represents an upward diffusion of lower-class attitudes and practices;[40] but are lower-class patterns all that are diffused? To what extent are children on all class levels conditioned not just by lower-class values but by mass stimuli which emphasize violence, toughness, protest, kicks, and expedience? These are certainly important aspects of our "brawling" American history, a part of our cultural tradition. If we pay too little heed to them then we may be inclined to overemphasize the narrowness and autonomy of delinquent subculture, especially as the sole possession of the lower class. It is seductively easy to overemphasize the uniqueness of problem people and thereby to obscure their similarities to non-problem people. For example, studies of self-reported delinquency reveal that the extent of hidden law violation is widespread,[41] so widespread, indeed, that Murphy, Shirley, and Witmer were led to remark that "even a moderate increase in the amount of attention paid to it by law enforcement authorities could create the semblance of a 'delinquency wave' without there being the slightest change in adolescent behavior."[42] This finding, coupled with the questionable strength of the theory of an inverse relationship between social class and delinquency, suggests that, unless we are to assume that deviant traditions actually predominate, they must occupy a symbiotic tie of some kind with conformist traditions.

Conventional Values and Deviance

In order to investigate the matter further, several factors should be considered. One important factor is the nature of adult-youth relationships. What perspectives, for example, are transmitted from adults to youth? Is the youthful search for "kicks" or the irresponsible acquisition of wealth and leisure profoundly different from adult desires for the same things or, rather, a projection of them? A double standard for judging adult and youth-

[40] William C. Kvaraceus and Walter B. Miller, *Delinquent Behavior, Culture and the Individual* (Washington: National Education Association, 1959), pp. 77–79.

[41] Erickson and Empey, *op. cit. supra* note 27; and Gold, *op. cit. supra* note 27.

[42] Fred J. Murphy, M. Shirley, and Helen L. Witmer, "The Incidence of Hidden Delinquency," *American Journal of Orthopsychiatry*, October 1946, pp. 686–96.

ful behavior is certainly not uncommon and could be far more influential than a double standard distinguishing between the sexes. Personal access to various adult role models, as contrasted to a vague and abstract relationship with them, would likely affect the selection of deviant or conformist behavior. The absence of a strong personal relationship would make the juvenile more dependent upon the images projected by such secondary sources as the movies or television.

A second important factor has to do with the relative valences of delinquent and conformist values for different populations of adolescents. How do they balance? Short and Strodtbeck found that, while conventional prescriptions were generally accepted, subterranean, deviant values were accepted differentially. While gang boys were as willing as lower- and middle-class nongang boys to legitimate official *pre*scriptions, they were not as inclined to support official *pro*scriptions.[43] This particular research failed to explore other important aspects of the issue.

Besides obtaining some indication of the general valences of both deviant and conventional values, we need to explore their valences in various specific contexts. We know, for example, that if changes in group context or social situation occur, both behavior and the espousal of particular values are likely to change also. The citizen who is in favor of racial equality in a general way is often one of the first to sell his home when integration occurs in his neighborhood. Specific considerations alter his behavior. Similarly, the delinquent boy, when placed in the context of having to exercise leadership over his peers in a conventional setting, will often act remarkably like a conventional adult. His actions are surprisingly stereotyped, a response not to norms in general but to norms as they apply in a specific context.

In studying the relative valences of conventional and deviant *pro*scriptions we also need to compare not only lower-class gang boys with others, as Short and Strodtbeck did, but excessively delinquent boys from other classes with their peers as well. We need a better indication of the extent to which deviant values are diffused either throughout the entire class structure or through subgroups on all class levels.

Finally, we need more careful study of the way official and societal responses to juvenile behavior contribute to definitions of delinquency and delinquent subcultures, either by overemphasizing their uniqueness or by contributing to their development. Becker argues that the process by which some juveniles but not others are labeled may be as crucial in defining the problem as the behavior of the juveniles themselves.[44] For example, as mentioned earlier, there are those who think that the coalescence and persistence of delinquent gangs may be due as much to external pressure from

[43] Short and Strodtbeck, *op. cit. supra* note 8, pp. 59–76.
[44] Howard S. Becker, *Outsiders: Studies in the Sociology of Deviance* (Glencoe: Free Press, 1963), ch. 1.

official and other sources as to the internal gratifications and supposedly unique standards of those groups.

The contribution which could be made by a study of official systems— the police, the courts, the correctional agencies—would be clarification of the total *gestalt* to which officials respond: how legal statutes, official policies, and perceptual cues affect the administration of juvenile justice.[45] It seems apparent that official and societal reactions to juveniles are due not entirely to criminalistic behavior but also (1) to acts which, if committed by adults, would not warrant legal action and (2) to a number of "social disabilities" that are popularly associated with deviance: unkempt appearance, inappropriate responses due to lack of interpersonal skills, and educational deficiencies.[46]

These are characteristics which traditionally have been more closely associated with lower- than middle-class juveniles and are characterized in legal terms by truancy, dependency, or incorrigibility. It would be important to learn the extent to which these identifying characteristics, as contrasted to demonstrably delinquent *values*, contribute to the definition of some groups, but not others, as seriously delinquent. Since only a small fraction of their time and attention is devoted to law violation, even among the most seriously delinquent, the meanings which these juveniles assign to themselves are usually far less sinister than the meanings which officials assign to them.

CONCLUSION

It seems apparent that, in order to complete the picture of the total phenomenon, we need a series of related studies which would, first, identify a representative population of adolescents, their class positions, their value-beliefs and commitments, various measures of delinquent acts (self-reported and official), their symptoms of disability, and their group affiliations; and, second, follow these adolescents through the institutional paths—educational, economic, or correctional—along which they are routed by officials. Which juveniles are processed legally and on what criteria? In what ways are they

[45] See Irving Piliavin and Scott Briar, "Police Encounters with Juveniles," *American Journal of Sociology*, September 1964, pp. 206–15; Joseph D. Lohman, James T. Carey, Joel Goldfarb, and Michael J. Rowe, *The Handling of Juveniles From Offense to Disposition* (Berkeley: University of California, 1965); and Nathan Goldman, *The Differential Selection of Juvenile Offenders for Court Appearance* (National Research and Information Center, National Council on Crime and Delinquency, 1963).

[46] For conflicting evidence, see A. W. McEachern and Riva Bouzer, "Factors Related to Disposition in Juvenile Police Contacts," *Juvenile Gangs in Context: Theory, Research and Action*, Malcolm W. Klein and Barbara G. Myerhoff, eds. (New York: Prentice-Hall, 1967).

the same or different from nonprocessed juveniles in terms of values, class position, group affiliations, actual delinquent acts, and so on.

Given such research we might then be in a better position to know not only what the consequences are for those who are apprehended and processed by legal and correctional institutions but also what the consequences are for those who are *not* processed. This would most certainly apply to middle-class as well as lower-class juveniles. Hopefully, we might gain better insight into the total mosaic composed of delinquent values, actual behavior, and official reaction. Are delinquent values widely shared and is delinquent behavior common? Does legal or semilegal processing contribute to the solidification of delinquent groups? Is there differential treatment of juveniles based not on actual behavioral or value differences but on other identifying characteristics? Information of this type would help to indicate whether delinquent subculture is *contra*culture or *infra*culture.

We are only recently becoming aware of the extent of the symbiotic and mutually supporting characteristics of official and client roles in a long list of social systems; for example, policeman-offender, captor-captive, teacher-pupil, therapist-patient, caseworker-client. These are inextricably tied together by a host of traditional expectations and definitions. Change one and you are likely to change the other. We need to know more clearly the extent to which these definitions and the systems of which they are a part make delinquency and delinquents appear to be what they are, as well as the standards, beliefs, and behavior which may be unique to delinquents. Interactive relations between and among juveniles and official agencies may be as important as the behavior exhibited by juveniles in delimiting delinquency for purposes of both etiological inquiry and social control.

6 The Sociology
of the Deviant Act:
Anomie Theory
and Beyond*

ALBERT K. COHEN

My concern in this paper is to move toward a general theory of deviant behavior. Taking "Social Structure and Anomie"[1] as a point of departure, I shall note some of the imperfections and gaps in the theory as originally stated, how some of these have been rectified, some theoretical openings for further exploration, and some problems of relating anomie theory to other traditions in the sociology of deviance. It is not important, for my purposes, how broadly or narrowly Merton himself conceived the range of applicability of his anomie theory. Whatever the intention or vision of the author of a theory, it is the task of a discipline to explore the implications of a theoretical insight, in all directions. Many of the points I shall make are, indeed, to be found in Merton's work. In many instances, however, they either

Reprinted from *American Sociological Review*, 30 (February, 1965), 5–14, by permission of the American Sociological Association and the author.

* A revised version of a paper read at the annual meeting of the American Sociological Association, August, 1963.

[1] Robert K. Merton, "Social Structure and Anomie," *American Sociological Review*, 3 (October, 1938), pp. 672–682, *Social Theory and Social Structure*, Glencoe, Ill.: The Free Press, 1957, Chs. 4 and 5, and "Conformity, Deviation, and Opportunity-Structures," *American Sociological Review*, 24 (April, 1959), pp. 177–189; Richard A. Cloward, "Illegitimate Means, Anomie, and Deviant Behavior," *American Sociological Review*, 24 (April, 1959), pp. 164–176; and Robert Dubin, "Deviant Behavior and Social Structure: Continuities in Social Theory," *American Sociological Review*, 24 (April, 1959), pp. 147–164.

appear as leads, suggestions, or *obiter dicta*, and are left undeveloped, or they appear in some other context and no effort is made systematically to link them with anomie theory.[2]

THE ANOMIE THEORY OF DEVIANT BEHAVIOR

Merton's theory has the reputation of being the pre-eminently *sociological* theory of deviant behavior. Its concern is to account for the distribution of deviant behavior among the positions in a social system and for differences in the distribution and rates of deviant behavior among systems. It tries to account for these things as functions of system properties—*i.e.*, the ways in which cultural goals and opportunities for realizing them within the limits of the institutional norms are distributed. The emphasis, in short, is on certain aspects of the culture (goals and norms) and of the social structure (opportunities, or access to means). The theory *is*, then, radically sociological. And yet, as far as the formal and explicit structure of Merton's first formulation is concerned, it is, in certain respects, atomistic and individualistic. Within the framework of goals, norms, and opportunities, the process of deviance was conceptualized as though each individual—or better, role incumbent—were in a box by himself. He has internalized goals and normative, regulatory rules; he assesses the opportunity structure; he experiences strain; and he selects one or another mode of adaptation. The bearing of others' experience—their strains, their conformity and deviance, their success and failure—on ego's strain and consequent adaptations is comparatively neglected.

Consider first the concept of strain itself. It is a function of the degree of disjunction between goals and means, or of the sufficiency of means to the attainment of goals. But how imperious must the goals be, how uncertain their attainment, how incomplete their fulfillment, to generate strain? The relation between goals as components of that abstraction, culture, and the concrete goals of concrete role incumbents, is by no means clear and simple. One thing that is clear is that the level of goal attainment that will seem just and reasonable to concrete actors, and therefore the sufficiency of available means, will be relative to the attainments of others who serve as

[2] I am not here concerned with empirical applications and tests of anomie theory, on which there is now a large literature. In view of the sustained interest in anomie theory, its enormous influence, and its numerous applications, however, it is worth noting and wondering at the relatively slow and fitful growth of the substantive theory itself. It is of some interest also that, with respect to both substantive theory and its applications, there has been little follow-up of Merton's own leads relative to the implications of anomie theory for intersocietal differences in deviant behavior. Almost all of the work has been on variations in deviance within American society.

reference objects. Level of aspiration is not a fixed quantum, taken from the culture and swallowed whole, to lodge unchanged within our psyches. The sense of proportionality between effort and reward is not determined by the objective returns of effort alone. From the standpoint of the role sector whose rates of deviance are in question, the mapping of reference group orientations, the availability *to others* of access to means, and the actual distribution of rewards are aspects of the social structure important for the determination of strain.[3]

Once we take explicit cognizance of these processes of comparison, a number of other problems unfold themselves. For example, others, whom we define as legitimate objects of comparison, may be more successful than we are by adhering to legitimate means. They not only do better than we do, but they do so "fair and square." On the other hand, they may do as well as we or even better by cutting corners, cheating, using illegitimate means. Do these two different situations have different consequences for the sense of strain, for attitudes toward oneself, for subsequent adaptations? In general, what strains does deviance on the part of others create for the virtuous? In the most obvious case ego is the direct victim of alter's deviance. Or ego's interests may be adversely but indirectly affected by the chicanery of a competitor—unfair trade practices in business, unethical advertising in medicine, cheating in examinations when the instructor grades on a curve. But there is a less obvious case, the one which, according to Ranulf,[4] gives rise to disinterested moral indignation. The dedicated pursuit of culturally approved goals, the eschewing of interdicted but tantalizing goals, the adherence to normatively sanctioned means—these imply a certain self-restraint, effort, discipline, inhibition. What is the effect of the spectacle of others who, though their activities do not manifestly damage our own interests, are morally undisciplined, who give themselves up to idleness, self-indulgence, or forbidden vices? What effect does the propinquity of the wicked have on the peace of mind of the virtuous?

In several ways, the virtuous can make capital out of this situation, can convert a situation with a potential for strain to a source of satisfaction. One can become even more virtuous letting his reputation hinge on his righteousness, *building his self out of invidious comparison to the morally weak*. Since others' wickedness sets off the jewel of one's own virtue, and one's claim to virtue is at the core of his public identity, one may actually develop a stake in the existence of deviant others, and be threatened should they pretend to moral excellence. In short, another's virtue may become a

[3] See, for example, how Henry and Short explicitly incorporate reference group theory and relative deprivation into their theory of suicide. Andrew Henry and James F. Short, Jr., *Suicide and Homicide*, Glencoe, Ill.: The Free Press, 1954, pp. 56–59.

[4] Svend Ranulf, *Moral Indignation and Middle-Class Psychology: A Sociological Study*, Copenhagen: Levin and Munksgaard, 1938.

source of strain! One may also join with others in righteous puritanical wrath to mete out punishment to the deviants, not so much to stamp out their deviant behavior, as to reaffirm the central importance of conformity as the basis for judging men and to reassure himself and others of his attachment to goodness. One may even make a virtue of tolerance and indulgence of others' moral deficiencies, thereby implicitly calling attention to one's own special strength of character. If the weakness of others is only human, then there is something more than human about one's own strength. On the other hand, one might join the profligate.

What I have said here is relevant to social control, but my concern at present is not with social control but with some of the ways in which deviance of others may aggravate or lighten the burdens of conformity and hence the strain that is so central to anomie theory.

The student of Merton will recognize that some of these points are suggested or even developed at some length here and there in Merton's own writing. Merton is, of course, one of the chief architects of reference group theory, and in his chapter on "Continuities in the Theory of Reference Groups and Social Structure," he has a section entitled "Nonconformity as a Type of Reference Group Behavior."[5] There he recognizes the problems that one actor's deviance creates for others, and he explicitly calls attention to Ranulf's treatment of disinterested moral indignation as a way of dealing with this problem.[6] In "Continuities in the Theory of Social Structure and Anomie," he describes how the deviance of some increases the others' vulnerability to deviance.[7] In short, my characterization of the earliest version of "Social Structure and Anomie" as "atomistic and individualistic" would be a gross misrepresentation if it were applied to the total corpus of Merton's writing on deviance. He has not, however, developed the role of comparison processes in the determination of strain or considered it explicitly in the context of anomie theory. And in general, Merton does not identify the complexities and subtleties of the concept strain as a problem area in their own right.

Finally, in connection with the concept strain, attention should be called to Smelser's treatment of the subject in his *Theory of Collective Behavior*.[8] Although Smelser does not deal with this as it bears on a theory of deviance, it is important here for two reasons. First, it is, to my knowledge, the only attempt in the literature to generate a systematic classification of types of strain, of which Merton's disjunction between goals and means is only one. The second reason is Smelser's emphasis that to account for

[5] *Social Theory and Social Structure, op. cit.*, pp. 357–368.

[6] *Ibid.*, pp. 361–362.

[7] *Ibid.*, pp. 179–181.

[8] Neil J. Smelser, *Theory of Collective Behavior*, New York: The Free Press of Glencoe, 1963, esp. Ch. 3.

collective behavior, one must *start with* strain, but one's theory must also specify a hierarchy of constraints, each of which further narrows the range of possible responses to strain, and the last of which rules out all alternatives but collective behavior. If the "value-added" method is sound for a theory of collective behavior, it may also be useful for a theory of deviance, starting from the concept strain, and constructed on the same model.

Now, *given strain*, what will a person do about it? In general, Merton's chief concern has been with the structural factors that account for variations in strain. On the matter of choice of solution, as on other matters, he has some perceptive observations,[9] but it has remained for others to develop these systematically. In particular, in the original version of his theory each person seems to work out his solution by himself, as though it did not matter what other people were doing. Perhaps Merton assumed such intervening variables as deviant role models, without going into the mechanics of them. But it is one thing to assume that such variables are operating; it is quite another to treat them explicitly in a way that is integrated with the more general theory. Those who continue the anomie tradition, however—most notably Merton's student, Cloward—have done much to fill this gap. Cloward, with Ohlin,[10] has accomplished this in large part by linking anomie theory with another and older theoretical tradition, associated with Sutherland, Shaw and McKay, and Kobrin—the "cultural transmission" and "differential association" tradition of the "Chicago school." Cloward and Ohlin also link anomie theory to a more recent theoretical development, the general theory of subcultures, and especially the aspect of the theory that is concerned with the emergence and development of new subcultural forms.[11] What these other theories have in common is an insistence that deviant as well as nondeviant action is typically not contrived within the solitary individual psyche, but is part of a collaborative *social* activity, in which the things that other people say and do give meaning, value, and effect to one's own behavior.

The incorporation of this recognition into anomie theory is the principal significance of Cloward's notion of illegitimate opportunity structures. These opportunity structures are going social concerns in the individual's milieu, which provide opportunities to learn and to perform deviant actions and lend moral support to the deviant when he breaks with conventional norms and goals.

This is the explicit link with the cultural transmission—differential association tradition. The argument is carried a step farther with the recognition that, even in the absence of an already established deviant culture and

[9] *Social Theory and Social Structure, op. cit.,* p. 151.

[10] Cloward, *op. cit.*, and Richard A. Cloward and Lloyd E. Ohlin, *Delinquency and Opportunity, A Theory of Delinquent Gangs,* Glencoe, Ill.: The Free Press, 1960.

[11] *Ibid.*

social organization, a number of individuals with like problems and in effective communication with one another may join together to do what no one can do alone. They may provide one another with reference objects, collectively contrive a subculture to replace or neutralize the conventional culture, and support and shield one another in their deviance. This is the explicit link to the newer theory of subcultures.[12]

There is one more step in this direction that has not been so explicitly taken. Those who join hands in deviant enterprises need not be people with like problems, nor need their deviance be of the same sort. Within the framework of anomie theory, we may think of these people as individuals with quite variant problems or strains which lend themselves to a common solution, but a common solution in which each participates in different ways. I have in mind the brothel keeper and the crooked policeman, the black marketeer and his customer, the desperate student and the term paper merchant, the bookie and the wire services. These do not necessarily constitute solidary collectivities, like delinquent gangs, but they are structures of action with a division of labor through which each, by his deviance, serves the interests of the others. Theirs is an "organic solidarity," in contrast to the "mechanical solidarity" of Cloward and Ohlin's gangs. Some of Merton's own writing on functionalism—for example, his discussion of the exchange of services involved in political corruption—is extremely relevant here, but it is not explicitly integrated into his anomie theory.[13]

THE ASSUMPTION OF DISCONTINUITY

To say that anomie theory suffers from the assumption of discontinuity is to imply that it treats the deviant act as though it were an abrupt change of state, a leap from a state of strain or anomie to a state of deviance. Although this overstates the weakness in Merton's theory the expression, "the assumption of discontinuity," does have the heuristic value of drawing attention to an important difference in emphasis between anomie theory and other traditions in American sociology, and to the direction of movement in anomie theory itself. Human action, deviant or otherwise, is something that typically develops and grows in a tentative, groping, advancing, backtracking, sounding-out process. People taste and feel their way along. They begin an act and do not complete it. They start doing one thing and end up by doing another. They extricate themselves from progressive involvement or become further involved to the point of commitment. These processes of progressive involvement and disinvolvement are important

[12] Albert K. Cohen, *Delinquent Boys, The Culture of the Gang*, Glencoe, Ill.: The Free Press, Ch. 3, and Merton, *Social Theory and Social Structure, op. cit.*, p. 179.
[13] *Social Theory and Social Structure, op. cit.*, pp. 71–82.

enough to deserve explicit recognition and treatment in their own right. They are themselves subject to normative regulation and structural constraint in complex ways about which we have much to learn. Until recently, however, the dominant bias in American sociology has been toward formulating theory in terms of variables that describe initial states, on the one hand, and outcomes, on the other, rather than in terms of processes whereby acts and complex structures of action are built, elaborated, and transformed. Notable exceptions are interaction process analysis,[14] the brand of action theory represented by Herbert Blumer,[15] and the descriptions of deviance by Talcott Parsons[16] and by Howard Becker.[17] Anomie theory has taken increasing cognizance of such processes. Cloward and Merton both point out, for example, that behavior may move through "patterned sequences of deviant roles" and from "one type of adaptation to another."[18] But this hardly does justice to the microsociology of the deviant act. It suggests a series of discontinuous leaps from one deviant state to another almost as much as it does the kind of process I have in mind.

RESPONSES TO DEVIANCE

Very closely related to the foregoing point is the conception of the development of the act as a feedback, or, in more traditional language, interaction process. The history of a deviant act is a history of an interaction process. The antecedents of the act are an unfolding sequence of acts contributed by a set of actors. A makes a move, possibly in a deviant direction; B responds; A responds to B's responses, etc. In the course of this interaction, movement in a deviant direction may become more explicit, elaborated, definitive—or it may not. Although the act may be socially ascribed to only one of them, both ego and alter help to shape it. The starting point of anomie theory was the question, "*Given* the social structure, or ego's milieu, what will ego do?" The milieu was taken as more-or-less given, an independent variable whose value is fixed, and ego's behavior as an adaptation, or perhaps a series of adaptations, to that milieu. Anomie theory has come increasingly to recognize the effects of deviance upon the very vari-

[14] Robert F. Bales, *Interaction Process Analysis: A Method for the Study of Small Groups*, Cambridge: Addison-Wesley, 1950.

[15] Herbert Blumer, "Society as Symbolic Interaction," in Arnold M. Rose (ed.), *Human Behavior and Social Processes*, Boston: Houghton, Mifflin, 1962, pp. 179–192.

[16] Talcott Parsons, *The Social System*, Glencoe, Ill.: The Free Press, 1951, Ch. 7.

[17] Howard S. Becker, *Outsiders: Studies in the Sociology of Deviance*, New York: The Free Press of Glencoe, 1963, esp. Ch. 2.

[18] Merton, *Social Theory and Social Structure, op. cit.*, p. 152; Cloward, *op. cit.*, p. 175; Cloward and Ohlin, *op. cit.*, pp. 179–184; Merton, "Conformity, Deviation, and Opportunity-Structures," *op. cit.*, p. 188.

ables that determine deviance. But if we are interested in a general theory of deviant behavior we must explore much more systematically ways of conceptualizing the *interaction* between deviance and milieu.[19] I suggest the following such lines of exploration.

If ego's behavior can be conceptualized in terms of acceptance and rejection of goals and means, the same can be done with alter's responses. Responses to deviance can no more be left normatively unregulated than deviance itself. Whose business it is to intervene, at what point, and what he may or may not do is defined by a normatively established division of labor. In short, for any given role—parent, priest, psychiatrist, neighbor, policeman, judge—the norms prescribe, with varying degrees of definiteness, *what* they are supposed to do and *how* they are supposed to do it when other persons, in specified roles, misbehave. The culture prescribes goals and regulates the choice of means. Members of ego's role set can stray from cultural prescriptions in all the ways that ego can. They may overemphasize the goals and neglect the normative restrictions, they may adhere ritualistically to the normatively approved means and neglect the goals, and so forth. I have spelled out the five possibilities on alter's side more fully elsewhere.[20] The theoretical value of applying Merton's modes of adaptation to responses to deviant acts is not fully clear; yet it seems worthy of exploration for at least two reasons.

First, *one* determinant of ego's response to alter's attempts at control, and of the responses of third parties whom ego or alter might call to their aid, is certainly the perceived legitimacy of alter's behavior. Whether ego yields or resists, plays the part of the good loser or the abused victim, takes his medicine or is driven to aggravated deviance, depends in part on whether alter has the right to do what he does, whether the response is proportional to the offense, and so on.

Normative rules also regulate the deviant's response to the intervention of control agents. How the control agent responds to the deviant, after the first confrontation, depends on his perception of the legitimacy of the deviant's response *to him*, and not only on the nature of the original deviant act. For example, this perceived legitimacy plays an important part in police dispositions of cases coming to their attention.

This approach also directs attention to strain in alter's role, the adequacy of *his* resources relative to the responsibilities with which he is charged by virtue of his role, and the illegitimate opportunities available to *him*. A

---

[19] Dubin, *op. cit.*, esp. p. 151, and Merton's remarks on "typology of responses to deviant behavior," in his "Conformity, Deviation, and Opportunity-Structures," *op. cit.*, pp. 185–186.

[20] Albert K. Cohen, "The Study of Social Disorganization and Deviant Behavior," in Robert K. Merton, Leonard Broom, and Leonard S. Cottrell, Jr. (eds.), *Sociology Today*, New York: Basic Books, 1959, pp. 464–465.

familiar example would be the normative restrictions on the means police may consider effective to do the job with which they are charged, and variations in the availability to them of various illegitimate means to the same end.

The disjunction between goals and means and the choice of adaptations depend on the opportunity structure. The opportunity structure consists in or is the result of the actions of other people. These in turn are in part reactions to ego's behavior and may undergo change in response to that behvaior. The development of ego's action can, therefore, be conceptualized as a series of responses, on the part of ego, to a series of changes in the opportunity structure resulting from ego's actions. More specifically, alter's responses may open up, close off, or leave unaffected legitimate opportunities for ego, and they may do the same to illegitimate opportunities. The following simplified table reduces the possibilities to four.

RESPONSES OF THE OPPORTUNITY
STRUCTURE TO EGO'S DEVIANCE

	Legitimate Opportunities	Illegitimate Opportunities
Open up	I	II
Close off	III	IV

I. *Open up legitimate opportunities.* Special efforts may be made to find employment opportunities for delinquents and criminals. On an individual basis this has long been one of the chief tasks of probation officers. On a mass basis it has become more and more prominent in community-wide efforts to reduce delinquency rates.

Black markets may sometimes be reduced by making more of the product available in the legal market or by reducing the pressure on the legal supply through rationing.

Several years ago the Indiana University faculty had a high rate of violation of campus parking regulations, in part because of the disjunction between the demand for parking spaces and the supply. The virtuous left early for work and hunted wearily for legitimate parking spaces. The contemptuous parked anywhere and sneered at tickets. One response to this situation was to create new parking lots and to expand old ones. Since the new parking spaces were available to all, and not only to the former violators, this provides a clear instance where the virtuous—or perhaps the timid—as well as the deviants themselves are the beneficiaries of deviance.[21]

II. *Open up illegitimate opportunities.* Alter, instead of fighting ego, may facilitate his deviance by joining him in some sort of collusive illicit

[21] William J. Chambliss, *The Deterrent Influence of Punishment: A Study of the Violation of Parking Regulations*, M.A. thesis (sociology), Indiana University, 1960.

arrangement from which both profit. The racketeer and the law enforcement officer, the convict and the guard, the highway speeder and the traffic policeman, may arrive at an understanding to reduce the cost of deviance.

Alter, whether he be a discouraged parent, a law enforcement official, or a dean of students, may simply give up efforts systematically to enforce a rule and limit himself to sporadic, token gestures.

An important element in Cloward and Ohlin's theory of delinquent subcultures is that those who run the criminal syndicates are ever alert for promising employees, and that a certain number of those who demonstrate proficiency in the more juvenile forms of crime will be given jobs in the criminal organization.

III. *Closing off legitimate opportunities.* The example that comes most readily to mind is what Tannenbaum calls the "dramatization of evil."[22] A deviant act, if undetected or ignored, might not be repeated. On the other hand, others might react to it by publicly defining the actor as a delinquent, a fallen woman, a criminal. These definitions ascribe to him a social role, change his public image, and activate a set of appropriate responses. These responses may include exclusion from avenues of legitimate opportunity formerly open to him, and thus enhance the relative attractiveness of the illegitimate.

IV. *Closing off illegitimate opportunities.* This is what we usually think of first when we think about "social control." It includes increasing surveillance, locking the door, increasing the certainty and severity of punishment, cutting off access to necessary supplies, knocking out the fix. These measures may or may not achieve the intended effect. On the one hand, they make deviance more difficult. On the other hand, they may stimulate the deviant, or the deviant coalition, to ingenuity in devising new means to circumvent the new restrictions.

The table is a way of conceptualizing alter's actions. The same alter might respond simultaneously in different cells of the table, as may different alters, and these responses might reinforce or counteract one another. Responses might fall in different cells at different stages of the interaction process. In any case, as soon as we conceive of the opportunity structure as a dependent as well as an independent variable, this way of thinking suggests itself as a logical extension of the anomie schema.

Parsons' paradigm of social control is in his opinion applicable not only to deviance, but also to therapy and rehabilitative processes in general. According to this paradigm, the key elements in alter's behavior are support, permissiveness, denial of reciprocity, and rewards, judiciously balanced, and strategically timed and geared to the development of ego's behavior.[23] To

---

[22] Frank Tannenbaum, *Crime and the Community*, New York: Ginn, 1938, Ch. 7.
[23] *Op. cit.*, pp. 297–325.

exploit the possibilities of this and other paradigms of control, one must define more precisely these categories of alter's behavior, develop relevant ways of coding ego's responses to alter's responses, and investigate both theoretically and empirically the structure of extended interaction processes conceptualized in these terms.

Finally, the interaction process may be analyzed from the standpoint of its consequences for stability or change in the normative structure itself. Every act of deviance can be thought of as a pressure on the normative structure, a test of its limits, an exploration of its meaning, a challenge to its validity. Responses to deviance may reaffirm or shore up the normative structure; they may be ritual dramatizations of the seriousness with which the community takes violations of its norms. Or deviance may prompt re-examination of the boundaries of the normatively permissible, resulting in either explicit reformulation of the rule or implicit changes in its meaning, so that the deviant becomes redefined as nondeviant, or the nondeviant as deviant. Thus deviance may be reduced or increased by changes in the norms.[24] These processes go on within the household, courts of law, administrative agencies, and legislative chambers, but also in the mass media, the streets, and the other forums in which "public opinion" is shaped. Although these processes may be punctuated by dramatic, definitive events, like the passage of a new law or the promulgation of a new set of regulations on allowable income tax deductions, the pressure of deviance on the normative structure and the responses of the normative structure to deviance constitute continuing, uninterrupted, interaction processes. One goal of deviance theory is to determine under what conditions feedback circuits promote change and under what conditions they inhibit change in the normative structure.

In this connection, one of Merton's most perceptive and fruitful distinctions is that between the "nonconformist" and other types of deviant.[25] Whereas the criminal and others typically *violate* the norms in pursuit of their own ends, but in no sense seek to *change* those norms (though such change might very well be an unanticipated consequence of their cumulative deviance), the nonconformist's objective is precisely to change the normative system itself. This distinction suggests, in turn, the concept of the "test case" (which need not be limited to the context of legal norms and the formal judicial system)—*i.e.*, the act openly committed, with the intention of forcing a clarification or redefinition of the norms. What we must not overlook, however, is that *any* deviant act, whatever its intention, may, in a sense, function as a test case.

[24] Theodore M. Mills, "Equilibrium and the Processes of Deviance and Control," *American Sociological Review*, 24 (October, 1959), pp. 671–679.

[25] Merton, *Social Theory and Social Structure, op. cit.*, pp. 360–368; Robert K. Merton and Robert A. Nisbet, *Contemporary Social Problems*, New York: Harcourt, Brace, 1961, pp. 725–728.

DEVIANCE AND SOCIAL IDENTITY

There is another piece of unfinished business before anomie theory, and that is to establish a more complete and successful union with role theory and theory of the self. The starting point of Merton's theory is the means-ends schema. His *dramatis personae* are cultural goals, institutional norms, and the situation of action, consisting of means and conditions. The disjunction between goals and means provides the motive force behind action. Deviance is an effort to reduce this disjunction and re-establish an equilibrium between goals and means. It issues from tension; it is an attempt to reduce tension. Roles figure in this theory as a locational grid. They are the positions in the social structure among which goals, norms and means are distributed, where such disjunctions are located and such adaptations carried out.

Another starting point for a theory of deviant behavior grows out of the social theory of George Herbert Mead. This starting point is the actor engaged in an ongoing process of finding, building, testing, validating, and expressing a self. The self is linked to roles, but not primarily in a locational sense. Roles enter, in a very integral and dynamic way, into the very structure of the self. They are part of the categorical system of a society, the socially recognized and meaningful categories of persons. They are the kinds of people it is possible to be in that society. The self is constructed of these possibilities, or some organization of these possibilities. One establishes a self by successfully claiming membership in such categories.[26]

To validate such a claim one must know the social meaning of membership in such roles: the criteria by which they are assigned, the qualities or behavior that function as signs of membership, the characteristics that measure adequacy in the roles. These meanings must be learned. To some degree, this learning may be accomplished before one has identified or even toyed with the roles. Such learning Merton has called anticipatory socialization. To some degree, however, it continues even after one has become more or less committed to a role, in the process of presenting one's self, experiencing and reading the feedback, and correcting one's notion of what it is to be that kind of person. An actor learns that the behavior signifying membership in a particular role includes the kinds of clothes he wears, his posture and gait, his likes and dislikes, what he talks about and the opinions he expresses—everything that goes into what we call the style of life. Such aspects of behavior are difficult to conceptualize as either goals or means;

[26] George Herbert Mead, *Mind, Self, and Society*, Chicago: University of Chicago Press, 1934; Erving Goffman, *The Presentation of Self in Everyday Life*, New York: Doubleday Anchor, 1959, and *Stigma, Notes on the Management of Spoiled Identity*, Englewood Cliffs, N.J.: Prentice-Hall, 1963.

in terms of their relation to the role, at least, their function is better described as expressive or symbolic. But the same can be said even of the goals one pursues and the means one employs; they too may communicate and confirm an identity.

Now, *given* a role, and *given* the orientations to goals and to means that have been assumed because they are part of the social definition of that role, there may be a disjunction between goals and means. Much of what we call deviant behavior arises as a way of dealing with this disjunction. As anomie theory has been formally stated, this is where it seems to apply. But much deviant behavior cannot readily be formulated in these terms at all. Some of it, for example, is directly expressive of the roles. A tough and bellicose posture, the use of obscene language, participation in illicit sexual activity, the immoderate consumption of alcohol, the deliberate flouting of legality and authority, a generalized disrespect for the sacred symbols of the "square" world, a taste for marijuana, even suicide—all of these may have the primary function of affirming, in the language of gesture and deed, that one is a certain kind of person. The message-symbol relationship, or that of claim and evidence, seems to fit this behavior better than the ends-means relationship.

Sexual seduction, for example, may be thought of as illicit means to the achievement of a goal. The point is, however, that the seduction need not be an adaptation to the insufficiency of other means, a response to disjunction. One may cultivate the art of seduction because this sort of expertise is directly significant of a coveted role. Indeed, the very value and meaning of the prize are conferred by the means employed. One could, of course, say that the expertise is itself the goal, but then it is still a goal that expresses and testifies to a role. Finally, one could say that the goal of the act is to validate the role, and all these kinds of behavior are means to this end. I think this statement is plausible and can be defended. If it *is* the intent of anomie theory, then the language of tension reduction does not seem to fit very well. The relation I have in mind, between deviant act and social role, is like the relation between pipe and elbow patches and the professional role. Like the professor's behavior, it is not necessarily a *pis aller*, a means that one has hit on after others have failed. It commends itself, it is gratifying, because it seems so right—not in a moral sense, but in the sense that it fits so well with the image one would like to have of oneself.

One important implication of this view is that it shifts the focus of theory and reseach from the disjunction and its resolution to the process of progressive involvement in, commitment to, and movement among social roles, and the processes whereby one learns the behavior that is significant of the roles. One may, like the child acquiring his sex identity, come to accept and identify with a role before he is quite clear what it means to be that sort of person, how one goes about being one. But once one has established the identity, he has an interest in learning these things and making use of that learning. Thus Howard Becker's dance band musicians arrive at that estate by various routes. For many of them, however, it is only as this identity is crystallizing that they fully learn what being a musician means within the world of musicians. They discover, so to speak, what they are, and what they are turns out to be highly unconventional people.[27] We seek roles for various reasons, some of them having little to do with tension reduction, and having found the role, come into unanticipated legacies of deviant behavior.

The same processes operate in movement in the other direction, toward restoration to conformity. They are most dramatically illustrated in religious conversion. As the sinner is born again, with a new identity fashioned out of new roles, whole bundles of behavior, not all of them deviant, are cast aside, and new bundles are picked up. Relatively little may be learned by examining, one at a time, the items these bundles contain, the sense in which they constitute means to ends, and their adequacy to their respective goals. The decisive event is the transformation of self and social identity. At that moment a wholesale transformation of behavior is determined.

Anomie theory is, perhaps, concerned with *one* structural source of deviance, while the ideas just presented are concerned with another. Neither one need be more faithful to reality than the other, and the defense of one need not be a challenge to the other. But those who are interested in the development of a general theory of deviance can hardly let matters stand at that. Is it possible to make any general statements about the kinds of deviance that may be attributed to anomie and the kinds that may be attributed to role validation through behavior culturally significant of membership in the role? Or may two instances of *any* sort of deviant behavior, identical in their manifest or "phenotypic" content, differ in their sources or "genotypic" structure?

Ultimately, however we must investigate the possible ways in which the two kinds or sources of deviance interact or interpenetrate. For example, does role symbolism function as a structural constraint on the choice of means, and instrumental or means-ends considerations as a structural constraint on the choice of expressive symbolism? Does behavior that originates as a characteristic adaptation to the anomie associated with a particular role, come in time to signify membership in that role and thereby to exercise a secondary or even independent attraction or repulsion, depending on one's orientation toward the role itself? Finally, is it possible that in any instance of deviant behavior, or, for that matter, *any* behavior, both processes are intertwined in ways that cannot be adequately described in terms of presently available modes of conceptualization? I suggest that we must bring the two schemes into more direct and explicit confrontation and try to evolve a formulation that will fuse and harness the power of both.

[27] Howard S. Becker, *op. cit.*, Ch. 5.

PART VIII

Formal and Informal Organizations of Delinquents and Criminals

Introduction

It is sometimes assumed that lawbreakers have common values, common attitudes, and common rules for behavior. This assumption is usually apparent whenever the word "underworld" is used, for this term signifies a different (and baser) society with its own culture and social organization. We have seen, however, that the rules of conduct among criminals are somewhat specific, one set of rules supporting one kind of criminality and another set of rules supporting a different variety of criminal behavior.

The interaction of delinquents and criminals which maintains the varied delinquent subcultures and criminal value systems described in preceding sections has also produced a variety of stabilized patterns of interaction that give continuity and structure to certain delinquent and criminal enterprises. In some cases, "structure" means a cluster of role-relationships that are established as interaction patterns become routinized. "Street corner groups" have structures of this kind. In other cases, "structure" means a particular collection of role-relationships that has come to be seen by the role incumbents as serving express purposes. Such structures may then allocate certain tasks to certain members, limit entrance, and influence the rules established for their own maintenance and survival. As structures move toward this later stage of development, they become "formal" organizations rather than "informal" organizations.

A structure of role-relationships, criminal or otherwise, that has moved to the point where it can be designated a "formal" organization has three characteristics: (1) It has a division of labor (occupational specialization). (2) The members' activities are coordinated by rules, agreements, and understandings which support the structure. (3) The entire enterprise is rationally designed to achieve announced objectives.[1]

These features are matters of degree. In the selections that follow, it will be seen that variations in the degree to which they are present affect the character of the criminal or delinquent organization involved. There is, for example, the criminal syndicate in which members' organizational activities are tightly coordinated and controlled, not only by the structure itself, but also by a criminal code, the values and rules of which govern many of the interpersonal relationships in which members engage off the job. Then there is the pickpocket mob which has a rather precise division of labor and rather careful coordination of organizational activities, but where controls over job responsibilities and daily activities are not as extensive or as precise as they are in criminal syndicates. And there is the illegitimate cartel made up of legitimate businesses acting illegitimately; here the members retain their identities as "good citizens" and "respected businessmen" while engaging in a specific kind of organized illegal activity "only when necessary."

In structures of role-relationships which have more to do with social relationships and life styles than with occupational specialization, the term "informal organization" is most appropriate. The group activities of "righteous dope fiends," of "retreatist gangs," and of "cool cats" are examples of ongoing informal social structures with distinctive styles of language, clothing, and definitions of appropriate behavior all of which are underwritten by special vocabularies of motives. The distinction between these informally organized structures and formal organizations becomes evident when it is noted that in none of these three groups of drug users are the activities organized around a rationally planned and coordinated effort to achieve specific goals. The groups are not even organized to secure a constant and safe source of drugs. The distribution and sale of drugs is the business of formally organized criminal groups, but those who use drugs are not necessarily members.

Somewhere between criminal syndicates and social groups of drug users is the delinquent gang oriented to theft. These organizations have both formal and informal aspects. Criminal activities are rationally planned and coordinated, and assignments to perform specific tasks related to theft are given to gang members. But the ultimate ambition of the members is to move out of the gang and into a career in criminal syndicates. The stealing gang is an organization comprised of lower-class boys who

---

[1] Cf. S. J. Udy, Jr., "The Comparative Analysis of Organizations," Chapter 16 in James G. March, ed., *Handbook of Organizations* (Chicago: Rand McNally, 1965), p. 687.

find in joint activity not only agreeable social relationships but also the satisfaction of learning skills which make them eligible to participate in illegitimate opportunity structures. Although the stealing gang is not purposively designed to educate boys in the ways of theft, it nevertheless does so. The theft gang shows clearly that the transition from generalized social activity to occupational careers and efforts to achieve specific goals involves rational planning and thus the establishment of formally organized structures.

Gangs are significant in delinquency causation and crime causation because they are ongoing systems which exist independently of their current membership. As organizations they are not, to be sure, as rational as, say, General Electric. But they do consist of divisions of labor designed to facilitate certain ends such as stealing, fighting, or drug use. Cloward and Ohlin point out that lower-class boys are able to achieve these objectives through the formation of juvenile gangs, and that, in addition, gangs enable the boys to resolve status frustrations. Some lower-class boys who find themselves at a competitive disadvantage in gaining access to the legitimate routes to success attribute to their own conduct their failure to achieve the goals of conventional society. To cope with this "inadequacy," they learn to revise their aspirations downward and to accommodate themselves to the world of inconsistencies in which they live. Other boys, on the other hand, develop the sense of injustice that springs from knowledge that they are being discriminated against. But even status frustration followed by feelings of unjust deprivation does not require that delinquency or the structure of roles making up a delinquent gang must appear. If a boy has learned to attribute his failure to injustices in the social system, he might take one of at least three paths: (1) He might bend his efforts to reforming the social order by peaceful and legal means; (2) he might dissociate himself from the social order in a manner which is not illegal, such as becoming a hermit or a member of a religious cult; or (3) he might react against the system in a manner which is illegal, such as resorting to theft, to violence, or to drug use.

There are, then, alternatives to delinquency, and the course taken by any individual boy will depend first of all upon which behavior patterns are available as models. Secondly, no matter which path the frustrated boy takes, he may find reassurance for his action by, as Cloward and Ohlin put it, "searching out others who have faced similar experiences and who will support one another in common attitudes of alienation from the official system."[2] The gang-formation process becomes complete when a frustrated individual becomes delinquent and joins with others who have reacted to frustrating conditions in the same way. Similarly, when a frus-

---

[2] See "The Evolution of Delinquent Subcultures" in Part VII, above.

trated individual becomes a social reformer or a religious fanatic and joins with others like himself, different, but nevertheless organized, groups are also established. In all of these cases, an organization has been purposely designed to achieve limited objectives.

An important question here is the same one raised in our introduction to Part V, namely to what degree do delinquent gang members consciously identify and attribute their need to engage in illegal behavior to "status frustration"? Several selections have included discussions of this question, notably Hartung's review of Sykes and Matza's "techniques of neutralization" and the Schwendingers' discussion of delinquent vocabularies of motive.[3] Here it can be noted that delinquent and criminal vocabularies have come to include the language of sociologists and psychologists—from "minority group discrimination" to "problems with authority figures." The constant public debate and discussion of minority group problems, poverty programs, and the disadvantages of dropping out of school have enabled delinquents to "explain" their activities, whether they be devoted to stealing, fighting, or using drugs, in much more sophisticated language than that contained in old-fashioned phrases such as "for the fun of it" or "for kicks." The new language of delinquents stresses social, economic, political, and psychological justifications for behavior. It should not be assumed, however, that these conditions are consciously identified and constitute the basis for organizing delinquent activity. Gang members are not necessarily aware that gangs may be a way of combating status frustration. This function is based on analysis by sociologists, not by participants.

Cloward and Ohlin and Spergel treat delinquent gangs as rational systems whose goals and structures are affected, if not determined, by the social environment in which they arise. Gangs oriented to committing property offenses develop in areas in which the criminality of adults makes readily available both the norms and rules favorable to the commission of property offenses and the opportunities for displaying endorsement and adoption of these rules. Gangs oriented to "bopping" (gang fighting) develop in areas where access to legitimate channels to success goals is denied, as in the case of gangs oriented to stealing, but where the conduct norms support violent actions rather than property crimes. Gangs oriented to "retreatism" in the form of drug use develop among persons faced with failure both in their efforts to use legitimate means and in their efforts to use illegitimate means for achieving success.[4] These three types of gangs should not be regarded as mutually exclusive, since there is overlap of the kinds of activities in some gangs, and the areas from which

[3] See "A Vocabulary of Motives for Law Violations" and "Delinquent Stereotypes of Probable Victims" in Part V, above.

[4] See "Illegitimate Means, Anomie, and Deviant Behavior in Part IV, above.

the three types emerge contain some norms relevant to the development of each type.

The selections by Finestone and Sutter, however, question the notion that drug users are essentially "double failures" who are trying to get away from it all. Finestone agrees that the role of the young Negro "cat" is the product of a subculture which arises in response to status deprivation and exclusion from many middle-class socializing experiences. But the "cat" can hardly be viewed as a retreatist. The main features of his world are the "hustle" and the "kick." The former involves his activities as a pimp; the latter involves relationships related to drug use. Both are essential elements of a "cool" style of living and require that the "cat" be involved with, not withdrawn from, the people around him. He must struggle to get what he needs and keep what he has—just as a nonaddict struggles to maintain his style of living. Finestone points out that the common stereotype of the young Negro addict as a pitiful figure does not correspond to the addict's self-image nor to the image of himself that he tries to convey to others. Current conceptions of an "addict subculture," thus, do not adequately depict the world of the "righteous dope fiend," who has mastered the art of "hustling." The notion that members of the addict subculture always select a retreatist role does not fit the "player" nor the "hustler," social types described in the selection written especially for this volume by Sutter. There are several addict subcultures, but the "righteous dope fiend" becomes a retreatist only when he becomes a "sick addict" or an "ex-dope fiend."

Further evidence that few real retreatist gangs actually exist has been provided by Short and his associates, who had to search Chicago for a year before locating a gang that could be so identified.[5] Perhaps this means that the rules for retreating to drugs are not as clearly formulated as are, say, the rules for "bopping." It seems likely that such groups are harder to find than the theory would suggest because some forms of drug use do not involve retreatism in the sense of withdrawal from active participation in ongoing social structures.

The selection by Spergel notes that there is a continuum of informal and formal structure—a continuum of rationality—even within delinquent gangs. Gangs oriented to "bopping" have a hierarchal structure, including a president, a vice-president, a war chief, and an armorer. Their activities are systematic and ritualized, but their goals are not precise. Accordingly, their structure is not tightly integrated. Gangs oriented to stealing and robbery are more rational, but even here the degree of rationality varies with the traditions of the people in the social areas sup-

[5] James F. Short, Jr., Ray A. Tennyson, and Kenneth I. Howard, "Behavior Dimensions of Gang Delinquency," *American Sociological Review, 28* (June, 1963), 411–428.

porting them. As Spergel says, "The burglary or theft pattern represented a more systematic and purposeful orientation in Haulburg than in other areas." Finally, boys oriented to the "rackets" (Spergel does not describe them as "gangs") are rationally organized for making illegal profits. While upper-echelon positions in organized crime are not necessarily available to lower-class delinquent boys, these boys know of the criminal organization and aspire to membership in it. A few of the boys in some neighborhoods are given opportunities to prepare for roles in organized crime by performing seemingly minor errands. The delinquents growing up in the Racketville area where organized criminals were present developed a keen business sense which was not characteristic of the other two types studied by Spergel. The influence of organized crime also is seen in the fact that Racketville youth were "criminally oriented" to a much greater degree than were the youth of the other areas studied. Further, the young men of Racketville believed to a greater degree that having "connections" (as opposed to having "ability," "luck," and "education") is the most important quality for getting ahead. On the other hand, drug use and gang fighting were not regarded as commensurate with the cool, rational approach to life demanded of organized criminals, and these activities occurred in Racketville less frequently than in either Slumtown or Haulburg.

Juvenile gangs, working groups of criminals, criminal syndicates, and legitimate corporations behaving illegitimately—all can be differentiated from less formal criminal groups by the fact that the members of the latter do not participate in a set of positions rationally developed with an eye to efficiency and to continuing operations. Sutherland observed the rationality behind the operations of working groups of criminals in three different contexts.[6] First, the crimes committed by teams of criminals tend to be those whose nature makes it difficult to apprehend and prosecute the perpetrators. Second, the division of labor is such that all incumbents must be skilled in the use of specific techniques which in combination make the whole group's work safe and therefore profitable. And third, in some groups of working criminals, rational organization for safety and profit involves the establishment of at least one position for a "corrupter" and one or more positions for "corruptees." The corruptee position is occupied by public officials who, for a fee, will insure that the group can operate with relative immunity from the penal process. It is as much a part of the criminal organization as is any other position. (The corruptee will be considered further in Part IX.)

Small working groups of criminals are, then, to a greater degree than

---

[6] Edwin H. Sutherland, *The Professional Thief* (Chicago: University of Chicago Press, 1937), pp. 217–218.

juvenile gangs, formal systems with divisions of labor based upon the requirements of specific team operations. Maurer's selection indicates that the fundamental form of organization among pickpockets is the "tribe," "troupe," or "team" of two, three, or four members. The relationships between the men occupying the positions making up the "tribe" are "loose, ephemeral, and highly insecure," but there is organization nevertheless. The duties and responsibilities of each position are finely detailed. There is, for example, a position for a man whose duty it is to locate the prospective victim and distract his attention; a second position calls for a specialist skilled in actually removing the wallet from the victim's pocket; a third position requires skills in receiving the wallet from the man who took it; and a fourth position involves disposal of the stolen goods in legitimate, semilegitimate, or illegitimate channels. The men who fill these positions are specialists, just as in any other organization where a variety of skills are required for effective operations.[7]

The last three selections indicate that American syndicated crime (including some forms of white-collar crime) is a system based on further extension of this rational design for safety and profit. Although it is true that the divisions of labor in La Cosa Nostra and the electrical industry have been designed for the perpetration of crimes, which cannot be profitably undertaken by small working groups of criminals, let alone by criminals working outside an organization, the critical difference is not merely a difference in size. Small firms selling illicit goods and services must, if they are to capitalize on the demand for their wares, expand by establishing a division of labor which includes positions for financiers, purchasing agents, supervisors, transportation specialists, lawyers, accountants, and employee-training specialists. The next rational move is

---

[7] Such specialization by small working groups of criminals was apparent in a "steal-to-order car ring" discussed in a *New York Times* report on November 15, 1967. Ten men were indicted as members of a group that stole automobiles according to prospective customers' specifications.

A "salesman" would get in touch with a prospective customer and give him a choice of make, model, color and such accessories as air-conditioning and whitewall tires. When they had agreed on a purchase price—usually between $2,000 and $3,000 for a car actually worth up to $7,500—the purchaser would pay a downpayment of about $300.

A thief would then steal the car, using either master keys or ignition jumper wires, and deliver the car to the "salesman."

The next day a "paper man" would file a stolen MV 50 certificate of sale with the Motor Vehicle Department. In some cases one digit of the car's serial number would be changed on the form, and in about half the cases, false names and addresses were used for the purchasers.

The "paper man" would then obtain a registration for the car and turn it over to the "salesman." The "salesman" would then deliver the car, providing a false "bill of sale," and receive payment in cash . . .

consolidation and integration of separate operations or organizations into a cartel which minimizes competition and maximizes profits.

This is the kind of organization existing in the United States in the form of geographically-based "families" of criminals of Italian and Sicilian descent, described in the selection by Cressey. Each "family" has its position for "Boss," "Underboss," "Lieutenants," "Soldiers," and other functionaries, and each has a position in the larger cartel or confederation called La Cosa Nostra or, loosely, "organized crime."

This also was the kind of organization involved in the electrical company conspiracy which, as Smith reports, involved at least 45 top management executives of 29 electrical equipment corporations. These men occupied positions in an organization dedicated to systematic violation of the laws prohibiting fixing of prices, rigging of bids, and dividing of markets. It may be argued that the corporations created organizational positions whose incumbents had to violate the law if they were to do their job. In fact, some of the executives occupying these positions claimed that when they violated the law, they were merely carrying out their duties. The federal prosecutors argued that the corporations themselves were guilty of breaking the law and that they were rationally organized for this purpose. It is worth noting, in the light of this argument, that the Internal Revenue Service permitted the corporations to list as "business expenses" the substantial fines they paid.

Cohen has theorized that the pattern of deferred gratification, traditionally a characteristic of the middle class, is breaking down.[8] Even middle-class boys are not as willing as were their fathers and grandfathers to defer gratifications to the distant future. In an economy of scarcity, it "paid" a boy to defer a desire for, say, a new suit or a new car, to save the money and to spend it later for a college education or the expenses of setting up a household. But in an era of affluence, when the status symbols and other good things of life going to persons who defer gratification are barely different from those going to persons who do not, the practice might not seem worth the candle. The distinctions between the "conventional" and the "unconventional," the "respectable" and the "unrespectable," and the "responsible" and the "irresponsible" ways of achieving things are less clear. In effect, more alternative means, some of them delinquent or criminal, for achieving status symbols have been made available to middle-class persons. Conceivably, a structural change of this order is somewhere in the background of white-collar crimes such as those described in the selection by Smith.

[8] Albert K. Cohen, "Middle-Class Delinquency and Social Structure," in Edmund W. Vaz, ed., *Middle-Class Juvenile Delinquency* (New York: Harper and Row, 1967), pp. 203–207.

1 The Differentiation of Delinquent Subcultures

RICHARD A. CLOWARD
LLOYD E. OHLIN

[In the following discussion we shall examine] the specific social conditions that make for the emergence of distinctive delinquent subcultures. Throughout this analysis, we shall make extensive use of [two] concepts of social organization; namely, integration of . . . different age-levels of offenders, and integration of carriers of conventional and deviant values. Delinquent responses vary from one neighborhood to another, we believe, according to the articulation of these structures in the neighborhood. Our object here is to show more precisely how various forms of neighborhood integration affect the development of subcultural content.

THE CRIMINAL SUBCULTURE

The criminal subculture, like the conflict and retreatist adaptations, requires a specialized environment if it is to flourish. Among the environmental supports of a criminal style of life are integration of offenders at various age-levels and close integration of the carriers of conventional and illegitimate values.

Reprinted with permission of The Macmillan Company from *Delinquency and Opportunity: A Theory of Delinquent Gangs* by Richard A. Cloward and Lloyd E. Ohlin. Copyright by The Free Press, a Corporation 1960, pp. 161–186.

Integration of Age-Levels

Nowhere in the criminological literature is the concept of integration between different age-levels of offender made more explicit than in discussions of criminal learning. Most criminologists agree that criminal behavior presupposes patterned sets of relationships through which the requisite values and skills are communicated or transmitted from one age-level to another. What, then, are some of the specific components of systems organized for the socialization of potential criminals?

CRIMINAL ROLE-MODELS. The lower class is not without its own distinctive and indigenous illegitimate success-models. Many accounts in the literature suggest that lower-class adults who have achieved success by illegitimate means not only are highly visible to young people in slum areas but often are willing to establish intimate relationships with these youth.

Every boy has some ideal he looks up to and admires. His ideal may be Babe Ruth, Jack Dempsey, or Al Capone. When I was twelve, we moved into a neighborhood with a lot of gangsters. They were all swell dressers and had big cars and carried "gats." Us kids saw these swell guys and mingled with them in the cigar store on the corner. Jack Gurney was the one in the mob that I had a fancy to. He used to take my sis out and that way I saw him often. He was in the stick-up rackets before he was in the beer rackets, and he was a swell dresser and had lots of dough. . . . I liked to be near him and felt stuck up over the other guys because he came to my home to see my sis.[1]

Just as the middle-class youth, as a consequence of intimate relationships with, say, a banker or a businessman, may aspire to *become* a banker or a businessman, so the lower-class youth may be associated with and aspire to become a "policy king": " 'I want to be a big shot. . . . Have all the guys look up to me. Have a couple of Lincolns, lots of broads, and all the coppers licking my shoes.' "[2] The crucial point here is that success-goals are not equally available to persons in different positions in the social structure. To the extent that social-class lines act as barriers to interaction between persons in different social strata, conventional success-models may not be salient for lower-class youth. The successful criminal, on the other hand, may be an intimate, personal figure in the fabric of the lower-class area. Hence one of the forces leading to rational, disciplined, crime-oriented delinquency may be the availability of criminal success-models.

[1] C. R. Shaw, "Juvenile Delinquency—A Group Tradition," *Bulletin of the State University of Iowa*, No. 23, N. S. No. 700, 1933, p. 8.
[2] *Ibid.*, p. 9.

AGE-GRADING OF CRIMINAL LEARNING AND PERFORMANCE. The process by which the young acquire the values and skills prerequisite for a stable criminal career has been described in many studies. The central mechanism in the learning process is integration of different age-levels of offender. In an extensive study of a criminal gang on the Lower East Side of New York City, Bloch and Niederhoffer found that

. . . the Pirates [a group of young adults] was actually the central organizing committee, the party headquarters for the youthful delinquents in the area. They held regular conferences with the delegates from outlying districts to outline strategy. . . . The younger Corner Boys [a gang of adolescents in the same vicinity] who . . . were trying to join with the older Pirates . . . were on a probationary status. If they showed signs of promise, a couple of them were allowed to accompany the Pirates on tours of exploration to look over the terrain around the next "job."[3]

At the pinnacle of this age-graded system stood an adult, Paulie.

Paulie had real prestige in the gang. His was the final say in all important decisions. Older than the other members [of the Pirates] by seven or eight years, he maintained a certain air of mystery. . . . From talks with more garrulous members, it was learned that Paulie was the mastermind behind some of the gang's most impressive coups.[4]

The basis of Paulie's prestige in the gang is apparent in the following account of his relationship with the full-fledged adult criminal world:

From his contacts, information was obtained as to the most inviting locations to burglarize. It was he who developed the strategy and outlined the major stages of each campaign of burglary or robbery. . . . Another vital duty which he performed was to get rid of the considerable loot, which might consist of jewelry, clothing, tools, or currency in large denominations. His contact with professional gangsters, fences, bookies, made him an ideal choice for this function.[5]

Learning alone, as we have said, does not ensure that the individual can or will perform the role for which he has been prepared. The social structure must also support the actual performance of the role. To say that the individual must have the opportunity to discharge a stable criminal role as well as to prepare for it does not mean that role-preparation necessarily takes place in one stage and role-performance in a succeeding stage. The apprentice may be afforded opportunities to play out a particular role at various points in the learning process.

[3] H. A. Bloch and Arthur Niederhoffer, *The Gang: A Study in Adolescent Behavior* (New York: Philosophical Library, 1958), pp. 198–99.

[4] *Ibid.*, p. 201.

[5] *Ibid.*

When we were shoplifting we always made a game of it. For example, we might gamble on who could steal the most caps in a day, or who could steal in the presence of a detective and then get away. This was the best part of the game. I would go into a store to steal a cap, by trying one on when the clerk was not watching, walk out of the store, leaving the old cap. With the new cap on my head I would go into another store, do the same thing as in the other store, getting a new hat and leaving the one I had taken from the other place. I might do this all day. . . . It was the fun I wanted, not the hat. I kept this up for months and *then began to sell the things to a man on the West Side. It was at this time that I began to steal for gain.*[6]

This quotation illustrates how delinquent role-preparation and role-performance may be integrated even at the "play-group" stage of illegitimate learning. The child has an opportunity to actually perform illegitimate roles because such activity finds support in his immediate neighborhood milieu. The rewards—monetary and other—of successful learning and performance are immediate and gratifying at each age level.

Integration of Values

Unless the carriers of criminal and conventional values are closely bound to one another, stable criminal roles cannot develop. The criminal, like the occupant of a conventional role, must establish relationships with other categories of persons, all of whom contribute in one way or another to the successful performance of criminal activity. As Tannenbaum says, "The development of the criminal career requires and finds in the immediate environment other supporting elements in addition to the active 'criminal gangs'; to develop the career requires the support of middlemen. These may be junk men, fences, lawyers, bondsmen, 'backers,' as they are called."[7] The intricate systems of relationship between these legitimate and illegitimate persons constitute the type of environment in which the juvenile criminal subculture can come into being.[8]

An excellent example of the way in which the content of a delinquent subculture is affected by its location in a particular milieu is afforded by the "fence," a dealer in stolen goods who is found in some but not all lower-class neighborhoods. Relationships between such middlemen and criminals are not confined to adult offenders; numerous accounts of lower-class life

[6] Shaw, *op. cit.*, p. 3. Emphasis added.

[7] Frank Tannenbaum, *Crime and the Community* (New York: Columbia University Press, 1938), p. 60.

[8] In this connection, see R. A. Cloward, "Social Control in the Prison," *Theoretical Studies of the Social Organization of the Prison*, Bulletin No. 15 (New York: Social Science Research Council, March 1960), pp. 20–48, which illustrates similar forms of integration in a penal setting.

suggest not only that relationships form between fences and youngsters but also that the fence is a crucial element in the structure of illegitimate opportunity. He often caters to and encourages delinquent activities among the young. He may even exert controls leading the young to orient their stealing in the most lucrative and least risky directions. The same point may be made of junk dealers in some areas, racketeers who permit minors to run errands, and other occupants of illegitimate or semilegitimate roles.

As the apprentice criminal passes from one status to another in the illegitimate opportunity system, we should expect him to develop an ever-widening set of relationships with members of the semilegitimate and legitimate world. For example, a delinquent who is rising in the structure might begin to come into contact with mature criminals, law-enforcement officials, politicians, bail bondsmen, "fixers," and the like. As his activities become integrated with the activities of these persons, his knowledge of the illegitimate world is deepened, new skills are acquired, and the opportunity to engage in new types of illegitimate activity is enhanced. Unless he can form these relationships, the possibility of a stable, protected criminal style of life is effectively precluded.

The type of environment that encourages a criminal orientation among delinquents is, then, characterized by close integration of the carriers of conventional and illegitimate values. The *content* of the delinquent subculture is a more or less direct response to the local milieu in which it emerges. And it is the "integrated" neighborhood, we suggest, that produces the criminal type of delinquent subculture.

Structural Integration and Social Control

Delinquent behavior generally exhibits a component of aggressiveness. Even youth in neighborhoods that are favorable learning environments for criminal careers are likely to engage in some "bopping" and other forms of violence. Hence one feature of delinquency that must be explained is its tendency toward aggressive behavior. However, aggressiveness is not the primary component of all delinquent behavior; it is much more characteristic of some delinquent groups than of others. Therefore, we must also concern ourselves with the conditions under which the aggressive component becomes ascendant.

The importance of assessing the relative dominance of expressive and instrumental components in delinquent patterns is often overlooked. Cohen. for example, stresses the aggressive or expressive aspect of delinquent behavior, remarking that "it is non-utilitarian, malicious and negativistic," although he also asserts that these traits may not characterize all delinquency. Cohen's tendency to neglect relatively nonaggressive aspects of delinquency is related to his failure to take into account the relationships between delinquent behavior and adult criminality. However, *depending upon the pres-*

ence or absence of those integrative relationships, behavior that appears to be "non-utilitarian" in achieving access to conventional roles may possess considerable utility for securing access to criminal roles. Furthermore, these integrated systems may have important consequences for social control.

To the extent that delinquents take as their primary reference group older and more sophisticated gang boys, or even fully acculturated criminals or racketeers, dramatic instances of "malicious, negativistic" behavior may represent efforts to express solidarity with the norms of the criminal world. Delinquents who so behave in an attempt to win acceptance by older criminals may be engaging in a familiar sociological process; namely, over-conformity to the norms of a group to which they aspire but do not belong. By such overconformity to the norms of the criminal world, delinquents seek to dramatize their eligibility for membership. To an observer oriented toward conventional values, aggressive behavior of this kind might appear to be purposeless. However, from the perspective of the carriers of deviant values, conspicuous defiance of conventional values may validate the "rightness" of the aspirant. Once he has been defined as "right," he may then be selected for further socialization and preparation for mature criminal activity.

Once the delinquent has successfully demonstrated his eligibility for acceptance by persons higher in the criminal structure, social controls are exerted to suppress undisciplined, expressive behavior; there is no place in organized crime for the impulsive, unpredictable individual. A dramatic illustration of the emphasis upon instrumental performance is offered by the case of Murder, Inc. Abe Reles, a former member of the syndicate who turned state's evidence, made certain comments about Murder, Inc. which illustrate perfectly Max Weber's famous characterization of the norms governing role performance and interpersonal relationships in bureaucratic organizations: *"Sine ira et studio"* ("without anger or passion").

The crime trust, Reles insists, never commits murder out of passion, excitement, jealousy, personal revenge, or any of the usual motives which prompt private, unorganized murder. It kills impersonally, and solely for business considerations. Even business rivalry, he adds, is not the usual motive, unless "somebody gets too balky or somebody steps right on top of you." No gangster may kill on his own initiative; every murder must be ordered by the leaders at the top, and it must serve the welfare of the organization. . . . The crime trust insists that that murder must be a business matter, organized by the chiefs in conference and carried out in a disciplined way. "It's a real business all the way through," Reles explains. "It just happens to be that kind of business, but nobody is allowed to kill from personal grievance. There's got to be a good business reason, and top men of the combination must give their okay."[9]

[9] Joseph Freeman, "Murder Monopoly: The Inside Story of a Crime Trust," *The Nation,* Vol. 150, No. 21 (May 25, 1940), p. 648. This is but one of many sources in which the bureaucratization of crime is discussed.

The pressure for rational role performance in the adult criminal world is exerted downward, we suggest, through interconnected systems of age-graded statuses. At each point in this illegitimate hierarchy, instrumental rather than expressive behavior is emphasized. In their description of the Pirates, for example, Bloch and Niederhoffer observe that Paulie, the adult mastermind of the gang, avoided expressive behavior: "The younger Pirates might indulge in wild adolescent antics. Paulie remained aloof."[10] Paulie symbolized a mode of life in which reason, discipline, and foresight were uppermost. To the extent that younger members of the gang identified with him, they were constrained to adopt a similar posture. Rico, the leader of a gang described in a recent book by Harrison Salisbury, can be characterized in much the same way:

This youngster was the most successful kid in the neighborhood. He was a dope pusher. Some weeks he made as much as $200. He used his influence in some surprising ways. He persuaded the gang members to stop bopping because he was afraid it would bring on police intervention and interfere with his drug sales. He flatly refused to sell dope to boys and kicked out of the gang any kid who started to use drugs. He sold only to adults. With his money he bought jackets for the gang, took care of hospital bills of members, paid for the rent on his mother's flat, paid most of the family expenses and sometimes spent sixty dollars to buy a coat as a present for one of his boys.[11]

The same analysis helps to explain a puzzling aspect of delinquent behavior; namely, the apparent disregard delinquents sometimes exhibit for stolen objects. Some theorists have concluded from this that the ends of stealing are not utilitarian, that delinquents do not steal because they need or want the objects in question or for any other rational reason. Cohen, for example, asserts that "were the participant in the delinquent subculture merely employing illicit means to the end of acquiring economic goods, he would show more respect for the goods he has thus acquired."[12] Hence, Cohen concludes, the bulk of stealing among delinquents is "for the hell of it" rather than for economic gain. Whether stealing is expressive or instrumental may depend, however, on the social context in which it occurs. Where criminal opportunities exist, it may be argued that stealing is a way of expressing solidarity with the carriers of criminal values and, further, that it is a way of acquiring the various concrete skills necessary before the potential criminal can gain full acceptance in the group to which he aspires. That is, a certain amount of stealing may be motivated less by

10 Bloch and Niederhoffer, *op. cit.*, p. 201.

11 H. E. Salisbury, *The Shook-up Generation* (New York: Harper & Bros., 1958), p. 176.

12 A. K. Cohen, *Delinquent Boys: The Culture of the Gang* (Glencoe, Ill.: Free Press, 1955), p. 36.

immediate need for the objects in question than by a need to acquire skill in the arts of theft. When practice in theft is the implicit purpose, the manner of disposing of stolen goods is unimportant. Similarly, the status accruing to the pickpocket who can negotiate a "left-front-breech" derives not so much from the immediate profit attaching to this maneuver as from the fact that it marks the individual as a master craftsman. In other words, where criminal learning environments and opportunity structures exist, stealing beyond immediate economic needs may constitute anticipatory socialization. But where these structures do not exist, such stealing may be simply an expressive act in defiance of conventional values.

Shaw pointed to a related aspect of the social control of delinquent behavior. Noting the prestige ordering of criminal activities, he commented on the way in which such definitions, once internalized, tend to regulate the behavior of delinquents:

> It is a matter of significance to note . . . that there is a general tendency among older delinquents and criminals to look with contempt upon the person who specializes in any form of petty stealing. The common thief is not distinguished for manual dexterity and accomplishment, like the pickpocket or mobsman, nor for courage, ingenuity and skill, like the burglar, but is characterized by low cunning and stealth—hence the term "sneak thief." . . . It is possible that the stigma attaching to petty stealing among members of older delinquent groups is one factor which gives impetus to the young delinquent's desire to abandon such forms of petty delinquency as stealing junk, vegetables, breaking into freight cars . . . and to become identified with older groups engaged in such crimes as larceny of automobiles and robbery with a gun, both of which are accredited "rackets" among older delinquents. . . .[13]

To the extent that an area has an age-graded criminal structure in which juvenile delinquents can become enmeshed, we suggest that the norms governing adult criminal-role performance filter down, becoming significant principles in the life-organization of the young. The youngster who has come into contact with such an age-graded structure and who has won initial acceptance by older and more sophisticated delinquents will be less likely to engage in malicious, destructive behavior than in disciplined, instrumental, career-oriented behavior. In this way the adult criminal system exerts controls over the behavior of delinquents. Referring to urban areas characterized by integration of different age-levels of offender, Kobrin makes an observation that tends to bear out our theoretical scheme:

> . . . delinquency tends to occur within a partial framework of social controls, insofar as delinquent activity in these areas represents a tolerated means for the

[13] Shaw, *op. cit.,* p. 10.

acquisition of an approved role and status. Thus, while delinquent activity here possesses the usual characteristics of violence and destructiveness, there tend to develop effective limits of permissible activity in this direction. Delinquency is, in other words, encompassed and contained within a local social structure, and is marginally but palpably related to that structure.[14]

In summary, the criminal subculture is likely to arise in a neighborhood milieu characterized by close bonds between different age-levels of offender, and between criminal and conventional elements. As a consequence of these integrative relationships, a new opportunity structure emerges which provides alternative avenues to success-goals. Hence the pressures generated by restrictions on legitimate access to success-goals are drained off. Social controls over the conduct of the young are effectively exercised, limiting expressive behavior and constraining the discontented to adopt instrumental, if criminalistic, styles of life.

THE CONFLICT SUBCULTURE

Because youngsters caught up in the conflict subculture often endanger their own lives and the lives of others and cause considerable property damage, the conflict form of delinquency is a source of great public concern. Its prevalence, therefore, is probably exaggerated. There is no evidence to suggest that the conflict subculture is more widespread than the other subcultures, but the nature of its activities makes it more visible and thus attracts public attention. As a consequence, many people erroneously equate "delinquency" and "conflict behavior." But whatever its prevalence, the conflict subculture is of both theoretical and social importance, and calls for explanation.

. . . [We question] the common belief that slum areas, because they are slums, are necessarily disorganized. [There are] forms of integration which give some slum areas unity and cohesion. Areas in which these integrative structures are found . . . tend to be characterized by criminal rather than conflict or retreatist subcultures. But not all slums are integrated. Some lower-class urban neighborhoods lack unity and cohesiveness. Because the prerequisites for the emergence of stable systems of social relations are not present, a state of social disorganization prevails.

The many forces making for instability in the social organization of some slum areas include high rates of vertical and geographic mobility; massive housing projects in which "site tenants" are not accorded priority in occupancy, so that traditional residents are dispersed and "strangers"

14 Solomon Kobrin, "The Conflict of Values in Delinquency Areas," *American Sociological Review*, Vol. 16 (Oct. 1951), p. 657.

reassembled; and changing land use, as in the case of residential areas that are encroached upon by the expansion of adjacent commercial or industrial areas. Forces of this kind keep a community off balance, for tentative efforts to develop social organization are quickly checked. Transiency and instability become the overriding features of social life.

Transiency and instability, in combination, produce powerful pressures for violent behavior among the young in these areas. First, an unorganized community cannnot provide access to legitimate channels to success-goals, and thus discontent among the young with their life-chances is heightened. Secondly, access to stable criminal opportunity systems is also restricted, for disorganized neighborhoods do not develop integration of different age-levels of offender or integration of carriers of criminal and conventional values. The young, in short, are relatively deprived of *both* conventional and criminal opportunity. Finally, social controls are weak in such communities. These conditions, we believe, lead to the emergence of conflict subcultures.

Social Disorganization and Opportunity

Communities that are unable to develop conventional forms of social organization are also unable to provide legitimate modes of access to culturally valued success-goals. The disorganized slum is a world populated with failures, with the outcasts of the larger society. Here families orient themselves not toward the future but toward the present, not toward social advancement but toward survival. The adult community, being disorganized, cannot provide the resources and opportunities that are required if the young are to move upward in the social order.

Just as the unintegrated slum cannot mobilize legitimate resources for the young, neither can it provide them with access to stable criminal careers, for illegitimate learning and opportunity structures do not develop. The disorganized slum, populated in part by failures in the conventional world, also contains the outcasts of the criminal world. This is not to say that crime is nonexistent in such areas, but what crime there is tends to be individualistic, unorganized, petty, poorly paid, and unprotected. This is the haunt of the small-time thief, the grifter, the pimp, the jackroller, the unsophisticated "con" man, the pickpocket who is all thumbs, and others who cannot graduate beyond "heisting" candy stores or "busting" gas stations. Since they are unorganized and without financial resources, criminals in these areas cannot purchase immunity from prosecution; they have neither the money nor the political contacts to "put in the fix." Hence they are harassed by the police, and many of them spend the better part of their lives in prison. The organized criminal world is generally able to protect itself against such harassment, prosecution, and imprisonment. But professional crime and organized rackets, like any business enterprise, can thrive only in a stable, predictable, and integrated environment. In this sense, then, the unintegrated area does not constitute a promising launching site for lucrative and protected criminal careers. Because such areas fail to develop criminal learning environments and opportunity structures, stable criminal subcultures cannot emerge.

Social Disorganization and Social Control

As we have noted, social controls originate in both the conventional and the illegitimate sectors of the stable slum area. But this is apparently not the case in the disorganized slum. The basic disorganization of the conventional institutional structure makes it impossible for controls to originate there. At the same time, Kobrin asserts, "Because adult crime in this type of area is itself unorganized, its value system remains implicit and hence incapable of generating norms which function effectively on a groupwide basis." Hence "juvenile violators readily escape not merely the controls of conventional persons in the community but those of adult violators as well." Under such conditions,

. . . [the] delinquencies of juveniles tend to acquire a wild, untrammelled character. Delinquents in this kind of situation more frequently exhibit the personality traits of the social type sometimes referred to as the hoodlum. Both individually and in groups, violent physical combat is engaged in for its own sake, almost as a form of recreation. Here groups of delinquents may be seen as excluded, isolated conflict groups dedicated to an unending battle against all forms of constraint. The escape from controls originating in any social structure, other than that provided by unstable groupings of the delinquents themselves, is here complete.[15]

Unlike Kobrin, we do not attribute conflict behavior in unorganized urban areas to the absence of controls alone. The young in such areas are also exposed to acute frustrations, arising from conditions in which access to success-goals is blocked by the absence of any institutionalized channels, legitimate or illegitimate. They are deprived not only of conventional opportunity but also of criminal routes to the "big money." In other words, precisely when frustrations are maximized, social controls are weakened. Social controls and channels to success-goals are generally related: where opportunities exist, patterns of control will be found; where opportunities are absent, patterns of social control are likely to be absent too. The association of these two features of social organization is a logical implication of our theory.

[15] *Ibid.*, p. 658.

Social Disorganization and Violence

Those adolescents in disorganized urban areas who are oriented toward achieving higher position but are cut off from institutionalized channels, criminal as well as legitimate, must rely upon their own resources for solving this problem of adjustment. Under these conditions, tendencies toward aberrant behavior become intensified and magnified. These adolescents seize upon the manipulation of violence as a route to status not only because it provides a way of expressing pent-up angers and frustrations but also because they are not cut off from access to violent means by vicissitudes of birth. In the world of violence, such attributes as race, socioeconomic position, age, and the like are irrelevant; personal worth is judged on the basis of qualities that are available to all who would cultivate them. The principal prerequisities for success are "guts" and the capacity to endure pain. One doesn't need "connections," "pull," or elaborate technical skills in order to achieve "rep." The essence of the warrior adjustment is an expressed feeling-state: "heart." The acquisition of status is not simply a consequence of skill in the use of violence or of physical strength but depends, rather, on one's willingness to risk injury or death in the search for "rep." A physically immature boy may find a place among the warrior elite if, when provoked, he will run such risks, thus demonstrating "heart."

As long as conventional and criminal opportunity structures remain closed, violence continues unchecked. The bulk of aggressive behavior appears to be channeled into gang warfare; success in street combat assures the group that its "turf" will not be invaded, that its girls will not be molested, that its members will otherwise be treated deferentially by young and old in the local community. *If new opportunity structures are opened, however, violence tends to be relinquished.* Indeed, the success of certain efforts to discourage violent, aggressive behavior among warrior gangs has resulted precisely from the fact that some powerful group has responded deferentially to these gangs. (The group is powerful because it can provide, or at least hold out the promise of providing, channels to higher position, such as jobs, education, and the like.) The most dramatic illustration of this process may be seen in programs conducted by social group workers who attach themselves to street gangs. Several points should be noted about the results of these programs.

First, violent behavior among street gangs appears to diminish rapidly once a social worker establishes liaison with them. Reporting on the outcome of detached-worker programs in Boston, for example, Miller notes, "One of the earliest and most evident changes . . . was that groups worked with directly [by social workers] relinquished active participation in the [established] network of conflict groups. . . ."[16] The reduction in conflict may reflect the skill of the social workers, but another explanation may be that *the advent of the street-gang worker symbolized the end of social rejection and the beginning of social accommodation.* To the extent that violence represents an effort to win deference, one would logically expect it to diminish once that end has been achieved.

Secondly, a detached-worker program, once initiated, tends to give rise to increased violence among groups to which workers have *not* been provided. In the Boston experience, to the extent that they interpreted having a street-club worker as an act of social deference, gangs came to compete for this prestigeful symbol. As Miller notes, "During later phases of the Program [there was] an upsurge in gang fights involving Program groups. . . . These conflicts did not involve Program groups fighting one another but represented for the most part attacks on Program groups by corner groups in adjacent areas which did not have an area worker." Miller suggests that such attacks took place in part because "the outside groups knew that Program groups were given a social worker in the first place because they were troublesome; so they reasoned, 'They were bad, and they got a social worker; if we're bad enough now, we'll get a social worker, too.' " An attack by an outside gang on a Program gang was not, therefore, simply an expression of the traditional hostility of one gang toward another but an attempt on the part of the non-Program gang to win "rep." Thus Miller is led to observe, "A program aiming to 'clean up' the gang situation in a single section of the city cannot count on limiting its influence to that section but must anticipate the fact that its very successes in its home district may increase difficulties in adjacent areas." This suggests that programs aimed at curbing violence constitute a new opportunity structure in which gangs compete for social deference from the conventional world.

Finally, a resurgence of violent behavior may be observed when the liaison between the street worker and the gang is terminated if the members of the gang have not been successfully incorporated in a conventional opportunity system. Continuing to lack conventional economic opportunity, the gang fears the loss of the one form of recognition it has achieved from conventional society, symbolized by the street worker. Hence the group may reassert the old patterns of violence in order to retain the social worker. Under these conditions, the conventional society will continue to accommodate to the group for fear that to do otherwise would result in renewed violence, as indeed it so often does. A successful street-gang program, in short, is one in which detached workers can create

[16] This quotation and those that follow are from W. B. Miller, "The Impact of a Community Group Work Program on Delinquent Corner Groups," *Social Service Review,* Vol. 31, No. 4 (Dec. 1957), pp. 390–406.

channels to legitimate opportunity; where such channels cannot be opened up, the gang will temporize with violence only as long as a street worker maintains liaison with them.

In summary, severe limitations on both conventional and criminal opportunity intensify frustrations and position discontent. Discontent is heightened further under conditions in which social control is relaxed, for the area lacking integration between age-level of offender and between carriers of conventional and criminal values cannot generate pressures to contain frustrations among the young. These are the circumstances, we suggest, in which adolescents turn to violence in search of status. Violence comes to be ascendant, in short, under conditions of relative detachment from all institutionalized systems of opportunity and social control.

THE RETREATIST SUBCULTURE

The consumption of drugs—one of the most serious forms of retreatist behavior—has become a severe problem among adolescents and young adults, particularly in lower-class urban areas. By and large, drug use in these areas has been attributed to rapid geographic mobility, inadequate social controls, and other manifestations of social disorganization. In this section, we shall suggest a hypothesis that may open up new avenues of inquiry in regard to the growing problem of drug use among the young.

Pressures Leading to Retreatist Subcultures

Retreatism is often conceived as an isolated adaptation, characterized by a breakdown in relationships with other persons. Indeed, this is frequently true, as in the case of psychotics. The drug-user, however, must become affiliated with others, if only to secure access to a steady supply of drugs. Just as stable criminal activity cannot be explained by reference to motivation alone, neither can stable drug use be fully explained in this way. Opportunity to use drugs must also be present. But such opportunities are restricted. As Becker notes, the illegal distribution of drugs is limited to "sources which are not available to the ordinary person. In order for a person to begin marihuana use, he must begin participation in some group through which these sources of supply become available to him."[17]

Because of these restrictions on the availability of drugs, new users must become affiliated with old users. They must learn the lore of drug use, the skills required in making appropriate "connections," the controls which govern the purchase of drugs (e.g., drugs will not generally be

17 H. S. Becker, "Marihuana Use and Social Control," *Social Problems*, Vol. 3, No. 1 (July 1955), pp. 36–37.

made available to anyone until he is "defined as a person who can safely be trusted to buy drugs without endangering anyone else"), and the like. As this process of socialization proceeds, the individual "is considered more trustworthy, [and] the necessary knowledge and introductions to dealers [then become] available to him." According to Becker, the "processes by which people are emancipated from the larger set of controls *and become responsive to those of the subculture*" are "important factors in the genesis of deviant behavior."[18] The drug-user, in other words, must be understood not only in terms of his personality and the social structure, which create a readiness to engage in drug use, but also in terms of the new patterns of associations and values to which he is exposed as he seeks access to drugs. The more the individual is caught in this web of associations, the more likely that he will persist in drug use, for he has become incorporated in a subculture that exerts control over his behavior.

Despite these pressures toward subcultural formation, it is probably also true that the resulting ties among addicts are not so solidary as those among participants in criminal and conflict subcultures. Addiction is in many ways an individualistic adaptation, for the "kick" is essentially a private experience. The compelling need for the drug is also a divisive force, for it leads to intense competition among addicts for money. Forces of this kind thus limit the relative cohesion which can develop among users.

"Double Failure" and Drug Use

We turn now to a discussion of the social conditions which give rise to retreatist reactions such as drug use among adolescents. According to Merton,

> Retreatism arises from continued failure to near the goal by legitimate measures and from an inability to use the illegitimate route because of internalized prohibitions, this process occurring while the supreme value of the success-goal has not yet been renounced. The conflict is resolved by abandoning both precipitating elements, the goals and the norms. The escape is complete, the conflict is eliminated and the individual is asocialized.[19]

---

[18] *Ibid.*, p. 35. Emphasis added.

[19] R. K. Merton, *Social Theory and Social Structure*, Rev. and Enl. Ed. (Glencoe, Ill.: Free Press, 1957), pp. 153–54. For discussions of drug use among juveniles, see D. L. Gerard and Conon Kornetsky, "Adolescent Opiate Addiction—A Study of Control and Addict Subjects," *Psychiatric Quarterly*, Vol. 29 (April 1955), pp. 457–86; Isidor Chein *et al.*, *Studies of Narcotics Use Among Juveniles* (New York University, Research Center for Human Relations, mimeographed, Jan. 1956); Harold Finestone, "Cats, Kicks, and Color," *Social Problems*, Vol. 5, No. 1 (July 1957), pp. 3–13; and D. M. Wilner, Eva Rosenfeld, R. S. Lee, D. L. Gerard, and Isidor Chein, "Heroin Use and Street Gangs," *Criminal Law, Criminology and Police Science*, Vol. 48, No. 4 (Nov.-Dec. 1957), pp. 399–409.

Thus he identifies two principal factors in the emergence of retreatist adaptations: (1) continued failure to reach culturally approved goals by legitimate means, and (2) inability to employ illegitimate alternatives because of internalized prohibitions. We take it that "internalized prohibitions" have to do with the individual's attitudes toward norms. Retreatists, according to Merton, do not call into question the legitimacy of existing institutional arrangements—a process which might then be followed by the use of illegitimate alternatives. Rather, they call into question their own adequacy, locating blame for their dilemma in personal deficiencies. One way of resolving the intense anxiety and guilt which ensue is to withdraw, to retreat, to abandon the struggle.

This definition of the processes giving rise to retreatist behavior is useful in connection with some types of retreatism, but it does not, we believe, fit the facts of drug use among lower-class adolescents. It is true that some youthful addicts appear to experience strong constraints on the use of illegitimate means; the great majority of drug-users, however, had a history of delinquency before becoming addicted. In these cases, unfavorable attitudes toward conventional norms are evident. Hence we conclude that internalized prohibitions, or favorable attitudes toward conventional norms, may not be a necessary condition for the emergence of retreatist behavior.

If internalized prohibitions are not a necessary component of the process by which retreatism is generated, then how are we to account for such behavior? We have noted that there are differentials in access both to illegitimate and to legitimate means; not all of those who seek to attain success-goals by prohibited routes are permitted to proceed. There are probably many lower-class adolescents oriented toward success in the criminal world who fail; similarly, many who would like to acquire proficiency in the use of violence also fail. We might ask, therefore, what the response would be among those faced with failure in the use of *both* legitimate and illegitimate means. We suggest that persons who experience this "double failure" are likely to move into a retreatist pattern of behavior. That is, retreatist behavior may arise as a consequence of limitations on the use of illegitimate means, whether the limitations are internalized prohibitions or socially structured barriers. For our purpose, the two types of restriction are functional equivalents. Thus we may amend Merton's statement as follows:

Retreatism arises from continued failure to near the goal by legitimate measures and from an inability to use the illegitimate route because of internalized prohibitions *or socially structured barriers,* this process occurring while the supreme value of the success-goal has not yet been renounced.

This hypothesis permits us to define two general classes of retreatist: those who are subject to internalized prohibitions on the use of illegitimate means, and those who seek success-goals by prohibited routes but do not succeed. If we now introduce a distinction between illegitimate opportunity structures based on the manipulative use of violence and those based on essentially criminal means, such as fraud, theft, and extortion, we can identify four classes of retreatist.

Types I and II both arise in the manner described by Merton—that is, as a consequence of internalized restrictions on the use of illegitimate means. The two types differ only with respect to the content of the internalized restraints. In type II, it is the use of criminal means that is precluded; in type I, it is the use of violence. Resort to illegitimate means, violent or criminal, apparently evokes extreme guilt and anxiety among persons in these categories; such persons are therefore effectively cut off from criminal or violent routes to higher status. For persons of types III and IV, access to illegitimate routes is limited by socially structured barriers. They are not restrained by internal prohibitions; they would employ illegitimate means if these were available to them.

RETREATIST ADAPTATIONS

	Restrictions on Use of Illegitimate Means	
Basis of Illegitimate Opportunity Structure	Internalized Prohibition	Socially Structured Barriers
Violence	I	III
Criminal Means	II	IV

Generally speaking, it has been found that most drug addicts have a history of delinquent activity prior to becoming addicted. In Kobrin's research, conducted in Chicago, "Persons who become heroin users were found to have engaged in delinquency *in a group-supported and habitual form* either prior to their use of drugs or simultaneously with their developing interest in drugs."[20] And from a study of drug addicts in California, "A very significant tentative conclusion [was reached]: namely,

[20] Solomon Kobrin, *Drug Addiction Among Young Persons in Chicago* (Illinois Institute for Juvenile Research, Oct. 1953), p. 6. Harold Finestone, in a study of the relationship between addicts and criminal status, comments: "The impression gained from interviewing . . . was that these addicts were petty thieves and petty 'operators' who, status-wise, were at the bottom of the criminal population of the underworld" ("Narcotics and Criminality," *Law and Contemporary Problems*, Vol. 22, No. 1 [Winter 1957], pp. 69–85).

that the use of drugs follows criminal activity and criminal association rather than the other way around, which is often thought to be the case."[21] In other words, adolescents who are engaged in group-supported delinquency of the criminal or conflict type may eventually turn to drug use. Indeed, entire gangs sometimes shift from either criminal or conflict to retreatist adaptations.

We view these shifts in adaptation as responses to restrictions on the use of illegitimate means. Such restrictions, as we have seen, are always operative; not all who would acquire success by violence or criminal means are permitted to do so. It is our contention that retreatist behavior emerges among some lower-class adolescents because they have failed to find a place for themselves in criminal or conflict subcultures. Consider the case of competition for membership in conflict gangs. To the extent that conflict activity—"bopping," street-fighting, "rumbling," and the like—is tolerated, it represents an alternative means by which adolescents in many relatively disorganized urban areas may acquire status. Those who excel in the manipulation of violence may acquire "rep" within the group to which they belong and respect from other adolescent groups in the vicinity and from the adult world. In areas which do not offer criminal opportunities, the use of violence may be the only available avenue to prestige. But prestige is, by definition, scarce—just as scarce among adolescents who seek to acquire it by violence as it is elsewhere in the society. Not only do juvenile gangs compete vigorously with one another, but within each gang there is a continual struggle for prestigeful positions. Thus some gangs will acquire "rep" and others will fail; some persons will become upwardly mobile in conflict groups and others will remain on the periphery.

If the adolescent "failure" then turns to drugs as a solution to his status dilemma, his relationships with his peers become all the more attenuated. Habitual drug use is not generally a valued activity among juvenile gangs. Ordinarily the drug-user, if he persists in such behavior, tends to become completely disassociated from the group. Once disassociated, he may develop an even greater reliance upon drugs as a solution to status deprivations. Thus adolescent drug-users may be "double failures" who are restrained from participating in other delinquent modes of adaptation because access to these illegitimate structures is limited.

Our hypothesis states that adolescents who are double failures are more vulnerable than others to retreatist behavior; it does not imply that *all* double failures will subsequently become retreatists. Some will respond to failure by adopting a law-abiding lower-class style of life—the "corner boy" adaptation. It may be that those who become retreatists are incapable of revising their aspirations downward to correspond to reality. Some of

[21] *Narcotics in California* (Board of Corrections, State of California, Feb. 18, 1959), p. 9.

those who shift to a corner-boy adaptation may not have held high aspirations initially. It has frequently been observed that some adolescents affiliate with delinquent groups simply for protection in gang-ridden areas; they are motivated not by frustration so much as by the "instinct of self-preservation." In a less hostile environment, they might simply have made a corner-boy adjustment in the first place. But for those who continue to exhibit high aspirations under conditions of double failure, retreatism is the expected result.

Sequences of Adaptation

Access to success-goals by illegitimate means diminishes as the lower-class adolescent approaches adulthood. Illegitimate avenues to higher status that were available during early adolescence become more restricted in later adolescence. These new limitations intensify frustration and so create pressures toward withdrawal or retreatist reactions.

With regard to criminal means, late adolescence is a crucial turning point, for it is during this period that the selection of candidates for stable adult criminal roles takes place. It is probably true that more youngsters are exposed to criminal learning environments during adolescence than can possibly be absorbed by the adult criminal structure. Because of variations in personality characteristics, criminal proficiency, and capacity to make "the right connections," or simply because of luck, some persons will find this avenue to higher status open and some will find it closed off. In effect, the latter face a dead end. Some delinquents, therefore, must cope with abrupt discontinuity in role-preparation and role-performance which may lead to retreatist responses.

In the case of conflict patterns, a similar process takes place. As adolescents near adulthood, excellence in the manipulation of violence no longer brings high status. Quite the contrary, it generally evokes extreme negative sanctions. What was defined as permissible or tolerable behavior during adolescence tends to be sharply proscribed in adulthood. New expectations are imposed, expectations of "growing up," of taking on adult responsibilities in the economic, familial, and community spheres. The effectiveness with which these definitions are imposed is attested by the tendency among fighting gangs to decide that conflict is, in the final analysis, simply "kid stuff": "As the group grows older, two things happen. Sports, hell raising, and gang fights become 'kid stuff' and are given up. In the normal course of events, the youthful preoccupations are replaced with the more individual concerns about work, future, a 'steady' girl, and the like."[22] In other words, powerful community expectations emerge

22 Wilner et al., op. cit., p. 409.

which have the consequence of closing off access to previously useful means of overcoming status deprivations. Strains are experienced, and retreatist bebavior may result.

As we have noted, adolescents who experience pressures leading to retreatist reactions are often restrained by their peers. Adolescent gangs usually devalue drug use (except on an experimental basis or for the sake of novelty) and impose negative sanctions upon those who become "hooked." The very existence of the gang discourages the potential user:

The activities of the gang offer a measure of shared status, a measure of security and a sense of belonging. The boys do not have to face life alone—the group protects them. Escape into drugs is not necessary as yet.[23]

In the post-adolescent period, however, the cohesiveness of the peer group usually weakens. Those who have the requisite skills and opportunities begin to make the transition to adulthood, assuming conventional occupational and kinship roles. As the solidarity of the group declines, it can no longer satisfy the needs or control the behavior of those who continue to rely upon it. These members may try to reverse the trend toward disintegration and, failing this, turn to drugs:

This group organized five years ago for self-protection against other fighting groups in the area. Recently, as the majority grew cool to bopping, a group of three boys broke off in open conflict with the president; *soon after, these three started using heroin and acting "down with the cats."* They continue making efforts to get the gang back to fights. . . . The three users are still out and it is unlikely that they will be readmitted.[24]

For some adolescents, the peer group is the primary avenue to status as well as the primary source of constraints on behavior. For these youngsters, the post-adolescent period, during which the group may disintegrate or shift its orientation, is one in which social controls are weakened precisely when tensions are heightened.

Whether the sequence of adaptations is from criminal to retreatist or from conflict to retreatist, we suggest that limitations on legitimate and illegitimate opportunity combine to produce intense pressures toward retreatist behavior. When both systems of means are simultaneously restricted, it is not strange that some persons become detached from the social structure, adandoning cultural goals and efforts to achieve them by any means.

[23] *Ibid.*
[24] *Ibid.*, p. 405. Emphasis added.

2 Patterns of Delinquent Subcultural Behavior

IRVING SPERGEL

The purpose of [this paper] is to describe the patterns of delinquent behavior and orientation which are characteristic of various types of delinquent social systems and subcultures. The discussion is focused on the constellations of delinquent behavior that differentiate delinquent subcultures, rather than on behavior patterns that may be common to delinquents regardless of type of lower-class neighborhood. A wide variety of provocative and aggressive behavior, such as brawling or unorganized and spontaneous fighting, is common among youths in lower-class areas. Such behavior apparently is more prevalent among lower-class than among middle-class youths. It is more typical of the delinquent than the non-delinquent adaptation. An activity such as fist fighting need not, however, necessarily reflect a delinquent orientation. It represents, at least partially, normal adolescent behavior. Its high incidence among lower-class delinquent youths may be in considerable measure a function of the greater need and striving for status and prestige and the relative lack of means, other than personal, by which to achieve them. Aspirations for success status are higher among delinquents than among non-delinquents. . . . The conventional means to success-goals, however, such as academic preparation or vocational training, have not been acquired by delinquents. The gang or peer group provides the means—more significantly for the delin-

Reprinted from *Racketville, Slumtown and Haulburg* by Irving Spergle, pp. 29–53, 61–62, by permission of The University of Chicago Press, © 1964 by The University of Chicago. Also by permission of the author.

quent than for the non-delinquent—by which some kind of success status may be obtained. Delinquent-group interaction and activity develop pressures and provide opportunities for testing physical strength and courage —the simplest and most readily available attributes of a status of prestige. It is much less necessary for the non-delinquent to be "somebody" in his group through fighting, since a significant status can be more easily secured by him through conventional means.

Nevertheless, dominant patterns of delinquent activity, including aggressive behavior, seem to vary from one type of neighborhood to another. Certain acts of delinquency which are common in one area may occur infrequently in another. Outwardly similar kinds of delinquent behavior may be organized for different purposes in the various neighborhoods.

Not only delinquent behavior but delinquent norms and values may be distributed differently in the three neighborhoods [studied]. However, delinquent orientation and delinquent behavior may not be necessarily commensurate or correlative at a given time and place. Delinquent or criminal attitudes may be considered just as basic, in the long run, to the determination of the criminal-adult life style as is delinquent behavior. Conversely, the relative lack of current involvement by youths in delinquent behavior does not preclude the possibility of criminal-adult adjustments later.

An understanding of the delinquent adjustment requires attention to both the antisocial behavior and to the antisocial orientation. The delinquent adjustment must be viewed within a broad sociocultural framework over a sufficiently long-term perspective. For instance, a youth who does not perform delinquent acts but who has a delinquent orientation may become an adult who performs criminal acts.

THE RACKET SUBCULTURE

The rackets in Racketville and in the other neighborhoods signify highly organized criminal activities such as policy or numbers, off-track betting, loan-shark operations, narcotics-selling, and organized prostitution. These criminal operations, particularly in Racketville, involved large numbers of persons in a bureaucratic structure. There were various echelons of responsibility, power, and opportunity. Significant upper-echelon opportunities were not open to the youth of Racketville. It was anticipated, however, that some delinquents, by virtue of access to criminal means, would engage in significant apprentice racketeer roles, if on a limited basis. Undoubtedly, many delinquents in this type of area would be able to assume, in due time, significant racketeer roles without necessarily starting at the bottom.

POLICY RACKET. The interview evidence did not make it clear that more delinquents from Racketville than from the other areas were engaged in such operations as taking numbers or making pickups of numbers receipts. Of the ten delinquents in each area sample, only four from Racketville, two from Slumtown, and one from Haulburg said that they had ever been involved in the policy racket.[1] There was a strong indication, however, that of the few who reported participation in such activities, the median involvement was highest for the delinquents from Racketville—135 days in their entire delinquent careers. In Slumtown and Haulburg, the median participation was merely 1 or 2 days. The risks of serving time for this kind of law violation were minimal.

There was observational evidence from Racketville that delinquents were invloved in policy operations mainly through family connections. Since relatives were often in the upper reaches of the racket structure, it was natural for delinquents to be exposed and drawn into illegitimate activity in some fashion:

Davey said to the street club worker that he had Uncle Joey's Cadillac outside and asked if he would like to be driven home. Davey went on to say that he was on an errand to pick up some money from the —— Luncheonette. . . . This was the first time that he openly acknowledged to the worker that he spent part of each day in making calls at various bars, luncheonettes, and restaurants in order to pick up the day's receipts from policy. On the way home, the worker remarked that the Cadillac was beautiful and that Davey handled it extremely well. Davey replied that someday he would own a car as fine as this and go around in style.

The delinquent was given opportunities to prepare for organized criminal roles by performing seemingly minor errands. Such assignments served to put him in a position to do a small favor for the racketeer, thus showing him that he was willing and trustworthy. The communication of criminal norms and values and the opportunity to establish useful contacts with racketeers was made possible by completion of these little jobs.

Butch explained that he had to pay a fine for someone at traffic court next morning. It was for a vehicle violation. The person had given him a twenty-

---

[1] It should be pointed out that no formal checks on the truthfulness of responses of informants and subjects were made. The researcher assumed that the delinquent would tend to be honest and accurate in his responses when interviewed in a relaxed, non-threatening, open community situation, by a "streetwise" skilled interviewer. Non-systematic and, at times, informal checking of responses was made through conversations with street-club workers and other delinquents who knew the respondents and through a review of agency records and materials, where such were available and relevant. The validity of the responses of only two of the interviewed subjects was strongly questioned—by street-club workers. The original responses were, nevertheless, used.

dollar bill. Since he wasn't going to school tomorrow anyway, Butch didn't mind doing this person a favor. He said that the guy who gave him the money had a big fat bankroll and just pulled the twenty dollars from the top. This man wasn't related to the boy but he was supposed to be a "big" man in the numbers. Butchie said this man owned, in addition, two dump trucks and an ice cream and meat-delivery business. He said this might be a break for him. . . . Someday he might get a job making a couple of hundred dollars a week hardly doing anything, which is what he wanted. He would be employed by this "big shot." He would be able to take it easy, get up late in the morning, have girls, go to night clubs . . . no one to tell him what to do.

Field observation indicated that such criminal opportunities either were not available or were not sought as much by delinquents in other kinds of areas.

SHYLOCK OR LOAN-SHARK RACKET. The practice of money-lending at usurious or illegal rates of interest, often 20 percent or higher—the Shylock or loan-shark racket—appeared to be more common to delinquents from Racketville than from the other areas. While six delinquents from Racketville had participated in money-lending, only one delinquent in each of the two other neighborhoods had done so.

Field data suggested that this type of illegal business might be conducted on the job outside as well as in the neighborhood. Involvement in loan-shark activities apparently started early. Two youths from Racketville who were still attending school were apprehended by school authorities for systematic loan-shark activities. There was little doubt that the loan-shark operator was considered "a respectable businessman" and was highly admired by delinquent youths in the area:

Jackie, Freddie, and Louie once discussed with the researcher the advantages of being a loan shark. They felt that this was a very good kind of racket to be in. It was safe. The main thing to worry about was the income-tax people, since, of course, you couldn't report all the money you would be making. Most of the fellows who borrowed money at high rates of interest paid back. The only drawback was that you had to have a little money to start with. Jackie said that he was definitely interested in becoming a loan shark when he got a little older.

Delinquents from Racketville were highly business-oriented. Indeed, they seemed to develop a keen business sense which was not characteristic of delinquents from the other areas.

NARCOTICS-SELLING OR "PUSHING." The interview data did not reveal that more delinquents from Racketville were involved in the sale of narcotics than were delinquents from other areas. Indeed, while two delinquents from Slumtown and one delinquent from Haulburg admitted that they sold narcotics, no delinquents from Racketville admitted such activity.

"Pushing" was perhaps not a common offense among delinquents. The interview data seemed to contradict expectations.

However, the observational data supported expectations, at least at the adult level. The findings here indicated that, just prior to the researcher's arrival in the neighborhood, two major raids by treasury agents resulted in the arrest of a drug-selling ring consisting of at least fifteen adults who were distributing heroin, mainly. Also, there was evidence that although the sale of drugs on a wholesale level was approved by these adults, there was great concern about petty trafficking, particularly in the immediate area. In previous years, when drug-selling had been permitted in the neighborhood, the racketeers themselves were "hurt" when their own sons and nephews, in certain instances, succumbed to the use of drugs. Drug-selling was now prohibited in the area. Racketeers had even gone to the extreme of setting the police on the trail of small-time drug peddlers who would not obey their injunctions.

Thus the observational and interview data were not entirely contradictory. They merely indicated different patterns of involvement, depending on which segment of the drug market was studied. Upper-echelon or large-scale drug-selling was considered permissible and appropriate, but not petty trafficking, especially in the Italian neighborhood. Furthermore, it was unlikely that delinquents would be trusted with responsibility at the upper level of the drug racket.

Value-Norm Index

A value-norm index was constructed on the basis of nineteen items. Three directly indicated values—whether racketeers were good or bad, whether it was all right to cheat, and whether people should be honest. Sixteen items sought to establish the likelihood of participation in such acts as "kill someone"; "beat up a guy"; "gang-fight"; "steal a car"; "steal a bicycle"; "steal groceries, candy, etc."; "burglary of an apartment"; "hold up a store"; "be a pimp"; "get involved in numbers"; "push narcotics"; "use narcotics"; "rape"; "con a few bucks"; "Shylock or loan shark"; "extort money." Four responses were possible—"very likely," "likely," "hardly," or "not at all."

The responses of the subjects were added to obtain a group response for each item. Then, since it was assumed that all questions tapped a single legitimacy or illegitimacy variable, the responses to the nineteen items were added for each of the groups. The resultant four intensity scores ("very likely," "likely," "hardly," or "not at all") were collapsed into two: The total illegitimate ("very likely," "likely") and the total legitimate ("hardly," "not at all") responses for each group. A criminal value score was obtained by computing the percentage of the total responses of each group which indicated an illegitimate orientation.

The findings showed marked differences in criminal orientation between delinquents from Racketville and delinquents from Slumtown or Haulburg. The delinquents° from Racketville were most highly criminal in orientation; 71 per cent of their responses were illegitimately oriented (see Table 1).

Nevertheless, an inspection of the data on antisocial activity did not reveal a greater delinquency rate for delinquents from Racketville than for those in the other areas. In other words, there did not appear to be a strict correlation between criminal value orientation and general involvement in delinquent behavior. It is possible, however, that the criminal value orientation of the delinquent from the racket subculture merely made him a likely candidate for future organized criminal activity. Although it was important for the young delinquent to develop a reputation for being tough, it was at the same time necessary that he minimize his risks of arrest. Racketeers placed a premium on smooth and unobstrusive operation of their employees. The undisciplined, trouble-making young "punk" was not acceptable. The primary condition for admission to the racket organization was not necessarily previous involvement in delinquent acts but training in attitudes and beliefs which would facilitate the smooth

TABLE 1. VALUE ORIENTATIONS*

Neighborhood and Component Group	Number of Responses		Percentage of Illegitimate Responses
	Legitimate	Illegitimate	
Racketville			
Non-delinquent†	138	50	27
Delinquent	56	134	71
Drug addict	107	83	44
Slumtown			
Non-delinquent	153	37	19
Delinquent	103	87	46
Drug addict	122	68	36
Haulburg			
Non-delinquent‡	152	33	18
Delinquent	100	90	47
Drug addict	125	65	34

* The number of respondents in each component group was ten, and total responses expected per group were 190.

† Two subjects refused to answer the item on evaluation of racketeers.

‡ Five subjects did not know any racketeers.

operation of the criminal organization. Prior development of specific skills and experiences seemed less necessary than the learning of an underlying illegitimate orientation or point of view conducive to the development of organized crime.

ROLE-MODELS. The kind of adult a young person aspires to be is manifested by the values and the way of life which he esteems highly. The role-model such a young person selects provides an indication of his current orientation to life and is suggestive of the type of adult he himself may well turn out to be.

Responses to the question, "What is the occupation of the adult in your neighborhood whom you would most want to be like ten years from now?" indicated that more delinquents from Racketville identified with the role of the racketeer than did delinquents from Slumtown or Haulburg. The sharpest contrast existed between Racketville, where eight of ten delinquents interviewed, and Haulburg, where only one of ten delinquents interviewed, considered the racketeer as a role-model. Indeed, more subjects generally from each of the three component groups of Racketville (non-delinquents, delinquents, drug addicts) identified with racketeers than those from either of the other two areas. Furthermore, it should be noted that of the nine youngsters in a total sample of ninety subjects who could not find any adult to identify with in any of the three types of neighborhoods, five were non-delinquents from the racket subculture (see Table 2). This finding suggested that the non-delinquents in this area were to some

TABLE 2.   ROLE-MODELS*

Neighborhood and Component Group	Racketeer	Non-Racketeer
Racketville		
Non-delinquent†	1	4
Delinquent	8	1
Drug addict	5	5
Slumtown		
Non-delinquent	0	10
Delinquent	3	7
Drug addict‡	4	5
Haulburg		
Non-delinquent	0	10
Delinquent§	1	7
Drug addict	0	10

* The number in each sample or component group per neighborhood is ten.
† Five subjects responded "Nobody."
‡ One subject responded "Nobody."
§ Two subjects responded "Nobody."

extent *deviant* in relation to their own neighborhood and local culture. They would have had to be in order to develop a social or conventional orientation.

GETTING AHEAD—EDUCATION VERSUS CONNECTIONS. The subjects were asked to rank what they considered the most important quality in "getting ahead." There were four categories from which to select: "ability," "good luck," "connections," and "education." The term "connections" had a criminal connotation, particularly in Racketville.

The data revealed that delinquents from the racket subculture were highly oriented toward the use of connections as the most important factor, and education and ability as the least important factors in attaining goals. Delinquents from the other areas, particularly from Slumtown, were less oriented toward the use of connections and much more oriented to the importance of education in getting ahead (see Table 3).

It was possible, particularly in the racket subculture, that the concepts of education and connections were antithetical. A strong value association with connections precluded an emphasis on an educational orientation. In a larger sense, the pursuit of education was the pursuit of that which was highly legitimate. The pervasive use of connections was in essence a commitment to the deviant, or that which was culturally regarded as unacceptable. Such an orientation was preeminently illegitimate. Confirmation of the validity of this deduction was obtained through an examination of the second, third, and fourth choices of attributes which were considered important in getting ahead; seven out of ten delinquents from the racket subculture chose education as the least important factor in achieving success.

TABLE 3. ATTRIBUTE CONSIDERED MOST NECESSARY TO GET AHEAD*

Neighborhood and Component Group	Ability	Good Luck	Connections	Education
Racketville				
Non-delinquent	7	0	2	1
Delinquent	0	1	9	0
Drug addict	1	0	5	4
Slumtown				
Non-delinquent	2	0	1	7
Delinquent	2	3	0	5
Drug-addict	2	0	3	5
Haulburg				
Non-delinquent	3	0	0	7
Delinquent	1	0	3	6
Drug addict	3	0	5	2

* The number in each sample or component group per neighborhood is ten.

THE CONFLICT SUBCULTURE

GANG FIGHTING OR "BOPPING." Gang fighting in its most repetitive and virulent form characterized the behavior of delinquents in Slumtown, and it could be described as group-based, systematic, and ritualized. Just the same, it was a somewhat nebulous and fluid phenomenon, difficult to observe or to identify consistently from one situation to the next. It could be un-planned, consisting of youngsters running down the street firing shots in-discriminately at one or two, ten, or twenty members of an opposing gang gathered on a front stoop, on a street corner, or in a candy store. Gang fighting sometimes was a series of planned attacks in which youngsters who were organized into squads armed themselves with sticks, knives, rifles, revolvers, zip guns, chains, can openers, bricks, ash-can covers, lead pipes, brass knuckles, or home-made bombs and converged on a large group who were similarly armed and waiting or, perhaps, not waiting and unaware of the planned attack. It could be, on rare occasions, a prearranged affair between one hundred or more youngsters from each group, meeting, head on in a park, at a dance, in a playground, or on a beach. Weapons such as revolvers, automatics, shotguns, and rifles were the preferred means of combat.

The group "brawl" was distinguished from the gang fight by being a less destructive and generally more spontaneous form of aggression in which the crucial element of gang reputation, or "rep," was not at stake. This type of fighting, found with about the same frequency among delinquents in each of the areas, occurred most often on Friday or Saturday nights after several members of a group had got drunk and had become embroiled in an argument with peers or with adults. Usually such fights were broken up quickly and did not affect group prestige. Subjects in each area were clear about the differences between a gang fight and a brawl.

The interview data revealed that delinquents from Slumtown appeared to have been involved in more gang fighting than delinquents from either of the other two areas. Although each delinquent, regardless of neighbor-hood, admitted to or claimed a history of gang-fighting activity, the fre-quency of such involvement was greater in Slumtown than in Racketville of in Haulburg, but it was not statistically significant (see Table 4). The difference in the incidence of gang fighting in Slumtown and Racketville was objectively established, however, through an analysis of agency records.[2] The frequency of major gang fights or threats of gang fights sufficiently serious to alert the police was examined in regard to four typical delinquent

[2] The Youth Board in the city where the research was done makes use of a twenty-four-hour-a-day, seven-day-a-week telephone and secretarial service to record all in-cidents of gang fights or threats of gang fights reported by the street-club workers.

TABLE 4. REPORTS OF GANG FIGHTS BY MEMBERS OF GROUPS IN EACH NEIGHBORHOOD*

Racketville			Slumtown			Haulburg		
Non-Delinquent	Delinquent†	Drug Addict	Non-Delinquent	Delinquent†	Drug Addict	Non-Delinquent	Delinquent	Drug Addict
0	3	2	0	15	0	0	5	1
2	25	3	0	20	0	0	6	2
3	25	3	0	50	3	0	7	3
3	30	7	0	50	3	0	13	10
3	50	15	0	50	10	0	20	10
5	50	20	0	50	30	0	20	10
5	50	40	1	100	50	1	20	12
6	50	70	2	100	100	1	30	20
7	55	100	25	205	500	3	50	20
15	100	300	50	1,000	1,000	4	100	150

* The number in each sample or component group per neighborhood is ten. Each figure represents the number of gang fights in which a subject said he had been involved. Every gang foray, skirmish, aggressive or .defensive action was included in the estimate of the subject. Figures are arranged in order of magnitude.

† Difference between Racketville and Slumtown delinquents, using a Mann-Whitney U Test, is not statistically significant — z = 1.13.

groups: two from Racketville—the Vultures, the observation group, and the Stompers, the formal interview group—and two from Slumtown—the Regals, the observation group and part of the formal interview group, and the Noble Lords, the other part of the formal interview group. The results indicated that there was little difference between delinquent groups from the same type of area, but that differences between delinquent groups from Racketville and Slumtown were marked and statistically significant. The frequency of gang fights reported for the Slumtown groups was approximately four times as great as the number reported for the Racketville groups (see Table 5).

Although gang fighting was a less frequent phenomenon in Racketville, when it did occur it could be just as destructive as in Slumtown.

Ralphie said the fellows used to go uptown to play around with some of the girls. One day some of the guys uptown telephoned for ten Vultures to come and meet ten of their fellows and they'd have it out. The Vultures were so upset that eight of them jumped into a car right away. When they got uptown, a dance was in progress with a hundred or more of the fellows from the other neighborhood present. The Vultures had garrison belts and a couple of machetes. One of them had a blank pistol. Ralphie remembered that there was a big fellow who was not really involved and wanted to settle things between the groups. One of the Vultures got sore at him, took off his garrison belt, and slashed the big fellow across the face with the buckle, cutting deeply. Ralphie said the boy deserved it. When he went down, some of the Vultures cut him on the back with machetes . . . "not too badly" . . . "just sliced him a little." Then the fight started, but the other fellows got "real scared" when one of the Vultures took out the blank pistol and made believe he was going to shoot. This gave the Vultures a chance to get back to the car and drive off.

However, the street-club worker explained:

"These boys don't orient themselves to 'bopping.' Every few months they may decide to go out and get a 'spick,' but there isn't a constant tension or pressure to participate in a gang fight as in other neighborhoods. Fighting isn't the usual subject of conversation among the Italian kids."

A staff worker in the settlement house frequented by the Vultures stated that the delinquent groups in the area did not talk about gang fighting. They were mainly interested in girls, a good time, and money. A gang fight, when it occurred, was "just one of those things." The nature of the gang fighting which took place from time to time appeared to be largely defensive and grew out of fear of attack, based on reality or fancied.

Some of the Vultures spoke excitedly about "a whole mess of" Puerto Ricans coming to the park about forty minutes before and about how all the fellows (the Vultures) and one of the cops from the neighborhood chased them. Some of the older boys grabbed some of the Puerto Ricans and beat them up, and three of them (the Puerto Ricans) were then picked up by the police.

TABLE 5. MAJOR GANG-FIGHT THREATS AND ACTUAL GANG FIGHTS*

Neighborhood and Group	Major Threats of Gang Fights	Major Gang Fights	Total
Racketville			
Vultures	2	4	6
Stompers	3	5	8
Slumtown			
Regals	10	17	27
Noble Lords	8	19	27

* Calculated from answering service messages and street-club worker estimates, Big City Youth Board, for a twelve-month period, with age of group members and size of groups held approximately constant. A major gang-fight threat was any threat important enough to be telephoned in to the answering service.

Differences between Racketville and Slumtown groups are statistically significant, using a t test, $p(s) < .05$.

Among the delinquent groups in Slumtown, the Vultures had a reputation mainly as a defensive club. Papo from the Regals commented:

"I don't like the Vultures. I always wanted to bop against the Vultures for certain reasons that everytime they catch one of us alone they want to beat us or stab us or something, but they really ain't nothing because they never hardly ever come down on us. They always wait until we come down on them. So the Vultures, I think—they got a big reputation of staying in their block, but for me they don't have no reputation at all because they never come down."

Perhaps more typical of the aggressive activity of the delinquent group in Rocketville was brawling or fist fighting among several youngsters of the same or different groups over strictly momentary grievances, where group honor or "rep" was not at stake.

Big Freddie recalled that when he was fourteen years old and was with some of the older guys in the Vultures, they got into trouble with a bunch of guys who were sitting in front of them at the movies. They had a real free-for-all, Big Freddie said boastfully. He was pretty big for his age and fought three of the other guys at once. Then the cops came, broke up the fight, and he was almost picked up, but somebody said he wasn't involved, and the cops let him go. He thought this was just clean fun and loved it.

Gang fighting or "diddy bopping" in Slumtown was of a different character and frequency. For the delinquents in this area, gang fighting was a full-time preoccupation, typifying a way of life in which the achievement and maintenance of status or "rep" were paramount goals. The fighting group generated, more completely and directly than other types of delinquent groups, the means to achieve prestige and recognition:

Chico said he joined the Regals about five years ago. He joined them because he wanted to be "bad" (notorious). He wanted a reputation. He said that most guys belonged to a "bopping" club because they wanted to impress guys, girls—but also adults. The researcher asked him what he meant by that. He said that if you were not a member of a "bopping" gang, you were nobody. If you walked "four-by-four" with the other guys in the club down the street and looked everybody straight in the eye, then they noticed you. They said you were a Regal, and they respected you.

Every opportunity was sought, particularly by the up-and-coming young delinquent clique or group, to develop a reputation and to achieve the all-important status of a "down," or tough, gang-fighting group. A member of a younger segment of a fighting group described the process of achieving a "rep":

"I remember a summer when Dillinger, me, and little Lulu, we formed a club. Dillinger became the president; Cheyenne, that's me, became the vice-president. Little Lulu became the war counselor—only us three—we had a club. All the old Regals were in jail. Dillinger, the first time he took us down, we got a rep. We burned King Kong and Count Shadow of the Noble Lords. They were all a bunch of punks, so Papo came in, and Husky Louie and a whole lot of guys wanted to join the Regals and the Tims—that's us. We went down every day. We shanked the Noble Lords. We kicked their ass. Every day we used to go down. We went down once, twice, three times, four times . . . eleven times. The eleventh time we got busted. Dillinger got busted—he was the one who got the rep for us. He went to Youth House . . ."

The crucial component in the acquiring of a gang-fighting "rep" or reputation, was "heart," signifying toughness, daring, bravery, adventurous foolhardiness. To be called a "guy who had heart" symbolized the achievement of the sought-after ultimate goal. It was the pinnacle, the Distinguished Service Cross for performance, by the standards of the conflict subculture:

Billy the Kid spoke of the importance of having "heart." He spoke of one of the Gonzales brothers, a former president of the Regals, who would go down with another fellow and tell him where and when to "burn" (fire a weapon). This would be a kind of training. If the other fellow became frightened or wasn't sure, this fellow would take the gun from him and "burn" for him. He wasn't afraid of anything.

The possession or lack of "heart" distinguished the worthy from the unworthy in the gang-fighting group:

Bobby said, "Just about three guys, Billy the Kid, Tito, and myself had heart . . ." All put together there were about twelve or thirteen in the club, but a lot of them "weren't worth a damn." He said they were "chicken" and would run.

Since gang fighting was the means by which to attain significant status, it was important to create a crisis, particularly if relations between groups had been quiet for too long. By calling a member of another gang a "punk," or by insulting his girl friend, or by bringing up an unsettled grievance which might be two days or two years old, a member of a group could cause a crisis. The specific factor precipitating the onset of hostilities was usually insignificant. The major consideration was that reputation, the sense of group, and, thereby, individual importance was denied or impugned. Group prestige had to be maintained or re-established. It was also important to guard against conditions which might destroy opportunities to have gang fights:

Bobby said, "It was best if the Noble Lords didn't go to the Regal's territory or the Regals to the Noble Lord's territory, otherwise we would get to know each other and become too friendly, and then it would be hard to bop."

"Bopping" was the most exciting, satisfying, and worthwhile part of life for a great many delinquents in Slumtown. It was so considered even by former delinquent group members. In a moment of stone-cold sobriety the gang member, past or present, might say "This is crazy, bopping is no good, it only gets you busted." Yet the typical view among delinquents from Slumtown was that gang fighting was a source of satisfaction, a means of overcoming the constrictions of slum life, and was useful in learning the ways of the world:

"When you're a jitter-bug (gang fighter) that's the best part of your life. . . . You have fun. It's true you go down. I think when you're jitter-bugging you learn more about life than when you don't, or when you go to community centers, or when you do nothing. In jitter-bugging you learn what's happening like. . . . You ain't doing nothing—you don't learn nothing. When you're jitter-bugging you learn a whole lot. You learn about jury . . . court. In a way, you could learn about court when you take up a lawyer . . . but take someone else, they don't even know what a courtroom is. You see, when you're jitter-bugging you know . . ."

Gang fighting occurred least frequently in Haulburg. The difference in gang-fighting patterns among the various neighborhoods was recognized by the delinquents themselves:

Recalling his own participation in fighting, a delinquent from Haulburg reported that certainly he was not in as many gang fights as guys from other neighborhoods. The fellows here did not get into many gang fights. Once in a while there was talk of a gang "bust," but this kind of talk "comes and goes." He remembered the time when the fellows were interested in becoming a division of a citywide fighting gang. This talk lasted a few weeks, and the guys were never sure who was in or out of the gang.

The low incidence of gang fights in Haulburg did not mean that delinquents who had a theft orientation were inherently less aggressive than delinquents from other types of areas. Aggression was merely manifested in other ways. Impulsive brawling, usually involving a small number of participants, was the characteristic way of settling differences:

"Here we have one-man or two-men fights like me against you and him against him, more than up in the other neighborhood. Up there they have six or seven guys or more on one other guy or many other guys . . ."

Fighting in this area rarely resulted in serious injury. Weapons were seldom used. Occasionally a stick, a brick, or a bottle was impulsively used in a fight. Once in a while, when relations between two groups deteriorated and a gang fight seemed to threaten, feeble efforts at arms preparations were made. Indeed there was indication that the delinquent code called for and accorded higher respect to the youngster or youngsters who employed physical prowess only:

Tony said he used to be president of the Devils, and they were going to fight a group on —— Street. These guys had a reputation for being the toughest bunch in their part of the neighborhood. The Devils had a gun and a few knives, but the fellows from the other street came into their block and only had their fists and beat them up anyway. After that they dropped their club name and gave up their weapons.

In Haulburg, brawling was common on Friday and Saturday evenings after long drinking sessions. Pretexts were used to justify fighting other peers and even adults who wandered into the block. Such fighting was consistent with general lower-class norms about fighting as a permissible and approved form of behavior. Delinquents from this area recalled with pleasure the noteworthy "donnybrooks" in which they were involved or those in which others participated. Several stories glorifying the prowess of fighters were part of the folklore of the neighborhood. Some of the fights even involved their own parents:

Stan boasted that when his father was younger, right after World War II, he used to go down to the bar and get into a lot of fights. He spoke proudly of the times his father used to "string out" the other guys. "Once he took care of three guys at one time. He knocked the guy across the bar, and the other down on a table, and third into the cellar—all by himself." Stan also said that on a Friday night, like tonight, the bar would be hopping. Chairs would be broken;

mirrors smashed; bottles thrown against the counters. Not quite eighteen years old, the boy spoke with anticipatory glee of the time when he would go along with the older fellows to the bar.

In general, the data showed a difference in fighting patterns in the three types of area. Gang fighting in its most organized and offensive form was prevalent in Slumtown. It occurred less frequently and more defensively in Racketville, especially when delinquents and grownups viewed themselves as threatened from outside. In Haulburg, gang fighting was not a significant phenomenon.

Values

Delinquents from Slumtown were considerably less oriented to criminal or illegitimate norms and values than were delinquents from Racketville. According to the data obtained from the interviews (see Table 1), delinquents from Slumtown, as those from Haulburg, were principally oriented to the standards of the legitimate or conventional culture. Delinquents from Slumtown were far less oriented to careers in the rackets than were delinquents from Racketville (see Table 2). (This does not obviate the fact that there were many criminals, including racketeers, in the neighborhood. They were in the low echelons of the criminal hierarchy, however, and possessed relatively little power or influence.) Delinquents in the conflict subculture were mainly oriented to conventional working-class and lower-middle-class occupations, such as grocery or candy-store proprietor, plumber, or photographer. Formal education, despite the uniformly negative experiences which the delinquents from this area had encountered in school, still appeared to them as the major means by which success status could be achieved.

Luck, relatively more in Slumtown than in the other areas, was valued as a means for getting ahead (see Table 3). However, the factor of luck appeared generally not to be held as significant among young people in the three neighborhoods. From the data obtained it appeared that believing in luck was not as important an aspect of lower-class culture as some writers had indicated.[3]

THE THEFT SUBCULTURE

Stealing was a pervasive activity among delinquents in the theft subculture. Although as a rule not carefully planned or executed, acts of theft

[3] See, for example, Robert K. Merton, *Social Theory and Social Structure* (rev. ed.; Glencoe, Ill.: Free Press, 1957), pp. 147–49; Walter B. Miller, "Lower Class Culture as a Generating Milieu of Gang Delinquency," *Journal of Social Issues*, XIV (Fall, 1958), 11–12.

appeared, nevertheless, to provide the opportunity to learn skills and attitudes which might be useful for the few who chose to pursue careers of adult crime later in life.

CAR THEFT. "Joy riding," or car theft by delinquents, i.e., breaking into a parked automobile and going for a ride, was common in Haulburg. While the appropriation of the car itself occurred rarely, its parts or accessories were often illegally taken and disposed of by the delinquent clique or small group. The interview data showed that whereas only three out of ten delinquents from Slumtown and six out of ten delinquents from Racketville were minimally involved in car theft, nine out of ten delinquents from Haulburg reported quite frequent participation in this kind of illegitimate activity. In Haulburg, the median involvement for delinquents in car theft was thirty instances; in Racketville, two instances; and in Slumtown, three instances. For many in this particular area, therefore, car theft appeared to be a highly repetitive and patterned preoccupation.

In Haulburg car theft appeared to have a function similar to gang fighting in Slumtown or being a "tough guy" in Racketville. In each neighborhood, delinquent behavior was a way of demonstrating conformity with the model of "big shot" or "important guy." In the theft subculture the possession of material goods, including flashy cars, fine clothes, and money, was the criterion of successful status. Yet it was not so much the money as what the money could buy that was significant. Car-stealing provided, most directly, an opportunity to fulfill a desired mode of existence. A young adult of the theft subculture discussed car-stealing as follows:

Karl said of course the younger kids were all involved in stealing cars, but he wasn't sure they sold the cars. The researcher asked why the kids stole the cars. He said it was to be a "big shot." The kids would drive around—say they got the car from their uncles or brothers-in-law—and invite the girls or other fellows to go along with them. They'd ride around for a while and then abandon the car—maybe a couple of blocks from where they'd picked it up. The kids on the street didn't make any money—not at first, anyway. Karl said that he noticed that the kids who did a great deal of "joy riding" hung around the used-car lots which were also good outlets for stolen car parts.

Although "joy riding" was for "kicks," or excitement, according to the youths themselves, and did not necessarily result in misappropriation of the car or its parts; the theft of cars was on occasion an act of conscious criminal intent. The director of a local settlement house in the area who held this point of view reported that:

Not infrequently, when the boys stole the cars and, occasionally, a truck, they went out to other neighborhoods where either the whole vehicle was sold or parts were stripped and then sold to any of a number of secondhand car dealers with whom the boys had regular business dealings. These boys were mainly interested in the money they could make rather than in the fun that riding in the car provided.

Knowledge derived from breaking into cars and driving or from disposing of the parts of the vehicles could be useful to delinquents in later years in more sophisticated illegal operations of purchase, sale, maintenance, and repair of automobiles.

APARTMENT BURGLARY.   Unlawful entry into apartments and the taking of valuables such as clothes, money, radios, TV's, and hi-fi sets was a common activity among Haulburg delinquents. Whereas in Slumtown and Racketville, respectively, two out of ten delinquents reported participation in acts of apartment burglary, in Haulburg, eight out of ten delinquents did so. Illegal entry into apartments appeared not to be limited to the luxury apartment buildings, where, although the "takings" were good, the risks were higher. It seemed to occur as often in the lower-rental apartment houses, where the advantages of knowing the layout and taking more portable goods existed.

The delinquents in Haulburg were engaged in apartment burglary generally on a planned basis. They knew who the fences in the neighborhood were and sometimes arrangements were made in advance of the staging of certain apartment burglaries. Some of the boys, even at a fairly young age, brought well-developed skills to these assigned tasks:

Karl said that he knew a group of youngsters who were involved in a whole lot of burglaries in the neighborhood. The kids broke into apartments systematically and took stuff that they knew they could sell. . . . In fact, some of them were very good at it. They had special keys for the doors. A few could even pick locks. Karl said that he himself had learned to pick locks from one of the older guys in the neighborhood.

STICKUPS OF STORES.   Robbery of stores at knife- or gun-point by delinquents was not a common phenomenon in any of the areas. This type of activity was not reported by delinquents from either Racketville or Slumtown. However, five of ten delinquents interviewed from Haulburg reported at least one holdup. When delinquents from Haulburg participated in stickups, there was evidence that usually two boys were involved together and that some planning had taken place beforehand.

In general, the pattern of thievery was more systematic and organized in Haulburg than in the other areas. Social agency personnel and the local youth patrolman were in agreement that stealing was a serious problem in the locality. The youth partolman had established a rating system for groups of youngsters engaged in theft. One group of twelve- and thirteen-year-olds had a particularly high score.

Patrolman K. showed me a list of names of boys from —— Street who constituted a serious problem during the last three years. These boys, seven or eight of them, were repeatedly picked up for breaking into the coin boxes of public washing and drying machines in the building basements. They also broke into parking meters. They were constantly appearing in court but the judges were reluctant to send them to the training school at so early an age. Patrolman K. said that he had been able to persuade the local settlement house to assign a street-club worker, half-time, to this group.

Petty thievery, in particular, seemed to be common among children and younger adolescents in all three types of areas. However, it was the researcher's impression that as the delinquents got older, thieving generally diminished in Slumtown and Racketville. Other types of delinquent orientation, such as gang fighting and involvement in racket activities, would then develop with greater momentum.

This did not preclude occasional instances of thievery during middle and late adolescence in the racket and conflict subcultures. The following is an extract of a report by a street-club worker assigned to a group in Racketville. He had just started working with this group:

After a while the boys got tired of merely sitting on the swings in the playground and "shooting the breeze," so Jerry suggested that they try to put into operation the plan they had decided upon for that night. As the worker wondered about this and saw the boys gradually drifting off in pairs, Carl remarked that they were on their way to what he jokingly referred to as some "supplies." He pointed to the stacked building materials to be used for construction of a new roadway. Although Jerry was masterminding the operation, he did not take a direct part in it. Joey and Philip, who previously had been drinking, were leading the rest of the boys in their attempt to steal whatever they could find. About ten minutes later, the boys began to return with their loot. Although the worker was sure each boy was capable of carrying off bricks, cement blocks, or cement building implements, they had taken only three saws. Jerry directed that the saws be buried and that they return for them later in the evening, when the watchman was no longer suspicious. While plans were being made to go back for a second haul, the worker tried to intervene and suggested that Jerry and Philip, as well as Joey, go with him for sodas or coffee.

In the store Jerry explained that the guys went on "raids" like these just for "kicks." He said that sometimes the guys sold or used the tools they took. But the main purpose was to have a little fun. Philip then went on to tell about their raiding the A&P and other grocery chain stores to get cake, which they ate with milk stolen from the milkman. Jerry repeated that they did this just for "kicks" and said that they really did not need the money or the stuff they took.

In Slumtown it was rare that the entire group or a substantial part of it was engaged in organized burglary, even for "kicks." When stealing occurred, it tended to be a peripheral activity of one of two youngsters. However, in Slumtown, too, such actions could be quite serious in plan and consequences:

Superman, seventeen years old, told the researchers that recently he was in trouble. In fact, he was on probation for it now. He said that he was picked up for gang fighting, but this was not the whole story. The cops found $400 in his pocket and forced him to confess that he participated in a liquor-store burglary. Superman said that an older guy he knows worked in the liquor store and had loosened part of the wall at the rear of the store. Superman came back at night when the store was closed and squeezed through this opening and took a lot of money. He gave part of the money to his family. He did not give any of it to his partner. He "pulled a bomb" (swindle).

The burglary or theft pattern represented a more systematic and purposeful orientation in Haulburg than in the other areas. Although at first it was part of a game, within a short time it might serve as a start in learning important skills that would be useful to the older adolescent and young-adult thief:

Pete said that when he was a kid the guys used to go around from car to car and see if they could break into glove compartments. They did this mainly to see who was the best "stealer." Pete recalled that he was "busted" when he was fifteen years old for stealing hubcaps. Actually, he didn't get much money out of it. Much of it was a matter of who could steal the most hubcaps. Richie said that you couldn't help learning while you were doing these things . . . and when you got older you didn't rob for "kicks" but for money. That's what most of the guys who were in trouble did now.

While the "fun" component in stealing was common in each of the lower-class areas, the organization of a deliberate income-producing theft pattern was most developed in Haulburg.

Values

Delinquents from Haulburg, like those from Slumtown, were considerably less oriented to criminal or illegitimate norms and values than were delinquents from Racketville (see Table 1). At the same time, the observational data suggested, on the whole, that the conventional standard of respectability was more firmly established in delinquents from Haulburg than in delinquents from the other two areas. Hardly any delinquents from Haulburg were oriented to careers in the rackets. Only a small number of them had ever had any contact with adult racketeers or seen them as role-models (see Table 2). Delinquents from this area attributed high status to professional people. Occupations such as those of engineer, military officer, and social worker were highly desired. Local business proprietors, such as garage owners or even landlords, were also attractive role-models. In Haulburg, as in Slumtown, formal education was considered the key to the achievement of adult success status. Connections were considered important but not nearly so important as they were regarded in Racketville (see Table 3). At the same time, partial access to criminal opportunities was available, and they were considered somewhat more important than they were in Slumtown.

. . .

SUMMARY

Characteristic subcultures and concomitant behavioral systems appeared to have developed in the three areas under discussion. Delinquent behavior was highly aggressive, regardless of neighborhood. However, aggressive orientation and activities were differently organized in each area. For example, the racket subculture "toughness" was directly associated with preparation for careers in the rackets. In the conflict subculture, aggressive behavior was highly organized for purposes of group conflict. In theft subculture, aggressive orientations tended to be more indirect and were expressed through acts of theft.

In Racketville, there was little question that the value orientation of delinquents was highly criminal or illegitimate; a large proportion of delinquents aspired to be racketeers. A guide to success in this area was expressed as: "It isn't *what* you know but *whom* you know that counts." While the data did not establish a heavy involvement of delinquents from this area in racket activity, it did demonstrate the anticipatory readiness of delinquents to participate in organized criminal behavior when such opportunities became available to them. In Slumtown, systematic and continual fighting was prescribed as the means of obtaining prestige and reputation. Other types of delinquent behavior or orientation, such as involvement in theft or racket activity, were relatively minimal. This conflict subculture was not fundamentally organized within a criminal context. True, the gang-fighting response was essentially deviant, but it was not preparatory to a criminal way of life. Delinquents who subscribed to this type of orientation were largely, if weakly, governed by conventional norms and values. They aspired to legitimate careers. They saw formal education as the surest road to achievement.

In Haulburg, orientation to various types of thievery afforded the possibility of illegally appropriating the means to desired success status. Perhaps the chief characteristic of the theft subculture was its evasiveness. The commitment to conventional norms and values was verbalized, but its actual implementation was not achieved. The culture of the middle-class society, with its standards of responsibility, orderliness, and self-control, was fully recognized but only partially acceptable, and a system of illicit orientation was developed which permitted an indirect and partial attack on the established value systems. While acts of theft were permitted, acts of extreme violence were not acceptable.

. . .

Finally, it is important to stress that [this paper] has emphasized the *differences* in delinquent orientation and behavior of each area. Delinquent subcultures are not totally mutually exclusive. They may exist side by side and interpenetrate each other. What this [paper] has pointed out is the dominant character of delinquent subcultural patterns and how they are distinctively associated with certain neighborhood conditions.

3 Cats, Kicks, and Color[*]

HAROLD FINESTONE

Growing recognition that the most recent manifestation of the use of opiates in this country has been predominantly a young peoples' problem has resulted in some speculation as to the nature of this generation of drug users. Is it possible to form an accurate conception as to what "manner of man" is represented by the current species of young drug addict? Intensive interviews between 1951 and 1953 with over fifty male colored users of heroin in their late teens and early twenties selected from several of the areas of highest incidence of drug use in Chicago served to elicit from them the expression of many common attitudes, values, schemes of behavior, and general social orientation. Moreover, since there was every reason to believe that such similarities had preceded their introduction to heroin, it appeared that it was by virtue of such shared features that they had been unusually receptive to the spread of opiate use. Methodologically, their common patterns of behavior suggested the heuristic value of the construction of a social type. The task of this paper is to depict this social type, and to present a

Reprinted from *Social Problems*, Volume 5, Number 1 (July, 1957), 3–13, by permission of The Society for the Study of Social Problems and the author.

* This investigation was supported by research grant 3M 9030 from the National Institute of Mental Health, Public Health Service, and was carried on under the direction of Clifford R. Shaw and Solomon Kobrin. The writer acknowledges the generous assistance received in the clarification of the problems dealt with in this paper through discussions with Clifford R. Shaw, Henry D. McKay, and Solomon Kobrin, supervising sociologists at the Illinois Institute for Juvenile Research and the Chicago Area Project.

hypothetical formulation to account for the form it has taken.

No special justification appears to be necessary for concentrating in this paper on the social type of the young colored drug user. One of the distinctive properties of the distribution of drug use as a social problem, at least in Chicago, is its high degree of both spatial and racial concentration. In fact, it is a problem which in this city can be pinpointed with great accuracy as having its incidence preponderantly among the young male colored persons in a comparatively few local community areas. The following delineation of the generic characteristics of young colored drug users constitutes in many respects an ideal type. No single drug addict exemplified all of the traits to be depicted but all of them revealed several of them to a marked degree.

The young drug user was a creature of contrasts. Playing the role of the fugitive and pariah as he was inevitably forced to do, he turned up for interviews in a uniformly ragged and dirty condition. And yet he talked with an air of superiority derived from his identification with an elite group, the society of "cats." He came in wearing a non-functional tie clip attached to his sport shirt and an expensive hat as the only indications that he was concerned with his appearance and yet displayed in his conversation a highly developed sense of taste in men's clothing and a high valuation upon dressing well. He came from what were externally the drabbest, most overcrowded, and physically deteriorated sections of the city and yet discussed his pattern of living as though it were a consciously cultivated work of art.

Despite the location of his social world in the "asphalt jungle" of the "Blackbelt" he strictly eschewed the use of force and violence as a technique for achieving his ends or for the settling of problematic situations. He achieved his goals by indirection, relying, rather, on persuasion and on a repertoire of manipulative techniques. To deal with a variety of challenging situations, such as those arising out of his contacts with the police, with his past or potential victims, and with jilted "chicks," etc., he used his wits and his conversational ability. To be able to confront such contingencies with adequacy and without resort to violence was to be "cool." His idea was to get what he wanted through persuasion and ingratiation; to use the other fellow by deliberately outwitting him. Indeed, he regarded himself as immeasurably superior to the "gorilla," a person who resorted to force.

The image of himself as "operator" was projected onto the whole world about him and led to a complete skepticism as to other persons' motives. He could relate to people by outsmarting them, or through open-handed and often ruinous generosity, but his world seemed to preclude any relationship which was not part of a "scheme" or did not lend itself to an "angle." The most difficult puzzle for him to solve was the "square," the honest man. On the one hand the "square" was the hard-working plodder who lived by routine and who took honesty and the other virtues at their face value. As such he constituted the prize victim for the cat. On the other hand the cat harbored the sneaking suspicion that some squares were smarter than he, because they could enjoy all the forbidden pleasures which were his stock in trade and maintain a reputation for respectability in the bargain.

The cat had a large, colorful, and discriminating vocabulary which dealt with all phases of his experience with drugs. In addition, he never seemed to content himself with the conventional word for even the most common-place objects. Thus he used "pad" for house, "pecks" for food, "flicks" for movies, "stick hall" for pool hall, "dig the scene" for observe, "box" for record player, "bread" for money, etc. In each instance the word he used was more concrete or earthier than the conventional word and such as to reval an attitude of subtle ridicule towards the dignity and conventionality inherent in the common usage.

His soft convincing manner of speaking, the shocking earthiness and fancifulness of his vocabulary, together with the formidable gifts of charm and ingratiation which he deployed, all contributed to the dominant impression which the young drug user made as a person. Such traits would seem to have fitted naturally into a role which some cats had already played or aspired to play, that of the pimp. To be supported in idleness and luxury through the labors of one or more attractive "chicks" who shoplifted or engaged in prostitution or both and dutifully handed over the proceeds was one of his favorite fantasies. In contrast with the milieu of the white under-world, the pimp was not an object of opprobrium but of prestige.

The theme of the exploitation of the woman goes close to the heart of the cat's orientation to life, that is, his attitude towards work. Part of the cat's sense of superiority stems from his aristocratic disdain for work and for the subordination of self to superiors and to the repetitive daily routine entailed by work, which he regards as intolerable. The "square" is a person who toils for regular wages and who takes orders from his superiors without complaint.

In contrast with the "square," the cat gets by without working. Instead he keeps himself in "bread" by a set of ingenious variations on "begging, borrowing, or stealing." Each cat has his "hustle,"[1] and a "hustle" is any non-violent means of "making some bread" which does not require work. One of the legendary heroes of the cat is the man who is such a skillful con-man that he can sell "State Street" to his victim. Concretely, the cat is a petty thief, pickpocket, or pool shark, or is engaged in a variety of other illegal activities of the "conning" variety. A very few cats are actually living off the proceeds of their women "on the hustle."

The main purpose of life for the cat is to experience the "kick." Just

---

[1] Harold Finestone, "Narcotics and Criminality," *Law and Contemporary Problems*, 22 (Winter, 1957), pp. 60–85.

as every cat takes pride in his "hustle," so every cat cultivates his "kick." A "kick" is any act tabooed by "squares" that heightens and intensifies the present moment of experience and differentiates it as much as possible from the humdrum routine of daily life. Sex in any of its conventional expressions is not a "kick" since this would not serve to distinguish the cat from the "square," but orgies of sex behavior and a dabbling in the various perversions and byways of sex pass muster as "kicks." Some "cats" are on an alcohol "kick," others on a marihuana "kick," and others on a heroin "kick." There is some interchangeability among these various "kicks" but the tendency is to select your "kick" and stay with it. Many of these young drug users, however, had progressed from the alcohol to the marihuana to the heroin "kick." Each "kick" has its own lore of appreciation and connoisseurship into which only its devotees are initiated.

In addition to his "kick" the cat sets great store on the enjoyment of music and on proper dress. To enjoy one's "kick" without a background of popular music is inconceivable. The cat's world of music has a distinctive galaxy of stars, and the brightest luminaries in his firmament are performers such as "Yardbird" (the late Charlie Parker) and disc jockeys such as Al Benson. Almost every cat is a frustrated musician who hopes some day to get his "horn" out of pawn, take lessons, and earn fame and fortune in the field of "progressive music."

The cat places a great deal of emphasis upon clothing and exercises his sartorial talents upon a skeletal base of suit, sport shirt, and hat. The suit itself must be conservative in color. Gaiety is introduced through the selection of the sport shirt and the various accessories, all so chosen and harmonized as to reveal an exquisite sense of taste. When the cat was not talking about getting his clothes out of pawn, he talked about getting them out of the cleaners. With nonchalant pride one drug user insisted that the most expensive sport shirts and hats in the city of Chicago were sold in a certain haberdashery on the South Side. The ideal cat would always appear in public impeccably dressed and be able to sport a complete change of outfit several times a day.

The cat seeks through a harmonious combination of charm, ingratiating speech, dress, music, the proper dedication to his "kick," and unrestrained generosity to make of his day-to-day life itself a gracious work of art. Everything is to be pleasant and everything he does and values is to contribute to a cultivated aesthetic approach to living. The "cool cat" exemplifies all of these elements in proper balance. He demonstrates his ability to "play it cool" in his unruffled manner of dealing with outsiders such as the police, and in the self-assurance with which he confronts emergencies in the society of "cats." Moreover, the "cat" feels himself to be any man's equal. He is convinced that he can go anywhere and mingle easily with anyone. For example, he rejects the type of music designated "the blues" because for him it symbolizes attitudes of submission and resignation which are repugnant and alien to his customary frame of mind.

It can be seen now why heroin use should make such a powerful appeal to the cat. It was the ultimate "kick." No substance was more profoundly tabooed by conventional middle-class society. Regular heroin use provides a sense of maximal social differentiation from the "square." The cat was at last engaged, he felt, in an activity completely beyond the comprehension of the "square." No other "kick" offered such an instantaneous intensification of the immediate moment of experience and set it apart from everyday experience in such spectacular fashion. Any words used by the cat to apply to the "kick," the experience of "being high," he applied to heroin in the superlative. It was the "greatest kick of them all."

In the formulation now to be presented the cat as a social type is viewed as a manifestation of a process of social change in which a new type of self-conception has been emerging among the adolescents of the lower socio-economic levels of the colored population in large urban centers. It is a self-conception rooted in the types of accommodation to a subordinate status achieved historically by the colored race in this country, a self-conception which has become increasingly articulated as it responded to and selected various themes from the many available to it in the milieu of the modern metropolis. Blumer's classification of social movements into general, specific, or expressive, appears to provide a useful framework for the analysis of the social type of the cat.[2]

In terms of these categories the cat as a social type is the personal counterpart of an expressive social movement. The context for such a movement must include the broader community, which, by its policies of social segregation and discrimination, has withheld from individuals of the colored population the opportunity to achieve or to identify with status positions in the larger society. The social type of the cat is an expression of one possible type of adaptation to such blocking and frustration, in which a segment of the population turns in upon itself and attempts to develop within itself criteria for the achievement of social status and the rudiments of a satisfactory social life. Within his own isolated social world the cat attempts to give form and purpose to dispositions derived from but denied an outlet within the dominant social order.

What are these dispositions and in what sense may they be said to be derived from the dominant social order? Among the various interrelated facets of the life of the cat two themes are central, those of the "hustle" and the "kick." It is to be noted that they are in direct antithesis to two

[2] Herbert Blumer, "Social Movements," in Robert E. Park, ed., *An Outline of the Principles of Sociology* (New York: Barnes & Noble, 1939), pp. 255-278.

of the central values of the dominant culture, the "hustle" versus the paramount importance of the occupation for the male in our society, and the "kick" versus the importance of regulating conduct in terms of its future consequences. Thus, there appears to be a relationship of conflict between the central themes of the social type of the cat and those of the dominant social order. As a form of expressive behavior, however, the social type of the cat represents an indirect rather than a direct attack against central conventional values.

It is interesting to speculate on the reasons why a type such as the cat should emerge rather than a social movement with the objective of changing the social order. The forces coercing the selective process among colored male adolescents in the direction of expressive social movements are probably to be traced to the long tradition of accommodation to a subordinate status on the part of the Negro as well as to the social climate since the Second World War, which does not seem to have been favorable to the formation of specific social movements.

The themes of the "hustle" and "kick" in the social orientation of the cat are facts which appear to be overdetermined. For example, to grasp the meaning of the "hustle" to the cat one must understand it as a rejection of the obligation of the adult male to work. When asked for the reasons underlying his rejection of work the car did not refer to the uncongenial and relatively unskilled and low-paid jobs which, in large part, were the sole types of employment available to him. He emphasized rather that the routine of a job and the demand that he should apply himself continuously to his work task were the features that made work intolerable for him. The self-constraint required by work was construed as an unwarranted damper upon his love of spontaneity. The other undesirable element from his point of view was the authoritarian setting of most types of work with which he was familiar.

There are undoubtedly many reasons for the cat's rejection of work but the reasons he actually verbalized are particularly significant when interpreted as devices for sustaining his self-conception. The cat's feeling of superiority would be openly challenged were he to confront certain of the social realities of his situation, such as the discrimination exercised against colored persons looking for work and the fact that only the lowest status jobs are available to him. He avoided any mention of these factors which would have forced him to confront his true position in society and thus posed a threat to his carefully cherished sense of superiority.

In emphasizing as he does the importance of the "kick" the cat is attacking the value our society places upon planning for the future and the responsibility of the individual for such planning. Planning always requires some subordination and disciplining of present behavior in the interest of future rewards. The individual plans to go to college, plans for his career, plans for his family and children, etc. Such an orientation on the part of the individual is merely the personal and subjective counterpart of a stable social order and of stable social institutions, which not only permit but sanction an orderly progression of expectations with reference to others and to one's self. Where such stable institutions are absent or in the inchoate stages of development, there is little social sanction for such planning in the experience of the individual. Whatever studies are available strongly suggest that such are the conditions which tend to prevail in the lower socio-economic levels of the Negro urban community.[3] Stable family and community organization is lacking in those areas of the city where drug use is concentrated. A social milieu which does not encourage the subordination and disciplining of present conduct in the interests of future rewards tends by default to enhance the present. The "kick" appears to be a logical culmination of this emphasis.

Accepting the emergence of the self-conception of the cat as evidence of a developing expressive social movement, we may phrase the central theoretical problem as follows: What are the distinctive and generic features of the cat's social orientation? Taking a cue from the work of Huizinga as developed in *Homo Ludens*,[4] we propose that the generic characteristics of the social type of the cat are those of play. In what follows, Huizinga's conception of play as a distinctive type of human activity will be presented and then applied as a tool of analysis for rendering intelligible the various facets of the social orientation of the cat. It is believed that the concept of play indicates accurately the type of expressive social movement which receives its embodiment in the cat.

According to Huizinga the concept of play is a primary element of human experience and as such is not susceptible to exact definition.

"The *fun* of playing resists all analysis, all logical interpretation . . . Nevertheless it is precisely this fun-element that characterizes the essence of play."[5] The common image of the young colored drug addict pictures him as a pitiful figure, a trapped unfortunate. There is a certain amount of truth in this image, but it does not correspond to the conception which the young colored addict has of himself or to the impression that he tries to communicate to others. If it were entirely true it would be difficult to square with the fact that substantial numbers of young colored persons continue to become drug users. The cat experiences and manifests a certain zest in his mode of life which is far from self-pity. This fun element seemed to come particularly to the fore as the cat recounted his

---

[3] St. Clair Drake and Horace R. Cayton, "Lower Class: Sex and Family," *Black Metropolis* (New York: Harcourt, Brace & Co., 1945), pp. 564–599.

[4] Johan Huizinga, *Homo Ludens, A Study of the Play Element in Culture* (Boston: Beacon Press, 1955).

[5] *Ibid.*, p. 3.

search for "kicks," the adventure of his life on the streets, and the intensity of his contest against the whole world to maintain his supply of drugs. Early in the cycle of heroin use itself there was invariably a "honeymoon" stage when the cat abandoned himself most completely to the experience of the drug. For some cats this "honeymoon" stage, in terms of their ecstatic preoccupation with the drug, was perpetual. For others it passed, but the exigencies of an insatiable habit never seemed to destroy completely the cat's sense of excitement in his way of life.

While Huizinga declines to define play, he does enumerate three characteristics which he considers to be proper to play. Each one of them when applied to the cat serves to indicate a generic feature of his social orientation.

(a) "First and foremost . . . all play is a voluntary activity."[6] "Here we have the first main characteristic of play: that it is free, is in fact freedom."[7] The concept of an expressive social movement assumes a social situation where existing social arrangements are frustrating and are no longer accepted as legitimate and yet where collective activity directed towards the modification of these limitations is not possible. The cat is "free" in the sense that he is a pre-eminent candidate for new forms of social organization and novel social practices. He is attempting to escape from certain features of the historical traditions of the Negro which he regards as humiliating. As an adolescent or young adult he is not fully assimilated into such social institutions as the family, school, church, or industry which may be available to him. Moreover, the social institutions which the Negroes brought with them when they migrated to the city have not as yet achieved stability or an adequate functioning relationship to the urban environment. As a Negro, and particularly as a Negro of low socio-economic status, he is excluded from many socializing experiences which adolescents in more advantaged sectors of the society take for granted. He lives in communities where the capacity of the population for effective collective action is extremely limited, and consequently there are few effective controls on his conduct besides that exercised by his peer group itself. He is fascinated by the varied "scenes" which the big city spreads out before him. Granted this setting, the cat adopts an adventurous attitude to life and is free to give his allegiance to new forms of activity.

(b) . . . A second characteristic is closely connected with this (that is, the first characteristic of freedom), namely, that play is not "ordinary" or "real" life. It is rather a stepping out of "real" life into a temporary sphere of activity with a disposition all of its own. Every child knows perfectly well that he is "only pretending," or that it was "only for fun." . . . This "only pretending" quality

6 *Ibid.*, p. 7.
7 *Ibid.*, p. 8.

of play betrays a consciousness of the inferiority of play compared with "serious-ness," a feeling that seems to be something as primary as play itself. Nevertheless . . . the consciousness of play being "only a pretend" does not by any means prevent it from proceeding with the utmost seriousness, with an absorption, a devotion that passes into rapture and, temporarily at least, completely abolishes that troublesome "only" feeling.[8]

It is implicit in the notion of an expressive social movement that, since direct collective action to modify the sources of dissatisfaction and restless-ness is not possible, all such movements should appear under one guise, as forms of "escape." Persons viewing the problem of addiction from the perspective of the established social structure have been prone to make this interpretation. It is a gross oversimplification, however, as considered from the perspective of the young drug addict himself. The emergence of the self-conception of the cat is an attempt to deal with the problems of status and identity in a situation where participation in the life of the broader community is denied, but where the colored adolescent is becoming increas-ingly sensitive to the values, the goals, and the notions of success which obtain in the dominant social order.

The caste pressures thus make it exceedingly difficult for an American Negro to preserve a true perspective of himself and his own group in relation to the larger white society. The increasing abstract knowledge of the world outside—of its opportunities, its rewards, its different norms of competition and coopera-tion—which results from the proceeding acculturation at the same time as there is increasing group isolation, only increases the tensions.[9]

Such conditions of group isolation would appear to be fairly uniform throughout the Negro group. Although this isolation may be experienced differently at different social levels of the Negro community, certain fea-tures of the adaptations arrived at in response to this problem will tend to reveal similarities. Since the struggle for status takes place on a stage where there is acute sensitivity to the values and status criteria of the dominant white group, but where access to the means through which such values may be achieved is prohibited, the status struggle turning in on itself will assume a variety of distorted forms. Exclusion from the "serious" concerns of the broader community will result in such adaptations manifesting a strong ele-ment of "play."

Frazier in *Black Bourgeoisie* discusses the social adaptation of the Negro middle class as "The World of Make-Believe."[10]

---

[8] *Ibid.*, p. 8.

[9] Gunnar Myrdal, *An American Dilemma* (New York: Harper & Brothers, 1944), p. 760.

[10] E. Franklin Frazier, *Black Bourgeoisie* (Glencoe, Illinois: Free Press, 1957).

The emphasis upon "social" life or "society" is one of the main props of the world of make-believe into which the black bourgeoisie has sought an escape from its inferiority and frustrations in American society. This world of make-believe, to be sure, is a reflection of the values of American society, but it lacks the economic basis that would give it roots in the world of reality.[11]

In the Negro lower classes the effects of frustrations deriving from subordination to the whites may not be experienced as personally or as directly as it is by the Negro middle class, but the massive effects of residential segregation and the lack of stable social institutions and community organization are such as to reinforce strong feelings of group isolation even at the lowest levels of the society.

It is here suggested that the function performed by the emergence of the social type of the cat among Negro lower class adolescents is analogous to that performed by "The World of Make-Believe" in the Negro middle class. The development of a social type such as that of the cat is only possible in a situation where there is isolation from the broader community but great sensitivity to its goals, where the peer group pressures are extremely powerful, where institutional structures are weak, where models of success in the illegitimate world have strong appeals, where specific social movements are not possible, and where novel forms of behavior have great prestige. To give significance to his experience, the young male addict has developed the conception of a heroic figure, the "ideal cat," a person who is completely adequate to all situations, who controls his "kick" rather than letting it control him, who has a lucrative "hustle," who has no illusions as to what makes the world "tick," who is any man's equal, who basks in the admiration of his brother cats and associated "chicks," who hob-nobs with "celebs" of the musical world, and who in time himself may become a celebrity.

The cat throws himself into his way of life with a great deal of intensity but he cannot escape completely from the perspective, the judgments, and the sanctions of the dominant social order. He has to make place in his scheme of life for police, lockups, jails, and penitentiaries, to say nothing of the agonies of withdrawal distress. He is forced eventually to confront the fact that his role as a cat with its associated attitudes is largely a pose, a form of fantasy with little basis in fact. With the realization that he is addicted he comes only too well to know that he is a "junky," and he is fully aware of the conventional attitudes towards addicts as well as of the counter-rationalizations provided by his peer group. It is possible that the cat's vacillation with regard to seeking a cure for his addiction is due to a conflict of perspectives, whether to view his habit from the cat's or the dominant social order's point of view.

[11] *Ibid.*, p. 237.

(c) Play is distinct from "ordinary" life both as to locality and duration. This is the third main characteristic of play: its secludedness, its limitedness. It is "played out" within certain limits of time and place. It contains its own course and meaning.[12]

It is this limited, esoteric character of heroin use which gives to the cat the feeling of belonging to an elite. It is the restricted extent of the distribution of drug use, the scheming and intrigue associated with underground "connections" through which drugs are obtained, the secret lore of the appreciation of the drug's effects, which give the cat the exhilaration of participating in a conspiracy. Contrary to popular conception most drug users were not anxious to proselyte new users. Of course, spreading the habit would have the function of increasing the possible sources of supply. But an equally strong disposition was to keep the knowledge of drug use secret, to impress and dazzle the audience with one's knowledge of being "in the know." When proselyting did occur, as in jails or lockups, it was proselyting on the part of a devotee who condescended to share with the uninitiated a highly prized practice and set of attitudes.

As he elaborates his analysis of play, Huizinga brings to the fore additional aspects of the concept which also have their apt counterpart in the way of life of the cat. For instance, as was discussed earlier, the cat's appreciation of "progressive music" is an essential part of his social orientation. About this topic Huizinga remarks, "Music, as we have hinted before, is the highest and purest expression of the *facultas ludendi*."[13] The cat's attitude toward music has a sacred, almost mystical quality. "Progressive music" opens doors to a type of highly valued experience which for him can be had in no other way. It is more important to him than eating and is second only to the "kick." He may have to give up his hope of dressing according to his standards but he never gives up music.

Huizinga also observes, "Many and close are the links that connect play with beauty."[14] He refers to the "profoundly aesthetic quality of play."[15] The aesthetic emphasis which seems so central to the style of living of the cat is a subtle elusive accent permeating his whole outlook but coming to clearest expression in a constellation of interests, the "kick," clothing, and music. And it certainly reaches a level of awareness in their language. Language is utilized by the cat with a conscious relish, with many variations and individual turns of phrase indicating the value placed upon creative expression in this medium.

It is to be noted that much of the description of the cat's attributes did

---

[12] Johan Huizinga, *op. cit.*, p. 9.
[13] *Ibid.*, p. 187.
[14] *Ibid.*, p. 7.
[15] *Ibid.*, p. 2.

not deal exclusively with elements unique to him. Many of the features mentioned are prevalent among adolescents in all reaches of the status scale. Dress, music, language, and the search for pleasure are all familiar themes of the adolescent world. For instance, in his description of the adolescent "youth culture" Talcott Parsons would appear to be presenting the generic traits of a "play-form" with particular reference to its expression in the middle class.

It is at the point of emergence into adolescence that there first begins to develop a set of patterns and behavior phenomena which involve a highly complex combination of age grading and sex role elements. These may be referred to together as the phenomena of the "youth culture". . . .
Perhaps the best single point of reference for characterizing the youth culture lies in its contrast with the dominant pattern of the adult male role. By contrast with the emphasis on responsibility in this role, the orientation of the youth culture is more or less specifically irresponsible. One of its dominant roles is "having a good time." . . . It is very definitely a rounded humanistic pattern rather than one of competence in the performance of specified functions.[16]

Such significant similarities between this description and the themes of the social type of the cat only tend to reinforce the notion that the recent spread of heroin use was a problem of adolescence. The cat is an adolescent sharing many of the interests of his age-mates everywhere but confronted by a special set of problems of color, tradition, and identity.

The social orientation of the cat, with its emphasis on non-violence, was quite in contrast to the orientation of the smaller group of young white drug users who were interviewed in the course of this study. The latter's type of adjustment placed a heavy stress upon violence. Their crimes tended to represent direct attacks against persons and property. The general disposition they manifested was one of "nerve" and brashness rather than one of "playing it cool." They did not cultivate the amenities of language, music, or dress to nearly the same extent as the cat. Their social orientation was expressed as a direct rather than an indirect attack on the dominant values of our society. This indicates that the "youth culture" despite its generic features may vary significantly in different social settings.

In his paper, "Some Jewish Types of Personality," Louis Wirth made the following suggestive comments about the relationship between the social type and its setting.

A detailed analysis of the crucial personality types in any given area or cultural group shows that they depend upon a set of habits and attitudes in the group for their existence and are the direct expressions of the values of the group.

[16] Talcott Parsons, "Age and Sex in the Social Structure," *Essays in Sociological Theory Pure and Applied* (Glencoe, Illinois: Free Press, 1949), pp. 220–221.

As the life of the group changes there appears a host of new social types, mainly outgrowths and transformations of previous patterns which have become fixed through experience.[17]

What are some of the sources of the various elements going to make up the social type of the cat which may be sought in his traditions? The following suggestions are offered as little more than speculation at the present time. The emphasis upon non-violence on the part of the cat, upon manipulative techniques rather than overt attack, is a stress upon the indirect rather than the direct way towards one's goal. May not the cat in this emphasis be betraying his debt to the "Uncle Tom" type of adjustment, despite his wish to dissociate himself from earlier patterns of accommodation to the dominant white society? May not the "kick" itself be a cultural lineal descendant of the ecstatic moment of religious possession so dear to revivalist and store-front religion? Similarly, may not the emphasis upon the exploitation of the woman have its origin in the traditionally greater economic stability of the colored woman?

W. I. Thomas in one of his references to the problems raised by the city environment stated, "Evidently the chief problem is the young American person."[18] In discussing the type of inquiry that would be desirable in this area he states that it should

. . . lead to a more critical discrimination between that type of disorganization in the youth which is a real but frustrated tendency to organize on a higher plane, or one more correspondent with the moving environment, and that type of disorganization which is simply the abandonment of standards. It is also along this line . . . that we shall gain light on the relation of fantastic phantasying to realistic phantasying. . . .[19]

Posed in this way the problem becomes one of evaluating the social type of the cat in relation to the processes of social change. This social type is difficult to judge according to the criterion suggested by Thomas. Since many of the cat's interests are merely an extreme form of the adolescent "youth culture," in part the problem becomes one of determining how functional the period of adolescence is as preparation for subsequent adult status. However, the central phases of the social orientation of the cat, the "hustle" and the "kick," do represent a kind of disorganization which indicates the abandonment of conventional standards. The young addicted cat is "going nowhere." With advancing age he cannot shed his addiction the way he can

[17] Louis Wirth, "Some Jewish Types of Personality," in Ernest W. Burgess, ed., *The Urban Community* (Chicago: University of Chicago Press, 1926), p. 112.

[18] William I. Thomas, "The Problem of Personality in the Urban Environment," in Ernest W. Burgess, ed., *The Urban Community* (Chicago: University of Chicago Press, 1926), p. 46.

[19] *Ibid.*, p. 47.

many of the other trappings of adolescence. He faces only the bleak prospect, as time goes on, of increasing demoralization. Although the plight of the young colored addict is intimately tied to the conditions and fate of his racial group, his social orientation seems to represent a dead-end type of adjustment. Just as Handlin in *The Uprooted* suggests that the first generation of immigrant people to our society tends to be a sacrificed generation,[20] it may be that the unique problems of Negro migrants to our metropolitan areas will lead to a few or several sacrificed generations in the course of the tortuous process of urbanization.

The discussion of the social type of the cat leads inevitably to the issue of social control. Any attempt to intervene or modify the social processes producing the "cat" as a social type must have the objective of reducing his group isolation. For instance, because of such isolation and because of the cat's sensitivity to the gestures of his peers, the most significant role models of a given generation of cats tend to be the cats of the preceding age group. Where, in a period of rapid change, the schemes of behavior of the role-models no longer correspond to the possibilities in the actual situation, it is possible for attitudes to be transmitted to a younger generation which evidence a kind of "cultural lag." Thus the condition of the labor market in Chicago is such as to suggest the existence of plentiful employment opportunities for the Negro in a variety of fields. But because such openings are not mediated to him through role-models it is possible that the cat is unable to take advantage of these opportunities or of the facilities available for training for such positions.

The social type of the cat is a product of social change. The type of social orientation which it has elaborated indicates an all too acute awareness of the values of the broader social order. In an open-class society where upward mobility is positively sanctioned, an awareness and sensitivity to the dominant values is the first stage in their eventual assimilation. Insofar as the social type of the cat represents a reaction to a feeling of exclusion from access to the means towards the goals of our society, all measures such as improved educational opportunities which put these means within his grasp will hasten the extinction of this social type. Just as the "hoodlum" and "gangster" types tend to disappear as the various more recently arrived white ethnic groups tend to move up in the status scale of the community,[21] so it can confidently be expected that the cat as a social type will tend to disappear as such opportunities become more prevalent among the colored population.

[20] Oscar Handlin, *The Uprooted* (New York: Grosset & Dunlap, 1951), p. 243.
[21] Daniel Bell, "Crime as an American Way of Life," *Antioch Review*, 13 (June, 1953), pp. 131–154.

4 Worlds of Drug Use on the Street Scene*

ALAN G. SUTTER

The introduction of new chemical agents affecting the central nervous system, repressive drug control policies, and changing patterns of drug use among young people, raise problems for theoretical analysis and point to unexplored territory in the sociology of deviance. The "subculture" of drug use on the streets of large urban ghettos is often viewed as a "retreatist" role adaptation which provides security and status for people who reject the norms and values of the dominant culture, give up the quest for success, and ultimately escape from the requirements of society. It is also fashionable to picture the young drug user as an inadequate personality who begins his career with marijuana use, later experiments with a variety of other drugs, eventually gets "hooked" on opiates, and thereafter supports a degenerate habit through crime. Scholars have lumped different patterns of drug use into one package by positing the existence of a uniform cultural adaptation made by frustrated or handicapped people who move along a single career line.

It is the task of this essay to illuminate a drug community which is

* This paper was prepared especially for this volume. The study on which it is based was supported in part by a grant from the American Social Health Association, by grants #65029 and #66022 from the President's Committee on Delinquency and Youth Crime, and by an Intern Fellowship in Criminology from the National Institute of Mental Health. The research was carried out under the direction of Herbert Blumer at the Institute of Social Sciences, University of California, Berkeley. The writer acknowledges the generous help in clarifying the problems dealt with in this paper through discussions with Herbert Blumer and Richard Korn.

not homogeneous in composition and reflects anything but a retreatist role adaptation. The culture of drug use on the street scene is constituted by different types of drug users, different sets of practices, different life styles and perspectives. Furthermore, a vast selective process differentiates people at major turning points as they enter into and move through different worlds of drug use, fall into different patterns and sequences of patterns of use, form different kinds of associations, and have different runs of experience which orient them along different career lines. Any attempt to describe or analyze the phenomenon of street-level drug use in terms of a cultural system must account for different social types of users, must grasp the nature of this selective process, and must recognize that worlds of drug use are subject to great fluctuations over time.

During the past three years, informal conversations were held with over 40 heroin users and over 100 adolescents using non-opiate drugs.[1] Most of the participants were met in their own settings while living in the San Francisco Bay Area. Others were seen in jail awaiting trial or while serving time in correctional institutions. Intimate associations were established with drug users in their full round of daily life. This made it possible to ask meaningful questions in the light of their own experiences and to obtain ethnographic descriptions of daily patterns of life. Information gained through participant observation was checked for its authenticity by submitting every account to panels of drug users representing different age, sex, and racial groups, different neighborhood areas, and different social strata. However, the following account will concentrate on the street life of young people from 16 to 25, situated in low-income neighborhoods in the East Bay Area. The portrait of different social worlds was guided by the analogy of a drama,[2] laying special emphasis on language.[3] Action takes place on a "set"—the street scene where users gossip freely in different

[1] This project is currently in progress. The methodology and some of the following material on adolescent drug use are elaborated in Herbert Blumer, Alan Sutter, Roger Smith, and Samir Ahmed, "The World of Youthful Drug Use," *Add Center Project, Final Report*, Berkeley: School of Criminology, University of California.

[2] A dramatic perspective was derived from the following sources: Kenneth Burke, *The Philosophy of Literary Form, Studies in Symbolic Action*, rev. ed. (New York: Vintage Books, Random House, 1957); *A Grammar of Motives and a Rhetoric of Motives* (New York: Meridian Books, World, 1962), and *Permanence and Change, An Anatomy of Purpose* (Indianapolis: Bobbs-Merrill, 1965); Herbert Blumer, "Sociological Implications of the Thought of George Herbert Mead," *American Journal of Sociology*, 71 (March, 1966), pp. 535–548, and "Society as Symbolic Interaction," in Arnold M. Rose, ed., *Human Behavior and Social Processes* (Boston: Houghton Mifflin, 1962), pp. 179–192; Orrin E. Klapp, *Heroes, Villains and Fools* (Englewood Cliffs, N.J.: Spectrum Book, Prentice-Hall, 1962), and *Symbolic Leaders, Public Dramas and Public Men* (Chicago: Aldine, 1964); Erving Goffman, *The Presentation of Self in Everyday Life* (Garden City, N.Y.: Anchor Book, Doubleday); Alfred Schutz, "The Problem of Social Reality," in *Collected Papers*, Vol. I, Maurice Natanson, ed., (The Hague: Mar-

circles, coin prosaic slang expressions, label the types of people in their world, and reflect their status in the drug community.

BEING COOL AND THE ILLUSION OF RETREATISM

Harold Finestone's illuminating picture of young Negro addicts belonging to Chicago's "elite society of cats,"[4] has often been advanced to support the idea that drug use is a retreatist role adaptation.[5] The ideal "cat" was "cool" in the face of threatening encounters. He valued charm, sharp dress, non-violence, ingratiating speech, progressive music, manipulative ability, and generosity which in combination gave his daily life routine an artistic flavor and made for a "cultivated approach to living." In the search for "ecstatic" experiences through drugs, cats were detached and aloof from the preoccupations of "squares." Facing typical adolescent problems of adjustment as well as having to deal with problems of color, tradition, and identity, cats rejected the norms and values of the larger society and found security and status within a separate cultural system. If a cat had a lucrative "hustle" or lived idly off the labor of a few "chicks," he could center his entire life around the essentially private, esthetic experience of the "kick." The characteristics of "play" were posited as the generic features of the cat's orientation.

Relying on Finestone's description, Cloward and Ohlin interpreted being cool as "the sense of apartness and detachment which the retreatist experiences in his relationship with the conventional world . . . the retreatist subculture provides avenues to success-goals, to the social admiration and the sense of well-being or oneness with the world which the members feel

---

tinus Nijhoff, 1962); and Harold Garfinkel, "Studies in the Routine Grounds of Everyday Activities," *Social Problems*, 11 (Winter, 1964), pp. 225–250.

[3] See: Edward Sapir, *Culture, Language, and Personality, Selected Essays*, D. G. Mandelbaum, editor, Berkeley: University of California Press, 1949; David Maurer, *Whiz Mob, A Correlation of the Technical Argot of Pickpockets with their Behavior Pattern*, (New Haven, Conn.: College & University Press, 1964), and *The Big Con: The Story of the Confidence Man and the Confidence Game* (Indianapolis: Bobbs-Merrill Co., 1940); and Jacob E. Schmidt, *Narcotics Lingo and Lore* (Springfield, Ill.: Charles C. Thomas, 1959).

[4] Harold Finestone, "Cats, Kicks, and Color," *Social Problems*, 5 (July, 1957), pp. 3–13.

[5] "Defeatism, quietism and resignation are manifested in escape mechanisms which ultimately lead him to 'escape' from the requirements of society." Robert K. Merton, *Social Theory and Social Structure*, rev. ed. (New York: The Free Press of Glencoe, 1963), p. 153.

are otherwise beyond their reach."[6] However, Finestone observed that many features of the "cool society of cats" were "prevalent among adolescents in all reaches of the status scale." Dress styles, music, and the search for pleasure are familiar aspects of adolescent life.[7] This would immediately suggest that the "cool cat" hipster represents only one of many expressive types oriented toward a cool form of existence, and that the cool style is not to be arbitrarily equated with retreatism.

In order to account for why certain lower-class urban slum dwellers move into a retreatist subculture, Cloward and Ohlin advanced the "double-failure" hypothesis.[8] Accordingly, some adolescents who are unable to find a place for themselves in a violent gang subculture, a criminal subculture, or a conventional youth subculture are faced with a status dilemma. If they continue to aspire toward success and repeatedly fail, adolescents are likely to select a retreatist role adaptation and may use drugs as one of the more serious forms of escape. Either because of "internalized prohibitions" or "socially structured barriers," a youngster who cannot make it as a criminal or a square escapes the double-failure by using drugs. Presumably if he gets "hooked" on narcotics, self-esteem and social status can be found in an addict subculture where the escape is complete. But it is clear from Finestone's account that he was depicting the culture of "cats" and certainly not the culture of addicts. After the cat became addicted to narcotics he faced the "exigencies of an insatiable habit," increasing demoralization, and struggled to *maintain* his cool, esthetic approach to life.[9] Interestingly enough, marijuana, not heroin, is the preferred drug among cool adolescent drug users in the East Bay Area. These two areas of drug use do not comprise a single homogeneous culture, nor is there a natural "progression" from the former into the latter. For the most part there are barriers separating non-opiate users from opiate addicts, and the lines of access to heroin circles are restricted, depending on special runs of experience. Three major social types in the cool pattern will be discussed: the "Mellow Dude," the "Pot Head," and the "Player."

The Mellow Dude

The most common type of adolescent drug user encountered was recognized as a "mellow dude" or "mellow fellow"—one who centers his

[6] Richard A. Cloward and Lloyd E. Ohlin, *Delinquency and Opportunity* (New York: The Free Press of Glencoe, 1960), p. 27.

[7] *Op. cit.*, p. 11.

[8] *Op. cit.*, pp. 178–186.

[9] Finestone, *op. cit.*, p. 8.

daily life around "partying," "fine music," sexual conquests, and varieties of sensual experience. Marijuana is the most popular drug in the "mellow crowd"; although amphetamine pills are often "dropped" in the course of "getting loaded," and less frequent LSD "trips" are taken. A mellow person is "game to try anything once," but he always "maintains his cool" during the quest for experience; he "knows what's happening" on the street scene, and is very selective in his choice of associates. The primary difference between a "mellow fellow" and a "pot head" lies in the regularity of drug use and the degree of participation in the adolescent drug market.

Mellow dudes distinguish themselves from pot heads in that they take no special pride in using drugs; their drug use is relatively inexpensive and constitutes a small portion of their round of life; they do not often "go out of their way" to buy drugs, and they may use any number of drugs when the situation is "appropriate."

I'd say that I get loaded when it comes my way, but I don't consider myself a pot head, you know. I'm not going out of my way to look for it. Ain't no big thing to me . . . I mean it's a boss high (pleasant experience), mellow off, listen to music, just groove you know. 'Cause when you get loaded your conversation gets strong, man. You really get down with a broad. You want this girl, and this weed's going to make you want to pile (have sexual intercourse) right now. . . .

Parties stand in sharp contrast to wild affairs. "People mind their own business, getting loaded, tripping on different things." Everything is under control, no windows are broken, no fights occur. The atmosphere is casual, similar to adults at a cocktail party among very intimate friends. During larger gatherings, youngsters will "get loaded" first in a car, or at a particular friend's home. After smoking a few "joints" (marijuana cigarettes) and dropping a few pills, they attend the party and initially size up the situation to see if there will be trouble. If things look all right, everyone "falls in the groove" and has a good time. A mellow dude will calmly enjoy himself in an attempt to "rap" (give a line) to a girl. If any trouble arises, he "splits" to avoid the possibility of arrest. Great value is placed on the enjoyment of music, and during any social gathering, a few "sides" (records) are brought out while everyone "just sits back and digs on the music." It is generally believed that one is not sensitive to music, or "not really *in* the music" unless he is "high." The favored types of "sounds" include Rhythm and Blues (Soul Music), Progressive Jazz, certain types of Latin music, and less frequent preferences for Folk-Rock.

A "trip" can be anything which intensifies the present moment of experience, but it normally involves a shifting of attention, re-perception, and re-interpretation of objects from a different vantage point. "Trips" take one out of the "world taken for granted," may allow one to impute occult meanings to common words, may release a person's usual inhibitions, or may allow one to take an attitude of playful pretense toward roles which are usually performed seriously. There are "good trips" and "bum trips." A "lousy party" or unpleasant situation is not made pleasant merely because one is "loaded," but a "good party is even better when you're loaded." Among other things, the trust and confidence in other people present will alter a person's "trip."[10] For example, the presence of a "stranger" can turn a "beautiful trip" on LSD into a terrifying experience; a "rowdy, loud mouth poop butt" making trouble at a party will shatter the common mood of sociability by putting everyone else on a "bum trip." Ideally things should be "mellow" and relaxed. While one is sharing drug experiences, it often happens that particular "trips" are associated with various drugs, almost as if an informal "road map" is devised to plot the journey one can take while intoxicated. The impulse to share one's drug experience with other like-minded people does in fact exist; however, such an impulse is *never* translated into active proselytism among "cool people."

To "turn someone on" means to introduce him to a drug, usually marijuana. It is an expression of trust, friendship, and acceptance. Most lower-strata youth were introduced to drugs in the normal course of living by a close friend or relative. After they learned to use drugs for pleasure,[11] being turned on and turning others on became an established social practice, similar to the convention of buying a friend a drink or offering a drink to a guest when he comes to your home. Since mellow people feel no dependence on drugs and do not deal for profit, it is more common to exchange "joints" with a close friend, "bum" cigarettes for a while, then give joints away, all the time "maintaining one's cool," and "coasting" from party to party. Contrary to the newly emergent drug users in "hippie" and intellectual circles who often "turn on" strangers as an expression of

[10] One cannot fully understand the meaning of drug use in human group life until one grasps the difference between the pharmacological action of different drugs and the way these effects are altered by personal and collective interpretations. "Trips" are radically altered by one's mood, the particular setting, the expected impact of the drug, the purpose for which the drug is used, the amount and frequency of use, and naturally the biographical situation of the person. Since there has been little systematic research on drug use in natural settings, almost nothing is known about the changing subjective responses to different drugs under different conditions. See: David Ebin, ed., *The Drug Experience* (New York: Grove Press, 1965).

[11] Howard Becker observed that before one is able to use marijuana for pleasure, he must learn how to smoke the drug "properly," a very simple process of holding the inhaled smoke in the lungs for a longer period than with a regular cigarette. He must learn to recognize the effects and associate them with being "high," and he must learn to enjoy the effects he has experienced. Unless all three of these conditions are present, one will not be able to use marijuana for pleasure. This sequential model also helps to illuminate the way people come to experience the effects of drugs other than marijuana. See Howard S. Becker, *Outsiders, Studies in the Sociology of Deviance* (New York: The Free Press of Glencoe), pp. 41–78.

love,[12] in cool crowds, one must "establish himself on the set" before he will be turned on.

Concrete images are formed of people who are dangerous, and the structure of the drug community acts as a selective device. If an initiate arrives on the scene and presents an image of being "rowdy," "lame," or "uncool," he is immediately "put on the shine" (shunned). To be "rowdy" is to express oneself in unlimited, nervy, public displays of violence. Physical prowess is aimed at "wowing" an adolescent audience or building up a reputation as the "baddest." "Rowdy dudes" have no set of understandings that impose order over their conduct. Drug use is fluid and unstructured, with no attachment to a particular drug and no shared scheme to control and regulate its use. Alcohol is the preferred intoxicant in the "rowdy set." If no alcohol is available, they will turn to inhalation of glue, gasoline, cotton inserts from sinus inhalers, and so forth. Rowdy dudes are likely to cause "trouble" and are often fair game for police action. On the other hand, a "lame dude" does not "know what's happening." He is "out of it" by not sharing the common schemes of interpretation held by cool people. His parents regulate most of his leisure time activity. One of the most severe threats is a potential "snitch" (informer). Anyone who looks and acts lame, who talks loud in public, who is considered to be "weak minded," who becomes "too inquisitive about drugs," or who cannot "maintain his cool" at the right time is shunned. He is likely to be seen as one who might panic under the threat of arrest. A good test of a person's worth lies in how well he handles himself while in the presence of police.

The mellow dude will use a variety of drugs, especially marijuana, to place him in a mood of sociability or to give him a "sexual boost." He will use a drug as an aphrodisiac, to intensify his own sexual feelings, to arouse the sexual desires in another, to heighten the pleasures of sexual intercourse, or merely to enjoy himself. More interestingly, one can be genuinely "cool" without using drugs and still enjoy the friendship and

[12] Recent drug involvement by adolescents from middle-class backgrounds reflects a radically different scene. College-age drug users and "teeny boppers" or high school "hippies" are not "street people." Drug experience is part of a strained and self-conscious attempt to be authentic, spontaneous, and "hip"; LSD is the drug of increasing popularity, and protest takes on a stylized form. A youth living in poverty need not discover the existential here and now; he lives it. He has experienced fear, suffering, "authentic reality," and the ever present danger of incarceration from the time he was a child running in alleys, drinking wine and learning to survive. Cool people in the lower strata seek to control their drug experience; LSD is often viewed as "too dangerous"; they view "trippers" and "happeners" as fools—as dangerous and "uncool." For a contrast to the cool style, see J. L. Simmons and Barry Winograd, *It's Happening, A Portrait of the Youth Scene Today* (Santa Barbara: Marc-Laird Publications, 1966); J. Larner, "The College Drug Scene," *Atlantic Monthly*, 216 (November, 1965), pp. 127–130; and R. Goldstein, *1 in 7: Drugs on Campus*, New York, 1966.

company of drug-using associates. Drug involvement is not a condition regulating social interaction. It is merely woven into the round of life. If one "knows what's happening," "holds his mug" (does not snitch), and does not "rank" people who get loaded, he is accepted as "one of the fellas." It is clear that mellow dudes approach the usual, pleasure-seeking, sociable adolescent. They go along with the "fellas" who move within a prestige-laden cool pattern of living. Aside from the use of illegal drugs, they are essentially conventional in orientation, staying clear of criminal activity, shunning public displays of violence and delinquency, being totally uninterested in opiate use, and generally fitting into a major stream of youth life:

See the people in my set, after they started getting loaded they squared off completely you know. They wanted to enjoy themselves instead goin' out terrorizing, getting busted (arrested). I'm not going to be no chump . . . I don't see how anyone can get any satisfaction out a drinking, man. In fact, I don't think there's a person in this world that likes the taste of whisky. . . . In the future I'll keep getting loaded when it's there, but then after I move out from my peoples' (parents' home) and get my own pad and get what I want out of school, I might just flat out, cut it loose all together. Pills too. In fact, you can say I only get loaded maybe everyday. Just smoke a joint here and there. I don't hardly buy anything. . . .

The Pot Head

The "pot head," in the course of his daily round of life, represents the generic features of the cool pattern. He is seen by other adolescents as "ultra-cool," one who "knows what's happening," one who handles himself well on the set, one who has complete control over his drug use. In his daily contacts he projects an image of a calm, sensible, solitary figure, soft-spoken and personable. He takes great pride in his appearance, always wearing sharp slacks and sweaters, spit-shined shoes, and a neat, inconspicuous hair style. Interwoven with his speech pattern is a colorful vocabulary of drug argot, combined with slight hand gestures and facial expressions which make him appear loose, good-natured, and self-confident. When he is strolling down the street, his eyes continually dart about. His sensitivity to the presence of the police is often remarkable. Although lodged in an area where violence readily occurs, he will only resort to violence if "pushed" or "sounded on" to the point where he must defend his self-respect. He participates in many conventional activities, often keeping up his studies, sharing in school functions, perhaps engaging in athletics or in conventional forms of employment.

The pot head confines his drug use essentially to smoking marijuana; some even prefer drinking soda pop to liquor. As opposed to mellow dudes who "get loaded on weed to be sociable," the pot head consciously seeks out marijuana, "scores" his own drugs, and may deal on a small-time basis for a "connection" who handles larger quantities. He uses marijuana for a trip, to make him alert in whatever dealings he may be carrying on, to put him in the proper mood for a party or dance, or merely as an integral part of his daily existence. Notice how the following youth takes a second look at the "world-taken-for-granted" by more conventional adolescents and assumes an attitude of playful pretense during school activities; yet, he participates in the full round of conventional adolescent life:

I got sort of a reputation around school. Everybody used to call me Mr. Cool and stuff, but I wouldn't never let it go to my head. . . . 'Cause I used to get loaded and go to school just to wig out on all the people, just a big trip I was on all the time. . . . Like in school, say, during lunch period . . . might go around by the hot dog stand . . . smoke a few joints with the fellas, go back and sit in class and wait for the teacher to make a mistake so you can debate or something . . . After school I go to baseball practice, or in the winter everybody will be trying to find out what's happening on the weekend. . . .

I might be hooked on grass, but I think I'm pretty cool about it, you know . . . I know what's happening. I don't try to get in nobody else's business. I don't want to snitch on anybody neither . . . and I don't run around the streets like them crazy-ass punks, man. People lose respect for you. . . . I don't use nothing else neither. 'Cause if you want to get loaded and stay bright, the only way you can make it is smoking grass. If you drop a lot of pills, or you mess around with stuff, you ain't gonna make it, man. . . .

The pot head considers himself the antithesis of the heroin addict. There is very little association between pot heads and addicts, outside of isolated incidents where family members are addicted to heroin or when an addict drops in on a casual party. Such casual contact is rarely sufficient for a person even to try heroin. The cool pattern acts to limit drug use rather than being favorable to drug dependence:

You know what, man, people like myself, and even younger kids than me right now, they figure an addict is uncool. He's righteously uncool, man, strung out behind that shit. He's lame . . . he's a chump to get off in that bag. He should know a little bit better that if he keeps fucking around with it, he's gonna get on it, gonna get hooked. . . .

While youngsters can buy a matchbox of marijuana for five dollars, exchange joints with friends, then wait to be "turned on" by others, a pot head is more involved in the traffic and normally has more "connections" than the average user. He may buy marijuana by the ounce or in half-pounds, or a number of youths may pitch in their money to buy a pound. If they do pool their money, the pot head will "score" at the next level of the traffic. It is at this level that the risk of arrest is greatest. If a youth is cool, as pot heads are, he will make very few purchases, will try to buy the largest amount possible, and will avoid too many contacts with dealers. In turn, he will deal to a very small number of intimate friends who have been known for years and can be trusted to "hold their mug" in case of arrest. It is to be noted that most pot heads do not make a profit from drugs; they only mediate the flow of marijuana from older adolescent dealers to the general population of adolescent consumers. However, being able to "score" at will brings considerable respect and admiration among friends; not everyone has access to higher levels of the adolescent traffic, knows the right people, and is willing to take the risk of purchasing larger quantities.

Like the mellow fellow, the pot head shares in the general round of conventional adolescent life. His personal traits equip him well for such participation, and there is good reason to believe that he will use his in- genuity to "advance himself": continue with his education, marry, get a conventional job, and raise a family. Many stay clear of criminal activity other than their use of marijuana. Barring unfortunate runs of experience, many pot heads may even diminish their drug use with increasing age. On the other hand, some pot heads are attracted by the money to be made from drugs. The attraction of coming to possess a lucrative "hustle" combines with the existence of petty dealing opportunities at the lower level of the drug traffic to launch a number of people in the direction of hustling. Ironically, there were some pot heads who never sold marijuana for the purpose of making a profit, but after being arrested and incarcer- ated for dealing, they viewed themselves as "chumps" who risked "getting busted without even getting anything out of it." Also, by virtue of in- carceration, some were thrown into intimate association with zealous hustlers, picked up the enterprising spirit of the hustling world, and began to "play."

The Player

The "player" performs a crucial role in the adolescent marketplace and mediates the flow of drugs and hot merchandise from adult hustlers to adolescent consumers. Herman Schwendinger's discovery of an adoles- cent marketplace in Los Angeles[13] prompted observation of a similar market

[13] Schwendinger takes a major theoretical departure from differential association and means-ends explanations by explaining the passage from delinquent to criminal careers in terms of the formation of an illegal adolescent marketplace within the lower strata of the adolescent community and division of labor within this marketplace. See Herman Schwendinger, *The Instrumental Theory of Delinquency: A Tentative Formu- lation.* Unpublished Ph.D. dissertation, University of California, Los Angeles, 1963 (Ann Arbor, Mich.: University Microfilms, Inc., 1964), p. 336.

among adolescents in the East Bay Area. The major suppliers of marijuana, pills, smaller amounts of LSD, and methedrine crystal, together with stolen merchandise (clothes, transistor radios, jewelry, and auto parts) are older youths in the "cool set" who occupy key positions in the lower strata of the adolescent community. Schwendinger hypothesized that "the modal type of criminality-oriented delinquent is the delinquent of the adolescent marketplace" who is not fully integrated into adult arrangements.[14] The specific activities engaged in or the particular type of commodities handled by youth depend upon "prevailing differences in police pressure on different kinds of criminal acts, the available opportunities, and the current demands of the market."[15] These and other factors operate in selecting out people with appropriate background experience to perform various marketplace roles.

While pot heads and mellow dudes are primarily interested in using drugs "socially," the player also uses drugs to help him "game" (hustle). Money is the player's first desire; drug use takes an instrumental slant; the theme of enterprise gradually supplants the theme of sociability. Players tend to see themselves living "slick" and become sensitive to the opportunities to exploit for their monetary gain. They are "light-weight hustlers."

Two types of "playing" or "gaming" are recognized on the "set": "playing hard" and "playing easy." Playing hard refers to the more violent, more dangerous and physical forms of illegal activity taking place in the marketplace—armed robbery, extortion, serving as a bodyguard for a hustler, even engaging in physical violence for hire. What are called the "hustling drugs" by the hard player include methedrine crystal (taken intravenously) and often barbiturate and hypnotic compounds:

Now a lot of dudes on the set will drop a roll of them reds (seconal) . . . and go out terrorizing. . . . But actually I'm all the time testing myself for my conversation and want to see how good I really am. . . . I was wiggin' behind them crystals when I ripped off that warehouse, TVs and radios, you know. . . . I served penitentiary time for that (Youth Authority Institution), and I fell out (was released) and was steady pushing that dope. I was beginning to play now, you know. I was trying to be sharp, trying to get myself together playin' hard . . . crystal makes me play hard.

The easy player selects games which require less physical work and entail a minimal risk of serving "penitentiary time"—selling phony jewelry, pimping, shoplifting, dealing drugs, and pool hustling. Easy players are more likely to use marijuana and amphetamines to help them game. The following account by a light-weight hustler illustrates the enterprising spirit, the suc-

14 *Ibid.*, p. 360.
15 *Ibid.*, p. 337.

cess ideology, and the way motives for using a drug change in the course of one's experience with its effects and changes in one's social world:

Let me tell you, man, life ain't nothing without weed. . . . When I'm high on weed and I'm looking at my clothes, and I got on $65 suede shoes and $3 silk socks, and $5 silk shorts, and I got on this bad shark skin slack suit, great big old diamond ring, this Omega watch, and I'm loaded off this weed, I'm more aware of how good I really am. I think, "Look how I got this," you know, "I got it hustling," and my mind gets sharp. . . .

Like when I first started, I smoked dope just to be happy, yeah, have fun and all. Then I began seeing that weed can do more, you know. . . . Then you see yourself and the way the world really is and the way people be really front-ing. That weed makes me aware so I can game. 'Cause if you're loaded, it seems like you do a lot of things other people can't do. They staggering around from that wine and you feel gooder than they feel and still you can hold your own. . . . I think that they should rename marijuana *future*, 'cause if I get loaded at one o'clock I'm thinking about how I'm going downtown and boost at three o'clock . . . and about them three holes (girls) I got out there. I'm not thinking about the past when I made that hundred dollars yesterday. . . . I may sit down and think: "When I get thirty, I'll own three restaurants, five apartment build-ings and three cafes, and I'll have a gang of holes out there." I'm twenty now and I got a long way to go, man, and I'm gonna make it, man. Weed is part of my progress. . . .[16]

Even players view heroin addicts with contempt, not because they use heroin, but because they are addicted. In their eyes, a heroin addict has lost his cool, has no respect for himself, is quick to "burn" his best friend, and is most likely to "snitch":

Yeah, I shot up some stuff a few times. It was a trip, man, but I don't mess with dope fiends. They steal from you, and they just terrible. I hate people that shoot dope. Oh yeah, they get you busted quick 'cause they can't hold their cool. They foul people, man. . . .

Barriers to the Opiate World

Finestone's picture of the "cool society of cats" cannot be equated with an "addict subculture." On the contrary, the essence of the cool style

[16] This account, one of many, is a good commentary on the frequent attempts by scholars to explain drug use as an expression underlying "motives." Drug use is a developing experience and the defining response of associates shapes whatever "motives" are imputed to the actor. In this sense, motivation does not precede action and cannot be used to account for action. In Mill's terms, it is more useful to view motives as "typical vocabularies having ascertainable functions in delimited societal situations." C. Wright Mills, "Situated Actions and Vocabularies of Motive," *American Sociological Review*, 5 (December, 1940), p. 904, and Herbert Blumer, *op. cit.*

is self-control. The cool motif reflects a system of built-in controls which act to prevent adolescents from "progressing" to opiate use. It serves to limit drug use instead of being favorable to drug dependence. Most cool drug users viewed heroin addicts with disdain, as having "blown their cool," as "punks," "burn artists," "snitches," "dirty," "untrustworthy," and "foul" people. More important, the lines of access to heroin circles are restricted; there was very little association with addicts; many had never even seen a heroin addict. Even youngsters who knew people who were "hooked," or who observed a relative "fixing stuff" and "nodding" were more often disgusted with the sight, not attracted to heroin. Some even tried heroin for the "trip" on isolated occasions and were unimpressed:

I don't appreciate heroin, man. I vomited the first time. I vomited the second time, and the third time I was higher than I ever been before in my life you know, but it wasn't Me. I'd nod, and sex, I didn't want it. . . . I just wanted to sit down, listen to music and be there you know. No, I don't dig it. Weed and crystals is my bag. See you lose everything when that stuff get to you. The habit gets larger and your pocket gets smaller. People healthy get sick and shaggy fast. No, I don't dig it. . . .[17]

Barriers to addict circles, stereotypic views of addicts, unfavorable images of heroin, and experiences entering into the interpretation of the drug effects were factors in a selective process making very few cool drug users disposed to use heroin on a regular basis. The drugs used by youth were limited to marijuana, pills, and much smaller amounts of LSD and methedrine crystal. The popular idea that marijuana users automatically glide along a single path into heroin addiction is fanciful. Access to heroin use was fairly well limited to "players"—light-weight hustlers who were already moving out of the adolescent marketplace into the world of hustlers. Once they began associating with hustlers in the adult marketplace they were exposed to heroin addicts. Some were surprised by particular hustlers who appeared to support an opiate habit as a "luxury"; others were impressed by the hustling ability of some addicts; some got involved with a "dope fiend broad" who "pulled them down." In almost every case, young hustlers were drawn into heroin circles, not merely out of a desire to use narcotics, but out of admiration for a particular addict and the attraction of his life world.

[17] Even with heroin, the interpretation of the situation can radically alter one's initial experience. "Pleasure and pain are elusive, relativistic, subjective phenomena." Alfred R. Lindesmith and John Gagnon, "Anomie and Drug Addiction," in Marshall B. Clinard, ed., *Anomie and Deviant Behavior: A Discussion and Critique* (New York: The Free Press of Glencoe), p. 182, citing Beecher's work with non-addicted subjects. Henry K. Beecher, *Measurement of Subjective Responses* (New York: Oxford University Press), 1959, pp. 321–341.

THE LURE OF THE HUSTLING WORLD

Street addicts who make themselves known to official agencies are most often seen as miserable, petty, "snatch-and-grab junkies" who, status-wise, are at the bottom of the criminal population.[18] Similarly, addicts seen in clinical settings are invariably classified as "inadequate personalities," who become dependent on narcotics because drugs fulfill various passive, dependent, oral-erotic, and narcissistic needs in the psychic economy.[19] In fact, most recent studies lend support to the "double-failure" hypothesis and the retreatist vision of the "addict subculture." In their study of heroin use in New York street gangs, researchers found that "normal" gang members were preoccupied with steady girls and jobs. The emotionally disturbed and "already defeated" gang members turned to narcotics when the gangs began to break up.[20] The same investigators compared a group of delinquents and drug users with a group of squares in the same neighborhood and found that squares more often had cohesive families, could talk to a father, teacher, or priest about their personal problems, could perceive a "meaningful and productive future," worked toward the future, and resisted their deprived neighborhoods.[21] However, when the self-esteem of five groups of prisoners was examined, one finding revealed that early-starting adult addicts in prison had the same level of self-esteem as teen-age prisoners. According to Chein, "It seems that they could preserve their self-esteem by taking to narcotics as an alibi for failure."[22] An outstanding feature of these and similar studies is the attempt to understand addiction by debunking, or even worse, ignoring the addict's own experience. Terms

[18] Harold Finestone, "Narcotics and Criminality," *Law and Contemporary Problems*, 22 (Winter, 1957), pp. 69–85.

[19] See David P. Ausubel, *Drug Addiction: Physiological, Psychological, and Sociological Aspects* (New York: Random House, 1966); Donald L. Gerard and Conan Kornetsky, "Adolescent Opiate Addiction: A Study of Control and Addict Subjects," *Psychiatric Quarterly*, 29 (March, 1955), pp. 457–486, and "A Social and Psychiatric Study of Adolescent Opiate Addicts," *Psychiatric Quarterly*, 28 (January, 1954) pp. 113–125; Paul Zimmering, *et al.* "Heroin Addiction in Adolescent Boys," *Journal of Nervous and Mental Diseases*, 114 (July, 1951), pp. 19–34; Martin Hoffman, "Drug Addiction and 'Hypersexuality' Related Modes of Mastery," *Comprehensive Psychiatry*, 5 (August, 1964), pp. 262–270; and Robert A. Savitt, "Psychoanalytic Studies on Addiction: Ego Structure in Narcotic Addiction," *The Psychoanalytic Quarterly*, 32 (January, 1963), pp. 43–57.

[20] I. Chein, D. L. Gerard, R. S. Lee, and E. Rosenfeld, *The Road to H: Narcotics, Delinquency, and Social Policy* (New York: Basic Books, 1964), pp. 177–178; and I. Chein, "The Use of Narcotics as a Personal and Social Problem," in *Narcotics*, D. Wilner and G. Kassebaum, eds. (New York: McGraw-Hill, 1965), p. 110.

[21] *Ibid.*, p. 111. See also Chein, *et al.*, *The Road to H, op. cit.*, pp. 141–145.

[22] *Ibid.*, p. 111. See also Chein, *et al.*, *The Road to H, op. cit.*, pp. 188–192.

like "inadequacy," "failure," "defeatism," "immaturity," merely convey an ethnocentric, middle-class view of social reality.

Without understanding the romantic pull of the hustling world, the colorful life of "successful" hustlers, the sportlike challenge of the hustling games, and the nature of the illegal marketplace, it is impossible to grasp fully the nature of opiate use in the United States. Hustling enterprise plays a central role in both the initiation into opiate use and abstinence from opiate use. Outside of prison experience, lower-class adolescents are drawn into hustling when they begin to mediate the flow of drugs and hot merchandise from adult hustlers to other adolescent consumers. A player becomes a hustler when his games are converted into the polished works of a craftsman. Commitment to his action gradually shifts from playful pretense and a preoccupation with the immediate present to "serious business" and preoccupation with a master crime scheme for the future. Hustling appeals to many as the road to an elite type of existence, success, prestige, and luxury.

The Ideal Hustler

On the basis of his experience, a successful hustler believes that "life is a racket," "everyone has a front," and "everyone is running a game." All bona fide hustlers strive for a life of conspicuous wealth and leisure time. Visible evidence of a hustler's success is communicated by first showing no visible means of income. Any man who works laboriously for a regular salary is a fool. At the same time, the successful hustler will drive an expensive car, wear gold watches, diamond rings, alligator skin shoes, and mohair or silk suits, which he changes twice daily. He carries a large bankroll, and a bodyguard protects him. Of course during "working hours" on the streets, a hustler will not dress too conspicuously or wear flashy jewelry, but during social gatherings and parties he will display his wealth and occupational success. He owns a number of apartment buildings and invests his money through a working family member. He may also have two or three parties at his home each month. During such an exclusive party ("Hustler's Ball"), a variety of drugs are literally "served" to guests. A matchbox of marijuana and a roll of pills for each guest is not uncommon.

The outstanding feature among drug-using hustlers is their frequent claim to be using "different dope for different hustles." The introduction of new amphetamine compounds on the streets during the past five years[23]

---

[23] See John W. Rawlin, " 'Street Level' Abusage of Amphetamines," *A presentation to the Conferees Attending the First National Institute on Amphetamine Abuse at Southern Illinois University*, February 21–25, 1966; Seymour Fiddle, "Circles Beyond the Circumference: Some Hunches about Amphetamine Use and Addiction," *ibid.*; and John D. Griffith, "Psychiatric Implications of Amphetamine Drug Use," *ibid.*

has radically altered the nature of drug use in hustling circles. Methedrine crystal ("speed") has come to be used as a "boost" to a hustler's action. A good illustration of this practice is the "mackman" or "sweet-back" (pimp). The image of a passive, parasitic individual who lives idly off a few down-and-out prostitutes is probably the most fanciful stereotype ever constructed. Young girls compete ruthlessly for the favors of their "Man," and the enterprise of a successful pimp is time consuming, dangerous, and extremely competitive. Nearly all young Negro players aspire to reach the position of a "big mack," but few are qualified to be anything more than a "lousy pop corn pimp" who "claims" to have a "gang of holes" (prostitutes).

A mackman may have a few "bitches" on the streets turning tricks and taking care of customers; he may, as a male prostitute, be sharing a working girl's salary; he may have a woman "boosting" (shoplifting) merchandise from stores, or even a "gang" of female boosters. At the same time, he may be dealing "heavy narcotics." The mackman faces a number of problems, and the strain involved in his work often requires that he go for days without sleep. Other aspiring pimps are continuously trying to "steal his holes," take merchandise from his boosters, and make love to his working women. His life is frequently in danger of being "snuffed" by a jealous husband or another hustler wanting to kill him. He has many enemies and the exigencies of his job has led to the widespread use of pep-pills and methedrine crystal, which enables him to work around the clock "taking care of business," and seeing that his "bitches" are protected against the onslaughts of competing hustlers.

If a pimp can do so, he will stay clear of narcotics and "keep his holes" wired on pills or crystals.[24] The only drawback in the widespread use of "speed" lies in the tendency of women to get "strung-out," and exhausted from lack of proper food and sleep. Ideally, a woman must keep healthy, free from "liver trouble" caused by an unsterile "spike" (needle), well dressed, well fed, and attractive to be profitable. In the same light, because of the stimulating effect on the central nervous system, those who use "speed" regularly experience agitated depression, rapid flights of ideas, hallucinations, paranoid delusions, and extreme hypertension. These erratic side effects are controlled by mixing barbiturate compound and amphetamines or by "speed-balling" crystal and heroin (interspersing heroin and

[24] One hustler commented on this statement after reading parts of the manuscript: "Very few of them broads that's making any money are hooked. Any guy that's got one of them old broads that's dope fiends, he's just got a fixing partner. Ain't nothing else happening. Nowadays you find more of them younger, enterprising little broads out there on the scene using crystals. Now a smart dude won't let his bitches stick no needle in their arm. Most of 'em are not built too heavy so they'll drop a few cartwheels (amphetamine pills, usually dexedrine)."

crystal), but there is always the danger of turning into a "crystal freak," getting careless, and running the risk of arrest.

A good hustler is always alert for new techniques which can be incorporated into his working games. The preferred hustles are those which yield the most cash profit and also carry the shortest jail sentences. Hustlers rank themselves on a fixed prestige hierarchy based on "moneymaking power," ingenuity, and versatility in different games—people who go after straight cash (dope dealers, pimps, con artists, money burglars) rank highest. Those who go after property (boosters, fences, merchandise burglars, etc.) occupy the lower level of the hierarchy. Strong-arm robbers and thugs are not respected in hustling circles, and they in turn distinguish themselves from the more "sneaky" hustlers and dope fiends without any "heart." Those who are essentially committed to forms of violent crime as a means of living claim that if a man wants money, the easiest way is with a gun. They have contempt for addicts and hustlers; but few hustlers will stoop to such activity because violent crime does not involve the ingenuity, finesse, and sportlike challenge required for a good hustler. Yet thugs are in demand by some hustlers who need extra protection, and these types are often called on to enforce the informal sanctions against "snitching." It is not by accident that in many prisons, violence and "heart" are the ingredients of status. Strong-arm criminals rarely last long on the streets. Most are likely to be "raised by the state" after their earlier street-gang activities. This group is often the source from which scholars derive a criterion for "success" in the criminal world, when in fact, every good hustler and even young players consider "getting busted and doing time" the essence of "failure."

In spite of the prestige allocated to a successful hustler, a large part of the hustling enterprise is anything but romantic. Few see themselves living the life of conspicuous leisure they dream about, but it would be a serious mistake to believe that the life of a successful hustler is merely a dream. Some hustlers are so good they become "legends" on the streets. This is in part due to the contrast between the hustler's life and the routinized existence of most poor people. It should also be noted that many youngsters "claim" to be "hustling" when in fact they are merely "scuffling" around picking up "pocket money." Others hold regular jobs or attend school and "hustle" part time on the weekends. One can appreciate the attraction of coming to possess a lucrative "hustle," but a player who drifts out of the adolescent marketplace and begins to "run in hustling circles," soon realizes that his dealings are nothing like the amiable transactions among previous friends. Techniques of survival must be learned quickly. Very often older addicts who are at the time "down" will literally "sell" their knowledge of the hustling world for a shot of heroin. If their clothes are in the pawnshop and they look "strung-out," it is impossible to make any decent money hustling. Thus, if a young player is smart, like the following youth, he will try to "get the games" from the "old heads" who in turn charge consultation fees. Notice how one youth paid an older addict to "run the game down":

So I paid this dude to run the game down and tell me what was happening, and the dude ran it down to me. He say, "If somebody beats you, man (selling adulterated drugs), don't be too scared to go back and get your stuff and your money 'cause if you don't, they be beating you the rest of your life." . . . And I started running with him then, and he was taking me to all these places, man, and we was making some money, man. . . .

Then this one night I took a half spoonful of crystal for myself and took me a whammie (shot). It hit me hard, man, like sawdust all in my mouth. The dude beat me, man; he beat me! I got mad, man, and I didn't know what to do, but I knew what the Man had told me. So I got back to the pad and got my .45 out and caught a cab back to Frisco see. Went up to the dude and told him, "Man, you beat me!" You know, I roared at him. Pulled my .45 out and told him I was gonna kill him, just fronting, you know, to see what he was gonna do. And the dude, he do exactly what the Man had told me. He gave me a spoon of dope, and then he gave me a whammie of dope, and the dude thought I was sharp then. He say, "You a cold dude, brother, you all right, man." . . .

In short, the organization of the hustling world sets many obstacles as well as opportunities to an enterprising player and may be fraught with bitter as well as gratifying consequences.

Faith in the "Chippy Habit"

On the West Coast anyone with an automobile and the proper contacts can deal narcotics by driving to Mexico and purchasing whatever he wants.[25] Dealing "heavy narcotics" is a lucrative hustle, and the "big-time dope dealer" will buy heroin in pound units ($3,500 to $4,000 a pound) from "runners" who bring it to the Bay Area from Los Angeles. The heroin is "cut" with milk sugar to from 2 to 6 percent pure heroin and distributed to other dealers at about $250 per ounce. The "piece man" deals in ounces to a "spoon man," who cuts the ounces and deals to a "bag man," who may in turn cut the spoons into $10 balloons, or "five-cent papers" ($5 balloons). Heroin dealers very seldom handle anything but heroin or crystals; although at the lower levels of the traffic some act as middlemen or "connections" to other drug markets.

[25] For an illuminating description of the narcotics traffic see: D. Lyle, "Logistics of Junk," *Esquire*, 65 (March, 1966), pp. 59–68.

An addict moves so fast in the streets that he may pass several people looking for "grass" or crystals, in which case he may take their money, score from a friend, bring back the drugs, and use the extra money to buy "stuff" (heroin) for his habit. It is not a general practice to handle both marijuana and heroin because marijuana bulk is too large, the profit is very small compared to heroin or crystal, and the prison sentence is almost the same if arrested. Addicts on the streets occupy different positions in the hustling world, and a player who is well on his way to a hustling career will come in contact with heroin. By this time, however, he is out of the adolescent market. This accounts for the low visibility of addicts among the vast majority of adolescent drug users.

At the point where a young hustler is moving fast in the streets, using heroin intermittently on the weekends, or "speed-balling" crystal and heroin, he often changes his image of heroin addicts. Young drug users who have never experienced addiction, and addicts who will not admit their addiction, have a magical belief that one can "chippy around" (use heroin intermittently) without getting hooked. The firmness of this belief is communicated to players. Not all "dope fiends" are "uncool"— only those who are "weak minded" and "let the drug get to them" are uncool. Some addicts, while on the street, present the image of using heroin as a "luxury," not as a necessity. If a person knows from experience that he has always been able to control his drug use and still "take care of business," he will be convinced of his strong "will power" and will believe that only "weak-minded people get hooked." This very belief lays the groundwork for addiction. Opiates are viewed by the young hustler as a "luxury drug," "taking a whammie" once in a while is experienced as a "trip," and each incident of use is viewed as an isolated episode. But when he shortens the intervals between shots, tolerance develops and he may increase the dose of heroin to receive the initial effect. After going without the drug for a while, the illusion of will power is shattered by the awareness of physical dependence. Addicts often comment that heroin "sneaks up" or it "grabs." The following account by a young hustler illustrates clearly a developing experience of "getting hooked" which takes place inside a social world known only to hustlers:

And the thing came down to where I'm a cold dude now. I'm playing hard, body guarding a little bit, starting to cut dope, doing a little bit of everything. . . . I draw my respect from the mackman. He wants to keep sharp so he can get out there and steal them holes. So I get out there and dress the rest of them and keep them in business, then stand out there doing the same thing they doing. Nothin' to worry about see. (He took pride in his shoplifting ability, and he fenced his merchandise with a pimp who in turn kept his women dressed sharp.) Then too, I draw my respect from the dope man 'cause I'm so young, and I can get out there and make money from the weed man, the crystal man, and money from the gow (heroin) man too. Get anything I want and nobody can game on me. . . .

I ran into this gow dealer you know, and he had a batch of holes man, and the dude busted me, you know (asked him if he wanted to deal heroin). "How would you like to deal for me, man?" And I seen a chance where I can be father (big-time dope dealer). So I begin dealing, you know, and this is when the busts (arrests) started coming down on me, you know, and things started getting warmer. I had to cool it a little bit, but I wouldn't never stay in one place and deal. I'd go all through and deal everywhere, man. Didn't mind too much about 'cause I was steady running. . . .

And it came down that we went over and scored some stuff and I had me some crystal, and this gow fiend offered me some gow, you know. I said, "No man, fuck it." I didn't dig it 'cause I never did it before and I was leery behind it. "Can you get hooked on it?" He says, "No, man, just speed-ball it, man, speed-ball it and just take a little taste." So I took me a whammie, and it was out a sight, out a sight, man, and we went over to the dude's pad and I was wiggin out on all them people. Them gow fiends, man, the way they was holdin' theirselves, too much. This one hole was cutting her fingernails, just wiggin man, dressed all up, nodding, and me, I stand up and go into my crystal trip, runnin' around when they was just holdin' their cool. . . . So I started speed-balling a lot, but I was starting to put more gow in than anything, and pretty soon I just cut the crystal loose period, you know. I love that gow, man. It is most definitely out of sight. . . .

Well this big mack I was taking care of had lost everything, man, his apartment buildings, his car, and all his holes. He was down see, and it hurt me to see him like that, man. All he could do was sit there and talk that stuff. He'd say, "I'm a dope fiend, and she's a dope fiend, they all dope fiends, and we ain't doin nothing but making a little change to support our habit, man. Don't get in that bag, man, don't get in that bag." But it was too late. I was in that bag deep. . . .

We had copped about twenty suits one night, and I had me a five-cent paper. Did it in (injected the heroin) about 3:00 and about 8:00 I started to come down. Was standing waiting for somebody to come around, anybody to get me a little fix and avoid it. Kind of figured that the gow had got to me. Nobody came around and it started getting worse, but finally I got this dude and fixed. It set me straight, man; it set me straight and I knew that the gow had got to me. I was in that bag deep then. . . .

If one can verbalize an awareness of the relationship between withdrawal distress and the absence of opiates, he will realize that he is "hooked," and thereafter assumes a number of characteristic attitudes which *reinforce* the addiction.[26] The continued experience of using heroin to eliminate withdrawal suffering also has consequences for the recently addicted which could not have been anticipated. He is faced with the bleak prospects of "shooting up stuff" merely to remain "normal." It is extremely rare for a

[26] Alfred R. Lindesmith, "Problems in the Social Psychology of Addiction," in Wilner and Kassebaum, *op. cit.*, p. 134.

person to resume a "chippy habit" once he has experienced being hooked, and addicts often relapse because of their continued faith in the capacity to use heroin "socially."[27] One may try repeatedly to take a few "joy pops" and believe that he is controlling his habit, but invariably he ends up with full physical dependence on the drug.

The process of relapse has been explained in terms of the trace effects of an earlier conditioning process which is established in the course of using opiates to eliminate withdrawal distress.[28] Even though an addict is not physically dependent at the time, he tends to verbally associate the slightest discomforts of life in terms of withdrawal distress. The phrase "I was on a bummer," or "I was bum kicked," may refer to distress from a cold or merely being near unpleasant people. Although such discomforts may appear trivial to an outsider, they are experienced by addicts in terms of withdrawal symptoms calling for a "fix." Also, the sharp contrast between withdrawal symptoms and the ease of curing them with a shot of heroin makes an addict generalize his conception of heroin as a drug with the power to cure anything.

The Righteous Dope Fiend

Lindesmith and Gagnon point out the naive, indeed ridiculous, nature of the double-failure hypothesis and the retreatist vision of the addict subculture. Given the social situation of an addict which is brought into being by the law and the public conception of addiction, opiate use hardly provides an escape from the requirements of society. Instead, it "plunges the newly recruited addict into an abrasive contact with the world. . . ."[29] For the most part, regular heroin use on the street scene takes place inside a world known only to hustlers. Prestige in the hierarchy of street addicts is allocated by the size of a person's habit and his prosperity as a hustler. The drug experience is only half the picture. When questioned privately, older addicts who were "hooked" and "running" said they were miserable with their habit. But when some of the very same people were observed among associates on the set, they pretended to be satisfied and even proud of their addiction. A "righteous dope fiend," or bona fide addict, prefers heroin to any other drug and ranks himself among the elite in the drug com-

---

[27] One experienced addict made the following observation: "After I got hooked, the years of 'social drug addiction' were over, man. I could never go back and use again the way I'd used that first seven months when I could take it or leave it alone . . . I'd go back and use again and figure I was going to cool it, and by the end of the week I was pumping as much stuff into my arm as I could hustle."

[28] Lindesmith, op. cit., pp. 134–135; and Abraham Wikler, "Conditioning Factors in Opiate Addiction and Relapse," in Wilner and Kasselbaum, op. cit., pp. 85–97.

[29] Lindesmith and Gagnon, op. cit., p. 179.

munity.[30] Since heroin is the most expensive drug on the illegal market, the size of a person's habit indicates his moneymaking power and his versatility as a hustler. Other types of drug users must be content with a less expensive chemical and a lower-class existence.[31] He "ranks" other "freaks" in the drug community who merely play with drugs and clutter up the hustling scene by attracting police. Also, once a person has experienced being hooked, only morphine-like agents will "fix" him or satisfy his craving, and he experiences non-opiate drugs as "weaker." Anyone who can support an opiate habit as a "luxury" without letting it interfere with his hustling schemes will be the "father" to all other dope fiends on the set.

The process of "scoring" includes hustling for money, buying narcotics, and "fixing." All three activities symbolize the cure for withdrawal distress, the return to "normal" functioning, and the maintenance of self-esteem and social status. When his eyes begin to water, his nose runs, and a burning feeling grips his stomach, a dope fiend knows it is time for "work." He calls on previous experience, sizes up the immediate situation with a hustling partner, and decides where to go into his act. After "making a sting," the image of a "connection" comes to mind. At this time his mental life is fused with tension and excitement. The anticipation of getting "fixed," impending danger of arrest, and thoughts of whether his connection will deal him "bum stuff" clutter his mind. Back at his apartment or a tattered rooming house, three or four other addicts may be waiting for him to score, hoping that he comes back with "good stuff." In order not to put a "hex" on him, nobody argues over who will "get the first fix" until he returns with the stuff in his hands. If he makes it back, other dope fiends may be nudging each other to get that "first fix." Fixing holds a fascination for dope fiends and often takes ritualistic forms. After the heroin is portioned out, each person takes himself a "whammie," or "geezes" by sticking the needle in his arm, leg, or anywhere he can find a vein.

A heroin addict does not "trip" in the sense that other types of drug users "trip." The word "trip" comes from experience with hallucinatory drugs. Addicts speak of a "flash" or "call" and then "going on the nod." If the quality of heroin is good, the initial effect of an injection will throw one into a stuporous, dreamy state with short periods of sleep. When four dope fiends had finished "shooting up" one night, they merely sat slumped, with slight grins, periodically snorting, scratching, twitching, yawning, or sneezing. A person can be talking and his eyelids begin to droop. He appears

[30] For a detailed description of this social type of addict, see Alan G. Sutter, "The World of the Righteous Dope Fiend," *Issues in Criminology*, 2 (Fall, 1966), pp. 177–222.

[31] See Seymour Fiddle, " 'The Pills' and the Heroin Addict," Statement prepared for the Joint Legislative Committee on Health Insurance Plans, *Hearings on the Public Health Laws and Penal Laws to Regulate the Sale and Possession of Dangerous Drugs*, March 26, 1965.

drowsy, speaks clearly and softly, but may pause between sentences, stare into space, and later resume his sentence. When his head slumps on his chest, he is "on the nod," in a satiated state of complete relaxation. But this is not an "ecstatic" experience or a "kick"; rather, it is a state of nothingness. A person who takes an LSD trip may go on a voyage of discovery through the depths of his own consciousness. Feelings are intensified.[32] In contrast, an addict feels best when he does not feel. Being on the "nod" is being "fixed," a temporary suspension of tension, pain, hunger, or sexual urges.[33] It is indeed a paradox that dope fiends "run" the fastest, "hustle the hardest," suffer the most agony for an experience of nothingness. However, a street addict's life loses its depravity once it is realized that he is fixing merely to "stay normal," not for an "out-of-this-world experience."[34]

While a number of hustlers now experiment with crystal upon being released from prison, a righteous dope fiend or "bona fide addict" is not impressed by any drug other than heroin. Crystal is only used periodically when one is taking a "vacation" from an opiate habit, when he is speedballing the heroin effect by mixing it with an amphetamine, when he is forced to "clean up" before taking a Nalline test while on parole, or when his habit gets beyond his ability to support it. Anyone using methedrine crystal regularly for the sole purpose of experiencing its effects (for the "trip") is labeled a "crystal freak." The rapid flight of a crystal user's associations, the intensity of his speech pattern, and frequent paranoid delusions make him easy to single out in public places, and he is dangerous to have as a hustling partner. Also, when a dope fiend is "on the nod" he does not want to be around erratic or excited people who put him on a "bum kick." He merely wants to sit back and relax.

A similar tendency is apparent in the case of pills. Only while on parole, or when trying to "kick" the opiate habit will a righteous dope fiend use drugs in rotation by interspersing opiate and non-opiate drugs. Those who use pills on a repetitive or continuous basis are viewed as "drug store hyps" or "pill freaks" by heroin addicts. A pill freak, although he is often addicted, cannot afford a "respectable habit," and is more likely to divert his conning

[32] David Solomon, ed., *LSD: The Consciousness-Expanding Drug* (New York: Putnam, 1964).

[33] See Abraham Wikler, *Opiate Addiction: Psychological and Neurophysiological Aspects in Relation to Clinical Problems* (Springfield, Ill.: Charles C. Thomas, 1953).

[34] One addict put it this way: "You know I been hearing this for years, 'Oh, man, I was on, I'm tripping,' and that's bull shit; they lying. You don't get no cherry feeling after you fix; this is just something to say, you know. I mean after you've had your righteous fix, you can nod for three or four hours and you feel good, but you're completely in a world of oblivion. Now when you got some cinch money and don't have to worry about hustling for a while, then you can sit there and nod all them six hours, but if you haven't got any money, then you fix and you're right back out on the street hustling."

ability to "making a croaker" (physician) by simulating bodily illnesses, depression, or severe headaches.

The lowest level of drug user in the dope fiend hierarchy is a "garbage junkie" who is forced to set up a "shooting gallery" to make enough money to "fix." Dope fiends seldom carry their "outfits" (needle fixed to the end of an eye dropper) while running in the streets. More commonly, they carry a small piece of wire to be used for cleaning the "spike" if it clogs up while fixing. "Outfits" are often provided at the "shooting gallery." A garbage junkie will rent a cheap hotel room and loan out four or five outfits in exchange for a few "drops" or used "cottons" from another man's "stuff." This type of drug user will use any substance available to him at the time. He is ranked along with "winos" and "lushes," at the bottom of the general hierarchy of respectable drug users.

Survival

The career of a dope fiend may alternate between periods of unusual success and periods of extreme deprivation. It is misleading, however, to form a picture of the heroin addict's world solely on the basis of his appearance in hospital or prison settings. A few addicts on the street support their habit as a "luxury" and keep up the appearance of prosperity. But it is difficult enough to survive in the hustling world without having to carry the miserable burden of addiction. For the most part, the vision of a "luxury habit" remains a dream. As an addict gets progressively "strung out" behind the scene, his health deteriorates. He begins to look skinny, dirty, hollow-faced, and his bones begin to ache. In order to hustle well, a person must look sharp. A "ragged" appearance is the first sign that a dope fiend is "going down." When he is "down," an addict can no longer afford to score high-quality heroin. Dealers begin to take advantage of him by adulterating his drug with larger quantities of milk sugar. The risk of "getting a case" is increased because he passes more people on the streets and confronts more informers who cooperate with the police. After getting a case and doing time, he is confronted with the conditions of parole and Nalline testing, which he continuously tries to "beat" by rotating different drugs to prevent physical dependence and tolerance. In other words, he begins to transform into the type of drug user he once despised. The theme of enterprise changes to that of survival, and circumstances begin to conspire against him. At this time a street addict may view his entire life as a "bum kick."

Charles Winick's findings suggest that "addiction may be a self-limiting process for perhaps two-thirds of addicts."[35] To account for the apparent

[35] Charles Winick, "Epidemiology of Narcotics Use," in Wilner and Kassebaum, op. cit., pp. 6–9.

abstinence from opiates with increasing age, Winick advanced the "maturing out" hypothesis. The typical user begins his career in his early or late teens because he is unable to face normal adult decisions. Addiction provides the youth with something to do, gives him a special vocabulary, a special in-group, and allows him to absorb sex and aggression. By the early 30's these needs are not experienced with such intensity, and people seem to drift away from use with longer periods of abstinence.[36] Interestingly enough, Winick found that a minority of addicts who used opiates for fifteen years or more did not "mature out." When the question of abstinence is phrased in the light of the world of street-level opiate use, an equally plausible explanation for abstinence would assert that most addicts, as well as hustlers, "burn out" with increasing age. It is clear that the hustling world is a world for young athletes or hunters, not for older men and women. A "burning out" hypothesis might account for the fact that some addicts select a "retreatist role adaptation" when they *quit* using drugs, not when they start using drugs. That is, a bona fide addict, a righteous dope fiend, selects a retreatist role adaptation only if he takes the social role of an "ex-dope fiend," or a "sick addict."

ILLEGAL DRUG USE AS A CULTURAL SYSTEM

This essay points out a highly neglected dimension of human action in the sociology of deviance—the immediate experience world of the participants. Concepts like "subculture," "norms," and "values" lose their descriptive and analytic power if they reduce the developing experiences of people in their daily round of life. A "subculture" presumably develops when people effectively interact with one another to resolve "common problems of adjustment."[37] In the course of interaction, certain stable patterns of behavior and artifacts of behavior emerge that differentiate a subculture from the general culture. A person's commitment to the values and norms of his subculture gives him a certain status and a personal identity within that subculture, as well as a certain position and social image within the larger culture. The danger of this imagery lies in a tendency to assume that a deviant

---

[36] Charles Winick, "Maturing Out of Narcotic Addiction," *Bulletin on Narcotics* (United Nations, Department of Social Affairs), 14 (1962), pp. 1–7, and "The Life Cycle of the Addict and of Addiction," *ibid.* 16 (1964), pp. 1–10. Also see Marshal B. Ray, "The Cycle of Abstinence and Relapse Among Heroin Addicts," *Social Problems*, 9 (Fall, 1961), pp. 132–140.

[37] Albert K. Cohen and James F. Short, Jr., "Research in Delinquent Subcultures," *The Journal of Social Issues*, XIV (1958), pp. 20–37; and David J. Bordua, "Delinquent Subcultures: Sociological Interpretations of Gang Delinquency," *The Annals of the American Academy of Political and Social Science*, 338 (November, 1961), pp. 120–136.

subculture consists of a homogeneous group of people who make a uniform adaptation to the social structure and move along a single career line. How meaningful is it to assert that various norms and values, positions and roles of a subculture regulate the action of participants, or that strain in the "social structure" determines the form and content of a "subculture?"

"Mellow dude," "pot head," and "player" indicate different types of drug users, different sets of practices, and different runs of experience taking place within a prestige-laden "cool" round of life. Cool adolescent drug users are not all lodged in a self-contained subculture, let alone a "retreatist subculture." They have not given up the quest for success, nor have they withdrawn from the requirements of society. Woven into the cool style is a pervasive quest for experience, a repertory of practical knowledge, a set of strategies and protections against law enforcement. The social poise, esthetic grace, and elusive "awareness" of cool people are atractive to the less-cultivated "rowdy" youngsters and the more conventional "lame" youth. Drug use, especially marijuana use, is a function of a socializing movement into a major stream of adolescent life. To be admired by those whom one respects, to be sociable, to participate in parties, to avoid "hassle" with the police, to share in the cool round of life is anything but a retreatist role adaptation. Unless one can assess how "functional" adolescent life is a preparation for entrance into conventional adult roles or show that "youth culture" as a whole is a retreatist role adaptation, it is meaningless to speak of cool adolescent drug users as retreatists.

The process of building up a style of life oriented toward being cool involves a deliberate, self-conscious attempt to control oneself in all aspects of one's daily routine. Some youngsters spend hours in front of the mirror practicing their conversation, combing their hair, imagining themselves in a variety of encounters with the opposite sex, viewing their posture, experiencing themselves from the standpoint of their image of being cool. Some even write out lines and memorize passages to be verbalized during the day. Outside of being "turned on" by an older brother or sister, or through an experience during incarceration, the most typical way of beginning to use marijuana is to emulate an "older crowd" of "cool people." But one has to "establish himself on the set" before he can be turned on. At the same time, one can be genuinely cool and not even use drugs. Entrance into drug use is a developing experience and a highly selective process that depends on access to drugs, acceptance by drug-using associates, kinds of images which youngsters form of drug use, and the runs of experience which affect their interpretation of the drug effects ("trips").

This selective process continues *within the same cultural system* as people are differentiated out at major turning points, enter different social worlds, fall into different patterns and sequences of patterns of drug use, form different kinds of associations, take on the features of different social types, come to occupy different positions and roles, and have different runs of experience which orient them along different career lines. Marijuana, not heroin, is the preferred drug among cool adolescent drug users. These two areas of drug use do not comprise a single homogeneous subculture, nor is there a natural "progression" from the former into the latter. Very few adolescents enter into and move through the hustling world. Those who are differentiated out form new associations; themes running through their lives transform; "motives" for using drugs change. Even after becoming addicted to narcotics, people have different runs of experience and are thereby oriented along different career lines. To by-pass these individual and collective experiences by positing a homogeneous, "retreatist" role adaptation to "failure" is to be led up a blind alley.

An analysis of addict life in terms of the general system attributes of an "addict subculture" is appropriate and illuminating only if it captures different social types and the selective process of drug involvement. Indeed, the behavior of illegal drug users is significantly influenced by public policy.[38] The operation of the Harrison Act transformed addicts into criminals, shifted the concentration of heroin use to members of lower-class, urban slum dwellers with easiest access to the illegal market, changed the popular idea of addiction to a degenerate practice, and created the stereotype of a raging dope fiend.[39] It would follow that an addict culture has emerged to deal with common problems which any street addict has in adjusting to his status as a criminal, to his popular stereotype as a dope fiend, and to the illegal marketplace for opiates. Fiddle has observed that the addict culture contains within it a "circulatory system" of role relationships through which addicts buy, sell, and use illegal drugs.[40] It also contains within it a

[38] For recent considerations of the policy question see: Alfred R. Lindesmith, *The Addict and the Law* (Bloomington: Indiana University Press, 1965); Edwin M. Schur, *Narcotic Addiction in Britain and America: The Impact of Public Policy*, (Bloomington: Indiana University Press, 1962); Rufus G. King, "The Naroctics Bureau and the Harrison Act: Jailing the Healers and the Sick," *Yale Law Journal*, 62 (April, 1953), pp. 736–749; William B. Eldridge, *Narcotics and the Law—A Critique of the American Experiment in Narcotic Drug Control* (New York: American Bar Foundation, 1962); and Roger Smith, "Status Politics and the Image of the Addict," *Issues in Criminology*, 2 (Fall, 1966), pp. 157–175.

[39] The criminalizing process of addiction is discussed in Edwin M. Schur, *Crimes Without Victims: Deviant Behavior and Public Policy*, (Englewood Cliffs, N.J.: Prentice-Hall, 1965); Leslie T. Wilkins, "A Behavioral Theory of Drug Taking" *Howard Journal of Penology*, 11 (1965), pp. 269–273; and Alfred R. Lindesmith, " 'Dope Fiend' Mythology," *Journal of Criminal Law and Criminology*, 31 (July-August, 1940), pp. 199–208.

[40] Seymour Fiddle, "The Addict Culture and Movement Into and Out of Hospitals," as reprinted in U.S. Senate, Committee on the Judiciary, Subcommittee to Investigate Juvenile Delinquency, *Hearings*, Part 13, New York City, September, 1962 (Washington, D.C.: Government Printing Office, 1963), pp. 3154–3162.

"survival system" which wards off destructive forces emanating from the larger social system. An "ideology of justification" helps street addicts to explain their predicament, deal with their stigmatized social and legal status, and sustain morale. A "reproductive process" operates to recruit new members into the addict culture by a magnetic pull which attracts lower-class adolescents, by "subterranean values" implicit in the addict culture, or by other, still undiscovered, mechanisms. "Defensive communication" develops in the form of addict argot, a grapevine system that anticipates police and informer threats, and counter informer sanctions that minimize the risk of exposure. A "neighborhod warning system" operates to protect addicts from police and comes into being as a result of services which street addicts provide to ghetto residents. Ritualistic, magical, and cyclical patterns regulate the time, place, and manner of obtaining money, buying, and selling drugs. Finally, the addict culture generates forces which make it relatively easy for people to form intense interpersonal relations. This type of analysis is meaningful only if it faithfully depicts the different life styles and perspectives of people acting, modifying, redefining, and building up new cultural forms as they meet their conditions of life. The recognition of a dramatic dimension in human group life compels one to refine existing concepts or develop new concepts in order to capture the developing experiences of people acting and to incorporate a realistic image of social change.

5 Different Types of Pickpocket Mobs

DAVID W. MAURER

A mob is a working unit of pickpockets. The minimum is two; a lone pickpocket, working without any support, is hardly classed as a mob. He is usually referred to as a *single o tool*, a *single handed tool*, or a *single o cannon*. Mobs are usually referred to by the number of persons composing them; that is, they are *two handed*, *three handed*, or *four handed*, which is the maximum number used in this country, with perhaps some temporary or unusual exceptions. In general, mobs are also known as *tribes*, *troupes*, or *teams*, the last two being terms often used by the police, though not exclusively so. Sometimes a *team* is *two handed*, while a *troupe* is *three handed* or larger. "So this dick come over, and I know that this troupe over here got nailed and that troupe over there got nailed. Right out from under me. . . . Well, that don't make no difference. . . . I got to make a living." Within the profession, mobs are classified in numerous ways, several of which will be discussed here.

In order to avoid confusion, perhaps we should indicate immediately that all mobs belong simultaneously to more than one of the categories which we are setting up. Thus there are *three handed local mobs*, *road mobs* that are *four handed*, *organized mobs* that work *locally*, *class mobs* who work *on the road*, *jig mobs* who operate on a *knockabout* basis, *cannon broads*

Reprinted from Irving Spergel, *Whiz Mob: A Correlation of the Technical Argot of Pickpockets with Their Behavior Pattern*, American Dialect Society, 24 (1955), 83–102, by permission of College and University Press Services, Inc., and the authors.

who work *two handed,* either *locally* or *on the road,* etc. Likewise, several different kinds of pickpocket may be found in any given type of mob. A *mocky jew mob* might *fill in* a *jig tool,* a *hungry tool* might work with any kind of mob, a *class cannon* (white) might work with a *jig mob* on *put ups,* or a *makeshift mob* may operate with two bums for stalls and a pretty good *wire. Rough tools* may be *class cannons* and *careful tools* may never make the grade or vice versa, depending upon personalities. These terms will all be explained as the discussion progresses.

Furthermore, the mob in its various forms is the heart of the pickpocket subculture. It would fall within Trager's Cultural Index No. 2, Association. In the pickpocket subculture it appears that the mob is often more important than the family as a stabilizing influence; sometimes mob and family are combined, as we shall show. These two are the only formal aspects in the subculture, with the family usually being secondary. In fact, because of the importance of the mob in the economics and technology, it is the primary and basic associational factor in the subculture; all other aspects of association are peripheral and relatively nonessential except when they impinge upon the activities of the mob. Thus the pickpocket's loyalties, as well as his fortunes, are tied up with a fundamental type of association which, to members of the dominant culture, appears to be loose, ephemeral, and highly insecure. Yet the thief respects it and participates in it because it is all he knows; furthermore, tradition says that it works; and so it does, within limits.

TRAVEL

Perhaps the first major division made by pickpockets themselves is on the basis of travel. If a mob goes out of town to *hustle* and if it has a policy of traveling from place to place, working in each *spot* for varying periods, it is known as a *road mob.* "Road mobs that are always on the tear, always hustling, they never take time to enjoy their money; so it don't do them no good, 'cause they are always on the hustle." If it stays more or less permanently in one locality, working that city or the immediate vicinity, it is known as a *local mob.* While there are skilled operators in each type of mob, there is a certain status enjoyed by *road mobs* which *locals* do not generally share, largely because there is a much higher percentage of *class cannons* among *road mobs* than among *locals.* Also, there is a certain social distinction observable, with some *road mobs* wondering how their *local* brethren stand the boredom of a permanent life in one city; at the same time, other *road mobs* develop the same aversion to travel that some legitimate traveling salesmen express; they envy anyone who can settle down—or at least they say they do. Actually a pickpocket who has been on the road for years is seldom happy to live and work permanently in one city, though he may do so for various reasons. Likewise, *local* pickpockets, once established, do not seem to gravitate to the road, with its hazards and uncertainties. As a matter of fact, one can discern two different kinds of thief and two philosophies of thievery underlying this dichotomy: the *road man* is the more venturesome, the more restless, the more interested in change and variety; also, because of the stresses and strains of *road work*, he is usually a sharp, alert thief, with an eye to all the angles; sometimes he has auxiliary *rackets*, such as the *hype* or some form of the *short con* which he practices occasionally, or on which he can fall back in an emergency. The *local*, on the other hand, likes his security and is sometimes incapable of facing the hazards of *road work*. Some are simply afraid to work outside their own city. It is obvious that, while many *locals* enjoy a high professional standing in all ways, some *locals* may be simply lazy, dilatory, or somewhat shiftless professionals who make a good thing of police protection in a given locality.

Now you take Willie Anderson. He never left New York in all his life. He wouldn't get out of the subway, and you couldn't make him get out of the subway. The only time he ever got out of the subway was when he went out on the road one time. I was with the String Kid. We was going to Jefferson City, Missouri, and he was doing the pinching. Willie and his mob was all on the same train. They was four handed and Willie Anderson is doing the pinching for this mob. So we're in Kansas City, and here's a guy that got on at Topeka and I want to make a play for him. Because the presidential special train would stop at every capital, you know.

So this guy is an Associated Press correspondent, and he's got a billfold like that. It was an insider. Willie had him spotted, too. When this guy come off the train, Willie was figuring on getting that for hisself, see. And he couldn't get up there to the steps where the correspondent was leaving the coach. I wiggled through there. . . . I'm as good as the next one, you know. It was perfect for a fast and furious. The Kid got right in there, too. So we clipped this guy and the score was six or six and a half.

We walked away. We jumped in a cab and went downtown and went in a restaurant. That's the only score I wanted to get, you know. I didn't want to be around there after that. We went on down there to the restaurant and in a few minutes Willie came in. He said, "Well, I have had nothing but bad luck. I've made more money in New York in one goddamned day than I could make on the road in all my life. This is my first, last, and only time. I'm going over and get me a plane." And he did. This was at Topeka, Kansas. He said, "You knew I had that mark spotted. I wanted to get that score."

I said, "Yes, but I've got to make a living too. Do you need anything? Do you need any money?"

"No," he said, "I don't need anything, but I'm going back to New York and if I leave again, it'll be in a wooden box. I'm not going on the road any more." And it's a fact, he never did.

Road mobs are usually *organized mobs*. That is, they specialize their duties and responsibilities down to fine details. They adjust their number to the minimum (usually two or three members) and each member is a specialist in his work. One of them is always a *steer*, a specialty for which a *local mob* has little necessity. Some mobs call him a *folder man* because he handles the timetables and rail or bus schedules. The *steer* plans the itinerary and handles the details of transportation; he knows all the events en route which the *road mob* should *make*, he knows what cities the mob should *buy through*, and he has a vast personal knowledge of persons and places which are important to the mob if they are to work efficiently. He must be able to read and should head the newspapers. Also, since the *road mob* must arrange the *fix* as it goes, he has the duty of contacting the detectives, the *fixers*, or other intermediaries in each locality in order to arrange for the mob to work for one, two, three, or more days under police protection. The details of this will be discussed under the chapter entitled *The Thief and the Law*. Also, if the *road mob* decides to work *on the sneak*, that is, without advance arrangements in any given locality, the *steer* must be prepared to handle any trouble which arises as a result of this lack of protocol. Of necessity, he either carries a part of the mob's total emergency capital or *fall dough* (sometimes amounting to several thousands of dollars) or he knows where and how he can get it into his hands with a minimum of delay.

Usually a good stall is also a good steer, as a rule. He knows all the get ons, he knows all the fixers, he knows all the transfer points, he knows the country, he knows the topography, he knows the geography, he knows where you're going, he's got all your plans laid out. He knows that Jim Sweeney's the fix over here, and Jack Little's the fix over there, and who can get you here, and who's bondsman, and this and that and the other thing. He knows all these things. That's what makes him so valuable to a mob, because actually stealing a pocketbook . . . there's a million guys that can steal a pocketbook. But it don't mean nothing. They just keep the wolf from the door, that's all.

The *steer* is usually also a stall. If the mob operates *two handed*, the other member will be a tool. If the mob is *three handed*, there will be two stalls and one tool. Often one of the stalls is a woman, and on occasion the tool may be female.

A woman stall uses her arms and elbows to keep a mark in position, the same as a male stall. But of course there's a sex angle that comes in there with a woman, where it doesn't with a man. Of course with a woman stall she uses her buttocks in order to distract his attention . . . to keep his mind where she wants his mind to be. That's about all there is to it.

Usually, however, *road mobs* use the woman, if any, for stalling, as previously described. Rarely both stalls are women, except in a *four handed* mob, which is less common now than formerly.

If the stall handles the mark right, there's no question about what the tool . . . the tool's work is easy then. The hardest work, the hardest part of the whiz is the stall. That's the hardest part there is. Once a stall becomes a good stall, he very seldom becomes a wire . . . because he's so much in demand, there's so many mobs that are willing to fill him in that he can be filled in without dough, without fall dough.

A *single handed* pickpocket, male or female, while actually a functioning unit—and usually a very efficient one—is not referred to as a mob. However, he—or she—may be quite versatile because the *single handed worker* must operate without a stall; also, he is more flexible since he does not have to get other people, and usually highly individualistic people at that, to agree upon an itinerary, working hours, and other technical matters. It is also to his advantage to work alone, especially if he is expert, for he does not have to divide the proceeds of the day with anyone. A *single o tool* traveling over the country has an additional advantage, especially if he is not well known to the police, because he does not attract so much attention, nor does he run the risk of being arrested because he is with someone else who is known. He often has auxiliary *rackets* such as the *hype* or the *heel*, at which he may be quite proficient. Many police officers have never seen a pickpocket working alone, and so do not look for one. The reason for this is that such pickpockets are rare, are difficult to see working because there is no *frame*, and are not often booked by the police. *Road mobs* also, it should be noted, are not so common as they were in former years. The following statement will give a good general distinction between *local* and *road mobs*:

There's a lot of guys that are local pickpockets. You know what I mean. I don't know whether it's fear or what it is, but they don't want to get out of town. They just stay in one locality. But then there's other mobs, you know, that want to work on the road all the time. You work on the road, you get all the spots . . . where you pay off, you know. And you can always find smebody to pay off. There are some pickpockets that never leave the town right where they are. I don't know whether it's fear or what. But they just will not leave town. It's the same in Philadelphia, or Cincinnati, or any town.

There's just some guys that have got the fear. They must have fear, because . . . well, there ain't any way they can leave there. Of course, they get pinched here and there, and that's to be expected. There's some kind of a fear that if they get away from where they're known. . . . Let me explain this to you. Every good cannon, he's got a bondsman, you know, and there's nine out of ten of these guys I'm talking about have got a bondsman and they're afraid to get away from him. They can't get out . . . see, it's some sort of fear. One of the best in the country I know of is in Pittsburgh, and he . . . I mean he's really good. He's tops. This guy, he is one of the best, but you just can't get him out of Pittsburgh to save your neck.

Local mobs, on the other hand, are not so closely *organized*. They may be *three handed* this week and *two handed* next week. They may use this tool now and have another one later. They may be *pick ups* or *pick up mobs* in that they get together a varying personnel to work at irregular intervals anywhere that the picking seems good. "Yeah, strictly class mobs. I'm not talking about makeshifts and pick ups and this and that. I'm talking about knowing what your're going after." Because all members live in the same vicinity, it is easy to operate on this rather casual basis. Their relations with the local law are generally quite good—otherwise they would be in prison. In fact, it has been said that some detectives protect certain *locals* in order to use them as informers or stoolpigeons. *Local mobs,* especially the lower-class ones, do not always pay for police protection, but count on the fact that they are not well known and the fact that they prey largely on transients in large cities to keep them from the attention of the police. Some *locals* operate on a small scale, irregularly, in certain cities for months or even years without much difficulty. Other *local mobs* are very well *organized,* and have a minimum of turnover in personnel.

Working consistently in a certain area has great social and personal advantages for this type of thief, since he can maintain a home and numerous contacts with people who are useful to him or with whom he likes to associate. His *connection* for narcotics is also usually local, and he fears to go away from a safe and reliable source for drugs. He can work regularly or irregularly, with the same mob, or as a temporary *fill in* or *pick up* for several mobs if the occasion arises. "He was telling me about a character he filled in with—you wouldn't know him—one time in St. Louis." It is notable, also, that there are a few very capable women working *single handed* on a *local* basis, though few old-timers still work *single handed* on the *road.* For instance, a "sharply" dressed Negro woman, uniformed as a maid and using a child as a front, can get in some very effective work on crowded buses or city railway systems. This is known as *grifting with a squealer* or *hustling with a brat.*

There is also a sort of in-between type of mob which operates locally but which also covers the surrounding area in short trips, or makes occasional trips to large gatherings such as political conventions, inauguration ceremonies, etc. although they do not travel consistently or far from home. These are known as *knock-about mobs;* as a general thing, they do not have any particular specialty, nor do they have a restricted territory away from home. "Knockabout mobs are usually low-class. One good guy and a couple of bums."

PROFESSIONAL STATUS

Mobs are also classified according to the professional status of the members. Thus a *class mob* will be composed of *class cannons*, and usually exclusively so, since this type of operator will not take the risks of working with inferiors, or with people whose reputation for integrity (according to the standards of the subculture) is not established. "Class mobs don't declare you out, because you have your fall dough up. You never discharge a man. He always discharges himself. If he's always late, he discharges himself and he takes down the fall dough." These mobs are contrasted to *pick ups*, *makeshifts*, *locals*, etc., which reflect lesser stability and lower professional rating. A *cannon mob* is usually a highly *organized mob*, though not necessarily a *class mob*. Says a con man, "Never play for a lop-eared apple; they love to be trimmed by a cannon mob." The designation *cannon* itself has a kind of internal or built-in status, since it has, within the past twenty or twenty-five years, supplanted older terms such as *dip* (used today largely by Britishers or Colonials, policemen, and men on some other *rackets*), which simply means a pickpocket. "Dips very seldom make a roper. Once a dip, always a dip." *Cannon*, an intensification or augmentative of *gun* was, and still is, used with some sense of indicating a better-than-ordinary pickpocket. *Gun* still used largely by old-timers, derives from the Yiddish *gonif* 'thief.' We see a similar process operating among Negro pickpockets, who use the term *shot* to refer to the same class of professional which white thieves call a *cannon*.

RACIAL, NATIONAL, AND SEX CLASSIFICATIONS

Racial, national or ethnic classification is reflected also in the names applied to types of mobs based on these divisions. All-Negro mobs are called *boon mobs*, *burr heads*, or *jig mobs*, especially on the East Coast. "There's jig mobs. The jigs, they work a lot different from us. I mean, you stick one for me and I'll stick one for you." Although some individual Negro pickpockets are not only expert professionally but in every way *class cannons*, Negro mobs generally speaking do not have a very high rating in the fraternity of white pickpockets, or among the few topnotch Negro operators, for that matter. Here the status depends not upon race but upon professional reputation, it being rather a sociological and economic accident that so many of the less accomplished pickpockets belong to the Negro race. Negro mobs, also, lack the specialization and organization necessary to effective operation. It is common for white pickpockets to disclaim any race prejudice, acknowledge the abilities of certain Negro *shots* with whom they have worked or with whom they have associated, and then to discount all other Negro operators.

I said, "There's one swell jig," I said. I can borrow money from him and he's a nice guy; and he had a broad, oh she was a beautiful broad. Must have been part Polynesian, or something. She had jig in her, you know, but she must have been part Polynesian, or something like that, for she was a very beautiful woman. Maybe part Chink or something like that, with them almond eyes. And my girl, she said to me, "You mean you let a nigger set down at the table along side of me?" I like to . . . lost my own broad over that.

Likewise, Jewish organizations are referred to as *mocky mobs* or *mocky jew mobs*. "Mocky is not a Jew. It's a Sixth Avenue Jew. There is lots of very fine, high-class Jews on the whiz." There are a few good Chinese and Japanese pickpockets, but not many. "Shorty the Jap was one of the best cannons I ever knew." A very sharp observer among pickpockets tells me that he suspects that Orientals have a dislike for bodily contact with Occidentals which keeps them off the *whiz*. Although some American Indians are expert thieves along the traditional lines of their own subculture, I have never heard of one becoming a pickpocket.

There is something of the same ambivalence of feeling about Jewish mobs that we have noted above regarding Negro mobs, except that it is notably less prevalent, with many Jewish operators working with Gentiles, and vice versa. There are also numerous Roman Catholic pickpockets, though no mobs organized on this basis have been observed; it is notable that there is a sort of mutual recognition or tolerance of religious scruples amongst Jews, Gentiles, Greek Orthodox, and Roman Catholics. A Roman Catholic, for instance, will be permitted to drop out of the mob while a Catholic priest is being robbed (much thievery takes place in the crowds at various shrines and religious congresses) and such a scrupulous pickpocket naturally wants no part of the proceeds from this theft. Likewise, if a Rabbi is being robbed, Jewish members may be excused, though it is reported that they do not so generally respect the cloth as do the Catholics.

Nationality also plays a part in labeling mobs, such as *spik* or *spick mob* (Cubans, Puerto Ricans, or Mexicans) or *old country mobs* (Europeans not yet Americanized); usually these *old country mobs* consist of Germans, Russians, Austrians, or other Central Europeans. These are much less numerous than they were twenty-five or thirty years ago, although there still are some, and individual *old country guns* still operate or *fill in* with modern native American mobs. There are also many French-Canadian mobs operating in Canada, with some crossing the border into the United States. Montreal seems to be the headquarters for pickpockets in Canada; in fact, it is known as the "Home of the Chirps." French-Canadians, however, do not rate very high professionally among *class cannons* in this country, nor do Latins, the Mexicans rating highest in this group.

Women are accepted on an equal footing with men so far as mob membership is concerned, and there are some all-female mobs who as often as not specialize in other peripheral *rackets* such as the *boost* and *binging hangers*, which will be discussed in a later chapter. All-women mobs are known as *moll mobs* or *twist mobs*. Some of them are highly effective and seem to have less trouble with the law than male mobs or than women who work with male mobs.

You meet some good women on the whiz. Two Jewish gals, Sarah and Rachel, and the best broad outfit I ever seen. I was coming down the elevator one time in John Wanamaker's and got to the bottom and heard a woman scream. She fell over in a dead faint. Some big pigeon-breasted gal. She screamed because her pocketbook was open and they didn't have a chance to close it. So I closed her pocketbook up and helped her off the elevator. And got her outside and then called a floor walker and everything.

They said, "We'll take care of her, she just fainted."

I said, "I don't know what happened—high altitude or something."

I seen those two gals, so I tailed them on out. I got outside and said, "How about my end?" I was just kidding, you know.

They said, "What are you talking about?"

I said, "I know you beat that broad." And two nice looking gals—I mean real nice looking—and both about five foot or along in there.

They said, "Then come up the street if you are that smart. Come on up the street and we'll turn that thing over." So we turned it over and they had a pretty fair score—$150 or $170, I forget which. So that's the reason this broad fainted, you see; she had that money in her poke. So I got their address.

I monkey around with this one, this Sarah. She had a guy, but I didn't have no gal. I was on the outs, you know, so I went up to her apartment. We had coffee and drinks, and this and that. I monkey around with them for quite awhile. There was nobody with them. When they worked, they wouldn't take me, they wouldn't take you, they wouldn't take nobody. They were strictly two handed. They knew each other's actions. They could beat a man, they could beat a woman, they could beat anybody. They were moll buzzers and whiz at the same time. They could handle anything that came up and boy they had a ton of money. They had the swellest apartment you ever seen. Rugs that thick on the floor; some of them must have cost $1500. And closets full of groceries and everything. Of course, they boosted all that stuff.

Occasionally one encounters a *single o broad,* and she is likely to be very skillful. Some of these are well up in years. In this connection I have a report showing the intrusion of a young woman from the dominant culture into the criminal subculture, but only insofar as her criminal techniques are concerned; she was entirely self-taught, but her methods were sufficiently effective to impress the skilled international operator who discovered her; she had no contacts with other professionals, although she had observed them working in crowds in the city where she lived. . . .

WORKING HABITS

Some mobs are known by their tactics, especially when these are rough or unorthodox. Thus a *heist mob* is one which brooks no interference and robs the victim willy-nilly. The irony of this label is broad if we stop to recall that real "heist mobs" are stick-up gangs who rob banks and payrolls and armored trucks; they operate with violence and at gun-point. They belong to the *heavy rackets*, which are at the opposite pole from the pickpocket. The hyperbole here is characteristic of the pickpocket's imagery; an operator who tugs a bit hard at a victim's wallet, or who purloins a pocketbook without first establishing the appropriate misdirection is likened to a tough stick-up artist who uses naked violence. These mobs may simply be clumsy or inept; on the other hand, they may feel so secure in the *fix* that they need not be subtle; or they may simply not care. They do not constitute the upper echelons of the profession. They are also known as *clout and lam mobs*, *hijackers*, or *rip and tear mobs*. "It was pitiful the way the mob got away with the rip and tear stuff." *Hit and run* and *root and toot* are also used, though some *whiz* claim that the last is more of a *con* term than a pickpocket word.

PLACES TO WORK

Pickpockets also classify mobs according to the places they work, or the kind of work they do. Thus a *third rail mob* is one which consistently works the subways; this is largely New York usage, and these mobs are fewer now than formerly. In all large cities there are *jug mobs* who work the banks; these mobs are usually transients, although some *local mobs* will work *jugs* at certain times and under certain conditions. "In L.A. I filled in with a jug mob for a while." *Jug mobs* are selective workers; that is, they watch the customers withdraw money from a bank, or have information that a certain customer will withdraw a considerable sum of money and then *take him out* (*bring him out*) where they rob him. A mark who is robbed on the basis of advance information is called a *put up*. Because this is delicate work, the professionals who do it are usually *class cannons*, and they take very few *scores*, perhaps only one a day or less. "Only mobs with class can stand that jug grift. They can afford to wait. They don't have to get that touch every day. Those junker mobs have to keep it coming in. If they take ten scores of $25, that's $250, but they get the town all heated up. Only class mobs have money in reserve and can wait for the one or two big ones."

The mobs who formerly infested railroad and bus stations and who rode the trains are now practically nonexistent; in fact, one now seldom sees a *whiz copper* or pickpocket detective in a railroad station; ten years ago all stations were heavily protected. "This old kayducer was as right as rain and would not start his elevated train unless there was a whiz mob on with him, and at that time, he would not have to hold his rattler long." Likewise the *circus grift* and the *carnival grift*, while still surviving here and there, are nothing like what they were before World War II, when some of the big circuses carried their own *whiz mobs* to trim the crowds along the way.

KINDS AND VARIETIES OF PICKPOCKETS

There are many different kinds of individual pickpocket as recognized by the profession. These have certain predominant characteristics of technique, personality, or behavior recurring with great enough frequency to constitute recognizable types. There are, of course, many more kinds of pickpocket which are not recognized as types, or only partially recognized; these are individuals who get a name for certain things within a limited circle, or who fancy themselves as specialists in this or that, or who believe that they constitute a special breed of cat for personal reasons. There are also several other types of pickpocket which cannot be included in this study.

The pickpocket is essentially egocentric almost to the point of megalomania. When we consider the high percentage of illiteracy or semiliteracy among them, we can understand why many of them have horizons sufficiently limited to throw their own self-image into high relief. No pickpocket thinks of himself as an inferior operator; in fact it is a safe guess that there is no pickpocket who does not consider himself near the top of his profession and who does not rationalize this assumption in one of several ways. Most pickpockets are able to observe and recognize this tendency in others, but never recognize it in themselves; in this way they prove not only their basic humanity, but verify the pattern which most of the professions follow, and with good precedent, for thievery is very old. The fact is that the pickpocket has to believe that he is one of the best; if he admits his own limitations, he loses his nerve (*blows his moxie*) and will eventually find it impossible to work. His constant preoccupation with thievery and its imagery in his own thoughts, together with the perpetual rehashing of each *touch* with his partners (*cutting up touches, chopping them up*, etc.) tends to reënforce in his own mind the infallibility of his technique, the daring of his nerve, the irresistibility of his personality. "We're very fortunate today to hear about this, Doc, because Doc always enjoys chopping them up. He likes to hear them." Among *class cannons*, however, braggadocio is notably infrequent, and the individual will have an impressive external reserve.

In any consideration of these types, the question of status is inevitably intruded, and that question becomes increasingly complicated if we attempt to discuss it with deference to all points of view within the profession. Therefore, we shall assume something approximating the point of view of the *class cannon*, simply because that kind of individual has more perspective than, say, a *hit and run* pickpocket from Harlem who works with anyone who will *throw the hump* for him. To attempt any sort of representation of all or even several points of view in this study would complicate it out of all proportion to its practicality. Also, indications of relative status, as they are expressed, will be understood to be statements colored by the entire class-consciousness of the top men in the profession; they are not intended to reflect either favorably or unfavorably on any other levels of professional operators whose point of view, unfortunately, cannot be included here.

Since there is no convenient principle of analysis by which we can subdivide the various types, perhaps an alphabetical one is as good as any. Furthermore, this method will avoid the necessity for putting one type above another, unless that type has definite status-value.

A *bang up* operator is an accomplished one. This implies that his excellence lies in his techniques; he may or may not be a *class cannon;* that is, he might be skilled and capable, but lack status for some other personal reason, such as having a reputation for cheating his partners. The term, as I have recorded it, usually applies to tools, as a *bang up wire*, a *bang up tool* or a *bang up hook*, but may refer to stalls also.

Cannon and *cannon broad* or *cannon moll* we have discussed briefly above in connection with types of mob. This label carries status, though perhaps not so much as it did several years ago when it was new as a substitute for the older *gun*, which has gradually weakened and generalized; it also included some other types of thief, but *cannon* reënforced the older term, made it sharper and more specialized, and it immediately became acceptable to the more competent professionals. Within the past few years it has become increasingly popular, but may eventually go the way of *gun*. A *careful tool* is one who works gently but expertly, who takes no chances, who lets every questionable victim go, for he would rather lose a *score* than endanger the mob. "Some careful tools reef every score." "He was a careful tool. He didn't take so many scores, but he'd go for weeks without a rumble." There is a distinction between a *careful tool* and a tool who is cautious; the latter may be neither expert nor recognized as a good operator; he may simply be timid or fearful.

When a pickpocket works with a carnival, he is known as a *carnival louse*, a *carnival cootie*, a *carnival bum*, or a *sure thing grafter*, which is an older and less pejorative term, though it is rapidly becoming synonymous with *louse*. "Show me a sure thing grafter and I'll show you a carnival louse." This term has a definitely negative status-value and is always applied by others to someone not present, or someone who is being abused; a man might use it ironically or humorously about himself, but hardly seriously. Probably the negative implications of the term stem from the fact that *carnival bums* often cannot work except under the protection of a carnival and all that this implies; they are looked down on for this reason, as well as because carnivals do not attract the highest type of *grifting* personnel. This stigma does not apply so strongly to pickpockets who *work* the *circus grift* (now almost obsolete) or who *work behind the big top*. Here there is a marked difference in status between *circus grifters* and *carnival grifters*.

When a pickpocket is unduly careful or shy about making close contact with the victim, he is called a *center fielder*. This is especially applicable to a stall who fears to take his share of the risk, but who always wants his share of the take. "Sometimes we call a center fielder a 'mile away' or we say he's 'sneeze shy.'" Note again the degree of hyperbole involved here; the distance involved in the operator's relation to the mark is a few inches or at most a foot or two, but the image visualizes him as working out in center field or within a mile. *Sneeze shy* implies that he has an inordinate fear of arrest. Some mobs refer to a *center fielder* as *playing safety first*, which is a kind of play on another baseball term, though the addition of the *first* has its sarcastic implication.

When a pickpocket is financially embarrassed, he is said to be *c.o.d.* This is especially applicable to one who has just been released from prison, or who has just been *filled in* in an insolvent condition. The implication is that, as soon as he arrives, the mob starts paying his way. "When I filled him in, he was strictly c.o.d. but when I took a fall he didn't spring with a dime." Of course, any thief might find himself in this condition temporarily, but if he turns up *c.o.d.* consistently, he soon loses status, even though some mobs might feel an obligation to use him as a *pick up* for a few days to enable him to get on his feet. This is called *giving him a day's work*, even though he might work as an extra man for several days, or even weeks.

When a pickpocket operates consistently on a *petty larceny* basis, or is never anything more than a very small-timer, he is called a *doormat thief*, the sarcastic implication being that he steals doormats (or that he can't even steal a doormat), though of course such a profession or specialty is entirely mythical. A *dynamiter* is a very *rough tool* who may get by without too many *beefs*, but whose technique associates him with the "tear off Kids" or the *snatch and grab* type of theft. Note again the hyperbole; an operator who does not observe the proper finesse is imaged as blasting the wallet away from the victim. This type of tool naturally does not expect immunity, but he had better operate under very sound *fixing* arrangements or have excellent stalls, or both, unless he wants to spend half his life in *stir*. A tool who is *dynamite*, on the other hand, is tops, and is anything but a *snatch and grab* man.

Anyone asleep in a public place is, in the thieves' argot, a *flop*. While this may seem to the lay reader an unconventional situation in which only bums and riffraff would be involved, let him be assured that many otherwise decorous people doze in public; this is particularly true of senior citizens who find that, once they sit down and relax, the next step is a nap. Pickpockets are ever watchful for these marks, and there is a specialty in the *racket* which preys exclusively on *flops*. "He hustles the flops." He is called a *flop worker*, and he prowls the parks, the subways, the railroad stations and, more frequently, the stations for subways or elevated trains. Some invade hotel lobbies; in fact, I have in my files some photographs of a dozing postprandial mark who is being stripped of everything including his wrist watch and jewelry. These *flop workers*, while recognized as part of the profession, are not highly regarded by better-class pickpockets, who think of a mark as someone who is up on his feet and going somewhere; in fact, many of the best operators cannot work successfully on a victim unless he is moving naturally. "That's the psychology of it. He [the *flop worker*] can't stand my racket. He said, "How in the *goddamned* hell can you put your hand in that man's pocket when he's walking and talking? And I can't see how he could put his hand in a man's pocket when he's sound asleep." A *forty-second street thief* is one who cannot *work* anywhere but in one city or one locality. Perhaps this is because he cannot *work* unless he is *hustling behind a shade*, and the only shade he knows how to manipulate is in one locality. Perhaps he has a psychological block against *working* in other localities. "A Forty-Second Street thief might work in New Orleans or Los Angeles, not necessarily in New York. He is a one-spot hustler, and he's afraid to grift when he's not in that spot."

Among old-timers, a *grifter* denotes a pickpocket or *sneak thief*, and some still so call themselves. The term *grifter* has, however, in recent years so generalized that it now includes all sorts of nonviolent criminals from carnival *flat jointers* to *big con men*. The *grifter* in this older sense is the *gentle grafter* of the fiction of O. Henry, written shortly after the turn of the century before *grifter* had become sufficiently popular to have replaced *grafter*.

We have already mentioned *hijackers* (or *high jackers*). The individual tool using very rough techniques is called a *hijacker*. This may be regarded as a specialty by some pickpockets—usually those who have little else to claim as a specialty. "Johnny may not be a good sneak, but he's one hell of a fine hijacker." A *home guard* is simply the name which *road mobs* apply to a *local* pickpocket; it is not a term which *locals* would apply to themselves, except whimsically. "They will say about home guards, they'll say, 'Pay no attention to him . . . he's just a local character.'" A *hungry tool* is one who is always working; he is said to be *money hungry* because he thinks only of making money. There are also *hungry mobs*, though this classification is largely accidental in that two or three *hungry* operators work together, probably by choice. "A hungry tool doesn't necessarily mean that he is determined, but it means that he is money hungry. He could be ever so determined to take his score and still not be money hungry."

When a tool is very fast and dextrous—but not *rough*—he is called a *lightning tool*. "Joey Fay is a lightning tool. That's why they call him the Electric Kid." This is a label which indicates professional status, especially when used by *class cannons*. The Eastern police use the term *live cannon* to distinguish a pickpocket from other related operators; while it is not a pickpocket term, many pickpockets, especially those in the East, know it and may use it ironically or humorously. Says a detective from a pickpocket detail: "In New York City a live cannon is a pants pocket worker who hustles crowds, while a lush-worker rolls drunks." In this quotation we see another police word, *pants pocket worker*, which is used by pickpockets seldom if at all. An accomplished tool, smooth and fast, is called a *live wire*. "Abie Lesser was a live wire if I ever seen one."

Another term for an excellent tool is *mechanic*, a term preferred by the more conservative old-timers; this word, meaning a skilled worker, has spread throughout the underworld from safecrackers to professional gamblers. A woman pickpocket is, of course, a *moll*, or *moll whiz*. "Some say Owney Madden's broad was a real moll whiz, but when I knew her she was mainly a booster." In this connection perhaps the term *gun moll* should be mentioned ("The sharpest gun molls are mockies"), although it has left the underworld for Hollywood and the crime magazines, where it is often erroneously used to mean a girl accomplice of a *heavy worker* who carries his pistol, and sometimes uses it; in fact, this character has been created out of whole cloth and has no counterpart among the thieves who call themselves *guns* and their female accomplices, *gun molls*. As has been pointed out, the *gun* element stems from the Yiddish *gonif* and does not, as Hollywood likes to believe, mean "pistol."

A diligent and skilled operator may be called a *money getter*, especially if he is a tool; this term is complimentary, whereas *hungry*, discussed above, is not; the difference lies in the attitudes implied toward money and work by the two words. At the risk of seeming facetious, we might say that a *hungry tool* devotes his life to the taking and hoarding of money; a *money getter* can take it or let it alone. Actually, the *money getter* is more of a "playboy"; he likes to spend money as well as make it. When a pickpocket (usually a tool but not always) who normally works with a mob decides to work by himself now and then, he is said to be *muzzling around*, and such an operator may be called a *muzzler*. This indicates only occasional departure from the normal relationship of tool and stall and a *muzzler* should not be confused with a *single o tool*, who works consistently alone. This term is interesting in that it is probably borrowed from a certain type of sex pervert who gets gratification from manual and bodily contact with women in a crowd; while the similarity in movement is perhaps close, there the analogy ends, for pickpockets as a group are overtly and conventionally heterosexual, with little understanding and no tolerance for so-called perversions of any kind. The following quotation is characteristic, even to the point that the informant thinks that *muzzlers* (the sexual kind) must be homosexuals because they are perverts. "No, a muzzler ain't a faggot. His line—I'll tell you—he's a guy that will muzzle around single o."

A very small-time pickpocket who fears to take risks is referred to as a *petty larceny bum*, often shortened to *petty larceny*, as "He's petty larceny." This kind of thief likes to keep his *scores* within the limit for petit larceny, thereby avoiding the much heavier penalties incurred for grand larceny; in many states anything over $20 constitutes grand larceny. Obviously, no professional pickpocket can accept a $20 limit on the proceeds of free enterprise and maintain his self-respect. When one pickpocket reaches for a term of deep contempt for another, it is likely to be *pocketbook snatcher*. "Sheeny Augie . . . that pocketbook snatcher." *Poke glommer* is also used, with the added pejorative implications.

All pickpockets like to think of themselves as specialists of one kind or another, the specialty sometimes changing from time to time. Sometimes they fancy their specialty lies in the particular pocket which they can pick best, or which they find easier than others. Really topnotch thieves, I have observed, have few illusions about a specialty, but are completely versatile. Therefore, one wonders if the concept of specialization may not actually be a rationalization of one's limitations. The terms *prat digger* and *prat worker* reflect this situation. Both mean a tool who specializes in hip pockets. Some pickpockets have never seen anyone rob any other kind of pocket, and perhaps do not even know that it is practical to try to do so; such an operator would see nothing derogatory in being termed a *prat worker*, but when either *prat worker* or *prat digger* is used by a *class cannon* to refer to another pickpocket, the term definitely suggests his limitations. Following are three quotations from different types of pickpocket which show varying attitudes toward the *prat digger*, and at the same time reveal something of the techniques and professional status of the speakers. "Kid Shelton had fingers five inches long. He was the sharpest prat digger I ever stole with." "A prat digger isn't a good one if he can't make a bridge or a pit." "We have summer cannons [in New York City] who are hooks and can nail a prat poke when they don't have to go in under a tog." A *producer*, on the other hand, is a pickpocket, usually a tool but not necessarily so, who has a reputation as a money-maker without meriting the label *hungry;* he is a good man to have in the mob.

When a youngster who has just been *turned out* begins to feel overconfidence in his own abilities, or when a newcomer to the *whiz* talks too much about his exploits, he is called behind his back—and on occasion to his face—a *sensational punk*, which we might render into the language of the dominant culture as "the boy wonder," although the argot phrase has more bite and more sarcasm than the legitimate idiom. A Negro professional is called a *shine cannon*, which is generally a term used by whites showing acceptance and sometimes respect; it is not applied to every Negro who calls himself a pickpocket. The good Negro pickpocket prefers to be called a *shot*, and is so designated by his own race. A *sneak tool* is a very capable operator who normally works with a mob, but who can operate by himself after the fashion of a *solo cannon* or *single o tool*; with a *sneak tool* it is more than just *muzzling around* now and then, for he can operate alone much of the time, even though he has stalls with him. He seems to rely more on his own skill, daring, and *grift know* than he does upon his stalls. He is not a lone wolf, but rather an aggressive, productive worker who does not always depend on the support of the mob, even when the stalls are present. Another name rarely used for a stall is a *stick*, so-called because he *sticks the mark* or *sticks the mark down* so that the tool can do his work. "You see, you got only a second. You got to come away with it when the stick comes through." Another kind of stall is a *straphanger*, which term adequately suggests a dilatory, inactive, uninterested, nonaggressive pickpocket who moons along, unaware of what goes on around him; he resembles the typical *sucker* straphanger in a subway or elevated car. Usually this term is applied to a stall, but it may also refer to a tool, in which case he is about as ineffective as a tool can be. A pickpocket who cannot go under a topcoat or overcoat is called a *summer cannon* or *summertime tool*; during the winter these tools like to stall for someone who can go under the *togs*, or go to the South or Southwest where they can find marks who are not unduly encumbered with outer vestments. "Now, of course, if a guy's a summertime tool and one of them guys that we call, pardon my French, a half-assed pickpocket—half the time he sees a kickout, a guy's poke sticking half out of his pocket and he's falling down drunk hanging on a lamppost, and he walks over and gives him the Mary and calls hisself a pickpocket."

When a pickpocket *works* the subways, especially during the rush hours, he is known as a *third rail*; this is New York and Boston usage largely. Note here again the implication of power and violence which the picketpocket focuses in himself, the third rail being actually the center rail which carries the tremendous voltage necessary to run the subway system.

If one pickpocket says of another that he *wears the gloves* he means that the one referred to is afraid to take hold of a situation, he is not aggressive toward the mark, he is a *center fielder*, a *mile away*, or *playing safety first*. When this term is applied to a tool it is very sarcastic, for it evokes the ludicrous image of a thief performing this most delicate of all thieving operations with gloves on. A successful professional, either stall or tool, may be called a *winner*, but one hears the term more often than not applied to tools, probably because the tool must *produce* if the mob is to make any money, and any success that the mob has directly reflects his abilities. And, of course, any pickpocket is a *whiz* or *whizzer*, though this is usually expressed as being *on the whiz*, which is the name for the profession. "I never knew he was on the whiz." "If you have a hot thimble on you in Boston and somebody puts the finger on you for being whiz, they can do you in."

There are, of course, many more names applied to individual pick-pockets, the number and variety being limited only by the experience and observations of the various groups. Those included here are pertinent because they have been in use for some years and are, generally speaking, known throughout the fraternity.

6 The Activities and Location of Organized Criminals

THE PRESIDENT'S COMMISSION
ON LAW ENFORCEMENT
AND ADMINISTRATION OF JUSTICE

Organized crime is a society that seeks to operate outside the control of the American people and their governments. It involves thousands of criminals, working within structures as complex as those of any large corporation, subject to laws more rigidly enforced than those of legitimate governments. Its actions are not impulsive but rather the result of intricate conspiracies, carried on over many years and aimed at gaining control over whole fields of activity in order to amass huge profits.[1]

Reprinted from "Organized Crime," *Task Force Report: Organized Crime*, Annotations and Consultants' Papers, Task Force on Organized Crime—The President's Commission on Law Enforcement and Administration of Justice (Washington: Government Printing Office, 1967), pp. 1–7.

[1] The Kefauver committee found that:

"1. There is a Nation-wide crime syndicate known as the Mafia, whose tentacles are found in many large cities. It has international ramifications which appear most clearly in connection with the narcotics traffic.

"2. Its leaders are usually found in control of the most lucrative rackets in their cities.

"3. There are indications of a centralized direction and control of these rackets, but leadership appears to be in a group rather than in a single individual.

"4. The Mafia is the cement that helps to bind the Costello-Adonis-Lansky syndicate of New York and the Accardo-Guzik-Fischetti syndicate of Chicago as well as smaller criminal gangs and individual criminals throughout the country. These groups have kept in touch with Luciano since his deportation from this country.

"5. The domination of the Mafia is based fundamentally on 'muscle' and 'murder.'

The core of organized crime activity is the supplying of illegal goods and services—gambling, loan sharking, narcotics, and other forms of vice—to countless numbers of citizen customers.[2] But organized crime is also extensively and deeply involved in legitimate business and in labor unions.[3] Here it employs illegitimate methods—monopolization, terrorism, extortion, tax evasion—to drive out or control lawful ownership and leadership and to exact illegal profits from the public.[4] And to carry on its many activities secure from governmental interference, organized crime corrupts public officials.[5]

Former Attorney General Robert F. Kennedy illustrated its power simply and vividly. He testified before a Senate subcommittee in 1963 that the physical protection of witnesses who had cooperated with the Federal Government in organized crime cases often required that those witnesses change their appearances, change their names, or even leave the country.[6] When the government of a powerful country is unable to protect its friends from its enemies by means less extreme than obliterating their identities surely it is being seriously challenged, if not threatened.

The Mafia is a secret conspiracy against law and order which will ruthlessly eliminate anyone who stands in the way of its success in any criminal enterprise in which it is interested. It will destroy anyone who betrays its secrets. It will use any means available —political influence, bribery, intimidation, etc., to defeat any attempt on the part of law-enforcement to touch its top figures or to interfere with its operations."
Sen. Special Comm. to Investigate Organized Crime in Interstate Commerce [hereinafter cited as Kefauver Comm.], *3d Interim. Rep.*, s. REP. NO. 307, 82d Cong., 1st Sess. 150 (1951). See also OFFICE OF THE N.Y. COUNSEL TO THE GOVERNOR, COMBATING ORGANIZED CRIME —A REPORT OF THE 1965 OYSTER BAY, NEW YORK, CONFERENCES ON COMBATING ORGANIZED CRIME (1966).

[2] Johnson, *Organized Crime: Challenge to the American Legal System* (pts. 1–3), 53 J. CRIM. L., C. & P.S. 399, 402–04 (1962), 54 J. CRIM. L., & P.S. 1, 127 (1963).

[3] See generally Sen. Select Comm. on Improper Activities in the Labor or Management Field [hereinafter cited as McClellan, Labor-Mgt. Reps.], *1st Interim Rep.*, s. REP. NO. 1417, 85th Cong., 2d Sess. (1958), *2d Interim Rep.* (pts. 1 & 2), s. REP. NO. 621, 86th Cong., 1st Sess. (1959), *Final Rep.* (pts. 1–4), s. REP. NO. 1139, 86th Cong., 2d Sess. (1960), *Index to Reports*, 86th Cong., 2d Sess. (1960).

[4] "A gangster or racketeer in a legitimate business does not suddenly become respectable. . . . [E]vidence was produced before the committee concerning the use of unscrupulous and discriminatory business practices, extortion, bombing and other forms of violence to eliminate competitors and to compel customers to take articles sold by the mobsters." Kefauver Comm., *3d Interim Rep.*, s. REP. NO. 307, 82d Cong., 1st Sess. 170 (1951).

[5] Johnson, *supra* note 2, at 412–14, 419–22; Kefauver Comm., *3d Interim Rep.*, s. REP. NO. 307, 82d Cong., 1st Sess. 181–86 (1951).

[6] *Hearings Before the Permanent Subcomm. on Investigations of the Senate Comm. on Government Operations* [hereinafter cited as McClellan, *Narcotics Hearings*], 88th Cong., 1st Sess., pt. 1, at 25 (1963).

What organized crime wants is money and power. What makes it different from law-abiding organizations and individuals with those same objectives is that the ethical and moral standards the criminals adhere to, the laws and regulations they obey, the procedures they use are private and secret ones that they devise themselves, change when they see fit, and administer summarily and invisibly. Organized crime affects the lives of millions of Americans, but because it desperately preserves its invisibility many, perhaps most, Americans are not aware how they are affected, or even that they are affected at all. The price of a loaf of bread may go up one cent as the result of an organized crime conspiracy, but a housewife has no way of knowing why she is paying more.[7] If organized criminals paid income tax on every cent of their vast earnings everybody's tax bill would go down, but no one knows how much.[8]

But to discuss the impact of organized crime in terms of whatever direct, personal, everyday effect it has on individuals is to miss most of the point. Most individuals are not affected, in this sense, very much. Much of the money organized crime accumulates comes from innumerable petty transactions:[9] 50-cent bets, $3-a-month private garbage collection services, quarters dropped into racketeer-owned jukeboxes, or small price rises resulting from protection rackets. A one-cent-a-loaf rise in bread may annoy housewives, but it certainly does not impoverish them.

Sometimes organized crime's activities do not directly affect individuals at all. Smuggled cigarettes in a vending machine cost consumers no more than tax-paid cigarettes, but they enrich the leaders of organized crime. Sometimes these activities actually reduce prices for a short period of time, as can happen when organized crime, in an attempt to take over an industry, starts a price war against legitimate businessmen. Even when organized crime engages in a large transaction, individuals may not be directly affected. A large sum of money may be diverted from a union pension fund to finance a

7 Kefauver Comm., *3d Interim Rep.*, s. REP. NO. 307, 82d Cong., 1st Sess. 170–71 (1951): "There can be little doubt that the public suffers from gangster penetration into legitimate business. It suffers because higher prices must be paid for articles and services which it must buy . ... The public suffers because it may have to put up with shoddy and inferior merchandise in fields where gangsters have been able to obtain a monopoly."

8 One indication of the amount of tax revenue lost is found in the testimony of Comm'r of Internal Revenue Sheldon S. Cohen before the Senate Subcommittee on Administrative Practice and Procedure on July 13, 1965. He stated that during the period between February 1961 and March 13, 1965, more than $219 million in taxes and penalties had been recommended for assessment against subjects of the Federal organized crime drive. *Hearings Before the Subcomm. on Administrative Practice and Procedure of the Sen. Comm. on the Judiciary* [hereinafter cited as *Long Comm. Hearings*], 89th Cong., 1st Sess., pt. 3, at 1119 (1965).

9 See generally McClellan, Labor-Mgt. Reps., *Final Rep.*, s. REP. NO. 1139, 86th Cong., 2d Sess., pt. 4 (1960).

business venture without immediate and direct effect upon the individual members of the union.[10]

It is organized crime's accumulation of money, not the individual transactions by which the money is accumulated, that has a great and threatening impact on America. A quarter in a jukebox means nothing and results in nothing. But millions of quarters in thousands of jukeboxes can provide both a strong motive for murder and the means to commit murder with impunity.[11] Organized crime exists by virtue of the power it purchases with its money. The millions of dollars it can invest in narcotics or use for layoff money give it power over the lives of thousands of people and over the quality of life in whole neighborhoods.[12] The millions of dollars it can throw into the legitimate economic system give it power to manipulate the price of shares on the stock market,[13] to raise or lower the price of retail merchandise, to determine whether entire industries are union or nonunion, to make it easier or harder for businessmen to continue in business.[14]

The millions of dollars it can spend on corrupting public officials may give it power to maim or murder people inside or outside the organization with impunity; to extort money from businessmen; to conduct businesses in such fields as liquor, meat, or drugs without regard to administrative regulations; to avoid payment of income taxes or to secure public works contracts without competitive bidding.[15]

The purpose of organized crime is not competition with visible, legal government but nullification of it. When organized crime places an official in public office, it nullifies the political process. When it bribes a police official, it nullifies law enforcement.

There is another, more subtle way in which organized crime has an impact on American life. Consider the former way of life of Frank Costello, a man who has repeatedly been called a leader of organized crime. He lived

[10] Such bootlegging activities cost the city and State of New York about $40 million a year in lost tax revenues. N.Y. Times, Feb. 2, 1967, p. 21.

For a discussion of the problems of cigarette smuggling in New York State, see Weintraub, A Report on Bootlegging of Cigarettes in the City and State of New York, Jan. 1966 (prepared for Cigarette Merchandisers Ass'n, Inc., New York, N.Y.); Weintraub & Kaufman, Bootlegged Cigarettes, Jan. 1967 (prepared for Wholesale Tobacco Distributors of New York, Inc., New York, N.Y.). See also Weintraub, The Bootlegging of Cigarettes Is a National Problem, Oct. 1966 (prepared for Wholesale Tobacco Distributors of New York, Inc., New York, N.Y.).

[11] Peterson, *Chicago: Shades of Capone*, Annals, May, 1963, p. 30.

[12] Kefauver Comm., *3d Interim Rep.*, s. REP. NO. 307, 82d Cong., 1st Sess. 171 (1951).

[13] See Lefkowitz. *New York: Criminal Infiltration of the Securities Industry*, Annals, May 1963, p. 51. See also excerpt from Porter, *On Wall Street*, N.Y. Post, Aug. 3-7, 1959, in ORGANIZED CRIME IN AMERICA 298 (Tyler ed. 1962).

[14] Johnson, *supra* note 2, at 406.

[15] Kefauver Comm., *3d Interm Rep.*, s. REP. NO. 307, 82d Cong., 1st Sess. 30-144 (1951).

in an expensive apartment on the corner of 72d Street and Central Park West in New York. He was often seen dining in well-known restaurants in the company of judges, public officials, and prominent businessmen. Every morning he was shaved in the barbershop of the Waldorf Astoria Hotel. On many weekends he played golf at a country club on the fashionable North Shore of Long Island. In short, though his reputation was common knowledge, he moved around New York conspicuously and unashamedly, perhaps ostracized by some people but more often accepted, greeted by journalists, recognized by children, accorded all the freedoms of a prosperous and successful man. On a society that treats such a man in such a manner, organized crime has had an impact.

And yet the public remains indifferent. Few Americans seem to comprehend how the phenomenon of organized crime affects their lives. They do not see how gambling with bookmakers, or borrowing money from loan sharks, forwards the interests of great criminal cartels.[16] Businessmen looking for labor harmony or nonunion status through irregular channels rationalize away any suspicions that organized crime is thereby spreading its influence. When an ambitious political candidate accepts substantial cash contributions from unknown sources, he suspects but dismisses the fact that organized crime will dictate some of his actions when he assumes office.[17]

President Johnson asked the Commission to determine why organized crime has been expanding despite the Nation's best efforts to prevent it. The Commission drew upon the small group of enforcement personnel and other knowledgeable persons who deal with organized crime. Federal agencies provided extensive material. But because so little study and research have been done in this field, we also secured the assistance of sociologists, systems analysts, political scientists, economists, and lawyers.[18] America's limited response to organized crime is illustrated by the fact that, for several of these disciplines, our call for assistance resulted in their first concentrated examination of organized crime.

THE TYPES OF ORGANIZED CRIMINAL ACTIVITIES

Catering to Public Demands

Organized criminal groups participate in any illegal activity that offers maximum profit at minimum risk of law enforcement interference. They

---

[16] See generally COOK, THE TWO DOLLAR BET MEANS MURDER (1961).

[17] For an excellent discussion of the influences of underworld money in politics, see HEARD, THE COSTS OF DEMOCRACY 154–68 (1960).

[18] Selected papers of Commission consultants appear in the appendices to this volume.

offer goods and services that millions of Americans desire even though declared illegal by their legislatures.

GAMBLING.[19]   Law enforcement officials agree almost unanimously that gambling is the greatest source of revenue for organized crime.[20] It ranges from lotteries, such as "numbers" or "bolita," to off-track horse betting, bets on sporting events, large dice games and illegal casinos. In large cities where organized criminal groups exist, very few of the gambling operators are independent of a large organization.[21] Anyone whose independent operation becomes successful is likely to receive a visit from an organization representative who convinces the independent, through fear or promise of greater profit, to share his revenue with the organization.[22]

Most large-city gambling is established or controlled by organized crime members through elaborate hierarchies.[23] Money is filtered from the small operator who takes the customer's bet, through persons who pick up money and slips, to second-echelon figures in charge of particular districts, and then into one of several main offices.[24] The profits that eventually accrue to or-

[19] See generally Permanent Subcomm. on Investigations of the Sen. Comm. on Gov't Operations, *Gambling and Organized Crime* [hereinafter cited as McClellan, *Gambling Rep.*], S. REP. NO. 1310, 87th Cong., 2d Sess. (1962). See also N.Y. TEMPORARY COMM'N OF INVESTIGATION, SYNDICATED GAMBLING IN NEW YORK STATE (1961).

[20] "Gambling is the principle source of income for organized criminal gangs in the country." Kefauver Comm., *2d Interim Rep.*, S. REP. NO. 141, 82d Cong., 1st Sess. 11 (1951).

"According to major Federal, state and local law enforcement officials who have made studies and who are known to the subcommittee staff, organized crime in the United States is primarily dependent upon illicit gambling, a multibillion dollar market, for the necessary funds required to operate other criminal and illegal activities or enterprises." McClellan, *Gambling Rep.*, S. REP. NO. 1310, 87th Cong., 2d Sess. 43 (1962).

[21] Information submitted to Commission by a Federal agency.

[22] Statement by then Deputy Inspector Arthur C. Grubert, New York City Police Dep't, In-Service Training Program, Apr. 19, 1965, New York, N.Y.

[23] "Number gambling follows the general pattern of organization of all large scale vice and crime. This pattern consists of four basic elements: (1) an elaborate hierarchical organization of personnel, (2) a spatial organization in which a wide territory is controlled from a central metropolitan area, (3) the 'fix,' in which public officials, principally police and politicians, are drawn into and made a part of the organization, (4) legal aid in which members of the legal profession become the advisors and consultants of the organization." Carlson, Numbers Gambling, A Study of a Culture Complex 68, 1940, unpublished Ph.D. dissertation, Univ. of Mich. Dep't of Sociology.

[24] It was reported, for example, that in Detroit there were almost 100 positions involved in the operation of one lottery enterprise. Bet slips were delivered by 50 "pick up" men to substations where they were tabulated. After a "bookkeeper" determined the winning slips, the proceeds were taken to a "section chief" who passed a portion up through the hierarchy. McClellan, *Narcotics Hearings*, 88th Cong., 1st Sess., pt. 2, at 460–62 (1963).

ganization leaders move through channels so complex that even persons who work in the betting operation do not know or cannot prove the identity of the leader. Increasing use of the telephone for lottery and sports betting has facilitated systems in which the bookmaker may not know the identity of the second-echelon person to whom he calls in the day's bets. Organization not only creates greater efficiency and enlarges markets,[25] it also provides a systematized method of corrupting the law enforcement process by centralizing procedures for the payment of graft.[26]

Organization is also necessary to prevent severe losses. More money may be bet on one horse or one number with a small operator than he could pay off if that horse or that number should win. The operator will have to hedge by betting some money himself on that horse or that number. This so-called "layoff" betting is accomplished through a network of local, regional, and national layoff men, who take bets from gambling operations.[27]

There is no accurate way of ascertaining organized crime's gross revenue from gambling in the United States. Estimates of the annual intake have varied from $7 to $50 billion.[28] Legal betting at racetracks reaches a gross annual figure of almost $5 billion, and most enforcement officials believe that illegal wagering on horse races, lotteries, and sporting events totals at least

[25] In his statement to the Temporary Commission of Investigation of the State of New York on Apr. 22, 1960, Charles R. Thom, Comm'r of Police of Suffolk County (Eastern Long Island), N.Y., said: "The *advantages* of syndicate operation to the previously independent bookie included: (1) unlimited resources with absolute backing which eliminated the need to lay off, thus permitting vast expansion, and the average bookie quickly discovered he was making a bigger net on a 50–50 basis than he formerly made when he controlled the entire operation; (2) New York City telephone numbers could be passed along to regular bettors and players, which made the bookie merely a collector of money, credited on the books of the syndicate through an efficient bookkeeping system, and adding the tremendous factor that use of telephones was thus changed, greatly reducing the efficiency of telephone taps; and (3) the syndicate agreed to provide 'stand-up men' where feasible." Mimeo. p. 2.

[26] "It is somewhat startling to learn that the syndicates are particularly happy with the consolidation of the nine police departments into the Suffolk County Police Department, as they feel that protection is easier to arrange through one agency than through many. The intensive campaign against gamblers instituted by this Department commencing January 1st had the astounding side effect in solving the recruitment problem of the syndicate, as our drive successfully stampeded the independents into the arms of the syndicate for protection, and the syndicate can now pick and choose those operators which they wish to admit." *Ibid.*

[27] See Cressey, "The Functions and Structure of Criminal Syndicates," *Task Force Report: Organized Crime*, President's Commission on Law Enforcement and Administration of Justice, Washington: Government Printing Office, 1967, Appendix A, pp. 35–36.

[28] "[G]ambling is the leading source of organization revenue, accounting for probably half of organization profits. It has been estimated that illegal gambling grosses from seven to twenty billion dollars annually." Johnson, *supra* note 2, at 402. For some estimates on the volume of illegal gambling, see *id.* at 402 n.22.

$20 billion each year. Analysis of organized criminal betting operations indicates that the profit is as high as one-third of gross revenue—or $6 to $7 billion each year. While the Commission cannot judge the accuracy of these figures, even the most conservative estimates place substantial capital in the hands of organized crime leaders.[29]

LOAN SHARKING.[30]   In the view of most law enforcement officials loan sharking, the lending of money at higher rates than the legally prescribed limit, is the second largest source of revenue for organized crime.[31] Gambling profits provide the initial capital for loan-shark operations.[32]

No comprehensive analysis has ever been made of what kinds of customers loan sharks have, or of how much or how often each kind borrows. Enforcement officials and other investigators do have some information. Gamblers borrow to pay gambling losses;[33] narcotics users borrow to pur-

[29] "Gambling profits are the principal support of big-time racketeering and gangsterism. These profits provide the financial resources whereby ordinary criminals are converted into big-time racketeers, political bosses, pseudo businessmen, and alleged philanthropists." Kefauver Comm., *3d Interim Rep.*, S. REP. NO. 307, 82d Cong., 1st Sess. 2 (1951).

[30] For an excellent treatment of the subject in New York State, see N.Y. TEMPORARY COMM'N OF INVESTIGATION, THE LOAN SHARK RACKET (1965).

[31] "[S]hylocking . . . represents a substantial portion of the multibillion dollar take of organized crime." Johnson, *supra* note 2, at 403.

[32] Permanent Subcomm. on Investigations of the Sen. Comm. on Gov't Operations, *Organized Crime and Illicit Traffic in Narcotics* [hereinafter cited as McClellan, *Narcotics Rep.*], S. REP. NO. 72, 89th Cong., 1st Sess. 18 (1965); testimony of J. Edgar Hoover, *Hearings Before the Subcomm. on Dept's of State, Justice, and Commerce, the Judiciary, and Related Agencies Appropriations of the House Comm. on Appropriations*, 89th Cong., 2d Sess. 272 (1966).

[33] In his statement to the Temporary Commission of Investigation of the State of New York on Apr. 22, 1960, Comm'r Charles R. Thom described how loan sharking provided the means for organizing previously independent bookmakers:

"Speaking generally, prior to 1958, professional gambling in Suffolk County was conducted primarily by independent operators. There was no known pattern of organized gambling beyond the usual facilities for laying off, and no reported rackets or collateral criminal activities.

"About two years ago, representatives of one or more syndicates began approaching these independent gambling operators with a view to incorporating them into syndicated operations. By and large, these independent gamblers refused to be so organized, and the syndicates withdrew their efforts without resort to rough tactics. The syndicates then commenced an insidious campaign of infiltration, wherein the principle M.O. was *finance*. With open pocketbook, the syndicate recruited a number of independent operators, by financing their operations until these bookies were hooked. Part of this system included the notorious 6 for 5 plus 5 per cent per week, which meant simply that they financed the bookies on the basis that the gambling operator had to return $6.00 for every $5.00 borrowed, plus the staggering interest of 5 per cent per week. It follows that a bookie who had a couple of bad weeks was completely hooked and fell under the control of the syndicate. Most of these independent bookies were small businessmen,

chase heroin. Some small businessmen borrow from loan sharks when legitimate credit channels are closed.[34] The same men who take bets from
employees in mass employment industries also serve at times as loan sharks,
whose money enables the employees to pay off their gambling debts or meet
household needs.[35]

Interest rates vary from 1 to 150 percent a week, according to the
relationship between the lender and borrower, the intended use of the
money, the size of the loan, and the repayment potential.[36] The classic "6-
for-5" loan, 20 percent a week, is common with small borrowers. Payments
may be due by a certain hour on a certain day, and even a few minutes'
default may result in a rise in interest rates. The lender is more interested in
perpetuating interest payments than collecting principal; and force, or threats
of force of the most brutal kind, are used to effect interest collection,
eliminate protest when interest rates are raised, and prevent the beleaguered
borrower from reporting the activity to enforcement officials.[37] No reliable
estimates exist of the gross revenue from organized loan sharking, but profit
margins are higher than for gambling operations, and many officials classify
the business in the multi-billion-dollar range.[38]

NARCOTICS.[39]   The sale of narcotics is organized like a legitimate importing-wholesaling-retailing business. The distribution of heroin, for example, requires movement of the drug through four or five levels between the
importer and the street peddler.[40] Many enforcement officials believe that
the severity of mandatory Federal narcotics penalties has caused organized
criminals to restrict their activities to importing and wholesale distribution.[41]
They stay away from smaller-scale wholesale transactions or dealing at the
retail level. Transactions with addicts are handled by independent narcotics
pushers using drugs imported by organized crime.[42]

---

including the typical barber, candy store operator and the like, without the financial
resources to withstand this squeeze, which was effectively accomplished by the money
men of the syndicate. Once hooked, the bookies now worked for the syndicate on a
50–50 basis."

[34] N.Y. TEMPORARY COMM'N OF INVESTIGATION, THE LOAN SHARK REPORT 45 (1965).

[35] Information submitted to Commission by a Federal agency.

[36] See McClellan, Labor-Mgt. Reps., *Final Rep.*, S. REP. NO. 1139, 86th Cong., 2d Sess.,
pt. 4, at 772 (1960).

[37] Information submitted to Commission by a Federal agency.

[38] N.Y. TEMPORARY COMM'N OF INVESTIGATION, THE LOAN SHARK REPORT 17 (1965).

[39] See generally McClellan, *Narcotics Hearings*, 88th Cong., 1st Sess., pts. 1 & 2
(1963), 1st & 2d Sess., pts. 3 & 4 (1963–64), 2d Sess., pt. 5 (1964). McClellan, *Narcotics
Rep.*, S. REP. NO. 72, 89th Cong., 1st Sess. (1965).

[40] See Cressey, *op. cit.*, p. 35.

[41] McClellan, *Narcotics Rep.*, S. REP. NO. 72, 89th Cong., 1st Sess. 120 (1965).

[42] *Id.* at 121–22.

The large amounts of cash and the international connections necessary for large, long-term heroin supplies can be provided only by organized crime. Conservative estimates of the number of addicts in the Nation and the average daily expenditure for heroin indicate that the gross heroin trade is $350 million annually,[43] of which $21 million are probably profits to the importer and distributor.[44] Most of this profit goes to organized crime groups in those few cities in which almost all heroin consumption occurs.

OTHER GOODS AND SERVICES. Prostitution and bootlegging play a small and declining role in organized crime's operations.[45] Production of illegal alcohol is a risky business. The destruction of stills and supplies by law enforcement officers during the initial stages means the loss of heavy initial investment capital. Prostitution is difficult to organize and discipline is hard to maintain. Several important convictions of organized crime figures in prostitution cases in the 1930's and 1940's made the criminal executives wary of further participation.[46]

Business and Labor Interests

INFILTRATION OF LEGITIMATE BUSINESS. A legitimate business enables the racket executive to acquire respectability in the community and to establish a source of funds that appears legal and upon which just enough taxes may be paid to avoid income tax prosecution.[47] Organized crime invests the profit it has made from illegal service activities in a variety of businesses throughout the country.[48] To succeed in such ventures, it uses accountants, attorneys, and business consultants, who in some instances work exclusively

[43] *Id.* at 120.

[44] Information submitted to Commission by a Federal agency.

[45] "Gambling has supplanted prostitution and bootlegging as the chief source of revenue for organized crime. Before the First World War, the major profits of organized criminals were obtained from prostitution. The passage of the Mann White Slave Act, the changing sexual mores, and public opinion, combined to make commercialized prostitution a less profitable and more hazardous enterprise." Kefauver Comm., *2d Interim Rep.*, s. REP. NO. 141, 82d Cong., 1st Sess. 11 (1952).

For a recent investigation of commercialized prostitution, see N.Y. TEMPORARY COMM'N OF INVESTIGATION, AN INVESTIGATION OF LAW ENFORCEMENT IN BUFFALO (1961).

[46] People v. Luciano, 277 N.Y. 348, 14 N.E.2d 433, *cert. denied sub nom.*, Luciano v. New York, 305 U.S. 620 (1938). See also POWELL, NINETY TIMES GUILTY (1939), and for a brief description of Charles Luciano's role in organized crime, see excerpt from SONDERN, BROTHERHOOD OF EVIL (1959), in ORGANIZED CRIME IN AMERICA 302 (Tyler ed. 1962).

[47] See Kefauver Comm., *3d Interim Rep.*, s. REP. NO. 307, 82d Cong., 1st Sess. 170 (1951).

[48] "[C]riminals and racketeers are using the profits of organized crime to buy up and operate legitimate enterprises." Kefauver Comm., *3d Interim Rep.*, s. REP. NO. 307, 82d Cong., 1st Sess. 170 (1951).

on its affairs.[49] Too often, because of the reciprocal benefits involved in organized crime's dealings with the business world, or because of fear, the legitimate sector of society helps the illegitimate sector.[50] The Illinois Crime Commission, after investigating one service industry in Chicago, stated:

There is a disturbing lack of interest on the part of some legitimate business concerns regarding the identity of the persons with whom they deal. This lackadaisical attitude is conducive to the perpetration of frauds and the infiltration and subversion of legitimate businesses by the organized criminal element.[51]

Because business ownership is so easily concealed, it is difficult to determine all the types of businesses that organized crime has penetrated.[52] Of the 75 or so racket leaders who met at Apalachin, N.Y., in 1957, at least 9 were in the coin-operated machine industry, 16 were in the garment industry, 10 owned grocery stores, 17 owned bars or restaurants, 11 were in the olive oil and cheese business, and 9 were in the construction business. Others were involved in automobile agencies, coal companies, entertainment, funeral homes, ownership of horses and race tracks, linen and laundry enterprises, trucking, waterfront activities, and bakeries.[53]

Today, the kinds of production and service industries and businesses that organized crime controls or has invested in range from accounting firms to yeast manufacturing. One criminal syndicate alone has real estate interests with an estimated value of $300 million.[54] In a few instances, racketeers control nationwide manufacturing and service industries with known and respected brand names.[55]

Control of business concerns has usually been acquired through one of four methods: (1) investing concealed profits acquired from gambling and other illegal activities; (2) accepting business interests in payment of the

[49] "Mobsters and racketeers have been assisted by some tax accountants and tax lawyers in defrauding the Government." *Id.* at 4.

[50] "In some instances legitimate businessmen have aided the interests of the underworld by awarding lucrative contracts to gangsters and mobsters in return for help in handling employees, defeating attempts at unionization, and in breaking strikes." *Id.* at 5.

[51] 1965 ILL. CRIME INVESTIGATING COMM'N REP. 11.

[52] "Using dummy fronts, the real owners of a business, the men who put up the money, never have to list themselves as owners or partners or as even being involved in any way in the business." Grutzner, *Mafia Steps Up Infiltration and Looting of Businesses*, N.Y. Times, Feb. 14, 1965, p. 1, col. 3, at 65, col. 1.

[53] McClellan, Labor-Mgt. Reps., *Final Rep.*, S. REP. NO. 1139, 86th Cong., 2d Sess., pt. 3, at 487–88 (1960). The report of the Kefauver Committee provides a discussion of the degree of infiltration into legitimate business, including a list of 50 types of business enterprises in which organized crime is involved. Kefauver Comm., *3d Interim Rep.*, S. REP. NO. 307, 82d Cong., 1st Sess. 170–81 (1951).

[54] Information submitted to Commission by a Federal agency.

[55] *Ibid.*

owner's gambling debts; (3) foreclosing on usurious loans; and (4) using various forms of extortion.[56]

Acquisition of legitimate businesses is also accomplished in more sophisticated ways. One organized crime group offered to lend money to a business on condition that a racketeer be appointed to the company's board of directors and that a nominee for the lenders be given first option to purchase if there were any outside sale of the company's stock.[57] Control of certain brokerage houses was secured through foreclosure of usurious loans, and the businesses then used to promote the sale of fraudulent stock, involving losses of more than $2 million to the public.[58]

Criminal groups also satisfy defaulted loans by taking over businesses, hiring professional arsonists to burn buildings and contents, and collecting on the fire insurance. Another tactic was illustrated in the recent bankruptcy of a meatpacking firm in which control was secured as payment for gambling debts. With the original owners remaining in nominal management positions, extensive product orders were placed through established lines of credit, and the goods were immediately sold at low prices before the suppliers were paid. The organized criminal group made a quick profit of three-quarters of a million dollars by pocketing the receipts from sale of the products ordered and placing the firm in bankruptcy without paying the suppliers.[59]

Too little is known about the effects on the economy of organized crime's entry into the business world, but the examples above indicate the harm done to the public[60] and at least suggest how criminal cartels can undermine free competition.[61] The ordinary businessman is hard pressed to compete with a syndicate enterprise. From its gambling and other illegal revenue —on most of which no taxes are paid—the criminal group always has a ready source of cash with which to enter any business. Through union connections, the business run by organized crime either prevents unionization or secures "sweetheart" contracts from existing unions.[62] These tactics are used effec-

---

[56] *Ibid.*

[57] *Ibid.*

[58] *Ibid.* See also Grutzner, *supra* note 5, at 65, cols. 5–6.

[59] *Id.* cols. 1–3. *Hearings Before the Subcomm. on Criminal Laws and Procedures of the Sen. Comm. on the Judiciary*, 89th Cong., 2d Sess., at 204–06 (1966).

[60] "There can be little doubt that the public suffers from gangster penetration into legitimate business. It suffers because higher prices must be paid for articles and services which it must buy. . . . The public suffers because it may have to put up with shoddy and inferior merchandise in fields where gangsters have been able to obtain a monopoly." Kefauver Comm., *3d Interim Rep.*, s. rep. no. 307, 82d Cong., 1st Sess. 170–71 (1951).

[61] See Johnson, *Organized Crime: Challenge to the American Legal System* (pt. 1), 53 j. crim. l., c. & p.s. 399, 406–07.

[62] See generally McClellan, Labor-Mgt. Reps., *1st Interim Rep.*, s. rep. no. 1417, 85th Cong., 2d Sess. (1958), *2d Interim Rep.* (pts. 1 & 2), s. rep. no. 621, 86th Cong., 1st Sess. (1959), *Final Rep.* (pts. 1–4), s. rep. no. 1139, 86th Cong., 2d Sess. (1960).

tively in combination. In one city, organized crime gained a monopoly in garbage collection by preserving the business's nonunion status and by using cash reserves to offset temporary losses incurred when the criminal group lowered prices to drive competitors out of business.[63]

Strong-arm tactics are used to enforce unfair business policy and to obtain customers.[64] A restaurant chain controlled by organized crime used the guise of "quality control" to insure that individual restaurant franchise holders bought products only from other syndicate-owned businesses. In one city, every business with a particular kind of waste product useful in another line of industry sold that product to a syndicate-controlled business at one-third the price offered by legitimate business.

The cumulative effect of the infiltration of legitimate business in America cannot be measured.[65] Law enforcement officials agree that entry into legitimate business is continually increasing and that it has not decreased organized crime's control over gambling, usury and other profitable, low-risk criminal enterprises.

LABOR RACKETEERING.[66]   Control of labor supply and infiltration of labor unions by organized crime prevent unionization of some industries, provide opportunities for stealing from union funds and extorting money by threats of possible labor strife, and provide funds from the enormous union pension and welfare systems for business ventures controlled by organized criminals. Union control also may enhance other illegal activities. Trucking, construction, and waterfront shipping entrepreneurs, in return for assurance that business operations will not be interrupted by labor discord, countenance gambling, loan sharking, and pilferage on company property. Organized criminals either direct these activities or grant "concessions" to others in return for a percentage of the profits.

Some of organized crime's effects on labor union affairs, particularly in the abuse of pension and welfare funds, were disclosed in investigations by Senator John McClellan's committee. In one case, almost immediately after

[63] Information submitted to Commission by a Federal agency.

[64] "When organized crime embarks on a venture in legitimate business it ordinarily brings to that venture all the techniques of violence and intimidation which are employed in its illegal enterprises." Johnson, *Organized Crime: Challenge to the American Legal System* (pt. 1), 53 J. CRIM. L., C. & P.S. 399, 402–04 (1963).

[65] For a discussion of the criminal infiltration of legitimate activities, see Woetzel, *An overview of Organized Crime: Mores versus Morality*, Annals, May 1963, pp. 1, 6–7. For an excellent discussion of criminal infiltration into business in Chicago, see Peterson, *Chicago: Shades of Capone*, Annals, May, 1963, pp. 30, 32–39.

[66] For a detailed examination of labor racketeering, see McClellan, Labor-Mgt. Reps., *1st Interim Rep.*, s. REP. NO. 1417, 85th Cong., 2d Sess. (1958), *2d Interim Rep.* (pts. 1 & 2), s. REP. NO. 621, 86th Cong., 1st Sess. (1959), *Final Rep.* (pts. 1–4), s. REP. NO. 1139, 86th Cong., 2d Sess. (1960).

receiving a license as an insurance broker, the son of a major organized crime figure in New York City was chosen as the broker for a number of such funds, with significant commissions to be earned and made available for distribution to "silent partners." The youthful broker's only explanation for his success was that he had advertised in the classified telephone directory.[67]

In New York City, early in 1966, the head of one organized crime group was revealed to be a partner in a labor relations consulting firm. One client of the firm, a nationally prominent builder, said he did not oppose unions but that better and cheaper houses could be built without them. The question of why a legitimate businessman would seek the services of an untrained consultant with a criminal record to handle his labor relations was not answered.

LOCATION OF ORGANIZED CRIME ACTIVITIES

Organized criminal groups are known to operate in all sections of the Nation. In response to a Commission survey of 71 cities, the police departments in 80 percent of the cities with over 1 million residents, in 20 percent of the cities with a population between one-half million and a million, in 20 percent of the cities with between 250,000 and 500,000 population, and in over 50 percent of the cities between 100,000 and 250,000, indicated that organized criminal groups exist in their cities. In some instances Federal agency intelligence indicated the presence of organized crime where local reports denied it.[68] Of the nine cities not responding to the Commission survey,[69] six are known to Federal agencies to have extensive organized crime problems.[70] Where the existence of organized crime was acknowledged, all police departments indicated that the criminal group would continue even though a top leader died or was incarcerated.

Organized crime in small cities is more difficult to assess. Law enforcement personnel are aware of many instances in which local racket figures controlled crime in a smaller city and received aid from and paid tribute to organized criminal groups located in a nearby large city. In one Eastern

[67] Interview with James P. Kelly, former investigator for Sen. Select Comm. on Improper Activities in the Labor or Management Field, Nov. 23, 1966.

[68] Information submitted to Commission by a Federal agency. The Kefauver Committee encountered similar inconsistencies in responses of certain local law enforcement officials: "Whether out of ignorance or indolence is not clear, but some local authorities insisted, orally and in writing, that there was no organized crime in their jurisdiction, although the subsequent testimony proved them pathetically in error." Kefauver Comm., 2d Interim Rep., s. REP. NO. 141, 82d Cong., 1st Sess. 7 (1951).

[69] Buffalo, N.Y.; Flint, Mich.; Kansas City, Kans.; Milwaukee, Wisc.; Mobile, Ala.; Nashville, Tenn.; New Orleans, La.; Oakland, Calif.; Youngstown, Ohio.

[70] Information submitted to Commission by a Federal agency.

town, for example, the local racket figure combined with outside organized criminal groups to establish horse and numbers gambling grossing $1.3 million annually, an organized dice game drawing customers from four states and having an employee payroll of $350,000 annually, and a still capable of producing $4 million worth of alcohol each year. The town's population was less than 100,000.[71] Organized crime cannot be seen as merely a big-city problem.

CORRUPTION OF THE ENFORCEMENT
AND POLITICAL SYSTEMS[72]

Today's corruption is less visible, more subtle, and therefore more difficult to detect and assess than the corruption of the prohibition era. All available data indicate that organized crime flourishes only where it has corrupted local officials.[73] As the scope and variety of organized crime's activities have expanded, its need to involve public officials at every level of local government has grown. And as government regulation expands into more and more areas of private and business activity, the power to corrupt likewise affords the corrupter more control over matters affecting the everyday life of each citizen.

Contrast, for example, the way governmental action in contract procurement or zoning functions today with the way it functioned only a few years ago. The potential harm of corruption is greater today if only because the scope of governmental activity is greater. In different places at different times, organized crime has corrupted police officials, prosecutors, legislators, judges, regulatory agency officials, mayors, councilmen, and other public officials, whose legitimate exercise of duties would block organized crime and whose illegal exercise of duties helps it.[74]

[71] *Ibid.*

[72] "Finally, the public suffers because the vast economic resources that gangsters and racketeers control [enable] them to consolidate their economic and political positions. Money, and particularly ready cash, is power in any community and over and over again this committee has found instances where racketeers' money has been used to exercise influence with Federal, state, and local officials and agencies of government . . . The money used by hoodlums to buy economic and political control is also used to induce public apathy." Kefauver Comm., *3d Interim Rep.*, s. REP. NO. 307, 82d Cong., 1st Sess. 171 (1951).

[73] "[C]orruption by organized crime is a normal condition of American local government and politics." Moynihan, *The Private Government of Organized Crime*, The Reporter, July 6, 1961, p. 14.

[74] See, for example, United States v. Kahaner, 317 F.2d 459, *cert. denied*, 375 U.S. 836 (1963), in which a State judge, a Federal prosecutor, and a racketeer were involved in a conspiracy to obstruct justice in connection with the sentencing of a Federal law violator. See also Johnson, *supra* note 61, at 419–22.

Neutralizing local law enforcement is central to organized crime's operations. What can the public do if no one investigates the investigators, and the political figures are neutralized by their alliance with organized crime? Anyone reporting corrupt activities may merely be telling his story to the corrupted; in a recent "investigation" of widespread corruption, the prosecutor announced that any citizen coming forward with evidence of payments to public officials to secure government action would be prosecuted for participating in such unlawful conduct.

In recent years some local governments have been dominated by criminal groups. Today, no large city is completely controlled by organized crime, but in many there is a considerable degree of corruption.[75]

Organized crime currently is directing its efforts to corrupt law enforcement at the chief or at least middle-level supervisory officials. The corrupt political executive who ties the hands of police officials who want to act against organized crime is even more effective for organized crime's purposes.[76] To secure political power organized crime tries by bribes or political contributions to corrupt the nonoffice-holding political leaders to whom judges, mayors, prosecuting attorneys, and correctional officials may be responsive.

It is impossible to determine how extensive the corruption of public officials by organized crime has been. We do know that there must be more vigilance against such corruption, and we know that there must be better ways for the public to communicate information about corruption to appropriate governmental personnel.

MEMBERSHIP AND ORGANIZATION OF CRIMINAL CARTELS[77]

Some law enforcement officials define organized crime as those groups engaged in gambling, or narcotics pushing, or loan sharking, or with illegal business or labor interests. This is useful to the extent that it eliminates certain other criminal groups from consideration, such as youth gangs, pickpocket rings, and professional criminal groups who may also commit many types of crimes, but whose groups are ad hoc. But when law enforcement officials focus exclusively on the crime instead of the organization, their

[75] Information submitted to Commission by a Federal agency.

[76] "The largest single factor in the breakdown of law enforcement agencies in dealing with organized crime is the corruption and connivance of many public officials." ABA, REPORT ON ORGANIZED CRIME AND LAW ENFORCEMENT 16 (1952).

[77] See generally Cressey, *op. cit.* For detailed information on organized crime members and their activities in various areas of the country, see McClellan, *Narcotics Hearings,* 88th Cong., 1st Sess., pts. 1 & 2 (1963), 1st & 2d Sess., pts. 3 & 4 (1963–64), 2d Sess., pt. 5 (1964).

target is likely to be the lowest-level criminals who commit the visible crimes. This has little effect on the organization.[78]

The Commission believes that before a strategy to combat organized crime's threat to America can be developed, that threat must be assessed by a close examination of organized crime's distinctive characteristics and methods of operation.

National Scope of Organized Crime

In 1951 the Kefauver Committee declared that a nationwide crime syndicate known as the Mafia operated in many large cities and that the leaders of the Mafia usually controlled the most lucrative rackets in their cities.[79]

In 1957, 20 of organized crime's top leaders were convicted (later reversed on appeal)[80] of a criminal charge arising from a meeting at Apalachin, N.Y. At the sentencing the judge stated that they had sought to corrupt and infiltrate the political mainstreams of the country, that they had led double lives of crime and respectability, and that their probation reports read "like a tale of horrors."

Today the core of organized crime in the United States consists of 24 groups operating as criminal cartels in large cities across the Nation. Their membership is exclusively men of Italian descent, they are in frequent communication with each other, and their smooth functioning is insured by a national body of overseers.[81] To date, only the Federal Bureau of Investigation has been able to document fully the national scope of these groups, and FBI intelligence indicates that the organization as a whole has changed its name from the Mafia to La Cosa Nostra.

In 1966 J. Edgar Hoover told a House of Representatives Appropriations Subcommittee:

La Cosa Nostra is the largest organization of the criminal underworld in this country, very closely organized and strictly disciplined. They have committed almost every crime under the sun . . .

La Cosa Nostra is a criminal fraternity whose membership is Italian either by birth or national origin, and it has been found to control major racket activities in many of our larger metropolitan areas, often working in concert with criminals representing other ethnic backgrounds.

It operates on a nationwide basis, with international implications, and until recent years it carried on its activities with almost complete secrecy. It functions

---

[78] "Minor members . . . may be imprisoned, but the top leaders remain relatively untouched by law enforcement agencies." ABA, *op. cit. supra* note 76, at 13.

[79] Kefauver Comm., *3d Interim Rep.*, s. REP. NO. 307, 82d Cong., 1st Sess. 150 (1951).

[80] United States v. Bufalino, 285 F.2d 408 (2d Cir. 1960).

[81] See testimony of J. Edgar Hoover, *supra* note 32, at 272–74.

as a criminal cartel, adhering to its own body of "law" and "justice" and, in so doing, thwarts and usurps the authority of legally constituted judicial bodies . . .[82]

In individual cities, the local core group may also be known as the "outfit," the "syndicate," or the "mob."[83] These 24 groups work with and control other racket groups, whose leaders are of various ethnic derivations. In addition, the thousands of employees who perform the street-level function of organized crime's gambling, usury, and other illegal activities represent a cross section of the Nation's population groups.

The present confederation of organized crime groups arose after Prohibition, during which Italian, German, Irish, and Jewish groups had competed with one another in racket operations. The Italian groups were successful in switching their enterprises from prostitution and bootlegging to gambling, extortion, and other illegal activities. They consolidated their power through murder and violence.[84]

Today, members of the 24 core groups reside and are active in the States shown on the map [Figure 10]. The scope and effect of their criminal operations and penetration of legitimate businesses vary from area to area. The wealthiest and most influential core groups operate in States including New York, New Jersey, Illinois, Florida, Louisiana, Nevada, Michigan, and Rhode Island.[85] Not shown on the map are many States in which members of core groups control criminal activity even though they do not reside there. For example, a variety of illegal activities in New England is controlled from Rhode Island.[86]

Recognition of the common ethnic tie of the 5,000 or more members of organized crime's core groups[87] is essential to understanding the structure of these groups today. Some have been concerned that past identification of Cosa Nostra's ethnic character has reflected on Italian-Americans generally. This false implication was eloquently refuted by one of the Nation's outstanding experts on organized crime, Sgt. Ralph Salerno of the New York City Police Department. When an Italian-American racketeer complained

[82] *Id.* at 272.

[83] See testimony of former New York City Police Comm'r Michael J. Murphy, McClellan, *Narcotics Hearings*, 88th Cong., 1st Sess., pt. 1, at 63 (1963); testimony of Capt. William Duffy, *id.* pt. 2, at 506; OFFICE OF THE N.Y. COUNSEL TO THE GOVERNOR, COMBATING ORGANIZED CRIME—A REPORT OF THE 1965 OYSTER BAY, NEW YORK, CONFERENCES ON COMBATING ORGANIZED CRIME 24 (1966).

[84] See generally ORGANIZED CRIME IN AMERICA 147–224 (Tyler ed. 1962).

[85] Information submitted to Commission by a Federal agency.

[86] *Ibid.*

[87] Testimony of J. Edgar Hoover, *Hearings Before the Subcomm. on Dep'ts of State, Justice, and Commerce, the Judiciary, and Related Agencies Appropriations of the House Comm. on Apppropriations*, 89th Cong., 2d Sess. 273 (1966).

States in Which Organized Crime Group Members Both Reside and Operate

Figure 10

to him, "Why does it have to be one of your own kind that hurts you?", Sgt. Salerno answered:

> *I'm not your kind and you're not my kind. My manners, morals, and mores are not yours. The only thing we have in common is that we both spring from an Italian heritage and culture—and you are the traitor to that heritage and culture which I am proud to be part of.*[88]

Organized crime in its totality thus consists of these 24 groups allied with other racket enterprises to form a loose confederation operating in large and small cities. In the core groups, because of their permanency of form, strength of organization and ability to control other racketeer operations, resides the power that organized crime has in America today.

---

[88] Grutzner, City Police Expert on Mafia Retiring from Force, N.Y. Times, Jan. 21, 1967, p. 65, col. 3.

7 The National and Local Structures of Organized Crime

DONALD R. CRESSEY

The structure of the nationwide cartel and confederation which today operates the principal illicit businesses in America, and which is now striking at the foundations of legitimate business and government as well, came into being in 1931. Further, even the skeleton structure of the local units of the confederation, the "families" controlling illicit businesses in various metropolitan areas, came into being in 1931. These structures resemble the national and local structures of the Italian-Sicilian Mafia, but our organization is not merely the old world Mafia transplanted. The social, economic and political conditions of Sicily determined the shape of the Sicilian Mafia, and the social, economic and political conditions of the United States determined the shape of the American confederation.

To use an analogy with legitimate business, in 1931 organized crime units across the United States formed into monopolistic corporations, and these corporations, in turn, linked themselves together in a monopolistic cartel. To use a political analogy, in 1931 the local units formed into feudal governments, and the rulers of these governments linked themselves together in a nation-wide confederation which itself constitutes a government. Feudalism was the system of political organization prevailing in Europe from the

Reprinted from Donald R. Cressey, "The Functions and Structure of Criminal Syndicates," *Task Force Report: Organized Crime,* The President's Commission on Law Enforcement and Administration of Justice (Washington: Government Printing Office, 1967), Appendix A, pp. 31–36, 54–56. Figure 11 (see page 873) is from the *Task Force Report,* p. 9.

ninth to the fifteenth centuries. Basically agricultural, the system meant that a vassal held land belonging to a lord on condition of homage and service under arms. The servant deferred to the lord and in other ways paid homage to him; the lord, in turn, protected the servant. The system was "hereditary" in the sense that the lord had custody of the heirs' property.

The structure of the Sicilian Mafia resembles that of ancient feudal kingdoms, and the Mafia probably is a lineal descendant of feudalism. The structure of the American confederation of crime resembles feudalism also, as it resembles the structure of the Sicilian Mafia. Like feudal lords and Sicilian Mafia chieftains, the rulers of American, geographically-based, "families" of criminals derive their authority from tradition in the form of homage and "respect." They allocate territory and a kind of license to do business in return for this homage. Nevertheless, the feudal local governments formed in 1931, and the confederation between them, are American innovations.

Certain American criminals, law-enforcement officials, political figures, and plain citizens have known from the beginning that a nation-wide confederation was established in 1931. Some of them have denied the existence of the apparatus because they are members of it. Others have for over thirty years been trying to convince the American public that the nation-wide apparatus does in fact exist. We shall quote three such attempts to convince, occurring about a decade apart.

In a series of articles appearing in 1939, the former attorney for an illicit New York organization, a man who had occupied a position of "corrupter" for the organization, but who later testified for the state, observed that a nation-wide alliance between criminal businesses in the United States was in operation. This was not the first time such an allegation was made, but it dramatically foreshadowed statements which have been made in more recent years. . . .

When I speak of the underworld now, I mean something far bigger than the Schultz mob. The Dutchman was one of the last independent barons to hold out against a general centralization of control which had been going on ever since Charlie Lucky became leader of the Unione Siciliana in 1931 . . . The "greasers" in the Unione were killed off, and the organization was no longer a loose, fraternal order of Sicilian blackhanders and alcohol cookers, but rather the framework for a system of alliances which were to govern the underworld. In Chicago, for instance, the Unione no longer fought the Capone mob, but pooled strength and worked with it. A man no longer had to be a Sicilian to be in the Unione. Into its highest councils came such men as Meyer Lansky and Bugs Siegel, leaders of a tremendously powerful mob, who were personal partners in the alcohol business with Lucky and Joe Adonis of Brooklyn. Originally the Unione had been a secret but legitimate fraternal organization, with chapters in various cities where there were Sicilian colonies. Some of them were operated openly, like any lodge. But it fell into the control of the criminal element, the Mafia, and with the coming of prohibition, which turned thousands of law-abiding Sicilians into boot-leggers, alcohol cookers and vassals of warring mobs, it changed.

It still numbers among its members many old-time Sicilians who are not gangsters, but anybody who goes into it today is a mobster, and an important one. In New York City the organization is split up territorially into districts, each led by a minor boss, known as the '*compare*,' or godfather . . . I know that throughout the underworld the Unione Siciliana is accepted as a mysterious, all-pervasive reality, and that Lucky used it as the vehicle by which the under-world was drawn into co-operation on a national scale.[1]

More than a decade after this statement appeared in a popular magazine of the time, many members of the public (and some law enforcement offi-cers) still had no notion that an illicit cartel performed some types of crime across the nation. If they heard of "the Mafia," or "the syndicate," or "the outfit," or "the mob," they did not believe what they heard, or did not believe in its importance. They were shocked when in 1951 the Kefauver Committee was able to draw the following four conclusions from the testi-mony of the many witnesses who had appeared before it.

(1) There is a Nation-wide crime syndicate known as the Mafia, whose tentacles are found in many large cities. It has international ramifications which appear most clearly in connection with the narcotics traffic.

(2) Its leaders are usually found in control of the most lucrative rackets in their cities.

(3) There are indications of a centralized direction and control of these rackets, but leadership appears to be in a group rather than in a single individual.

(4) The Mafia is the cement that helps to bind the Costello-Adonis-Lansky syndicate of New York and the Accardo-Guzik-Fischetti syndicate of Chicago as well as smaller criminal gangs and individual criminals throughout the country. These groups have kept in touch with (Lucky) Luciano since his deportation from this country.[2]

In the next decade, investigating bodies were able to overcome some of the handicaps of the Kefauver Committee, which "found it difficult to obtain reliable data concerning the extent of Mafia operation, the nature of Mafia organization, and the way it presently operates."[3] While *all* such handicaps will not be overcome for some years to come, there no longer is any doubt that several regional organizations, rationally constructed for

[1] J. Richard Davis, "Things I Couldn't Tell Till Now," *Collier's*, July 22, July 29, August 5, August 12, August 19, and August 26, 1939. The quote is from pp. 35–36 of the August 19 issue.

[2] Special Committee to Investigate Organized Crime in Interstate Commerce (Ke-fauver Committee), *Third Interim Report*, U.S. Senate Report No. 307, 82nd Congress, 1951, p. 150. See also Sid Feder and Burton B. Turkus, *Murder, Inc.*, (New York: Permabooks, 1952), pp. 86–115.

[3] *Id.* at p. 149.

the control of the sale of illicit goods and services, are in operation. Neither is there any doubt that these regional organizations are linked together in a nation-wide cartel and confederation.

In 1957 about seventy-five of the nation's leading illicit businessmen were discovered at a meeting in Apalachin, New York. They came from all parts of the country, and most of them had criminal records relating to the kind of offense customarily called "organized crime." Beside their illicit businesses, at least nine of them were in the coin-machine business; 16 were in the garment industry; 10 owned grocery stores; 17 owned bars or restaurants; 11 were in the olive oil and cheese importing business; nine were in the construction business. Others were involved in automobile agencies, coal companies, entertainment, funeral homes, ownership of horses and race tracks, linen and laundry enterprises, trucking, waterfront activities and bakeries.[4] No one has been able to prove the nature of the conspiracy involved, but no one believes that the men all just happened to drop in on the host at the same time. Two of the men attending the meeting had met at a somewhat similar meeting of criminals in Cleveland in 1928. The discovery of the Apalachin conference convinced many officials that a nation-wide apparatus does in fact exist and that law-enforcement intelligence is inadequate; that the procedures for studying the organization controlling the sale of illicit goods and services in the United States, and governing the lives of the participants, are inadequate; and that the procedures for disseminating hard facts about organized crime to law-enforcement agencies and the public are inadequate.

One response to the discovery of the Apalachin meeting was increased investigative action by the U.S. Attorney General, the Federal Bureau of Narcotics, the Federal Bureau of Investigation, the Internal Revenue Service, and several state and local agencies. In 1960 there were 17 attorneys in the Organized Crime and Racketeering Section of the United States Department of Justice; in 1963 there were 60. Beginning in about 1961 the investigating agencies began to receive information about the existence of the criminal confederation now commonly labelled "Cosa Nostra," a large-scale criminal organization complete with a board of directors and a hierarchial structure extending down to the street level of criminal activity. The McClellan Committee and a nation-wide television audience in 1963 heard Mr. Joseph Valachi, an active member of the confederation, describe the skeleton of the structure of the organization, its operations, and its membership. These data, and supplementary data, enabled Senator (then Attorney General) Kennedy to testify as follows before the Committee:

[4] Select Committee on Improper Activities in the Labor or Management Field, *Final Report*, U.S. Senate Report No. 1139, 86th Congress, 1960, pp. 487–488.

Because of intelligence gathered from Joseph Valachi and from informants we know that Cosa Nostra is run by a commission and that the leaders of Cosa Nostra in most major cities are responsible to the commission. We know that membership in the commission varies between 9 and 12 active members and we know who the active members of the commission are today.

We know, for example, that in the past two years, at least three carefully planned commission meetings had to be called off because the leaders learned that we had uncovered their well-concealed plans and meeting places.

We know that the commission makes major policy decisions for the organization, settles disputes among the families and allocates territories of criminal operations within the organization.

For example, we now know that the meeting at Apalachin was called by a leading racketeer in an effort to resolve the problem created by the murder of Albert Anastasia. The racketeer was concerned that Anastasia had brought too many individuals not worthy of membership into the organization. To insure the security of the organization, the racketeer wanted these men removed. Of particular concern to this racketeer was that he had violated commission rules in causing the assault, the attempted assassination of Frank Costello, deposed New York rackets boss, and the murder of Anastasia. He wanted commission approval for these acts—which he received.

We know that the commission now has before it the question of whether to intercede in the Gallo-Profaci family gangland war in New York. Gang wars produce factionalism, and continued factionalism in the underworld produces sources of information to law enforcement. Indications are that the gangland leaders will resolve the Gallo-Profaci fight . . .

Such intelligence is important not only because it can help us know what to watch for, but because of the assistance it can provide in developing and prosecuting specific cases . . . Thus we have been able to make inroads into the hierarchy, personnel, and operations of organized crime. It would be a serious mistake, however, to over-estimate the progress Federal and local law enforcement has made. A principal lesson provided by the disclosures of Joseph Valachi and other informants is that the job ahead is very large and very difficult.[5]

Now, three years later, and almost ten years since the Apalachin meeting, the job ahead is still "very large and very difficult." While law-enforcement officials now have detailed information about the criminal activities of individual men of Italian and Sicilian descent, and others, who are participating in illicit businesses and illicit governments, knowledge of the structure of their confederation remains fragmentary and impressionistic. Since the time of the Apalachin meeting, and especially since the McClellan Committee hearings, law-enforcement officers have shown conclusively that

[5] Permanent Subcommittee on Investigations of the Committee on Government Operations (McClellan Committee), *Organized Crime and Illicit Traffic in Narcotics*, Part I, 1963, pp. 6-8.

"families" of criminals of Italian and Sicilian descent either operate or control the operation of most of the illicit businesses—including gambling, usury, and the wholesaling of narcotics—in large American cities, and that these "families" are linked together in a nation-wide cartel and confederation. Nevertheless, some officials, and some plain citizens, remain unconvinced.

THE STRUCTURAL SKELETON

Since the McClellan Committee hearings, there has been a tendency to label the nation-wide cartel and confederation "Cosa Nostra" and then to identify what is known about its division of labor as the structure of "organized crime" in America. This tendency might be responsible for some of the misplaced skepticism about whether a dangerous organization exists. In the first place, calling the organization "Cosa Nostra" lets citizens believe that they are safe from organized criminals because their local bookie, lottery operator, or usurer is not of Italian or Sicilian descent. The term directs attention to membership rather than to the power to control and to make alliances. In the second place, using "Cosa Nostra" as a noun implies that the total economic and political structure involved is as readily identifiable as that of some other formal organization, such as the Elk's Lodge, the Los Angeles Police Department, or the Standard Oil Company. This is obviously not the case. We know very little. Our knowledge of the structure which makes "organized crime" organized is somewhat comparable to the knowledge of Standard Oil which could be gleaned from interviews with gasoline station attendants. Detailed knowledge of the formal and informal structures of the confederation of Sicilian-Italian "families" in the United States would represent one of the greatest criminological advances ever made, even if it were universally recognized that this knowledge was not synonymous with knowledge about all organized crime in America. Since we know so little, it is easy to make the assumption that there is nothing to know anything about.

But we do know enough about the structure to conclude that it is indeed an organization. When there is a board of directors or governors, a president, a vice-president, some works managers, foremen and lieutenants, and some workers and plain members, there is an organization.

As the former Attorney General's testimony before the McClellan Committee indicated, the highest ruling body in the confederation is the "Commission." This body serves as a combination board of business directors, legislature, supreme court, and arbitration board, but most of its functions are judicial, as we will show later. Members look to the Commission as the ultimate authority on organizational disputes. It is made up of the rulers of the most powerful "families," which are located in large cities. At present,

An Organized Crime Family

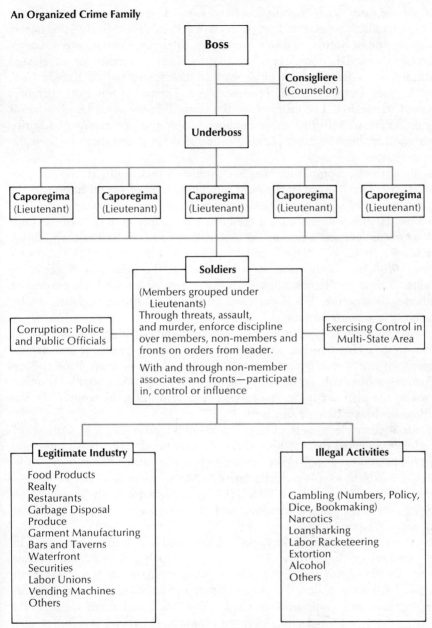

SOURCE: After the President's Commission on Law Enforcement and Administration of Justice, "Organized Crime," in *Task Force Report: Organized Crime* (Washington, D. C.: Government Printing Office, 1967), p. 194.

Figure 11

nine of the many such "families" are represented on the Commission. Three of the "families" represented are in New York City, one in Buffalo, one in Newark, one in Boston, and one each in Philadelphia, Detroit, and Chicago. The Commission is not a representative legislative assembly or an elected judicial body—"families" in cities such as Baltimore, Dallas, Kansas City, Los Angeles, Pittsburgh, San Francisco, and Tampa do not have members on the Commission. The members of the council do not regard each other as equals. There are informal understandings which give one member authority over another, but the exact pecking order, if there is one, has not been determined.

Beneath the Commission are 24 "families," each with its "Boss." (See Figure 11.) The "family" is the most significant level of organization and the largest unit of criminal organization in which allegiance is owed to one man, the Boss. (Italian words often are used interchangeably with each of the English words designating a position in the division of labor. Rather than "Boss," the words "Il Capo," "Don," and "Rappresentante" are used.) The Boss's primary function is to maintain order while at the same time maximizing profits. Subject to the possibility of being overruled by the Commission, his authority is absolute. He is the final arbiter in all matters relating to his branch of the confederation.

Beneath each Boss of at least the larger "families," is an "Underboss" or "Sottocapo." This position is, essentially, that of vice-president and deputy director of the "family" unit. The man occupying the position often collects information for the Boss; he relays messages to him; and he passes his orders down to the men occupying positions below him in the hierarchy. He acts as Boss in the absence of the Boss.

On the same level as the Underboss there is a position for a "Counselor" or adviser, referred to as "Consiglieri" or "Consulieri." The person occupying this position is a staff officer rather than a line officer. He is likely to be an elder member who is partially retired after a career in which he did not quite succeed in becoming a Boss. He gives advice to family members, including the Boss and Underboss, and he therefore enjoys considerable influence and power.

Also at about the same level as the Underboss is a "Buffer" position. The top members of the "family" hierarchy, particularly the Boss, avoid direct communication with the lower-echelon personnel, the workers. They are insulated from the police. To obtain this insulation, all commands, information, money, and complaints generally flow back and forth through the Buffer, who is a trusted and clever go-between. However, the Buffer does not make decisions or assume any of the authority of his Boss, as the Underboss does.

To reach the working level, a Boss usually goes through channels. For example, a Boss's decision on the settlement of a dispute involving the activities of the "runners" (ticket sellers) in a particular lottery game, passes first to his Buffer, then to the next level of rank, which is "Lieutenant" or "Capodecina" or "Caporegima." This position, considered from a business standpoint, is analogous to works manager or sales manager. The person occupying it is the chief of an operating unit. The term "Lieutenant" gives the position a military flavor. Although "Capodecina" is translated as "head of ten," there apparently is no settled number of men supervised by any given Lieutenant. The number of such leaders in an organization varies with the size of the organization and with the specialized activities in that organization. The Lieutenant usually has one or two associates who work closely with him, serving as messengers and buffers. They carry orders, information, and money back and forth between the Lieutenant and the men belonging to his regime. They do not share the Lieutenant's administrative power.

Beneath the Lieutenants there might be one or more "Section Chiefs." Messages and orders received from the Boss's buffer by the Lieutenant or his buffer are passed on to a Section Chief, who also may have a buffer. A Section Chief may be deputy lieutenant. He is in charge of a section of the Lieutenant's operations. In smaller "families," the position of Lieutenant and the position of Section Chief are combined. In general, the larger the regime the stronger the power of the Section Chief. Since it is against the law to consort for criminal purposes, it is advantageous to cut down the number of individuals who are directly responsible to any given line supervisor.

About five "Soldiers," "Buttons," or just "members" report to each Section Chief or, if there is no Section Chief position, to a Lieutenant. The number of Soldiers in a "family" varies; some "families" have as many as 250 members, some as few as 20. A Soldier might operate an illicit enterprise for a Boss, on a commission basis, or he might "own" the enterprise and pay homage to the boss for "protection," the right to operate. Partnerships between two or more Soldiers, and between Soldiers and men higher up in the hierarchy, including Bosses, are common. An "enterprise" could be a usury operation, a dice game, a lottery, a bookie operation, a smuggling operation, or a vending machine company. Some Soldiers and most upper-echelon "family" members have interests in more than one business.

"Family" membership ends at the Soldier level, and all members are of Italian or Sicilian descent. Between 2,000 and 4,000 men are members of "families" and, hence, of the confederation. But beneath the Soldiers in the hierarchy of operations are large numbers of employees and commission agents who are not necessarily of Italian-Sicilian descent, although some of them are Italian-Sicilian aspirants. These are the persons carrying on most of the work "on the street." They have no "buffers" or other forms of insulation from the police. They are the relatively unskilled workmen who actually take bets, answer telephones, drive trucks, sell narcotics, etc. In Chicago, for example, the workers in a major lottery business who operated in a Negro neighborhood were Negroes; the bankers for the lottery were Japanese-Americans; but the game, including the banking operation, was licensed, for a fee, by a "family" member. The entire operation, including the bankers, was more or less a "customer" of the Chicago "family," in the way any enterprise operating under a franchise is a "customer" of the parent corporation.

The positions outlined above constitute the "organizational chart" of the American confederation as it is described by members. Two things are missing. *First,* there is no description of the many positions necessary to the actual street level operation of an illicit enterprise such as a book-making establishment or a lottery. While we cannot outline the basic structure of all these enterprises, we must at least mention three principal operations—lotteries, bookmaking, and narcotics distribution. Mr. Arthur Sage, District Inspector of the Detroit Police Department and supervisor of police work in vice, liquor and gambling in Detroit, presented to the McClellan Committee a chart showing the hierarchy of the lottery enterprise supervised by one Detroit Section Chief.[6] Over one hundred positions are involved, but they are not unique and, further, some personnel occupy more than one position. Included on the chart or mentioned in the testimony are about fifty positions for "pick-up men," divided into five groups, each reporting to a substation supervisor. After the bet slips are collected at the substation, presumably by the substation supervisor, one or more of the trusted employees plays the role of messenger by taking them to the main office. The main office is depicted as having six workers, but their roles are not specifically identified. Someone at the main office tabulates the amounts bet, and someone determines which slips are winners, a role described as "bookkeeper." Another trusted person takes the proceeds to the Section Chief, who in turn passes a share up through the hierarchy.

The positions just described are in reference to what might be called "curbstone betting." In the operation of off-track bets on horse races and other contests, a similar set of positions is essential. In some such enterprises a bookie, working on a commission basis, accepts bets verbally and telephones them to his supervisor. Other bookies accept bids from customers who telephone to place the bet. A bookie of this kind might employ six to ten telephone operators, and a similar number of "runners" to collect bets and pay winners. The substation and messenger positions are similar to those in lottery enterprises.

Narcotics enterprises are organized like any importing-wholesaling-retailing business. At the top level are importers of multi-kilo lots. At the next level are "kilo-men" who handle nothing less than a kilogram of heroin at a time. A kilo-man makes his purchase from an importer-supplier and re-

6 *Id.* at Part II, pp. 461–465.

ceives delivery from a courier. He dilutes the heroin by adding 3 kilograms of milk sugar for each kilo of heroin. The product is then sold to "quarter-kilo men" and then to "ounce-men" and then to "deck-men," there being further adulteration at each stage in this process. Eventually, street peddlers dispense it in 5-grain packets called "bags" or "packs." The cost to the consumer is in excess of 300 times the cost of the original kilo.

Second, and more important, the structure described by members of the confederation is primarily the *formal* structure of the organization. The informants have not described, probably because they have not been asked to do so, the many *informal* positions any organization must contain. To put the matter in another way, there is no description of the many functional roles performed by the men occupying the formally-established positions making up the organization. Businessmen and managers know that identifying a position as that of, say, "Vice President" is rather meaningless unless there is a description of what the person occupying the position *does*. And what he does is a response to an informal position he occupies at the same time he occupies the formal one—he may be "expediter" or "troubleshooter" or "psychotherapist" as well as Vice President. In the confederation, one position of this kind is Buffer. This position has been identified by the New York policemen who watch "family" and confederation operations, not by the members themselves. The position is occupied by men who might also be occupying an "official," formal, position such as Underboss, Lieutenant, or even some lower position. Later we will discuss other informal positions of this kind, and the informal roles of the men who occupy them. "Corrupter," "Corruptee," "Enforcer," "Executioner," and "Money Mover" are some of these. Here we shall mention three informal or "unofficial" positions essential to the curbstone betting enterprise just described. The positions for "Lay-off Man," for "Large Lay-off Man," and for "Come Back Man" are essential to gambling enterprises, and the fact that they are included in the division of labor indicates why a gambling enterprise cannot be a "mom and pop" operation for long.

The division of labor essential to bookmaking does not stop at the street level. It is essential that the bookie insure himself against loss by making bets himself, in much the way a casualty insurance company re-insures a risk that is too great for it to assume alone. So that this is possible, the Lay-off Man position has been established. The bookie, sometimes called a "handbook operator," does not gamble. He pays the same odds as does the race track, but at the track these odds are calculated after deducting about fifteen to eighteen per cent of the gross, this amount going to the track operators for taxes, expenses, and profits. The bookie pockets the entire fifteen to eighteen per cent, less a percentage going to a "family" member for a license to operate, for corruption of police and political figures, and for "welfare" benefits such as bail and an attorney in time of need. However, since the bookie's customers do not necessarily bet on the same horses selected by bettors at the track, the amount of money bet with him on losing horses sometimes is not enough to pay off those of his customers who have selected winners. He notes, before a race is run, that his books are out of balance. To get them in balance, he takes some of the money and makes a large bet with a Lay-off Man, who, like the bookie himself, operates on a percentage basis.

But when a number of bookies use the services of the same Lay-off Man, the latter's books may get out of balance also. Since he, like the bookie, is a commission agent rather than a gambler, he seeks a man occupying a position at the third level up the enterprise hierarchy, the Large Lay-off Man. The men occupying this position reside in all parts of the country, but they keep in close touch with each other so that the over-all amount of money handled by each of them will be bet on the various horses in the same proportions as is the total amount bet at the track. When this is the case, the bookie, the "family" members who license him, the Lay-off Man, the Large Lay-off Man cannot lose—they simply split up the fifteen to eighteen per cent of the gross. One Large Lay-off Man takes in about $20 million a year, and his annual profit before expenses is about four per cent of the gross, or $800,000.

If, just before a horse race, it looks as if there is some possibility that the persons occupying positions for Large Lay-off Men might lose because their books are out of balance with the legitimate books at the track, they employ the services of a man occupying still another position in the division of labor, the Come Back Man. Persons occupying this position function in such a way that the legitimate track bettors themselves re-insure the bets taken by Large Lay-off Men. The Come Back Man is an "odds changer" who stands by at the race track. Just before each race he opens a telephone line to a representative of the syndicated Large Lay-off Men. When the latter's books are out of balance with those at the track, the person occupying the position of Come Back Man is instructed to bet large amounts on specific horses, thus making the track odds approximately the same as the odds based on the proportions bet with the Large Lay-off Men on each of the horses. "Lay-off action," together with the "come back money" system, is a principal device used by rulers of "families" and of the confederation to control all gambling of any consequence in the United States. Another device is coercion—extortion, muscle, and murder.

The skeleton structure we have outlined is by no means the structure of the organization operating America's illicit businesses. Even the skeleton has more bones than those we have described, as our discussion of informal positions and roles indicates. The structure outlined is sufficient to demonstrate, however, that a confederation of "families" exists. Investigating agencies have, since the time of the Apalachin meeting, documented the fact that the apparatus is tightly knit enough to have a corporate chain of command. Moreover, the names of the men occupying the major positions have been known for at least five years. The next important task for these agencies is that of depicting the numerous functional positions, formal and informal, making up the structure of the organization whose authority structure has been sketched out. Some aspects of the structure can be deduced from studies of function; details can be learned only by close observation of the interaction of members with each other.

. . .

RECRUITMENT

If it is to survive, every organization must have an institutionalized process for inducting new members and inculcating them with the values and ways of behaving in the social system. In the Italian-Sicilian confederation and cartel, the process of admitting new members is called "opening the books." It is reasonably certain that the books were "open" until about 1958 and that they have been "closed" since that time. Taken literally, this would indicate that no new members have been admitted for about a decade. It is tempting to take such a literal position, for it carries the assurance that the "family" cartel and confederation organization is on the way out, that an important decline in membership and influence will occur as soon as the current leaders, who tend toward old age, die or are deposed. This is not the case. While it may be true that the "books are closed," it also is true that in some neighborhoods all three of the essential ingredients of an effective recruiting process are in operation: inspiring aspiration for membership, training for membership, and selection for membership. Some recruits are deliberately sought out and trained on the assumption, implicit or explicit, that without the induction of youngsters the organization will founder. Other recruits, usually mature college graduates, are sought out because they possess the expert skills needed for modern large-scale business operations. Both kinds of recruits must now remain for years in a kind of probationary status because inducting them into a "family" might change the balance of power between "families," thus disturbing the peace.

The most successful recruitment processes are those which do not appear to be recruiting techniques at all. These are the processes by which membership becomes highly desirable because of the rewards and benefits the prospective members believe it confers on them. Some boys grow up knowing that it is a "good thing" to belong to a certain club or to attend a certain university, and they know it is a "good thing" because men they emulate have or have had membership. Other boys grow up knowing that it is a "good thing" to become a member of a criminal "family," for the same reason. Because the activities of the cartel and confederation are illegal, it is necessary for aspirants to abandon some of the values of conventional society as they learn to aspire to membership. They do so because they grow up in social situations in which the desire for membership comes naturally and painlessly. It is still an honor to be taken into the society of "stand-up guys," and, moreover, not all the best things in life are free.

It has long been known that in a multi-group type of society such as that of the United States, conflicting standards of conduct are possessed by various groups. Discovery of the processes leading to the invention of criminal subcultures which conflict with the standards of conventional groups is now the focus of the research of many social scientists. It has for some time been acknowledged that the condition of conflicting standards, which anthropologists and sociologists call "normative conflict," is not distributed evenly through the society. Simply stated, persons growing up in some geographic or social areas have a better chance than do others to come into contact with norms and values which support legitimate activities, in contrast to criminal activities, while in other areas the reverse is true. Individuals who come into intimate association with legitimate values will use legal means of striving for "success," while individuals having such associations with criminal values will use illegitimate means. McKay has referred to the acquisition of desires for membership in either non-criminal or criminal groups as an "educational" process, and he has pointed out that in many neighborhoods alternative educational processes are in operation, so that a child may be educated in either conventional or criminal means of achieving success.[7]

Martin has referred to these alternative processes for education in the values of conventional society and the values of the society of organized crime by reporting that in some neighborhoods of South Brooklyn boys grow up under two "flags." One is the flag of the United States, symbolizing conventional institutions, traditions, and culture, and the other is the flag of organized crime, symbolizing traditions quite different from conventional American ones.[8] For syndicate members, recruitment of boys who grow up under the "syndicate flag" is no real problem, for the boys have in a sense recruited themselves. Helpful, however, is what Martin calls the "legend" of the importance of syndicate men in political, economic, and social affairs. A story about the virtues of the members of a social group need not be true in order to be effective; it can be wholly false or it can be an elaboration of some incident that occurred in the past, as most legends are. A "stand-up guy" can be made into a revered hero, even if that "stand-up guy" also kills

[7] Henry D. McKay, "The Neighborhood and Child Conduct," *Annals of the American Academy of Political and Social Science*, 261:32–42, January, 1949.

[8] Raymond V. Martin, *Revolt in the Mafia* (New York: Duell, Sloan and Pearce, 1963), p. 60.

and "works over" his devoted subjects. A powerful illicit cartel can, similarly, become so respectable, once it has undermined legitimate political and economic processes, that aspirants do not even have to experience any psychological conflict as they transfer their allegiance from conventional society to criminal society in order to achieve its economic rewards.

In his testimony before the McClellan Committee, Mr. Valachi argued, in effect, that in the 1930's the boys who were to become recruits to Italian-Sicilian "families" of organized criminals trained themselves. As they participated in boys' criminal activities such as burglary, they were observed by the syndicated criminals in the neighborhood, who paid special attention to the behavior of the boys when they were jailed. A boy who revealed nothing about himself or his criminal associates was a likely candidate for membership; other boys were not. Thus, the recruits trained themselves to adhere to a code which put them under the domination of the recruiters. This process is still in operation. It is old fashioned and inefficient, however. Syndicate members now deliberately set out to help boys obtain skills that will be valuable to the syndicate. These include skill in crime and personal values about silence, honor, and loyalty—values which make them controllable, as ex-convicts who cannot find legitimate employment are controllable. On the streets of Brooklyn the important attribute sought is the orientation of the "stand-up guy":

Some hoodlums are assigned to recruiting . . . He learns which kids are good prospects and which are not. Like a telephone company public-relations man enrolling Amherst seniors or a California airplane plant personnel manager looking over graduate engineers from M.I.T., he wants the best and the smartest. He also wants the strongest, the meanest, and the most vicious. He starts testing boys at sixteen or seventeen. They are put into teams of six, eight, or ten for training. There are rules to be followed by the trainees and rewards to be won. Mob injunctions begin with *omerta*, the heart of the syndicate code of honor. Silence on pain of death; say nothing, know nothing. Drink if you wish, but don't get drunk. Avoid narcotics; they are all right to sell, no good to use. The rewards include money, status, and release from the yoke of morality . . . Eventually, the mob men plan burglaries for the recruits. There are techniques to be taught.[9]

Nowadays, being a "stand-up guy" and being skilled in the perpetration of lower-class crimes like robbery and burglary is not enough, however.[10] One must have the business skills of a purchasing agent, an accountant, a lawyer, or an executive. No longer do these skills come "automatically" as one climbs the ladder from the shop floor to the executive office of legitimate business. Neither do they come "automatically" in organized

---

[9] *Ibid.*, pp. 61–62.

[10] *Cf.* Daniel P. Moynihan, "The Private Government of Crime," *Reporter,* July 6, 1961, pp. 14–20.

crime if slum boys are recruited because they are "honorable" and skilled in burglary. College training is needed. "Family" members are now sending their sons to college to learn business skills, on the assumption that these sons will soon be eligible for "family" membership. One particular college has in its student body an over-representation of the sons and other relatives of "family" members. Accounting and business administration are the favorite major subjects of the males.

Not everyone who wants to participate in the businesses conducted by crime syndicates can do so. One cannot "just decide" to become a "family" member, or to participate in business affairs controlled by a "family," any more than he can "just decide" to become a professional baseball player, a policeman, or a banker. His desires must be matched by his competence, and by the desires of those who control membership in the profession he wants. Until recently, "competence" was judged by estimates of loyalty and a certain toughness made evident in the condition of being "right." But the procedures for selecting men for highly desired positions are always more stringent than those for positions which are less desirable. Martin tells how the selection process operates on the streets of South Brooklyn:

> From a safe distance the mob instructors observe the operation [of a burglary] and prepare for a subsequent critique of the job . . . A team that shows capacity for avoiding trouble is allowed eventually to operate on its own, though it must still get mob clearance on each job. Frightened kids are weeded out, tougher ones move closer to the day when they join the syndicate and achieve the good life.[11]

Again we point out that the skills now needed and sought are not merely those necessary to "avoiding trouble." Relatively unskilled men will always be needed to conduct street operations, and these men must of necessity be honorable and, thus, exploitable. But because organized crime is becoming increasingly respectable there is less "trouble" to avoid. The pattern of authority can therefore shift from "rank" to "expertise." The man who relies alone on the old fashioned virtues of honor and obedience will not go far in the organized crime of the future, because these virtues are not essential when the organization is so powerful that it need not be kept secret. Identive power is still prevalent, but we are witnessing a shift from respect for a patriarch to respect for a "stand-up guy," regardless of age. Respect for men of rank is still an important control device, but the deference now seems to be as much to a man of wealth as to "the old man," as much to a leader of a business as to a governor.

As organized crime has gained power and respectability by moving out of bootlegging and prostitution and into gambling, usury, and control of legitimate businesses, the need for secrecy and security has decreased and

11 Martin, *op. cit.*, p. 62.

the need for expertise has increased. If this trend continues, the pattern of extreme totalitarian control will change. Even now, neither the multimillion-aire Boss nor the millionaire Soldier is able to handle alone the complicated problems of business organization and finance. In criminal life as in non-criminal life, fewer and fewer jobs are simple and routine. Soon there will be no place in the higher levels of organized crime for high school dropouts. As the technical competence of even lower-echelon members increases, decision-making will be decentralized, and individual freedom of action will expand. There already are signs that each member's frontiers of action are expanding. They probably will continue to expand as organized crime continues to move away from profit and control by violence and toward profit and control by fraud.

Perhaps, however, we should expect a new wave of violence in organized crime before the lines between membership and non-membership become blurred by the increasing need for workers with the kind of business skills which only legitimate society can provide. As the shift to the authority of the expert occurs and, concurrently, as decision-making is decentralized, opportunities for the present unskilled participants to achieve positions of power will decrease.

In legitimate life, government officials, and others, are urging that each individual citizen must be given his rights as a member of society and as a human being, to justice, to a living wage, to human dignity. Most respectable citizens are now demanding those rights, primarily in the form of opportunities to achieve, and they are rejecting governments which will not or cannot make the opportunities available. We expect that within the next decade the disrespectable citizens who are the underlings of organized crime will similarly demand, from the unofficial governments that rule them, their opportunities to achieve. We can expect them to grow tired of a system which denies equal opportunities to low-status personnel, even if everyone in the system is relatively rich. If these men begin demanding their rights we will witness in the ranks of organized crime rebellions comparable in principle to the current rebellions of Negroes.

8 The Incredible Electrical Conspiracy

RICHARD AUSTIN SMITH

As befitted the biggest criminal case in the history of the Sherman Act, most of the forty-five defendants arrived early, knocking the snow of Philadelphia's Chestnut Street from their shoes before taking the elevator to federal courtroom No. 3. Some seemed to find it as chill inside as out, for they kept their coats on and shifted from one foot to another in the corridor, waiting silently for the big mahogany doors to open. On the other side of those doors was something none of them relished: judgment for having conspired to fix prices, rig bids, and divide markets on electrical equipment valued at $1,750,000,000 annually. The twenty indictments, under which they were now to be sentenced, charged they had conspired on everything from tiny $2 insulators to multimillion-dollar turbine generators and had persisted in the conspiracies for as long as eight years.

As a group, they looked like just what they were: well-groomed corporation executives in Ivy League suits, employed by companies ranging in size from Joslyn Manufacturing & Supply Co., whose shop space is scarcely larger than the courtroom itself, to billion-dollar giants like General Electric and Westinghouse. There was J. E. Cordell, ex-submariner, sales vice president of Southern States Equipment Corp., pillar of the community in a small

Richard Austin Smith, "The Incredible Electrical Conspiracy," *Fortune*, April, 1961, pp. 132–180; May, 1961, pp. 161–224 (Editorial Adaptation). Reprinted from the April and May 1961 issues of Fortune Magazine by special permission; © 1961 Time, Inc.

Georgia town, though his net worth never exceeded $25,000, and urbane William S. Ginn, G.E. vice president at $135,000 a year, a man once thought to be on his way to the presidency of the corporation. There was old, portly Fred F. Loock, president of Allen-Bradley Co., who found conspiring with competitors quite to his taste ("It is the only way a business can be run. It is free enterprise."), and G.E.'s Marc A. de-Ferranti, who pocketed his repugnance on orders from his boss. There was M. H. Howard, a production manager of Foster Wheeler, who found it hard to stay in the conspiracy (his company's condenser business ran in the red during two years of it), and C. H. Wheeler Manufacturing's President Thomas, who found it hard to quit— he'd been told his firm couldn't survive if he left the cartel.

At nine-thirty the courtroom doors opened and everyone trooped in. It was a huge room, paneled in mahogany with carved pilasters that reached up thirty feet or more to a white ceiling; yet big as it was it very soon filled with tension. What the defendants were thinking of was not hard to guess: the possibility of prison; the careers ruined after decades of service; the agile associates who weren't there, the ones who had saved their hides by implicating others.

Shortly after ten o'clock, Judge J. Cullen Ganey, chief judge of the U.S. District Court, entered the courtroom. He had earned a reputation in his twenty years on the bench for tolerance and moderation. But it was clear almost immediately that he took a stern view of this conspiracy: "This is a shocking indictment of a vast section of our economy, for what is really at stake here is the survival of the kind of economy under which this country has grown great, the free-enterprise system." The first targets of his censure were the twenty-nine corporations and their top management. He acknowledged that the Justice Department did not have enough evidence to convict men in the highest echelons of the corporations before the court, but in a broader sense the "real blame" should be laid at their doorstep: "One would be most naive indeed to believe that these violations of the law, so long persisted in, affecting so large a segment of the industry and finally involving so many millions upon millions of dollars, were facts unknown to those responsible for the corporation and its conduct . . ." Heavy fines, he said, would be imposed on the corporations themselves.

Next he turned a cold blue eye on the forty-five corporation executives who had not escaped the nets of Antitrust. Many of the individual defendants he saw "torn between conscience and an approved corporate policy . . . the company man, the conformist, who goes along with his superiors and finds balm for his conscience in additional comforts and the security of his place in the corporate set-up." The judge said that individuals "with ultimate responsibility for corporate conduct, among those indicted," were going to jail.

By midafternoon of that first day E. R. Jung, Clark Controller vice president, was ashen under a thirty-day prison sentence and a $2,000 fine. Gray-haired Westinghouse Vice President J. H. Chiles Jr., vestryman of St. John's Episcopal Church in Sharon, Pennsylvania, got thirty days in prison, a $2,000 fine; his colleague, Sales Manager Charles I. Mauntel, veteran of thirty-nine years with the corporation, faced thirty days and a $1,000 fine; Ginn of G. E. (indicted in two conspiracies), thirty days and a $12,500 fine; G.E. Divisional Manager Lewis Burger, thirty days plus a $2,000 fine; G.E. Vice President George Burens, $4,000 and thirty days. "There goes my whole life," said this veteran of forty years with G.E., waving his arm distractedly as he waited to telephone his wife. "Who's going to want to hire a jailbird? What am I going to tell my children?"

By lunchtime the second day it was all over. The little game that lawyers from G.E. and Westinghouse had been playing against each other—predicting sentences and total fines—was ended. G.E. had "lost," receiving $437,500 in total fines to Westinghouse's $372,500. All told, $1,924,500 worth of fines were levied, seven jail sentences and twenty-four suspended jail sentences handed down. But sentencing, far from closing the case, has raised it to new importance.

THE PROBLEMS OF PREDOMINANCE

No thoughtful person could have left that courtroom untroubled by the problems of corporate power and corporate ethics. We live in a corporate society. Big business determines institutionally our rate of capital formation, technological innovation, and economic growth; it establishes the kind of competition that is typical of our system and sets the moral tone of the market place. The streets of every city in the U.S. are crowded with small businesses that take their cue from great corporations, whether it trickles down from what some executive tells a crop of college graduates about free enterprise or the way he himself chooses to compete. Their lawyers pleaded that the way the electrical-equipment executives did compete was not collusion at its *worst*. To be sure, it was not so vulgar as the strong-arm price fixing of the Gulf Coast shrimpers or the rough scuff employed by a certain Philadelphia linen-supply company. But by flouting the law, the executives of the great companies set an example that was bound to make small companies feel they had similar license, and never mind the kid gloves. As Robert A. Bicks, then head of Antitrust, declared early in the proceedings, "These men and companies have in a true sense mocked the image of that economic system which we profess to the world."

This being so, it is highly important to understand what went wrong with the electrical-equipment industry and with General Electric, the biggest company of them all and the one without which the conspiracies could not have existed.

"SECURITY, COMPLACENCY, MEDIOCRITY"

When Ralph Cordiner took over the presidency of G.E. from Charles E. Wilson in December of 1950, it was clear from the outset that the corporation was in for some teeth-rattling changes. Cordiner had spent the previous five years working up a reorganization plan that would give G.E. the new plants, the new additions to capital, and the new management setup he thought essential to its revitalization. Moreover, he had long made plain his distaste for running any big company the way G.E. had been run by his predecessors, with authority tightly concentrated in the president's office. Decentralization was a thing with him: he had never forgotten how the "layers of fat" in a centralized G.E. had slowed his own incessant drive for recognition to a point where he'd once quit to take the presidency of Schick. The simple fact was that intellectually and temperamentally a centralized organization went against his grain, whether it be run with Electric Charlie Wilson's relaxed conviviality or the clockwork autocracy of Gerard ("You have four minutes") Swope.

The corporation at large learned almost immediately what the new boss had in store for it and from Cordiner himself. Within six weeks he rode circuit from New York to Bridgeport, Chicago, Lynn-Boston, Schenectady, spreading the word to some 6,000 G.E. executives. The gist of his message could be divided into three parts. First, G.E. was in sorry shape. It was dedicated principally to "security, complacency, and mediocrity." Second, decentralization and rewards based on performance were going to be relied on in the rapid transformation of his "sinecure of mediocrity" into a dynamic corporation. G.E. would be split into twenty-seven autonomous divisions comprising 110 small companies. The 110 would be run just as if they were individual enterprises, the local boss setting his own budget, even making capital expenditures up to $200,000. But with authority and responsibility would go accountability and measurement, measurement by higher, harder standards. Third, G.E.'s new philosophy of decentralized management specifically prohibited meeting with competitors on prices, bids, or market shares. Charlie Wilson's General Instruction 2.35[1] on compliance with the antitrust laws, first issued in 1946 and re-issued in 1948 and 1950, would remain very much in force.

[1] "It has been and is the policy of this Company to conform strictly to the antitrust laws . . . special care should be taken that any proposed action is in conformity with the law as presently interpreted. If there is any doubt as to the legality of any proposed action . . . the advice of the Law Department must be obtained."

There was good reason for stressing this last point. Antitrust was then a very sore subject at G.E. In the decade just ended (1940–50), the corporation had been involved in thirteen antitrust cases, the offenses ranging from production limitation and patent pooling to price fixing and division of markets. Moreover, G.E. had long been something of a battleground for two divergent schools of economic thought. One school was straight Adam Smith and dedicated to the classical concept that corporate progress, like national progress, was best secured by freedom of private initiative within the bonds of justice. Its advocates believed that nothing was less intelligent than entering into price restrictions with competitors, for this just put G.E. on a par with companies that had neither its research facilities nor its market power. Ralph Cordiner, the company's most articulate advocate of this viewpoint, prided himself on the fact that it was at his insistence that the three G.E. employees implicated in illegal price fixing got the sack in 1949; his philosophy, at its most eloquent, was simply: "Every company and every industry—yes, and every country—that is operated on a basis of cartel systems is liquidating its present strength and future opportunities."

The second school of thought held that competition, particularly price competition, was for the birds. Getting together with competitors was looked on as a way of life, a convention, "just as a manager's office always has a desk with a swivel chair." It was considered easier to negotiate market percentages than fight for one's share, less wearing to take turns on rigged bids than play the rugged individualist. Besides, the rationale went, they were all "gentlemen" and no more inclined to gouge the consumer than to crowd a competitor. Admittedly, all of them knew they were breaking the law— Section 1 of the Sherman Act is as explicit as a traffic ordinance. Their justification was on other grounds. "Sure, collusion was illegal," explained an old G.E. hand, "but it wasn't *unethical*. It wasn't any more unethical than if the companies had a summit conference the way Russia and the West meet. Those competitor meetings were just attended by a group of distressed individuals who wanted to know where they were going."

One important reason for the strength of G.E.'s anticompetition school was a change that occurred in the electrical industry after World War II. Smaller companies were becoming bigger and they were broadening their product lines. Customers had a wider choice of heavy electrical equipment, alike in quality and design. Price, consequently, became the decisive selling point. To turn this situation to their best advantage, buyers adopted a new technique: the competitive bid. When the utilities took it up, it became so prevalent that some manufacturers came to believe certain types of equipment would be treated like commodities with prices expected to fluctuate from day to day. This produced serious instability in the market and made profit planning difficult. The conspiracies proliferated at G.E. and elsewhere because the manufacturers lacked the gumption to shift the buyers' attention from price to higher quality, better service, and improved design.

Precisely what numerical strength the anticompetition school commanded at the time Cordiner took office in 1950 is of course a controversial point. G.E. prefers to talk of it as "a pocket," while the collusionists themselves like to think nine G.E. executives out of ten shared their point of view. A fact to keep in mind is that thirty-two G.E. executives implicated themselves before the grand juries in addition to those general managers and vice presidents, clearly involved, but not called to testify. There can be no doubt that the collusionists' influence was formidable and pervasive. And now, despite what Cordiner said about over-all company policy on cartels, under his decentralization plan the head of each of the 110 units comprising the company was being given power to set his own marketing policies and to raise or lower prices as he saw fit. Under the circumstances, anyone might have foreseen the results.

A WAY OF LIFE FOR CLARENCE BURKE

One of the more attentive listeners to what the incoming president had to say about antitrust was Clarence Burke, a hard-driving, tenacious executive in his middle forties (who was to become the $42,000-a-year general manager of the High Voltage Switchgear Department and one of fifteen G.E. executives sentenced in Philadelphia). Burke had come to the heavy-equipment end of G.E. in 1926, fresh from the Georgia Institute of Technology (B.S. in electrical engineering), and his entire corporate life had been spent there. The heavy-equipment division was more than just the group that accounted for some 25 per cent of G.E. sales; it was the oldest division, and the foundation upon which the whole company had been built. Moreover, it was the stronghold of the collusionists. All of the nineteen indictments to which G.E. pleaded either guilty or no contest in Philadelphia sprang from price fixing, bid rigging, market division in heavy equipment.

Burke's introduction to the heavy-equipment conspiracies was easy as falling off a log. It occurred when he reported to Pittsfield, Massachusetts, on June 1, 1945, as sales manager of distribution transformers. A month or so after Burke's arrival, H. L. "Buster" Brown, sales manager of the whole Transformer Department, called the new man in and told him he'd be expected to attend a Pittsburgh meeting of the transformer section of the National Electrical Manufacturers' Association. It was a regularly scheduled affair, held during OPA days, in what is now the Penn-Sheraton Hotel, and it was attended by thirty or forty industry people plus the N.E.M.A. secretaries from New York. But after adjournment—when the N.E.M.A.

secretaries had departed—the company men reassembled within the hour for a cozier meeting. The talk this time was about prices, OPA-regulated prices, and how the industry could best argue Washington into jacking up the ceilings. Burke didn't consider this illegal, and he took part in several subsequent monthly meetings before OPA was abolished.

The convenient price klatsches following the regular N.E.M.A. meetings continued after OPA's demise. But instead of discussing pricing under government controls, the conspirators turned to fixing prices among themselves. "In that conspiracy," Burke recalled this winter, "we didn't try to divide up the market or prorate the sealed-bid business. We only quoted an agreed-upon price—to the penny." Nor did the post-OPA agreements seem to some of the participants like Burke to put them any more outside the law than agreements under the OPA. "We gradually grew into it. Buster Brown assured us that [the company's antitrust directive] didn't mean the kind of thing we were doing, that Antitrust would have to say we had *gouged* the public to say we were doing anything illegal. We understood this was what the company wanted us to do."

For a while this comfortable rationale sustained Burke and any conspirators who had qualms about the matter, but in 1946 it was demolished by the company lawyers. Teams of them made the rounds of G.E. departments, no doubt in response to federal probings that were to result in the successful antitrust prosecutions of G.E. two years later. The lawyers put everyone in G.E. on notice that it certainly was illegal to discuss prices with competitors, whether the public was gouged or not. Then the head office followed this up by barring anybody who had anything to do with pricing from attending N.E.M.A. meetings. Engineering personnel were substituted for people like Buster Brown and Clarence Burke. The G.E. conspirators called such enforced withdrawal from active participation "going behind the iron curtain." This situation continued for about nine months, during which everyone received a copy of Electric Charlie's antitrust admonition and during which G.E.'s competitors kept the Pittsfield shut-ins informed by telephone of their own price agreements. Then, abruptly, the iron curtain was raised.

"Word came down to start contacting competitors again," Burke remembers. "It came to me from my superior, Buster Brown, but my impression was that it came to him from higher up. I think the competitive situation was forcing them to do something, and there were a lot of old-timers who thought collusion was the best way to solve the problems. That is when the hotel-room meetings got started. We were cautioned at this time not to tell the lawyers what we were doing and to cover our trails in our expense-account reports." Part of Burke's camouflage: transportation entries never showed fares to the actual city where the meeting was held but to some point of equivalent distance from Pittsfield.

The conspiracy operated, although sporadically, for the next several years of Burke's Pittsfield assignment (he was reassigned February 1, 1950). Every so often, the G.E. participants would retire behind the iron curtain, until it seemed necessary to bring about some general price increases. Then there would be a resumption of quiet talks with the men from other major manufacturers like Westinghouse. The antitrust-compliance directives they had all initialed? "When anybody raised a question about that, they would be told it doesn't apply now." . . .

By 1951, however, at the time Burke was listening to Ralph Cordiner's antitrust exhortations, the Pittsfield conspiracy had closed down—to make matters simpler if, as everyone correctly suspected, Cordiner was going to clamp down on such cabals. But bigger and better conspiracies were in the offing. In September, 1951, not very long after the Cordiner meeting, Clarence Burke walked into a new job at G.E.—and into membership in probably the oldest conspiracy then extant. The conspiracy was in circuit breakers[2] and it had been operative over the span of a quarter-century. Burke's new job was manager of all switchgear marketing, which included circuit breakers, switchgear, and other items of heavy electrical equipment. This particular spot was open because the previous incumbent had been troubled ever since signing a restatement of Charlie Wilson's "Policy Concerning the Antitrust Laws" the year before. As Burke got the story from Robert Tinnerholm, who interviewed him for the job: "I was to replace a man who took a strictly religious view of it; who, because he had signed this slip of paper [the Wilson directive] wouldn't contact competitors or talk to them—even when they came to his home." Burke got the job, an important step up the G.E. ladder, because he had become something of a conspiratorial wheel by then: "They knew I was adept at this sort of thing. I was glad to get the promotion. I had no objections." No objections then or subsequently, as it turned out, for he had found it easy to persuade himself that what he was doing in defiance of the letter of the antitrust directive was not done in defiance of its spirit.

Burke's boss when he first went to switchgear in 1951 was Henry V. Erben, to whom Buster Brown had reported in the cozy old days at Pittsfield. Erben had risen to the No. 3 spot in G.E.—executive vice president, Apparatus Group—and as Burke recalls, "he was saying then that he had talked to Cordiner about this policy, that Cordiner was not pleased with [the idea of getting together with competitors] but that he, Erben, had said he would do it in a way that would not get the company into trouble. And I'd been told by others that Erben had said things like this earlier than that."

Burke's initial assignment in Philadelphia was to get to know the local marketing executives of Westinghouse, Allis-Chalmers, and Federal Pacific,

[2] Like their household counterparts, circuit breakers are used to interrupt the flow of electricity when it reaches dangerous voltages. The industrial versions are sometimes forty feet long, twenty-six feet high, and weigh eighty-five tons.

and then to see they met the other new members of G.E.'s switchgear management. (This department had been restaffed in anticipation of being split into three parts, the separate companies called for by Cordiner's decentralization plan.) He was also expected to take a hand at indoctrination in conspiracy. "Erben's theory had been live and let live, contact the competitors. He gave us that theory at every opportunity and we took it down to other levels and had no trouble getting the most innocent persons to go along. Mr. Erben thought it was all right, and if they didn't want to do it, they knew we would replace them. Not replace them for that reason, of course. We would have said the man isn't *broad* enough for this job, he hasn't grown into it yet."

One man, ironically enough, who had not yet "grown" into the job was George Burens, the new boss of the whole switchgear operation. Burens had started out in G.E. as a laborer; he had the additional disadvantage of being a junior-high-school man in a corporate world full of college men, but during the next thirty years he had steadily risen by sheer competitive spirit. Part of his zest for competition had been acquired in the Lamp Division, where he had spent the bulk of his career. Lamps had long been noted as the most profitable of G.E. divisions and the most independent, a constant trial to Gerard Swope in the days when he tried to centralize all administrative authority in G.E.'s New York headquarters. But most of Buren's competitive spirit was simply in the nature of the man. "He had grown up hating competitors," was the way a colleague put it. "They were the enemy."

"THIS IS BOB, WHAT IS 7'S BID?"

Burens arrived on the scene in September of 1951 and busied himself solely with the job of splitting switchgear into three independent companies (high, medium, and low voltage), each with a general manager and himself as general manager of the division. Once decentralization was accomplished, he was content for a time to let his new departmental general managers like Clarence Burke run the conspiracy. And some conspiracy it was.

Some $650 million in sales was involved, according to Justice Department estimates, from 1951 through 1958. The annual total amounted to roughly $75 million and was broken down into two categories, sealed bids and open bids. The sealed-bid business (between $15 million and $18 million per year) was done with public agencies, city, state, and federal. The private-sector business was conducted with private utilities and totaled some $55 million to $60 million per annum.

The object of the conspiracy, in so far as the sealed-bid business was concerned, was to rotate that business on a fixed-percentage basis among four participating companies, then the only circuit-breaker manufacturers in the U.S. G.E. got 45 per cent, Westinghouse 35, Allis-Chalmers 10, Federal Pacific 10. Every ten days to two weeks working-level meetings were called in order to decide whose turn was next. Turns were determined by the "ledger list," a table of who had got what in recent weeks, and after that the only thing left to decide was the price that the company picked to "win" would submit as the lowest bid.

Above this working-level group was a second tier of conspirators who dealt generally with the over-all scheme of rigging the sealed bids but whose prime purpose was maintenance of book prices (quoted prices) and market shares in the yearly $55 million to $60 million worth of private-sector business. Once each week, the top executives (general managers and vice presidents) responsible for carrying out the conspiracy would get the word to each other via intercompany memo. A different executive would have the "duty" over each thirty-day period. That involved initiating the memos, which all dealt with the same subject matter: the jobs coming up that week, the book price each company was setting, comments on the general level of equipment prices.

The conspiracies had their own lingo and their own standard operating procedures. The attendance list was known as the "Christmas-card list," meetings as "choir practices." Companies had code numbers—G.E. 1, Westinghouse 2, Allis-Chalmers 3, Federal Pacific 7—which were used in conjunction with first names when calling a conspirator at home for price information ("This is Bob, what is 7's bid?"). At the hotel meeting it was S.O.P. not to list one's employer when registering and not to have breakfast with fellow conspirators in the dining room. The G.E. men observed two additional precautions: never to be the ones who kept the records and never to tell G.E.'s lawyers anything.

WHERE TO CUT THROATS

But things were not always smooth even inside this well-oiled machine, for the conspirators actually had no more compunction at breaking the rules of the conspiracy than at breaching the Sherman Act. "Everyone accused the others of not living up to the agreement," Clarence Burke recalled, "and the ones they complained about tried to shift the blame onto someone else." The most constant source of irritation occurred in the sealed-bid business, where chiseling was difficult to detect. But breaks in book price to the utilities in the open-bid business also generated ill will and vituperation. Indeed, one of the many ironies of the whole affair is that the conspiracy couldn't entirely suppress the competitive instinct. Every so often some company would decide that cutthroat competition outside was preferable to the throat-cutting that went on in the cartel; they would break contact and sit out the conspiracy for a couple of years.

What prompted their return? Chronic overcapacity, for one thing, overcapacity that put a constant pressure on prices. Soon after he went to Washington as defense mobilization chief in 1950, Electric Charlie Wilson announced that the nation's electric-power capacity needed to be increased 30 per cent over the next three years. The equipment industry jumped to match that figure, and added a little more as well. Thus an executive, who ebulliently increased capacity one year, a few years later might join a price conspiracy to escape the consequences of that increase. "This is a feast or famine business," summed up Clarence Burke. "At one time everybody was loaded with orders, and ever since they wanted to stay that way. When utilities decide they need more generating capacity, they start buying and we have three years of good business—and then three years of bad. The decision to build capacity was delegated down to the managers [under decentralization]."

A more human explanation of why the conspiracy snarled on for eight years was corporate pressure, the pressure to perform. "All we got from Lexington Avenue," said Burke, "was 'get your percentage of available business up, the General Electric Co. is slipping.'" Cordiner himself has remarked: "I would say the company was more than slightly nervous in 1951–52–53."

Certainly corporate pressure no more exculpates an executive who enters into an illegal conspiracy than the relatively low pay of a bank clerk justifies his dipping into the till. But that is not to say it didn't carry weight with the conspirators from G.E. For the company was not only experiencing the increased pressure that goes with new presidents but was adjusting to a whole new organizational setup. Said one observer of the scene, Vice President Harold Smiddy, G.E.'s management expert: "Some thought . . . that he was going too fast. But Cordiner's asset is stretching men. He can push them and he did." Said another observer, G.E. director Sidney Weinberg: "If you did something wrong, Cordiner would send for you and tell you you were through. That's all there would be to it."

Down the line, where the pressure must have been intense, Clarence Burke had this to say of it as a factor in continuing the conspiracy: "We did feel that this was the only way to reach part of our goals as managers. Each year we had to budget for more profit as a per cent of net sales, as well as for a larger percentage of available business. My boss, George Burens, wouldn't approve a budget unless it was a 'reach' budget. We couldn't accomplish a greater per cent of net profit to sales without getting together with competitors. Part of the pressure was the will to get ahead and the desire to have the good will of the man above you. He had only to get the approval of the man above *him* to replace you, and if you wouldn't cooperate he could find lots of other faults to use to get you out."

CORDINER TAKES THE PLUNGE

By May of 1953, Clarence Burke had been promoted to general manager of one of the three new switchgear departments (high voltage), a post that made him in effect the president of a small company with some $25 million worth of sales. He felt he had a bellyful of the cartel because "No one was living up to the agreements and we at G.E. were being made suckers. On every job some one would cut our throat; we lost confidence in the group." So he got out.

The G.E. boycott of that cartel continued on through 1954. To be sure, Westinghouse, Allis-Chalmers, and the other competitors would still call Royce Crawford, Burke's marketing man, to tell him the prices that the high-level group had decided on, and express the heartfelt hope he would honor it. Crawford did honor it pretty much, though maintaining a free hand to go after all the business available.

This was the situation when, in mid-September 1954, Ralph Cordiner replaced the Wilson directive of antitrust compliance with a stronger one of his own. Far more explicit than Wilson's directive, Cordiner's Directive Policy 20.5 went beyond the compliance required by the law and blanketed the subject with every conceivable admonition.

But 1954 was a bad year for the industry and for G.E. The company's sales slumped for the first time since Cordiner had taken the helm, dropping almost $176 million. Moreover, profits as a per cent of sales were still well below the 8 per cent achieved by Charlie Wilson in 1950. The result was that Cordiner and Robert Paxton, executive vice president for industrial products, began putting more heat on one division after another.

"We were told," as one general manager remembered it, "that G.E. was losing business and position because our prices weren't competitive." Then, in the latter part of 1954, Paxton heard a report that moved him from words to the action his blunt Scottish temperament favored. Westinghouse had beaten G.E. out of a big turbine order and had done it at considerably off book price. Determined that no more of the big ones were going to get away, Paxton decided he'd instruct the fieldmen personally. Thus, when the next big job came along, a $5-million affair for transformers and switchgear with Ebasco, the New York district manager knew he was not to let the competition underbid him. But Westinghouse and the others were hungry too, and the price breaks came so fast it was difficult to keep track of them: one day the price was 10 per cent off book, the next 20 per cent, finally 40 per cent.

So began the celebrated "white sales" of 1954–55. Before it was over, the electrical industry was discounting price as much as 40 to 45 per cent off book. Delivery dates began stretching out, got as far as five years away from date of sale. This of course meant that the impact of 1955's giveaway prices was not confined to that one year; the blight they put on profits persisted down to 1960.

MIXING CONSPIRACY WITH GOLF

General Electric, with its broad product lines, was not hit as hard by the "white sale" as some of its smaller competitors, but it was just as anxious as anyone else to call a halt. The word went out from headquarters on Lexington Avenue that prices had to be got back up, and stability restored. Sales responsibility was being returned to the general managers. They certainly welcomed the news, for all during the period that Paxton had taken over sales nobody had relieved the general managers of the companion responsibility of turning in the profit demanded. Now with power over sales restored, they could strike a better balance between the irreconcilables of getting more market and getting more profit.

At the Switchgear Division, the pressure was so great that George Burens, the lifelong believer in tough competition, underwent a remarkable conversion. He called department manager Clarence Burke into his office and told him the old cartel was going to be cranked up again. More than that, Burens was going to do the job of re-establishing it himself. Shortly thereafter, he and Burke trotted off to mix in a little conspiracy with a little golf in Bedford Springs, Pennsylvania. Burens and Burke formed a foursome with Landon Fuller and J. B. McNeill, key men in sales at Westinghouse. They concluded that it might take more than the combined market power of G.E. and Westinghouse (some 70 to 75 per cent) to get things back to normal; other companies would have to be brought in. Fuller agreed to contact Allis-Chalmers and Burens agreed to get in touch with I–T–E Circuit Breaker—but only at a high level. Everyone was concerned at the danger of low-level contacts and rightly so, for, as Burke remembers what happened subsequently: "It got so that people who worked for people who worked for me knew about pricing arrangements."

About January, 1956, another high-level meeting was held in Cleveland. Fuller's call on Allis-Chalmers had been successful; he had Joseph W. McMullen in tow. But at I–T–E, George Burens, trying to keep the contact at a high level, apparently hadn't got to the right man. Joe McMullen, however, had his eye on somebody in I–T–E (Harry Buck, as it turned out) and volunteered to bring him into camp. Then there was a round of golf and a couple of rounds of drinks and the conspirators went their separate ways, after agreeing to keep in touch by memorandums. Every month that year one company conspirator would initiate a memorandum to the others (who now included I–T–E's Buck), listing every pending job whether sealed bid or open and stating what the calculated book price would be. Then the conspirators would reassemble and compare calculations to forestall any chiseling from the agreed-upon book. There were nine much meetings in 1956, held in various hotel suites. These and the memorandums worked fairly well, until the first part of 1957. Then a one-man gang named McGregor Smith lit the fuse that blew them up.

THE MALIGN CIRCLE

"Mac" [McGregor] Smith, chairman of the Florida Power & Light Co., personally handled some of the buying for his dynamic utility. As he went marketing for equipment, it struck him that the manufacturers had set artificially high profit goals for themselves, had priced their products accordingly, and then had got together to see that the prices stuck. In other words, a malign circle of manufacturers was short-circuiting what Ralph Cordiner liked to call the "benign circle of power producers and power consumers." Smith was buying a lot of transformers, switchgear, and other equipment in 1957, but the manufacturers were defending book price as if life depended on it and, despite heavy pressure from Mac Smith and his purchasing agents, were giving little in the way of discounts.

Then one Monday, Smith closed his transformer purchases with a number of companies, including G.E. and Westinghouse; on Tuesday Clarence Burke got a worried report from one of his switchgear salesmen in Miami: Westinghouse had proposed to Florida Power that it add all its circuit-breaker order (about a million dollars worth) to its order for Westinghouse transformers. In return, Westinghouse would take 4 per cent off circuit-breaker book and hide the discount in the transformer order. Telling his man to be sure of the facts first, Burke gave him authority to meet the Westinghouse terms. A grateful Mac Smith then decided to split the circuit-breaker order, half to Westinghouse, which had broken the price, and half to G.E., which had matched the break.

This unexpected turn of the wheel brought the Westinghouse salesman boiling into Florida Power's executive suite. There he raised Mac Smith's hackles to a point where the latter called G.E. and asked it to do him the favor of taking the whole order. G.E. naturally obliged.

Retaliation was not long coming. "Westinghouse went to Baltimore Gas & Electric," says Burke, shaking his head in recollection of the chaos that ensued, "and said they'd give them 5 per cent off on switchgear and circuit breakers, and a week later Allis-Chalmers gave Potomac Electric 12 per cent off. A week after that, Westinghouse gave Atlantic City Electric 20 per cent off, and it went on down to much worse than the 'white sale'—in the winter of 1957–58 prices were 60 per cent off book."

That was the end of that cartel. It did not, of course, mean the end of the other conspiracies G.E. was involved in. Far from it. Each general manager of a division or department took a strictly personal view of his participation in any cartel. Thus while circuit breakers was at daggers drawn, industrial controls was enjoying an amiable conspiracy. . . .

CORDINER'S "PIECES OF PAPER"

G.E. was involved in at least seven other conspiracies during the time the circuit-breaker cartel was inoperative. The one in power transformers (G.E. Vice President Raymond W. Smith) was going, for G.E. had yet to develop the "black box" (a design breakthrough using standard components to produce tailor-made transformers), which two years later would enable it to take price leadership away from Westinghouse. The one in turbine generators (G.E. Vice President William S. Ginn) was functioning too. In the fall of 1957 it was agreed at the Barclay Hotel[3] to give G.E. "position" in bidding on a 500,000-kilowatt TVA unit.

The question that naturally arises, the cartels being so numerous, is why didn't G.E.'s top management stop them? Cordiner has been criticized within the company, and rightly so, for sitting aloofly in New York and sending out "pieces of paper"—his 20.5 antitrust directive—rather than having 20.5 personally handed to the local staff by the local boss. But there was also a failure in human relations. A warmer man might have been close enough to his people to divine what was going on. According to T. K. Quinn (*I Quit Monster Business*), the G.E. vice president who had helped him up the ladder, Ralph Cordiner, was "first class in every aspect of management except human relations."

After the conspiracy case broke, the question of top-level complicity came up. G.E. hired Gerhard Gesell of the Washington law firm of Covington & Burling to come to a conclusion one way or another as to whether Cordiner, Paxton, or any other member of the Executive Office had knowledge of the cartels. No corroborated evidence ever came to light that Cordiner knew of them; quite the opposite. As Clarence Burke put it last month: "Cordiner was sincere but under-sold by people beneath him who rescinded his orders."

[3] On February 2, 1960, the hotel jocularly described its *spécialité de maison* in a small *New York Times* ad: "Antitrust-corporation secrets are best discussed in the privacy of an executive suite at the Barclay. It's convenient, attractive, and financially practical."

Robert Paxton, however, is something else again. The fifty-nine-year-old G.E. president, who resigned this February for reasons of health, was in the unenviable position of having worked most of his corporate life in those vineyards of G.E. where cartels thrived. He was in switchgear for twenty-one years, five of them as works manager, went to Pittsfield with his close friend Ray Smith (later one of the convicted conspirators), and eventually became manager of the Transformer and Allied Product Division there. A conspiracy had started before he got to Pittsfield and one was operating (first under Ginn, then under Smith) after he left. Paxton was not then *responsible* for marketing, as G.E. points out, but he has always shown a lively interest in the subject: "I found myself, even as a very young engineer working for General Electric, dealing with the very practical daily problem of how to minimize cost and how to maximize profit."

Gesell discovered there was violent disagreement within G.E. about Paxton and the cartels: "Things were said about his having knowledge. I interviewed Ray Smith and made every effort to pin down what he thought he had, but it was always atmospheric. The government investigated and didn't have any better luck."

Judge Ganey, however, expressed a more definite view: "I am not naive enough to believe General Electric didn't know about it and it didn't meet with their hearty approbation." In Ganey's opinion, Directive 20.5 was "observed in its breach rather than in its enforcement." To say the least, there was a serious management failure at G.E.

COLD TURKEY AND THE PRESSURE FOR PROFITS

In 1958 the circuit breaker-switchgear conspiracy started up again. George Burens and his three departmental general managers, Burke, H. F. Hentschel, and Frank Stehlik, were all dead set against resumption. But the pressure was too great. Pressure had already produced some profound changes in Burke. "He used to be hail fellow well met," said a colleague who witnessed the transformation over the years, "until he was put under that great pressure for profits. Then he simply shrank into himself; everything got to be cold turkey with him—without any warmth at all." Now the pressure was redoubling, as it always did after the market went to pieces. Burens and some of the other apparatus executives were summoned to New York in 1958 for a talk with the boss, Group Executive Arthur F. Vinson. This affair became known to Burens' subordinates as the "Beat Burens" meeting, for at it were aired angry complaints by G. E.'s customers that, with switchgear selling at 40 to 45 per cent off book, other G.E. departments should be offering their products at substantial discounts. The solution: stabilize switchgear prices; in other words, get back in the cartel.

Burens returned to Philadelphia, battered but unshaken in his resolve to keep clear of the cartel. He expected to do it by keeping up quality and efficiency, and by pricing the product so that there was a fair profit. Ironically enough, in view of his subsequent indictment, he was firmly of the belief that, given six months time, he could bring prices up in the free market without messing around with any conspiracy. But at the annual business-review meeting of apparatus people, held on July 30 and 31 in Philadelphia, he underwent a further hammering from other divisional general managers about the way switchgear prices were hurting them. He seemed morose at the following banquet, held in a private dining room at the Philadelphia Country Club; indeed, he got into a heated argument about prices with Paxton, who had succeeded Ralph Cordiner as president that April.

What happened next to change George Burens' mind about getting back into the conspiratorial rat race is a matter of great controversy. It concerns whether he got a direct order to rejoin the cartel from Arthur Vinson. If Vinson did so instruct Burens, and others, then General Electric's complicity extended to the highest corporate level, for Vinson was a member of the fifteen-man Executive Office, a group that included Cordiner and Paxton. . . .

Suffice it to say here that Burens did rejoin and was confronted by a delicate problem of face. He didn't want to have to crawl back, particularly after having given everyone such a hard time when he quit. But as matters turned out, G.E. was holding its quadrennial Electric Utility Conference in California that fall and there Burens ran into Fischer Black, the amiable editor of *Electrical World*. Black reported that a lot of people in the industry were sour on G.E. in general and Burens in particular because Burens had refused to go along with new pricing agreements. To end this insalubrious state of affairs, Black would be happy to set up a meeting— if Burens would just attend. The latter agreed.

On October 8, 1958, the cartel set gathered at the Astor Hotel in New York. The G.E. contingent was there, headed by Burens and Burke, Landon Fuller for Westinghouse, Harry Buck for I–T–E Circuit Breaker, Frank Roby for Federal Pacific. L. W. "Shorty" Long had called in to say he couldn't make it but anything they decided was okay with Allis-Chalmers. Black himself popped in to chirp that he was paying for the suite and to be sure and order up lunch. Then he left them to business. Not much of it was transacted. There was a lot of crepe-hanging over what had happened in the past and a number of hopeful ideas for the future were discussed. The net of it was that everybody agreed to go home, check their records, and come up with proposals on November 9, at the Traymore Hotel in Atlantic City.

A PARTY FOR BURENS

Whatever watery cordiality prevailed at the Astor vanished into the steam of conflict at the Traymore. Circuit-breaker prices had been dropping alarmingly ever since September, so much so that G.E., Westinghouse, Allis-Chalmers, and Federal Pacific extended options to some utilities to purchase large numbers of circuit breakers at 40 to 55 per cent below book. Moreover, I–T–E Circuit Breaker had got into the business via the purchase of Kelman Electric and wanted a slice of the sealed-bid market; Federal Pacific had a slice but wanted a fatter one.

Deciding what to do about prices was not particularly trying; an agreement was reached to keep them substantially identical at book. The real trouble came over changing the percentages of sealed-bid business. G.E., Westinghouse, and Allis-Chalmers knew that anything done to accommodate the demands of Federal Pacific and I–T–E would have to come out of their hides. But at the end of ten hours of angry argument they decided the only way to get the cartel going again was to submit to the knife: General Electric's percentage was sliced from 45 to 40.3. Westinghouse's from 35 to 31.3, Allis-Chalmers from 10 to 8.8. I–T–E was cut in for 4 per cent and Federal Pacific got a 50 per cent boost, its percentage of the market was raised from 10 to 15.6.

So began the final circuit-breaker cartel, born in recrimination and continued in mistrust. George Burens struggled with it for the next three months, a round of meetings at the old hotels and some swanky new places. Circuit-breaker prices inched up. Then in January, 1959, Burens was promoted out. It was a gay party that celebrated his departure to head up G.E.'s Lamp Division, and nobody was gayer than Burens, the tough competitor returning to free competition. Paxton was on hand with an accolade; the Lamp Division, he said, needed Burens' admirable talents to get it back where it belonged.

But there was no gay party for the incoming general manager of switch-gear. Lewis Burger was simply told his job was "at risk" for the next two years. If he performed, he could keep it and become a vice president to boot. If he was found wanting, he wouldn't be able to go back to his old job. He'd just be out. Burger promptly joined the circuit-breaker conspiracy. But the day was not far off, indeed it was only nine months away, when a phone call would set in motion the forces that would shatter the conspiracy and send Burger along with Burens off to prison.

Shortly before ten o'clock on the morning of September 28, 1959, an urgent long-distance call came in to G.E.'s vast Transformer Division at Pittsfield, Massachusetts. It was for Edward L. Dobbins, the divisional lawyer, and the person on the line was another attorney, representing Lapp Insulator Co. He just wanted to say that one of Lapp's officers had been subpoened by a Philadelphia grand jury and was going to tell the whole story. "What story?" said Dobbins pleasantly, then listened to an account that sent him, filled with concern, into the office of the divisional vice president, Raymond W. Smith.

At that time, Vice President Smith was a big man in G.E., veteran of twenty-eight years with the corporation, and one of President Robert Paxton's closest personal friends; he was also a big man in Pittsfield, where the Transformer Division employs 6,000 people out of a population of 57,000, director of a local bank, active member of the hospital building board. Smith heard Dobbins out, his six-foot-five frame suddenly taut in the swivel chair and a frown deepening on his forehead; he got up and began pacing back and forth. "It's bad," he said, "very bad." Then he added, shaking his head grimly, "You just don't know how bad it is!"

The story Dobbins had, which the man from Lapp was about to spill before a Philadelphia grand jury, was that Paul Hartig, one of Ray Smith's departmental general managers, had been conspiring with Lapp Insulator and a half-dozen other manufacturers to fix prices on insulators. Such news was unsettling enough to any boss, but Smith's alarm had its roots in something deeper than the derelictions of a subordinate. He was himself "Mr. Big" of another cartel, one involving $210 million worth of transformers a year, and he didn't need the gift of prescience to sense the danger to his own position. Nevertheless, Smith concluded that he had no choice but to report the trouble to Apparatus Group Vice President Arthur Vinson, in New York.

That very night Vinson flew up to Pittsfield. A cool, dynamic executive, boss of G.E.'s nine apparatus divisions, Vinson was used to hearing the word "trouble" from his general managers, but the way Smith had used it permitted of no delay, even for a storm that made the flight a hazardous one. He had dinner with the Smiths at a nearby inn, and then back in Smith's study, heard the story. Vinson's concern centered immediately on the extent of G.E.'s involvement. His recollection today is that after discussing Hartig, he asked Ray Smith whether the Transformer Division was itself involved in a cartel and received assurances to the contrary. Hartig's case appeared to be just that of a young manufacturing executive whose inexperience in marketing matters had got him compromised.

By sheer coincidence, G.E. Chairman Ralph Cordiner showed up in Pittsfield the next day. He had come, ironically enough, to hear an account of the new market approach by means of which Smith's Transformer Division expected to beat the ears off the competition, foreign and domestic. G.E. had worked out a method of cutting the formidable costs of custom-made transformers by putting them together from modular (standard) components. Westinghouse, long the design and cost leader in the transformer field, had been put on notice only the previous month that new prices reflecting the 20 per cent cost reduction were in the making.

Told of Hartig's involvement in the insulator cartel, Cordiner reacted with shock and anger. Up until then he had reason to think his general managers were making "earnest efforts" to comply with both the spirit and the letter of the antitrust laws; he had so testified in May before a congressional antitrust subcommittee. When the Tennessee Valley Authority had complained that it was getting identical bids on insulators, transformers, and other equipment, and the Justice Department had begun to take an active interest in this charge, he had sent G.E.'s amiable trade-regulation counsel, Gerard Swope Jr., son of the company's former chief executive, to Pittsfield. Swope considered it his mission to explore "a more dynamic pricing policy to get away from the consistent identity of prices." He had, however ventured to say, "I assume none of you have agreed with competitors on prices," and when nobody contested this assumption, he came away with the feeling that any suspicion of pricing agreements boiled down to a competitor's voicing a single criticism at a cocktail party. Cordiner had been further reassured by a report from G.E.'s outside counsel, Gerhard Gesell of Covington & Burling, who had burrowed through mountains of data and couldn't find anything incriminating. Gesell's conclusion, accepted by the top brass, was that G.E. was up against nothing more than another government attack on "administered" prices such as he and Thomas E. Dewey had beaten off earlier that year in the Salk vaccine case.

It was no wonder, then, that Cordiner was upset by what he heard about the insulator department. And this was only the beginning. G.E.'s general counsel, Ray Luebbe, was brought into the case, and within a matter of days Paul Hartig was in Luebbe's New York office implicating Vice President Ray Smith. Smith made a clean breast of things, detailing the operation of the transformer cartel (bids on government contracts were rotated to ensure that G.E. and Westinghouse each got 30 per cent of the business, the remaining 40 being split among four other manufacturers; book prices were agreed upon at meetings held everywhere from Chicago's Drake Hotel to the Homestead at Hot Springs, Virginia; secrecy was safeguarded by channeling all phone calls and mail to the homes, destroying written memoranda upon receipt).

Then Smith implicated a second G.E. vice president, William S. Ginn. Head of the Turbine Division at forty-one, Ginn was considered a comer in the company. Unfortunately for him, he was just as much of a wheel in conspiracy, an important man in two cartels, the one in transformers, which he had passed on to Ray Smith, and the one in turbine generators, which only the year before had aroused the suspicions of TVA by bringing about some very rapid price increases.

The involvement of divisional Vice Presidents Smith and Ginn put G.E.'s whole fifteen-man Executive Group—a group including Cordiner and Paxton—in an understandable flap. By now, the corporation was plainly implicated in four cartels, and an immense number of questions had to be answered, questions of how to ferret out other conspiracies, what legal defense to make, whether there was any distinction between corporate and individual guilt. For the next few weeks—from early October to late November—the executive office was to devote itself almost exclusively to searching for dependable answers.

BIG FISH IN SMALL COMPANIES

The Justice Department was also looking for answers. It had got started on the case because of TVA's suspicions and because Senator Estes Kefauver had threatened an investigation of the electrical industry, putting the executive branch of government on notice that if it didn't get on with the job, the legislative branch would. Robert A. Bicks, the most vigorous chief of Antitrust since Thurman Arnold, certainly had plenty of will to get on with the job, but the way was clouded. The Antitrust Division had once before —in 1951–52—tried to find a pattern of collusive pricing in the maze of transformer bids, but had wound up with no indictments. Now, as Bicks and William Maher, the head of the division's Philadelphia office, moved into the situation, proof seemed as elusive as ever.

The tactics of the Antitrust Division were based on using the Philadelphia grand jury to subpoena individuals—the corporation executives who would logically have been involved if a conspiracy existed. The ultimate objective was to determine whether the biggest electrical manufacturers and their top executives had participated in a cartel, but the approach had to be oblique. As Maher put it: "Even if we had proof of a meeting where Paxton [president of G.E.] and Cresap [president of Westinghouse] had sat down and agreed to fix prices, we would still have to follow the product lines down through to the illegal acts. You have to invert it, start with what happened at a lower level and build it up step by step. The idea is to go after the biggest fish in the *smallest* companies, then hope to get enough information to land the biggest fish in the biggest companies."

In mid-November a second Philadelphia grand jury was empaneled, and Justice Department attorneys began ringing doorbells across the land. As more of these rang and the trust busters took more testimony (under grand-jury subpoena), a sudden shiver of apprehension ran through the industry. The grapevine, probably the most sensitive in American business, began to buzz with talk that the feds were really on to something—moreover, that jail impended for the guilty. Everyone by then was only too well aware that an Ohio judge had just clapped three executives behind bars for ninety days for participating in a hand-tool cartel.

CORDINER'S COMMAND DECISION

Back at G.E., meanwhile, Cordiner had issued instructions that all apparatus general managers, including those few who so far had been implicated, were to be interviewed by company attorneys about participation in cartels. Most of the guilty lied, gambling that the exposures would not go any further than they had. Cordiner, accepting their stories, began to formulate what he thought would be G.E.'s best defense. It would have two principal salients: first, the company itself was not guilty of the conspiracies; what had occurred was without the encouragement or even the knowledge of the chairman, the president, and the Executive Office. G.E.'s corporate position on antitrust compliance was a matter of record, embodied in Directive 20.5, which Cordiner had personally written and promulgated five years before. Furthermore, illegal conduct of any individuals involved was clearly beyond the authority granted to them by the company, and therefore the company, as distinguished from the individuals, should not be held criminally responsible. Second, those employees who had violated Directive 20.5 were in for corporate punishment. "Stale offenses" were not to be counted, but a three-year company "statute of limitations" would govern liability (the federal limitation: five years).

Punishment of necessity had to go hand in hand with a corporate not-guilty stance. If G.E.'s defense was to be that the conspiracies had taken place in contravention of written policy (Directive 20.5), then unpunished offenders would be walking proof to a jury that 20.5 was just a scrap of paper. On the other hand, here was a clear management failure on the part of the Executive Office—a failure to detect over a period of almost a decade the cartels that were an open secret to the rest of the industry. As G.E. was to learn to its sorrow, lots of people who approved of punishment for the offenders did not think this permitted G.E. to wash its hands of responsibility. Westinghouse's president, Mark W. Cresap Jr., spoke for many executives both inside the industry and out when he stated his position this January: "Corporate punishment of these people . . . would only be self-serving on my part . . . this is a management failure."

But aside from the moral question, the legal basis of G.E.'s not-guilty stance was shaky to say the least. Its lawyers felt bound to inform the Executive Office: "The trend of the law appears to be that a business corporation will be held criminally liable for the acts of an employee so long as these acts are reasonably related to the area of general responsibility entrusted to him notwithstanding the fact that such acts are committed in violation of instructions issued by the company in good faith . . ." Under the decentralization policy, distinguishing between an "innocent" corporation and its "guilty" executives would be tough, for Cordiner himself had given the general managers clear pricing powers.

The Cordiner position had another weakness: it was based on the assumption that G.E. was involved in only four cartels—at the most. Yet wider involvement could reasonably have been expected. That very month general counsel Luebbe (who retired on October 1, 1960) had been warned by one of the general managers who had confessed that collusion would be found to have spread across the whole company front. ("I tried to tell Luebbe to stop the investigation," reflected the general manager, "and try to make a deal with the government. I told him in November, 1959, that this thing would go right across the board. He just laughed at me. He said, 'You're an isolated case—only you fellows would be stupid enough to do it.' ") Thus when wider involvement actually did come to light—the four cartels multiplied into nineteen and accounted for more than 10 per cent of G.E.'s total sales—the company found itself in the ludicrous position of continuing to proclaim its corporate innocence while its executives were being implicated by platoons.

THE AX FALLS

But vulnerable or not, G.E.'s posture was officially established in November, and management moved to put it into effect. Ray Smith was summoned to Arthur Vinson's big, handsome office and told he was going to be punished. His job was forfeit and his title too. There was a spot for him abroad, at substantially less money, if he wanted to try to rebuild his career in General Electric. Smith was stunned. Once implicated, he had leveled with the company to help it defend itself, and there'd been no hint of punishment then or in the succeeding two months. He decided he'd had it, at fifty-four, and would just take his severance pay and resign.

It was probably a wise move. Those conspirators who didn't quit on the spot had a very rough go of it. Initial punishment (demotion, transfer, pay cuts) was eventually followed by forced resignation, as we shall see. But the extra gall in the punishment was the inequality of treatment. William Ginn had been implicated at the same time as Ray Smith, and his case fell well within G.E.'s statute of limitations. Yet he was allowed to continue in his $135,000 job as vice president of the Turbine Division—until he went off to jail for that conspiracy, loaded with the biggest fine ($12,500) of any defendant.

Widespread resentment over this curious partiality to Ginn and over the meting out of discipline generally was destined to have its effect: willing G.E. witnesses soon began to turn up at the trust busters' camp; among them was an angry Ray Smith, who claimed he had been acting on orders from above. His mood, as a government attorney described it, was that of a man whose boss had said: "I can't get you a raise, so why don't you just take $5 out of petty cash every week. Then the man gets fired for it and the boss does nothing to help him out."

There was, however, an interval of some three months between Smith's resignation in November and his appearance in Philadelphia with his story. And eventful months they were. The first grand jury was looking into conspiracies in insulators, switchgear, circuit breakers, and several other products. The second grand jury was hearing four transformer cases and one on industrial controls. With a score of Justice men working on them, cases proliferated, and from December on lawyers began popping up trying to get immunity for their clients in return for testimony. Scarcely a week went by that Picks and company didn't get information on at least two new cases. But what they still needed was decisive data that would break a case wide open. In January, 1960, at just about the time Ralph Cordiner was making an important speech to G.E.'s management corps ("every company and every industry—yes, and every country—that is operated on a basis of cartel systems is liquidating its present strength and future opportunities"), the trust busters hit the jackpot in switchgear.

"THE PHASES OF THE MOON"

Switchgear had been particularly baffling to the Antitrust Division, so much so that in trying to establish a cartel pattern in the jumble of switchgear prices the trust busters got the bright idea they might be in code. A cryptographer was brought in to puzzle over the figures and try to crack the secret of how a conspirator could tell what to bid and when he'd win. But the cryptographer was soon as flummoxed as everyone else. One of the government attorneys in the case, however, made a point of dropping in on a college classmate who was the president of a small midwestern electrical-equipment company. This executive didn't have chapter and verse on the switchgear cartel but what he did have was enough for Justice to throw a scare into a bigger company, I–T–E Circuit Breaker. Indicating that subpoenas would follow, antitrust investigators asked I–T–E's general counsel, Franklyn Judson, to supply the names of sales managers in specific product lines. Judson decided to conduct an investigation of his own. When the subpoenas did come, a pink-cheeked blond young man named Nye Spencer, the company's sales manager for switchgear, was resolutely waiting —his arms loaded with data. He had decided he wasn't about to commit another crime by destroying the records so carefully laid away in his cellar.

There were pages on pages of notes taken during sessions of the switchgear conspiracy—incriminating entries like "Potomac Light & Power O.K. for G.E." and "Before bidding on this, check with G.E."; neat copies of the ground rules for meetings of the conspirators: no breakfasting together, no registering at the hotel with company names, no calls to the office, no papers to be left in hotel-room wastebaskets. Spencer, it seems, had been instructed to handle some of the secretarial work of the cartel and believed in doing it right; he'd hung onto documents to help in training an assistant. But the most valuable windfall from the meticulous record keeper was a pile of copies of the "phases of the moon" pricing formula for as far back as May, 1958.

Not much to look at—just sheets of paper, each containing a half-dozen columns of figures—they immediately resolved the enigma of switchgear prices in commercial contracts. One group of columns established the bidding order of the seven switchgear manufacturers—a different company, each with its own code number, phasing into the priority position every two weeks (hence "phases of the moon"). A second group of columns, keyed into the company code numbers, established how much each company was to knock off the agreed-upon book price. For example, if it were No. 1's (G.E.'s) turn to be low bidder at a certain number of dollars off book, then all Westinghouse (No. 2), or Allis-Chalmers (No. 3) had to do was look for their code number in the second group of columns to find how many dollars they were to bid *above* No. 1. These bids would then be fuzzed up by having a little added to them or taken away by companies 2, 3, etc. Thus there was not even a hint that the winning bid had been collusively arrived at.

With this little device in hand, the trust busters found they could light up the whole conspiracy like a switchboard. The new evidence made an equally profound impression on the grand juries. On February 16 and 17, 1960, they handed down the first seven indictments. Forty companies and eighteen individuals were charged with fixing prices or dividing the market on seven electrical products. Switchgear led the list.[4]

A LEG UP FROM ALLIS-CHALMERS

These initial indictments brought about two major turning points in the investigation. The first was a decision by Allis-Chalmers to play ball

[4] The other six: oil circuit breakers, low-voltage power circuit breakers, insulators, open-fuse cutouts, lightning arresters, bushings. Each indictment covered one product and listed all the corporations and individuals charged with conspiracy to fix prices on that product.

with the government. This move came too late to save L. W. (Shorty) Long, an assistant general manager—he was one of the eighteen already indicted—but the trust busters were willing to go easier on Allis-Chalmers *if* the company came up with something solid. It did. Thousands upon thousands of documents were turned over to the government. Further, the testimony of Vice President J. W. McMullen, and others was so helpful (attorney Edward Mullinix had coached them many hours on the importance of backing up allegations with receipted hotel bills, expense-account items, memorandums, telephone logs, etc.) that a number of new cases were opened up. Only two of those first seven indictments retained their Justice Department classification as "major" cases. To them were added five new major indictments—power transformers, power switching equipment, industrial controls, turbine generators, and steam condensers—culled from thirteen to follow that spring and fall.

The second major turning point came through a decision in March by Chief Federal Judge J. Cullen Ganey, who was to try all the cases. That decision concerned whether the individuals and companies involved in the first seven indictments would be permitted to plead *nolo contendere* (no contest) to the charges. The matter was of vital importance to the companies, which might well be faced by treble-damage suits growing out of the conspiracies. (A G.E. lawyer had advised the Executive Office: "If a criminal case can be disposed of by a *nolo* plea, the prospective damage claimant is given no assistance in advancing a claim; it must be built from the ground up.) The matter was also of great importance to a determined Robert Bicks, who argued that *nolo* pleas would permit the defendants "the luxury of a 'Maybe we did it; maybe we didn't do it' posture. 'Oh, yes, technically before Judge Ganey we admitted this, but you know we weren't guilty. You know we didn't do this.' "

Actually, in the opinion of one veteran antitrust lawyer, everybody in the industry and 99 per cent of the government thought the court would accept *nolos*. Indeed, the Justice Department was so worried about the matter, and so anxious to forfend such a development, that for the first time in the history of the department an attorney general sent a presiding judge an affidavit urging rejection of *nolos*.

"Acceptance of the *nolo* pleas tendered in these cases," William Rogers deposed to Judge Ganey, "would mean [that] . . . insistence on guilty pleas or guilty verdicts would never be appropriate in any antitrust case—no matter the predatory nature of the violation or the widespread adverse consequences to governmental purchasers. This result would neither foster respect for the law nor vindicate the public interest. These interests require, in the cases at bar here, either a trial on the issues or pleas of guilty."

But Judge Ganey didn't need to be impressed with the seriousness of the cases. He ruled that *nolo contendere* pleas were inacceptable (unless, of course, the Justice Department had no objections). The corporations and individuals would either have to plead guilty or stand trial. At the arraignment in April, Allis-Chalmers and its indicted employees promptly pleaded "guilty"; most others, including G.E. and its employees, pleaded "not guilty." They intended at that time to take their chances before a jury, no matter how bleak the prospects.

. . .

G.E. [eventually] pleaded "guilty" to all the major indictments against it, and with the government's consent, *nolo contendere* to the thirteen "minor" ones. The other major companies followed suit. The way thus cleared, judgment was swift in coming. On February 6, executives from every major manufacturer in the entire electrical-equipment industry sat in a crowded courtroom and heard Judge Ganey declare: "What is really at stake here is the survival of the kind of economy under which this country has grown great, the free-enterprise system." Seven executives went off to a Pennsylvania prison; twenty-three others, given suspended jail sentences, were put on probation for five years; and fines totaling nearly $2 million were handed out.

Twenty-nine companies received fines ranging from $437,500 for G.E. down to $7,500 each for Carrier Corp. and Porcelain Insulator Corp. The others, for the record, were Allen-Bradley Co., Allis-Chalmers Manufacturing Co., A. B. Chance Co., Clark Controller Co., Cornell-Dubilier Electric Corp., Cutler-Hammer, Inc., Federal Pacific Electric Co., Foster Wheeler Corp., Hubbard & Co., I–T–E Circuit Breaker Co., Ingersoll-Rand Co., Joslyn Manufacturing & Supply Co., Kuhlman Electric Co., Lapp Insulator Co., McGraw-Edison Co., Moloney Electric Co., Ohio Brass Co., H. K. Porter Co., Sangamo Electric Co., Schwager-Wood Corp., Southern States Equipment Corp., Square D Co., Wagner Electric Corp., Westinghouse Electric Corp., C. H. Wheeler Manufacturing Co., and Worthington Corp.

IS THE LESSON LEARNED?

So ended the incredible affair—a story of cynicism, arrogance, and irresponsibility. Plainly there was an egregious management failure. But there was also a failure to connect ordinary morals and business morals; the men involved apparently figured there was a difference.

The consent decrees now being hammered out by the Justice Department are partial insurance that bid rigging and price fixing won't happen again. Yet consent decrees are only deterrents, not cures. The fact is that the causes which underlay the electrical conspiracies are still as strong as they ever were. Chronic overcapacity continues to exert a strong downward pressure on prices. The industry's price problem—outgrowth of an inability to shift the buyer's attention from price to other selling points like higher quality, better service, improved design—could hardly be worse: many items of electrical equipment are currently selling for less than in the ruinous days of the "white sale." Corporate pressure is stronger than ever on executives, who must struggle to fulfill the conflicting demands of bigger gross sales on the one hand and more profit per dollar of net sales on the other. These are matters that require careful handling if conspiracy is not to take root again in the electrical-equipment industry.

The antitrust laws also confront the largest corporations with a special dilemma: how to compete without falling afoul of Section 2 of the Sherman Act, which makes it unlawful to "monopolize, or attempt to monopolize." It will take plenty of business statesmanship to handle this aspect of the law; one way, of course, is simply to refrain from going after every last piece of business. If G.E. were to drive for 50 per cent of the market, even strong companies like I–T–E Circuit Breaker might be mortally injured.

Has the industry learned any lessons? "One thing I've learned out of all this," said one executive, "is to talk to only one other person, not to go to meetings where there are lots of other people." Many of the defendants *Fortune* interviewed both before and after sentencing looked on themselves as the fall guys of U.S. business. They protested that they should no more be held up to blame than many another American businessman, for conspiracy is just as much "a way of life" in other fields as it was in electrical equipment. "Why pick on us?" was the attitude: "Look at some of those other fellows."

This attitude becomes particularly disturbing when one considers that most of the men who pleaded guilty in Judge Ganey's court (to say nothing of the scores given immunity for testifying before the grand juries) are back at their old positions, holding down key sales and marketing jobs. Only G.E. cleaned house; out went Burens, Burke, Hentschel, and Stehlik, plus ten others, including the heretofore unpunished William S. Ginn. (Although the confessed conspirators at G.E. had been assured that the transfers, demotions, and pay cuts received earlier would be the end of the corporate punishment, this was not the case. In mid-March they were told they could either quit or be fired, and were given anywhere from a half hour to a few days to make their decision.)

DISJOINTED AUTHORITY, DISJOINTED MORALS

But top executive officers of the biggest companies, at least, have come out of their antitrust experience determined upon strict compliance programs and possessed now of enough insight into the workings of a cartel to make those programs effective. Allis-Chalmers has set up a special compliance section. G.E. and Westinghouse, without which cartels in the industry could never endure, are taking more elaborate preventive measures. Both are well aware that any repetition of these conspiracies would lay them open to political pressure for dismemberment; size has special responsibilities in our society, and giants are under a continuous obligation to demonstrate that they have not got so big as to lose control over their far-flung divisions.

This case has focused attention on American business practices as nothing else has in many years. Senator Kefauver says he intends to probe further into the question of conspiracy at the top levels of management. Justice Department investigations are proliferating. Said Attorney General Robert Kennedy: "We are redoubling our efforts to convince anyone so minded that conspiracy as 'a way of life' must mean a short and unhappy one."

The problem for American business does not start and stop with the scofflaws of the electrical industry or with antitrust. Much was made of the fact that G.E. operated under a system of disjointed authority, and this was one reason it got into trouble. A more significant factor, the disjointment of morals, is something for American executives to think about in all aspects of their relations with their companies, each other, and the community.

PART IX

Symbiotic Relationships Between Criminals and Others

Introduction

Generally speaking, the criminal law and many criminological studies pay attention to only one part of the total situational complex called a "crime." That is the part dealt with officially by the machinery of criminal justice or selected out for research and study—the individual offender. The criminal law fixes responsibility and blame for illegal acts upon individual criminals. Occasionally a person is convicted of "aiding," "abetting," or "conspiring in" the crime of another criminal, and in such cases the contribution to the crime of a person other than the principal actor is acknowledged legally. However, the acknowledgment usually takes the form of a separate prosecution of the contributing party. Because the individual offender is seen as a complete and self-contained unit of action, explanations of why he violated the law are likely to be made in terms of his individual qualities, traits, or characteristics. Attention is diverted from consideration of reciprocal relations between his activities and the activities of other persons, including other criminals. This legal perspective is found both in popular modes of thought and in much criminological research. It has been supported by Freudian psychology and other individualistic theories which view behavior as if it were determined by personality traits. Consequently, it has been customary to assume that such conduct as "uncooperativeness," "loyalty," "aggressiveness," "homosexuality," "dishonesty," and "criminality" is the personal property of the individual exhibiting the behavior. Deviant behavior is viewed as a consequence of something "in" the deviant.

But many such behaviors might well be the properties of organizations, subcultures, and groups—not of individuals—as we have seen in preceding Parts. Further, the perpetration of some crimes requires the active cooperation of persons who, in many cases, are not blamed or held legally responsible for playing this role. Part IX deals with such crimes. Each selection is an example of a symbiotic relationship that exists between the principal actors (the criminals) and the supporting players in the drama of crime. In some cases the supporting actors are themselves criminals; in others they are respectable citizens, customers buying a service, and victims.

Not all criminals fit the stereotyped picture of the young, tough, slum dweller. We have seen that some dress in white collars and business suits, some in the expensive garb of the hustler and mackman. Furthermore, some law violators receive assistance from persons ordinarily regarded as the official protectors of legitimate society, such as policemen, politicians, and court officials. The persons giving such assistance are, of course, violating laws themselves. Some criminals, then, look like slum dwellers or businessmen or labor union officials, but others look like policemen, politicians, or civil servants.

For every "corrupter" (criminal) there must be a "corruptee" (criminal). The selections by Poston and Gardiner indicate that most of the crimes committed by corrupt officials are perpetrated in order to facilitate the crimes perpetrated by the corrupters. An example of this is the police official who, for a fee, makes it possible for someone to operate a dice game or a house of prostitution or a bookmaking establishment. The police official in such a case is a criminal in uniform, but the laws he breaks are different from those violated by the gambler, pimp, or bookie. Occasionally, a significant proportion of all the functionaries of the legislative, judicial, and executive branches of a local government derive income from shares of the illegal fees paid by corrupters for the privilege of violating the law. Such was the case in "Wincanton," the fictitious name given by Gardiner to a city in the eastern part of the United States.

But corrupt officials are not always merely minor actors in the crimes in which they are involved, as is the case when they issue "crime-committing licenses" to persons to whom we assign the blame and responsibility for "real" crime. In a second kind of corruption, corrupt officials are the star actors playing the major role in the criminal drama. The politician who charges an under-the-table fee for a building permit or a liquor license is an example of such a criminal. The supporting actors here are the "honest citizens" who bribe the corrupt officials into performing their ordinary duties. The official is responsible for violating the law, but the person paying the fee is also at fault. Gardiner gives several examples of such malfeasance in Wincanton, including the system of charging fees for employment in city hall and demanding kickbacks from the men who supply and service city hall. The selection by the late Senator Robert Kennedy, written while he was Counsel for the Senate Select Committee on Improper Activities in the Labor or Management Field (the McClellan Committee), indicates that some labor union officials are guilty of this same type of malfeasance. A corrupt union official might, for instance, charge a fee for a labor contract that management should be able to acquire through routine legitimate negotiation.

The symbiotic relationship between criminals can also be seen in a third kind of corruption. In this form, a government official conspires with a businessman or labor leader to cheat the citizens represented by the officials. In Wincanton, for example, it was alleged that companies with a franchise to tow away illegally parked cars charged citizens an extra dollar for the service, then paid the dollar to a city official for the privilege of holding the franchise. The persons granting the franchises and the persons holding them were co-stars in this crime. Similarly, the Kennedy selection indicates that perhaps the most frequent kind of labor-management corruption occurs when a dishonest businessman joins with a dishonest union official in order to cheat the businessman's competitors and to exploit rank-and-file union members. The businessman here is not the corrupter of a union official, nor is he the victim of extortion by a corrupt union official. He is a partner in a crime designed to cheat other businessmen and the union members who are "represented" by the union official. The perpetration of this crime requires two actors working closely together. In Senator Kennedy's words, "Labor-management corruption is a crooked two-way street." Significantly, of the 150,000 persons complaining to the McClellan Committee about being victims of labor-management corruption, the vast majority were labor union members, not businessmen or consumers.

In still a fourth kind of corruption, the symbiotic relationship is between a corruptee and a corrupter who is also a victim. The small shopkeeper is sometimes the victim of simple extortion on the part of officials. When a policeman for a fee grants a merchant the privilege of violating the law (the first kind of corruption), he supports the more important criminal role of the merchant, who is the principal actor. But when a policeman threatens the merchant with harrassment until a bribe is paid, the merchant becomes a supporting actor rather than a star. Further, in this case the merchant's role is that of both criminal (briber) and victim.

The symbiotic relationships between a criminal and others need not be a relationship with another criminal. The supporting actors in the perpetration of some crimes are quite respectable and generally honest citizens. The selection from a CBS radio program documents the fact that businessmen try to create good will among their suppliers and customers by buying sex for them, just as the Kennedy selection documents the fact that some businessmen try to create good will among their suppliers (labor union officials) by handing them hard cash. The second is a crime on the part of the businessman; the first need not be. Nevertheless, the businessman who purchases a prostitute's services for a client obviously contributes to the prostitute's crime. The businessman, the client, the prostitute, and the pimp or mackman make up the cast of characters for the crime. Each contributes to the situational complex.

The problem of determining the essentiality of various roles in law violations can be seen in Reiss's selection describing the symbiotic relationship between delinquent boy prostitutes and male homosexuals. This study indicates that the boys are oriented to delinquency but not to homosexuality. They do not define themselves either as homosexuals or as prostitutes. Saying, "I am not a homosexual or a prostitute" to himself enables the boy to define the abnormal as normal. Because of their self-definitions, and because they are minors, the boys are likely to be considered the victims of the homosexual's deviant interest. The homosexual is regarded as the principal actor in a crime in which a boy delinquent is a minor actor. This is not the case according to Reiss. The boys and the homosexuals have equally important parts in the drama. Nevertheless, blame and responsibility for the crime tend to be fixed upon the homosexual, not upon the boy prostitute. Perhaps it is correct to say that some male homosexuals need male prostitutes in the same way that call girls need male customers. At any rate, the two sets of populations under discussion here—"executive types" and female prostitutes, and homosexuals and male prostitutes—understand each other's role, know where to find each other and, in fact, need each other. The existence of customers is a boon to prostitutes, and the existence of prostitutes is a boon to "executive types" and male fellators.

It is difficult to determine who, if anyone, is "victimized" in certain types of criminal enterprises where all of the actors are willing participants. For example, the prostitute commits a crime when she services a customer, but the customers described in the CBS selection are by no means victims. The stockholders of the companies whose executives buy the services of prostitutes in order to influence clients are not victims either, because they indirectly earn money from the increased sales to the client. The stockholders of the buying companies, whose executives are entertained by the prostitutes, are not victims, because their companies need the goods purchased for them. Perhaps the real victim, in the long run, is the consumer, because he must pay a higher price for merchandise if the cost of producing and selling it includes the fees for sexual services. Someone must pay because prostitution is an economic enterprise. But not even consumers are victimized when a man simply pays for a prostitute's services with his own personal funds. These crimes are committed against norms governing "decency" or "morality," not against people.[1]

But some victims contribute so directly to the crime that it is proper to assign to them some degree of the blame and responsibility for the criminal act. In confidence games, victims frequently contribute to their victimization, as the Maurer selection shows. The success of some confidence games depends upon the dishonesty of the "mark," who believes he is allied with a friend in a conspiracy to swindle a third party. Not all confidence games are based on this principle, but confidence men are hard-pressed to believe "you can't beat an honest man," because so many of their victims are trying to cheat someone else. Confidence men also believe that most men have "larceny in their veins," even if they think they are honest. In his selection, Wolfgang uses the term "victim-precipitated homicide" to refer to killings in which victims directly help move criminals toward their crimes. A large number of the victims of murder are would-be-murderers.

It is not essential that we be able to assign blame or responsibility to a person before concluding that his role, or at least his existence, was necessary to the crime perpetrated by a convicted criminal. It is clear that a victim is both in part responsible and in part at fault if he tries to win an argument by resorting to physical violence and then winds up the loser— murdered. The assignment of responsibility and blame to the victim of a car theft who left the key in the ignition of his unlocked car is more difficult, but still possible. Such assignment becomes more questionable when participation in the criminal event is indirect. Nevertheless, indirect participation is a necessary ingredient in some crimes. The selection by Poston indicates that the direct victims of the lotteries called "numbers games" are relatively poor people who each lose a dollar or two a day by taking a 1,000 to 1 chance on picking a number in the hope of getting a 600 to 1 payoff if they are lucky enough to win. Victims or not, these gamblers contribute to crime by demanding the illegal service which the lottery operator has for sale, in the manner of prostitutes' customers. As described in "The Business of Sex," some citizens of Beatty, Nevada, demanded the secondary economic and social benefits brought to the town by prostitutes. Poston goes on to show that the less direct victims of illegal lottery operators are the honest citizens who lose their voice in the democratic process when lottery operators corrupt their elected and appointed officials. While it is difficult to assign blame and responsibility to honest and respectable citizens who wink at illegal gambling, such gambling could not exist without these citizens. Gardiner's selection

[1] See Edwin M. Schur, *Crimes Without Victims* (Englewood Cliffs, N.J.: Prentice-Hall, 1965).

shows that, during the time when Wincanton officials were corrupted by gambling game operators, honest citizens shared gambling profits with the criminals who controlled the gambling. The officials only tolerated what most citizens wanted. Nevertheless, a 1966 survey of the residents of Wincanton revealed that during the period of corruption the citizens' perception of some kind of wrongdoing was quite limited, perception that city officials were protecting illegal enterprises was even more restricted, and knowledge that specific officials were paid off was quite rare. Gardiner observes that a significant number of the residents still want to be able to gamble and to make improper deals with city government, but now they also want to keep out racketeers and corrupt politicians. He concludes that residents of Wincanton fail to see that a community cannot have one without the other.

1 The Numbers Racket

TED POSTON

This is the story of the Pad.

It is the story of a multi-million dollar collaboration between members of the police vice squad and powerful policy barons, many of them with Mafia connections, to control and perpetuate the numbers racket in the five boroughs.

It is the story of day-by-day, week-by-week, month-by-month graft which is so vast as to stagger the imagination of the men actually on the take.

Before we tell the story, let us make one point clear. Not all police officers in the various divisions of the Police Dept. are venal. Most of the men are honest enforcers of the law—even in areas where the policy racket flourishes. But this is not to minimize the effect on department morale where the minority fattens on graft in the open view of honest policemen—and the public.

Veteran police officials told The Post during this newspaper's investigation of the policy racket that there are men who have accumulated so much money from The Pad that they can scarcely find ways to spend it without getting in trouble. There are others who are trying desperately to get out of the department before the bubble bursts, but their superiors won't let them.

And there are others, these officials say, who never rose above the rank

Ted Poston, "The Numbers Racket," *New York Post*, February 29–March 10, 1960. Reprinted with permission of the New York Post. Copyright 1960, N.Y. Post Corp.

of plainclothesman before they retired but now own prosperous businesses in the South and West—businesses set up with their own capital.

What is The Pad?

The Pad is the police-approved list of spots or locations where "official protection" is guaranteed in the six-day-a-week operation of the numbers racket.

A spot might be a grocery store or a tailor shop, a luncheonette or a poolroom. It might be a bank of elevators in a Wall Street office building. It might be an elevator or a newsstand in the Garment Center.

It can be any agreed-upon place where a numbers player can openly place his daily wager without being molested by the cops. It might be even a specified hallway in a Harlem tenement.

A spot or location, however, is not to be confused with a policy bank. A bank may—and many of them do—have a score of spots in just one police precinct. But each spot must be approved by the police for The Pad. And each spot on The Pad must be paid for in cash.

And who shares in fixed fees collected for this "legal" operation of an illegal racket? The payoffs are not limited to vice squad plainclothesmen assigned to the suppression of vice and gambling but are distributed regularly to sergeants, lieutenants, captains and, in many cases, to some of their superiors.

This is how the cash flows:

The cop on the beat—low man on the totem pole—collects from each "spot" on The Pad in his area daily. There are three daily shifts; each cop on each shift makes his own collection.

The two men in the squad car whose patrol includes The Pad collect their "blanket payment" weekly. This frees them from the task of daily collection.

The men on the take in the precincts, the divisions, the borough commands and the special squads, on up to officials in Police Headquarters itself, receive their share of the payoffs from their own special pick-up men once each month.

To operate on a "Full Pad"—that is, to buy protection from the bottom to the top—costs each spot, even if it's just a tenement hallway, about $2500 a month. The tariff is scaled proportionately higher for those spots and locations where the daily play is greater.

And here is why veteran police officials call the graft take "astronomical":

The Post investigation of just 90 "approved" spots in a single section of Harlem indicated that specified payments to the police involved exceeded $220,000 a month, or an annual take of more than $2,500,000.

"But you must remember," one official expert told The Post, "that, contrary to popular belief, the numbers play in Harlem comprises only a fraction of the daily play in all boroughs. You have to multiply the Harlem take many times to get anywhere near the real figure for the 'ice' paid out by policy.

"There are 80 precincts in New York City, and in my experience in all five boroughs, I have not found a single one in which a Pad for policy isn't maintained in one form or another.

"Of course, Harlem is the happy-hunting-ground for the boys who get greedy. They can get their regular take from the operators of The Pad and their shakedown from some of the small fry for an additional taste-something-extra-without risking too much of a squawk."

The Post began digging into the numbers game in January after Rep. Adam Clayton Powell Jr. charged that the police in Harlem were running Negro bankers out of business and turning the game over to whites—mainly Italians, although Powell also spoke of Jewish policy racketeers in one speech from his Harlem pulpit.

The inquiry spread to all sections of the city as it became apparent that Harlem furnished only a fraction of the astounding sums bet daily on a sucker's game.

The Post team established that the gross numbers business written every day on the waterfront—in Manhattan, in Brooklyn, on Staten Island—exceeds Harlem's "action" on its best days. They also found that it was easier to "get down on the figure" in any section of the Garment Center at that moment than it was to get similar action on, say, Lenox Av. (*The heat happened to be on uptown, of course, as a result of Powell's blasts at the police from his pulpit and on the floor of Congress.*)

In staid Wall St., few people had to walk further than a designated elevator or a newsstand in his building or around the corner to make a daily bet. Such big numbers bets are placed in the financial district that the total play there appears to exceed the entire take in the Bedford-Stuyvesant section of Brooklyn.

The Bronx—once the stamping ground of the late Dutch Schultz—was found to be organized into a tightly closed duchy which probably would have made the Dutchman himself proud.

Most New Yorkers are vaguely familiar with the numbers game, certainly one of the simplest forms of mass gambling ever devised.

The bettor takes a 1,000-to-one chance that he can pick a set of three digits anywhere between 000 and 999 which will appear in an agreed-upon tabulation at a race track, clearing house, or elsewhere. If he wins, the most he can get is 600-to-one (really 599 to one, since the original wager is included in the pay-off). Some banks pay as little as 300-to-one in the case of certain numbers which the policy operators consider "hot" at a given time.

The general conception (or misconception) is that numbers racket is a harmless little game dreamed up in Harlem and played only by poor people who hope to cash 600-to-one bets on pennies and nickels filched from their relief allotments. The newspapers down through the years have fortified this conception by calling the game "poor man's policy," "the welfare client's Wall St.," "the dream of the destitute" or "the opiate of the paupers."

Nothing could be further from today's truth. And no one knows it better than those Vice Squad cops who profit by it.

For more than a quarter of a century, the police brass has been "estimating" that New Yorkers bet an average of $100,000,000 a year on the numbers. That figure may have been valid back in 1935; the gross at that time did contain a lot of penny, nickel and dime bets on the daily lottery.

But those days are gone forever.

Today's numbers bets usually begin at a quarter. A flat, $1 bet is no longer unusual. Regular $10 bets are accepted by some collectors, and the sky is the limit where the larger banks are concerned.

(*Of course, a long-time addict can get down a nickel or dime bet, or even a series of bets for pennies, but most banks' regular operators scorn such wagers whenever possible.*)

One authoritative source, who has watched the phenomenal growth of the game over the past quarter century, said frankly:

"Nobody can really know how much money is bet on the numbers yearly, not even the big operators or the police themselves.

"But it is my opinion that the annual take in the five boroughs here is closer to a quarter billion dollars than to the $100,000,000 figure so commonly used."

He cited reasons for his conclusion.

"Back in 1935," he recalled, "there was only one official number for all boroughs. It was based then, as now, on the three figures derived from the total parimutuel bets on the third, fifth and seventh races at a specified race track (Hialeah now).

"But in Brooklyn, for instance, the player can bet on two sets of numbers every day—the usual one based on the third, fifth and seventh races, and a brand new number based on the total parimutuel handle at the track that same day."

This Post informant cited another reason why he believed that the daily take from numbers had doubled or even tripled during recent years.

"In the old days," he said, "there was only the 'day number' available. I mean that the wagers were only paid off on races run during the daytime. Now there is also a 'night' number for a large part of the year.

"I think this is almost exclusively a New York development, but night numbers are taken daily for the full run of the trotting races at Yonkers and Roosevelt Raceways.

"Again, no one except the policy banks which book the night number can know how much is wagered, but the night numbers, for the months they run, probably take in almost as much as the day game took in in 1935."

There is also a variation of the numbers game which has added to the "racket's" gross. This innovation, first popular around 1940, is called Single Action and permits the player to make individual bets on each of the three separate digits composing that day's full figure.

Say, for instance, that the player has already made his bets for the day on the number 671. He then can make Single Action bets—the payoff is 8-to-1—that the first number that day will be 6 or the second number will be 7 or the third will be 1.

Single Action is most popular in areas of Negro and Puerto Rican concentration and is often banked and operated by the runners and collectors in the employ of the big policy banks.

One former policy banker, forced out of business by the rising costs of The Pad, operated recently on Single Action alone. He estimated that Single Action, controlled mainly by Negroes, grosses between $15,000,000 and $25,000,000 a year.

"The big white banks haven't moved in on Single Action," he said, "mainly because it's too complicated to handle and they're afraid they might get cheated. There's nothing too complicated about it for the cops, though. Nobody cheats them. You've got to get on The Pad to stay in business. And if the bite gets so big it drives you out of business, that's just too bad for you."

"If you write $1,000 worth of numbers a day," a recently retired policy operator said bitterly, "then the first 12 days of the month you work for the cops.

"The cops are the only ones who are guaranteed to make their taste (profit, that is) no matter what happens."

The operator was discussing The Pad, the list of spots and locations in all five boroughs sanctioned by corrupt policemen, where the mobs behind the numbers racket are permitted to operate wide open six days a week in return for specified payoffs totaling millions upon millions of dollars a year.

Here, in detail for the first time, is what policy operators must pay crooked cops to operate just one "full open spot"—that is, an agreed-upon location where numbers bets may be handled without police molestation:

$300 a month to a squad connected with high-echelon officialdom, with $25 of this going to the "bag man," who is usually a retired cop like ex-Sgt. Joseph Luberda.

$300 a month to the group connected with the next highest official, again with $25 going to the "bag man."

$300 a month to the ranking squad in the department hierarchy. This sum may often be picked up by a member of the squad, obviating the $25 cut for a "bag man."

$300 a month to a group operating out of a top office, based on geographical location.

$350 to $615 a month to a smaller geographic subdivision office.

The $350 figure is the basic sum for all such groups in the city, but the $615 figure was cited as the current Pad in one group which covers several precincts.

Police operating from the smaller subdivision, which now has some 30-odd plainclothesmen, originally set their price at $350 monthly also. But the bite has gone up twice—first to $470 and then to $615 a month because of policy scandals and a wholesale transfer of members of the old squad in one of Police Commissioner Stephen Kennedy's periodic shakeups.

But back to the monthly payments for the operation of a "spot," which, not to be confused with a policy bank, may be merely a Brooklyn grocery store, a Staten Island tailor shop, a Wall Street newsstand, a Garment Center elevator, or even an agreed-upon hallway in a Harlem apartment.

To be on The Pad for a "full open spot," the operators must also pay, on top of what is listed above:

$250 a month to be divided among detectives in the precinct where the spot is located.

$10 a month for each of the precinct lieutenants involved.

$100 a month to be split among the racket precinct sergeants.

If a precinct captain must be paid, the sum varies, but it is usually about $75 per month per spot. And from this sum, the captain must take care of his own "bag man" and a precinct warrant officer.

But this doesn't end the payments. For each spot—and some banks have as many as 20 spots or more in a single precinct—the cops also collect $35 a week to be split between the two patrolmen assigned to the squad cars on the beat. These men pick up their own take at a specified place in person weekly.

The final "official" payment for The Pad goes to the cop on the beat.

It is $2 a day, accepted personally, and paid to each of the beat cops on the three shifts from Monday through Saturday. Thus, a cop with only a half dozen spots on his beat is assured of at least $12 each day in "legal payments."

One policy operator, who discussed The Pad, was asked why the cop on the beat had to be paid.

"He knows you are on The Pad," the reporter said, "and he knows his superiors may raise hell if he arrests you. So why pay?"

The policy man smiles at the question.

"Of course he knows he can't arrest me," he said, "and I know it too. But he doesn't have to. All he needs to do is just stand in front of my spot and nobody is going to come in and play any numbers as long as a uniformed cop is standing out front.

"So you just slip him his two bucks and send him on his way. After all, he's got to visit other spots on his beat for his taste also. You don't want to be a bad fellow by delaying this messenger on the swift completion of his appointed rounds."

It was not easy to flush out the exact details of The Pad, although Post reporters learned about it shortly after Rep. Adam Clayton Powell charged that Harlem police were turning the Negro bankers' business over to whites —mainly Italians.

The 10-week investigation started in Harlem but quickly extended to all five boroughs since even preliminary study showed that the numbers game, like the organized graft and corruption which it spawned, was not just a Harlem pastime but citywide.

The existence of The Pad was well known throughout the multi-million-dollar industry. Even before Joseph Luberda, the retired cop, was picked up drunk with The Pad for one section of Harlem, everyone in the industry knew that such lists existed.

And Luberda, now serving a contempt term in prison for refusing to name the police squads and officials for whom he had been collecting, admitted that much when asked before the grand jury:

"In other words, police officers would go around to different places and visit these people who are operating these gambling places and collect money in return for their refraining from interfering with their operations?"

"Yes, sir," said Luberda, "could be."

But few known policy operators in Harlem or elsewhere were willing to go into details on the actual Pad in the early days of The Post's investigation.

Even men who had spent their lives in the game only to be reduced from bankers to controllers and even down to runners because of increasing vice squad demands were reluctant to discuss The Pad.

Similarly, HONEST members of the Police Dept.—and the vast majority on the force have little opportunity to get on The Pad—would admit the existence of the organized graft and corruption involving the numbers racket, but would give no details.

One police official said frankly:

"If you knew the actual amount of money involved, you wouldn't believe it. And even if you believed it, The Post wouldn't dare print it. The thing is just that big."

One long-time former banker whose bank has been taken over by the East Side Harlem mob, which now dominates the citywide game, asked a reporter half-jokingly:

"You want to be killed?"

Then, more soberly, he remarked: "Look, this thing is much bigger than you think. Anybody who talks about it too much is out of business for good.

And I'm too old to learn anything else now."

As The Post team continued digging, however, it became obvious that the police too had learned of their inquiries.

Two men who had discussed the payoffs quite frankly with reporters suddenly decided to leave town—one on an extended Caribbean vacation. A former banker who now has a legitimate business was called in by a member of a vice squad inspector's staff and questioned about the passing presence of a Post reporter in his establishment.

"If any of you fellows go around shooting off your mouth," he was told, "we are going to close down the whole operation."

The suspected men reportedly retorted: "and then what will *you* do? Starve to death?"

A few days after this incident, a source close to an influential police official called one Post reporter to inform him that his home telephone had been tapped.

"There's nothing you can do about it, but just be careful," he said. "It's not a legal tap and nobody in the department or the Telephone Company will admit that it exists, no matter how much hell The Post might raise about it. But the boys know what you are doing and they want to know how much you know."

The Post reporters were able to obtain Pads first from one source in one borough and then from two other sources in another and the payoff lists checked in all major details.

Once confronted with the actual schedule of police-set payments, several policy operators confirmed the figures. Then well-informed sources familiar with the department not only confirmed the "official" Pad but filled in other details of the vice squad's lucrative participation in the rich numbers game.

A police-connected source, who had never denied the existence of The Pad but had refused to discuss its operations until The Post obtained the "official" list of graft payments from other sources, explained how the money is distributed to members of the ring.

"Beginning in the precinct," he said, "and extending on up the line through the special squads, the take is divided on the basis of shares. The plainsclothesmen involved each get the basic share with two or more shares being given monthly to their superiors.

"Take the —— Division, for instance, where the monthly take is listed at $615 per spot. There are some 30 plainclothesmen there now and each gets a basic share of $15 per spot. The lieutenants' share comes to $25.

"Now take the —— Division, which covers three precincts, has 50 spots on its pad—and you and I both know that there are far more than 50 spots involved in that area. But take 50 spots as an example. That means that each of the plainclothesmen who are on the take there gets $750 each a month for these 50 spots alone and the lieutenants involved are in for $1,250 each."

The source, stressing the point that not all policemen share in the policy graft ring, added:

"I'm not saying that every man in the —— Division is in on The Pad. But that makes little difference to the operators of the approved spots. The pay-off must be made on the basis of the personnel assigned to the division, to the precinct and to the special squads above them. How it is split up in the squad is sometimes another matter."

Another source familiar with another borough furnished further light on the matter as he described "pay day" in one station house.

"I had gone there on a matter not connected in any way with vice or gambling. I had to see a plainclothesman who once had been assigned to my precinct and who had some information about a suspect in a burglary ring.

"We were sitting there in the squad room discussing my case when a fellow pushed open the door and yelled 'pay day!' And everybody stopped what they were doing as this fellow went around the room calling out each name and taking sealed envelopes from a box under his arm.

"The plainclothesman with whom I was talking broke off our conversation and took his envelope. He split it open right in front of me and started counting the crisp sheaf of $10 and $20 bills. I stopped counting when he passed $180. But he finally finished his count and resumed our conversation as if nothing had happened."

The source added:

"Of course this happened several years ago. I don't think they are quite as open about it now, especially when the heat is on. The fact is, the take has grown so large now that they are forced to take more precautions, for they all know that a real bad break can eventually blow them and the whole department sky high."

One retired banker—and most of them claim retirement in any discussion of the racket—reinforced the suggestion that the police are not always honest with The Pad.

"For several months when I was active," he recalled, "they had me down for 31 men in the Division office. One of the plainclothesmen involved was a good friend of mine. He finally felt that they were cheating him on his share, so he came and told me the truth.

"There were really only 26 men on my Pad for that Division, and either the boss or the bag man had been taking me every month for an extra $75 a spot, and I had several going then.

"I tried to see the brass about it but that was no dice. The big guys always avoid any kind of contact which would tip their hands. But the next time the bag man came around, I squawked to him. He denied that he was ringing in 5 extra shares a spot on my Pad but the next month he only picked up for 26 men."

Other policy operators pointed out that only the real big banks can afford the "full open spot" payments for their various spots because of the amount of police graft involved. One Harlem banker, also claiming retirement, complained:

"I don't think that there has been a Negro banker—what few there are of us left—on a full Pad for the last few years.

"Most of us are down from the beat cop on through the precinct, and in some cases, most cases I would say, for the Division also.

"I'm told you can still make a living at this—if you don't get too big, although you are still liable to raids by all of the guys on the special squads above the Division level if they are not getting their taste.

"There was a time when you could make a personal Pad with individual members of these squads, but the big boys cut that out. Now all contracts must be made with the squad itself in behalf of all those involved and any plainclothesman making a personal deal will find himself busted to uniform in a minute.

"But the real danger in being on only a partial Pad is that you can't afford to expand too much. If the local cops find you've got a real good business, they'll try to force you to give the business to one of the East Side mob."

This former banker, a Negro, was reminded of Powell's charge that the cops were hounding Negro bankers while protecting the Italian big shots.

"There's some truth in what he says," the source observed, "but I don't think it's just racial. You see, these cops know that the East Side mob can afford a full open Pad for each of their spots. And in many cases the banks will collect the pay-off in a lump sum and give it in bulk to the pay-off men.

"No, I don't think it's all racial. From the cop's point of view, it's just more efficient business."

One inevitable result of the operation of The Pad—the multi-million-dollar police-protection set-up in the numbers game—has been to give major control of the policy racket to the underworld here.

Call them what you like—the East Harlem Mob, the Syndicate, the Mafia—The Post's investigation of policy showed that these are the people who now control what once was a comparatively harmless, penny-ante lottery and is now a major racket.

Today, for the first time in the 150 years that it has existed here in one form or another, the numbers game is now a means as well as an end.

The end is obvious—the once-fabulous profits reaped by numbers bankers from suckers who take a 1,000 to 1 chance on picking a number in the hope of getting a 600 to 1 payoff if they're lucky enough to win.

The profits are still there but the rigidly organized graft of dishonest vice squad policemen has made a heavy dent in the take enjoyed by the policy banks.

The means became equally obvious when Post reporters began a two-month investigation of the numbers game here in the wake of Rep. Adam Clayton Powell's charges that Negro numbers bankers were being forced out of the game by the police so that whites—mainly Italians—could take over.

For the numbers industry—with its thousands of collectors, hundreds of controllers and other thousands of full and part time employees—provides an already established apparatus for other uses by unscrupulous racket bosses.

Here is what the Brooklyn Grand Jury reported last year after its investigation of gambling and police corruption:

"If you scratch the professional operator of gambling ventures you will find the narcotics peddler, the loan shark, the dice game operator, the murderer.

"Brooklyn has been the scene of a number of unsolved gangland homicides over the past few years. Almost every one of those killings is involved with gambling ventures in one form or another.

"In one case where seven leading narcotics dealers were convicted in Kings County last year, six were actively engaged in gambling activities, including bookmaking and policy, which they used as the source of funds for their deadly trade in narcotics."

A veteran numbers banker who insisted on using an obviously fictitious name told The Post a story which vividly illustrated the Grand Jury's findings.

"It happened around Christmas a year or so ago," this man said. "I was paid up on The Pad (the list of police-protected policy spots) and would've been in good shape if all the cops on The Pad, past and present, hadn't doubled back for a 'Christmas taste.' I had to shell out.

"And then, just before New Year's, I get hit heavy by some of my biggest players. I was out about $18,000 and I just couldn't raise that kind of money. Then the bag man for one of the special squads set up a meet for me with the East Harlem boys. He said they'd let me have the money until I got back on my feet.

"But when we finally had our meet, I found they wanted something in return. They said that if I would use my setup to handle about $18,000 worth of hoss (heroin) that I wouldn't even have to pay any interest on the $18,000 they were lending me.

"Well, I wasn't going to get mixed up in that kind of rap this late in life. So I just walked out. They didn't like it a bit, and the bag man told me later I was a fool. Of course, they took over my bank anyhow—and they've still got it."

Unfortunately, other bankers pressed to the wall by limited capital and mounting vice squad graft demands, evidently have taken the other road. During its investigation, The Post found strong indications that at least one major "independent" bank in Manhattan is closely allied with the narcotics trade, as is another in Brooklyn and at least two in The Bronx.

The connection is becoming increasingly evident as narcotic agents more frequently find themselves tracking down dope peddling suspects only to find them also employed in numbers operations.

The Syndicate, or Mafia, has long been active in the numbers game on the waterfront, but policy then was only an adjunct to such other activities as loan sharking and other waterfront rackets.

It was not until 1949 or so that the late Albert Anastasia, chief assassin of Murder, Inc., decided to expand from the waterfront and take over the policy game in other profitable areas.

First to feel the weight of the new decision was Louis Weber, Brooklyn's then admitted policy king and a pal of James Moran, Mayor O'Dwyer's right-hand man and a political power in his own right in Kings County.

One night in 1949, Weber received a visit in a South Brooklyn tavern from Anastasia and Frank (Frankie Shots) Abbatemarco, who had handled the policy operation for Anastasia's syndicate on the Brooklyn and Staten Island waterfronts.

The conversation was short and to the point. Weber was out; Frankie Shots was taking over.

Weber was a man of standing. He had a vice squad payroll nearing that of Harry Gross' still-to-be-exposed bookmaking empire. He had defied a long list of District Attorneys (when defiance was necessary) and could depend on the immense political power of Moran in the O'Dwyer Administration.

But Weber knew this was all to no avail when the Syndicate decided to move in. So he gave up a life-long policy empire in Brooklyn without an argument and fled to West Harlem to try to re-establish himself. He never attained his former eminence.

For the next decade, Frankie Shots, a boastful, high-living thug, became Brooklyn's biggest policy operator, although the real power for the borough's operation was held by Carmine Lombardozzi, a representative of the East Harlem mob which even then was consolidating its spreading policy power.

Lombardozzi, soft-spoken and unobtrusive, was only faintly known to the public until his participation in the 1957 underworld conclave at Apalachin put him on the front pages.

Brooklyn underworld sources said that Lombardozzi was demoted after Apalachin, presumably for not being diligent in pushing the Syndicate to take over all the major policy banks in Brooklyn, and Mike Miranda, still a major policy figure in Brooklyn, took over his behind-the-scenes role.

(Frankie Shots, loud-mouthed to the end, wasn't as lucky as Lombardozzi. Suspected of holding out on the Syndicate, he was mowed down in Brooklyn by two gunmen on Nov. 4, 1959 in the very same tavern where Louis Weber had been handed his walking papers.)

The Syndicate's plan, duplicated in other boroughs, was quite simple. The major banks were swept up by the mob, with all direction coming from the East Harlem empire of Vito Genovese, Anthony (Fat Tony) Salerno, Trigger Mike Coppola and Joseph (Joe Stretch) Stracci.

The remaining "independent" banks, run mainly by veteran Negro and Puerto Rican bankers, were to be supervised by the Syndicate at a flat fee of 1 per cent of the gross take.

Each "independent" bank had to permit a Syndicate representative to check its "ribbon" (the daily adding machine tabulation of the total play) so that the Syndicate could be assured of its 1 per cent "off the top."

At the same time, the mob undertook to put all policy spots and locations on The Pad—the vice squad's list of police-protected places.

The conquest of Brooklyn by the Syndicate was almost complete by early 1958 when District Attorney Edward Silver began a secret two-month investigation which in April of that year led to the smashing of the $5,000,000 bank of Angel F. Calder, the city's largest Puerto Rican policy banker. The raid also revealed an open connection between Calder's bank and what Silver called "the Manhattan Syndicate."

Working so quietly that even the clerical staff in his office didn't know when he planned to act, Silver assembled 82 detectives and picked plain-clothesmen an April 1, 1958, and made a series of simultaneous mass raids which netted Calder and 67 of his associates, along with policy paraphernalia, the day's play and several thousand dollars in cash.

The prize catch of the raid proved to be an obscure East Side mobster, Emannuel (Nappy) Frazetta, 40, of 160 Mott St. Frazetta was seized in the basement of a three-story brownstone at 693 Lafayette St. in Bedford-Stuyvesant, which Silver said was the temporary headquarters of Calder's main bank. The raiders found Frazetta holding the "ribbon" for the day's policy play and surmised that he was checking for the Syndicate to guarantee its 1 per cent take.

Frazetta would only admit that he was "a messenger" sent over from Manhattan to "pick up something" to turn over to "somebody" in a subway.

Urbano (Benny) DeMucci, 41, seized while checking the take there at a Calder annex, also was suspected to be a Syndicate representative.

Calder himself, along with his son, Angelo, and his brother, Julio (One-Eyed Red) Calder, was charged with contriving a lottery—a felony—and released on $25,000 bail each.

Forty-four other persons seized among the 68 with the Calders were also booked and released on bail. Most of them went directly back into business.

On April 9, just eight days after the big April Fool's Day raid, Silver's Rackets Bureau detectives struck again—in the absence of any action by the police who regularly covered the area.

The DA's men seized Otis Spain Jr., of 110 Cambridge Pl. and charged him with possession of 22 numbers slips containing 1,800 plays. One of the 45 booked in the big Brooklyn raid, Spain had been plying his trade industriously since his release on bail.

With Spain in custody, the Rackets Bureau detectives struck again that night at 924 Lafayette St., just three blocks from the basement at 693 Lafayette where Calder's main bank had been smashed.

The raiders acted on information that 20 of Calder's controllers and runners were assembled there to set up a new operation, but apparently the policy boys had been tipped by their own sources, for the DA's squad found just two men there.

But the raid was not in vain. One of the two men turned out to be the aforementioned Angel Calder himself, a durable veteran of 22 years in the business and the other was Fitz Sealy, 70, another old time policy operator.

The 45 men seized in the Calder ring are still awaiting trial after two years.

Silver and Asst. DA Koota told The Post this week that the trial was being held up awaiting clarification of a 1957 U. S. Supreme Court decision which indicated that evidence obtained by wire-tapping might not be admissible in local courts.

One year after the raid, the State Court of Appeals upheld the use of wiretap evidence in state courts, but Koota pointed out that the Court of Appeals did not rule on the legality of wire-tapping under Section 605 of the Federal Communications Act, on which the Supreme Court based its ruling.

"We are still concerned," Koota said, "about the possibility of having a policeman admit to an act which the U. S. Supreme Court has held to be illegal. Such testimony by a policeman might expose him to possible indictment by a Federal Grand Jury."

Meanwhile, it can be assumed that the Calder bank is back in business as usual—probably trying to lay up a reserve for the day when the court showdown finally comes and Silver—as he expects—sends most of the 45 to jail.

But a Brooklyn Negro policy banker, whose operation was once closely associated with that of Calder, predicted that there wouldn't be much reserve left.

"The only boys who made anything out of the Calder business," he said, "are the vice squad boys on The Pad. They were around the day after the first raid to say that everybody's payments had to go up because 'We're taking more chances now.' And I'll be damned if they didn't try to get a second hike just 8 days later when Calder was picked up again.

"So the old man will be lucky if he can keep his head above water until the trial comes up. I doubt if they'll leave him much more than that."

2 Gambling and Political Corruption

JOHN A. GARDINER
With the assistance of DAVID J. OLSON

This study focuses upon the politics of vice and corruption in a town we have chosen to call Wincanton, U.S.A.[1] Although the facts and events of this report are true, every attempt has been made to hide the identity of actual people by the use of fictitious names, descriptions and dates.

Following a brief description of the people of Wincanton and the structure of its government and law enforcement agencies, a section outlines

Reprinted from John A. Gardiner, with the assistance of David J. Olson, "Wincanton: The Politics of Corruption," *Task Force Report: Organized Crime*, Annotations and Consultants' Papers, Task Force on Organized Crime—The President's Commission on Law Enforcement and Administration of Justice (Washington: Government Printing Office, 1967), Appendix B, pp. 61–79.

[1] This study, part of a larger investigation of the politics of law enforcement and corruption, was financed by a grant from the Russell Sage Foundation. All responsibility for the contents of this report remains with the senior author. The authors wish gratefully to acknowledge the assistance of the people and officials of Wincanton who will, at their request, remain anonymous. The authors wish particularly to acknowledge the assistance of the newspapers of Wincanton; Prof. Harry Sharp and the staff of the Wisconsin Survey Research Laboratory; Henry S. Ruth, Jr., Lloyd E. Ohlin, and Charles H. Rogovin of the President's Commission on Law Enforcement and Administration of Justice; and many National, State, and local law enforcement personnel. The authors shared equally in the research upon which this report is based; because of the teaching duties of Mr. Olson, Mr. Gardiner assumed the primary role in writing this report. Joel Margolis and Keith Billingsley, graduate students in the Department of Political Science, University of Wisconsin, assisted in the preparation of the data used in this report.

the structure of the Wincanton gambling syndicate and the system of protection under which it operated. A second section looks at the corrupt activities of Wincanton officials apart from the protection of vice and gambling.

The latter part of this report considers gambling and corruption as social forces and as political issues. First, they are analyzed in terms of their functions in the community—satisfying social and psychological needs declared by the State to be improper; supplementing the income of the participants, including underpaid city officials and policemen, and of related legitimate businesses; providing speed and certainty in the transaction of municipal business. Second, popular attitudes toward gambling and corruption are studied, as manifested in both local elections and a survey of a cross-section of the city's population. Finally, an attempt will be made to explain why Wincanton, more than other cities, has had this marked history of law-breaking and official malfeasance, and several suggestions will be made regarding legal changes that might make its continuation more difficult.

WINCANTON

In general, Wincanton represents a city that has toyed with the problem of corruption for many years. No mayor in the history of the city of Wincanton has ever succeeded himself in office. Some mayors have been corrupt and have allowed the city to become a wide-open center for gambling and prostitution; Wincanton voters have regularly rejected those corrupt mayors who dared to seek reelection. Some mayors have been scrupulously honest and have closed down all vice operations in the city; these men have been generally disliked for being too straitlaced. Other mayors, fearing one form of resentment or the other, have chosen quietly to retire from public life. The questions of official corruption and policy toward vice and gambling, it seems, have been paramount issues in Wincanton elections since the days of Prohibition. Any mayor who is known to be controlled by the gambling syndicates will lose office, but so will any mayor who tries completely to clean up the city. The people of Wincanton apparently want both easily accessible gambling and freedom from racket domination.

Probably more than most cities in the United States, Wincanton has known a high degree of gambling, vice (sexual immorality, including prostitution), and corruption (official malfeasance, misfeasance and nonfeasance of duties). With the exception of two reform administrations, one in the early 1950's and the one elected in the early 1960's, Wincanton has been wide open since the 1920's. Bookies taking bets on horses took in several millions of dollars each year. With writers at most newsstands, cigar counters, and corner grocery stores, a numbers bank did an annual business in excess of $1,300,000 during some years. Over 200 pinball machines, equipped to pay off like slot machines, bore $250 Federal gambling stamps. A high stakes dice game attracted professional gamblers from more than 100 miles away; $25,000 was found on the table during one Federal raid. For a short period of time in the 1950's (until raided by U.S. Treasury Department agents), a still, capable of manufacturing $4 million in illegal alcohol each year, operated on the banks of the Wincanton River. Finally, prostitution flourished openly in the city, with at least 5 large houses (about 10 girls apiece) and countless smaller houses catering to men from a large portion of the State.

As in all cities in which gambling and vice had flourished openly, these illegal activities were protected by local officials. Mayors, police chiefs, and many lesser officials were on the payroll of the gambling syndicate, while others received periodic "gifts" or aid during political campaigns. A number of Wincanton officials added to their revenue from the syndicate by extorting kickbacks on the sale or purchase of city equipment or by selling licenses, permits, zoning variances, etc. As the city officials made possible the operations of the racketeers, so frequently the racketeers facilitated the corrupt endeavors of officials by providing liaison men to arrange the deals or "enforcers" to insure that the deals were carried out.

· · ·

To understand law enforcement in Wincanton, it is necessary to look at the activities of local, county, State, and Federal agencies. State law requires that each mayor select his police chief and officers "from the force" and "exercise a constant supervision and control over their conduct." Applicants for the police force are chosen on the basis of a civil service examination and have tenure "during good behavior," but promotions and demotions are entirely at the discretion of the mayor and council. Each new administration in Wincanton has made wholesale changes in police ranks—patrolmen have been named chief, and former chiefs have been reduced to walking a beat. (When one period of reform came to an end in the mid-1950's, the incoming mayor summoned the old chief into his office. "You can stay on as an officer," the mayor said, "but you'll have to go along with my policies regarding gambling." "Mr. Mayor," the chief said, "I'm going to keep on arresting gamblers no matter where you put me." The mayor assigned the former chief to the position of "Keeper of the Lockup," permanently stationed in the basement of police headquarters.) Promotions must be made from within the department. This policy has continued even though the present reform mayor created the post of police commissioner and brought in an outsider to take command. For cities of its size, Wincanton police salaries have been quite low—the top pay for patrolmen was $4,856—in the lowest quartile of middle-sized cities in the Nation. Since 1964 the commissioner has received $10,200 and patrolmen $5,400 each year.

While the police department is the prime law enforcement agency within Wincanton, it receives help (and occasional embarrassment) from other groups. Three county detectives work under the district attorney, primarily in rural parts of Alsace County, but they are occasionally called upon to assist in city investigations. The State Police, working out of a barracks in suburban Wincanton Hills, have generally taken a "hands off" or "local option" attitude toward city crime, working only in rural areas unless invited into a city by the mayor, district attorney, or county judge. Reform mayors have welcomed the superior manpower and investigative powers of the State officers; corrupt mayors have usually been able to thumb their noses at State policemen trying to uncover Wincanton gambling. Agents of the State's Alcoholic Beverages Commission suffer from no such limitations and enter Wincanton at will in search of liquor violations. They have seldom been a serious threat to Wincanton corruption, however, since their numbers are quite limited (and thus the agents are dependent upon the local police for information and assistance in making arrests). Their mandate extends to gambling and prostitution only when encountered in the course of a liquor investigation.

Under most circumstances, the operative level of law enforcement in Wincanton has been set by local political decisions, and the local police (acting under instructions from the mayor) have been able to determine whether or not Wincanton should have open gambling and prostitution. The State Police, with their "hands off" policy, have simply reenforced the local decision. From time to time, however, Federal agencies have become interested in conditions in Wincanton and, as will be seen throughout this study, have played as important a role as the local police in cleaning up the city. Internal Revenue Service agents have succeeded in prosecuting Wincanton gamblers for failure to hold gambling occupation stamps, pay the special excise taxes on gambling receipts, or report income. Federal Bureau of Investigation agents have acted against violations of the Federal laws against extortion and interstate gambling. Finally, special attorneys from the Organized Crime and Racketeering Section of the Justice Department were able to convict leading members of the syndicate controlling Wincanton gambling. While Federal prosecutions in Wincanton have often been spectacular, it should also be noted that they have been somewhat sporadic and limited in scope. The Internal Revenue Service, for example, was quite successful in seizing gaming devices and gamblers lacking the Federal gambling occupation stamps, but it was helpless after Wincantonites began to purchase the stamps, since local officials refused to prosecute them for violations of the State antigambling laws.

The court system in Wincanton, as in all cities in the State, still has many of the 18th century features which have been rejected in other States. At the lowest level, elected magistrates (without legal training) hear petty civil and criminal cases in each ward of the city. The magistrates also issue warrants and decide whether persons arrested by the police shall be held for trial. Magistrates are paid only by fees, usually at the expense of convicted defendants. All serious criminal cases, and all contested petty cases, are tried in the county court. The three judges of the Alsace County court are elected (on a partisan ballot) for 10-year terms, and receive an annual salary of $25,000.

GAMBLING AND CORRUPTION: THE INSIDERS

The history of Wincanton gambling and corruption since World War II centers around the career of Irving Stern. Stern is an immigrant who came to the United States and settled in Wincanton at the turn of the century. He started as a fruit peddler, but when Prohibition came along, Stern became a bootlegger for Heinz Glickman, then the beer baron of the State. When Glickman was murdered in the waning days of Prohibition, Stern took over Glickman's business and continued to sell untaxed liquor after repeal of Prohibition in 1933. Several times during the 1930's, Stern was convicted in Federal court on liquor charges and spent over a year in Federal prison.

Around 1940, Stern announced to the world that he had reformed and went into his family's wholesale produce business. While Stern was in fact leaving the bootlegging trade, he was also moving into the field of gambling, for even at that time Wincanton had a "wide-open" reputation, and the police were ignoring gamblers. With the technical assistance of his bootlegging friends, Stern started with a numbers bank and soon added horse betting, a dice game, and slot machines to his organization. . . .

. . .

. . . [I]n the early 1950's, Irv Stern was able to establish a centralized empire in which he alone determined which rackets would operate and who would operate them (he never, it might be noted, permitted narcotics traffic in the city while he controlled it). What were the bases of his control within the criminal world? Basically, they were three: First, as a business matter, Stern controlled access to several very lucrative operations, and could quickly deprive an uncooperative gambler or numbers writer of his source of income. Second, since he controlled the police department he could arrest any gamblers or bookies who were not paying tribute. (Some of the local gambling and prostitution arrests which took place during the Stern era served another purpose—to placate newspaper demands for a crackdown. As one police chief from this era phrased it, "Hollywood should have given us an Oscar for some of our performances when we had to pull a phony raid to keep the papers happy.") Finally, if the mechanisms of fear of financial loss and fear of police arrest failed to command obedience, Stern was always able to keep alive a fear of physical violence. As we have seen, numbers writers, pinball distributors, and competing gamblers were brought into line after outside enforcers put in an appearance. Stern's regular collection agent, a local tough who had been convicted of murder in the 1940's, was a constant reminder of the virtues of cooperation. Several witnesses who told grand juries or Federal agents of extortion attempts by Stern, received visits from Stern enforcers and tended to "forget" when called to testify against the boss.

. . . An essential ingredient in Irv Stern's Wincanton operations was protection against law enforcement agencies. While he was never able to arrange freedom from Federal intervention (although, as in the case of purchasing excise stamps for the pinball machines, he was occasionally able to satisfy Federal requirements without disrupting his activities), Stern was able in the 1940's and again from the mid-1950's through the early 1960's to secure freedom from State and local action. The precise extent of Stern's network of protection payments is unknown, but the method of operations can be reconstructed.

Two basic principles were involved in the Wincanton protection system —pay top personnel as much as necessary to keep them happy (and quiet), and pay something to as many others as possible to implicate them in the system and to keep them from talking. The range of payoffs thus went from a weekly salary for some public officials to a Christmas turkey for the patrolman on the beat. Records from the numbers bank listed payments totaling $2,400 each week to some local elected officials, State legislators, the police chief, a captain in charge of detectives, and persons mysteriously labeled "county" and "State." While the list of persons to be paid remained fairly constant, the amounts paid varied according to the gambling activities in operation at the time; payoff figures dropped sharply when the FBI put the dice game out of business. When the dice game was running, one official was receiving $750 per week, the chief $100, and a few captains, lieutenants, and detectives lesser amounts.

While the number of officials receiving regular "salary" payoffs was quite restricted (only 15 names were on the payroll found at the numbers bank), many other officials were paid off in different ways. (Some men were also silenced without charge—low-ranking policemen, for example, kept quiet after they learned that men who reported gambling or prostitution were ignored or transferred to the midnight shift; they didn't have to be paid.) Stern was a major (if undisclosed) contributor during political campaigns—sometimes giving money to all candidates, not caring who won, sometimes supporting a "regular" to defeat a possible reformer, sometimes paying a candidate not to oppose a preferred man. Since there were few legitimate sources of large contributions for Democratic candidates, Stern's money was frequently regarded as essential for victory, for the costs of buying radio and television time and paying poll watchers were high. When popular sentiment was running strongly in favor of reform, however, even Stern's contributions could not guarantee victory. Bob Walasek, later to be as corrupt as any Wincanton mayor, ran as a reform candidate in the Democratic primary and defeated Stern-financed incumbent Gene Donnelly. Never a man to bear grudges, Stern financed Walasek in the general election that year and put him on the "payroll" when he took office.

Even when local officials were not on the regular payroll, Stern was careful to remind them of his friendship (and their debts). A legislative investigating committee found that Stern had given mortgage loans to a police lieutenant and the police chief's son. County Court Judge Ralph Vaughan recalled that shortly after being elected (with Stern support), he received a call from Dave Feinman, Stern's nephew. "Congratulations, judge. When do you think you and your wife would like a vacation in Florida?"

"Florida? Why on earth would I want to go there?"

"But all the other judges and the guys in City Hall—Irv takes them all to Florida whenever they want to get away."

"Thanks anyway, but I'm not interested."

"Well, how about a mink coat instead. What size coat does your wife wear? * * *"

In another instance an assistant district attorney told of Feinman's arriving at his front door with a large basket from Stern's supermarket just before Christmas. "My minister suggested a needy family that could use the food," the assistant district attorney recalled, "but I returned the liquor to Feinman. How could I ask a minister if he knew someone that could use three bottles of scotch?"

Campaign contributions, regular payments to higher officials, holiday and birthday gifts—these were the bases of the system by which Irv Stern bought protection from the law. The campaign contributions usually ensured that complacent mayors, councilmen, district attorneys, and judges were elected; payoffs in some instances usually kept their loyalty. In a number of ways, Stern was also able to reward the corrupt officials at no financial cost to himself. Just as the officials, being in control of the instruments of law enforcement, were able to facilitate Stern's gambling enterprises, so Stern, in control of a network of men operating outside the law, was able to facilitate the officials' corrupt enterprises. As will be seen later, many local officials were not satisfied with their legal salaries from the city and their illegal salaries from Stern and decided to demand payments from prostitutes, kickbacks from salesmen, etc. Stern, while seldom receiving any money from these transactions, became a broker: bringing politicians into contact with salesmen, merchants, and lawyers willing to offer bribes to get city business; setting up middlemen who could handle the money without jeopardizing the officials' reputations; and providing enforcers who could bring delinquents into line.

From the corrupt activities of Wincanton officials, Irv Stern received little in contrast to his receipts from his gambling operations. Why then did he get involved in them? The major virtue, from Stern's point of view, of the system of extortion that flourished in Wincanton was that it kept down the officials' demands for payoffs directly from Stern. If a councilman was able to pick up $1,000 on the purchase of city equipment, he would demand a lower payment for the protection of gambling. Furthermore, since Stern knew the facts of exortion in each instance, the officials would be further implicated in the system and less able to back out on the arrangements regarding gambling. Finally, as Stern discovered to his chagrin, it became necessary to supervise official extortion to protect the officials against their own stupidity. Mayor Gene Donnelly was cooperative and remained satisfied with his regular "salary." Bob Walasek, however, was a greedy man, and seized every opportunity to profit from a city contract. Soon Stern found himself supervising many of Walasek's deals to keep the mayor from blowing the whole arrangement wide open. When Walasek tried to double the "take" on a purchase of parking meters, Stern had to step in and set the contract price, provide an untraceable middleman, and see the deal through to completion. "I told Irv," Police Chief Phillips later testified, "that Walasek wanted $12 on each meter instead of the $6 we got on the last meter deal. He became furious. He said, 'Walasek is going to fool around and wind up in jail. You come and see me. I'll tell Walasek what he's going to buy.'"

Protection, it was stated earlier, was an essential ingredient in Irv Stern's gambling empire. In the end, Stern's downfall came not from a flaw in the organization of the gambling enterprises but from public exposure of the corruption of Mayor Walasek and other officials. In the early 1960's Stern was sent to jail for 4 years on tax evasion charges, but the gambling empire continued to operate smoothly in his absence. A year later, however, Chief Phillips was caught perjuring himself in grand jury testimony concerning kickbacks on city towing contracts. Phillips "blew the whistle" on Stern, Walasek, and members of the city council, and a reform administration was swept into office. Irv Stern's gambling empire had been worth several million dollars each year; kickbacks on the towing contracts brought Bob Walasek a paltry $50 to $75 each week.

OFFICIAL CORRUPTION

Textbooks on municipal corporation law speak of at least three varieties of official corruption. The major categories are nonfeasance (failing to perform a required duty at all), malfeasance (the commission of some act which is positively unlawful), and misfeasance (the improper performance of some act which a man may properly do). During the years in which Irv Stern was running his gambling operations, Wincanton officials were guilty of all of these. Some residents say that Bob Walasek came to regard the mayor's office as a brokerage, levying a tariff on every item that came across his desk. Sometimes a request for simple municipal services turned into a game of cat and mouse, with Walasek sitting on the request, waiting to see how much would be offered, and the petitioner waiting to see if he could obtain his rights without having to pay for them. Corruption was not as lucrative an enterprise as gambling, but it offered a tempting supplement to low official salaries.

Nonfeasance

As was detailed earlier, Irv Stern saw to it that Wincanton officials would ignore at least one of their statutory duties, enforcement of the State's gambling laws. Bob Walasek and his cohorts also agreed to overlook other illegal activities. Stern, we noted earlier, preferred not to get directly involved in prostitution; Walasek and Police Chief Dave Phillips tolerated all prostitutes who kept up their protection payments. One madam, controlling more than 20 girls, gave Phillips et al. $500 each week; one woman employing only one girl paid $75 each week that she was in business. Operators of a carnival in rural Alsace County paid a public official $5,000 for the privilege of operating gambling tents for 5 nights each summer. A burlesque theater manager, under attack by high school teachers, was ordered to pay $25 each week for the privilege of keeping his strip show open.

Many other city and county officials must be termed guilty of nonfeasance, although there is no evidence that they received payoffs, and although they could present reasonable excuses for their inaction. Most policemen, as we have noted earlier, began to ignore prostitution and gambling completely after their reports of offenses were ignored or superior officers told them to mind their own business. State policemen, well informed about city vice and gambling conditions, did nothing unless called upon to act by local officials. Finally, the judges of the Alsace County Court failed to exercise their power to call for State Police investigations. In 1957, following Federal raids on horse bookies, the judges did request an investigation by the State Attorney General, but refused to approve his suggestion that a grand jury be convened to continue the investigation. For each of these instances of inaction, a tenable excuse might be offered—the beat patrolman should not be expected to endure harassment from his superior officers, State police gambling raids in a hostile city might jeopardize State-local cooperation on more serious crimes, and a grand jury probe might easily be turned into a "whitewash" in the hands of a corrupt district attorney. In any event, powers available to these law enforcement agencies for the prevention of gambling and corruption were not utilized.

Malfeasance

In fixing parking and speeding tickets, Wincanton politicians and policemen committed malfeasance, or committed an act they were forbidden to do, by illegally compromising valid civil and criminal actions. Similarly, while State law provides no particular standards by which the mayor is to make promotions within his police department, it was obviously improper for Mayor Walasek to demand a "political contribution" of $10,000 from Dave Phillips before he was appointed chief in 1960.

The term "political contribution" raises a serious legal and analytical problem in classifying the malfeasance of Wincanton officials, and indeed of politicians in many cities. Political campaigns cost money; citizens have a right to support the candidates of their choice; and officials have a right to appoint their backers to noncivil service positions. At some point, however, threats or oppression convert legitimate requests for political contributions into extortion. Shortly after taking office in the mid-1950's, Mayor Gene Donnelly notified city hall employees that they would be expected "voluntarily" to contribute 2 percent of their salary to the Democratic Party. (It might be noted that Donnelly never forwarded any of these "political contributions" to the party treasurer.) A number of salesmen doing business with the city were notified that companies which had supported the party would receive favored treatment; Donnelly notified one salesman that in light of a proposed $81,000 contract for the purchase of fire engines, a "political contribution" of $2,000 might not be inappropriate. While neither the city hall employees nor the salesmen had rights to their positions or their contracts, the "voluntary" quality of their contributions seems questionable.

One final, in the end almost ludicrous, example of malfeasance came with Mayor Donnelly's abortive "War on the Press." Following a series of gambling raids by the Internal Revenue Service, the newspapers began asking why the local police had not participated in the raids. The mayor lost his temper and threw a reporter in jail. Policemen were instructed to harass newspaper delivery trucks, and 73 tickets were written over a 48-hour period for supposed parking and traffic violations. Donnelly soon backed down after national news services picked up the story, since press coverage made him look ridiculous. Charges against the reporter were dropped, and the newspapers continued to expose gambling and corruption.

Misfeasance

Misfeasance in office, says the common law, is the improper performance of some act which a man may properly do. City officials must buy and sell equipment, contract for services, and allocate licenses, privileges, etc. These actions can be improperly performed if either the results are improper (e.g., if a building inspector were to approve a home with defective wiring or a zoning board to authorize a variance which had no justification in terms of land usage) or a result is achieved by improper procedures (e.g., if the city purchased an acceptable automobile in consideration of a bribe paid to the purchasing agent). In the latter case, we can usually assume an improper result as well—while the automobile will be satisfactory, the bribe giver will probably have inflated the sale price to cover the costs of the bribe.

In Wincanton, it was rather easy for city officials to demand kickbacks, for State law frequently does not demand competitive bidding or permits the city to ignore the lowest bid. The city council is not required to advertise or take bids on purchases under $1,000, contracts for maintenance of streets and other public works, personal or professional services, or patented or copyrighted products. Even when bids must be sought, the council is only required to award the contract to the lowest responsible bidder. Given these permissive provisions, it was relatively easy for council members to justify or disguise contracts in fact based upon bribes. The exemption for patented products facilitated bribe taking on the purchase of two emergency trucks for the police department (with a $500 campaign contribution on a $7,500 deal) three fire engines ($2,000 was allegedly paid on an $81,000 contract), and 1,500 parking meters (involving payments of $10,500 plus an $880 clock for Mayor Walasek's home). Similar fees were allegedly exacted in connection with the purchase of a city fire alarm system and police uniforms and firearms. A former mayor and other officials also profited on the sale of city property, allegedly dividing $500 on the sale of a crane and $20,000 for approving the sale, for $22,000, of a piece of land immediately resold for $75,000.

When contracts involved services to the city, the provisions in the State law regarding the lowest responsible bidder and excluding "professional services" from competitive bidding provided convenient loopholes. One internationally known engineering firm refused to agree to kickback in order to secure a contract to design a $4.5 million sewage disposal plant for the city; a local firm was then appointed, which paid $10,700 of its $225,000 fee to an associate of Irv Stern and Mayor Donnelly as a "finder's fee." Since the State law also excludes public works maintenance contracts from the competitive bidding requirements, many city paving and street repair contracts during the Donnelly-Walasek era were given to a contributor to the Democratic Party. Finally, the franchise for towing illegally parked cars and cars involved in accidents was awarded to two garages which were then required to kickback $1 for each car towed.

The handling of graft on the towing contracts illustrates the way in which minor violence and the "lowest responsible bidder" clause could be used to keep bribe payers in line. After Federal investigators began to look into Wincanton corruption, the owner of one of the garages with a towing franchise testified before the grand jury. Mayor Walasek immediately withdrew his franchise, citing "health violations" at the garage. The garageman was also "encouraged" not to testify by a series of "accidents"—wheels would fall off towtrucks on the highway, steering cables were cut, and so forth. Newspaper satirization of the "health violations" forced the restoration of the towing franchise, and the "accidents" ceased.

Lest the reader infer that the "lowest responsible bidder" clause was used as an escape valve only for corrupt purposes, one incident might be noted which took place under the present reform administration. In 1964, the Wincanton School Board sought bids for the renovation of an athletic field. The lowest bid came from a construction company owned by Dave Phillips, the corrupt police chief who had served formerly under Mayor Walasek. While the company was presumably competent to carry out the assignment, the board rejected Phillips' bid "because of a question as to his moral responsibility." The board did not specify whether this referred to his prior corruption as chief or his present status as an informer in testifying against Walasek and Stern.

One final area of city power, which was abused by Walasek et al., covered discretionary acts, such as granting permits and allowing zoning variances. On taking office, Walasek took the unusual step of asking that the bureaus of building and plumbing inspection be put under the mayor's control. With this power to approve or deny building permits, Walasek "sat on" applications, waiting until the petitioner contributed $50 or $75, or threatened to sue to get his permit. Some building designs were not approved until a favored architect was retained as a "consultant." (It is not known whether this involved kickbacks to Walasek or simply patronage for a friend.) At least three instances are known in which developers were forced to pay for zoning variances before apartment buildings or supermarkets could be erected. Businessmen who wanted to encourage rapid turnover of the curb space in front of their stores were told to pay a police sergeant to erect "10-minute parking" signs. To repeat a caveat stated earlier, it is impossible to tell whether these kickbacks were demanded to expedite legitimate requests or to approve improper demands, such as a variance that would hurt a neighborhood or a certificate approving improper electrical work.

All of the activities detailed thus far involve fairly clear violations of the law. To complete the picture of the abuse of office by Wincanton officials, we might briefly mention "honest graft." This term was best defined by one of its earlier practitioners, State Senator George Washington Plunkitt who loyally served Tammany Hall at the turn of the century.

There's all the difference in the world between [honest and dishonest graft].
Yes, many of our men have grown rich in politics. I have myself.

I've made a big fortune out of the game, and I'm gettin' richer every day, but
I've not gone in for dishonest graft—blackmailin' gamblers, saloonkeepers, disorderly people, etc.—and neither has any of the men who have made big fortunes
in politics.

There's an honest graft, and I'm an example of how it works. I might sum up
the whole thing by sayin': "I seen my opportunities and I took 'em."

Let me explain by examples. My party's in power in the city, and it's goin' to
undertake a lot of public improvements. Well, I'm tipped off, say, that they're
going to lay out a new park at a certain place.

I see my opportunity and I take it. I go to that place, and I buy up all the
land I can in the neighborhood. Then the board of this or that makes its plan
public, and there is a rush to get my land, which nobody cared particular for
before.

Ain't it perfectly honest to charge a good price and make a profit on my
investment and foresight? Of course, it is. Well, that's honest graft.[2]

While there was little in the way of land purchasing—either honest or
dishonest—going on in Wincanton during this period, several officials who
carried on their own businesses while in office were able to pick up some
"honest graft." One city councilman with an accounting office served as
bookkeeper for Irv Stern and the major bookies and prostitutes in the city.

Police Chief Phillips' construction firm received a contract to remodel
the exterior of the largest brothel in town. Finally one councilman serving
in the present reform administration received a contract to construct all
gasoline stations built in the city by a major petroleum company; skeptics
say that the contract was the quid pro quo for the councilman's vote to give
the company the contract to sell gasoline to the city.

. . . This cataloging of acts of nonfeasance, malfeasance, and misfeasance by
Wincanton officials raises a danger of confusing variety with universality,
of assuming that every employee of the city was either engaged in corrupt
activities or was being paid to ignore the corruption of others. On the
contrary, both official investigations and private research lead to the conclusion that there is no reason whatsoever to question the honesty of the
vast majority of the employees of the city of Wincanton. Certainly no more
than 10 of the 155 members of the Wincanton police force were on Irv
Stern's payroll (although as many as half of them may have accepted petty
Christmas presents—turkeys or liquor). In each department, there were a few
employees who objected actively to the misdeeds of their superiors, and the
only charge that can justly be leveled against the mass of employees is that

2 William L. Riordan, "Plunkitt of Tammany Hall" (New York: E. P. Dutton,
1963), p. 3.

they were unwilling to jeopardize their employment by publicly exposing what was going on. When Federal investigators showed that an honest (and possibly successful) attempt was being made to expose Stern-Walasek corruption, a number of city employees cooperated with the grand jury in aggregating evidence which could be used to convict the corrupt officials.

Before these Federal investigations began, however, it could reasonably appear to an individual employee that the entire machinery of law enforcement in the city was controlled by Stern, Walasek, et al., and that an individual protest would be silenced quickly. This can be illustrated by the momentary crusade conducted by First Assistant District Attorney Phil Roper in the summer of 1962. When the district attorney left for a short vacation, Roper decided to act against the gamblers and madams in the city. With the help of the State Police, Roper raided several large brothels. Apprehending on the street the city's largest distributor of punchboards and lotteries, Roper effected a citizen's arrest and drove him to police headquarters for proper detention and questioning. "I'm sorry, Mr. Roper," said the desk sergeant, "we're under orders not to arrest persons brought in by you." Roper was forced to call upon the State Police for aid in confining the gambler. When the district attorney returned from his vacation, he quickly fired Roper "for introducing politics into the district attorney's office."

If it is incorrect to say that Wincanton corruption extended very far vertically—into the rank and file of the various departments of the city—how far did it extend horizontally? How many branches and levels of government were affected? With the exception of the local Congressman and the city treasurer, it seems that a few personnel at each level (city, county, and State) and in most offices in city hall can be identified either with Stern or with some form of free-lance corruption. A number of local judges received campaign financing from Stern, although there is no evidence that they were on his payroll after they were elected. Several State legislators were on Stern's payroll, and one Republican councilman charged that a high-ranking State Democratic official promised Stern first choice of all Alsace County patronage. The county chairman, he claimed, was only to receive the jobs that Stern did not want. While they were later to play an active role in disrupting Wincanton gambling, the district attorney in Hal Craig's reform administration feared that the State Police were on Stern's payroll, and thus refused to use them in city gambling raids.

Within the city administration, the evidence is fairly clear that some mayors and councilmen received regular payments from Stern and divided kickbacks on city purchases and sales. Some key subcouncil personnel frequently shared in payoffs affecting their particular departments—the police chief shared in the gambling and prostitution payoffs and received $300 of the $10,500 kickback on parking meter purchases. A councilman controlling one department, for example, might get a higher percentage of kickbacks than the other councilmen in contracts involving that department.

. . .

GAMBLING AND CORRUPTION:
THE GENERAL PUBLIC

. . . The social life of Wincanton is organized around clubs, lodges, and other voluntary associations. Labor unions have union halls. Businessmen have luncheon groups, country clubs, and service organizations, such as the Rotary, Kiwanis, the Lions, etc. Each nationality group has its own meeting-house—the Ancient Order of Hibernians, the Liederkranz, the Colored Polit-ical Club, the Cristoforo Colombo Society, etc. In each neighborhood, a PTA-type group is organized around the local playground. Each firehall is the nightly gathering place of a volunteer firemen's association. Each church has the usual assortment of men's, women's, and children's groups.

A large proportion of these groups profited in one way or another from some form of gambling. Churches sponsored lotteries, bingo, and "Las Vegas nights." Weekly bingo games sponsored by the playground associations paid for new equipment, Little League uniforms, etc. Business groups would use lotteries to advertise "Downtown Wincanton Days." Finally, de-pending upon the current policy of law enforcement agencies, most of the clubs had slot machines, payoff pinball machines, punchboards, lotteries, bingo, poker games, etc. For many of these groups, profits from gambling meant the difference between financial success and failure. Clubs with large and affluent membership lists could survive with only fees and profits from meals and drinks served. Clubs with few or impecunious members, however, had to rely on other sources of revenue, and gambling was both lucrative and attractive to nonmembers.

The clubs therefore welcomed slots, pinball machines, punchboards, and so forth, both to entertain members and to bring in outside funds. The clubs usually divided gambling profits equally with machine distributors such as Stern or Klaus Braun. Some clubs owed even more to gamblers; if Braun heard that a group of men wanted to start a new volunteer firemen's associa-tion, he would lend them mortgage money simply for the opportunity to put his slot machines in the firehall. It is not surprising, therefore, to find that the clubs actively defended Stern, Braun, and the political candidates who favored open gambling.

Gambling in Wincanton also provided direct and indirect benefits to churches and other charitable organizations. First, like the other private groups, a number of these churches and charities sponsored bingo, lotteries, etc., and shared in the profits. Second, leading gamblers and racketeers have been generous supporters of Wincanton charities. Klaus Braun gave away literally most of his gambling income, aiding churches, hospitals, and the underprivileged. In the late 1940's, Braun provided 7,000 Christmas turkeys to the poor, and frequently chartered buses to take slum children to ball games. Braun's Prospect Mountain Park offered free rides and games for local children (while their parents were in other tents patronizing the slot machines). Irv Stern gave a $10,000 stained glass window to his synagogue, and aided welfare groups and hospitals in Wincanton and other cities. (Since the residents of Wincanton refuse to be cared for in the room that Stern gave to Community Hospital, it is now used only for the storage of bandages.) When Stern came into Federal court in the early 1960's to be sentenced on tax evasion charges, he was given character references by Protestant, Catholic, and Jewish clergy, and by the staff of two hospitals and a home for the aged. Critics charge that Stern never gave away a dime that wasn't well publicized; nevertheless, his contributions benefited worthwhile community institutions.

(Lest this description of the direct and indirect benefits of gambling be misleading, it should also be stressed that many ministers protested violently against gambling and corruption, led reform movements and launched pulpit tirades against Stern, Walasek, et al.)

One final social function of Wincanton gambling might be termed the moderation of the demands of the criminal law. Bluntly stated, Irv Stern was providing the people with what at least a large portion of them wanted, whether or not State lawmakers felt they should want it. It is, of course, axiomatic that no one has the right to disobey the law, but in fairness to local officials it should be remembered that they were generally only tolerating what most residents of the city had grown up with—easily accessible numbers, horsebetting, and bingo. When reform mayor Ed Whitton ordered bingo parlors closed in 1964, he was ending the standard form of evening recreation of literally thousands of elderly men and women. One housewife interviewed recently expressed relief that her mother had died before Whitton's edict took effect; "It would have killed her to live without bingo," she said.

In another sense, Wincanton law enforcement was also moderated by the aid that the gambling syndicates gave, at no cost to the public, to persons arrested by the police for gambling activity. Stern provided bail and legal counsel during trials, and often supported families of men sent to jail. A large portion of the payments that Stern sent to the east coast syndicates (as discussed earlier) was earmarked for pensions to the widows of men who had earlier served in the Stern organization. In light of the present interest in the quality of legal services available to the poor, this aspect of Wincanton gambling must be regarded as a worthy social function.

In these ways, Wincanton gambling provided the financial basis for a network of private groups, filling social, service, and quasi-governmental functions. Leading the list of latent functions of gambling, therefore, we must put the support of neighborhood and other group social life and the provision of such important services as recreation and fire protection. Providing these services through private rather than public mechanisms not only reduced tax burdens but also integrated the services into the social structure of the neighborhood served. While it is hard to give profits from gambling sole credit for maintaining these clubs, it must be noted that a number of firemen's and political associations were forced to close their doors when law enforcement agencies seized slot and pinball machines.

. . . Just as the proceeds from gambling made possible, or at least less expensive, an extensive series of social relationships and quasi-public services, so also did gambling and corruption affect the local economy, aiding some businesses while hindering others. Their manifest function, of course, was to increase the incomes of the providers of illicit services (members of the Stern syndicate, individual number writers and pinball machine distributors, madams, prostitutes, etc.), the recipients of payoffs (elected officials and policemen, for whom these payments were a welcome addition to low salaries), and the businessmen who secured unwarranted contracts, permits, variances, etc. On the other hand, these arrangements provided entertainment for the consumers of gambling and prostitution.

In describing the latent functions of Wincanton illegality, we can begin with two broad phenomena. First, gambling permitted a number of outmoded businesses to survive technological change. As a quotation at the beginning of this chapter indicated, a "mom and pop" grocery store or a candy or cigar store could make more from writing numbers or taking horse bets than they did from their nominal source of support. When reform mayors cracked down on betting, many of these marginal shops went out of business, not being able to compete with the larger, more efficient operations solely on the basis of sales. Second, the system provided an alternate ladder of social mobility for persons who lacked the educational or status prerequisites for success in the legitimate world. Irv Stern came to this country as a fruit peddler's son and is believed by the Internal Revenue Service to be worth several millions of dollars. Gene Donnelly was a bartender's son; Bob Walasek grew up in a slum, although he was able to attend college on an athletic scholarship. Many Wincantonites believe that each of these men collected at least a quarter of a million dollars during his 4 years in city hall. As Daniel Bell has pointed out,[3] and as these men illustrate, organized crime in America has provided a quick route out of the slums, a means of realizing the Horatio Alger dream.

[3] Daniel Bell, "The End of Ideology" (New York: Free Press, 1960), ch. 7, "Crime as an American Way of Life."

A number of legitimate enterprises in Wincanton profited directly or indirectly when gambling was wide open. Eight or ten major bingo halls provided a large nighttime business for the local bus company. In one year, for example, 272,000 persons paid to play bingo, and most of them were elderly men and women who were brought to the games on regular or chartered buses. Prizes for the bingo games were purchased locally; one department store executive admitted that bingo gift certificates brought "a sizable amount" of business into his store. Several drugstores sold large quantities of cosmetics to the prostitutes. As in Las Vegas, one Wincanton hotel offered special weekend rates for the gamblers at the dice game, who would gamble at night and sleep during the daytime. Finally, several landlords rented space to Stern for his bookie parlors and accounting offices. Worried that legislative investigations might terminate a profitable arrangement, one landlord asked the investigating committee, "Who else would pay $150 a month for that basement?" Being the center of gambling and prostitution for a wide area also meant increased business for the city's restaurants, bars, and theaters. One man declared that business at his Main Street restaurant was never as good as when gamblers and bingo players were flocking to the downtown area. (Many of these restaurants and bars, of course, provided gambling as well as food and drink for their customers.)

Corruption, like gambling, offered some businessmen opportunities to increase sales and profits. If minor building code violations could be overlooked, houses and office buildings could be erected more cheaply. Zoning variances, secured for a price, opened up new areas in which developers could build high-rise apartment buildings and shopping centers. In selling to the city, businessmen could increase profits either by selling inferior goods or by charging high prices on standard goods when bidding was rigged or avoided. Finally, corruptible officials could aid profits simply by speeding up decisions on city contracts, or by forcing rapid turnover of city-owned curb space through either "10-minute parking" signs or strict enforcement of parking laws. (Owners of large stores, however, sought to maximize profits by asking the police to ignore parking violations, feeling that customers who worried about their meters would be less likely to stay and buy.)

This listing of the latent benefits of gambling and corruption must be juxtaposed against the fact that many Wincanton businessmen were injured by the Stern-Walasek method of operations and fought vigorously against it. Leaders of the Wincanton business community—the bankers, industrialists, Chamber of Commerce, etc.—fought Walasek and Stern, refusing to kickback on anything, and regularly called upon State and Federal agencies to investigate local corruption.

It is somewhat misleading, however, to use the single term "business" in analyzing responses to corruption. It will be more fruitful to classify businesses according to the nature of their contact with the city of Wincanton. Some industries had a national market, and only called upon the city for labor and basic services—water, sewage, police and fire protection, etc. Other companies such as sales agencies or construction firms did business directly with city hall and thus were intimately concerned with the terms upon which the city government did business. Because of the looseness of State bidding procedures, these businesses had to be careful, however, not to alienate officials. A third group, while not doing business with the city, had primarily a local clientele. Under these conditions, businesses in this group were frequently interested in corruption and gambling policies.

Official corruption affected each of these groups differently. Businesses whose markets lay primarily outside the city usually had to be concerned only with the possibility that Walasek might force them to pay for building permits. Companies dealing with City Hall, however, were exposed to every extortionate demand that the mayor might impose. As an example, agencies usually able to underbid their competitors were ignored if they refused to abide by the unofficial "conditions" added to contracts. Businessmen in the third category were in an intermediate position, both in terms of their freedom to act against the system and in terms of the impact that it had upon them. Like the others, they suffered when forced to pay for permits or variances. Legitimate businesses, such as liquor stores, taverns, and restaurants, whose functions paralleled those of the clubs, lost revenue when the clubs were licensed to have gambling and slot machines. Those businesses, such as banks, whose success depended upon community growth, suffered when the community's reputation for corruption and gambling drove away potential investors and developers. (Interestingly, businessmen disagree as to whether it is the reputation for corruption or for gambling that discourages new industry. Several Wincanton bankers stated that no investor would run the risk of having to bribe officials to have building plans approved, permits issued, and so forth. One architect, however, argued that businessmen assume municipal corruption, but will not move into a "sin town," for their employees will not want to raise children in such circumstances.)

The last detrimental aspect of gambling and corruption seems trivial in comparison with the factors already mentioned, but it was cited by most of the business leaders interviewed. Simply stated, it was embarrassing to have one's hometown known throughout the country for its vice and corruption. "I'd go to a convention on the west coast," one textile manufacturer recalled, "and everyone I'd meet would say, 'You're from Wincanton? Boy, have I heard stories about that place!' I would try to talk about textiles or opportunities for industrial development, but they'd keep asking about the girls and the gambling." An Air Force veteran recalled being ridiculed about his hometown while in boot camp. Finally, some insiders feel that a Wincanton judge was persuaded to act against Irv Stern when he found that his daughter was being laughed at by her college friends for being related to a Wincanton official.

. . .

THE FUTURE OF REFORM IN WINCANTON

When Wincantonites are asked what kind of law enforcement they want, they are likely to say that it is all right to tolerate petty gambling and prostitution, but that "you've got to keep out racketeers and corrupt politicians." Whenever they come to feel that the city is being controlled by these racketeers, they "throw the rascals out." This policy of "throwing the rascals out," however, illustrates the dilemma facing reformers in Wincanton. Irv Stern, recently released from Federal prison, has probably, in fact, retired from the rackets; he is ill and plans to move to Arizona. Bob Walasek, having been twice convicted on extortion charges, is finished politically. Therefore? Therefore, the people of Wincanton firmly believe that "the problem" has been solved—"the rascals" have been thrown out. When asked, recently, what issues would be important in the next local elections, only 9 of 183 respondents felt that clean government or keeping out vice and gambling might be an issue. (Fifty-five percent had no opinion, 15 percent felt that the ban on bingo might be an issue, and 12 percent cited urban renewal, a subject frequently mentioned in the papers preceding the survey.) Since, under Ed Whitton, the city is being honestly run and is free from gambling and prostitution, there is no problem to worry about.

On balance, it seems far more likely to conclude that gambling and corruption will soon return to Wincanton (although possibly in less blatant forms) for two reasons—first, a significant number of people want to be able to gamble or make improper deals with the city government. (This assumes, of course, that racketeers will be available to provide gambling if a complacent city administration permits it.) Second, and numerically far more important, most voters think that the problem has been permanently solved, and thus they will not be choosing candidates based on these issues, in future elections.

. . . When the voters have called for clean government, they have gotten it, in spite of loose bidding laws, limited civil service, etc. The critical factor has been voter preference. Until the voters of Wincanton come to believe that illegal gambling produces the corruption they have known, the type of government we have documented will continue. Four-year periods of reform do little to change the habits instilled over 40 years of gambling and corruption.

3 The Respectables

ROBERT F. KENNEDY

1. BUSINESSMEN

One day in the fall of 1958 I received an invitation to speak about the work of our Committee[1] to an association of businessmen at a dinner at the Waldorf in New York.

A week before the dinner I received a second letter from the association. It read:

DEAR MR. KENNEDY:

. . . I am most embarrassed to be confronted with a situation which necessitates the withdrawal of that invitation. Our members have a very real and deep interest in the subject on which you were expected to speak. . . . They would very much like to hear you be the one to discuss it, but it now develops some of the members of the industry feel that the subject is one which probably should be discussed in a meeting of a more general character than a single industry meeting.

I am certain that you, too, realize, as do we upon reflection, that it might be a mistake for one single industry to sponsor a speech at this time by one in your

[1] Senate Select Committee on Improper Activities in the Labor or Management Field (Senator John L. McClellan, D., Ark.). Robert F. Kennedy was Committee counsel.

official position. There is too much opportunity for misunderstanding arising therefrom. Such would not be so if the speech were delivered before a general meeting, such as the Chamber of Commerce or Association of Manufacturers, etc.

Accordingly it is necessary for me to ask you to disregard my letter of October 31 and to accept my apologies for having to withdraw the invitation.

Some otherwise honest businessmen look on the relationship between labor and management as a great power struggle in which "anything goes." In their anxiety to gain the upper hand in this struggle they resort to unethical and dishonest tactics on the mistaken theory that they must do this to win.

The great concentration of power that rests in some of the unions in this country should be a matter of concern, just as should the great concentrations of power in some companies and businesses in certain sections of the country. But the answer to the problem of powerful unions is not to be found in a breakdown of morality in the nation's business community. Unfortunately this is the answer too many businessmen are willing to accept.

I recognize that the majority of American businessmen are above crookedness and collusion in labor-management negotiations. But we found that with the present-day emphasis on money and material goods many businessmen were willing to make corrupt "deals" with dishonest union officials in order to gain competitive advantage or to make a few extra dollars.

Because of limited jurisdiction our Committee could not go into improper activities of business per se, but only where there was some direct connection with labor. Even thus restricted, we came across more than fifty companies and corporations that had acted improperly—and in many cases illegally—in dealings with labor unions. Here it was not a matter of an employer's being whipped into line by fear or fright or abuse. Such things happen, as in the case in New York, for example, where an employer was told that his children would be killed on the way to school if he did not give in to union demands. We found management representatives who were threatened and maltreated by union officials. Where this occurred the Committee did not find it difficult to understand that a man afraid for his life or for the welfare of his family might act unwisely. Such an employer deserves sympathy and help.

But in the companies and corporations to which I am referring the improprieties and illegalities were occasioned solely by a desire for monetary gain. Furthermore we found that we could expect very little assistance from management groups. Disturbing as it may sound, more often the business people with whom we came in contact—and this includes some representatives of our largest corporations—were uncooperative. For some it was a question of not wanting to involve themselves; for others, such as the writer of the letter mentioned above, it was a question of not having the courage to speak out—because "there is too much opportunity for misunderstanding."

We found there is often a thin line between bribery and extortion, shakedown and pay-off. Labor-management corruption is a crooked two-way street. That is why company officials who conspire with union officials won't talk. They have bought something, just as the labor leader has sold something. And those management officials who aren't involved themselves are usually satisfied to let things go along with everybody happy. They don't want anyone to rock the boat.

Frank Hogan, the able New York District Attorney, told me of his difficulties in dealing with so-called respectable management people during his investigation into labor racketeering in the 1940's. Company officials even fled his jurisdiction and hid out in states beyond his reach.

Fifteen years later I found the situation had not changed—not even the faces had changed.

We called before the Committee S. A. Healey, owner of one of the major construction firms in the United States. He had hidden out from Hogan for over a year before he finally came in and admitted having paid $125,000 to "Big Mike" Carozza, the head of the Hod Carriers Union. We wanted to know about Healey's relationship with William E. Maloney, the International president of the Operating Engineers. But rather than discuss it with the Committee, he took the Fifth Amendment.

During Joey Fay's trial in the forties officials of the Walsh Construction Company in New York admitted having made a pay-off to him. In our hearings in 1959, the Committee found this same company had awarded a contract to Charley Johnson of the Carpenters Union under circumstances that made it clear that this too was a pay-off.

By and large, little or no accurate information came to us from the business community. We received 150,000 complaints during the Committee's life. Seventy-five per cent of them came from representatives of organized labor, mostly rank-and-filers. Some came from people outside the labor-management field. Only a handful came from people in the business world. Certainly no investigation was touched off by any voluntary help we received from management. And this was not because management had no information to give. I believe 90 per cent of the corrupt deals between business and labor could be eliminated if business officials would simply talk to proper authorities.

It was encouraging to see the AFL–CIO move against certain unions—notably the Teamsters and the Bakers—as a result of corrupt practices found within the unions. But not one management group or association has made a single move to rid itself of members who were found to be involved in collusive deals. Not one firm has been barred from any business organization for wrongdoing that officials of the firm often admitted existed. These corrupt businessmen are still sitting down to luncheon and dinner meetings with business groups across the country, and they are getting encouragement and admiration—not censure.

Often we found that corrupt deals involving management were handled through attorneys who played the role of "middleman" or, as we came to think of them, "legal fixers" or "legal prostitutes." More often it was the labor relations consultant who played the "middleman" role. And America's most notorious middleman was Nathan W. Shefferman, some of whose activities we discussed earlier in connection with Dave Beck.

As our investigations moved from Beck and the Teamsters into other areas we ran across Shefferman and his operatives repeatedly—most often where a company was resisting unionization. One of his assets as a labor relations consultant was, of course, his friendship with labor leaders, which he used to get favorable treatment for his management clients in their negotiations with the unions. (Naturally the favors were reciprocal.)

His methods of rescuing a firm from the dreadful prospect of legitimate unionization were various and devious. We discovered in his files an outline of what must have been one of his favorite methods of attack (judging by the frequency with which the pattern cropped up) when dealing with labor leaders who could not be bought. This was his advice to one company that was facing organization:

"Don't dignify them. Call them bums and hoodlums. Cheap common bums. Don't argue wage differential. Don't answer it. Stay away from it. Ridicule leaders."

He urged his client to find an employee who would work with a lawyer to organize an anti-union group:

"Find lawyer and guy who will set up 'vote no' committee. Give American Legion material we have and let 'vote no' committee get it from American Legion."

The memo continued: "Material to use: Communism, un-Americanism, destroying our country . . . Attack them and pin them down when they get closer to an issue. Hit leaders toward last. . . ."

One of Shefferman's clients was Sears, Roebuck, which paid him approximately $250,000 during the period from 1953 to 1956 alone.

Sears, Roebuck officials were amazingly frank. Wallace Tudor, a vice president of Sears, Roebuck & Company, admitted to the Committee that:

Many of the activities engaged in by Labor Relations Associates and certain company personnel acting with them were inexcusable, unnecessary and disgraceful. A repetition of these mistakes will not be tolerated by this company. . . .

Mr. Tudor said the relationship with Shefferman had been terminated in 1957. He could not explain why it had not been broken off earlier.

His attitude and forthright admission blunted the sharp criticism the company might otherwise have received from the Committee. As a practical matter, when someone says that mistakes have been made, asks for no sympathy and pledges in good faith that the errors will not be repeated, it is difficult to be critical.

As we went into the efforts of other companies to stave off unionization, or to get a union that would "deal" with them, the same pattern was apparent again and again. At times our investigators would spot the Shefferman imprint almost immediately. One interesting case involved the Morton Frozen Food Company in Webster City, Iowa.

When the United Packinghouse Workers started an organizing drive there in June, 1955, immediately a "spontaneous" opposition group called "We the Morton Workers" sprang up. From the outset, union officials were certain that the company was supporting this group financially, but could not obtain proof.

Looking into the case, we found that their suspicion was justified. A middleman lawyer, a man named Stewart Lund, hired by the company's regular attorney, had worked with a Shefferman representative in the usual way to defeat the union. When first interviewed, Lund told Pierre Salinger that all he ever received by way of compensation was a set of steak knives from the grateful "We the Morton Workers"; later—after we proved that he had been well paid by the company's attorney—he admitted that he had lied. He excused his falsehood on the grounds of a "confidential relationship" with the company.

I recognize the real need for a bond between lawyer and client. But, as we pointed out at the hearing, if Mr. Lund felt that by talking to Salinger he would have been betraying this relationship, he should have said so, instead of lying to him.

The hearings showed that for keeping the union out, Shefferman got $12,000. The next year, 1956, he got $8,000 for bringing a union in. During the year Morton Frozen Foods had become a division of the Continental Baking Company. Continental's general counsel was George Faunce, a close friend of James Cross of the Bakers Union. So with the help of a Shefferman operative, Cross and his Bakers Union took over, in an "organizing drive" that was more a conspiracy against the employees than a legitimate organizing program. The officers of the new local were chosen in the office of the general manager of the Morton Company, and the contract was drawn up and signed in Shefferman's office. It was a very bad contract. It did away with the wage incentive and contained no seniority provision. But the members were not consulted, and only parts of the contract were read to them.

We asked George Faunce about this, and he said: "I think you normally make a contract with a union leader. You don't make a contract with a mob of people."

Nevertheless, in order to give the contract some appearance of legitimacy, Shefferman's man, James T. Neilsen, alias James Guffey, had wanted the new union to go through the farce of a negotiating session. Merle Smith, a field organizer for the International, and a legitimate union leader, had objected.

"These people are not that stupid," he told Guffey.

At the hearings the Continental Baking Company had swarms of public relations men all over the hearing room. They had employed Tex McCrary's publicity firm and there seemed to be more of their people around than there were witnesses. After George Faunce made his remark about "the mob"— a reference to Morton workers—McCrary's public relations men seemed to double. They put out a new statement every hour in an effort to kill the bad publicity the company was getting.

In my estimation the Morton firm showed bad judgment in not following the example of Sears, Roebuck and admitting what the facts clearly proved. Their failure to do so made their position much more difficult before the Committee.

We also found Shefferman's muddy footprints at the Whirlpool Company in Ohio, which was being organized by the UAW. "Spontaneous" anti-union committees handed out literature paid for by the company; lists were made of pro-union employees, and workers were bribed to vote against the UAW.

At one point during this investigation, we drew up at the request of several Committee members a complete list of Shefferman's clients. Shortly thereafter, John Herling, an outstanding Washington labor reporter, obtained a copy and printed it. Senator Goldwater and several other Republican Senators exploded, mistakenly holding me responsible.

One of Shefferman's agents, George Kamenow, was extremely close to Hoffa and other union officials. Many of his clients were able to avoid unionization. However, the middleman who turned up most often in deals where Hoffa was concerned was Jack (Babe) Bushkin, the Detroit labor consultant. During the period that Hoffa controlled the Detroit local of the Retail Clerks, Bushkin was able to get substandard contracts with them for a number of his clients.

A year after the Committee had exposed Bushkin's operations and he had pleaded the Fifth Amendment before us, we found some of the most reputable firms in Detroit—Federal Department Stores, Cunningham Drug Stores, the ACF Wrigley Grocery chain—still had him on their payrolls as a "consultant" and they had no intention of getting rid of him. While this would have been disillusioning for me in 1957, by 1959 it no longer seemed surprising.

On the role of the "middleman" in labor-management affairs, Senator McClellan, after listening to accounts of the activities of Shefferman, Kamenow, Babe Bushkin and others, had this to say:

THE CHAIRMAN: I am compelled to observe that I see nothing wrong in seeking counsel and employing legal counsel, and employing even experts in labor-management relations . . . but it looks to me like we are developing a pattern of what amounts to a payoff to union officials to have them disregard the rights of the workingmen or to be reluctant, if not to refuse, to press any drive for unionization. . . .

The labor relations "middleman" was not always a necessary ingredient in the deals some companies cooked up with unions. Sometimes management officials acted for themselves without a "consultant."

In 1955, Food Fair Stores, the sixth largest food chain in the country, created an affiliate to be known as Food Fair Properties, Inc. Bonds and stocks were issued the latter part of 1955 and "stock rights" were given to all those who already owned stock in Food Fair Stores. Holders of the stock rights had preferred treatment in the purchase of a debenture bond and eleven shares of stock.

Mr. Samuel Friedland, Chairman of the Board of Food Fair Stores, made 136,000 of his own "rights" available to twenty individuals who otherwise would not have been entitled to them. Of the twenty, four were labor officials, who received as a gift a total of twelve thousand "rights," which at the time were worth approximately $9,000. This enabled them to purchase for $30,000 units that actually were worth $42,000.

In addition to the units, common stock was issued, for which a tremendous demand built up. The offering of 650,000 shares became greatly oversubscribed. Nevertheless, through the courtesy of Mr. Lou Stein, president of Food Fair, twenty labor leaders were permitted to buy 12,100 shares of this already oversubscribed stock for $12,000—though at the time of purchase these shares were actually worth $48,000. Altogether, Food Fair officials made available to labor officials for $42,100 bonds and stocks worth $90,400.

Some of the major stock rights went to Max and Louis Block of the Meat Cutters Union. In a nice *quid pro quo*, Food Fair was granted an eighteen-month grace period before having to pay into the union's pension and welfare fund in New York. This saved the firm a tidy $142,000. The two major competing firms in its area were not similarly blessed.

To Ben Lapensohn, a union leader of Local 107 of the Teamsters, Stein made available—in addition to the Food Fair stock—$15,000 worth of stock in another company of which he was a director. This cost Lapensohn only $10,000.

When I asked Stein why he wanted to favor Mr. Lapensohn, he said, "Because if anyone is in business, and you know that a person stands well in labor circles, you don't try to incur any ill will. If it did not mean anything to me, and he came and asked me for a favor, certainly I ought to try to do it for him, because that is human nature, and that is the way business is done, not to get any benefits that you are not entitled to . . . but merely to be sure that you don't create ill will but try to get good will of people insofar as your business is concerned."

Good will, the Committee found, is what Mr. Stein got—approximately $300,000 worth—when in the contract negotiations with Lapensohn's local in 1954 Food Fair was given extremely advantageous terms regarding the unloading of merchandise that were not granted to its competitors.

Although I thought I had become case-hardened, I discovered I still was not shockproof when I studied the results of our investigation of the A & P—the Great Atlantic & Pacific Tea Company. This is the largest retail organization in the world, with 4,500 stores in the United States and Canada, and an income of approximately $4,700,000,000. For many years, a number of different unions had tried to organize the A & P employees and for many years the company had fought the unions off—and in the process had several times been found guilty of unfair labor practices. Eventually, however, the Meat Cutters and Butchers Union succeeded in organizing the people in the stores' meat departments.

But, for the company, the real D-day came when in the summer of 1952 the Safeway Stores signed a contract with the CIO Clerks Union calling for a forty-hour week. This put the heat on the A & P, because it was obvious that in the next negotiating session, at the end of the year, the Meat Cutters would demand a forty-hour week for its members. It was also obvious that when some union succeeded in organizing the rest of the A & P employees—a day that could not be far off—it too would demand a forty-hour week.

So, the Committee found, representatives of the A & P got together with the Meat Cutters' Max Block to see what could be "arranged." The A & P, the giant of big business, secretly agreed to turn over to the Meat Cutters some ten thousand of its unorganized workers—in return for a five-year contract with a forty-five-hour week.

Walter May and George Martin, our investigators on the case, suspected from the beginning that a secret agreement had been made, though both company and union officials denied it. All copies had been destroyed—they thought. But digging into the union's files, May found a copy of it. It extended the previous two-year contract an extra three years. And in the A & P files we found a memorandum showing that the five-year deal saved the company at least $2,000,000 a year. The company thus got what it wanted.

The union got ten thousand new members—and $500,000 a year in dues.

The employees of the Atlantic & Pacific—the hapless new members of Max Block's union—got virtually nothing, and lost the chance of legitimate representation.

They were told only that a two-year contract had been signed; nothing was said about extending the present forty-five-hour work week for another five years in all.

Senator Ervin and Senator Church made their feelings plain when they questioned Charles A. Schimmat, attorney for the A & P Company.

SENATOR ERVIN: In other words, you agreed with him that it was all right, since your company got such a big advantage out of it, it was all right for him to conceal, and that you would assist him in concealing it, the knowledge of the five-year agreement from the very persons who were to be bound by the five-year agreement?

MR. SCHIMMAT: May I point out to you that the International name was also on that document with Max Block's name on it.

SENATOR ERVIN: That does not change it. You tell me that your conscience would approve conduct like that . . . ?

MR. SCHIMMAT: That is what we did in this case.

SENATOR ERVIN: Yes, sir; you sure did.

Senator Church pressed the point.

SENATOR CHURCH: You would think then when representatives of the labor union ask you to keep certain terms of the contract concealed, that since it is their responsibility to expose the terms of this contract, you can enter into such an agreement and your hands are not soiled by doing it; is that right . . . ?

MR. SCHIMMAT: I did not see anything wrong with it, sir. . . .

SENATOR CHURCH: Well, I do. . . .

It is not possible here to relate in detail every corrupt practice that our investigation placed at the doorstep of the so-called respectable business community, but these self-serving deals cropped up constantly from the very beginning of our investigation. I have already shown, for example, how the power of Dave Beck induced Anheuser-Busch and other companies to deal with him; how Martin Philipsborn enabled James Cross to profit personally at the expense of his union members; how a number of oil companies made mutually beneficial arrangements with Charley Johnson's Penn Products; and there were many other cases. The Niagara-Mohawk Corporation of New York, for example, paid $93,000 to Ben Lapensohn, the Teamster official and labor "fixer" from Philadelphia, supposedly for ads in a yearbook he was publishing. Lapensohn, we found, raked off $84,700 of the $93,000, though corporation officials told us they thought the money was going to the New York state labor federation. Then there was Harold Roth, the New York businessman who loaned or arranged for more than $200,000 in loans, some unsecured and interest free, for Milton Holt, a Teamster official with whom Roth interests had contracts. Mr. Roth told us he saw nothing wrong with the loans—but admitted he would not make them again.

In addition, we found many small businesses that made deals with racket locals simply to keep their workers in line and to keep legitimate unions out. This was true especially in New York City, where the likes of Johnny Dio and others were allowed to come in and "organize" the employees.

More often than not these were illiterate Negro workers, or Puerto Ricans who could neither speak nor understand English. There are tens of thousands of them living in squalor, sometimes on as little as $32 a week. The ones we interviewed could not understand what was happening to them. They only knew they were faced with severe hardships and that providing food and clothing for a family on less than $40 a week was nearly impossible in New York, or in any other industrial community.

We heard from one witness, Miss Bertha Nunez, who told of a woman who contracted pneumonia and lost a child because of the coldness of the plant where she worked. Miss Nunez was an attractive and intelligent Puerto Rican who knew that she and her fellow workers were being exploited. But she was helpless to do anything about it.

2. LAWYERS

No one could listen to the testimony before our Committee, or read the record, and not be deeply concerned and badly disillusioned about the practices some attorneys engaged in while representing labor and management. From the first, we found lawyers who considered that their clients were not the rank and file but the union officials who held the purse strings.

I have already mentioned some, but consider also the attorneys who represented union officials in the following cases—again just to take a sampling from the many in our files:

Lou Berra, a Teamster official in St. Louis who paid for his house with union money, was indicted for income tax evasion. Some $35,000 of union funds were used to defend him, with the argument that he had embezzled the money and embezzled funds do not constitute income. The attorneys who made this argument knew their fee was coming from union funds.

Similarly, the attorneys defending Jimmy James, a vice president of the Laundry Workers Union, who was charged with taking over $600,000 from the pension and welfare fund, and was indicted for income tax evasion, argued their case on the same grounds, and accepted their compensation from the union.

Even more disturbing was the behavior of the attorney for Hoffa's own local, George Fitzgerald. He got a $100,000 Teamsters loan for a construction firm in which he had a major interest, and a $135,000 loan to go into the insurance business.

But what really concerned the Committee was his connection with a land development company in Michigan. He had recommended that the Teamsters lend $1,000,000 to a group of land speculators known as Winchester Village Land Company to develop some property on which the union held a mortgage. But the borrowers, with Fitzgerald's approval, invested so much of the money in a quite different plot, in which the Teamsters had no interest, that the whole deal turned into a financial bust which cost the union at least $600,000.

We found that Fitzgerald and his law partners received a $35,000 fee from the Winchester Village Land Company for arranging this loan from the Teamsters.

Hoffa told the Committee that he never knew that George Fitzgerald had shared in this fee of $35,000.

Fitzgerald, questioned about the propriety of his action, said: "Hindsight is better than foresight. If I knew this inquiry was going to be made about it, it would have made a difference."

A different kind of situation is that which concerned Carney Matheson of Detroit, the chief negotiator for the over-the-road truckers. He wields immense power and has been remarkably successful in obtaining favorable contracts for those he represents. Albert Matheson, his brother, was also in the trucking business. Both of them have performed legal work for Hoffa for which they have received no reimbursement and Carney Matheson has been in a number of financial deals with Hoffa.

Just as this kind of operation is improper for Hoffa, so is it improper for the two Mathesons.

The Committee was also highly critical of lawyers who accepted payment from the union treasury while representing officials who refused on the ground of self-incrimination to answer questions about the misuse or misappropriation of union funds. It was perfectly proper for them to represent these men, but they should have received their fees from the individual officials, not from the union members' dues.

I think that bar associations have a strong obligation in cases such as this. Leading members of bar associations across the country are eloquent in denouncing the corruption within the labor unions and the betrayal of trust by certain union officials. But they are silent about the betrayal of trust by their fellow lawyers. And while the AFL–CIO has taken action against the union leaders whose corruption we exposed, the bar associations have done virtually nothing about attorneys whose duplicity we also exposed. One exception is the Bar in Tennessee, which sought to disbar a judge who had been impeached.

But William Langley, a former district attorney in Portland, Oregon, whom our Committee showed was working hand in glove with the city's gangster elements, is still a practicing lawyer. It would also seem that the

Bar Association of Indiana might look into the situation regarding Holovachka, the former prosecuting attorney of Lake County, Indiana.

Time and again the Committee was disillusioned to discover that lawyers had lied to our investigators. In New York, while investigating the Teamsters' connection with the Akros Dynamics firm, we ran into a father-son team of lawyer and accountant in Herbert and George Burris who were certainly less than truthful. When our investigators asked Herbert about a certain important document related to the case, he denied that it ever existed. When we produced it, he said, startled: "I thought it had been destroyed."

The Committee also showed that Martin J. Quigley, a businessman in Washington, D.C., and a member of the Bar of the District of Columbia, knowingly accepted union funds to make payments on two houses for officials of the Textile Workers Union. In order to hide these transactions from the trustees of the union Quigley, on two separate occasions, wrote completely untruthful letters to conceal the real use to which the money had been put.

However, labor has been fortunate enough to attract the active assistance of many wise and skillful lawyers, men like Arthur Goldberg, counsel for the AFL–CIO, who have been drawn to the growing labor movement by a sense of idealism and a dedication to the cause of economic justice and a better way of life for the working man. They are men of high principle, who recognize that their profession carries with it certain responsibilities and obligations; they are completely loyal to the best interests of their clients—within the bounds of sound professional ethics.

Jim Rowe, a Washington, D.C., lawyer, comes to mind as one of these. For a time, he represented James Cross, president of the Bakers Union. At first he was convinced that the Committee's investigation of Cross was inspired only by the complaint of a faction within the union, and that the hearing would simply air an inter-union rivalry. But before we opened hearings he came to my office and, complimenting the staff on its work in the case, told me he was withdrawing as Cross's counsel. He did not tell me why; I did not ask him. Mr. Rowe, I knew, had done substantial preparatory work before the hearings; but as we later found, the union's records showed that he did not charge a fee for his services.

Another man who gave his time and talent was Abraham Freedman of Philadelphia, who represented Roy Underwood and his followers in their fight against the corrupt leadership of the Operating Engineers. Mr. Freedman knew that his clients were men with little money. He acted as their attorney at a personal sacrifice, because he hoped to achieve for Underwood some measure of justice. Dave Rabinovitz, the UAW attorney, was another whose ability and integrity have contributed greatly to the labor movement.

We did not meet Asher Schwartz, of New York, the general counsel of the Mail Deliverers Union there. We went into this union's activities and discovered corruption among some of its leaders. Mr. Schwartz resigned his job and gave up a substantial retainer rather than represent officials of the union who took the Fifth Amendment on questions pertaining to a sellout of the union members. He believed in the cause of his clients—and as he saw it the clients were the rank-and-file union men whose dues made up the treasury that paid him his retainer. Any other course, he felt, would involve him in a conflict of interest.[2]

His was a rarely found point of view, in our experience.

In 1934 Supreme Court Justice Harlan Stone gave a speech at the University of Michigan in which he referred to lawyers of that day who were serving large corporations:

I venture to assert that when the history of the financial era which has just drawn to a close comes to be written, most of its major mistakes and its major faults will be ascribed to the failure to observe the fiduciary principle, the precept as old as holy writ, that "a man cannot serve two masters." . . . There is little to suggest that the Bar has yet recognized that it must bear some of the responsibility for these evils. But when we know and face the facts we should have to acknowledge that such departures from the fiduciary principle do not actually occur without the active assistance of some member of our profession; and that their increasing recurrence would have been impossible but for the complaisance of a Bar, too absorbed in the work-a-day care of private interests to take account of these events of profound import—or to sound the warning that the profession looks askance on these things that "are not done."

Now twenty-five years later, history has given us an interesting parallel. Though Justice Stone was talking about evils that had developed in corporations, not labor unions, his words are just as pertinent today.

I feel very strongly that our bar associations should deal with these problems. But as matters presently stand the bar associations are not meeting their responsibilities. And if they continue to ignore such practices as our Committee encountered, as well as the unethical tactics of some attorneys engaged in the practice of criminal law, they will simply be asking for stricter regulation.

The sooner lawyers face up to this situation, the sooner we will have a profession of which we can properly be proud.

3. THE PRESS

The high editorial ideals fostered by American newspapers do not alter the basic fact that to exist as great instruments of information, newspapers

[2] When the leadership of the union changed, Mr. Schwartz resumed his connection with the union.

must be successful business enterprises. As such they are subject to the same economic pressures, the same financial pitfalls and the same management problems that confront other corporations.

This was forcefully brought home to the Committee—and to the press itself—in a series of hearings beginning in May, 1959, when it was disclosed that associates of Mr. Hoffa had practiced shakedown on management people engaged in newspaper distribution.

The papers were: the *New York Times*, the New York *Daily Mirror*, the Detroit *Times*, the Pittsburgh *Sun-Telegraph*, and *The American Weekly*.

Deeply involved in the pay-offs by the *New York Times*, the *Mirror* and *The American Weekly* was the Neo-Gravure Printing Company of Weehawken, New Jersey.

Strangely, this investigation began in Miami—far from the New York-New Jersey scene where the pay-offs occurred. We were investigating Harry Gross, the ex-convict-extortionist, who in October, 1958, many months after Hoffa had promised to clean up the union, had been given a Teamster charter in Miami. The union, Local 320, had only thirty-two members but Gross was receiving $14,000 a year in salary and expenses. The local was also paying for a red Thunderbird for his comfort. We found that Hoffa was sending International funds to the local to support him. Gross also maintained two Florida residences and one in New York, and seemed generally to have a limitless source of ready money.

During the course of his investigation, Walt Sheridan talked with a filling station operator who had had some dealings with Gross, and he mentioned that he had cashed a number of checks for him; some of them, he said, were from a printing company in New Jersey. Sheridan became curious. The operator said he happened to have one with him. It was this minor incident that broke the investigation wide open.

The checks were from the Neo-Gravure Company of Weehawken, New Jersey, and within a few hours Sheridan was on a plane north to discover what lay behind them. But the Neo-Gravure Company executives were wary and evasive. Yes, they said, Harry Gross was on their payroll. He was a platform foreman in their Shipping Department. He was worth his pay. They were satisfied with his work.

We could not possibly understand how a foreman for Neo-Gravure—with the record and reputation of Harry Gross—could earn his money on a New Jersey shipping platform while running a Teamsters local in Miami, Florida. Then a secret source who knew the inside workings of the company told Sheridan that a close study of the company's books would indicate that Mr. Gross was far more than a platform straw boss.

Placed under Committee subpoena, the company officials employed an attorney, former Governor George Craig of Indiana, who advised them to offer complete co-operation. I interviewed them in my office Monday, May 4, from 8:00 P.M. until nearly midnight.

The Neo-Gravure Company, it turned out, had been paying Gross over $1,000 a month to insure "labor peace" since shortly after his release from Sing Sing. At one time or another it had also had on its payroll Gross's two sons, a brother and brother-in-law. Over a period of a few years the combined salaries totaled $226,000. Gross, the company officials said, worked in league with Cornelius (Connie) Noonan, president of Local 1730 of the International Longshoremen's Association, with whom they had a contract.

"Had he received any other payments?" I asked.

Yes. From 1952 to 1958 he had been paid an additional $4,000 annually for "outside work."

What was "outside work"? In 1952 Neo-Gravure had started printing *The American Weekly* for the Hearst organization. However, a union jurisdictional dispute blew up and Hearst could not get its magazine delivered. Officials at *The American Weekly* asked the officers of the Neo-Gravure firm if they could do anything to help. Neo-Gravure in turn called on Harry Gross. Yes, he could fix it—for $4,000 a year for ten years, which he said he would spread around to the various labor officials concerned. *American Weekly* agreed, and the pay-offs were made through Neo-Gravure. Finally in 1958, acting on a request from *American Weekly* executives, Neo-Gravure asked Harry Gross if, in view of cost pressures, the payment could not be dropped. A few days later Mr. Gross agreed.

"Were there any other payments?" I asked.

In 1954 and 1955 they had made two payments to Gross of $2,500 each for settling a contract with Noonan's ILA Local 1730 platform workers at below-scale wage increases.

"Had any other pay-offs been made to Gross?"

"Yes."

In 1948 a Teamsters Union strike had hit the entire city of New York. But the *New York Times*, which then was having its Sunday magazine section printed by the Neo-Gravure Company, and the *New York Mirror*, which was receiving a Sunday supplement from the same firm, were able to obtain distribution.

That night in my office in the Senate we found out how.

Through the Neo-Gravure Company, these two newspapers made a $45,000 pay-off to Gross and Noonan in order to get their supplements delivered. Approximately $35,000 came from the *Times;* some $10,000 from the *Mirror.* Moreover, two years before, the same two papers had made a pay-off amounting to some $10,000 and for the same purpose. I could only think as I drove home that night of the little boy's reputed plea to Shoeless Joe Jackson in the 1919 World Series, "Joe, say it ain't so."

Several days later when we held our hearings, the Neo-Gravure people appeared as witnesses and deviated in no way from the story they had told in my office.

Senator McClellan told Charles Chenicek, vice president and general manager of the Neo-Gravure Printing Company: "What it actually amounted to is that you acted as agent, in a sense of go-between, between *The American Weekly* and the racketeers; is that true?"

Without flinching Mr. Chenicek answered: "That is true."

Both Gross and Noonan took the Fifth Amendment when questioned. Between the two of them and Gross's family they had received $307,000 as pay-offs for labor peace.

Senator McClellan expressed his appreciation to the Neo-Gravure witnesses for their testimony. He said: "The time has come in this country, if we are going to stop this racketeering and rascality that is going on . . . it is going to require that businessmen, honest labor people, their leaders, all of us stand up and be counted in this thing."

After our conversation in my office that Sunday night, Jerome Adlerman and Walter Sheridan called on business officials of the *New York Times* and the *Daily Mirror*. From the outset the *Times*'s business department co-operated. They furnished documents that we did not know existed, setting forth the details of the pay-off, which the memorandum referred to as a "tribute." The man who had handled it was no longer alive and the *Times* could have pleaded ignorance. They chose rather, like the representatives of Neo-Gravure, to tell the truth.

Amory H. Bradford, vice president and business manager of the *Times*, appeared before the Committee and summarized the history of the 1948 strike. He said that had the magazine section not been delivered, the cost to the *Times*, because of advertising commitments, would have been $160,000. He admitted that a similar problem in 1946 had also been taken care of by a pay-off. Through Neo-Gravure, he said, Harry Gross had passed the word along that "Connie Noonan can reach the proper people."[3]

But he added: "This is not the kind of payment that we would make today . . . in order to obtain deliveries of this kind."

On the day after Mr. Bradford testified, the *New York Times* played the story on the front page of the newspaper. Objectively written by an Associated Press reporter, it gave complete details of the *Times*'s involvement in the pay-off as exposed by the Committee. This, and the straightforward admission of error and co-operative attitude of the *Times*'s representatives, helped us greatly to recover from the shock of discovering that a paper of

[3] Gross and Noonan are under Federal indictment on charges growing out of the Committee's investigation. In December, 1959, Gross was convicted of income-tax evasion and resigned as president of Local 320.

the *Times*'s reputation should have been concerned in such a deal in the first place.

When we questioned Joseph E. Fontana, business manager of *The American Weekly*, regarding their $28,000 pay-off to Gross, he insisted that he had never bothered to ask Neo-Gravure where the $4,000 was going each year. He just paid it. The Committee could call it payment for labor peace, said Mr. Fontana, but he was going to call it payment to assure delivery of *The American Weekly*. He did say it was an action that the paper would never repeat.

Warren Kelly, vice president and advertising manager of the *Daily Mirror*, testified that his company had paid $13,856 in shakedown money through Neo-Gravure at the same time the *Times* had.

Did he worry about who got his money as long as his papers were delivered?

"I did not," he said.

"Do you think that is the proper attitude for a business executive?"

"I think it is the proper attitude for an executive that wants to sell two million papers."

And if he held the same position today that he had had then, and the same situation arose, would he still pay a bribe in order to assure delivery of his paper?

MR. KELLY: "That I would have to give more thought to."

Senator McClellan later raised the same question with him.

SENATOR MCCLELLAN: You know it is the wrong thing to do, do you not? Your paper editorially would condemn it in others just like that.

MR. KELLY: Exactly.

SENATOR MCCLELLAN: Don't you condemn it when you do it?

MR. KELLY: Yes, sir.

MR. KENNEDY: You wouldn't do it again if you were in the same position?

MR. KELLY: I would not.

In Pittsburgh, the Committee found that the *Sun-Telegraph* had on its payroll as a driver President Theodore Cozza of Local 211, one of Mr. Hoffa's union leaders, who had been convicted three times—of obstructing public justice, entering a building to steal, and operating a lottery. According to company officials, Cozza performed "very little" work for the money the paper paid him. Yet each week he pocketed a check for working fifty-six hours, plus the highest amount of overtime paid to any driver who really worked for the company. From January, 1950, until May, 1959, he received a total of slightly more than $100,000—including some $20,000 he was paid for a truck he rented to the newspaper.

Why had the payments to Cozza continued?

"I would say it was continued for fear of disturbing our labor relations and labor peace," said Mr. Poch, business manager of the paper.

A month before Mr. Poch testified, the paper had fired Cozza for roughing up its efficiency expert when he questioned Cozza's usefulness.

Cozza then called a strike and the newspaper was shut down. The strike was settled when the paper agreed to hire a substitute for Cozza, but with the understanding that he would actually work.[4]

The Committee also found that Cozza was getting a 5 per cent rake-off from the firm that leased trucks to the newspaper. This, the truck company said, was to "control drivers and prevent damage and abuse of their equipment."

In Detroit, Joe Prebenda, head of Teamsters Local 372, the union that handled delivery of the Detroit *Times*, was also serving two employers: the local and the *Times*. He drew substantial salaries from both.

Charles Obermeyer, business manager of the paper, said Prebenda did do "some work" for the paper, but only on Saturday nights. For this he drew a full week's salary, $36,000 over a five-year period. He received $14,000 a year from the union.

Mr. Obermeyer told the Committee that he planned to end Prebenda's employment with the *Times* immediately after the hearing. He was a quiet, soft-spoken man. It obviously disturbed him to have to admit that his company paid Joe Prebenda for doing little or no work.

Senator McClellan asked Mr. Obermeyer if he could construe the money paid to Prebenda as anything but a shakedown.

"I don't think so," answered the newspaper official.

"Do you think it is a proper payment?"

"Absolutely not."

As he got to his feet to leave the witness chair, I called for Joe Prebenda to appear. Walking to the table, he passed Mr. Obermeyer on his way out of the hearing room.

I saw him step directly in front of Mr. Obermeyer, and it was obvious even in the crowded hearing room that Prebenda had spoken sharply to him. When the Teamster took the stand and was under oath, I asked: "What did you just say to Mr. Obermeyer as he left?"

Joe Prebenda, unaware that he had been observed, hesitated. Then he grinned: "I just said, 'I think you made a mistake,'" he answered.

Before Mr. Obermeyer left the witness stand, Senator Ervin made this comment: "Your evidence indicates to me that the press in the United States is not quite as free as it is supposed to be."

[4] Cozza is now under Federal indictment on charges growing out of our Committee's investigation.

It cannot help but be disquieting that gangsters like Cozza or Gross are in a position to shut down great newspapers merely because they are not receiving their pay-offs. It is an intolerable situation; for this is a power that the Constitution denies even to the Federal Government. I hope that the hearings aroused concern among people about the tremendous power presently wielded by such people; certainly we shall have to have a far different attitude than we have had in the past if we are to lick the problem.

The Committee was unhappy to learn during our investigation that besides the cases I have mentioned, Teamsters Union money had contaminated a few reporters, a few columnists, a few feature writers. We found that in a number of cases Hoffa's union had paid cash, or given gifts or "expenses" to get favorable press coverage. Nevertheless, these few cases were more than overshadowed by the integrity of the vast majority of the newspapers of the nation, and by the idealism of a number of reporters whose vigilance contributed in many ways to the work of the Committee.

Pulitzer Prizes were awarded to such men as Clark Mollenhoff of the Cowles Publications, who, more than anyone else, was responsible for the existence of the Committee; to Wally Turner and Bill Lambert of the Portland *Oregonian;* to Harold Brislin of the Scranton, Pennsylvania, *Scrantonian* for outstanding investigative reporting, which led in more than one instance to hearings by our Committee. And the assistance and advice of men like Ed Guthman of the Seattle *Times* and John Seigenthaler of the Nashville *Tennesseean* were essential in our investigation of bad situations in their areas. Columnists such as John Herling, the late Fred Othman, Fred Perkins, and Victor Reisel frequently used their talent and space to raise significant questions.

And above and beyond the individual work of these and many others, the newspapers, national magazines, television and radio performed a substantial and constructive task in sifting the maze of day-to-day testimony and flashing it out across the nation, making the public aware of the enemy within.

4 The Business of Sex

COLUMBIA BROADCASTING SYSTEM

ANNOUNCER: The subject matter of the following program, THE BUSI-
NESS OF SEX, is addressed to adults and is recommended for adult listening
only.

WOMAN: My name is Hillary. I go out with men from many different
businesses. You understand that this is business for them as it is business for
me and they pay me and the result for them is profit and it makes it worthwhile for us all.

MODERATOR: The voice you have just heard was the voice of a call girl.
The name of this program is THE BUSINESS OF SEX. In its preparation, our reporters spent the last three months querying individuals across the
country; questioning law enforcement officials; meeting with welfare officers
and interviewing people from every walk of life, including procurers and call
girls. In the gathering of this information our staff encountered considerable
resistance on the one hand, and on the other, a surprising willingness to talk
about even the most personal and intimate matters.

The subject we are investigating is an old one . . . that of prostitution.
But in today's industrial society, it has appeared in a new form, with new
consequences. That form is encompassed in the words "call girl," and tonight's report will attempt to examine the extent and significance of this

phenomenon. . . . Anthropologist Margaret Mead.

DR. MEAD: Prostitution is an old potentiality of human beings; an old weakness which each generation in each society has to deal with over and over again. But every society has to consider how these practices which exploit and degrade human beings, are to be controlled; to be isolated; and to be reduced in magnitude.

Every society depends upon a certain degree of clarity about what it regards as good and what it regards as evil.

MODERATOR: Call girls, or "party girls" as they are sometimes known, are the aristocrats of the prostitute world. Their income permits them a way of life far above that of the ordinary prostitute. But like their poorer sisters, their role is a largely passive one. And even though they are an integral part of THE BUSINESS OF SEX, their active concern stops with the fees they receive. They are a commodity, and in the transaction play the part of a catalyst. We asked how some of them had got a start in "the life," as they call it.

MONTAGE: I had worked as a check-room girl and observed the other girls around the boss . . . getting fifty dollars, a hundred dollars, two hundred dollars, and here I was working for quarters and it came about one date, and then another date, and then before I knew it, I didn't mind it at all.

And I was invited on a date and received fifty dollars for an hour's services, and the money was very attractive compared to the forty dollars I had been making working in an office.

I started when I was about 17 years old. I went out with some friends of mine and they met these men and they offered some money and it was enough. I didn't need it at that particular time but that started me, 'cause I like pretty clothes.

I needed money to take care of my children. My baby was very ill and he needed an operation at the time. So they asked me whether I'd be interested in making some money, and I told them yes.

MODERATOR: We discovered that call girls come from all walks of life . . . they are secretaries, receptionists, school teachers, models, society girls, dancers, fledgling actresses, or housewives in need of extra money. Their clients are men from equally varied professions. Here is how a call girl defines *her* customers.

WOMAN: My clients are usually referred to in the trade between the girls as "Johns." The large majority are of the executive type; men in the higher income bracket with better positions because they're the only ones that can afford to spend that kind of money, fifty dollars for an hour's entertainment or a hundred dollars for several hours. I don't think that these

"Johns" are too wealthy, but they must have an income of ten-thousand dollars a year and up.

MODERATOR: In this business nothing can be left to chance, but as our reporters discovered, it is not possible to find a pattern in the way arrangements are made for the entertainment of customers. This much can be said when arrangements *are* made: they vary from industry to industry, from company to company, from one level of society to another. In some cases top executives are directly involved—giving instructions as to the type and extent of the entertainment their company will provide. In other cases only the middle or lower echelon of the company is aware of the entertainment that is planned. But whatever the arrangements, they must be made carefully; the risks for all concerned are far too great. In some cases there is no question that this type of entertainment *must* be provided, as this executive points out.

EXECUTIVE: We have to produce sex for some of the buyers. The buyers will say, "Do you have any good numbers for this trip?" Call girls that we can get for them or models that will supply entertainment for the buyers.

MODERATOR: The reasons and the methods for the entertainment of a client may vary. In some instances, procedures are greatly simplified to avoid embarrassment and needless contacts. This man, himself often approached to provide the services of top call girls, explains how selections can be made by individuals in some corporations.

MAN: There's a very famous madam in New York who takes care of your multi-millionaires only. She is a famous famous name in New York. She puts out a book every year, pictures of the girls she has working for her. And sends this book to her very very exclusive clients. Now this woman is one who really works with big business, you know, when big corporations have a party, they'll contact this woman. She'll make a flat fee, three-thousand, five-thousand, all according to how many girls they want. And she'll send them a book, they'll pick out the girls. There's no guesswork here. And she deals with the largest corporations in the United States.

MODERATOR: More usual in the making of selections for clients, is the use of lists. This man knows of the existence of two: A and B.

MAN: An "A" list would be the very expensive, very beautiful girls that can be taken out any place, and look completely respectable, charming, alluring, enticing, etc. And the "B" list are more a type that just drop into a hotel room for an hour or so, and then leave and the man is never seen in public with them. And the difference, of course, is the difference in price and the girl herself.

MODERATOR: To this executive, the reasons for the use of female entertainment in business by his company are quite clear.

EXECUTIVE: We need the people that are in a position to tip the scales in one direction or another. These are bank presidents and mortgage officers, real estate, vice presidents in large chain store companies and people of that kind who have to evaluate deals that are proposed to them. You have to understand that in making of mortgage loans that any bank or mortgage lender, insurance companies, as well as banks, have many demands made upon them for money and in many cases the loans are equally as good and they have just so much money to lend at this time. In cases of this kind, the people that have the best personal relationships will get more consideration than a stranger walking in. You don't let more than a week go by before there is some contact of some kind. You have lunches, you have dinners, theatre, you meet them at conventions where you entertain them there, take them to dinner; and then there are others where you'll go away for week-ends with them or spend a night with them in the city and go to a party and then later provide female entertainment for them.

MODERATOR: Our reporters were told that some companies maintain one or two call girls on their payroll as part of their public relations staff. The girls use the five- to six-thousand dollars of their yearly salary as a drawing account. *This* call girl also has accounts, even though she is on no one's payroll.

GIRL: I have accounts with manufacturers who will call me and advise me of the fact that one of their buyers is coming into town and that I should proceed. Usually they will send me a check the next day. This is ordinarily the head of the company or the manufacturer who wants to keep these buyers happy so that they will give him a large order. Many times there is a large party of oh, perhaps eighteen to twenty individuals involved, in which case I will get in contact with two or three of my girl friends, tell them of the final arrangements, and make an appointment to meet them at the hotel. We girls will be there to satisfy whatever whim each of these buyers might have. In turn, the manufacturers will give each girl twenty dollars per individual. Usually the girls want a guarantee of one-hundred dollars before they will go there. Sometimes if a buyer is very important, he will increase the price to the girl accordingly, so that she will spend more time and give him more consideration than others. This happens so frequently that it seems to me to be a standard way of conducting business through feminine company.

MODERATOR: She found that her presence helped to improve the atmosphere.

GIRL: I have been present during business conferences which are usually conducted at the end of the evening. After quite a bit of liquor has been consumed, and in this case the fee is one-hundred dollars, I will first be invited out to dinner. The man who is doing the entertainment will get tickets for whatever shows the buyer requests and then I will go back to the hotel with the man and usually we'll spend till two o'clock in the morning with him. He will often give a verbal agreement, subject to confirmation the next morning. This is done before I have gone to bed with him. They believe that this is a psychological moment when a person is in a very anxious mood.

MODERATOR: She recalls a specific deal.

GIRL: A man who was selling electronics was especially interested in getting a large order from the distributing organization. He had been trying for at least three or four years to entertain this man. The man had always refused until one particular evening when they had gone out to dinner. He told me to stand by, that he would probably give me a ring a little later after he got the man into a more receptive mood. I did stand by, and they both came to my apartment. We had quite a number of drinks and both men had relationships with me. This was at four o'clock in the morning. And the men had such a hilarious evening that he confirmed a very large order while we were all sitting here.

MODERATOR: It would seem that conventions provide suitable arenas for all types of business activities. *This* call girl describes the arrangements which are made for her when she is present at a convention.

GIRL: They usually have a number of rooms or suites in a hotel or hotels and they usually have one or two girls in one suite and these suites usually consist of a living room and two bedrooms and one girl will be in one bedroom and the other girl will be in the other bedroom and if there are maybe five or six men in that suite, then they just take turns and when that's finished with, if there's anybody else they know in other suites or rooms, then you go into another suite and room and this may go on or continue on till five or six in the morning and then the girl goes home. You'd be pretty tired by four o'clock, believe me.

MODERATOR: She remembers one specific convention evening.

GIRL: I went into a suite and there were say maybe five or six businessmen there. One man that you would see first, would explain to you, in the bedroom, "Don't ask anybody you see for money. I'll look after you when it's finished and you're ready to leave." And this is what he does. They usually give me twenty-five a piece, and my taxi fare. And if the man is very nice, he'll throw maybe a twenty-dollar tip in . . . a bonus . . . or whatever it is. After you leave there, once you get out into the air, it just feels like you haven't done anything at all.

MODERATOR: In our competitive economy the middle man is in a position all his own. This broker is in a position all his own. This broker describes the particular appeal of his methods of operation.

MAN: You can be a big company and steelers don't recognize you . . . they want to know what your background is . . . well you never bought steel from us before. That's where a fellow like me comes in. I know somebody who knows somebody and we split the pie. But there was this very large company going into the manufacture of deep freezers which call for the use of a lot of steel and being a steel broker I like to reach out for fellas like that. You just can't get them by knocking on their door or sending your card in. This isn't the approach. There are many occasions . . . on a thing like that where we gotta use a little finesse. So I called up long distance and invited them to New York with his staff. He was the head purchasing agent and one of the members of the firm. When they arrived, it was summertime. And this one man was quite elderly you know, and I was afraid he'd die on me; the heat was terrific. So I got an air conditioning unit for him and I got this tremendous living room. Then, he had his two assistants who I noticed after one or two days were very influential. He listened to their advice on many matters. So I had served a few cocktails parties, but when I wanted to make my move I found that the two younger men were the men to be impressed. So I had these girls, I met them, told them, told them, "Now look. There's no mention of money. You're show girls. I'll arrange to have them meet you after eleven, and you're separated or divorced, and go along with the bit . . . I'll pay all the tabs, but give them that stare, you know . . . like they remind you of somebody and just get gaga over the whole thing." Which was what happened and made these fellas; their egos were just at the bursting point. So naturally, I was their fair-haired boy, you know. They started calling me by my first name, you know. So I was recommended for the deal. My prices were within bounds. And I got it . . . I beat about six other men that were after this contract, and the deal netted me about $60,000.

MODERATOR: Call girls are often given specific assignments by the men who hire them. The client, or target of her attentions must somehow not be made to realize that he is being treated to a paid professional performance. In this case, a man named Harry footed the bill.

GIRL: Harry's not too straight-laced, and he doesn't play to be, but he did, amongst these people who sent six men there, and I knew he wanted to do business with them, and he wanted me to seek out one in particular. Harry had said to me on the telephone, "Now when I introduce you to so-and-so, be very pleasant. Be just as nice to everybody else, as to him. But when you can get him on the side, slip him your phone number, and tell him you'd like to meet him later." Harry was giving me the hundred dollars, so it was all right with me. So I did. Oh, and he was thrilled, very flattered and I said the usual, "Oh, I really go for you. You do something to me." And, "Let's go up to your room and have a drink." And you don't let him know that you're a call girl. And make whoopee with him, and he's very flattered and at the same time, you keep plugging Harry; what a great guy he is; what a terrific businessman he is; and always makes such legitimate deals; such big deals; and you practically talk the fellow into signing the next morning. They had some big order on hand, a hundred-thousand anyhow, 'cause Harry wouldn't put himself out, and he wouldn't part with a hundred for me—if it wasn't something big—'cause Harry's pretty cheap.

MODERATOR: Call girls interviewed by our reporters told them that their assignments bring them in contact with the highest levels of business.

GIRL: I have a lot of dealings with large corporations. The majority of the men that I do entertain are in the top businesses in this country. They all use the services of call girls. They want somebody who can carry on a converation; who can enjoy a joke without being rowdy and boisterous; somebody who doesn't get drunk and blabber all over. And a few of them'll entertain somebody who's worth a lot to you in the business. You don't want his picture in the paper for any reason or anything like that. You don't want anything to go wrong. You want somebody that you know is going to handle it right.

MODERATOR: This woman was the madam of a busy call house.

MADAM: I met one sales manager for one of the larger companies who did a great deal of entertaining. Usually, his parties require from two to four to five, some girls. They were in the afternoon mostly. This was a combination of cocktail hour, go to bed for a little while, and wake up with a new thought on the subject and usually some sales. All of this bill was taken care of through expense account tabs. Later on, it got to the place where I billed them once a month, and it was paid that way. Another company that I had this same arrangement with, was a large equipment company that had branches all over the world, and I had some quite prolonged parties that didn't all consist of just girls. I mean it was important in these cases not to have a girl that was going to take up all of the man's time. Of course, the point of the things was to make sales or to buy merchandise.

MODERATOR: A gambling casino can be big business, and there, as in most businesses, a basic creed is to keep the customer happy. But in gambling there are winners and losers, and this call girl recalls how her particular talents were used.

GIRL: This one particular night I received this call to go to one of the casinos with another girl. Then there was two distinguished guys. They picked on us as the girls to spend the evening with these gentlemen. We were not to receive any money from these men, no gifts, and that we would be paid by the casino around fifty dollars an hour. These particular men had won quite a bit of money from the casino and they wanted us to try and get them back to the tables so the casino could win back their money. We'd go to the show, we'd dance, we'd drink, we'd gamble, and later we'd go back to the hotel room to go to bed with these people. Most of them are losers, but they don't care if you get them back to the tables. But they want you to make them happy to keep the good-will toward that club so that when they come back the next time, they'll come to the same club. The pit-bosses have us entertain the guys, to have us do anything they wish. All the clubs use this technique. The funny thing is that some of these clients of ours don't even know that we're getting paid. They think that we're show girls or girls just out for a good time.

MODERATOR: *This* girl was instrumental in the signing of a contract.

GIRL: My boyfriend who was a theatrical manager, he wanted to get one of the stars to sign a contract with him. This was a rock 'n' roll star. The star asked him if he knew me. He said, yes he did. The manager told me if I could talk these people into signing the contract he would give me seventy-five dollars. The party agreed to do it if he could have me. I did what he wanted me to do that same night. The manager gave me seventy-five dollars, and he went to the office and signed the contract the following day. Afterwards, I felt guilty about it. I didn't think it was right for them . . . I mean, I figure if a person really wanted to work for a person, he'd just go ahead and do it. I knew the manager was just trying to get his money or something like that. He would make a hundred times more than what he gave me. And the boy would be losing.

MODERATOR: There is, as we said earlier, no standard formula in business entertainment. Here is one man's description of how men of importance to his company's business were entertained.

MAN: On several occasions we have gone out and we have rented for the weekend a boat which will sleep six or eight people, and have taken along two or three people from one chain store or one mortgage banking institution or maybe it will be two of them, and two from our company. And we will have four girls that will go along. We'll leave perhaps on a Friday night, and come back in on a Sunday night. Of course, they've explained home that they're going off fishing for the weekend with the boys and identify the boys. And one thing is that we normally have, on other social occasions met the wives and created a good relationship so that they feel that when their husbands go away they're in very good hands; that if they're going fishing, they're going fishing. So that it all falls into a pattern. And then we will have an equal number of girls aboard. These girls are either professional prostitutes who are extremely attractive and intelligent and good company, or else on some occasions they are girls that have other jobs during the week and are not averse to this kind of relationship of going off and keeping their anonymity during the kind of relationship. They're meeting extremely interesting people. They're meeting top people in the business world who are good company, have good minds, and it's very entertaining as well as profitable.

MODERATOR: Why would a businessman decide that a client required special handling?

MAN: A man is coming in from out-of-town, to approve a budget, and the budget is a little bit higher than they quoted him when they went after the account. Now, in order to justify the extra fifteen- or twenty-thousand dollars that they've tacked on the budget, they decided to wine and dine the man and show him a good time before he comes into the office the following day and sees this alarming rise in budget.

MODERATOR: Men are not the only targets of those selling public relations or good will practices . . . or so it would appear from this account by a man who helped to engineer this sale, to an important woman executive.

MAN: These fellows had this chemist . . . and he had this great formula and this woman who was un-approachable to them; very domineering type of a person. So we got a tall, handsome man that had every requisite that a man should have. And he was made a salesman for the express purpose of seeing this woman. And he went up and called on her, and instead of calling on her in her office, he waited till she was through and on her way out. She accepted his invitation to a cocktail and he told her what his mission was and told her a lot about himself. Just in from another part of the country, the southwest. She figured well, I got myself a private little exclusive prize here and once you know a person's weakness, why you just let nature take its course; which was what happened. And in about ten days, his formula was used and that was a tremendous two- three-million deal.

MODERATOR: Some executives denied that it was a widespread practice, other expressed amazement that anyone should not know how common the practice was. This publicist for his part, had few doubts of the widespread acceptance of the practice, particularly in our larger cities.

PUBLICIST: The use of call girls in industry is pretty widespread at this time. There are a lot of industries that use them, that are not suspect, such as industrial corporations. I think that in places like Chicago or St. Louis or Cleveland, the use of these girls is much greater than in New York.

MODERATOR: As for the girls themselves, the majority we interviewed shared this opinion.

GIRL: Based on my own experience a very wide variety of businesses are involved in these practices.

MODERATOR: What is the result of such business relations? We asked one company vice-president for his opinion.

MAN: When you reach the point where they're ready to go away with you for a weekend where you're going to bring girls along or for a night where you're going to have girls there, you have created a very very close personal relationship which cannot be replaced. Everything else you do with them, nothing is illegal or immoral. This is a stage of relationship, when you have reached this point with a person that you sleep together in effect, and have girls together, you couldn't get any closer to them personally.

And you realize in this kind of a business relationship that although when you walk in with a deal you don't say to him, "I want you to do something for me." He knows damn well when you walk in that you're hoping that he will do everything he can and you know that he will do everything within his power to be able to help you.

MODERATOR: This man is president of a large international firm; he seemed to agree with the vice-president.

MAN: There is absolutely no doubt that prostitution per se does help business. This is the fastest way that I know of to have an intimate relationship established with a buyer. It's an experience which has been shared, whether it's together or not makes no difference. The point is, that I know that the buyer has spent the night with a prostitute that I have provided. In the second place, in most cases the buyers are married, with families. It sort of gives me a slight edge; well, we will not call it exactly blackmail, but it is a subconscious edge over the buyer. It is a weapon that I hold, and I could discreetly drop it at any time when the wife is present, and the buyer subconsciously mulls it over. He knows I will not do it; is aware of it. Since there are many occasions thereafter where I and my family, and his family will be together—such as conventions and whatnot—where we all gather, all the people of the same industry . . . it is a weapon, there's no doubt about it—and it is a good weapon to have.

MODERATOR: But even under this implied threat it would appear that some individuals still expect to be supplied with the sex commodity, as an integral part of their business dealings . . . and they will not hesitate to say so.

MAN: Nowadays the clients who come in to town to conclude a business deal expect it and very often these girls work in the detriment of your own interests because the client may be dissatisfied with the girl.

MODERATOR: In addition to her role in furthering business deals, this madam and sometime call girl told our reporter how she had been used by a man with a more than usual interest in politics.

GIRL: Some time ago, when I was operating a call house, I was approached by a man that I had done business with before. I'm going to call him Burt. He gave me the name and the occupation and a little material on a particular individual that he wanted me to make a contact with. He told me he has some aspirations to run this man for a political office. He wanted us to get on a real good basis. I made this contact and I arranged a meeting then between the two men. From the beginning, he was told that he was to take absolutely no donations from any outside source other than the one- or two-dollar donations that might be from housewives that might be backed up with a vote. But he was to make no commitments whatsoever. The financier on this project, which was Burt, had enough money to finance the campaign completely. He could have walked up to the man and shook his hand and told him that he thought he was a good citizen, would make a good mayor, and he wanted to back him. If everything had been on the up and up, that was all that would have needed to be done. He wanted someone who would have a hold on him to make sure that the man, should he be elected, would not appropriate all the funds into playgrounds and swimming pools for children. We wanted him to stay in line after he was elected mayor, and it would certainly be a mark against him, his association with me on the basis that it was on. It would have been enough for the man to play ball if he had gotten in office. . . .

MODERATOR: Thus far, our illustrations have been concerned with "The Big Deal," and "The Big Operator," who is making money, aided by feminine company, to the tune of thousands, and sometimes millions of dollars. We are going to turn our attention now, to a smaller scale version of the same phenomenon: the relationship between prostitution and profit, as it involves a small town, and people in the lower income brackets. The name of the town is Beatty. It is roughly one hundred miles northwest of Las Vegas, in Nye County, Nevada.

MONTAGE: This town is around 250 population, and it's strictly a tourist town. We're on the main highway from Canada to Mexico. And we're thirty-eight miles from the heart of Death Valley, and they bring around 500-thousand people a year through there.

We don't have too much to offer. It's more or less of a stopover point in the middle of the desert.

MODERATOR: In the state of Nevada, prostitution as such is not prohibited by statute. Brothels have existed in Nye County for as long as the residents can remember. However, county authorities are empowered to halt the practice of prostitution, as a "nuisance," whenever they receive formal notification of its existence. Up until about a year ago, there were two brothels in the town of Beatty. These were closed after formal complaints were received by Nye County's District Attorney, William Beko.

BEKO: They were situated just across the street from a playground area for school children and children that age. The other factors that involved the closure of those houses was the lack of cooperation between the operators of the houses and the girls working there. We found flagrant examples of where there was no fingerprinting nor any medical check of the girls prior to the time they went to work. The fingerprinting from the law enforcement standpoint was important to keep track of the movements of the girls and as a possible basis for Mann Act violations under federal law, where there's the unlawful transportation of the female across the state line for immoral purposes. We were continually getting complaints from some of the residents in Beatty because the areas were so well lighted or so conspicuous. There was little doubt in the minds of the children there what was going on in those particular houses.

MODERATOR: When District Attorney Beko closed the brothels in Beatty, the impact on the town was immediately noticeable.

MONTAGE: Well, it damn near made a ghost town out of the place.

Night club business, I would say, dropped off about eighty per cent. The service station business dropped off about fifty per cent. Around a fifty to eighty per cent drop-off on business.

MODERATOR: But some residents of Beatty blame not the closing of the brothels, but the resulting publicity.

MAN: It brought the wrong element in the killing of our tourist business. Since all of this bad publicity has been in the paper.

MODERATOR: Some of the citizens decided to give their reaction a concrete form.

BEKO: Within just a very few days after the closure, petitions were received by the county commissioners, not signed only by people who made it a practice to go in those places, but by very prominent and highly respected business people in Beatty that objected to the closure. They felt that with the large atomic energy base there at Mercury, and all of the construction that was incidental to that station that they would attract a great number of men that were not known, might cause possible danger to their children being assaulted. That is, the young girls being assaulted. They feel, that by having an establishment of that type that it lessens the danger of that. The business houses were hurt by it financially, there's no doubt about that, because it did attract quite a great deal of traffic to Beatty.

MODERATOR: Not all of the residents backed the petition, and our reporters found that even today, a year after the closure, there is still bitter disagreement over the whole question of open prostitution.

MONTAGE: It's bad morale for the children and the tourists frown on it —especially women tourists—and I think they should be closed up, cleaned up, specially when we're on a main highway and dealing strictly with tourist trade.

Well, I think that we should have them. As a matter of fact, I believe we need them. If it's policed right, well, I don't object.

I've always been raised in a place that was wide open. I don't consider that it has ruined me.

It got out of line, got a lot of syndicates in, and too many operators. There was nothing left for a legitimate businessman, only sit here and starve.

MODERATOR: There are some who are torn by an inner conflict: they support the District Attorney as an official of the law, but they regret the closure of the brothels.

MONTAGE: In my opinion, Mr. Beko has always been very fair and tried to do the things that the people in Beatty wanted him to do. He knows we're having a hospital problem here. Our closest doctor is ninety-six miles away.

We have absolutely no Red Cross. We have, I believe, one registered nurse from World War I is all we have in town. There's no medicines. If there's any car wrecks or anything else, you have to leave the patient there until an ambulance comes 114 miles to get them. Or if you have an emergency yourself, you've got to get the person with the fastest car and just hope and pray that you get to a hospital or a doctor in time. I mean, there's no other way.

There was two doctors came out here and they couldn't make a living and they left about ninety days ago.

MODERATOR: What is the connection between the operation of the brothels and the hospital problem?

MAN: Well, each girl that works in any of these houses has to be inspected once a week and they have to be transported to Tonopah for that purpose. If the hospital were here, of course, they could just tell what they need locally, and avoid that long trip each week.

MODERATOR: But there's another way in which the brothels contributed to the welfare of the town.

MONTAGE: It was more or less agreed that houses of prostitution in the town were to make substantial donations to the hospital fund.

They help out the hospital fund and Girl Scouts, the Boy Scouts and the P.T.A. and Christmas fund; everything, I mean that, you know, would just help the community.

We need the doctor very badly here and if that's what we have to do to get it, well, that's all right. And although we're not exactly proud of this method of obtaining one, why it is a method. It's one way.

I sure wouldn't want to patronize a hospital that anybody stoops so low to sell a woman's body to support a hospital.

MODERATOR: The petition from Beatty now rests in District Attorney Beko's safe. He says it will remain there, and he will not act upon it. As for Beatty itself, the incident has left in its wake a continuing controversy, marked by anger and ethical confusion. . . .

5 The Social Integration of Queers and Peers*

ALBERT J. REISS, JR.

Sex delinquency is a major form of behavior deviating from the normative prescriptions of American society. A large number of behaviors are classified as sex delinquency—premarital heterosexual intercourse, pederasty, and fellation, for example.

Investigation of sex behavior among males largely focuses on the psychological structure and dynamic qualities of adult persons who are described as "sexual types" or on estimating the incidence, prevalence, or experience rates of sex acts for various social groups in a population. There is little systematic research on the social organization of sexual activity in a complex social system unless one includes descriptive studies of the social organization of female prostitution.

An attempt is made in this paper to describe the sexual relation between "delinquent peers" and "adult queers" and to account for its social organization. This transaction is one form of homosexual prostitution between a young male and an adult male fellator. The adult male client pays a de-

Reprinted from *Social Problems*, Volume 9, Number 2 (Fall, 1961), 102–120, by permission of The Society for the Study of Social Problems and the author.

* The word "queer" is of the "straight" and not the "gay" world. In the "gay" world it has all the qualities of a negative stereotype but these are not intended in this paper. The paper arose out of the perspective of boys in the "straight" world.

I am particularly indebted to Howard S. Becker, Evelyn Hooker, Everett Hughes, John Kitsuse, Ned Polsky, H. Laurence Ross and Clark Vincent for their helpful suggestions and encouragement in publishing this article.

linquent boy prostitute a sum of money in order to be allowed to act as a fellator. The transaction is limited to fellation and is one in which the boy develops no self-conception as a homosexual person or sexual deviator, although he perceives adult male clients as sexual deviators, "queers" or "gay boys."

There has been little research on social aspects of male homosexual prostitution; hence the exploratory nature of the investigation reported here and the tentative character of the findings. Although there are descriptions of "marriage" and of the "rigid caste system of prison homosexuality"[1] which contribute to our understanding of its social organization in the single sex society of deviators, little is known about how homosexual activity is organized in the nuclear communities of America.

A few recent studies discuss some organizational features of male prostitution.[2] Ross distinguishes three types of male homosexual prostitutes on the basis of the locus of their hustling activity:[3] (1) the *bar-hustler* who usually visits bars on a steady basis in search of queer clients; (2) the *street-hustler*, usually a teen-aged boy who turns "tricks" with older men; (3) and, the *call-boy* who does not solicit in public. The street-hustler has the lowest prestige among hustlers, partly because his is the more hazardous and less profitable form of activity. One might expect their prestige status in the organized "gay world" to be low since they apparently are marginal to its organization. Street-hustlers, therefore, often become bar-hustlers when they are able to pass in bars as of legal age.

The boys interviewed for this study could usually be classified as street-hustlers, given the principal locus of their activity. Yet, the street-hustlers Ross describes are oriented toward careers as bar-hustlers, whereas none of the boys I studied entered hustling as a career. For the latter, hustling is a transitory activity, both in time and space.

There apparently are crucial differences among hustlers, however, in respect to the definition of the hustler role and the self-concept common to occupants in the role. The hustlers Ross studied are distinguished by the fact that they define themselves as both prostitute and homosexual. The boys I studied *do not define themselves either as hustlers or as homosexual.* Most of these boys see themselves as "getting a queer" only as a substitute activity

---

[1] Arthur V. Huffman, "Sex Deviation in a Prison Community," *The Journal of Social Therapy*, 6 (Third Quarter, 1960), pp. 170–181; Joseph E. Fishman, *Sex in Prison*, New York: The Commonwealth Fund, 1930; Donald Clemmer, *The Prison Community*, Boston: The Christopher Publishing House, 1940, pp. 260–273.

[2] William Marlin Butts, "Boy Prostitutes of the Metropolis," *Journal of Clinical Psychopathology*, 8 (1946–1947), pp. 673–681; H. Laurence Ross, "The 'Hustler' in Chicago," *The Journal of Student Research*, 1 (September, 1959), pp. 13–19; Jens Jersild, *Boy Prostitution*, Copenhagen: C. E. Gad, 1956 (Translation of *Den Mandlige Prostitution* by Oscar Bojesen).

[3] H. Laurence Ross, *op. cit.*, p. 15.

or as part of a versatile pattern of delinquent activity.[4] The absence of a shared definition of one another as hustlers together with shared definitions of when one "gets a queer" serve to insulate these boys from self-definitions either as street-hustlers or as homosexual.

The boys interviewed in this study regard hustling as an acceptable substitute for other delinquent earnings or activity. Although the sexual transaction itself may occur in a two-person *or* a larger group setting, the prescribed norms governing this transaction are usually learned from peers in the delinquent gang. Furthermore, in many cases, induction into the queer-peer transaction occurs through participation in the delinquent group. They learn the prescribed form of behavior with adult fellators and are induced into it as a business transaction by means of membership in a group which carries this knowledge in a common tradition and controls its practices. In particular, it will be shown that the peer group controls the amount of activity and the conditions under which it is permitted. Finally, it is postulated that this is a shared organizational system between peer hustlers and adult fellators.

There apparently exist the other possible types of males who engage in homosexual sex acts based on the elements of self-definition as homosexual and hustler. John Rechy in several vignettes describes a third type who conceive of themselves as hustlers but do not define themselves as homosexual.[5]

> . . . the world of queens and male-hustlers and what they thrive on, the queens being technically men but no one thinks of them that way—always "she"—their "husbands" being the masculine vagrants—"fruithustlers"—fleetingly sharing the queens' pads—never considering they're involved with another man (the queen), and as long as the hustler goes only with queens—and with fruits only for scoring (which is making or taking sexmoney, getting a meal, making a pad) *he is himself not considered queer*." (italics mine)[6]

The importance of being defined as nonhomosexual while acknowledging one's role as a hustler is brought forth in this passage:

> "Like the rest of us on that street—who played the male role with other men —Pete was touchy about one subject—his masculinity. In Bickford's one afternoon,

---

[4] The dinstinction made here is not intended to suggest that other types of hustlers do not also define themselves in other deviant roles. Hustlers may occupy a variety of deviant roles which are classified as delinquent or criminal; they may be "hooked," blackmailers, thieves, etc.

[5] I am indebted to Ned Polsky for bringing Rechy's stories to my attention.

[6] John Rechy, "The Fabulous Wedding of Miss Destiny," *Big Table* I, Number 3 (1959), p. 15.

a good looking masculine young man walked in, looking at us, walks out again hurriedly. 'That cat's queer,' Pete says, glaring at him. 'I used to see him and I thought he was hustling, and one day he tried to put the make on me in the flix. It bugged me, him thinking I'd make it with him for free. I told him to f . . . off, go find another queer like him.' He was moodily silent for a long while and then he said almost belligerently: 'No matter how many queers a guy goes with, if he goes for money, that don't make him queer. You're still straight. It's when you start going for free, with other young guys, that you start growing wings.' "[7]

The literature on male homosexuality, particularly that written by clinicians, is abundant with reference to the fourth possible type—those who define themselves as homosexual but not as hustlers.

THE DATA

Information on the sexual transaction and its social organization was gathered mostly by interviews, partly by social observation of their meeting places. Though there are limitations to inferring social organization from interview data (particularly when the organization arises through behavior that is negatively sanctioned in the larger society), they provide a convenient basis for exploration.

Sex histories were gathered from 18.6 of the 1008 boys between the ages of 12 and 17 who were interviewed in the Nashville, Tennessee, SMA for an investigation of adolescent conforming and deviating behavior. These represent all of the interviews of one of the interviewers during a two-month period, together with interviews with all Nashville boys incarcerated at the Tennessee State Training School for Boys.

As Table 1 discloses, the largest number of interviews was taken with lower-class delinquent boys. There is a reason for this: when it was apparent that delinquents from the lowest social class generally had some contact with adult male fellators, an attempt was made to learn more about how this contact was structured and controlled. Sex histories, therefore, were obtained from all of the white Nashville boys who were resident in the Tennessee State Training School for Boys during the month of June, 1958.

The way sex history information was obtained precludes making reliable estimates about the incidence or prevalence of hustling within the Nashville adolescent boy population. Yet the comparisons among types of conformers and deviators in Table 1 provide an informed guess about their life

[7] John Rechy, "A Quarter Ahead," *Evergreen Review*, Vol. 5, No. 19 (July-August, 1961), p. 18.

TABLE 1. TYPE OF SEX EXPERIENCE BY CONFORMING-DEVIATING TYPE OF BOY

Per Cent by Conforming-Deviating Type

Type of Sex Experience	Lower Class				Middle Class				All Classes			Total
	Org. career delinquent	Peer-oriented delinquent	Con-forming non-achiever	Con-forming achiever	Peer-oriented delinquent	Con-forming non-achiever	Con-forming achiever	Hyper-conformer	Non-conforming isolate	Con-forming isolate		
Total	73	166	250	81	38	86	193	56	24	41		1008
Queers, masturbation, and heterosexual	32.5	27.3	5.1	20.0	—	10.0	—	—	37.5	—		17.6
Queers, masturbation, hetero and animal	30.2	4.5	—	—	5.0	—	—	—	—	—		8.5
Heterosexual only	4.7	11.4	—	—	70.0	30.0	—	—	12.5	—		13.4
Heterosexual and masturbation[a]	25.6	34.1	33.3	40.0	15.0	10.0	40.0	—	25.0	—		27.3
Masturbation only	2.3	15.9	48.7	40.0	—	10.0	40.0	57.1	25.0	100.0		21.9
Denies sex experience	4.7	6.8	12.8	—	10.0	40.0	20.0	42.9	0.0	—		11.2
Subtotal	43	44	39	5	20	10	10	7	8	1		187
No sex history	41.1	73.5	84.4	93.8	47.4	88.4	94.8	87.5	66.7	97.6		81.4

[a] Includes 3 cases of heterosexual, masturbation, and animal (2 lower class organized career delinquent and 1 peer oriented delinquent).

chances for participation in such an activity.[8]

Only two middle-class boys report experience in the peer-queer trans-action. In one case, the boy acquiesced once to solicitation; in the other, the boy had acquired experience and associations in the State Training School for Boys which led to continued participation following his release. Within the lower-class group, it seems clear that the career-oriented delinquent is most likely to report sex experiences with fellators. Roughly three of every five boys report such experiences as contrasted with the peer-oriented de-linquent, the type with the next highest relative frequency, where only about one in three report such experiences.

Taking into account the proportional distribution of types of conformers and deviators in a school population of adolescent boys and applying in a very rough way the proportional distribution for type of sex deviation set forth in Table 1, the experience rate with fellators is quite low in a popula-tion of all adolescent boys. The peer-queer relationship seems almost ex-clusively limited to lower-class delinquent boys—particularly career-oriented delinquent boys, where the experience rate is probably very high.

While not of direct concern here, it is of interest that the conformers in Table 1 seem to consist about equally of boys who either report a history of heterosexual and masturbation experience, or masturbation only experi-ence, while hyperconformers either report no sex experience or that they masturbate only.

It might also be inferred from Table 1 that the adolescent conforming boy of lower-class origins in our society is very unlikely to report he never masturbates, though a substantial proportion of middle-class conforming boys maintain they never masturbate and never have masturbated. Although there may be age differences among the class levels in age of onset of mas-turbation, the class difference may yet be genuine. It is possible, of course, that this difference in masturbation experience reflects only a difference in willingness to report masturbation to a middle-class investigator, i.e., middle-class boys are more likely to hide their sexual experience, even that of masturbation, from others. Nevertheless, there may be class differences in the social organization of sexual experiences, since lower-class boys reported masturbating in groups when they first began to masturbate, while this ex-perience was reported much less frequently by middle-class boys, for whom it is more likely a private matter. The same thing is true for heterosexual experience: lower-class boys, particularly delinquent ones, frequently report they participate in group heterosexual activity in "gang-bangs," while hetero-

[8] For a definition of the types of conformers and deviators see Albert J. Reiss, Jr., "Conforming and Deviating Behavior and the Problem of Guilt," *Psychiatric Research Reports*, 13 (December, 1960), pp. 209–210, and Albert J. Reiss, Jr. and Albert Lewis Rhodes, "The Distribution of Juvenile Delinquency in the Social Class Structure," *American Sociological Review*, Vol. 26, No. 5 (October, 1961), pp. 720–732.

sexual experience appears to be a more private experience for the middle-class boy, who does not share his sexual partner with peers. All of this may reflect not only greater versatility in the sex experience of the lower-class male but perhaps a greater willingness to use sex as a means to gratification.

HOW PEERS AND QUEERS MEET

Meetings between adult male fellators and delinquent boys are easily made, because both know how and where to meet within the community space. Those within the common culture know that contact can be established within a relatively short period of time, if it is wished. The fact that meetings between peers and queers can be made easily is mute evidence of the organized understandings which prevail between the two populations.

There are a large number of places where the boys meet their clients, the fellators. Many of these points are known to all boys regardless of where they reside in the metropolitan area. This is particularly true of the central city locations where the largest number of contact points is found within a small territorial area. Each community area of the city, and certain fringe areas, inhabited by substantial numbers of lower-class persons, also have their meeting places, generally known only to the boys residing in the area.

Queers and peers typically establish contact in public or quasi-public places. Major points of contact include street corners, public parks, men's toilets in public or quasi-public places such as those in transportation depots, parks or hotels, and "second" and "third-run" movie houses (open around the clock and permitting sitting through shows). Bars are seldom points of contact, perhaps largely because they are plied by older male hustlers who lie outside the peer culture and groups, and because bar proprietors will not risk the presence of under-age boys.

There are a number of prescribed modes for establishing contact in these situations. They permit the boys and fellators to communicate intent to one another privately despite the public character of the situation. The major form of establishing contact is the "cruise," with the fellator passing "queer-corners" or locations until his effort is recognized by one of the boys. A boy can then signal—usually by nodding his head, a hand gesticulation signifying OK, following, or responding to commonly understood introductions such as "You got the time?"—that he is prepared to undertake the transaction. Entrepreneur and client then move to a place where the sexual activity is consummated, usually a place affording privacy, protection and hasty exit. "Dolly," a three-time loser at the State Training School, describes one of these prescribed forms for making contact:

"Well, like at the bus station, you go to the bathroom and stand there pretendin' like . . . and they're standin' there pretendin' like . . . and then they motions their head and walks out and you follow them, and you go some place. Either they's got a car, or you go to one of them hotels near the depot or some place like that . . . most any place."

Frequently contact between boys and fellators is established when the boy is hitchhiking. This is particularly true for boys' first contacts of this nature. Since lower-class boys are more likely than middle-class ones to hitch rides within a city, particularly at night when such contacts are most frequently made, they perhaps are most often solicited in this manner.

The experienced boy who knows a "lot of queers," may phone known fellators directly from a public phone, and some fellators try to establish continued contact with boys by giving them their phone numbers. However, the boys seldom use this means of contact for reasons inherent in their orientation toward the transaction, as we shall see below.

We shall now examine how the transaction is facilitated by these types of situations and the prescribed modes of contact and communication. One of the characteristics of all these contact situations is that they provide a *rationale* for the presence of *both* peers and queers in the *same* situation or place. This rationale is necessary for both parties, for were there high visibility to the presence of either and no ready explanation for it, contact and communication would be far more difficult. Public and quasi-public facilities provide situations which account for the presence of most persons since there is relatively little social control over the establishment of contacts. There is, of course, some risk to the boys and the fellators in making contact in these situations since they are generally known to the police. The Morals Squad may have "stake-outs," but this is one of the calculated risks and the communication network carries information about their tactics.

A most important element in furnishing a rationale is that these meeting places must account for the presence of delinquent boys of essentially lower-class dress and appearance who make contact with fellators of almost any class level. This is true despite the fact that the social settings which fellators ordinarily choose to establish contact generally vary according to the class level of the fellators. Fellators of high social class generally make contact by "cruising" past street-corners, in parks, or the men's rooms in "better" hotels, while those from the lower class are likely to select the public bath or transportation depot. There apparently is some general equation of the class position of boys and fellators in the peer-queer transaction. The large majority of fellators in the delinquent peer-queer transaction probably are from the lower class ("apes"). But it is difficult to be certain about the class position of the fellator clients since no study was made of this population.

The absence of data from the fellator population poses difficulties in interpreting the contact relationship. Many fellators involved with delinquent boys do not appear to participate in any overt or covert homosexual

groups, such as the organized homosexual community of the "gay world."[9]
The "gay world" is the most visible form of organized homosexuality since
it is an organized community, but it probably encompasses only a small proportion of all homosexual contact. Even among those in the organized homosexual community, evidence suggests that the homosexual members seek
sexual gratification outside their group with persons who are essentially
anonymous to them. Excluding homosexual married couples, Leznoff and
Westley maintain that there is ". . . a prohibition against sexual relationships
within the group . . ."[10] Ross indicates that young male prostitutes are chosen,
among other reasons, for the fact that they protect the identity of the
client.[11] Both of these factors tend to coerce many male fellators to choose
an anonymous contact situation.

It is clear that these contact situations not only provide a rationale for
the presence of the parties to the transaction but a guarantee of anonymity.
The guarantee does not necessarily restrict social visibility as both the boys
and the fellators may recognize cues (including, but not necessarily, those
of gesture and dress) which lead to mutual role identification.[12] But
anonymity is guaranteed in at least two senses: anonymity of presence is assured in the situation and their personal identity in the community is protected
unless disclosed by choice.

There presumably are a variety of reasons for the requirement of
anonymity. For many, a homosexual relationship must remain a secret since
their other relationships in the community—families, business relationships,
etc.—must be protected. Leznoff and Westley refer to these men as the
"secret" as constrasted with the "overt" homosexuals,[13] and in the organized
"gay world," they are known as "closet fags." For some, there is also a necessity for protecting identity to avoid blackmail.[14] Although none of the peer
hustlers reported resorting to blackmail, the adult male fellator may nonetheless hold such an expectation, particularly if he is older or of high social
class. Lower-class ones, by contrast, are more likely to face the threat of

---

[9] See, for example, Maurice Leznoff and William A. Westley, "The Homosexual
Community," *Social Problems*, 4 (April, 1956), pp. 257–263.

[10] *Ibid.*, p. 258.

[11] H. Laurence Ross, *op. cit.*, p. 15.

[12] The cues which lead to the queer-peer transaction can be subtle ones. The literature on adult male homosexuality makes it clear that adult males who participate in
homosexual behavior are not generally socially visible to the public by manner and dress.
Cf., Jess Stearn, *op. cit.*, Chapters 1 and 3.

[13] *Op. cit., pp.* 260–261.

[14] Ross notes that, failing in the conman role, some hustlers resort to extortion
and blackmail since they provide higher income. See Ross, *op. cit.*, p. 16. Sutherland
discusses extortion and blackmail of homosexuals as part of the practice of professional
thieves. The "muzzle" or "mouse" is part of the role of the professional thief. See Edwin
Sutherland, *The Professional Thief*, Chicago: University of Chicago Press, 1937, pp.
78–81. See also the chapter on "Blackmail" in Jess Stearn, *op. cit.*, Chapter 16.

violence from adolescent boys since they more often frequent situations where they are likely to contact "rough trade."[15] The kind of situation in which the delinquent peer-queer contact is made and the sexual relationship consummated tends to minimize the possibility of violence.

Not all male fellators protect their anonymity; some will let a boy have their phone number and a few "keep a boy." Still, most fellators want to meet boys where they are least likely to be victimized, although boys sometimes roll queers by selecting a meeting place where by prearrangement, their friends can meet them and help roll the queer, steal his car, or commit other acts of violence. Boys generally know that fellators are vulnerable in that they "can't" report their victimization. Parenthetically, it might be mentioned that these boys are not usually aware of their own institutional invulnerability to arrest. An adolescent boy is peculiarly invulnerable to arrest even when found with a fellator since the mores define the boy as exploited.[16]

Situations of personal contact between adolescent boys and adult male fellators also provide important ways to *communicate intent* or to carry out the transaction *without* making the contact particularly visible to others. The wall writings in many of these places are not without their primitive communication value, e.g., "show it hard," and places such as a public restroom provide a modus operandi. The entrepreneur and his customer in fact can meet with little more than an exchange of non-verbal gestures, transact their business with a minimum of verbal communication and part without a knowledge of one another's identity. In most cases, boys report "almost nothing" was said. The sexual transaction may occur with the only formal transaction being payment to the boy.

INDUCTION INTO THE PEER-QUEER TRANSACTION

The peer-queer culture operates through a delinquent peer society. Every boy interviewed in this study who voluntarily established contacts with fellators was also delinquent in many other respects. The evidence shows that contact with fellators is an institutionalized aspect of the organization of lower-class delinquency-oriented groups. This is not to say that boys outside these groups never experience relationships with adult male fellators: some do, but they are not participants in groups which sanction the activity according to the prescribed group standards described below. Nor is it to say that all delinquent groups positively sanction the peer-queer transaction since its distribution is unknown.

[15] Jess Stearn, *op. cit.*, p. 47.
[16] Albert J. Reiss, Jr., "Sex Offenses: The Marginal Status of the Adolescent," *Law and Contemporary Problems*, 25 (Spring, 1960), pp. 322–324 and 326–327.

How, then, do lower-class delinquent boys get to meet fellators? Most boys from the lowest socioecinomic level in large cities are prepared for this through membership in a delinquent group which has a knowledge of how to make contact with fellators and relate to them. This is part of their common culture. Often, too, the peer group socializes the boy in his first experiences or continuing ones with fellators. The behavior is apparently learned within the framework of differential association.

The peer group actually serves as a school of induction for some of its members. The uninitiated boy goes with one or more members of his peer group for indoctrination and his first experience. Doy L., a lower-class boy at a lower-class school and a two-time loser at the State Training School explains how he got started:

> I went along with these older boys down to the bus station, and they took me along and showed me how it was done . . . they'd go in, get a queer, get blowed and get paid . . . if it didn't work right, they'd knock him in the head and get their money . . . they showed me how to do it, so I went in too.

In any case, boys are socialized in the subcultural definitions of peer-queer relations by members of their group and many apply this knowledge when an opportunity arises. Within the group, boys hear reports of experiences which supply the cultural definitions: how contacts are made, how you get money if the queer resists, how much one should expect to get, what kind of behavior is acceptable from the queer, which is to be rejected and how. Boys know all this *before* they have any contact with a fellator. In the case of street gangs, the fellators often pass the neighborhood corner; hence, even the preadolescent boy learns about the activity as the older boys get picked up. As the boy enters adolescence and a gang of his own which takes over the corner, he is psychologically and socially prepared for his first experience, which generally occurs when the first opportunity presents itself. Lester H. illustrates this; his first experience came when he went to one of the common points of convergence of boys and fellators—the Empress Theatre—to see a movie. Lester relates:

> I was down in the Empress Theatre and this gay came over and felt me up and asked me if I'd go out . . . I said I would if he'd give me the money as I'd heard they did, and I was gettin' low on it . . . so he took me down by the river and blowed me.

In a substantial number of cases, a brother introduces the boy to his first experience, much as he introduces him to other first experiences. Jimmie M. illustrates this pattern. Jimmie describes how he was led into his first heterosexual experience:

> When I was almost 14, my younger brother said he'd screwed this woman and he told me about it, so I went down there and she let me screw her too.

His induction into the peer-queer transaction also occurred through his younger brother:

> Well, my younger brother came home and told me this gay'd blowed him and he told me where he lived . . . And, I was scared to do it, but I figured I'd want to see what it was like since the other guys talked about it and my brother'd done it. So I went down there and he blowed me.

Not all boys belonging to groups which sanction peer hustling accept the practice. Some boys reject the peer-queer transaction while retaining membership in the group. It is not too surprising that such exceptions occur. Although in most delinquent groups some forms of sex activity confer status, it is rarely an absolute requisite for participation in such groups. Some boys in gangs which frequently gang shag, for example, refuse to participate in these activities. "I don't like my meat that raw" appears to be an acceptable "out." Exemption appears possible so long as the boy is acceptable in all, if not most, other respects. A lower-class delinquent boy apparently doesn't "chicken-out" or lose his "rep" if he doesn't want to engage in sex behaviors which most of his peers practice. (The same condition may hold for other practices, such as the use of narcotics.) Jerry P. from a lower-class school is in a group where all the other boys go with fellators; but he refuses to become involved, though he goes so far as to ride in the car with one of the gang's "regular queers." Jerry is in a gang which often gets picked up by a well known "local gay," a David B. Jerry admits: "I ride with B. a lot, but he's never done anything to me; I just can't go for that." When asked how he knew B. was a queer, he replied, "Oh, all the guys say so and talk about doin' it with him. . . . I could, but I just don't want to." Joe C., at a school which crosscuts the class structure, was asked if he had any other kind of sex experiences. His reply shows his rejection of his peer group's pattern of behavior with fellators. "You mean with queers?" "Uh huh." "I don't go with any. Most of my friends queer-bait, but I don't." A friend of his, Roy P., also rejects the activity: "Ain't no sense in queer-baitin'; I don't need the money that bad."

The impression should not be gained that most lower-class boys who are solicited by fellators accept the solicitation. A majority of all solicitations are probably refused when the initial contact is made unless several other conditions prevail. The first is that the boy must be a member of a group which permits this form of transaction, indoctrinates the boy with its codes and sanctions his participation in it. Almost all lower-class boys reported they were solicited by a queer at least once. A majority refused the solicitation. Refusal is apparently easy since boys report that queers are seldom insistent. There apparently is a mutual willingness to forego the transaction in such cases, perhaps because the queer cannot afford the risk of exposure, but perhaps also because the probability of his establishing contact on his next try is sufficiently high so that he can "afford" to accept the refusal. Looked at another way, there must be a set of mutual gains and expectations for the solicitation to be accepted and the transaction to proceed. Boys who refuse to be solicited are not vulnerable for another reason: they usually are members of groups which negatively sanction the activity. Such groups generally "bug" boys who go out with fellators and use other techniques of isolation to discourage the transaction. There also are gangs which look upon queers as "fair game" for their aggressive activity. They beat them, roll, and otherwise put upon them. A third condition that must prevail is that the boy who accepts or seeks solicitation from fellators must view the offer as instrumental gain, particularly monetary gain (discussed below).

There are boys, however, particularly those who are quite young, who report a solicitation from a man which they were unable to refuse but which they subsequently rejected as neither gratifying nor instrumentally acceptable. It is these boys who can be said to be "exploited" by adult fellators in the sense that they are either forced into the act against their will, or are at least without any awareness of how to cope with the situation. One such instance is found in the following report:

> This guy picked me up down at Fourth and Union and said he was going over to East Nashville, so I got in . . . but he drove me out on Dickerson Pike. (What'd he do?) . . . Well, he blowed me and it made me feel real bad inside . . . but I know how to deal with queers now . . . ain't one of 'em gonna do that to me again . . . I hate queers. . . . They're crazy.

There is an important admission in the statement, "But I know how to deal with 'em now." The lower-class boy as he grows older learns how to deal with sexual advances from fellators. Boys exchange experiences on how they deal with them and it becomes quite difficult to "exploit" a lower-class boy who is socialized in a peer group. It is perhaps largely the very young boy, such as the one in the case above, or those isolated from peer groups, who are most vulnerable to solicitation without previous preparation for it.

Lower-class boys, as we have seen, have the highest probability of being in situations where they will be solicited by fellators. But, *the lower-class boy who is a member of a career-oriented gang which positively sanctions instrumental relationships with adult male fellators and which initiates members into these practices, and a boy who at the same time perceives himself as "needing" the income which the transaction provides, is most likely to establish personal contact with adult male fellators on a continuing basis.*

It is suggested that the peer-queer transaction is behavior learned through differential association in delinquent gangs. This cannot be demonstrated without resort to a more specific test of the hypothesis. But, as Sutherland has pointed out, "Criminal behavior is partially a function of opportunities to commit special classes of crimes. . . . It is axiomatic that persons who commit a specific crime have the opportunity to commit that crime. . . . While opportunity may be partially a function of association with criminal patterns and of the specialized techniques thus acquired, it is not entirely determined in this manner, and consequently differential association is not a sufficient cause of criminal behavior."[17] Middle-class boys are perhaps excluded from the peer-queer transaction as much through lack of opportunity to commit this special class of crime in their community of exposure as through any criterion of differential association. The structure of the middle-class area is incompatible with the situational requirements for the peer-queer transaction.

NORMS GOVERNING THE TRANSACTION

Does the peer society have any norms about personal relations with fellators? Or, does it simply induct a boy into a relationship by teaching him how to effect the transaction? The answer is that there appear to be several clear-cut norms about the relations between peers and queers, even though there is some deviation from them.

The first major norm is that *a boy must undertake the relationship with a queer solely as a way of making money; sexual gratification cannot be actively sought as a goal in the relationship.* This norm does not preclude a boy from sexual gratification by the act; he simply must not seek this as a goal. Put another way, a boy cannot admit that he failed to get money from the transaction unless he used violence toward the fellator and he cannot admit that he sought it as a means of sexual gratification.

The importance of making money in motivating a boy to the peer-queer transaction is succinctly stated by Dewey H.:

This guy in the Rex Theatre came over and sat down next to me when I was 11 or 12, and he started to fool with me. I got over and sat down another place and he came over and asked me, didn't I want to and he'd pay me five bucks. I figured it was *easy money* so I went with him . . . I didn't do it before that. That wan't too long after I'd moved to South Nashville. I was a pretty good boy before that . . . not real good, but I never ran with a crowd that got into trouble before that. But, I met a lot of 'em there. (Why do you run with queers?) It's *easy money* . . . like I could go out and break into a place when I'm broke and get money that way . . . but that's harder and *you take a bigger risk* . . . with a queer it's *easy money.*

Dewey's comments reveal two important motivating factors in getting money from queers, both suggested by the expression, "easy money." First, the money is easy in that it can be made quickly. Some boys reported that

---

[17] Albert Cohen, Alfred Lindesmith and Karl Schuessler (editors), *The Sutherland Papers*, Bloomington, Indiana: The University of Indiana Press, 1956, p. 31.

when they needed money for a date or a night out, they obtained it within an hour through the sexual transaction with a queer. All a boy has to do is go to a place where he will be contacted, wait around, get picked up, carried to a place where the sexual transaction occurs, and in a relatively short period of time he obtains the money for his service.

It is easy money in another and more important sense for many of these boys. Boys who undertake the peer-queer transaction are generally members of career-oriented delinquent groups. Rejecting the limited opportunities for making money by legitimate means or finding them inaccessible, their opportunities to make money by illegitimate means may also be limited or the risk may be great. Theft is an available means, but it is more difficult and involves greater risk than the peer-queer transaction. Delinquent boys are not unaware of the risks they take. Under most circumstances, delinquents may calculate an act of stealing as "worth the risk." There are occasions, however, when the risk is calculated as too great. These occasions occur when the "heat" is on the boy or when he can least afford to run the risk of being picked up by the police, as is the case following a pick-up by the police, being put on probation or parole, or being warned that incarceration will follow the next violation. At such times, boys particularly calculate whether they can afford to take the risk. Gerald L., describing a continuing relationship with a fellator who gave him his phone number, reflects Dewey's attitude toward minimizing risk in the peer-queer transaction: "So twic'd after that when I was gettin' real low and couldn't risk stealin' and gettin' caught, I called him and he took me out and blowed me." Here is profit with no investment of capital and a minimum of risk in social, if not in psychological, terms.

The element of risk coupled with the wish for "easy money" enters into our understanding of the peer-queer relationship in another way. From a sociological point of view, the peer-queer sexual transaction occurs between two major types of deviators—"delinquents" and "queers." Both types of deviators risk negative sanctions for their deviant acts. The more often one has been arrested or incarcerated, the more punitive the sanctions from the larger social system for both types of deviators. At some point, therefore, both calculate risks and seek to minimize them, at least in the very short run. Each then becomes a means for the other to minimize risk.

When the delinquent boy is confronted with a situation in which he wants money and risks little in getting it, how is he to get it without working? Illegitimate activities frequently provide the "best" opportunity for easy money. These activities often are restricted in kind and number for adolescents and the risk of negative sanctions is high. Under such circumstances, the service offered a queer is a chance to make easy money with a minimum of risk.

Opportunities for sexual gratification are limited for the adult male fellator, particularly if he wishes to minimize the risk of detection in locating patrons, to avoid personal involvement and to get his gratification when he wishes it. The choice of a lower-class male, precisely because of his class position somewhat reduces the risk. If the lower-class male also is a delinquent, the risk is minimized to an even greater degree.

This is not to say that the parties take equal risks in the situation. Of the two, the fellator perhaps is less able to minimize his risk since he still risks violence from his patron, but much less so if a set of expectations arise which control the use of violence as well. The boy is most able to minimize his risk since he is likely to be defined as "exploited" in the situation if caught.

Under special circumstances, boys may substitute other graitfications for the goal of money, provided that these gratifications do not include sexual gratification as a major goal. These special circumstances are the case where an entire gang will "make a night (or time) of it" with one or more adult male fellators. Under these circumstances, everyone is excepted from the subcultural expectations about making money from the fellator because everyone participates and there is no reason for everyone (or anyone) to make money. For the group to substitute being given a "good time" by a "queer" for the prescribed financial transaction is, of course, the exception which proves the rule.

Several examples of group exemption from the prescribed norm of a financial gain were discovered. Danny S., leader of the Black Aces, tells of his gang's group experiences with queers: "There's this one gay who takes us to the Colonial Motel out on Dickerson Pike . . . usually it's a bunch of us boys and we all get drunk and get blowed by this queer . . . we don't get any money then . . . it's more a drinking party." The Black Aces are a fighting gang and place great stress on physical prowess, particularly boxing. All of its members have done time more than once at the State Training School. During one of these periods, the school employed a boxing instructor whom the boys identified as "a queer," but the boys had great respect for him since he taught them how to box and was a game fighter. Danny refers to him in accepting terms: "He's a real good guy. He's fought with us once or twice and we drink with him when we run into him. . . . He's taken us up to Miter Dam a coupla times; he's got a cabin up there on the creek and he blows us. . . . But mostly, we just drink and have a real good time." These examples illustrate the instrumental orientation of the gang members. If the expense of the gang members getting drunk and having a good time are borne by a "queer," each member is released from the obligation to receive cash. The relationship in this case represents an exchange of services rather than that of money for a service.

The second major norm operating in the relationship is that *the sexual transaction must be limited to mouth-genital fellation. No other sexual acts are generally tolerated.*[18] The adult male fellator must deport himself in such a way as to re-enforce the instrumental aspects of the role relationship and to insure affective neutrality.[19] For the adult male fellator to violate the boy's expectation of "getting blowed," as the boys refer to the act, is to risk violence and loss of service. Whether or not the boys actually use violent means as often as they say they do when expectations are violated, there is no way of knowing with precision. Nevertheless, whenever boys reported they used violent means, they always reported some violation of the subcultural expectations, Likewise, they never reported a violation of the subcultural expectations which was not followed by the use of violent means, unless it was clearly held up as an exception. Bobby A. expresses the boys' point of view on the use of violent means in the following exchange: "How much did you usually get?" "Around five dollars; if they didn't give that much, I'd beat their head in." "Did they ever want you to do anything besides blow you?" "Yeh, sometimes . . . like they want me to blow them, but I'd tell them to go to hell and maybe beat them up."

Boys are very averse to being thought of in a queer role or engaging in acts of fellation. The act of fellation is defined as a "queer" act. Most boys were asked whether they would engage in such behavior. All but those who had the status of "punks" denied they had engaged in behavior associated with the queer role. Asking a boy whether he is a fellator meets with strong denial and often with open hostility. This could be interpreted as defensive behavior against latent homosexuality. Whether or not this is the case, strong denial could be expected because the question goes counter to the subcultural definitions of the peer role in the transaction.

A few boys on occasion apparently permit the fellator to perform other sexual acts. These boys, it is guessed, are quite infrequent in a delinquent peer population. Were their acts known to the members of the group, they would soon be defined as outside the delinquent peer society. Despite the limitation of the peer-queer sexual transaction to mouth-genital fellation, there are other sexual transactions which the peer group permits members to perform under special circumstances. They are, for example, permitted

[18] It is not altogether clear why mouth-genital fellation is the only sexual act which is tolerated in the peer-queer transaction. The act seems to conform to the more "masculine" aspects of the role than do most, but not all possible alternatives. Ross has suggested to me that it also involves less bodily contact and therefore may be less threatening to the peers' self-definitions. One possible explanation therefore for the exclusiveness of the relationship to this act is that it is the most masculine alternative involving the least threat to peers' self-definition as nonhustler and nonhomosexual.

[19] Talcott Parsons in *The Social System* (Glencoe: The Free Press, 1951, Chapter III) discusses this kind of role as ". . . the segregation of specific instrumental performances, both from expressive orientations other than the specifically appropriate rewards and from other components of the instrumental complex." (p. 87).

to perform the *male* roles in "crimes against nature," such as in pederasty ("cornholing" to the boys), bestiality (sometimes referred to as buggery) and carnal copulation with a man involving no orifice (referred to as "slick-legging" among the boys) provided that the partner is roughly of the same age and not a member of the group and provided also that the boys are confined to the single-sex society of incarcerated delinquent boys. Under no circumstances, however, is the female role in carnal copulation acceptable in any form. It is taboo. Boys who accept the female role in sexual transactions occupy the lowest status position among delinquents. They are "punks."

The third major norm operating on the relationship is that *both peers and queers, as participants, should remain affectively neutral during the transaction.* Boys within the peer society define the ideal form of the role with the fellator as one in which the boy is the entrepreneur and the queer is viewed as purchasing a service. The service is a business deal where a sexual transaction is purchased for an agreed-upon amount of money. In the typical case, the boy is neither expected to enjoy or be repulsed by the sexual transaction; mouth-genital fellation is accepted as a service offered in exchange for a fee. It should be kept in mind that self-gratification is permitted in the sexual act. Only the motivation to sexual gratification in the transaction is tabooed. But self-gratification must occur without displaying either positive or negative affect toward the queer. In the prescribed form of the role relationship, the boy sells a service for profit and the queer is to accept it without show of emotion.

The case of Thurman L., one of three brothers who are usually in trouble with the law, illustrates some aspects of the expected pattern of affective neutrality. Thurman has had a continuing relationship with a queer, a type of relationship in which it would be anticipated that affective neutrality would be difficult to maintain. This relationship continued, in fact, with a 21-year-old "gay" until the man was "sent to the pen." When queried about his relationship with this man and why he went with him, Thurman replied:

> Don't know . . . money and stuff like that I guess. (What do you mean? . . . stuff like that?) Oh, clothes. . . . (He ever bought you any clothes?) Sure, by this one gay. . . . (You mind being blowed?) No. (You like it?) Don't care one way or the other. I don't like it, and I don't not like it. (You like this one gay?) Nope, can't say that I liked anythin' about him. (How come you do it then?) Well, the money for one thing. . . . I need that. (You enjoy it some?) Can't say I do or don't.

More typical than Thurman's expression of affective neutrality is the boy who accepts it as "OK" or, "It's all right; I don't mind it." Most frequent of all is some variant of the statement: "It's OK, but I like the money best of all." The definition of affective neutrality fundamentally requires only that there be no positive emotional commitment to the queer *as a person.* The relationship must be essentially an impersonal one, even though the pure form of the business relationship may seldom be attained. Thus, it is possible for a boy to admit self-gratification without admitting any emotional commitment to the homosexual partner.

Although the peer group prescribes affective neutrality toward the queer in the peer-queer transaction, queers must be regarded as low-prestige persons, held in low esteem, and the queer role is taboo. The queer is most commonly regarded as "crazy, I guess." Some boys take a more rationalistic view, "They're just like that, I guess" or, "They're just born that way." While there are circumstances under which one is permitted to like a particular fellator, as in the case of all prejudices attached to devalued status, the person who is liked must be the exception which states the rule. Though in many cases both the boy and the fellator are of very low-class origins, and in many cases both are altogether repulsive in appearance, cleanliness and dress by middle-class standards, these are not the standards of comparison used by the boys. The deviation of the queers from the boy's norms of masculine behavior places the fellator in the lowest possible status, even "beneath contempt." If the fellator violates the expected affective relationship in the transaction, he may be treated not only with violence but with contempt as well. The seller of the service ultimately reserves the right to set the conditions for his patrons.

Some boys find it difficult to be emotionally neutral toward the queer role and its occupants; they are either personally offended or affronted by the behavior of queers. JDC is an instance of a boy who is personally offended by their behavior; yet he is unable to use violence even when expectations governing the transaction are violated. He does not rely very much on the peer-queer relationship as a source of income. JDC expresses his view: "I don't really go for that like some guys; I just do it when I go along with the crowd. . . . You know. . . . That, and when I do it for money. . . . And I go along. . . . But . . . I hate queers. They embarrass me." "How?" "Well, like you'll be in the lobby at the theatre, and they'll come up and pat your ass or your prick right in front of everybody. I just can't go for that—not me." Most of the boys wouldn't either, but they would have resorted to violent means in this situation.

Two principal types of boys maintain a continuing relationship with a known queer. A few boys develop such relationships to insure a steady income. While this is permitted within peer society for a short period of time, boys who undertake it for extended periods of time do so with some risk, since in the words of the boys, "queers can be got too easy." The boy who is affectively involved with a queer or his role is downgraded in status to a position, "Ain't no better'n a queer." There are also a few boys affectively committed to a continuing relationship with an adult male homosexual. Such boys usually form a strong dependency relationship with him and are kept much as the cabin boys of old. This type of boy is clearly outside the peer society of delinquents and is isolated from participation in gang activity. The sociometric pattern for such boys is one of choice into more than one gang, none of which is reciprocated.

Street-hustlers are also downgraded within the peer society, generally having reputations as "punk kids." The street-hustler pretty much "goes it alone." Only a few street-hustlers were interviewed for this study. None of them was a member of an organized delinquent group. The sociometric pattern for each, together with his history of delinquent activity, placed them in the classification of nonconforming isolates.

A fourth major norm operating on the peer-queer relationship serves as a primary factor in stabilizing the system. This norm holds that *violence must not be used so long as the relationship conforms to the shared set of expectations between queers and peers.* So long as the fellator conforms to the norms governing the transaction in the peer-queer society, he runs little risk of violence from the boys.

The main reason, perhaps, for this norm is that uncontrolled violence is potentially disruptive of any organized system. All organized social systems must control violence. If the fellator clients were repeatedly the objects of violence, the system as it has been described could not exist. Most boys who share the common expectations of the peer-queer relationship do not use violent means unless the expectations are violated. To use violence, of course, is to become affectively involved and therefore another prescription of the relationship is violated.

It is not known whether adult male fellators who are the clients of delinquent entrepreneurs share the boys' definition of the norm regarding the use of violence. They may, therefore, violate expectations of the peer society through ignorance of the system rather than from any attempt to go beyond the set of shared expectations.

There are several ways the fellator can violate the expectations of boys. The first concerns money: refusal to pay or paying too little may bring violence from most boys. Fellators may also violate peer expectations by attempting to go beyond the mouth-genital sexual act. If such an attempt is made, he is usually made an object of aggression as in the following excerpt from Dolly's sex history:

(You like it?) It's OK. I don't mind it. It feels OK. (They ever try anything else on you?) They usually just blow and that's all. (Any ever try anything else on you?) Oh sure, but we really fix 'em. I just hit 'em on the head or roll 'em . . . throw 'em out of the car. . . . Once a gay tried that and we rolled him and threw him out of the car. Then we took the car and stripped it (laughs with glee).

Another way the fellator violates a boy's expectations is to introduce considerable affect into the relationship. It appears that affect is least acceptable in two forms, both of which could be seen as "attacks on his masculinity." In one form, the queer violates the affective neutrality requirement by treating the adolescent boy as if he were a girl or in a girl's role during the sexual transaction, as for example, by speaking to him in affectionate terms such as "sweetie." There are many reasons why the feminine sex role is unacceptable to these lower-class boys, including the fact that such boys place considerable emphasis on being "tough" and masculine. Walter Miller, for example, observes that:

> . . . The almost compulsive lower class concern with "masculinity" derives from a type of compulsive reaction-formation. A concern over homosexuality runs like a persistent thread through lower class culture—manifested by the institutionalized practice of "baiting queers," often accompanied by violent physical attacks, an expressed contempt for "softness" or frills, and the use of the local term for "homosexual" as a general pejorative epithet (e.g., higher class individuals or upwardly mobile peers are frequently characterized as "fags" or "queers").[20]

Miller sees violence as part of a reaction-formation against the matriarchal lower-class household where the father often is absent. For this reason, he suggests, many lower-class boys find it difficult to identify with a male role, and the "collective" reaction-formation is a cultural emphasis on masculinity. Violence toward queers is seen as a consequence of this conflict. Data from our interviews suggests that among career-oriented delinquents, violation of the affective-neutrality requirement in the peer-queer relationship is at least as important in precipitating violence toward "queers." There are, of course, gangs which were not studied in this investigation which "queer-bait" for the express purpose of "rolling the queer."

The other form in which the fellator may violate the affective neutrality requirement is to approach the boy and make suggestive advances to him when he is with his age-mates, either with girls or with his peer group when he is not located for "business." In either case, the sexual advances suggest that the boy is not engaged in a business relationship within the normative expectations of the system, but that he has sexual motivation as well. The delinquent boy is expected to control the relationship with his customers. He is the entrepreneur "looking" for easy money or at the very least he must appear as being merely receptive to business; this means that he is receptive only in certain situations and under certain circumstances. He is not in business when he is with girls and he is not a businessman when he is cast in a female role. To be cast in a female role before peers is highly unacceptable, as the following account suggests:

---

[20] Walter Miller, "Lower-Class Culture as a Generating Milieu of Gang Delinquency," *The Journal of Social Issues,* 14 (1958), No. 3, p. 9.

This gay comes up to me in the lobby of the Empress when we was standin' around and starts feelin' me up and callin' me Sweetie and like that . . . and, I just couldn't take none of that there . . . what was he makin' out like I was a queer or somethin' . . . so I jumps him right then and there and we like to of knocked his teeth out.

The sexual advance is even less acceptable when a girl is involved:

I was walkin' down the street with my steady girl when this gay drives by that I'd been with once before and he whistles at me and calls, "hi Sweetie." . . . And, was I mad . . . so I went down to where the boys was and we laid for him and beat on him 'til he like to a never come to . . . ain't gonna take nothin' like that off'n a queer.

In both of these instances, not only is the boys' masculinity under attack, but the affective neutrality requirement of the business transaction is violated. The queer's behavior is particularly unacceptable, however, because it occurs in a peer setting where the crucial condition is the maintenance of the boy's status within the group. A lower-class boy cannot afford to be cast in less than a highly masculine role before lower-class girls nor risk definition as a queer before peers. His role within his peer group is under threat even if the suffers *no* anxiety about masculinity. Not only the boy himself but his peers perceive such behavior as violating role expectations and join him in violent acts toward the fellator to protect the group's integrity and status.

If violence generally occurs only when one of the major peer norms has been violated, it would also seem to follow that *violence is a means of enforcing the peer entrepreneurial norms of the system.* Violence or the threat of violence is thus used to keep adult male fellators in line with the boy's expectations in his customer role. It represents social control, a punishment meted out to the fellator who violates the cultural expectation. Only so long as the fellator seeks gratification from lower-class boys in a casual pick-up or continuing relationship where he pays money for a "blow-job," is he reasonably free from acts of violence.

There is another, and perhaps more important reason for the use of violence when the peer-defined norms of the peer-queer relationship are violated. The formally prescribed roles for peers and queers are basically the roles involved in all institutionalized forms of prostitution, the prostitute and the client. But in most forms of prostitution, whether male or female, the hustlers perceive of themselves in hustler roles, and furthermore the male hustlers also develop a conception of themselves as homosexual whereas *the peer hustler in the peer-queer relationship develops no conception of himself either as prostitute or as homosexual.*

The fellator risks violence, therefore, if he threatens the boy's self-conception by suggesting that the boy may be homosexual and treats him as if he were.

Violence seems to function, then, in two basic ways for the peers. On the one hand, it integrates their norms and expectations by controlling and combatting behavior which violates them. On the other hand, it protects the boy's self-identity as nonhomosexual and reinforces his self-conception as "masculine."

The other norms of the peer society governing the peer-queer transaction also function to prevent boys in the peer-queer society from defining themselves as homosexual. The prescriptions that the goal is money, that sexual gratification is not to be sought as an end in the relationship, that affective neutrality be maintained toward the fellator and that only mouth-genital fellation is permitted, all tend to insulate the boy from a homosexual self-definition. So long as he conforms to these expectations, *his "significant others" will not define him as homosexual;* and this is perhaps the most crucial factor in his own self-definition. The peers define one as homosexual not on the basis of homosexual *behavior* as such, but on the basis of participation in the homosexual *role*, the "queer" role. The reactions of the larger society, in defining the *behavior* as homosexual is unimportant in their own self-definition. What is important to them is the reactions of their peers to violation of peer group norms which define roles in the peer-queer transaction.

TERMINATING THE ROLE BEHAVIOR

Under what circumstances does a boy give up earning money in the peer-queer transaction? Is it altogether an individual matter, or are there group bases for abandoning the practice? We have little information on these questions since interviews were conducted largely with boys who were still participants in the peer-queer culture. But a few interviews, either with boys who had terminated the relationship or spoke of those who had, provide information on how such role behavior is terminated.

Among lower-class adolescent boys, the new roles one assumes with increasing age are important in terminating participation in the peer-queer relationship. Thus older boys are more likely to have given up the transaction as a source of income. Several boys gave as their reason, "I got a job and don't need that kind of money now." An older boy, who recently married, said that he had quit when he was married. Another responded to the question, "When do you think you'll quit?" with, "When I quit school, I reckon. . . . I don't know a better way to make money afore then." A few boys simply said that they didn't care to make money that way any more, or that since they got a steady girl, they had quit.

The reasons older boys have for giving up the peer-queer transaction as a means of making money is perhaps different for the career-oriented than for the peer-oriented delinquent boy. As career-oriented delinquents get older, the more serious crimes direct their activity and the group is more actively involved in activities which confer status. The boy has a "rep" to maintain. The peer-hustler role clearly contributes nothing to developing or maintaining a reputation, and the longer one gets money this way, the more one may risk it. The older career-oriented delinquent boy perhaps gives up peer-hustling activity, then, just as he often gives up petty theft and malicious destruction of property. These are activities for younger boys.

As peer-oriented delinquents get older, they enter adult groups where a job becomes one of the acceptable ways of behaving. Many of them may also move out of the "tight little island" of the peer group which inducted them into the activity. If one gets enough money from a job, there is no socially acceptable reason for getting money in the peer-queer transaction. One risks loss of status if one solicits at this age, for this is the age to move from one steady girl to another and perhaps even settle on one and get married, as often one "has to."

Regardless of the reasons for moving out, it seems clear that most boys do move out of their roles as peer hustlers and do not go on to other hustling careers. The main reason perhaps that most boys do not move on in hustling careers is that they never conceived of themselves in a hustling role or as participants in a career where there was a status gradation among hustlers. Hustling, to the peer hustler, is simply another one of the activities which characterizes a rather versatile pattern of deviating acts. It is easier, too, to move out when one has never defined oneself as homosexual. It is in this sense, perhaps, that we have reason to conclude that these boys are not involved in the activity primarily for its homosexual basis. Peer hustlers are primarily oriented toward either delinquent, and later criminal, careers, or toward conventional conformity in lower-class society. They become neither hustlers nor queers.

SUMMARY

This paper explores a special form of male prostitution in American society, a homosexual relationship between adult male fellators and delinquents. It is seen as a financial transaction between boys and fellators which is governed by delinquent peer norms. These norms integrate the two types of deviators into an institutionalized form of prostitution and protect the boys from self-definitions either as prostitutes or as homosexuals.

The conclusions offered in this paper must be regarded as tentative, because of limitations inherent in the data. Study of the fellator population might substantially change the conclusions. Cross-cultural studies also are necessary. Discussion of these findings with criminologists in Denmark and Sweden and exploratory investigations in several larger American cities, however, suggest that the description and explanation offered in this paper will hold for other American cities and for some other social systems.

6 The Mark

DAVID W. MAURER

People who read of con touches in the newspaper are often wont to remark: "That bird must be stupid to fall for a game like that. Why, anybody should know better than to do what he did. . . ." In other words, there is a widespread feeling among legitimate folk that anyone who is the victim of a confidence game is a numskull.

But it should not be assumed that the victims of confidence games are all blockheads. Very much to the contrary, the higher a mark's intelligence, the quicker he sees through the deal directly to his own advantage. To expect a mark to enter into a con game, take the bait, and then, by sheer reason, analyze the situation and see it as a swindle, is simply asking too much. The mark is thrown into an unreal world which very closely resembles real life; like the spectator regarding the life groups in a museum of natural history, he cannot tell where the real scene merges into the background. Hence, it should be no reflection upon a man's intelligence to be swindled. In fact, highly intelligent marks, even though they may tax the ingenuity of the con men, respond best to the proper type of play. They see through the deal which is presented, analyze it, and strike the lure like a flash; most con men feel that it is sport of a high order to play them successfully to the gaff. It is not intelligence but integrity which determines whether or not a man is a good mark.

Reprinted from David W. Maurer, *The Big Con*, copyright 1940 by David W. Maurer, reprinted by permission of the publishers, The Bobbs-Merrill Company, Inc. Also by permission of the author.

Stupid or "lop-eared" marks are often played; they are too dull to see their own advantage, and must be worked up to the point again and again before a ray of light filters through their thick heads. Sometimes they are difficult or impossible to beat. Always they merit the scorn and contempt of the con men. Elderly men are easy to play because age has slowed down their reactions.

Most marks come from the upper strata of society, which, in America, means that they have made, married, or inherited money. Because of this, they acquire status which in time they come to attribute to some inherent superiority, especially as regards matters of sound judgment in finance and investment. Friends and associates, themselves social climbers and syco-phants, help to maintain this illusion of superiority. Eventually, the mark comes to regard himself as a person of vision and even of genius. Thus a Babbitt who has cleared half a million in a real-estate development easily forgets the part which luck and chicanery have played in his financial rise; he accepts his mantle of respectability without question; he naïvely attrib-utes his success to sound business judgment. And any confidence man will testify that a real-estate man is the fattest and juiciest of suckers.

Businessmen, active or retired, make fine marks for big-con games. In fact, probably the majority of marks fleeced by the big-time confidence men are businessmen. Their instincts are sound for the confidence game, they respond well to the magnetic personalities of roper and insideman, and they have or can raise the necessary capital with which to plunge heavily. "In prohibition days," notes one con man whose identity cannot be re-vealed, "a businessman turned bootlegger was a prize package. You couldn't miss. Do you remember the big bootlegger from Cincinnati? R——— was his name. He got tangled up with a government dick while he was in stir at Atlanta. He blew $200,000 against the pay-off. After beating him out of that money, we turned him over to a faro-bank mob from Chicago and they gave him the best of it for about fifty G. They gave him the last turn. There were hundreds taken the same way. It was a perfect in to the mark."

Bankers, executors in charge of estates, trustees and guardians in charge of trust funds sometimes succumb with surprising alacrity. To the con men, anyone who has access to funds with which he might speculate is a potential mark. Even church funds frequently find their way into grifters' pockets. Several years ago Big W——— roped a pious and respectable church trustee from New Britain, Connecticut. Gondorff was said to have played him against the big store and he was reputed to have yielded over $300,000. Ironically enough, the con men were acquitted—or rather Gondorff was acquitted and his roper took it on the lam and was never tried—but the church trustee got a good stiff jolt in prison for misappropriating funds. "He was a very religious man," said Gondorff, dryly, "but I guess the temptation for the dough was too much for his scruples."

Religious scruples often seem to fail a mark at the crucial moment. One confidence man who has contributed liberally to this study attributes his facile knowledge of the Bible to the long nights spent in solemn prayer with devout marks who sought moral support from a Divine Providence which, so it might appear to the pious mind, may sometimes select confidence men as instruments of vengeance against one who covets his neighbor's goods.

Professional men who have prospered in their work or who have married money also contribute their share of marks. Doctors, lawyers and dentists sometimes yield good results, though most operators do not like to play for lawyers. Even an occasional college professor is played for, with scores which are said to be quite discouraging. Con men feel that professional men as a class are notoriously gullible; they readily fancy themselves as adept at financial manipulation as they are in their own fields of specialization. One dentist from New York state, fortunately having married very well, has been played against the big store more than half a dozen times. He has become somewhat of an institution among grifters. One meets another on the road and asks, "Do you have anything good in tow?" "No," says his colleague. "Well," suggests the other, "why not go up and rope that dentist? He'll always go for twenty grand."

One would naturally expect bankers to be well aware of the nature of confidence games, and consequently to be too wary to be taken in by them. Most of them are, but some make perfect marks. With a Yellow Kid Weil or a Charley Gondorff on the inside, any one of them will meet his match in wit, financial sagacity and shrewdness. Bankers, if they can be played at all, can be counted on to plunge heavily, for they can dip into bank funds with a view to reimbursing the bank once they have taken their profit. Several instances of that ironical spectacle, one mark roping another, are reported by a mob operating in Florida. When a mark who is brought in expresses a desire to talk the matter over with his banker, he is (under certain circumstances) encouraged to do so. Sometimes, the banker comes back with him, both of them well heeled for the play. Thus two marks flourish where only one grew before.

Wealthy or retired farmers are putty in the hands of competent operators. Many ropers specialize in retired farmers, ranchers or fruit-growers, and one distinguished confidence man, Farmer Brown, devoted most of his checkered career to nefarious bucolic swindling; his rural make-up, his pastoral manners, his back-country speech, and his unbelievable clothing, reinforced by an open and naïve personality, proved to be deadly to literally hundreds and hundreds of farmers throughout the West and Midwest. In the years following the World War they poured millions into the hands of willing confidence men.

An occasional police officer is taken—though that practice is generally frowned upon by professionals. However, within very recent years a Los Angeles captain of detectives was roped in Europe by Stewart Donnelly, brought to the United States for his money, then moved to Montreal, where Kent Marshall played the inside for him. He yielded $38,800 according to Marshall, but that figure does not check with the amount made public in the newspapers. "He wasn't dumb," said Marshall, "he just thought he knew all the angles to the big con. He had headed the con-detail for years. It was two weeks after he got back home before he suddenly tumbled that he had been played for the pay-off."

Other tales regarding the fleecing of police officers float about, but cops seem to react much the same as any other mark. One comes to me from Havana which is interesting because of the method used to rope and tie a Texas sheriff who was vacationing there. He frequented the hotel lobbies, where he did a good deal of boasting about how many thieves and criminals he had shot in the course of his term as peace officer. The grifters in Havana decided to trim him properly. So an expert pickpocket was commissioned to pick his pockets clean. The grifters tore up his boat tickets for home and gave his wallet to the pickpocket. Meanwhile he discovered his loss and "beefed gun" at a great rate. He yelped about the hotel, telling everyone his tale of woe. Then a smooth roper approached him, listened to his troubles, and loaned him money to go home on. Just before he sailed, he was given the point-out, the insideman told him the tale, and he was given the convincer. He returned to Havana within a few weeks with $80,000 in a money belt. Also, rumor has it that the great fixer, Lou Blonger, was once given a fine trimming on the big con, but I have been unable to unearth any very definite information about it.

Not all marks are men. Since the World War, big-con men have played for women with increasing success. Middle-aged women—married or single —are especially susceptible, for sooner or later the element of sex enters the game. Some ropers are particularly adept at picking up women because they know how to use their personalities, their clothes, their manners, all to the best advantage. Most of them deliberately compromise their victim by inducing her to sign the hotel register for both of them, then sharing a room or suite with her. Thus the con men usually preclude any retaliatory action on her part, for often she is a woman whose position would be damaged by the evidence on the hotel register, regardless of whether or not she had actually been intimate with the roper. One successful roper tells me that he often finds, when he is playing for a man accompanied by his wife, that a little amorous by-play with the wife facilitates the play. "I always treat charwomen like duchesses," he laughs, "and the duchesses like charwomen."

But no profession, occupation, race or sex has a corner on the never-failing supply of marks. "Anyone with money," reflected old Buck Boatwright, dean of modern confidence men, "is worth playing for. Just bring him in, and I'll take something from him."

II

The mark is wary game. Like most game, he migrates, and his migration is his undoing. The wily roper, armed only with a smooth tongue, a deep disillusion regarding the motives of mankind, and some notes on human psychology which are not to be found in the textbooks, knows how to stalk his quarry.

Although marks may be plentiful, they do not walk heedlessly into the traps of the confidence men. They must be stalked for days and even weeks before the kill. This strenuous field-work is done by the roper, who travels far and wide, in this country and abroad, in his diligent search for promising material.

Ropers employ various methods for flushing their game. But most of them depend solely upon chance and casual contacts to provide them with marks. A con man never meets a stranger. Within a quarter of an hour he can be on good terms with anyone; in from twenty-four to forty-eight hours he has reached the stage of intimate friendship. And so most ropers swing back and forth across the country or ride the passenger liners, knowing full well that sooner or later they will meet their man. And they do. Most marks are gathered into the net on one or another of our transportation systems as a result of what appears to be a most casual contact.

A few years ago, before the American public turned wholesale to travel by automobile, the Pullman car was the roper's best hunting ground. "If you were on a train bound for Florida," said Old Man Russell, a fine wireman of the old school, "you might notice a clean-cut man traveling alone. You would tab him and when he went into the smoker or lounge car you would tail him there. That would be your first contact."

This one contact is all a first-class roper needs, provided the mark has the necessary cash and the proper temperament. And it doesn't take a skillful roper long to find that out. For a good roper is first of all a good listener. In a short time he knows where the mark is going, what business he is in, what his financial standing is, and has collected an amazingly intimate fund of information regarding the mark's hobbies, his family, his friends, his extra-marital exploits. Many ropers agree that often marks can be played for the same day they are picked up, but most con men feel safer to allow the mark plenty of time to become thoroughly hooked.

The ease with which people make traveling acquaintances may account for the great number of marks which are roped on trains or ships. When a mark is off his home ground, he is no longer so sure of himself; he likes to impress important-looking strangers; he has the leisure to become expansive, and he likes to feel that he is recognized as a good fellow. The natural barriers to friendships with strangers come down. He idles away time chatting and smoking in a way he would not do at home. And the roper knows how to play upon the festive note which is always latent in a traveler away from home.

Occasionally it happens that a fortunate roper has more than one mark in tow on the same train or boat. If he cannot handle both of them, he may turn one of them over to another roper with whom he gets in touch along the way. If the second roper scores with his victim, the first of course collects the standard fee—ten per cent—for "putting the mark up."

"You can't always tell which mark is better," wailed one roper, who once turned a most unprepossessing mark over to his friend, Joe Furey. "The mark I kept was a fat-looking baby, but he blew up and didn't yield a cent. The one I put up for Joe was the kind you don't bump into. He went for a hundred grand and didn't think anything about it. All I got was a measly ten per."

Vacation cruises are often fine hunting grounds for ropers. The High Ass Kid was once riding a boat to Cuba when a friendly, talkative gentleman came up to him in the bar and started a conversation. He practically roped himself. "That egg just blowed a hundred and fifty grand for tying into the wrong man," laughed the Kid. Almost every roper has had a similar experience at some time in his life.

Summer resorts catering to a high type of vacationers, golf links, health spas and country clubs also furnish their quota of lucrative marks. The Hashhouse Kid, a roper from Minneapolis, was playing golf on a private course adjoining a country club outside Ottawa. He played a few rounds with a visiting Englishman, then steered him to Montreal where he played him against the store and took $375,000 from him on the pay-off. Many of the best con men include slacks and golf clubs as a regular part of their traveling wardrobe.

One roper reports that he operates with some success wherever vacation cruises come ashore. "In Havana," he says, "I meet each cruise ship that comes in. When the tourists are herded off for a shore excursion, I fall right in and mingle with them. I talk about the trip and they naturally think I'm one of the party. Then I tie into a mark and stay with him until I sound him out. If he looks good, we play the point-out for him and tie him up on the pay-off. The last time I worked there, I cut out a fine old Scotchman and sent him right home to Dingwell, Scotland, for $100,000."

The roper who depends upon casual contacts will find marks anywhere that well-to-do folk congregate. Sometimes they fall right into his lap. Says Bill Howard, a con man from Detroit, "I was standing one night in the bar room of the Tod House in New York. Just as I was leaving, a stranger asked me for a match. That match cost him $100,000." Needless to say, Bill made friends with him, let Gondorff tell him the tale, and the next day he went home for his money, which he lost like a gentleman. "When Charley put him on the train, he was satisfied that a great mistake had been made," said Bill.

While luck plays a large part in bringing the mark and the con men together, not all ropers are willing to wait for the law of averages to operate. Many of them have agents who "put up" marks for them for ten per cent of the score. Any professional criminal may put up a mark if he locates one; some have permanent connections with confidence men and collect a steady income from this source. For instance, Overcoat Kelly acted for many years as general agent for ropers working out of Minneapolis. Many good con men got their start by first putting up the marks for established con men to trim. Most fruitful of these agents are the professional gamblers who ride the trains and steamships and, as a convenient source of additional revenue, put up marks for the big store. From the many itinerant gamblers who act in this capacity, we might cite the two most skillful and prosperous old-timers—Eddie Mines of Hamilton, Ontario, and Wildfire John of Chicago. Mines is strictly a gambler—and a fine one—but Wildfire occasionally ropes and steers a mark on his own.

Some grifters will put up other underworld folk as readily as they will legitimate marks, and on occasion this cannibalistic tendency backfires with amusing and embarrassing results. Once A—— C—— sent for a con mob to come to Little Rock to trim a sucker gambling house which was taking some of her husband's business. They were instructed to register at the hotel and wait for A——'s husband, who would give them the necessary information. When they arrived at the hotel, the roper wandered out into the dining room and found gambling going on behind a screen. He played for a short time, then left, saying that he would bring in a friend later in the evening. Up in the room the roper said, "Boys, I have spotted the joint. It is so soft you can put your finger in it." After dinner they gave it a play and cleaned up more than $5,000. The next morning they called A—— and she aroused her husband. "We certainly found that sucker joint easy enough," said one of the con men. "We took them for five grand last night."

"Where did you find it?" asked C——.

"Right down in the hotel dining room," said the con man.

"Jesus Christ!" howled C——, "that's my joint."

While most men who put up marks are grifters or other underworld folk, it is an interesting and significant fact that often con men have good marks put up for them by legitimate citizens who have no underworld connections except an acquaintance with the con men whom they assist. Many of these respectable agents take no commission, but put up the mark only to help the con man, or, more frequently, to secure revenge upon someone. It is a strange fact that some marks will put up another mark for a con game on which they have just been beaten; they may even beg for permission to watch the process; they seem to feel that they would get a sort of satisfaction from knowing that someone else has taken the bait and found a hook in it; probably nothing would bolster up their deflated egos more than watching the play, but no non-professionals ever get into the big store.

One of the proprietors of the old Bon Ton Livery Stable in Des Moines seemed to get pleasure out of putting up marks for the men who swindled him. After being fleeced himself on *the tip*, he looked up the con men and asked them to fleece some of his acquaintances, refusing any commission. A prosperous cattle-buyer who once ran for mayor of Sioux City, Iowa, hung around with con men and located fat marks as a favor to them.

However, the ten-per-cent arrangement extends beyond a simple agreement among ropers. Many persons from the respectable and legitimate world accept their commission with never a qualm. F—— H——, one-time proprietor of two hotels in Chicago, purloined promising-looking guests from his own registers and put them up for con men at a commission. One Dr. A—— of Des Moines located fat marks among his patients and put them up for ropers. A traveling representative for a well-known Cincinnati safe manufacturer, one W—E—B—, ferreted out wealthy marks (to which his business gave him ready access) throughout Iowa and Nebraska; because of the sure-fire quality of his marks, he received the rather high commission of 33⅓ per cent. But sometimes he seems to have lacked the courage of his convictions. One roper says of him: "B—— always introduced me to the mark and then lit a rag out of town. He seemed to have an unholy fear that something would go wrong." A former railroad executive who was later interested in a prominent midwestern baseball club also acted as agent for con men for many years. W—— S——, originally from Paris, Kentucky, bought a hotel in Kansas City; a pair of con men took him there for a nice round sum which ruined him and his business. Later on in a St. Louis hotel he accosted the man who had roped him. S—— was a husky, flaxen-haired Kentuckian who had the reputation of being dangerous; the roper was much relieved to discover that S—— only wanted to recoup his losses by putting up several wealthy marks in St. Louis. The con men obliged him, and S—— went happily on his way with his commission tucked in his pocket.

But enough of these hypocritical folk who pimp away the purses of their friends. They are mentioned only as illustrations of the fact that larceny makes strange bedfellows.

Other lambs are brought to the slaughter through newspaper advertisements. The roper puts an ad like this in a metropolitan newspaper:

BUSINESS OPPORTUNITY: For an honest, reliable business man with $20,000 to invest for a large return. References exchanged.

From the surprisingly large number of persons who claim to have the character and the money to qualify for this investment, the roper selects those who seem to merit an interview, then from these selects one or more to be played.

Sometimes a mark is found by answering bona fide advertisements seeking purchasers for farms, real estate or established businesses. The roper pretends an interest in purchasing the property, offers the victim a high price, then under the pretense of consummating the deal, steers the owner to the city where the big store is located and "switches" him over to the pay-off, the wire or the rag. Prosperous farmers and small-town merchants who have laid by comfortable nest eggs are often visited at home after they have been investigated and found suitable.

Strange as it may seem, there are authenticated instances of a man's looking up a con man in the hope that he can profit from a con game. "I remember one winter in Miami," said the Postal Kid, "when there was a mark hanging around trying to meet someone who played the pay-off. He had read about it in the papers and had brought along a bank roll to see if he could make some money at it. But none of the grifters would pay any attention to him. They thought he was batty, until one day the Leatherhead Kid found out that he really had the money. So the Kid played the point-out for him right there. They moved him to the store and he went for twenty-five grand. When it was all over, the mark said, 'I'll go home and raise some more money, and we'll clean up next time.' This savage just thought things broke that way. You couldn't knock him."

The Square Faced Kid tells a tale in similar vein. "One day I went into Dan the Dude's place," he said, "and Dan gave me what he thought was a good subject for the wire. He was an old gentleman about seventy years old. So I went over to Plainfield to see him. He was a spunky old boy and looked like a good mark. So I moved him to the City and we told him the tale of the wire. Then he blew up. 'Young man,' he said, 'I've been swindled by that game. Not only that, but I've been swindled by every other crooked game in the country—the gold brick, the green-goods game, three-card monte, the shell game, the eight-dice game, and a braced faro game. And do you know, they all took me good. Now I've been reading in the papers that there is a new game out. It must be all right, for it's the only game where they pay you off. It's called the pay-off and I'd be interested to take a whack at it if you can dig one up.' He thought the game was on the up and up because they paid you off. He was the only perfect sap that ever was born."

And Joe Furey—whose statements must be discounted because of his

reputation for tall talk—adds, "At that time [1925–1929] marks were so thick
in Florida that you had to kick them out of your way."

III

The sagacity of Buck Boatwright's philosophy that any man with money
is worth playing for would not be questioned by any experienced con man.
The first thing a mark needs is money.

But he must also have what grifters term "larceny in his veins"—in other
words, he must want something for nothing, or be willing to participate in an
unscrupulous deal. If a man with money has this trait, he is all that any con
man could wish. He is a mark. "Larceny," or thieves' blood, runs not only
in the veins of professional thieves; it would appear that humanity at large
has just a dash of it—and sometimes more. And the con man has learned that
he can exploit this human trait to his own ends; if he builds it up carefully
and expertly, it flares from simple latent dishonesty to an old-consuming lust
which drives the victim to secure funds for speculation by any means at
his command.

If the mark were completely aware of this character weakness, he
would not be so easy to trim. But, like almost everyone else, the mark thinks
of himself as an "honest man." He may be hardly aware, or even totally
unaware, of this trait which leads to his financial ruin. "My boy," said old
John Henry Strosnider sagely, "look carefully at an honest man when he
tells the tale himself about his honesty. He makes the best kind of mark. . . ."

In most big-con games the initial approach is made to the mark on the
basis of his fundamental honesty. When ropers interview prospective marks
who have answered "come-on" advertisements it is customary to insist upon
character references which will establish the mark's honesty beyond all
doubt. Plunk Drucker tells this anecdote which is so typical that one version
or another of it is repeated each time a mark is roped. "I had advertised in a
Chicago paper for an honest and reliable man with $50,000 to invest for a
quick, sure profit," he said. "A redheaded Jew answered the ad. I interviewed
him in his office and raised the question of his character. He said, 'Mr. Ban-
nester, to show you how honest I am, I found a pocketbook with $220 in it
on the street the other day. I spent three dollars advertising to try to find
the owner.' I shook hands with him and congratulated him on his integrity.
I said that showed that he was just the party for a large and confidential
transaction." The mark's honesty is always a standing joke among grifters.

Without raising the fundamental problem of the pot and the kettle, it
can be reliably said that this attitude among con men is universal and that
this almost childish insistence upon dealing with an honest man gets very
gratifying results. Thus the mark's ego is flattered at the start, while at the

same time he feels a sense of security in the deal because he is convinced that the men he deals with trust and admire him for his honesty. And once a man admits complete and unshakable faith in his own integrity, he is in an excellent frame of mind to be approached by con men. The larceny begins to percolate ever so gently, and by the time it reaches the boiling point, he is helpless to cope with it—even assuming that he sincerely wishes to do so. Often his rationalization mechanisms are so perfectly developed that he never admits, even to himself, that he is fundamentally dishonest.

Many con men feel that marks have one characteristic in common— they are all liars. Whether this is true or not, I have no way of knowing first-hand, but we may assume that, if anyone is capable of giving expert testimony on this point, con men are, since lying is their profession. It is the consensus of opinion among many operators that marks usually lie about how much money they have, what kind of investments they make, how aristocratic their family connections are, and how good they are to their wives and families. Many marks love to dwell on the magnitude of their sexual adventures. These topics might be said to be universal, or almost so, as prevaricatory grist to the mill of most marks. The breadth of variation from these norms is limited only by the ingenuity of the mark and the daring with which he chooses to navigate the uncharted seas of the imagination. Individual forays into fabrication may be amusing or spectacular, but they hardly contribute to the general picture. This tendency of marks to fourflush is, in the end, helpful to the con men. If marks were not so anxious to impress strangers, they would keep their bank accounts intact much longer.

The mark may usually be counted upon to lie (if only by omission) about the way in which he was swindled. This type of dissimulation, of course, takes place when the mark is telling his troubles to newspapermen, the police, or his family. It may be explained in two ways, either of which may be justifiable. First, he may feel that he must protect himself against publicly displaying his own chicanery; that is, he must carefully conceal that fact for business, social or purely egotistic reasons. No con man would hold a mark in contempt for this sort of protective lying. Second, a mark often does not understand exactly how he was swindled, and feels called upon to explain in some logical fashion, both to himself and to others, how he happened to lose so much money. So he fabricates the parts which are not clear to him and builds up a story which he himself comes to believe. This is regarded by con men as natural and looked upon indulgently. But sometimes a mark shows singular daring and originality. He denies he has been swindled, or never mentions the fact; then he swears out a warrant for the con men charging armed robbery, and tells a story which convinces the prosecutor and the grand jury. This is known as a "bum rap" and is contrary to all established canons of lying; it is looked upon by con men in much the same light as a fly-fisherman regards dynamiting fish.

Con men do not assume that fundamental dishonesty is universal in human nature. Any one of a number of simple tests will reveal to the grifter how well his prospect likes "the best of it" and enable him to judge the strength of this motive with uncanny accuracy.

Sometimes he finds otherwise promising prospects whose concepts of honesty and dishonesty are very clearly defined; these men refuse to respond to the lure because their own consciences speak in a still small voice—and they harken. Most con men have met this kind of man, and few of them show any tendency to ridicule him—their only feeling is one of being baffled because the man cannot be beaten. The Big Alabama Kid, proprietor of some of the most successful stores in Alabama and Florida during the most prosperous days of the big-con games, has this to say about honest marks: "Yes, I have seen men who were too honest to have anything to do with the pay-off, and most of them were the nicest men I've ever met. And they weren't knockers either. You could say to them, 'Just don't say anything about this,' and their word was good. Just really folks."

This sentiment is echoed, often in almost identical phrases, by experienced con men. Truly, "you can't beat an honest man."

But we must remember that, first of all, marks are human beings. As such, their reactions to being swindled are unpredictable, though they do fall into something of a pattern and con men depend upon their "grift-sense" to tell them roughly what those reactions will be. For instance, a mark who is hard to hook frequently exhibits a bulldog tenacity and, once he has taken the hook, can be played for all he has; on the other hand, a mark who is very easily led into a con game may "blow up" before the play has gone far. An "easy mark" sometimes lets his emotions get the better of him and, forgetting himself, sympathizes with the poor roper who has to face the insideman's wrath when the mark is fleeced. Marks who immediately start to cry and complain are easy to handle. Some get violent immediately; some do foolish or ridiculous things. "I remember a redheaded fellow we beat in a Chicago hotel," recalls John Henry Strosnider. "He went haywire in the lobby after we cleaned him on the wire. I remember he had a little red stash, and he pulled it all out a few hairs at a time when he blew his chunk." Some marks are tough and can cause plenty of trouble if they get out of hand. Some are well-bred and take their medicine like men. Laughing marks are usually considered the most dangerous; and there is an iron-clad maxim current among big-con men: "Never beat a mark when he is drunk."

Some marks are mean, grasping and cunning. Just as soon as the insideman tells them the tale, they begin to scheme and connive for a way by which the roper can be done out of his share in the profits, or squeezed out of the deal entirely. Of course, there are really no profits—except what the mark ultimately furnishes—but con men feel that the mark's attitude toward these hypothetical and never-to-be realized profits is justification for a good and proper skinning. In their eyes he is just as much a "tear-off rat" as if he were holding out on actual cash. "Grifters get a kick out of trimming a fink like that," said one con man. "But," he added, "on the other hand, some marks are fine fellows and it is a shame to trim them."

"That's exactly right," said John Henry Strosnider, who, in his thirty-odd years of playing the inside on all rackets, had ample opportunity to study marks first-hand. "Why, some marks are the finest men you would want to meet, and I have heard grifters say, 'It was hard to beat a good man like him, as he was no beefer, and when he blew his cush, he just laughed it off and said it might have been worse. And all the time he knew he had been trimmed. . . .' "

Many con men have fleeced marks who remained good fellows throughout the entire procedure, men whose good nature and restraint seemed inexhaustible.

Once in Shreveport, Louisiana, a con mob made up of Johnny Tolbert, Jerry Mugivan, and others trimmed a Dutchman named Palmy Rinky on a con game. Palmy had a large saloon just across the street from the police station, and was well connected locally. Sometime later the con men were back in Shreveport beating a gambling house from the outside. They had just collected $3,000 of checks when the management was tipped off. "Stop the play," said the dealer. "These men are cheaters." The house refused to cash the checks. The con men found themselves outside. Two detectives immediately picked them up. They knew that the gambling house operated under very powerful local protection, and it looked bad. Then, too, they remembered the Palmy Rinky business. As the con men were being arraigned, who should come into the police court but Palmy. Their hearts sank. But Palmy had a big smile on his face. He was immediately pleased that the con men had taken the gamblers. "I lost my money and didn't squawk," he said, "why can't they do the same?" Then he used his influence to have the con men freed and, with the aid of the local fixers, he persuaded the gambling house to cash in the $3,000 in checks. Forever afterward those con men had a warm spot in their hearts for Palmy.

Suspicious marks are not unusual; in fact all marks are suspicious at first, but once they fall under the spell of the con men, and once they become fascinated by the play in the big store, most of their suspicions are laid. "Marks don't often get suspicious, or if they do, they get suspicious of details that really don't matter," said Claude King. "When they have a good insideman telling them the merits of the send, and how their paper will be handled by the insideman, who always knows what's best to do, they follow his advice. An insideman is like your mother. Mother knows best. . . ."

Maybe all insidemen do not have the natural touch which Claude King cultivated. At any rate, the mark's suspicions are not always so easily allayed. The roper really bears the brunt of the mark's suspicions while he is tied up; it is during this period that the "sucker feel-out" reaches its peak. The poor roper must be prepared to be awakened from a sound sleep at any moment during the night by some startling question, and promptly invent an answer to it.

In this connection there is a tale told of a crotchety old mark whom Red Lager once had tied up in a hotel in Havana. Frank MacSherry, who was playing the inside, gave the mark the customary instructions to watch the roper so that he could not get out and talk about the deal. Red tried putting on a little play with the mark, pleading all sorts of excuses to get out, but the mark stood pat. As soon as the mark's money came, Red made the "mistake" which cost the old man $75,000. After the roper had gone, the mark looked ruefully at MacSherry and wailed, "Now I wish I'd let him go out. Maybe a car would have hit him and then we would have saved our money. Even if he did talk, you and I could have gone somewhere else and put over the deal. But things happen that way when you've got an airtight thing. I know, because it happened to me right here in Havana! It made a difference to me of about $200,000 just because I wouldn't let that flighty guy out of the room for a week."

But not all marks are so easily quieted. Some grow restive and take precipitous leave without further ado. "Any mark might get a brain-blow," said Jackie French, "and take a powder any time. You just can't do anything about it. He just blows—a message from Heaven."

Mean and vicious marks are sometimes encountered. There are instances of marks who went so far as to plot with one con man against the life of another for profit. Eddie Mines, perhaps one of the best ropers for the tip who ever lived, once found himself in such a situation. Eddie, a kindly, dignified man, interviewed a real-estate man in St. Louis and told him the tale. He was traveling, he said, with the scapegrace son of a very dear friend. The young man had just inherited half a million dollars in securities from his father and was rapidly dissipating the estate. In fact, he was carrying at the time more than $200,000 in a money belt. He was a fool for gambling and the roper feared that his charge (played by Johnny on the Spot) would run through his fortune before he could persuade him to invest it soundly. Eddie sought the real-estate broker's aid in getting some of this money into property. The real-estate man was impressed; he became more than cooperative.

"I have a big farm away up in the country," he told Eddie. "Let's bump him off, and split the two hundred thousand. We can bury him on this farm and no one will ever know what happened to him."

Eddie talked this proposal over with Johnny and their moral indignation was aroused to such an extent that they trimmed their mark unmercifully.

It is only natural to expect that some marks become incensed when they learn that they have been swindled and try to kill or injure the con men, although it is very seldom that any mark actually hurts a con man. Never-theless, because this is always a possibility; a con man always guards himself as best he can. His greatest danger threatens from other underworld charac-ters. For instance, it is rumored that a well known East Coast gambler tried to have Stewart Donnelly put on the spot for swindling him of $38,000. He hired Legs Diamond to have the killing done, but Diamond was a friend of Donnelly and prevented the execution. On the whole, however, con men show little fear of physical violence from the marks they trim.

Some con men have observed that marks respond to con games dif-ferently according to nationality, with well-to-do American businessmen being the easiest. "Give me an American businessman every time," declared one of the most successful of the present generation of ropers, "preferably an elderly executive. He has been telling other people what to do for so long that he knows he can't be wrong." Perhaps it naturally follows that, if a mark has made money in a speculative business, his acquisitive instincts will lead him naturally into a confidence game; in the light of his past experience and his own philosophy of profit, it is a natural and normal way of increasing his wealth; to him, money is of value primarily for the purpose of making more.

"All Latin races like the best of it," says Limehouse Chappie, distin-guished British con man working both sides of the Atlantic and the steamship lines between all with equal ease, "but when they lose their dust, they lose it the hard way and are hard to cool out. They get highly excited when they blow, and it takes a good man to see that they are cooled out properly."

The large number of Britishers and Canadians who are swindled on big-con games in America would seem to indicate that the Latins are not alone in liking the "best of it." "People of Anglo-Saxon and Scandinavian extrac-tion have always been easy for me," said Plunk Drucker, one of the Postal Kid's best ropers. "Germans and Swedes are easy. Irish are hard to beat, and, boy, how they can beef! For my part, give me an Englishman, and you can have all the rest. Our dear country cousin just blows his money like the gen-tleman he is supposed to be. An Englishman is so different from other marks that there is no comparison. He just takes hold with that bulldog tenacity and holds on—until he is trimmed good and proper."

Jews are difficult, but there is a con man's proverb which says, "It takes ten Jews to trim one Greek." And all con men agree that it is next to im-possible to trim a Chinese. "I don't know any grifter who would be dumb enough to try to trim a Chink," said Little Chappie Lohr. "I've often seen them watching flat-joints down in Chinatown [San Francisco] that were playing for tourist suckers. They would look on for about five minutes, then walk on with a kindly grin. They're a fly lot, those Chinks. They can smell a crooked joint." Nevertheless, Chinese do occasionally fall victim to confidence men.

IV

"Once a mark, always a mark," and "You can't knock a good mark" are not meaningless sayings; they have been born of long experience, and express a good deal more of the grifter's philosophy about marks than appears on the surface.

It is easy for the layman to understand why some marks "blow up" when they realize that they have been trimmed. If these marks are not properly cooled out, they may get the mob into serious trouble, or, more rarely, kill or injure the roper. The average reader can readily sympathize with the mark whom Christ Tracy once trimmed for a large chunk in New York. "I've been calling you Mr. Bennett for the past week," said the mark, "but now I'm going to call you the biggest s—— of a b—— in New York." Some years later Christ encountered the mark on the street in Boston. "What are you calling me now, my friend?" he kidded. "I haven't changed my mind since I saw you last in New York," snapped the mark and walked away.

But it is difficult for the legitimate citizen (and sometimes for the mark himself) to understand why a man, once trimmed on a con game, will go back for another dose of the same medicine. Yet it happens all the time. Grifters have an endless fund of stories which illustrate this fact.

"I roped a mark for the last turn at faro-bank in Chicago," said a fine short-con man named Scotty. "Old Hugh Brady played for him. The mark went for about ten grand—all he had at the time. About two years later Old Hughey was strolling down Clark Street and he met Mr. Mark, who was tickled to see him again. He said, 'I've been looking for you for a long time. I've raised some more money and I'd like to play that faro game again.' Brady told the mark that he had moved to another hotel. He rented another room and framed the gaff and took the mark all over again."

The Big Alabama Kid tells of a mark they had beaten in Miami for $50,000. "We figured he was good for a second play," said the Kid, "so we sent him from Miami to Vancouver, B. C., for $30,000 more. He was gone for nearly three months. The store had given him up for lost, strayed or stolen. But one day who should come in smiling but Mr. Bates with a lot of apologies for keeping me waiting so long. He said that his banker had tried to tell him that this deal was a swindle, and wouldn't let him have his money. So he waited until things had cooled off at home and the banker had forgotten all about it. Then he went to the bank, drew out his money, and caught the first train for the South."

The Big Alabama's mark is typical of the man who leaves the big store beaten, only to return as soon as possible with a fresh bank roll, determined to correct the mistake which was made the first time and recoup his losses. It is also quite indicative of the strength of the "con" which has been put into the mark. Some marks would return even years later if they could raise the money and locate the insideman. This is well illustrated by a mark whom the High Ass Kid roped in Texas. He was put on the send and came through with about $45,000. The Kid figured that he would not be good for another play and "blew him off." Some time later, another roper picked up the mark on a train. He steered him to the hotel, when the mark recognized the approach and confided to the roper that he had been through this once before, and that he was looking for the insideman. The roper convinced the mark that he worked for the High Ass Kid with another branch of the same syndicate. The mark said that he already had the money in his home bank, so that he could go ahead with the deal as soon as he found the High Ass Kid. Then the roper, finding his work all done for him, steered his man to another store and took him for $20,000 more. The mark said he would have been back much sooner, but for the fact that it had taken him some time to borrow the $20,000 here and there from friends.

A mark, once hooked, is often most difficult to "unhook." If the operators once get his confidence completely, he is so sure of the deal in which he is involved that he will not listen to reasonable advice even if it is given to him. Many a banker has dissuaded one of his clients from withdrawing his money only with difficulty; some marks proceed with the deal in the face of sound advice to do otherwise. Con men report many instances of this phenomenon. And District Attorney Van Cise* of Denver, in prosecuting the Denver confidence ring, cites the case of one C. H. Hubbell of McPherson, Kansas, who was tied up with the Christ Kid when the officers arrested the Kid. He was being played for $50,000 and was most indignant at the interruption. Even when he learned that he was being played on the rag, he refused to believe it and insisted on posting bond for both the Christ Kid and his insideman.

Once the "con" takes effect on the mark, its strength is surprising. The mark may believe in the validity of the con deal even after the con men have told him it is a swindle; part of this is doubtless wishful thinking, and part the comforting fact to which he always returns when he doubts the scheme —hasn't he already made money by this method? And so he often does ludicrous things because he is unwilling or unable to shake off the "con" which has been put into him. Claude King tells an experience to illustrate this point.

"I had a store in Florida," said he, "and played for a savage who lost ten grand. That was all the jack he could get his mitts on at that time, so I sent him on his way and eased him up. I thought I'd knock him good, so I wrote him that he'd been trimmed and that it was no use looking for us as we were going to Europe. About a year later I bumped into him on the

* Cf. Philip S. Van Cise, *Fighting the Underworld* (Boston: Houghton Mifflin, 1930), p. 207.

street. He shook my hand and said, 'Mr. MacAllister, you can't get away with it. You can't let me down now. You know, I didn't make that mistake. It was that crazy fellow who introduced me to you. Now I have dug up ten thousand more. You can't keep me out of the deal this time. Just you and I alone will get the money from that poolroom, and we won't let anyone else in on it.'

"I said, 'You've got something there, my boy. We'll do it.' I took him again and he said, 'Well, I guess that is just the breaks of gambling. I'll see if I can't make some more money.' Off he went and I felt sorry for him because he was such an understanding winchell."

Of course, not all marks come back. Many of them, realizing or suspecting that they have been swindled, immediately cause trouble and all the ingenuity and persuasiveness of the insideman is required to prevent serious repercussions; sometimes all that fails and the con men are indicted. But not very often, considering the large number of marks who are beaten.

It is a rather common experience among con men to encounter a mark who knows about con games, or who has known someone who has been fleeced, and to find that the mark is good for a play himself. An old-timer tells a story which shows this type of mark in action. "Jerry Daley and I had an 8 die store [a short-con game much used by old-timers] in Charleston, South Carolina. We had a famous jockey in our boost. One day he said to Daley, 'Jerry, if I had the money I once had, I'd break that game of yours. I've watched you beat a lot of marks and I notice that you freeze out the players who can't put up the money. Your game is on the level, but you know you have to have money to beat it.' "

Two other old-timers cap this anecdote with a similar one. They tell how they had rented space from a saloon-keeper in Mattoon, Illinois, for an 8 die cloth. All week the saloon-keeper watched the con men trim the suckers who came into the saloon. When Saturday night's business was over, the con men "mitted him in" and took him for $800—his week's receipts.

There are simply no statistics available on the number of marks who are swindled on the big-con games. However, it is estimated by experienced con men that only from five to ten per cent of those swindled ever go to the police.

7 Victim-Precipitated Criminal Homicide

MARVIN E. WOLFGANG

In many crimes, especially in criminal homicide, the victim is often a major contributor to the criminal act. Except in cases in which the victim is an innocent bystander and is killed in lieu of an intended victim, or in cases in which a pure accident is involved, the victim may be one of the major precipitating causes of his own demise.

Various theories of social interaction, particularly in social psychology, have established the framework for the present discussion. In criminological literature, however, probably von Hentig in *The Criminal and His Victim*, has provided the most useful theoretical basis for analysis of the victim-offender relationship. In Chapter XII, entitled "The Contribution of the Victim to the Genesis of Crime," the author discusses this "duet frame of crime" and suggests that homicide is particularly amenable to analysis.[1] In *Penal Philosophy*, Tarde[2] frequently attacks the "legislative mistake" of concentrating too much on premeditation and paying too little attention to motives, which indicate an important interrelationship between victim and offender.

[1] Hans von Hentig, *The Criminal and His Victim* (New Haven: Yale University Press, 1948), pp. 383–385.

[2] Gabriel Tarde, *Penal Philosophy* (Boston: Little, Brown and Company, 1912), p. 466.

And in one of his satirical essays, "On Murder Considered as One of the Fine Arts," Thomas DeQuincey[3] shows cognizance of the idea that sometimes the victim is a would-be murderer. Garofalo,[4] too, noted that the victim may provoke another individual into attack, and though the provocation be slight, if perceived by an egoistic attacker it may be sufficient to result in homicide.

Besides these theoretical concepts, the law of homicide has long recognized provocation by the victim as a possible reason for mitigation of the offense from murder to manslaughter, or from criminal to excusable homicide. In order that such reduction occur, there are four prerequisites.[5]

(1) There must have been adequate provocation.

(2) The killing must have been in the heat of passion.

(3) The killing must have followed the provocation before there had been a reasonable opportunity for the passion to cool.

(4) A causal connection must exist between provocation, the heat of passion, and the homicidal act. Such, for example, are: adultery, seduction of the offender's juvenile daughter, rape of the offender's wife or close relative, etc.

Finally (4), a causal connection must exist between provocation, the heat of passion, and the homicidal act. Perkins claims that "the adequate provocation must have engendered the heat of passion, and the heat of passion must have been the cause of the act which resulted in death."[6]

DEFINITION AND ILLUSTRATION

The term *victim-precipitated* is applied to those criminal homicides in which the victim is a direct, positive precipitator in the crime. The role of the victim is characterized by his having been the first in the homicide drama to use physical force directed against his subsequent slayer. The victim-precipitated cases are those in which the victim was the first to show and use a deadly weapon, to strike a blow in an altercation—in short, the first to commence the interplay or resort to physical violence.

[3] Thomas DeQuincey, "On Murder Considered as One of the Fine Arts," in Edward Bulwer-Lytton, Douglas Jerrold, and Thomas DeQuincey, *The Arts of Cheating, Swindling, and Murder* (New York: The Arnold Co., 1925), p. 153.

[4] Baron Raffaele Garofalo, *Criminology*, (Boston: Little, Brown and Company, 1914), p. 373.

[5] For an excellent discussion of the rule of provocation, from which these four requirements are taken, see: Rollin M. Perkins, "The Law of Homicide," *Jour. of Crim. Law and Criminol.*, (March-April, 1946), 36: 412–427; and Herbert Wechsler and Jerome Michael, *A Rationale of the Law of Homicide*, pp. 1280–1282. A general review of the rule of provocation, both in this country and abroad, may be found in "The Royal Commission on Capital Punishment, 1949–1952 Report," Appendix II, pp. 453–458.

[6] *Ibid.*, p. 425. The term "cause" is here used in a legal and not a psychological sense.

In seeking to identify the victim-precipitated cases recorded in police files it has not been possible always to determine whether the homicides strictly parallel legal interpretations. In general, there appears to be much similarity. In a few cases included under the present definition, the nature of the provocation is such that it would not legally serve to mitigate the offender's responsibility. In these cases the victim was threatened in a robbery, and either attempted to prevent the robbery, failed to take the robber seriously, or in some other fashion irritated, frightened, or alarmed the felon by physical force so that the robber, either by accident or compulsion, killed the victim. Infidelity of a mate or lover, failure to pay a debt, use of vile names by the victim, obviously means that he played an important role in inciting the offender to overt action in order to seek revenge, to win an argument, or to defend himself. However, mutual quarrels and wordy altercations do not constitute sufficient provocation under law, and they are not included in the meaning of victim-precipitated homicide.

Below are sketched several typical cases to illustrate the pattern of these homicides. Primary demonstration of physical force by the victim, supplemented by scurrilous language, characterizes the most common victim-precipitated homicides. All of these slayings were listed by the Philadelphia Police as criminal homicides, none of the offenders was exonerated by a coroner's inquest, and all the offenders were tried in criminal court.

A husband accused his wife of giving money to another man, and while she was making breakfast, he attacked her with a milk bottle, then a brick, and finally a piece of concrete block. Having had a butcher knife in hand, she stabbed him during the fight.

A husband threatened to kill his wife on several occasions. In this instance, he attacked her with a pair of scissors, dropped them, and grabbed a butcher knife from the kitchen. In the ensuing struggle that ended on their bed, he fell on the knife.

In an argument over a business transaction, the victim first fired several shots at his adversary, who in turn fatally returned the fire.

The victim was the aggressor in a fight, having struck his enemy several times. Friends tried to interfere, but the victim persisted. Finally, the offender retaliated with blows, causing the victim to fall and hit his head on the sidewalk, as a result of which he died.

A husband had beaten his wife on several previous occasions. In the present instance, she insisted that he take her to the hospital. He refused, and a violent quarrel followed, during which he slapped her several times, and she concluded by stabbing him.

During a lover's quarrel, the male (victim) hit his mistress and threw a can of kerosene at her. She retaliated by throwing the liquid on him, and then tossed a lighted match in his direction. He died from the burns.

A drunken husband, beating his wife in their kitchen, gave her a butcher knife and dared her to use it on him. She claimed that if he should strike her once more, she would use the knife, whereupon he slapped her in the face and she fatally stabbed him.

A victim became incensed when his eventual slayer asked for money which the victim owed him. The victim grabbed a hatchet and started in the direction of his creditor, who pulled out a knife and stabbed him.

A victim attempted to commit sodomy with his girlfriend, who refused his overtures. He struck her several times on the side of her head with his fists before she grabbed a butcher knife and cut him fatally.

A drunken victim with knife in hand approached his slayer during a quarrel. The slayer showed a gun, and the victim dared him to shoot. He did.

During an argument in which a male called a female many vile names, she tried to telephone the police. But he grabbed the phone from her hands, knocked her down, kicked her, and hit her with a tire gauge. She ran to the kitchen, grabbed a butcher knife, and stabbed him in the stomach.

THE PHILADELPHIA STUDY

Empirical data for analysis of victim-precipitated homicides were collected from the files of the Homicide Squad of the Philadelphia Police Department, and include 588 consecutive cases of criminal homicide which occurred between January 1, 1948 and December 31, 1952. Because more than one person was sometimes involved in the slaying of a single victim, there was a total of 621 offenders responsible for the killing of 588 victims. The present study is part of a much larger work that analyzes criminal homicide in greater detail. Such material that is relevant to victim-precipitation is included in the present analysis. The 588 criminal homicides provide sufficient background information to establish much about the nature of the victim-offender relationship. Of these cases, 150, or 26 percent, have been designated, on the basis of the previously stated definition, as VP cases.[7] The remaining 438, therefore, have been designated as non-VP cases.

Thorough study of police files, theoretical discussions of the victim's contribution, and previous analysis of criminal homicide suggest that there may be important differences between VP and non-VP cases. The chi-square test has been used to test the significance in proportions between VP and non-VP homicides and a series of variables. Hence, any spurious association which is just due to chance has been reduced to a minimum by application of this test, and significant differences of distributions are revealed. Where any expected class frequency of less than five existed, the test was not ap-

[7] In order to facilitate reading of the following sections, the *vicitim-precipitated* cases are referred to simply as VP cases or VP homicides. Those homicides in which the victim was not a direct precipitator are referred to as non-VP cases.

plied; and in each tested association, a correction for continuity was used, although the difference resulting without it was only slight. In this study a value of P less than .05, or the 5 percent level of significance, is used as the minimal level of significant association. Throughout the subsequent discussion, the term *significant* in italics is used to indicate that a chi-square test of significance of association has been made and that the value of P less than .05 has been found. The discussion that follows (with respect to race, sex, age, etc.) reveals some interesting differences and similarities between the two. (Table 1.)

Race

Because Negroes and males have been shown by their high rates of homicide, assaults against the person, etc., to be more criminally aggressive than whites and females, it may be inferred that there are more Negroes and males among VP victims than among non-VP victims. The data confirm this inference. Nearly 80 percent of VP cases compared to 70 percent of non-VP cases involve Negroes, a proportional difference that results in a *significant* association between race and VP homicide.

Sex

As victims, males comprise 94 percent of VP homicides, but only 72 percent of non-VP homicides, showing a *significant* association between sex of the victim and VP homicide.

Since females have been shown by their low rates of homicide, assaults against the person, etc., to be less criminally aggressive than males, and since females are less likely to precipitate their own victimization than males, we should expect more female *offenders* among VP homicides than among non-VP homicides. Such is the case, for the comparative data reveal that females are twice as frequently offenders in VP slayings (29 percent) as they are in non-VP slayings (14 percent)—a proportional difference which is also highly *significant*.

The number of white female offenders (16) in this study is too small to permit statistical analysis, but the tendency among both Negro and white females as separate groups is toward a much higher proportion among VP than among non-VP offenders. As noted above, analysis of Negro and white females as a combined group does result in the finding of a *significant* association between female offenders and VP homicide.

Age

The age distributions of victims and offenders in VP and non-VP homicides are strikingly similar; study of the data suggests that age has no ap-

TABLE 1. VICTIM-PRECIPITATED AND NON-VICTIM-PRECIPI-
TATED CRIMINAL HOMICIDE BY SELECTED VARIABLES
PHILADELPHIA, 1948–1952

	Total Victims		Victim-Precipitated		Non-Victim-Precipitated	
	Number	Percent of Total	Number	Percent of Total	Number	Percent of Total
Race and Sex of Victim						
Both Races	*588*	*100.0*	*150*	*100.0*	*438*	*100.0*
Male	449	76.4	141	94.0	308	70.3
Female	139	23.6	9	6.0	130	29.7
Negro	*427*	*72.6*	*119*	*79.3*	*308*	*70.3*
Male	331	56.3	111	74.0	220	50.2
Female	96	16.3	8	5.3	88	20.1
White	*161*	*27.4*	*31*	*20.7*	*130*	*29.7*
Male	118	20.1	30	20.0	88	20.1
Female	43	7.3	1	0.7	42	9.6
Age of Victim						
Under 15	28	4.8	0	—	28	6.4
15–19	25	4.3	7	4.7	18	4.1
20–24	59	10.0	18	12.0	41	9.4
25–29	93	15.8	17	11.3	76	17.3
30–34	88	15.0	20	13.3	68	15.5
35–39	75	12.8	25	16.7	50	11.4
40–44	57	9.7	23	15.3	34	7.8
45–49	43	7.3	13	8.7	30	6.8
50–54	48	8.2	11	7.3	37	8.5
55–59	26	4.4	6	4.0	20	4.6
60–64	18	3.1	7	4.7	11	2.5
65 and over	28	4.7	3	2.0	25	5.7
Total	588	100.0	150	100.0	438	100.0
Method						
Stabbing	228	38.8	81	54.0	147	33.6
Shooting	194	33.0	39	26.0	155	35.4
Beating	128	21.8	26	17.3	102	23.3
Other	38	6.4	4	2.7	34	7.7
Total	588	100.0	150	100.0	438	100.0
Place						
Home	301	51.2	80	53.3	221	50.5
Not Home	287	48.8	70	46.7	217	49.5
Total	588	100.0	150	100.0	438	100.0
Interpersonal Relationship						
Relatively close friend	155	28.2	46	30.7	109	27.3
Family relationship	136	24.7	38	25.3	98	24.5
(Spouse)	(100)	(73.5)	(33)	(86.8)	(67)	(68.4)
(Other)	(36)	(26.5)	(5)	(13.2)	(31)	(31.6)
Acquaintance	74	13.5	20	13.3	54	13.5
Stranger	67	12.2	16	10.7	51	12.8

TABLE 1 (*Continued*)

	Total Victims		Victim-Precipitated		Non-Victim-Precipitated	
	Number	Percent of Total	Number	Percent of Total	Number	Percent of Total
Paramour, Mistress, Prostitute	54	9.8	15	10.0	39	9.8
Sex rival	22	4.0	6	4.0	16	4.0
Enemy	16	2.9	6	4.0	10	2.5
Paramour of Offender's mate	11	2.0	1	.7	10	2.5
Felon or police officer	6	1.1	1	.7	5	1.3
Innocent bystander	6	1.1	—	—	6	1.5
Homosexual partner	3	.6	1	.7	2	.5
Total	550	100.0	150	100.0	400	100.0
Presence of alcohol during Offense						
Present	374	63.6	111	74.0	263	60.0
Not Present	214	36.4	39	26.0	175	40.0
Total	588	100.0	150	100.0	438	100.0
Presence of alcohol in the victim						
Present	310	52.7	104	69.3	206	47.0
Not Present	278	47.3	46	30.7	232	53.0
Total	588	100.0	150	100.0	438	100.0
Previous Arrest record of victim						
Previous arrest record	277	47.3	93	62.0	184	42.0
Offenses against the person	150	25.5 (54.2)	56	37.3 (60.2)	94	21.4 (50.1)
Other offenses only	127	21.6 (45.8)	37	24.7 (39.8)	90	20.5 (49.9)
No previous arrest record	311	52.7	57	38.0	524	58.0
Total	588	100.0	150	100.0	438	100.0
Previous arrest record of Offender						
Previous arrest record	400	64.4	81	54.0	319	67.7
Offenses against the person	264	42.5 (66.0)	49	32.7 (60.5)	215	45.6 (67.4)
Other offenses only	136	21.8 (34.0)	32	21.3 (39.5)	104	22.1 (32.6)
No previous arrest record	221	35.6	69	(46.0)	152	32.3
Total	621	100.0	150	100.0	471	100.0

parent effect on VP homicide. The median age of VP victims is 33.3 years, while that of non-VP victims is 31.2 years.

Methods

In general, there is a *significant* association between method used to inflict death and VP homicide. Because Negroes and females comprise a larger proportion of offenders in VP cases, and because previous analysis has shown that stabbings occurred more often than any of the other methods of inflicting death,[8] it is implied that the frequency of homicides by stabbing is greater among VP than among non-VP cases. The data support such an implication and reveal that homicides by stabbing account for 54 percent of the VP cases but only 34 percent of non-VP cases, a difference which is *significant*. The distribution of shootings, beatings, and "other" methods of inflicting death among the VP and non-VP cases shows no significant differences. The high frequency of stabbings among VP homicides appears to result from an almost equal reduction in each of the remaining methods; yet the lower proportions in each of these three other categories among VP cases are not separately very different from the proportions among non-VP cases.

Place and Motive

There is no important difference between VP and non-VP homicides with respect to a home/not-home dichotomy, nor with respect to motives listed by the police. Slightly over half of both VP and non-VP slayings occurred in the home. General altercations (43 percent) and domestic quarrels (20 percent) rank highest among VP cases, as they do among non-VP cases (32 and 12 percent), although with lower frequency. Combined, these two motives account for a slightly larger share of the VP cases (3 out of 5) than of the non-VP cases (2 out of 5).

Victim-Offender Relationships[9]

Intra-racial slayings predominate in both groups, but inter-racial homicides comprise a larger share of VP cases (8 percent) than they do of non-VP cases (5 percent). Although VP cases make up one-fourth of all criminal homicides, they account for over one-third (35 percent) of all interracial slayings. Thus it appears that a homicide which crosses race lines is often likely to be one in which the slayer was provoked to assault by the vic-

---

[8] Of 588 victims, 228, or 39 percent, were stabbed; 194, or 33 percent, were shot; 128, or 22 percent, were beaten; and 38, or 6 percent, were killed by other methods.

[9] Only 550 victim-offender relationships are identified since 38 of the 588 criminal homicides are classified as unsolved, or those in which the perpetrator is unknown.

tim. The association between inter-racial slayings and VP homicides, however, is not statistically significant.

Homicides involving victims and offenders of opposite sex (regardless of which sex is the victim or which is the offender) occur with about the same frequency among VP cases (34 percent) as among non-VP cases (37 percent). But a *significant* difference between VP and non-VP cases does emerge when determination of the sex of the victim, relative to the sex of his specific slayer, is taken into account. Of all criminal homicides for which the sex of both victim and offender is known, 88 involve a male victim and a female offender; and of these 88 cases, 43 are VP homicides. Thus, it may be said that 43, or 29 percent, of the 150 VP homicides, compared to 45, or only 11 percent, of the 400 non-VP homicides, are males slain by females.

It seems highly desirable, in view of these findings, that the police thoroughly investigate every possibility of strong provocation by the male victim when he is slain by a female—and particularly, as noted below, if the female is his wife, which is also a strong possibility. It is, of course, the further responsibility of defense counsel, prosecuting attorney, and subsequently the court, to determine whether such provocation was sufficient either to reduce or to eliminate culpability altogether.

The proportion that Negro male/Negro male[10] and white male/white male homicides constitute among VP cases (45 and 13 percent) is similar to the proportion these same relationships constitute among non-VP cases (41 and 14 percent). The important contribution of the Negro male as a victim-precipitator is indicated by the fact that Negro male/Negro female homicides are, proportionately, nearly three times as frequent among VP cases (25 percent) as they are among non-VP cases (9 percent). It is apparent, therefore, that Negroes and males not only are the groups most likely to make positive and direct contributions to the genesis of their own vimtimization, but that, in particular, Negro males more frequently provoke females of their own race to slay them than they do members of their own sex and race.

For both VP and non-VP groups, close friends, relatives, and acquaintances are the major types of specific relationships between victims and offenders. Combined, these three relationships constitute 69 percent of the VP homicides and 65 percent of the non-VP cases. Victims are relatives of their slayers in one-fourth of both types of homicide. But of 38 family slayings among VP cases, 33 are husband-wife killings; while of 98 family slayings among non-VP cases, only 67 are husband-wife killings. This proportional difference results in a *significant* association between mate slayings and VP homicide.

---

[10] The diagonal line represents "killed by". Thus, Negro male/Negro male means a Negro male killed by a Negro male; the victim precedes the offender.

Finally, of VP mate slayings, 28 victims are husbands and only 5 are wives; but of non-VP mate slayings, only 19 victims are husbands while 48 are wives. Thus there is a *significant* association between husbands who are victims in mate slayings and VP homicide. This fact, namely, that *significantly* more husbands than wives are victims in VP mate slayings—means that (1) husbands actually may provoke their wives more often than wives provoke their husbands to assault their respective mates; or, (2) assuming that provocation by wives is as intense and equally as frequent, or even more frequent, than provocation by husbands, then husbands may not receive and define provocation stimuli with as great or as violent a reaction as do wives; or (3) husbands may have a greater felt sense of guilt in a marital conflict for one reason or another, and receive verbal insults and overt physical assaults without retaliation as a form of compensatory punishment; or, (4) husbands may withdraw more often than wives from the scene of marital conflict, and thus eliminate, for the time being, a violent overt reaction to their wives' provocation. Clearly, this is only a suggestive, not an exhaustive, list of probable explanations. In any case, we are left with the undeniable fact that husbands more often than wives are major, precipitating factors in their own homicidal deaths.

Alcohol

In the larger work of which this study is a part, the previous discovery of an association between the presence of alcohol in the homicide situation and Negro male offenders, combined with knowledge of the important contribution Negro males make to their own victimization, suggests an association (by transitivity) between VP homicide and the presence of alcohol. Moreover, whether alcohol is present in the victim or offender, lowered inhibitions due to ingestion of alcohol may cause an individual to give vent more freely to pent up frustrations, tensions, and emotional conflicts that have either built up over a prolonged period of time or that arise within an immediate emotional crisis. The data do in fact confirm the suggested hypothesis above and reveal a *significant* association between VP homicide and alcohol in the homicide situation. Comparison of VP to non-VP cases with respect to the presence of alcohol in the homicide situation (alcohol present in either the victim, offender, or both), reveals that alcohol was present in 74 percent of the VP cases and in 60 percent of the non-VP cases. The proportional difference results in a *significant* association between alcohol and VP homicide. It should be noted that the association is not necessarily a causal one, or that a causal relationship is not proved by the association.

Because the present analysis is concerned primarily with the contribution of the victim to the homicide, it is necessary to determine whether an association exists between VP homicide and presence of alcohol in the victim. No association was found to exist between VP homicide and alcohol in the offender. But victims had been drinking immediately prior to their death in more VP cases (69 percent) than in non-VP cases (47 percent). A positive and *significant* relationship is, therefore, clearly established between victims who had been drinking and who precipitated their own death. In many of these cases the victim was intoxicated, or nearly so, and lost control of his own defensive powers. He frequently was a victim with no intent to harm anyone maliciously, but who, nonetheless, struck his friend, acquaintance, or wife, who later became his assailant. Impulsive, aggressive, and often dangerously violent, the victim was the first to slap, punch, stab, or in some other manner commit an assault. Perhaps the presence of alcohol in this kind of homicide victim played no small part in his taking this first and major physical step toward victimization. Perhaps if he had not been drinking he would have been less violent, less ready to plunge into an assaultive stage of interaction. Or, if the presence of alcohol had no causal relation to his being the first to assault, perhaps it reduced his facility to combat successfully, to defend himself from retaliatory assault and, hence, contributed in this way to his death.

Previous Arrest Record

The victim-precipitator is the first actor in the homicide drama to display and to use a deadly weapon; and the description of him thus far infers that he is in some respects an offender in reverse. Because he is the first to assume an aggressive role, he probably has engaged previously in similar but less serious physical assaults. On the basis of these assumptions several meaningful hypotheses were established and tested. Each hypothesis is supported by empirical data, which in some cases reach the level of statistical significance accepted by this study; and in other cases indicate strong associations in directions suggested by the hypotheses. A summary of each hypothesis with its collated data follows:

(1) In VP cases, the victim is more likely than the offender to have a previous arrest, or police, record. The data show that 62 percent of the victims and 54 percent of the offenders in VP cases have a previous record.

(2) A higher proportion of VP victims than non-VP victims have a previous police record. Comparison reveals that 62 percent of VP victims but only 42 percent of non-VP victims have a previous record. The association between VP victims and previous arrest record is a *significant* one.

(3) With respect to the percentage having a previous arrest record, VP victims are more similar to non-VP offenders than to non-VP victims. Examination of the data reveals no significant difference between VP victims and non-VP offenders with a previous record. This lack of a significant difference is very meaningful and confirms the validity of the proposition above.

While 62 percent of VP victims have a police record, 68 percent of non-VP offenders have such a record, and we have already noted in (2) above that only 42 percent of non-VP victims have a record. Thus, the existence of a statistically *significant* difference between VP victims and non-VP victims and the *lack* of a statistically significant difference between VP victims and non-VP offenders indicate that the victim of VP homicide is quite similar to the offender in non-VP homicide—and that the VP victim more closely resembles the non-VP offender than the non-VP victim.

(4) A higher proportion of VP victims than of non-VP victims have a record of offenses against the person. The data show a *significant* association between VP victims and a previous record of offenses against the person, for 37 percent of VP victims and only 21 percent of non-VP victims have a record of such offenses.

(5) Also with respect to the percentage having a previous arrest record of offenses against the person, VP victims are more similar to non-VP offenders than non-VP victims. Analysis of the data indicates support for this assumption, for we have observed that the difference between VP victims (37 percent) and non-VP victims (21 percent) is *significant;* this difference is almost twice as great as the difference between VP victims (27 percent) and non-VP offenders (46 percent), and this latter difference is not significant. The general tendency again is for victims in VP homicides to resemble offenders in non-VP homicides.

(6) A lower proportion of VP offenders have a previous arrest record than do non-VP offenders. The data also tend to support this hypothesis, for 54 percent of offenders in VP cases, compared to 68 percent of offenders in non-VP cases have a previous police record.

In general, the rank order of recidivism—defined in terms of having a previous arrest record and of having a previous record of assaults—for victims and offenders involved in the two types of homicide is as follows:

	Percent with Previous Arrest Record	Percent with Previous Record of Assault
(1) Offenders in non-VP Homicide	68	46
(2) Victims in VP Homicide	62	37
(3) Offenders in VP Homicide	54	33
(4) Victims in non-VP Homicide	42	21

Because he is the initial aggressor and has provoked his subsequent slayer into killing him, this particular type of victim (VP) is likely to have engaged previously in physical assaults which were either less provoking than the present situation, or which afforded him greater opportunity to defer attacks made upon him. It is known officially that over one-third of them assaulted others previously. It is not known how many formerly provoked others to assault them. In any case, the circumstances leading up to the present crime in which he plays the role of victim are probably not foreign to him since he has, in many cases, participated in similar encounters before this, his last episode.

SUMMARY

Criminal homicide usually involves intense personal interaction in which the victim's behavior is often an important factor. As Porterfield has recently pointed out, "The intensity of interaction between the murderer and his victim may vary from complete non-participation on the part of the victim to almost perfect cooperation with the killer in the process of getting killed. . . . It is amazing to note the large number of would-be murderers who become the victim."[11] By defining a VP homicide in terms of the victim's direct, immediate, and positive contribution to his own death, manifested by his being the first to make a physical assault, it has been possible to identify 150 VP cases.

Comparison of this VP group with non-VP cases reveals *significantly* higher proportions of the following characteristics among VP homicide:
(1) Negro victims;
(2) Negro offenders;
(3) male victims;
(4) female offenders;
(5) stabbings;
(6) victim-offender relationship involving male victims of female offenders;
(7) mate slayings;
(8) husbands who are victims in mate slayings;
(9) alcohol in the homicide situation;
(10) alcohol in the victim;
(11) victims with a previous arrest record;
(12) victims with a previous arrest record of assault.

In addition, VP homicides have slightly higher proportions than non-VP homicides of altercations and domestic quarrels; inter-racial slayings, victims who are close friends, relatives, or acquaintances of their slayers.

---

[11] Austin L. Porterfield and Robert H. Talbert, "Mid-Century Crime in Our Culture: Personality and Crime in the Cultural Patterns of American States, (Fort Worth: Leo Potishman Foundation, 1954), pp. 47–48.

Empirical evidence analyzed in the present study lends support to, and measurement of, von Hentig's theoretical contention that "there are cases in which they (victim and offender) are reversed and in the long chain of causative forces the victim assumes the role of a determinant."[12]

In many cases the victim has most of the major characteristics of an offender; in some cases two potential offenders come together in a homicide situation and it is probably often only chance which results in one becoming a victim and the other an offender. At any rate, connotations of a victim as a weak and passive individual, seeking to withdraw from an assaultive situation, and of an offender as a brutal, strong, and overly aggressive person seeking out his victim, are not always correct. Societal attitudes are generally positive toward the victim and negative toward the offender, who is often feared as a violent and dangerous threat to others when not exonerated. However, data in the present study—especially that of previous arrest record—mitigate, destroy, or reverse these connotations of victim-offender roles in one out of every four criminal homicides.

PART X
Loners in a Criminal World

Introduction

The preceding Parts of this book, especially Parts V–VIII, have described varieties of criminal and delinquent behavior which are "owned" by groups rather than by individuals. Verbalizations in the form of values, attitudes, norms, and rationalizations are properties of groups. Some groups share verbalizations that make it "proper" for individual members to behave in ways that are violations of the laws of the larger society. Such "criminal behavior patterns," "rules for delinquency" or "rules for criminality" are used by white-collar criminals, delinquent gangs, marijuana users, "cats," "hustlers," professional thieves, pickpockets, confidence men, prostitutes, male homosexuals, gamblers, members of criminal syndicates, and many others. But what of solitary offenders? It has long been maintained that differential association theory does not adequately explain all criminality because some criminals do not learn the methods of committing their crimes or their vocabularies of motives in interaction with criminal behavior patterns. Some forms of criminality seem to be the property of individuals, the result of something *within* the offender. Part X makes clear, however, that the symbolic interactionist perspective can be helpful in explaining several important aspects of the criminality of "loners." We do not contend that sociological theory, including symbolic interaction theory, provides a complete explanation of all types of crime.

Three basic statements will help place the selections which follow into the framework of arguments used in the preceding Parts. First, the commission of some crimes does not require the learning of special skills and techniques from other *offenders*. The skills may be learned in the course of training for a legitimate job or profession or they may simply be learned in the process of being socialized into the conventional society. Second, the elements of the vocabulary of motives for some crimes can be taken from the culture of the larger society. A vocabulary of motives for committing some crimes need not come from a deviant subculture or group. Third, a good part of the difficulty in explaining so-called "individual crimes" is related to a major issue confronting all criminologists: determination of the degree to which the offender is responsible for his criminal behavior and the degree to which he is "compelled" to behave in an illegal manner by biochemical, genetic, psychic, or socio-cultural forces.

When phrased as a question, the first of these statements asks how the knowledge to commit crimes is acquired. How does one learn the techniques for committing rape? The socialization process through which most American males pass includes the establishment of a role which directs sexual interests toward certain females and calls for certain ways of behaving in relationships with females. In playing this role a man may learn sophisticated techniques of seduction and love-making from experienced males. But such fine points in the art are not relevant to forcible rape. Rape requires only the rather basic knowledge of how to commit the act of sexual intercourse.

The need for specialized knowledge and training is clearer in the case of physician drug addicts and embezzlers than it is in the case of rapists. However, the knowledge and skills necessary to commit these crimes are not learned from criminal associates. They are obtained in the course of legitimate preparation to become a physician or the occupant of a position of financial trust such as a bookkeeper, accountant, or treasurer. Similarly, the type of check forger described in the selection by Lemert is not highly skilled in his craft, works alone, and does not pick up his abilities to forge or pass checks from other check-writers. While some kinds of check-passing involve very sophisticated training and techniques in forgery and a well-organized system for passing the instruments, some check passers pass bad checks with the same skills used to cash good checks. Some forms of murder, arson, and theft also require sophisticated techniques, but the techniques which are required to commit "compulsive" murder, pyromania, and kleptomania are not complex, and they are not based upon learning experiences associated with participation in criminal groups or delinquent subcultures.

The second of the points made above poses a more complex theoretical problem. Each "loner" or "individual offender" has acquired a vocabulary of motives which permits him to engage in forms of behavior which are not only illegal, but in some cases are subject to the most severe sanctions society can exercise against its members. It is clear, however, that these vocabularies of motive are not learned through association or identification with other offenders.

The behavior of rapists, for example, seems to be "individual," to be prompted by something "in" the rapist rather than in conduct norms learned from others. But if the behavior is entirely individual, stemming "from within" the actor, why is it not idiosyncratic? The study by the staff of the Institute for Sex Research at Indiana University reveals that there is a good deal of similarity in the conduct of rapists, despite the fact that the acts of one rapist are carried out quite independently of the acts of another rapist. The great majority of rapists try to avoid detection, do not join together to commit their crimes, and do not act "compulsively." They plan their crimes, and they give similar rationales for their behavior. The vocabularies of motives of rapists, according to the Indiana University researchers, include "seemingly plausible accounts of their actions to prove their innocence." It is reported for instance that some rapists really believed that their victims willingly cooperated—"she didn't struggle," "she voluntarily removed her clothes," "she enjoyed it," "she didn't act mad afterward," "she encouraged me." "Cooperation" was interpreted by these men to mean a lack of violent physical resistance by the victims. This view of the conditions under which it is "all right" to have sexual intercourse with a woman was not merely expressed as an after-the-fact justification of the rapists' conduct. That some rapists held this belief while committing their crimes is attested to by the fact that in a number of cases the rapist returned for a second visit. Other verbalizations by rapists are efforts to neutralize the condemnation of the community, either after the crime or before the crime—"She was just a whore," "I didn't want to hurt anybody, but I just had to get a piece," "I was drunk at the time," etc.

The selection by Winick does not explicitly discuss a vocabulary of motives used by physicians who become drug addicts. However, some hints are given. It is reported that each physician-addict has used verbalizations similar to those used by other physician-addicts. These include beliefs and rationalizations such as "Demoral gives me relief from overwork," "Medical work is so rigorous that some kind of relief is necessary," "I need drugs for my illness," and "A drug user does not become an addict unless he is emotionally disturbed or stupid." The idea that overwork can be eased by narcotics could be "invented" by each physician-addict, as could the idea that only disturbed persons become addicts. On the other hand, the physician-addicts used these notions so frequently that it is possible to conclude that the verbalizations were readily available in the language of physicians and were merely adopted by individuals who found themselves with similar problems.

Winick's descriptive report does not explain what it was about the physicians who became addicts that differentiated them from physicians who did not become addicts. The Hartung and Cressey selections provide clues about the processes which the physician-addicts went through as they became addicted, but not about the question of why only some physicians go through these processes. Both these selections make the point that symbolic interaction includes conversations an individual has with himself in everyday language—conversations that make a specific form of deviance somehow acceptable under the circumstances. One of Winick's main findings was that the physician-addicts had no association with other addicts or with a drug subculture, so if the process occurred, the everyday language must have been available in the language of physicians generally. However, the question of why only some physicians utilize this language in their own circumstances remains unresolved. Interactionist theory is in this case more helpful in explaining *how* an individual comes to take on the role of a lawbreaker than in explaining *why* he did so.

Like physician-addicts, the check forgers studied by Lemert worked alone and avoided associations with other criminals. Their language did not include criminal argot. Perhaps in their conversations with themselves the check forgers used verbalizations available in middle-class culture. Some of them expressed middle-class values and referred to themselves as "black sheep" and as " a Dr. Jekyll–Mr. Hyde type person." The process by which some persons become systematic check forgers is understandable in the framework of symbolic interaction, but explanation of why only certain persons become forgers of this kind still is not clear.

Many of the verbalizations favorable to criminality which are presented to an individual in his lifetime are not presented by criminals. Hartung indicates that even the author of a book intending to condemn embezzlement presents verbalizations which can be used by trusted persons to "excuse" their embezzlements. These verbalizations even include a vocabulary used by confidence men and other professional thieves— "everyone has larceny in his heart," and "everyone has his own racket." They also include verbalizations that create roles freeing the potential embezzler of his responsibility—verbalizations that make embezzlement appear to be a "disease," "compulsive," or in some other way is "beyond control." Hartung draws on Cressey's analytic study which describes the vocabulary of motives actually used by embezzlers. He contends that before a person in a position of financial trust can embezzle he must be able to reconcile his image of himself as a criminal with the image of himself as a trustworthy person. Verbalizations such as "I will borrow the money temporarily" or "they don't pay me enough," enable the trusted person to steal his employer blind while continuing to regard himself as an honest and trustworthy person. Such verbalizations are drawn from the store of motives—in the form of patterns of thought and action— which the trusted person has acquired in his everyday associations with friends, relatives, and colleagues. The final selection, by Cressey, argues that even crimes identified as "personal," "emotional," "irrational," "impulsive," "irresistible," and "compulsive" are controlled by verbalizations which the actor has learned from his social groups. The selection was written without reference to the conduct of solitary offenders like rapists, physician-addicts, and check forgers. Yet, as we indicated earlier, its basic thesis—that conduct is determined by verbalizations which affect self-identification and which, by definition, are social in nature—might be used to "make sense" of such conduct.

Cressey's article deals explicitly with the third statement above, the one concerned with the issue of criminal responsibility. Sociologists have not been much involved in the legal-psychiatric controversies about "insanity," about whether defendants know right from wrong at the time they commit offenses, and about whether defendants are subject to "irresistible impulses." Their involvement has been pretty much limited to criticism of the principal assumption underlying this controversy, namely that the causes of crime are to be found "in" individual offenders. Perhaps sociologists have avoided the area of "insanity" and "irresistible impulse" because it has not been shown that sociological theories of criminality can efficiently be used to explain the types of crimes most frequently involved in "insanity" and "irresistible impulse" cases—sex offenses, arson, kleptomania, and homicide. The conclusion of Part X, and this book, is that symbolic interactionist theory should increasingly be used in attempts to explain "individualistic" criminal behavior as well as in attempts to explain other forms of delinquent and criminal conduct.

1 Sexual Aggression Against Adult Females

PAUL H. GEBHARD,
JOHN H. GAGNON,
WARDELL B. POMEROY,
AND CORNELIA V. CHRISTENSON

This report is based on a study of the sexual case histories obtained by interviewing the following: (a) 1,356 white males who had been convicted of one or more sex offenses (the sex offender group); (b) 888 white males who had never been convicted of a sex offense, but who had been convicted of some other misdemeanor or felony (the prison group); and (c) 477 white males who had never been convicted of anything more serious than traffic violations (the control group).

The offenses of the convicted sex offenders were classified as heterosexual offenses, peeping, exhibitionism, heterosexual aggressions, incest offenses, and homosexual offenses. Heterosexual offenses, heterosexual aggressions, incest offenses and homosexual offenses were further broken down into three categories according to the age of the victim—offenses against children under the age of twelve, against minors aged twelve to fifteen, and against adults. In this selection a sub-sample of 146 persons convicted of heterosexual aggression against adults is analyzed and compared with the prison group, with the control group, with heterosexual aggressors against children and minors, and with sex offenders convicted of offenses other than heterosexual aggression.

Heterosexual aggressors vs. adults are adult males convicted of sexual contact, accompanied by force or threat, with females aged sixteen or over who were not their daughters. Ordinarily force or threat can be easily identified in these cases, but there remain some instances in which the alleged force or threat may have been a post-factum invention on the part of the woman. The police and courts are well aware of this and not infrequently manifest some cynicism toward women who claim they have been sexually assaulted or raped; nevertheless, in the absence of witnesses or evidence, her word weighs more than that of the man.

The phenomenon of force or threat in sexual relations between adults is beclouded by various things.[1] In the first place, there may be the ambivalence of the female who is sexually aroused but who for moral or other reasons does not wish to have coitus. She is struggling not only against the male but against herself, and in retrospect it is exceedingly easy for her to convince herself that she yielded to force rather than to persuasion. This delusion is facilitated by the socially approved pattern for feminine behavior, according to which the woman is supposed to put up at least token resistance, murmuring, "No, no" or "We mustn't!" Any reasonably experienced male has learned to disregard such minor protestations, and the naive male who obeys his partner's injunction to cease and desist is often puzzled when she seems inexplicably irritated by his compliance.

Secondly, there is a certain masochistic streak in many women: they occasionally desire to be overpowered and treated a little roughly. It is, after all, very ego-satisfying for a female to feel she is so sexually attractive that the male cannot maintain social restraints and reverts to "caveman" tactics. Indeed, some women complain that their partners are too gentle; "Why do you always ask me, why don't you just take me sometimes?" they protest. Our literature, cartoons, and advertisements are ample testimony that a male is supposed to be physically forceful in his sexual behavior and that the female is supposed to respond favorably. Actually there is some sound biology behind this supposition. In many mammals coitus is ordinarily preceded by a physical struggle that ranges from the extreme (as in the mink), to something akin to playful wrestling. The physiological by-products of excitement and exertion—the increased heart rate, increased breathing, muscle tension, the greater supply of blood to the body surfaces, etc. —all of these are also a part of sexual response, and it is easy to see how these physiological conditions could facilitate a subsequent sexual response. The marriage counselor knows how often a fight between husband and wife changes rather suddenly into an almost simultaneous reconciliation and coitus. The "fight and make up" sequence is common in courtship and mar-

[1] The psychological aspects of aggressive sexual offenses against women were analyzed by Walter Bromberg in his *Crime and the Mind* (Philadelphia: Lippincott, 1948), pp. 86 ff.

riage. A standard gambit in feminine flirtation is to irritate the male and provoke him into physical contact; this ranges from the childhood "Ha, ha, you can't catch me" to the more subtle machinations of adult females.[2]

Another source of the female desire to be forced is a psychological defense and projection mechanism that enables an inhibited woman to enjoy sexual activity without feeling guilty about it. "He made me do it" salves the conscience very readily. Unfortunately this excuse can have disastrous consequences if it is offered by the girl not only to herself but to her outraged parents. As Dr. Kinsey often said, the difference between a "good time" and a "rape" may hinge on whether the girl's parents were awake when she finally arrived home.

The heterosexual aggressors vs. adults are well aware of public skepticism concerning rape, and make use of it in offering their own versions of their offenses. Perhaps more than any other group they give seemingly plausible accounts of their actions to prove their innocence, and while we are interviewing them it is often quite easy to be persuaded of the validity of their stories. Later, upon examining official records, we may discover that the allegedly willing female had to have five stitches taken in her lip.

Aside from instances of deliberate deceit, a considerable number of aggressors vs. adults believe in their innocence and are honestly mystified about why the woman brought charges against them. These men are victims of self-delusion and projection; they have in their minds minimized the violence and wishfully interpreted the woman's ultimate acquiescence as cooperation and forgiveness. Such a man will dwell on the fact that the woman made no protest and "voluntarily" removed her clothing, and seemingly consider as unimportant the fact that he had initially displayed a knife. His rationale frequently is that his threat or violence proved unnecessary because of the female's subsequent willingness, and hence should be disregarded. These men express the belief that the woman enjoyed the relationship; one gains the impression that their logic runs thus: sex is enjoyable, I enjoyed it, therefore she must have enjoyed it also. "She didn't act mad afterwards" is a common comment. In a few cases the victim purposely arranged another meeting with the man, who was so blinded by his own wishful thinking that he kept the appointment, and consequently we met him in prison.

Many aggressors vs. adults feel that a lack of violent physical resistance indicates some degree of assent. They point out that, without rendering her unconscious, it is physically almost impossible to have coitus with an adult female who is determined to prevent it at any cost. This is true, but they overlook the fact that fright may make her incapable of real resistance, and

[2] The unconscious tempting of the offender by the potential rape victim was discussed by Ralph Slovenko and Cyril Phillips in "Psychosexuality and the Criminal Law," *Vanderbilt Law Review*, XV (June 1962), pp. 807–808.

that a woman who keeps a level head prefers to have unwanted coitus rather than to suffer physical injury.

Some convicted offenders maintain that the woman claimed rape because they did not pay her the sum agreed upon in advance. This may be true in rare instances, but it is probable that few prostitutes would be willing to bring themselves to police attention and appear in court solely to avenge one loss of revenue. Some aggressors vs. adults wish to label their victims as prostitutes in the mistaken belief that her occupation somehow, wholly or partially, exempts him from punishment.

Lastly, of course, some aggressors vs. adults admitted without equivocation that they forced sexual relationship and were under no delusions about their victim's response. We have the impression that many of these men had a curiously impersonal, almost mechanistic, attitude toward their activity: they needed a woman so they got one, willing or not. Her age and physical attributes seem to have been of secondary importance; she was female and that was sufficient. Often in their eyes the compulsive need was great enough to justify their behavior: "I didn't want to hurt anybody, but I just had to get a piece." There are intimations that such men consider woman's main role in life is to provide sexual pleasure for men, and think a refusal to do so is a feminine perversity that deserves to be overridden if a man is in real need.

Sadistic aggressors vs. adults to whom violence and pain are consciously desirable ingredients of a sexual relationship, and who require contrived sadistic preliminaries, are rare: we found only a few of these. However, unnecessary (and probably unconsciously motivated) brutality was common.

EARLY LIFE

While most of the aggressors vs. adults were intermediate in rank-order of birth, they do display a small tendency to be the youngest children of the family (28 per cent). A similar tendency was seen in the aggressor vs. children, but the reverse was inexplicably true of the aggressor vs. minors. A very small percentage of aggressors vs. adults—but still a larger percentage than obtains for other groups—were raised alone despite having had siblings. They are also unusual in having fewer brothers than sisters, a characteristic of all three aggressor groups.

The aggressors vs. adults are not distinctive in their relationships to their fathers at ages fourteen to seventeen; about all that can be said is that they got along better with their fathers than did the aggressors vs. children and minors. This is in keeping with the general trend for heterosexual sex offenders whose objects were older to have had better paternal relationships than did sex offenders with younger objects. Their adjustment to their mothers is also unremarkable (although inferior to that of the prison and control groups) but better than that of the other heterosexual aggressors. In a rank-order of good adjustment with either father or mother, the aggressors are always in the lower half of the scale.[3]

More aggressors vs. adults got along better with their mothers than equally well with both parents. As is true of all groups, fewest were partial to the father. This preference for the mother is shared by all the heterosexual aggressors.

Sixty per cent of the aggressors vs. adults came from broken homes, the third highest number of any of the groups and double the number of the control group. They differ from the other heterosexual aggressors only in having an unusually large number (24 per cent) of cases in which the breakup came after the age of nine. The relationship of their parents was about average when the boys were in their early and midteens, neither particularly better nor worse than that of parents of sex offenders as a whole. It was, however, inferior to the relationship that existed between the parents of the control- and prison-group individuals.

Largely because of the high percentage from broken homes, the aggressors vs. adults spent fewer of their early years in a home in which both a husband and wife were present. Sixty per cent had 15 or more such years, while the equivalent figure for the control group is 80 per cent. About 7 per cent had lived ten or more years of their early lives in households in which the adults were all women. In absolute terms this is a small figure, but there may be some significance in the fact that it is the highest percentage manifested by any group guilty of heterosexual or homosexual offenses against adults. Also, a rather large proportion went to institutions after the breakup of the home.

.   .   .

There is a tendency for the aggressors vs. adults to have had more years of prepubertal heterosexual play than most other groups; for 48 per cent it continued for three or more years. A study of the prepubertal heterosexual techniques reveals some interesting facts. In a rank-order of those who had coitus during this period, the heterosexual aggressors rank second, fourth, and fifth—the fourth being the aggressors vs. adults, with 69 per cent. With respect to mouth-genital contact, the aggressors vs. children ranked first with 15 per cent, and the aggressors vs. adults third with 12 per cent. To those of a psychoanalytic bent, this might suggest an oral-aggressive type, but this assumption is weakened by the fact that a similar proportion

[3] A psychoanalytic interpretation of the relationship of rapists to their mothers by Rose Palm and David Abrahamsen revealed a seductive but rejecting maternal figure. See "A Rorschach Study of the Wives of Sex Offenders," *Journal of Nervous and Mental Disease*, 119 (February 1954), pp. 170–171.

is shared by the peepers and the incest offenders vs. adults, and the fifth rank is occupied by the exhibitionists—these three types of sex offenders being the least aggressive of any.

The homosexual play of the aggressors vs. adults was of moderate duration: for 44 per cent of them it lasted three or more years. Nevertheless, the future aggressors vs. adults were prone to engage in the more specific and developed techniques. Twenty-seven per cent of those with homosexual play had had mouth-genital contact (fourth rank); a relative predilection for this technique was seen in the heterosexual play. Twenty-nine per cent had had anal intercourse, this percentage placing them in fourth rank just below the three homosexual offender groups. In this anal coitus these aggressors are generally the ones who inserted their penes into other boys and are seldom in the recipient role only.

About 10 per cent of the aggressors vs. adults had, while prepubescent, been sexually approached by adult females. Such overtures led to noncoital physical contact in 9 per cent of the cases (fifth in rank-order) and to coitus in between 4 and 5 per cent (fourth rank). Relatively speaking, the future aggressors vs. adults were an experienced group insofar as contact with older females was concerned, and far more experienced than the control group. Regarding homosexuality with adult males, they are intermediate in the rank-order.

Like the aggressors vs. minors, the aggressors vs. adults enjoyed good health during childhood. Here in percentage terms they are essentially identical with the aggressors vs. minors, who occupy third rank.

There is nothing distinctive about the aggressors vs. adults as far as their prepubertal masturbatory experience is concerned. As in the case of heterosexual offenders against females aged twelve or more, the incidence of those with prepubertal masturbation is below average.

MASTURBATION

The incidence of postpubescent masturbation among aggressors vs. adults, and the median age at which it began, are in no way noteworthy.

The tendency to have high frequencies of masturbation before marriage, which we saw in the aggressors vs. minors, is seen again among the aggressors vs. adults.

. . .

Like the heterosexual aggressors vs. minors, the aggressors vs. adults were unusually prone to fantasy. Moreover, they rank second only to the aggressors vs. minors in the percentage with sadomasochistic (9 per cent) fantasies—an omen of the offenses for which they were ultimately convicted. This high rank with regard to sadomasochistic fantasy we shall see parallels their responsiveness to sadomasochistic stories and pictures.

The aggressors vs. adults were less prone than other aggressors to worry over their masturbation, but nevertheless fall in the upper half of a rank-order of "worriers."

SEX DREAMS

There are three salient points concerning the nocturnal emissions and dreams of the heterosexual aggressors vs. adults: first, a relatively large per-centage had heterosexual dreams (a trait of aggressors), and second, the highest percentage of any group (4 per cent) had sadomasochistic dreams. This latter phenomenon, as we have said, coincides with the relatively large percentage of aggressors vs. adults who had sadistic fantasies during mastur-bation, and is in keeping with the overt behavior that resulted in their con-viction. No such coincidence was observed in the other aggressors. The third notable feature is that the proportion of total outlet (total orgasms) constituted by emissions is always very small for both the single and married aggressors vs. adults. . . .

HETEROSEXUAL PETTING

All but two males in our sample of heterosexual aggressors vs. adults had had petting experience. By the age of twelve some 38 per cent (a moderate number) had petted; by the age of fourteen, 62 per cent (fourth in rank-order); by sixteen, 83 per cent (again fourth); and by eighteen, nearly 91 per cent. The median individual began petting at 14.9 years of age. . . .

The aggressors vs. adults share with the aggressors vs. minors the char-acteristic of having had a large number of petting partners. They are fourth in a rank-order of those with 31–50 partners, second in the 51–100 category, and fourth in the 101+ category (20 per cent). This sexual success is in keeping with their records of excellent socialization with females of sixteen and seventeen; over half (the second largest percentage) reported having had numerous girl companions (not necessarily sexual partners) at that age, and only 13 per cent (the second smallest percentage) reported having had none.

While not equal to the aggressors vs. minors, a large proportion of the aggressors vs. adults had petted to orgasm. By the time they were sixteen, a quarter (the second largest proportion) were thus experienced; two fifths (again second in rank) by the time they were twenty; and 46 per cent (third largest) by twenty-three.

. . .

Again like the other aggressors, they are particularly given to mouth-genital contact: about 41 per cent had performed cunnilingus and 66 per cent had experienced fellation by females at some point in their lives. These figures are nearly double those of the control group. In comparison to other groups, this oral activity was concentrated in premarital life and in prostitute relationships. One fourth had cunnilingus with companions before marriage (a percentage exceeded only by the aggressors vs. minors); and 34 per cent had experienced fellation prior to marriage (the highest percentage, just above that of the aggressors vs. minors). In mouth-genital contact of both sorts with prostitutes the offenders vs. adults also rank high: 6 per cent (third in rank) with cunnilingus and 59 per cent (first in rank-order) with fellation. This stress on mouth-genital contact is evident in their marital sex lives as well, the aggressors vs. adults ranking third in cunnilingus (46 per cent) and third in fellation (49 per cent). The control-group individuals rank eighth or lower in both respects.

We have previously mentioned that an unusually large number of aggressors vs. adults had sadistic dreams and masturbatory fantasies. In this connection it is worth noting that a rather large proportion of them (15 per cent, the fourth largest percentage) frequently bit or nibbled their sexual partners.

PREMARITAL COITUS

The aggressors vs. adults rather rapidly gained experience in premarital coitus. By age fourteen some 40 per cent (fifth rank) had had coitus with companions or with prostitutes; by sixteen, 64 per cent; by eighteen, 84 per cent (fourth rank); and by twenty, 91 per cent (second rank). At the time of interview, the figure was 96 per cent.

. . .

Nearly four fifths had had coitus with prostitutes at some point in their lives, mainly before marriage. A study of the accumulative incidence clearly indicates that this percentage would be substantially higher were it not for the fact that the sample includes many young individuals. Actually, in terms of accumulative incidence, the aggressors vs. adults are one of the most experienced groups: by age sixteen, 21 per cent had paid for coitus (third in rank-order); by eighteen, 54 per cent (second); by twenty, 68 per cent (second); and by twenty-six, 84 per cent (first in rank-order). . . .

Up to age twenty-five the aggressors vs. adults rank moderately high in frequency of premarital coitus with companions, the frequencies being below those of the prison group and the heterosexual offenders vs. minors, and markedly less than those of offenders vs. adults. The average (median) aggressor vs. adults had premarital coitus 30 to 40 times a year from puberty until he was twenty-five; the equivalent frequencies for the control group are 12 to 20 times a year.

The frequency of premarital coitus with prostitutes was neither high nor low. Before marriage, the average aggressor vs. adults had 14 coital companions, the fifth largest number. The number of premarital partners who were prostitutes is again moderate—11.

As a result of the rather high frequencies mentioned earlier, these aggressors derived fairly large proportions of their total sexual outlet from premarital coitus with companions; they are nearly always in the upper half of any rank-order. The proportion of total outlet so derived begins at 23 per cent in the early teens and increases to 41 per cent by age-period 31–35. The proportion of total outlet from premarital coitus with prostitutes is moderate, never exceeding 17 per cent.

A study of the factors they reported as having substantially impeded their premarital coitus shows that they are similar to the aggressors vs. minors in a lack of moral considerations, as well as in indifference to pregnancy and venereal disease. Fifty-nine per cent, the fourth highest percentage, claimed that they had lacked opportunity for more premarital coitus. A moderate proportion (33 per cent) stated that they did not have more premarital coitus because they were not interested in more. Nine per cent, again a moderate number, were restrained by fear of the opinion of others if they were found out.

Whereas the aggressors vs. minors were singularly indifferent about whether their brides were virgins or not, the aggressors vs. adults were more inclined to have definite opinions. Ten per cent, a somewhat small number, strongly desired virgins; 47 per cent were wholly indifferent; but 13 per cent, the largest percentage recorded, wanted experienced brides.

MARRIAGE

Not quite three fifths of our sample of aggressors vs. adults had married before they contributed their case histories to our research. The accumulative incidence curve indicates that by age thirty-five roughly three quarters would have married. The average aggressor vs. adults married five months after his twenty-first birthday. None of these figures are at all unusual.

On the whole, the aggressors vs. adults showed a definite tendency to marry more than once, although not to the same extent as the aggressors vs. minors. Roughly one third of them had married twice, a proportion exceeded by only two other groups, one of which is the aggressors vs. minors. Also, a relatively large number of them had had brief marriages (two years' duration or less) that ended in divorce or separation.

The aggressors vs. adults had known their wives for a little over five months, on the average, before marriage. This seems a brief courtship, and, in fact, falls in the shortest third of a rank-order of brevity. However, the aggressors vs. adults cannot be called impetuous when compared with the other aggressors, for a hasty marriage is typical of the group as a whole.

Within this admittedly limited period of acquaintance some 65 per cent had premarital coitus with their future wives—a figure exceeded by only two groups, one being the aggressors vs. minors. Aggressiveness is a decidedly effective factor in obtaining coitus, as the success of these two groups attest; this is particularly true outside of wedlock.

Since a relatively large number of aggressors vs. adults had premarital coitus with their future wives, and presumably rather often (the total premarital coital frequency with companions is rather high), a proportionately large number (24 per cent, the second largest number) of brides were pregnant when they married.

There is nothing remarkable about the subsequent fertility of these aggressors.

Like the aggressors vs. minors, the aggressors vs. adults devoted an unusually large amount of time to petting preliminary to coitus. Thirty-seven per cent, the largest proportion recorded, ordinarily spent 30 or more minutes in this way. Again like the aggressors vs. minors, a large percentage of aggressors vs. adults included mouth-genital contact in their precoital play —an activity that, as we have observed, was also evident in their premarital lives. Only one other group had more members experienced in marital mouth-genital contact. It is noteworthy that in those cases where mutuality (i.e., both fellation and cunnilingus) was not obtained, the desire was such that the aggressors vs. adults rank second among those with only fellation and those with only cunnilingus. The aggressors vs. minors also rank high in this respect.

Up to the age of thirty-five, which is as far as our data will let us go, the aggressors vs. adults have the greatest frequency of marital coitus. The average (median) aggressor vs. adults is also unusual in twice defying the frequency-depressing effects of age: he had intercourse more often at twenty-one to twenty-five than at sixteen to twenty, and still more often between thirty-one and thirty-five than between twenty-six and thirty. Indeed, his 3.75 per week frequency between thirty-one and thirty-five is the highest recorded in any age-period. He also ranks first in age-periods

21–25 and 26–30. The tendency of aggressors vs. adults toward high coital frequencies in premarital life—despite the complaint of a large proportion that lack of opportunity seriously impeded their efforts to obtain still more coitus—is seen in retrospect as an omen of their marital coital performance.

.   .   .

One quarter of the aggressors vs. adults, the second largest percentage recorded, had had anal coitus with their wives, and an additional 8 per cent had attempted it. This is not unexpected in a group which, as we have seen, had an unusual amount of heterosexual activity, was little troubled by moral restraints, and had a strong proclivity toward taboo sexual techniques (e.g., mouth-genital contact). Since anal coitus is initially almost always painful, and since many females feel humiliated by it, there is probably a sadistic component here that is in keeping with aggression.

Whereas the wives of the aggressors vs. minors reportedly reached orgasm in coitus with unusual frequency, the wives of the aggressors vs. adults were not so fortunate; in fact, if one accepts their husbands' estimates, they made a rather mediocre showing. A moderate number reached orgasm regularly, but nearly one fifth of their married years were marred by low (less than 10 per cent) orgasm rates.

As for how they evaluated the happiness of their marriages, the aggressors are in no way unusual; their marriages were not especially happy or unhappy in comparison to those of the other groups.[4]

EXTRAMARITAL COITUS

Seventy-seven per cent of the ever-married individuals, while married, had coitus with females other than their wives. This is the third largest percentage and not far below the record of the aggressors vs. minors. All the heterosexual aggressors fall within the first five ranks in this respect. . . .

Although the frequency of extramarital coitus was moderate to low, a comparatively large amount of it was with prostitutes. While in most groups the frequency with companions far exceeds that with prostitutes, for the aggressors vs. adults the two figures are often closer. For example, the average individual with extramarital coitus in age-period 21–25 had coitus 0.14 times per week with companions as against 0.10 with prostitutes.

.   .   .

_____

[4] A poor marital adjustment accompanied by a masochistic submissiveness on the part of the wives was noted in the Palm and Abrahamsen study of the wives of eight rapists. *Ibid.*, p. 170.

HOMOSEXUAL ACTIVITY

In the rank-order of percentages of those with homosexual experience in or out of prison, the aggressors vs. adults are in sixth place (57 per cent), just below the prison group, and in sixth place in a rank-order of those with more than incidental homosexual experience in or out of prison. They owe this moderately high position to their prison experience, as is evident when one examines the percentages of those with homosexual experience outside prison; here the aggressors vs. adults occupy an intermediate position (45 per cent) in the rank-order.

. . .

ANIMAL CONTACTS

Nearly 19 per cent of the aggressors vs. adults had had, since puberty, sexual contact with animals other than human. This earns them sixth place in a rank-order of incidence, above the prison group (14 per cent), and far above the control group which has the lowest incidence of all (8 per cent). It should immediately be added that these three groups are very similar in the percentages who had a rural background.

. . .

As in the case of aggressors vs. minors, this activity is not reflected in their dream content (not one reported dreams of animal contact) or in their masturbation fantasy. The sexual contact with animals was confined in every case except one to the years between puberty and twenty, and seems to have been, as usual, a seldom-repeated experiment, devoid of much emotional content. The quantitative unimportance of animal contact is seen in the proportion of total sexual outlet, where it never constitutes as much as 1 per cent of the total orgasms experienced in a given age-period.

CRIMINALITY

The aggressors vs. adults had a rather substantial record of juvenile convictions: 22 per cent, the fourth largest proportion. Five per cent, a moderate figure, had been convicted for juvenile sex offenses.

These aggressors came into conflict with society more rapidly than most sex offenders, essentially paralleling the prison group up to age twenty and then outstripping them. By age twenty-six some 87 per cent had been convicted for some crime—a figure exceeded only by the aggressors vs. minors. By age thirty the proportion had risen to 96 per cent—the largest proportion recorded by that age. Compared with other groups, many of these aggressors were convicted of serious crimes; by the time they were twenty-six over two-thirds of them had committed at least one offense that cost them a full year or more of prison time. Again, only the aggressors vs. minors surpass this figure, and no other group comes near equaling it.

Approximately half of the convictions were for sex offenses and slightly fewer were for other offenses; this is a somewhat, though not markedly, low percentage of sex offenses. One third of the men had *only* sex offense convictions, and again this is a relatively small percentage; the aggressors rank one, two, and three in having fewest "pure" sex offenders.

With this relative stress on nonsex offenses one might expect to find the aggressors vs. adults specializing in some type of antisocial activity, but actually their convictions show no marked concentration. However, they do show, like other aggressors, a predilection for crimes against the person: in these they rank fourth, with 14 per cent of their convictions being for such behavior, and the per capita incidence being 0.27. Again like other aggressors they had few crimes against order.

Considering now the other sex offenses committed by these men, one finds that aside from aggression against adult females the most frequent offenses were against willing or acquiescent females (27 per cent), exhibition (21 per cent), and peeping (19 per cent). Only rarely was there aggression against minors or children; these men were strongly oriented toward adult females. As we mentioned in discussing the aggressors vs. minors, the proclivity to exhibit is not incompatible with aggression, since exhibition may in these cases be a hostile act designed to shock and frighten. Similarly, the stereotype of the timid, harmless peeper need not interfere with our finding that nearly one fifth of these aggressors' sex-offense convictions were for peeping: after all, a certain amount of reconnaissance is necessary in selecting the object, time, and place for rape.

Concerning recidivism for all types of crime the aggressors vs. adults are remarkable in only one respect: few (17 per cent) were not recidivists. However, they are far less recidivistic than their brothers, the aggressors vs. children, and are more like the aggressors vs. minors.

OTHER FACTORS

While the aggressors vs. minors were quite distinctive in the incidence and intensity of response to nonphysical stimuli such as sight and thought, the aggressors vs. adults were undistinguished in all except one of our measurements. This one exception, appropriately enough, was response to pictures or stories of sadomasochistic activity. In the proportion of men reporting sexual arousal from this source (15 per cent), the aggressors vs. adults were second only to the aggressors vs. minors. Similarly a relatively large number (7 per cent, fourth in rank-order) stated that their arousal was strong or frequent.

CIRCUMSTANCES OF THE OFFENSE

The average aggressor vs. adults was twenty-four and one-half years old at the time of his offense. Between one quarter and one third were married at the time of the offense, one quarter had been separated, divorced, or widowed, and 46 per cent had never married. As a group they were "less married" than their counterparts, the offenders vs. adults, but about the same proportion were currently married when they committed their offense.

For slightly more than half, the offense was their first sex offense; for about one quarter, their second; for 7 per cent their third; and 9 per cent had had three or more previous sex-offense convictions. This record is lower than for the aggressor vs. children, but somewhat greater than for the aggressor vs. minors.

About 5 per cent had either been institutionalized for mental or emotional disorders, or had been evaluated as neurotic by the interviewer. This is a modest percentage. However, the number who were drunk at the time of the offense is large: 39 per cent (the second largest percentage). An additional 15 per cent had been mildly to moderately intoxicated—a large proportion of the men in all the aggressor groups claimed they were intoxicated at the time of offense—and four men had been using an opiate, but drugs obviously are a minor factor. The "drug-crazed sex fiend" or the "sex-crazed drug addict" are figments of journalistic imagination.

In 12 per cent of the cases two or more men were involved, which is not unusual in aggression offenses; in fact, the aggressor groups rank first (aggressors vs. minors) and third (aggressors vs. adults) in this respect. A couple of young men cruising about looking for a girl or girls to pick up is a common thing in our culture. A relatively large number of the offenses were opportunistic (10 per cent, the third largest percentage) or committed while the subject was *non compos mentis* (8 per cent, second in rank-order). Only 70 per cent, the smallest proportion in any of the offense groupings, were premeditated.

The offenses occurred most often in residences (26 per cent), chiefly in the home of the female, and outdoors (38 per cent), mainly in urban areas such as parks, vacant lots, and alleys.

The average girl involved was twenty-four years old, the same age as the average aggressor at the time of his conviction. Between one quarter and one third of the girls, however, were under age twenty. Older women are definitely more immune to rape: only 3 per cent of the victims were fifty-one or over. As one would anticipate, a high percentage of the females (72 per cent) were strangers to the offender. However, 17 per cent of the cases (a relatively small number) involved friends and 9 per cent involved acquaintances. These percentages of strangers, acquaintances, and friends present, we realize, a false picture of rape and other sexual aggression. It is known that many rape cases go unreported, especially if the two people concerned have been dating. No girl likes to advertise her misfortune through court action, and she is especially loath to do so if the defendant is someone with whom she has been friendly, lest there may be some question about the validity of her charge. To be raped by a stranger makes one a martyr; to be raped by a friend makes one an object of suspicion.

Nearly half of the aggression offenses resulted in coitus, and in one fourth coitus was definitely attempted. In comparison to other groups the aggressors include large percentages of males who unsuccessfully attempted coitus; they occupy the first three ranks in this respect with the aggressors vs. adults in first place. All aggressors also rank high in a category we label "general attack." This term describes violent and aggressive activity which, while presumably sexually motivated, appears aimed not at obtaining coitus, but at inflicting physical damage. More aggressors vs. adult offenses were general attacks (13 per cent) than was true for any other offense category.

We have 146 cases in which the degree of the victim's participation was described both in the official records and by the offender. In about two thirds of the cases both the records and the offenders agree that the females resisted; in another 9 per cent the offenders claim that resistance was preceded by encouragement. In one fifth of the cases the records state that the females resisted, while the offenders say that the women were encouraging or acquiescent. By no means were all these men consciously lying; we believe that normal male conceit led some of them to mistake the passivity of fear for acquiescence. Still others evidently encountered females who paid heed to the general admonition that it is wiser to cooperate in the rape than to resist, be beaten up, and raped anyway. The rapist in these instances often looks upon grudging and reluctant cooperation as evidence of enthusiasm. Often we heard the plaint, "It wasn't rape—she took her clothes off!" In only about 4 per cent of the offenses does there seem to have been initial encouragement by the female followed by a change of heart.

In half of the offenses the offender had made at least some of the overtures males customarily make in attempting to obtain a sexual relationship, or, to put it another way, half of the time there were attempts to gain a voluntary rather than a forced relationship. When these preliminaries failed,

the men resorted to force and threat. In two fifths of the offenses considerable physical force was employed; in slightly more (45 per cent) only
moderate to little force was exerted; and in a small number of cases (7 per
cent) threat alone sufficed. In the few remaining offenses we know that force
was used, but we do not know to what degree.

Although differentiation is not always easy, there appear to be two
major varieties of aggressive offenses: (1) those in which the aggression is a
means to an end, and no more force is used than is necessary to achieve the
end (coitus, usually), (2) those in which violence is an end in itself or at
least a secondary goal; in these cases the female is either subjected to more
force than is necessary or she is mistreated *after* coitus or other direct sexual
activity has ended. The first variety of aggression is by far the more common.

In slightly over half of the offenses threats were made or implied in
order to coerce the females. Threats of a major sort, e.g., threats of serious
physical damage or threats of injuring the victim's children, were involved
in two fifths of the cases. In about the same number of cases no threats
were made at all, and in only a few instances (10 per cent) were minor
threats employed.

At this juncture it is worth noting that the aggressors vs. adults used
physical force to a markedly greater degree than the other aggressors, and
employed threat less often than the aggressors vs. minors. These facts reflect
not so much the habits of the offender, but the differences in the victims:
older females are not so readily intimidated by threats and, therefore, the
offender must resort to force. Moreover, with mature females he must employ a greater degree of physical force.

Because of our cultural attitudes toward fighting and because physical
aggression is particularly discouraged in females, the great majority of girls
and women do not know how to fight effectively. In addition, the few who
do know how sometimes fear to try lest they fail and only infuriate their
attacker, or in other instances they simply cannot bring themselves to commit the effective brutalities. For instance, in most rapes there are moments
when the offender's eyes and genitalia could easily be damaged. At any rate,
the aggressors we have interviewed emerged from their rapes either un-
scathed or with only scratches. They were seldom even bitten. The ineffectual resistance put up by most victims is sometimes taken as an indication
that they have a conscious or unconscious desire to submit. This is undoubtedly true in some undetermined number of cases, but we feel such cases
constitute a definite minority. It is more probable that the ineffectuality
results from fright or from a realistic appraisal of the danger involved in
making a determined resistance.

The aggressors vs. adults are more vulnerable to arrest than any other
type of sex offender. We estimate that in nearly three fifths of the offenses

apprehension by the police was probable rather than merely possible. In the first place, since the female did not willingly participate, she is not going to assist the offender in evading punishment; on the contrary, she is interested in having him captured. In over three quarters of the cases it was the female herself who reported the matter to the authorities—by far the largest percentage of offenses reported by the object of the offense. Secondly, the offender is not involved with a juvenile whose naiveté may facilitate his escape, but with an adult who often has enough presence of mind to look for identifying marks, license plate numbers, etc. Thirdly, the screaming and struggling often associated with rape or attempted rape is likely to attract attention. Lastly, a number of aggressors vs. adults delude themselves into believing their victims have become sexually interested in them and the aggressor therefore agrees to subsequent meetings.

Only about half (52 per cent) fully admitted their aggression to the authorities and a few more (57 per cent) to us. This is a relatively small percentage, as is usual among aggressors. Another 18 per cent made qualified admissions to the authorities, and 24 per cent to our interviewers. Twenty-five per cent flatly denied their guilt to the authorities, and 14 per cent to us. Roughly 4 per cent were so drunk or upset at the time of offense that they could neither confirm nor deny the act with which they were charged. Despite the relatively small number who made full admissions, about two thirds pleaded guilty when they came before the court, but this is not a large percentage compared to other groups.

VARIETIES OF OFFENDERS

Examination of the aggressors vs. adults leads us to feel that the majority can be classified into seven varieties, and that the classification is scientifically and clinically useful.[5]

The commonest variety, accounting for between one quarter and one third of our sample, we have labeled the assaultive variety. These are men whose behavior includes unnecessary violence; it seems that sexual activity alone is insufficient and that in order for it to be maximally gratifying it must be accompanied by physical violence or by serious threat. In brief, there is a strong sadistic element in these men and they often feel pronounced hostility to women (and possibly to men also) at a conscious or unconscious level. They generally do not know their victims; they usually commit the offense alone, without accomplices; preliminary attempts at seduction are

[5] A classification of types of rapists and their variant personalities can be found in Manfred S. Guttmacher and Henry Weihofen, *Psychiatry and the Law* (New York: Norton, 1952), pp. 116–117; Paul Plaut, *Der Sexualverbrecher und seine Persönlichkeit* (Stuttgart: Ferdinand Enke, 1960), pp. 75–81.

either absent or extremely brief and crude; the use of weapons is common; the man usually has a past history of violence; he seemingly selects his victim with less than normal regard for her age, appearance, and deportment. Lastly, there is a tendency for the offense to be accompanied by bizarre behavior including unnecessary and trivial theft. Aside from the drunken variety of aggressor, the assaultive type has more cases involving erectile impotence than do the others. In some instances the violence seems to substitute for coitus or at least render the need for it less. In other cases there appears to have been a conflict between sexual desire and hostility resulting in some measure of erectile (less often ejaculatory) impotence.

An example of the type of assaultive aggressor whom the newspapers label "sex maniac" is a man aged forty-two when interviewed. The repetitive and compulsive element is particularly strong in this case. Beginning at age seventeen he had an uninterrupted list of arrests for indecent exposure, molestation, and indecent assault, culminating in a flurry of forced rapes after his marriage broke up when he was about thirty. He accosted his victims chiefly on the street, but sometimes sought them out in their rooms. He intimidated them by displaying a long knife. He never injured any of the women and his statement that he would not fulfill his verbal threats is probably correct, since when one woman refused to comply with his order to undress he simply departed. The impotence which is not unusual in assaultive aggressors was in this man manifested in some erectile difficulty. The prison psychologist found the man to have an "acceptance of and obsession with sex fantasies."

A second illustrative case reveals a more sadistic bent. This man had since puberty been sexually excited by stories of rape and he had developed a particularly gratifying fantasy of breaking into a house at night and tearing the clothes from a girl who, in the process, became sexually aroused and finally cooperative. His overt assaultive behavior developed a few years after puberty. While window-peeping he saw a woman undress and go to bed; aroused by the sight he broke into her house and struck her on the head with the handle of a knife, hoping to make her unconscious and vulnerable for coitus. However, the woman screamed when struck and the subject, then aged fifteen, ran away. There appear to have been no other overt aggressions until he was twenty-two, the year before his marriage, when he broke into the house of a neighboring woman whom he believed to be promiscuous and whose husband was away. He found her asleep in bed, nude. Placing his hand over her mouth he warned her to be quiet and then began to caress her. According to his statement, which parallels his fantasy suspiciously well, she became sexually aroused and the consequent coitus was by mutual desire. She subsequently recognized him and asked him to return on the following night. However, she informed the police who made the arrest the next morning. Then the woman, who was a friend of the young man's mother, suffered another change of heart and refused to press charges and he was released with the suggestion that he seek psychiatric help.

He did not follow this advice, but married. The marriage did not end either his fantasy or his desire to assault women: during the two years of his marriage he twice seized females at night, once on a deserted street and once in the woman's backyard, but in both instances his victim's screams caused him to abandon his efforts. Also while married he entered two houses at night, but departed when he found the beds occupied by males as well as females. Soon after his marriage broke up he made three attempts at rape. The first consisted of grabbing a girl at night on a residential street; her screams caused people to turn on porch lights and he fled. The second was an attempt to pull a woman into his car. She struggled and finally offered him money to let her go, an offer he declined until her cries and struggles attracted some passers-by; at this point he seized the money and fled. This episode did not deter him. He drove until he saw a lone female in a car, followed her to an apartment house, and watched to find out which was her apartment. After waiting an hour, he took the screen off her window and entered, noticing a purse which he immediately appropriated—a typical instance of the petty theft which one finds among assaultive aggressors. This was the second time within a few hours that he had obtained money from an intended victim. Finding the woman asleep in bed (as in the earlier instance), he put his hand over her mouth, told her to be quiet, and began to caress her. She told him she was menstruating and showed him the tampon; this caused him to lose his erection (an instance of the impotence not uncommon in this variety of aggressor) and he was unable to continue. After talking a while he left under the impression that the woman would welcome his return. He did subsequently return some nights later and was welcomed by the waiting police. This wishful self-delusion that their victims have become desirous of seeing them again is frequent among aggressors vs. adults, and they seem to find it difficult to believe that the women bear them any ill will.

In these two cases, there was really rather little physical violence despite the obvious or implied threats. The assaultive aggressor who seemingly requires violence for his gratification is exemplified by a semiskilled laborer with two marriages and seven prison sentences behind him when he was interviewed in his late forties. While no conscious sadism appeared in his dreams, fantasies, or reactions to stories of brutality, all or nearly all his four rapes or attempted rapes were marked by unnecessary violence. The first rape, committed when he was in his early twenties, was a case of two young men picking up two girls, one of whom fled when the men refused to take them home. While it seems clear that the other girl could have been easily subdued and restrained by the two sturdy males, the subject felt it necessary to beat her and, after placing her on the ground, to kick her in the mouth before having coitus. Data are incomplete regarding his second rape when he was in his late twenties, but he entered the bedroom of a sleeping woman and attempted to have coitus with her. His third rape was committed, when he was in his thirties, upon his mother-in-law who was nearly twenty years his senior. He raped her twice and in the process beat her so severely that she was hospitalized for a month. He evaded prosecution by fleeing the state. His fourth rape, when he was in his late thirties, consisted of forcing a girl into his motel cabin and threatening her with a knife. When she tried to escape he struck her with a bottle and beat her up. Before coitus was accomplished, she did manage to run, nearly nude, from the cabin to seek help. The man solaced himself by taking her purse before he fled, but made the error of returning to salvage a bottle of whiskey which he had forgotten to take with him. After serving some years for this offense he was paroled but extradited to another state to stand trial for having raped his former mother-in-law.

The second commonest variety of aggressors vs. adults are the amoral delinquents previously described under aggressors vs. minors and offenders vs. children. These men pay little heed to social controls and operate on a level of disorganized egocentric hedonism, and consequently have numerous brushes with the law. They are not sadistic—they simply want to have coitus and the females' wishes are of no particular consequence. They are not hostile toward females, but look upon them solely as sexual objects whose role in life is to provide sexual pleasure. If a woman is recalcitrant and will not fulfill her role, a man may have to use force, threat, weapons, or anything else at his disposal. The amoral delinquent may or may not have previously known his victim, but this too is a minor point to someone who regards women as mere pleasantly shaped masses of protoplasm for sexual use. It appears that one eighth to one sixth of the aggressors vs. adults may be classed as amoral delinquents.

One case is that of a semiskilled man of twenty-two with a tenth-grade education. The descriptions of him contain terms such as "lazy," "drifter," "reckless," "restless," and "a chronic nuisance in his area." Almost half of his brief army career was spent in the stockade for having been absent without leave. About two years later, by which time he was tattooed and running with local gangs, he and two companions picked up two girls and, instead of giving them the promised ride to their destination, took them to a rural area where they forced sexual activity by threatening the girls with a knife. After serving slightly more than a year for this offense, the young man was released on parole. Shortly thereafter he was arrested along with a large group of males and females who were engaged in some sort of street fight. He was also suspected of encouraging a girl to write bad checks. In the year he came of age his parole was revoked when he and a friend broke a window and stole several hundred dollars worth of tools.

An example of an older amoral delinquent is a thirty-seven-year-old in our sample. There was nothing unusual about his life until impending fatherhood forced his marriage at age nineteen. He made his living through semiskilled labor and also got into the entertainment world. His first marriage ended in divorce after three years and his second marriage, when he was in his early twenties, lasted only one year. His wife, complaining of his too frequent sexual demands, made the following highly significant remark, ". . . he treated me as though I were a child," i.e., not as a real person, but as an inferior of use only as a sexual object. Soon after the collapse of this second marriage the man held up a number of stores, in one of which he found a young saleswoman and opportunistically forced her to undress and have coitus. These acts resulted in a long prison term. He was paroled in his early thirties and within about a year was back in prison for petty theft. Paroled again, he supported himself by managing an eating place staffed by waitresses who doubled as prostitutes while he served as the pimp. This remunerative situation came to an end when his attempts to persuade a woman to have coitus resulted in some sort of struggle during which the woman fell, or was pushed, down a flight of stairs, at least partially forced coitus occurred, and the man was injured in his left eye. In any event, he returned to prison on a charge of assault with intent to commit rape.

About as common as the amoral delinquent variety of aggressor is the drunken variety. The student of sex offenders soon comes to realize that drunks are omnipresent, appearing in all offense categories to a greater or lesser degree. The drunk's aggression ranges from uncoordinated grapplings and pawings, which he construes as efforts at seduction, to hostile and truly vicious behavior released by intoxication.

The simplest and least aggressive sort of drunken offense is exemplified by a ninetten-year-old farm laborer of borderline intelligence. The case is summed up in the words of the prison psychologist: "The subject is a dull boy of nineteen. . . . While drunk, he tried to force the young wife of his former employer into a bedroom in an attempt to have sexual intercourse. She resisted and later told her husband. . . ." This resulted in a 90-day sentence for assault and battery. The boy was under the impression that the wife was more amenable than she actually was.

A more bizarre, but still relatively harmless case is one of a forty-two-year-old, previously married man of average intelligence who was living in a motel and was feeling sexually deprived. He had in the past once forced coitus on a girl friend with whom he had had a mutually voluntary coital relationship and also had once forced coitus on his ex-wife. Both women had resisted, wrestling ensued, and both had finally yielded in order to get it over with and get rid of him. It seems probable that the man looked upon the use of minor force as both effective and safe. He became intoxicated and re-called that a young, unmarried woman lived in a motel cabin nearby. He decided to peep in her window to see if she was with a man, his logic being that if she were with a man this would be evidence that she was sexually loose and, hence, worth cultivating. He peered in and saw her alone asleep in bed and at this moment conceived the idea of having coitus with her then and there. He cut the window screen and then with drunken logic recalled that he was not properly clothed for bed, so he returned to his own cabin and changed into his pajamas. Thus properly dressed, he went back to the girl's cabin, removed the cut screen, opened the window, and crawled in. He tiptoed to the bed, turned off the bed lamp which had been left on, and tried to slip unobtrusively into the bed. The girl awoke and screamed. The man, frightened, clapped his hand over her mouth and the girl became quiet and immobile—possibly fainting. He then crawled on top of her and re-moved his hand from her mouth in order to kiss her. The girl galvanized into action, screaming and scratching. The man was severely scratched before he managed to get out of bed and stumble out of the door into the grasp of a man attracted by the screams.

In contrast to these two examples which involved no physical harm of any consequence and which were not without some humorous aspects, the cases where intoxication releases a violent pathological response are ex-tremely serious. One of the best illustrations is the case of a young man who up to the time of his offense seemed in no way unusual except for his above-average intelligence, his hatred for his abusive father, and a tendency to want to bite his sexual partners as he reached orgasm. Following graduation from high school he enlisted in military service where he served well and had just re-enlisted before his offense. He had gone on a drunken binge and was frequenting bars in order to pick up girls. He finally found one; they drank and left together. They went into an alley and began petting. According to the man, while they were deep-kissing she suddenly bit his tongue severely, and subsequent medical examination disclosed a deep cut nearly halfway through his tongue. This intense pain coming on top of erotic arousal and extreme intoxication precipitated a sadistic assault in which he not only beat the woman but repeatedly bit her face, breasts, and genitals. Portions of flesh were actually bitten off. He claimed only vague memory of this and had no memory of taking the woman's wristwatch and dental plate when he left her. The psychologists and psychiatrists who examined him reported deep underlying hostile impulses which were released during intoxication, and one psychologist believed that he had "displaced his hostility toward his father on to women."

The next commonest variety of aggressor, constituting perhaps 10 to 15 per cent of the aggressors vs. adults, might be termed the explosive variety. These are men whose prior lives offer no surface indications of

what is to come. Sometimes they are average, law-abiding citizens, sometimes they are criminals, but their aggression appears suddenly and, at the
time, inexplicably. As one would expect in situations where individuals snap
under hidden emotional stresses, there are often psychotic elements in their
behavior. The stereotype of this variety of aggressor is the mild, straight-A
high school student who suddenly rapes and kills. For total unexpectedness,
one of our cases is equally dramatic. A small, physically delicate, devoutly
religious eighteen-year-old had been reared by his mother, who seems to have
dominated him. While heterosexually oriented, he never developed sociosexually with girls of his own age; instead, on rare occasions he engaged
female children in what would be called childhood sex play had he been
preadolescent rather than fifteen or older. He was never able to achieve
coitus, but usually ejaculated when the children struggled or when his penis
touched their genital area. This behavior resulted in his being sent to a
juvenile institution for about a year. On his return home and only a few
days after his eighteenth birthday, during his mother's absence he asked a
neighbor woman to come into the kitchen and light the oven for him. When
she entered he struck her on the head with a hammer, hoping to knock her
unconscious so that he could have coitus. She was not rendered unconscious by the blow and succeeded in escaping.

While the above case is unusual in that the subject was so sociosexually
underdeveloped, in the following case the man's sexual history was normal.
He was a hard-working, semiskilled laborer described by the prison psychologist as having "many fine traits, . . . deep respect for authority, family
pride, sense of personal responsibility, a knowledge of right and wrong and
a willingness to abide by the same, . . . etc." His dossier contained numerous
and various letters attesting to his good character and respectability. The only
negative note was his wife's statement that he tended to worry excessively
and became emotionally upset easily. This statement is biased by the fact
that the behavior of the wife and her relatives directly led to the sex offense.
This conservative and respectable man had made the error of marrying a girl
from a very low socioeconomic stratum who brought with her to marriage
not only an unborn child, but a number of shiftless, drunken, parasitic relatives. The resultant bitter arguments essentially destroyed the marriage, and
the man decided to make the best of a bad situation by having extramarital
coitus with some of his promiscuous female in-laws. He chose his mother-in-
law, having interpreted her behavior toward him as provocative; the psychologists say that this choice also was unconsciously motivated by a desire
for revenge against his wife and all her relatives. In any case, coitus occurred
and the woman was at least partly forced.

The next variety of aggressor vs. adult, and one accounting for perhaps
as much as 10 per cent of the group, is the double-standard variety. The
males so classified divide females into good females whom one treats with

some respect and bad females who are not entitled to consideration if they become obstinate. While one would not ordinarily think of maltreating a good girl, any girl one can pick up easily has in essence agreed to coitus and can legitimately be forced to keep her promise. These double-standard aggressors are somewhat like the amoral delinquents in attitude, but differ from them in being less criminal, in resorting to force only after persuasion fails, and in not being so generally asocial. In brief, the double-standard variety may be described as rather average males of lower socioeconomic background who feel that with provocation the use of moderate threat or force is justifiable when applied to females judged to be sexually lax or promiscuous. There are strong philosophical parallels with the Latin-American "machismo" phenomenon. These double-standard males share with the amoral delinquents a penchant for group activity, the logical result when several males cruise about looking for female pickups. This trend may include a sort of man-to-man generosity, the female being shared much as men would share food or liquor, and with about the same emotional affect. Indeed, we have one case in which the man left a pickup girl and his friend in his car to go to a nearby parked car containing three other men and suggested sharing the girl in exchange for a gallon of wine. Yet this man strongly desired to marry a virgin and had refrained from coitus with his fiancée.

Another man of limited intellect and education who had a clear record, save for juvenile car theft (not uncommon behavior in his social milieu), helped a woman get her stalled auto started, mistook her appreciation and offer of a lift for an indication of sexual willingness and then threatened and struck her when she refused coitus. The prison report is illuminating: "[The subject has] habitually a naive expression . . . anxious to have everyone understand that he was neither brutal nor violent with his victim . . . admits that when he could not persuade her in friendly fashion he uttered threats. . . . Frank to admit he sees nothing wrong with what he did, for the victim was not harmed in any way and it was nothing more than what he has done on many occasions in the past to other girls. . . ."

The rationalization of a double-standard aggressor might often be in the following vein, to quote one of them: "Man, these dumb broads don't know what they want. They get you worked up and then they try to chicken out. You let 'em get away with stuff like that and the next thing you know they'll be walking all over you." If a large segment of the population of any socioeconomic class subscribed to this view, we might regard this variety as a "subculture" variety like the offenders vs. minors. However, no large social segment approves of force although it is easily forgiven.

After subtracting the above varieties, nearly one third of the aggressors vs. adults remain. A few of them may be recognized as clear cases of mental defectives and a few others as unquestionable psychotics, but the others strike one as being mixtures of the varieties described.

SUMMARY

The majority of aggressors vs. adults may be succinctly described as criminally inclined men who take what they want, whether money, material, or women, and their sex offenses are by-products of their general criminality.

Aside from their early involvement in crime, there are no outstandingly ominous signs in their presex-offense histories; indeed, their heterosexual adjustment is quantitatively well above average. There are occasional hints of underlying violence and sadism, but these are manifest in only a minority of individuals. In the sex offense itself, however, one can frequently see a basic pathology revealed by unnecessary violence, bizarre behavior, and self-delusion.

A minority of the aggressors vs. adults are not the amoral and antisocial individuals often involved in criminal activities, but are seemingly rather ordinary citizens leading conventional or even restrained lives. Actually many are suffering from personality defects and stresses which ultimately erupt in a sex offense. A few aggressors vs. adults appear to be statistically normal individuals who simply misjudged the situation.

2 Physician Narcotic Addicts

CHARLES WINICK

This study was undertaken in order to explore what would appear to be the anomaly of the substantial incidence of drug addiction among physicians. It is an anomaly because addiction is generally perceived as a degraded and visibly pathological form of deviant behavior which is associated with the lower socioeconomic classes. In contrast, physicians are usually perceived as constituting one of the most prestigious and honored and wealthy occupations in our society.[1] A further anomaly is the extent to which the physician is clearly a person who early learns to defer gratifications during his very lengthy training. In contrast, the addict's orality and need for his drug frequently make it very difficult for him to defer gratifications.

The incidence of opiate addiction among physicians has been estimated by the U.S. Commissioner of Narcotics as being about one addict among every 100 physicians, in contrast to a rate of one in 3,000 in the general population.[2] According to official records of the Federal Bureau of Narcotics, 1,012 physicians were reported as addicts and 659 were found guilty of

Reprinted from *Social Problems*, Volume 9, Number 2 (Fall, 1961), pp. 174–186, by permission of The Society for the Study of Social Problems and the author.

[1] National Opinion Research Corporation, "Jobs and Occupations: A Popular Evaluation," *Opinion News*, 9 (September 1, 1947), pp. 3–13.

[2] "Interview with Hon. Harry J. Anslinger," *Modern Medicine*, 25 (October 15, 1957), pp. 170–191.

illegal narcotics sales or prescription activity from 1942 through 1956. One report identified the dean of a university medical school and other well-known physicians who became addicted.[3] The head of a leading state medical society became addicted and committed suicide. The number of physicians becoming addicted each year is roughly equivalent to the graduating class of a medical school. It is of course possible that there are physician addicts who are not known to the authorities, so that the incidence may be even higher.

A substantial incidence of addiction among physicians has been reported from several other countries, suggesting that there may be something about the physician's role independent of his nationality which is related to his use of narcotics. England has reported that physicians are the occupational group most heavily represented among addicts, accounting for 17 per cent of the country's addicts.[4] One authority, summarizing United Nations reports on the subject, has said that in England one physician in every 550 and in Germany one physician in every 95 was an addict.[5] Another study reported that addiction in the 1930's among German physicians was 100 times more frequent than in the general population, and that the typical physician addict used more drugs than other addicts.[6]

There have been two statistical studies of physician addicts, both conducted at the U.S. Public Health Service hospitals. One study of 47 addict physicians conducted 20 years ago at the U.S. Public Health Service Hospital at Fort Worth reported that the typical addict physician was a native-born, 52-year-old, white male, engaged in general practice in a small town.[7] He began using morphine at the age of 39 for the relief of a painful condition, and came from comfortable economic circumstances. He had sought a voluntary cure in sanitaria on three occasions and been in jail once. He was married and had two children. He had approximately the same prospects for cure as the average addict. A study of 457 consecutive admissions to the U.S. Public Health Service Hospital at Lexington for meperidine ("Demerol") addiction reported that 32.7 per cent of these cases of primary addiction were physicians and osteopaths.[8]

[3] J. DeWitt Fox, "Narcotic Addiction Among Physicians," *Journal of the Michigan State Medical Society*, 56 (February, 1957), pp. 214–217.

[4] Her Majesty's Government, *Report to the United Nations on the Working of the International Treaties on Narcotic Drugs*, London, 1955.

[5] Lawrence Kolb, "The Drug Addiction Muddle," *Police*, 1 (January-February, 1957), pp. 57–62.

[6] Alfred R. Lindesmith, *Opiate Addiction*, Evanston: Principia Press, 1947, p. 60.

[7] Michael J. Pescor, "Physician Drug Addicts," *Diseases of the Nervous System*, 3 (June, 1942), pp. 173–174.

[8] Robert W. Rasor and H. James Crecraft, "Addiction to Meperidine," *Journal of the American Medical Association*, 157 (February 19, 1955), pp. 654–657.

PROCEDURE

The purpose of this study was to explore the social and personality correlates of addiction in addict physicians. In order to explore these correlates, interviews were conducted in New York, Pennsylvania, Massachusetts, Rhode Island, New Jersey, and Connecticut, with 98 physicians who either were or had been opiate addicts. All the physicians had been addicts during a period of at least ten years prior to the interview, and some may have been addicts at the time of the interview. Access to the physicians was obtained through a variety of non-law-enforcement sources. The physicians had previously been asked by an intermediary if they would consent to be interviewed about their use of opiates, and all those interviewed had agreed to meet with the investigator who conducted the interviews.

The interviews were generally conducted in the office or home of the respondent and took an average of two hours. The format of the interview was simple: the respondent was asked to discuss his career, beginning with his first interest in medicine. If he did not mention his experience with opiates, he was asked to discuss it. Specific questions about the respondent's attitudes toward medicine and his early life were asked if he did not discuss these subjects in detail. He was asked about his youth, parents, career aspirations, health, and current family situation. The interviewer took notes on the physician's comments and these notes were content-analyzed into various content categories, which are summarized below.

DESCRIPTION OF INTERVIEWEES

The physicians interviewed ranged in age from 28 to 78, with an average age of 44. There were 93 men and five women, 61 general practitioners and 37 specialists. All but one were married and 84 per cent had children.

The average age at which drug use began was 38. The average length of time since the addiction of the physicians interviewed had begun was six years. The range was one year to 22 years.

Of the physicians interviewed, 53 per cent had their practices in cities of over a million population, 33 per cent worked in communities of 250,000 to a million, and 12 per cent in communities of under 250,000. In contrast, 22 per cent were born in cities over a million, 23 per cent in cities of 250,000 to a million and 55 per cent were born in communities of under 250,000.

Every physician interviewed was in private practice and had some kind of hospital affiliations. None had been involved in any official or institutional research project on narcotics. The physicians interviewed ranged from a few who were less successful than the average in their professional careers to some who were extraordinarily successful national figures. The typical physician interviewed was more successful than the average, in terms of income, honorific and institutional affiliations, and general professional activity. Most were useful and effective members of their community. For example, one physician was brought to a private hospital for treatment by the public prosecutor in his community in order to avoid charges being preferred against him by the prosecutor.

Eighty per cent of the subjects were meperidine ("Demerol") addicts, nine per cent took dilaudid, seven per cent used morphine, and four per cent took codeine. Every subject interviewed was an addict and not a user, in terms of the traditional addiction criterion of daily use of an opiate. Some of the physicians took as much as 50 or 100 cc of meperidine daily, which is several times the amount given a hospital patient in considerable pain. Some physicians (two per cent) turned themselves in for treatment because they were almost saturated with meperidine and it was having less and less effect. One man who was taking 50 cc a day said, "It's like drinking four or five gallons of water a day."

Most (74 per cent) of the respondents said that their wives had known of their addiction. Many (61 per cent) said that their nurses knew of their addiction, although there were no cases of contamination of the wife or nurse by the physician.

There appeared to be no significant socioeconomic differences between the respondent who was a minimal addict, taking a small dosage daily, and the heavy user who took a large dosage. It is possible to speculate that the minimal addict may be "more" addicted than the heavy user, because he is taking so little of the drug that he might be able to stop it altogether—yet he cannot do so.

In New York, meperidine is often called "the doctor's drug." Its label clearly states that its use should be discontinued if euphoria is noted. In spite of this caveat, the drug was selected by so many physicians for a number of reasons. They thought it less addicting and less toxic than other opiates. It is relatively available. The users thought its effects would be less visible than those of other narcotics. Its medical connotations made it more acceptable. There was a feeling that it was somehow easier for a physician to cure himself of meperidine addiction than of addiction to other drugs. Its being a synthetic opiate made it more attractive to some.

LAW ENFORCEMENT AND THE PHYSICIAN

Eight of the interviewees had had their license to practice revoked, 38 were on probation, 51 had completed probation, and one had not received any formal punitive action.

A small proportion of the physicians interviewed (4 per cent) sought help for their condition before they were apprehended or before some official or government functionary discussed their drug use with them. The rest (96 per cent) of those who were in trouble with the law did not seek help until they were apprehended or could tell that they were just about to be apprehended.

The physicians who had run afoul of the law enforcement agencies were treated relatively kindly by the law. One reason for this was probably that none had attempted to prescribe drugs for other addicts. Every physician who was taking drugs could have been charged with a crime. Only one, however, actually had been so charged, and only a few were arrested. The reason for the leniency afforded these physicians was perhaps not only the feeling that they would be punished enough by having their licenses to practice suspended for varying periods of time. It was probably also the assumption that they could be salvaged for the community and not lose their years of training and preparation for their careers.

Once a physician has begun taking drugs himself, he is likely to have difficulties in concealing his activities for any considerable length of time. The pharmacists and nurses or wives who observe their activities may report the physicians to state or federal authorities, who may have already observed unusual prescription activity on the part of a physician. None of the physicians interviewed was reported by either a colleague or a patient.

The physicians exhibited considerable ingenuity in obtaining drugs illegally. The most frequent method was to write prescriptions in a real or imaginary patient's name and use the drugs themselves. Others would give a patient a fraction of a dose and keep the rest for themselves. Some might order a standard 30 cc vial of meperidine for a patient in a hospital, give the patient a few cc, and keep the rest for themselves. Or they took what might be left from a hospital patient and withdrew it for "office use." Some might get drugs "in an emergency" from a friendly pharmacist without a prescription. Others might go to their hospital and feign having absent-mindedly left their prescription pads at their offices. All of these procedures are, of course, illegal, and state and federal narcotics inspectors are on the alert for them.

A number of physicians (15 per cent) said that they were aware of the negative connotations of the way in which they got narcotics. "I've never done anything that has made me feel so degraded," said one respondent. "I went back to the hospital and told my nurse I had forgotten my prescription pad. She gave me some drugs and I took a shot. I knew it was wrong."

Federal or state narcotics law enforcement officials usually confront addict physicians with the evidence against them and turn them over to state licensing authorities who decide on the circumstances, if any, under which the physician will be able to practice. Some physicians were required to pay a fine and to demonstrate that they were not using drugs for a period of some years. Apprehended physicians are required to surrender their tax stamp which permits them to prescribe narcotics. The New York authorities have developed a procedure designed to protect the public against the addict physician while it assists the physician to rehabilitate himself. He usually has his license suspended and must demonstrate non-drug use for a year. He must agree to be treated by an approved physician and examined to check on his abstinence every three months for several years. A physician who has not demonstrated abstinence may have his license revoked.

Once confronted by state or federal authorities, the physicians usually said that they were relieved to be caught. They often said that they had been hoping someone would help them to stop drug use. No physician interviewed attempted to deny his use of narcotics once he had been caught.

Eighty-nine per cent of the physicians interviewed remained in the community in which they had been practicing, after being apprehended. There was practically no publicity about any of the cases. Where the physician had to leave his practice, he generally turned the practice over to a colleague and resumed it upon his return.

PHYSICIAN ADDICTS AND "STREET" ADDICTS

The physician addicts interviewed differed in a number of ways from the typical "street" addict who buys drugs from a "pusher." The most obvious difference is that the age at which the physicians began to use drugs is just about the age that the typical addict stops using drugs, whether by "maturing out" or for other reasons. The "street" addict typically begins drug use in adolescence, while the physician begins when he is an established community and professional figure. The "street" addict takes heroin, while the typical physician addict took meperidine. The physician can get a pure quality of his drug, although it is not as strong as heroin. The "street" addict gets a diluted drug. He often starts with marijuana, although none of the physicans ever smoked marijuana.

The physician is usually discovered by the indirect evidence of a check of prescription records, while the "street" addict is usually arrested either because he has narcotics in his possession or has been observed making an illegal purchase. The physician is usually not arrested, while the typical "street" addict is arrested. Money to obtain drugs was not a problem for the physicians, as it usually is for the typical addict who must steal in order to obtain money to buy drugs illegally. The physicians could use their professional access to narcotics to obtain drugs without much money. Even if they paid, the legal prices of narcotic drugs are very low.

Most non-physician addicts associate with other addicts. In contrast, the physicians interviewed almost never associated with other physician addicts, or did not do so knowingly. They did not have any occasion for doing so, either for the purpose of getting drugs or for passing time, or for emotional support. They were solitary about their addiction. The "street" addict usually talks in a special jargon and often has a kind of wry insight into drug use, which stems from his extended discussions with his peers. The physicians did not talk in jargon and manifested very little insight into their drug use.

The typical "street" addict is not withdrawn in a medical setting. The physicans had almost all withdrawn in relatively comfortable medically supervised situations, so that there was little withdrawal distress. Seventy-four per cent had gone to a private hospital, usually under an assumed name; eleven per cent had gone to Lexington, and 15 per cent had made informal arrangements with friends and others.

"Street" addicts are likely to have been introduced to drugs by a contemporary. In contrast, none of the physicians interviewed had introduced anyone else to narcotic drugs or had "turned on" other physicians. It is possible to speculate that an addict physician, although he may not consciously wish to recruit addicts, may be unconsciously receptive to a patient who is especially eager for the physician to prescribe pain-killing drugs. He may identify with the patient's need and project his own need. Such a physician might possibly prescribe more drugs than the patient needs. It is possible, of course, that some addict physicans may be unusually sensitive to the possibility of patients becoming addicted and strive to prevent it. Twelve per cent of the respondents had come into contact with "street" addicts in hospitals. A typical reaction to such contact was, "I feel so degraded when I realize I'm like those people."

FACTORS RELATED TO DRUG USE

It took an average of two months of drug use for the physician to realize that he was addicted. The physician's professional knowledge of the qualities of opiates is certainly a factor in his using them himself, in terms of his knowledge of what effects they might have. His accessibility to drugs is not a complete explanation, because pharmacists are practically never addicted, even though they have much easier access to opiates than do physicians and can more easily manipulate their records.

It was possible to code several factors mentioned by the respondents as having been associated with their use of narcotics. In order of their incidence these themes could be categorized as overwork, physical ailments, self-concept, wives, level of aspiration, euphoric or depressing effect, liquor, insomnia, and age. A brief discussion of each theme follows, along with the proportion of respondents mentioning it. The total proportion of physicians interviewed who cited these themes came to 216 per cent, because many respondents mentioned more than one theme. Thus, the genesis of their drug use would appear to be multi-factorial.

Overwork (41 per cent)

Almost all of these respondents had come from lower class homes in communities of under 250,000, and practiced in big cities. These physicians usually mentioned their feeling low and depressed as a result of their overwork, and there appeared to be an association in their thinking between fatigue and depression. "Demerol builds up my resistance when I am working hard so quickly it is tremendous," said one respondent. "If I take some dilaudid, I might do eight perfect operations under pressure instead of two," said another who had said that he was overworked.

Overwork may mean different things to different physicians. Some of those interviewed were working so hard that, as one said, they might "end up as the richest doctor in the cemetery." Those who became addicted may have had some reasons either for working hard or for leading themselves to think that they were working hard, and for using their heavy schedules as the rationale for their drug use. Some seem to have almost created a situation of overwork so that they could use the overwork as an excuse for narcotics use. "Anyone who worked as hard as I did was entitled to a half of a grain of morphine each day," said one. Most of these physicians seem to have had an unrealistic notion of how long they could take drugs without becoming addicted.

Some of the respondents who talked of working very hard conveyed a feeling of resignation that medicine was so demanding, and some expressed negative feelings about having entered the profession. "I wonder why I ever got into medicine at all," or "This is not a field I'd recommend to anyone," were comments typical of these respondents. A number of these respondents mentioned that a parent, usually the mother, had wanted them to be physicians.

Physical Ailment (36 per cent)

Five-sixths of the physical ailments reported by the physicians who said that their drug use was related to the ailment was gastrointestinal disorders, like ulcers and colitis. The others reported a variety of ailments. The ailments were all chronic conditions. All but one of the physicians who had reported physical complaints were treating the ailments by themselves, although a few had undergone surgery. The drugs they took usually alleviated both their pain and symptoms. It is curious that practically none of the physicians with ailments commented on the unusualness of opiates alleviating the symptoms of the relatively serious ailments which they had.

Although none of these physicians discussed their addiction with physician colleagues, some (27 per cent) said that when they discussed their physical ailments with colleagues they mentioned the narcotics they were taking for pain relief. "I told a friend I was taking Demerol for my stomach," said one respondent. This kind of disclosure to a physician may have been one way in which the addict physician justified his regular use of narcotics to himself.

Self Concept (32 per cent)

About a third of these interviewed said that they were surprised at becoming addicted. "I felt I could take a shot when a crisis arose." "I felt I could stop at any time," and "I thought I'd toy with it because I knew enough about it to inhibit its reaction and control its use," were typical comments made by this group. "I thought I was above getting addicted," said another physician. Their professional familiarity with the effects of drugs appears to have provided a rationale for their semi-magical belief that the drugs would somehow have a different effect on them than they had on non-physicians. Addicts other than physicians often believe that they can control the effects of drugs, or "take just one more shot," or reduce their intake. The physicians cited many of these rationalizations in clarifying their surprise at becoming addicted. The majority of these physicians believed that they were too smart to become "hooked."

Marital Problems (31 per cent)

These physicians voiced a wide range of marital difficulties. The largest proportion of these respondents said that their wives were too aggressive and driving. A number said that they should have gotten a divorce, and some expressed other kinds of dissatisfaction with their wives. None of these physicians had taken any action toward a divorce or separation. A number of these physicians were also among those who reported physical ailments.

Level of Aspiration (24 per cent)

These physicians generally had a history of disaffection toward and disagreement with their profession, usually coupled with a record of considerable achievement within the profession. They often were officers of their college pre-medical society, and tended to be good students in both college and medical school. Their level of aspiration and competitive spirit tended to be high.

For the physicians in this group who developed physical symptoms, the illness appeared to have been perceived as a very threatening interference with their fantasies about their success. The pain associated with their illness may have occasioned almost a panic in the physicans, and one way in which they may have coped with the panic was to begin taking drugs. The drugs they took were usually effective in the physicans' attempts to cope with their pain. This diminution of pain may have provided the physicians with a variety of further rationalizations for drug use.

It is possible to speculate that the high level of aspiration and competitive spirit of these physicians was so integral a part of their personality that it may have been very difficult for them to express their disaffection toward medicine because their medical career was the embodiment of their level of aspiration. The aggressiveness and disaffection may have thus been partially drained off by drug use.

Euphoric or Depressing Effect (21 per cent)

These physicians specifically mentioned the drug's effect on their mood. Most of these physicians said that the drugs made them feel good and improved their work. "I realized that here was something I'd been looking for all my life, and the last piece of the jigsaw puzzle fell into place," said one.

There were others who said that the drug lost its stimulus effect after a while, and "I just took it to keep alive. It made me feel depressed and slow." These physicians tended to say that the continued use of opiates interfered with their work.

Liquor (17 per cent)

These physicians said that they had been drinking fairly heavily before they began using drugs. Most of these respondents had been drinking by college and medical school days. Some began narcotics use because "You can't walk into an operation reeking of liquor on your breath." Two had switched from alcohol to barbiturates before using opiates. Others began because "Alcohol makes you fumble," and they could function with opiates but not with alcohol. Some began opiate use, either self-prescribed or prescribed by others, as one way of coping with hangovers from liquor. Whatever needs were met by alcohol were apparently also met by narcotics, since none of these physicians continued drinking after beginning narcotics use. None of the physicians who had been heavy drinkers before their addiction had returned to liquor after stopping drug use. Few of those who drank also reported somatic complaints. A number of the drinkers generally had negative things to say about their profession.

Insomnia (11 per cent)

The physicians who were insomniacs were among the most intelligent interviewed. They seemed to have special difficulties in talking about their feelings. They were likely to report marital difficulties and disaffection toward medicine. Some of the physicians who cited their overwork said that they began drug use because they fell asleep more easily after taking a shot, and thus saved time in falling asleep and thus had more time available for their practice.

Age (3 per cent)

A small number of the physicians interviewed were older men, in their 60's and 70's, who became addicted during World War II. These men said that they had retired or semi-retired and were called back to practice, over their objections, because of the wartime shortage of physicians. Most of them were from non-urban areas, whose practices covered a fairly extended geographic area. They reported difficulties in meeting the increasing demands on them and in getting along with little sleep. They began taking a small dose of morphine in order to relieve fatigue and keep going. All of these physicians had ceased taking narcotics fairly soon after they returned to retirement, after the war.

RETURN TO DRUG USE

Over half the respondents had stopped drug use and then reverted, at least once. The circumstances of return to drug use varied. The physicians did not generally appear able to explain it. One said, "I got into a taxi to go to the hospital for an operation. Suddenly, as if it were another person inside me, I stopped the taxi at a pharmacy and got a shot." Another had gone to a ranch "cure" for three months, said he "felt great" there, and taken some drugs within an hour after his return to his office. Some physicians returned to drug use after a period of abstinence while in the middle of an investigation by an official agency, which could not help but uncover their reversion. One physician had been withdrawn and spent a month at a hospital, and went to a movie in a nearby city one afternoon. When he returned to the hospital that evening, he said that he had actually gone to his private office for the purpose of getting a shot. One physician returned to drug use after 19 years of abstinence. As in the case of non-physician addicts, logic did not appear to be very influential in assisting many of these physicians in remaining off drugs.

Of the respondents who had been to the U.S. Public Health Service

Hospital at Lexington, most had remained off drugs. One said of the hospital: "Lexington cured me forever. It made we acutely aware of how sick I was, and I decided never again. I was so shaken that I never even got another narcotic tax stamp." One of the few Lexington patients who reverted said, "The hospital helped me. I realized I could get a shot in my vein that would be better than one in my arm."

PROGNOSIS

The prognosis for many of these physicians can only be regarded as guarded. A licensed physician who has to engage in subterfuge to get drugs and who is aware of the implications of drug use, and who only seeks help when crisis or the law threatens, may not be a good risk for abstinence. "You have to fudge so much to get your drugs," as one physician said, that an addict physician who has been so willing to "fudge" may have difficulties in giving up narcotics. He has to do so many things that are destructive in order to get drugs that his addiction may be relatively salient.

However, it has been estimated by one student that 85 per cent of addicted physicians return to their practice and to drug-free life, with the other 15 per cent deteriorating or committing suicide.[9] This high recovery rate is attributed to a considerable extent to the physician's recollection of the agreeable way of life that he enjoyed before addiction.

A variety of methods of abstinence was mentioned by the physicians who had stayed off drugs successfully for a period of several years. Most had had several periods of relapse, with the periods of time between reversion becoming longer and longer. Many took "milder" drugs like paregoric to ease the transition. Some adjusted their external schedules in order to minimize temptation: "I made up my mind to handle only the amount of practice I could handle without fatigue." Those in pain decided to be uncomfortable and live with pain rather than take drugs. Others had a version of the Coué method: "Every morning I make up my mind that nothing will make me take drugs today." A very few of the physicians had sought psychiatric help. Wives and colleagues did not seem to have much of a role in assisting the physician to get off drugs.

DISCUSSION

The established sociological theories of deviant behavior and of addiction do not completely explain the narcotics use of these physicians. The Mer-

---

[9] Edward R. Bloomquist, "The Doctor, The Nurse, and Narcotic Addiction," *GP*, 18 (November, 1958), pp. 124–129.

tonian theory of deviant behavior as a reflection of differences in the legitimate means of access to culturally prescribed goals does not appear to be
relevant to these physicians, who had achieved such goals publicly and legitimately. The traditional explanation of addiction as the result of socialization
in a particular kind of delinquent sub-culture does not appear to be immediately useful in explaining the addiction of these physicians. It was not possible
to find even one addicted physician who was either Peurto Rican or Negro,
the two sub-cultural groups most heavily represented in the general addict
population. In general, the social correlates of the physicians' addiction
emerged less clearly than did the personality correlates.

There did appear to be some elements which a number of the physicians
interviewed might have in common with other addicts. The physicians whose
addiction appeared to have been related to their self concept (32 per cent)
and to their high level of aspiration (24 per cent) were essentially expressing
fantasies of a kind common in other addicts. Opiate use enables the user to
remove himself temporarily from the world of demanding external reality to
a world in which his fantasies of achievement and power can be exercised.

The physicians who mentioned marital difficulties (31 per cent) were reflecting a common theme in the lives of many addicts. Although the typical
addict is relatively unlikely to marry, when he does, he is often likely to
marry the kind of aggressive wife described by these physicians.

Another dimension mentioned by the physicians was the actual euphoric
or depressing effect of the drug (21 per cent), which is similar to what is
reported by other addicts. Like other addicts, a number of respondents (11
per cent) reported insomnia. Addicts often have difficulties in falling asleep,
possibly for the same reasons that they have difficulties in recalling dreams—
perhaps because the free expression of feelings possible during sleep via
dreams may be perceived as threatening.

There were a number of themes in the physicians' discussions of their
addiction which are not usually found in other addicts. Most non-physician
addicts do not complain of overwork, and are not even likely to have a regular job. Most addicts do not have an associated physical ailment. Since the
addict often regards the alcoholic as an inferior "wino," drinking is not too
frequently associated with addiction, although 17 per cent of the physicians
were drinkers before they became drug users. There is probably also no
analogue in the general addict population for the older physicians who began
using narcotics during World War II.

These physicians do have some similarity to the addicted jazz musicians
seen since 1957 at the Musicians' Clinic in New York. The musicians were all
fairly successful in their profession and began to use heroin in their twenties
as one way of coping with various reality problems, like those stemming from
their work or marriage. The musicians also showed considerable interest in
liquor. A number of them used drinking as one way of cushioning their

leaving the use of drugs, whereas none of the physicians did this. The musicians had all sought psychiatric help at the Clinic, whereas practically none of the physicians had sought such help.

It is possible to speculate that there are probably several basic and different reasons for physicians' use of drugs, and that there is probably no one addict physician for whom all of the reasons are relevant. The factors that appear to be related to physicians' drug use, as reported by the physicians, are all problems that have confronted many other physicians. Yet only a small proportion of the physicians confronted by these problems became drug users. Perhaps there are some underlying threads that may run through a number of the external reasons for drug use cited by the respondents. We may speculate that there may be perhaps four such underlying threads: the addict physician's role strain, his passivity, his omnipotence, and the effects of the drug.

Role Strain

In the sample interviewed there were a number of respondents who had negative attitudes toward being physicians. Most of them are likely to have grown up in a small community and moved to a big city, to have been pushed into medicine by a parent, and to have moved up and out of the lower classes when they became physicians. They thus may have found themselves occupying a role which posed a variety of kinds of role strain. One way in which they could respond to such strain was by overwork, which may have provided less and less time to think about their dissatisfaction with their occupation. Another way of responding was by drinking. It is perhaps more than a coincidence that most of the drinkers had begun using liquor around college and medical school, at just about the time that their career commitment was made. Insomnia was another way of expressing role strain. The few older physicians who returned to practice during World War II clearly exhibited role strain.

If this hypothesis of role strain as an important underlying contributor to physician drug use is correct, it helps to explain some of the intermediate steps that seem to be related to narcotics use and that were identified by the respondents. About two-thirds of the physicians were following individualistic careers and one-third were following colleague careers, in Hall's terminology.[10] Preoccupation with success, status, and income, characterized the group interviewed, whereas there was not one example of Hall's person-centered friendly career. The struggle to get recognition professionally may have been so difficult and demanding that the physicians could barely experience their negative feelings about their profession while becoming estab-

[10] Oswald Hall, "Types of Medical Careers," *American Journal of Sociology,* 55 (November, 1949), pp. 243–253.

lished. By their late 30's, these respondents could confront the fruits of their hard work and of their status and role. Perhaps one effect of this kind of confrontation was related to their beginning drug use.

Passivity

It is well established that many narcotic addicts have an underlying passivity, which they reinforce by taking drugs. Physicians are so active and busy that it is difficult to see how they could be described as passive. The substantial number of physicians interviewed reporting physical ailments and marital difficulties suggests that their passivity may have manifested itself in significant but indirect ways.

The majority of the physicians with ailments had gastrointestinal disorders like ulcers or colitis. It has been fairly well established that these ailments are often methods by which certain conflicts are handled by some passive people. Ulcers seem to be related to a typical conflict situation involving a dependent person's seeking accomplishment and self-sufficiency, and colitis often first manifests itself when the individual faces a life situation which requires an outstanding accomplishment for which he feels unprepared.[11] Perhaps as one way of sustaining their illness, most of the respondents were treating themselves, in spite of the established medical principle that physicians ought not to treat their own illnesses. The physician's illness may thus have been a socially approved form of deviant behavior through which he could express the conflict between his passivity and the demanding and active role of the physician, until his use of narcotics provided him with another avenue for the expression of the conflict.

Passivity also manifested itself indirectly in the respondents who reported marital problems. These problems were generally related to their wives' being domineering. It is usually relatively passive men who marry domineering women. In spite of their complaints, none of these respondents had taken any action to improve their marriage situation, thus further underscoring their passivity.

Omnipotence

The self concept of a number of the interviewees appeared to have been very high, and in some cases to have included fantasies of omnipotence. Such fantasies are common in other addicts. They may have been especially congenial to physicians because the physician's work makes it easy for him

---

[11] Franz Alexander, *Psychosomatic Medicine*, New York: W. W. Norton, 1950, pp. 102–132.

to have feelings of power over others and of grandiosity. It is perhaps an easy step from such feelings to believing that he can control the effect of an opiate.

The high level of aspiration of some of the respondents also may reflect feelings of omnipotence. Although they generally demonstrated considerable ability and achievement in their profession, their fantasies of what they might achieve left many dissatisfied. One physician, for example, dated his drug use from the day that he was told that he would not be getting attending privileges as a specialist at a particular hospital. He was so sure he would be granted these privileges that the disappointment of not doing so was directly related to his use of drugs.

It is possible that achievement was as much of a threat as non-achievement to some respondents. One said, "I was fighting to be top man for all those years, but when I reached the top, what did I have?" He began drug use because he felt that his victories were hollow, and there were no more conquests to make. No matter how successful such a man might be, his omnipotence would leave him restless. A number of these physicians began drug use when they had reached a stage in life at which they could begin to implement their omnipotence, and such implementation seemingly posed grave problems. Not one of the respondents reported any interest in drugs in the early stages of his career, even amidst the stress and demands of internship and the early stages of establishing a practice.

Effects of the Drug

One ultimate dimension of drug use by physicians is the drug's effect on its users. The effect of the opiate appears to be mediated by the personality of the physician user. Some users feel better and othe users feel worse after taking opiates. The relationships between either the euphoric or depressing effect of the opiate and other factors related to its use are not clear.

Some combination of these factors of role strain, passivity, omnipotence, and effects of the drug, appear to underlie the narcotics use of the physicians interviewed. These factors may predispose physicians to addiction in a wide variety of external situations and environments. If these or similar factors are not present, the physician may not become addicted even in extremely taxing environments. No external situation, by itself, can be taxing enough to drive a physician to becoming addicted. Thus, there is not one recorded case of a Jewish physician who was in a Nazi concentration camp who became a drug addict during or after his incarceration. It would be difficult to imagine a more demanding situation than experience in a concentration camp.

The external situations that faced the physician addicts interviewed, however, were perceived and experienced by the physicians themselves in a manner that gave rise to the deviant behavior of drug use. These physicians appear to have been addiction-prone through some combination of role strain, passivity, omnipotence, and effects of the drug. It is of course possible that the physicians interviewed are not typical of other addict physicians, or that they may be reflecting regional or other special factors.

3 The Behavior of the Systematic Check Forger

EDWIN M. LEMERT

The concept of behavior systems in crime was first approximated in this country in Hall's analysis of several types of larceny in terms of their historical, legal, and social contexts.[1] Later the concept was made explicit and formulated into a typology by Sutherland and by Sutherland and Cressey.[2] Although this has hitherto inspired only a few monographic studies, there seems to be a growing consensus that focusing attention on specific orders of crime or making behavior systems the unit of study holds considerable promise for criminological research.[3]

Because this paper proposes to assess the usefulness of Sutherland's

Reprinted from *Social Problems*, Volume 6, Number 2 (Fall, 1958), pp. 141–148, by permission of The Society for the Study of Social Problems and the author.

[1] Jerome Hall, *Theft, Law and Society*, 2nd ed. (Indianapolis: Bobbs-Merrill, 1952).

[2] E. H. Sutherland, "The Professional Thief," *Journal of Criminal Law and Criminology*, 28 (July-August, 1937), pp. 161–163; E. H. Sutherland and D. Cressey, *Principles of Criminology*, 5th ed. (New York: Lippincott, 1955); A. R. Lindesmith and H. W. Dunham, "Some Principles of Criminal Typology," *Social Forces*, 19 (March, 1941), pp. 307–314; L. Puibaraud, *Les Malfaiteurs de profession* (Paris: E. Flammarion, 1893); A. W. Gruhle and L. Wetzel, eds., "Verbrechentype" (cited in Bonger, W. A., *Criminality and Economic Conditions*, Boston: Little, Brown, 1916, p. 581); and W. A. Bonger, *Criminality and Economic Conditions* (Boston: Little, Brown, 1916), pp. 579–589.

[3] W. C. Reckless, *The Crime Problem*, 2nd ed. (New York: Appleton, Century, 1955), p. 134.

formulation of the behavior system in analyzing or understanding the behavior of the systematic check forger, the typology outlined in his study of
the professional thief will be employed. The five elements of the behavior
system of the thief are as follows: (1) stealing is made a regular business;
(2) every act is carefully planned, including the use of the "fix"; (3) technical skills are used, chiefly those of manipulating people; this differentiates
the thief from other professional criminals; (4) the thief is migratory but
uses a specific city as a headquarters; (5) the thief has criminal associations
involving acquaintances, congeniality, sympathy, understandings, rules, codes
of behavior, and a special language.[4]

Altogether seventy-two persons currently serving sentences for check
forgery and writing checks with insufficient funds were studied. Three
additional check offenders were contacted and interviewed outside of
prison. The sample included eight women and sixty-seven men, all of whom
served time in California correctional institutions.

Thirty of the seventy-five check criminals could be classified as systematic in the sense that they (1) thought of themselves as check men; (2)
had worked out or regularly employed a special technique of passing checks;
(3) had more or less organized their lives around the exigencies or imperatives of living by means of fraudulent checks. The remaining forty-five cases
represented a wide variety of contexts in which bogus check passing was
interspersed with periods of stable employment and family life, or was simply
an aspect of alcoholism, gambling, or one of a series of criminal offenses
having little or no consistency.

FINDINGS

Projected against the typology of professional theft, the behavior of the
persons falling into the systematic check forgery category qualified only
in a very general way as professional crime. In other words, although it is
possible to describe these forgeries as *systematic*, it is questionable whether
more than a small portion of them can be subsumed as *professional* under the
more general classification of professional theft. A point-by-point comparison
will serve to bring out the numerous significant differences between systematic forgery and professional theft.

---

[4] E. H. Sutherland, *The Professional Thief* (Chicago: University of Chicago,
1937); E. H. Sutherland, "The Professional Thief," *op. cit.*; M. B. Clinard, *Sociology
of Deviant Behavior* (New York: Rinehart, 1957), pp. 256–262; W. C. Reckless, *op. cit.*;
R. S. Cavan, *Criminology* (New York: Crowell, 1948), Chapter V; M. Elliott, *Crime
in Modern Society* (New York: Harper and Bros., 1942), Chapter IV; D. W. Maurer,
Whiz Mob (Gainesville, Florida: American Dialect Society, No. 24, 1955); and
H. Von Hentig, "The Pickpocket: Psychology, Tactics and Technique," *Journal of
Criminal Law and Criminology*, 34 (May-June, 1943), pp. 11–16.

1. Forgery as a "Regular Business"

It is questionable whether check men look upon their crimes as a "regular business" in the same way as do members of "other occupational groups" who "wish to make money in safety."[5] In virtually all cases the motivation proved to be exceedingly complex. This fact was self-consciously recognized and expressed in different ways but all informants revealed an essential perplexity or conflict about their criminal behavior. The following statement may be taken as illlustrative:

> Nine out of ten check men are lone wolves. Those men who work in gangs are not real check men. They do it for money; we do it for something else. It gives us something we need. Maybe we're crazy. . . .

The conflicts expressed involved not merely the rightness or wrongness of behavior; they also disclosed a confusion and uncertainty as to the possibility of living successfully or safely by issuing false checks. All of the cases, even the few who had a history of professional thieving, admitted that arrest and imprisonment are inevitable. None knew of exceptions to this, although one case speculated that "It might be done by an otherwise respected business man who made one big spread and then quit and retired."

The case records of the systematic check forgers gave clear testimony of this. Generally they had but short-lived periods of freedom, ranging from a few months to a year or two at the most, followed by imprisonment. Many of the cases since beginning their forgery careers had spent less total time outside prisons than within, a fact corroborated by the various law-enforcement officers queried on the point.

Many of the check men depicted their periods of check writing as continuous sprees during which they lived "fast" and luxuriously. Many spoke of experiencing considerable tension during these periods, and two cases developed stomach ulcers which caused them to "lay off at resorts." A number gambled and drank heavily, assertedly to escape their internal stress and sense of inevitable arrest. A number spoke of gradual build-up of strain and a critical point just before their arrest at which they became demoralized and after which they "just didn't care any more" or "got tired of running." The arrests of several men having a very long experience with checks resulted from blunders in technique of which they were aware at the time they made them. Some of the men gave themselves up to detectives or F.B.I. agents at this point.

In general the picture of the cool, calculating professional with prosaic, matter-of-fact attitudes towards his crimes as a trade or occupation supported by rationalizations of a subculture was not valid for the cases in question.

[5] E. H. Sutherland and D. Cressey, *op. cit.*, p. 240.

2. Planning as an Aspect of Forgery

In regard to the second element of professional theft—planning—the behavior of check forgers is again divergent. Actually the present techniques of check passing either preclude precise planning or make it unnecessary. Although systematic check passers undeniably pay careful attention to such things as banking hours, the places at which checks are presented, and the kinds of "fronts" they employ, these considerations serve only as generalized guides for their crimes. Most informants held that situations have to be *exploited as they arise*, with variation and flexibility being the key to success. What stands out in the behavior of systematic check forgers is the rapid tempo—almost impulsiveness—with which they work.

The cases seemed to agree that check forgers seldom attempt to use the "fix" in order to escape the consequences of their crimes. The reason for this is that although one or a small number of checks might be made good, the systematic forger has too many bad checks outstanding and too many victims to mollify by offering restitution. Although the forger may be prosecuted on the basis of only one or two checks, ordinarily the prosecuting attorney will have a choice of a large number of complaints upon which to act. About the best the check forger can hope for through fixing activities is a short sentence or a sentence to jail rather than to prison.

3. Technical Skills

Although the systematic check man relies upon technical skills—those of manipulating others—these are usually not of a high order, nor do they require a long learning period to master. From the standpoint of the appearance of the check or the behavior involved at the time of its passing, there need, of course, be no great difference between passing a bad check and passing a good check. This is particularly true of personal checks, which are at least as favored as payroll checks by check men.

When check men impersonate others or when they assume fictitious roles, acting ability is required. To the extent that elaborate impersonations are relied upon by the forger, his check passing takes on qualities of a confidence game. Most of the check men showed strong preference, however, for simple, fast-moving techniques. A number expressed definite dislike for staged arrangements, such as that of the "out of town real estate buyer" or for setting up a fictitious business in a community, then waiting several weeks or a month before making a "spread" of checks. As they put it, they "dislike the slow build-up involved."

4. Mobility

Like the thief, the systematic forger is migratory. Only one check man interviewed spoke of identifying himself with one community, and even he was reluctant to call it a headquarters. Generally check men are migratory within regions.

5. Associations

The sharpest and most categorical difference between professional theft and systematic forgery lies in the realm of associations. In contrast to pickpockets, shoplifters, and con men, whose criminal techniques are implicitly cooperative, most check men with highly developed systems work alone, carefully avoiding contacts and interaction with other criminals. Moreover, their preference for solitude and their secretiveness gives every appearance of a highly generalized reaction; they avoid not only cooperative crime but also any other kinds of association with criminals. They are equally selective and cautious in their contacts and associations with the noncriminal population, preferring not to become involved in any enduring personal relationships.

A descriptive breakdown of the thirty check forgers classified as systematic bears out this point. Only four of the thirty had worked in check passing gangs. Two of these had acted as "fences" who organized the operations. Both were close to seventy years old and had long prison records, one having been a receiver of stolen property, the other having worked as a forger. Both had turned to using gangs of passers because they were too well known to detectives either to pass checks themselves or to permit their handwriting to appear on the checks. The other two forgers who had worked in gangs were female drug addicts who had teamed up with other female addicts.[6]

Three other systematic check forgers did not work directly with other criminals but had criminal associations of a *contractual* nature. One old-time forger familiar with the now little-used methods for forging signatures and raising checks usually sold checks to passers but never had uttered (passed) any of his own forgeries. Two men were passers who purchased either payroll checks from a "hot printer" or stolen checks from burglars. Apart from the minimal contacts necessary to sell or obtain a supply of checks, all three men were lone operators and very seclusive in their behavior.

Six of the thirty systematic forgers worked exclusively with one other person, usually a girl or "broad."[7] The check men seemed to agree that

[6] One may question whether they were systematic check forgers in a true sense: other informants state that "such people are not real check men; they are just supporting a habit." Their self-definitions and the organization of their lives center around drug addiction rather than forgery.

[7] One of the "pair" workers consisted of two homosexual females. The other non-man-woman pair was made up of two brothers, both of whom had substantial prison records. They worked up and down the West Coast, alternating in making out checks and playing the part of passer.

working with a girl was equivalent to working alone. These pairs ordinarily consisted of the check man and some girl not ordinarily of criminal background with whom he had struck up a living arrangement and for whom he felt genuine affection. The girl was used either to make out the checks or to pass them. In some cases she was simply used as a front to distract attention. Some men picked up girls in bars or hotels and employed them as fronts without their knowledge.

The remaining seventeen of the thirty systematic check forgers operated on a solitary basis. The majority of these argued that contact with others is unnecessary to obtain and pass a supply of checks. Most of them uttered personal checks. However, even where they made use of payroll or corporation checks they contrived to manufacture or obtain them without resorting to interaction with criminal associates or intermediaries. For example, one Nisei check man arranged with a printer to make up checks for a fraternal organization of which he represented himself as secretary-treasurer. Another man frequented business offices at noon time, and when the clerk left the office, helped himself to a supply of company checks, in one instance stealing a check-writing machine for his purposes.

It was difficult to find evidence of anything more than rudimentary congeniality, sympathy, understandings, and shared rules of behavior among the check forgers, including those who had worked in gangs. Rather the opposite seemed true, suspicion and distrust marking their relationships with one another. One organizer of a gang, for example, kept careful account of all the checks he issued to his passers and made them return torn off corners of checks in case they were in danger of arrest and had to get rid of them. Only two of the thirty forgers indicated that they had at times engaged in recreational activities with other criminals. Both of these men were lone wolves in their work. One other lone wolf stated that he had on occasion had dinner with another check man he happened to know well and that he had once or twice entered into a rivalry with him to see who could pass a check in the most difficult place.

The two men who had organized gangs of check passers worked with a set of rules, but they were largely improvised and laid down by the fence rather than voluntarily recognized and obeyed by the passers. The other check men with varying degrees of explicitness recognized rules for passing checks—rules learned almost entirely on an individual trial-and-error basis. The informants insisted that "you learn as you go" and that one of the rules was "never use another man's stunt."

Such special morality as was recognized proved to be largely functional in derivation. Thus attitudes toward drinking and toward picking up women for sexual purposes were pretty much the result of individual perceptions of what was likely to facilitate or hamper the passing of checks or lead to arrest. Many of the men stated that since they were dealing primarily with business, professional, and clerical persons, their appearance and behavior had to be acceptable to these people. "Middle class" is probably the best term to describe their morality in most areas.

Careful inquiries were made to discover the extent to which the check men were familiar with and spoke an argot. Findings proved meager. Many of the men had a superficial acquaintance with general prison slang, but only four men could measurably identify and reproduce the argot of check forgery or that of thieves. Three more could be presumed to have some familiarity with it. Only one of these spoke the argot in the prison setting. Another said that he never used the argot either in prison or on the outside, except years previously when once in a great while he had "let down at a thieves' party." There were only two men who spoke of themselves as being "on the scratch."[8]

INTERPRETATION

How can these findings be reconciled with the specific statement of Sutherland's informant[9] that "laying paper" is a form of professional theft most often worked in mobs? The answer to this apparent contradiction requires that a distinction be made between forgery of *the nineteenth and early twentieth centuries and that of the present day*. In the past forgery was a much more complex procedure in which a variety of false instruments such as bank notes, drafts, bills of exchange, letters of credit, registered bonds, and post office money orders as well as checks were manufactured or altered and foisted off. A knowledge of chemicals, papers, inks, engraving, etching, lithography, and penmanship as well as detailed knowledge of bank operations were prime requisites for success. The amounts of money sought were comparatively large, and often they had to be obtained through complex monetary transactions.[10] The technological characteristics of this kind

[8] The attitude of the lone wolf check man toward the argot is illustrated by the following quotation:

It's just the older man in here San Quentin who used argot, or some of the young guys who think they are tough. I know the argot but when I hear it I tell them to talk English. Most people on the outside know it anyway. Why call a gun a heater? What is gained by it . . . ?

These findings coincide with Maurer's. D. W. Maurer, "The Argot of Check Forgery," *American Speech*, 16 (December, 1941), pp. 243–250. He states that the argot of check forgery is relatively unspecialized and that forgers seldom have an opportunity to use it.

[9] E. H. Sutherland, *The Professional Thief, op. cit.*, p. 77. Maurer refers to check forgery as a branch of the "grift," and also speaks of professional forgers without, however, defining the term. Yet he recognizes that check forgers are usually lone wolves. D. W. Maurer, "The Argot of Check Forgery," *op. cit.*, pp. 243–250.

[10] G. Dilnot, *The Bank of England Forgery* (New York: Scribner, 1929).

of forgery made planning, timing, specialization, differentiation of roles, morale, and organization imperative. Capital was necessary for living expenses during the period when preparations for the forgeries were being made.[11] Intermediates between the skilled forger and the passers were necessary so that the latter could swear that the handwriting on the false negotiable instruments was not theirs and so that the forger himself was not exposed to arrest. A "shadow" was often used for protection against the passer's temptation to abscond with the money and in order to alert the others of trouble at the bank.[12] "Fall" money was accumulated and supplied to assist the passer when arrested. Inasmuch as forgery gangs worked together for a considerable length of time, understandings, congeniality, and rules of behavior, especially with regard to the division of money, could and did develop. In short, professional forgery was based upon the technology of the period.

Although precise dating is difficult, the heyday of professional forgery in this country probably began after the Civil War and lasted through the 1920's.[13] It seems to have corresponded with the early phases of industrialization and commercial development before business and law-enforcement agencies developed methods and organization for preventing forgery and apprehending the offenders. Gradually technological developments in inks, papers, protectographs, and check-writing machines made the forging of signatures and the manufacture of false negotiable instruments more difficult. According to one source, for example, raised drafts have been virtually nonexistent since 1905.[14] Similarly, at the present time raising of checks is quite rare. The establishment of a protective committee by the American Bankers Association in 1894, related merchants' protective agencies, and improvements in police methods have made the risks of organized professional forgery exceedingly great.[15]

Check gangs have always been vulnerable to arrest but this vulnerability has been multiplied many times by the large amounts of evidence left behind

---

[11] W. A. Pinkerton, "Forgery," paper read before Annual Convention of the International Association of Chiefs of Police, Washington, D.C., 1905; W. A. Pinkerton, *Thirty Years a Dectective* (New York: G. W. Carleton, 1884), pp. 338–441; and G. Dilnot, *op cit.*

[12] W. A. Pinkerton, "Forgery," *op. cit.* Pinkerton enumerates the following roles of the forgery gang: (1) backer, (2) forger, (3) middleman, (4) presenter, (5) shadow; Maurer ("The Argot of Check Forgery," *op. cit.*) without specifying the historical period to which his description applies, distinguishes the following as check forger roles: (1) connection, (2) fence, (3) passer.

[13] J. W. Speare, *Protecting the Nation's Money* (Rochester: Todd Protectograph Co., 1927).

[14] *Ibid.*

[15] W. A. Pinkerton, "Forgery," *op. cit.*; D. W. Maurer, "The Argot of Check Forgery," *op. cit.*

them in the form of countless payroll checks. Vulnerability is also heightened by the swiftness of communication today. If one person of a check-passing gang is arrested and identifies his associates, it becomes a relatively simple matter for police to secure their arrest. A sexually exploited and angered female companion may easily do the same to the check man. This goes far to explain the extreme seclusiveness of systematic check forgers and their almost abnormal fear of stool pigeons or of being "fingered." The type of persons who can be engaged as passers—unattached women, bar waitresses, drug addicts, alcoholics, petty thieves, and transient unemployed persons—also magnifies the probabilities that mistakes will be made and precludes the growth of a morale which might prevent informing to the police. These conditions also explain the fact that when the forger does work with someone it is likely to be one other person upon whom he feels he can rely with implicit confidence. Hence the man-woman teams in which the woman is in love with the man, or the case of the two homosexual girls, or of the two brothers mentioned previously.

Further evidence that organized forgery is a hazardous type of crime, difficult to professionalize under modern conditions, is indicated by the fact that the organizer or fence is apt to be an older criminal with a long record, whose handwriting methods are so well known that he has no choice other than to work through passers. Even then he does it with recognition that arrest is inevitable.

A factor of equal importance in explaining the decline of professional organized forgery has been the increasingly widespread use of business and payroll checks as well as personal checks. Whereas in the past the use of checks was confined to certain kinds of business transactions, mostly involving banks, today it is ubiquitous. Attitudes of business people and their clerical employees have undergone great change, and only the most perfunctory identification is necessary to cash many kinds of checks. Check men recognize this in frequent unsolicited comments that passing checks is "easy." Some argue that the form of the check is now relatively unimportant to passing it, that "you can pass a candy bar wrapper now days with the right front and story."[16] It is for this reason that the systematic check man does not have to resort to criminal associates or employ the more complex professional procedures used in decades past.

These facts may also account for the presence among lone-wolf check forgers of occasional persons with the identification, orientation, skills, codes, and argot of the thief. Case histories as well as the observations of

[16] Detectives in Santa Monica, California, showed the writer a collection of checks successfully passed with such signatures as: "I. M. A. Fool," "U. R. Stuck," and others not printable. For a discussion of the crudeness of bogus checks accepted by business people see, J. L. Sternitsky, *Forgery and Fictitious Checks* (Springfield: Charles C. Thomas, 1955).

informants show that older professional criminals in recent decades have
turned to check passing because they face long sentences for additional
crimes or sentencing under habitual criminal legislation. They regard checks
as an "easy racket" because in many states conviction makes them subject
to jail sentences rather than imprisonment. Check passing may be a last resort
for the older criminal.

The presence of the occasional older professional thief in the ranks of
check forgers may actually token a general decline and slow disappearance
of professional thieving. One professional thief turned check passer had this
to say:

I'm a thief —a burglar—but I turned to checks because it's getting too hard
to operate. Police are a lot smarter now, and they have better methods. People
are different nowadays too; they report things more. It's hard to trust anyone
now. Once you could trust cab drivers; now you can't. We live in a different
world today.[17]

THE CHECK FORGER AS AN ISOLATE

The preference of many systematic check forgers for solitary lives and
their avoidance of primary-group associations among criminals may also
be explicable in terms of their educational characteristics and class origins.
The history of forgery reveals that in medieval times it was considered to
be the special crime of the clerical class, as indeed it had to be inasmuch
as the members of this class monopolized writing skills.[18] It also seems to be
true from the later history of the crime that it has held a special attraction
for more highly educated persons, for those of higher socioeconomic status
and those of "refined" or artistic tastes.[19] The basic method of organized

[17] There is evidence that there has been a sharp absolute decline in the number
of pickpockets in recent years and that most of the so-called "class cannons" (highly
skilled) operating now are fifty years of age or over. D. W. Maurer, *Whiz Mob, op. cit.*

[18] T. F. Tout, *Medieval Forgers and Forgeries*, Bulletin of the John Rylands
Library, 5, 3, 4, 1919, pp. 5–31.

[19] This is the thesis of Rhodes. A. T. F. Rhodes, in *The Craft of Forgery* (London:
J. Murray, 1934). Two of the four participants in the famous Bank of England forgery
in 1873 were college-educated, one being a Harvard graduate. See G. Dilnot, *op cit.*;
forgers coming from "good" families are described by H. L. Adam, *Oriental Crime*
(London: T. Werner Laurie, 1908); fourteen of the nineteen persons tried for forgery
at Newgate Prison in England during the later eighteenth and early nineteenth
centuries were what can be termed "middle" and "upper" class, including three army
or navy officers (one who commanded the royal yacht of Queen Caroline, consort
of George IV), one banker, one physician Cambridge graduate, one prosecuting attorney,
two engravers (one by appointment to George III), three "gentlemen" of good connections, and three bank clerks. Two of the three men who had "poor parents" had
married women of "good means." T. Tegg, *The Chronicles of Crime*, Vols. I, II (Lon-

forgery is stated to have been invented and perfected in England, not by criminals but by a practicing barrister of established reputation in 1840.[20] An early gang of forgers organized by a practicing physician is also described by Felstead.[21] A number of studies directed to the differentiating characteristics of check criminals point to an "above average" intelligence and formal education. This refers to the general population as well as to the criminal populations with which they have been compared.[22]

All of this is not to say that less-educated persons do not frequently pass bad checks but rather that the persons who persist in the behavior and develop behavior systems of forgery seem much more likely than other criminals to be drawn from a segment of the population distinguished by a higher socioeconomic status. Generally this was true of the systematic forgers in this study. Eight of the thirty had completed two or more years of college. Fourteen of the thirty had fathers who were or had been in the professions and business, including a juvenile court judge, a minister, a postmaster of a large city, and three very wealthy ranch owners. One woman came from a nationally famous family of farm implement manufacturers. Four others had siblings well established in business and the professions, one of whom was an attorney general in another state. Two of the men had been successful businessmen themselves before becoming check men.

The most important implication of these data is that systematic check forgers do not seem to have had criminal antecedents or early criminal associations.[23] For this reason, as well as for technical reasons, they are not likely to seek out or to be comfortable in informal associations with other criminals who have been products of early and lengthy socialization and

---

don: Camden Pelham, 1841), and W. A. Bonger, *op. cit.*, pp. 429, 430, 437, give data from France and Italy which support this idea. A number of writers have commented on the fact that forgery has been quite common among the educated classes of India, particularly the "wily Brahmins." H. L. Adam, *Oriental Crime, op. cit.*; S. M. Edwards, *Crime in India* (London: Oxford University Press, 1924), pp. 3–6; and Hardless and Hardless, *Forgery in India* (Chunar: Sanctuary, 1920).

[20] H. T. F. Rhodes, *op. cit.*; and G. Dilnot, *The Trial of Jim the Penman* (London: Geoffrey Bles, 1930).

[21] T. S. Felstead, in *Famous Criminals and Their Trials* (New York: Doran, 1926).

[22] I. Berg, "A Comparative Study of Forgery," *Journal of Applied Psychology*, 28 (June, 1944), pp. 232–238; V. Fox, "Intelligence, Race and Age as Selective Factors in Crime," *Journal of Criminal Law and Criminology*, 37 (July-August, 1946), pp. 141–152; E. A. Hooton, *The American Criminal*, Vol. I (Cambridge: Harvard University, 1939), p. 87; and L. Lawes, *Life and Death in Sing Sing* (New York: Sun Dial Press, 1938), p. 40.

[23] E. Lemert, "An Isolation and Closure Theory of Naive Check Forgery," *Journal of Criminal Law and Criminology*, 44 (September-October, 1953), pp. 296–307; and E. Lemert, "Generality and Specificity in Criminal Behavior: Check Forgery Considered," paper read before American Sociological Society, September, 1956.

learning in a criminal subculture. It also follows that their morality and values remain essentially "middle" or "upper" class and that they seldom integrate these with the morality of the professional criminal. This is reflected in self-attitudes in which many refer to themselves as "black sheep" or as a kind of Dr. Jekyll–Mr. Hyde person. Further support for this interpretation comes from their status in prison where, according to observations of themselves and others, they are marginal so far as participation in the primary groups of the prison is concerned.

CONCLUSION

The cases and data presented suggest that present-day check forgery exists in systematic form but does not appear to be a professional behavior system acquired or maintained through associations with other criminals. The technical demands of contemporary check forgery preclude efficient operation on an organized, cooperative basis. In addition to these factors the class characteristics and backgrounds of systematic forgers incline them to avoid intimate association with other criminals.

4 The White-Collar Thief

FRANK E. HARTUNG

The development and the use of vocabularies of motives are by no means confined to some juveniles learning to be delinquent and some others learning to be be lawful. The same process characterizes both the criminal and the lawful adult, and may be observed with particular clarity in the adult offender commonly known as the "embezzler." Before analyzing the sociological research dealing with this type of offender, we shall find it useful, by way of comparison, to see him through the perspective of a recent popular study, *The Thief in the White Collar*, by Jaspan and Black.[1] According to the claim made on the dust-jacket of the book, Jaspan is one of the foremost management consultants in the United States, president of Norman Jaspan Associates, management engineers, and of its "fact-finding" division, Investigations, Inc. His firm's clients include many large and small manufacturing, service, and retail establishments; and his firm operates throughout Canada and the United States. With hardly more than one exception the cases in the book were drawn from the files of his firm. It may be that the book was written for business firms and the potential embezzlers whom they employ. Jaspan does establish one thing beyond

Reprinted from *Crime, Law and Society*, pp. 125–136, by Frank E. Hartung, by permission of The Wayne State University Press. Copyright © 1965 by The Wayne State University Press, Detroit 2, Michigan. Also by permission of the author.

[1] Norman Jaspan with Hillel Black, *The Thief in the White Collar*, Philadelphia: J. B. Lippincott Co., 1960.

question, to judge from his interpretation of his firm's experience; embezzlement has become endemic in American business. White-collar employees, both rank-and-file, and supervisory and executive, steal about four million dollars from their employers every working day. More than one billion dollars was stolen in 1960. The United States Department of Justice's *Uniform Crime Reports* shows that in 1960 American police departments reported that burglars, pickpockets, robbers, and automobile thieves stole only 570 million dollars worth. Jaspan estimated that as of today employees of banks have embezzled between ten million to twenty-five million dollars still to be discovered. Such estimates are statistically worthless because they cannot be checked.

When I first began to read *The Thief in the White Collar*, I decided merely to sample it here and there, because it seemed, at first glance, to be only another hastily—which is to say, badly—written book. I had not read very far in it, however, before it became fascinating. As a result of his company's experience in finding that such things as embezzlement, the theft of goods, kickbacks, and cheating on expense-accounts are so common as to have become an integral part of the culture of business, Jaspan has a message for employers. Even though never explicitly stated, it is perhaps the more forcefully communicated for being implicit. The message is: pay your employees adequately or your niggardliness will cause them to embezzle; treat them decently and ascertain their personal problems or your indifference and ignorance may cause them to embezzle; always distrust both them and the security personnel whom you hire to check on them; conduct your own personal and unannounced checks on your security personnel. Mr. Jaspan never asks or considers the question, Who will check on the honesty of the employers?

This book may serve an end never intended by its author. By their sympathetic interpretation of the embezzler they may help to perpetuate the vocabulary of motives employed by such people since time out of mind. Their conception of *cause* constitutes, in my judgment, a vocabulary of motives for the committing of embezzlement! It seems to me, for example, that in the first pages of the book Jaspan provides a white-collar formulation of two often-repeated motives used by delinquents, and also by adults who commit serious crimes. He asserts not only that "everyone has larceny in his heart," or that "everyone has his own racket," but also (p. 12) that "most people will try to cheat on their income tax if they think they can get away with it." He presents no supporting evidence. Perhaps he had his own clients in mind. We read (p. 101) that a Mrs. Burton was possessed by an "irrational hunger" for "conspicuous consumption," the "senseless desire that we all have."

In addition to learning that crooks and honest people all have the same senseless desires and motives, the man or woman contemplating embezzlement may take heart when reading of "the fact" that "chance and luck are responsible for the detection of most white-collar thieves."[2] An interesting project would be a comparative study of vocabularies of motives according to social class and education. It will be recalled that delinquents make use of *irresponsibility* and *a higher loyalty*. They present themselves as being subjects moved around by agencies beyond their control, such as the slum, a broken home, a drunken mother or a worthless father; or they might claim, "I did it for a friend." Jaspan presents these two motives to the embezzler in a more elegant and esthetic form. "The Honest Crooks" of his fifth chapter "have in common the fact that circumstances over which they had no control forced them to commit their dishonest acts." We should understand "the forces that drive" the white-collar thief.[3] Continuing the discussion with reference to the white-collar accomplice in crime, who also is an "honest crook," Jaspan notes that "there is often a mitigating circumstance, for the individual he is protecting usually is a close relative, friend or loved one."

The creation of a role that the potential embezzler can enact frees him of responsibility, supplying further motivation for his offense. In this instance the role is that of a sick person and—as everyone knows—the sick person is not responsible for his sickness. Thus we are informed that a thief by the name of Jean "couldn't help herself. She was a kleptomaniac."[4] If Jaspan were familiar with the psychiatric literature he would know that the diagnosis of kleptomania depends at least as much on what goes on in the head of the psychiatrist as on what goes into the pocket of the thief. White-collar crime, we are told, is a disease; perhaps "it may be possible to detect the first symptoms of the disease, and perhaps, in many instances even prevent the original infection."[5] The medical metaphor is misleading, even if it does help a man to talk himself into being a thief. Jaspan seems to take it literally. We are informed (p. 154) that "horses, cards and dice have become the largest single causative factor in white collar crime." On the next page we find that "gambling is a disease, the causes of this bacillus are numerous. . . . The bacillus of this disease, of course, feasts on a ready supply of cash." Jaspan even quotes from a bank teller in grammar typical of a third-grade street-corner boy, "It got like a disease." That quotation, of course, presents the embezzling bank teller as the passive subject of an active agent that he could not control. Six pages later gambling has grown so large that "it is a national disease." "The Insecure Executive" (the title

[2] *Ibid.*, p. 37.
[3] *Ibid.*, pp. 92 and 26.
[4] *Ibid.*, p. 93.
[5] *Ibid.*, p. 26.

of Chapter 7) will be interested in the motivation supplied to John Russell Cooney: "The cause of his thefts was the promise of a salary raise that was fulfilled too late."

It seems to me that Jaspan and Black understand neither Sutherland's conception of white-collar crime nor Cressey's analysis of the violation of financial trust. Sutherland studied white-collar crime as perpetrated by businessmen in the conduct of their *business* and not of their *personal* affairs. Jaspan makes no reference to this conception and type of white-collar crime. Perhaps the reason is that the United States Department of Justice may investigate Jaspan's employers (that is, his firm's clients), whereas Jaspan investigates their employees.[6]

Cressey's book, *Other People's Money* [see note 9], is a study in the criminal violation of financial trust. Where Cressey's book is scientific and analytical, Jaspan and Black's is sympathetic and moralistic, and may contribute to the criminal's vocabulary of motives.[7]

Cressey's research on the criminal violation of financial trust is of great significance for both a general theory of criminality and for a general theory of human, or sociocultural, behavior. The theory of differential association has been attacked on several grounds. One of the criticisms is that some types of criminals are exceptions to it. Two of the supposed exceptions are (1) persons such as embezzlers, with no previous criminal record and no known past or present criminal friends and (2) murderers, nonprofessional shoplifters, and persons who commit crimes of passion under emotional stress.[8] These two classes do not, in my opinion, constitute exceptions to the social-psychological and sociological analysis of human conduct. One great merit of that analysis is that it makes possible the bringing within the purview of a single theory the widest range of sociocultural behavior. It renders unnecessary the postulation of invention of pathologies in order to explain morally disapproved behavior. It cannot, however, account for cases of strict liability and negligence which, Jerome Hall has suggested, should be excluded from the rules of criminal law.

The legal category "embezzlement" does not, Cressey found, refer to a homogeneous class of criminal behavior, because of variations in the

[6] See Frank E. Hartung, "A Vocabulary of Motives for Embezzlers," *Federal Probation*, 25, December 1961, pp. 68–69.

[7] The comments on Jaspan's book are concerned with the validity of its analysis. While they indicate that the book may provide motivation to potential embezzlers, that is not relevant to its evaluation. The logico-empirical validity of a theory, and the actual or potential uses made of that theory, are two quite different things. The scientific evaluation of a theory can, as a matter of course, be concerned only with validity, and not with possible misuse.

[8] For an enumeration of supposed exceptions to the theory of differential association, and a bibliography of the criticisms, see the article by Donald R. Cressey, "Epidemiology and Individual Conduct: A Case from Criminology," *Pacific Sociological Review*, 3 Fall 1960, pp. 47–58, esp. pp. 37–49.

definitions of legal terms from one state to another. He developed the concept "criminal violation of financial trust" to refer to a homogeneous class. Two criteria must be met in order for a given case to be included. First, a person must have accepted a position of financial trust in good faith. This criterion is practically identical with the legal definition that the "felonious intent" in embezzlement must be formulated *after* taking the position. Second, the person must have violated that trust by committing a crime.[9] The central problem of Cressey's research was to ascertain whether a definite sequence or concurrence of events is always present when the criminal violation of trust occurs and never present when that violation is absent, and the correlated problem, to explain genetically the presence or absence of those events. Cressey formulated the following hypothesis, which he subsequently tested and confirmed:

> Trusted persons become trust violators when they conceive of themselves as having a financial problem which is nonshareable, are aware that this problem can be secretly resolved by violation of the position of financial trust, and are able to apply to their own conduct in that situation verbalizations which enable them to adjust their conceptions of themselves as trusted persons with their conception of themselves as users of the entrusted funds or property.[10]

The nonshareable financial problem was so defined by the violator. Another person might not have defined it thus. *A*, for example, could lose a considerable amount of money at the race track daily; but the loss, even if it constituted a personal problem for him, would not be defined by him as being a nonsharable problem. For *B*, however, the financial problem created by his loss would be defined as nonshareable. He would thus find it impossible to discuss the problem with his wife, best friend, or employer. People may have nonshareable problems of a nonfinancial character, for example, whether or not to obtain a divorce. Such nonfinancial, nonshareable problems are usually not solvable by obtaining more money either legitimately or through the violation of financial trust. Thus not all trusted persons who have nonshareable problems become trust violators; but according to the present research and theory, all criminal violators of financial trust have what *they* define as nonshareable financial problems. All of the situations involved in producing nonshareable financial problems were concerned with either status-seeking or status-maintaining activities. Since, however, status-seeking or -maintaining seems to be universal, engaging in these activities does not differentiate the trust-violators from nonviolators.[11]

[9] Donald R. Cressey, *Other People's Money: A Study in the Social Psychology of Embezzlement*, Glencoe: Free Press, 1953, p. 20.

[10] *Ibid.*, p. 30.

[11] "Status-seeking, status-gaining, status-maintaining, irrespective of the unit, time and place is universal insofar as human relationships are concerned." Samuel Haig Jameson, "Principles of Human Interaction," *American Sociological Review*, 10, February 1945, pp. 6–7.

In addition to defining a financial problem as nonshareable the violator of trust must identify his position and knowledge *to himself* as providing the means of solving it. He must also apply certain motives to his own conduct that will allow him to use this means. The identification of the opportunity for trust violation and the development of motivation occur together.[12] The realization by the violator that he can solve his problem criminally is indicated by his use of such phrases as "it occurred to me," or "it dawned on me," that the entrusted funds or property could be used personally. Trusted persons know that positions of trust can be criminally violated, even when they have no nonshareable financial problem, and so do most other adults. I have already referred to a small part of the literature dealing with fraud and embezzlement in particular and white-collar crime in general.[13] In many cases of trust violation, the people trained to discharge the routine duties of a position have at the same time been trained in the skills necessary for the violation of trust. The technical skill necessary to the violation is the same technical skill necessary to hold the position in the first place. When violators perpetrate their criminal violations, they do not depart from ordinary occupational routines in which they are skilled. Thus, "Accountants use checks which they have been entrusted to dispose of, sales clerks withhold receipts, bankers manipulate seldom-used accounts or withold deposits, real estate men use deposits entrusted to them, and so on." As an example Cressey quotes from an accountant who "never even thought of stealing" the money that passed across his desk outside of normal routine. "It was a matter of routine with me; I simply followed out the routine I had every day."[14]

If a person in a position of financial trust defines his financial problem as being nonshareable, realizes that he can solve it illegally, and at the same time applies to his own conduct verbalizations enabling him to adjust his conception of himself as a trusted person with his conception of himself as a user of the entrusted funds, he will violate that trust. When these three components are in conjunction, the criminal violation of trust will occur; when any one of them is absent there will be no such violation.

This hypothesis makes use of the social-psychological theory of motivation mentioned briefly in the discussion of the development of a vocabulary of motives by delinquent boys and boys who are becoming delinquent. The process through which the criminal violator of financial trust develops and uses motives is basically the same process through which the boys proceed. The adult violator uses a language enabling him to conceive of the violation of trust as being essentially noncriminal and also as either justified or as

[12] The following paragraphs are a brief summary of the complex third and fourth chapters in Cressey, *op. cit.*

[13] Cressey cites other references. *Ibid.*, pp. 79, 173–74.

[14] *Ibid.*, p. 84.

irresponsible behavior over which he can exert no control. Cressey uses the term "rationalization" to refer to this use of language by the violator. As we indicated previously, this use of the term emphasizes that the behavior in question is deliberate and purposive and in part results from the way in which the actor conceives of himself in relation to others. The rationalization is the actor's motivation, as we said before, and this applies to the criminal violator. His motive is a linguistic construct organizing his behavior in a particular situation. The use of the motive makes his behavior intelligible to himself. Its use may or may not make his behavior understandable to others, depending on whether they accept or reject his vocabulary of motives. If they accept his rationalization they will define his behavior as "understandable," even if they disapprove of or condemn it, and even if they may think him "stupid," or "not very smart." If others reject the criminal violator's rationalization, they will define his behavior as "unintelligible," or "senseless," or "impulsive," or "unmotivated."

Significant rationalizations were always present *before* the criminal violation of financial trust in all the cases in the study now being discussed. It was often found that the rationalization was abandoned after the violation was discovered. The trusted person can violate his trusted position because he is able to rationalize. The use of these rationalizations in trust violation is not separable from their sources. Just as the delinquent boys were able to draw upon the cultural store of motives, the trust violators "discovered" or "rediscovered" the cultural store of motivations sanctioning trust violation and applied them to their own conduct. The trust violators thus came into effective contact with cultural patterns of thought and action. Association with other criminals was unnecessary, and, as Cressey has said, could not be demonstrated. He has suggested the following definitions of situations calling for the violation of financial trust, and thus amounting to justifications for the crime: "Some of our most respectable citizens got their start in life by using other people's money temporarily." He quotes from Alexander Dumas' *The Money Question*, "What is business? That's easy. It's other people's money, of course." "In the real estate business there is nothing wrong about using deposits before the deal is closed." "All people steal when they are in a difficult position."

The trust violator gives a personal touch to the above rationalizations: "My intent is only to use this money temporarily so I am 'borrowing,' not 'stealing' "; "My immediate use of real estate deposits is 'ordinary business' "; "I have been trying to live an honest life but I have had nothing but troubles so 'to Hell with it.' "[15] In applying motives such as these to his behavior, the violator of financial trust may have some comfort in the knowledge that reactions by others to "borrowing" in order to solve a nonshareable problem are very different from their reactions to "stealing." Thus, like the delin-

15 *Ibid.*, p. 96.

quent drawing upon the rationalizations of his peers and the larger community, and like the business executives in the electrical industry conspiracy mentioned above, the trust violator can observe himself as being "all right" because the rationalizations upon which he has drawn sanction and support him in his actions.

The criminal violator of financial trust is a man who almost by definition has had no criminal record, no known criminal friends and associates, and who for a greater or lesser number of years has been well established as a respectable member of his community. And still he becomes a criminal. As I have tried to indicate above, this does not constitute an exception to the theory of differential association. The violator of trust is involved in the sociocultural process from the beginning to the end of his crime. Starting with his having learned his occupation socioculturally, he has encountered a financial problem. By linguistic means—a conversation confined wholly to himself—he has defined his problem as being nonshareable. He cannot even discuss it with his wife! The definition of his problem is based upon his system of values, and upon his conception of himself in relation to others who are significant to him—"What *will* they think of me?"—and his values and self-conception are purely sociocultural.

Through the continued private use of language he informs himself that he knows how to solve his problem. By the same means he draws upon cultural resources in the form of motives applicable in his situation, finds a vocabulary of adjustment, and criminally violates his position of financial trust. Through his private conversation he has "conned" or talked or verbally manipulated himself into a situation in which he can perpetrate his crime.

Physical contact with others already criminal is therefore not always necessary to the development of criminality in a given individual. It seems, however, that effective contact with appropriate sociocultural sources and processes, in the form of patterns of thought and action, is always necessary. This type of offender's criminality is learned socioculturally, in the process of symbolic communication, including his self-conversations.

It will have been noticed that the criminal violator of financial trust and the career delinquent have one thing in common: Their criminality is learned in the process of symbolic communication, dependent upon cultural sources for patterns of thought and action, and for systems of values and vocabularies of motives. The criminality and the life-history of the two types of offenders is, however, quite different. The delinquent who engages in delinquency as a financial means is most likely to be a more completely developed criminal than the trust violator. A boy who is reared in an area with a high rate of delinquency might have a well-developed pattern of criminality, Sutherland and Cressey say, "by age twelve or fourteen." Some might object that twelve years is a bit too young, and it could be that one should set the years at twelve to sixteen, or fourteen to sixteen. But whatever the range of years, the significant fact is that by about twelve to about sixteen years such a boy is criminally developed in the sense that criminal conceptions of law, person, and property have been accepted by him as values upon which to act.

Such a boy is deliberate in committing his crimes: he plans how to perpetrate them, plots possible escape routes, and soon learns to consider securing immunity if caught. If his precautions are inadequate—as they often are—his apprehension and subsequent possible detention and commitment to a juvenile correctional institution do not constitute crises for him. He does not like detection or detention but he can accept them as part of his life, an occupational hazard, so to speak, "just as a newsboy who has made what provision he could against the rain takes the rain as a part of his life." He may, and in fact often does, gain in prestige among his peers if he is committed to a correctional institution. In addition, the career delinquent of sixteen years of age is likely to have had about five to six years, and it seems in many cases as much as about eight years, of active and intensive experience with other delinquents. If the boy is on the way to becoming an adult burglar or robber, there is considerable evidence to show that his delinquency has had a typical development: from trivial to serious offenses, from a game to a livelihood, and from membership in a loosely organized boy's gang to a rather tightly organized gang of adolescents.[16] In those years he will have engaged in a wide range of

[16] See a short bibliography for this in Sutherland and Cressey, *Principles of Criminology*, 6th ed., pp. 219–20. The two brief quotations in this and the previous paragraph are from the same source. Their Chapter 12, "Processes in Criminal Behavior," presents a more detailed comparison of the life histories of the career delinquent and the trust violator.

McCleery has presented a vivid description of a different although related result of the continued private use of language that supports the present analysis of the vocabulary of motives. The thief in the white collar talks himself into a criminal violation of his position of financial trust. The isolated inmate in the incorrigible unit of a maximum security prison—which is physically separate from the other units—may talk himself into a mental hospital. The days and months during which his illusions are developed are seldom interrupted by contact with reality or by challenging skepticism. The isolate has no one but himself to convince that he is blameless and the victim of a complex plot.

McCleery says that

A fairly common product of this condition is a note written to the Warden [which] with minor variations, will express the idea that the inmate has complete power over the prison system. It will assert that unless the Warden stops "them" from trying to poison or hurt him, the inmate and God will destroy the system. If these notes find their way through official channels, the inmate may be transferred to a mental hospital where his condition is diagnosed apart from the situation that produced it. Prison inmates, however, recognize it as an extreme form of a common affliction they call "stir crazy." In its extreme form it manifests itself in the individual's not wanting to be released from prison, or from the incorrigible unit, or from his isolation cell. More rational inmates fear and resist going "stir crazy," but they do not resent it in others. They recognize

offenses. Usually they begin with petty pilfering and truancy, and proceed to such offenses as shoplifting, purse-snatching, strong-arming, robbery, and burglary.

The career of the trust violator is quite different. First, as we said before, he is most likely not to have had a previous record, even though typically he is middle-aged when detected. Second, his education, occupation, residence, friends, and leisure-time activities usually set him in a social class higher than that of the delinquent. Third, even though his crime is deliberate and he attempts to avoid detection, he fails to plan for the securing of immunity if caught. Fourth, even though he may be three or four times as old as the career delinquent, his arrest constitutes a serious crisis for him that he cannot take in his stride. His arrest and conviction, and the attendant publicity, are a disgrace to him. He loses status even though some segment of the community may sympathize with him without condoning what he did. The trust violator is therefore typically not as fully developed a criminal as a sixteen-year-old delinquent is likely to be.

The career delinquent and the criminal violator of financial trust are like and unlike each other in ways significant to our further discussion. They are similar in that both are dependent upon and make use of culturally supplied vocabularies of motives. They are different in that the delinquent makes use of a more systematized and widely held vocabularly of motives openly and explicitly discussed and accepted by his peers. At least one important motive —the denial of responsibility—is also widely accepted by persons in positions of legal authority who use that motive to explain the delinquency of the boy. Furthermore, the conception of cause and effect that marks mechanistic theories imparts to this motive the respectability and persuasive power of science. The delinquent has a relative psychical advantage in that his motivation is constantly validated by other, significant people. Knowledge that he is conforming to acceptable motives helps him to justify his delinquency to himself. Policemen, reporters, parents, and newspapers confirm the delinquent's motive when, in a case involving adolescent offenders from the middle class and upper class, a parent says, "I don't understand why he stole; my boy had everything he needed."[17] Those boys have no motive that is acceptable to respectable society; hence, their delinquency is described as "having no cause," or as "senseless," or as "unmotivated."

---

it as a way of adjusting to confinement and distinguish it from the "cracking up" which comes with [the] inability to take punishment.

Richard H. McCleery, "Authoritarianism and the Belief System of Incorrigibles," in Donald R. Cressey, ed., *The Prison*, New York: Holt, Rinehart & Winston, Inc., 1961, p. 289.

[17] For an example, see the New York *Times*, June 25, 1961, and the photograph accompanying the story, "14 Who Had no Cause for Crime in Court for 'Trial of Plenty.'"

Because the delinquent is conforming to an acceptable and independently validated motive he does not have to contend with his conscience very much. This state of affairs is one reason why he is sometimes described as "displaying no remorse." Another and perhaps major reason is that "displaying no remorse" is an interpretation made by an examiner. The criminal violator of financial trust, in contrast, does not find such a constant validation in his personal experience. He has only himself and the impersonal cultural source of his motivation. The sanction for his behavior is not systematized and not as widely accepted as the delinquent's. The trust violator is therefore not as emancipated from his conscience. When apprehended he may experience great shame and guilt through rejecting his previous criminal rationalization, and agreeing with respectable society that what he did was criminal.

5 Role Theory, Differential Association, and Compulsive Crimes

DONALD R. CRESSEY

The important point in Sutherland's theory of differential association is the principle that all criminal behavior is learned in a process of social interaction,[1] and to prove or disprove the theory we must carefully examine behavior to which the label "crime" is applied but which does not appear to have been learned in such interaction. "Compulsive crime" is the best example of such behavior.

Before such re-examination of compulsive crime can be made, however, it is necessary to review briefly the three fundamental points in the legal-psychiatric controversy about whether behavior said to be "compulsive" also is "crime." The issues are fairly clear. First, in the criminal law, under the M'Naghten rules, the stigma "insanity," not "crime," is applied to legally harmful behavior perpetrated under circumstances such that the defendant

Editorial adaptation by Donald R. Cressey of his "Role Theory, Differential Association and Compulsive Crimes," in *Human Behavior and Social Processes*, Arnold M. Rose, ed. (Boston: Houghton Mifflin, 1962), pp. 447–467, used by permission of the publisher. Some sections of the chapter appeared originally in Donald R. Cressey, "The Differential Association Theory and Compulsive Crimes," *The Journal of Criminal Law, Criminology, and Police Science*, Volume 45, Number 1 (June, 1954), pp. 29–40. Reprinted by special permission from *The Journal of Criminal Law, Criminology and Police Science*, Copyright © 1954 by the Northwestern University School of Law, Volume 45, Number 1.

[1] Edwin H. Sutherland and Donald R. Cressey, *Principles of Criminology*, 7th ed. (Philadelphia: J. B. Lippincott Co., 1966).

was unable to distinguish between right and wrong. This is to say, in more sociological terms, that he was unable to contemplate the normative consequences of his acts. If it is observed that a so-called "compulsive criminal" *did* contemplate the normative consequences of his behavior, the behavior is classed as crime, rather than insanity.

Second, psychiatrists insist that some of the behavior which results in legal harm ("compulsive crime") has essentially the same characteristics as does compulsive behavior generally. As a general category of neuroses ("psychasthenia," "anankastic reactions," etc.), compulsive acts are described as irresistible behavior which the person in question often recognizes as irrational but is subjectively compelled to carry out.[2] Such acts are considered as irrational because they are thought to be prompted by a subjective morbid impulsion which the person's "will" or "judgment" or "ego" cannot control. Malamud, for example, states that psychasthenias or anankastic reactions "have in common the fact that the patients feel themselves compelled by some inner force and against their own will or reason to think, act or feel in an abnormal manner," and that compulsive acts are "forms of behavior which the person carries out consciously without knowing the reason for such activity or for reasons which he knows have no logical foundation."[3] In other words, behavior described as compulsive is thought to be completely determined by the inner impulse or compulsion, and while the genesis of the compulsion might lie in a social context, once it has been formed it apparently operates as an entity, agent, or element in itself. Thus, the overt act is considered as prompted entirely "from within," and present contact with values concerning morality, decency, or correctness of the overt behavior in no way affects the actor, in the last analysis, either in deterring him from acting or in encouraging him to act.[4]

It is argued by psychiatrists, then, that in cases of "compulsive crime" the actor *does* know right from wrong and does contemplate the normative consequences of his acts (that is, he recognizes the behavior as irrational, foolish, wrong, illegal, etc.), but *nevertheless* exhibits the behavior because it is prompted from within by a force which he is powerless to resist. Lorand, for example, cites three case histories as evidence that "compulsive stealing" is a subconscious act of aggression against the parents or parent surrogates. He points out that there were faults in the critical appreciation of the factors of

---

[2] Roy M. Dorcus and G. Wilson Shaffer, *Textbook of Abnormal Psychology* (Baltimore, Md.: The Williams and Wilkins Company, 1941), p. 364.

[3] William Malamud, "The Psychoneuroses," in Joseph McV. Hunt (ed.), *Personality and the Behavior Disorders* (New York: The Ronald Press Company, 1944), pp. 851–852; cf. Franz Alexander and Hugo Staub, *The Criminal, the Judge, and the Public* (New York: The Macmillan Company, 1931), pp. 149–150.

[4] Cf. Gregory Zilboorg, "Misconceptions of Legal Insanity," *American Journal of Orthopsychiatry*, Vol. 9 (July 1939), pp. 540–553.

reality, and that "all showed an overwhelmingly strong instinctual drive which clouded the function of the critical faculty. They were unable, consciously, to resist, and they could not prevent the breaking through of strong drives from within that lead to stealing."[5] If the legal harm resulting from such behavior actually is crime, then it obviously is exceptional to the differential-association theory. The "criminality" in "compulsive crime" would depend not upon former contacts with differential values concerning law-abidingness, but upon a non-social agent or process.

Third, some jurists have adopted a position similar to that of the psychiatrist. This is apparent from the fact that the courts of about fourteen states hold that the consequences to the actor of the perpetration of a legal harm can be avoided by showing that while the defendant knew right from wrong his behavior was prompted by an "irresistible impulse."[6] The "irresistible impulse" and "compulsive crime" concepts seem to have at their base the same assumptions inherent in the old faculty psychology concepts "moral perversion," "moral imbecility," "inhibitory insanity," "affective mania," "monomania," and so on, each of which implied a psychological disorder which has no connection with the "intellect" or "knowing" or "reasoning" faculties.[7] Most modern psychiatrists claim that theirs is not a faculty psychology since what was formerly considered as emotional and intellectual faculties is now considered as one—the total personality. But while this "integration" theory is affirmed by psychiatrists as they oppose the M'Naghten rules, it is denied when they support notions of "compulsive crime" or "irresistible impulse."[8] While there is disagreement among psychiatrists, it appears that most of them agree with the legal theory of those jurisdictions allowing the irresistible impulse defense, and many of them contend that those judges not allowing it are backward, ignorant, or stubborn. Wertham is a noteworthy exception. He writes that "the criminal law which makes use of the conception of irresistible impulse is not an advance belonging to the present 'scientific social' era. It is a throwback to, or rather a survival of, the previous 'philosophical psychological' era. The concept of irresistible impulse derives from a philosophical, speculative, synthetic psychology. It forms no part of and finds no support in the modern dynamic psychoanalytic study of

---

[5] Sandor Lorand, "Compulsive Stealing," *Journal of Criminal Psychopathy*, Vol. 1 (January 1940), pp. 247–253; cf. Malamud, *op. cit.*, pp. 851–852.

[6] E. R. Keedy, "Irresistible Impulse as a Defense in Criminal Law," *University of Pennsylvania Law Review*, Vol. 100 (May 1952), pp. 956–993.

[7] Lawson G. Lowrey, "Delinquent and Criminal Personalities," in Joseph McV. Hunt (ed.), *Personality and the Behavior Disorders* (New York: The Ronald Press Company, 1944), pp. 799–801.

[8] See Jerome Hall, *Principles of Criminal Law* (Indianapolis, Ind.: The Bobbs-Merrill Company, Inc., 1947), pp. 523–524.

mental process."[9] Elsewhere, the same author has stated that there is nothing in the whole field of psychopathology which corresponds to the irresistible impulse, and that compulsions play no role in criminal acts.[10] Bromberg and Cleckley recently took a similar position: "The concept of sudden 'irresistible impulse' in an otherwise perfectly normal organism is unsupported by modern psychiatric knowledge."[11]

MENTALISTIC ASSUMPTIONS OF LAW AND PSYCHIATRY

This divergence in opinion and viewpoint is enhanced by the fact that an assumption of "mind" is implicit in the psychological orientations of both psychiatry and criminal law, so that each discipline has a "mentalistic" approach to human behavior. In criminal law, the "right and wrong test" assumes the existence of a mind which, when normal and mature, operates in such a way that the human has conscious freedom to choose rationally whether or not a crime shall be committed. The mind impels the person only in the direction "he" wishes to be impelled. But a mind which is immature or "diseased" cannot make intelligent choices, and a defendant possessing such a mind is considered incapable of entertaining criminal intent. Such an assumption tends to equate rationality and sanity, and it is necessary to fix "responsibility" for acts.[12] Although psychiatrists often denounce this jurisprudential assumption on the ground that it ignores the facts of science[13] their denunciation is possible only because of emphasis on a different mentalistic construct. In writing of "compulsive crime," at least, most psychiatrists assume a mind with only one significant difference from the one assumed by most jurists. Here, the mind is said to be subject to casual emotional experiences, especially early sexual experiences, which give it characteristics such that at the present moment of action it completely

[9] New York University School of Law, *Social Meaning of Legal Concepts—Criminal Guilt* (New York: New York University School of Law, 1950), p. 164.

[10] Fredric Wertham, *The Show of Violence* (Garden City, N.Y.: Doubleday & Company, Inc., 1949), pp. 13–14.

[11] Walter Bromberg and Hervey M. Cleckley, "The Medicolegal Dilemma—A Suggested Solution," *Journal of Criminal Law and Criminology*, Vol. 42 (March-April 1952), pp. 729–745.

[12] Cf. Bromberg and Cleckley, *op. cit.*, pp. 729–745; and Arnold W. Green, "The Concept of Responsibility," *Journal of Criminal Law and Criminology*, Vol. 33 (February 1943), pp. 392–394.

[13] See, e.g., Edward Glover, "The Diagnosis and Treatment of Delinquency," in L. Radzinowicz and J. W. C. Turner (eds.), *Mental Abnormality and Crime*, Vol. 2 of *English Studies in Criminal Science* (London: Macmillan and Co., Ltd., 1949), pp. 279–280.

determines the person's choice—and, consequently, his overt behavior—in a manner which usually is completely unconscious and unknowable without the help of a psychiatrist. The deeply hidden emotional forces of the mind are thought to compel the actor even if "he" knows the action is illegal, and "he" has no choice in whether the action shall be undertaken. The chief difference between such psychological forces or "mainsprings of action," and instinctive "mainsprings of action" is that the former are "unconscious."[14] Foote has pointed out that in spite of the seductive appeal which is exerted by the hope of reducing human behavior to some simple and permanent order through finding certain "basic" imperatives underlying it, criticism has negated every naming of the "mainsprings of action."[15]

Mentalistic assumptions of both kinds must be clarified and supplemented in order to determine whether "compulsive criminality" is an exception to the differential-association theory. As long as criminality is said to have its etiology in a rather mysterious "mind," "soul," "will," or "unconscious," there will be no possible way for generalizations about criminality to be subjected to empirical tests or observations which would settle the issue. Also, so long as "compulsiveness," as traditionally described, must be determined by specialists rather than judges or juries, jurists will resist discussion of it in their courts and the legal-psychiatric controversy will continue.

A SOCIOLOGICAL THEORY OF MOTIVATION

Behavior traditionally considered as "compulsive crime" can be handled and clarified without the assumption of "mind" or a basic biological or psychic imperative by application of the sociological hypothesis that there are differences in the degree to which acts are controlled by the linguistic constructs (words or combinations of words) which the actor has learned from his social groups. Since the use of linguistic constructs depends upon contacts with social groups, this amounts to differences in the degree to which the actor participates in group experiences. In sociological role theory, differences of this kind are considered differences in the *motivation* of the actor, although this concept is used in a sense quite different from the use in psychiatry. Motivation here refers to the process by which a person, as a participant in a group, symbolically (by means of language) defines a problematic situation as calling for the performance of a particular act, with

[14] See Benjamin Karpman, "An Attempt at a Re-evaluation of Some Concepts of Law and Psychiatry," *Journal of Criminal Law and Criminology*, Vol. 38 (September-October 1947), pp. 206–217.

[15] Nelson N. Foote, "Identification as the Basis for a Theory of Motivation," *American Sociological Review*, Vol. 16 (February 1951), pp. 14–22.

symbolically anticipated consummation and consequences.[16] Motives are not inner, biological mainsprings of action but linguistic constructs which organize acts in particular situations,[17] the use of which can be examined empirically. The key linguistic constructs which a person applies to his own conduct in a certain set of circumstances are motives; the complete process by which such verbalizations are used is motivation.

The great difference between this conception of motivation and the notion that motives are biological or are deeply hidden in the "unconscious" may be observed in the use of the concept "rationalization" in the two systems. In psychiatry it usually is said that one "merely rationalizes" (*ex post facto* justification) behavior which "has really been prompted by deeply hidden motives and unconscious tendencies."[18] In the other system, which uses a non-mentalistic conception of motivation, it is held that one does not necessarily "merely rationalize" behavior already enacted but acts because he has rationalized. The rationalization is his motive. When such rationalizations or verbalizations are extensively developed and systematized the person using them has a sense of conforming because they give him a sense of support and sanction.[19] An individual in our society, for example, may feel fairly comfortable when he commits an illegal act in connection with his business for, after all, "business is business." But not all verbalizations are equally developed or systematized, and in some instances the use of the verbalizations does not, therefore, receive such extensive support and sanction. The individual in these instances does not have a comfortable sense of conforming. The person in the above example probably would not feel as comfortable if his illegal act were perpetrated according to the verbalization "all businessmen are dishonest." Motives can be treated, then, as "typical vocabularies (linguistic constructs) having ascertainable functions in delimited societal situations"[20] and, as such, they may be examined empirically.

Using this conception of motivation, it is immediately apparent that not all behavior is equally motivated; there are differences in the degree to which behavior is linguistically controlled. Certainly some behavior is performed with almost no social referent, that is, with the use of no shared verbalization. For instance, behavior which is physiologically autonomous is

[16] *Ibid.*

[17] Cf. C. Wright Mills, "Situated Actions and Vocabularies of Motive," *American Sociological Review,* Vol. 5 (December 1940), pp. 904–913.

[18] Arthur P. Noyes, *Text-Book of Modern Psychiatry* (Philadelphia: W. B. Saunders Company, 1940), p. 49; see also Karpman, *op. cit.,* pp. 206–217; and William A. White, *Insanity and the Criminal Law* (New York: The Macmillan Company, 1923), p. 9.

[19] Alfred R. Lindesmith and Anselm Strauss, *Social Psychology* (New York: The Dryden Press, 1949), pp. 307–310.

[20] Mills, *op. cit.,* pp. 904–913.

clearly non-motivated since the release of energy appropriate to performing the behavior does not depend upon the application of a linguistic construct. Similarly, if one's behavior has been so conditioned by his past experiences that he behaves automatically, in the way that Pavlov's dogs behaved automatically at the sound of the bell, he is not motivated. Genuinely fetishistic behavior probably is of this kind. However, it is equally certain that other behavior cannot be enacted unless the actor has had rather elaborate and intimate contact with linguistic constructs which are, by definition, group products. Such behavior is motivated, and it may be distinguished from automatic behavior by the fact that it has reference to means and ends. If a person defines a situation as one in which there are alternatives, if there is evidence of planning, evidence of delaying small immediate gains for larger future gains, or evidence of anticipation of social consequences of acts, he is motivated.

APPLICATION OF THE MOTIVATION THEORY
TO "COMPULSIVE CRIME"

When this theory of motivation is applied to the problem at hand, it may be seen that if behavior traditionally considered as "compulsive crime" were clearly non-motivated or autonomous then the legal-psychiatric controversy would have been resolved long ago since, if such were the case, the behavior easily could be subsumed under the legal concept "insanity." If "compulsions" "in" a person "came out" in the same way that his whiskers "come out," then even in the most "anti-psychiatric" court there would be no question of his legal responsibility, and his behavior would not, in fact, be designated as crime. In this case, there would be no problem about whether the behavior were an exception to the differential-association theory but, instead, the behavior would lie outside the definition of the phenomenon (crime) with which the differential-association theory is concerned. Non-motivated behavior of this kind which resulted in legal harm would not be unlike the behavior of a sleeping or drugged person whose hand was guided by another to the trigger of a gun aimed at a victim's head. Such behavior is not planned by the actor, and precautions against detection are not taken because the ability to use the language symbols normally pertinent to the situation is absent or deficient.[21] If behavior is non-motivated

[21] Although it is not recommended, because it probably would lead to even more confusion than now exists, the criminal law theory which exempts some persons from liability because they lack "responsibility" might easily be restated in these terms. Those persons—generally psychotics and very young children—who are now excused on the grounds that they cannot distinguish between right and wrong either have not acquired or have lost the ability to control language symbols. In fact, on a level that now seems very unsophisticated, this principle was recognized as early as the thirteenth century, when Bracton formulated what erroneously has been called the "wild beast test."

the actor cannot possibly entertain "criminal intent."

In most cases now labeled "kleptomania," "pyromania," and the like, however, the actors appear to be motivated in the same way that other criminals are motivated. Consequently they are, in the terminology of the criminal law, "responsible." They select secluded places in which to perpetrate their acts, plan their activities in advance, realize that they will be arrested if detected, and do many other things indicating that there is a conscious normative referent in their behavior. Certainly most acts traditionally decribed as "compulsive crime" are clearly quite different from autonomous behavior having no normative components, in spite of the fact that the two are usually assumed to be identical or at least very similar. Possibly it was observation of the significant difference between the two that led Alexander and Staub to argue that while the impulse in kleptomania, pyromania, and compulsive lying is an unconscious one, an impulse foreign to the ego, yet the act is not completely unconscious, as is the case, they hold, in compulsive neuroses generally.[22] Gault uses kleptomania and pyromania as illustrations of the psychopathic personality. That is, they are considered as

> . . . a form of outlet for a nature that is unbalanced by reason of the dominance of the egocentric disposition. . . . They take what does not belong to them not so much as a result of blind impulsion; not *quite* "blind impulsion" because the kleptomaniac is at pains to conceal not only his act but the products of his stealing. . . . We are forced to conclude that in the general run of instances of this nature we are dealing with unreasoned impulsion to get goods to amplify one's store, to gratify one's desire for possession, and therefore magnify one's self. In other words, here is the egocentric disposition. This language suggests a purposive character of the behavior—and it is so that it results in obtaining goods.[23]

However, many other authorities claim that the evidence of deliberation and intent in acts of pyromaniacs and kleptomaniacs does not in and of itself signify sanity.[24] Thus, while it is not easy to classify precisely certain acts as motivated or non-motivated, since men do not always explicitly articulate motives, the sociological framework at least affords an opportunity to classify correctly the great proportion of the acts ordinarily labeled "compulsive crime." Using that framework, illegal conduct which is motivated would be classed as "crime" and illegal acts which are non-motivated would be classed as "compulsion" and would fall within the legal category "insanity."

[22] Alexander and Staub, *op. cit.*, pp. 95–97.

[23] Robert H. Gault, *Criminology* (Boston: D. C. Heath and Company, 1932), pp. 163–166.

[24] Perry M. Lichtenstein, *A Doctor Studies Crime* (Princeton, N.J.: D. Van Nostrand Co., Inc., 1934), p. 182; Wilhelm Stekel, *Peculiarities of Behavior* (New York: Liveright Publishing Corp., 1924), Vol. 1, p. 258.

NON-SCIENTIFIC CRITERIA OF COMPULSIVE CRIMINALS

Accurate classification of this kind would be valuable, since in the current system it appears that compulsive-crime concepts are no less "wastebasket categories" than is the "psychopathic personality" concept. Casual observation indicates, at least, that the application of the "compulsive crime" label often accompanies the inability of either the subject or the examiner to account for the behavior in question *in terms of motives which are current, popular, and sanctioned in a particular culture or among the members of a particular group within a culture.* For example, one criterion, usually overlooked, for designating behavior "kleptomania" rather than "theft" is apparent lack of economic need for the item on the part of the person exhibiting the behavior. This may be observed in at least two different ways. First, the probability that the term "kleptomania" will be applied to a destitute shoplifter is much lower than the probability that it will be applied to a wealthy person performing the same kind of acts. "Kleptomania," then, often is simply a short-hand way of saying, as the layman does, "That woman is rich and can buy almost anything she desires. She does not need (economic) to steal. She must be crazy."[25] An interesting but erroneous assumption in such logic is that the behavior of normal persons committing property crimes is explainable in terms of economic need. This assumption, coupled with the empirical observation that wealthy persons sometimes do commit major property crimes, led to the erroneous conclusion by two sociologists that such crimes must be prompted by "greed" rather than "need."[26] Among psychiatrists, contradiction of the same assumption, through observation of the fact that wealthy persons do sometimes commit minor property crimes, results in the notion that larcenous behavior of wealthy persons must be "compulsive." The economic status of the observer probably is of great importance in determining whether he

[25] Compare: 'In kleptomania we have individuals who steal, but their stealing has a number of important differences from ordinary theft. For one thing, the purely predatory element present in common theft is lacking here. The subject steals not because of the value and the money he gets from the stolen articles—that is, not for their mercenary value—but entirely for what they mean to him emotionally and symbolically. One often observes this in rich women who have no need for the article they steal and, in point of fact, dispose of it almost immediately after the article has been stolen. While the symbolic nature of such stealing is often evident on the surface, we not infrequently come across cases of stealing the nature of which is not so obvious, so that one is puzzled to figure out whether we are dealing with kleptomania or ordinary theft. Many such cases are found in our prisons." Benjamin Karpman, "Criminality, Insanity and the Law," *Journal of Criminal Law and Criminology*, Vol. 39 (January-February 1949), pp. 584–605.

[26] Harry E. Barnes and Negley K. Teeters, *New Horizons in Criminology*, 1st ed. (Englewood Cliffs, N.J.: Prentice-Hall, Inc., 1959), p. 43.

thinks a person is not in economic need and is consequently compulsive. Whether or not the misconduct is considered "disproportionate to any discernible end in view"[27] conceivably will depend a great deal upon the attitudes of the examiner rather than upon those of the offender. That is, a poor person might consider that a middle-class person had no need to steal and that his stealing must be the result of "greed" or a "compulsion," while a middle-class person probably will entertain this notion only as it refers to upper-class persons whose incomes far exceed his. If all psychiatrists were poverty-stricken, the proportion of shoplifters called "kleptomaniacs" probably would be much higher than it is. And if it is assumed that the larcenous behavior of wealthy persons is, because they are wealthy, "compulsive" then there is little opportunity for determination of possible contacts with behavior patterns conducive to crime.

Second, the absence, from the observer's standpoint, of economic need is used as a criterion for designating persons as "kleptomaniacs" in cases in which the particular articles taken appear to be of no immediate use to the subject. For example, Alexander and Staub do not consider as kleptomanic the behavior of a physician (a "neurotic criminal") who had been taking medical books and supplies, but his "theft of porcelain figures which were new and actually of no value is more in the nature of a kleptomaniac act," and Wallerstein has stated that a case "was hardly kleptomania in the usual sense because the articles were pawned or sold for money."[28] Although they have not been explored in this connection, Veblen's arguments about the great desirability in our culture of acquiring money merely as a means of accumulating economically "useless" goods might have a bearing here.[29] If his thesis were followed it would seem, at least, that there is little logical justification for designating as "criminal" the behavior of one who stole money with which to buy "useless" goods while at the same time designating as "compulsive" the stealing of the goods themselves.

This criterion also is used for designating even poor persons as "kleptomaniacs" in instances of repetitive taking of what appear to be economically useless goods. However, the fact that mere repetitive taking need not indicate a compulsion may be illustrated by the case of a gang of boys who went from store to store in a large city stealing caps. They would enter a store and each boy would steal a cap, leaving his own on the counter. The group would then move to another store where the stolen caps would be

---

[27] William Healy, *The Individual Delinquent* (Boston: Little, Brown and Co., 1918), p. 771.

[28] Alexander and Staub, *op. cit.*, p. 168; James S. Wallerstein, "Roots of Delinquency," *Nervous Child*, Vol. 2 (October 1947), pp. 399–412.

[29] Louis Schneider, *The Freudian Psychology and Veblen's Social Theory* (New York: King's Crown Press, 1948); Thorstein Veblen, *The Theory of the Leisure Class* (New York: Modern Library, Inc., 1934).

left on the counter, and new ones would be stolen. This practice would continue until the gang members became bored with the game. It is not difficult to distinguish such behavior from what is called kleptomania because it was perpetrated by a number of boys acting together, because it appears to have been done as play[30] and, most important, because it was perpetrated by boys closely approaching the cultural stereotype of the delinquent or criminal. Even a psychoanalyst probably would not assume that the caps were sex symbols or fetishes, although it is not inconceivable that he would do so.[31] However, if one of the boys at a later date repeated alone the same kind of thefts, the probability that he would be labeled a kleptomaniac would be high. And if the boy were a member of a wealthy family the probability of his being labeled a kleptomaniac would be even higher.

In fire-setting cases the absence of obvious economic need also is used, in the traditional system of thought, as a criterion for applying the term "pyromania," but here the absence of other popular motives is used as well. If it can be determined easily that one burned property in order to collect insurance, in order to get revenge, or in an attempt to conceal a criminal act, or if there is ground for believing that he had some other conventional motive, then the probability that he will be designated a "pyromaniac" is low. However, if one of these is immediately apparent, and especially in instances where the thing burned has no great economic value, the probability that the term will be applied is much higher. Traditionally, pyromania has been, then, like kleptomania, a residual category. One investigator states that of all the varieties of incendiarists, the pyromaniac is the most difficult to detect "because of the lack of motive."[32]

---

[30] Jerome Hall, *op. cit.*, p. 517; H. M. Tiebout, and M. E. Kirkpatrick, "Psychiatric Factors in Stealing," *American Journal of Orthopsychiatry*, Vol. 2 (April 1932), pp. 114–123.

[31] Karpman, *op. cit.*, reports the case of a man who burglarized women's apartments, taking both money and female intimate garments. By using the case as an illustration of "fetishistic kleptomania," he puts great emphasis upon the taking of the garments and almost ignores the taking of money.

Gault, *op. cit.*, pp. 163–166, has made the following significant statement about such psychiatric practices: "*The attempt that some have made to lay the foundation for cases of this nature in repressed sex motives and to interpret the objects stolen as so many symbols that they have in relation to the sex aspect of experience is a very unconvincing procedure. . . .* The case is doubtless not so simple. The sex urge is only one of many that actuate the human organism. For instance, let us assume that a clothespin or a rubber hose found among the stolen goods of a kleptomaniac is a symbol. Symbol of what? The answer, according to the present writer's opinion, is that *its symbolic character depends upon what the investigator is interested in finding.*" (Italics added)

[32] Camille F. Hoyek, "Criminal Incendiarism," *Journal of Criminal Law and Criminology*, Vol. 41 (March–April, 1951), pp. 836–845. Psychoanalysts make much of the assumed sex symbolism in cases of non-economically motivated incendia-

In contrast to what appears to be current practice, when a sociological theory of motivation is used, the apparent inability of a person to explain his actions to the police, to a psychiatrist, or even to himself is not considered sufficient for classifying those actions "compulsive." Using that theory, it may be observed that most criminals, in fact, when asked to explain their acts either recite the popular motives involved or respond that they do not know. For example, one might say, as did a criminal who had stolen a whole truckload of groceries, "I didn't want to take them but I had to because I was hungry." This response may be compared with that of a person arrested for taking small objects from a store: "I didn't want to take them but I just had to take them," and with that of a person who had burned an automobile, "I just wanted to stir up some excitement." As indicated above, such rationalizations are not necessarily *ex post facto* justifications for acts —and if they are not, then there is no logical justification for classifying one person as a "thief" and the others as "compulsive." Motives are circumscribed by the actor's learned vocabulary.

SOCIOLOGICAL ROLE THEORY APPLIED TO "COMPULSIVE CRIME"

But sociological theory can do more than correctly classify the large proportion of defendants said to be compulsive. The literature on role theory provides a framework not only for understanding the behavior of such defendants, but for understanding their inability to account for their behavior as well. Closely related to the theory of motivation which has been outlined is that aspect of role theory which deals with the relationship between the person's identification of himself as a "social object" and his subsequent behavior. In order to play a social role, one must anticipate the reactions of others by taking the role implicitly before it is taken overtly. He must look at himself from another's point of view. By hypothesizing the reactions of others, the person looks upon himself as an object and, consequently, identifies himself as a particular kind of object. He then performs the role which is appropriate to the kind of social object with which he has

---

rism. Thus, in one case of repeated burning of grass on vacant lots it was asserted that the lots symbolized the subject's father, that by driving onto the lot with his father's automobile the subject identified himself with his father and his sex organ and performed the act of incest on his mother, that the subject's effort to help in extinguishing the fires was symbolic of an unconscious wish to atone for his sin, and that the splashing of water on the fire was a symbolic repetition of a regression to the urethral phase of his libidinal development, in which phase the subject was said to have had erections which he relieved by urinating. Ernst Simmel, "Incendiarism," in Kurt R. Eissler (ed.), *Searchlights on Delinquency* (New York: International Universities Press, 1941), pp. 90–101.

identified himself. The vocabulary of motives employed in the performance of the role also is a corollary of this self-identification. But at various times and in different situations the person may identify himself differently, so that he is able to play many, often even conflicting, social roles. Again, his identification of who he is and what he is determines the roles he plays.[33]

For example, one might in the course of a day identify himself as a father in one situation, as a husband in another situation, and as a property owner in another situation. The motives employed in the performance of each role will reflect his particular identification. A similar phenomenon may exist in respect to so-called "compulsive crime." For example, a person might in some situations identify himself as a kleptomaniac, since that construct is now popular in our culture, and a full commitment to such an identification includes the use of motives which, in turn, release the energy to perform a so-called compulsive act. The more positive the conviction that one is a kleptomaniac the more automatic his behavior will appear. The subject's behavior in particular situations, then, is organized by his identification of himself according to the linguistic construct "kleptomania" or its equivalent. In the framework of role theory, it is this kind of organization which makes the behavior recognizably recurrent in the life history of the person. The fact that the acts are recurrent does not mean that they are prompted from within but only that certain linguistic symbols have become usual for the person in question.

If this theory were applied, we would not expect apprehended shoplifters, some of whom conceive of themselves as kleptomaniacs, to provide a logically consistent or even "correct" explanation of their behavior. For example, one who has behaved according to a set of linguistic constructs acceptable to himself in one role (kleptomaniac) might later discover that both the behavior and the constructs are unacceptable to himself in another role he is playing or desires to play (father, property owner). In that case there will be a high probability of denial to himself in the second role that "he" behaved at all. His conception of himself from one point of view results in denial of the action: "I wasn't myself when (or if) I did that," "I wasn't feeling well that day," "I couldn't be the criminal you seek—I couldn't do a thing like that," etc. On the other hand, his continued conception of himself according to the symbolic constructs which were used in behaving in the first place probably will result in open confession that "he" behaved: "Stop me before I do it again," "I have no control of myself," "That which is 'in' me comes out in situations like that," "I did it and I'm glad," etc.

In interviewing persons who, according to role theory, have identified themselves with "compulsive criminals" of some sort, we should not expect

[33]Foote, *op. cit.*, pp. 14–22.

them to realize that "who they are" depends upon language symbols and, hence, upon arbitrary ascriptions by others. One who identifies himself as a "kleptomaniac," for example, will be prone to accept such a conception of himself as ultimate reality. Even those observers or examiners who use the traditional notion that compulsive behavior is an expression of an "inner spring of action" have considered the subject's conception of himself as absolute rather than as a group product. As one sociologist has pointed out, "Because our learning has more often than not been perfected to the point where cognitive judgments in standardized situations are made instantaneously, and the energy for performing the appropriate behavior is released immediately, it has been an easy mistake for many observers to suppose that the organic correlates came first and even account for the definition of the situation, rather than the reverse.[34]

In our present state of knowledge we cannot be entirely sure how one gets committed to particular identities and motives in the first place, but, as indicated, the process certainly is one of social learning. Differential association is a theory of social learning specifically applied to criminal behavior, and it contends that, in the terminology used above, the identifications and motives of criminals are acquired through direct personal contacts with persons sharing those identifications and motives. This theory may have many defects, in that it does not precisely or adequately describe or integrate all the aspects of the processes by which criminality is learned, but it describes the processes by which one becomes a "compulsive" criminal as well as it describes the processes by which one becomes a "non-compulsive" criminal. "Compulsive criminality," as traditionally described, is not of such a nature that it necessarily is an exception to the differential-association theory.

SUMMARY AND CONCLUSIONS

1. The assertion that "latent forces of such phenomena as compulsive stealing and fire-setting are understood"[35] is not warranted.

2. If the traditional assumption that all "compulsive crime" is motivated entirely "from within" is correct, then the use of the words "compulsive" and "crime" together is erroneous. If the behavior actually were prompted "from within" it would be subsumed under the legal concept "insanity," not "crime."

3. Re-examination of "compulsive crime" concepts in the framework of sociological theories of motivation, identification, and role-playing in-

[34] *Ibid.*

[35] Robert M. Lindner, *Stone Walls and Men* (New York: The Odyssey Press, 1946), p. 323.

dicates that most of the legally harmful behavior traditionally labeled "compulsive" actually is "motivated" and has a developmental history which is very similar to that of other "motivated" behavior. That legally harmful behavior which is automatic ("non-motivated") cannot be considered as crime.

4. Since the developmental processes in so-called "compulsive criminality" are the same as the processes in other criminality, "compulsive crimes" are not, because of something in their nature, exceptional to the differential-association theory. Upon closer empirical examination it probably will be demonstrated that criminality which has traditionally been assumed to be "personal" is actually a group product, and this criminality will become of more concern to the sociologist than has been the case in the past.

Indices

Name Index

Subject Index